HV
9950
.B36
2000

Criminal Justice in America

Hugh D. Barlow

Southern Illinois University at Edwardsville

Prentice Hall
Upper Saddle River, New Jersey 07458

KVCC KALAMAZOO VALLEY COMMUNITY COLLEGE LIBRARY

OCT 0 5 2000

Library of Congress Cataloging-in-Publication Data
Barlow, Hugh D.
Criminal Justice in America / Hugh D. Barlow.
p. cm.
Includes bibliographical references and index.
ISBN 0-13-083271-5
1. Criminal justice. Administration of—United States. 2. Crime—Government policy—United States. 3. Juvenile justice. Administration of—United States. 4. Law enforcement—United States. 5. Trials—United States. I. Title.
HV9950.B36 2000 99-12555
364.973-dc21 CIP

Publisher: Dave Garza
Acquisitions Editor: Neil Marquardt
Development Editor: Cheryl Adam
Managing Editor: Mary Carnis
Production Management: Linda Zuk, WordCrafters
Interior Design: Jill Yutkowitz
Production Liaison: Adele M. Kupchik
Director of Manufacturing and Production: Bruce Johnson
Manufacturing Manager: Ed O'Dougherty
Creative Director: Marianne Frasco
Cover Design: Jill Yutkowitz
Typesetting: Clarinda Company
Editorial Assistant: Susan Kegler
Marketing Manager: Shannon Simonsen
Marketing Assistant: Adam Kloza
Printer/Binder: R. R. Donnelley & Sons, Inc., Salem, Virginia
Cover Illustration: Andrea Ventura
Director, Image Resource Center: Lori Morris-Nanzt
Photo Researcher: Beaura Kathy Ringrose/Beth Boyd
Permissions Coordinator: Charles Morris

©2000 by Hugh D. Barlow
Published by Prentice Hall
Upper Saddle River, New Jersey

All rights reserved. No part of this book may be reproduced, in any form or by any means, without permission.

Printed in the United States of America
10 9 8 7 6 5 4 3 2 1

ISBN 0-13-083271-5

Prentice-Hall International (UK) Limited, London
Prentice-Hall of Australia Pty. Limited, Sydney
Prentice-Hall Canada Inc., Toronto
Prentice-Hall Hispanoamericana, S.A., Mexico
Prentice-Hall of India Private Limited, New Delhi
Prentice-Hall of Japan, Inc., Tokyo
Pearson Education Asia Pte. Ltd., Singapore
Editora Prentice-Hall do Brasil, Ltda., Rio De Janeiro
Prentice-Hall, Upper Saddle River, New Jersey

Gift 1-20-00 $72.45

Brief Contents

CONTENTS

Each chapter begins with What Do You Think? critical learning questions and concludes with What Do You Think Now?, Summary, Key Terms, Active Learning Challenges, and Internet Challenges.

Part II: THE POLICE: FIRST LINE OF DEFENSE AGAINST CRIME 157

Chapter 5: History, Organization, and Functions of Police 158

Chapter 6: Culture and Styles of Policing 194

CHAPTER 11: PRE-TRIAL DECISIONS IN THE JUDICIAL PROCESS 384

CHAPTER 12: THE COURTS AND THE CRIMINAL TRIAL 420

CHAPTER 15: THE HISTORY AND USE OF PRISONS 546

CHAPTER 16: LIFE IN PRISON 588

CHAPTER 17: COMMUNITY-BASED CORRECTIONS 632

PREFACE

Criminal justice is a modern society's system of roles and activities for defining and dealing with crime. The goal of this text is to introduce students to the workings of the criminal justice system in the United States. They will learn what is expected of the system, what the system actually delivers, how it does so, and what the consequences are for Americans and their communities. *Criminal Justice in America* covers the material found in other prominent texts, but does so in a language and style that is accessible to all students and does not assume any prior knowledge of the subject. On the other hand, students who are already employed in criminal justice will find plenty to identify with in this text.

Criminal Justice in America also departs from other texts in some other important ways:

* **Seven criminal justice themes** help bring the system alive by emphasizing its dynamic quality. A historical theme links the present with the past, while a comparative theme encourages students to consider how criminal justice in America compares with practices in other countries. An innovations theme reflects the continual changes that are occurring within criminal justice and highlights some of the latest developments. An insider theme emphasizes the insights and interpretations of people who work in the various criminal justice fields, bringing a personal touch to the discussion. A diversity theme acknowledges the cultural diversity of American society and pays special attention to the experiences of minorities and women as offenders, victims, and criminal justice employees.

* **Unique pedagogical features** are included that facilitate learning and help students (and instructors) assess their progress throughout the course. Each chapter contains:

- A statement of learning objectives
- Before and after questions, *What do you think?* and *What do you think now?*
- A list of key terms and cases
- Active Learning Challenges that invite students and instructors to collaborate on learning projects and class exercises
- Internet Challenges that encourage students to use the Internet as a research tool for exploring specific criminal justice issues.

Finally, each chapter in Parts 2 through 4 opens with a short vignette that dramatizes some of the major issues to be discussed in the chapter. Together, these pedagogical features should enhance the learning experience of students while making the course more enjoyable for students and instructors alike.

ACKNOWLEDGMENTS

Many people helped me in writing this text, and I am most grateful for their efforts. Without Alan McClare's persistence, the book would never have been written. Early in the project, Michael Kimball gave me helpful advice on writing styles and pedagogy. As the writing progressed, I received constructive criticism from colleagues across the country who teach criminal justice in a variety of different learning environments. Their ideas helped make the book accessible to a wide range of students and their many suggestions on things to include, delete, or change certainly improved the final product—though the responsibility for any mistakes or omissions is mine alone. These colleagues are:

James F. Albrecht, John Jay College of Criminal Justice
Stephen J. Bahr, Brigham Young University
Michael L. Barrett, Ashland University
Steve Brandl, University of Wisconsin, Milwaukee
Velmer S. Burton, Jr., Washington State University
Charles Chastain, University of Arkansas at Little Rock
Tere Chipman, Fayetteville Technical Community College
Joseph L. Ciccone, Berkeley College
Paul V. Clark, Philadelphia Community College
Ellen G. Cohn, Florida International University
Gary F. Cornelius, George Mason University
Dana C. DeWitt, Chadron State College
Thomas G. Eynon, Southern Illinois University, Carbondale
Gayle Fisher-Stewart, John Jay College of Criminal Justice
Andrew Giacomazzi, University of Texas at El Paso
Julia Glover Hall, Drexel University
Kathrine A. Johnson, Kentucky State University
William E. Kelly, Auburn University
Lydia M. Long, Indiana State University
Rich Mancuso, Buffalo State College
Frank Morn, Illinois State University
David L. Parry, Endicott College
Debra E. Ross, Buffalo State College
William F. Wagner, Mankato State University
Wayne L. Wolf, South Suburban College, South Holland, Illinois

I am lucky to have a group of wonderful colleagues and students at Southern Illinois University, Edwardsville. Over the past four years they have been gracious in their understanding and support, for at times I know I tested their patience. The same is true of the departmental office staff, particularly Barbara Hickman, to whom I owe a special debt of gratitude; she shouldered many burdens with fortitude and grace, often beyond the call of duty. A note of thanks, too, must go to Associate Dean Dixie Engelman and professors Tom Regulus and John Farley, who kindly read parts of the manuscript and gave much-needed encouragement during a difficult period in its gestation. Tina Federer, supervisor of the Peck copy center, made room for me even when overwhelmed by other work. The following graduate assistants helped me in various ways, sometimes on short notice: Erin Ercoline, Joseph Fiorenza, Teri Kapp, Nicholas Karidis, Steve McLean, Krista Thien, Cindy Thomas, and Mark Webb. I wish to single out graduate assistant Omar Nagi, who worked diligently on various aspects of the project and made many helpful suggestions.

A special thanks goes to the many people who shared with me their personal experiences working in criminal justice and allowed me to pass those experiences on to the readers of this book. Those wishing to remain anonymous know who they are; the others are Special Agent-in-Charge Jack Fox, United

States Secret Service; Elizabeth Watson, former Chief of Police in Austin, Texas; Officer Todd Ramirez, Edwardsville Police Department; Donald Wolff, attorney-at-law and municipal judge; Joseph Brown, attorney-at-law and former prosecutor, Madison County, Illinois; Billy Hahs, Assistant Public Defender, Madison County, Illinois; William Beatty, Senior U.S. District Judge for the Southern District of Illinois; Dr. Dora Schriro, Director of the Missouri Department of Corrections; Philip White, probation officer, Madison County, Illinois; Richard Asperger, Human Services Administrator, Madison County Probation Services, formerly Assistant Supervisor of Juvenile Detention.

The editorial staff at Prentice Hall have been a joy to work with. Criminal justice editor Neil Marquardt's enthusiasm and support are gratefully acknowledged. My development editor, Cheryl Adam, did an outstanding job in a very short space of time and her creative ideas were outdone only by her sense of humor. It is hard to find laughter around a subject so important and serious as criminal justice, yet laughter is just what this author needed. Thank you, Cheryl! Also, thanks to the folks at WordCrafters, in particular Linda Zuk, who kept the book's production on schedule; to Karen Winget, who composed the indexes; and to Amy Schneider, who did a wonderful job as copyeditor. The wonderful website for this book has been created by Steven Brandl, of the University of Wisconsin, Milwaukee; and Tere Chipman, of Fayetteville Technical Community College, created 142 PowerPoint slides for the Active Learning Challenges. Finally, Ellen Cohn, of Florida International University, did a masterful job writing the instructor's manual and test bank. Thank you all! Thanks also to my Omaha friends who have provided a different type of support as together we challenged the boundaries of skill and luck: Norman "Bert" Bertagnolli, Douglas Bock, Vito Casucci, Michael Cohen, Tom Dolan, Doyle Featherston, William Obermoeller, and Royce Powell.

Last, but certainly not least, are the thanks I owe my family. At different times, writing this book meant that I could not enjoy time with my mother, brother, and sister, all of whom live far away but are always in my thoughts. My daughters Alison and Melissa could have done with more time and support from their dad while they studied at the University of Texas, Austin. My wife, Karen, assisted with the pedagogical elements in the text, bringing fresh ideas at just the right time, and she and our children Eric, Colin, Chelsea, and Kelsey allowed me the space and time I needed without resentment. There is no better love than that.

[illegible] Elizabeth Warren, [illegible] of Police in Austin, Texas; Officer Karl Ramirez, [illegible]; [illegible] attorneys; and municipal judges [illegible].

Madison County, Illinois: [illegible], senior U.S. District Judge for the southern District of Illinois; [illegible], Director of the Missouri Department of Corrections; [illegible], prosecuting officer, Madison County, Illinois; Richard [illegible], Court Services Administrator, Madison County Corrections; [illegible], assistant superintendent of Juvenile Detention.

The editorial staff at Prentice Hall have been a joy to work with. Criminal justice editor Neil Marquardt's enthusiasm and support are gratefully acknowledged, as are [illegible] Karen Kramer, who [illegible].

[illegible] University of Wisconsin [illegible] at Edwardsville [illegible] Michael [illegible], and Robert Lowell.

Lastly but certainly not least, [illegible] better than that.

About the Author

Hugh D. Barlow

Hugh D. Barlow, Ph.D., is professor of sociology and chair of the Department of Sociology at Southern Illinois University, Edwardsville. After an undergraduate education in economics and sociology at the University of Southampton, England, Dr. Barlow received his M.A. and Ph.D. degrees from the University of Texas at Austin. His interest in criminology and criminal justice was sparked by the upward trend in crime during the late 1960s and the national debate over the death penalty. With encouragement from Professor Jack P. Gibbs, Barlow focused his attention on the relationship between crime and punishment, culminating in a Ph.D. dissertation titled "A Formal Theory of Crime and Punishment."

From 1971 to 1973, Dr. Barlow was a member of the founding faculty at Sangamon State University (now the University of Illinois at Springfield), where he taught his (and the university's) first courses in criminology and criminal justice. Since 1973, Barlow has been a faculty member at Southern Illinois University, Edwardsville. From 1977-1978, Barlow was Visiting Assistant Professor at the University of Wisconsin, Milwaukee; in Fall, 1979, he was Visiting Associate Professor at the University of North Carolina, Chapel Hill; and in Spring, 1981, he was Visiting Scholar at Cambridge University's Institute of Criminology. At SIUE, Dr. Barlow has developed a variety of courses in crime and delinquency, victimology, and criminal justice, and in 1997, he designed a new undergraduate major in criminal justice. Students have nominated Barlow for teaching awards on numerous occasions, and in 1995 he received the SIUE Teaching Recognition Award.

Hugh D. Barlow has maintained an active research agenda over the years, including published articles on homicide and assaults, the spatial aspects of crime, and on white collar crime. He is also the author of *Introduction to Criminology*, now in its 7th edition (HarperCollins, 1996). He is coauthor with

Theodore N. Ferdinand of *Understanding Delinquency* (HarperCollins, 1992), and editor of a collection of original essays titled *Crime and Public Policy: Putting Theory to Work* (Westview Press, 1995). The journal *Federal Probation* rated this book one of the top ten published works of 1995.

In addition to teaching and research, Barlow has been active in applied areas and in service to the profession. From 1976 to 1980 he was an Assistant Director of Public Safety with the Madison County Sheriff's Reserve; from January, 1986, to December, 1989, Barlow was Editor of *The Criminologist,* published by the American Society of Criminology. In 1993, he received the prestigious Herbert A. Bloch Award from the ASC for "outstanding service contributions to the American Society of Criminology and to the professional interests of criminology."

On a less serious level, Dr. Barlow enjoys driving country roads, snow skiing, and playing poker. All these ventures involve luck and skill, although perhaps in different combinations. He recently added painting to this list, which seems to involve no luck at all—but a great deal of satisfaction when the work is completed.

PART I

THE STUDY OF CRIMINAL JUSTICE

Most people have opinions and beliefs about criminal justice, yet few have the opportunity to seriously study it. The four chapters that make up Part One help acquaint readers with issues and problems associated with the study of criminal justice. Chapter 1 lays the foundation for the book by introducing important concepts and definitions, and by showing how criminal justice emerged as a modern society's system of roles and activities for defining and dealing with crime. This chapter also introduces readers to the seven themes emphasized in the text. Chapter 2 explores the ways in which information about crime and justice are produced, and discusses their strengths and weaknesses. The chapter also reviews important resources that students can use for class projects and independent research. Chapter 3 considers how theories of crime differ in their underlying assumptions about human nature and social order, and explores the relationship between theory and public policy. Order and justice are identified as twin goals of criminal justice policy in America, and the chapter argues that order is given more emphasis than justice. Finally, Chapter 4 provides an overview of the adult and juvenile justice systems in America, including differences between them. The system is described as a set of interlocking functional areas that do not always work well together. The major decision stages are explored so that readers understand the key actions that bring the system to life.

CHAPTER 1

CRIME, LAW, AND CRIMINAL JUSTICE

LEARNING OBJECTIVES

- Describe media coverage of crime and justice and explain why it portrays extremes rather than the everyday reality.
- Understand what is meant by the terms *crime* and *criminal.*
- Explain the labeling perspective and the four meanings of *crime.*
- Distinguish between types of crimes and categories of criminals.
- Understand the place of criminal law in systems of social control.
- Distinguish between functionalist and conflict perspectives on law.
- Describe the foundations of American criminal law.
- Understand the seven themes emphasized in this text.

The recent trials of O. J. Simpson and Timothy McVeigh have heightened American interest in the criminal justice system, but have not necessarily improved the public's understanding of the typical *criminal trial. What was unusual about the Simpson and McVeigh trials? What seemed "normal" about them?*

PHOTO OF SIMPSON COURTESY OF AP/NICK UT, STF.; PHOTO OF MCVEIGH BY BOB DAEMMRICH, COURTESY OF /SYGMA

Law must be stable, and yet it cannot stand still.

ROSCOE POUND, LEGAL SCHOLAR AND FORMER DEAN OF HARVARD LAW SCHOOL

The group that defines the law and controls public opinion is the group that will define criminal images and control the punishment for all groups. . . .

MARK S. HAMM, PROFESSOR OF CRIMINOLOGY, INDIANA STATE UNIVERSITY

I think they should get life in prison. In fact, I think life is too good for them.

MARY ANN BETTS, GRANDMOTHER OF ONE OF THE FIVE VICTIMS KILLED BY TWO BOYS IN A JONESBORO, ARKANSAS, SCHOOLYARD IN MARCH 1998

My client today does not understand the nature of the proceedings.

VAL PRICE, DEFENSE LAWYER FOR 12-YEAR-OLD ANDREW GOLDEN, ONE OF THE BOYS CONVICTED OF THE JONESBORO KILLINGS

"Criminals Becoming More Brazen, Officials Fear" was the headline in a story released by the *New York Times* News Service and published in newspapers across the country in April 1997. The story focused on a series of violent bank robberies in Los Angeles, Detroit, and St. Louis over a three-week period earlier that year. In all three cases, robbers were clad in full body armor and carried assault rifles or shotguns. In each incident the robbers opened fire inside the bank but their escape was foiled by police. In Los Angeles the gun battle with police was videotaped by circling TV news helicopters. Six police officers and three bystanders were wounded. Temporarily outgunned, the police borrowed high-powered semi-automatic weapons from a nearby gun store and eventually killed the robbers. Observers saw a close parallel with the climactic robbery in the 1995 movie *Heat,* starring Al Pacino and Robert DeNiro. According to the news article, unidentified law enforcement officials were worried that more "copycat" robberies would occur.

WHAT DO YOU THINK?

- Do you think that crime is usually violent? Committed by hardened criminals? Why or why not?
- Do you think that certain types of media, such as movies, sensationalize crime more than do other types of media such as newspapers and television news? If so, to what extent?
- How much do you feel that media events such as the O. J. Simpson trial teach the public about criminal justice? What do they teach that is valuable? Not valuable?
- Where do you think criminal laws come from? Who decides what will be a crime?

IMAGES OF CRIME AND JUSTICE IN AMERICA

Most people learn about crime and justice through the news media. Unfortunately, the picture presented in the headlines is a highly distorted one. For example, the highly publicized robberies mentioned earlier are the exception to the rule—and this is one reason they attract so much attention. Bank robberies today are rarely the work of organized gangs or professional robbers and even more rarely result in death or injury. During 1996, for example, in the more than 8,000 bank robberies reported by police, the FBI recorded only 2 deaths—19 if you count the robbers who were killed—and only 204 injuries to customers or employees (Maguire and Pastore, 1998; Tables 3.149 and 3.151). The typical bank robbery involves a lone robber who hands a teller a note demanding money and then flees with a relatively small amount of cash.

MEDIA IMAGES RAISE IMPORTANT QUESTIONS ABOUT CRIMINAL JUSTICE IN AMERICA

Some important questions about criminal justice emerge when we look behind the media images. Although it is now rather old news, the O. J. Simpson murder trial provides a very good example. The nationally televised arrest, trial, and acquittal of Simpson mesmerized the nation for over a year. People who followed the case day by day learned a lot about the criminal process in that particular case, but they learned little about criminal justice as it is played out in most criminal cases, even those involving murder. Most criminal defendants are not celebrities; most criminal trials last a few hours or days at most; most criminal suspects are prosecuted and defended by attorneys working alone—usually young, poorly paid assistant prosecutors and equally young, poorly paid public defenders or lawyers from small firms; and most defendants plead guilty, even those charged with serious crimes such as murder, robbery, or rape.

Although the O. J. Simpson case was an exception to the rule in many ways, it nevertheless stimulated some important questions about criminal justice in America. For example, can "ordinary" offenders get a fair trial? Is racism a pervasive problem in police work? Do the news media influence the course of justice? Is it ever possible to select an unbiased jury? Are criminal investigations routinely tainted by incompetence? Should jury consultants, DNA experts, and other professional trial witnesses be available in all criminal trials, or only when the defense and prosecution can afford them?

Many of the same questions were raised during the trial of Timothy McVeigh. Along with Terry Nichols, who was tried later, McVeigh was charged with the greatest mass murder in U.S. history—the bombing of the Alfred P. Murrah federal building in Oklahoma City on April 19, 1995. The blast killed 168 people. McVeigh's trial did not match the media circus created by the

Simpson trial, for cameras were not allowed in the courtroom. Nevertheless, the news media found many juicy tidbits to report. For example, the FBI crime lab was accused of mishandling crucial bomb evidence, and days before the trial began, it was widely reported that McVeigh had confessed to his attorneys as well as to a cellmate. Not surprisingly, McVeigh's attorneys requested a postponement of the trial on grounds of prejudicial pretrial publicity. The request was denied by a federal appeals court, and the trial began as scheduled on March 31, 1997. McVeigh was convicted of all charges, and sentenced to death on June 13, 1997. The McVeigh case was by no means over, however; the state of Oklahoma immediately began proceedings to try McVeigh on state murder charges, and his attorney said he would launch "an extensive appeal" of McVeigh's federal conviction and death sentence (Reuters, June 16, 1997).

The Simpson and McVeigh cases were extraordinary events that generated a considerable amount of public discussion about crime and justice in America. This is a good thing because public debate helps keep the justice system open to scrutiny. There is a tendency for criminal justice agencies to maintain a veil of secrecy over their operations, and this is especially true of the police and the prison system. A closed system of justice encourages abuses of power, which in turn weakens democracy and threatens the civil rights of citizens. From this point of view, extensive media coverage of crime and justice helps preserve our democratic form of government and serves the interests of the citizenry.

The Media Image Shows a World of Extremes

The public must be given a balanced and accurate account of crime and justice in order for this debate to be an informed one. However, headline news tends to accentuate extremes, to focus on crimes or the actions of criminal justice agencies that are newsworthy precisely because they are exceptional. Such events sell the news, which brings in more customers and more advertising dollars.

Consider the murder of 6-year-old JonBenet Ramsey; it has continued to make national headlines for over three years. Ramsey, a child beauty queen and model, was strangled sometime during Christmas night, 1996. Early the next day, her mother discovered an apparent kidnap note demanding money; a short time later her father found JonBenet's body in the basement of their fashionable home in Boulder, Colorado. From the beginning, the parents refused to cooperate with police and prosecutors, and hired their own detectives to investigate the case. News reporters from all over the world descended on Boulder. The police chief and local prosecutor held numerous press conferences over the following months, and the city even maintained a Web site on the Internet that catalogued the important events in the case. Newspapers from the *New York Times* to the *National Enquirer* kept Americans enthralled with the case. By June 1998, the case had cost the Boulder Police Department over $275,000 in overtime pay and other expenses. As of March 1999, the little girl's murder still was unsolved.

Such crime stories dominate the headlines because they stir up anger, fear, uncertainty, sympathy, or disbelief. People turn to each other and say "Did you hear about that little girl? Isn't that awful!" Or, they might wonder: "Why haven't the police arrested anyone? It's been over two years! Imagine what the family must be going through!" There is no sign that an arrest is near in the JonBenet Ramsey case. If there is an arrest, people will be anxious to learn what happens next—and this will make more media dollars.

The Ramsey case raises another issue that can be addressed in the form of a question: Why did this particular murder become national news and not the hundreds of other child murders that occur during any given year? Was it because Ramsey was from a wealthy family, not normally associated with violent crime? Was it because she was a beauty queen? Was it the timing of the murder on Christmas Day? Or the peculiar circumstances of the killing, suggesting a botched kidnapping? It was probably all of these things, and more. The case is now newsworthy because it has remained unsolved for so long.

The problem of extremes is clearly revealed when we compare what is emphasized in the media with what criminological research shows to be the case. For example, far from being violent, carefully planned, or complex, the bulk of crime is petty and opportunistic: Small-time thefts, petty drug deals, vandalism, and minor assaults are the rule. If we include crimes that occur in the workplace, such as fraud and employee theft, then many of these are petty, too (Gottfredson and Hirschi, 1990). As portrayed by the media, criminals are exceptionally violent, exceptionally greedy or exceptionally corrupt people who pick on exceptionally vulnerable victims. Yet consistent with their crimes, the bulk of criminals are actually nonviolent offenders looking for quick and easy rewards.

On the justice side of the crime scene, the picture presented in the headlines is again a world of extremes. The police are portrayed as either excessively violent, exceptionally talented, completely outclassed by criminals, or willfully corrupt. Prosecutors are portrayed as tenacious guardians of the law, or glory seekers, or cruelly indifferent to injustice, or downright incompetent. Judges fare no better; their courtroom behavior and sentencing decisions are portrayed as grossly unfair or ridiculously lenient. Criminal justice professionals who work with offenders in prison or on probation and parole get much less attention—unless some outrage or atrocity occurs. In 1997 it was revealed that the infamous killer Richard Speck had made videotapes in prison showing him having sex with other inmates. At times like this, correctional officials are portrayed as incompetent, as barbaric, as blundering fools, or as willfully ignorant of public safety.

Television series such as *Cops* and *Court TV* may appear to present a more accurate view of crime and justice because they record events as they occur in real life. However, the picture they show is also a distorted one. Their producers search for material that will attract new viewers and keep old viewers coming back for more. The programs are heavily edited and the expert commentary often used glosses over the complexities of the criminal justice process. Yet viewers of these shows do get an opportunity to hear things from the perspective of people directly involved with a criminal case, including offenders and victims. Insights into how crime and justice are experienced by participants are useful for uncovering the truth about crime. Two fundamental truths about crime and justice are apparent if you listen carefully to those involved: there is very little glamour in crime, and justice is a matter of opinion.

UNCOVERING THE TRUE, AND TIMELY, STORY OF CRIMINAL JUSTICE

This textbook tries to uncover the true story of criminal justice in America. We may not always agree on what we are seeing, and certainly we will not always agree on what it means. That is what makes social and behavioral science challenging, and sometimes frustrating. But I hope you will find that the journey you are about to take is well worth the effort and the frustration.

Our journey will take us through a complex system of agencies and activities whose purpose is to identify and respond to crime and criminals. We shall look at how and why activities, events, and people are labeled criminal. We shall consider how criminal justice is experienced by offenders, by those who work in the justice system, and also by crime victims. How and why are decisions made? What are the consequences of decisions for the people involved, for the criminal justice system, and for society as a whole?

criminal justice A society's system of roles and activities for defining and dealing with crime.

Criminal justice is a modern society's system of roles and activities for defining and dealing with crime. The police, the courts, and correctional agencies are the three pillars of the criminal justice system; each is crucial in its own right and each is affected by the others. Together they determine the nature and quality of American justice. Chapters 5 through 17 of the text explore in detail how the various parts of the system have worked in the past, how they work today, and what changes may be in store for tomorrow.

Before embarking on that exploration, criminal justice students need to know some basic things. For example, what exactly is crime? And who is the criminal? Are there differences among criminals? Why do societies have laws, and how are they created? Where do facts and theories about crime and justice come from? Where can criminal justice students look for help in researching criminal justice topics? What are the basic goals of the criminal justice system? How is it organized, and where are the key decision points? What are the basic differences between the adult and juvenile justice systems? These questions are addressed in this chapter and the next three. Let us begin by tackling the issue of definitions.

WHAT IS CRIME AND WHO IS THE CRIMINAL?

When people are asked to define crime they often come up with responses like these:

- Crime is an act forbidden by society.
- Crime is something that goes against the norms of society.
- Crime is what murderers, rapists, and robbers do.
- Crime is behavior that harms people or their property.

When it comes to defining criminals, these are common responses:

- Criminals are people who commit crimes.
- Criminals are people who violate the law.
- Criminals are people arrested by the police.
- Criminals are people who commit violent acts such as murder, rape, or robbery.

These definitions are fine for everyday conversation, and we could probably agree with all of them. But they are about as useful as saying: "I know it when I see it." Common as they are, the definitions have no foundation in law, and the following discussion will show that they are actually misleading. Although there is no single compelling definition of crime or criminals that is acceptable to all criminologists, we should be able to improve on the examples just given. In the next two sections we shall explore two different ways of defining *crime* and *criminal*: the legalistic and the sociological. Here are the main points that distinguish the two perspectives:

Legalistic definition:

- Identifies crime and criminal in terms of a body of written law.
- Emphasizes legal elements in actions or events.
- Emphasizes responsibility and intent.
- Recognizes specific situations in which responsibility may be challenged or waived.

Sociological definitions:

- Recognize similarities between acts or events that are illegal and those that are not.
- Recognize that law in action is substantially different from law on the books.
- Distinguish between crime as something people do and crime as a label that may be attached to certain acts, people, or events.
- Emphasize the role of social variables such as class, power, and race/ethnicity in the creation and application of criminal labels.

THE LEGALISTIC DEFINITION OF *CRIME*

legalistic definition of crime Crime is a human act that violates the criminal law.

substantive criminal law A body of written law that defines crimes and specifies the criminal penalties associated with them.

procedural criminal law A body of written law that specifies the rules to be followed by the state when dealing with crimes and criminals

actus reus The wrongful conduct, or activity, that constitutes a crime.

mens rea The intent, or "guilty mind," behind the wrongful conduct.

The **legalistic definition of crime** says that *crime is a human act that violates the criminal law.* This definition has two important components: (1) crime involves behavior: someone has actually to do something—or fail to do something required by law, such as file an income tax return; and (2) the behavior in question is specifically identified as crime in a body of written law. The law that identifies crimes is called **substantive criminal law.** This is distinguished from **procedural criminal law,** which sets down the rules the state must follow when processing crimes and criminals—for example, the legal procedures used to investigate crimes and to prosecute criminals.

An action or event is legally a crime if all the following elements exist:

- *There must be wrongful conduct.* Referred to as ***actus reus,*** literally, a "guilty or evil act." Pulling out a loaded pistol and pointing it at someone, falsifying a signature, dumping toxic waste, filing through the bars of a prison cell, or drawing up plans to rob a bank are examples. Mere thoughts, no matter how terrible, are not crimes.
- *The wrongful conduct must be intentional,* expressed in the concept ***mens rea,*** or guilty mind. It is not just the physical act that is taken into account but also the mental state of the person performing it. To quote the famous U.S. Supreme Court Justice Oliver Wendell Holmes, "Even a dog distinguishes between being stumbled over and being kicked." However, unintentional acts resulting from negligence or omission may qualify as crimes in some cases. For example, a charge of negligent homicide might be brought against someone who caused a fatal accident by failing to maintain proper control while driving down the highway. Together, *actus reus* and *mens rea* constitute the *corpus delicti,* which literally means "body of the offense."
- *The conduct and the intent must be concurrent.* This means that the conduct must coincide, or be consistent with, the underlying intent. To use Justice Holmes' example of the dog, if I went looking for the dog with the intention of kicking it but I accidentally stumbled over it instead, the dog would be right to assume I had committed no crime. If I then turned around and kicked it, that would be a different story—and both the dog and the courts would recognize the difference.
- *The conduct must constitute a social harm.* This means that the conduct must be injurious to the state, the "body politic" or "the people." Something that harms an individual private citizen—adultery or gambling, for example—might not qualify as a social harm. The distinction mirrors the long-standing legal doctrine that the state—historically in the body of the king or ruler—is the true victim of crime. This doctrine recognized a distinction between the individual citizen and the collective. In theory the law is concerned with the interests of society as a whole, but if it also serves the interests of people as individuals, all the better.

It is sometimes claimed that certain activities harm only the people doing them, and therefore should not be crimes. Marijuana users have made this claim, as have gamblers and prostitutes. The common counterargument is that these acts are socially harmful because they undermine the family or have economic costs that society must bear. From this point of view there are no so-called "victimless" crimes.

inchoate offenses Incomplete or partial acts that could cause harm if they were actually carried out.

Yet another complication relating to harm concerns actions that have not actually occurred, but could cause harm if they did. In law these are called **inchoate offenses,** meaning that they are incomplete or partial. They include unsuccessful attempts to commit a crime, and (in most states) conspiracies. For

An important consideration when labeling an act a crime is the social harm caused by it. In some places gambling is illegal or highly restricted, yet many people believe that it should not be a crime because it is a consensual act with no clear-cut victim. What do you think?

Photo by Tom Campbell, courtesy of Liaison International

example, if you and a fellow student were overheard planning to steal a criminology book from your professor's office, you could be charged with conspiracy even if you did not go through with the theft.

- *The harm must be caused by the conduct.* In assessing whether a particular act is a crime, the law also requires that the harm is caused by that act, and not by some other. Causation may be obvious—a person is stabbed and quickly dies from loss of blood—or it may be unclear—a person is stabbed and dies six months later from an infection. While no one would dispute that the stabbing occurred and caused an injury, a judge or jury might decide in the second case that the stabbing did not cause the victim's death, and thus find the defendant innocent of murder—but perhaps guilty of aggravated assault.
- *The conduct must be prohibited by law.* Conduct that is lawful, even though socially harmful and committed intentionally, is not a crime. Neither is conduct prohibited by families, schools, churches, or other groups, unless it is also prohibited by the criminal law.
- *The conduct must be punishable by law.* In fact, the punishment must be specified in advance of the conduct. A person who intentionally commits a harmful act for which there is no lawfully designated punishment has not committed a crime. This legal element in crime recognizes that a person cannot be held criminally liable today for conduct that may be prohibited tomorrow.

The Legalistic Definition of *Criminal*

Consistent with the legalistic definition of crime, a *criminal* is someone who is *legally capable of behavior that violates the criminal law and who has intentionally engaged in such behavior.* Prominent defenses against criminal charges are shown in Box 1.1.

To say that a criminal must be "legally capable" implies that some people are not. The law recognizes that some people are incapable of committing a crime due to their young age or their mental state. For centuries, and throughout the Western world, children under age 7 have generally been considered incapable of committing crime. The belief is that logical reasoning does not develop until that age,

Box 1.1

JUSTICE AND THE LAW

MAJOR DEFENSES AGAINST CRIMINAL CHARGES

There are various legal defenses that, if successful in court, mean that a person is legally blameless of the crime he or she is charged with. Although the defendant may have engaged in socially harmful conduct, criminal responsibility is waived. Some of the major defenses are as follows:

DEFENSE	DEFINITION AND EXAMPLE
Age	The person is below the age of criminal responsibility, usually 7 years.
Insanity	The defendant lacks the mental capacity for criminal responsibility or suffers from a mental disease or illness that renders the defendant insane or of unsound mind. Five prevalent tests for insanity are as follows: (1) *M'Naghten Rule.* It must be competently shown that the defendant did not know what he or she was doing or did not know that it was wrong. (2) *"Wild Beast" Test.* The defense must show that the defendant was acting like a "raving maniac," having no more knowledge of what he or she was doing than a wild beast. (3) *Irresistible Impulse Test.* Defendants may be declared innocent if irresistible impulses make them incapable of controlling their behavior. (4) *Substantial Capacity Test.* The defendant was unable to understand the wrongfulness of his or her conduct, or to control it according to the requirements of the law. (5) *Severe Mental Disease.* The defendant, as a result of severe mental disease or defect, was unable to appreciate the nature and quality of the wrongfulness of the act. Used in federal courts.
Self-Defense	Use of force is deemed justifiable if it is established that the defendant was in fear of injury or death, was unable to escape the situation, and was not the instigator of aggression. The belief that force was necessary to prevent harm to self need only be *reasonable* given the circumstances.
Necessity	An illegal act is committed in the belief that doing so will prevent harm to self or others or avoid a greater evil. This defense has been used to excuse cannibalism by dying sailors and also for much more common acts such as breaking into someone's home to escape a snowstorm or to call 911 in an emergency.
Defense of Property	Most states allow a person to use counterforce to prevent someone from forcibly entering his or her residence. Generally, *deadly* force may

Box 1.1 (continued)

	not be used unless the property owner reasonably fears for his or her life. In this case, the situation merges with one of self-defense. However, the so-called "Make My Day" laws adopted in Colorado and a few other states have broadened the conditions under which deadly force may be justified.
Statutes of Limitation	Statutes of limitation exist for most offenses (except crimes carrying the death penalty), and they specify the time limit during which criminal responsibility lasts. If the time has expired, an offender cannot be prosecuted for the crime. This is not a defense in the true sense, but has the same effect of absolving the offender of responsibility.
Mistake	In general, "ignorance of the law is no excuse," but there are times when a person truly believes that the law does not apply. For example, a person may take someone else's property believing it to be their own. This is a mistake of *fact.* In this case, there was no intent to steal. A mistake of *law* is a defense if it is shown that the defendant did not, and could not, have known of a specific law that requires a certain action, such as registering with police.
Entrapment	This defense involves showing that a law enforcement agent posed as a participant in a crime and persuaded the defendant to commit a crime when he or she would not normally do so. It is used most often as defense in consensual crimes such as drug sales and prostitution, where detection of criminal activity often requires police to go undercover or set up opportunities for crime.
Involuntary Act	An example of this defense is a person doing injury to another while sleepwalking, hypnotized, or in a state of near unconsciousness.
Duress	Duress or coercion is a defense *if* the defendant, through no personal fault, is put in fear for his or her life or the life of another. Most states require that the threat is of greater magnitude than the crime itself. For example, while robbing a service station because your life is threatened by someone if you don't might be excused, killing the service station operator during the robbery probably would not be. In addition, a duress defense is generally not accepted if it shown that the defendant had the opportunity to get out of the situation but chose not to.
Alibi	An alibi is a witness-supported defense based on the claim that the defendant was not present at the scene of the crime during the time it was carried out.

and therefore children under 7 cannot be held responsible for their actions, no matter how serious. However, in response to growing public concern over rising rates of juvenile violence, most states now have no specified minimum age of criminal responsibility (Griffin, Torbet, and Szymanski, 1998: 16).

The issue of mental state is best illustrated by the *insanity defense.* Essentially, the insanity defense is a claim that an offender lacks the mental capacity for criminal responsibility. A closer look will show how this defense can be used to challenge a criminal charge, but also that it is a controversial—and usually unsuccessful—defense. It most often surfaces when defense attorneys see no other valid defense.

Challenging Criminal Charges: The Insanity Defense. Before 1843 there was no such thing as an insanity defense, although differences in mental capacity had been recognized since the days of ancient Greece (Robinson, 1996). In 1843, Daniel M'Naghten was found not guilty of murder by reason of insanity. M'Naghten killed Edward Drummond, secretary to British prime minister Sir Robert Peel. It was a case of mistaken identity, for M'Naghten was trying to assassinate Peel, not Drummond. Defense attorneys successfully claimed that M'Naghten *did not know what he was doing at the time of the crime.* This became part of the so-called **M'Naghten Defense** (or *M'Naghten Rule*). It was the first time a court had found a defendant not guilty by reason of insanity. As subsequently applied in practice, this insanity defense also included the alternative test: *an inability to distinguish right from wrong.*

M'Naghten Defense The defendant did not know what he or she was doing at the time of the crime or was unable to distinguish right from wrong.

substantial capacity test The defendant is unable to understand the wrongfulness of an act or to conform to the requirements of the law.

Figure 1.1 shows that most American states use either the M'Naghten Defense—or a modified version of it—or the substantial capacity test (Simon and Aaronson, 1988). The **substantial capacity test** rests on a person's inability to understand the wrongfulness of an act, or to conform to the requirements of the law. It was proposed in 1962 by the American Law Institute in its Model Penal Code (MPC). The MPC is often used as a reference point for discussions of criminal definitions and procedure, but its provisions have no legal force.

Criticism and Reform of the Insanity Defense. The insanity defense has come under increasing criticism in recent years, with some people calling for its removal altogether. The highly publicized 1982 acquittal of John Hinckley, Jr. for the attempted assassination of President Ronald Reagan put the insanity defense center stage. Psychiatrists hired by the defense successfully convinced the court that Hinckley was psychotic and suffering delusions at the time of the shooting. Using the substantial capacity test, Hinckley was found not guilty by reason of insanity.

Many people were outraged, and Congress quickly moved to restrict use of the insanity defense in federal cases. The *Insanity Defense Reform Act of 1984* specifies that severe mental disease or defect must have caused a defendant to be unable to appreciate the wrongfulness of the act. The new law also shifted the burden of proof from the prosecution to the defense, which must show "clear and convincing evidence" of insanity. The law also limited the role of expert witnesses, who could no longer express an opinion as to whether a defendant's mental state was an element in the crime. That conclusion must be left to the judge or jury alone.

The Hinckley case and growing public concern about violent crime spurred many states to reconsider the insanity defense. Three states—Idaho, Montana, and Utah—abolished the insanity defense altogether, and a dozen others introduced the new plea of *guilty, but mentally ill* as a supplement to the traditional insanity defenses. This defense permits the court to find a defendant guilty as charged and to impose a prison sentence. However, correctional authorities are required to provide psychiatric treatment during the term of imprisonment.

The insanity defense is especially controversial when it is used in highly publicized trials involving despicable crimes that the accused admits commit-

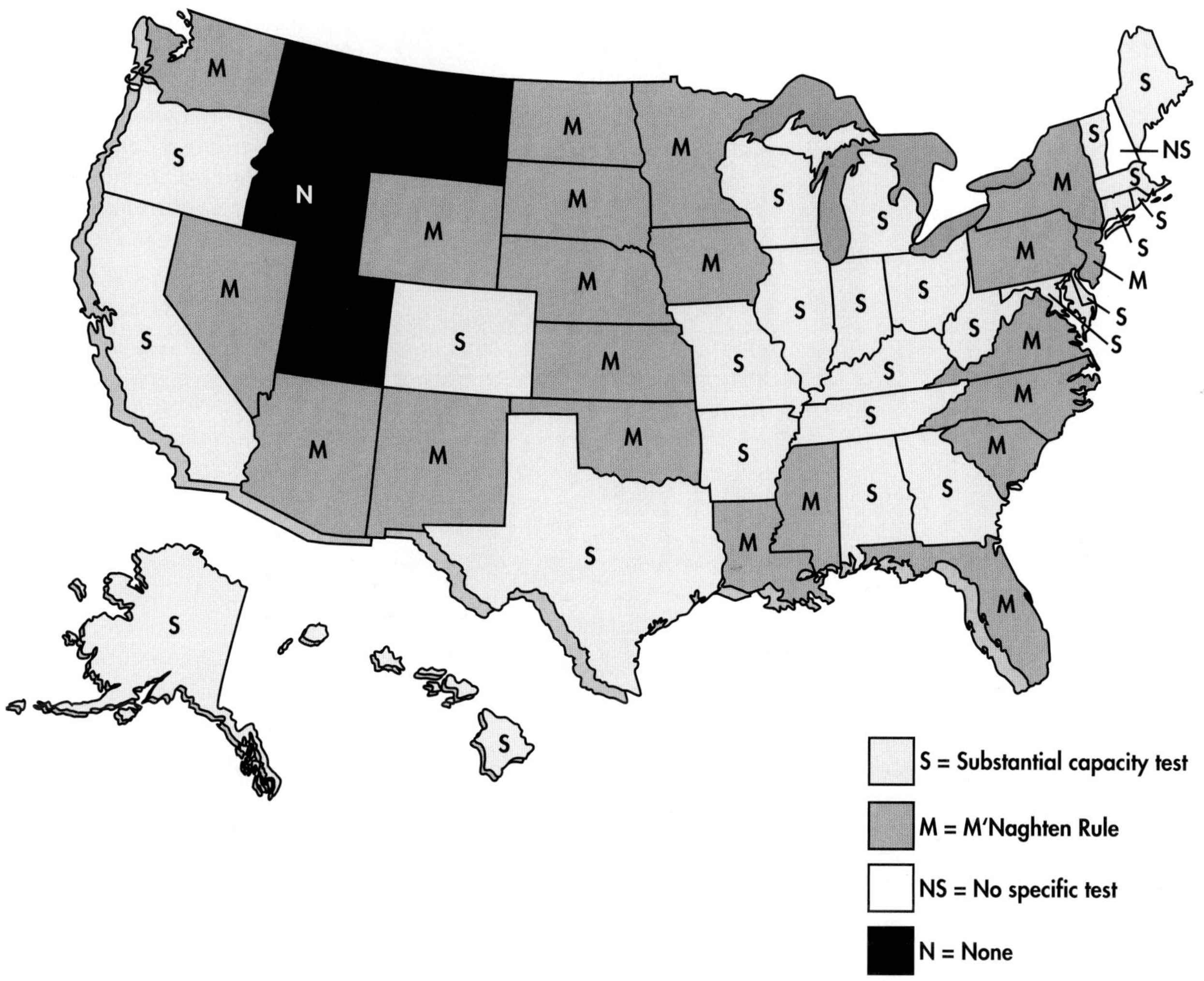

FIGURE 1.1 TYPES OF INSANITY DEFENSES USED BY THE STATES
Most states use either the M'Naghten Rule or the substantial capacity test to determine whether an offender is insane. Some states allow for both methods, or modified versions of either method.

Source: Figure created from data in Rita Simon and David Aaronson (1988). *The Insanity Defense* (pp. 251–263). Copyright © 1988 by Praeger Publsihers. New York: Praeger. Reprinted with permission.

ting. When the lawyer for 12-year-old schoolyard mass murderer Andrew Golden tried to use the substantial capacity defense, the judge rejected it (Associated Press, August 12, 1998). Even a finding of guilty but mentally ill may be objectionable to a judge or jury. This was apparently so in the 1991 trial of Jeffrey Dahmer, who admitted killing seventeen men, most of whom he then dismembered. Police found genitalia stuffed in a kettle, two heads in a freezer, and four torsos jammed in a barrel (*Newsweek,* August 5, 1991:40–42). Testimony showed that Dahmer had anal intercourse with some of the dead bodies. Since Dahmer did not dispute that he had killed the men, the only issue for the jury was his mental state at the time. The jury decided that Dahmer was sane. He was sentenced to fifteen life terms without parole—and was subsequently beaten to death in November 1994 by another inmate.

To complicate the insanity issue, insanity is generally regarded as a legal term, not a psychiatric one. However, psychiatrists give expert testimony in

One defense against criminal charges is insanity; however, it is rarely used and rarely successful. Jeffrey Dahmer, who admitted killing 17 men and committing atrocities on the dead, was found to be sane by a jury.

PHOTO COURTESY OF AP/WIDE WORLD PHOTOS

court to help the judge or jury understand different mental states according to current medical knowledge. Lawyers and psychiatrists who represent the defense invariably find their testimony contradicted by lawyers and psychiatrists representing the state. It is no wonder that judges and jurors often have difficulty deciphering all the technicalities involved in insanity cases, and the more complex the crime, the harder it becomes.

Other Defenses against a Criminal Charge. Insanity and age are only two possible defenses against accusations of a crime. Box 1.1 lists a variety of other legal defenses. Some of these are **situational defenses,** in the sense that they relate to the circumstances surrounding an incident. Examples are duress, mistake, self-defense, and necessity. These defenses are raised by the defendant's counsel, who bears the burden of proof. Lawyers call this an **affirmative defense.** Basically, the defense counsel tries to present the undisputed facts of the offense in a new light based on an alternative interpretation of the circumstances surrounding the alleged crime. In a murder case, for example, attorneys might try to show that their client killed the victim accidentally or in self-defense.

situational defense A defense against criminal charges based on circumstances surrounding the incident.

affirmative defense A defense raised by the defendant's counsel, who has the burden of proof and tries to present the undisputed facts of a case in a new light.

procedural defense The claim that a defendant's rights were violated by police or other criminal justice personnel.

Another category consists of **procedural defenses.** These are based on claims that a defendant's rights were violated during the process leading up to prosecution for the alleged crime. For example, the defense may claim *entrapment.* This defense is most often used in drug and prostitution cases, and it is both a situational and a procedural defense. Entrapment occurs when police officers induce someone to commit a crime that the person would not ordinarily have committed. A successful procedural defense usually means that the person who actually did the crime goes free—at least this time. Some people get very angry when they think of offenders going free on "technicalities," but the existence of procedural defenses is a check against the power of the state, and against abuses of authority by its agents.

The New "Innovative Defenses." A whole new category of defenses has emerged in recent years, sometimes called *innovative* or *exotic* defenses. They include the "black rage" defense, "urban survival syndrome," "battered wife syndrome," "abused child syndrome," and "rape trauma syndrome"; more will be said about them in Chapter 12. Generally, these defenses argue that the abusive and oppressive conditions under which some people live create such mental distress that they are driven to criminal acts. Basically, the abuse defense turns the offender into a victim who is acting in self-defense.

Defense attorneys in some recent high-profile trials have had mixed success in using these innovative defenses. In 1994, Lorena Bobbitt was acquitted of malicious wounding after cutting off her husband's penis while he slept; the jury was told of a history of sexual and physical abuse by John Wayne Bobbitt. In this case, defense attorneys successfully linked the abuse to the more conventional irresistible impulse insanity defense. In the case of Lyle and Erik Menendez, who killed their parents in a gruesome shotgun slaying, the defense said years of sexual abuse by their father was part of an abusive home environment that had driven the boys to murder. The abuse defense produced a hung jury at the first trial, but in 1996 a second trial resulted in a conviction; the brothers are now in prison.

The "black rage" defense was first used to defend Colin Ferguson, charged with murdering six passengers and wounding nineteen others on the Long Island Rail Road in 1993. The victims were all white or Asian American, and Ferguson is African American. The late celebrated civil rights attorney William Kunstler was one of the lawyers originally representing Ferguson. Kunstler did not contest that Ferguson committed the murders, but claimed that the massacre was triggered by an insane rage resulting from the racial injustices of an oppressive white society. We do not know whether this defense would have succeeded in court because Ferguson fired his attorneys and represented himself during the trial. He was convicted of all charges.

The issue of racial injustice was prominent during the O. J. Simpson murder trial. Although "black rage" was not used as a defense, racism was raised by the defense in cross-examination of detective Mark Fuhrman, a white police officer who had gathered crucial evidence against Simpson. The defense team, led by African American attorney Johnnie Cochran, showed that Fuhrman had lied under oath when he denied using the word *nigger* in reference to blacks. The jury apparently wondered: With his credibility destroyed, why should any of his other testimony be believed? Cochran made a convincing case that a racist white cop was lying—and might even have planted evidence—in order to convict a black hero.

Much of the African American community apparently believed him. Opinion polls taken after Fuhrman's testimony but before the verdict came in showed that 77 percent of white respondents thought Simpson was guilty; *almost the same percentage of African Americans thought he was innocent* (Associated Press, October 1, 1995). The Simpson case brought the issue of race and criminal justice to the forefront of public debate, and its long-term impact is yet to be assessed. It is important to keep in mind that if black and white Americans have significantly different views of how American justice works, they will tend to behave differently as victims, witnesses, and members of juries. A "social reality" of criminal justice is constructed out of the everyday experiences people have with crime and criminals, and with police, courts, and corrections. This text will show that the reality of justice is not the same for all groups of Americans. For example, Table 1.1 shows how black and white Americans differ in their opinions about police behavior. Black Americans are more likely than white Americans to think that racism is common among police, that police overreaction to crime is a threat to citizen rights, and that police treat black citizens worse than white citizens; but black Americans are less likely than white Americans to approve of police striking suspects.

TABLE 1.1 Opinions about Police Behavior among Black and White Americans

Americans differ in their experiences with and perceptions of criminal justice. This table shows substantial differences among black and white Americans in their opinions about police behavior. The findings were compiled from various recent national surveys.

QUESTION	GENERAL PUBLIC	BLACKS	WHITES
From what you know, is racism and falsification common among members of your local police force?			
Yes, common	20%	53%	15%
No, not common	64	32	70
How serious a threat to Americans' rights and freedoms is police overreaction to crime?			
Very serious threat	27%	43%	24%
Moderate threat	20	27	42
Not much of a threat	32	28	32
As far as you know, do the police in your community mostly treat blacks worse then whites, or both races about equally?			
Black worse than white	14%	42%	11%
Mostly equally	74	47	76
Would you approve of a policeman striking a citizen who was attempting to escape from custody?			
Yes	75%	57%	78%
No	21	36	18
Are their situations you can imagine in which you would approve of a policeman striking an adult male citizen?			
Yes	71%	45%	76%
No	26	48	22

Note: Percentages do not add up to 100 because "don't knows" and mixed responses have been omitted.
Source: Jean Johnson (1997). "Americans' Views on Crime and Law Enforcement." *NIJ Journal* (September) 9–14.

SOCIOLOGICAL APPROACHES TO THE DEFINITION OF CRIME

Successful or not, the innovative defenses against criminal charges just discussed draw attention to sociological issues that lurk in the background of the legalistic perspective. Let us then consider alternative sociological perspectives on the definitions of *crime* and *criminal.*

Many criminologists believe that the legal definition of crime is too restrictive (Sellin, 1938; Reiman, 1984; Gottfredson and Hirschi, 1990). A prominent argument is that many socially harmful acts that are not considered crimes under the law have similar or worse consequences in terms of loss of life, physical injury, or property loss, yet no one is arrested or goes to prison for committing them. The current controversy over the regulation of tobacco products illustrates the debate. The workplace, the environment, political campaigns, and international banking are other arenas where legal distinctions between crimes and other harms are uncertain and have been hotly debated. When compared with the legalistic approach, this perspective expands the range of behaviors defined and studied as crimes.

The Labeling Perspective. An alternative to the emphasis on crime as behavior is represented by the so-called **labeling perspective,** or *societal reactions perspective.* This view argues that crimes are distinguished from other acts because they have been defined as crimes by people whose reactions matter. In other words, the meaning and social impact of behavior are established by the reactions to it (Durkheim, 1964 [1893]; Becker, 1963). The perspective draws attention to the behavior, attitudes, and characteristics of the people *doing the labeling,* not just the people being labeled.

labeling perspective The meaning and social impact of behavior is established by the reactions to it.

The social transformation of behavior into crime and people into criminals is called **criminalization.** The opposite process—when the label *criminal* is removed from an action, event, or person—is called **decriminalization.** Supporters of the labeling perspective believe that to understand the social reality of crime, we must learn why and how this transformation occurs. How people perceive the actions of others, and what they do about it, should be central issues in the study of crime and justice. From this point of view, the goal is to describe and explain variations in criminalization, and to assess the consequences of those variations for the individuals involved and for society as a whole.

criminalization The labeling of acts, events, or people as criminal.

decriminalization The removal of the criminal label from acts, events, or people.

Some People Are More Likely to Be Labeled Criminal than Others. According to the labeling perspective, people acquire their social identities through other people's reactions to them. Basically, people are "criminal" because someone in authority has applied a criminal label to them, and other people are "law abiding" because that label has not been applied. As we shall see time and again, criminal labels are not applied uniformly. As a rule, people who are young, poor, less educated, or members of minority groups are more likely than others to be labeled criminal.

As will be shown in Chapters 2 and 6, one reason for this is that the police concentrate their energies in areas of towns and cities where such people tend to live and congregate. Another reason is that the process of criminalization is tied up with politics and the power structure. Low-status people tend to have less say in the political process, and this reduces their influence on the creation and enforcement of criminal law. As more powerless members of society, they are more vulnerable to being labeled criminal, whether or not they have actually committed any crimes.

To illustrate, consider the "Mariel Boat People" (Hamm, 1995). In 1980, over 120,000 Cubans left the Port of Mariel for the United States under an agreement between the Cuban and American governments. Most were entrepreneurs and professionals, but a few were ex-inmates and former mental patients. Three hundred and fifty of the Cuban immigrants were immediately imprisoned as "dangerous criminals," and between 1980 and 1987 a further 7,000 were imprisoned on various charges. However, an in-depth investigation of inmate files found that in many cases "their criminalization was not the product of their own behavior; rather, it came through the actions of overeager warriors of the state. . . . [N]umerous accounts indicated that . . . Cubans were incarcerated because they had no visible means of support, or because they did not have an appropriate sponsor" (Hamm, 1995:66).

The Saints and the Roughnecks: A Study of Delinquent Labeling. An important thing about criminalization is that the status of "criminal" is rarely determined solely by what a person does. Equally important, some people escape criminalization even though they are known to have committed offenses. A now-classic study by William Chambliss (1973) illustrates. Chambliss followed the experiences of two small-town juvenile gangs whose members were students at "Hannibal High" (a pseudonym). Both gangs regularly broke the law. However, only the members of one gang, the "Roughnecks," were considered delinquent by officials and repeatedly arrested. The other gang, which the author aptly calls the "Saints," largely escaped criminalization, and no members were ever arrested. Why the difference?

Four factors played an important role, and all related to the fact that the Roughnecks came from lower-class families, while the Saints came from "respectable" upper-middle-class families. First, the Roughnecks were more visible. Unlike the Saints, whose members had access to cars and could escape the local community, the Roughnecks had little choice but to hang out under the surveillance of neighbors and local authorities.

Second, the outward demeanor of the Saints deceived parents and officials. Around authority figures they were courteous and obedient, and if accused of misbehavior they were apologetic. The Roughnecks, in contrast, made no attempt to apologize when accused, and they made no effort to hide their hostile feelings. They also engaged in disturbances and fights. In short, the Roughnecks misbehaved openly while the Saints largely kept their misbehavior hidden.

Third, when responding to misbehavior, the authorities and community members clearly favored the Saints. The Saints were characterized as typical adolescents who were merely sowing their wild oats as normal boys do; the Roughnecks were defined as "trouble." Fourth, by defining the Roughnecks as trouble, the community reinforced their deviance and helped produce a self-fulfilling prophecy: Delinquent self-images emerged that promoted further delinquency, and Roughnecks found themselves seeking out, and being sought by, kids with similar self-images. As time went by, the escalating delinquency of the Roughnecks was matched and reinforced by escalating community disapproval and punishment. The Saints, meanwhile, remained respectable in the eyes of the community, although in fact they continued to maintain a high level of delinquency.

Whenever you hear that people have been labeled criminal by the authorities, ask not only, "What did they do?" but also, "What prompted the authorities to apply the label to these particular people?" If "what they did" adequately explains the label, then ask, "Why did this particular behavior become a crime?" The answer to this question may have more to do with characteristics of the people associated with the behavior than with the behavior itself.

Four Distinct Meanings of Crime. From these studies we can see that the labeling perspective views "criminal" as a status assigned to certain acts and certain people. Viewed in this way, crime actually has four distinct meanings:

1. *The creation of criminal labels.* Legislatures and government agencies create legal definitions of behavior through statutes and regulations. These statutes and rules identify acts that violate them and that therefore are crimes. Sometimes statutes are developed to cover new forms of behavior—use of ATMs, for example, or communication via the Internet—and sometimes statutes create new crimes out of old behaviors. The crime of *stalking* is an example (Krueger, 1997). California passed the first stalking law in 1990; by 1998 all 50 states had created the crime of stalking (Tjaden and Thoennes, 1998). Box 1.2 presents an overview of this new crime.
2. *The application of criminal labels through enforcement.* Those who enforce criminal law—such as police and prosecutors—also define crime. This idea recognizes that some laws on the books are never enforced and that others are enforced selectively. It stimulates the question "Why?" In practice, enforcement of a law does not necessarily result in arrest or prosecution. When it does, the acts of making an arrest and filing formal

Box 1.2

JUSTICE AND THE LAW

THE CRIME OF STALKING

"Stalking" is a new crime that many states rushed to enact following the 1989 murder of actress Rebecca Schaeffer and reports that comedian David Letterman had been harassed by a fan. In 1990, California passed the first law making stalking a crime; by 1998 all 50 states had followed suit.

WHAT IS STALKING?

Stalking is defined differently in different states. A typical definition is "willful, malicious, and repeated following and harassing of another person." However, three states include "lying in wait," and seven include "surveillance." Many states require a pattern of behavior, and some require that victims have a "reasonable" fear for their safety. Texas requires that the victim continue to be stalked *after* law enforcement officials have been notified. A model definition of stalking developed by the National Institute of Justice is as follows: "a course of conduct directed at a specific person that involves repeated visual or physical proximity, nonconsensual communication, or verbal, written or implied threats, or a combination thereof that would cause a reasonable person fear." Applying this definition, a national survey of 8,000 men and 8,000 women estimated that 1 in 12 American women and 1 in 45 American men had been stalked at some time in their lives.

WHAT ARE THE LEGAL ELEMENTS OF THE CRIME?

Most stalking statutes require that the defendant engage in threatening behavior and possess criminal intent. If an action would cause a reasonable person to feel threatened, it satisfies this threat requirement in most states. However, thirteen states require not just threat, but also the apparent ability to carry it out. To show intent, most states require evidence that the defendant intended to cause reasonable fear. Twelve states, however, do not require intent if it is shown that the defendant's behavior actually caused fear.

WHAT IS THE PENALTY FOR STALKING?

Most states treat stalking as a misdemeanor, carrying a penalty of up to a year in jail. However, many states have enhancement provisions that turn stalking into a felony and permit courts to sentence offenders to many years in prison and to pay large fines. Typically, stalking is treated as a felony when it is a repeat offense, involves the same victim, or occurs within five or ten years of a previous conviction.

Sources: National Institute of Justice (1993). *Project to Develop a Model Anti-Stalking Law.* Washington, D.C.: U.S. Department of Justice; Kenneth R. Thomas, (1993). "How to Stop the Stalker: State Antistalking laws." *Criminal Law Bulletin* (March–April): 124; Patricia Tjaden and Nancy Thoennes (1998). "Stalking in America: Findings from the National Violence Against Women Survey." *NIJ Research in Brief* (April): 1–19.

charges also apply the crime label. In effect, people who are not arrested escape criminalization.

3. *The confirmation of criminal labels through conviction.* When defendants are convicted, they are once again criminalized within the framework of criminal law. Yet the personal and social consequences of criminalization at this stage are different from those at earlier stages. From a legalistic standpoint, people who are not convicted are not criminals. This is where the narrow legalistic definition of *criminal* shows a major weakness: It tends to take earlier phases of the criminalization process for granted.

4. *The validation of criminal labels through punishment.* Conviction makes an offender eligible for the imposition of criminal penalties. As we shall see in Part Four of the text, different kinds of penalties are imposed on offenders; some are unofficial—and may even be illegal (torture, for instance).

Criminalization is thus a complex process that cannot be taken for granted at any of its stages. Using these four meanings of crime encourages critical examination of all stages of the criminalization process, from defining acts as crimes to punishing people as criminals.

To summarize, definitions of *crime* and *criminal* that are alternatives to the legal definition can be stated as follows:

- *Crime* is a label that is attached to behavior and events by those who create and administer criminal law.

Consistent with this definition,

- A *criminal* is a person whose behavior has been labeled crime by those who create and administer criminal law.

You may still be wondering: Why focus on the actions of people who create and enforce the law when surely people are criminals because of something *they* do. The idea emphasized in this text is that criminalization represents a social process through which behavior and people are defined as criminal and made eligible for punishment. *No behavior is inherently criminal; someone must label it so.* As the Saints and Roughnecks study showed so well, criminalization sometimes occurs not because of something a person has done, but because of how they look, where they live, or the people they hang around with.

DISTINCTIONS AMONG TYPES OF CRIMES AND CRIMINALS

The law recognizes differences among crimes and criminals and so do the people who play a role in criminalization. This section introduces the major distinctions among crimes and criminals that will be recognized throughout this book.

Distinctions Relating to the Seriousness of Crime. The labeling of an act as crime is often noncontroversial (Braithwaite, 1989:38–42), because there is general agreement among members of society that certain acts should be designated as crimes. Who would disagree that robbery should be a crime, or murder, or child molesting? Yet there is less consensus about some other behaviors. What about marijuana use, gambling, or prostitution? Should cigarette smoking be criminalized? How about displaying pornography via the Internet? These questions are likely to produce disagreement, even heated disagreement. Ask your classmates, friends, or family.

Surveys have been conducted to tap opinions on the seriousness of crimes. In the early 1960s, for example, there was much agreement among a sample of judges, police officers, and university students asked to rate the seriousness of 141 offenses (Wolfgang and Sellin, 1964). A later survey of adults in Baltimore, Maryland, again found overall consensus on a similar list of illegal acts (Rossi, Waite, Bose, and Berk, 1974). However, this study also found a prominent difference between black and white respondents: Black respondents rated violence among family and friends lower in seriousness than did their white counterparts. So although there may be general agreement on crime seriousness, subgroups of the population may not share the general attitude toward a particular crime.

These findings were confirmed by a more recent study (Wolfgang, Figlio, Tracy, and Singer, 1985). A total of 204 crimes were rated on a scale of 0–100 by a national sample of 60,000 respondents (though no one person rated more than 25 offenses). Some of the specific crimes and their seriousness scores are shown in Table 1.2. Overall, there was broad consensus. Violent crimes were rated as more serious than property offenses, and drug dealing was taken very seriously. The survey also showed that people who had been victims of crime tended to assign higher seriousness scores than did others.

Some studies have looked at what people think the penalties should be for different crimes. Again, there is much consensus about the crimes people think should receive the harshest penalties—murder, robbery, rape, child molesting, burglary, and drug trafficking. Many people also support rehabilitation alongside punishment (McCorkle, 1993). Yet similar opinions may obscure important differences. Some of these differences fall along racial lines. For example, in one survey both black and white respondents supported harsher penalties for crime; however, among white respondents this view appeared to reflect racial prejudice, while among black respondents it was fueled by fear of being victimized by crime (Cohn, Barkan, and Halteman, 1991). These findings underscore just how important it is to consider the social context of criminalization—particularly the beliefs, social position, and experiences of people doing the labeling.

The Distinction between *Mala in Se* and *Mala Prohibita* Offenses. Criminalization has usually been linked with moral beliefs: Early criminal codes were a sort of catalog of sins. Even the extensive legal codes of ancient Greece and Rome fused morality with law. In some languages—Hungarian is one—the word for *crime* means not only an act that is illegal but also one that is evil or sinful (Schafer, 1969). As life grew more complex, however, the link between crime and sin weakened. Laws were passed to regulate activities in business, politics, and the family. Refusing to file an income tax return or agreeing with competitors to sell a product at a certain price would not be thought of as sins by most people. Yet today they are crimes.

Two legal concepts emerged to reflect these changes. Acts came to be designated either ***mala in se***—meaning evil in themselves—or ***mala prohibita***—meaning evil because they are forbidden. Examples of *mala in se* crimes, acts that are inherently evil, include incest, murder, arson, and robbery; examples of *mala prohibita* crimes include cocaine use, traffic violations, antitrust offenses, and embezzlement. Generally, crimes that are *mala in se* are thought of as more serious than *mala prohibita* offenses; the many Americans now serving long prison terms for drug crimes would rightly point to their offenses as exceptions. Another exception is found in the criminalization in many states of consensual sex involving homosexual acts, oral sex, and other sexual "deviance." These acts have been termed "unnatural" and "perverse," and offenders have faced potentially severe punishments. Today, although consensual sex offenses are still on the books in most American jurisdictions, the penalties are less severe than for many *mala prohibita* crimes, and the prohibitions are rarely enforced.

mala in se Acts that are evil in themselves.

mala prohibita Acts that are evil because they are forbidden.

The Distinction between Misdemeanors and Felonies. This distinction will be familiar to most readers, but you may not know just how significant it is. In most jurisdictions, **misdemeanors** are relatively minor crimes that carry maximum sentences of one year or less in a local jail. **Felonies** are more serious offenses that carry maximum penalties of death or imprisonment for more than one year in a state or federal prison. Conviction of a felony may also carry what are called **collateral consequences.** These include loss of the right to vote or hold public office, loss of license or ability to practice a profession, and loss of the right to purchase a firearm. Most of this text will be concerned with felonies and felony offenders.

misdemeanor A relatively minor offense punishable by up to one year in jail.

felony A more serious offense punishable by more than one year in a state or federal prison.

collateral consequences Automatic penalties such as loss of citizenship or loss of the right to hold public office.

TABLE 1.2 Seriousness Scores from the National Survey of Crime Severity

Score	Offense
HIGHEST SCORES (ON A SCALE OF 0–100)	
72.1	A person plants a bomb in a public building. The bomb explodes and 20 people are killed.
52.8	A man forcibly rapes a woman. As a result of physical injuries, she dies.
47.8	A parent beats his young child with his fists. As a result, the child dies.
43.2	A person robs a victim at gunpoint. The victim struggles and is shot to death.
39.2	A man stabs his wife. As a result she dies.
39.1	A factory knowingly gets rid of its waste in a way that pollutes the water supply of a city. As a result, 20 people die.
35.7	A person stabs a victim to death.
35.6	A person intentionally injures a victim. As a result, the victim dies.
33.8	A person runs a narcotics ring.
33.0	A person plants a bomb in a public building. The bomb explodes and one person is injured but no medical treatment is required.
32.7	An armed person skyjacks an airplane and holds the crew and passengers hostage until a ransom is paid.
30.0	A man forcibly rapes a woman. Her physical injuries require hospitalization.
27.9	A woman stabs her husband. As a result he dies.
LOWEST SCORES	
0.2	A person under 16 years old plays hooky from school.
0.3	A person is a vagrant, that is, he has no home and no visible means of support.
0.5	A person takes part in a dice game in an alley.
0.6	A person trespasses in the backyard of a private home.
0.7	A person under 16 years old breaks a curfew law by being out on the street after the hour permitted by law.
0.8	A person is drunk in public.
0.8	A person knowingly trespasses in a railroad yard.
0.8	A person under 16 years old runs away from home.
0.9	A person under 16 years old is reported to police by his parents as an offender because they are unable to control him.
1.1	A person under 16 years old illegally has a bottle of wine.
SOME OTHER SCORES	
1.3	Two person willingly engage in a homosexual act.
1.4	A person has some marijuana for his own use.
1.6	A person breaks into a parking meter and steals $10 worth of nickels.
1.6	A person is a customer in a house of prostitution.
2.1	A person engages in prostitution.
2.2	A person steals $10 worth of merchandise from the counter of a department store.
3.1	A person breaks into a home and steals $100.
3.6	A person knowingly passes a bad check.
6.2	An employee embezzles $1,000 from his employer.
6.7	A person, using force, robs a victim of $10. The victim is hurt and requires treatment by a doctor, but not hospitalization.
7.4	A person illegally gets monthly welfare checks.
7.9	A teenage boy beats his father with his fists. The father requires hospitalization.
9.0	A person armed with a lead pipe robs a victim of $1,000. No physical harm occurs.
9.2	Several large companies illegally fix the retail prices of their products.
10.3	A person operates a store where he knowingly sells stolen property.
10.5	A person smuggles marijuana into the country for sale.
12.0	A police officer takes a bribe not to interfere with an illegal gambling operation.
13.9	A legislator takes a bribe from a company to vote for a law favoring the company.
14.6	A person using force robs a victim of $10. The victim is hurt and requires hospitalization.
16.4	A person attempts to kill a victim with a gun. The gun misfires, and the victim escapes injury.
17.7	An employer orders one of his employees to commit a crime.
18.3	A man beats his wife with his fists. She requires hospitalization.
20.6	A person sells heroin to others for resale.
21.7	A person pays another person to commit a serious crime.

Source: Marvin E. Wolfgang, Robert M. Figlio, Paul E. Tracy, and Simon L. Singer (1985). *The National Survey of Crime Severity,* (pp. vi–x). Washington, D.C.: U.S. Department of Justice.

Violence in the nation's schools is fueling calls for tougher treatment of juveniles. Trying them as adults may not be the best approach, but it is growing in popularity.

Illustration by Barrie Maguire, courtesy of The Creative Workshop

In the United States, the creation of criminal law is primarily the responsibility of states—although more and more federal crimes are created or expanded each year. Under this system, a misdemeanor offense in one state may be a felony offense in another, or it may not be a criminal offense at all. The best examples come from a category of crimes often referred to as "public order offenses." Prostitution and other consensual sex, gambling, loitering, vagrancy, drug sales, and many alcohol-related offenses fall into this category.

The distinction between felonies and misdemeanors has important consequences, not only for punishment but also for how arrests are made. Regardless of the seriousness of an offense, the basis for making an arrest is probable cause that a crime has been, is being, or is about to be committed. (The legal elements of probable cause are discussed in detail in Chapter 9). However, in misdemeanor cases, police do not normally arrest a suspect without first obtaining an arrest warrant, unless the misdemeanor was committed in the officer's presence. For example, if someone reports a misdemeanor crime, the police will interview witnesses and collect other evidence to determine whether there is probable cause to make an arrest. The police will then seek an arrest warrant. In some states the police have up to 18 months to complete their investigation and make an arrest. In the case of felonies, however, an officer who has not observed the offense but has probable cause to believe that a particular person committed the crime may arrest the individual without a warrant.

The Distinction between Adult and Juvenile Offenses. We have already seen that children under age 7 are generally considered incapable of committing crimes. In all states another distinction is made between juvenile offenders and adult offenders. Children between ages 7 and 18 are regarded as having criminal responsibility, but they are handled more informally than adults. Since the late 1800s they have been called *juvenile offenders* or *juvenile delinquents*—not criminals—and the offenses they commit have been called *delinquencies,* even though they may involve exactly the same behavior and harm as a crime. Because most of our attention will be focused on adult offenders, the terms *delinquent* and *delinquency* are rarely used in this text.

This is not meant to minimize the volume or significance of juvenile offenses. In fact, although juveniles represent less than 10 percent of the United States population, they represent over 20 percent of all arrests (Federal Bureau of Investigation, 1996). Even among arrests for serious crimes, juveniles make up around 40 percent of all arrests for property crimes, and just over 20 percent of all arrests for violent crime. It is predicted that juvenile arrests for violent crimes will double by the year 2010 (Office of Juvenile Justice and Delinquency Prevention, 1995).

Recognizing the significant contribution that juveniles make to the nation's crime problem, some states have moved away from use of terms such as *delinquent* and *delinquency* and have framed their juvenile codes around the seriousness of offenses assuming they were committed by an adult. The State of Washington is an example (Weis, Crutchfield, and Bridges, 1996:16–20). Its 1994 Juvenile Justice Act incorporated all the usual distinctions between misdemeanors and felonies and used the terms *crime* and *offense,* and *criminal* and *offender,* interchangeably. All references to delinquents or delinquency were removed; a juvenile offender is simply "any juvenile who has been found by the juvenile court to have committed an offense."

As of 1997, all states and the District of Columbia allow juveniles to be prosecuted as adults (Griffin, Torbet, and Szymanski, 1998). In most states, the process is called *waiver of jurisdiction;* this means that the juvenile court is giving up its authority over the child and passing that authority on to the criminal court. There is no consensus among states as to the minimum age at which a juvenile may be transferred to adult court (see Figure 1.2). Sixteen states have no statutory minimum age at all.

Juvenile court jurisdiction is generally waived for one of two reasons: (1) The offense is a violent felony that if committed by an adult would result in a lengthy prison term, or execution; or (2) the security and/or treatment in juvenile facilities is not considered in the best interests of the juvenile or the public. This generally applies to older juveniles and those with long criminal histories.

In response to rising rates of juvenile violence and perceptions that juveniles often get away with murder, many state legislatures have reformed the rules governing waivers. These statutory revisions have taken various forms: lowering the minimum age for waivers, broadening the range of offenses for which waivers may be sought, lowering the age of juvenile court jurisdiction from 18 to 16, and even excluding certain offenses—murder, for example—from the jurisdiction of juvenile court. These changes are reflected in the rising numbers of juveniles tried as adults: From 1985 to 1994, waivers increased from 7,200 to 12,300 cases (Butts, 1997a:1).

In addition, 31 states have created a special transfer provision covering juveniles who have previously been tried as adults. This "once an adult/always an adult" provision requires criminal prosecution of all subsequent offenses committed while the suspect was still technically a juvenile. Most states require that the juvenile must have been convicted in the earilier case; and Michigan, Minnesota, and Texas restrict use of once an adult/always an adult laws to juveniles accused of felonies (Griffin, Torbet, and Szymanski, 1998:10–11).

Although there is tremendous support among politicians and the general public for trying some juvenile offenders as adults—especially after highly publicized violent crimes by children such as the 1998 schoolyard murders in Jonesboro, Arkansas, by a 13-year-old boy and his 12-year-old friend—the

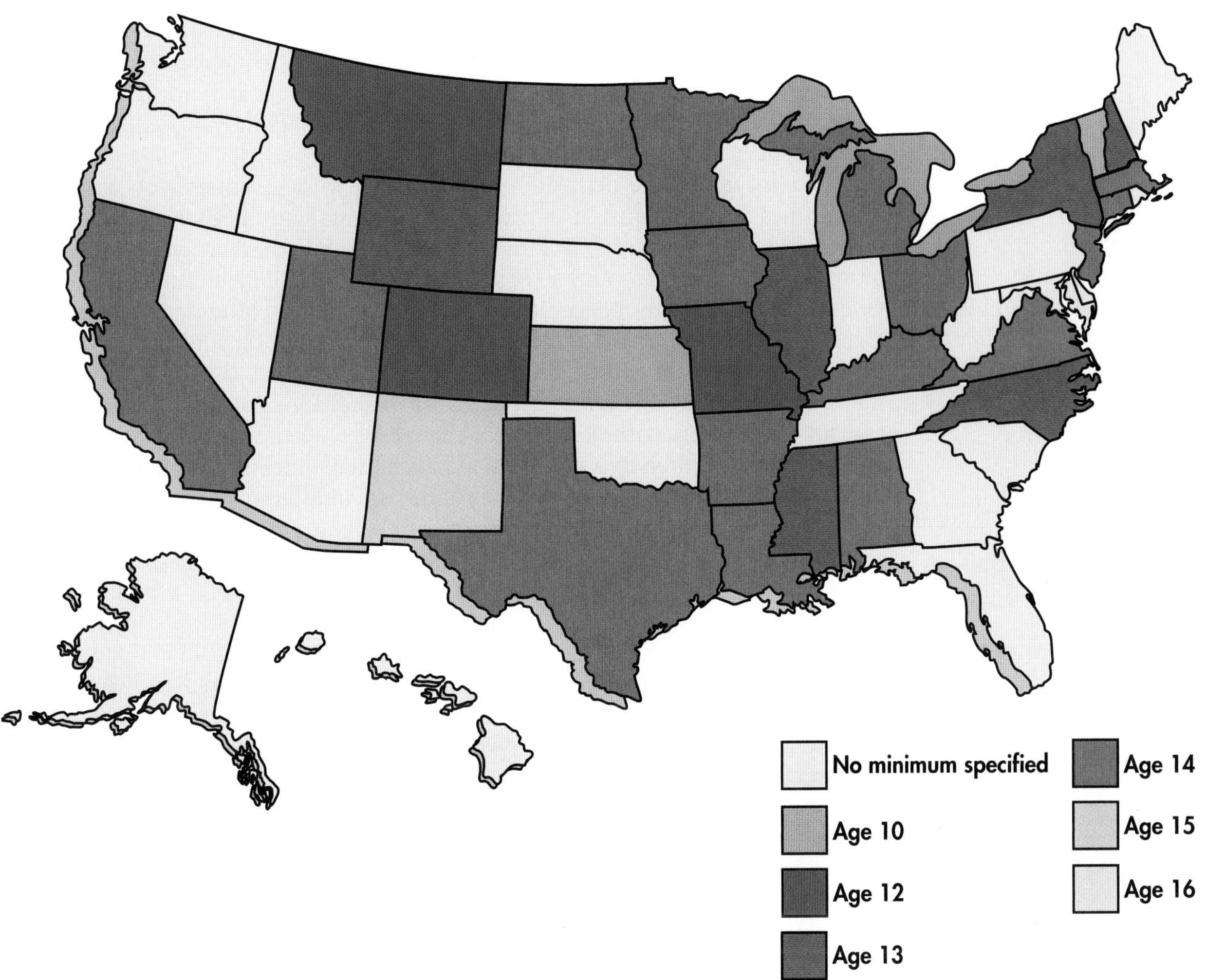

FIGURE 1.2 Minimum Age at Which Juveniles May Be Transferred to Criminal Courts

All states allow juveniles to be tried as adults, but the age at which this is permitted varies from state to state and usually depends on the offense. The lowest specified age is 10 (Kansas and Vermont) and the highest is 15 (New Mexico). In some states a lower minimum age is permitted for violent offenses; for example, Indiana sets the minimum age at 14 for most offenses, but at 10 for murder. In 23 states, the law allows juveniles to be transferred to criminal court under special circumstances where no minimum age is specified. These states are marked NS in figure above.

Source: Patrick Griffin, Patricia Torbet, and Linda Szymanski (1998). *Trying Juveniles as Adults in Criminal Court* (pp. 14–15). Washington, D.C.: U.S. Dept. of Justice.

practice is not without its critics. Some experts believe that the criminalization of juveniles is arbitrary and helps neither society nor the juvenile (Feld, 1993): Most juveniles waived to adult court are in fact charged with property crimes, and since they appear in adult courts as first offenders they typically escape imprisonment.

One answer to the problem of what to do with juveniles who commit violent crimes lies in devising a process of criminalization that recognizes *both* that they have committed serious offenses *and* that they are younger and vary more in maturity than adults (Feld, 1993). A juvenile criminal court that provides at least as many procedural safeguards as adult offenders enjoy but also gives juveniles somewhat "discounted" penalties in recognition of their age may be a step in the right direction.

Our examination of the concepts of *crime* and *criminal* has shown that criminalization is a complex process that results when attitudes, beliefs, behavior, and law converge in a certain way. To better understand what criminal justice is, we must first consider the broader societal context in which this convergence takes place. The next section of the chapter examines social control and the origins and development of criminal law.

SOCIAL CONTROL AND CRIMINAL LAW

All groups try to ensure that individual members behave predictably and in accordance with the expectations and values of the other group members. This is accomplished through a variety of mechanisms that are referred to collectively as *social control.* Societies are no different, although the task is usually far more complicated because of population size, geography, and differences among people in their backgrounds, daily activities, wealth, prestige, and power. Successful social control creates order in society, just as it creates order in school, neighborhoods, or the family.

TYPES AND SOURCES OF SOCIAL CONTROL

Social control may be informal or formal. Informal control appears in many forms: facial expressions such as a frown or a smile, physical gestures such as a friendly wave or an angry finger, or gossip. Informal social control is present in a kind word and in a nasty comment; it is also seen in gift giving, as well as in the withholding of favors. Figure 1.3 shows that sources of informal social controls may be close to or more distant from everyday activity. Close sources of control are found in family settings and among our friends. More distant sources of control are found in neighborhoods, communities, cities, and regions—in fact, all the way out to national and even international culture.

Formal social control is characterized by (1) explicit rules of conduct, (2) planned use of rewards and penalties to support the rules, and (3) designated officials who create, interpret, and enforce the rules (Davis, 1962). Formal social control also appears in different forms. Close sources of formal control are school and work; increasingly more distant from everyday activities are police, courts, and corrections. Law is a type of social control, and since its content is relayed and interpreted by intermediaries such as lawyers, police, and judges, it is the most distant type of formal social control. Figure 1.3 also illustrates these points.

THE ORIGINS AND DEVELOPMENT OF CRIMINAL LAW

civil law A body of written law governing the relationships among individuals and organizations.

Today, a variety of different kinds of law make up formal social control. The most extensive is **civil law.** Civil law deals with relationships among individuals and organizations, including disputes arising from accidents, medical mal-

INFORMAL CONTROLS				
Close ——————————— Distant				
Family/Peers	**Street**	**Neighborhood**	**Community**	**National Culture**
FORMAL CONTROLS				
Close ——————————— Distant				
Teachers/Employers	**Police**	**Courts**	**Corrections**	**Law**

FIGURE 1.3 SOURCES OF SOCIAL CONTROL

practice, libel, and other actions for which damages may be awarded victims under a branch of civil law known as the *law of torts.* Some torts are also crimes, such as assaults and destruction of property. Although O. J. Simpson was acquitted of criminal homicide, he was found liable for damages in civil court under the law of torts. The young English nanny Louise Woodward was punished for manslaughter in the killing of baby Matthew Eappen, but also faced a civil suit for damages *(USA Today,* June 17, 1998, p. 3A).

Another example of the links between civil and criminal law are the civil laws dealing with sex offenders that have sprung up around the country in recent years. In 1995, New Jersey passed the so-called Megan's Law, named after 7-year-old Megan Kanka, who was raped and murdered by a known child molester who had moved in across the street. Megan's Law requires authorities to notify communities of convicted sex offenders in their neighborhoods. By 1998, 36 other states had enacted similar laws (*Washington Post,* February 24, 1998, p. 3). Megan's Law has been upheld by the U.S. Supreme Court despite objections that it violates the constitutional rights of people who have already been punished for their crimes. Some states have also passed new laws allowing certain repeat sex offenders to be committed to secure mental facilities indefinitely after they have completed their prison sentences. A civil proceeding is held, and the burden of proving why commitment should not occur rests with the defendant.

Criminal law is concerned with the definition of crime and the designation of rules and procedures for dealing with it. Criminal law has its roots in the earliest legal codes, although the most important developments occurred in England between the twelveth and thirteenth centuries.

criminal law A body of written law dealing with the definition of crimes and procedures for dealing with them.

The Decline of Primitive Law. It is generally agreed that **primitive law**—the system of rules and obligations in preliterate and semiliterate societies—represents the foundation on which modern legal systems were built. Primitive law contains three important features:

primitive law A system of rules and regulations identifying private wrongs and based on self-help justice through retaliation.

- Acts that injured or wronged others were considered "private wrongs"—that is, injuries to particular individuals rather than the group or tribe as a whole. Exceptions to this were acts deemed harmful to the entire community, such as treason or witchcraft.
- Typically, the injured party took personal action against the wrongdoer, creating a kind of self-help justice. Today, the idea of self-help justice conjures up images of vigilantes. In primitive societies, there was no one to represent victims or to protect them.
- This self-help justice usually took the form of retaliation in kind: If you steal a farm animal from me, I will take one of yours; if you kill my son or daughter, I will kill a member of your family. Blood feuds were not uncommon under systems of primitive justice.

As the centuries passed, technological change brought about a growing division of labor, and populations began to increase. Strongly held customs and traditions gave way to new ideas and new ways of behaving. The family began to lose some of its autonomy and authority. Growing differences in wealth, prestige, and power meant new patterns of authority and decision making. The rise of chieftains and kings set the stage for the centralization of political authority, the establishment of territorial domains, and the emergence of the civil state. The handling of disputes slowly moved out of the hands of the people and into the hands of the state. The creation and enforcement of laws eventually became the dominant mechanism of formal social control.

These changes did not happen overnight. Today's criminal law is a product of centuries of change. The earliest known code of written law dates back to the 21st century B.C. This is the code of Ur-Nammu, the Sumerian king who founded the Third Dynasty of Ur. The famous Code of Hammurabi was discovered in 1901 in Susa, near the Persian Gulf. This code dates from around 1750 B.C. Other ancient codes of law include the Twelve Tables of Rome, the Mosaic code, the laws of ancient Greece, and the laws of Tacitus. All these codes show strong ties with the self-help justice typical of primitive law. Early forms of criminal law were contained in the law of torts—or private wrongs (Maine, 1905:341–342). The Twelve Tables treated theft, assault, and violent robbery as *delicta* (private wrongs), along with trespass, libel, and slander. The person, not the state or the public, was the injured party.

The maturing legal systems of ancient Greece and Rome eventually created offenses against the state (public wrongs, or *crimena*), as well as mechanisms for administration and enforcement. The establishment of permanent criminal tribunals around the first century B.C. represented a crucial step in the emergence of true criminal law (Maine, 1905). One of the most interesting features of these early codes is the number of activities they covered. The Code of Hammurabi was particularly wide ranging. The laws covered such diverse areas as kidnapping, unsolved crimes, price fixing, rights of military personnel, the sale of liquor, marriage and the family, inheritance, and slavery. Some of the laws would probably strike the modern reader as barbaric, while others might seem very reasonable. Table 1.3 illustrates some of the code's provisions. As in all early codes, the penalties were physical punishments such as death or mutilation, but compensation in goods or money was also permitted. The penalties also were varied according to the social status of the victim: the higher the victim's status, the greater the penalty. Women were considered inferior to men, children inferior to adults.

The early legal codes restated in formal, written terms many long-standing customs and traditions. But they also included new rules that were an attempt to regulate and coordinate increasingly complex economic activities and social relationships.

Historically, people with little wealth or power have been labeled criminals more often and punished more severely for their crimes than people higher up in the social order. The most powerful have been the most privileged. This is especially evident in matters relating to business and government, but it also applies to laws regarding sexual assault. Still today, women and poor people find it hard to protect their interests through law.

This can be illustrated by two examples. First, consider laws against rape. Far from meeting the needs of society as a whole—the functionalist view of law—rape laws have historically served the interests of males, the dominant group. They have actually victimized the women they are ostensibly designed to protect. Although there is clearly broad agreement that rape should be a crime—a consensus that has probably existed for centuries—rape laws are

TABLE 1.3 A Sample of Laws from the Code of Hammurabi

The Code of Hammurabi (sometimes spelled Hammurapi) was written around 1750 B.C. and discovered in 1901 in Susa, near the Persian Gulf. It was one of the first written codes of law. The code contained laws covering all sorts of things, from acts that we would today recognize as crimes to the relationship between employers and employees and between doctors and patients. Here are some examples of Hammurabi's laws:

- If someone kidnaped another's son, he was executed.
- If a boy struck his father, his hand was cut off.
- If an assailant caused a miscarriage, the penalty increased with the victim's status.
- If a woman killed her husband over another man, she would be impaled on a stake. (No law appears to have covered a man killing his wife over another woman).
- A person who stole from another paid compensation to the victim—the amount geared to the victim's status.
- A person who lent grain or silver and charged more than 20 percent interest would forfeit the principal.
- A builder who built a house that collapsed and killed the owner would be put to death; if the son of the owner was also killed, the builder's own son would also be put to death.
- A physician who operated on a member of the nobility and caused death or loss of sight had his hand cut off.

Source: Paraphrased from laws cited in Cyrus H. Gordon (1957), *Hammurapi's Code: Quaint or Forward Looking?* New York: Holt, Rinehart, and Winston.

written and enforced in such a way that males benefit. For example, until recently a husband could not rape his wife. In fact, throughout most of history rape was so narrowly defined, and the evidence needed to convict so specific, that successful prosecution of rape was almost impossible. The victim's behavior and character—whether she struggled or cried out, for example, or whether she was a virgin—was at least as important as the behavior of the rapist.

Conflict theorists, who see law as resulting from and protecting special interests rather than as an instrument of harmony and compromise, view rape not as an unfortunate consequence of otherwise functional arrangements such as dating, but as a reflection of gender differences in authority and power. Throughout history most societies have been patriarchal societies where men rule. Some psychologists have described rape as an assertion of male control and domination (Groth, 1979). Other writers argue that rape extends patriarchy into the most intimate and private realm: Men not only control how women behave in general, they also control how their bodies will be used (Russell, 1982; Messerschmidt, 1986; Matoesian, 1993).

The second illustration of how the law often undermines the interests of women and poor people is a controversy over the conflicting interests of a multinational corporation and Third World mothers. Some years ago the Nestlé Company launched an international campaign to promote its infant formula (Post and Baer, 1978). Ads proclaiming "Give your baby love and Lactogen" were used to promote the product in less-developed countries, where families are typically large and poor. However, the promotion discouraged mothers from breastfeeding and encouraged practices that were more expensive, irreversible, and, because of contaminated water supplies, potentially harmful. Many babies became ill, and some died. But Nestlé had committed no crime, nor were any sanctions imposed on the company. In effect, the law protected the company despite the harmful consequences of its actions.

Despite evidence such as this, it is conventional to argue that law is based on consensus—and lacking consensus, on compromise—and that it also reflects and supports the needs of society. Certainly, to some extent this is correct. In *The Leviathan,* published in 1651, English philosopher Thomas Hobbes warned that without law and a government to enforce it, life would be "solitary, poore, nasty, brutish, and short." The functionalist perspective on law asks us to think about how law and its enforcement serve societal needs and contribute to the smooth functioning of other social institutons—the family, the economy, and education, to name but three. It is essentially a conservative perspective, because it emphasizes stability and order. Conflict theory, on the other hand, says that if we also look behind the consensus and appearance of order, we will find that there is much dissent. Law—and social control in general—are shaped by differences in power and in the ability to participate in or influence law in action. Both perspectives are useful in the study of criminal justice.

ANGLO-AMERICAN CRIMINAL LAW

Criminal law in the United States draws mainly from Greek, Mosaic, and Roman law via English law. The common law of England can be traced to the reign of Henry II (1154–1189). For centuries English law had been a system of tribal justice, the primitive law of private wrongs and self-help retaliation. As feudalism took hold in the eighth and ninth centuries, Anglo-Saxon society underwent important changes. The family lost its autonomy; kings and kingdoms emerged; and the blood feud was replaced by a system of material compensation (usually money), controlled by individuals with special status such as kings, lords, and bishops. Equally important, political unification was underway, as territorial acquisitions by the new kings transformed a patchwork of small family-dominated territories into fewer, larger kingdoms. With the Norman conquest of 1066, complete political unification was but a short step away.

common law A body of national laws created by traveling courts in the twelfth century.

precedent A feature of common law in which prior court rulings guide future judgments; also known as *stare decisis.*

The Common Law. The Normans centralized their administrative machinery, including the courts. During the reign of Henry II, a court of **common law** was established. Representing the king, the courts decided which customs, social practices, and rules should be national laws that all citizens would follow—hence the designation "common." People with complaints and individuals charged with offenses were brought before courts that traveled around a specific route—called a circuit. The royal justices ruled on each case as it was brought before them. Their decisions were recorded and became a body of legal **precedent**—also known as *stare decisis*—to guide future judgments. Much of American criminal law has roots in English common law.

The Carrier's Case: A New Law to Meet New Economic Interests. Common law continually evolved as new cases came before the court. Often, the court would be faced with a situation where existing precedent didn't quite fit the current case. The judges could find the defendant innocent, which they sometimes did, or they could decide that the law should be extended to fit the new circumstances. One of the most famous examples of this was the so-called *Carrier's Case,* decided in 1473.

The Carrier's Case illustrates how both functional and conflict perspectives help us understand law in action (Hall, 1952; Chambliss, 1975a). This case involved a man hired to deliver bales of wool to Southampton, an English port city. Instead of doing so, he broke open the bales and took their contents. He was subsequently arrested and charged with felony theft. As theft law then stood, however, the man's actions did not legally constitute theft because he had lawful possession of the bales in the first place. Under existing rules he could not steal from himself or from the merchant who hired him. After much debate, a majority of the judges in the case found him guilty, and in doing so extended theft law to cover cases of "breaking bulk," as it was called.

Most people would probably agree that the verdict and the legal precedent it established were reasonable. After all, if you hire a truck driver to deliver goods and the driver steals them, you would probably expect the law to step in. At the time the Carrier's Case was decided, many important social changes were occurring that necessitated new rules, and this was especially true in the area of commerce and trade. The growing English textile industry needed a healthy international trade. It was important not only for the country but for the trading companies themselves. In this case, the functional interdependence of the economy and the law and their relationship to societal needs seems fairly clear.

Yet the functionalist view only partly explains what was going on. Although under existing common law the carrier had committed no crime, the law of torts allowed the merchant to sue for civil damages. Apparently, this was not enough, and the merchant class had become strong enough to press its case successfully: "The judges deciding the Carrier's Case had, then, to choose between creating a new law to protect merchants who entrusted their goods to a carrier or permitting the lack of such legal protection to undermine trade and the merchant class economic interests. The judges decided to act in the interests of the merchants despite the lack of a law" (Chambliss, 1975a:7). Because the new law made breaking bulk a crime against the state, it put carriers on notice that they could now be sued *and* imprisoned for breaking bulk. Imprisonment added no material benefit for the merchant, but represented a major symbolic victory for class interests.

The Development of Criminal Law in America. The Puritans brought English law to the New World, including common law. Over the next 400 years English common law was slowly "Americanized." The single most important event was the creation of the U.S. Constitution, which laid down the law of the United States. The U.S. Constitution is the final authority on the rights of individuals, the powers of state and federal governments to create and enforce laws, and the imposition of penalties on people who violate the law. The first ten amendments to the Constitution are known as the **Bill of Rights;** they lay out the rights that all citizens enjoy. The specific amendments of the Bill of Rights are listed in Chapter 9. Many of its provisions affect criminal justice. For example, among the criminal justice rights Americans enjoy are the following:

Bill of Rights Ten amendments added to the U.S. Constitution in 1791 that specify the rights of all citizens.

- the right against unreasonable searches and seizures (fourth Amendment)
- the right against being arrested without probable cause (fourth Amendment)
- the right against self-incrimination (fifth Amendment)
- the right not to be tried again for the same offense (fifth Amendment)
- the right to an attorney (sixth Amendment)
- the right to trial by jury (sixth Amendment)
- the right to cross-examine witnesses (sixth Amendment)
- the right to a speedy trial (sixth Amendment)
- the right not to be subjected to cruel and unusual punishment (eighth Amendment)

Courts have interpreted and reinterpreted the Bill of Rights many times over the years, and this important process will probably continue for centuries to come. As the nation's most powerful court, the U.S. Supreme Court has the last word on what these rights are in practice. Because the Court sometimes changes its mind, specific details of our constitutional rights may change from one generation of Americans to the next. This has great impact on law in action, and on the criminal justice system, as we shall see in later chapters.

The rules embodied in American criminal law come from four sources: (1) *federal and state constitutions;* (2) *decisions by courts,* including decisions of precedent and Supreme Court rulings; (3) *administrative regulations*—procedures developed by federal and state agencies as they carry out their legal duties; and (4) *statutory enactments by legislatures*—today the primary source of new criminal laws. Although courts create crime by establishing new precedents—for example, a court may decide that a particular magazine violates a state's obscenity law, or that a site on the World Wide Web is engaged in fraudulent practice—each state has a published list of statutes that make up the state's *criminal code.* Each year statutes are added, revised, or dropped, which is why these laws are usually called *revised statutes.* In Illinois, for example, the state's criminal law is found in Chapter 38 of the *Illinois Revised Statutes.* You will find a similar chapter in the statutes for your state. Many are now available on the World Wide Web.

The U.S. Congress also passes criminal laws that become part of the federal criminal code. Even though the U.S. Constitution reserves the bulk of criminal matters to the jurisdiction of states, the number of federal laws—and consequently the size of the federal enforcement machinery—has grown tremendously over the last 100 years. Some of the details and consequences of this expansion will be examined in Chapter 5. Suffice it to say that whenever an activity crosses state borders it becomes eligible for criminal labeling under federal statutes. As the nation's economic and urban life has grown in scope and complexity, so has the scope and complexity of the federal criminal code. In recent years, the drug trade has been the focus of many new federal laws, which have further expanded the reach of the criminal law.

Conflicts between Federal and State Law. At times, federal and state laws come into conflict. This is illustrated in the case of a new California law legalizing the medical use of marijuana. Passed in 1996, Proposition 215 allows people with illnesses such as AIDS, glaucoma, and cancer to use marijuana with the written approval of a licensed physician. Box 1.3 shows the main provisions of the law. Under federal law, however, it is illegal for private individuals to grow, distribute, or sell marijuana. Early in the morning on April 24, 1997, federal agents of the Drug Enforcement Administration (DEA) broke into a San Francisco warehouse owned by a group that regularly dispensed small amounts of marijuana to patients with properly signed authorization from their physicians. Marijuana plants were removed along with equipment and records. However, no arrests were made, and both the California attorney general and the San Francisco city attorney requested that the U.S. Attorney refrain from filing federal charges. The incident illustrates how overlapping state and federal jurisdiction in criminal matters makes it possible for some activities and people to be criminal and law abiding at the same time.

WHAT IS CRIMINAL JUSTICE?

criminal justice A society's system of roles and activities for defining and dealing with crime.

Now that the groundwork is laid, it is time to ask: What is criminal justice? **Criminal justice** is a modern society's system of roles and activities for defining and dealing with crime. In the United States today, criminal justice involves the actions of:

Box 1.3

JUSTICE AND THE LAW

THE COMPASSIONATE USE ACT OF 1996

Passed by California voters in November, 1996, Proposition 215 established the Compassionate Use Act, which puts California law in direct conflict with federal statutes dealing with marijuana. The California law was written "to ensure that seriously ill Californians have the right to obtain and use marijuana for medical purposes [when] recommended by a physician who has determined that the person's health would benefit from the use of marijuana in the treatment of cancer, anorexia, AIDS, chronic pain, spasticity, glaucoma, arthritis, migraine, or any other illness for which marijuana provides relief."

The law provides that neither patients nor their primary caregivers who obtain and use marijuana upon the recommendation of a licensed physician will be prosecuted or punished. The law also contains a provision "encouraging federal and state governments to implement a plan to provide for the safe and affordable distribution of marijuana to all patients in medical need of marijuana. . . ."

The law also protects physicians who dispense marijuana for medical purposes from punishment or the denial of any rights or privileges associated with their profession.

Federal and state laws sometimes conflict. The Compassionate Use Act of 1996, passed by California voters, allows the ill to use marijuana for medicinal purposes. This law conflicts with federal anti-drug laws, which federal authorities continue to enforce in California.

PHOTO BY MARK RICHARDS, COURTESY OF PHOTO EDIT

- State and federal legislatures, where rules governing crime and justice are enacted into law.
- Administrative agencies such as the Internal Revenue Service and the Food and Drug Administration, which create rules that carry criminal penalties if violated.
- Local, state, and federal law enforcement agencies.
- Prosecution and defense, made up of attorneys who practice criminal law and handle criminal cases in the courts.
- Municipal, state, and federal trial courts where criminal cases are handled.
- State and federal appellate courts, which rule on the constitutionality of actions taken by lower courts and by police and correctional agencies.
- Probation and parole agencies that provide services to the courts and to correctional agencies.
- Local, state, and federal correctional agencies, which carry out the punishment of convicted criminal offenders and oversee the operation of jails and prisons.
- Justice professionals such as private detectives, medical examiners, expert witnesses, jury consultants, criminologists, and law professors.
- Social service agencies providing treatment, counseling, and rehabilitation.
- Private companies that provide goods or services to individuals and agencies involved in criminal justice or employ criminal justice personnel.
- Special-interest groups such as the National Rifle Association (NRA), the American Civil Liberties Union (ACLU), the National Association for the Advancement of Colored People (NAACP), and the National Organization for the Repeal of Marijuana Laws (NORML).
- Private citizens who are crime victims, witnesses, or complainants, or who have ties with offenders or criminal justice personnel.

And, of course,

- Criminal suspects, defendants, and offenders.

The relationship between these different actors is shown in Figure 1.4, a "road map" of criminal justice in America. Decisions made at one point in the road flow along it and influence decisions made at other points. Notice again that the core agencies, or pillars, of the criminal justice system, are the police, the courts, and corrections. However, actions taken outside the core influence what happens inside, and vice versa. For example, in March 1997, the United States Supreme Court, the nation's highest appellate court, ruled unconstitutional a legislative decision by the State of Florida to take away from certain prison inmates the "good time" they had earned toward their release. Florida was forced to release hundreds of offenders who had served portions of lengthy sentences for murder, robbery, rape, and other serious crimes. The Court had upheld the rights of prisoners, but many private citizens and justice officials were concerned by the prospect of a mass release of violent criminals. In response, special-interest groups and the state legislature immediately sought ways to stop the release, and police organizations geared up for trouble.

The map in Figure 1.4 shows that probation and parole is partially inside and partially outside the core. Departments of probation and parole are usually part of county government and are attached to circuit courts. They enforce regulations governing the behavior of offenders sentenced to probation or released from prison on parole. In addition, they work closely with justice professionals and social service agencies whose primary work takes place in the community. These same agencies often provide services to noncriminal-justice clients, such

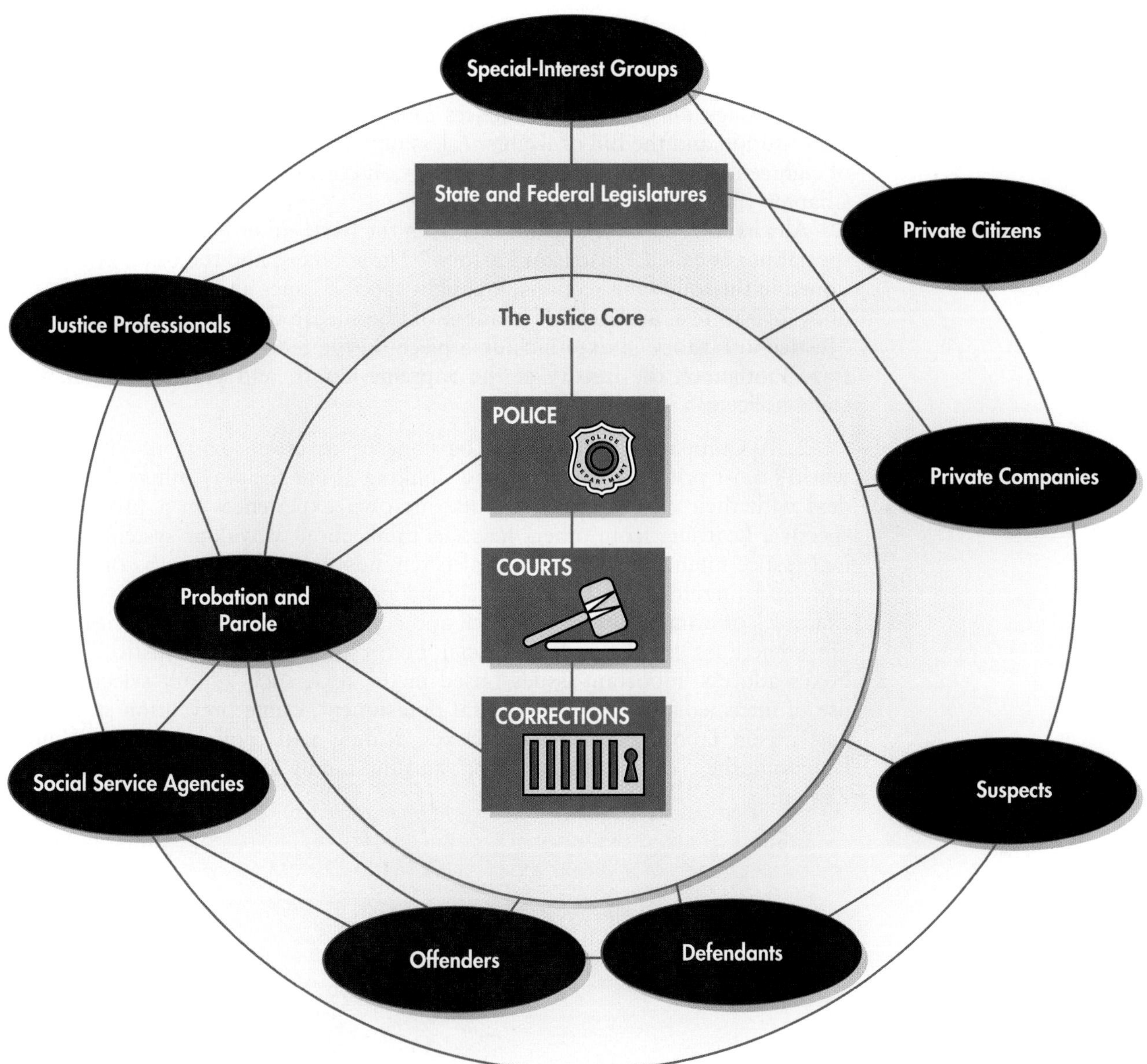

FIGURE 1.4 A "ROAD MAP" OF CRIMINAL JUSTICE

as the mentally ill, alcoholics, the unemployed, and those with various other treatment or counseling needs.

The emergence of **intermediate sanctions**—penalties that lie between prison and simple probation—has enlarged the responsibilities of probation and parole agencies in the community while also drawing them closer to the "hard" end of punishment represented by confinement and surveillance. This is discussed in detail in Chapter 17. The map in Figure 1.4 reflects the straddling of probation and parole across the boundaries of the justice core.

intermediate sanctions Penalties that lie between prison and simple probation.

CRIMINAL JUSTICE THEMES EMPHASIZED IN THIS TEXT

This text uses seven themes to help bring the criminal justice system to life. These themes will help you think about criminal justice as a system whose parts are in a state of continual interaction and adjustment; *dynamic* is the word when thinking about criminal justice. Here are the seven themes:

1. A Historical Theme. Criminal justice in America today is different from what it was 50 years ago, and vastly different from the days of the American Revolution and the founding of the country. Yet things that happened over 200 years ago are still vital influences today. One obvious example is the U.S. Constitution and the Bill of Rights. A less obvious one, perhaps, is the influence of eighteenth-century ideas on modern prison construction. This is discussed in Chapter 15.

All chapters contain illustrations from the past, either in the text itself or in special boxes called "Justice in History." These boxes, and the other ones mentioned in the following sections, highlight specific issues and topics raised in the body of the text and remind readers of the major themes of the book. The "Justice in History" boxes include a piece on the federal penitentiary at Alcatraz, another on the history of the Supreme Court, and yet another on how some police get around Miranda.

2. A Comparative Theme. The concept of crime exists in all but the world's most primitive societies, and thinking about the way others define and deal with their crime problems puts our own experiences in a broader perspective. Learning from others helps us think about ways our system of criminal justice might be improved; it also reminds us of the strengths of our system, and therefore the things we should not change. Most chapters contain examples of criminal justice practice and research from other countries. These are sometimes highlighted in special boxes called "Global Justice." These boxes address important issues raised in the text, such as jury selection, the use of intermediate sentences, capital punishment, crime prevention strategies, and prison labor. Examples are boxes dealing with policing in the United Kingdom, the court system in China, and the family group conference in New Zealand.

Innovative criminals take advantage of changing technology and new opportunities for crime. This requires innovative counter-responses by the criminal justice system.

PHOTO BY SPENCER GRANT, COURTESY OF PHOTO EDIT

3. An Innovations Theme. The 20th century has been a century of great and rapid change. Technological advances have made countless things obsolete, and now that word processors are commonplace and portable, some people hardly ever write by hand. Crime has changed, too, as new devices such as automatic teller machines (ATMs) have created new opportunities for fraud and theft. The rise of a global economy has created many new social, political, and economic relationships, and with them the emergence of transnational criminal organizations involved in political corruption, money laundering, drug running, smuggling, terrorism, and all sorts of frauds (Steffensmeier, 1995).

Changes in crime call for innovations in criminal justice. But even without a significant change in crime, there will be changes in criminal justice as new ideas and new technologies rise to the surface. Sometimes change is welcomed; at other times it is strongly resisted. Resistance may come from inside criminal justice organizations, as employees are asked to change long-standing behaviors. Community policing, heralded in many quarters as a way to foster mutually supportive relationships between neighborhoods and the police who patrol them, has been resisted by police themselves, as we shall see in Chapter 6. Resistance to change may also come from outside criminal justice organizations. For example, attempts to create more stringent gun controls have been vigorously opposed by special-interest groups such as the National Rifle Association.

Important historical innovations in criminal justice are identified during discussions of historical trends. Contemporary innovations are also discussed throughout the book, and some are highlighted in special boxes called "Justice Innovations." Today, for example, urban gangs are receiving a lot of attention, and the police are not the only ones who are introducing innovative ways of identifying and addressing the problem. A box in Chapter 11 highlights the new gang crimes prosecution units that have sprung up in some major cities; two boxes in Chapter 8 demonstrate innovations in policing drugs and terrorism; and a box in Chapter 2 discusses new methods of mapping crime hot spots, while another highlights research via the World Wide Web. These boxes show where some of the important changes in the field of criminal justice are taking place, and they describe the ideas and activities that are involved.

4. An Insider Theme. It is impossible to understand criminal justice in action without the insights and interpretations of participants themselves. Although most of the information in the text is drawn from scholarly research and the publications of criminal justice agencies, the personal perspectives of insiders are also presented. Personal accounts are given throughout the text and in special boxes called "Inside Criminal Justice." These autobiographical glimpses inside criminal justice come from a variety of sources: the nation's first female police chief of a major city, a black police chief, a veteran criminal defense attorney, a public defender, a city patrol officer, a U.S. district judge, an executioner, members of a chain gang, the head of a state department of corrections, and a man in boot camp. You will learn how these individuals see themselves in the context of their work or experiences with criminal justice. Their opinions, needless to say, are personal, and not necessarily shared by others.

A second set of boxes, called Justice Professionals at Work, highlight the daily work roles and responsibilities of different criminal justice professionals. They give us a glimpse of the routines involved in doing criminal justice work. Students considering a career somewhere in criminal justice should find the insights in these boxes especially interesting. In Chapter 11, for example, there is

Box 1.4

CAREERS IN CRIMINAL JUSTICE

SPECIAL AGENT OF THE U.S. SECRET SERVICE

The U.S. Secret Service was founded in 1865 as a bureau of the U.S. Treasury Department; it is currently the ninth largest federal law enforcement agency. The Secret Service protects U.S. presidents and vice-presidents, presidential candidates, specified government officials, and visiting foreign dignitaries and also conducts criminal investigations into a wide range of activities, including fraud and forgery of U.S. checks and bonds; frauds related to false IDs; frauds involving credit cards and bank cards; computer, ATM, and telecommunications frauds; and crimes against federally insured banks and savings and loans. Today, the Secret Service employs 2,000 special agents, 1,200 uniformed officers, and 1,200 support staff. Its agents are stationed in field offices around the United States, and in Paris, London, Bonn, Rome, and Bangkok. Here are the salary, duties, and qualifications of a special agent of the U.S. Secret Service as of September 1998:

Salary Range (entry level): $22,000 to $31,000 plus law enforcement availability pay.

Duties: Special agents engage in all facets of policing except routine patrolling: protective techniques, investigative procedures, criminal law, rules of evidence, surveillance techniques, undercover operations, interviewing techniques, defensive measures. Special agents are also trained in emergency medicine. Throughout their careers agents are rotated between investigative and protective assignments. Newly appointed agents may be assigned anywhere in the United States, and they will travel extensively throughout their careers.

Qualifications: Bachelor's degree from an accredited institution or an equivalent combination of education and experience in criminal investigation.

Conditions of Employment: Include U.S. citizenship; 21 to 37 years of age; must pass the Treasury Enforcement Agent Examination, be in excellent health, and pass polygraph examination and background investigation.

Source: Adapted from official publications of the U.S. Secret Service.

a box describing the typical day of probation officers working in an intensive pretrial supervision program; in Chapter 12 a box highlights the work of jury consultants; and in Chapter 2 ethnographic research is highlighted, and also the work of crime survey interviewers.

5. A Diversity Theme. If one issue deserves close attention in discussions of criminal justice, it is the cultural diversity of American society. While most Americans would like to think that justice is neutral when it comes to gender, race, or ethnicity, the facts say otherwise. Bias, and the prejudice and stereotypes that give rise to it, are found at all levels of the system, from criminal legislation itself to the treatment of prison inmates. Employees of the justice system may also feel the sting of gender, ethnic, and racial bias. In extreme forms, bias results in cruelty and violence, even death. Sixty years ago, blacks in the South who were accused of sexually assaulting a white woman stood a good

Most of us like to think that justice is neutral. Despite some progress over the past 30 years, there is plenty of evidence that it is not, particularly where race is concerned.

Illustration by Dean Rohrer

chance of being lynched, with or without a trial, innocent or guilty. Closer to the present we have the 1991 videotaped beating of Rodney King and the riots in South Central Los Angeles that followed the acquittal of three white police officers by an all-white jury. Aside from the extensive injuries to King, hit more than 50 times over a two-minute period following a high-speed chase, the riot resulted in 57 deaths, 14,000 arrests, and nearly $1 billion in property damage. The Christopher Commission, set up to investigate the beating, documented long-standing racial bias within the patrol ranks of the Los Angeles Police Department, and tacit if not open approval of that bias by command officers, including then-chief Daryl Gates.

Most of the time, ethnic, gender, and racial biases are nonviolent and more hidden. This does not lessen the harm to the people victimized by bias and to the cause of justice. The experience of bias is reacted to differently by different individuals, and some victims manage to overcome discrimination where many others fail. For most victims, the problem may be too overwhelming or too entrenched to overcome. Any challenge to the status quo requires influence and power, all the more so if the people in charge resist change. Affirmative action programs have helped more women and minorities get jobs and promotions in criminal justice, but the bulk of decision-making positions are still held by white males. Over the next 50 years, the United States population will change dramatically; no longer will whites of European heritage be in the majority; Hispanics, African Americans, and Asian Americans will make up over half the population. How the criminal justice system responds to the changing demographic picture will be a major challenge facing the 21st century. Some of the special boxes titled "Justice and the Law" highlight important laws and U.S. Supreme Court rulings that have shaped criminal justice responses to poor and minority populations over the years.

6. A Discretion Theme. A sixth theme of this book concerns the role of *discretion* in criminal justice decision making (see Table 1.4). A good definition of discretion is "authority to make decisions based on one's own judgment rather than on specified rules" (Champion, 1997:42). Virtually every aspect of criminal procedure can be associated with some rule, whether it is a law passed by a state or federal legislature, an amendment to the U.S. Constitution, a procedural ruling by a court, or a requirement imposed on employees by the agency they work for. Some of these rules carry significant consequences if they are violated, and use of discretion tends to be discouraged; others are viewed more as guidelines, and criminal justice personnel are expected and encouraged to exercise discretion.

Examples of situations where there is a clear expectation of discretion include decisions to interrogate a suspect, to make an arrest, to prosecute a defendant, to negotiate a plea, to follow the recommendations in a pre-sentence report, and to release an inmate onto parole. Examples of situations where the exercise of discretion is discouraged, and even prohibited, are generally those relating to *how* a procedure is followed. For example, criminal justice

TABLE 1.4 Discretion in the Criminal Justice System

The exercise of discretion by criminal justice officials is a major theme of this text. Here are some examples of the discretionary decisions exercised by different criminal justice personnel.

WHO EXERCISES DISCRETION? THESE CRIMINAL JUSTICE OFFICIALS. . .	MUST OFTEN DECIDE WHETHER OR NOT OR HOW TO—
Police	Enforce specific laws Investigate specific crimes Search people
Prosecutors	File charges or petitions for adjudication Seek indictments Drop cases Reduce charges
Judges or magistrates	Set bail or conditions for release Accept pleas Determine delinquency Dismiss charges Impose sentence Revoke probation
Correctional officials	Assign to type of correctional facility Award privileges Punish for disciplinary infractions
Paroling authorities	Determine date and conditions of parole Revoke parole

Source: Bureau of Justice Statistics (1998). Report to the Nation on Crime and Justice. 2nd Edition. Washington D.C.: U.S. Department of Justice.

officials do not have discretion to violate the U.S. Constitution when carrying out their duties.

There are both positive and negative aspects to the exercise of discetion. On the positive side, discretion allows criminal justice personnel to take into consideration the individual characteristics and circumstances of people who come into contact with the system. Another potential benefit of discretion is that it permits the system to adjust to changing demands and pressures. The exercise of discretion inevitably results in some individuals and groups being treated differently than others, and this points up a major problem: Discretion undermines the constitutional right of all Americans to be treated equally under the law. While some people "get away with crime," others do not; while some prisoners are released early, others are not; while some Americans are treated as suspicious persons by police, others are not; while the complaints of some victims are treated seriously, those of some other victims are not. Discretion means power, and if it is abused justice is compromised and respect for the law—and its enforcers—is diminished.

7. An Individual Rights Theme. In recent years there has been a conservative shift in the dominant thinking about crime and justice. Calls for faster justice, harsher punishments, and the removal of restrictions on the police have pitted the protection of individual rights against the state's interest in curbing crime and maintaining order. The state has awesome power that conceivably could be turned against any of its citizens. In America, the Constitution and especially the Bill of Rights seek to balance the state's obligation to protect the interests of society with the right of individuals to live their lives as freely as possible from government interference.

Drug enforcement brings the issue of individual rights versus state power into sharp relief because the crimes involved are often consensual, they are often ongoing, and they are often committed in private. Countermeasures must of necessity involve surveillance, undercover work, informants, and continuous intrusions into the private lives of citizens. In addition, the drug trade generates vast amounts of cash that must be "laundered" through banks and other businesses that also have legitimate operations. This draws otherwise respectable people into collusive relationships with criminals, and muddies the line between legitimate and illegitimate enterprise. Here, too, the effort to construct effective countermeasures threatens the right to privacy and other constitutional protections.

These seven themes unite the material in the text and also provide important topics for research and discussion. Do not imagine that everyone agrees with all the ideas expressed in this text. Criminal justice is both complex and controversial, and there are many different opinions about it, even among experts. Coupled with the expertise and guidance of your instructor, the aim of this book is to make the subject matter accessible and interesting without glossing over things that are controversial and sometimes disturbing.

SUMMARY

This opening chapter has laid the groundwork for the material you will read in the next sixteen chapters. Criminal justice is a challenging field of study whose subject matter is both intriguing and complex. Probably all students come to this introductory course with firm ideas and strong opinions about crime and justice. The entertainment and news media have surely played a role in the development of those ideas and opinions, but we have seen that the media picture of criminal justice is a distorted one that tends to portray extremes. It is wise to be wary of media images of criminal justice in America.

The study of criminal justice begins with definitions of *crime* and *criminal*. No single definition adequately conveys the complexity of the subject matter, so we reviewed legal and sociological definitions and spent some time examining criminalization, the process by which acts and people are transformed into crimes and criminals. We saw that criminalization is influenced not only by what people do, but also by who they are.

There are many useful distinctions that can be drawn among crimes and criminals. For example, the distinction between misdemeanors and felonies reflects differences in the seriousness of crimes as measured by the prescribed penalties; the distinction between criminals and delinquents is based mainly on the age of offenders, although more and more juveniles are being tried as adults and some states have dropped the term *delinquent* altogether.

Criminal justice is a modern society's system of roles and activities for defining and dealing with crime and criminals. It is a formal system of social control resting on a foundation of law. Modern American law has roots in primitive systems of self-help justice and in the ancient codes of the Middle East and Europe. Later, English common law grew out of the decisions of traveling courts, and this became the basis of early American criminal law. Today, most criminal law is created by state and federal legislatures, although courts and regulatory agencies contribute to it as well.

The themes that unite the exploration of criminal justice in this text deal with seven issues: criminal justice in the past; criminal justice in other countries; criminal justice innovations; the experiences and perspectives of insiders, including criminals; the relationship of criminal justice to human diversity; the exercise of discretion in criminal justice decision making; and balancing of state power and individual rights. As we continue our journey through the next sixteen chapters we shall see that these seven themes help explain the world of crime and justice in America.

WHAT DO YOU THINK *NOW*?

- Based on what you read, what is your impression of the role of violence in everyday crime? How have your views changed?
- Which types of media are most responsible for reporting crime accurately? Do you feel that they live up to that standard? Why or why not?
- Based on what you are learning about the average crime and criminal, do you feel that there are benefits to following highly publicized trials such as O. J. Simpson's? What might those be?
- Do criminal laws reflect the will of the people? Are they based on consensus or do they reflect conflict as well?

KEY TERMS

legalistic definition of crime
substantive criminal law
procedural criminal law
actus reus
mens rea
inchoate offenses
M'Naghten defense
substantial capacity test
situational defense
affirmative defense
procedural defense
labeling perspective
criminalization
decriminalization
mala in se
mala prohibita
misdemeanor
felony
civil law
criminal law
primitive law
collateral consequences
common law
precedent
Bill of Rights
criminal justice
intermediate sanctions

ACTIVE LEARNING CHALLENGES

1. Break up into groups and have each group identify what it sees as the most significant court case in the media today. Then discuss what is significant about each case and what you have learned about criminal justice.
2. Discuss the use of the insanity defense. Which method of defense does the class favor and why? What should the punishment be for offenders who are defined as insane?
3. Have the class break into two groups: "Formal Controllers" and "informal controllers" (notice any difference?). Each group is charged with reducing crime. Use one class period to come up with a plan that utilizes the groups' primary method of control (formal or informal), and have the groups present their plan for discussion during the next class period.
4. Divide the class into seven groups and assign each group one of the seven themes emphasized in this text. Each group identifies an issue that is important to them within the theme, and suggests one that is not listed in the text's discussion.

INTERNET CHALLENGES

1. Your first Internet Challenge: Click on Search to reach Yahoo, Excite, Lycos, or any other search engine (some Web browsers allow you to choose one from a list). Then type in "criminal justice" (without the quotation marks). You will see a listing of "hits" using the words "criminal" and/or "justice." There may be lots of pages. Scroll down a page and click on a site that looks interesting. Briefly note down the main topics discussed on the site(s) you visit. If you have plenty of time, explore one of the links from the site you chose to other sites that have something to do with criminal justice. Write down something you learn that relates to the topics discussed in this chapter. *Note:* Always "bookmark" the criminal justice Web sites you like so that you can visit them again without searching.
2. Visit your local newspaper on the Web. Check out the stories on crime and justice. List the stories receiving the most attention. What do they have in common?
3. Personal experiences with the criminal justice system provide many insights into how things are perceived to work in real life. Using Search, see if you can find some personal experiences of victims, offenders, or criminal justice employees that illustrate one or more of the seven themes emphasized in this text.

CHAPTER 2

Getting a Line on Crime and Justice in America

LEARNING OBJECTIVES

- Describe the steps involved in compiling crime statistics, and understand the limitations of official police tallies such as the Uniform Crime Reports.
- Explain how victimization and self-report studies probe the "dark figure of crime," and understand their shortcomings.
- Understand the meaning of crime rates, clearance rates, and victimization rates and how they are constructed.
- Explain why overpolicing and underpolicing of certain groups of people occurs, and understand its impact on crime data.
- Describe some of major sources of information on the criminal justice system.
- Understand how to use the Internet as a resource for studying criminal justice.

Generally, the police decide whether or not an incident is a crime. This is called the founding decision, *and it is the first official step taken by the criminal justice system. Unless an incident is founded, there are in effect no suspects, and there will be no arrests and no prosecutions.*

PHOTO COURTESY OF AP PHOTO/POOL

The statistics about crime and delinquency are probably the most unreliable and most difficult of all social statistics.

EDWIN H. SUTHERLAND AND DONALD R. CRESSEY,
CRIMINOLOGISTS WHO DEVOTED LONG AND DISTINGUISHED CAREERS TO UNDERSTANDING CRIME AND JUSTICE

We had to do more than find offenders; we also had to convince them to cooperate. This was easier said than done because most of them were deeply suspicious of our motives.

RICHARD T. WRIGHT AND SCOTT H. DECKER, COMMENTING ON THEIR FIELD WORK WITH ACTIVE ARMED ROBBERS, 1997

In order to understand how criminal justice works, we need appropriate information. In this chapter we will explore how information on crime and justice is collected and what it means. We will also examine the resources that are available for student research and where to find them. By the end of the chapter you should be able to tell your friends what is missing in media reports on crime, and to explain how they can construct a more accurate picture of crime and justice in America.

? WHAT DO YOU THINK?

- Are all or most crimes reported? Are most criminals caught and prosecuted? Why or why not?
- Do you think that all groups in American society are treated equally by the criminal justice system? If not, why not?
- What are the best sources for information on crime and criminals? What are other good choices?

THE PRODUCTION OF INFORMATION ON CRIME

An important part of the public record on crime comes from official reports created by the police. Yet the police are usually not the first people to define an act or event as a crime. That honor belongs to the public at large. The production of information on crime begins when someone—anyone—labels an act or event as crime and does something about it. When a member of the public calls the police about a possible crime, he or she is called a **complainant.** Each day, thousands of Americans take on the role of complainant.

complainant A person who calls police about a possible crime.

But many possible crimes go unreported. Suppose you hear a burglar alarm go off as you are walking past a house. You know that alarms sometimes go off accidentally, but this could signal a burglary in progress. You decide to ignore it. Why? Perhaps you thought that someone else must have heard the alarm and would notify the police. You might have worried about getting hurt. Or perhaps you were in a hurry and didn't want to spend time looking for a phone and waiting around for the police to arrive. Worse still, if the police did catch a burglar at work, you might have to testify in court. The burglar might even be a friend or relative of yours! Or perhaps you figured the police would not want to be bothered. Anyway, since the alarm had sounded, you imagined that the burglar, if there was one, would be long gone before the police arrived. And so you do nothing.

A little later the homeowner returns and discovers that a rear window is open and a VCR is missing. Now something will surely be done—or will it? It turns out that many apparent victims of crime do nothing, even when the crime is a serious one. We will see in a moment why that is so, but the consequence of doing nothing is that the act or event is "lost": It cannot become part of the public record on crime. Instead, it becomes part of the **dark figure of crime.** This is the portion that cannot be seen by reading official police reports. Crime is like an iceberg: For most crimes the dark figure is much larger than the figure we can see. There are two exceptions to this: murder and auto theft. Can you guess why these crimes are exceptions? The answer is given a little later on.

dark figure of crime All the crimes that do not become part of the official police record.

Of course, police see many crimes themselves. Some of these would never become part of the official record if police did not see them. So-called public order crimes such as prostitution and drug sales, and many alcohol-related offenses, are examples. Loitering and vagrancy also fall into this category. The public generally does not rush to call the police, and police must use informants and undercover agents to discover many of these offenses. In other cases, the crimes are discovered during routine police patrol. Still, the police only see the tip of the iceberg: A vast but unknown amount of public order crime is never recorded as crime.

REPORTING CRIME TO THE POLICE

The police generally learn about serious crimes involving property loss or injury from complainants. It is estimated that only 3 percent of reported violent crimes and 2 percent of reported household crimes are actually discovered by the police themselves (Bureau of Justice Statistics, 1985). If researchers had to rely on police observation of serious crime, the information base would be small indeed. Yet national surveys indicate that only around 35 percent of all serious crimes are reported *to* the police, and the situation is not much different in other countries such as Canada, Australia, and Britain (Bureau of Justice Statistics, 1998a; Bastion, 1995; Mirrlees-Black, Mayhew, and Percy, 1996). There is thus a vast amount of crime that the police do not know about even when someone else does.

Various reasons for deciding not to report a burglar alarm have already been listed. But what if people are victims or witnesses in rapes or robberies?

Most felony crimes are not observed by the police but are reported to them. A complainant is a person who reports a possible crime.

Photos by Bob Daemmrich, courtesy of The Image Works

Surely that would change their inclination to call the police. Perhaps, but the situation is complicated. Although it is true that more serious crimes tend to be reported more often than less serious crimes, differences among serious crimes make some more likely to be reported than others. For example, crimes resulting in high losses or injuries that require medical attention tend to be reported more often than other crimes. Murders are reported most often—it is hard to ignore a dead body. Among other serious offenses, motor vehicle theft heads the list at around 75 percent being reported, followed by robbery (55 percent) and aggravated assault (54 percent). [Bureau of Justice Statistics, 1998a].

It has long been assumed that insurance is the key reason high-value property crimes such as auto theft are reported to the police. But even here the picture is not a simple one. In a recent British national survey, some people with insurance decided not to call police because they feared the insurance company would increase their premium (Mirrlees-Black, Mayhew, and Percy, 1996:26). Others had high deductibles, making claims too costly.

The reporting situation with violent crimes is also complicated. On the whole, violent crimes are more likely to be reported if they involve female victims or weapons, or result in injuries (Gottfredson and Gottfredson, 1988; Bureau of Justice Statistics, 1994f). Surprisingly, assaults involving strangers are no more likely to be reported than incidents involving people who know each other. This is a recent change and may be due to the fact that domestic violence has received a lot of negative publicity over the past few years. The major exception to this pattern is sexual assault: Assaults by strangers are more likely to be reported than assaults by acquaintances or family members.

Reasons for Not Reporting Serious Crimes. Why do many violent crimes go unreported to the police? The most frequent reason given by victims is that the incident is "personal" or "private." This reason is less likely to be given when the victim is attacked by a stranger (Harlow, 1991:3); in these cases victims who don't report the crime usually say they feel nothing could be done. In fact, this is the most common reason for not reporting any type of serious crime. The second most common reason is that the victim felt the police would not want to be bothered. These responses sometimes reflect unpleasant prior experiences with the police, or a belief that the police are uncaring or incompetent.

Sometimes a decision not to call the police is stimulated by fear of reprisal by the offender. This is most likely to arise with domestic violence or incidents involving friends. Victims feel that reporting the offender to police will result in more violence against them—if not immediately, then later on. Yet national surveys have shown that calling the police may actually prevent future domestic violence (Bureau of Justice Statistics, 1994e). Victims who reported being assaulted by their husbands were three times less likely to be assaulted again than victims who did not call the police. This crime-preventing aspect of the complainant role is recognizd by some crime victims: Among those who reported a crime to police, 1 out of 5 did so because they believed it would prevent a similar incident from happening again (Bureau of Justice Statistics, 1998a).

Sometimes people who are witnessing a serious crime in progress fail to call the police. They may assume that someone else has done so, or they may underestimate the true seriousness of the situation. These reactions often happen when more than one witness is involved. A famous case occurred in New York City in 1964: A young woman, Kitty Genovese, was repeatedly stabbed within view of dozens of people; nobody intervened and nobody called the police until after she had died. A similar case occurred in St. Louis in 1984; this time a crowd of people leaving Busch Stadium kept walking by a woman as she was being attacked. Again, nobody interfered or called the police. Sociologists explain this phenomenon with two concepts: *diffused responsibility* and *pluralistic ignorance* (Farley, 1998:459). Diffused responsibility suggests that in situations where more than one witness is involved, people do not feel individually responsible for taking action, assuming that someone else will do so instead. If everyone makes this assumption, of course, no action will be taken. Pluralistic ignorance suggests that in group situations, each person treats the inaction of others as a cue that the situation is not really an emergency.

The Police Role in the Production of Information on Crime

Although the public has a very important role in producing official data on crime, the police have the last word. This is true of both data on crime and data on criminals. Recall from Chapter 1 that criminalization at the arrest stage of the criminal process must occur for a criminal suspect to be eligible for criminalization at later stages. But first the police must decide that a crime has in fact occurred and then what to do about it. Neither decision can be taken for granted.

The "Founding" Decision. A complainant may call the police to report a crime, but the police decide whether or not the incident will be treated as a crime. This is called the **founding decision.** Since the police have considerable discretion in deciding whether to treat a complaint as a crime, the amount of crime officially recorded is directly shaped by how that discretion is exercised. This means that a rise (or decrease) in published crime rates may reflect changes in police founding decisions rather than changes in the amount of crime itself. One study of this issue has shown that a 20-year upward trend in violent crime rates from 1973–1992 was largely due to greater police productivity in recording and reporting crime (O'Brien, 1996).

founding decision Occurs when investigating police decide whether a particular incident should be treated as a crime (founded) or not (unfounded).

The founding decision is important for other reasons as well. The public does not know all the technicalities of criminal law, a fact reflected in the vast number of emergency calls that turn out to be false alarms. Sometimes complainants describe events that police dispatchers initially record as robberies, aggravated assaults, and even murders; however, investigating officers cannot later verify that a crime occurred. In one of the few studies of crime verification, only 73 percent of nearly 25,000 crimes classified as violent offenses were subsequently verified, or founded (Maxfield, Lewis, and Szoc, 1980:225). In another study, founding decisions varied by alleged offense, from only 30 percent of reported bicycle thefts to 70 percent of reported burglaries (Bottomley and Coleman, 1981).

Underrecording of Crime by the Police. The founding decision is sometimes inaccurate and may even be intentionally falsified. Internal audits of police founding practices in Chicago and in Portland, Oregon, found that 50 to 70 percent of "unfounded" felony crimes had been incorrectly labeled (Schneider, 1977; *Chicago Sun-Times,* April 12, 1983). Accusations of deliberate falsification are difficult to document, but not hard to imagine. In one study of founding behavior by English police, the authors discovered several reasons why the police would not record an incident as founded even though it was in fact a crime (Kinsey, Lea, and Young, 1986):

- The police considered it too trivial.
- The victim was unlikely to prosecute the offender.
- The incident was "not police business."
- The crime was too difficult to investigate or prosecute.
- The incident was not "real" crime.

The last reason deserves comment. Many people believe that behaviors such as marijuana use, prostitution, and gambling should not be crimes. If people believe offenses are not "real" crime they are less likely to report them to police. When the police also take this approach it reinforces the public's view and contributes to nonreporting.

Underrecording of crime by police is related to the type of crime involved and the people victimized by it (Kinsey, Lea, and Young, 1986; Elias, 1993). Fights among lower-class and minority individuals, or domestic assaults involving female victims, are examples of underrecorded crimes. In Canada, some police officers in one large city made a distinction between the public—whom they served—and "the dregs," or "scum" (Shearing, 1979). The scum, drawn mainly from lower-class minority groups, were often not taken seriously when they complained of crime. Chapters 6 and 8 look more closely at police definitions of real crime and their impact on criminal justice.

Largely because of the influence of civil rights activists and the women's movement, police in many cities are more sensitive about minority victimization and domestic violence than they used to be, and departments try to address racism and other prejudices in their training programs. However, such positive steps must overcome two things. First, the police receive little reward for catering to victims, especially those without political influence. Second, stereotypes are remarkably enduring, and police labeling practices will be influenced by them until officers see a compelling reason to change. Under these circumstances, the dark figure of crime continues to grow: The unresponsiveness of some officers leads people to feel that the police don't care about their problems, so why bother reporting a crime? The flow of information about crime is reduced, further distorting the picture of crime that is drawn from official sources.

Recording of Crime Is Influenced by Police-Citizen Encounters. Police recording decisions are influenced primarily by the legal seriousness of an offense: The more serious the crime, the more likely the police are to record it. But even serious crimes are sometimes ignored by the police, and therefore remain unrecorded. This outcome may result from the nature of encounters between police and citizens in the field.

The first and most famous study of police recording behavior in the field was published in 1970 (Black, 1970). Researchers rode around with the police in Chicago, Boston, and Washington, D.C., recording the interactions that occurred between police and complainants. They discovered that police recording practices were influenced by four factors. First and foremost was the legal seriousness of the crime, as noted previously. But three other factors helped explain why 20 to 30 percent of legally serious crimes went unrecorded:

- The demeanor of the complainant: Victims and witnesses who showed respect and were deferential to the police were more likely to get their complaints officially recorded.
- The complainant's preference: Complainants who expressed a strong preference for or against the police taking formal action generally got their way.
- The relational distance between the complainant and the suspect: When incidents involved victims and suspects who were relatives or close friends, the police were less likely to officially record them as crimes.

Studies of police behavior at crime scenes generally agree that a complaint or call for assistance is no guarantee that the police will do much. In one survey, victims reported that the police asked few questions, even in cases of violent crime, and in the case of burglaries, the police did not even "look around" in nearly half the incidents (Whitaker, 1989). The recording of crime by the police is obviously a good example of discretion at work, and it will be discussed again in Chapter 7. Suffice it to say that the number of **crimes known to the police**—the term usually used to refer to officially recorded offenses—is a poor approximation of the true amount of crime.

crimes known to the police The official count of criminal offenses recorded and reported by police agencies.

THE PRODUCTION OF OFFICIAL INFORMATION ON CRIMINALS

All sorts of people commit crimes, and some do so many times. To become part of the official record, people must be officially identified as suspects and then arrested by the police. Once an arrest is made and the suspect is turned over to the court for prosecution, an offense is considered "cleared," and the offender's name is entered into police records. In most jurisdictions, if the arrested suspect is over age 17 the person's name appears on the daily "police blotter," and is available to the press. The names of juvenile arrestees generally remain sealed—unless the offender is subsequently tried as an adult in criminal court. However, some states have recently made juvenile records more accessible to the press and public as part of a "get tough on juvenile crime" policy.

The arrest data compiled by the police are the only official count of criminals. This does not mean that every arrested individual is in fact guilty of the crime for which he or she is arrested; that is determined at later stages of the criminalization process. Arrest data simply provide a count of the people who have been arrested and charged as suspects in a crime. Arrest data probably tell us more about the activities of the police than they do about the activities and characteristics of criminals. This is because a majority of crimes never result in an arrest. Nor can arrest data tell us anything about the dark figure of crime.

We noted earlier that poor and minority neighborhoods tend to experience an underrecording of crime. It may come as a surprise, therefore, to learn that police also tend to concentrate law enforcement efforts in the same neighborhoods. These areas become overpoliced relative to other parts of the city (Hagan, Gillis, and Chan, 1978; Smith, 1986). To some extent this reflects the distribution of crime itself: Violent crimes such as robbery, aggravated assault, and murder tend to be concentrated in the inner city. But it also reflects stereotypes held by both police and public about the origins, characteristics, and dangers of "real" crimes and "real" criminals. Police go where they expect to find real criminals committing real crime. Using computerized Geographic Information Systems (GIS) to map crime locations, many large urban police forces today keep track of crime "hot spots" and concentrate their personnel in those areas (Sherman, Gartin, and Buerger, 1989). A hot spot may be a city block, a bar, an intersection, or even a residence. Box 2.1 illustrates the use of GIS by Chicago police to map crime hot spots in that city.

Since urban police generally concentrate enforcement in poor and inner-city neighborhoods they discover not only more serious criminals there, but also more drunks, loiterers, vagrants, and other petty offenders. The result is that arrest data in general are heavily weighted by poor and minority individuals. The people most likely to be victimized by crime are also the people most vulnerable to arrest. Table 2.1 shows that in 1996, for example, even though African Americans made up just over 12 percent of the U.S. population, they represented nearly half of all arrests for serious violent crime, and around one-third of those arrested for property crimes and drug abuse violations; they also represented over one-third of all arrests for vagrancy, disorderly conduct, and prostitution—and well over half of all arrests for gambling (Maguire and Pastore, 1998:338–339).

TABLE 2.1 Arrests by Selected Offenses and Race, 1996

Police made an estimated 15,168,100 arrests in 1996. This table shows the breakdown of arrests for which information was available on age and race. It represents 13,172,829 arrests by 9,661 police agencies serving an estimated population of 189,885,000. Whether adults or juveniles, black suspects are arrested in disproportionate numbers, considering they make up roughly 12 percent of the U.S. population.

	Adult Arrests			Juvenile Arrests (Under age 18)		
Offense	White*	Black	Other**	White*	Black	Other**
All crimes	66.2%	31.5%	2.3%	69.7%	27.3%	3.0%
Index crimes***	59.9	37.7	2.3	66.8	29.7	3.5
Violent crimes	55.6	42.2	2.1	50.3	47.2	2.5
Property crimes	61.9	35.6	2.5	69.9	26.4	3.7
Gambling	50.1	45.3	4.5	14.8	84.7	0.5
Prostitution	59.0	38.4	2.6	58.9	37.3	3.8
Drug crimes	60.1	38.8	1.1	62.2	36.2	1.6
Disorderly conduct	62.1	35.9	2.0	63.1	35.1	1.8
Vagrancy	52.9	44.6	2.4	63.5	34.9	1.5

* The FBI includes Hispanics in this category.
** American Indians, Alaskan Natives, and Asian or Pacific Islanders
*** There are 8 index crimes: murder and negligent manslaughter, forcible rape, robbery, aggravated assault, burglary, larceny-theft, motor vehicle theft, and arson. Violent crimes are the first four index crimes; property crimes consist of the other four. Because of incomplete reporting, the FBI does not include data on arson in its count of index crimes.

Source: Kathleen Maguire and Ann L. Pastore (1998). *Sourcebook of Criminal Justice Statistics 1997* (pp. 338–339). Washington, D.C.: U.S. Department of Justice.

Box 2.1

JUSTICE INNOVATIONS

MAPPING CRIME "HOT SPOTS"

The police tend to concentrate enforcement activities in areas where they expect to find crime. This leads some people and neighborhoods to be overpoliced relative to others, and more crimes are recorded in those areas. Could this be a self-fulfilling prophecy?

ILLUSTRATION BY JOHN OVERMYER

The Chicago Police Department is a leader in the use of computer mapping techniques to identify crime "hot spots." A hot spot is an intersection, block, or neighborhood with an unusually high number of crime incidents. When these are identified, the police can concentrate their enforcement activities in the hot spot.

The Chicago mapping system, called ICAM2, allows patrolling police to select a particular offense, beat, time, and date for investigation. ICAM2's mapping function allows crime data to be viewed spatially. Each incident is plotted on the map and assigned a particular symbol representing the type of incident and number of occurrences.

A beat officer may use ICAM2 to help solve crime and disorder problems. The officer looks for clusters or patterns of incidents to see whether there is any visual relationship between the incidents. The officer can then analyze this information to determine whether there is a visual correlation between crimes and community factors such as vacant buildings, schools, ATMs, liquor stores,

clearance rate The proportion of crimes that result in arrests.

Constructing Police Clearance Rates. The **clearance rate** represents the proportion of crimes that result in arrests. It is conventionally defined as the number of arrests during a period of time divided by the number of recorded crimes. Thus, if there were 1,000 robberies in your city during 1998, and 200 robbery suspects were arrested, the clearance rate would be

Box 2.1 (continued)

or public housing estates. If the officer determines that crimes are tending to occur around a particular community factor, then patrol efforts can be directed to that area.

Finally, maps are resourceful tools when officers attend community beat meetings. Maps are passed out to citizens so they can see graphically where the incidents are occurring. Heightened awareness also allows citizens to look out for one another, and maps can promote more effective dialogue between the police and the community, leading to partnership-based problem-solving.

The maps in Figure 2.1 show a hot spot involving motor vehicle theft. The incidents occurred in the 10th District, Beat 1033, from May 26, 1998, to June 18, 1998.

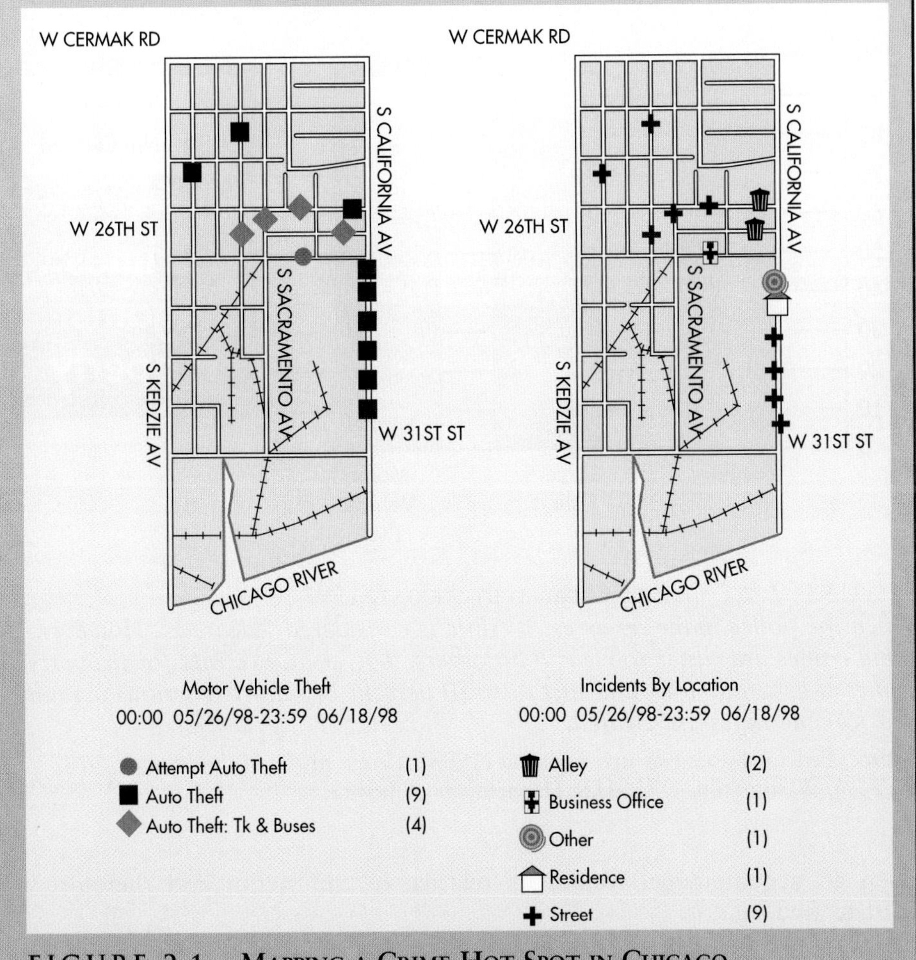

FIGURE 2.1 MAPPING A CRIME HOT SPOT IN CHICAGO
Source: Chicago Police Department, ICAM2. Used with permission.

200/1,000. This is 0.20 or 20 percent. Figure 2.2 shows the clearance rate for various offenses as computed by the FBI for 1997. As you can see, the clearance rates for violent crimes are generally higher than those for property crimes. Murder tops the list. This should come as no surprise since murder is a heinous crime that people want to see solved, and the murderer is

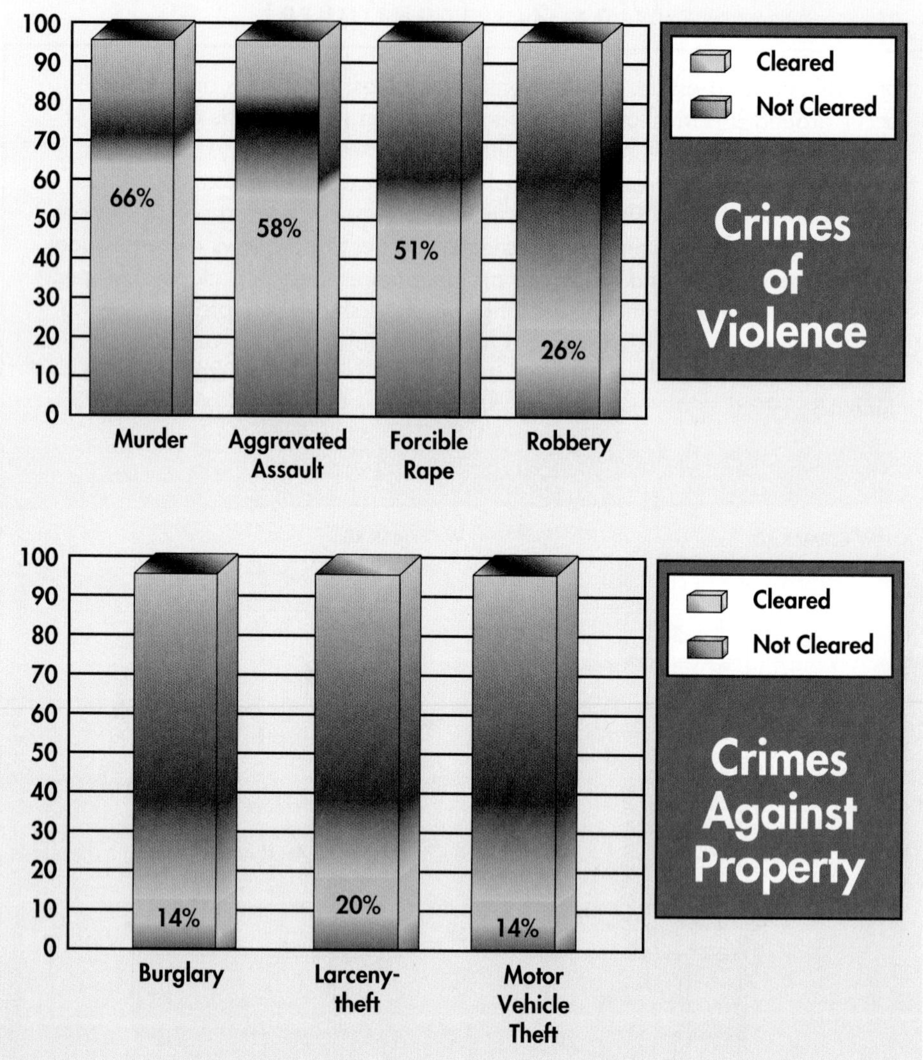

FIGURE 2.2 CRIMES CLEARED BY ARREST, 1997
When the police make an arrest a crime is considered "cleared." However, some crimes are easier to clear than others. The clearance rate for property crimes is generally low, and just over 50 percent of reported serious assaults and forcible rapes are cleared.

Source: Federal Bureau of Investigation (1998). *Crime in the United States, 1997* (p. 212). Washington, D.C.: U.S. Department of Justice.

often an acquaintance, friend, or relative of the victim and therefore not hard to find.

Since overpolicing and underrecording of crime tend to occur in the same parts of the city, the impact on police clearance rates is substantial. Overpolicing inflates the numerator of the clearance rate (the numbers of arrests) while underrecording of crime lowers the denominator (the number of crimes known to the police). The resulting clearance rate is thus artificially inflated, suggesting that there is greater police efficiency in a community than is really the case. It distorts the true picture of a community's experiences with crime: Underrecording downplays the suffering that occurs in inner-city areas and poorer neighborhoods, while overpolicing subjects residents to increased surveillance and risk of arrest. The result can be a sense of neglect on one hand and a sense of abuse on the other (Elias, 1993; Kinsey, Lea, and Young, 1986). In any case, the true clearance rate is typically lower than the published statistics indicate.

Figure 2.3 summarizes our discussion of the production of information on crime and criminals. The numbers at the end of the process are much smaller than those at the beginning. Most crimes are lost to the official record, becoming part of the dark figure of crime. Needless to say, the number of arrested criminals is even smaller. In the next section we look at the data sources available to researchers (as well as to the media and the public at large), and consider how some of these help reveal parts of the dark figure of crime.

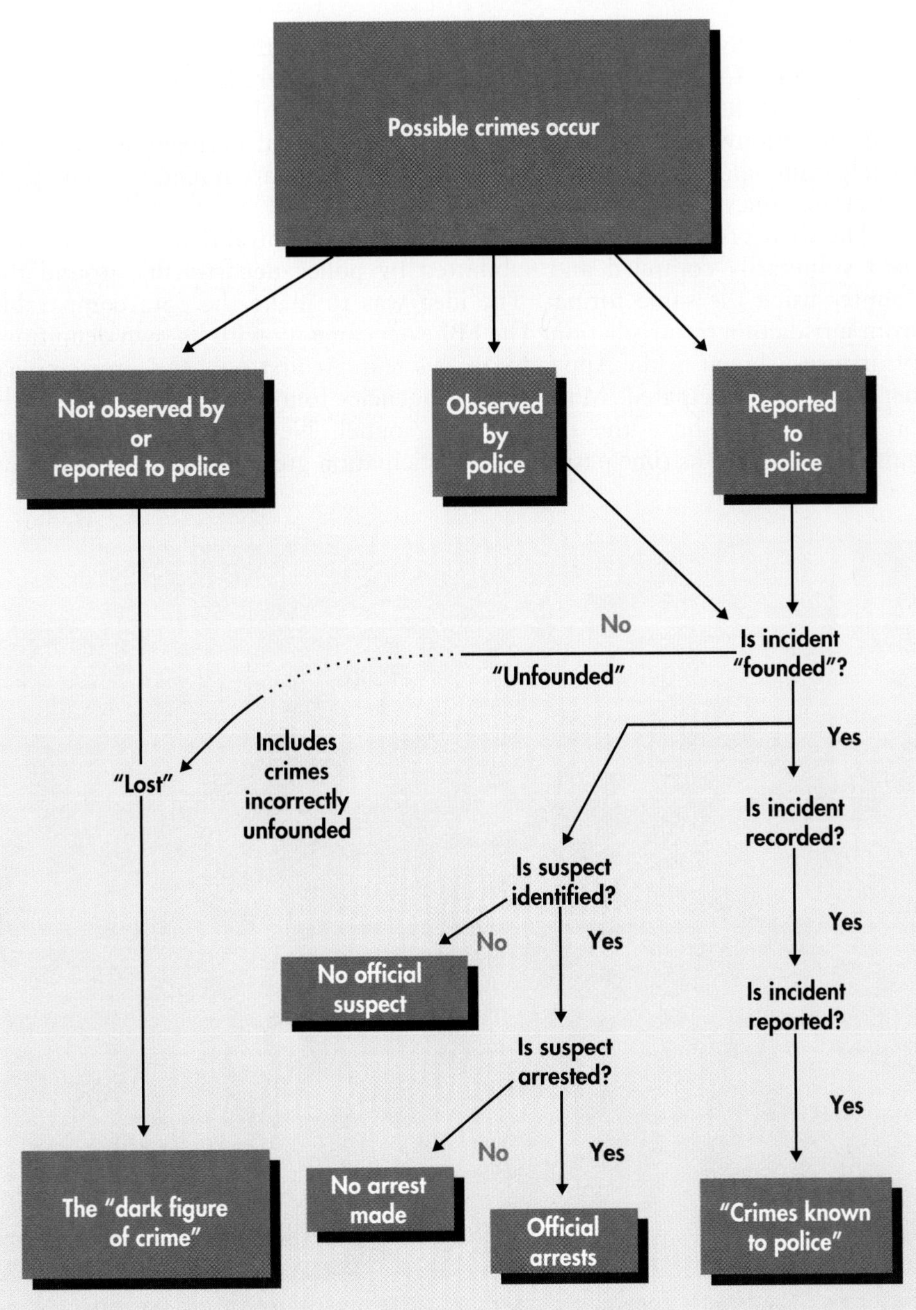

FIGURE 2.3 Production of Official Police Data on Crimes and Criminals

SOURCES OF INFORMATION ON CRIME AND CRIMINALS

The first places most people turn to for data on crime and criminals are official publications of the U.S. government and state and local law enforcement agencies. However, this is not the only place to look for information on crime. This section of the chapter explores three data sources: (1) information supplied by government agencies; (2) information on crime victimization gathered through interviews with the general public; and (3) information on criminal activity gathered through interviews with citizens who admit they have committed offenses.

THE FBI'S UNIFORM CRIME REPORTS

Uniform Crime Reports (UCR) An FBI program that collects and disseminates national data on crimes known to the police and on arrests.

The most widely used source of national data on crime and criminals is the FBI's **Uniform Crime Reports (UCR)**. These reports were begun in 1929 as the brainchild of the new FBI director, J. Edgar Hoover. Hoover recognized the need for nationwide data on crime as an aid to law enforcement agencies and to help criminological research. He thought the information might also help direct crime policy.

The UCR program was originally designed as a central depository of crime data voluntarily compiled and submitted by police departments around the country using the same format. The idea was to make the data comparable from jurisdiction to jurisdiction. The FBI even came up with its own definitions of offenses, shown in the Appendix of this text. At first only the largest police departments participated. Many smaller agencies found the process too costly or simply didn't have the necessary personnel. Nevertheless, the program gained acceptance as time passed, and participation grew. Today, almost all law

The FBI started its Uniform Crime Reports (UCR) in 1929. The UCR was the first nationwide database on crime, and has helped countless law enforcement agencies and crime researchers learn more about crime in America.
PHOTO COURTESY OF CORBIS-BETTMANN

enforcement agencies participate, representing over 96 percent of the U.S. population (Federal Bureau of Investigation, 1997a). Each month local police, sheriff's departments, and state police agencies report information on the offenses known to them and the arrests they have made. The FBI's annual report, titled *Crime in the United States,* is now available on the Internet at **http://www.fbi.gov/.** (Most larger police departments also maintain their own internal records of crime in their jurisdictions, and these can usually be obtained directly from the department.)

The FBI's Index Crimes. A major portion of the UCR deals with **index offenses.** Index offenses are serious crimes that are considered representative of the worst crimes as well as a measure of crime in general. The assumption is that if index offenses go up, the crime problem is getting worse; if they go down, the crime problem is easing. There are now eight index offenses: criminal homicide (murder and nonnegligent manslaughter), forcible rape, robbery, aggravated assault, burglary, larceny-theft, motor vehicle theft, and arson. Arson was added to the list in 1978, but the FBI has not yet included the data in the UCR because of incomplete reporting. Arrests are reported for an additional 21 crime categories. The Appendix gives the definitions of these and all other offenses included in the Uniform Crime Reports. State figures on some crimes are sometimes estimated because they are not reported according to the FBI's guidelines (Federal Bureau of Investigation, 1997a:62).

index offenses Eight serious crimes that the FBI uses as a measure of crime in America: criminal homicide, forcible rape, robbery, aggravated assault, burglary, larceny-theft, motor vehicle theft, and arson.

Computing the Crime Rate. The UCR provides a variety of information on index crimes, from trends over time to comparisons across states, counties, and cities of different sizes. Figure 2.4 shows trends in index offenses from 1980 to 1996. The information is presented in the form of a rate. A **crime rate** is a very important concept, as we shall see. It is conventionally computed by dividing the number of crimes known to police in a jurisdiction by the popula-

crime rate A measure of crime conventionally expressed as the number of crimes known to the police for a given year divided by the population for the same year and multiplied by 100,000.

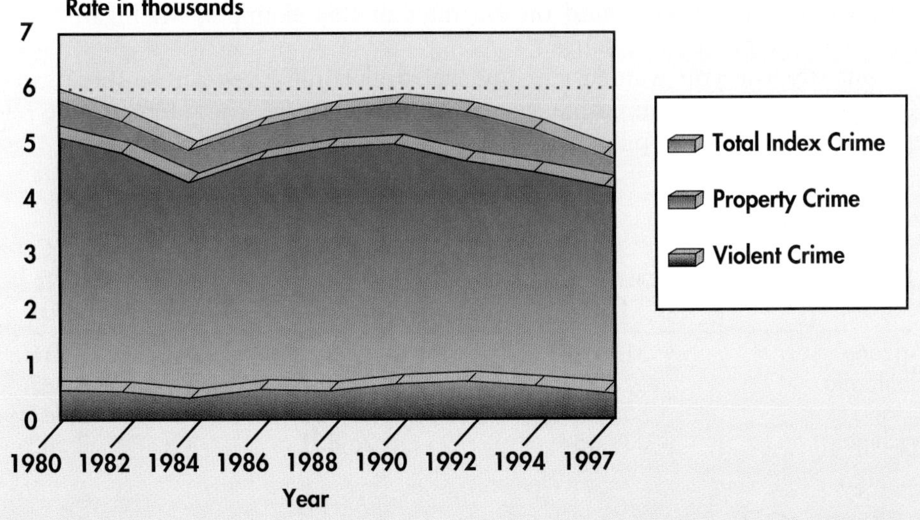

FIGURE 2.4 TRENDS IN INDEX OFFENSES, 1980–1997
Figures are rates of total index crimes, violent crimes, and property crimes expressed as the number of recorded crimes per 100,000 population. Violent crimes are murder and non-negligent manslaughter, forcible rape, robbery and aggravated assault; property crimes are burglary, larceny-theft, and motor vehicle theft.

Source: Federal Bureau of Investigation (1998). *Crime in the United States, 1997* (p. 66). Washington, D.C.: U.S. Department of Justice.

tion of the jurisdiction. The result is multiplied by 100,000 to avoid fractions. To illustrate, suppose we look at the states of Arizona, California, Florida, and Michigan in 1994. Here are the relevant figures (Maguire and Pastore, 1996:326–329):

STATE	POPULATION (1)	NUMBER OF INDEX CRIMES (2)	INDEX CRIME RATE (3)
Arizona	4,075,000	322,926	7,924.6
California	31,431,000	1,940,497	6,173.8
Florida	13,953,000	1,151,121	8,250.0
Michigan	9,496,000	517,076	5,445.2

The index crime rate for Arizona, shown in column 3, was computed as follows:

$$\frac{322{,}926}{4{,}075{,}000} \times 100{,}000 = 7{,}924.6$$

Using a hand-held calculator and the same equation, you can easily check the crime rate figures for the other three states.

Rates are more useful for comparative purposes than are absolute numbers. This can be illustrated by using the preceding information. If you heard that California had six times as many crimes as Arizona and nearly twice as many as Florida you might think California a less safe place to live than either of the other states, especially compared to Arizona. But the overall chances of being victimized by crime were actually *higher* in Arizona and Florida than in California. Column 3 shows that California had the lowest crime rate of the three states, even though column 2 shows that it had the most official crime. Rates take population size into account, making them a better basis for comparisons than absolute numbers. Based on the rates in this example, Michigan seems safer than the other three states.

But suppose you wanted to compare rural crime rates across these same four states. The Uniform Crime Reports could help here, too. Here are the relevant figures for the population living in rural areas:

STATE	POPULATION (1)	NUMBER OF INDEX CRIMES (2)	INDEX CRIME RATE (3)
Arizona	312,726	7,249	2,318
California	621,211	21,043	3,387
Florida	756,471	29,962	3,961
Michigan	1,039,484	26,851	2,583

Look at what has happened. According to these FBI figures, the number of crimes per 100,000 residents of rural Arizona is lower than the number per 100,000 residents of rural Michigan.

Since these data cover only one year—1994—you probably wouldn't pull up stakes and move to Arizona. In fact, even if the rural crime rates in Arizona were lower than those in Michigan over a number of years one might still hesitate to move. The reason is this: The rates are fairly close and crime labeling practices might differ in the two states. If the public or the police are more inclined to label events as crimes in Michigan than in Arizona, this might explain some of the difference. The true crime threat could be similar, or even greater in Arizona.

This exercise is meant to show that even when crime rates are computed, it is difficult to make meaningful comparisons across time or across jurisdictions. Generally, when criminologists compare published rates such as those in the Uniform Crime Reports, they hope that variations in labeling practices are minimal across jurisdictions. In effect, crime rate comparisons assume that the public who report crimes, the police who record them, and the clerks in police departments who transcribe them for the FBI all make similar judgments and mistakes, or if not, that the variations are random. Comparisons also assume that the population estimates used in rate calculations are accurate. None of these assumptions is probably correct, but the alternative is to give up doing comparative research with FBI crime figures. Because of this, efforts to improve the comparability of data on crime and criminals continue.

The National Incident-Based Reporting System. In 1991, the FBI initiated a more comprehensive and detailed reporting system known as the **National Incident-Based Reporting System (NIBRS).** All 17,000 state and local enforcement agencies now report their crime data to NIBRS. The plan is to replace the UCR with this incident-based system in 1999.

National Incident-Based Reporting System (NIBRS) A nationwide database consisting of individual police records on crimes and related arrests, slated to replace the UCR in 1999.

The difference between the traditional UCR and NIBRS is basically this: Under NIBRS, individual police records on each official criminal incident and related arrest—rather than monthly summaries—will make up a database that can be used by criminal justice practitioners, policymakers, and researchers to answer a wide variety of questions. Information on crime incidents will be taken directly from the reports officers make at the scene, as well as from reports maintained by prosecutors and the courts. An immediate advantage of NIBRS is that all offenses within a given crime incident can now be recorded, as opposed to only the most serious offenses, which is the case with the UCR. Another advantage concerns the breadth of information that will be available. Under NIBRS, information will be available on a wide range of details, from demographic information, time of day, weapon use, victim resistance, location of offense and residence of victims and suspects, to police response times, whether the crime was completed, and what eventually happened to the suspect, if there was one. In addition, NIBRS will contain incident-based data on the entire list of Part 1 and Part 2 offenses shown in the Appendix.

The promise of NIBRS is substantial but as yet unfulfilled. In 1997, the U.S. Department of Justice reported that NIBRS was not moving along as quickly as hoped and began a study to find out why (Bureau of Justice Statistics, 1997f). Even when fully operational, NIBRS will still capture only official police-generated data. Many crimes and many criminals will never appear in the data for the reasons we discussed earlier. Comparative analyses will still be affected by variations in the crime-labeling practices of the public and the police. But many agree that NIBRS is a step in the right direction.

Uncovering the Dark Figure of Crime I: Victimization Surveys

The gap between the official police count of crimes and criminals and the true count can never be known. But criminologists have developed two other sources of crime data that help uncover the dark figure of crime. One source is represented by **victimization surveys.** As the name indicates, these surveys are designed to determine whether people have been victimized by crime. They are based on the belief that unrecorded crimes may be uncovered through direct interviews with members of the public. The second source is represented by **self-report studies,** which uncover crime by asking people whether they have committed offenses. The self-report study is discussed later on.

victimization surveys Surveys that ask people whether they have been victims of crime during a given period of time.

self-report studies Surveys that ask people whether they have committed crimes during a given period of time.

National Crime Victimization Survey (NCVS) An annual survey of 100,000 people age 12 and older to determine the nature and extent of their victimization by crime.

The National Crime Victimization Survey (NCVS). Every year since 1973 the U.S. Department of Justice has sponsored a nationwide survey of 49,000 households to find out more about crime in America. Called the National Crime Survey until 1991, and now called the **National Crime Victimization Survey (NCVS)**, the program has become an international model. The Bureau of Justice Statistics (BJS), which runs the survey, calls NCVS "the only national forum for victims to describe outcomes of crime and characteristics of violent offenders" (Bureau of Justice Statistics, 1997b:21). Approximately 100,000 individuals age 12 and older are interviewed each year by trained personnel from the U.S. Bureau of the Census.

The NCVS begins with a series of screening questions done by telephone or in face-to-face interviews with respondents. These questions identify whether the respondent recalls being personally involved in a crime during the previous year. For example, here is Question 42 from the NCVS Basic Screen Questionnaire used in the 1996 survey:

> 42a. People often don't think of incidents committed by someone they know. Other than incidents already mentioned, did you have something stolen from you or were you attacked or threatened by:
> (a) Someone at work or school?
> (b) A neighbor or friend?
> (c) A relative or family member?
> (d) Any other person you've met or known?
> 42b. Did any incidents of this type happen to you?
> 42c. How many times?

These questions help jog the respondent's memory and the answers tell interviewers where to go next. The more specific questioning that follows is designed to pinpoint the specifics of incidents that respondents recall. Box 2.2 shows some of the questions used to uncover details about rape.

Sometimes an incident is revealed not to be a crime; other times it turns out to be a different crime than initially believed. For example, a broken window may at first suggest a case of attempted burglary but further questioning could reveal that it was more likely vandalism. In addition, detailed questioning provides information about such things as the actions of offenders and victims, the extent of injury or loss, the type of weapon used, and the reasons for reporting or not reporting the incident to police. Indeed, without the NCVS our earlier discussion of nationwide crime reporting by victims would have been entirely speculative.

Limitations of Victimization Surveys. Victimization surveys have their limitations. First, findings are based only on recall, and people's memories are often flawed. Second, respondents may intentionally deceive interviewers, although carefully constructed questionnaires and well-trained interviewers can reduce this risk. Deception is more likely to be a problem for some crimes and some victims than for others. For example, it is likely that victimization of women and children is underreported by victimization surveys because of embarrassment or fear. "Indeed, their assailant may be in the room at the time of the interview" (Hough and Mayhew, 1983:21). It has been found that the simple step of using female interviewers in a nonthreatening setting helps uncover more domestic violence (Mirrlees-Black, 1995).

Another problem with victimization surveys is the possibility that they overestimate the proportion of crimes involving black suspects. This is less likely to result from victims intentionally lying about a suspect's race than from the fact that some victims hold stereotypical images of criminals. In one interesting study of this issue, white and black subjects were asked to describe a picture they had been shown of a white man holding a razor during an argument

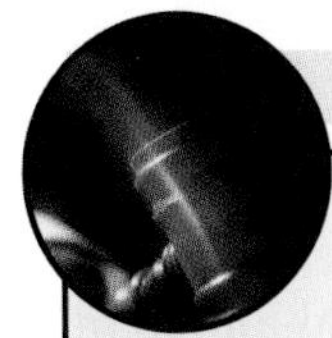

Box 2.2

JUSTICE PROFESSIONALS AT WORK

FINDING RAPE VICTIMS

The NCVS Questionnaire and the Reporting of Rape As a household survey, the NCVS directs interviewers to ask each household member age 12 or older whether he or she experienced a crime in the previous six months. If an individuals says that he or she has been victimized by a crime, whether or not the incident was reported to the police, the interviewer collects information on the crime.

Each respondent is asked whether he or she was attacked; and if so, how. If the respondent says that he or she was raped, the incident is classified as a completed rape. If the victim reports an offender's attacking and trying to rape him or her, the incident is classified as an attempted rape, even if the victim incurred injuries. If the offender threatened to rape the victim but did not attack, the incident is classified as an attempted rape. Rapes committed by nonstrangers, particularly those intimate with the victim, were less likely to be reported to the NCVS than rapes by strangers.

7b. Did the person(s) hit you, knock you down, or actually attack you in any way?

- ☐ Yes
- ☐ No

7c. Did the person(s) threaten you with harm in any way?

- ☐ Yes
- ☐ No

7d. How were you threatened? Any other way?

- ☐ Verbal threat of rape
- ☐ Verbal threat of attack other than rape
- ☐ Weapon present or threatened with weapon
- ☐ Attempted attack with weapon
- ☐ Object thrown at person
- ☐ Followed, surrounded
- ☐ Other (specify) ____________

7f. How did the person(s) attack you? Any other way?

- ☐ Raped
- ☐ Tried to rape
- ☐ Shot
- ☐ Knifed
- ☐ Hit with object in hand
- ☐ Hit by thrown object
- ☐ Hit by thrown object
- ☐ Hit, slapped, knocked down
- ☐ Grabbed, held, tripped, pushed, etc.
- ☐ Other (specify) ____________

Source: Caroline Wolf Harlow (1991). *Female Victims of Violent Crime* (p. 10). Washington, D.C.: U.S. Department of Justice.

with a black man; a majority of the white subjects recalled that the black man had been holding the razor (McNeely and Pope, 1981)! It is possible, too, that errors in racial identification could be made if some white offenders conceal their race by wearing masks and gloves, or by blackening their hands and face when committing crimes at night.

Victimization surveys nevertheless provide useful information on a broad range of issues. For example, researchers can learn about the protective measures victims take when they are assaulted, robbed, or raped; about relationships between victims and offenders; about the distribution of crimes in time and space; about the risks of victimization and the costs suffered by different segments of the population; and about the nature and timeliness of the police response.

By maintaining comparability from year to year, the NCVS surveys allow us to look at short-term changes and long-term trends. For example, Figure 2.5 shows victimization trends from 1975 to 1992 (the data after 1992 are not directly comparable with previous years due to changes in NCVS methods). Overall, crime showed a long and continuous decline, while some crimes showed little movement at all. Rape—which is close to zero—is an example.

A Peek at NCVS Findings on Violent Crime in America. Violent crime is of great concern to many people, and so recent NCVS reports showing that violent crime victimization rates remained stable from 1992 to 1994 and then declined by 12.4 percent from 1994 to 1995 were greeted with cautious optimism (Bureau of Justice Statistics, 1997b:1). This was the largest drop in the history

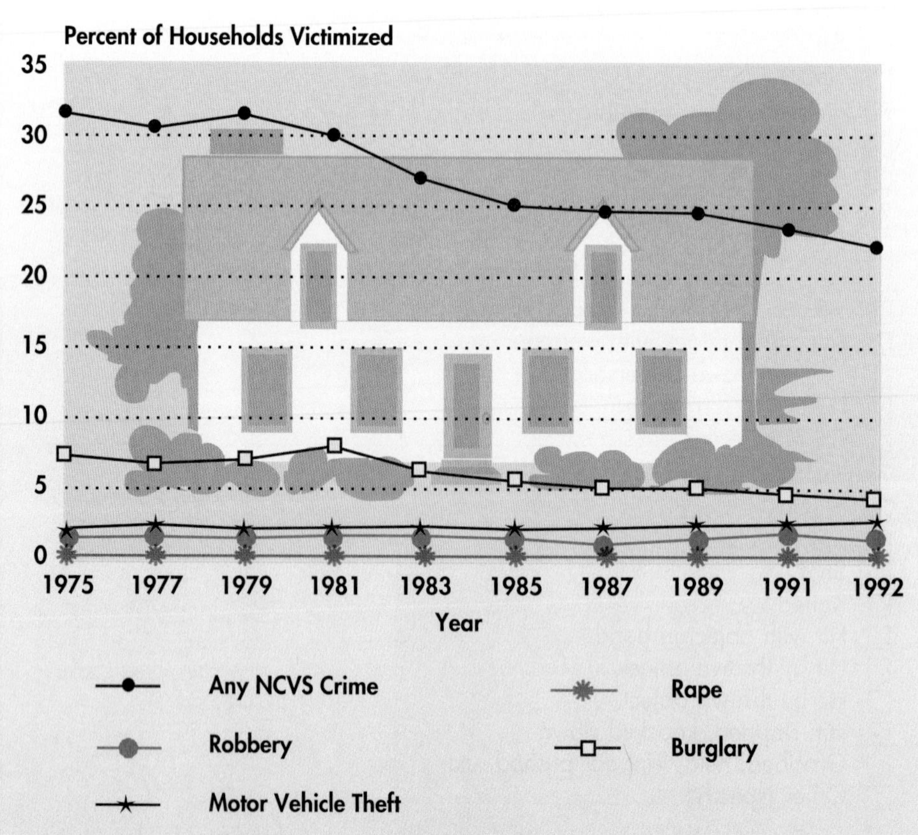

FIGURE 2.5 TRENDS IN CRIME VICTIMIZATION, 1975–1992
Over this 20-year period, the trend in crime victimization has generally been downward. This figure shows overall trends and trends in rape, robbery, burglary, and motor vehicle theft. Note that data collected through NCVS after 1992 are not directly comparable with earlier years due to changes in NCVS procedures.

Source: Michael R. Rand (1993). "Crime and the Nation's Households, 1992." BJS Bulletin (August):2.

of the NCVS, and it represents 1.2 million fewer reported victimizations. Still, an estimated 9.6 million individuals were victims of violent crime in 1995—and this does not include murder, since the victim cannot be questioned. This represents 46.2 victimizations per 1,000 persons age 12 or older, the usual way rates are expressed using NCVS data.

When the overall NCVS figures on violence are broken down to represent different population groups or offense circumstances—a process called *disaggregation*—interesting patterns emerge. Table 2.2 shows some of this information. Notice that the burdens of crime victimization are not born equally. Young men experience more violence than other groups, as do poorer people, blacks, and people living in cities; women are much more likely than men to report being victims of rape or sexual assault.

TABLE 2.2 Who Is Victimized Most by Violent Crime?

The burden of crime victimization is not borne equally. This is particularly true of violent crime. NCVS reports for 1994 and 1995 show which Americans are more likely and which are less likely to be victimized by violent crimes.*

- In 1994, violent crime struck:

  1 in 17 males
  1 in 24 females

  1 in 9 young people age 12 to 15
  1 in 8 teenagers age 16 to 19
  1 in 10 young adults age 20 to 24
  1 in 16 adults age 25 to 34
  1 in 25 adults age 35 to 49
  1 in 66 adults age 50 to 64
  1 in 196 adults age 65 and older

  1 in 20 whites
  1 in 17 Hispanics
  1 in 16 African Americans

  1 in 12 households with incomes less than $7,500
  1 in 25 households with incomes of $75,000 or more

  1 in 16 urban residents
  1 in 20 suburban residents
  1 in 26 rural residents

- Women are six times more likely than men to experience violence committed by a spouse, an ex-spouse, or an intimate friend.
- The risks of a woman being assaulted by a spouse or former spouse, or by a current or former boyfriend or girlfriend, are about equal across ethnic and racial lines.
- In 1995, the rate of rape and sexual assault of women was almost 10 times the rate for male victims.
- Consistently over the history of NCVS, the least likely victims of any type of violent crime are people age 65 and older; the most likely victims are people age 12 to 24.

*Violent crimes are rape, sexual assault, robbery with or without injury, aggravated assault with injury, and simple assault with minor injury. The data includes attempts to commit robbery or rape, and threats of assault involving weapons.

Source: Bureau of Justice Statistics (1997). *Changes in Criminal Victimization, 1994–1995.* Washington, D.C.: U.S. Department of Justice; Bureau of Justice Statistics (1996). *Fiscal Year 1996 at a Glance.* Washington, D.C.:U.S. Department of Justice; Ronet Bachman and Linda E. Saltzman (1995). "Violence against Women: Estimates from the Redesigned Survey." *BJS Special Report,* August:1–8.

Violence in the Workplace. The NCVS has also provided the first national data on violence in the workplace. Survey respondents were asked if they had been a victim of a crime while working or on duty. Between 1992 and 1996, an estimated 2 million violent victimizations occurred in the workplace each year (Warchol, 1998). Figure 2.6 shows how various occupations rank in terms of the number of nonfatal victimizations that occur for every 1,000 workers. People in criminal justice occupations experienced the highest rates, followed by taxi drivers, people in retail sales, and people working in mental health. Most of the victimizations involved assaults, but over 80,000 robberies and over 50,000 sexual assaults were reported on average each year. Men were more often victimized than women, and a third of the time victims faced armed offenders. Not surprisingly, commercial establishments and public locations were more dangerous than any other workplace locale. When attacked, most victims offered no resistance or took actions that were nonconfrontational, such as trying to persuade or bargain with the offender, or fleeing or hiding. Even so, nearly 10 percent of all workplace crimes resulted in the victim needing medical attention.

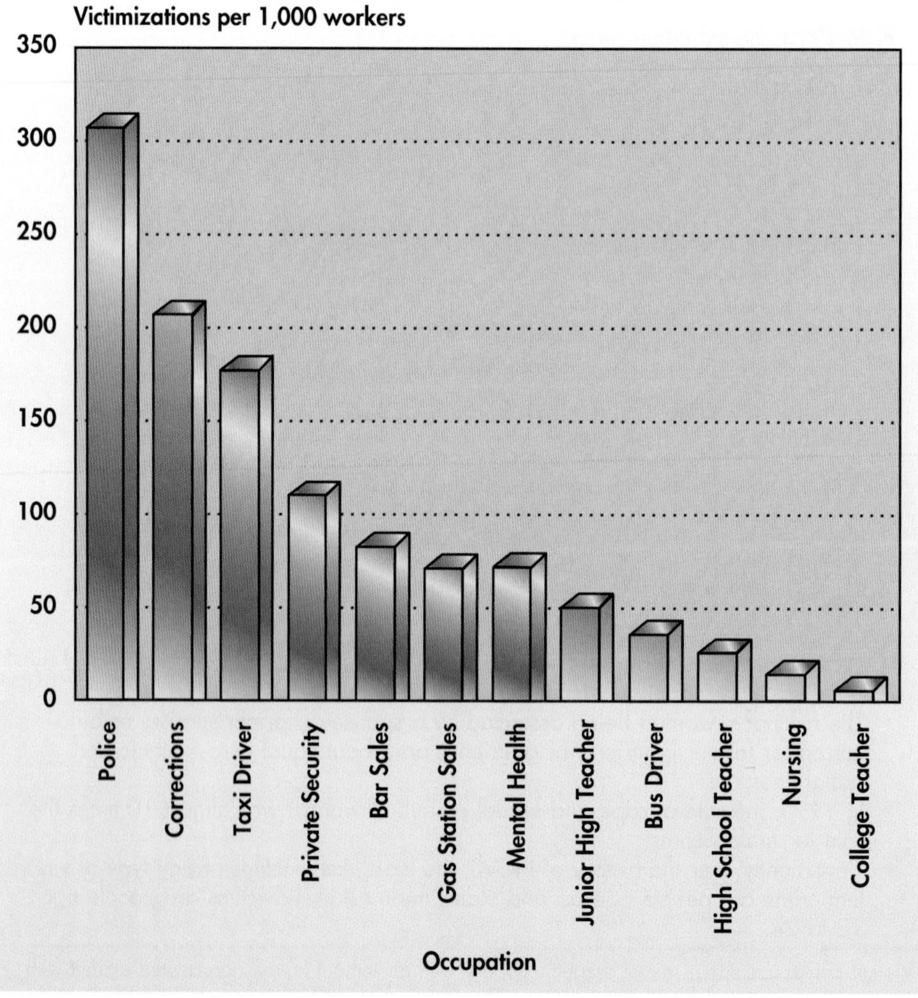

FIGURE 2.6 Nonfatal Workplace Violence by Occupations
The figure shows the number of violent victimizations per 1,000 workers in each occupation.

Source: Greg Worchol (1998). "Workplace Violence, 1992–1996." *BJS Special Report,* July: p. 3.

Violence in the workplace affects millions of Americans each year. Those most at risk work in commercial establishments or in the open—which includes the police and people who make deliveries.

Photo by Lenny Ignelzi, courtesy of AP Laserphoto

Comparing the UCR and the NCVS. The NCVS was designed to complement the UCR (U.S. Department of Justice, 1995). The two programs are not directly comparable; as we have seen, they use different methods, calculate crime rates differently, and provide different kinds of information. However, sometimes it is possible to manipulate the data from both programs to overcome some of the differences between them. Even though the NCVS still records more crimes, long-term trends in some offenses look remarkably similar in both UCR and NCVS data sets. For example, if robberies of commercial establishments such as gas stations, convenience stores, and banks are excluded from the UCR, the long-term rates closely correspond with those of the NCVS, which measure noncommercial robbery.

Not surprisingly, the National Crime Victimization Survey provides virtually no information on crimes that victimize society rather than individuals—for example, drug offenses, treason and espionage, or environmental crimes. Nor does it collect information on crimes committed in connection with a person's job, such as embezzlement, price-fixing, or bribery. The UCR hardly does any better in this regard, reporting only on fraud and embezzlement. In fact, it would not be easy to collect information on "white-collar" or "occupational" crimes under either format. There is little systematic policing of the workplace, and agencies that investigate such crimes do not generally report them to the FBI's UCR program—and probably would not do so even if there were a category to put them in. In addition, people often have no idea what to call it or where to report it if they are victimized. Being the target of consumer fraud at an appliance store is different from having one's purse snatched or coming home to a ransacked house.

The Costs of Missing Crime: White-Collar and Environmental Offenses. The absence of a regular national data collection effort designed to measure white-collar and environmental crime—which often overlap—is unfortunate because the costs to individuals and society are far above those associated with street crimes and personal offenses against individuals. The most recent estimate of yearly financial costs associated with crimes such as burglary, robbery,

Occupational crimes such as offenses against the environment are more costly to society than conventional street crimes. Yet occupational crime is not as visible nor is it as often punished. Why might this be?

PHOTO BY BOB DAEMMRICH, COURTESY OF UNIPHOTO

homicide, rape, physical and sexual assault, drunk driving, and arson is $105 billion (Miller, Cohen, and Wiersema, 1996).

Now consider the financial costs of white-collar crime. Although there has been no comprehensive study, here are some estimates of the yearly financial losses to victims and society (Levi, 1987; Rockwell, 1990; Maguire and Pastore, 1998): tax evasion, up to $300 billion; securities fraud, $5 billion; bank fraud, $20 billion; insurance fraud, $40 billion; employee theft, $25 billion; and computer-related crimes, $10 billion and rising every year. Together, these costs are four times greater than those associated with common personal crimes. And the figures do not include price fixing and other restraint-of-trade practices, bribery, political corruption, industrial espionage, or violations of occupational health and safety regulations. Nor do the figures include environmental crimes. A major part of the dark figure of crime will remain hidden as long as there is no systematic national effort to collect victimization data on white-collar crime.

Combining National Data Sources on Crime: BJS *Selected Findings*. In a series of publications entitled *Selected Findings*, the Bureau of Justice Statistics uses UCR and NCVS data as well as other national data sources to shed light on particular crime problems for which no single data source alone is adequate. Table 2.3 shows some examples of the kinds of information available through these publications; in this case the focus is on weapons-related offenses.

UNCOVERING THE DARK FIGURE OF CRIME II: SELF-REPORT STUDIES

Researchers can also explore the dark figure of crime by asking people to recount their participation in criminal activities. The main purpose of these *self-report studies* is to assess the extent and type of criminality among different groups of people. Some people who admit committing offenses may already be part of the official record because they have been arrested by police. However,

Table 2.3 Combining Data Sources: BJS *Selected Findings* on Weapons Offenses

The Bureau of Justice Statistics publishes a variety of reports on crime topics called *Selected Findings.* These reports usually combine national data from different government sources, including the NCVS and the UCR. Here are some illustrative findings from reports on weapons-related offenses.

- Most crime is not committed with a firearm, but when it is, handguns are most often used: In 1993, 4 out of 5 reported victimizations involving firearms, and 3 out of 5 recorded murders involved handguns; in 1991, 25 percent of state prisoners who used a weapon to commit crime said they used a handgun.
- Offenders who use firearms prefer easily concealed, large-caliber guns.
- During a 28-month period following the passage of the Brady Handgun Violence Prevention Act of 1994, over 186,000 illegal over-the-counter gun sales were blocked by background investigations. In the first six months of 1996, around 34,000 handgun buyers were rejected; 72 percent of them were convicted or indicted felons.
- The majority of victims of intentional but nonfatal shootings are male (90 percent), black (60 percent), and aged between 15 and 29 (60 percent). Almost half of the victims are shot in the arm, hand, leg, or foot.
- Arrest rates for weapons offenses have more than doubled since 1965, though they vary considerably among states—from less than 25 arrests per 100,000 in Maine, New Hampshire, Montana, and Vermont to over 150 in Wisconsin and Missouri. Four out of 5 weapons arrests occur in urban areas, and black arrest rates are five times higher than those among whites.
- From 1990 to 1992, the average prison sentences for weapons offenders increased from 47 months to 77 months in federal courts, but decreased slightly in state courts, from 47 to 45 months.

Sources: Bureau of Justice Statistics (1994). "Violence between Intimates," *BJS Selected Findings* (November):1–10; Marianne W. Zawitz (1995), "Guns Used in Crime." *BJS Selected Findings* (July):1–7; Lawrence A. Greenfeld and Marianne W. Zawitz (1995). "Weapons Offenses and Offenders." *BJS Selected Findings* (November): 1–8; Marianne W. Zawitz (1996). "Firearm Injury from Crime." *BJS Selected Findings* (April):1–7; Diane Craven (1996). "Female Victims of Violent Crime." *BJS Selected Findings* (December): 1–3; Don Manson (1997). "Presale Firearms Checks." *BJS Selected Findings* (February): 1–5.

most offenders escape official labeling most of the time, so the self-report study is an important way of uncovering hidden crime and hidden criminals. Self-report studies also have some advantages over victimization surveys: They can uncover public order crimes, consensual offenses, and victimless offenses; they can also look at offenses committed by juveniles, including delinquencies that would not be crimes if committed by an adult—for example, running away, truancy, and curfew violations. These are called **status offenses.** We shall learn more about them in Chapter 4. Self-report studies have commonly focused on adolescents because much juvenile crime is hidden from official records and because the schools provide easy access to samples of youth.

status offenses Delinquent acts such as truancy and running away that only juveniles can commit.

The National Youth Survey (NYS) and Other Self-Report Surveys. A well-known nationwide survey illustrates the self-report technique. In the mid-1970s, criminologists at the Behavioral Research Institute of the University of Colorado interviewed a representative sample of American youth born from 1959 through 1965 to find out about their delinquent activity (Dunford and Elliott, 1984). A group of 1,725 adolescents were surveyed in 1977, making up the first "wave" or "panel" of the study, called the **National Youth Survey (NYS).** The youths were interviewed again in 1978, 1979, 1980, and 1981. Now adults, they were again interviewed in 1984, 1987, 1990, and 1993. As you would expect, some of the original sample dropped out of the study because researchers could not find them or they refused to participate further. By 1993,

National Youth Survey (NYS) A repeat survey of adolescents who were interviewed each year from 1978 to 1981, and then four more times as adults through 1993.

only 78 percent of the original sample remained. This respondent loss is referred to as *attrition,* and it is a problem faced in all studies that follow the same group of people over time.

The subjects of the National Youth Survey were asked whether they had committed any of an extensive list of delinquent and criminal activities during the year preceding the survey. Table 2.4 lists the items and, where appropriate,

TABLE 2.4 Self-Reported Delinquency Items from the National Youth Survey

The following items make up the self-report delinquency measure used in the 1976–1993 National Youth Survey. This list omits status offenses but includes some items added to the original 1977 questionnaire with dates shown in parentheses.

Question: "How many times in the last year have you:"

1. Purposely damaged or destroyed property belonging to your parents or other family members
2. Purposely damaged or destroyed property belonging to a school
3. Purposely damaged or destroyed other property that did not belong to you
4. Stolen (or tried to steal) a motor vehicle, such as a car or motorcycle
5. Stolen (or tried to steal) something worth more than $50
6. Knowingly bought, sold, or held stolen goods (or tried to do any of these things)
7. Carried a hidden weapon other than a plain pocket knife
8. Stolen (or tried to steal) an item worth $5 or less
9. Attacked someone with the idea of seriously hurting or killing them
10. Been involved in gang fights
11. Sold marijuana or hashish ("grass," "pot," "hash")
12. Stolen money or other things from your parents or from other members of your family
13. Hit (or threatened to hit) a teacher or adult at school
14. Hit (or threatened to hit) one of your parents
15. Hit (or threatened to hit) other students
16. Sold hard drugs such as heroin, cocaine, and LSD
17. Taken a vehicle for a ride (drive) without the owner's permission
18. Had (or tried to have) sexual relations with someone against their will
19. Used force (strong-arm methods) to get money or things from other students
20. Used force (strong-arm methods) to get money or things from a teacher or other adult at school
21. Used force (strong-arm methods) to get money or things from other people (not students or teachers)
22. Stolen (or tried to steal) things worth $5 to $50
23. Stolen (or tried to steal) something at school such as someone's coat from a classroom, locker, or cafeteria, or a book from the library
24. Broken into a building or vehicle (or tried to break in) to steal something or just to look around
25. Used or tried to use credit cards without the owner's permission (1978)
26. Used checks illegally or used phony money to pay for something (includes intentional overdrafts) (1979)
27. Tried to cheat someone by selling them something that was worthless or not what you said it was (1979)
28. Purposely set fire to a building, car, or other property or tried to do so (1980)
29. Hit or threatened to hit your supervisor or other employee (1986)
30. Forged or copied someone else's signature on a check or legal document without their permission (1993)
31. Made fraudulent insurance claims, that is, falsified or inflated medical bills or property or automobile repairs or replacement costs (1993)
32. Beaten up on someone so badly they probably needed a doctor (1993)

Source: Kathleen Maguire and Ann L. Pastore, eds. (1996). *Sourcebook of Criminal Justice Statistics, 1995.* (Appendix 11). Washington D.C.: U.S. Department of Justice.

the year they were added to the original 1977 survey. The list shows a mixture of serious and less serious offenses, from joyriding and minor theft to assault, strong-arm robbery, and weapons offenses. The original survey also included some status offenses—for example, cheating on school tests, skipping classes, and running away from home.

The NYS has produced a wealth of information about delinquency and crime, and criminologists are still learning new things from it. Because the study collected information on both the prevalence and incidence of delinquency and crime over a number of years, it is possible to identify the frequency of offending as well as its seriousness and duration (Barlow and Ferdinand, 1992:45–49). The NYS confirmed, for example, that although most delinquency is sporadic and minor in nature, a small group of "chronic delinquents" is responsible for a disproportionate amount of all types of self-reported delinquency (Dunford and Elliott, 1984). Although some authors have criticized general youth surveys because they underrepresent truly serious chronic offenders who are incarcerated during the interview periods (Cernkovich, Giordano, and Pugh, 1985), the NYS is generally recognized as one of the best.

Shortcomings of Self-Report Surveys. In the early days of self-report studies, especially those using adolescents, the surveys were full of questions about status offenses, with only one or two tapping participation in serious crimes. Not surprisingly, the prevalence of self-reported delinquency turned out to be similar across class, race, and gender lines (Hindelang, Hirschi, and Weis, 1979). Critics argued that the surveys trivialized juvenile crime by underemphasizing serious offenses. More recent surveys have tried to correct this imbalance by including more questions dealing with major crimes such as robbery and assaults involving injuries or weapons. Although overall rates of self-reported delinquency still do not vary much by class, race, or gender, serious offending involving violence is more commonly reported by males, lower-class individuals, and African American youth (Barlow and Ferdinand, 1992:60–69).

Although self-report studies now tap more serious crimes, they have largely neglected white-collar crimes, especially corporate crimes. There are two major reasons for this. First, it is difficult to penetrate the "protective walls of secrecy behind which corporate executives conspire to commit crime" (Box, 1983:86). Second, even if corporate executives were willing to consider being questioned about illegal activity, the researcher has little to offer in the way of inducement. Adolescents in school no doubt enjoy the momentary distraction from regular studies, but the situation is surely different for executives, who may also feel that they are taking unnecessary risks by opening up to strangers. The few in-depth studies of corporate crime that have involved personal interviews were completed only after elaborate steps had been taken to ensure confidentiality and to gain the trust of respondents (Jackall, 1988; Clinard and Yeager, 1980).

Trust is important in all interview situations, but especially with crime, a topic that is often embarrassing or humiliating, or involves behavior that would ordinarily get a person into serious trouble. An interview subject may well wonder whether cooperation is worth it, so interviewers must be adequately trained to overcome such negative reactions. Even then, problems may remain. For example, those people who agree to be interviewed may have had different experiences with crime from those who refuse; clearly, this would bias the results. Some respondents may conceal past criminal activities, and others may exaggerate them. Some youths think it "cool" to report doing things that in fact they never have done. Although all these problems create potential pitfalls in the use and interpretation of self-report studies, the knowledge gained still adds new pieces to the puzzle of crime in America and helps uncover the dark figure of crime.

Autobiographical Accounts of Crime and Justice. Self-reports can also be used for in-depth examination of the long-term experiences of individual offenders and victims, as well as those employed by criminal justice agencies. These "autobiographical accounts," or "life histories," provide insights on crime and justice that only detailed questioning over many hours can uncover. Two pioneers of American criminology, Clifford Shaw (1930) and Edwin Sutherland (1937b) were among the first to use autobiographical interviews. Shaw interviewed a "career" delinquent he called "Stanley." Box 2.3 describes this work. Sutherland interviewed a professional thief. Their work influenced later research on diverse crimes, from fencing stolen property (Klockars, 1974;

Box 2.3

JUSTICE PROFESSIONALS AT WORK

CLIFFORD SHAW AND THE JACK-ROLLER

In the 1920s, a sociologist at the University of Chicago named Clifford Shaw was studying delinquency in Chicago. As part of his research he conducted interviews with delinquents. Many were short oral histories but three of the longer ones were turned into books: The *Jack-Roller: A Delinquent Boy's Own Story* (1930), *The Natural History of a Delinquent Career* (1931), and *Brothers in Crime* (1938).

Jack-Roller has become a classic in criminology. It is the story of "Stanley," who was 12 when he first met Shaw in 1921. Stanley had already run up an extensive arrest history and had spent almost half his life in juvenile institutions of one sort or another. By the time he was 17, Stanley had 38 arrests. Most of these were for petty offenses, but later arrests were for more serious crimes such as assault, robbery, and "jack-rolling." Jack-rolling involved locating a drunk, or sometimes a homosexual, assaulting him, and then stealing whatever took Stanley's fancy. "We sometimes stunned the drunks by 'giving them the club,' in a dark place near a lonely alley. It was bloody work, but necessity demanded it—we had to live" (Shaw, 1930:85).

Through stories like Stanley's, Shaw showed how delinquent attitudes and practices develop and are transmitted from boy to boy, and also how individual delinquent careers develop. Shaw decided that the acquisition of delinquent attitudes and practices is encouraged through friendships, neighborhood traditions, and the breakdown of parental controls. In addition, Shaw used autobiographical accounts to suggest appropriate treatment strategies. In Stanley's case, this included finding a "sympathetic and informal" foster home; obtaining employment as a salesman (which did not last); helping him develop contacts with new, nondelinquent friends; and maintaining weekly contact with him.

Later, in his seventies, Stanley recollected that Shaw's efforts helped turn him away from crime, despite occasional relapses (Snodgrass, 1982). On a larger scale, Shaw's work with Stanley and other youths helped him construct the delinquency prevention project known as the Chicago Area Project. This program focused on changing the delinquent child's social environment through neighborhood reconstruction and community self-help projects. It is still regarded by many as one of the best delinquency prevention programs ever developed.

Steffensmeier, 1986), safecracking (King, 1972), and female gang delinquency (Campbell, 1984) to drug offenses (Hills and Santiago, 1992).

An autobiographical account is a first-person description of experiences with crime that is usually given orally under the guidance of a researcher. Such accounts may be a few pages long or run to volumes. This life history research explores experiences and relationships in a subject's personal biography that may be decades old. It can be amazing what subjects recall once they get started, and the picture that emerges helps researchers understand the evolution of delinquent and criminal practices and their transmission from one person or group to another (Bennett, 1981:189).

Ethnographic Research. A great deal of criminological research is based on another kind of self-report study—the **ethnography.** Ethnographic research involves "open-ended" interviews and discussions—sometimes over many hours or days—during which subjects give detailed accounts of their criminal lifestyles. Ethnographers often spend considerable time in the natural environments of their subjects, as participant observers. Criminologist Paul Cromwell (1996) has assembled a remarkable volume of ethnographic studies titled *In Their Own Words: Criminals on Crime.* It covers thieves of all sorts, gang members, rapists, murderers, drug dealers, and doctors who defraud the Medicaid system.

ethnography A descriptive account of a culture or lifestyle that is obtained through participant observation and/or in-depth conversations with the people involved.

A recent example of this methodology is a study of the street life of residential burglars in St. Louis (Wright and Decker, 1994). Some of the problems mentioned earlier were also experienced in this study: convincing subjects to participate, gaining trust, assessing the truthfulness of what subjects said—and protecting the researchers' own safety. Safety is often a problem in field research dealing with crime, all the more so if researchers spend hours and hours with their subjects on their own turf. A social researcher who was studying Chicago area gangs in the 1950s told how boys would constantly test him by frightening, "baiting," or "ranking" him, and subjecting him to minor acts of violence (Spergel, 1964).

Even locating the interview subjects in the first place was a problem for the St. Louis researchers. The authors solved this by using the *snowball technique:* A former student of theirs was a retired criminal with hundreds of offenses—but very few arrests. The authors hired him to put the word on the street that active burglars were being sought for interviews. One person told another, and through these informal referrals the authors eventually built up a sample of 105 active burglars (Wright and Decker, 1994). These burglars described their lives and crimes, and 70 of them agreed to visit sites of successful burglaries they had committed to reconstruct the crime. The researchers were able to place targets in their neighborhood context, and also develop a clear picture of how these offenders typically went about their business of residential burglary.

There is not room here to examine all the interesting findings from self-report studies, but one seems to emerge time and time again: Although self-reports show that crime is widespread and crosses all social boundaries, they also show that a relatively small percentage of individuals are responsible for a large percentage of the crime, especially serious crime. These individuals commit many offenses during their active criminal careers, sometimes hundreds each year. One famous study of California prison inmates asked them to recount their criminal activity in the year immediately prior to their incarceration (Peterson, Braiker, and Polich, 1980). The researchers found that a typical group of 100 inmates would have committed 490 armed robberies, 310 assaults, 720 burglaries, 70 auto thefts, 100 forgeries, and 3,400 drug sales in one year of street freedom.

SOURCES OF INFORMATION ON THE CRIMINAL JUSTICE SYSTEM

Suppose you want to know the number of Americans serving prison sentences, the reasons they are in prison, and how long they have been there. Suppose you are interested in the physical, social, and health conditions in the nation's jails. Or perhaps you want to compare the post-incarceration experiences of prison inmates with those in community-based correctional programs. All these issues will be examined in this book, but where does the information come from?

Much of the information comes from reports issued by agencies within the U.S. Department of Justice, which oversees all federal law enforcement operations and coordinates the collection and dissemination of national data on the justice system. However, it was not until the 1960s that federal authorities showed much interest in national data beyond the FBI's Uniform Crime Reports. Before that time, data collection was left to individual states and there was virtually no standardization in reporting or in the kinds of information being collected. In 1968 Congress passed the Omnibus Crime Control and Safe Streets Act, part of which created the Law Enforcement Assistance Administration (LEAA). Over the next few years the LEAA's budget grew to more than $1 billion. While most of this money went to policing, millions of dollars poured into data collection and research. Periodic fact-finding surveys of the nation's courts, jails, and prisons were conducted, and some of these eventually became annual reports.

PROGRAMS OF THE U.S. DEPARTMENT OF JUSTICE

As is the case with police and victimization data on crime, the federal government now acts as a national clearinghouse for information gathered by state and federal justice agencies. This effort is handled by agencies within the U.S Department of Justice. The **Office of Justice Programs (OJP)** oversees data collection; federal training grants to police, courts, and correctional agencies; government research on crime and justice; juvenile justice programs; and support of specialized justice programs such as gang investigation, prison drug treatment, criminal records, and missing children. OJP was established by the 1984 Justice Assistance Act to replace the LEAA and OJARS, the Office of Justice Assistance, Research, and Statistics.

Office of Justice Programs (OJP) A Justice Department agency that oversees criminal justice research, data collection, and training programs for the federal government.

The Bureau of Justice Statistics. Within OJP, the **Bureau of Justice Statistics (BJS)** collects, analyzes, publishes, and disseminates information on all aspects of criminal justice. The previous section introduced you to the NCVS; the BJS also produces specialized publications and statistical reports on a variety of justice topics, some of them on an annual basis (see Table 2.5). The following list illustrates the scope of the Bureau's efforts (Bureau of Justice Statistics, 1998b):

Bureau of Justice Statistics (BJS) Collects data, conducts research, and disseminates results on all aspects of criminal justice.

- Annual publications on Americans under correctional supervision
- Annual reports on the processing of offenders through the federal courts
- Annual reports on capital punishment
- Periodic data series dealing with:
  - Felony convictions
  - Processing of defendants through state courts
  - Characteristics of correctional populations
  - Prosecutorial practices and policies
  - Administration of law enforcement agencies and correctional facilities
  - Criminal justice expenditures and employment

TABLE 2.5 Annual Publications of the Bureau of Justice Statistics

The Bureau of Justice Statistics publishes a variety of annual statistical reports on the justice system at work. Many can be found on the Internet, as listed in Box 2.5. Here is the list as of 1997:

Sourcebook of Criminal Justice Statistics—compiled from more than 150 separate data sources; almost all data are nationwide in scope, and many tables show figures for regions and states. A most useful source of information, referred to many times in this text.

Federal Justice Statistics Series—data on the workload, activities, and outcomes associated with federal criminal cases.

National Corrections Reporting Program—data on all prison admissions and releases and on all parole entries and discharges in participating jurisdictions. Individual prisoner records are used to provide conviction offense, sentence length, minimum time to be served, credited jail time, and other information.

Capital Punishment Series—data on persons sentenced to death and those executed. Includes demographic characteristics, prior criminal histories, and time spent on death row.

Annual Survey of Jails—data providing estimates of number of inmates in local jails and on the relationship between populations and jail capacities.

National Probation and Parole Reporting Program—data on state and federal probation and parole counts and the movement and characteristics of persons under supervision.

Source: Bureau of Justice Statistics (1998). *Bureau of Justice Statistics Fiscal Year 1998: At a Glance.* Washington, D.C.: U.S. Department of Justice.

- Special studies on other criminal justice topics—for example, campus law enforcement agencies, local police and sheriffs' departments, sentences and time served in prison by violent offenders, lawsuits brought by prisoners, defense of indigent defendants, community-based corrections, AIDS in prisons and jails, and criminal justice systems around the world

The Bureau of Justice Statistics is America's primary source of national statistics on the justice system at work. Table 2.6 illustrates some of the findings from recent BJS publications. Many detailed tables and figures using BJS information will be used throughout this text to document important points. For example, in Chapter 1 the discussion of criminalization pointed out that some groups of Americans are more likely to be labeled criminals than others. People of color have disproportionately high rates of arrest, and they are more likely to end up in prison. Using confinement data from federal and state prisons, BJS statisticians have computed the lifetime probability of going to prison for different racial and ethnic groups of American males (Bonczar and Beck, 1997). At birth, black males have a 28.5 percent chance of going to prison during their lifetime, compared with a 16 percent chance for Hispanic males and a 4.4 percent chance for non-Hispanic white males.

The Bureau of Justice Statistics not only publishes statistical reports and disseminates data already collected by other justice agencies, but also sponsors special seminars and workshops to address data collection needs that stem from new federal legislation. In 1995, for example, BJS embarked on a joint effort with the National Institute of Justice—the research and development arm of the Office of Justice Programs—to collect national data on police use of force. This initiative was ordered by Congress through the U.S. Attorney General as part of the Violent Crime Control and Law Enforcement Act of 1994.

TABLE 2.6 Illustrative Findings from BJS Publications on the Justice System

The Bureau of Justice Statistics is the primary source of published information on the operations of America's justice system. Here are some recent findings from various BJS reports:

Law Enforcement on College Campuses

In 1995, more than 90 percent of four-year public universities and colleges serving 2,500 or more students employed sworn police officers, compared to less than half of private campuses.

Two-thirds of these campuses have armed officers, and one-half to one-third operated general crime prevention programs, rape prevention programs, and programs to combat drug and alcohol abuse.

The 1994 costs of campus police services were $181 per student on public campuses and $94 per student on private campuses.

Police and Sheriffs' Departments

A 1993 survey of 411 city police departments, 146 sheriffs' departments, 49 state police agencies, and 33 county departments found that men made up 90 percent of sworn personnel, and that more than 80 percent were white, non-Hispanic officers.

Expenditure and Employment Statistics

In 1992, 3.8 cents of every tax dollar went for police protection, jails or prisons, and the courts; 85.5 percent of this money was spent on state and local governments. However, per capita federal spending on justice rose 132 percent from 1987 to 1992, more than twice as fast as state and local spending.

Prosecution Statistics

Among prosecutors' offices that handle juvenile cases, almost two-thirds transferred at least one juvenile case to criminal court in 1994.

Half of 2,343 state prosecutors' offices surveyed in 1994 had a staff person—usually the chief prosecutor—who had been threatened or assaulted.

Court and Sentencing Statistics

In a survey of the nation's 75 most populous counties in 1992, nearly two-thirds of defendants charged with a felony were released from jail pending disposition of their case.

In 1994, over 870,000 adults were convicted in state courts of a felony offense—a 31 percent increase from 1988.

Nearly three-quarters of those convicted in 1994 were sentenced to incarceration.

Corrections Statistics

As of December 31, 1996, 5.5 million adults were on probation, in jail or prison, or on parole—about 2.8 percent of all adult U.S. residents.

Local jails held over 637,000 adults; prisons over 1.2 million.

The 1990 census of prisons showed an inmate-employee ratio of three inmates for every prison employee.

Source: Bureau of Justice Statistics (1998). *Bureau of Justice Statistics Fiscal Year 1998: At a Glance.* Washington, D.C.: U.S. Department of Justice.

Section 210402 of the act requires the Attorney General to collect and publish annual data "about the use of excessive force by law enforcement officers." Forty experts attended the workshop and concluded that "no single data collection mechanism can provide a full picture of police use of force" (McEwen, 1996:8).

The two agencies therefore set up two data collection strategies. One creates a comprehensive Police Use of Force Database that will be supervised by the International Association of Chiefs of Police (IACP); the second will involve a supplement to the National Crime Victimization Survey that will question respondents about their experiences with the police and, if relevant, the extent and circumstances of police use of force. It is too early to tell whether these efforts will produce useful national data on police use of force, but they are certainly welcome.

The Office of Juvenile Justice and Delinquency Prevention (OJJDP). A special agency within the Office of Justice Programs is responsible for statistical reports and research on juvenile crime and juvenile justice. Established by Congress in 1974, the **Office of Juvenile Justice and Delinquency Prevention (OJJDP)** sponsors a variety of programs aimed at improving juvenile justice and reducing juvenile crime. In 1984, its responsibilities were expanded to include the Missing and Exploited Children Program, which supports a nationwide network of organizations and agencies dealing with this important problem. In 1994, OJJDP began publication of a journal titled *Juvenile Justice.*

Office of Juvenile Justice and Delinquency Prevention (OJJDP) Sponsors programs, collects data, conducts research, and disseminates results specifically on juvenile crime and juvenile justice.

The Information Dissemination and Planning Unit within OJJDP is charged with disseminating data on juvenile justice. Much of the information is gathered through existing programs such as the FBI's Uniform Crime Reports, the NCVS, and nationwide self-report surveys. Two of the OJJDP's most important tasks are funding of the National Juvenile Justice Center, the research arm of the National Council of Family Court Judges, and the Juvenile Justice Clearinghouse, which is part of the National Criminal Justice Reference Service (NCJRS). Box 2.4 briefly describes the activities of these organizations.

Juvenile Justice: The National Picture. Two recent reports illustrate the kind of national information available through OJJDP (Poe-Yamagata and Butts, 1996; Snyder, 1997). They provide a glimpse of the nation's juvenile justice system at work:

- In 1995, there were 2.7 million arrests of people under age 18. Since 1986, overall arrests of juveniles increased by 30 percent, but arrests for violent crime increased 67 percent. However, the rate of increase

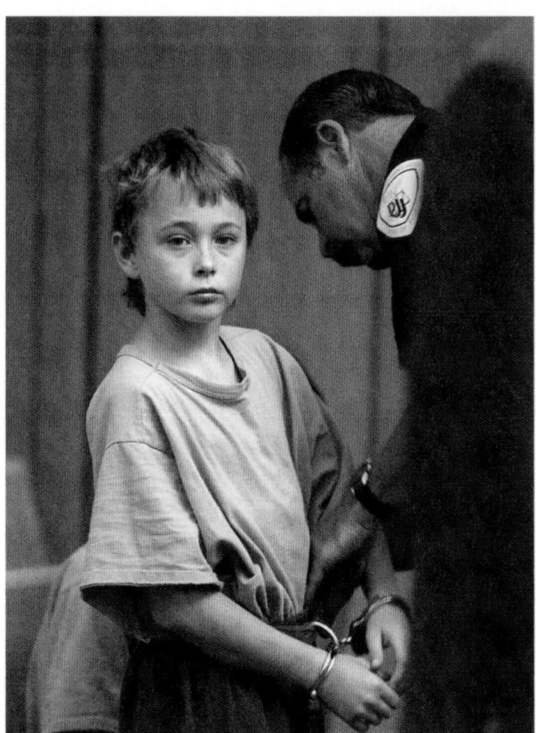

The National Juvenile Justice Center and the Juvenile Justice Clearinghouse are two important research agenices within the OJJDP. Due to rising juvenile crime and questions about whether more juvenile offenders should be treated as adults, research on juvenile delinquency is increasing in importance.

Photo by Scott Wheeler, courtesy of The Ledger/AP Photo

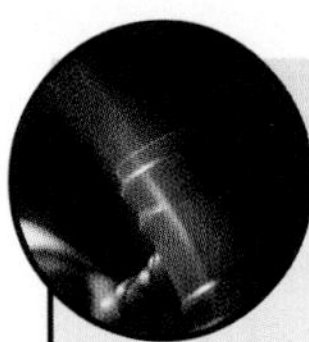

Box 2.4

JUSTICE PROFESSIONALS AT WORK

INSIDE THE OJJDP

The study of criminal justice depends on systematic and comprehensive data collection and dissemination. Since data collection is expensive, time-consuming, and often beyond the authority and capacity of private individuals and organizations, government agencies do the job or fund others to do it for them. The Office of Juvenile Justice and Delinquency Prevention (OJJDP) sponsors a variety of data efforts, two of which are described here.

The National Center for Juvenile Justice (NCJJ). This is the research arm of the National Council of Juvenile and Family Court judges. Among its current funded tasks is maintenance of the National Juvenile Court Data Archive and the Juvenile Justice Statistics and Systems Development (SSD) Program. The Data Archive collects and disseminates information from the nation's juvenile courts; SSD analyzes data and disseminates information gathered through existing federal statistical programs and other national studies. A recent example is the 1996 publication of *Female Offenders in the Juvenile Justice System,* which summarized the arrest, judicial management, and incarceration of female juvenile offenders. SSD also seeks ways to improve data collection efforts at the national level. Some of the projects include a national reporting program for juveniles waived to criminal court, and development of standardized techniques for self-report surveys.

The Juvenile Justice Clearinghouse (JJC). This is a component of the National Criminal Justice Reference Service. It is OJJDP's central resource for collecting, maintaining, producing, and sharing information on all aspects of juvenile justice. JJC disseminates OJJDP publications, research findings, program information, and literature reviews, and provides referrals and links to other resource materials on juvenile justice. JJC can be accessed from the World Wide Web at **http://www.ncjrs.org/ojjhome.htm**. Those with e-mail addresses can send inquiries or request documents by sending a message to **askncjrs@ncjrs.org**.

Source: Office of Juvenile Justice and Delinquency Prevention (1997). *Proposed Comprehensive Plan for Fiscal Year 1997.* Washington, D.C.: U.S. Department of Justice.

has been declining over the period, and from 1994 to 1995 the number of juvenile arrests for violent offenses actually decreased by 3 percent.

- Even though males are arrested four times as often as females, since 1991 female arrests have increased faster than male arrests in most offense categories.
- Juveniles make up a much larger proportion of the nation's arrests for property crime than for violent crime; the data are shown in Figure 2.7. In terms of arrests, there are some primarily adult offenses—DUI, drunkenness, fraud, forgery, embezzlement, and gambling—and some offenses for which juveniles are as likely to be arrested as adults—arson, vandalism, and motor vehicle theft.
- Most arrested juveniles are referred to court, and since 1980 the figure has been rising: from 58 percent to 66 percent in 1995. However, only about half are petitioned (the equivalent of prosecution in adult court), and of these just over half are adjudicated (that is, convicted). Among

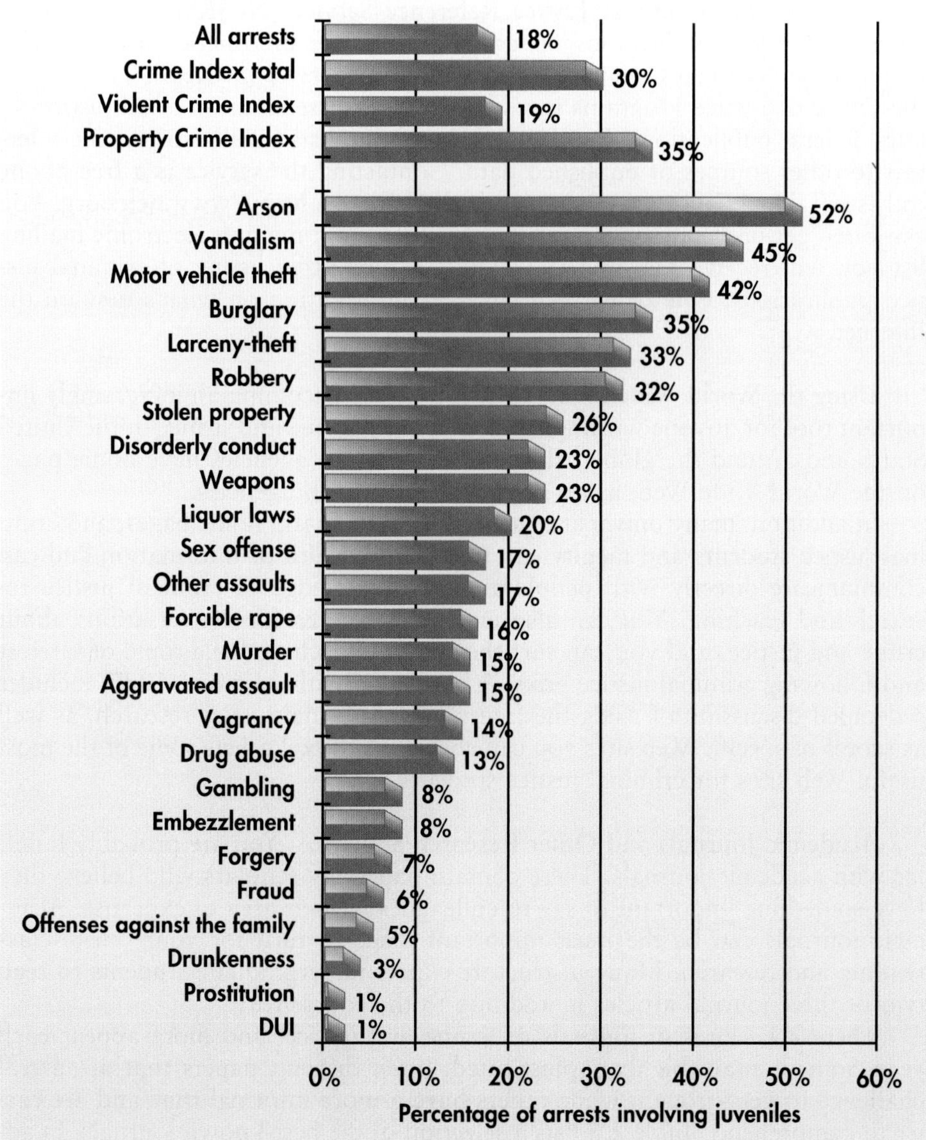

FIGURE 2.7 JUVENILE ARRESTS AS A PRECENTAGE OF ALL U.S. ARRESTS, 1995

Juveniles were involved in a much larger proportion of property crime arrests than violent crime arrests in 1995.

Source: Howard N. Snyder (1997). "Juvenile Arrests 1995." *OJJDP Juvenile Justice Bulletin* (February): p. 3.

adjudicated juveniles, roughly 30 percent of males and 25 percent of females are placed in detention or long-term custody.

RESOURCES FOR STUDENT RESEARCH ON CRIMINAL JUSTICE TOPICS

This chapter has explained the production of crime data and introduced you to the primary sources of national data on the criminal justice system at work. This last section gives you additional tips on where to look for information that will help you learn more about crime and justice, including the latest statistics and research findings.

National Criminal Justice Reference Service (NCJRS) Responsible for disseminating all justice-related federal publications and federally funded research.

The National Criminal Justice Reference Service (NCJRS). Virtually all federally funded publications on crime and justice in America are available through the **National Criminal Justice Reference Service (NCJRS).** This unit of the Office of Justice Programs is responsible for dissemination of all justice-related federal publications. Its "Information Specialists" will also provide referrals to other sources of published data. Contacting the service is a free phone call (see Table 2.7), or you may visit its Web site at **http://www.ncjrs.org.** You can often get publications free of charge. If you join the non-electronic mailing list you will receive the *NCJRS Catalog,* a bimonthly listing of criminal justice publications. One of its sections gives information on what's new on the Internet.

Using the World Wide Web. The Internet is becoming an increasingly important tool for anyone wishing to keep up with crime and justice in the United States and around the globe. All major U.S. justice agencies have home pages on the World Wide Web, as do many state and local agencies.

In addition, many universities and colleges maintain home pages, and criminal justice students and faculty can tap into a wealth of information and can communicate directly with people at the cutting edge of criminal justice research and teaching. You can also enter chat rooms for conversations about crime and justice, and you can surf the Net by searching for a topic of interest and following criminal justice links. A book by Cynthia Leshin (1997) includes a detailed discussion of using the Internet for criminal justice research, as well as scores of specific Web sites you can check out. Box 2.5 lists some of the most useful Web sites for criminal justice students.

Academic Journals and Other Research Sources. You are probably familiar with academic journals. These contain papers by scholars who believe they have something important to say to colleagues in their area of expertise. Academic journals can be the most important place to turn for your out-of-class reading and research. Many instructors expect undergraduate students to read two or three journal articles in addition to the course text.

There are scores of journals on crime and justice, and more appear each year. Some contain highly sophisticated, often difficult papers that are a real challenge to get through, while others have a more informal tone and are easier to comprehend. Table 2.8 lists a selection of the best-known journals. In ad-

TABLE 2.7 Criminal Justice Information Is a Free Phone Call Away

By calling any of the following numbers you can receive information about criminal justice topics, including statistical reports, current research programs and plans, and referrals to other data sources.

1-800-851-3420	National Criminal Justice Reference Service
1-800-732-3277	Bureau of Justice Statistics Clearinghouse
1-800-638-8736	Juvenile Justice Clearinghouse
1-800-666-3332	Drugs and Crime Clearinghouse
1-800-999-0960	National Archive of Criminal Justice Data
1-800-421-6770	Department of Justice Response Center
1-800-688-4252	Bureau of Justice Assistance Clearinghouse
1-800-394-3255	National Victim Center
1-800-627-6872	Office for Victims of Crime Resource Center

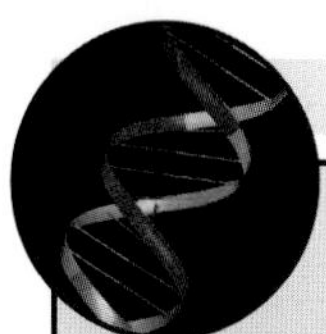

Box 2.5

JUSTICE INNOVATIONS

USEFUL WEB SITES FOR CRIMINAL JUSTICE STUDENTS

A vast array of criminal justice resources are now available on the Internet. Here is just a sampling of the sites you should check out for up-to-the-minute information, ideas, research, and discussions of criminal justice topics. All these sites have links to other criminal justice sites.

A word of advice: If you want to download government reports in their full-graphics, published form, you will need Adobe Acrobat Reader software. This can be downloaded free of charge by following the link at the Bureau of Justice Statistics home page.

URL	ORGANIZATION
http://www.ncjrs.org/	National Criminal Justice Reference Service (NCJRS)
http://www.ojp.usdoj.gov/bjs/	Bureau of Justice Statistics
http://www.ncjrs.org/ojjhome.htm	Office of Juvenile Justice and Delinquency Prevention
http://www.icpsr.umich.edu/nacjd/	National Archive of Criminal Justice Data
http://www.ncjrs.org/statwww.htm	Criminal Justice Statistics World Wide Web Sites
http://www.fbi.gov/	Federal Bureau of Investigation
http://www.usdoj.gov/	U.S. Department of Justice
http://www.ifs.univie.ac.at/~uncjin/uncjin.html	United Nations Crime and Justice Information Network
http://andromeda.rutgers.edu/~wcjlen/WCJLEN!.html	World Criminal Justice Library Perhaps the best network and criminal justice home page maintained by a university professor
http://www.criminology.fsu.edu/cj.html	Dr. Cecil Greek's Criminal Justice Links

dition to academic journals, students are encouraged to check out national newspapers such as the *New York Times* and *USA Today,* weekly news magazines such as *Time* and *Newsweek,* and their local newspapers. Notwithstanding problems with the accuracy and objectivity of media accounts of crime and justice, these sources provide information about current events that is unavailable anywhere else. Used with caution, they can provide interesting material for papers and class discussions.

TABLE 2.8 A Sampling of Academic Journals on Crime and Justice

Among the scores of journals dealing with crime and justice, here are some you will find useful for out-of-class reading and research:

General Criminology and Criminal Justice Journals

Criminology
Crime, Law, and Social Change
Journal of Research in Crime and Delinquency
Law and Society Review
British Journal of Criminology
Canadian Journal of Criminology
Journal of Criminal Law and Criminology
Crime and Justice
Crime and Delinquency
Journal of Criminal Justice
Justice Quarterly
Criminal Justice and Behavior
Crime and Social Justice
The Howard Journal of Criminal Justice

Law Enforcement

American Journal of Police, now called *Policing: An International Journal of Police Strategies and Management*
Enforcement Journal
FBI Law Enforcement Bulletin
Journal of Police Science and Administration (last issued in 1991)
Police Chief
Police Journal
Police Law Journal
Police Quarterly

Courts and the Law

American Criminal Law Review
American Journal of Criminal Law
Criminal Law Bulletin
Criminal Law Review
Federal Probation
Howard Civil Rights Civil Liberties Review
Harvard Law Review (and the journals of other major law schools)
Journal of Legal Studies
Law and Society Review
Law and Social Inquiry
Judicature

Corrections

American Jails
Corrections Today
Corrections Quarterly
Federal Probation
Journal of Correctional Education
Journal of Correctional Training
Journal of Offender Counseling and Rehabilitation
The Keeper's Voice
National Prison Project Journal
The Prison Journal
Probation Journal
Probation and Parole

Victimology

Victimology
Violence and Victims

SUMMARY

The study of criminal justice cannot proceed without information on crime and on the people, events, and organizations that deal with it. In this chapter we have explored how information on crime and justice is created and shared. We have also considered what it means and where its limitations lie.

Members of the general public have an important role in the production of information on crime, for they are usually the first to witness a possible crime and only if they report it to police can it become part of the official record. Many crimes go unreported, and even the police themselves fail to record many crimes that have been brought to their attention or that they have witnessed themselves. This explains why the official police picture of crime represents only the tip of the iceberg; the dark figure of crime is much larger.

Criminologists attempt to uncover the dark figure of crime through victimization studies and through self-reports, in which people describe their own involvement in crime. Self-report studies are particularly useful for finding out about juvenile crime. Both methods rely on memory, and this is one possible source of error. They also do not adequately tap white-collar crimes, which involve more people and cost the country more than conventional "street" crimes such as burglary, robbery, assault, and theft. This criticism applies also to the FBI's Uniform Crime Reports. However, victimization and self-report studies still provide a wealth of information on how people experience crime as victims and offenders. They also provide a picture of the nation's overall experience with street crime, which has shown a downward trend in recent years.

Information on the criminal justice system and its operations is primarily produced by government agencies, particularly the Office of Justice Programs, of which the Bureau of Justice Statistics (BJS) is a part. We saw that BJS publishes reports and statistical analyses on all sorts of criminal justice topics. These mostly concern the adult side of crime and justice. For information on juveniles, the Office of Juvenile Justice and Delinquency Prevention is the parallel agency.

The communications revolution has brought the power of the World Wide Web to the study of criminal justice. Students will find a wealth of information on the Internet, from government Web sites that publish official data to Web sites of police departments, probation and parole agencies, law firms, universities, private organizations, and individuals who work in criminal justice or merely have something to say about it. Chat rooms can be informative, too. However, when it comes to serious research, always be careful to check out the source of the information being shared.

WHAT DO YOU THINK *NOW*?

- Why is the "dark figure of crime" so large? What can be done to uncover it?
- What are the benefits of overpolicing certain areas? The dangers? What about underpolicing? How do overpolicing and underpolicing of different groups contribute to public perceptions about the "typical" criminal?
- How are U.S. government figures about crime and criminals useful? What are their possible drawbacks? What are the advantages and disadvantages of other sources?

KEY TERMS

complainant
dark figure of crime
founding decision
crimes known to the police
clearance rate
Uniform Crime Reports (UCR)
index offenses
crime rate
National Incident-Based Reporting System (NIBRS)
victimization surveys
self-report studies
National Crime Victimization Survey (NCVS)
status offenses
National Youth Survey (NYS)
ethnography
Office of Justice Programs (OJP)
Bureau of Justice Statistics (BJS)
Office of Juvenile Justice and Delinquency Prevention (OJJDP)
National Criminal Justice Reference Service (NCJRS)

ACTIVE LEARNING CHALLENGES

1. Each student in the class finds a criminal justice data source or publication available in the university or college that is not mentioned in the text. Discuss what the students found in class.
2. Divide the class into three groups: "Police," "Victims," and "Offenders." Provide Police with UCR data, Victims with NCVS data, and Offenders with data from the General Social Survey or other national self-report survey. Each group reports its conclusions about trends in violent crime over the past five years.
3. Groups of three to four students interview each other on their experiences with crime and the criminal justice system. Each group summarizes its experiences and shares them with the class. Discuss any patterns or exceptions that emerge. Please be careful to respect each other's sensitivity, recognizing that some students may have had embarrassing or humiliating experiences.
4. Every student finds a nongovernment Web site that contains information on criminal justice that tells the student something he or she didn't know and cannot find in this text. Bring the information to class and explain where it fits in the text.

INTERNET CHALLENGES

The Web pages mentioned here can all be accessed through the Web site for this textbook at **http://www.prenhall.com/barlow/**.

1. Visit the FBI's Web site and find the latest edition of the Uniform Crime Reports. Compare the listed count of index crimes in the city where you live, or the closest city listed, with those of another city of similar size in some other state where you would consider living. Compute the crime rates for the two cities. What do you see?
2. Think of some specific information you would like to know about crime or the justice system. After checking this text for relevant information, look for more stuff on the Web. A place to begin is the Web page of Dr. Cecil Greek, a criminology professor at Florida State University. Follow one of his links and write down what you find out.

3. More and more Web sites are appearing that carry stories of personal experiences with criminal justice. If you did not "bookmark" the sites you found in Internet Challenge 3 from Chapter 1, click on Search and look for a site representing victims, one representing offenders, and one representing criminal justice workers—for example, probation officers, prosecutors, or police officers. Briefly summarize what you learn at each site.
4. Learn about special steps being taken by individual police departments to improve the quality of their information on crime. The New York City Police Department Web site has many good links. Find two improvements and summarize them briefly.

CHAPTER 3

PUBLIC POLICY AND THEORIES OF CRIME

LEARNING OBJECTIVES

- Understand the link between policies and theories of crime.
- Distinguish between the different assumptions about human nature and social order underlying theories of crime.
- Understand the policy implications of those underlying assumptions.
- Explain what an integrated theory is, and be able to give an example.
- Understand the role of opportunities in the occurrence of criminal events.
- Distinguish between opposing ideological positions on the causes of crime, the methods for dealing with criminals, and the operations of criminal justice agencies.
- Understand the differences between the crime control and due process models of criminal justice at work.

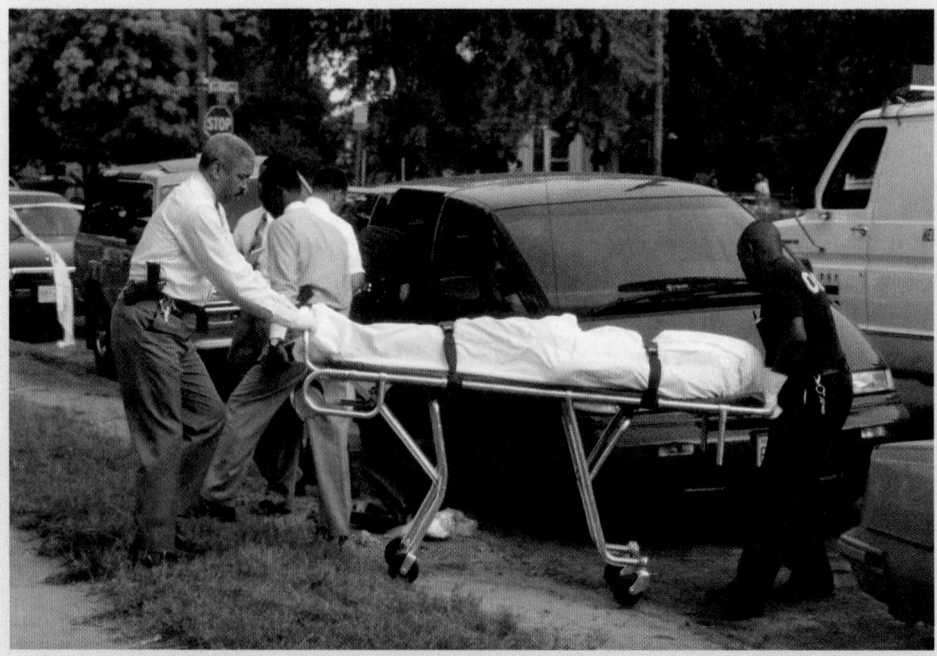

Theories of crime often differ in their "level of explanation." A theory that explains why individuals commit violent acts may not explain why there is more violent crime in some places than in others.

PHOTO BY JOHN GASTALDO, COURTESY OF AP PHOTO

The overwhelming bulk of the scientific evidence shows that incarceration has little impact on crime rates.

JAMES AUSTIN, EXECUTIVE VICE-PRESIDENT,
NATIONAL COUNCIL ON CRIME AND DELINQUENCY

There is less interest in what is correct or even in what "works" than in what sounds good.

JEROME G. MILLER, CO-FOUNDER OF THE NATIONAL
CENTER ON INSTITUTIONS AND ALTERNATIVES,
COMMENTING ON CURRENT CRIME POLICY

[W]hen it comes to the search for rational, workable crime policies, it's time to admit that the brain-dead law-and-order right is no better than the soft-in-the-head anti-incarceration left.

JOHN J. DIIULIO, JR., PROFESSOR OF POLITICS AND PUBLIC AFFAIRS

Persistent thieves, robbers, and other career criminals often say they spend little time worrying about getting caught (Shover and Henderson, 1995; Wright and Decker, 1994; Feeney, 1986). Their decision making is not driven by fear of negative consequences. They focus instead on the opportunities and rewards of crime, and think about what they are going to do with the money they expect to make. Even some thieves who have gone to prison say they do not dwell on the negative, but leave prison with new knowledge and skills they believe will make them better thieves. They describe themselves as more confident and more determined to succeed at crime, and the fact they survived the rigors of prison life reassures them as well.

These insights are based on in-depth interviews with relatively small numbers of criminal offenders, and they may not apply to other offenders. Yet they raise questions about current crime policy, which largely revolves around increasing the threat and severity of punishment. If criminals do not worry much about getting caught—especially those who have already been in prison—they probably do not dwell on the possible punishment, which is even more remote. Policies based on the idea that the threat or experience of severe punishment deters potential offenders from committing crimes will fail if many of the people they target don't care.

This inconsistency between crime policy and the behavior of criminals would not matter as much if policy had no impact on criminal justice practice, but this is not the case. Policies influence practice because policies determine what resources will be directed where. Hardly a day goes by without some government official or politician proclaiming the need to reduce or prevent crime. Since this is the official goal of crime policy, politicians ought to support strategies that address the underlying causes of crime and the immediate situations that bring it about. This approach requires knowledge of the theories of crime and their implications for strategies of prevention.

In this chapter we shall explore American crime policy and the varying degrees of influence enjoyed by different criminological theories. Many books and articles have been written on criminological theory, and if one conclusion can be drawn it is this: There is no consensus among policymakers, criminal justice professionals, or academics regarding the "best" explanation of crime. One reason for this is that people's receptiveness to a particular theory is influenced by **ideology**—the beliefs, opinions, and doctrines they subscribe to. It has been said that "ideology is the permanent hidden agenda of criminal justice" (Miller, 1973:142). This means that the formal policies and practices of criminal justice generally reflect and support the beliefs of those who shape them. This chapter also examines the implications of this view. As with all the chapters in this text, you are encouraged to explore the issues in more detail by following up the references cited throughout the discussion.

ideology The beliefs, opinions, and doctrines that influence the way people explain and deal with the world around them.

? WHAT DO YOU THINK?

- Do you believe that criminals are born with criminal tendencies or that these tendencies come from their environment—or both? Why?
- How much does crime rely on opportunity and how much on the offender's skills? Do you think this varies among different offenders and different circumstances? If so, how?
- What do you believe are the main goals of American crime policy today?

THEORIES OF CRIME AND CRIMINALITY

A theory of something is an attempt to explain it. Explanations are important because they help us figure out why things are the way they are, and they suggest what might be done to change things (if we want to).

Theories come in all forms, from loosely linked ideas to formally constructed models from which explicit hypotheses are derived. Some theories are called general theories because they attempt to explain a broad range of facts in a variety of social or historical settings. A successful **general theory** is the ultimate goal of any science because it promises the best returns—it explains more (Tittle 1995:20–27). Other theories are much narrower in the range of facts they explain; one might call them **restricted theories,** or *simple theories.* Restricted theories apply to one type of crime or to crimes occurring at one time or place, or involving specific groups of individuals, such as juveniles. Most criminological theories lie between these extremes, although in recent years a number of authors have proposed general theories of crime (Wilson and Herrnstein, 1985; Cohen and Machalek, 1988; Braithwaite, 1989; Gottfredson and Hirschi, 1990; Vila, 1994; Agnew, 1992, 1995).

general theories Theories that explain a broad range of facts in varied social or historical settings.

restricted theories Theories that explain a narrow range of facts occurring at one time or place, or involving specific groups of people.

LEVELS OF EXPLANATION

Another distinction among theories of crime is **level of explanation.** This concept recognizes that crime can be explained as the behavior of an individual, but also as the behavior or social characteristic of a group, community, or society. *Individual-level explanations* can address such questions as, "Why do some individuals commit crime and not others?" or "Why do some individuals commit crimes more often than others?" *Aggregate-level explanations* can address such questions as, "Why do crime rates vary from one group of people to another?" or "Why are murder rates higher in the South than elsewhere?" However, the things that account for variations in crime among individuals may not explain variations among communities, social classes, or societies. For example, although unemployment is often shown to be a strong predictor of individual criminality, societies with high rates of unemployment generally do not have high crime rates.

level of explanation Distinguishes between theories that explain the behavior of individuals and those that explain the behavior of groups, communities, or societies.

An Example: Explaining Violence. Let us consider level of explanation in relation to violent crime (Short, 1997:37–48). Table 3.1 will help. The table presents a matrix of risk factors for violence developed by the National Academy of Sciences Panel on the Understanding and Prevention of Violence (Reiss and Roth, 1993). Note that the "Units of Observation and Explanation" are divided into *Social* (or group) and *Individual* sections. Looking across the columns, we see that consistent with this distinction, the factors that predispose groups and individuals to violence differ in level of abstraction and in the immediacy of their impact. For example, a person's temperament or intellectual ability is generally more concrete and immediate in its impact on behavior than the more abstract opportunity structure or economic condition of the larger community.

But even within the realm of social factors that predispose people to violence, a distinction is drawn between *macro* and *micro* levels. This is a conventional sociological distinction recognizing that some groupings are more distant from the individual: "[G]angs and families are small and more immediate in the experience of their members, for example, whereas the effects of poverty concentration are more global and abstract and, in many instances, less consciously and immediately experienced" (Short, 1997:39). However, some sociologists see the microsocial level as even less abstract than in Table 3.1. They think of it in terms of "ongoing interaction within events" so that the unit of analysis is not the gang, say, but the criminal event itself and the interaction among the people involved in it. "The microsocial level asks the following questions: How did this event occur, and what was the nature of the interaction among event participants that led to the . . . violent act? . . . Note that micro-level questions may be addressed to events occurring in large or small groups, in crowds, in institutional settings (such as schools), or on city streets" (Short, 1997:42).

To summarize this brief discussion of levels of explanation, theories of crime that provide individual-level explanation focus on the characteristics of individuals and the criminal behaviors that result from them. For example, "John" and "Jane" commit crimes because they are psychologically predisposed to do so, or because of experiences within the family or with their friends. Theories of crime that provide aggregate-level explanation focus on the characteristics of population groups—communities, cities, ethnic and racial groups, social classes, or whole societies—and the crime rates associated with them. For example, crime rates are higher in cities compared with rural areas, or in certain parts of cities than in other parts, because of differences in criminal opportunities, or in the extent to which group life is effectively regulated. Some theories try to bridge individual and aggregate levels of explanation by

TABLE 3.1 A Matrix for Organizing Risk Factors for Violent Behavior

UNITS OF OBSERVATION AND EXPLANATION	PROXIMITY TO VIOLENT EVENTS AND THEIR CONSEQUENCES		
	PREDISPOSING	SITUATIONAL	ACTIVATING
SOCIAL			
Macroscial	Concentration of poverty Opportunity structures Decline of social capital Oppositional cultures Sex role socialization	Physical structure Routine activities Access: weapons, emergency medical services	Catalytic social event
Microsocial	Community organization Illegal markets Gangs Family disorganization Pre-existing structures	Proximity of responsible monitors Participants' social relationships Bystanders' activities Temporary communication impairments Weapons: carrying, displaying	Participants' communication exchange
INDIVIDUAL			
Psychosocial	Temperament Learned social responses Perceptions of rewards/penalties for violence Violent deviant sexual preferences Social, communication skills Self-identification in social hierarchy	Accumulated emotion Alcohol/drug consumption Sexual arousal Premeditation	Impulse Opportunity recognition
Biological	Neurobehavioral* "traits" Genetically medicated traits Chronic use of psychoactive substances or exposure to neurotoxins	Transient neurobehavioral* states Acute effects of psychoactive substances	Sensory signal processing errors

*Includes neuroanatomical, neurophysiological, neurochemical, and neuroendocrine. "Traits" describe capacity as determined by status at birth, trauma, and aging processes such as puberty. "States" describe temporary conditions associated with emotions, external stressors, etc.

Source: Albert J. Reiss, Jr., and Jeffrey A. Roth, eds. (1993). *Understanding and Preventing Violence.* Washington, D.C.: National Academy Press.

incorporating biological or psychological factors with interactional aspects of criminal events, as well as with macrosocial conditions. So-called life-course perspectives on crime (Sampson and Laub, 1993b) are one example, and another is the theory of "reintegrative shaming" (Braithwaite, 1989). Both will be discussed in a later section of this chapter.

UNDERLYING ASSUMPTIONS ABOUT HUMAN NATURE

Underlying all theories of human behavior are assumptions about human nature. Sometimes these assumptions are explicitly stated; sometimes they are merely implied. Over the centuries, different views of human nature have gained prominence. Some remain influential today, and guide current thinking about crime and criminality. Four prominent views of human nature are discussed in this section; the criminological theories that incorporate them are

Cesare Beccaria (1738–1794), author of Essay on Crimes and Punishment, *was a founder of the classical school of criminology. His followers believed that humans act of their own free will and can be deterred from crime by swift, certain, and appropriately severe punishment.*

ILLUSTRATION COURTESY OF THE GRANGER COLLECTION

briefly mentioned here, but will be discussed in more detail later, along with their implications for criminal justice.

Human Beings Are Free to Choose Their Actions. When commenting on people who have broken the law or other rules, people sometimes say, "Nobody makes people do something bad; they choose to do it." The idea here is that human behavior represents the exercise of free will that all normal people supposedly possess. The **free will doctrine** gained prominence during the eighteenth century. Sometimes referred to as *voluntarism,* the doctrine emphasizes the ability of human beings to recognize alternative courses of behavior and to choose among them. The choice is made according to the relative attractiveness of each alternative. People choose the course of action they believe is most likely to result in positive outcomes. In most versions of the free will doctrine, therefore, the choice is presumed to be a *rational* one.

free will doctrine Human behavior reflects free choices that individuals have made from among alternative courses of action.

Theories of crime that incorporate free will assumptions about human nature span 240 years (Einstadter and Henry, 1995:44). Early examples are referred to as *classical theory* or the *classical school of criminology;* one is Cesare Beccaria's famous book titled *Essay on Crimes and Punishment* and published in 1764. The most recent versions are found in the rational-choice theories that achieved prominence during the 1980s and early 1990s (Clarke and Mayhew, 1980; Cornish and Clarke, 1986; Clarke, 1992). In between are works by economists, among them 1993 Nobel Prize winner Gary Becker, whose 1968 article "Crime and Punishment: An Economic Approach" stimulated much interest in his field. Becker argued that individuals choose to commit crimes, and do so when that course of action promises maximum satisfaction, or "utility," compared with noncriminal alternatives. The utility of crime is the expected gain weighed against the probability and costs of being caught, convicted, and punished. The policy implication of rational-choice theory and other voluntaristic perspectives is to devise ways to reduce the attractiveness of the decision to commit crime and/or to increase the attractiveness of alternatives to crime.

determinism Human beings are pushed or pulled into behaving a certain way by forces over which they have no control.

Human Beings Are Pawns in the Hands of External Forces. This sounds melodramatic, but the idea is simple and directly contradicts the free will doctrine. This view of human nature, called **determinism,** sees people as naturally vulnerable to forces over which they have no control. They are pushed or pulled into acting a certain way. This point of view rejects the notion that choices are freely made; rather, its advocates believe that human behavior is shaped by biological, cultural, social, economic, or even supernatural forces that determine not only what the choices are, but who can take advantage of them.

In its most extreme form, determinism allows no room for individual choice. The belief that people may be "possessed" by evil demons or the devil represents extreme determinism: "Once possessed, a person may be viewed as no longer responsible—as no longer able to choose between good and evil, sin or conformity" (Pfohl, 1985:21). Only through exorcism—chasing out or removing the evil force—could a person be returned to a normal, but still inherently vulnerable state. In medieval Europe and colonial America, ritual exorcisms were widely used and "if exorcism failed . . . 'sinners' . . . were turned over to civil authorities and capital punishment and other brutal punishments were used to eradicate the devil" (Masters and Roberson, 1990:54). We may laugh at this today, but remnants of demonic theories of human behavior remain influential in some quarters. Some Christian psychologists and pastors, for example, see mental illness as the work of the devil (Einstadter and Henry, 1995:34–36). A 1990 Gallup poll found that 49 percent of respondents believed people are sometimes possessed by the devil (*Newsweek,* April 15, 1990:62). The policy implication of deterministic assumptions is to devise ways to make individuals less vulnerable to the criminogenic influence of external forces. This could mean strengthening the resistance of the individual or weakening the power of the external force.

Most contemporary views of human nature reject extreme determinism but vary in the emphasis they place on the power of external forces to influence behavior. Generally speaking, most biological, psychological, and sociological theories about the causes of crime assume a large measure of determinism, but allow for individual choice and reason within the constraints imposed by external forces and genetic makeup. The more deterministic theories advanced by psychologists and psychiatrists argue that the key cognitive processes of the human mind are constructed during early childhood through socialization and other developmental processes. These processes may be disrupted by mental disorders brought on by chemical imbalances in a child's brain, or by ineffective socialization by parents and other caretakers. Criminals are thus "poorly adjusted" or "defective" individuals whose personalities have not developed the internal controls necessary for conformity. According to some versions of psychological determinism, this maladjustment is the result of a combination of inherited deficiencies in the individual and poor environmental controls.

As noted, most contemporary theories of crime lie between the extremes of voluntarism and determinism. Even sociologists who lean toward the deterministic view of human behavior nevertheless agree that people are not doomed to inevitable responses to social forces. Rather, "they have individual moral choice within the context of circumstances that beset them. After all, even though crime is distinctly related to poverty, only a tiny proportion of the poor at any given time commit crimes. Crime is a subjective choice in an objective situation" (Kinsey, Lea, and Young, 1986:75). And certainly, many people who are not poor commit crimes.

For those who lean toward rational-choice perspectives, here again the key assumption is often tempered in the end. It is usually agreed, for example, that most people cannot know all the information necessary to evaluate all possible actions, and therefore rationality itself is limited. Their behavior is not so much the result of a rational choice, but more a reflexive reaction to opportunities that arise in ordinary and repetitive situations (Trasler, 1986:20). This limited-rationality view holds that behavioral choices routinely arise in people's lives and some involve crime. However, the choices are limited by such things as opportunity, individual capability, and the countermeasures taken by authorities or potential victims. The chosen actions are rational to the extent that they are conscious, goal oriented, and reasonable (that is, efficient) in light of those goals and the alternative courses of action that may be available.

Human Beings Are Basically "Good." This assumption lies behind the idea that normal people do not commit crime unless they are tempted into it by "bad" people. How often have children heard a parent say, "Don't hang around with so-and-so; he (or she) is a bad influence and will get you into trouble!" If people are good by nature they will not engage in acts that have harmful consequences. In sociological criminology, especially its more deterministic theories, the sources of criminal behavior are sometimes located in the bad influence of peer groups or adult role models—from neighborhood gangs to criminal parents.

This view appears similar to the deterministic approach discussed previously. However, the view that people are basically good does not rule out free will. A person can presumably choose not to respond to temptation or bad influence. Nevertheless, the policy implications of the assumption that people are naturally good is to devise ways to protect them from bad influences, including shoring up resistance.

Human Beings Are Basically "Bad." Some theories of crime rest on the assumption that people are by nature bad or evil. Unless constrained, they will tend to do bad things. A modified version of this view is found in a theory that criminal behavior is associated with low self-control (Gottfredson and Hirschi, 1990). This theory argues that human beings are naturally inclined to the immediate pursuit of pleasure, and that they will pursue this self-interest impulsively, with little concern for the well-being of others or for the long-term consequences, unless they have been socialized to the contrary. Put another way, "lack of self-control is the 'natural' condition that must be tempered by proper child-rearing practices" (Einstadter and Henry, 1995:189). Criminality is a manifestation of low self-control, as are other indulgent behaviors such as smoking, eating between meals, gambling, and premarital sex. The policy implication of the assumption that humans by nature pursue immediate gratification—and lack self-control—is to strengthen the desire and ability of society to properly socialize its members so they can delay gratification and think about the long-term consequences of their acts for themselves and for others. Many control theorists believe this is best accomplished in the family, during a child's first seven or eight years of life.

Clearly, then, the policy implications of these opposing views of human nature are quite different. We now turn to the policy implications of differing views of social order.

UNDERLYING ASSUMPTIONS ABOUT SOCIAL ORDER

Just as theories of criminal behavior rest on underlying assumptions about human nature, all criminological theory rests, at least implicitly, on ideas about **social order**—how society is held together. Three prominent ideas about social order will be examined in this section.

social order The forces that hold society together.

Social Order Is Based on Consensus. Some crime theories rest on the idea that social order is based more or less on consensus or agreement among members of society about basic values and appropriate ways of behaving. The functionalist model of law, which we encountered in Chapter 1, exemplifies this **consensus perspective.**

consensus perspective Social order rests on agreement among people about basic values and appropriate ways of behaving.

Theories of crime associated with this model explain crime as the product of a breakdown or disruption in the consensual basis of social order. For example, one prominent macrosocial theory of crime, first proposed in the 1930s, sees crime as one possible consequence of disharmony or "disjunction" between culturally approved goals of success and the acceptable means to achieve them (Merton, 1938). In the United States, according to this theory, material success is a goal all Americans are encouraged to believe in and strive for; a good education, a good job, and upward mobility are accepted as the proper means to achieve material success. For some groups of Americans, however, these acceptable routes to success are unavailable or highly restricted.

People react differently to this disjunction between goals and means, called *anomie.* Whereas some people conform to the rules despite the strain of blocked aspirations, some others substitute alternative, illegal behaviors such as theft, gambling, or pimping. In this adaptation, the criminal continues to accept the cultural goal of material success. An alternative adaptation used by some other people is rejection of *both* the goals *and* the means. This results in withdrawal from mainstream society and participation in "deviant" activities such as drug abuse. The policy implication of theories based on a consensus model of social order is to find ways to reduce disharmony and strain between goals and means, and to bolster controls that might inhibit criminal adaptations.

Social Order Is Based on Conflict. Even though at any given time members of a society may seem to agree on basic values, goals, and norms, the existence of scarce resources and the tendency for them to be allocated unequally means that someone—or some group—is benefiting at the expense of someone else. This "win-lose" condition is both a cause and a result of conflict. It causes conflict because people prefer to be on the winning side but everyone cannot be; it results from conflict because "winners" tend to protect the status quo, thus keeping "losers" in their place.

conflict perspective Social order rests on the ability of some people to dominate over others in the struggle for scarce resources.

Most supporters of the **conflict perspective** believe that conflict is a universal social condition. The conflict usually consists of a struggle over three related things: wealth, power, and influence. Winners become the "haves" and assume a dominant position in society; losers are the "have-nots," who assume a subordinate position. The dominant group makes the rules, controls the content and flow of ideas and information, and designs and imposes penalties for nonconformity. Dominance means that people are in a position to promote their self-interest, even at the expense of others. Explanations of crime based on conflict theory see criminality as an outgrowth of these structural inequities.

Sometimes the struggle over scarce resources is open and bloody, but more often it is subtle and restrained. Restraint is promoted by the dominant group in various ways. One way is through the control of ideas and information so that beliefs and values protecting the status quo are widely supported. The "have-nots" come to believe that the prevailing social conditions are in their interest, when in fact they are not. Karl Marx illustrated how this "false consciousness" works in the case of law. Law is presented to the masses as the "will of the people." Yet this is an illusion. If the people accept the illusion—which propaganda seeks to ensure—this will undermine the development of opposition and resistance among the disadvantaged (Marx and Engels, 1947:39). People feel uncomfortable challenging a law they believe reflects public consensus, even though in fact it may reflect and support only the interests of the ruling class.

A second way that the struggle over scarce resources is kept in check is through the "institutionalization of conflict." Special institutions such as courts, tribunals, and arbitration are set up to settle disputes. These institutionalized avenues of dispute resolution temper or moderate the underlying struggle, and may even obscure it altogether. People with grievances and complaints about exploitation and other crimes associated with inequity often find themselves overwhelmed by the institutionalized procedures they must follow (Elias, 1993). An example is the complete loss of purpose many crime victims experience in the face of interminable delays and the technical intricacies of the judicial process.

Whereas the functionalist/consensus view of social order sees law and other political arrangements as useful for society as a whole—which explains and justifies their existence—conflict theorists see them as useful for the dominant group or groups, but possibly harmful to other groups or to the larger society. As suggested in Chapter 1, laws and the political process tend to protect the interests of the powerful, who in turn resist efforts to modify them. The policy implication of the conflict view of social order is to devise strategies that reduce the inequities that encourage conflict and exploitation. The goal is to "achieve a more viable society—one in which people are increasingly able to survive and prosper without having to exploit or destroy one another" (Turk, 1995:20).

Social Order Is Constructed through Day-to-Day Social Interaction. Some theories of crime rest on the idea that social order is continually being constructed through the day-to-day interactions of individuals as they live their lives. This microsocial **interactionist perspective** sees human beings as active agents in the construction of the social world they experience. The idea is that during interaction, people construct meanings, expectations, and implications that shape everyone's behavior and thus create a certain social reality for participants. This experience influences what happens in later interactions, although each interaction creates its own social reality. Social order is therefore fluid and ever-changing.

interactionist perspective Social order is a continuous creation based on everyday interactions in which people respond to the actions and reactions of others.

One of the most important elements of the interactionist perspective is the idea that actions arise out of situations (Blumer, 1969:85). Whether people are at home with their families, in school, at work, or at play, each situation presents opportunities, demands, tasks, obstacles, pleasures—and sometimes dangers—that must be taken into account and evaluated by the actor. That assessment provides people with the basis for understanding the situation and forming their actions. Essentially, the meaning of a situation for each participant derives from the actions and reactions of the other participants.

For example, how do you decide that you are in control of a situation? By how others respond to you. Or consider how you know that a situation is safe or dangerous. You can "read" the situation through the actions of others, or you can put yourself in the shoes of another and imagine how he or she would act and what the likely results would be. Obviously, this becomes possible only when you have prior knowledge or experience of "situations and people like these." Social order is constructed as people agree on the meanings and implications of the situations they are in, and act accordingly.

This process may sound complicated, but it can be readily illustrated by a common adult activity—going to a bar for a drink. Whatever your motive for visiting the bar, bars are known to be places where fights sometimes break out and occasionally killings. Suppose you have a couple of drinks with a friend and during the conversation the friend says something you consider insulting. You react with indignation, and perhaps demand that your friend "take it back." The friend refuses, and then repeats the insult. What do you do? The situation has become difficult, and while you might decide to say nothing and hope it blows over, someone else might react differently, perhaps even pull out a knife or gun and threaten the friend with violence if the insult is not retracted. The friend may well interpret this as a challenge that cannot be ignored: A "face-saving" response is required. You can imagine what the friend might do. The point is this: During the face-to-face interaction, definitions of the situation have changed so that the parties are now on the verge of a fight (Luckenbill, 1977). What happens next could not have been predicted beforehand merely by knowing that you were going to a bar for a drink with a friend. The outcome is socially constructed as the interaction unfolds.

labeling theory Crime is a consequence of stigmatization.

With the interactionist view, the general assumption is that *both* consensus and conflict are factors framing any given social situation. However, some of the more prominent theories of crime drawing on the interactionist perspective have tended to emphasize conflict. **Labeling theory,** for example, sees crime as a consequence of the persistent application of negative labels to a person, which results in stigmatization (Erikson, 1966; Lemert, 1951; Braithwaite, 1989). Persistent labeling of a person as "no good," a "deviant," or a "criminal" can create a self-fulfilling prophecy: Once stigmatized, the person's behavior becomes consistent with the label—and so do the actions of others. As a used car dealer explains it, "They think because you're a used car dealer you're a liar. So they treat you like one and lie to you. Can you blame the dealer for lying back?" (Braithwaite, 1978).

People bring to situations all their prior learning and experiences, including stereotypes about "good" people and "bad" people, criminals and noncriminals. These stereotypes are usually rooted in conflicts. Ultimately, criminalization depends on authority and power, which are scarce resources. So the people most likely to emerge from interactions with the label *criminal* are those closest to the stereotype and least able to resist its application.

The interactionist perspective argues that social order is based on the reactions of people to the social situations in which they find themselves. Bars are often the scene of fights. How would the interactionist explain this?

PHOTO BY H. DRATCH, COURTESY OF THE IMAGE WORKS

TABLE 3.2 Policy Implications of Theoretical Assumptions in Criminology

All theories of crime rest on assumptions about the nature of human beings and the nature of society. Sometimes the assumptions are stated explicitly; often they are left unstated but implied. Since these assumptions influence the explanation of crime, they should have policy implications as well. Listed below are major theoretical assumptions in criminology and the policy implications that flow from them.

ASSUMPTION	POLICY IMPLICATION
Human beings are free to choose their actions (*voluntarism*).	Devise ways to reduce the attractiveness of the decision to commit crime and/or to increase the attractiveness of alternatives.
Human beings are pawns in the hands of the criminogenic influence of external forces (*determinism*).	Devise ways to make individuals less vulnerable to external forces—e.g., strengthen their resistance or weaken the power of the external force.
Human beings are basically "good."	Devise ways to protect them from bad influences.
Human beings are basically "bad."	Devise ways to create and maintain self-control.
Social order is based on consensus.	Devise ways to reduce disharmony and strain and to inhibit criminal adaptations.
Social order is based on conflict.	Devise ways to reduce the inequities that encourage conflict and exploitation.
Social order is constructed through day-to-day social interaction.	Devise ways to limit the imposition of criminal labels, or criminalization.

To summarize, the interactionist view of social order emphasizes how people react in social situations and the implications of those reactions for future conduct. It should come as no surprise that the policy implication of theories of crime based on this view is to devise strategies that limit criminalization. This can be done in various ways (Einstadter and Henry, 1995:220–223): by decriminalizing certain offenses; by diverting offenders from the criminal justice system; by finding alternatives to incarceration; and by instituting "restorative" programs such as restitution and reparation that seek to restore the situation to what it was before the offense. Each of these strategies is explained in detail in later chapters. For review, Table 3.2 lists the policy implications of the assumptions we have discussed in the last two sections.

LOCATING THE CAUSES OF CRIME AND CRIMINALITY

Theories are an attempt to explain something, to show why and how it occurs. Theories deal with causes; a theory of crime is a theory about its causes. The goal of all science is to identify causes, because once we know the cause of something we can predict when it will happen again, and perhaps control it. Criminologists who seek the causes of crime may not have a direct hand in controlling it, but the theories and evidence they provide may help others do so.

DISTANT AND PROXIMATE CAUSES

Causation is not a simple concept, especially in the social and behavioral sciences. Think about your own behavior for a moment. Right now you are reading this book. How and why you are reading could probably be explained in many different ways; in other words, various causes might be at work. Some of the causes are closer or more immediate—called **proximate causes**—while others are more distant. A proximate cause might be that your professor just

proximate causes Causes of behavior that are closer to the event or more immediate in their impact.

assigned this chapter to be read before your next class, which is tomorrow. An even more proximate (and perhaps more powerful!) cause might be that your mother just told you she would buy you a new car if you got an A in your criminal justice class. A more distant cause is the expectation that you will follow your father's footsteps and become a lawyer. An even more distant cause may lie in the fact that a university education is a requirement for many professional careers and increasingly for other jobs as well.

You look out the window and notice that a friend is not cracking the books like you. No surprise, since she's not a college student. But then you wonder why not. Because you know her, you comfortably reject personal explanations based on her intelligence, her drive, and her commitment to getting ahead, and start thinking about background factors. You remember that neither of her parents has a university education; you recall that she has four brothers and sisters and that only her father works outside the home, as a house painter. You remember that one of her brothers is disabled and that a few years ago the father had an accident and was out of work for two years. You start thinking about other university students you know and about high school friends who never went to college or dropped out.

Even though it is only a small sample of people, you begin to see patterns. You realize that a university education is explained by a combination of proximate and distant causes, some of which relate to the individual, some to the community and larger society, and some to the social situations people move in and out of in the course of their lives. You recognize, as well, that some causes seem to have a direct impact while the effect of others is more indirect, working through their impact on something else. Some causes are both direct and indirect. For example, the impact of poverty on behavior may be indirect through

Proximate causes are more immediate influences on behavior, but more distant, background, factors may be at work as well. These prostitutes (awaiting booking in Maricopa County Jail, Arizona) may be soliciting customers because their pimp has threatened them with harm if they do not, but their experiences in early childhood, running away from home, or the lack of alternative job opportunities may have set the stage for prostitution.

Photo by A. Ramey, coutresy of Photo Edit

its effects on family relationships, and direct through its impact on opportunities and access to them.

Social Structure and Social Process

All this applies to theories about the causes of crime. Some sociological explanations focus on distant background causes located in the organization and culture of societies, including its opportunity structures and the concentration and demographics of the population. These are sometimes called **social structure perspectives.**

social structure perspectives Theories of crime based on background causes located in the organization and culture of societies.

Criminologists have long recognized that people exposed to the same social structure or culture do not necessarily behave in the same way; sometimes the behavior of people from quite different backgrounds is remarkably similar. This suggests that crime is not adequately explained by distant background causes. Something else must be contributing to crime from the more proximate experiences of individuals. **Social process perspectives** look for causes in the microenvironment of group life, particularly the interactional experiences themselves. They focus on social-psychological processes and assume that people from all walks of life have the potential to be criminals.

social process perspectives Theories of crime based on more proximate causes located in the social experiences of individuals.

Some social process theories explain crime as the result of developmental processes individuals go through as they grow up from childhood; one prominent view is that crime is learned behavior and can be explained by the same processes that explain any other behavior. Other social process theories explain crime—or more correctly, criminality—as a social attribute acquired through interaction. Labeling theory, mentioned earlier, is an example. People acquire the stigma of criminality and then live up to it.

Perspectives That Integrate Causes

Social process theories deal with the dynamic aspects of the relationship between individuals and their immediate social environments. They consider how the actions of individuals and groups influence what people do and become. Social structure theories focus on the impact of social organization and culture, including values, norms, resources, and opportunities, on the behavior of individuals and groups. Though we distinguish the two conceptually, social structure and social process are actually connected.

One way to think about the connection is to visualize structure setting the stage for process, which in turn brings structure to life. In the case of crime, social structure promotes and restrains criminal activity among different segments of the population, while social process determines which individuals within these segments will become criminally active or be singled out for criminal labeling, and which will not.

Illustrations of Integrated Perspectives

It is helpful to illustrate how structure and process can be linked in theory and research. Three examples will be given. The first deals with the criminal behavior of people who live in different family and neighborhood environments (structure) and are exposed to different interactional experiences (process). The second looks at the influence of the life course (structure) and the social experiences of individuals as they move through it (process). The third looks at individual and aggregate rates of crime in terms of the social organization (structure) that facilitates different forms of social control (process), in this case shaming.

A Theory of Crime and Family Life. The first study is by sociologists John Laub and Robert Sampson (1988); it reanalyzes data gathered 40 years before by two psychologists, Sheldon and Eleanor Glueck (1950). The Gluecks collected data on 500 officially defined delinquents and 500 nondelinquents. All subjects were white males growing up in poor, deteriorated neighborhoods close to the industrial and commercial zones of Boston. Race and gender were not factors in this research. The average age of the subjects was just under 15. Information on all sorts of social, psychological, and biological variables was collected. The reanalysis by Laub and Sampson focused on the relationship between family factors and delinquency. Structural variables included household crowding, economic dependence, residential mobility, and parental criminality. Process variables included parental discipline and supervision of children and emotional support or rejection.

Figure 3.1 shows the model developed by these authors. Their theory predicted that child-rearing practices and other family management skills will be directly related to the delinquent behavior of a child, since they create the emotional atmosphere and control environment that a growing child experiences. Good parenting skills and a supportive emotional environment help prevent the emergence of delinquency because they enhance social control within the family. The model also predicted that parental discipline and the emotional environment are themselves influenced by structural factors such as irregular employment, family disruptions, and parental criminality. These structural variables influence delinquency through their impact on family process. For example, irregular employment makes supervising and monitoring children more difficult; family disruptions and other periodic crises also affect supervisory capacity and discipline practices, as well as the attachment of children to the home.

As predicted, the reanalysis of the Gluecks' data showed that the quality of family social control was directly and strongly related to serious and persistent delinquency among the boys. Equally important, the social structure variables helped set the stage for delinquency by directly influencing the ways in which parents supervised and disciplined their children, and the quality of their emotional relationship.

The relationship between family life and delinquency is one of the most researched issues in criminology. By integrating structure and process, Laub and Sampson put a new spin on old data and confirmed what hundreds of other

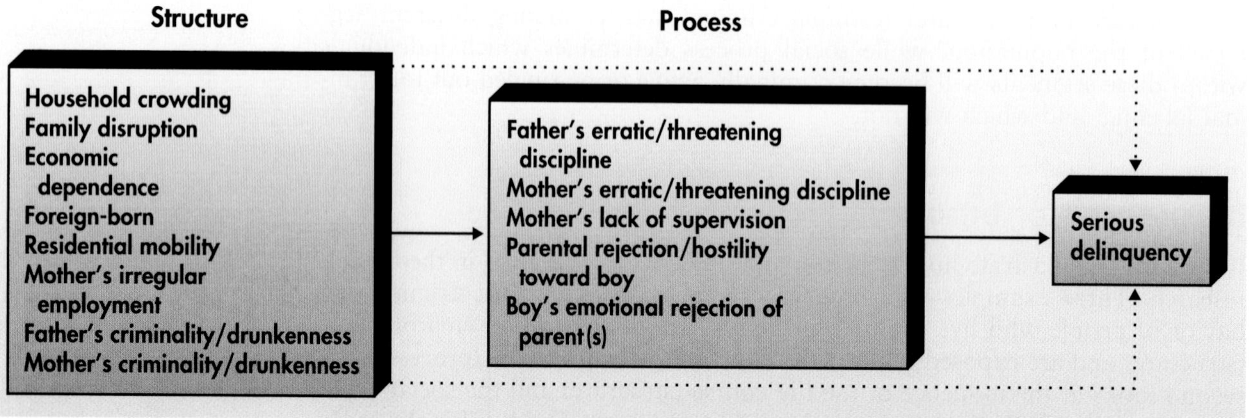

FIGURE 3.1 AN INTEGRATED MODEL OF FAMILY LIFE AND DELINQUENCY

Source: John H. Laub and Robert J. Sampson (1988). "Unraveling Families and Delinquency: A Reanalysis of the Gluecks' Data." *Criminology* 26:366.

studies have argued: Deviance begins at home (Wright and Wright, 1994). Even so, the nature of the relationship between delinquency, crime, and family life is clearly not a simple one, and few experts claim to understand all its intricacies. It is worth noting, as well, that most youths "mature" out of crime by their early twenties, suggesting that something halts or perhaps even reverses the impact of family-related factors that are important during childhood.

Some criminologists believe that key adult roles such as spouse, full-time worker, and parent make continued criminality too costly. As they age, people may become more concerned about their reputation in the community (Rowe, Lindquist, and White, 1989). Having a family bonds a person more closely to conventional society, including values and attitudes about marital, parental, and work responsibilities (Thornberry, 1987; Sampson and Laub, 1990). But what if criminality reflects impulsivity, the inability to delay gratification and think long-term, and other qualities of low self-control (Gottfredson and Hirschi, 1990)? People with these characteristics are unlikely to make successful marriage partners, parents, or workers as adults, just as they are unlikely to do well in school as children. In other words, those who make it in marriage or on the job succeed for the same basic reason some others do not: their degree of self-control.

The complex relationship between family life and crime is made all the more interesting by this observation: Some forms of crime—for example, crimes by small businesses, organized crime, and fencing stolen property—may actually thrive on strong family and work relationships (Barlow, 1993). Since the emphasis in most criminological theory and research—and certainly most policymaking—is on street crime, it is easy to forget that robbery, burglary, drug pushing, rape, assault, and murder are only the tip of a vast iceberg of crime. An adequate depiction and explanation of the relationship between family life and crime must surely encompass the world of business crime, money laundering, fraud, and bribery—offenses not usually committed by children or by people who exhibited low self-control as a child or lived a disadvantaged childhood.

A Life-Course Theory of Criminality. The same authors who reanalyzed the Gluecks' delinquency data have proposed an interesting theory of crime that accommodates both social structure and social process *and* explains why many delinquents mature out of crime as they grow older (Sampson and Laub, 1992, 1993b). The theory centers on the **life course** that individuals traverse from birth to death. A person's life course consists of *trajectories*, which are long-term sequences and patterns of behavior—for example, schooling, work life, marriage, parenthood, or criminal career—and *transitions*, which are specific life events within a trajectory, such as first job, first marriage, going to college, or joining a gang.

life course The long-term sequences (for example, work or parenthood) and specific life events (for example, first job or going to college) that people experience from birth to death.

The theory is that there are fairly stable characteristics of individuals that are established early in life and that provide continuity and consistency as people age: Aggression might be one, with adult manifestations in the form of spouse abuse and harsh physical discipline of children. But the authors also claim that a childhood trajectory may be modified or even halted by key life-course events, such as getting married, getting a job, or moving from one town to another. In the transition to adulthood, it is not so much the timing of discrete life events such as marriage that counts, but, rather, "the quality or strength of social ties" that result (Sampson and Laub, 1992:73). "When an individual has cohesive ties in marriage or work, these ties involve investments made by their spouses and employers" (Laub, Sampson, Corbett, and Smith, 1995:100–101). These "reciprocal investments" act as informal social controls: They deter individuals from acting in ways that would undermine or destroy the benefits associated with them.

The life-course theory of criminality is yet to be fully tested, and its dual focus on continuity and change hardly makes the task any easier. Sampson and Laub used autobiographical research to illustrate their theory, and the results show promising support. They have also outlined some of the public policy implications of the life-course perspective. They challenge current crime policies centered on harsher sentences, long-term imprisonment for repeat offenders, and renewed emphasis on the death penalty:

> A life-course perspective on crime offers a new way of thinking about crime control policy. The central theme of crime policy should be on developing and strengthening an individual's social bonds to society. The foundation of sound policy on crime is that strong social bonds provide informal social control, and this holds for each stage of the life course. . . .
>
> Although our thinking is currently unpopular, we believe that it is time to take a renewed look at social policies that focus on *prevention*. . . . Instead of cheap slogans [such as "Three Strikes and You're Out"], it is time for a broader crime policy that focuses on more than formal social control by the criminal justice system. Nongovernmental institutions such as families, schools, work settings, and neighborhoods must be the centerpiece of any crime reduction policy. (Laub, Sampson, Corbett, and Smith, 1995:103–104)

One of the ways social bonds can be strengthened is through the effective shaming of individuals when they misbehave. This idea has been developed by Australian criminologist John Braithwaite (1989).

Braithwaite's Integrative, General Theory of Crime. The central proposition of Braithwaite's theory is this: Crime rates of individuals and groups are influenced directly by processes of shaming. High crime rates result from shaming that stigmatizes. Here people are shamed *but not forgiven;* as a result they are more likely to become "outlaws" and to participate in subcultures of deviance and crime. In contrast, when offenders are shamed but then forgiven and welcomed back into the group, the unpleasant, punishing experience of being shamed is offset by the pleasant relief of discovering that one is still accepted despite the transgression. This is what Braithwaite calls **reintegrative shaming.** Its positive effect is twofold: The process of shaming and reintegrating *both* confirms the importance of the rule that has been broken *and* reestablishes the offender as a group member in good standing.

reintegrative shaming Punishment that includes forgiveness and attempts at reconciliation.

As a mechanism of social control, shaming works best among closely connected people whose fortunes, reputations, and futures are interdependent—as in families or among groups of workers, colleagues, and friends. Modern criminal justice in Western industrialized societies such as the United States rarely operates in this context; instead, its setting is formal, distinct, and independent from the everyday relationships of individuals. "Most of us will care less about what a judge (whom we meet only once in our lifetime) thinks of us than we will care about the esteem in which we are held by a neighbor we see regularly" (Braithwaite, 1989:87).

One of the theory's most interesting aspects is its implications for criminal justice policy in highly individualistic societies such as the United States. As suggested earlier, it complements the life-course theory. Given that reintegrative shaming works best in the informal contexts of family, friends, and neighborhood, a justice policy aimed at preventing or reducing crime should be a community-based, largely informal system. The formal criminal justice system and its punishments would be used as a last resort. With formal interventions minimized, attention would be paid to maximizing liberty, equality, fraternity, and

Box 3.1

CAREERS IN CRIMINAL JUSTICE

SOCIAL SCIENCE ANALYST

The National Institute of Justice (NIJ) and state criminal justice agencies such as the Illinois Criminal Justice Information Authority conduct research into a wide variety of criminal justice topics, the results of which are then disseminated to other criminal justice agencies and to the public. Researchers are generally trained in the social and behavioral sciences. If you are interested in applying to be a Social Science Analyst for NIJ, your salary, qualifications, and duties would be as follows:

Salary Range: $47,066 to $72,758

Qualifications: At least a bachelor's degree in behavioral or social sciences, or discipline related to the position; ability to develop, design, and conduct social and behavioral research; ability to manage research funded under government grants, contracts, and agreements; ability to present ideas, findings, and recommendations effectively, both orally and in writing; comprehensive knowledge of one or more fields of the social sciences, with expertise in one or more substantive areas of juvenile justice, juvenile delinquency, or both.

Duties: Assess and implement national-level research projects; integrate a wide variety of contemporary research studies and findings to identify critical programs of study; prepare research solicitations and requests for proposals; prepare and review grants and contracts; conduct evaluations; act as principal author and technical resource on special assignments, task forces, and committees.

dialogue among citizens (Braithwaite and Pettit, 1990; Makkai and Braithwaite, 1994; Braithwaite, 1995).

In this "republican" approach to criminal justice, the reintegrative aspects of shaming would be enhanced and offenders would be more likely to recognize that they have offended and shame themselves. In this way shaming becomes conscience building, which is the essence of crime prevention in Braithwaite's view. Braithwaite's ideas will be addressed again in Chapter 17 during our discussion of community-based corrections.

CRIME AS AN EVENT

We have seen that the causes of crime may be located both in structural factors and in social processes that determine how individuals see themselves and how they are seen by others. If the review of theory so far has left you with the impression that the explanation of crime is complex, that is a correct judgment. It follows that solutions to the crime problem are unlikely to be simple.

Since the early 1980s, some criminologists have moved away from thinking about the underlying causes of crime—for example, why some people are more predisposed or motivated to commit crimes than others—and have proposed a different way of analyzing crime (Cohen and Felson, 1979; Sparks, 1980; Brantingham and Brantingham, 1981; Roncek and Maier, 1991; Felson, 1998). This new perspective looks at crimes as events, occurrences, or happenings and explores the things that make them happen. The approach draws attention to the situations that facilitate crimes. It makes no assumptions about what motivates people to commit crimes, nor does it predict which individuals are more likely to commit crimes. Simply, crime results when the right mix of elements are present in a situation. As we shall see, this perspective has some very important implications for crime policy.

The Importance of Opportunities in Crime. If there is a common element in all events, criminal or otherwise, it is opportunity. An opportunity makes an event possible; a criminal opportunity makes a crime possible. Interestingly, criminal and noncriminal opportunities are often linked. Banks hold people's money and provide opportunities to earn interest and to transfer funds from one place to another; banks also provide opportunities for robbery, embezzlement, and other crimes. Functionalists would say that crime is a "latent dysfunction" of many useful objects and institutions. It is not their intended purpose, but arises in conjunction with it.

As societies grow increasingly complex and as knowledge and technology advance, both criminal and noncriminal opportunities expand. The range of what is possible grows, and so does crime. Technological change makes new activities possible, and some will be labeled criminal if those in authority decide that they should be. The United States government is obviously concerned: The Treasury Department recently changed its \$100, \$50, and \$20 bills because advances in copying machines have made counterfeiting easier! And the advent of automatic teller machines (ATMs) has made possible all sorts of new criminal activities, from unauthorized use to robbery of customers after they have withdrawn money.

The Routine Activity Approach. The impact of social change on crime has been explored in detail by criminologist Marcus Felson (1998) in his book *Crime and Everyday Life*. Felson explains crime as an event rather than as the result of the number or motivations of criminals. He uses a perspective he helped develop called the **routine activity approach** (Cohen and Felson, 1979). A routine activity is any recurring goal-seeking activity. Work is a routine activity, and so are sex, child rearing, eating, going to the movies, and vacationing. Much crime is also a routine activity.

routine activity approach Looks at how everyday activities create favorable conditions for crime by bringing motivated offenders and suitable targets together in the absence of capable guardians.

The routine activity approach argues that changes in noncriminal opportunities affect criminal opportunities when they bring together the elements necessary for a crime to occur. The basic proposition is that the "probability that a violation will occur at any specific time and place . . . is . . . a function of the convergence of likely [that is, motivated] offenders and suitable targets in the absence of capable guardians" (Cohen and Felson, 1979:590). For example, given a constant number of motivated offenders, there is likely to be more crime if people spend less time at home. When fewer people stay at home, more household property is left unguarded, and when more people leave home after dark or are alone, more people are unprotected.

Felson concludes that changes affecting where people live and work, where and when they interact, the type and storage of goods and services that are available, and the movement of goods and people have resulted in changing crime rates. For example, as cities became more dispersed, with more people living in single-family homes and in the suburbs, and more property being spread over larger and larger space, it also became more difficult for people to control—or handle—their environment to prevent crime. Cities that had previously been *convergent*, bringing people and property together, became *divergent*, spreading them apart. Work organizations and schools also became bigger, drawing thousands of people from miles away. People can less readily monitor their own families under such circumstances, let alone the activities of strangers. As a result, the effectiveness of both formal and informal social control is weakened.

The "routine activity" approach says that crime occurs when willing offenders have suitable targets that are not adequately guarded. How might this crime have been prevented?

Photo by Smith, courtesy of Monkmeyer Press

Some places are more dangerous than others because of variations in the level of guardianship (Newman, 1972; Roncek and Maier, 1991). A place that offers few opportunities to observe what is going on, where people are more anonymous, and where strangers can come and go is more prone to crime, including robbery and drug dealing. Although the built-environment itself helps set the structural conditions for crime, what goes on in and around buildings is the key. Anonymity and lowered guardianship are critical factors in places where people congregate for purposes of having a good time—more bars and taverns, for example, means more risk of crime.

The routine activity approach is a promising perspective on the relationship between criminal events and the organization of everyday activities. It correctly predicts, for example, that younger people are more likely to be offenders and victims than are older people, the active more than the inactive, and urban residents more than rural residents. It also correctly predicts that small but valuable pieces of property—stereos, car radios, VCRs, portable TVs—and property left unguarded are the items most vulnerable to theft.

Why Access to Criminal Opportunities Matters. An area where research is needed concerns how the organization of routine activities influences the type and range of crimes that are committed. This is a matter of *access* to criminal opportunities, and we know that access is not the same for everyone. Here are some illustrations:

- The opportunities for auto theft are greater where there are more cars, but getting to them, especially the more valuable ones, is not as easy for some thieves as for others.
- The opportunities for shoplifting are greater in areas where there are more stores, larger stores, and stores with open displays, but these

stores tend to be clustered in certain areas of the city, and are thus less accessible to people living in other areas.

- The opportunities to steal while on the job increase as more people work and as workplaces grow larger and more impersonal, but you have to be employed to commit such offenses, and some employees can steal much more valuable things than others.
- The opportunities for executive crimes such as price fixing, bribery, and corporate fraud increase as the economy expands, but relatively few people are in a position to take advantage of them.

Bear in mind, of course, that even though restricted access to criminal opportunities may limit the types of crimes different people can commit, it may actually increase the rate of some crimes. For example, higher rates of unemployment may lower rates of work-related crime such as embezzlement, but they may also result in higher rates of street crimes, including loitering and public intoxication.

Most criminals behave like other people most of the time; they grow familiar with certain parts of the city, and these parts become their "awareness" or "action" space (Brantingham and Brantingham, 1981). Regardless of where the best criminal opportunities are, criminals tend to commit crimes within their action space. The distance between an offender's home and the crime site is rarely more than two or three miles, and a person's rate of offending tends to be higher closer to home.

People motivated or predisposed to commit crimes but living in places with few criminal opportunities must either forego some potentially desirable crimes or move outside their action space. But moving outside one's action space raises the risks and costs of crime because it takes motivated offenders into unfamiliar territory; uses up more of their resources in travel, finding appropriate targets, and returning home; and makes them more visible as strangers.

These problems are intensified for people who lack the resources to find criminal opportunities in unfamiliar places or who stand out because of some characteristic that is not easily hidden, such as race or sex. A study of criminal decision making in Oklahoma City found that black offenders had to forgo areas they designated as having "easy marks" in favor of familiar places (Carter and Hill, 1979). For white offenders, easy marks and familiarity had equal weight in their selection of crime targets. Black offenders had a much more restricted image of the city than white offenders, who moved about more freely. The same was true in an earlier St. Louis study (Boggs, 1964). Homicides, assaults, and residential burglaries committed by black offenders were most often committed in the neighborhoods where offenders lived, whereas similar offenses committed by white offenders were more dispersed. Some individuals take for granted that committing crimes in certain parts of the city is out of the question, and so decision making is affected by other considerations—for example, ease of access to a target, anticipated profits, availability of partners, or required skills.

Needless to say, offenders do sometimes commit crimes outside their action space. This may occur because criminal opportunities are especially abundant—such as in "red light" districts or close to gambling casinos—or anticipated rewards are especially high. As we saw earlier, the rationality model of criminal behavior predicts selection of areas that maximize utility, and even high-risk target areas may be selected when the expected returns substantially outweigh those from safer areas.

A final point about access to opportunities concerns the availability of resources. In general, the greater the resources available to a person, the greater the range of crimes that person can commit. Some crimes require special skills—safecracking, counterfeiting, and con games; some crimes require special equipment—computer crimes, manufacturing counterfeit compact discs, bombing, and heroin production; some crimes require special planning—embezzlement, organized gambling, prostitution; some crimes require lots of money—large-scale drug smuggling, gambling, or loan sharking—or lots of muscle—extortion, hijacking, racketeering, terrorism; some crimes require prestige or social position—for example, bribery, corporate crime, police corruption; and some crimes require "connections"—drug dealing and fencing stolen property.

The resource aspect of criminal activity has not been explored carefully in relation to crime theory. Even so, the few studies that have been made point to its importance in shaping the nature, amount, and distribution of criminal events (Gibbs and Short, 1974; Shannon, 1982; Agnew, 1990). The crimes likely to occur most often, of course, are those requiring the least resources. However, the *range* and *frequency* of crimes committed by any particular person will tend to increase as that person's resources increase. This proposition produces an interesting prediction that challenges conventional wisdom: There should be *less*, not *more*, crime among people who are poor, unemployed, or otherwise disadvantaged in the competition for resources. This is because people with more wealth and "social capital" have the same access to criminal opportunities as poorer people *plus* what they can access because of their advantages. This idea is a key part of "power-control" theories of crime (Messerschmidt, 1986; Hagan, Gillis, and Simpson, 1985; O'Brien, 1991). Simply put, this view argues that more crime will be found among people with more power to control their own destinies as well as those of others; in most societies this means men, and in class societies it means higher-class individuals. The implication for crime prevention is that more attention should be paid to executive suites than inner-city streets.

Policy Implications of Viewing Crime as a Situated Event. This section began by looking at crime as an event arising out of situations that bring together motivated offenders and suitable targets in the absence of capable guardians. This perspective has given rise to crime prevention strategies that some policymakers find attractive because they make intuitive sense, can be relatively easily evaluated, and can be made cost effective. Furthermore, they do not require efforts to change people's motivations or predispositions, or to make any fundamental changes to the structure and culture of American society. In short, they don't address the deep-seated background factors in crime, but instead focus on the more proximate aspects of criminal events.

The term given to these strategies is **situational crime prevention**. Sixteen basic techniques of situational crime prevention have shown considerable promise (Clarke, 1997). They are based on the assumption that criminals engage in more or less rational decision making when faced with access to criminal opportunities and situational inducements. The goal is to remove opportunities and inducements by reducing rewards and making crimes more difficult and risky to commit, and less easily justified. Table 3.3 illustrates the sixteen techniques, grouped under three headings: "Increasing Perceived Effort," "Increasing Perceived Risks," "Reducing Anticipated Rewards," and "Removing Excuses."

situational crime prevention Attempts to reduce or prevent crimes by removing the opportunities and inducements associated with the situations in which they typically occur.

Increasing perceived effort involves making crimes more difficult to carry out successfully. One major technique is "target hardening," such as placing steering locks on cars and using bulletproof glass in stores and banks. Another technique is "controlling facilitators," which includes controlling gun sales, installing caller ID, and putting the user's photo an a credit card. In the absence of these controls, crimes involving guns, phones, and credit cards are easier to commit.

Table 3.3 Sixteen Techniques of Situational Crime Prevention

Increasing Perceived Effort	Increasing Perceived Risks	Reducing Anticipated Rewards	Removing Excuses
1. Target hardening Slug rejecter device Steering locks Bandit screens	*5. Entry/exit screening* Automatic ticket gates Baggage screening Merchandise tags	*9. Target removal* Removable car radio Women's refuges Phone cards	*13. Rule setting* Customers declaration Harassment codes Hotel Registration
2. Access control Parking lot barriers Fenced yards Entry phones	*6. Formal surveillance* Red light cameras Burglar alarms Security guards	*10. Identifying property* Property marking Vehicle licensing Cattle branding	*14. Stimulating conscience* Roadside speedometers "Shoplifting is stealing" "Idiots drink and drive"
3. Deflecting offenders Bus stop placement Tavern location Street closures	*7. Surveillance by employees* Pay phone location Park attendants CCTV systems	*11. Reducing temptation* Gender-neutral listings Off-street parking Rapid repair	*15. Controlling disinhibitors* Drinking-age laws Ignition interlock V-chip
4. Controlling facilitators Credit card photo Gun controls Caller ID	*8. Natural surveillance* Defensible space Street lighting Cab driver ID	*12. Denying benefits* Ink merchandise tags PIN for car radios Graffiti cleaning	*16. Facilitating compliance* Easy library checkout Public lavatories Trash bins

Source: Ronald V. Clarke, ed. (1997). *Situational Crime Prevention: Successful Case Studies* (2nd ed.). New York: Harrow and Heston. Reprinted by permission.

Increasing perceived risks involves such things as increasing *formal surveillance* by police and security guards and installing of cameras and alarms. In Australia and the United Kingdom, motorists see warnings that cameras have been installed on certain roads and freeways or at certain intersections to monitor speeding and other traffic violations. Photos of violating vehicles are taken and patrolling police alerted or summonses mailed to the vehicle's owner. While some motorists ignore the cameras, more appear to adjust their driving in response to the increased risk of being ticketed.

Reducing anticipated rewards includes *target removal*, such as using removable car radios, requiring payment by check, or reducing the amount of cash on hand, and *reducing temptations*, such as cleaning up neighborhood graffiti, repairing vandalized buildings as quickly as possible, and using gender-neutral phone lists that do not so readily stimulate the interest of con artists, pranksters, or obscene callers. Some forms of reward reduction act on the value of property: Branding or special marking often lowers the value of a stolen item, making it less profitable to steal.

Finally, removing excuses lessens the impact of temptations by making noncompliance with the law less easily justified under the circumstances. Roadside speedometers that show motorists' speed as they pass by stimulate conscience by publicly pointing out how fast they are going; easily accessible trash cans facilitate compliance among people who might simply drop trash when no cans are within easy reach.

The Dangers of Crime Displacement. These situational crime prevention techniques may have an undesirable side effect called **crime displacement**. Displacement means that a criminally motivated person decides to substitute one crime for another or to avoid a certain victim in favor of someone else. There are five kinds (Hakim and Rengert, 1981):

crime displacement Occurs when crime prevention efforts result in offenders changing the way they commit offenses or shifting from one type of crime to another.

- *Temporal displacement* means that an offender substitutes one time of day, week, or even season for another.
- *Spatial displacement* means that an offender substitutes one street, neighborhood, area, or region for another.
- *Target displacement* means that an offender substitutes an easier, less risky, or more rewarding target in the same location.
- *Tactical displacement* means that an offender substitutes one method of operation for another.
- *Type-of-crime displacement* means that an offender substitutes one type of offense for another, usually one that is less risky or more easily performed.

Displacement is one possible cost of crime prevention efforts, and it carries political risks as well. For example, when criminal opportunities are reduced by increased police surveillance in one jurisdiction, the net result may be an increase in crime in another jurisdiction. Criminally motivated individuals simply move to a "safer" area to commit crime. Therefore one community may benefit from crime prevention efforts at the expense of another.

Yet displacement is not an inevitable result of situational crime prevention. Sometimes it is a temporary response, until criminals adjust to it; at other times it may not happen at all (Cornish and Clarke, 1987; Tunnell, 1992). Sometimes, the introduction of a rule about one kind of behavior actually contributes to crime prevention of another sort. For example, the requirement in some countries that motorcyclists wear helmets for safety reasons has resulted in a reduction of motorcycle thefts, presumably because thieves must carry helmets around with them (Mayhew, Clarke, and Elliott, 1989). Displacement is a complex problem that researchers are just beginning to understand; the fact that there are at least sixteen distinct techniques of situational prevention hardly makes the task any easier.

IDEOLOGY AND PUBLIC POLICY

So far we have looked at theories of crime and their implications for criminal justice policy. The value of theory lies ultimately in its usefulness in helping society deal with the problem of crime. As we have seen, theory offers policymakers and criminal justice professionals ideas that have practical significance. Unfortunately, criminologists have not always done a good job of relaying their ideas to policymakers, who consequently may not be aware of their promise.

Even if they are aware of the differing explanations of crime, and recognize their practical significance, presidents, governors, legislators, and other policymakers often frame their decisions around political values and other ideological considerations. The opinions and beliefs of conservatives are different from those of liberals, and even though all may agree on the desirability of reducing crime, they tend to disagree on how that should be done. Inevitably, politicians are caught up in these disagreements, and the side they choose usually reflects the values of their party and the interests of those who put them in office. Criminal justice policy therefore reflects the values, opinions, and beliefs of the people in power, and those theories of crime that are consistent with them. The next two sections describe various ideological positions on crime and their implications for criminal justice in the United States.

Ideological Positions on Crime

Crime is one of those topics that most people have a position on, and the level of concern increased substantially in the early 1990s (see Figure 3.2). The explanation for this increase may lie in the behavior of politicians and the media: Both groups made sure that the 1994 Federal Crime Bill got tremendous publicity, and both made crime a major issue in 1992 and 1996 election campaigns. Few Americans could not recount the grisly details of the Simpson-Goldman double murder, the killing of Polly Klaas, the drowning of Susan Smith's children, the murder of Michael Jordan's father, a string of post office killings, and the Oklahoma City bombing. Despite declining crime rates, the belief that the crime problem is getting worse remains widespread among adults and teenagers (Maguire and Pastore, 1998:100). This encourages a lot of posturing among politicians who are keen to show that crime is high on their agenda. They want the public to know where they stand.

When asked for their opinions and beliefs about crime, most politicians share moderately liberal or moderately conservative views. These are ideologically safe positions, for they do not challenge basic American values or call for

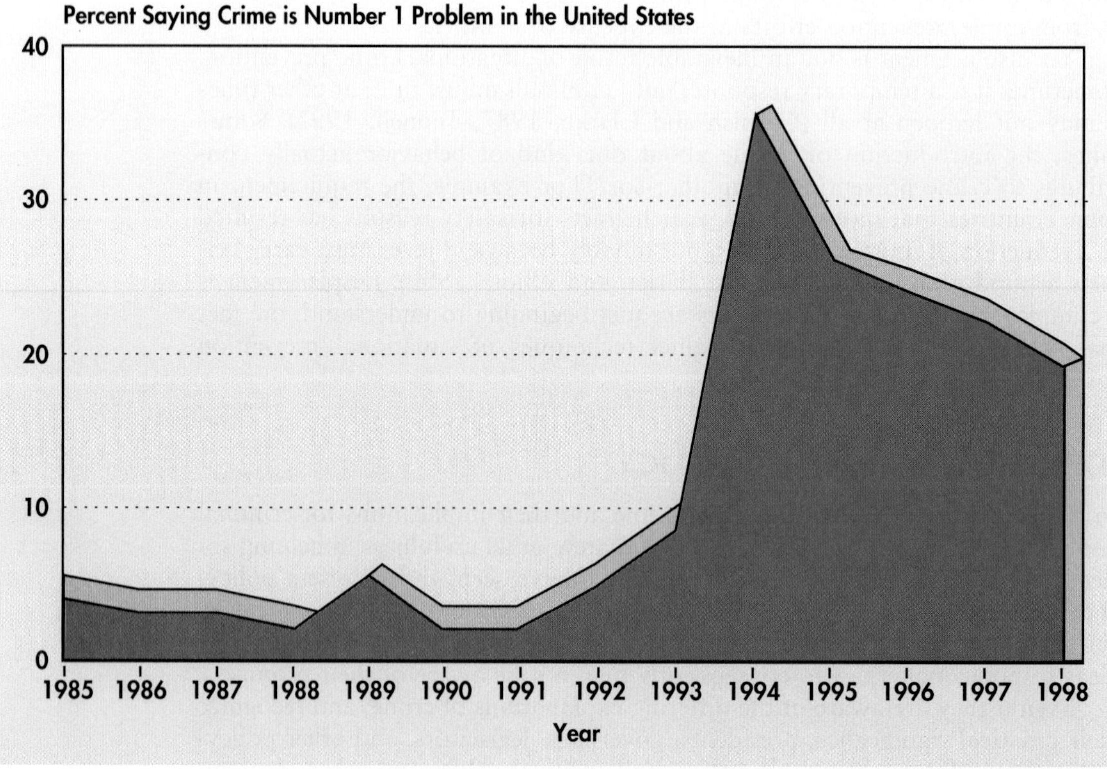

FIGURE 3.2 Changing Views of Crime as the Number One Problem Facing the United States, 1985–1998

Data were collected from Gallup polls conducted periodically during the years listed. Percentages indicate the proportion of respondents who said that crime is the number one problem in the United States.

Source: Kathleen Maguire and Ann L. Pastore (1998). *Sourcebook of Criminal Justice Statisics 1997* (p. 100). Washington, D.C.: U.S. Department of Justice.

fundamental reorganization of society. Illustrations of these ideological positions will be given in a moment. But far more controversial views can be found on both the left and the right of the political spectrum. The range of ideological positions extends from the radical left to the ultra conservative right. These, too, are illustrated in this section.

Although published over 20 years ago, a unique study of ideological positions on crime illustrates a range of opinions that is still relevant today (Miller, 1973). This study analyzed the public statements on crime made by government officials, labor leaders, novelists, journalists, clergy, academics, and criminal justice officials. Similar comments were grouped and then ranged along a scale as follows:

Leftist					Centrist					Rightist
5	4	3	2	1	0	1	2	3	4	5
Radical										Conservative

The most extreme ideological positions were given a value of 5; more moderate positions ranged in between. Thus, the ideological position "Left 3" is more leftist than "Left 1" but less leftist than position "Left 5." Each ideological position represents values, beliefs, and opinions about three issues: (1) the causes of crime and the locus of responsibility for it; (2) the proper methods for dealing with offenders; and (3) the proper operating policies of criminal justice agencies. Each issue is addressed here from opposing ideological positions at different points on the scale; as you read them, consider where you stand.

Ideological Positions on the Causes of Crime. The radical "Left 5" position sees crime as a product of a corrupt and unjust society governed by a ruling elite that perpetuates and profits from the exploitation of others. Criminals are forced into actions the state defines as crime as a justifiable response to deliberate policies of oppression, discrimination, and exploitation. The real criminals are those in power. The more moderate "Left 3" ideological position on the causes of crime blames public officials who allocate "pitifully inadequate resources to criminal justice agencies," as well as "damaging social conditions": poverty, urban decay, lack of jobs and educational opportunities, and racial segregation (Miller, 1973:156–157). Centrist views say crime is caused by a combination of adverse conditions in the family and neighborhood, the bad influence of criminal friends and relatives, and low self-control that results in inappropriate behavioral choices.

At "Right 5," the ideology of ultraconservatives blames crime and violence on a "massive conspiracy by highly organized and well-financed radical forces deliberately seeking to overthrow the society" through continuing attacks on fundamental moral values (Miller, 1973:156). Poorly educated, immoral individuals with low self-control are fooled into committing violent crimes on behalf of a radical agenda aimed at destroying the social order as we know it. More moderate, "Right 3" views also point to an erosion in fundamental moral values, and lay blame as well on the alternative values or "countercultures" that conservatives believe exist among young people, minorities, and the poor. Liberal educators, criminal justice officials, and journalists are also blamed for publicizing and supporting values and behaviors that attack the "American Way."

Ideological Positions on the Proper Methods for Dealing with Criminals. The "Left 4" position is that most criminals pose no threat to society and should be given unconditional freedom throughout the judicial process. Rehabilitation efforts inside prisons are rejected as policy objectives that do not work and never will. Since the policies and practices of police and corrections officials are often arbitrary and punishing, the full rights of all citizens must be protected, and criminal justice operations should be under citizen control. The moderately liberal "Left 2" position on dealing with offenders is that rehabilitation should replace punishment as the correctional objective, and that clinical services and social programs should be provided offenders so that they can overcome the social or psychological forces that drive them to commit crime.

The conservative "Right 4" position is that probation and parole should be abolished in favor of severe punishment of repeat offenders and those who commit violent crimes. Rehabilitation is seen as a "weakly disguised method of pampering criminals, and has no place in a proper system of criminal justice" (Miller, 1973:158). The principal mission of the criminal justice system is swift and certain removal and punishment of criminals. "To speak of rights of persons who have chosen deliberately to forfeit them by engaging in crime is a travesty" (Miller, 1973:158). The more moderate "Right 2" position argues for fair but firm penalties, aimed toward reforming offenders through rehabiliation and reeducation. The aim of criminal justice should be to instill respect for authority and basic moral values through hard work and strict discipline.

In between "Right 4" and "Right 2" positions lies what might be called the "classic conservative policy position," summarized in a recent book as follows:

> The police will act swiftly to remove criminals from the streets; prosecutors will vigorously bring their cases to court without plea-bargaining them to charges carrying lesser penalties; judges and juries will have less discretion in determining the penalties imposed; and more criminals will serve longer sentences for their crimes. (Messner and Rosenfeld, 1994:94)

People's views about the proper ways to deal with criminals are consistent with their views about the causes of crime. The more radical opinions stress the brutalizing strategies of government crime control, whereas more conservative views stress the dangerousness of offenders and the need for swift, certain, and severe punishment.

Ideological Positions on the Proper Operating Policies of Criminal Justice Agencies. From the perspective of the extreme radical left, "law enforcement" is simply a domestic military apparatus that the ruling elite uses to keep itself in power and to inflict pain or death on anyone who challenges that power. There is no talk of reforming such a system; rather, a total and forceful overthrow of the entire system is called for. The more moderate "Left 3" position advocates dismantling military-style criminal justice apparatus and replacing it with a democratic organizational model, including selection and promotion procedures that do not discriminate against minorities and other culturally disadvantaged groups. Furthermore, prisons are seen as dehumanizing schools for crime and should no longer form the core of correctional activities.

From the ultraconservative "Right 5" position comes a call for operating policies that increase the system's ability to maintain order and protect society: increases in staffing, improvements in weaponry, technological advances that improve surveillance and pursuit capability. The system must be able to deliver maximum force and control wherever needed. The more moderate "Right 3" ideology wants law enforcement agencies to have all the resources necessary to deal promptly and decisively with crime, and advocates less judicial control of the police and expansion of the scope of criminal law. Efforts to expand community corrections should be resisted as threats to neighborhood safety and stability.

"Left 1" and "Right 1" ideologies converge on policies relating to criminal justice operating procedures. Moderate liberals stress an overarching approach to crime, in which the criminal justice apparatus is coordinated with other agencies that serve the general welfare of the community, and where the federal government finances and oversees reforms. Moderate conservatives also stress system reform, but put more emphasis on increasing criminal justice efficiency through modern management and information processing techniques.

This managerial perspective has been very influential over the past few years (Feeley and Simon, 1992). The goal has been maximum management of unruly groups at minimum cost, and we shall see in Part Four how modern corrections, in particular, has incorporated this perspective.

THE TWIN GOALS OF CRIME POLICY: ORDER AND JUSTICE

The author of the study we have just reviewed believes that both left and right ideologies can be reduced to basic principles or values that few Americans would quarrel with:

> For the right, the paramount value is order—an ordered society based on a pervasive and binding morality—and the paramount danger is disorder—social, moral, and political. For the left, the paramount value is justice—a just society based on a fair and equitable distribution of power, wealth, prestige, and privilege—and the paramount evil is injustice—the concentration of valued social resources in the hands of a privileged minority. . . . Stripped of the passion of ideological conflict, the issue between the two sides could be viewed as a disagreement over the relative priority of two valuable conditions: whether order with justice, or justice with order should be the guiding principle of the criminal justice enterprise. (Miller, 1973:148)

In the last hundred years or so, government policies and practices have incorporated competing crime control and prevention strategies, but these can be

The crime control model focuses on the capacity of the criminal justice system to catch, prosecute, convict, and dispose of large numbers of offenders. American policy has long been dominated by this model, which emphasizes order first, justice second.

PHOTO BY MCGLYNN, COURTESY OF THE IMAGE WORKS

reduced to two "ideal type" models of the criminal justice system at work. One emphasizes *order*—with justice; the other emphasizes *justice*—with order. Although neither model exactly reproduces the real world, both are drawn from criminal justice in action and they display differences in assumptions and beliefs about the fundamental goals of the criminal justice system. The models were first suggested by Herbert L. Packer (1964, 1968), who calls them the **crime control model** and the **due process model.**

crime control model Emphasizes the capacity of the criminal justice system to promote order and safety by arresting, prosecuting, and convicting a high proportion of criminal offenders.

due process model Emphasizes the willingness of the criminal justice system to protect the constitutional rights of citizens and the formal fact-finding process.

Order with Justice: The Crime Control Model. According to the crime control model, the most important goal of the criminal justice system is to control criminals so that the rest of society is safe and secure. When people perceive that law enforcement is breaking down, that laws are not being enforced, the result is increased disregard for law among the general population. "The law-abiding citizen then becomes the victim of all sorts of unjustifiable invasions of his interests . . . [and] his liberty to function as a member of society [is] sharply diminished" (Packer, 1968:158).

To counteract this possibility, the crime control model focuses on the capacity of the criminal justice system to catch, prosecute, convict, and dispose of a high proportion of criminal offenders. A premium is placed on speed and finality: Procedures are standardized and cases handled informally whenever possible, and challenges are kept to a minimum. This requires that nonguilty suspects be efficiently screened out of the process and guilty offenders passed through quickly to final disposition. The system is like a conveyor belt along which flows an endless stream of cases processed by workers who perform routine, standardized tasks.

Justice with Order: The Due Process Model. Whereas the crime control model resembles an assembly line, the due process model is more like an obstacle course: "Each of the successive stages is designed to present formidable obstacles to carrying the accused any further along in the process" (Packer, 1968:163).

The due process model makes crime control a secondary goal. Emphasis is placed on making sure that evidence is carefully scrutinized in formal proceedings; on ensuring that the accused receives an impartial hearing; on protecting accused persons against violations of their civil rights; on maintaining a presumption of innocence until guilt is legally proven; on ensuring that all defendants are given equal protection under the law, including the chance to defend themselves adequately; and on ensuring that suspects and convicted offenders are treated with dignity. The emphasis, then, is on justice first.

American Crime Policy Puts Order First. In this country, crime policy has been dominated by the ideology underlying the crime control model—basically the ideology of the moderate right. Detection and apprehension of criminals in the defense of order and its underlying values has been the major emphasis. There have been continuing efforts to create and enforce criminal laws dealing with issues that some consider to be moral questions, from abortion to homosexuality to physician-assisted suicide (Meier and Geis, 1997). There has been an increasing effort to streamline the criminal justice process and coordinate procedures across local, state, and federal jurisdictions. The extensive use of enforcement discretion among police and plea bargaining among lawyers exemplifies the emphasis on informality. Finally, there has been a continuing effort to promote efficiency and productivity and to improve the technologies of law enforcement.

Congressional support for the crime control model came in 1968, when Congress passed the Omnibus Crime Control and Safe Streets Act. Through its various provisions, Congress extended the reach of the federal government in criminal justice matters and helped establish crime control policy for the states.

Although the U.S. Constitution specifically places the major responsibility for crime in the hands of the states, the federal government gained considerable power and influence through this act.

Its primary practical contribution—and source of its influence—was money. Through the Law Enforcement Assistance Administration (LEAA), the U.S. Department of Justice funneled millions of dollars to state and local criminal justice agencies—over a billion dollars in 1976 alone (U.S. Department of Justice, 1976:42). A period of downsizing followed in the face of rising criticism of the LEAA, including claims that large amounts of money were being wasted. However, the administrations of Presidents Ronald Reagan and George Bush soon started pumping money back into the federal fight against crime through a successor agency, the Office of Justice Programs (OJP). Federal outlays rose through the 1980s and early 1990s.

As Figure 3.3 shows, most of this money went to law enforcement and corrections, and this continues under the Clinton administration. In 1994, amid much fanfare, the president signed congressional bill HR3355, the Violent Crime Control and Law Enforcement Act, known as the Federal Crime Bill. Even though some Republican leaders faulted the bill for its "liberal social programs," over two-thirds of the $30 billion budget was earmarked for police ($13.3 billion) and corrections ($8.3 billion), most of it to build new prisons.

In addition, new "get tough" laws were included in the package: The death penalty was extended to more than 50 offenses, including terrorism, large-scale drug trafficking, drive-by shootings, and carjackers who kill; penalties were increased for a wide variety of other offenses, particularly those committed by

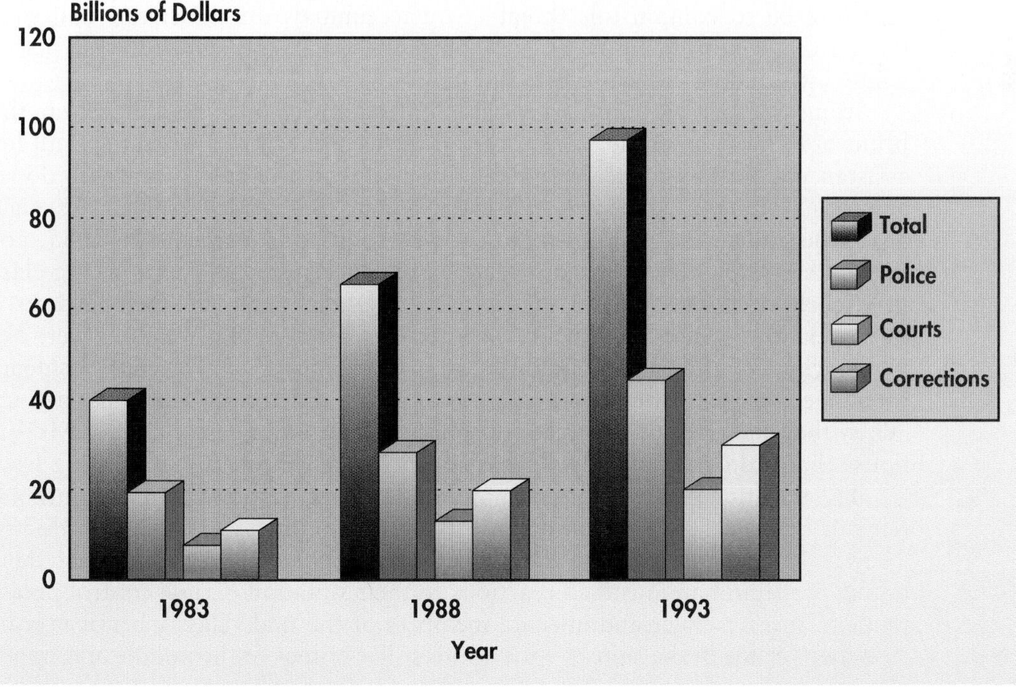

FIGURE 3.3 TRENDS IN GOVERNMENT EXPENDITURES ON POLICE, COURTS, AND CORRECTIONS, 1982–1993

Figures represent combined expenditures of federal, state, and local governments during the years shown.

Source: Kathleen Maguire and Ann L. Pastore (1998). *Sourcebook of Criminal Justice Statistics* (p. 3). Washington, D.C.: U.S. Department of Justice.

juveniles and those involving drugs or weapons; and life imprisonment was made a mandatory penalty for people convicted of three violent felonies or drug offenses—the so-called three-strikes rule. Many states have already passed similar legislation, including truth-in-sentencing laws that require felony offenders to spend at least 85 percent of their prison sentence behind bars.

Public Policy and Criminal Stereotypes. The 1994 Crime Bill emphasized the reduction of crimes involving violence, drugs, and/or juveniles as three of its major themes. To this extent it repeated a long-standing stereotype in criminal justice: The true crime threat lies in the streets.

Of course, there is some basis for concern about street crimes, especially those committed by the nation's youth. Over the past few years the average age of offenders has declined while victimization of juveniles and young adults has increased. Firearms are turning up more and more in homicides committed by youth, and more schools across the nation are reporting more violent crime than ever before. Violent crimes among strangers are also on the rise, according to the FBI (1994). And although accurate information is almost impossible to obtain, many police departments claim that gangs and gang crimes are growing across the nation (National Youth Gang Center, 1997). As we shall see in Chapter 8, this growth has been linked to the rising rates of violent crime among teenagers and young adults, especially minority males living in the inner city.

The 1994 Crime Bill targets the urban street criminal whose offenses are typically muggings, rapes, burglaries, armed robberies, assaults, homicides, and drug trafficking. This is the stereotypical criminal who threatens all law-abiding citizens. Small wonder, then, that the gang-banging and drive-by shootings of today are given so much press. People are encouraged to view the inner-city street as the unsafe turf of violent criminals. The task of any good government will therefore be to contain this threat—to get criminals off the streets and stop them from venturing into "decent" neighborhoods, the suburbs, and places where law-abiding citizens work and play.

Ironically, just as poor, lower-class, and minority people tend to bear the brunt of the war on crime, they may find themselves ignored when they call for assistance from the police. We talked about this in Chapter 2, and will do so again in Chapter 7. However, an event comes to mind that illustrates once again the under- and overpolicing of some groups of Americans. In 1985, police in Philadelphia were asked repeatedly by black residents of a working-class neighborhood to investigate the activities of neighbors who belonged to a quasi-religious group called MOVE. There were rumors that weapons were being stockpiled and that children were being abused. Only when residents threatened to go to the governor and the media did city officials take action. When they did they overreacted, dropping a bomb-like device on the MOVE house that ultimately destroyed an entire city block through the resulting fire.

The traditional targets of crime policy often feel oppressed by the authorities and see their own illegal actions as political crimes (Allen, 1974:74–76). They feel oppressed because they lack political power and believe that their crimes are legitimate, justified reactions to their situation. Crime control policy tends to further anger and alienate members of the underclass when it is realized that "crime in the suites"—the white-collar crimes of the middle and upper classes—get nowhere near the same attention. Even when middle- and upper-class people are convicted of common crimes, their criminality is somehow different: The view held by many people, including some criminal justice officials, is that they must be ill or disturbed because real criminals do not come from this class (Chapman, 1968): "[T]he wealthy do not need to commit crimes, especially crimes of theft, so . . . if they do it is because of physical ill health, mental illness, or evil influence" (Chapman, 1968:75).

Because existing criminal justice policies play down the detection, apprehension, and harsh punishment of people who commit white-collar crimes or other job-related offenses, they reinforce the idea that only the rare middle-class person turns to crime. This situation may be even more pronounced in more class-conscious countries such as England (Levi, 1995:259), but the consequence is the same: Crime is stereotypically—but not in reality—a problem born in the lower classes of society.

SUMMARY

No discussion of criminal justice can afford to ignore public policy, because policy, determines which ideas about crime and justice are officially supported. One of the practical goals of crime policy, and therefore of the criminal justice system, is the reduction and prevention of crime. Yet this chapter has argued that public policy is influenced by ideology and by stereotypes of crime and criminals as much as, if not more than, by an understanding of the underlying causes of crime and the immediate situations that bring it about. Public policy and the justice system that carries it out ought to be guided by theories of crime that are supported by good evidence.

Different theories of crime are based on competing assumptions about human nature and the basis of social order; their policy implications are therefore different. As we saw, theories that emphasize free will suggest policies that reduce the appeal of crime; those that suggest that human nature is basically good imply policies designed to protect people from bad influences; theories based on the conflict view of social order suggest policies aimed at reducing the inequities that encourage conflict and exploitation.

A variety of forces shape the social environment of individuals and groups, including their access to legal and illegal opportunities. Social structure theories of crime focus on these background factors, which may be cultural, economic, political, or social (for example, community, neighborhood, or family). They ask: How does social structure promote or restrain criminal activity? Social process theories focus on the experiences of individuals or groups as they interact with each other. These experiences include interactions with peers and parents, as well as with authority figures such as the police. This group of theories asks how social processes promote or restrain criminal activity. Some theories of crime incorporate both social structure and social process. The policy implication of these integrated theories, illustrated by life-course theory and by the theory of reintegrative shaming, is to develop criminal justice programs and procedures that draw on the strengths or assets of communities, neighborhoods, and families.

Ultimately, social structure and social process theories try to explain how some people become motivated to commit crimes. An entirely different approach focuses on the things that make criminal events more or less likely to occur. Opportunity-based theories of crime, such as the routine activities approach, see crime as an event that grows out of situations where motivated offenders have access to appropriate opportunities and where the inducements are strong enough to outweigh any disincentives, such as too much risk or too much effort. The policy implications of this approach are to devise ways to remove opportunities and reduce situational inducements. We reviewed sixteen promising crime prevention strategies based on this perspective.

In the end, the policies that drive criminal justice are heavily influenced by the ideology of the day, particularly the values and beliefs of powerful interest groups and the government officials in charge of allocating resources. A conservative ideology emphasizing order and control continues to dominate criminal justice in America. In recent years, it has given rise to tougher penalties for crime, more prisons to house a growing prison population, and less-tolerant treatment of juveniles who commit crimes involving violence or drugs. Even though crimes are committed across all ages, social classes, and ethnic/racial groups, and even though the costs of white-collar crime far exceed those of traditional street crimes, the criminal justice system in America continues to target young, poor, and minority individuals who commit mostly street crimes.

WHAT DO YOU THINK *NOW*?

- Compare the different explanations of crime and criminality that you read about. Which ones impressed you the most. Why?
- Consider the reliance of criminals on opportunity, and consider the value of crime prevention. Which types of crime prevention and deterrence seem to be most successful? Which do you think are less successful?
- How do the goals of maintaining order and serving justice summarize crime policy? Are there any other goals that might be important? If so, what?

KEY TERMS

ideology
general theories
restricted theories
level of explanation
free will doctrine
determinism
social order
consensus perspective
conflict perspective
interactionist perspective
labeling theory
proximate causes
social structure perspectives
social process perspectives
life course
reintegrative shaming
routine activity approach
situational crime prevention
crime displacement
crime control model
due process model

ACTIVE LEARNING CHALLENGES

1. Break the class into three groups: those who think social structure theories are more effective in explaining crime, those who think social process theories are more effective, and those who prefer interactionist perspectives. Have each group research at least two examples of each type of theory and develop arguments to support their case. Present the arguments for class discussion.
2. Contact your local elected state officials and invite them to class to defend or attack current crime policies. Afterward, try to identify the speakers' assumptions about human nature and social order and place each speaker on Miller's ideological continuum discussed in the chapter.
3. Break the class into two groups: those who think the "order with justice" model is preferable, and those who think the "justice with order" model is preferable. Have each side research and present points that support their views.
4. Watch an episode of *Law & Order, NYPD Blue*, or another TV show depicting criminal justice at work. How is crime explained in the show? What ideological position does the show represent? How much emphasis is placed on order, and how much on justice?

INTERNET CHALLENGES

The Web pages mentioned here can all be accessed through the Web site for this textbook at **http://www.prenhall.com/barlow/.**

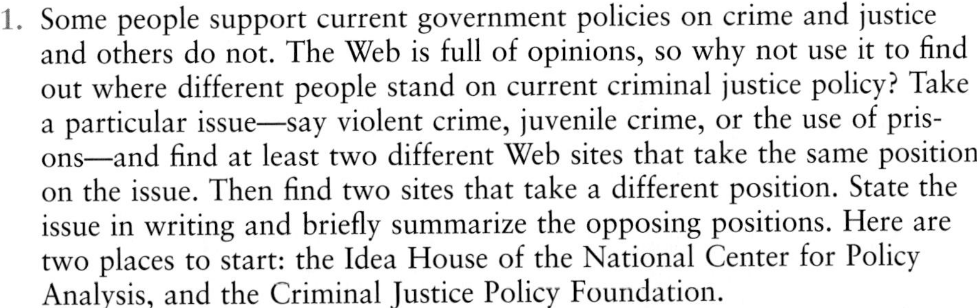

1. Some people support current government policies on crime and justice and others do not. The Web is full of opinions, so why not use it to find out where different people stand on current criminal justice policy? Take a particular issue—say violent crime, juvenile crime, or the use of prisons—and find at least two different Web sites that take the same position on the issue. Then find two sites that take a different position. State the issue in writing and briefly summarize the opposing positions. Here are two places to start: the Idea House of the National Center for Policy Analysis, and the Criminal Justice Policy Foundation.
2. The Council of State Governments promotes coordinated and standardized responses to major problems such as crime. Check out its latest criminal justice policy recommendations on its Web site. How well do they match your ideas?
3. The Vera Institute of Justice in New York City has been a leader in designing innovative programs in criminal justice for more than 35 years. Ideologically, Vera is between "Left 2" and "Left 3." Check out its latest ideas at its Web site. Then turn to the Right Side of the Web home page for ideas from "Right 2" and "Right 3."
4. Many police departments use the Internet to promote situational crime prevention. Check police department Web sites and find examples of four of the sixteen situational prevention strategies mentioned in this chapter.

CHAPTER 4

Overview of the Adult and Juvenile Justice Systems

LEARNING OBJECTIVES

- Understand the primary goals of the criminal justice system and the activities that support them.
- Describe the consensus and conflict models of criminal justice.
- Describe the basic organization and responsibilities of the police, the courts, and corrections.
- Describe the key decision points in the criminal justice process, and explain why they are important.
- Understand how the juvenile justice system came into being and how it differs from the adult system.
- Describe the recent trends in juvenile crime and the reforms being proposed to address them.

The three primary components of the criminal justice system are the police, the courts, and the corrections system. Although their specific roles are very different, together they determine the quality of justice in America.

PHOTO BY A. RAMEY, COURTESY OF PHOTO EDIT

Today, the grand jury is the total captive of the prosecutor who, if he is candid, will concede that he can indict anybody, at any time, for almost anything, before any grand jury.

WILLIAM J. CAMPBELL, U.S. DISTRICT COURT JUDGE

It's the end of the juvenile court.

DEAN IRA SCHWARTZ, UNIVERSITY OF PENNSYLVANIA, COMMENTING ON FEDERAL LEGISLATION TO INCREASE THE NUMBER OF JUVENILES TRIED AS ADULTS.

We learned in Chapter 1 how an act can become a crime and a person a criminal. We saw that crime is a label attached to an act or person through a rather complicated process involving the exercise of authority by officials who create and apply the criminal law. Even when essentially the same acts are committed, some people escape being labeled *criminal* because of who they are. As a result, stereotypes of "true" crime and "true" criminals emerge over time: Assaults, rapes, robberies, and burglaries committed by young, lower-class, minority males dominate the public image of crime.

In Chapter 2, we learned that the official count of crimes and criminals represents only the tip of a large iceberg. Through victimization and self-report studies, criminologists have found that the "dark figure of crime" includes millions of unreported offenses, many of them serious crimes involving property loss or injury. An even larger part of the dark figure is made up of minor offenses and so-called victimless crimes involving drugs, gambling, and consensual sex offenses such as prostitution. No adequate count exists of offenses committed within the family or by people on the job.

Considering these facts, it was probably no surprise to learn in Chapter 3 that explanations of crime and conventional crime policy have emphasized stereotypical offenses and offenders. Little attention has been paid to white collar crime or to crimes committed by business organizations. The theories that get the most play in government circles fit the ideology and political agendas of the people and parties in power. When the policy implications of crime theories suggest decriminalization, or significant changes in the social, economic, or political structure of society, or investments to increase the assets and dignity of the poor, minorities, and ex-offenders, those theories are generally discounted in favor of ones stressing low self-control, breakdown of family values, or the bad influence of criminal friends.

The remaining chapters of this text examine in detail how these realities of crime and policy are brought to life in the decisions and activities of the three major units or "functional areas" of the criminal justice system: the police, the courts, and corrections. Before we begin our journey into the criminal justice system at work, an overview of the system will help set the stage. This is the major purpose of this chapter. Although most of this book is concerned with adult offenders, half of this chapter and many examples throughout the text discuss the juvenile justice system. As we shall see, juveniles account for a significant portion of the crimes handled by criminal justice officials, yet there are important differences in how juvenile offenders experience the system compared with adults. As noted in Chapter 1, rising juvenile arrest rates for violent crimes are one reason these differences are currently under review in many states. We shall take a further look at proposed changes in the processing of juveniles and consider their implications for criminal justice.

? WHAT DO YOU THINK?

- What are the primary goals of the criminal justice system? How do the police, the courts, and corrections meet these goals?
- What are the main decisions made by the police? The courts? The corrections system?
- How are juvenile suspects and offenders treated differently from adults? What are some recent trends in juvenile crime?

THE CRIMINAL JUSTICE SYSTEM IN THE UNITED STATES

In Chapter 1 we defined criminal justice as a modern society's system of roles and activities for defining and dealing with crime. It is part of society's formal social control apparatus. All sorts of people and agencies are part of that system, but this book emphasizes the decisions and activities of the police, the courts, and corrections. There will be occasional historical and global illustrations of criminal justice at work in other times and places.

GOALS OF THE CRIMINAL JUSTICE SYSTEM

Three overall goals unite the three functional areas of the criminal justice system:

1. Track down and punish those found guilty of committing crimes
2. Maintain order
3. Promote justice.

Table 4.1 lists the immediate goals and primary activities of the police, the courts, and corrections. It is easy to see how one area relies on another. For example, a primary goal of the police is the detection and arrest of suspects. Unless that is accomplished, the courts have no one to process, and therefore cannot achieve their goals of determining guilt or innocence and promoting justice through fair punishments. Likewise, if no one is declared guilty by the courts, the goals of corrections cannot be achieved. Like any other system, the whole achieves its purpose only if the parts accomplish theirs. Viewed in this light, the criminal justice system is composed of a number of separate but interrelated subsystems that don't necessarily work well together.

TABLE 4.1 Goals and Primary Activities of the Criminal Justice System

OVERALL GOALS OF SYSTEM

Track down and punish those guilty of committing crime
Maintain order
Promote justice

THREE FUNCTIONAL AREAS OF THE SYSTEM

Police

Primary Goals

Enforce the law
Maintain order
Prevent crime

Primary Activities in Support of the Goals

Detection and investigation of crimes
Identification and arrest of suspects
Routine patrol, surveillance, and intelligence gathering
Education and training of officers and citizens, including children (e.g., bicycle safety, DARE)
Community and problem-oriented policing

Courts

Primary Goals

Determine guilt or innocence of suspects
Set the appropriate penalty upon conviction
Uphold the cause of justice, including due process

Primary Activities in Support of the Goals

Prosecution and defense of suspects
Pre-trial hearings
Impartial bench and jury trials
Plea negotiations
Sentencing
Appeals of conviction or sentence
Provide probation and parole services in conjunction with corrections

Corrections

Primary Goals

Apply court-ordered punishment
Maintain safety and security of correctional personnel and the community
Uphold due process and other constitutional rights of offenders

Primary Activities in Support of the Goals

Design, construct, and run prison and jail facilities with appropriate levels of security
Carry out the death penalty (in states where legal and prescribed)
Design and implement correctional programs
Provide probation and parole services in conjunction with courts

Consensus or Conflict in System Goals? It is useful to think of criminal justice as a system of interlocking functional areas or subsystems that contribute to the goals of the whole. This approach identifies the key parts and encourages us to examine how well they achieve their goals, and to contemplate the causes and consequences of problems that may arise. For example, if the police union in a particular city is fighting for improved benefits for its officers, it may encourage them to "play by the rule book" and enforce laws more strictly. This could mean less exercise of discretion, more arrests, and more paperwork. Not only would this tend to slow up the police process, it might even result in a reduction in the safety and security of citizens due to less frequent patrols, longer response times, and overcrowded jails. Overcrowded jails put pressure on the courts to process suspects more quickly or to release them into

Box 4.1

GLOBAL JUSTICE

THE ORGANIZATION OF POLICE IN ENGLAND AND WALES

Although American policing has roots in England, there are many differences between the two systems. Most people know that Enlish police officers do not generally carry firearms, but did you know that some officers do not drive because they have no driver's license?

© ANTMAN/THE IMAGE WORKS

Much of American criminal law and procedure has its roots in English history. Over the past 200 years, however, criminal justice has been slowly "Americanized," so that while similarities remain, more and more differences have emerged. One area where there are striking differences is in the organization and authority of the police. Here is a brief look at policing in England and Wales. Some of the major differences with the United States are summarized at the end.

There are 43 police forces in England and Wales, each responsible for a certain territory. Other police forces are responsible for policing particular

the community. Probation and corrections officials also find their programs affected by the overcrowding, including increased demand for community-based alternatives. Criminal suspects and offenders, meanwhile, may find that overcrowding undermines their constitutional rights, resulting in lawsuits putting yet further pressure on the courts.

consensus model Emphasizes cooperation and compromise based on shared values and goals.

Some experts see the system as a collection of agencies that are working together more or less effectively to achieve an agreed-upon set of goals. This model of criminal justice is known as the **consensus model**. Like the functional theory of law described in Chapter 1, the consensus model emphasizes order and stability. Conflicts are minimized because participants share common val-

Box 4.1 (CONTINUED)

places such as railway stations, ports, and defense installations. Police forces are maintained and funded by both central and local governments, under the immediate oversight of elected county council members and police magistrates. The Metropolitan Police is the law enforcement agency for the city of London, and is directly answerable to the Home Secretary, a government minister appointed by the prime minister and responsible for crime control and other domestic security affairs in the Home Office (the closest American counterparts are the U.S. Attorney General and the U.S. Department of Justice). Other police forces are directly run by a chief constable, who is not answerable to anyone on operational matters, but must account for resources to the local county or city council. Senior police appointments must be approved by the Home Secretary.

English police are generally armed only with a nightstick, called a truncheon. However, guns are available in special circumstances. Recent terrorist threats and fears that many professional criminals now carry firearms led to the development of special response squads armed with guns, and police carrying automatic weapons are now a fairly common sight at major airports. Nevertheless, only a small minority of specially trained officers have access to firearms. Some police forces do not require officers to have a driver's license. Driver training is offered, however.

In England and Wales, the police initiate the prosecution of a suspect by charging a defendant and passing case papers to the Crown Prosecution Service, which reviews the evidence and decides whether to prosecute. Until 1986, the police themselves prosecuted criminal cases. The change was made after criticism that police prosecution led to significant regional variations in rates of prosecution and high levels of dismissals. However, the new system appears to be doing little better, and is considered less accountable. There is pressure to revert to the older, traditional method of police prosecutions.

Some notable differences between U.S. and U.K. policing are as follows:

UNITED STATES	UNITED KINGDOM
Many jurisdictions	More centralized controls
Some elected police officials	No elected police officials
Officers armed and must be licensed to drive	Most officers not armed with guns and some not licensed to drive
Reduced police role in prosecution	Greater police role in prosecution

Sources: Coretta Phillips, Gemma Cox, and Ken Pease (1996). "England and Wales." In Graeme Newman, Adam C. Bouloukos, and Debra Cohen, eds., *World Factbook of Criminal Justice Systems.* Washington, D.C.: U.S. Department of Justice; U.K. police officers Nicola and David Newsome, personal communication, August 1997.

ues and goals; the system accommodates internal or external pressures by making small adjustments that maintain the integrity of the whole.

An alternative analytical approach suggests that conflict is inevitable, The **conflict model** of criminal justice recognizes that the interests, values, and needs of different players and organizations will bring them into conflict with each other or with the formal goals of the system. Consider the police. In the United States, unlike some other countries, different law enforcement agencies represent different levels of government as well as different areas of enforcement responsibility. (For example, Box 4.1 describes police organization in England and Wales.) There are federal police agencies such as the FBI, with jurisdiction

conflict model Emphasizes differences in interests, values, and needs, and the conflicts that arise as a result.

anywhere in the United States; state agencies such as the state police or highway patrol, with jurisdiction anywhere within a state; county agencies such as sheriff's departments, with jurisdiction anywhere within a county; and municipal agencies such as the St. Louis Metropolitan Police Department, with jurisdiction anywhere within city limits. There are also university police departments, whose jurisdiction is the campus. In addition, some federal and state law enforcement agencies have more limited or specialized policing responsibilities; for example, drug trafficking, transportation and commerce, parks, tax collection, or protection of the president. Although they may be operating in the same jurisdiction, these police agencies may report to a different department of state or federal government.

Clearly, this array of different police agencies makes coordination and cooperation more difficult to achieve. Just like any other organization, police agencies tend to be protective of their particular domain or "turf," and this can lead to conflicts. Consider also that each police agency is in competition with others for scarce resources. Once again we have a source of conflict.

Conflicts arise not only within functional areas of the criminal justice system but also across them. Just as police compete with each other for resources, they also compete with other criminal justice agencies. Conflicts may also arise when the goals of one agency are at odds with the practices of another. Poor police work may jeopardize the prosecution of cases; plea bargaining by lawyers may undermine the hard work of police; prison overcrowding may jeopardize the rehabilitative efforts of probation and parole officers, and early release puts more offenders back on the streets more quickly, perhaps making life more difficult for the police.

We shall see time and again throughout the text that both the consensus and conflict models have merit. However, the conflict approach invites students to look behind the surface of criminal justice, which may seem relatively calm and cooperative, to the tensions and strains associated with conflicting ideologies, needs, and interests that may exist among individuals and agencies supposedly pursuing the same goals.

Organization of Functional Areas in the Criminal Justice System

In the United States today, the organization of functional areas within the criminal justice system is governed by local, state, and federal laws, and by administrative regulations within the agencies themselves.

The Police. Law enforcement agencies operate at local, state, and federal levels; they are responsible for enforcing the laws that apply in their jurisdictions. At the federal level, agencies include the Federal Bureau of Investigation (FBI), the Drug Enforcement Administration (DEA), the Bureau of Alcohol, Tobacco, and Firearms (ATF), and the U.S. Secret Service. These agencies are headquartered in Washington, D.C., along with the rest of the federal government. The director of the FBI, the nation's premier law enforcement agency, is appointed by the president and approved by Congress.

Federal law enforcement agencies have field offices throughout the nation, and some—the DEA and Secret Service, for example—have offices abroad to facilitate work with international police agencies and foreign governments. They are organized along hierarchical lines, with commands flowing from the top through department heads and agents in charge of field offices to special agents working on assignments in the field. Their officers carry firearms and have powers of arrest.

State and local police agencies enforce state criminal laws and relevant local ordinances within their jurisdictions. University police departments are also included here. Most state agencies were created during the late 1800s and early 1900s. Local police agencies are authorized by state statute and are attached to county and city government. Sheriffs are usually elected, while chiefs of city departments are usually appointed. State and local police agencies are usually hierarchical organizations, except for small rural departments, which may have only one sworn employee who functions as chief, detective, and patrol officer.

Some states have centralized law enforcement, in which a state police force combines a variety of policing functions, from patrolling the state's highways to investigating crimes. Pennsylvania, Michigan, and New York are examples. Other states such as North Carolina and Texas follow a decentralized model, with separate bureaus handling highway patrol and criminal investigations. Most states provide assistance to local agencies in the form of criminal records management, police training, and assistance in carrying out criminal investigations.

Finally, large city police departments such as New York, Los Angeles, and Chicago employ thousands of officers and are highly bureaucratic organizations. Fiscal and operational control usually rests with city government, and sometimes a commission of appointed or elected representatives of the public oversees personnel decisions and approves budgets.

The Criminal Courts. Two court systems handle criminal complaints in the United States: federal courts and state courts. A number of other industrialized Western countries have both federal and state, or provincial, court systems, but the state systems are generally less autonomous than is the case in the United States. In Canada, for example, there is only one criminal code, and the federal government appoints judges to the highest provincial courts (Cohen and Longtin, 1996).

Most criminal matters begin in the state lower courts. These courts cover jurisdictions determined by county or municipal boundaries and sometimes by population size. They handle misdemeanors and ordinance violations ranging from assaults to drug possession, shoplifting, traffic violations, and disorderly conduct. The judges and magistrates in these courts also handle the first stages of many felony cases: They make bail decisions, for example, and hold preliminary hearings. In some states they are authorized to handle certain felony cases through to sentencing.

The highest court in the land is the U.S. Supreme Court; it is the court of last resort for all appeals. Box 4.2 gives a brief history of the Court. Eight associate justices and one chief justice sit on the court, although all nine are not required to hear a case. Supreme Court justices, like other federal judges, serve for life; in the current court, all but Justice Clarence Thomas were born before World War II, and Justice John Paul Stevens is almost 80 years old (Chapter 12 gives more details on the membership of the current Supreme Court). Approximately 6,000 cases a year are appealed to the Supreme Court, but only 100 or so are heard. Of these, less than half involve criminal cases. In recent years, conflicts of interest have resulted in some justices excusing themselves from a case. This practice, called a *recusal*, used to be rare, but from September 1994 to May 1997 it had been used a total of 192 times (*USA Today*, June 2, 1997, pp. 1–2). The absence of one justice can make a huge difference because there are few justices to begin with, and ties are more likely to result.

Corrections. The final functional area in the criminal justice system concerns the application of penalties to convicted offenders: state and federal correctional agencies. Today, the correctional population of the United States is at an all-time high. As of midyear 1997, state and federal prisons held over 1.2 million prisoners, and local jails another 67,000 (Gilliard and Beck, 1998:2). In addition, almost 4 million adult men and women were on probation or parole. Almost all of the nearly 700,000 offenders on parole had been convicted of a

Box 4.2

JUSTICE IN HISTORY

THE U.S. SUPREME COURT

This illustration reflects the political nature of Supreme Court appointees. For example, the current Chief Justice William Rehnquist is portrayed as President Richard Nixon (front row, center), who appointed him in 1971. Presidents appoint Supreme Court justices whose beliefs roughly match theirs. The political makeup of the Supreme Court at any given time has a profound effect on American law.

Illustration by Barrie Maguire, courtesy of The Creative Workshop

The U.S. Supreme Court was established in 1787 by Article III of the U.S. Constitution, which states: "The judicial Power of the United States, shall be vested in one supreme Court, and in such inferior Courts as the Congress may from time to time ordain and establish." The Supreme Court has ultimate jurisdiction over all cases arising under the Constitution, laws, and treaties of the United States. Originally set at six justices, since 1869 the Court has comprised 8 associate justices and one chief justice. The president appoints Supreme Court justices, who must be confirmed by Congress; they serve for life. The only qualification for the life term is "good behavior." By law, the Supreme Court begins its term on the first Monday in October and concludes nine months later at the end of June or in early July. Each justice is assigned to oversee one or more of the thirteen circuit courts of appeal.

felony, as had half of the 3.3 million adults on probation. Figure 4.1 shows just how much the correctional population grew from 1980 to 1997.

In the United States, as in most countries, corrections encompasses a large variety of activities. Figure 4.2 illustrates the major ones. At the "hard" end are maximum-security prisons such as the federal penitentiary at Marion, Illinois, and an array of state prisons from Attica and Sing Sing in New York to San Quentin in California. Some prisons, such as the federal penitentiary in Florence, Colorado, and Tamms Correctional Center in Illinois, are now referred to as *supermaximum*, or "maxi-maxi" prisons. As the name suggests, supermaximum prisons operate under the highest levels of security. They are built

Box 4.2 (continued)

The importance of the Supreme Court was not established until after John Marshall became chief justice in 1801. At that time, the justices had to meet in a small room in the basement of the Capitol because no space had been provided for the Court. Among Marshall's important contributions was the establishment of the notion of a "single opinion of the Court." Previously, the justices had followed the tradition in English courts of delivering separate opinions, with none designated as the Court's ruling. Today, opinions that a majority of the Court's justices agree on become the Court's ruling. Justices who agree with some aspect of this ruling, but for a different reason, can write a "concurring" opinion; justices who disagree with the majority ruling write a "dissenting" opinion.

Chief Justice Marshall also emphasized the Court's authority to undertake *judicial review* of legislation, and the extent of its power was demonstrated in various tests of the constitutionality of federal and state laws. From 1810 to 1860 many important rulings either supported the constitutionality of federal legislation or invalidated that of the states. This had the effect of increasing the power of the national government and curbing that of the states.

For many years the role of the Supreme Court in criminal cases was largely limited to appeals from state courts because no common-law crimes were recognized under federal law, and Congress passed very little criminal legislation until after the Civil War. Over the past 50 years, however, Congress has passed more and more criminal statutes, many of them dealing with drugs and violence. This means a greater role for the federal courts in criminal matters, and inevitably a larger role for the Supreme Court.

Because Supreme Court justices are political appointees, their ideological positions lean toward those of the presidents who appoint them. Over the years, the Court has tended to be conservative in its rulings. Under Chief Justice Earl Warren during the 1950s and early 1960s, however, the Court made many controversial decisions in support of minority rights and those of criminal suspects and defendants. The appointments of Presidents Nixon, Reagan, and Bush, and particularly the influence of Justice William A. Rehnquist, who became chief justice in 1986, turned the Court in a more conservative direction, resulting in the modification or reversal of some of the Warren Court's "liberal" rulings. The nature and implications of specific decisions are discussed in later chapters. Recalling the opposing models of criminal justice policy discussed in Chapter 3, the Warren Court might be called a "due process" court, while the Rehnquist Court has been a "crime control" court.

Sources: William H. Rehnquist, (1996). "The Future of the Federal Courts." Address to American University's Washington College of Law, April 9; William J. Brennan, Jr. (1986). "Guaranteeing Individual Liberty." *USA Today*, September, pp. 40–42.

solely to house inmates regarded as too dangerous or too likely to escape from "regular" maximum-security institutions. Inmates are kept under tight control at all times—often under *lockdown*, which means that inmates must stay in their cells for almost the entire day, and their privileges are severely curtailed. One of the primary goals of lockdown is to keep inmates from interacting with each other. Most death penalty inmates are housed in maximum or supermaximum prisons in a special block of cells known as Death Row, or simply the Row. Missouri is one of the few states that has no Death Row, mingling its condemned with the general prison population until two or three days before their scheduled execution.

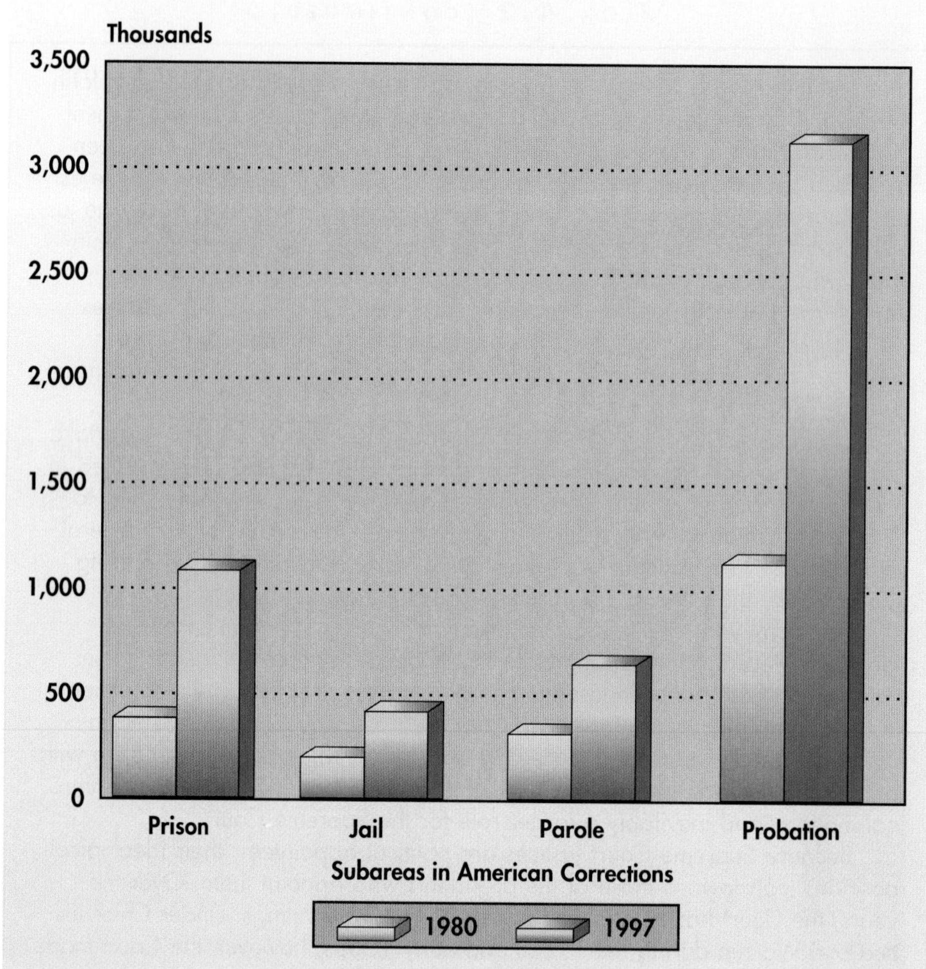

FIGURE 4.1 CORRECTIONAL POPULATIONS IN THE UNITED STATES, 1980 AND 1997
This figure shows the number of Americans confined in prisons or jails, on parole, or on probation.

Source: Kathleen Maguire and Ann L. Pastore (1998). *Sourcebook of Criminal Justice Statistics 1997* (p. 464). Washington, D.C.: U.S. Department of Justice.

Less restrictive, but still secure, are medium-security prisons; the least restrictive of all are minimum-security prisons, which sometimes look like a college campus. Nevertheless, inmates are not free to leave, and their lives are much more regimented than that of the typical student! Lying at the "soft" end of corrections is simple, unsupervised probation, where offenders are given a certain length of time, say six months, during which they must remain "clean," which really means not be arrested and charged with a crime. If they commit an offense while on probation and are caught, they risk getting a stiffer punishment for the original offense. For many offenders on probation, this means jail or prison time. Unsupervised probation is usually reserved for minor, nonviolent crimes. Offenders convicted of more serious misdemeanors and some nonviolent felonies are often placed on supervised probation. This usually means they must report in person to their probation officer on a regular basis and may have other requirements to fulfill, such as holding a job or attending a drug treatment program.

In between probation and prison lie other punishments, some of which are used together with other penalties. Fines are often used in conjunction with

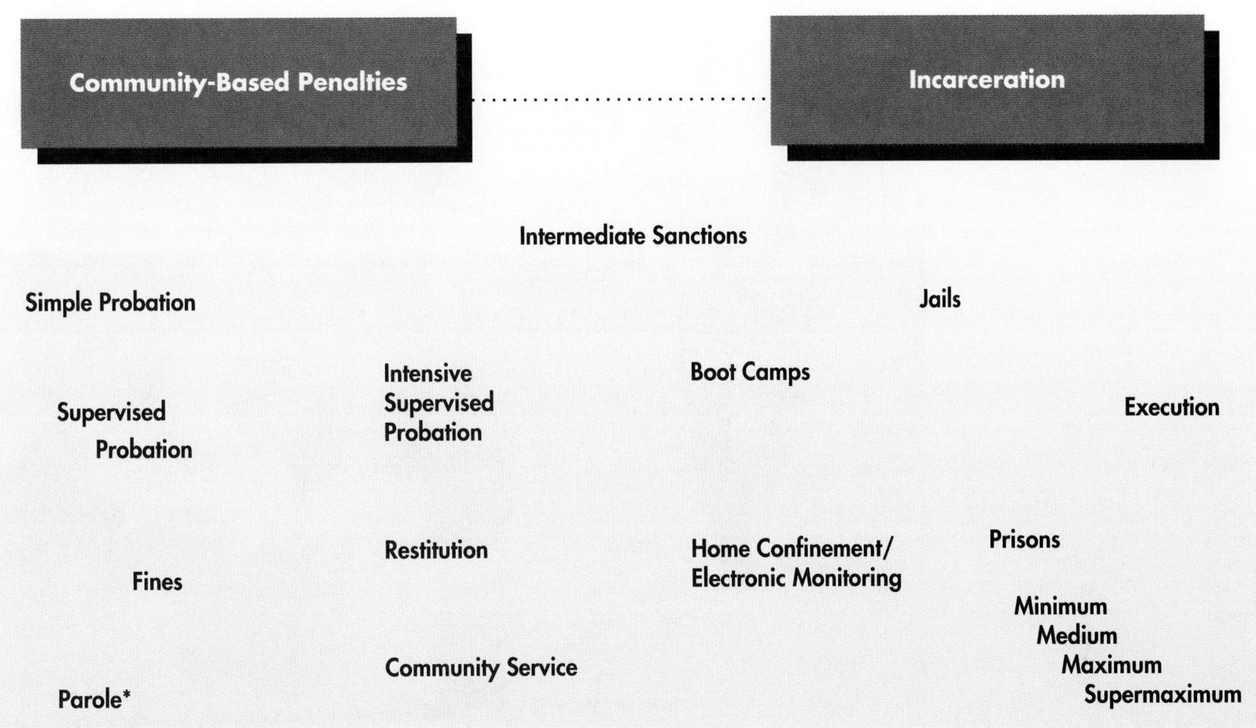

FIGURE 4.2 THE MAJOR ACTIVITIES OF CORRECTIONS
**Parole is community-based supervision of ex–prison inmates.*

probation or jail time. Jails are used not only to house convicted offenders sentenced to less than a year of incarceration, but also people awaiting trial or sentencing. Typically, over half of all jail inmates have not yet been convicted of the offense that put them there. Since 1985, jail incarceration rates have almost doubled for both white and black adults, although the rate for black adults is over five times that of white adults (Bureau of Justice Statistics, 1997c:Table 2.5). Thus, for every 100,000 adult white Americans, 122 were in jail during 1995; for every 100,000 adult black Americans, 700 were in jail:

	NUMBER OF JAIL INMATES		RATE PER 100,000 ADULTS	
DATE	WHITES	BLACKS	WHITES	BLACKS
Mid-year 1985	147,600	105,200	73	368
Mid-year 1995	266,200	232,000	122	700

The reasons for this disparity are addressed in Chapters 11, 13, and 15.

Jails are usually run by the county, although the cities of Baltimore and New York run their own jails. Many jails are overcrowded, posing not only a severe security risk but also a financial burden on taxpayers and an emotional and physical burden on inmates as well as staff. Of the 25 largest jails in the United States, 16 were filled over their rated capacity during the period 1993–1994 (Bureau of Justice Statistics, 1997c:25). Since 1988, the Cook County jail, which serves Chicago and the surrounding area, has been running more than 10 percent over its rated capacity, which was 9,317 inmates in 1995. One of the worst cases of overcrowding has been at the Orange County jail, serving 2.7 million residents just south of Los Angeles, California. This jail has been running 30 percent over capacity in recent years.

The extent of correctional control and supervision of offenders depends on the sentence they receive. The use of such "intermediate sanctions" as house arrest and boot camps is growing in popularity as an alternative to prison time for some offenders.

PHOTO BY SETH PERLMAN, COURTESY OF AP PHOTO

Jail and prison overcrowding is largely due to changes in policy rather than to changes in crime (Joyce, 1992). In recent years, many jurisdictions have cracked down on drunk driving and domestic violence, which has resulted in more arrests. In addition, states have introduced stiffer penalties for many crimes, resulting in overcrowded prisons; jails have been forced to take the overflow. More aggressive enforcement of drug laws together with the rise in crack cocaine use have also contributed to jail overcrowding. The pressure on jails and prisons has resulted in more offenders being released early and has encouraged the development of alternative penalties that do not involve incarceration—or involve less of it. These **intermediate sanctions** are discussed in detail in Chapters 13 and 17; they lie in between prison and probation, and include such things as boot camps, electronic monitoring, restitution, and community service. Can you see how jail overcrowding and the growth of intermediate sanctions illustrate both adaptation and conflict in the criminal justice system?

intermediate sanctions Penalties that lie between prison and simple probation.

COSTS OF THE CRIMINAL JUSTICE SYSTEM

You might well be wondering what all of this costs. Actually, the first things some people think of when they look at the criminal justice system are benefits such as jobs and profits. For criminologists and many lawyers—and for all those working in the system—crime and justice are like bread and water: They depend on them for subsistence. It is not hard to see that criminal justice is part of the fabric of society, and like any other system its health depends on its relation to other systems and to the whole—and vice versa. It is also true, however, that a society's resources are not infinite, and the more spent on one system, the less there is for others. This means that the functional areas of the criminal justice system must compete for resources not only with each other but with the functional areas of other systems, such as education, health, defense, and the economy.

The resources that are put into criminal justice reflect policy judgments made by public officials, and these are influenced by ideology as well as by public and private interests that are very practical. Public interests include the safety and security of the community and the health of the economy; private interests include personal safety and financial security. Although they are similar, public and private interests sometimes come into conflict. If a shopkeeper wants the police to spend more time patrolling her street because she is concerned that crime will affect her business, and if the police increase patrols as a result, it may mean fewer patrols somewhere else, affecting another person's interests and possibly those of the community as a whole.

Another example comes from the growing phenomenon of **privatization**, where private companies construct or manage correctional facilities, or provide police services on behalf of public agencies. There are immense profits to be made by the private sector through investments in prison construction and maintenance, and in various other areas of criminal justice, including law enforcement. However, private individuals and companies that take advantage of privatization opportunities may do so at the expense of public interests. Privatization is discussed in detail in Chapters 5 and 15.

privatization Occurs when activities and agencies traditionally run by the government are handed over to the private sector.

Employment in Criminal Justice. Figure 4.3 shows that the criminal justice system grew continually during the 1980s and early 1990s. This occurred at all levels of government, but most of all at the federal level. By 1995, a total of 167,115 federal workers had jobs in criminal justice, up from 139,799 in 1990, and 110,653 in 1985 (U.S. Bureau of the Census, 1997). This represents a 51 percent increase over that ten-year period. And apart from the U.S. Postal Service, criminal justice employment is the *only* area of federal government activity that has shown consistent increases since 1992, with corrections responsible for most of it. Government "downsizing" apparently does not apply when it comes to dealing with criminals. The drive to build and operate more and bigger jails and prisons, and the growing correctional population, has translated into many new corrections jobs.

Government Expenditures on Criminal Justice. Not surprisingly, as employment in criminal justice has risen, so have expenditures. Figure 4.4 shows the total justice expenditures made by local, state, and federal governments from 1983 to 1993. Payroll accounts for the bulk of the money spent, although new prison construction is a major factor in the growth of federal and state expenditures since the late 1980s. The 1994 Federal Crime Bill authorized billions of dollars more in prison construction money, so this trend should continue at least into the year 2000.

DECISION STAGES IN THE CRIMINAL JUSTICE SYSTEM

The criminal justice system comes alive through the actions of the people who work in it and those who are "processed" by it. In the following chapters we will explore these actions and the decisions that lie behind them in great detail. From the vantage point of criminal suspects, defendants, and victims, various key decision points have markedly different outcomes depending on the actions taken. This section briefly describes where those points are in the system, the actions that may be taken, and their consequences. Figure 4.5 presents a flow chart summarizing the formal criminal justice process. The arrows show where the suspect or defendant goes after each decision is made. Some decisions in-

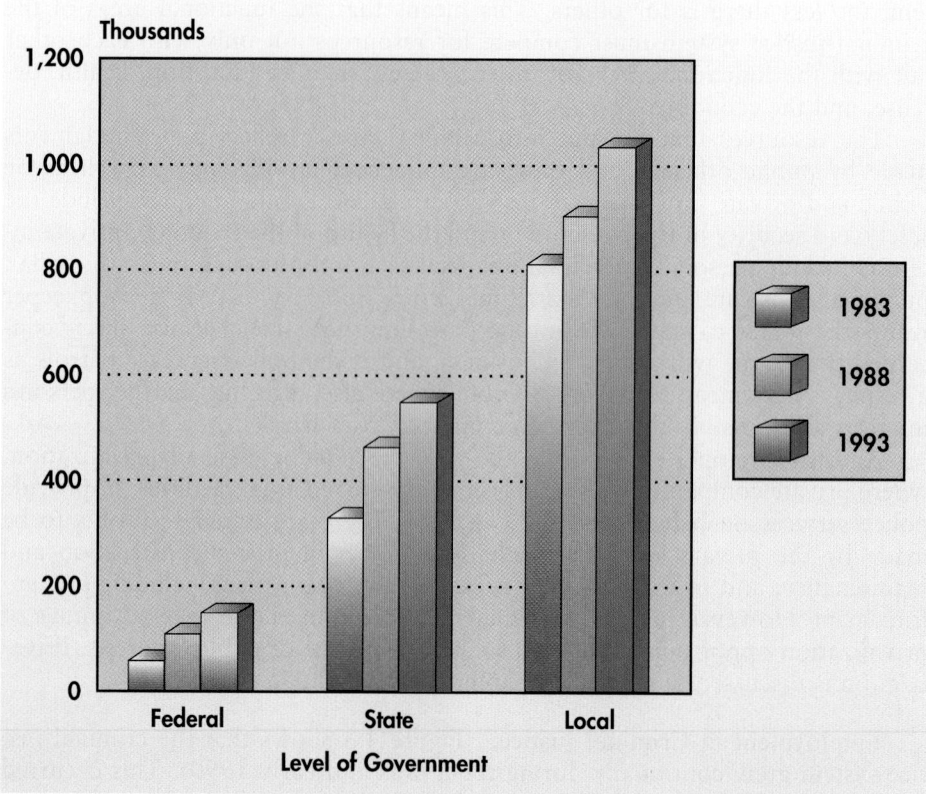

FIGURE 4.3 PUBLIC EMPLOYMENT IN THE CRIMINAL JUSTICE SYSTEM, 1983–1993

The number of Americans employed in criminal justice by federal, state, and local governments (in thousands).

Source: Kathleen Maguire and Ann L. Pastore, ed. (1998). *Sourcebook of Criminal Justice Statistics 1997* (p. 24). Washington D.C.: U.S. Department of Justice.

discretion Criminal justice officials may choose one action over another on the basis of their professional judgment.

volve considerable **discretion,** where criminal justice personnel act on the basis of their professional judgment; others are governed by strict rules allowing little leeway. Highly discretionary decisions are indicated by a $\surd+$.

KEY POLICE DECISIONS

The key decision points for police involve whether to do the following:

- Treat an event as a possible crime
- Investigate the crime
- Make an arrest
- Turn the suspect over to the prosecution

probable cause The constitutional standard for determining whether a search or an arrest is lawful.

Some of these decisions were discussed in Chapter 2, and they are the main topic of Chapter 7, which deals with the exercise of discretion. Most police decisions are highly discretionary. Even though the police rely heavily on complaints from the public, they must decide that an event is a possible crime and then investigate it in order to set the wheels of criminal justice in motion. It may be minutes or many months before a suspect is found, but only then can the police contemplate making an arrest. Arrest decisions are influenced by many things, but the essential legal criterion is **probable cause.** This means that a person exercising reasonable judgment would believe that a crime is being or has been committed and that the suspect is responsible for it. Technically, sus-

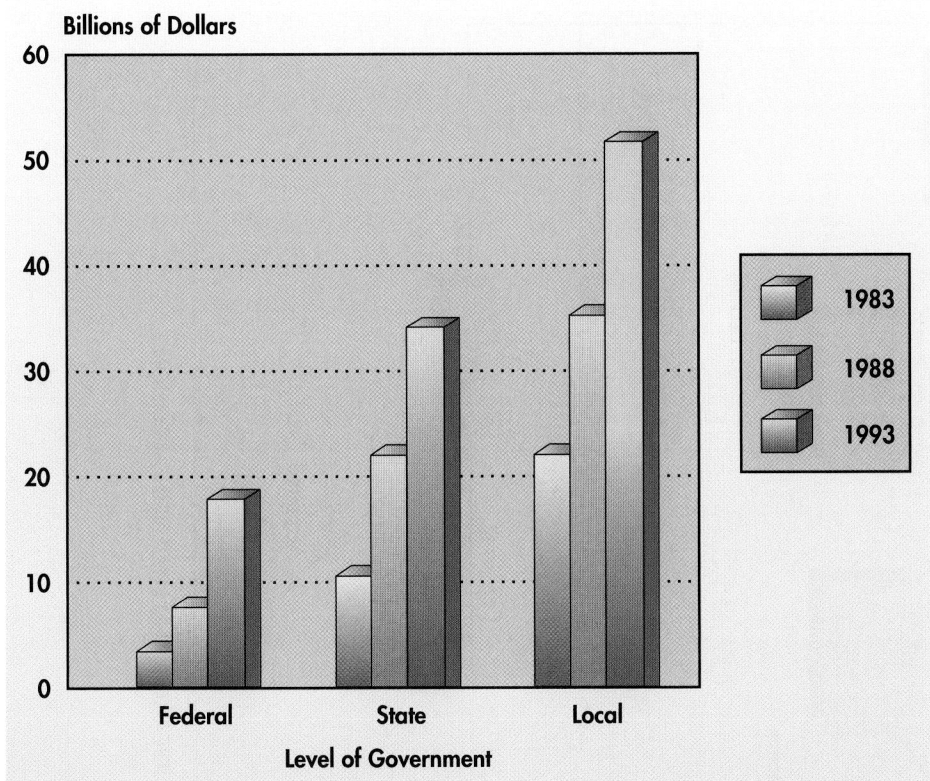

FIGURE 4.4 PUBLIC EXPENDITURES ON THE CRIMINAL JUSTICE SYSTEM, 1983–1993

Billions of dollars spent on criminal justice by federal, state, and local governments

Source: Kathleen Maguire and Ann L. Pastore, eds. (1998). *Sourcebook of Criminal Justice Statistics 1997* (p. 2). Washington, D.C.: U.S. Department of Justice.

pects are arrested when they have been deprived of their freedom, or believe that they have been placed in custody.

A suspect may be released quickly if the police realize they have made a mistake or believe they do not have probable cause. The same suspect can be rearrested if circumstances change, however. Suspects have the right to remain silent once they are arrested, but many end up talking to the police. Innocent or not, some suspects implicate others, and the police are trained to listen carefully to anything said by a suspect. Normally, the suspect must be formally charged with a crime or released within 48 hours of being arrested. Suspects who are charged are turned over to the prosecution, and thus enter the court phase of the criminal justice process.

KEY DECISIONS OF THE COURTS

Suspects who are turned over for prosecution become *defendants*. During the court phase of the criminal justice process, the key decisions involve the following:

- Filing a formal complaint or charge
- Granting or denying bail
- Issuing an *indictment* or *information*
- Entering a plea
- Plea negotiations

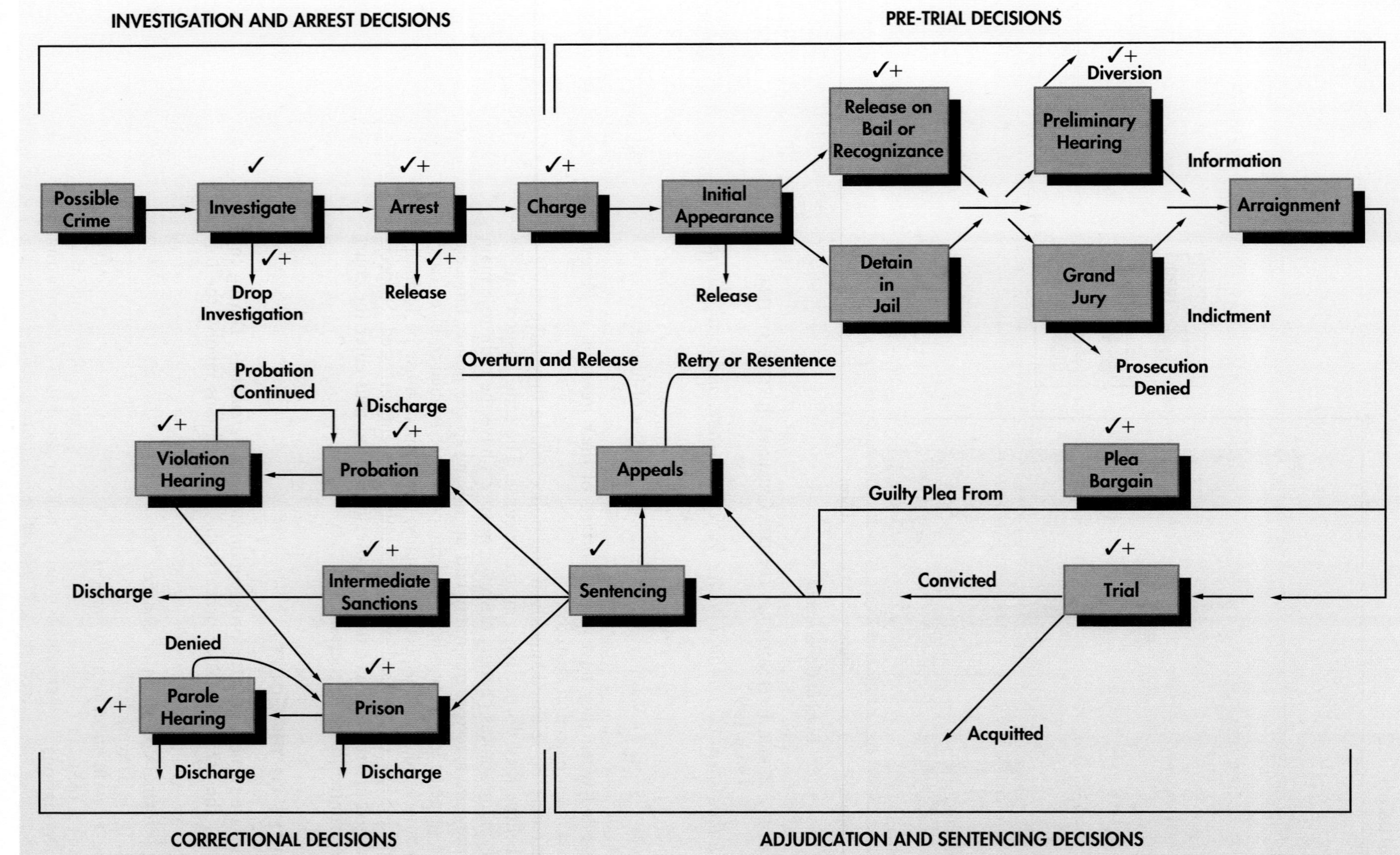

FIGURE 4.5 Key Decision Points in Criminal Case Processing
√Discretion usually exercised, but may be limited
√+Highly discretionary decsions involved

One of the most important decisions police make is to arrest someone. The legal basis for an arrest is probable cause, *meaning that a person exercising reasonable judgment believes that a crime is being or has been committed and that the suspect is responsible for it.*

Photo by A. Lichtenstein, courtesy of The Image Works

- Determining guilt or innocence at trial
- Filing an appeal
- Determining the sentence

One of the first decisions made in the court phase is bail. The U.S. Constitution does not guarantee a defendant's right to be released on bail pending trial, but it does prohibit "excessive" bail. Bail can be denied if the court has grounds to believe that a defendant will not return for trial, would pose a threat to the community if released, or will interfere with the police or prosecution in the preparation of the case. Bail turns out to be one of the most significant decisions for defendants because, among other things, freedom helps in the preparation of their defense, while detention generally hinders it.

Other crucial decisions are made in the charging process. Many cases are screened out early in the process as prosecutors concentrate on pursuing cases they feel they can win or that they believe are important to the community, the criminal justice system, or themselves. When prosecutors take no further action, the case is called *nolle prosequi*; sometimes they may decide to pursue less serious charges than the crime itself might warrant. Prosecutors thus exercise considerable discretion in the charging phase.

Most felony cases go through one of two kinds of pretrial review designed to establish that there is sufficient evidence to proceed against the defendant. One is a **preliminary hearing**, held before a lower court judge who summarizes the charge(s) listed by the prosecutor in a document called an *information* and reviews the evidence. Prosecution and defense may each present testimony. Police procedures are sometimes challenged at this stage. If the judge or magistrate finds there is enough evidence to support the charges, the defendant is bound over for trial. The other review process, held in about half the states and the federal system, is conducted in secret before a panel of citizens, usually 23,

preliminary hearing A court hearing to determine whether there is sufficient evidence to proceed with prosecution.

grand jury A group of citizens, usually 23, who are assembled to determine whether sufficient evidence exists to warrant prosecution.

called a **grand jury**. The grand jury dates back to the reign of Henry II in the twelfth century, when it was composed of a group of royal knights assembled by the sheriff to decide who should be brought before the traveling court. Over the years, the grand jury gained in popularity because it was not afraid to challenge the crown by refusing to indict political opponents of the king. This reputation helped make the grand jury popular in the American colonies.

Today, only the prosecutor presents testimony before the grand jury and there is no opportunity for cross-examination. To all intents and purposes the grand jury is an investigative arm of the prosecution. It sifts through the evidence presented and generates new evidence through the questioning of witnesses. If the grand jury accepts that there is probable cause to proceed with the case, it issues a *bill of indictment* listing the specific charges. In August 1998, President Clinton gave testimony before a federal grand jury investigating his relationship with Monica Lewinsky. The hearing was conducted via closed-circuit TV and videotaped for the record. With congressional authorization, and over the objection of Clinton's lawyers, the videotape was released to the public a month later. Although these were unprecedented events, this grand jury hearing had the same purpose as any other: to determine whether sufficient evidence of criminal wrongdoing existed to warrant prosecution.

Although the U.S. Constitution gives criminal defendants the right to a jury trial, approximately 90 percent of criminal convictions are the result of guilty pleas, and most of these are agreed upon by the prosecution and defense following some sort of negotiation. If the case goes to trial before a jury, the decision to convict must usually be a unanimous one. A guilty verdict sends the defendant on to sentencing; a not guilty verdict releases the defendant, who cannot normally be retried for the same offense. If the jury cannot make up its mind, it may be declared a *hung jury*, and the defendant may be retried at the discretion of the prosecution.

speedy trial The constitutional right to be tried within a reasonable time after arrest, usually 120 to 160 days.

continuance A request for a delay in trial proceedings that can be made by either defense or prosecution.

The court process sometimes takes many months. The Sixth Amendment to the U.S. Constitution gives defendants the right to a **speedy trial**, but there is little agreement among states as to what "speedy" means. Generally, defendants must be brought to trial within 120 to 160 days after arrest or the filing of charges. In federal courts, charges must be filed within 30 days of a suspect's arrest, and if the defendant pleads not guilty, the trial must commence within 70 days of the filing of an information or indictment. Speedy trial rules apply unless the defendant requests a delay in proceedings, called a **continuance**. Generally, if the prosecution requests a continuance, and the judge agrees to it, this could also extend the time of trial without violating speedy trial laws.

mandatory sentencing Occurs when the law requires judges to impose a certain penalty for a given offense.

Some convicted defendants may decide to appeal the conviction, which can take months or years to complete. The appellate court will be asked to consider whether the defendant's legal rights were violated in some way. If the court finds that they were, a new trial may be ordered or the defendant may be freed altogether. Defendants are usually sentenced even though an appeal is pending. In misdemeanor cases, convicted defendants are usually sentenced the same day; in felony cases, it may be three or four weeks before sentencing is carried out. Judges used to have considerable discretion in the sentences they handed down; today, many states have **mandatory sentencing**, which requires the court to impose a certain penalty for a given offense.

KEY DECISIONS OF CORRECTIONS

Even though the sentencing judge stipulates the penalties that will be imposed on a convicted offender, corrections officials have key decisions to make that affect offenders as well as the criminal justice system and the larger society. These decisions concern the following:

Box 4.3

CAREERS IN CRIMINAL JUSTICE

CORRECTIONAL CASE MANAGERS

Many prison systems employ case managers who are responsible for coordinating, supervising, and evaluating the treatment and release programs for individual inmates. Sometimes case managers are responsible for overall treatment, and sometimes they have a specialized responsibility—for example, drug treatment. The U.S. Bureau of Prisons employs both kinds of case managers. Here are the salary, qualifications, and duties for the position of Correctional/Drug Treatment Specialist, as advertised in July 1998:

Salary Range: $36,269 to $50,168

Qualifications: At least 24 semester hours of coursework in the behavioral or social sciences; higher grades must have at least two full years of graduate study in behavioral or social sciences *or* one year supervised casework experience. Candidates for drug treatment specialist must also show that they have the knowledge, skills, and abilities to perform the duties of the position, including ability to develop treatment planning and knowledge of psychological problems associated with addiction.

Duties: Case managers perform correctional casework in an institutional setting; evaluate progress of individual offenders; coordinate and integrate inmate training programs; develop social histories; provide case reports to the U.S. Parole Commission; and work with prisoners, their families, and interested persons in developing and implementing release plans or programs. Drug treatment specialists perform duties in substance abuse units within correctional facilities and are specially assigned caseloads of offenders who have histories of substance abuse.

- Classification of offenders
- Prison and jail management
- Type and extent of services provided
- Inmate release and postrelease

Some corrections decisions are more discretionary than others. For example, federal and state laws as well as court rulings may require that certain types of facilities be made available and that offenders receive certain services or be treated in a certain way. Increasing numbers of lawsuits filed by inmates and other offenders under correctional supervision continually test the constitutionality of practices and procedures. In 1980 a total of 42,781 suits were filed in U.S. district courts; by 1995 the figure had grown to 120,060 (Maguire and Pastore, 1996:Table 6.77). Although most suits are rejected, corrections officials know that their actions are subject to a level of public scrutiny that was unheard of 20 years ago.

Prison riots at state and federal facilities have escalated in recent years, some of them with deadly results. Prison gangs have proliferated as well. Prison officials have responded with lockdowns that keep inmates in their cells 23 hours a day, and many rehabilitative services have been curtailed. "Warehousing" of inmates convicted of violent crimes and other serious felonies has become widespread. Meanwhile, progressive wardens at medium-security prisons such as the federal correctional facility at Greenville, Illinois, have developed new management techniques to increase the safety and security of staff and inmates while building a prison environment that may help inmates turn their lives around.

Felony offenders headed to prison are generally classified according to the security risk they pose and their likely response to the available educational and treatment programs. In these times of mandatory sentencing, prison overcrowding, reduced support for rehabilitation and other "liberal" programs, classification decisions focus on security rather than inmate needs. But overcrowding is also forcing release of some inmates long before their time is served. This is seen by many people as a distinct threat to the community and it fuels calls for more prison beds.

The new hope in correctional circles today lies with intermediate sanctions. The bulk of criminal offenders do not pose a serious safety risk to the community, even though a majority of known felons are repeat offenders and many commit new offenses while on probation or parole. Correctional officials around the country are challenging public fears and the skepticism of many politicians by advocating increased use of community-based corrections. The American Correctional Association lobbied Congress in 1996 to support legislation that provides alternatives to incarceration for the bulk of felony offenders. Chapter 17 discusses these initiatives in detail.

parole Supervised release of inmates prior to the full completion of their prison term.

Many states and the federal system have done away with or are phasing out **parole**, the supervised release of inmates prior to the full completion of their prison term. Traditionally, parole was a discretionary judgment left up to state parole boards usually appointed by the governor. The new trend is for *mandatory release,* whereby inmates must be released once they have served a certain proportion of their sentence, and assuming they have earned the necessary "good time." Even so, some 700,000 Americans were on parole in 1995, a third of them in three states: Texas, California, and Pennsylvania (Bureau of

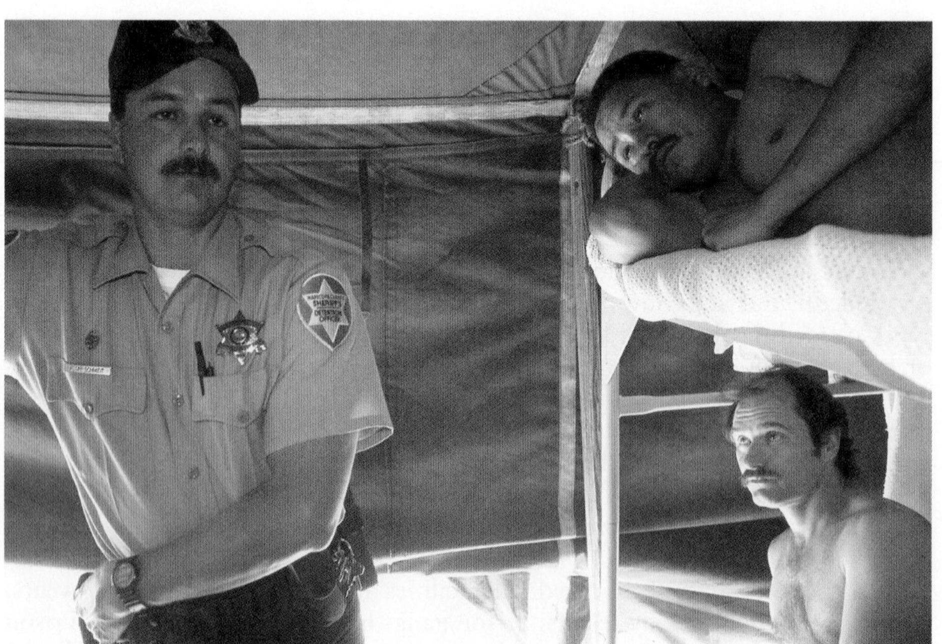

To protect against defendants languishing in jail for months or years before being tried, the U.S. Constitution gives them the right to a speedy trial. In most states, defendants must be brought to trial within 120 to 160 days after being arrested—unless they request a delay.

Photo by A. Lichtenstein, courtesy of The Image Works

Justice Statistics, 1997e). In states that have retained traditional parole, the decision to release or detain an inmate is made after the board hears from both the inmate and correctional officials, and sometimes from relatives, victims, and other concerned citizens.

An incarcerated offender's successful return into the community is never a foregone conclusion, and usually both offenders and correctional officials must work very hard at accomplishing it. More often than not the effort fails because offenders who leave prison have few marketable skills, few resources to fall back on, and few people willing and able to provide the emotional support and healthy companionship ex-inmates need to build a new life. Making matters worse is the stigma associated with street crime and prison time: Potential employers are reluctant to believe that ex-inmates are trustworthy, and the comment "once a criminal, always a criminal" sums up the view of many people. Notwithstanding the offense a person has committed—and ex-inmates have generally committed more serious ones—it is during the postrelease phase of the criminal justice system that some of the most crucial decisions are made. These decisions are made by members of the public, not criminal justice personnel.

THE CRIMINAL JUSTICE SYSTEM IS A LEAKY FUNNEL

Pour engine oil into a funnel with holes in it, and not much oil will reach the engine. Figure 4.6 illustrates this phenomenon using the criminal justice system as the funnel and criminal suspects as the oil. One can easily see that few of the people who start the journey through the system end up in prison.

Of course, it is unlikely that every one of the individuals arrested by the police for a felony crime actually committed it. But the picture is nonetheless sobering because it shows fairly convincingly that the system succeeds in weeding people out better than it does passing them through to the statutory punishment that defines a felony offense. This disturbs many people inside and outside criminal justice. However, other people are more disturbed by this fact: The people who get arrested in the first place are more likely to have committed conventional street crimes and are more likely to be from the lower classes and minority groups. These same people are the ones most likely to end up in prison. In this way, decisions made throughout the criminal justice system—including decisions about what constitutes serious crime in the first place—tend to have an accumulative, negative, impact on minority individuals, especially African Americans. It turns out this is true for juveniles as well as for adults (Pope and Feyerherm, 1991). We saw in previous chapters that a combination of factors are responsible for this state of affairs: stereotypes of real crime and real criminals; bias and discrimination in the labeling practices of some criminal justice personnel; the nonrandom distribution of criminal opportunities and access to them; get-tough-on-crime policies that target street crimes, particularly drug sales; and the higher rates of violent crime among minorities and the poor who live in inner-city neighborhoods.

THE JUVENILE JUSTICE SYSTEM

The year 1999 is noteworthy for at least two reasons: as the last year before the beginning of a new millennium, and as the 100th anniversary of the nation's first independent juvenile court system, established by the Illinois state legislature in 1899. From colonial times until that year, no separate system of justice existed for children accused of crimes; they were tried in adult courts as if they were adults. For the past 100 years, adults and juveniles charged with offenses have been treated differently. The remainder of this chapter examines

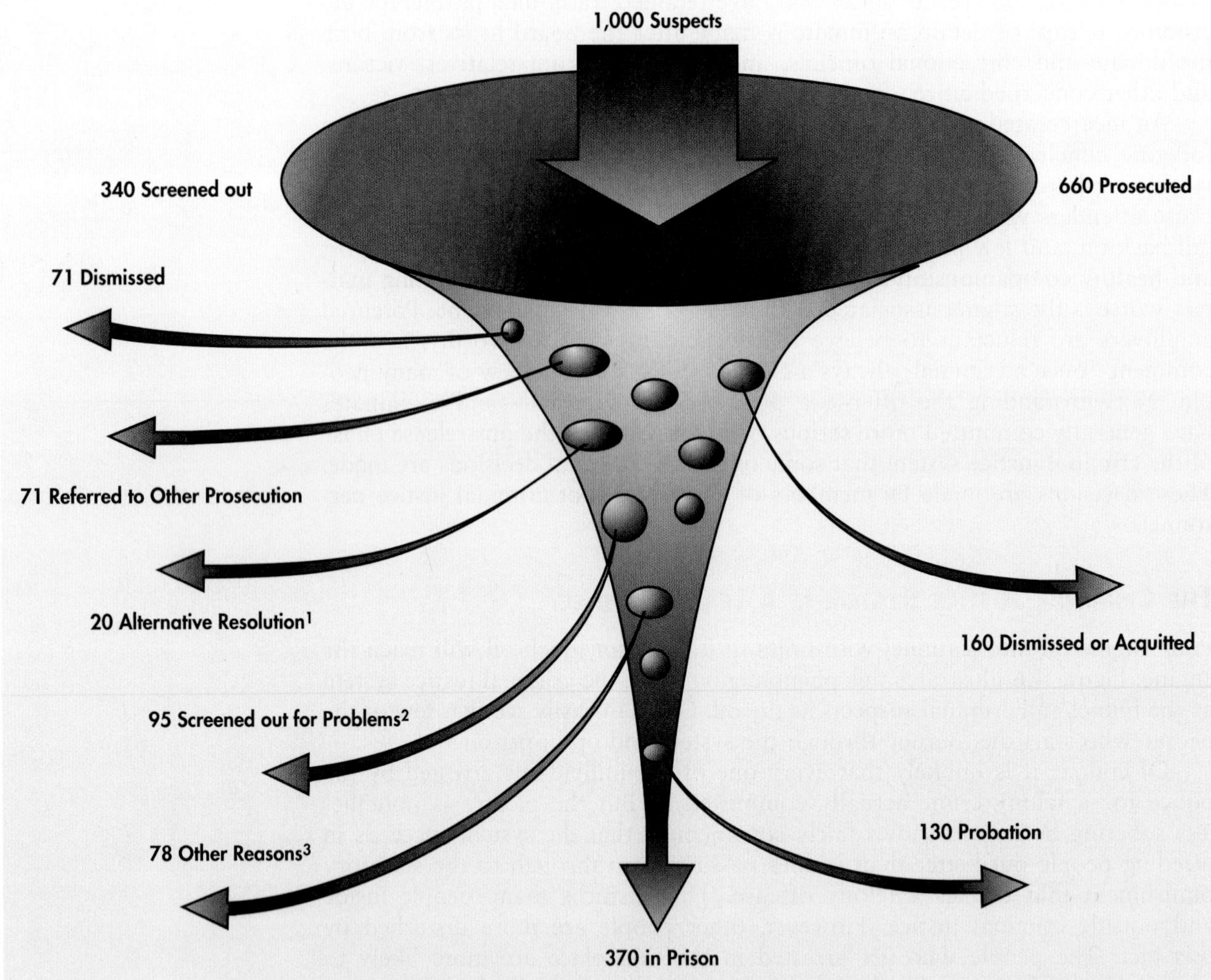

FIGURE 4.6 THE CRIMINAL JUSTICE FUNNEL
This figure is based on federal data; state data were not available.
[1] *Restitution, pre-trial diversion*
[2] *Problems with suspect, evidence, or witnesses*
[3] *Lack of resources, minimal federal interest*

Source: Data from Bureau of Justice Statistics (1996). *Compendium of Federal Justice Statistics, 1993.* Washington, D.C.: U.S. Department of Justice.

the juvenile justice system, past and present, and considers where it is headed in the year 2000.

JUVENILE DELINQUENCY AND JUVENILE JUSTICE

Children have always misbehaved, but the notion of juvenile delinquency was unheard of until the eighteenth century. Before that time, problem children had been handled mainly within the family, with the state getting involved only if the child was accused of committing a crime—in which case the child was treated just like an adult. However, the system of familial control began to break down during the sixteenth and seventeenth centuries as more and more people migrated from farms to cities in search of work and housing.

Many cities eventually became overburdened as their populations grew, and many poor families were prone to collapse. More and more children could be found wandering the streets and getting into trouble. By the late eighteenth century, "juvenile delinquency" was recognized everywhere as a major urban problem. Commenting on the situation in London, England, one observer wrote:

> There are, probably, 70,000 persons in the metropolis who regularly live by theft and fraud; most of these have women with whom they cohabit, and their offspring, as a matter of course, follow the example of their parents. . . . This is the chief source of juvenile delinquents. . . . Many of them belong to organized bands of [thieves] and are in the regular employ and training of older thieves; others obtain a precarious subsistence by begging, running errands, picking pockets, pilfering from shops and stalls. . . . It is a most extraordinary fact that half the number of persons convicted of crime have not attained the age of discretion [21 years]. During the last seven years, out of 16,427 commitments in the county of Surrey, 7,292 were under twenty years of age, and 370 under twelve years of age, and several of these no more than eight or ten years of age. . . . (Wade, 1829; cited in Sanders, 1970:135)

One response of authorities to the growing problem of delinquency among youth was to reinvent family controls through a system of apprenticeships. Poor, neglected, idle, and mischievous children were sent to private families, where they worked under strict discipline. Children convicted of murder, armed robbery, and other serious felonies were usually executed, transported to the colonies, or imprisoned.

In some parts of Europe and America, special institutions for wayward and delinquent children were established. Usually small, privately funded, and unregulated, these "homes," "houses," "schools," and "hospitals" often became known for exploitation and brutality. Children could be made to work long hours on a meager diet, and this gave them an obvious economic value (Platt, 1969; Mennel, 1973). While many child experts of the day spoke of promoting "virtuous industry" among the poor and delinquent, this was simply a euphemism for hard work under harsh conditions. The people benefiting from this "calculated philanthropy" (Mennel, 1973:xxvi) were often not the children nor the community at large, but the people who ran the homes, and their friends, relatives, and business partners.

The Rise of State Control. The thinly disguised profiteering and other abuses associated with these juvenile homes was one reason some people called for involvement by the state. Another factor was loss of faith in the ability of poor families to raise their own children. People started using the term *juvenile delinquency* to refer to the crimes and other misbehavior of poor and lower-class children. "The key to the solution of delinquency seemed to lie in the development of more institutions. A system of social control would have to be developed apart from the family which would discipline homeless, vagrant, and destitute children—the offspring of the poor" (Mennel, 1973:xxii). In its ideal form, such a system would avoid the cruelty of sending children to jail along with adults but would still correct and reform them.

Given that family controls were failing—demonstrated by the growing numbers of homeless and parentless children—one possible solution was for the state to take over the role of parent and provide shelter, support, and discipline. The British called this the *doctrine of* ***parens patriae***. In the United States there was no national strategy in support of *parens patriae*, although early in the nineteenth century some states sponsored new institutions for juvenile offenders. "Houses of refuge" were established in New York, Boston, and Philadelphia, and "reform schools" became widespread as the century progressed.

parens patriae The doctrine that the state should take over the role of parent in dealing with problem children.

Progressive Era A late nineenth century period in which criminal justice reforms took place, centered on rehabilitation and treatment.

The late nineteenth century ushered in the so-called **Progressive Era**, which included new ideas about crime causation and child delinquents. A central idea was that crime is caused by external factors, not free will, and that children were "corruptible innocents" who needed "special attention, solicitude and instruction" (Feld, 1984:144). The "Rehabilitative Ideal," discussed in Chapter 15, was a core theme of the Progressive Era. According to this perspective, the state should adopt a benevolent, constructive role in dealing with juveniles, with an emphasis on guidance and treatment, not punishment.

Enter the Juvenile Court. The juvenile court was a product of this thinking. Children, its founders believed, were not like adult criminals nor should they be dealt with by the same judicial process. As the U.S. Supreme Court stated many years later: "The early conception of the Juvenile Court proceeding was one in which a fatherly judge touched the heart and conscience of the erring youth by talking over his problems, by paternal advice and admonition, and in which . . . benevolent and wise institutions of the State provided guidance and help to save him from a downward career."

The first juvenile court was established in Chicago by the Illinois General Assembly. The 1899 law was titled "An Act to Regulate the Treatment and Control of Dependent, Neglected, and Delinquent Children." Under the act, delinquency was defined as a violation of "any law in this State or any City or Village ordinance." Dependency and neglect covered many things, including being destitute, homeless, or abandoned; being in need of public support; being deprived of parental care and guardianship; living with "vicious" or "disreputable" people or in an "unfit place"; and being a habitual beggar. Almost any poor child could fit into one of these categories. Indeed, the law was written so that the juvenile court could claim jurisdiction over every single poor child in Chicago (Bernard, 1992:90).

The official purpose of the juvenile court was to offer problem children specialized help and protection (as any good parent would), administered and regulated by the state. The Illinois lawmakers had adopted the doctrine of *parens patriae*, and gone a step further: The procedures for handling juveniles and the dispositions available would henceforth be different from those used for adult offenders. Furthermore, the new juvenile court would have jurisdiction over *all* juvenile offenders—murderers as well as vandals. This necessitated an important change: Jurisdiction over criminal children had to be removed from criminal court and established in the juvenile court (Bernard, 1992:89).

This change was accomplished by two legal steps: First, the age of criminal liability was raised from 7 to 16, and later to 17. This change effectively excused juveniles of the *mens rea* element in the legal definition of crime discussed in Chapter 1. Even though juveniles could still commit the act itself, whether a killing or an act of vandalism, they could not be charged with a crime. Juveniles were thus removed from the jurisdiction of the criminal court. The second legal step was to give the new juvenile court jurisdiction over all laws; by doing so the Illinois legislature gave it jurisdiction over children who committed acts that would be crimes if committed by adults.

By 1910, 32 states had followed Illinois's lead, and by 1945 every state had a juvenile court (McGarrell, 1988). The new court was hailed as a visionary institution that would bring intelligence, responsibility, and humanity to the emerging juvenile justice system. Few people noticed that the court had neither the authority nor the resources to mold juvenile institutions, or that it had only limited influence over treatment. However, the public was willing to give it a chance, at least for a while.

The Early Juvenile Court at Work. The new juvenile court had broad jurisdiction, and it soon became apparent that no juvenile court confined its definition of delinquency to violations of laws and ordinances (Rubin, 1949:1402).

All states included some of the following behaviors under the label "delinquency" (Barlow and Ferdinand, 1992:5–6):

- Growing up in idleness or crime
- Wandering the streets at night
- Habitually using vile, obscene, or vulgar language
- Being incorrigible or otherwise beyond parental control
- Jumping trains or entering them without authority
- Visiting a house of ill repute
- Habitually consuming alcohol
- Engaging in promiscuous sexual behavior
- Running away
- Being habitually truant from school
- Patronizing a poolroom
- Habitually gambling

Because they would not be crimes if committed by adults (and a few obviously could not be committed by adults), these offenses are conventionally referred to as **status offenses**. They are illegal by virtue of the offender's age. From its beginnings, then, the juvenile code was broader than the penal code governing the behavior of adults.

status offenses Delinquent acts such as truancy and running away that only juveniles can commit.

As the juvenile court responded to its broad mandate during the early years, an interesting thing happened. Instead of keeping juveniles out of custodial institutions, as had been envisioned by reformers, the number of children detained in public and private facilities in the United States grew significantly during the period 1890–1923 (Sutton, 1990). Far from private facilities withering away under *parens patriae*, their growth outpaced that of public institutions. Thus a period of much-publicized benevolence and reform actually resulted in more children being confined, the bulk of them in private institutions. Reform of juvenile justice was not as comprehensive—or benevolent—in its outcomes as in its promise.

Differences between the Juvenile and the Criminal Process

That promise is illustrated best in the terminology used by the juvenile court. A comparison of juvenile and criminal courts is shown in Table 4.2. Where criminal courts have indictments, juvenile courts speak of *petitions*. A petition is a formal request for the court to see whether it should take jurisdiction over a case involving a juvenile. In criminal court, the formal charges are read during an arraignment; in juvenile court there is an *intake hearing*, where the court determines whether the alleged facts about the child warrant further action by the court.

adversarial process In criminal trials, prosecution and defense are on opposing sides, each seeking to persuade the judge or jury to accept their version of the truth.

The criminal trial is an **adversarial process**; prosecution and defense battle over their versions of the truth. Although lawyers for both sides often claim victory, the adversarial process implies winners and losers. For the prosecution,

Table 4.2 Comparison of Terms Used in Juvenile and Criminal Courts

Juvenile Court	Criminal Court
Petition	Indictment or information
Intake hearing	Arraignment
In re John [or *Jane*] *Doe*	*State of Illinois v. John* [or *Jane*] *Doe*
Admit or deny the offense	Plead guilty or not guilty
Adjudicatory hearing	Trial
Social history	Pre-sentence investigation
Dispositional order	Sentence

conviction is victory, while for the defense acquittal is victory. This adversarial aspect of the criminal trial is reflected in the wording of the case: "State *versus* John (or Jane) Doe." In juvenile court, the case is referred to as *In re* John (or Jane) Doe, meaning "regarding" or "in the matter of." There is no sense of a contest. In addition, since the juvenile court process was designed to be non-adversarial, the constitutional guarantee of due process was thought to have little relevance in this environment. For example, until ***In re Gault*** (1967), juveniles had no right to counsel, no right to question witnesses, and no right against self-incrimination.

In re Gault Juveniles facing commitment to an institution are given the same formal rights of due process enjoyed by adult defendants in criminal court.

In juvenile court, children are not asked whether they plead guilty or not guilty, but are asked whether they admit or deny the facts alleged in the petition. If they admit the facts, the juvenile court judge will say that the case has been *adjudicated* and the facts are as stated in the petition. If they deny the alleged facts, there is a hearing during which the judge reviews the evidence presented and adjudicates the merits of the petition. If the judge finds in favor of the petition, the child is not convicted as in criminal court, but is adjudicated.

After conviction of a felony crime in criminal court, the judge usually orders a pre-sentence investigation. In juvenile court, the judge asks the juvenile probation department to develop a social history of the child, including such things as family history, educational progress, medical history, and police record. Instead of passing sentence, the judge enters a *dispositional order*, a term that does not imply punishment—although juveniles may be placed in detention or be required to do something they perceive as punishing. The disposition in juvenile court is supposed to be in the "best interests" of the child. Because of the more informal procedures and the commitment to *parens patriae*, juvenile court judges in the early part of the 20th century had considerable dis-

Unlike adult criminal court, juvenile proceedings are not considered adversarial. For many years juveniles were therefore denied the due process rights given to adult defendants. Only after 1967 did juveniles receive a right to counsel, a right to question witnesses, and a right against self-incrimination.

PHOTO BY SAOLA, COURTESY OF OLIVIER PICHETTI

cretion in their dispositional orders. Many adopted a fatherly approach, giving youth in trouble a "good talking to," as they tried to steer the child away from more trouble, or worse still, a career in crime.

Another important way in which juvenile procedures differ from criminal justice experienced by adult offenders concerns record keeping and privacy. Consistent with the philosophy of shielding the child, juvenile court records are sealed, and many states restrict access to a juvenile's police record. For many years, most states even forbade the police to photograph or fingerprint juveniles "taken into custody"—the term "arrested" was reserved for adult suspects. This does not mean there is no record keeping in the juvenile justice system—far from it. Police incident reports are kept on file because they are needed to develop a case. And juvenile court officials develop records on the juveniles they process. The tradition has been one of restricting record keeping to the minimum needed by police and courts to do their business, and to maintain the confidentiality of the records that are kept.

JUVENILE JUSTICE TODAY

Figure 4.7 shows the stages through which juveniles go when processed by the juvenile justice system today, and the possible outcomes. The flow chart is based on current Illinois statutes, but the process and terminology are similar across the country. From the very beginning, considerable discretion is exercised by justice officials. In the typical case, the likelihood that a juvenile taken into custody by police will actually be adjudicated delinquent in juvenile court is quite small; the likelihood that the juvenile will be placed in a detention facility is even smaller.

One author has calculated that only one-third of all juveniles who have contact with the police as suspects in jailable offenses will actually be arrested (Bernard, 1992:173–175). Of these, half will be released and half referred to juvenile court. Figure 4.8 shows the nationwide "leaky funnel" picture of what happened in 1,000 cases referred to juvenile court in 1994. Just under half were handled informally (*nonpetitioned*), and many of these were dismissed entirely. Of those handled formally (i.e., petitioned), 58 percent were adjudicated as delinquent; 18 juveniles were referred to criminal court. The remaining 42 percent were not formally found to be delinquent. Of the 277 youths who were adjudicated delinquent, just over half were put on probation, and 41 percent were placed in a juvenile facility outside the home. Most of those on probation would be ordered to pay restitution or a fine, to participate in community service, or to enter a treatment or counseling program (Butts, 1996:8). Some youths voluntarily agree to some supervision and counseling in exchange for no formal adjudication of delinquency. These youths make up the bulk of cases resulting in informal probation. The leaky funnel that describes the criminal process obviously applies to the juvenile justice process as well.

TRENDS IN JUVENILE JUSTICE STATISTICS

There has been much talk in recent years of rising rates of juvenile crime, and many criminal justice experts see an overburdened juvenile justice system that cannot cope with the growing demands placed upon it. Various reforms have been proposed, some of which are discussed in the next section. Let us briefly review some of the facts about trends in juvenile crime and juvenile justice in the United States. Most of the data come from publications of the Office of Juvenile Justice and Delinquency Prevention (OJJDP). For the latest information, check out OJJDP's home page listed in Box 2.5 in Chapter 2.

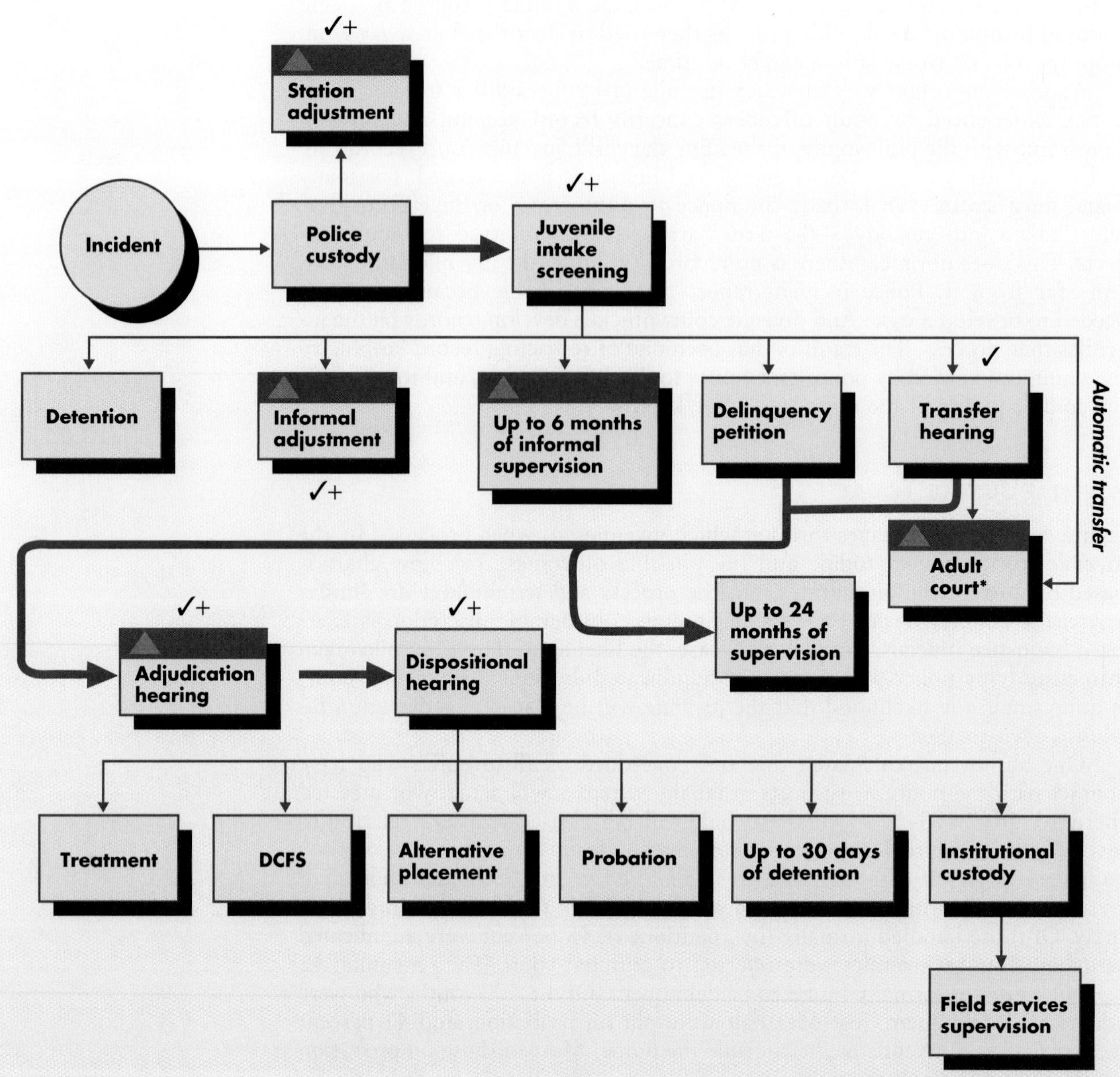

FIGURE 4.7 KEY DECISION POINTS IN JUVENILE CASE PROCESSING
This chart shows the stages through which juveniles may go once they have been taken into custody by the police. Although this chart is based on the system in Illinois, the process and terminology are similar across the country.
**Begin adult felony process at preliminary hearing.*
√Discretion usually exercised, but may be limited; √+Highly discretionary decisions involved; ▲ Minor discharged from juvenile process.

Source: Adapted from Sarah Dowse Wortham (1993). "Juvenile Justice in Illinois: An Overview." *The Compiler* (Summer):7.

Juvenile Arrest Trends. In 1995, an estimated 2.7 million arrests were made of people under age 18, representing about 18 percent of all U.S. arrests in that year (Snyder, 1997). For the first time in many years, juvenile arrest rates for violent crimes fell rather than rose. The largest declines were for murder (17 percent). Since almost all juvenile murders are shootings, it is encour-

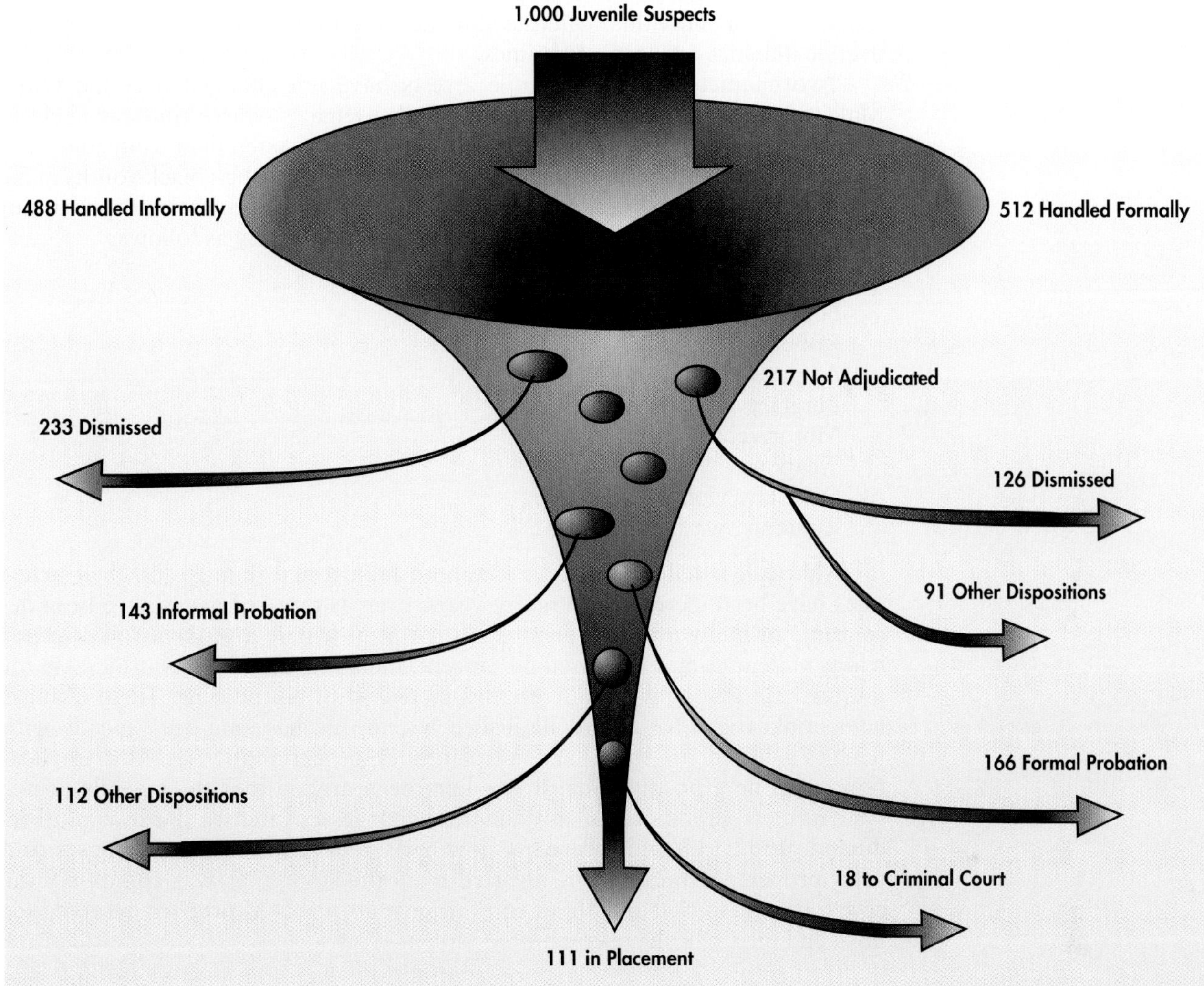

FIGURE 4.8 The Juvenile Justice Funnel
Source: Data from Howard N. Synder and Melissa Sickmund (1995). *Juvenile Offenders and Victims: A National Report* (p. 134). Washington, D.C.: U.S. Department of Justice.

aging to see that juvenile arrest rates for weapons law violations also declined by 16 percent from 1993 to 1995, after more than doubling since 1987. It is too early to tell whether a new downward trend is in the making. Some criminologists believe that inner-city drug markets are stabilizing, and this in turn may reduce the need for turf battles and the number of drive-by shootings. Juvenile arrest rates for drug law violations increased by 50 percent from 1993 to 1995, and this growing police presence may also have contributed to the decline in arrests on murder and weapons charges.

As with adults, most juvenile felony arrests involve property crimes. From 1980 to 1995, overall juvenile arrest rates for property crimes remained stable, at around 2,500 arrests for every 100,000 juveniles. However, this is mainly due to stability in the rate of larceny-theft arrests, which dominate the picture. Larceny-theft is a catch-all category that includes almost any kind of theft except burglary, motor vehicle theft, embezzlement, fraud, forgery, and confidence games. Juvenile arrest rates for burglary have declined consistently since 1985, while those for motor vehicle theft soared 130 percent between 1983 and 1990, but then declined 20 percent from 1990 to 1995. These differing arrest trends for individual offenses illustrate the importance of looking behind overall statistics on property crimes.

Two characteristics of juvenile arrests have not changed over the years: Males are far more likely to be arrested than females—three times as likely in 1995—and black juveniles are far more likely to be arrested than white juveniles, including those of Hispanic origin (Snyder, 1997:3). Although black youths make up around 15 percent of the U.S. population under age 18, their proportion of 1995 juvenile arrests for various crimes was approximately as follows:

Murder	60%
Forcible rape	46%
Robbery	61%
Aggravated assault	43%
Burglary	26%
Motor vehicle theft	41%
Weapons	36%
Drug law violations	35%
Running away	22%

Although females are far less likely to be arrested than males, their arrest rates have been increasing in recent years, even as those of males have been decreasing for many offenses. From 1991 to 1995, female juvenile arrest rates for felony violent crimes increased 34 percent, including an 18 percent increase for murder. Arrests for weapons offenses increased by 42 percent. These changes have implications for a juvenile justice system that has long dealt mostly with females referred for status and misdemeanor property offenses. One implication could be a positive one: It has long been argued that the juvenile justice system treats girls more harshly than boys for lesser offenses (Barlow and Ferdinand, 1992:132–143). Perhaps now girls referred for status offenses and petty property crimes will be diverted from the system, as was commonly the case for boys, so that the "hard end" of juvenile justice is properly reserved for boys and girls who have committed violent crimes.

Juvenile Court Caseloads. Notwithstanding recent declines in arrest rates, the upward trend over the past 20 years has resulted in significant increases in juvenile court caseloads. From 1986–1995 alone, delinquency cases increased by 45 percent (Stahl, 1998:1). Table 4.3 shows that the greatest increases involved aggravated assault (137 percent) and weapons offenses (132 percent). The smallest increases, and some decreases, occurred for property offenses, nonviolent sex offenses (−21 percent), and liquor law violations (−39 percent). While they accounted for less than 10 percent of all delinquency cases referred to juvenile court in 1994, the 159,100 drug offense cases represent a 120 percent increase from 1986 to 1995, and a 145 percent increase from 1991 to 1995 alone (Stahl, 1998:1).

Just as the number of serious offenses brought to the nation's juvenile courts showed an upward trend over the past few years, the number of petitioned status offenses such as underage drinking, truancy, and running away also grew substantially. For example, a total of 126,900 such cases were formally handled by the courts in 1994, compared with 76,300 in 1985 (Butts, 1996:8–9). This may surprise some readers, in light of the pressures placed on the juvenile justice system by more serious offenses. However, it seems to be consistent with the general hardening of attitudes toward youth misbehavior during the 1980s and early 1990s. Most of the increase in petitioned status offenses is accounted for by truancy and liquor law violations, two areas where schools, parent organizations, and law enforcement officials have been cracking down (Garry, 1996).

Table 4.3 Juvenile Cases Referred to Court by Most Serious Offense, 1986–1995

Offense	Number of Cases in 1995	Percent Change 1985–1995	1991–1995	1994–1995
Total	**1,714,300**	**45%**	**21%**	**7%**
Person Offenses	**377,300**	**98%**	**36%**	**8%**
Criminal homicide	2,800	84	20	−6
Forcible rape	6,800	47	19	4
Robbery	39,600	53	27	6
Aggravated assault	93,200	137	33	6
Simple assault	205,500	103	47	12
Other violent sex offenses	9,300	50	9	−3
Other person offenses	20,100	72	−2	−4
Property Offenses	**871,700**	**23%**	**3%**	**3%**
Burglary	139,900	−2	−9	−2
Larceny-theft	418,800	28	10	10
Motor vehicle theft	53,400	23	−26	−13
Arson	10,400	78	42	10
Vandalism	121,700	40	9	−2
Trespassing	64,400	18	9	1
Stolen property offenses	33,100	10	9	2
Other property offenses	29,900	46	−5	6
Drug Law Violations	**159,100**	**120%**	**145%**	**28%**
Public Order Offenses	**306,300**	**48%**	**37%**	**6%**
Obstruction of justice	110,100	53	45	8
Disorderly conduct	85,100	82	46	9
Weapons offenses	47,000	132	38	−9
Liquor law violations	12,200	−39	−1	2
Nonviolent sex offenses	10,500	−21	−8	−4
Other public order	41,300	19	31	17
Violent Crime Index*	**142,400**	**99%**	**30%**	**5%**
Property Crime Index**	**622,500**	**20%**	**1%**	**5%**

*Violent Crime Index includes criminal homicide, forcible rape, robbery, and aggravated assault.
**Property Crime Index includes burglary, larceny-theft, motor vehicle theft, and arson.
Note: Detail may not add to totals because of rounding. Percent change calculations are based on unrounded numbers.
Source: Anne L. Stahl (1998). "Delinquency Cases in Juvenile Courts, 1995," *OJJDP Fact Sheet* May:1–2.

Dispositional Trends. The most severe disposition faced in juvenile court is long-term confinement in a secure facility. For most juvenile offenders, long-term means on average around six months (Snyder and Sickmund, 1995:164). However, juveniles who have committed violent crimes or other serious offenses may be detained by juvenile authorities until their eighteenth birthday, and sometimes until they are 21 if so ordered by the juvenile court judge. The two boys convicted of the 1998 schoolyard killings in Jonesboro, Arkansas, will be held until they are 21, and then released. Like adult prisons, long-term juvenile facilities became overcrowded during the 1980s, with two-thirds of them operating above their official capacity by 1991.

A variety of public and private facilities are used for the custody of juvenile offenders. There are actually more private facilities than public ones, although they do not hold as many juveniles. Many private facilities have "open environments," meaning that there are no perimeter fences. In addition, private facilities more commonly house juveniles who have not been adjudicated delinquent. These youths are there voluntarily, or have been placed there by parents or by agencies outside the juvenile justice system. In 1995 almost 41 percent of all residents in private facilities were nonoffenders (Moone, 1997). However, this percentage has been dropping since 1992, while the percentage of delinquents held in private facilities has been increasing. Undoubtedly, overcrowding in public facilities partly explains this trend. Can you think of other reasons for it?

The guiding principle in housing juveniles is the "least restrictive placement alternative." However, high levels of security are available to ensure the safety of staff, other youths, and the general public. There are public and private juvenile facilities with razor wire fences, high walls, and surveillance equipment. Use of such devices has been increasing since 1987, although the primary method of providing security rests with staff rather than hardware. Raising staff-to-inmate ratios and reducing the number of youths within each living unit are among the methods used to increase security; some long-term facilities supplement these with security classifications of the juvenile population, physical isolation of troublemakers, and the use of mechanical restraints such as anklets, security belts, or straitjackets (Snyder and Sickmund, 1995:170–172).

One of the most striking dispositional trends during the 1980s and early 1990s involves juveniles placed in long-term custody. Between 1983 and 1991, the minority custody population rose, while the white custody population declined (Snyder and Sickmund, 1995:166). By 1991 the long-term custody rate for black youths was five times that for white youths—a total of 424 per 100,000 black juveniles in the U.S. population. Hispanic youths also had a higher custody rate than non-Hispanic white youths, though the difference was much smaller. Altogether, black and Hispanic juveniles made up 66 percent of publicly operated long-term closed facilities and 52 percent of open facilities. By comparison, the proportion of the 1991 U.S. population composed of Hispanic and black juveniles was approximately 24 percent. And the situation appears to be worsening: By 1995, minority youths made up "68 percent of the juvenile population in secure confinement and 68 percent of those in secure institutional environments such as training schools" (Hsia and Hamparian, 1998:1). It has been estimated that 1 in 7 African-American males will have been incarcerated before age 18, compared with 1 in 125 white males (DeComo, 1993). The disproportionate incarceration of minorities begins with juvenile offenders and continues with adults, as we shall see in Chapter 15.

JUVENILE JUSTICE REFORMS

Some people may look at the juvenile justice funnel in Figure 4.8 and see it as proof that the system works as intended: Children are handled informally and with considerable discretion; only very few find themselves removed from their families, schools, and neighborhoods and held in secure facilities. Other people, concerned about rising rates of teen violence, or angered and frightened by some highly publicized juvenile crime, see the system as a failure. Recent school shootings have heightened fears that the juvenile justice system cannot cope with teenage violence. In an eight-month period from October 1997 to May 1998, a rash of school shootings occurred: In Pearl, Mississippi, three people were killed, seven wounded; in West Paducah, Kentucky, three were killed and five wounded; in Jonesboro, Arkansas, five people were killed, ten wounded; in Edinboro, Pennsylvania, a teacher was killed and three other people were wounded; in Fayetteville, Tennessee, one student was killed; in Onalaska, Washington, a child was wounded; and in Springfield, Oregon, two people were killed and 22 wounded. From 1989 to 1995, the percentage of students aged 12 through 19 who report gangs, guns, and violence at school has increased, along with reports of being victimized by violence at school (Chandler, et al., 1998). Critics of the juvenile justice system outnumber supporters, and various efforts to reform the system are underway. In Chapter 1 we discussed one reform—making it easier for juveniles to be transferred to criminal court—but there are other reforms you should know about.

Due Process Reforms. One class of reforms, **due process reforms**, actually dates back to the 1950s and early 1960s. As noted earlier, the juvenile court was meant to be nonadversarial, everyone working instead toward the best interests of the child. Few people thought that the constitutional rights enjoyed by adult defendants in criminal court should apply also in juvenile court. However, in 1946 a legally trained criminologist, Paul Tappan, wrote an article titled "Treatment without Trial," pointing out that children were being sent to custodial institutions for treatment without the safeguards of formal due process, including a lawyer to represent them and the right to cross-examine witnesses. In many states, juveniles could also be transferred to adult courts without a formal hearing. Other criminologists took up the same argument in the late 1950s, and noted also that punishment was commonly hidden under therapeutic labels (Allen, 1964). For example, solitary confinement was called "quiet time." Some therapies, even when sincerely applied, were often more severe than outright punishments.

due process reforms Attempts in the 1950s and 1960s to strengthen the constitutional safeguards afforded juveniles, including right to counsel and to cross-examine witnesses.

The first major due process reform came with the U.S. Supreme Court's ruling in ***Kent v. United States*** (1966) that the juvenile court must provide the "essentials of due process" when transferring juveniles to the adult system. The Court also issued a scathing attack on the doctrine of *parens patriae*, referring to it as "murky" and of questionable historical relevance. This was followed by the famous case mentioned earlier, *In re Gault* (1967). In that case, the Court said juveniles were entitled to the same basic constitutional rights enjoyed by adults in any hearing that might result in their commitment to an institution.

Kent v. United States The juvenile court must provide the "essentials of due process" when transferring juveniles to adult court.

Although U.S. Supreme Court decisions over the past 30 years have generally expanded procedural safeguards for juveniles, the Court has also preserved some important differences between the adult and juvenile systems. For example, in *McKeiver v. Pennsylvania* (1970) the Court ruled that jury trials are not constitutionally required in juvenile court proceedings; in *Smith v. Daily Mail Publishing Company* (1979) it preserved the confidentiality of juvenile court records, although it agreed that information about a case that is lawfully obtained from an independent source could be published.

Another problem identified in the early 1960s concerned the indiscriminate mixing of status offenders with juveniles who had committed much more serious offenses. It is now recognized that childhood misbehaviors such as truancy and running away may be the first step to a lifetime of problems, but why hurry the process by mingling status offenders with more hardened, and usually older, offenders? New York state recognized this problem in 1962. Its Family Court Act renamed status offenders as PINS (Persons in Need of Supervision). By 1980 many other states had enacted similar statutes defining MINS (Minors . . .), JINS (Juveniles . . .) and CHINS (Children . . .), and separating them from delinquents.

Reforms in Handling Serious and Violent Juvenile Offenders. In 1994, Congress called for a new national strategy to address the problem of rising rates of serious and violent delinquency. In 1996, a National Juvenile Justice Action Plan was published by the Coordinating Council on Juvenile Justice and Delinquency, headed by U.S. Attorney General Janet Reno. Composed of nine representatives of the federal government and nine juvenile justice practitioners appointed by Congress and the president, the council concluded that while the future of the nation's children rests in the local community, state and local initiatives to reduce violence and prevent delinquency and to increase the capacity of the juvenile justice system to respond must be taken immediately.

The complete Action Plan is available at the OJJDP Web site listed in Chapter 2. Its major recommendations for the juvenile justice system are (1) strengthening the state's ability to successfully prosecute the small core of juveniles responsible for serious and violent crime, and (2) increasing the dispositional options that are available. The first step includes increasing the discretionary powers of prosecutors in making jurisdictional decisions—for example, whether to try a juvenile as an adult. The second step includes extending the jurisdiction of the juvenile court beyond age 21 if there is a reasonable expectation of successful treatment, and using **blended sentencing options** for juveniles processed by the criminal courts. Blended sentencing options incorporate traditional juvenile treatment strategies with sanctions traditionally imposed on adults. Examples are shown in Figure 4.9. In a similar vein, some criminologists are calling for a "restorative approach" to juvenile justice (Bazemore and Day, 1996). This approach combines offender accountability and competency building with community protection in an effort to heal the wounds caused by crime. It is being proposed for both adult and juvenile offenders, and is described in detail in Chapter 17.

blended sentencing Dispositions that incorporate traditional juvenile treatment strategies with punishments traditionally imposed on adults.

A review of actions taken at the state level shows that since 1992 nearly every state has made changes in the way its judicial system deals with serious and violent juvenile crime (National Center for Juvenile Justice, 1996). The following trends are apparent:

1. More serious and violent juvenile offenders are being removed from the juvenile justice system in favor of criminal court prosecution. A majority of states have added new crimes to the list of offenses for which juveniles may be transferred to criminal court; 15 states have lowered the age limit, with Missouri lowering it from 14 to 12 for *any* felony.
2. Traditional confidentiality provisions are being revised in favor of more open proceedings and records. By the mid-1990s, debate over the protection of the juvenile versus protection of the community, and over the juvenile's right to privacy versus the community's right to know, was being resolved in favor of the community. The comments in 1957 of then–FBI director J. Edgar Hoover have proved prophetic. He said: "Publicizing the names as well as crimes for public scrutiny, releases of past records to appropriate law enforcement officials, and fingerprinting for future identification are all necessary procedures in the war on flagrant violators, regardless of age. Local police and citizens have a right to know the identities of the potential threats to public order within their communities" (Bureau of Justice Statistics, 1997d:14).

   There are various ways that states are opening up juvenile records and reducing confidentiality of juvenile court proceedings. Some are allowing juvenile court proceedings to be public; some are releasing the names of offenders, and even the court record itself; most now allow photographs and fingerprints of juveniles to be deposited in a criminal history file; a few states now prohibit the sealing or removal of juvenile records, and roughly half the states have a state central repository for juvenile criminal histories (Bureau of Justice Statistics, 1997d:23).
3. State correctional administrators are faced with increasing pressures to develop new programs for juveniles. Since nearly all states now send juveniles sentenced as adults to the department of corrections, this means that there are more young inmates whose needs and vulnerabilities require special attention. In some states—Colorado, Kentucky, and New Mexico are examples—a special category of "youthful offenders" has been identified to distinguish more serious offenders from their delinquent peers. Although they have committed serious crimes and are

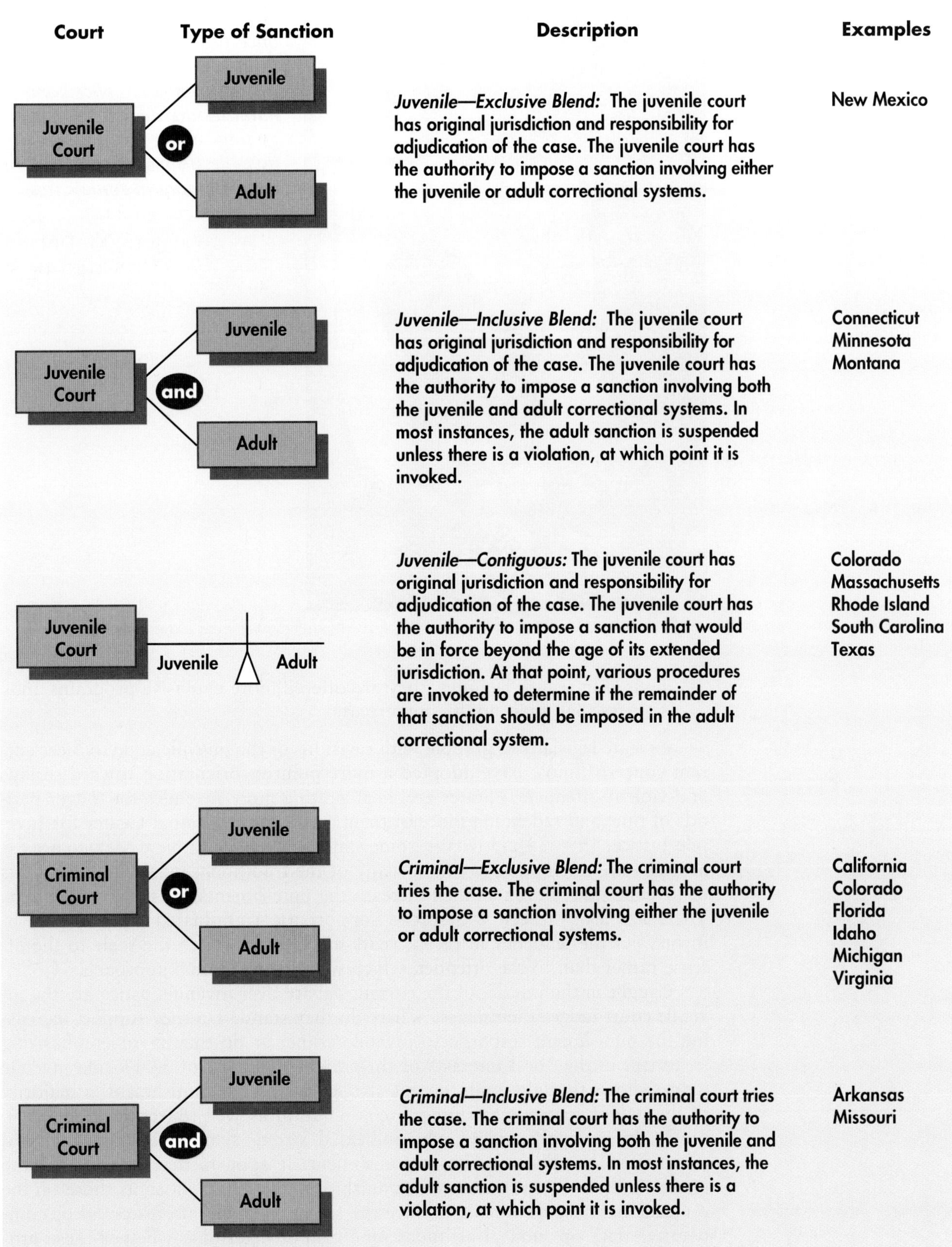

FIGURE 4.9 MODELS OF BLENDED SENTENCING

Source: Patricia Torbet, et al. (1996). *State Responses to Serious and Violent Juvenile Crime*. Washington, D.C.: Office of Juvenile Justice and Delinquency Prevention. Reprinted with permission.

Today, confidentiality laws that once protected offenders are disappearing. In the face of rising juvenile violence communities are demanding—and getting—more information on juvenile suspects and offenders, including in some cases the court record itself.

Photo by John M. Discher, courtesy of AP

housed in secure facilities, they are offered more extensive programs and services than their adult counterparts.

As state legislatures grapple with revisions of the juvenile code to meet current concerns, most have adopted a more punitive orientation toward serious and violent offenders. "States are incarcerating more juveniles for longer periods of time and redefining more of them as adults" (National Center for Juvenile Justice, 1996:34). However, some states—Florida and New Mexico are examples—are attempting to retain many of the traditional rehabilitative aspects of juvenile justice even as they increase the punishments for serious offenders. There has always been widespread support for a graduated scale of punishments, but the tendency in recent years has been to match the scale to the offense rather than to the offender, which was the traditional approach.

Caught in the middle of the current debate over juvenile justice are the juvenile court judges themselves. Where do they stand? Do they support increasing the punishment response to juvenile crime, or do they favor emphasizing treatment in the "best interests of the child"? A survey of 53 Florida juvenile judges shows that although there is strong support for punishment, a majority of the judges continue to support rehabilitation as well (Bazemore and Feder, 1997). Interestingly, judges who indicated strong sympathies for victims of crime were *less* likely to favor punishment. It appears that support for the crime victim need not mean more punishment for the offender, as those on the political right seem to believe. Since the study contained no historical or comparative data on judicial attitudes, one cannot determine whether these attitudes are new or apply elsewhere. Until we learn differently, it appears that juvenile court judges are not willing to discard entirely the ideal behind the original juvenile court.

To do justice to the subject of juvenile crime and the juvenile justice system would require an entire book. Since this text focuses primarily on the adult criminal justice system, issues pertaining to juveniles are discussed when they illustrate broader problems that are relevant for both systems.

SUMMARY

Criminal justice is a modern society's system of roles and activities for defining and dealing with crime. This chapter gave an overview of the goals of the criminal justice system in America, its organization, and the key decisions that determine whether and how criminal cases are processed. In addition, the history and current status of the juvenile justice system were also explored.

The American system of justice differs significantly from some others because of this country's complex political structure. Different police agencies operate at local, state, and federal levels; there are federal and state court and correctional systems; and local jails are usually run by counties, which also manage probation and parole services on behalf of the state. The highest court in the land is the U.S. Supreme Court, which hears appeals from the lower appellate and trial courts of both the federal and state systems. The Supreme Court interprets the meaning of the U.S. Constitution as it applies to criminal justice practice. Its decisions sometimes strengthen the hand of the state, and sometimes they increase the procedural safeguards enjoyed by suspects and defendants.

In practice, the criminal justice system is like a leaky funnel: Few suspects who start the journey through the system end up in prison. The same is true of the juvenile justice system, only more so. The decisions that are made at key points in the processing of cases—for example, whether to take official action, whether to make an arrest, whether to allow bail, whether to prosecute, whether to plea bargain, or whether to classify an offender as a high security risk—determine how justice will be experienced by those participating in it, and also how it will be judged by the politicians who make laws and create policy and by the general public. The trend in recent years is for policymakers to take an increasingly hard line with crime, especially drug trafficking and juvenile violence; this has resulted in rising prison populations and more juveniles being tried as adults.

This trend may plug some of the holes in the funnel, but not for all criminal suspects. Consistent with stereotypical images of real crime and real criminals, decisions made throughout the criminal justice system are having a cumulative, negative impact on minorities, especially African Americans, whose youth are filling up detention centers, jails, and prisons. Reforms proposed for the juvenile justice system are not likely to reverse this trend, although support is growing for a more balanced response to juvenile and adult criminals that does more than simply punish them more harshly for longer periods of time. The challenge for reformers is to devise strategies that promote peace and justice in an era of hard-line sentiment.

WHAT DO YOU THINK *NOW?*

- Consider the three main goals of the criminal justice system. How do the police, the courts, and corrections address these goals separately? Together?
- Now that you have studied the primary goals and decisions of the police, the courts, and corrections, explain how they are connected.
- How are juvenile crime and juvenile justice changing? What impact have these changes had on minority populations?

KEY TERMS AND CASES

consensus model
conflict model
intermediate sanctions
privatization
discretion
probable cause
preliminary hearing
grand jury
speedy trial
continuance
mandatory sentencing
parole
parens patriae
Progressive Era
status offenses
adversarial process
In re Gault
due process reforms
Kent v. United States
blended sentencing

ACTIVE LEARNING CHALLENGES

1. In small groups, find five state police agencies that follow a centralized model and five that are decentralized. List the major ways in which the two groups of agencies differ, and tell the class which model you prefer and why.
2. In pairs, trace the history of an actual felony case in your county, from filing of charges to final disposition. How long did it take? Was there a trial? Did the punishment handed down match the offense for which the defendant was initially arrested? If you were the victim, what would be your reaction to the outcome? Why?
3. Break the class into two groups to debate this statement: Less discretion in the hands of criminal justice officials would improve the quality of justice in America.
4. Invite a juvenile court judge and a juvenile probation officer into class to discuss current reforms and their implications for juvenile offenders, victims, and the people employed in the system.

INTERNET CHALLENGES

The Web pages mentioned here can all be accessed through the Web site for this textbook at **http://www.prenhal.com/barlow/.**

1. You have had a peek at policing in England and Wales. Now travel via the Web to Australia, New Zealand, and Canada and find out how their police are organized. How much of the English model have they retained? How do they differ?
2. Explore the latest challenges facing federal and state criminal court systems and find out how they are reacting to them. Visit the Federal Judiciary Homepage; check out the state courts by visiting state home pages or the home page of the National Center for State Courts. List the challenges you find and briefly summarize the results of your investigation.
3. Find out how corrections are organized in your state and in one other states. If your state does not have a Web site that provides the information, pick another that does. Try the Corrections Connection and Professor Tom Kerr's WWW Prison Links page at Syracuse University.
4. The juvenile justice system is undergoing policy reforms that will probably send more young people to prison for longer periods of time; at the same time, new ideas about delinquency prevention are being implemented around the country. Start at the Juvenile Justice page on the National Criminal Justice Reference Service's Web site and explore the link to "Delinquency Prevention." Briefly summarize one program that you believe has promise.

Part II

The Police

First Line of Defense against Crime

CHAPTER 5
HISTORY, ORGANIZATION, AND FUNCTIONS OF POLICE

CHAPTER 6
CULTURE AND STYLES OF POLICING

CHAPTER 7
THE EXERCISE OF DISCRETION

CHAPTER 8
SIX CRIME CHALLENGES FOR POLICE TODAY

CHAPTER 9
THE POLICE AND THE LAW

When people think of crime, they usually also think of the police. The police investigate crimes, pursue suspects, and make arrests—in short, they are society's first line of defense against crime. In the next five chapters we shall explore policing in detail. Chapter 5 examines the history, organization, and functions of modern police, and considers how the American model differs from its British counterpart. Chapter 6 explores what it means to be a police officer, including recruitment, training, and the police perspective; it also examines different styles of policing and the growing use of proactive policing strategies. In Chapter 7, we explore the use of discretion in police decision making, including the decision to interrogate suspects, make arrests, and use deadly force. Chapter 8 highlights six crime challenges that police face today: gangs, drugs, organized crime, hate crimes, terrorism, and domestic violence. This chapter briefly describes each of these problems, then evaluates police strategies in dealing with them. Finally, Chapter 9 tackles some difficult but very important questions dealing with the legal boundaries of police action and the problems that arise when police overstep them. Included are the rules of search and seizure, the law of arrest, the rights of suspects during questioning, and the "dark side" of policing—corruption and brutality.

CHAPTER 5

HISTORY, ORGANIZATION, AND FUNCTIONS OF POLICE

LEARNING OBJECTIVES

- Describe the progression of policing in England and America, from amateur systems of community surveillance, to the first use of professional police.
- Explain the influence of politics in law enforcement.
- Distinguish between federal law enforcement and state, county, and local policing.
- Understand the major positive and negative influences on cooperation between various levels of policing agencies.
- Describe the distinguishing features of rural policing.
- Understand why privatization of police operations has become more widespread, and why it is controversial.
- Describe the three major functions of modern policing.

This photo shows an adaptation that law enforcement officers made to survive in the Wild West: Western sheriffs often wore no uniform beyond the requisite badge.

PHOTO COURTESY OF WESTERN HISTORY COLLECTIONS, UNIVERSITY OF OKLAHOMA LIBRARY

In theory, the American police are apolitical. . . . In practice, however, police organizations function in a political context; they operate in a public political arena and their mandate is defined politically.

PETER K. MANNING, SOCIOLOGIST AND POLICE RESEARCHER

Police are police, and their obligation is to be fair and impartial. . . . [When officers are rented out] they are no longer being paid to be impartial.

AARON ROSENTHAL, VETERAN CITY COP AND CRIMINAL JUSTICE INSTRUCTOR, COMMENTING ON NEW YORK CITY'S "RENT-A-COP" PROGRAM

Orlando Winfield Wilson completed one of the first criminology degrees offered in the United States, at the University of California, at Berkeley, in 1924. While studying, he joined the Berkeley Police Department under Chief August Vollmer, the man history credits with bringing technology and professionalism to American policing. Vollmer also taught at the university, and Wilson soon became an ardent follower.

Wilson eventually moved to Wichita, Kansas, and was that city's police chief from 1928 to 1939. Wilson lost no time reorganizing the department, and he gained national attention for his innovations, which included using marked police cars and mobile crime labs that could be brought to the scene of a crime. From 1939 to 1960 Wilson was back in Berkeley as a professor of police administration. During that period he wrote important books on policing, and developed the theory that while police could not affect the underlying causes of crime, through careful organization and planning, and by aggressive patrolling, they could make it more difficult—and costly—for criminals to operate. Following Vollmer's leadership, Wilson also focused on developing police administration along scientific lines, to make it more efficient and to reduce the opportunities and incentives for corruption.

Wilson's work earned him an invitation to become superintendent of the Chicago Police Department, which he accepted in 1960. A notoriously corrupt and unwieldy department, the Chicago police force entered the modern era of policing under Wilson. He introduced one-officer patrols to bolster efficiency, and developed rapid-response tactics as part of his crime-fighting strategy. Wilson also advocated a high degree of professionalism among his officers, and to reduce the temptation and opportunities for corruption he rotated their beat assignments. Like his mentor, August Vollmer, O. W. Wilson believed that one of the most important steps toward professional policing was to get the police out of politics and politics out of policing. Although most experts would agree that Wilson and other reformers made some headway in that direction, the goal has remained elusive to this day.

In this and the next four chapters we explore the world that O. W. Wilson helped to shape. The day-to-day job of uncovering and responding to crimes, apprehending violators, and seeing that order is maintained rests with the police. The police bear the burden of translating law on the books into law in action. Without the police, the criminal justice system would quickly grind to a halt.

To most civilians, the police officer *is* the law. Not only are police officers expected to deal with crime and many other troubles that befall citizens, from barking dogs to difficult children, but they are also the civilian's most common and direct contact with the government. Once police officers are present, situations take on new meaning. The significance of their arrival is implied by the symbols they wear and carry: Their uniforms and badges symbolize their state authority; their weapons symbolize the availability of force to back up their commands; their handcuffs symbolize the state's power of detention. What the police do and don't do carries more weight in the legal process than the actions of any other single agency of criminal law—perhaps more than all others put together.

Arguably the most important decisions made by police are the negative ones: If they decide *not* to identify an act or event as a crime, if they choose *not* to label a person as a suspect, or if they decide *not* to take official action, then for all practical purposes the act, event, or person is not criminal. By taking no action the police effectively determine the limits of the law's reach. People whose actions are ignored by the police are for all practical purposes "law abiding." Looking at things from the other side, when police *do* take action they are generally the first to apply the official labels of *crime* and *criminal.* Whatever might happen at subsequent stages in the legal process can generally happen only after police have taken that initial defining action.

Police also shape the images we have of crime itself. The pictures we have of crime are based largely on the actions of the police on patrol and in their roles as detectives and investigators. The police create an "official" version of crime. This version shows us which crimes are considered serious; which crimes are on the increase; which offenders are getting caught most often; and which parts of the city, which days and times, and which groups of people are most crime prone. The picture is based on what the police do, rather than on what criminals do. It depends to a large extent on how the police keep track of their own activities, and on how they measure what they do.

In addition, aspects of police work such as patrolling practices and techniques, discretion, use of force, training, the "cop culture,"

Police work includes specialized details such as vice, traffic, and intelligence-gathering. Vice officers, such as the undercover officers shown here, often go undercover to catch lawbreakers. This includes posing as drug dealers or buyers, or as prostitutes or their customers. What are the benefits of undercover work? What sort of corruption could tempt undercover officers?

Photo by Michael Newman, courtesy of PhotoEdit

departmental norms and policies, and the operation of specialty details such as vice, traffic, or intelligence all contribute to the reality of crime that we experience. If all police officers treated every suspected criminal event or person the same way, this reality would be the same for everyone involved. But this is clearly not the case. As we shall discover in the next five chapters, there is a good deal of variation in police behavior, and much of that variation relates to who and what the police are dealing with.

People rarely stop to question the existence of police or to consider their impact on society. Although there has been much talk recently of the need for more police officers—the 1994 Federal Crime Bill included funding for 100,000 new recruits—how many of us have contemplated how society actually uses its police and what it might be like without them?

In this chapter we will explore these issues by examining the history, organization, and functions of policing. We will also consider the differences among federal, state, and local police agencies in the United States today and relations between them. Urban and rural policing will be compared, and we will also examine what has become an immense industry: private policing. The chapter concludes by outlining the functions of modern policing.

- How are law enforcement officials such as U.S. postal inspectors, FBI agents, and park police and rangers different from the average urban police officer? How are they similar?
- Do federal and local police forces work together smoothly when trying to solve cases that cross jurisdictions? Why or why not?
- What do you think are the main functions of policing today?

A BRIEF HISTORY OF POLICING

Policing as we know it in the United States today is of relatively recent origin. Most historians trace the origins of modern policing to the rapid industrial expansion and population growth in the eighteenth and early nineteenth centuries in western Europe, particularly England. However, we need to go further back in time to understand why this period in English history was so revolutionary for policing.

POLICING BEFORE THE INDUSTRIAL REVOLUTION

Prior to the Industrial Revolution, an assortment of different activities can be loosely thought of as policing in that they were connected to the law and its enforcement. Let us begin with the frankpledge system.

frankpledge system A medieval form of policing that required male citizens to form teams ("tythings") to deliver offenders to court.

The "Frankpledge" System. From at least the tenth to the thirteenth centuries, much of medieval England relied on the **frankpledge system.** Under this form of policing, citizens were *required* to form volunteer teams to police ten families in their village or neighborhood:

> The frankpledge police system required that every male above the age of twelve form a group of nine of his neighbors into a *tything*. Each tything was sworn to apprehend and deliver to court any one of its members who committed a crime. . . . One way to understand tything is to see it as a very special kind of promise that each adult had to make to the state. By being in tything each man promised, in advance of any wrongdoing, that he had already assembled a nine-man police force to apprehend, incarcerate, and deliver him to court if he did. The effectiveness of the frankpledge system of police rested on very severe fines, which were imposed upon all members of a tything if the tything failed to perform its required duties. (Klockars, 1985:23)

During this period much of the population was scattered throughout the countryside in small villages and towns. Maintaining order and protecting the village was considered a local responsibility, and policing was essentially a system of "surveillance-based discipline" (McMullan, 1998:95–97) that worked because people were highly visible and knew each other.

constable A local official responsible for keeping the peace.

sheriff The top county official authorized to collect taxes and to enforce the king's laws.

Constables and Sheriffs. After the Norman Conquest of 1066, the frankpledge system was supplemented by the services of constables and sheriffs, officials who were locally elected or specially appointed by or on behalf of the king. The **constable**—a name still used in British policing to refer to patrol officers and detectives in the lowest ranks—was an official of the village or local parish whose responsibilities were primarily to keep the peace and to represent local government in dealings with citizens and neighboring communities. One day the constable might help settle a dispute between neighbors; another day he might chase down a thief or deal with a charge of assault or robbery. The **sheriff**—earlier called the "Shire Reeve"—was the top official of a shire, or county, and was usually appointed by the landowner representing the king. Sheriffs spent much of their time and energy collecting taxes and making sure that villages and towns ran their affairs in accordance with the wishes of the landowner. In emergencies or to capture a particularly dangerous criminal, the sheriff had the authority to call upon all able-bodied men to form a **posse comitatus** (literally, "the power of the county"). However, in line with the tradition of self-help justice, the primary responsibility for doing something about crime remained on the shoulders of the citizenry. Individual towns and villages were held accountable for the enforcement of laws and prohibitions within their territories, so that policing was largely a communal affair.

posse comitatus A group of able-bodied men assembled to catch criminals or deal with local emergencies.

The Hue and Cry. Where crime was concerned, the citizenry had to be ready to spring into action at a moment's notice. This gave rise to the **hue and cry**, forerunner to the American posse, in which all able-bodied people chased after the suspect as quickly as they could. They made a lot of noise in order to arouse people to join in the chase. Speed was important because it was not easy to establish later on that a crime such as theft had actually been committed. In those days, establishing ownership through a bill of sale or receipt was almost unheard of: If people had things in their possession, such items were, to all intents and purposes, *their* things. To identify theft it was necessary to show first that the thief did not have lawful possession of the object in question, and second that the person who claimed lawful possession had the right to do so. In practical terms this meant that the thief had to be caught red-handed, that is, with the stolen item in his or her possession. Hence the importance of the chase. In 1285, the Statute of Winchester included a provision that citizens should maintain weapons in their homes so that they were adequately prepared to take up the chase.

hue and cry Able-bodied citizens chase noisily after fleeing suspects.

The Watch System. Through the Statute of Winchester, Edward I (1272–1307) established the first formal system of policing for the larger walled towns and cities of England. It strengthened the office of constable and created the **watch system**: Able-bodied men—especially property owners—were expected to volunteer for nighttime duty as "watchmen" to guard the town, look out for fires, and arrest people who committed offenses at night. The unpaid watchmen were also expected to look out for disruptions of public order and threats to property and were expected to uphold the moral standards of the day.

watch system The first formal system of policing in which property owners took turns guarding the town during the night.

Although constables and watchmen were granted the powers of arrest and in some towns were armed, little public protection and crime control was apparently expected of them, and little was delivered. As time passed, many property owners who had participated as watchmen tried to get out of the responsibility, considering it a thankless chore; those who stayed on the job made the most of it through a variety of corrupt and unlawful practices. Over the years, therefore, faith in the reliability of the constable and the watch system steadily declined.

The Impact of Capitalism and the Industrial Revolution

The rise of capitalism and the Industrial Revolution in Britain during the eighteenth century changed economic and social conditions dramatically and, for many citizens, painfully. The migration of thousands of hopeful workers into already crowded towns and cities added new tensions to the hardships suffered by the poor masses. Brutal living conditions, low wages and long hours for those lucky enough to have jobs, growing poverty in the midst of growing affluence, and the laissez-faire attitude that kept government out of economic relationships all contributed to social disorder. Add periodic crime waves, vagrants and beggars by the thousands, and an extremely punitive system of laws, and the scene was set for a breakdown in the existing police system.

Jonathon Wild and the "Thief Takers." By the 1700s, London was growing fast and policing was so ineffective that thieves and robbers moved freely about the city. Even as the government passed new laws in a desperate attempt to curb crime, enterprising thieves turned them into a source of profit. Notorious among these was Jonathan Wild (1682–1725), who along with others exploited the new Highwayman Act of 1692 (Pringle, n.d.; Critchley, 1972; Klockars, 1985). This new law created the infamous **thief taker**, a forerunner of the American bounty hunter, who received 40 pounds "blood money" (about $3,000 in today's money) for each thief captured, prosecuted, and convicted. He could also keep any of the thief's personal property, such as horses, guns, or money, provided they were not themselves stolen. The law also specified that a person's own thefts would be pardoned in exchange for information on at least two other thieves who were then convicted. Far from accomplishing the act's purpose, however, thief takers increased crime rather than controlled it; they used bribery, extortion, blackmail, perjury, and murder to line their own pockets.

thief taker A eighteenth-century version of the American bounty hunter.

Wild saw many opportunities to make money by exploiting the provisions of the law. He organized a band of thieves and then set himself up as a thief taker, advertising that he would help victims get their property back. He usually sold them back the same things he and his friends had stolen from them! He also returned stolen property he bought cheaply from other thieves, making a handsome profit. The risk that he might turn them in led other thieves to join his band rather than compete with him. Wild soon claimed to control most of the thieves in London. He was happy to take a bribe from any independent thief prepared to pay more than 40 pounds to avoid going to jail. But in 1725 the authorities caught up with Wild, whose escapades brought him to the hangman. He was hanged no doubt with grudging respect but also with much fanfare as one of England's most notorious criminals.

The Bow Street Runners. An important response to corrupt thief takers like Wild and to growing social unrest among the poor was an idea developed by Henry Fielding (1707–1754), author and chief magistrate at the court in London's Bow Street. Fielding established a small group of six salaried thief takers whose dedication and success in capturing criminals eventually became legendary. This small unit, supervised later by Henry's brother John Fielding (who succeeded him as magistrate), became known as the **Bow Street Runners.** Their name came from their crime-fighting strategy: Get to the crime scene as quickly as possible—usually by running—and begin an immediate investigation.

Bow Street Runners A famous eighteenth-century police unit in London composed of six salaried thief takers who usually ran to crime scenes.

This small unit certainly could not cope with the growing crime problem in London, nor could it address the deteriorating social and political conditions of the times. It was in the hope of containing and suppressing criminals, the unemployed, and poorer people in general—lumped together as the "dangerous classes" in some circles—that many people began to call for real police reforms (Critchley, 1972:34–42; Silver, 1967). The idea of creating an organized paramilitary police force began to take hold.

THE LONDON "NEW POLICE"

The English were reluctant to accept the notion of an organized paramilitary police force, however, feeling it would seriously threaten traditionally prized liberties such as freedom of movement (Banton, 1973:18). Despite this reluctance, the reform proposals of men such as Patrick Colquhoun (pronounced *Col-hoon*) eventually gained widespread support. In 1806, Colquhoun proposed that a well-regulated, full-time, centrally administered police organiza-

The Bow Street Runners were an innovative response to corruption and public unrest. Developed by author and chief magistrate Henry Fielding, the Runners were six salaried "thief takers" who had remarkable success at catching criminals. They were called Runners because they ran to crime scenes and began investigations immediately.

Photo courtesy of The Granger Collection, New York

tion be set up to prevent crime by patrolling the streets of London. Its officers were to be salaried men under the direction of commissioners accountable directly to the government. Colquhoun eventually created the Thames River Police as a compromise between private and public policing (Manning, 1992). In 1829, Parliament enacted the Metropolitan Police Act under the leadership of Home Secretary Robert Peel. This act followed the model for police organization and strategy long advocated by Colquhoun. The **"New Police,"** or **"Bobbies,"** (in reference to Peel's first name) had been born. They are the most immediate forerunner of our modern police.

"New Police" (Bobbies) A full-time, uniformed, salaried police organization developed by Sir Robert Peel in 1829 to patrol the streets of London.

The New Police were organized along military lines, with a clear hierarchy of control and an authoritarian system of command and discipline (Walker, 1992:5). Uniformed bobbies patrolled the streets in shifts, getting to know their beats and the people living there. They were not always well-received, however. Some citizens saw the continual presence of police in the neighborhood as a threat to their freedom and a way the government could spy on them. Clashes between citizens and police broke out from time to time, but eventually the bobbies became an accepted part of London life.

Policing the City in America

In America, meanwhile, the larger cities were facing some of the same problems as the English. Although industrialization and modern capitalism developed later in America, by the early 1800s many American cities were experiencing rising rates of poverty, unemployment, migration, and crime. Signs of growing unrest were all around. Riots and demonstrations erupted in Boston, New York, and Philadelphia, and the police came under attack for ineffectiveness in controlling the dangerous classes (Bacon, 1935; Lane, 1967, 1992). Before examining the response to these problems, however, we will learn about policing in the colonial period.

The Colonial Period. During the early colonial period, American towns and cities had relied on the English system of constables and watchmen. The protection of life, property, and public order was considered a civic responsibility, as it had been in England. Able-bodied property owners were expected to assume constable and watchman duties on a rotating basis. These policing methods soon acquired a dubious reputation. One reason had to do with the fee collection system. Not only were constables paid by the courts for each warrant issued or arrest made, but even the victims of crimes had to pay a fee before the constable would do anything (Ferdinand, 1980; Monkkonen, 1992). Here was a monetary incentive for constables to bend the rules, commit frauds, and take bribes. Meanwhile, night watchmen were regularly accused of falling asleep on the job or of running away from fires or other trouble. In any case, there is consensus that the watch system in colonial America was "not in any way a serious crime-fighting organization" (Monkkonen, 1992:550). As abuses of duty became commonplace, city officials tried to improve policing methods.

In 1772, Williamsburg, Virginia, instituted one of the first municipal night patrols, composed of four "sober and discreet people" who made up a permanent, paid patrol. Their job was "to patrol the streets of this city from ten o'-clock every night until daylight the next morning, to cry the hours, and use their best endeavors to preserve peace and good order, by apprehending and bringing to justice all disorderly people" (Weston and Wells, 1972:6). Boston and New York soon followed suit, and the new patrols were given authority to enforce all laws and to stop and question anyone suspected of criminal intentions (Bacon, 1935).

Policing in Nineteenth-Century American Cities. As American cities continued to grow, these moderate reforms failed to satisfy the growing demand for order and crime control voiced in many quarters. American authorities decided that the London bobbies seemed to be doing a good job, so why not try the same system in America? Compared with the constable watch system, three features of the English system were particularly attractive to American authorities:

- It had a hierarchical organization and military-style chain of command. "Even without an electronic communication system . . . the simple chain of command meant that a citizen could report an offense to an officer who would in turn relay the information to headquarters, which would then distribute the information back down the line" (Monkkonen, 1992:550).
- The greater visibility of the bobbies due to their uniforms made them accessible to all citizens—and more easily seen and supervised by higher ranks.
- The emphasis on active policing through regular patrols created a crime-*prevention* role for the police and encouraged citizens to report suspicious activities and people before crimes were actually committed.

In New York, an 1845 ordinance established a police force with around-the-clock patrol and law enforcement duties. The force was administered by a board of police commissioners composed of the mayor, the recorder, and a city judge. The same model was adopted by New Orleans in 1853; Cincinnati and San Francisco in 1859; Detroit, St. Louis, and Kansas City in 1861; and Buffalo and Cleveland in 1866.

It soon became clear that police commissions were little more than tools used to support the interests of the political parties in power. This was especially true around election time, when police officers in some departments were encouraged to commit bribery, intimidation, and fraud on behalf of their political bosses. Further, many police commissions proved ineffective in managing the administrative affairs of their departments, with the result that they quickly fell into disfavor. By the early 1900s many cities had abandoned commissions in favor of a single public official acting as police executive.

This nineteenth-century law enforcement official reflects the influence of the London New Police in his uniform and military-style rank.

Photo courtesy of Stock Montage, Inc.

Politicization of Law Enforcement

The New Police fared better in Britain than in America partly because they were organized under a central authority, the Crown, which was widely respected (Manning, 1992). Today, although local and regional authorities administer the day-to-day operations of British police forces, the police nevertheless retain a national character, in that Parliament and the Home Office oversee operations and local police also have jurisdiction in what here would be called federal matters. In the United States, the Constitution reserves the bulk of criminal law matters for state control and makes a clear distinction between federal and state laws and their enforcement. Law enforcement thus operates under a complicated system of jurisdictional controls, with local, county, state, and federal political units exercising varying degrees of authority and retaining varying amounts of autonomy in police affairs.

One consequence of this division of authority is the **politicization** of law enforcement. In America, police operations are entrenched in politics, and day-to-day political interference at all levels is almost inevitable even today. For example, in one major midwestern city in 1995, the mayor, state officials, the police union, the Board of Police Commissioners, and the police chief were embroiled in a war of words over who should control the police. The mayor wanted to take over control from the state, while other factions preferred the more distant state control and claimed that local control would embroil the department in dirty politics. Others feared that local control would eventually result in lower pay, fewer benefits, and a decline in police performance. Some police officers even took to picketing the mayor.

politicization Occurs when police operations are heavily influenced by politics.

The association between party politics and police work has been well documented in Chicago (Haller, 1976). At the turn of the century, when Chicago was experiencing unprecedented growth and industrial development, the law enforcement apparatus was an indispensable part of the political "machine." Police promotions as well as judgeships depended on the demonstration of party loyalty. All police employees paid a portion of their salaries into the party treasury and were required to do its bidding, even if this sometimes meant breaking the law.

Ethnic Dominance of Urban Policing in America. One demonstration of politicization is the ethnic composition of many nineteenth-century urban police forces. To the extent that a certain ethnic group controlled city hall, this group was likely to stack the police department with its own kind, especially relatives and friends. The ethnic composition of police and fire departments often reflected the ethnic heritage of the city: Over 75 percent of the employees of departments in New York City, Chicago, and Milwaukee, for example, were immigrants or children of immigrants. The group most associated with this process was composed of Irish immigrants. The New York City police department is a case in point. In that city in the mid-1800s, the Irish dominated city government through the democratic headquarters at Tammany Hall. However, even cities without large Irish populations had large numbers of Irish police officers: New Orleans, Vicksburg, Memphis and St. Louis are examples (Monkkonen, 1992:560). For a period in American history, it seems, being a policeman and being Irish was the natural order of things.

Police and the Labor Movement. A second illustration of the politicization of policing comes from studies of the labor movement. On balance, urban police forces in nineteenth- and early 20th-century America were used to undermine the union movement. They were often used as "shock troops for local capitalists" (Monkkonen, 1992:562; Harring, 1983). But it should also be kept in mind that in some cities—Boston was one—the police themselves were trying to organize unions, and in many smaller towns, policemen often had relatives in the union movement or prolabor officials in city hall, making police interference with labor actions less likely.

Today, the connection between politics and policing may no longer be so blatant, but it still exists; the progressive reforms and modernization that are ongoing in American policing have "had as a consistent primary objective the depoliticization of the police and their conversion to rational, professional norms of conduct. . . . The police and their leaders are inescapably political, however, especially in their localized American form" (Hunt and Magenau, 1993:23).

Size and Scope of Policing Today. Over the past few decades, American crime control agencies have mushroomed in number, personnel, and budgets. Today more than 40,000 federal, state, and local police agencies deploy over 660,000 officers and operate with a combined budget in excess of $40 billion. These figures do not include the more than 1 million people working in private police agencies such as Pinkerton's, and in the various inspection services employed by public authorities such as game wardens or bank examiners. In fact, ever since the early 1800s, private policing has played an important role in formal social control (Lane, 1992). We shall return to this issue later in the chapter.

One area where police services have grown tremendously over the past century has been the federal government's involvement in crime control. Although the Constitution reserves the bulk of criminal matters for the states, congressional action over the past century has made extensive federal participation in law enforcement inevitable. Not counting the various branches of the U.S. military, there are currently over 40 federal agencies with authority to carry firearms and to make arrests (see Table 5.1 for the major ones). Around 100,000 criminal suspects are now handled by the federal system each year, double the number handled in 1988. The 1997 budget for federal police agencies was almost $10 billion (Maguire and Pastore, 1998:14). The next section examines federal policing in more detail.

TABLE 5.1 Major Nonmilitary Federal Agencies with Officers Authorized to Carry Firearms and to Make Arrests

AGENCY OR DEPARTMENT	YEAR FOUNDED	NUMBER OF OFFICERS IN 1996*	CURRENT KEY RESPONSIBILITIES
U.S. Postal Inspection Service	1737	3,576	Enforce laws pertaining to the mails, e.g., frauds; use of mails to send dangerous materials; theft of mail; provide security for postal employees and facilities
U.S. Customs Service	1789	9,749	Seize contraband, including narcotics, farm produce, firearms, counterfeit goods; process baggage and persons at borders.
U.S. Marshal's Service	1789	2,650	Provide security in federal court; transport federal prisoners; manage Witness Protection Program; serve fugitive warrants; escort missile convoys
U.S. Capitol Police	1851	1,031	Police U.S. Capitol grounds and buildings
U.S. Secret Service	1865	3,185	Protect president, vice-president, presidential candidates, former presidents, and visiting heads of state; enforce counterfeiting and computer fraud laws; provide security at Treasury buildings.
Bureau of Investigation (named FBI in 1935)	1908	10,389	Broad policing powers covering over 250 federal crimes; shared jurisdiction with DEA over drug offenses
U.S. Park Police and Ranger Activities Division	1919	2,148	Investigate crimes and make arrests in the National Park system; provide crowd control in parks
IRS Criminal Investigation Division	1919	3,784	Investigate tax frauds
Border Patrol (within the Immigration and Naturalization Service)	1924	5,441	Seize aliens, drugs, and other contraband along borders between ports of entry
Bureau of Alcohol, Tobacco and Firearms (ATF)	1972	1,869	Investigate firearm offenses and enforce federal alcohol and tobacco laws
Drug Enforcement Administration (DEA)	1973	2,946	Enforce federal drug laws in cooperation with other federal, state, local, and international agencies; manage narcotics intelligence

*Full-time, sworn officers as of June, 1996

Sources: Adapted from William A. Geller and Norval Morris (1992). "Federal and Local Police" (Table A1). In Carl Klockars and Steven Mastrofski, eds., *Thinking About Police* (2nd ed.). New York: McGraw-Hill; Brian A. Reaves (1998). "Federal Law Enforcement Officers, 1996." *BJS Bulletin* (January): Table 1.

FEDERAL POLICING: GROWTH AND CURRENT STATUS

The first federal inroads into crime control came in 1737, when a plainclothes force of postal inspectors was established to enforce laws dealing with the mails, including the safety and security of employees, which today number over 750,000 in 40,000 facilities (Geller and Morris, 1992:332). Next, the U.S. Marshals Service was established in 1789; its duties include providing security to federal courts and court personnel, capturing fugitives and transporting federal prisoners, and overseeing the Federal Witness Protection Program. That same year the U.S. Customs Service was established, followed the next year by the Revenue Cutter Service (later the Coast Guard), both under the jurisdiction of the Treasury Department.

During the nineteenth century, more federal agencies joined the ranks of policing, including the Capitol Police (1851), the U.S. Secret Service (1865), the Bureau of Indian Affairs (1878), U.S. Probation Services (1870), and the

Immigration and Naturalization Service (1891). By far the greatest expansion of federal policing has occurred during this century, however. Thirty-one agencies received law enforcement authorization, including perhaps the most famous of all, the Federal Bureau of Investigation (FBI).

THE FBI: HIGH-PROFILE AGENCY WITH BROAD POLICE POWERS

Although the Department of Justice was formally established in 1879, it did not become actively involved in policing until 1908. In the interim, one of its primary tasks had been to collect information on federal crimes and criminals, for which it used agents attached to other federal agencies. In 1908, however, the Justice Department received authorization from Congress to establish its own enforcement agency; first called the Bureau of Investigation, its name was changed to the Federal Bureau of Investigation, or FBI, in 1935.

Originally established as an agency mainly concerned with interstate commerce and with enforcement of the Sherman Antitrust Act (1890), the Bureau soon acquired jurisdiction over a whole range of federal laws, from vice under the Mann Act (1910) to violations of copyright, espionage, and radical political activism. A continued expansion of responsibilities under the leadership of J. Edgar Hoover, who was appointed director in 1924, helps explain the phenomenal role this police agency has come to play in law enforcement in the United States.

From 1910 on, federal legislation added crime after crime to the enforcement responsibilities of the Bureau. Following the Mann Act—which outlawed the transportation of women across state lines for immoral purposes but was long used to deal with vice in general—other new federal legislation dealt with the distribution of narcotics under the Harrison Act (1914); alcohol under the Volstead Act (1919); interstate transportation of motor vehicles under the Dyer Act (1919); kidnapping under the Lindbergh Act (1932); escape across state lines to avoid prosecution under the Fugitive Act (1934); and bank robbery.

J. Edgar Hoover fashioned the Bureau into one of the best-equipped, best-trained, and best-financed police bureaucracies in the world. Under his leadership, the FBI sponsored numerous innovations in law enforcement techniques, developed a training academy unsurpassed in the world for its depth and sophistication of instruction, and garnered considerable acclaim for such programs as its Uniform Crime Reports, its "Ten Most Wanted" list of fugitives (see Figure 5.1), its maintenance of a national fingerprint file, and its comprehensive intelligence gathering capacity. The development in 1930 of the Uniform Crime Reports, discussed in Chapter 2, became a "crucial 'ice-breaker'" in the relationship between federal and local police agencies because it led to local police departments routinely sharing crime information with the feds, establishing a "powerful precedent for the collaboration to come" (Geller and Morris, 1992:283–284). Today, the FBI continues to be a leader in policing innovations (see Box 5.1).

The FBI has been a high-profile police agency since Hoover's early days as its director; today, what American older than nine or ten has not heard of the FBI? The FBI has received plenty of positive attention over the years, but also much criticism. The criticism peaked in the 1970s, not long before Hoover's death (Poveda, 1990). While Hoover's motives have remained a matter of debate, he led the agency into activities that outraged many members of Congress, as well as union leaders, journalists, members of minority groups, fellow law enforcement officers, and even some of his own agents, whom he could dismiss at will.

Some of the strongest criticisms concerned the Bureau's involvement in suppression of left-wing activism, its interference in management-worker relations

FIGURE 5.1 THE FBI'S "TEN MOST WANTED" LIST OF FUGITIVES
Since the 1940s, the FBI has maintained a published list of its ten most wanted fugitives. You can see the list posted in most post offices, along with photographs and descriptions of the suspects and their crimes. Today, the FBI also posts the list on its Web site at **http://www.fbi.gov/mostwant/tenlist.htm.** *Here are the fugitives on the list as of March 15, 1999. Some of the fugitives that week were wanted for terrorist attacks; Eric Rudolph was the object of a massive manhunt involving hundreds of federal, state, and local police. He was suspected of planting bombs at abortion clinics and at the Olympic Games in Atlanta.*

(usually on behalf of management), its extensive files on thousands of American citizens (many of whom had no criminal record), and the racism underlying many of its investigations during the Civil Rights era. There is a well-known story that Hoover responded to calls to hire more black agents by making his black driver a special agent—though he continued to drive Hoover around.

Box 5.1

JUSTICE INNOVATIONS

PROFILING OF SERIAL MURDERERS

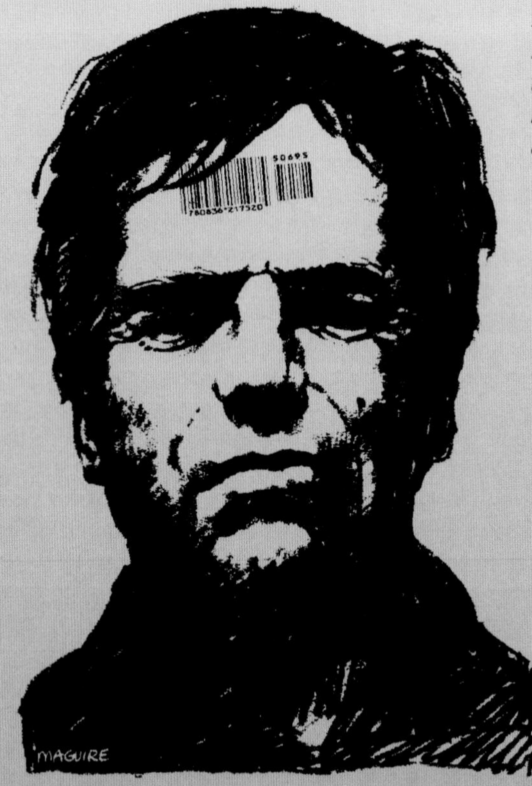

Profiling analyzes a serial killer's "personal signature," the unique marks that a killer leaves at the scene of a crime.

ILLUSTRATION BY BARRIE MAGUIRE, COURTESY OF THE CREATIVE WORKSHOP

Among the innovations in police investigations credited to the FBI is **profiling.** This technique has been applied to a wide range of offenders, including smugglers, an application discussed in Chapter 8. Here its application to serial murder is illustrated.

Profiling is an investigative technique that develops a behavioral composite of an offender who has yet to be caught. As first developed by FBI agent

profiling An investigative technique that develops a behavioral picture of an offender who is not yet caught.

Today, the FBI is viewed favorably by most Americans; many of its excesses under Hoover have faded from memory, and public opinion is now strongly in favor of law and order, including more police and fewer restrictions on police powers. Nevertheless, the dangers of abuses still lurk around the policing activities of this agency. Such dangers are inevitable, given the FBI's domestic intelligence-gathering function, its antiterrorist activities, and its proactive enforcement strategies that target individuals and groups *before* they actually commit any crimes. "The undercover operation is the principal mechanism for carrying out such investigations. . . . This strategy requires state intervention at a highly intrusive level, below the 'reasonable and probable cause' threshold for arrest [discussed in Chapter 9], and without any external checks and balances on police conduct" (Poveda, 1990:174).

The dangers resulting from this strategy include entrapment (when the police induce someone to commit a crime who would not otherwise have done so), damaged reputations, injury to third parties, wrongful arrest, falsification of criminal records, and even homicide. The 1992 shooting of right-wing militant

Box 5.1 (continued)

Howard Teten in the early 1970s, the technique emphasized the psychological characteristics of an offender based on a detailed examination of the homicide scene. The basic idea is that a killer leaves a kind of personal signature at the scene. Agents look for abnormalities or patterns in the crime scene, including the type of victim, the method of killing, and the probable motive.

Today, the profiling is done by members of the FBI's Behavioral Science Unit, and sociological as well as psychological characteristics of probable suspects are developed. However, the process is still based largely on the intuition and experience of the profiler. As of 1996 there had been no objective evaluation of the reliability or validity of the method. However, the FBI's own survey of 192 users of their profiles showed that less than half of the offenders had been caught, and the profiles had directly led to identification of the offender in less than 20 percent of the solved cases (Levin and Fox, 1985:176). Yet approximately 300 criminal profiles are prepared each year, usually at the request of local police departments.

Other profiling techniques have been developed during the past 20 years. One is *geographic profiling,* which tracks the spatial aspects of crime scenes that police believe are linked to the same offender in order to find the most probable area within which to locate the offender. It has been used successfully to investigate serial rape and serial murder. Another method, developed by English psychologist David Canter, relies on interpreting the "criminal's shadow," or personal story based on "cryptic signals" given off by the offender. These signals include the care taken to avoid capture, the experience shown in the crime, and unusual aspects of the offense. Canter has a database of information that relates known facts about offenders to those of their victims. These data become the basis for developing statistical probabilities that can be used to guide police.

Sources: David Canter (1994). *Criminal Shadows: Inside the Mind of a Serial Killer.* London: HarperCollins; Steven A. Egger (1998). *The Killer among Us: An Examination of Serial Murder and Its Investigation.* Upper Saddle River, N.J.: Prentice-Hall; Jack Levin and James Alan Fox (1985), *Mass Murder: America's Growing Menance.* New York: Plenum Press.

Randy Weaver's wife and child by FBI agents in a siege of Weaver's home in Ruby Ridge, Idaho, is one example. It resulted in a 1995 congressional hearing.

The siege began when U.S. marshals tried to apprehend Weaver on a weapons charge. A marshal shot Weaver's dog, prompting Weaver's 14-year-old son, Sammy, to fire at the marshal. Then another marshal fatally shot Sammy, and in a gun battle U.S. Marshal Michael Degan was killed. The FBI's Hostage and Rescue Team was called in, and the next day an FBI sharpshooter killed Weaver's wife as she stood in the doorway of the Weavers' home. Four FBI agents involved in the siege were suspended on August 11, 1995. In 1997 a federal appeals court concluded that the "shoot to kill" policy agents used was "a gross deviation from constitutional principles and a wholly unwarranted return to a lawless and arbitrary Wild West school of law enforcement" (*Los Angeles Times,* September 26, 1997, p. A1).

The neutralization and disruption of dissident groups continues to be a major thrust of the FBI's activities, and in the absence of effective safeguards and continuous public oversight, civil rights violations and other abuses of authority

Box 5.2

CAREERS IN CRIMINAL JUSTICE

SPECIAL AGENT OF THE FBI

The FBI is the primary investigative arm of the federal government, and is responsible for enforcing over 260 federal laws. As of June 1998, the FBI employed over 11,000 special agents and a similar number of civilians. Approximately 16 percent of its special agents are female, 5.6 percent are black, 7.1 percent are Hispanic, and 3 percent are Asian or Native Americans. Among the jobs available with the FBI are special agent, ballistics technician, fingerprint specialist, document expert, and criminalist. Here are the salary, qualifications, duties, and conditions of employment of a special agent:

Salary (entry level): $38,000

Qualifications: Four entry-level programs require different qualifications. The Law Program requires a JD degree; The Accounting Program requires a BS in acounting or related discipline and eligibility to take a CPA exam; the Language Program requires a BS or BA in any disipline and proficiency in a language that meets the needs of the FBI; the Diversified Program requires a BS or BA in any discipline plus three years of full-time work experience or an advanced degree and two years of full-time work experience.

Duties: Investigation of a broad range of illegal activities, including organized crime, white-collar crime, corruption, frauds of various sorts, bribery, bank robbery, civil rights violations, fugitive and drug trafficking matters, kidnapping, hate crimes, and foreign counterintelligence; work with other federal, state, and local law enforcement agencies investigating matters of mutual interest; make arrests, and be prepared to use deadly force if circumstances dictate.

Conditions of Employment: Include U.S. citizenship; 23–36 years of age; availability for assignment anywhere in the FBI's jurisdiction; must pass a color vision test and possess a valid driver's license.

are likely to occur from time to time (Box 7.2 in Chapter 7 contains another illustration of this problem).

STATE AND LOCAL POLICE AGENCIES

Despite the phenomenal growth of federal policing over the past century, most day-to-day criminal matters are still handled by the nation's 18,769 state and local police agencies. This is what the Constitution intended as part of the nation's system of checks against excessive federal involvement in local affairs. Let us, then, examine state and local police agencies.

STATE POLICE

At state and local levels, where most citizens have their dealings with police, there are approximately 25 sworn officers for every 10,000 residents (Reaves and Goldberg, 1998:1). New York has the highest ratio of officers to residents (49 per 10,000 in 1992), while West Virginia and Kentucky have the lowest (22).

All states but Hawaii have a uniformed state police force, and many states also have a criminal investigation division. State police academies, state crime labs, a centralized depository for crime information, and other specialized services are found in most states and are generally available to county and city police departments. Most state police agencies are also responsible for patrolling their state's highways.

Pennsylvania was one of the first states to unite all these operations under a centralized state police agency, and it served as a model for other states. Some states, however, have kept criminal investigation separate from the uniformed highway patrol. North Carolina and California are examples, as was Illinois until the late 1980s, when it merged the two. Illinois, North Carolina, and many other states also have separate enforcement units under the control of state agencies having more limited policing responsibilities. State departments dealing with wildlife, conservation, commerce, motor vehicles, alcohol, and education are examples. Officers employed by such agencies are generally armed and have arrest powers; most are distinguishable by their special uniforms and emblems, but some work undercover. It may come as a surprise to many students that state university police departments often have a detachment of plainclothes officers, some of whom work undercover.

State police are generally well trained, well equipped, and relatively well paid. In Illinois in 1998, for example, the starting salary for a state trooper was $39,960; local officers in a medium-sized city would expect to earn around $32,000 to start, while sheriff's deputies outside Chicago's Cook County earn around $30,000 at first. The uniformed state patrols are highly visible, and in many states have a well-earned reputation for professionalism. Many communities rely on the state police to supplement their own meager resources. This is especially true of rural areas and poorer cities. Sometimes, special crime problems can overwhelm a city and the state police are called in to help.

This happened a few years ago in a mid-sized Illinois city. Faced with a growing drug and gang problem and a rash of armed robberies of motorists stopped at red lights, the mayor asked the state police to provide routine patrolling. A gang crimes unit was also created in which local, county, and state police collaborated to fight youth crime and a growing trade in crack cocaine. One result of the state police patrols was that the city crime rate went up dramatically for the first couple of years, as did the number of arrests. Putting more police on patrol not only uncovered more crime, but when state police stopped motorists for traffic violations—which had been a low priority for the understaffed and poorly equipped city police—they found many people with outstanding arrest warrants against them (Barlow, 1989).

Like many other state patrols, those in Illinois are finding it increasingly difficult to meet the demands of a growing list of responsibilities, many of which are highly technical and require specialized training. Among the specialty police services provided by the Illinois State Police are the following:

- drug investigation
- truck and bus inspection
- accident reconstruction
- crime scene investigation
- protection of the governor and other VIPs
- airborne search and rescue
- tactical responses (SWAT)
- investigation of crimes by state employees
- underwater recovery
- probes of police shootings and public corruption
- community-oriented policing programs
- safety programs for schools and civic groups

Although state police agencies are best known for patrolling state highways, many also provide specialized police services such as a crime scene investigation, forensic laboratories, data collection, SWAT teams, search and rescue, and VIP protection.

PHOTO BY C. E. MITCHELL, 1998, COURTESY OF BLACK STAR

- riverboat casino detail
- general criminal investigation

These diversified services have taken a toll on state police resources, and have reduced the number of officers working the roads and patrolling in rural areas. The old philosophy of putting at least one car on patrol in every county is no longer followed in Illinois; the current policy is to put officers where they are needed, even if it means leaving some places unpatrolled (*St. Louis Post-Dispatch*, February 22, 1998, p. A10). The loneliness of patrol has increased, according to many troopers, but so too have the risks to officers. Backup is now 20 or 30 minutes away.

COUNTY POLICE

County police departments are generally "full-service" police agencies, but they vary considerably in staffing, resources, and expertise. Large police forces such as the sheriff's departments of Los Angeles County, California, and Cook County, Illinois, serve millions of citizens and cover the full range of law enforcement, including the county jail and courthouse security. Their budgets run into many millions of dollars. At the other end of the scale are small (in population) rural counties where serious crime is relatively rare and everyone knows the sheriff. Budgets are small, equipment is often old or passed down from the state police, and training may be on-the-job. Most of the nation's 3,088 county police agencies are somewhere in between, although as Table 5.2 shows, the typical department employs less than 25 full-time sworn officers.

Unlike most city and state police chiefs, county sheriffs are usually elected officials who serve for a few years and then must run for re-election. Their department's duties include running the county jail, maintaining security in the county courthouse, serving court papers, investigating crimes, and patrolling all

Table 5.2 Sworn Officers in County and City Police Departments*

Most of the nation's county and city police department's are fairly small, with less than 25 sworn personnel. On the other hand, 12 sheriff's departments and 41 city police departments account for 42 percent of the combined total of 564,000 full-time police officers.

Number of Sworn Personnel*	Number of Agencies	Total of Sworn Personnel*
	Sheriffs' Departments	
1,000 or more	12	27,211
500–999	23	15,508
250–499	72	25,477
100–249	188	28,769
50–99	282	19,520
25–49	471	16,247
10–24	904	14,088
5–9	722	4,886
2–4	367	1,176
1	40	40
Total	3,088	152,922
	City Police Departments	
1,000 or more	41	136,437
500–999	39	27,952
250–499	91	32,030
100–249	344	51,051
50–99	698	48,001
25–49	1,350	46,369
10–24	2,662	41,272
5–9	2,616	17,279
2–4	3,058	8,907
1	1,657	1,657
Total	13,578	410,956

*Includes only full-time officers.

Source: Brian A. Reaves and Andrew L. Goldberg (1998). "Census of State and Local Law Enforcement Agencies, 1996 (Tables 5, 6, 9, and 10). *BJS Bulletin* June: 1–15.

areas of the county except towns and cities that have their own police force. Their powers, however, extend to the entire county, so don't think that if a sheriff's deputy sees you commit an offense within city limits he or she will necessarily ignore it. In fact, in many counties, the sheriff is the chief law enforcement officer and exercises more power than local chiefs of police.

City Police

Municipal police agencies have jurisdiction within the political boundaries of a city. However, like county officers, city police are authorized to enforce all state laws and their arrest powers may be used anywhere within the state.

City departments vary in size and capability, just like their county cousins. Any municipality may establish a police force, consistent with state law. Some departments have only one or two part-time officers and a chief whose primary role is symbolic; other small towns maintain 24-hour police service with at least one officer on patrol at all times. Many smaller departments are housed in city hall, along with ambulance, fire, and other emergency services. In some communities the mayor doubles as police, fire, and ambulance chief; in others, the sworn personnel may all be part-timers or volunteers. In many small-town departments, police are usually generalists, which means they all share in routine duties: patrolling the streets, responding to calls for assistance,

Box 5.3

CAREERS IN CRIMINAL JUSTICE

DEPUTY SHERIFF

All U.S. counties have some form of law enforcement apparatus, usually a sheriff's department. Most sheriff's departments serve rural areas, patrolling the unincorporated areas of a county while municipal police departments provide law enforcement services to cities within the county; sheriff's departments also commonly run the county jail, transport prisoners, and provide security services to the courts. Here are the salary, qualifications, duties, and conditions of employment for the entry-level position of Deputy Sheriff as advertised in August 1998 by Lake County, California:

Salary Range: $25,373 to $33,492

Qualifications: Possession of knowledge and skills necessary for satisfactory job performance, including completion of a Basic Peace Officer Academy approved by the California Commission on Peace Officer Standards and Training (P.O.S.T.), or possession of a P.O.S.T. Basic, Intermediate, or Advanced Certificate. Ability to communicate in the English language both verbally and in writing.

Duties: Deputies patrol unincorporated areas of the county to prevent crime, enforce laws, and render aid or intervention where needed; they respond to calls for service, conduct investigations, act as bailiffs in court, and perform other law enforcement duties.

Conditions of Employment: Include 18 years of age or older; in good physical condition and health; must possess a valid California driver's license and a high school diploma or GED equivalent. Candidates undergo a complete physical examination and psychological testing, and a polygraph may be required.

investigating crimes, and taking care of paperwork. Even the chief takes a turn. This may sound like a "mom and pop" operation, but larger departments do not necessarily do a better job of policing merely because they have more staff. Many small departments fare just as well as large ones in terms of many measures of police performance, including handling complaints, making arrests, and solving crimes.

The vast majority of all local police agencies employ less than 25 full-time sworn officers, but 3 percent of them employ one-third of all city police officers (see Table 5.2). New York City Police Department (NYPD) is the nation's largest department—and the largest law enforcement agency of any kind. It employs 36,813 full-time sworn officers and 7,000 civilians (Reaves and Goldberg, 1998). Big-city departments also have hundreds of vehicles, equipment ranging from sophisticated computers to armored personnel carriers, forensic laboratories, jail facilities, and all sorts of specialized police units—from arson and bomb squads to horse and canine units, from homicide, narcotic and sex offender units to gang and organized crime units. Big-city police departments are complex, bureaucratic organizations that deal with thousands—in some cases millions—of emergency calls every year, and patrol thousands of miles of streets and sidewalks. The organizational chart of a typical big-city department is shown in Figure 5.2. It is similar to many other large organizations, including your university or college.

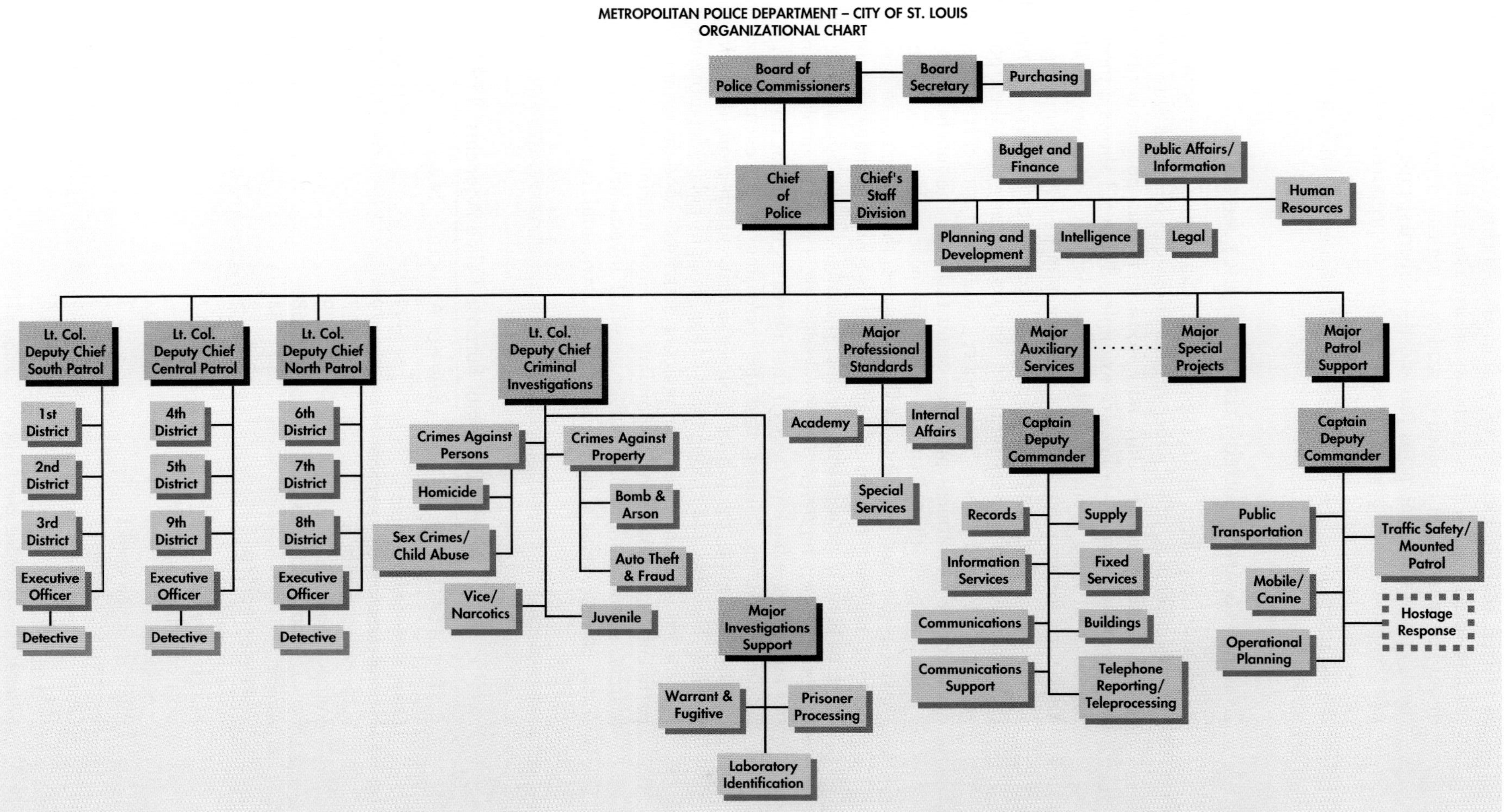

FIGURE 5.2 ORGANIZATIONAL CHART OF A BIG-CITY POLICE DEPARTMENT
Police departments differ in their internal organization, depending on their size, jurisdiction, and responsibilities. This figure shows the 1998 organizational chart of the Metropolitan Police of the City of St. Louis, Missouri. Compare it with a big-city department near you.

Given that 75 percent of municipal policing takes place in small and medium-sized towns, it is perhaps unfortunate that most of what we know about police in action is based on studies of big-city departments. On the other hand, crimes that Americans fear most—robberies, rapes, assaults, homicides, gang violence, and drug trafficking—occur disproportionately in our larger cities, and the demand for an efficient and effective police response inevitably draws attention to the organization and routine activities of big-city departments.

Specialized and Limited-Purpose Police Agencies

In addition to federal, state, county, and municipal agencies with broad policing responsibilities, other police organizations can be found with more specialized or limited purposes. University, housing, transit, port authority, park, public school, and airport police are examples. Table 5.3 shows a more complete list. Some of these agencies employ hundreds of full-time sworn officers. New York City, for example, employs *thousands* in its transit, housing, and public school police. But most special-purpose agencies are relatively small. Despite their firearms and powers of arrest, officers in many special-purpose agencies are often regarded as not "real" police, a view that for years was reinforced by questionable recruitment practices, scant training, and much lower pay.

Today, even though many special-purpose police officers may still be viewed as glorified security guards, it appears that the push to professionalize policing and raise standards is paying off in terms of image and expectations. Some of these improvements are due to changes in the populations served and the problems encountered. Campus police are a good example. Many universities and colleges have recognized that increases in student diversity, the advent of the commuting student, and the increasing use of evening and weekend classes have made the job of campus security much more difficult and challenging. The response among many larger campus police departments has been to broaden and improve their policing activities. Modern campus police departments are capable of responding to most policing needs: They monitor alarms, secure buildings, conduct criminal investigations, provide safety escorts, enforce vehicle traffic and safety laws, and control crowds (Reaves, 1996).

TABLE 5.3 Special-Purpose Police Agencies, 1996

Type of Special Purpose	Number of Agencies	Number of Sworn Personnel*
College/university campus	699	10,496
Natural resources/conservation	79	8,395
Public school district	117	5,247
Transportation	28	4,274
Parks/recreation facilities	68	2,595
Airport	84	2,407
Waterways/harbors	38	1,291
Public housing	13	1,245
Alcohol beverage control	17	1,199
State capitol/government buildings	24	988
Public sanitation district	3	193
Gaming/racing laws	5	190
Other	69	4,562
Total	1,316	43,082

Source: Brian A. Reaves and Andrew L. Goldberg (1998). "Census of State and Local Law Enforcement Agencies, 1996 (Table 14)." *BJS Bulletin* June:1–15.

Such is the case at Southern Illinois University, Edwardsville, a medium-sized state university of 11,000 students but with a large campus of 2,600 acres. Officers are trained at the Illinois State Police Academy alongside recruits from many other police departments around the state. The department is well equipped and capable of responding to almost any type of emergency. Its officers routinely participate in collaborative law enforcement efforts throughout the region. The department has also received federal grants to implement and test innovative policing programs.

RELATIONS BETWEEN FEDERAL, STATE, AND LOCAL POLICE

It is impossible to discuss policing in the United States without considering the relationship between federal and local police agencies. As noted previously, American police work at various jurisdictional levels: city, county, state, and federal. Overlap is inevitable, although only federal agencies have the authority to operate in *all* cities, counties, and states. The justification usually offered for the hodgepodge of American police forces is that "freedom, and a healthy system of checks and balances arising out of interagency competition, precludes the creation of a national police force. This is a deeply, one might say passionately, held belief, and it is for the time being politically unassailable" (Geller and Morris, 1992:233). So how do we make the best of this fragmentation in policing?

The first step is to see things in perspective. Even though the number of federal agencies has mushroomed over the past century, federal police are outnumbered 10 to 1 by their nonfederal colleagues; the FBI, which in 1991 had just over 10,000 special agents, has *less than half* the number of police officers assigned to the precincts of New York City. Yet without the presence and cooperation of federal agencies such as the FBI, ATF, and DEA, New York City police would find their crime-fighting efforts seriously hampered.

A second thing to keep in mind are agency conflicts *within* the federal system. Although the past two decades have seen much improvement in relations between federal and local agencies, turf wars among federal police have been rampant. One example is the competition among the FBI, the DEA, the Customs Service, and the Coast Guard in claiming credit for drug seizures. So what are the incentives for cooperation among local, state, and federal agencies?

Incentives for Cooperation and Coordination

First, and probably most important, is the fact that many criminals operate across multiple jurisdictions. It is both inevitable and desirable that agencies from different jurisdictions contribute to the law enforcement effort. It often turns out that each agency has particular benefits to contribute to a joint effort. For example, federal agencies can provide coordination and centralized intelligence gathering, while local police can offer specialized knowledge of local conditions as well as intelligence on the past crimes and criminal associations of local offenders.

A second incentive is the importance of avoiding collisions when operating on the same turf. Imagine the difficulties that are created when one police agency "unwittingly arrests or shoots another's informants or undercover agents or in some way impels another to take precipitate action in arresting or prosecuting suspects without adequate preparation" (Geller and Morris, 1992:250). Not only do such actions undermine the effectiveness of individual police agencies, but they may also result in lost cases, wrongful arrests, and a significant decline in public faith in the police.

Third, some criminals are highly organized and sophisticated, and the complex nature of their crimes requires that agencies team up and pool their knowledge and resources. Whether it is organized crime, environmental crime, white-collar crime, or high-tech crimes, local police generally consider themselves ill-equipped and lacking sufficient experience to get involved. Even gang-related crimes may be too much for some city departments. Cooperation from federal or state police agencies is often a precondition for local involvement. Local officers often benefit from on-the-job training by their state or federal colleagues, from whom they learn about new crime-fighting ideas and technologies.

A fourth incentive for cooperation and coordination is the danger of becoming the unwitting dupe of criminals who recognize the value of agency conflicts and disarray. Participants in ongoing criminal enterprises, from moonshiners to sophisticated organized criminals, have been known to play one agency against the other—for example, offering information or "deals" to the local police, while providing better information or deals to the feds. Better federal-local coordination and collaboration can help prevent such actions.

Finally, and especially in dealings with large city or county departments, federal law enforcement agencies find a substantial incentive to collaborate in the large number of talented and often highly motivated local police that can be called upon to assist them. In return, the local police often enjoy considerable kudos when they help crack a complex or high-profile federal case.

DISINCENTIVES FOR COOPERATION AND COORDINATION

Working against these incentives are various negative factors. For example, traditions of local independence are hard to shake, and some city officials are embarrassed when local crime problems attract federal attention. This independence is reinforced by various statutes, guidelines, and policy statements at both local and federal levels. These inhibit some forms of collaboration by prohibiting them altogether or by establishing priorities that curb interagency cooperation. For example, "the federal criminal justice system is not designed to handle juveniles. Cases involving adults are also declined if the dollar loss is not sufficient to meet federal prosecution requirements" (Conly, 1989:39).

Another disincentive for cooperation is the expectation, sometimes justified, among federal officers that local police will be insufficiently qualified or are not trustworthy enough to be of real help in an investigation (Geller and Morris, 1992:269–270). Similarly, local police may not be able to retrieve important data that may be needed in a cooperative investigation. Sometimes local police have the appropriate data but declare it nonsharable, perhaps because it relates to protection of local police informants, or perhaps because to do so would violate an individual's right to privacy.

One long-standing obstacle to cooperation and coordination across police agencies is the jealousy that sometimes results—most commonly, it seems, on the part of local police—when the "other" agency grabs the headlines and takes credit for arrests that result from a joint operation. Local police may also fear that a joint investigation will result in loss of control over their own cases. This fear is not unrealistic, given the broader jurisdictional powers of federal and state authorities, and the greater resources and skills they often bring with them.

asset forfeiture Property and cash are confiscated if they have been used in the commission of crimes or are the fruits of such activities.

Asset forfeiture, which occurs, for example, when the police confiscate the car, house, or other possessions of a suspected drug dealer, may act as either an incentive or a disincentive for cooperation among agencies. Asset forfeitures exceed $1 billion a year, and an incentive for cooperation is that a lot of that money is divided up among cooperating agencies. But the money often filters across jurisdictions very slowly. Recent efforts to simplify and speed up processing of forfeiture shares may result in *reduced* cooperation among local and state agencies (Geller and Morris, 1992:274). This is because the fewer partners there are, the more money each one gets.

Other disincentives to cooperation, collaboration, and coordination among police agencies include (1) the amount of time and effort often required in developing joint initiatives; (2) the reluctance of local departments with strapped resources to reassign officers, thereby losing their services; (3) political pressures to "get on with the job" instead of investing in long-term strategic planning among agencies; and (4) the reluctance of agencies to share intelligence, thereby risking loss of the capacity to safeguard its use. Clearly, long-term, effective cooperation among police agencies cannot be taken for granted, and the obstacles preventing it are formidable.

RURAL POLICING

As already emphasized, most of what we know about policing has come from studies of big-city police departments. However, the National Institute of Justice (NIJ), a research unit of the U.S. Department of Justice, is currently engaged in a long-term study of rural law enforcement, which should help clarify the picture (Bureau of Justice Assistance, 1994b:3).

One thing to keep in mind is that rural communities are by no means homogeneous with respect to law enforcement needs and problems. For example, some rural areas have very stable communities with long histories and strong ties among families residing there; other communities have transient populations, high poverty rates, and some of the same problems found in many large cities: increases in youth crime, drug trafficking, and rates of violent crime.

An NIJ-sponsored review of the sparse literature on rural crime and rural policing has identified some of the special problems facing rural police (Weisheit, Falcone, and Wells, 1994; Weisheit and Wells, 1998):

- Although county police in many rural areas are faced with declining population, declining resources, and deteriorating roads, they are expected to maintain full-service policing over a non-shrinking geographical area.
- Rural culture provides an operating environment for police in which outsiders, especially government agents, are likely to be mistrusted and in which problems are handled privately whenever possible. Informal social control is much preferred over bureaucratic, legalistic formality.
- Rural police are nevertheless expected to provide a wide range of services because other social services are more remote or nonexistent.
- Relations between rural residents and police are likely to be more personalized (people know each other as individuals) and responsive to the history and culture of the community. A study of drug enforcement in a rural community reports this comment from one rural officer describing an arrest:

> You can't act overly high and mighty with them, you won't get any cooperation. . . . This summer I went down and there was a guy with maybe 200 plants spread out over a small farm. I was fairly confident it was there and I pull up in his driveway. He was unloading wood. I'm in the pickup truck, and obviously he knows who I am. I walked up and told him what I was doing there. I said "I've come to get your marijuana and we're going to be doing an open field search. . . . I've just come up here to tell you what I'm doing." I helped him unload his wood and then I said, "I'm going down by the pond and look at this marijuana. I'll be back in a minute. I went down, looked at it and came back up. I said "Well, your marijuana is down there," and then I went ahead and helped him unload some more wood and talked about it. He went to jail with no problem. I think this was the kind of guy who

> would have liked to have fought you. But because of the way I handled it, he wasn't going to fight anybody. . . . A lot of times if you're dealing with people in these rural areas, they don't have a problem with you coming in and arresting them. They just want to be treated like human beings. (Weisheit, 1993:225)

- Rural policing tends to be highly visible; word spreads quickly and what the police do is soon known around the community. "Small town police enjoy less latitude in deviating from dominant community values as a result" (Weisheit, Falcone, and Wells, 1994:11).
- The greater informality of rural social control makes formal policies and detailed written guidelines for police procedures less important, although required cooperation from other agencies can be an obstacle to effective operations.
- Rural police are faced with highly technical and potentially very dangerous crimes involving the rural environment—including dumping of toxic wastes and sabotage of farms, lumber operations, and nuclear power facilities that they are ill-equipped to handle.

Because their resources are typically far more limited than their urban counterparts, cooperation between state and rural law enforcement agencies is becoming increasingly important (Dighton, 1998a). However, as noted earlier, many state agencies are finding their own resources stretched to the limit. This can pose problems for county and state police who are patrolling rural areas alone. One veteran state trooper commented that "it's lonelier out there than it's ever been in history. I pity the road trooper today" (*St. Louis Post-Dispatch*, February 22, 1998, p. A10). There are also greater personal risks for officers when the nearest backup may be many miles away.

The unique problems facing rural law enforcement will require innovative solutions backed up by research. Simply transplanting urban policing methods and technologies to the hills and farms of rural America is unlikely to be a successful strategy.

PRIVATE POLICING

One of the most interesting trends in policing in recent years has been the growth of private-sector involvement. Even though private policing has existed in the United States for over a century, the public is probably not aware that more people are employed and more money is spent today by private police operations than by all public police agencies combined (see Figure 5.3). The actual figures are staggering: the private security industry employs over 1.5 million people with a budget well over $80 billion a year; by the year 2000 the figures are projected to be 1.7 million and $100 billion, respectively (Cunningham, Strauchs, and Van Meter, 1990).

The growth of private-sector involvement in criminal justice is occurring in two ways: (1) private individuals and organizations are doing work traditionally thought of as the responsibility of governments; and (2) criminal justice personnel employed by the government are working for the private sector.

PRIVATIZATION

privatization Occurs when activities and agencies traditionally run by the government are handed over to the private sector.

The first situation involves private individuals or agencies doing work usually done by governments is often referred to as **privatization**. It is controversial, and its benefits are by no means established. Most controversial is the use of private-sector organizations to finance, build, run, and essentially control entire law enforcement operations. The typical setting for this type of privatization is in the correctional field, which will be examined in more detail in Chapter 15. Briefly, however, in 1988, there were thirteen private jails and prisons operat-

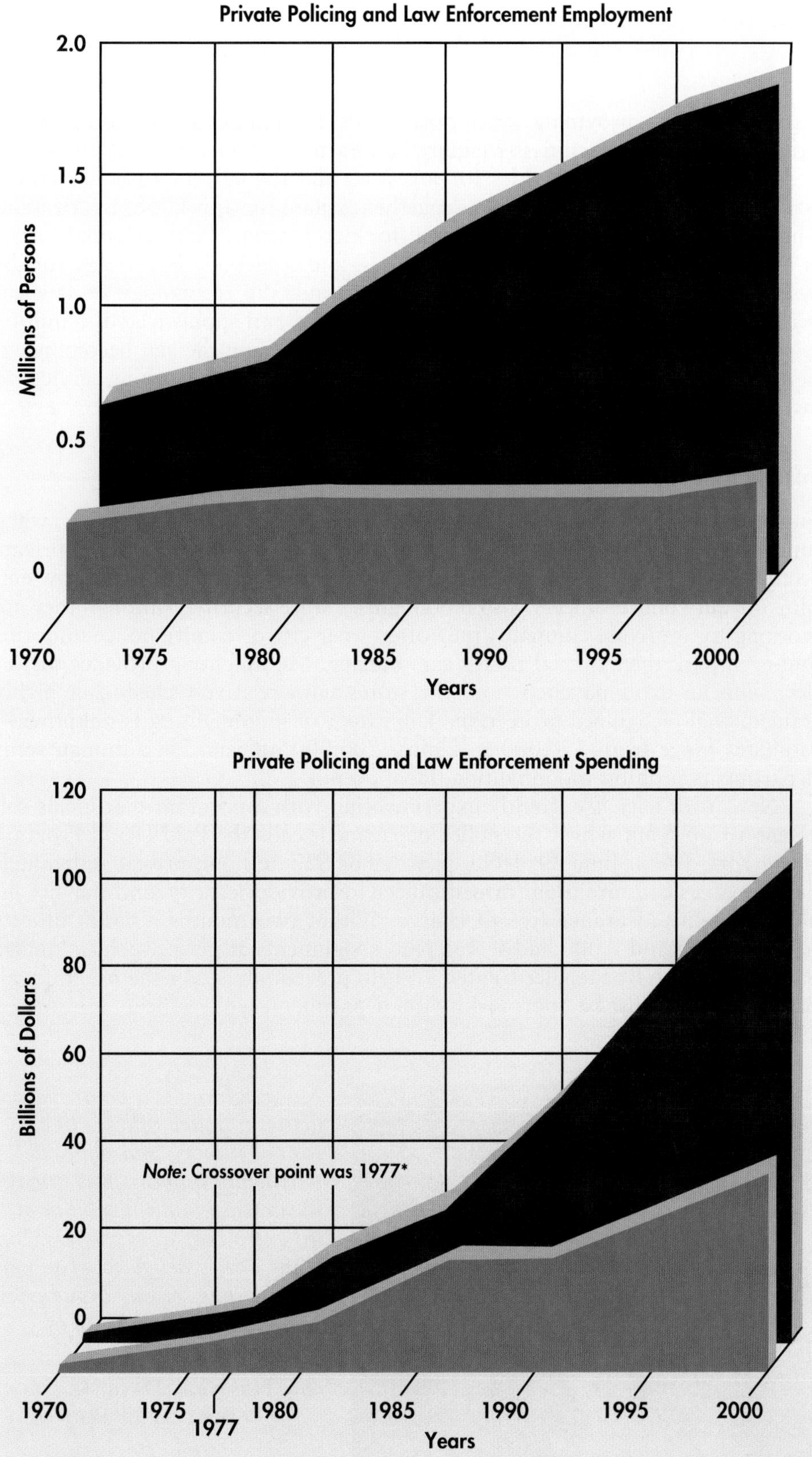

FIGURE 5.3 EMPLOYMENT AND SPENDING IN PRIVATE POLICING
While both public and private police employment and expenditures have increased dramatically since 1970, today more money is spent, and more people are employed, in private police operations than in the public sector.

*Crossover point is where annual spending on private police first exceeded spending on public police.

Source: National Institute of Justice (1991). *Research in Brief* (p. 3). Washington, D.C.: U.S. Department of Justice.

ing in nine states, providing 1,910 prison beds. By January 1994, there were 67 private correctional facilities (Maguire and Pastore, 1994:116–122).

The financial opportunities for investors and the current rush to "downsize" government and reduce taxes together explain the appeal of privatization. The financial incentives are substantial for two reasons. First, criminal justice is big business: There are a lot of criminals, and somebody has to pay for the system that catches and processes them. Second, the technology of law enforcement is becoming more and more specialized and sophisticated, requiring expensive experts and services. Even professors get in on the act, becoming expert witnesses, doing research for law firms, or providing consulting services to law enforcement agencies (Gitchoff, 1988).

"MOONLIGHTING"

moonlighting Off-duty police officers provide security services to private companies.

Financial considerations also dominate the other side of the coin, that is, when uniformed police officers and other justice personnel **moonlight** in the private sector. Grocery, department, and discount store chains in many states now employ off-duty police officers who moonlight as store security. Although they are working for a private company, they often wear city or county police uniforms and even park their official patrol cars outside. Moonlighting provides the officer with an extra paycheck and the stores with relatively cheap but highly trained, well-recognized protection. The extent of moonlighting is unknown—estimates range from 150,000 to almost 200,000 officers. Even though some departments prohibit moonlighting, most do not.

New York City is currently experimenting with a program that locals call "Rent-a-Cop," but which the police department calls the Paid Detail Program (*New York Times,* June 29, 1998, p. B1). For $27 an hour, private individuals or companies can hire a uniformed officer to provide security, and the city includes liability insurance free of charge. Within two months, 10,000 officers had signed on and 2,000 had served paid assignments at places such as Yankee Stadium and the Rockefeller Center. To help prevent abuses of the program, all private renters must be approved by the department, while officers are rotated

Moonlighting is a controversial activity; police officers like it for the money, and many departments support it as a way to increase police visibility at no extra cost to taxpayers. But some critics believe that moonlighting has serious drawbacks as well. What are some of them?

PHOTO BY DAVID K. CROW, COURTESY OF PHOTOEDIT

among renters to avoid the development of personal ties between renters and particular officers. The department sees the program as a way to provide more police services with no increased cost to the taxpayer; rank-and-file officers like it for the additional money they can earn. Yet there are negative aspects to police moonlighting, as we shall see in a moment.

The Private Security Industry

When people think of private police they most likely have in mind protection and detection agencies such as Pinkerton's, Wells Fargo, or the Brinks armored delivery service, all founded in the 1850s. These agencies, along with many others, provide security to banks, airports, shopping malls, nuclear facilities, and all manner of businesses and many public agencies as well. The scope of private policing is now immense: Large corporations, small businesses, and thousands of individuals now routinely hire the services of private police. Much of this policing is open and visible, but a lot is not: Many firms, concerned about becoming victims of employee pilfering, computer hackers, and competitors' spies now hire undercover police who work alongside employees; some even offer regular employees incentives to spy on each other, making police out of their own workforce. Security personnel have been known to engage in secret videotaping of employee lunchrooms and rest areas.

In contrast to the early days, when training, licensing, and regulation were virtually nonexistent, private security in most states today is a different story. Even so, many security guards are poorly trained by public police standards and their duties are limited; their low pay reflects this. Efforts to professionalize the private security industry have had some success: Many states now require licensing and special training, especially for armed guards, and background checks are more rigorous. The American Society for Industrial Security (ASIS) provides certification of "protection professionals." Topics covered include loss prevention (important in the retail industry), physical security, investigations, and security management. Specialized topics such as computer security and nuclear power security are also included in the examination for people planning careers in those areas (*Security Management,* 1990:97–104).

Unresolved Issues in Private Policing

A number of important issues have been raised regarding private policing, many of them still unresolved. Some concerns are practical—about costs, efficiency, performance, control—while others are ethical—about the prospects that fraud, extortion, or bribery will occur as profiteers seek to tap into this billion-dollar industry.

Equity and Hidden Justice. One ethical issue concerns equity: Is it fair that the rich should be able to buy security in addition to that provided through taxation? Furthermore, if the rich can buy their own security, perhaps they will be less inclined to support increased taxation to finance and improve public police. Another issue concerns the possibility of conflicts of interest that arise out of moonlighting: When police officers serve private interests, will they also be as diligent, professional, and alert in serving public interests? When private employers can provide quick pay increases, promotions, and special bonuses for loyalty and discretionary actions that put the company first, these incentives may undermine the public interest. This can happen in various ways:

- By drawing well-trained—at public expense!—officers away from public service
- By encouraging on-duty officers to provide better police services to the businesses that hire them off-duty

- By encouraging officers to structure their investigative and arrest actions according to company policy rather than public law
- By encouraging moonlighters to think of the private company as their "main" employer, and their public police work as secondary

Of great concern to many criminal justice professionals is an issue raised in the so-called *Hallcrest Report II*, published in 1990 (Cunningham, Strauchs, and Van Meter, 1990). Apart from documenting the tremendous growth in private policing, this report showed that many crimes and other law violations uncovered by private policing operations do not become part of the official record. If they do reach the official system, they are disposed of in proceedings that rarely come to light—for example, through back-room deals. There are, in essence, two criminal justice systems: one public and one private. The private system is less likely to be concerned about the public good; the interests of the paying client come first.

It seems inevitable that the scope of external control over individual behavior will continue to widen, especially now that private individuals and corporations are major players in criminal justice (Cohen, 1985). The real challenge facing policymakers concerned about the structure and delivery of policing services will be to devise strategies that provide protection and justice to *all* citizens, not just those with financial clout.

THE FUNCTIONS OF MODERN POLICING

Now that we have explored the history and organization of policing in America, it is time to consider this important question: How does a modern democratic society such as ours use its police? This question draws attention to the social functions of policing.

ORDER MAINTENANCE

Imagine a society in which chaos reigned. Little would get done; people would never be sure what was going to happen next; goals would be meaningless; organizations would be impossible to form or maintain; rules would be worthless; everything would be up for grabs; might would prevail and universal rights would be nonexistent. For a society to function smoothly, public order must be maintained. In modern societies, that job falls primarily on the shoulders of the police. Much police time and effort is therefore spent on **order maintenance**, also referred to as "peacekeeping."

order maintenance The peacekeeping function of policing: handling disputes, dealing with troublemakers, keeping things quiet.

When we see police officers patrolling the streets, dealing with disputes, handling juvenile troublemakers, responding to complaints about rowdy parties or boom boxes cranked up too high, we are witnessing order maintenance. Much of this peacekeeping is actually very informal, almost casual. Police officers understand that keeping things under control usually means nothing more than "fixing up" trouble or "handling the situation" so that no one complains that they are doing too little or too much (Wilson, 1968:31). Arrests are rarely made, and a lot of the time patrolling officers appear to be doing nothing specific (Cordner, 1989). Their presence and their ability to act when necessary carry a powerful message that helps peace prevail, at least in public places.

The informality of most peacekeeping activities reflects the fact that they are not focused on crime—particularly serious crime. This is evident when citizen calls for police service are analyzed. In one study, only 36 percent of calls involved a criminal complaint; in another, only 19 percent did so (Scott, 1981). But even when crime is involved, police exercise a considerable amount of discretion and decide in many cases not to make an arrest—and in some cases, not to respond at all. As long as officers feel that order is not seriously threatened or has been restored, they can claim to have met their peacekeeping obligations.

SERVICE

Up to 50 percent of police activity involves assisting citizens who have a problem and who turn to the police for help. As with order maintenance, the **service function** is not generally about crime. The police service role includes giving information, helping people find things, getting cats out of trees, helping stranded motorists, dealing with drug overdoses, helping ambulances reach patients, taking injured or ill people to the hospital, or helping young children, the disabled, or the elderly cross a street. Sometimes the service function overlaps with order maintenance, as seen in Box 5.4; this overlap seems to be increasing. In general, successful handling of personal problems helps prevent them from threatening the well-being of others, perhaps the entire community.

service function Providing assistance to citizens with problems.

LAW ENFORCEMENT AND CRIME PREVENTION

The police carry guns and handcuffs, wear bulletproof clothing, send officers undercover, purchase the services of informers, dust for fingerprints, testify at trials, enforce speeding laws, collect and maintain arrest records, employ high-tech detection equipment, and arrest people as part of their law enforcement and crime prevention roles. While some experts favor stressing law enforcement over crime prevention, and vice versa, a fusing of these two roles is advocated by others (Walker, 1992). They are therefore coupled in this discussion.

When police enforce speed laws, arrest suspects, or infiltrate a suspected drug trafficking operation, they are engaged in **law enforcement**. When police teach youngsters how to avoid being kidnapped or resist pressures to use drugs, or when they help business owners burglar-proof their premises or conduct neighborhood watch seminars, they are engaged in **crime prevention**. The visibility of patrolling officers provides the police patrol with a potential crime prevention aspect—people contemplating a crime may refrain from going through with it for fear of being caught and punished. Of course, some law enforcement activities also result in the prevention of crimes: Arresting a suspect may prevent a future crime, if not by that suspect, then by others who saw the arrest or know about it. This *deterrent* role of policing is discussed in more detail in Chapters 7 and 8.

law enforcement Arresting suspects, infiltrating criminal gangs, or giving traffic tickets.

crime prevention Teaching people how to avoid becoming victims of crime, aggressive patrolling of trouble spots, or teaching youngsters to resist drugs.

The law enforcement/crime prevention function of policing is the role that many police officers and many members of the public believe should be at the core of police operations. It certainly fits the media image of policing, and the great success of crime-fighting fiction on film and in books suggests that the public appetite for it is vast. Yet most of the time the police—or more precisely, patrolling police officers—are neither actively enforcing the law nor actively preventing crime. The bulk of traditional police work is taken up with such activities as the following (Felson, 1998:5):

- Driving around a lot
- Asking people to quiet down
- Hearing complaints about barking dogs
- Filling out paperwork
- Meeting with other police officers
- Waiting to be called up in court

Many patrolling officers see their enforcement activities as episodic and often crisis driven, as when something is defined by police managers as an emergency or pressing problem requiring immediate enforcement action. A gang war, for example, or a sudden rash of complaints about prostitution or trouble-making

Box 5.4

JUSTICE INNOVATIONS

POLICING SPECIAL POPULATIONS

Special populations such as the mentally ill, teenage runaways, and the homeless bring service and peacekeeping functions together and sometimes require a more specialized police response. Here are four locations around the country where police are making special efforts to address the challenge of policing special populations.

Springfield, Illinois. In 1998 the Illinois State Police revised its procedures for handling people suspected of suffering from mental illness after a 39-day standoff between police and a woman facing a court-ordered psychiatric examination. The police had tried unsuccessfully to coax the woman out of her home by methods ranging from playing Barry Manilow music to nonstop loudspeaker patter. The woman shot a police dog sent in to find her, and fired out of windows on other occasions. Police finally captured her when she stepped onto her back porch and was knocked down by rubber bullets. The standoff cost the state $650,000. All state police will now be given more training and special guidelines for dealing with the mentally ill, and full-time tactical teams will be established for dealing with crisis situations.

Los Angeles, California. The Los Angeles Police Department requires all 7,000 police officers to call an emergency Mental Evaluation Unit for 24-hour assistance in handling, screening, and transporting suspected mentally ill people. The unit is staffed by nine detectives and receives 550 to 600 calls a month from patrol officers.

A unit detective prescreens cases over the phone and suggests how to handle them. The detective then either goes to the scene to take over the case or tells the patrol officers to bring the person to the Mental Evaluation Unit office. Whether in the office or on the scene, the unit officer assesses the person's condition and, if appropriate, tells the patrol officers to take the person to the hospital.

youths, or an upsurge in robberies might constitute such a crisis. Police sometimes perceive enforcement activities, particularly making arrests, as primarily a means to fulfilling other goals: a weekly quota of arrests, getting a favorable assignment, being promoted, or simply relieving boredom.

Where exactly the balance lies among the three primary functions of policing is difficult to say. In any case, it is unlikely to remain stable from year to year or be the same across different departments. Rural and small-town departments tend to do more service activities than either law enforcement, crime prevention, or order maintenance; on the other hand, the balance across big-city departments is likely to vary considerably, depending on such things as crime rates, the average age of the population (more young people means more order maintenance *and* more crime), residential mobility, local economic and political conditions, and the size and resources of the police department.

SUMMARY

It is easy to take policing for granted. After all, most of us are used to the presence of police in our daily lives. As likely as not, our image of policing is based on a mixture of personal and vicarious experience coupled with what we have

Box 5.4 (CONTINUED)

Boston, Massachusetts. Police in a downtown Boston police precinct may take homeless people (including intoxicated and mentally ill street people) to the Pine Street Inn at any hour of the night. The Inn is the largest shelter for the homeless in the city.

The precinct captain keeps his officers informed about the small number of individuals—mainly those who are violent or have serious medical problems—whom the Inn will not accept. The captain also instructs officers to wait a few minutes at the Inn until unit staff admit the referral, rather than leaving the person at the door and driving off, as in the past.

The State Department of Welfare spends $148,000 a year to station an off-duty officer at the Inn during each shift. The special-duty officers often show other officers how to handle homeless people without inciting trouble, and they often double-check to make sure only appropriate referrals are brought in by on-duty officers. The police presence also helps keep the atmosphere calm at Pine Street.

Washtenaw County, Michigan. The 150 sheriff's deputies in Washtenaw County have 24-hour access to the County Community Mental Health Center for telephone consultation and on-site crisis intervention for encounters involving the mentally ill. Written protocols in the Sheriff's Policy and Procedures Manual describe each participating agency's responsibilities. Deputies carry wallet cards that list the steps for dealing with a suspected mentally ill person.

If a subject needs only outpatient health services, the deputy calls the mental health center for appropriate referrals. If the center's clinician believes the person may need hospitalization, the clinician telephones the psychiatric facility nearest the scene to arrange an evaluation. The sheriff's deputy transports the person to the facility. If the client's condition is volatile, however, the center dispatches a two-person team to the scene to provide crisis intervention and accompany the deputy sheriff in taking the person to the hospital. In extreme cases, deputies may transport the individual directly to the center for assistance.

Sources: Associated Press, May 16, 1998; Peter E. Finn, and Monique Sullivan (1988). "Police Respond to Special Populations." *NIJ Reports* (May–June):7–8.

picked up from radio, television, books, movies, and newspapers. If we ask any critical questions of policing, it is probably in reference to specific events rather than more abstract issues, such as its structure and functioning. Have you ever wondered what society would be like without police as we know them?

In this chapter we explored the history, organization, and functions of the police in America. Our brief history of policing showed that the police as we know them are a modern invention, going back barely 200 years. Before that time, towns and villages policed themselves through community-based surveillance. The rise of capitalism and the Industrial Revolution brought about tremendous growth in cities and a breakdown of the existing social order. The London "New Police" were formed in large part to counter growing urban unrest and threats to propertied interests posed by the so-called dangerous classes. In America, cities facing similar problems borrowed the English model, although modern policing in this country was far more politicized and has remained so to this day. The American police also operate under a highly complicated system of jurisdictional controls, with local, county, state, and federal governments exercising varying degrees of authority. Relations between agencies are complex, and we saw that cooperation and coordination cannot be taken for granted.

While the focus of discussion in the next four chapters will be mainly on urban police at work, rural policing was briefly addressed to show some of the special problems and issues that face police agencies in those areas. It is clear that much more research needs to be done. The same is true of private policing. Although there has been phenomenal growth in private policing over the past two decades, many important ethical and practical issues remain unresolved, such as whether society should continue to support two criminal justice systems, one public and one private, whose functions and goals may be at odds.

We discussed three main functions of modern policing: order maintenance or peacekeeping, service, and law enforcement/crime prevention. The job of maintaining public order, essential for the smooth functioning of society, falls mainly to patrolling police officers, who handle problems informally whenever they can. Crime, especially serious crime, is not the main focus of this activity. Nor is crime important within the service role, which is about giving assistance. The overlap between order maintenance and service functions is apparent, and it may be increasing due to the growth of populations with special problems. Although law enforcement and crime prevention take up the least time and energy of the typical patrol officer's day, it is the role that most police and many citizens believe should be at the core of police operations.

What do you think now?

- Based on what you read, what similarities and differences did you find between local, state, and federal police agencies?
- What keeps federal and local police forces from working together more efficiently? What approaches do you think would alleviate this problem?
- Are the three police functions given equal weight by police where you live? If not, why not?

Key terms

frankpledge system
constable
sheriff
posse comitatus
hue and cry
watch system
thief taker
Bow Street Runners
New Police (Bobbies)
politicization
profiling
asset forfeiture
privatization
moonlighting
order maintenance
service function
law enforcement
crime prevention

Active learning challenges

1. Have the class discuss the merits of reintroducing community-based surveillance as a cornerstone of modern policing. Suggest practical ways in which this might be done—and look at Chapter 6 for some ideas.
2. Discuss ways that cooperation could be enhanced between federal, state, and local police agencies. Also consider what cooperative steps might aid rural police in addressing their special problems.
3. Break the class into two groups: those who support increased privatization of policing, and those who oppose it. Have each group research their view and present arguments to support their position.

4. Divide the class into three groups: those who feel peacekeeping is the most important function of policing, those who feel service is the most important function, and those who feel crime prevention is most important. Have each group develop arguments, including research evidence, to support their position.

INTERNET CHALLENGES

The Web pages mentioned here can all be accessed through the Web site for this textbook at **http://www.prenhall.com/barlow/.**

1. Explore federal law enforcement activities through the Web sites of federal agencies. A good place to start is the FBI. Find out who is currently on the Ten Most Wanted List, and check out the latest Crime Alert.
2. Visit the Web sites of rural sheriff's departments in your state and see whether you can identify special problems they face, innovations they have made, and the nature of their relationship with other police agencies. Start with the home page of a county, and then follow the link to the sheriff.
3. Learn more about privatization of policing by visiting the Web sites of the American and British security industries: ASIS Online and BSIA. Check out their links; you will find interesting business opportunities.

CHAPTER 6

CULTURE AND STYLES OF POLICING

LEARNING OBJECTIVES

- Describe "cop culture" and its impact on the attitudes and behaviors of police officers.
- Explain the screening process involved in recruiting police officers, including hiring criteria, testing, and interviews.
- Describe recent trends in the employment of women and minorities in policing.
- Understand the purpose of affirmative action programs and why they are controversial in the hiring and promotion of police.
- Describe the elements of the police "working personality," and understand how training and on-the-job experiences shape behavior.
- Understand the role of stereotypes in shaping the patrolling practices of police.
- Distinguish between different styles of policing.
- Describe the various methods and successes of proactive policing, and explain why community policing remains controversial.

The legalistic approach to policing focuses on enforcing laws and maintaining order. While a service-oriented police department may give a warning for a small traffic infraction, a legalistic department is more likely to issue a citation.

PHOTO BY BOB DAEMMRICH, COURTESY OF UNPHOTO

Being a cop is solidarity personified. . . . [I]t is a sharing of identity. . . . Take an officer from the high deserts of Idaho and put him on the mean streets of Savannah, and it will not take long to work out the differences.

JOHN CRANK, *UNDERSTANDING POLICE CULTURE* (1998)

People don't like cops. People don't like us. I get a reaction when I see a cop—and I'm a cop. I'll be driving down the street in a police car. I look up, and there's a squad car in my rear view mirror. I think, what does this asshole want? What's he doing following me?

CONNIE FLETCHER, *WHAT COPS KNOW* (1990)

The idea of becoming a police officer was something that Phyllis Mann had kept to herself during high school. She had not even told her family, although the stories her father, a sheriff's deputy, had brought home had first kindled the idea. She had spent a lot of time around cops and saw them as a powerful force for good in society. Yet she also saw policing as a man's world, where masculinity is prized. She had often heard that police work was no place for women. Nevertheless, increasing numbers of women were entering police work, and she had even heard some veteran cops offer grudging praise of the way female officers had handled tense situations on the street.

Now in college, Phyllis had moved her idea forward by becoming a criminal justice major. She enjoyed learning about the history and problems of criminal justice, and particularly appreciated the contributions of part-time faculty drawn from local criminal justice agencies. These teachers brought their personal experiences into the classroom, and students learned about the perils and pleasures of working in the criminal justice system. It put a human face on the facts and theories learned in class.

The highlight of the degree program was the required internship, which Phyllis was to take the next semester. She had been accepted into the internship program run by the state police. This program was highly regarded by students and professors, and competition for the fifteen slots was always fierce. Phyllis would be assigned to a state police officer for the duration of the internship, and would be exposed to all aspects of the job, from routine highway patrol to criminal investigations. She looked forward to the challenge and expected the hands-on experience to confirm that she was making the right career choice.

Phyllis Mann is at an important threshold in her life; the career decision she makes will have long-term consequences. If she enters police work she will be drawn into a unique and complex world that mixes suspicion, fear, violence, tragedy, and boredom with generosity, pride, kindness, corruption, and unpredictability. She will find that her personal identity and her social relationships are redefined by the overwhelming influence of a **police culture**—the shared values, activities, and attitudes characteristic of people in law enforcement. Its presence is expressed bluntly by these words on a T-shirt worn by an off-duty officer: "It's a Cop Thing. You Wouldn't Understand" (Crank, 1998:13).

police culture Shared values, activities, and attitudes that are characteristic of people in law enforcement.

She will have considerable power by virtue of her position as an enforcer of the law; however, she will also be the target of verbal and physical abuse, and must constantly guard against temptations to abuse her authority and to violate the public's trust. Since the stakes are high for everyone involved, Phyllis's performance will be under intense scrutiny—by police administrators, by her fellow officers, by the courts, by the media, by her family and friends, and by the citizens she interacts with on the street. Every decision police officers make, including decisions to do nothing, is potentially a threat to themselves or to someone else. This makes police work unique. When students such as Phyllis Mann embark on a career in policing, they are entering a world that requires most of them to think and act in a whole new way. To the police, even everyday objects such as garbage cans take on new meaning: They are places where dead babies are thrown (Shearing and Ericson, 1991:490).

In this chapter and the next three we learn about the complexities of policing by exploring the police at work. This is not an easy task because of the mystery that surrounds real police work. This mystery results from a number of different things:

- Fear that sensitive information may get out to the "wrong" people
- A police culture that emphasizes "Us" (the police) versus "Them" (everyone else)
- A need to protect ongoing investigations
- Police vulnerability to lawsuits and to negative press
- The legal and bureaucratic jargon used in criminal justice circles
- The increasingly sophisticated technology of policing

As if to deepen the mystery, some police officers have difficulty identifying the goals of their work, or even what they do every day (Ryan, 1994). It is the aim of these chapters to peel back the veil of secrecy surrounding police work in America. We will begin our exploration of the police at work by examining the recruitment process. Our first question will be: Is there anything distinctive about people who become police officers?

WHAT DO YOU THINK?

- What sorts of people go into police work? Are they different from other people?
- Do you think that women or minorities have a harder time being hired and accepted by police departments? Why or why not?
- What do you feel is the main function of police: keeping watch (to ensure peace), offering services such as mediation and problem solving to the community, or crime solving/law enforcement? Why?

THE RECRUITMENT OF POLICE OFFICERS

There are few indications that police recruits are particularly different from those who enter many other occupations. Historically, police recruits usually came from a lower-middle or working-class background. They usually had no more than a high school education, and most had some previous work experience in clerical, sales, or manual jobs, or in the military. As for personality traits, no basis exists for distinguishing police recruits from people with similar backgrounds. It used to be thought that police recruits were more authoritarian and conservative than other people. Authoritarianism is a personality trait associated with bigotry, violence, cynicism, and suspicion. However, after exhaustive studies during the 1960s, psychologists concluded that there was "no self-selection among authoritarian personalities prior to appointment" (Niederhoffer, 1967:159). This conclusion has not changed over the past 30 years (Balch, 1977; Crank, 1998).

WHY BECOME A POLICE OFFICER?

Why, then, do individuals enter police work? They do so for reasons such as security, decent working conditions, adventure, and relatively good pay. These things make the job attractive to people with little formal education, few marketable skills, and family backgrounds in insecure lower-class occupations. When questioned about their reasons for joining the police, officers voice many of the same reasons that lead people to seek nonpolice jobs: variety of work performed, responsibility, security, benefits, and pay. However, since police work also conjures up images of adventure and public service, recruits also mention these as reasons for joining (Slater and Reiser, 1990). Even so, few officers say they took up police work solely because it promised them excitement or the opportunity to rid society of dangerous criminals.

Nevertheless, some police recruits are clearly predisposed to police work; they have grown up to embrace attitudes and beliefs about the world that fit with police work. For example, like Phyllis Mann, many Americans have grown up in families with connections to police, military, and firefighting organizations. In police families, "generational loyalties develop early and tend to be strong," so a "reservoir of solidarity [with police culture] is already well in place prior to formal recruitment" (Crank, 1998:192). Alternatively, some people have had positive experiences with neighborhood police officers while they were growing up, and this may have encouraged identification with police and policing. The values and traditions of rural and small-town America also support the development of positive attitudes toward the police, who are seen as "the last bastion of protection against the crime and decadence of large cities" (Crank, 1998:193). Finally, many older recruits have a military background, and military culture closely parallels police culture with its emphasis on loyalty, danger, togetherness, masculinity, duty, and the hierarchical command structure of its underlying organization.

SCREENING RECRUITS

Today, most law enforcement agencies carefully screen their applicants. The selection process starts with the specification of hiring criteria—the minimal qualifications necessary for the job—and includes testing and interviewing.

Hiring Criteria. Although the specific qualifications for admission to police work are not uniform throughout the country, the following criteria are fairly standard among city, county, and state police departments: (1) citizenship of the United States; (2) a minimum age of 21; (3) no prior felony convictions; (4) no prior convictions for "moral turpitude"—for example, sex offenses involving children, or acts of deceit or bribery; (5) a high school diploma or GED equivalency; and (6) physical ability to meet the demands of the job.

Testing. The typical police agency requires applicants to pass a standard civil service exam, undergo a battery of other tests and examinations, and pass investigations of their health, background, and character. None of these procedures is without controversy. For example, when background checks turn up illegal drug use in an applicant's past, should he or she be rejected? A survey of police department policies on this issue by *Law Enforcement News* found a virtual consensus among departments that they "would find it all but impossible to recruit if they had policies barring any prior use of drugs at any time in an applicant's past" (Rosen, 1997:11). One way to deal with this problem is to include the prior drug use as one element in the *overall* character of an applicant; if it was a short-lived behavior or is clearly outweighed by evidence of many positive attributes, then the recruit would not be rejected because of the past drug use.

The use of psychological testing of police applicants is perhaps most controversial of all. There are doubts about what the tests really show, and it is widely understood that personality evaluations cannot weed out all undesirable candidates. However, legal challenges to the use of psychological tests have failed largely because courts recognize the special responsibilities and dangers of police work (Inwald and Kenney, 1989:39). Psychological tests have been promoted as a way of predicting on-the-job performance. Yet this idea is not supported by most of the research, which shows that future success as a police officer cannot be predicted on the basis of personality tests of recruits (Burbeck and Furnham, 1985; Wright, Doerner, and Speir, 1990; Alpert, 1991; Walker, 1992; Doerner, 1998). At best, then, psychological tests may be useful in helping screen out potential recruits whose personality profiles suggest mental illness or disorder.

job-related exercises Real-world simulations and other tests that tap problem-solving skills, sensitivity to others, and reactions to stress.

In response to the difficulties of interpreting test results, some police departments have replaced psychological testing with **job-related exercises** that tap skills important in police work. Job-related exercises evaluate recruits' verbal and written skills while also tapping such things as their sensitivity to others, their skill in problem solving, their reactions under stress, and their ability to recall events. Sometimes these tests are conducted with recruits individually, sometimes in groups; the group strategy permits examiners to observe social interactions under a variety of simulated conditions. Job-related exercises and tests have also been promoted as a way to construct screening evaluations that are race and gender neutral. The United States Commission on Civil Rights (1981) has strongly criticized traditional tests of aptitude and ability on the grounds that they reflect the backgrounds, experiences, and attitudes of white males and are therefore biased against minority groups and women.

Interviewing. Interviews are generally carried out by senior officers, sometimes with outside consultants present. Interviews allow them to weed out undesirable recruits who have passed the various written and performance tests.

Traditionally, recruits are regarded as "undesirable" if they hold values, political attitudes, or backgrounds that differ significantly from those of most other officers on the force. The unspoken purpose, or hidden agenda, behind interviews has traditionally been to perpetuate the ethnic, gender, and attitudinal characteristics of people already in police work (Bent, 1974:16). Homogeneity among officers enables the police "brass"—top administrators—to keep existing policies and practices, reduce internal conflicts, and maintain more complete control over their operations. From the standpoint of police culture, the interview selection process is also a way of reinforcing distinctions between "Us" and "Them": Is this recruit one of Us?

Some departments use candidate rating sheets on which to score various qualities of each applicant being interviewed. Here are some of the qualities that might be evaluated (Doerner, 1998:49):

- Appearance: clean appearance, good physical bearing and grooming
- Self-confidence: ability to speak up forcefully with poise and self-assurance, use eye contact with questioner
- Verbal: Ability to express oneself: express thoughts logically and coherently, use proper English, show sincerity
- Written: ability to express oneself in logical, clear writing

Box 6.1

CAREERS IN CRIMINAL JUSTICE

CITY POLICE OFFICER

City police officers perform a wide range of law enforcement, order maintenance, and service activities. Qualifications for the position vary across the country, although most departments require a high school diploma and put recruits through at least 400 hours of academy training. Here are the salary, qualifications, duties, and conditions of employment for Police Officer with the Dallas, Texas, Police Department, as advertised in August 1998:

Salary: $28,498 (trainee) to $29,919 (starting)

Qualifications: 45 semester hours in an accredited college or university with a C average or better; strong communications skills; a firm, reassuring manner and sound judgment under pressure; commitment to public service, professionalism, and a peaceful community.

Duties: To provide law enforcement services to the city, including patrolling; investigations; interviewing suspects; victims, and witnesses; making arrests; responding to citizen requests for assistance; controlling crowds; and providing security services at special events. After completion of training and probationary periods and the required time on patrol, officers may be assigned to specialized operations such as criminal investigations, narcotics and vice investigations, K-9 unit, traffic enforcement, mounted patrol, bomb squad, bicycle squad, or gang unit.

Conditions of Employment: Include 21 years of age (or 19½ years of age and at least 60 semester hours with a C average or better); U.S. citizenship; valid driver's license; no felony convictions; successful completion of civil service test, physical agility exam, polygraph exam, background investigation, psychological evaluation, medical evaluation, and applicant interview.

- Understanding of job: understanding what the job entails, desire to become an officer
- Work history, education, background: interest in personal advancement, trainability, solid work background, self-discipline.

WOMEN AND MINORITIES IN POLICE WORK

The hiring practices of modern police departments are much more open than they used to be. Policing is no longer the preserve of the white male. Today, most departments have some female and minority members among their sworn personnel. Some big-city departments are now headed by women or minorities who have moved up through the ranks. These are significant changes, and they have come about largely because of strong political pressures and affirmative action policies. Many police observers believe that the changes, while slow in coming, have been extremely beneficial for all aspects of policing. Yet some controversies remain, as we shall see.

HOW FAR HAVE WOMEN COME?

Although there is some confusion as to exactly when the first woman was sworn in as a police officer in the United States, most accounts put it during the first decade of the 20th century. Certainly we know that in 1910, Alice Stubbin Wells was sworn in by the Los Angeles Police Department, albeit with restricted duties (Milton, 1972; Bell, 1982). She was not allowed to patrol the streets alone, nor was she permitted to make arrests without a male officer present. By 1919, over 60 departments had female officers. Even so, it took another 60 years before women had an equal legal right to a law enforcement career. Many court battles have been fought in a continuing effort to halt discriminatory employment practices.

Today there are two basic opinions about how far women have come since the 1972 amendments to the Civil Rights Act of 1964 (Martin, 1989, 1997; Fyfe, 1987). One argues that female entry into criminal justice professions has not kept pace with changes in other occupations such as law; the other says that dramatic changes have already occurred. There has certainly been growth in the number of female police officers over the past few years. However, that growth looks more impressive in absolute numbers than it does as a percentage, and some communities have fared much better than others. Although the number of female city police officers grew from 7,383 in 1980 to over 33,000 in 1994, by 1996 they still constituted only 10.1 percent of all city officers (Federal Bureau of Investigation, 1997a). The percentage increases for smaller cities and suburban counties have been smaller than those for large cities. This is largely because traditional views of gender roles are more powerful cultural forces in rural and small-town communities than in large cities. It is also likely that hiring practices that discriminate against women are more difficult to document, and complaints are less likely in smaller communities with little job turnover and heavy use of part-time officers.

Suburban communities and the small towns surrounding major metropolitan areas have experienced considerable growth over the past 20 years in many areas of the country. Population growth brings pressure on existing police services, resulting in the need to recruit new officers; it may also bring to light discriminatory hiring practices that previously went unnoticed. Such was the case in Belleville, Illinois, a community near St. Louis, Missouri. The United States Justice Department filed suit in 1993 claiming that the city had engaged in a pattern of discrimination against female and black applicants for jobs in the police and fire departments. The city denied the allegations—although it employed no black or female officers in either department—but entered into a highly publicized consent decree with the Justice Department that quickly resulted in the hiring of the city's first female and black officers.

Holding Women Back: The Glass Ceiling. One criminology professor who has also spent eighteen years as a part-time cop with the Tallahassee Police Department has written: "The biggest obstacle that female officers face are male officers. The antagonistic and chauvinistic attitudes that women encounter thrust them into the midst of a role conflict. They must choose between being either a *police*woman or a police*woman*" (Doerner, 1998:60). The first wants her co-workers to see her as a professional; she works very hard at being a cop, and answers more than her fair share of calls. The second emphasizes her femaleness; she favors service assignments over crime fighting, and enjoys police work that makes best use of the traditional female gender role—dealing with juveniles, women, and crime victims, for example.

Even when women are accepted into police work, they often find that they are held back despite good performance on the job. Few women achieve the highest administrative ranks, and men dominate in supervisory positions (Martin, 1997). Female officers are still largely found in police jobs that fit stereotypical images of the female role—dealing with juveniles, for example, or helping rape and sexual abuse victims, or being on mediation teams called out to deal with family violence. As important as they are, these jobs are often not the best track to promotion, and female officers who resist such assignments may find themselves fired or put in desk jobs. Even women who do well by accepted standards are often less likely to be promoted than their male counterparts (Martin, 1989:324–326). This is the so-called glass ceiling effect.

Women sometimes suffer from the design of performance evaluation itself (Morash and Greene, 1986). For example, evaluation of patrol performance is geared toward traits that males tend to value, such as physical strength, leadership initiative, and aggressiveness (Bloch and Anderson, 1974). Women do tend to make fewer arrests than men, but this finding is open to competing interpretations, some of which are favorable to women:

> For example, the women's lower arrest rates may mean that women are not taking enough initiative. Alternatively, it might indicate that women handled the situations better than male officers, if the latter caused incidents to escalate into confrontations which resulted in unnecessary arrests. A third explanation is that when a more experienced male patrols with a female rookie, he tends to take charge of the situation and take credit for arrests more frequently than with male rookies. Thus, it is necessary to look beyond the numbers to an interpretation of their meaning. (Martin, 1989:317)

Sexism and Sexual Harassment. Despite mounting evidence (discussed in a moment) that female officers perform their police duties as well as, and sometimes better than, their male counterparts, sexist attitudes and behavior persist among many male officers (Morash, 1986; Martin, 1989, 1997). While most of the opposition to women is expressed in terms of physical inadequacies, "women also pose a threat to work group solidarity by penetrating the emotional masks men wear and inhibiting their use of 'raunchy' language" (Martin, 1989:319). Because formal department policies today forbid gender abuse, the sexism is not as blatant as it once was, but it is there nonetheless. A female officer explains: "It is not very likely that . . . blatant [sexist] statements . . . would be made to my friends or to myself. Instead, they are made in the hallways or locker rooms or in more subtle tones and forms of behavior. You can't change attitudes through rules and regulations" (Herrington, 1997:388).

These observations about the status of women in policing are not confined to the United States. One high-ranking British policewoman claimed she was

Box 6.2

INSIDE CRIMINAL JUSTICE

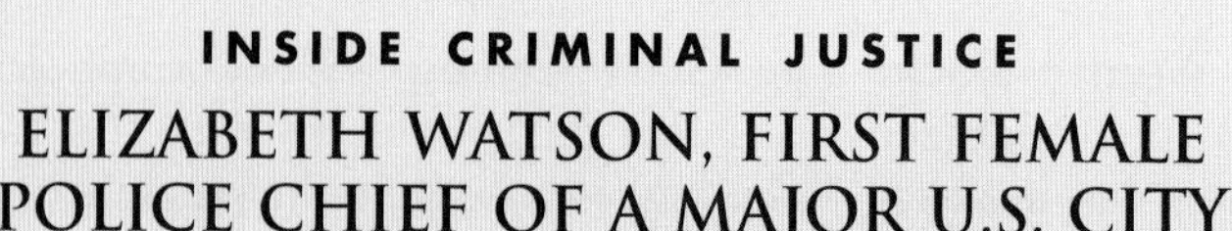

ELIZABETH WATSON, FIRST FEMALE POLICE CHIEF OF A MAJOR U.S. CITY

In June 1995, I had the pleasure of meeting and interviewing Elizabeth Watson, then chief of police of the City of Austin, Texas. Chief Watson entered the Houston, Texas, Police Academy in 1972, and subsequently rose through the ranks of detective, lieutenant, captain, and deputy chief before being appointed Houston's chief of police in January 1990. A change of mayors in 1992 resulted in her being replaced as chief, and she was unanimously appointed chief of police by the Austin city council in August 1992. Chief Watson was strongly influenced by her predecessor and former boss in Houston, Chief Lee Brown, one of the first African Americans to head a major police department.

Among Chief Watson's many accomplishments in policing are the design of Houston's Neighborhood Oriented Policing initiative, receipt of an award for achieving the largest reduction in auto theft among competing cities in the United States, and what she terms the "demilitarization" of policing in Austin, which included dismantling the old-fashioned command hierarchy.

Chief Watson's path to the top was strewn with obstacles, not all of which could be overcome merely by hard work and dedication. Although she recalls no blatant gender discrimination in her own recruitment or the procedures for gaining promotion—strict civil service laws were already in place—she knew of women in the department who had been pressured to waive their rights to take promotional tests. One woman who went ahead anyway achieved the rank of detective but was assigned as a "relief clerk," while other women were assigned to runaway detail or the police jail, and not allowed on the street. She recalled instances of sexual harassment, some of which may have delayed her own opportunities to move ahead; for example, she was involuntarily transferred to the sex crimes unit while a detective, and although some other patrolwomen would have gladly taken the assignment, it did not have to go to a woman and she ended up losing seniority because of the assignment.

On the street she found that women officers were more likely than their male counterparts to seek consensus in making decisions, and she believes that some male officers actually appreciated this. She feels she earned the respect of her partners on burglary detail despite their tendencies toward paternalistic protection and their initial apprehension. It was not uncommon to hear sexist jokes among the officers she worked with. She recalls one vividly, perhaps because her future burglary partner told it: "Says one officer to another, 'You could be replaced by a monkey.' Replies the other, 'Yes, but you could be replaced by a woman.'" And along came Detective Watson.

As chief, Watson sees part of her role as helping to break down the glass ceiling that still prevents many qualified women from moving into the highest ranks of policing. She also hopes to lessen some of the conflicts that come with putting men and women alone together for long periods of time. Early in her career, when women patrol officers were still rare, she found that male officers had trouble with wives who did not want women alone in cars with their husbands, and with fellow male officers who poked fun at them. This made it tough on the men, both on patrol and off. Those difficulties persist, and are one of the occupational hazards that Chief Watson believes good training, open communication, and an accessible management style can help reduce.

Source: Chief Elizabeth Watson, personal interview, June 1995.

denied promotion nine times because of her sex. In the aftermath of a suit she filed, she was accused of being a lesbian. "A few weeks later she was suspended for swimming in her underwear with other officers at a businessman's house while on duty; the others were not suspended" (Fielding, 1994:61). She was later accused of not having sufficient operational experience, of drinking too much, and of having affairs. The double standard is obvious: "If you don't have a drink with [the men] you're a lesbian, if you do you're an alcoholic" (*Guardian*, July 22, 1992; cited in Fielding, 1994:61). This is known as **defeminization**: Male officers neutralize perceived threats to male dominance by labeling female officers unfeminine, thereby denying women their gender (Berg and Budnick, 1986).

defeminization When male officers neutralize perceived threats to male dominance by calling female officers unfeminine.

Putting Sexism to Rest—Slowly. Various things have happened over the past few years to raise hopes that sexism and gender discrimination will eventually be put to rest. The women's rights movement, increasing numbers of lawsuits charging harassment or discrimination, the congressional hearings on the nomination of Supreme Court Justice Clarence Thomas, and more women in policing have all contributed to an increasing awareness of gender issues in criminal justice. Yet many male police officers still do not view women as equals. The common reference to female police officers as "girls" while male officers are called "men" accentuates the difference. Until sexist attitudes are overcome, women will continue to experience an uphill battle in their efforts to achieve equality and equity in policing. But over time, more and more women, such as former Chief Elizabeth Watson (see Box 6.2), will succeed in advancing through the ranks.

Women Perform as Well as Male Officers. Negative stereotypes about the work performance of female police officers are held by some male officers—and shared by many members of the public, male and female. But growing

Police work in a unique world where they have substantial authority and power, but are constantly vulnerable to abuse and attack. What are some of the special issues that female officers confront?

PHOTO BY BOB DAEMMRICH, COURTESY OF THE IMAGE WORKS

research, beginning with a 1972 Police Foundation study of 86 female recruits in Washington, D.C. (Bloch and Anderson, 1974), shows not only that female officers are as capable in the job as male officers, but also that the presence of women has many benefits to policing and to society at large (Charles, 1982; Homant and Kennedy, 1985; Morash and Greene, 1986; Grennan, 1988; Feinman, 1994). For example, compared with their male counterparts, female officers are more likely to prevent dangerous situations than to bring them on, and they are described by citizens as more sensitive, competent, and pleasant, thereby creating better relations between citizens and police.

How Far Have Minorities Come?

The overall situation is somewhat different for minority groups, though many have experienced an uphill battle to enter police work and gain acceptance once in it. Some ethnic groups had little trouble getting hired as police officers during the nineteenth and early 20th centuries. During those times police work was not a particularly respected occupation, nor did it promise good pay or prospects. But it was a steady job, and therefore appealing to people with few options. In New York City during the late 1800s, Irish Americans controlled city hall and the recruitment practices of all departments, including the police. That is why for many years most police officers in New York City had Irish roots.

Neither Hispanics nor African Americans were able to make significant inroads into policing until the late 1970s. This was true even in communities with large Hispanic or African American populations such as Los Angeles, Chicago, Cleveland, Detroit, and San Antonio. Following the Civil War, African Americans initially made significant gains in public employment, especially in the South. But these were short-lived. The U.S. Supreme Court's decision in ***Plessy v. Ferguson*** (1896), allowing "separate but equal" public facilities serving black and white citizens, effectively ended the postwar policy of Reconstruction. Public employment of black citizens dropped off dramatically, and police work was no exception. In New Orleans, for example, employment of black officers dropped from 177 in 1870 to 5 in 1900, and to none by 1910. It took another 40 years before a black officer was again appointed to the New Orleans police department (Williams and Murphy, 1990:44). Around the turn of the century, there were hardly more than 2,000 black police officers in the whole country (Kuykendall and Burns, 1980), almost none in small cities and rural areas.

Plessy v. Ferguson Allowed "separate but equal" facilities for white and black citizens.

Hispanics and blacks who wished to enter police work in the early 1900s suffered from widespread prejudice and discrimination and had no political clout to overcome it. Even when hired, black officers were confined to policing black areas, and their arrest powers were often restricted. In some departments, they had to call in white officers to make arrests. Fifty years would go by before significant changes occurred in the fortunes of minority recruits.

Native Americans are a special case in law enforcement. Although few Native Americans can be found in police careers outside reservations, the majority of the 304 federal reservations maintain law enforcement departments run by the tribes themselves. Over 1,100 tribal police officers are currently working (Melton, 1998:62). The federal Bureau of Indian Affairs (BIA) provides training through the federal Law Enforcement Training Center in Artesia, New Mexico. The tribal police are supplemented by BIA and FBI officers, some of whom are also Native American. However, the reservations are primarily rural and often vast, and neither the available resources nor the law enforcement training are adequate to meet the policing needs of Native American communities.

Minority officers face unique challenges, especially when policing their own communities and when dealing with prejudices within their police department. Although these challenges increase the stress levels experienced by many minority officers, job satisfaction is generally high.

PHOTO BY ROBERT BRENNER, COURTESY OF PHOTOEDIT

Recent Trends in Minority Recruitment. Race riots in the 1960s and growing numbers of lawsuits charging discrimination were among the forces that eventually brought about substantial changes in police hiring practices. In addition, African Americans began to mobilize as a political force and to develop organizations and police associations to represent their interests (Sullivan, 1989; Kuykendall and Burns, 1980). Together these events had a profound impact. To illustrate, Figure 6.1 shows that from 1970 to 1992 black representation among the nation's sworn police officers grew substantially. In fact, by 1992 there was almost the same percentage of adult African Americans in police service as in the U.S. population as a whole. The majority of African American police officers have been hired by large city departments and in the South. This largely reflects African American population patterns, and the change has reversed the long-standing underrepresentation of African Americans in cities with large minority populations such as Oakland, Detroit, Cleveland, and Chicago (Walker, 1992:314). Although Hispanic representation more than doubled over the same period, it merely kept pace with overall growth in the Hispanic population, and has yet to achieve the same degree of representation in police work as that of African-Americans. As of 1997, Hispanics still made up only 7.6 percent of the nation's police and detectives, whereas African Americans accounted for 18.1 percent (U.S. Bureau of the Cenus, 1998:419).

Racism and Discrimination on the Job. Like their female colleagues, some minority police officers experience prejudice and discrimination on the job, and minority officers generally find it harder to get favorable duty assignments and promotions (Sullivan, 1989:341; Walker and Martin, 1995). Despite highly publicized appointments of African Americans to the position of police chief in some of the nation's largest cities—for example, Detroit, Atlanta, Houston,

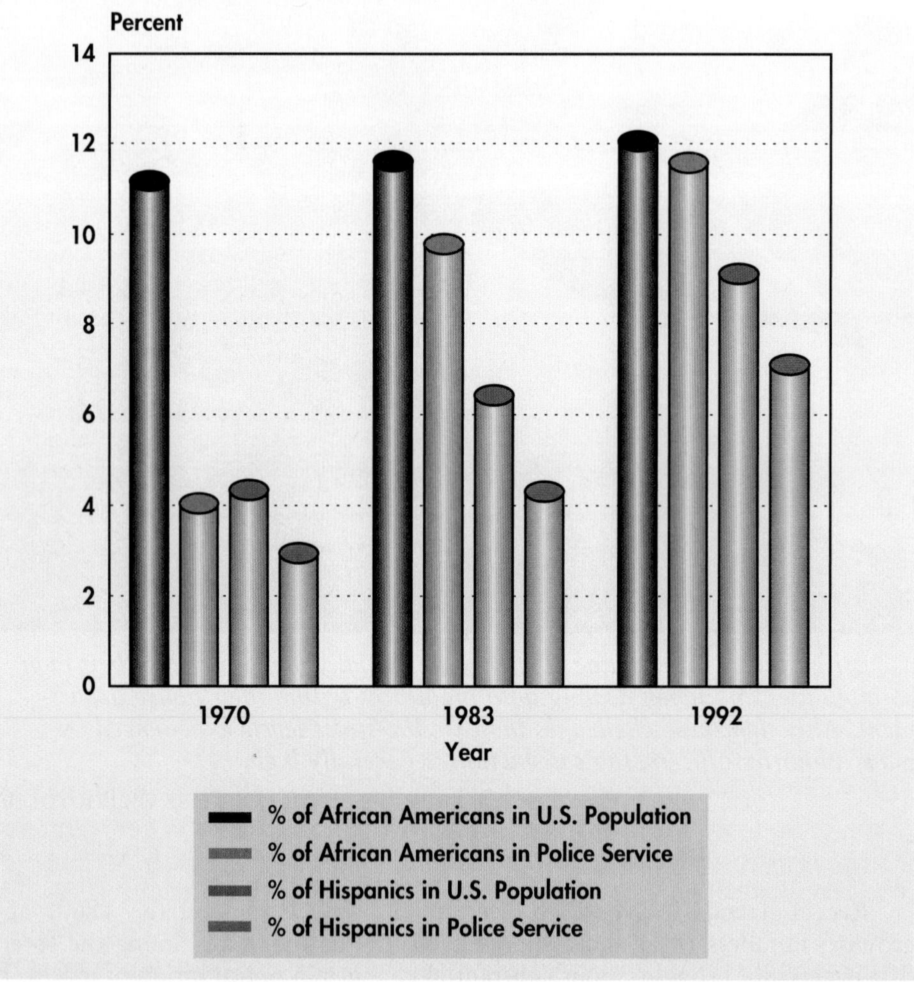

FIGURE 6.1 PERCENT OF AFRICAN AMERICANS AND HISPANICS IN THE U.S. POPULATION AND IN POLICE SERVICE, 1970–1992
Police figure is sworn officers only.

Source: U.S. Bureau of the Census (1994). *Statistical Abstract of the United States, 1993* (p. 407). Washington, D.C.: U.S. Government Printing Office.

New York City, Philadelphia, St. Louis, and Los Angeles following the Rodney King incident—African Americans and Hispanics are severely underrepresented in higher ranks. Court cases, many filed during the 1970s and 1980s, have confirmed this picture. The outcome of these cases has generally been favorable for African Americans, but suits charging reverse discrimination and other challenges have increased in recent years. In some communities black officers who qualify for promotion have been allowed to jump over white officers to the next higher rank; others have a policy that every time a white officer is promoted, a black officer will be too. Such practices are disquieting to many white officers, and therefore they carry the risk of increasing hostility and ill feelings among police officers.

One of the most difficult issues to resolve concerns written tests used in hiring and promotions. It has long been recognized that minority applicants do not compete well with white applicants in these tests. One argument is that poor scores on written tests may hide a person's interpersonal skills and potential for leadership. Some police and fire departments have moved away from multiple-choice and essay tests, replacing them with field simulations that require candidates to demonstrate relevant job skills. Even so, some experts charge that standards have been lowered at the risk of jeopardizing performance: "To fill positions, a department should never forsake procedures and standards or lower its qualifications" (Delattre, 1994:118).

Some authors believe that there is a *cultural disposition* in policing that fosters racism. The idea is that police culture itself promotes racist attitudes and behavior, and these are learned and manifested through concrete practices played out in everyday policing: "Shared in the form of stories, warnings, and officer training and safety exercises, racial biases become fixed into departmental traditions. . . ." (Crank, 1998:207). These "commonsense" biases are most often expressed in dealings with citizens, but they may also be directed toward African American, Hispanic, or female officers. Racism, by its nature, does not disappear merely because an individual puts on a uniform.

The very nature of police work demands that all minorities should be fairly represented among police ranks. Police are authorized to use *physical force*—the power to detain, to arrest, to overcome any resistance, and in some circumstances to kill. When used by a truly representative and able sample of adults, this power provides all groups with some voice in the policies and practices of policing, including the use of physical force against people from their own group. This alone is a powerful reason to fight for equal minority and gender representation in policing.

In addition, the bulk of police work involves responding to calls for assistance; helping, advising, and counseling people; observing, investigating and monitoring them; protecting them from each other, and arresting and detaining some of them. Even if all these activities were unaffected by racial, ethnic, and gender differences, the minority composition of police departments would still matter, because fair and effective police work requires officers to appreciate the history, culture, language, and experiences of *all* the people being policed. Whenever some groups are targeted for more policing than others, the greater police resources focused on them should include more personnel who share social characteristics with the people being policed. This strategy may reduce the misunderstandings, mistakes, and mistrust that have plagued the policing of minorities.

THE CONTROVERSY OVER AFFIRMATIVE ACTION

Few presidential actions in recent memory stirred as much controversy as Lyndon Johnson's 1965 Executive Order 11246, requiring all federal contractors to develop **affirmative action** programs. The order said: "The contractor will not discriminate against any employee or applicant because of race, color, religion, sex or national origin. The contractor will take affirmative action to ensure that employees are treated during employment without regard to their race, color, religion, sex, or national origin." Later orders added requirements that federal contractors establish specific plans for correcting deficiencies. An example of deficiency would be a federally funded organization of 98 white employees and 2 black employees doing business in a community where 25 percent of workers are black.

affirmative action A policy requiring employers to take positive steps to avoid discrimination and to remedy past discrimination.

Affirmative action means that employers should take positive steps to avoid discrimination *and* to remedy past discrimination. Specifically, they must "(1) make an active effort to increase the number of female and/or minority employees where they are underrepresented and (2) develop a specific set of goals and timetables that would serve as targets and as a measure of a contractor's success in hiring more minorities and women" (Farley, 1995:439).

Affirmative action programs quickly spread across the country, since any organization doing business with the federal government had to comply. Police agencies, as recipients of federal funds, were included, as were other criminal justice organizations. Many organizations adopted affirmative action plans voluntarily, including some private corporations.

Presidential orders can be changed by subsequent presidents, and they can be challenged in federal court. Affirmative action is no exception. The Reagan administration dropped the requirement for goals and timetables, and both President Reagan and President Bush ordered the U.S. Justice Department to argue against elements of affirmative action in various Supreme Court cases. The Clinton administration reversed this trend, but many politicians and increasing numbers of citizens are opposed to affirmative action. Why?

quotas Hiring by organizations of a certain number of women or minorities regardless of their qualifications.

The Problem of Quotas. One issue that has many people upset is the idea of **quotas**. The Reagan and Bush administrations portrayed affirmative action as nothing more than a quota system; in effect, they said, the law encourages organizations to hire a certain number of minorities or women, regardless of their qualifications. If a plan calls for having 10 percent of an organization's workforce composed of black workers within three years, for example, the organization could "end up having to hire some minimum number of blacks regardless of their qualifications" (Farley, 1995:441). Objections from white job applicants were soon heard, especially when they were passed over for seemingly less qualified black applicants. By the 1970s, affirmative action plans in Detroit, Chicago, and Omaha were being challenged in federal court by associations of white police officers.

United States v. Paradise Alabama is ordered to achieve racial balance in its Department of Public Safety without laying off any white officers.

In a landmark Supreme Court case, ***United States v. Paradise*** (1987), the Alabama Department of Public Safety was ordered to establish a pool of qualified applicants for entry-level positions and promotions, and then hire or promote an equal number of white and black employees until racial balance was obtained. The Supreme Court reasoned that past "blatant and egregious" discrimination had prevented qualified black applicants from being hired and promoted. Indeed, when the original suit was initiated, the Alabama State Patrol had no black officers above the rank of corporal, and only 4 of its 64 corporals were black. Knowing full well that its ruling would be unpopular in some circles and especially among opponents of quotas, the Court stipulated that its order would remain in force only until racial balance was reached, that only qualified people would be hired or promoted, and that no layoffs of white officers would be required.

reverse discrimination The charge that preferential treatment of minorities unfairly penalizes equally well-qualified white applicants.

The Charge of Reverse Discrimination. A popular argument against quotas and affirmative action plans in general is that they constitute **reverse discrimination**. The idea is that preferential treatment of minorities is simply discrimination in reverse; it penalizes whites who are passed over in favor of minorities who are no better qualified, and may even be less qualified, for the job at hand. However, the intent of affirmative action was never to force organizations to hire unqualified people, but merely to make a *good-faith effort* to reverse past discrimination and to ensure fair treatment of minorities and women. Today, many police departments continue to wrestle with the problem of how to achieve racial balance while honoring the achievements of white officers and recruits. In St. Louis, former police chief Clarence Harmon, who is black, struggled with this issue both before and after becoming chief (see Box 6.3).

U.S. Supreme Court rulings on affirmative action are often divided, many recent ones being based on five-to-four votes, some also containing four or five different legal opinions from the justices. The United States is still a long way from resolving all the difficulties surrounding the hiring and promotion of minorities and women in police work, and the battle against racism and sexism is still to be won. If the statistical picture continues to improve, the fact that females and minorities make just as good police officers as males and whites will be more widely recognized and will help dismantle prejudicial practices. However, the growing number of reverse discrimination suits, a conservative Supreme Court, and a Republican Congress have led many observers to contend that recent improvements in the fortunes of women and minorities may now be threatened. The future of female and minority officers is still uncertain, therefore, but there is hope for improvement.

Is Diversity Training an Answer to Race and Gender Inequities in Policing? A growing number of police departments—as well as other criminal justice agencies—have recognized the importance of cultural sensitivity in law enforcement and have introduced **diversity training** as one step toward improving race and gender relations on the job. The purpose of such training is to establish and maintain positive relationships with people from diverse backgrounds and to improve the capacity of the criminal justice system to serve diverse communities equally.

diversity training Training designed to improve race and gender relations by raising sensitivity to the cultural differences among individuals and groups.

Four basic models of diversity training are found among law enforcement agencies (Little, 1997:3):

1. Increase participants' awareness of their own culture by helping them to articulate their cultural values and to become more aware of how their lives have been shaped by that culture; increase awareness of the similarities and differences between their own culture and others; show how different cultures make significant contributions to society.
2. Examine the historical, socioeconomic, and political experiences of different groups; teach participants about prejudice, oppression, dominance, and institutional racism; emphasize information, awareness, and understanding of the minority experience.
3. Teach how attitudes are formed and reveal the participants' unexamined assumptions and tendencies to stereotype others; "[show p]articipants . . . how subtle forms of [prejudice and discrimination] pervade their culture and the systems in which they work" (Little, 1997:3); have participants confront their subconscious assumptions and learn to manage their attitudes in order to enhance nondiscriminatory job performance.
4. Emphasize problem solving and critical thinking so that trainees have the skills to interact effectively with diverse people; have participants complete exercises drawn from real-life on-the-job experiences so that they can recognize and correct actions that exclude or discriminate against other groups.

Although some experts believe that the fourth approach is likely to be most successful because it emphasizes changes in behavior rather than in underlying beliefs and attitudes, there is general uncertainty in law enforcement circles as to whether diversity training will solve discrimination problems. Diversity training cannot change the underlying social conditions that perpetuate racism and sexism, and a few hours in the classroom are unlikely to change police behavior or the legacy of discrimination transmitted by police culture (Barlow and Barlow, 1993; Bennett, 1995). While some of those who have been through diversity training comment positively on the new insights they have gained, others have come away with a hardened sense of differences that may inadvertently promote the very behavior the training is trying to prevent (Little, 1997:3). Instead of scrapping diversity training, however, the most promising route is one that builds multicultural sensitivity into the training of new recruits as well as the in-service training of veteran police officers.

THE POLICE PERSPECTIVE

Police officers often say that the only way to learn about police work is to do it. Although this view is by no means unique to policing, many features of police work not found in other occupations underscore the importance of on-the-

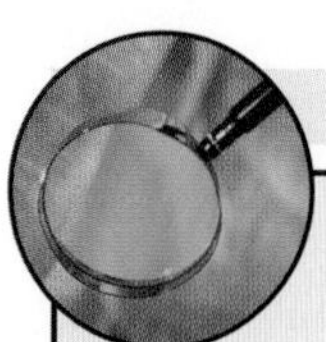

Box 6.3

INSIDE CRIMINAL JUSTICE

AFFIRMATIVE ACTION AND THE EXPERIENCES OF A FORMER BIG CITY POLICE CHIEF

Affirmative action plans have helped raise the proportion of minority police officers in many communities and have also helped ensure that more minority officers are promoted. As the text notes, these plans have come under increasing attack in recent years, and affirmative action seems to be on its last legs. Experience with affirmative action has led some former supporters to change their views; one is former St. Louis police chief Clarence Harmon.

Harmon joined the St. Louis Police Department in 1969, one of a small but growing number of black officers, and eventually rose through the ranks to become its first black chief in August 1991. While on the force he earned a bachelor's degree and then a master's degree in the administration of justice.

At his inauguration as chief, Harmon said "I take my blackness with pride, but I have a responsibility to the entire community. . . . In 1991, race should not be that big a deal" (*St. Louis Post-Dispatch,* November 18, 1995, p. 11A). But clashes over the department's affirmative action plan came to a head in late 1994 when the department announced the results of a promotion exam taken by officers seeking to become sergeants. Although black officers made up about 30 percent of the test takers, they had only 16 percent of the top scores.

The results were embarrassing for Harmon in a city where African Americans make up around half the population. Things got more complicated when stolen copies of the confidential exam were released to the press by Dennis McLin, the head of a local black police organization who claimed they had been circulated among white officers prior to the exam. "That's why we tend to score lower than whites," McLin said.

After an internal investigation found that the theft occurred after the officers took the exam, Harmon argued that the scores should stand. This position was well received by white officers, especially those who did well on the exam, but some black officers were appalled. One letter in a black newspaper from a retired police officer called the chief "a disgrace to your race" (*U.S. News & World Report,* February 13, 1995:43). St. Louis's black mayor, Freeman Bosley, Jr., unsuccessfully called for an independent investigation.

Chief Harmon found himself pitted against supporters of affirmative action even though he had been one of its staunchest supporters throughout his

job experience. Things can go terribly wrong if officers make mistakes or get carried away. Police carry potentially lethal weapons and are subject to other people's aggressions and hostilities just because they are police officers. Police are given special authority to act in situations where civilians are expected to stand back. In some jurisdictions, police are considered "on duty" 24 hours a day, even when technically their shift is over. For all these reasons the modern police training experience is an intense one, and it generally continues well after the recruit graduates from the police academy.

police perspective A special way of looking at people, things, and events that emerges from training and day-to-day experiences on the job.

Over the course of many months of training, the rookie police officer acquires a **police perspective**, a special way of looking at people (including themselves), things, events, and places that is the core of police culture. The themes within the police perspective include the following (Crank, 1998):

Box 6.3 (continued)

career. During the 1980s he had helped push through the department's first affirmative action plan, which resulted in the hiring and promotion of hundreds of black and female police officers. But now he found himself "almost 180 degrees from where I was" (*U.S. News & World Report,* February 13, 1995:46).

Yet Harmon's earlier experience with the department's affirmative action plan had already sowed seeds of doubt: He began noticing that in its efforts to meet the new affirmative action goals, the department was hiring black recruits who scored relatively poorly on entrance exams. Harmon and other high-ranking black officers worried that the new recruits would have trouble competing with their white counterparts for promotions. Like many black officers who joined the force in the 1960s and early 1970s, Harmon had taken pride in competing head-to-head with white officers even as they fought for affirmative action goals. Yet in the late 1980s he began to think that affirmative action was being used as a crutch.

The main mechanism of affirmative action in big-city police departments like St. Louis was something called "race norming": reworking test results to achieve racial balance. In St. Louis, race norming worked like this: Some black officers who scored in lower "clusters" (groups of candidates who achieved approximately the same scores) would be advanced ahead of some white officers who scored in higher clusters. While Harmon saw "cluster dipping" as a justified means of compensating black officers for years of being systematically held back by white commanders, he also saw the practice as detrimental to the white officers passed over for promotions. After Congress outlawed race norming in the 1991 Civil Rights Act, Harmon persuaded the St. Louis police board to stop cluster dipping.

In 1993, Chief Harmon began strengthening the department's efforts to recruit better-qualified minority cadets. Today, test scores among black and white recruits are much closer than they were in the late 1980s. Harmon believes that the narrowing of scores should translate into more promotions for minorities five years from now, when today's cadets are eligible to take the sergeant's exam. Harmon will no longer be able to view things from the inside, however, for he resigned as chief late in 1995, and is now mayor of the City of St. Louis.

Sources: "Black and Blue: A Top Cop's Rethinking of Race-Based Preferences," *U.S. News & World Report,* February 13, 1995:43, 46; "Police Chief Harmon's Goal Was to Make a Difference," *St. Louis Post-Dispatch,* November 18, 1995, p. 11A.

- *Dominion*—a sense of responsibility for and control over the territory you patrol
- *Force*—knowing when to use force, and how much force to use
- *Guns*—the handling, use, and importance of firearms
- *Suspicion*—a "sixth sense" that alerts you that something—or someone—is out of place, not right, or not to be trusted
- *Danger*—thinking about, preparing for, and defending yourself (and sometimes others) against violence
- *Unpredictability*—recognizing and dealing with uncertainty—"anything can happen on the street"; *edge control* is a related theme that emphasizes the strategies skilled officers use to keep things from getting out of hand (Crank, 1998:123–134).

- *Seduction*—dealing with the excitement, "high times," and sensuous temptations associated with police work, particularly undercover work involving illicit sex and drugs
- *Common sense*—applying the lessons of past police experiences and acquiring habits and routines that become taken for granted
- *Masculinity*—the association of police work with maleness, and the emphasis on physical conditioning, toughness, and bravery; tendency to demean women who "act like men".
- *Solidarity*—cultivation and protection of "Us" versus "Them," including emphasis on brotherhood, loyalty, superiority, and protection of partners.

TRAINING AND THE POLICE PERSPECTIVE

Police recruits are introduced to these themes during formal training, and they are reinforced throughout an officer's career. Because most recruits are ill prepared for the demands of police work, police agencies offer extensive training courses for their new recruits before they ever hit the street. This was not always the case: A mere 30 years ago, 85 percent of all officers in 4,000 police departments across America had received no training before going on patrol (Walker, 1992:317). State laws now mandate pre-service training for virtually all law enforcement officers. If there is no police academy nearby, departments send recruits to universities and colleges with special law enforcement programs. These training programs introduce the newcomer to the legal, organizational, and operational aspects of police work. Police academies also spend considerable time on the behavioral aspects of policing—the "how-to" of interacting with the public, other criminal justice personnel, and each other. An intensive socialization process begins in the academy, where the "cord binding the rookie to the civilian world is cut" (Niederhoffer, 1967:43).

Recruits Learn of Ambiguity and Conflicts in Police Work. In training by police instructors, rookies see for the first time the ambiguities and conflicts inherent in police work. They learn that they are expected to enforce all criminal laws, but that in practice they must be selective. They learn that the public can be their enemy—they are told to be suspicious, to be always on the lookout for a setup, and not to rely on any help from citizens—but also that they must serve and protect its members. They learn that crime fighting involves legal and bureaucratic procedures that sometimes produce the opposite result: the escape of a criminal, the commission of a crime, or even an innocent person's injury or death. They learn that police work is also public relations work. Normally valued attributes such as zeal and honesty may get them into trouble with the public or with their superiors; in other words, it is risky to be too enthusiastic or too sincere. Most important of all, perhaps, they learn that what they are told in class often differs markedly from what they know from experience as private citizens. Whatever idealism they brought with them is soon forgotten—often permanently. Training breeds cynicism.

Police War Stories. "War stories" are an important element of the training experience. Instructors know that stories about police officers under fire or arresting dangerous criminals or solving famous cases liven up the classroom and also make points that recruits are more likely to remember. The stories also encourage feelings of camaraderie and brotherhood, and they convey the history of the department. They are an important source of the common sense that police use to build their stock of everyday actions. War stories have been described as a soup of: "tradition, heroes, metaphors, ironies, bad

Danger is a core element in police work and it binds officers together. In this scene, officers are about to enter a room in search of a suspect believed to be armed. Mistakes can be very dangerous for police and citizens alike.

PHOTO BY ED LALLO, COURTESY OF LIAISON INTERNATIONAL

guys, trickery, assholes, coincidence, survival, and surreal events are what make stories interesting, what gives them a larger-than-life quality. Stories highlight the actions of particular individuals, and tell about what they did, what they didn't do, or something that happened to them. Stories are knowledge by example, concrete and specific—in response to a 'how-to' question, stories provide a concrete example about what someone did in the past" (Crank, 1998:166–167).

At a police training session I attended some years ago, the following war story got the undivided attention of recruits, and brought home the importance of staying alert, knowing one's location at all times, and following defensive procedures when making a traffic stop. A rookie deputy was on routine patrol in a squad car at night in a rural area of the county. She came upon a Ford Mustang parked by the side of a deserted road. She noticed what she thought were two heads in the back seat, and assumed it was two lovers taking advantage of the moon and the isolated setting. As she drove slowly past, she noted the car's make and license plate, and jotted down its location. The deputy drove on. About four hundred yards down the road the same car sped past the deputy at great speed, sliding from side to side and throwing up a shower of rocks and mud. The deputy flipped on her lights and siren and within minutes pulled the Mustang over. She called in the license plate number, gave her location, and told the dispatcher what had happened and that she was going to "check things out."

With flashlight in hand, the deputy approached the other car slowly, keeping its left rear roof pillar between herself and the occupants as best she could until she reached the side window. At this point she turned her body so that her right arm and shoulder faced the window and she shone her flashlight into the car. At that moment there was a flash and loud bang, neither of which reached the deputy's senses. The car sped off, leaving the deputy unconscious with part of her right arm torn off at the shoulder and a bullet lodged at the base of her skull. A few minutes later the dispatcher radioed the deputy with information on the car. Getting no response, the dispatcher quickly called for backup and gave the deputy's last location. Within minutes, the deputy's car was spotted, an ambulance dispatched and an all-points bulletin put out for the Mustang. The deputy survived, the Mustang was pulled over in a neighboring county, and two young men were arrested. It turned out they had been following the deputy at a distance during the evening with the intention of ambushing her. They got in front of the deputy, waited for her to show up, and then shot her as planned—all in revenge for the arrest she had made of one of their friends earlier in the week.

The moral of the story is that such events can never be predicted, but a well-trained police officer who uses common sense and is prepared for danger has a chance to survive an attack and help bring about an arrest even when he or she is injured and incapacitated.

War stories such as this are usually about skills, danger, and luck (good and bad). They confirm some of the recruits' expectations about the challenges of the job. But by the time the academy portion of the training is over, many recruits have completely altered their understanding of what police work is really all about. And as one recruit put it, there is a lot more to it than crime: "They expect us to be dogcatchers, lawyers, marriage counselors, boxers, firemen, doctors, baby-sitters, race-car drivers, and still catch a crook occasionally. There's no way we can do all that crap! They're nuts!" (Van Maanen, 1973:411).

DEFENSIVENESS, PROFESSIONALISM, AND DEPERSONALIZATION

One of the primary goals of formal police training is the development of uniform behavior among officers so that there is less room for personal judgment and individualized behavior. Recruits must be stripped of their previous identity and taught to assume a police identity—to think and act as a police officer in all situations. One classic study of a police academy shows that three themes emerge during training to help encourage adoption of the proper police perspective (Harris, 1973): defensiveness, professionalism, and depersonalization.

defensiveness Alertness to the many dangers of police work and building defenses against them.

Defensiveness. The first, perhaps most important theme is **defensiveness**: being alert to the many dangers of police work and building defenses against them. These dangers are not merely physical, however. They include the dangers of procedural violations that can lead to criminal charges, civil suits, reprimands, lost cases, and dismissal. They include the dangers of corruption, inefficiency, and emotional involvement in police-citizen encounters as well as the danger of provoking negative reactions by powerful or influential members of the public. How police handle or manage emotions, especially in the face of tragic events they witness, is only now being studied carefully. Initial work indicates that police culture restricts an officer's ability to deal with emotions, partly because the police are not expected to show emotions since this indicates a loss of control (Pogrebin and Poole, 1991).

A major California study documents the "schizophrenic existence" that embroils patrol officers and stimulates this defensiveness. The police "must cope not only with the terror of an often hostile and unpredictable citizenry, but also with a hostile—even tyrannical—and unpredictable bureaucracy" (Brown, 1988:9). One exasperated officer was heard to complain to his sergeant: "I'm getting jabbed in the ass by the public and jabbed in the ass by the department" (Brown, 1988:81). A police researcher who is also an officer with the Belmont, Massachusetts, police department recently wrote that "the most common sources of police officer stress involve the policies and procedures of law enforcement agencies themselves" (Finn, 1997:22).

Professionalization. The second theme is **professionalization**: developing a professional public image, specialized techniques, service ideals, a working knowledge of the law, and a shared technical language. These elements help promote a professional identity, a sense of "we, the professional police," who are clearly distinguishable from people in other occupations with investigative or arrest powers, such as security guards and private investigators. The message is this: Anyone can carry handcuffs and a gun, but only professional police go through the rigors of the police training academy and spend six months or more on probation working under the eye of a seasoned officer before they are allowed to truly practice their profession.

professionalization Development of specialized techniques, service ideals, shared language, and professional identity.

Depersonalization. The third theme is **depersonalization**, which has two sides. On one side, recruits learn that the public and their own supervisors often treat them as faceless: They are less human beings than impersonal objects. Until the last decade or so, it was traditional in English police departments for superiors to refer to police constables by their departmental number, such as PC275. The other side of depersonalization involves the officer's own adoption of stereotypes, black-and-white distinctions, and intolerance of "deviant" groups.

depersonalization Denying the personal qualities of individuals and avoiding relationships with members of the public.

Recruits learn that police work requires the denial of personal qualities—police officers dare not personalize their official relationships with the public and must be wary of those who do. A personal relationship is presumed to jeopardize an officer's ability to make objective interpretations of events and situations involving the other person. Friendship or even neighborliness symbolizes a degree of trust that only an incautious, unprofessional police officer would accept. Needless to say, this viewpoint tends to undermine the effectiveness of policing programs built on cooperation between police and the public. This point will be taken up again in the discussion of community policing later in the chapter.

One important by-product of defensiveness, professionalization, and depersonalization is the cultivation of solidarity among recruits, a sense of belonging and involvement that firms up and helps preserve the police identity fostered during training (Alpert and Dunham, 1988: Chapter 5). As mentioned earlier, these feelings of brotherhood, loyalty, and superiority constitute one of the major themes of police culture, and help protect it from outsiders. The "dark side" of solidarity is that loyalty can be used "to keep officers quiet in the face of corruption and lawbreaking" (Crank, 1998:201). This issue is one of the topics in Chapter 9.

THE POLICE "WORKING PERSONALITY"

Police officers typically develop a distinctive "**working personality**" (Skolnick, 1994:41–68). A unique combination of work elements fosters in police a certain way of looking at the world and responding to it. For example, suspicion and the development of a "sixth sense" are important elements of the police working personality. Although police see suspicion as part of self-protection and a way of coping with uncertainty, it also has a legal basis, as we shall see in more detail in Chapter 9. Briefly, the police may not interfere with the ordinary activities of citizens unless, on the basis of their training and experience, they have **reasonable suspicion** that an illegal act has been or is about to be committed. Police are therefore *required* to be suspicious in order to carry out their work.

working personality Develops when elements in police work such as suspicion and danger create a unique way of looking at the world and responding to it.

reasonable suspicion On the basis of their training and experience, police believe that an illegal act has been or is about to be committed.

Suspicion and the Problem of Social Isolation. As an aspect of self-protection, police learn to be suspicious of events, persons, and things that are associated with danger. However, suspicion creates a defensiveness that encourages barriers between police and the rest of the world. Even when they might prefer no barriers because their work makes them less desirable as a spouse, friend, or neighbor, police officers often find that barriers are there nonetheless. This produces social isolation: Police officers sense that they are not really included in the mainstream of society, and they stick to themselves; this, in turn, reinforces their rejection by others.

Perceptions of danger differ among the general population, from which all police recruits are drawn (Stanko, 1990). Police recruits who are not familiar with the signs of danger must be taught how to see them. These may be the way someone is dressed—for example, clothes suggesting gang affiliation or clothes inconsistent with the day's weather—or the way a person walks, indicating he or she may have a weapon; even the way a person talks may suggest lack of respect, or trouble (Skolnick, 1994; Crank, 1998). Unfortunately, once police have learned "the craft of suspicion" (Rubinstein, 1973), their quality of life, like that of many inner-city residents, is affected in a negative way; stress is increased (Cullen, 1983), and feelings of isolation are heightened.

The social isolation of police is increased by their authority to enforce laws, especially laws dealing with public morality and order: "Typically, the policeman is required to enforce laws representing puritanical morality, such as those prohibiting drunkenness, and also laws regulating the flow of public activity, such as traffic laws. In these situations, the policeman directs the citizenry, whose typical response denies recognition of his authority and stresses his obligation to respond to danger" (Skolnick, 1975:44).

As police are authorized and expected to enforce laws that they themselves may not agree with or that are resented by large segments of the population, the police role once again encourages feelings of suspicion and social isolation.

Besides the elements of danger and authority, police work involves persistent pressures to produce, to demonstrate that officers are living up to the expectations of the department. For example, traffic police in some cities and some state highway police are required to fill quotas for traffic tickets. And it is not uncommon among vice units to find that departments have quotas for vice arrests. Police officers in these situations find themselves further alienating the public as they seek to meet these demands.

Facing barriers between themselves and the general public, police seek support and reciprocity among themselves. To counteract the threat of danger and the effects of public hostility and to fulfill persistent demands from supervisors that they produce, officers are drawn together in relationships of mutual assistance and dependence (Manning, 1977). This solidarity becomes a key part of police working relationships. Patrol officers draw heavily on it to bolster their sense of belonging, their sense of comradeship and common purpose. Feeling that they can rely on neither the public nor their superiors, they turn to one another, further separating themselves from the public and from those giving the orders.

Loyalty and the Cop's Code. Loyalty becomes a core value of an informal police code of conduct. In return, the patrol officers receive protection and honor (Brown, 1988:83). Furthermore, suspicion and solidarity may take a "conspiratorial turn" in undercover police work, since officers often adopt a protective code of silence that cloaks their wide discretionary power and lack of close supervision (Marx, 1988). The informal **code of police conduct** covers the full range of police activities, from routine patrol and the use of force to relations among officers and between line officers and their supervisors. Box 6.4

code of police conduct Informal rules covering how police should behave in general and specific situations.

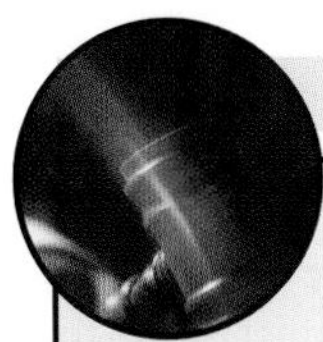

Box 6.4

JUSTICE PROFESSIONALS AT WORK

THE STREET COP'S CODE

Solidarity, suspicion, danger, and unpredictability are themes that draw police officers together and promote defenses against threats from inside and out. These defenses are specified as a set of informal rules of conduct—the cop's "code." Although specific provisions of the code differ from place to place, here are some of the code's rules that police researchers have documented over the past quarter century.

- Hold up your end of the work.
- Watch out for your partner first, and then the rest of the officers working your shift.
- Don't leave work for the next tour—for example, put gas in the car, finish your paperwork.
- Don't give up another cop—don't rat on a fellow officer.
- "Show balls"—don't back down when confronted.
- Don't be too eager.
- If you get caught in the wrong place or doing something forbidden by the department, don't implicate anybody else; take your punishment.
- Make sure the other officers know if another cop is dangerous or "crazy," but don't give that cop up to the bosses.
- Don't trust new officers until you have checked them out.
- Don't tell anybody else more than they have to know; it could be bad for you and it could be bad for them.
- Don't talk too much or too little.
- Protect your ass: "'If the system wants to get you, it will,' and so the prudent officer makes sure that his ass is covered" (Reuss-Ianni, 1983:15).
- Don't make waves—don't be a troublemaker and don't mess with the system.
- Keep out of the way of any boss from outside your precinct.
- Know your bosses; adjust your behavior to their expectations and style.
- Don't do the bosses' work for them—for example, telling them something they should find out for themselves.
- Don't trust the bosses to look out for your interest.

Sources: Elizabeth Reuss-Ianni (1983). *Two Cultures of Policing: Street Cops and Management Cops.* New Brunswick, N.J.: Transaction Books; Peter K. Manning (1977). *Police Work: The Social Organization of Policing.* Cambridge, Mass.: MIT Press; Victor E. Kappeler, Richard D. Sluder, and Geoffrey Alpert (1994). *Forces of Deviance: The Dark Side of Policing.* Prospect Heights, Ill.: Waveland Press; John P. Crank (1998). *Understanding Police Culture.* Cincinnati, Ohio: Anderson.

illustrates the code typically found among street cops; notice that much of it concerns how to deal with management.

"TROUBLE" AND THE EXERCISE OF POLICE AUTHORITY

As a means of making the world more manageable and simplifying their responses to it, police invariably stereotype certain people and places as "trouble." People or places identified as trouble call for police action. This means that police authority is sometimes exercised in situations that would not warrant it if all the facts were known. Police feel that the undesirable consequences of this are outweighed by the benefits. For one thing, facts often take time to establish. As long as police take actions that seem reasonable in the light of training and experience, the facts can wait. From the first day of training through the rest of their careers on the street, police officers discover that facts, while ultimately important, are less crucial than appearances; the best way to approach appearances is to have ready a set of categories to put them in.

As noted already, suspicion is a key element of the police personality. Police direct much of their attention toward people, objects, places, and events they have labeled suspicious. But the police cannot suspect everything and everyone. To simplify things and make the job more manageable—and to protect their sanity—police officers create their own versions of reality. Police may conclude, for example, that street crimes are more likely to be committed in certain sections of town and by certain groups of people. "On the basis of these conclusions, the police divide the population and physical territory under surveillance into a variety of categories, make some initial assumptions about the moral character of the people and places in these categories, and then focus attention on those categories . . . felt to have the shadiest moral characteristics" (Werthman and Piliavin, 1967:68–69). Those areas and groups that do not fit the stereotype remain "clean" and generally avoid concentrated police scrutiny unless residents request it.

Examples of Stereotyping at Work in Policing. To illustrate, here are two cases of stereotyping, one occurring in England, the other in the United States. Although both illustrations are 25 years old, they remain excellent examples of stereotyping at work. For six months, residents of an upper-middle-class English neighborhood removed building materials from a construction site: "Each evening and every weekend, after the workmen had departed, the site was visited by between 5 and 15 men with motor-cars or wheelbarrows. They removed bricks, tiles, paving slabs, timber, mortar, and other building materials systematically, and often in large quantities" (Chapman, 1968:56). When asked by an observer why he did not intervene, a police officer who witnessed one evening's thievery replied that he assumed they all had permission! Neither the thieves nor the circumstances fit his stereotype of trouble.

Contrast this case with an incident observed in Memphis, Tennessee (Bent, 1974). Some police officers were under pressure to produce following an uneventful evening. Acting on the assumption that when adolescents gather there will be trouble, officers in four cars descended on an area adjoining a converted warehouse in which a dance was being held. The officers made numerous attempts to uncover evidence of illegal activity by teenagers moving around the area or parked in their cars. Eventually four adolescents were discovered with a couple of marijuana joints, and a bust was made. The stereotype linking adolescents and crime (in this case illegal drugs) had worked and was thereby reinforced.

The Impact of Mainstream Attitudes and Values. Considering that police draw upon stereotypes to guide them in their work, most notably singling out young people, the poor, and especially minority males, it is tempting to conclude that these are *police* images, reflecting *police* bias or prejudice against such groups. It turns out, however, that police views are consistent with the widely held stereotypes of mainstream society. American police operate in a culture that generally rewards those who conform to mainstream (that is, white middle-class) values. Middle-class America doesn't look to its own kind for the criminal, but rather to the poor and especially to minorities.

Classic evidence shows police conformity with prevailing middle-class standards (Bent, 1974). Much similarity was found between the police and the white middle class despite the fact that most of the police officers surveyed came from lower-class backgrounds. Both the police and the typical white middle-class respondents stressed crime control, improved police efficiency and production, and enforcement patterns aimed at maintaining order. This value system contrasted sharply with that of minorities and students, which emphasized service responsibilities, social needs, due process, justice, human dignity, and respect for human differences. Since white middle-class individuals are typically in the best position to influence the activities of governments and their agencies, it should come as no surprise that police share a similar set of values and behave accordingly.

REDUCING STEREOTYPING THROUGH POLICE EDUCATION

In the 1970s programs of higher education were advocated as a means of broadening police attitudes and reducing prejudice, and to improve police performance and police-community relations. In 1966, 184 colleges and universities offered degree programs in criminal justice; by 1978, there were 816 such programs (Kobetz, 1978:1). According to a study commissioned by the Police Executive Research Foundation (PERF), by the end of the 1980s the average level of education among police officers was roughly equivalent to an associate degree from a community college—around fourteen years of education. Female officers tended to be more educated than their male counterparts: Almost one-third held graduate degrees, compared to less than 4 percent of male officers (Carter, Sapp, and Stephens, 1989).

Yet it appears far from conclusive that higher education for police greatly changes their attitudes and behavior or improves performance. Indeed, "there is strong evidence that the value of police education may be nullified by the realities of the police role as it is now constituted" (Weiner, 1974:323; Eskridge, 1989). Furthermore, while no conclusive evidence exists that law enforcement officers with degrees perform better than those without, there is some evidence to suggest that officers with degrees are more dissatisfied with police work and the career opportunities it affords (Walker, 1992:306–307). In addition, a college degree requirement would limit the pool of otherwise qualified applicants. Still, PERF's efforts on behalf of better-educated police have been influential, and some college-level work is being demanded by more and more departments—if not for initial hiring, then as a requirement for promotion.

Still, the nature of police work, especially the need to be suspicious and to pattern enforcement in terms of arrest-productive stereotypes, will discourage changes to police images of the world around them. Add to this the growing pressure from conservative law-and-order interests, and it is even less likely that any trend toward liberalization of police attitudes and behavior will occur in the foreseeable future.

THE RODNEY KING INCIDENT

The Los Angeles Police Department (LAPD), long regarded as one of the most professional and well-educated departments in the country (Brown, 1988: 60–64), illustrates the point just made. The 1991 Rodney King beating, videotaped by an onlooker and shown countless times on national television, involved members of this department. The Christopher Commission, which investigated the incident, remarked on "the frequency and bravado with which . . . many LAPD officers used the in-car Mobile Digital Terminal system to communicate their scurrilous racial, ethnic, and sexual sentiments. . . . These were conscious statements . . . typed on a keypad with little, if any, concern for the possibility that they would ever be disclosed or judged" (*Los Angeles Times*, September 14, 1991, p. M1).

This statement implies that police higher-ups condoned or ignored the rampant prejudicial slurs communicated among LAPD patrol officers, whose professional conduct reinforced existing prejudices and contributed to feelings of resentment and fear among African Americans and members of the community at large. It is hardly surprising that many black youths think of police attitudes and behavior in terms of violence (Sullivan, Dunham, and Alpert, 1987). Underclass poverty and racial inequality condemn many minority youths, especially African American youths, to a future of joblessness and uncertainty. What these same youths *can* expect is to have recurrent dealings with the criminal justice system. Some criminologists are suggesting that this is part of a general pattern of increased intolerance and punitiveness toward African Americans, and the police share in the responsibility for it (Mann, 1993; Hagan, 1994; Sampson and Laub, 1993a). The police are in a powerful position to reinforce negative messages about certain groups of Americans; if police culture embraces racism and sexism, these are the messages that will prevail.

VARIETIES OF POLICE BEHAVIOR

The discussion so far has referred to "police," "policing," and "police culture" as if there is more that is common than different among the people who police society. This is probably true, and yet important differences have also been found. In an influential book on policing, James Q. Wilson (1968) showed that the social and political characteristics of a community determine in large part how its police define and carry out their duties.

THREE STYLES OF POLICING

styles of policing Characteristic ways that police in different communities respond to the demands of the job.

Wilson describes three different **styles of policing**: watchman style, legalistic style, and service style.

Watchman Style. This harkens back to the days when police acted as reluctant maintainers of order. Watchman-style departments tend to be found in older cities with large populations of poor and minorities and traditions of political patronage. Patrolling officers avoid rather than seek out law violations (Lundman, 1980:43). Vice is tolerated, if not encouraged. When faced with serious crime, officers can be tough; on other occasions their enforcement is informal and follows no set pattern. Corruption is a frequent problem in watch departments, primarily because of the tolerance of vice and the dominance of machine politics, but also because patrolling officers are largely unsupervised. Chicago under Mayor Richard Daley, and Philadelphia under Mayor Frank Rizzo, had watchman-style departments.

Legalistic Style. This style of policing may also be found in some older cities with large concentrations of poor and minority residents, such as when reform-minded administrators replaced the old political machine in Los Angeles during the 1960s. However, the legalistic style is most often found in newer and more affluent communities—for example, Oakland, California, and Highland Park, Illinois (Lundman, 1980:46). Such communities want low-profile, yet professional policing; they want laws enforced and public disorder controlled without any fanfare. Police in legalistic departments are careful about their appearance and image, and they emphasize arrest and ticketing of violators without regard to race, affluence, or age. Organized corruption is rare, mainly because vice laws are routinely enforced.

Service Sytle. Service-style departments are found primarily in white middle- and upper-class suburbs. Lakewood, Colorado, and Burnsville, Minnesota have been identified as service-style departments (Lundman, 1980:47). In these departments, police are *proactive* (discussed in detail later) in generating contacts with citizens and suspects, but they also emphasize their duty to respond to all calls for assistance. Their response to less serious offenses is likely to be noncustodial: Warnings, counseling, mediation, and referrals to nonpolice agencies are typical. Service-style departments emphasize good community relations, and each officer is expected to work toward that end.

The three styles of policing have been examined in relation to domestic disputes and traffic violations (Lundman, 1980:47–49). The distinctions related to the three styles are summarized in Table 6.1. In domestic disputes, notice that while officers in watch departments tend to do nothing or issue warnings, officers in legalistic departments treat these incidents as potentially serious infractions of the law and look to make arrests, and officers in service departments see a domestic incident as an opportunity for crisis intervention. It is important to keep in mind that the three styles are ideal types, which means they may not exist in the real world exactly as depicted, and some departments may have elements of more than one style. The distinctions Wilson has drawn nevertheless help us understand the causes and contexts of variability in police practice—for example, its connection to community organization, political structures, and police-citizen relations.

OPERATIONAL STYLES OF POLICING

A more recent study looked at how patrolling officers respond to the pressures and demands of professional policing (Brown, 1988). The study used interviews, field observations, and official police statistics in developing a typology of operational styles. An "operational style" "represents a patrolman's initial response to the uncertainties of attempting to control crime and the demands of police administrators. . . . An operational style structures action, it leads a patrolman toward some alternatives and away from others, and it is frequently the decisive factor in determining his choices" (Brown, 1988:244–245). Four operational styles were constructed from the combination of two characteristics: "aggressiveness in pursuit of the goal of crime control, and selectiveness in the enforcement of the law" (Brown, 1988:223). The typology consists of (1) Old-Style Crime Fighters, (2) Clean-Beat Crime Fighters, (3) Professional-Style Officers, and (4) Service-Style Officers.

Old-Style Crime Fighters. These officers are high on aggressiveness and selective in their enforcement of laws. They regard felonies as the only crimes "worth" pursuing since they involve "real" police work involving technical skills and street sense. They are ruthless and aggressive in their street behavior: "Most of their free time is spent prowling down darkened streets, often with

TABLE 6.1 Typical Police Responses by Type of Department and Problem

	PROBLEM AND TYPICAL POLICE RESPONSES	
TYPE OF DEPARTMENT	DOMESTIC	TRAFFIC
Watch	Ignore/minimize/separate and warn not to call again	Ignore/honk horn and yell out window/opportunity for money
Legalistic	Potentially productive of serious criminality/law enforcement problem/arrest possible	Traffic citation
Service	Opportunity to counsel and refer citizen/"crisis intervention"	Counsel and advise

Source: Richard J. Lundman (1980). *Police and Policing: An Introduction* (p. 48). New York: Holt, Rinehart, and Winston. Reprinted by permission of the author.

their car lights out, and stopping any vehicle or individual that looks even remotely suspicious" (Brown, 1988:226). However, if they do stop someone for a minor violation, they rarely write a citation or make an arrest. They make themselves unavailable or find other ways to avoid such order-maintenance activities as breaking up fights and removing drunks, and they are unwilling to do service calls. The old-style crime fighter prospers in a large department such as LAPD, which permits independent action and values officers who demonstrate skill and ability in ferreting out serious crimes. "In a way, the old style crime fighters earn the right to flout the rules to which other policemen are subject," but the price is that they are "brutal and often given to the worst abuses of police power" (Brown, 1988:229).

Clean-Beat Crime Fighters. These officers are high on aggressiveness and dislike order-maintenance and service calls. Although they also agree with the old-style crime fighter that crime prevention and control is the primary function of patrolling, they look "for all kinds of violations . . . , from jaywalking to homicide, and make as many stops as [they] can." Their approach is similar to the legalistic style, but much more aggressive and intrusive. The clean-beat crime fighter possesses none of the skill and finesse of the old-style crime fighter but "is something of a rogue elephant . . . , the kind of officer who will make a lot of felony arrests but will be consistently in trouble" with management and resented by the public (Brown, 1988:230). He is always trying to "dig something up," always on the move, always stopping cars and people. Here is an example: "[T]wo clean-beat patrolmen in the course of an evening cited one jaywalker; made three traffic stops, two of which resulted in citations; arrested six drunks, although two were the result of backing up a vice unit in a bar; stopped and interrogated one suspected heroin addict; and made two other investigative stops in "suspicious" circumstances. This was in addition to handling a moderate number of calls for service" (Brown, 1988:231). Subjected to departmental constraints and a hostile public, the zealous clean-beat patrol officer is often frustrated and resentful.

Professional-Style Officers. Some patrol officers are broad in their enforcement of the law, but low on aggressiveness. Brown calls them "professional style." "These patrolmen are legalistic without being rigid" (Brown, 1988:233). They presume neither guilt nor innocence, but regard their role as serving a public that has a right to courtesy, impartiality, and compassion. Field interrogations are the exception rather than the rule, and all calls for service are treated with thoroughness, even ones that officers generally consider trivial. Police professionalism is emphasized, but unlike the clean-beat officer, the professional-style officer follows departmental rules and policies and believes "that a policeman can enforce the law and cope with crime while maintaining rapport with the people in the community" (1988:235).

Service-Style Officers. Finally, the "service-style" patrol officer comes in two forms, both low in aggressiveness and selective in enforcement of the law, although with different levels of commitment and passion. Either way, though, hunting out criminals is not a priority. In one form, officers take the line of least resistance and do the minimum work necessary to please their supervisors. "Their code was to take problems as they occur and above all stay out of trouble" (Brown, 1988:236). In their other form, service-style officers emphasize helping people solve their problems within the framework of the law: They "combine the best of the beat cop and the professional policeman" (Brown, 1988:236). Vice laws are downplayed, but violence is regarded as a serious problem calling for police intervention. Because service-style officers are skeptical of "present approaches to police work," they are not afraid to criticize fellow officers or department policy.

There is not space here to present Brown's intriguing work in detail; suffice it to say that because his work is based on field observations and interviews, it adds an experiential dimension to the analysis of styles of policing that was missing up to now.

PROACTIVE POLICING: A MODERN TREND

The traditional police response to crime is largely reactive: Crimes occur and the police respond. However, reactive policing is inappropriate for many types of crime, such as drug dealing and many forms of white-collar and organized crime. These crimes tend to happen behind closed doors, or they involve victims who are afraid to call police or who do not even realize that they are victims of crime. A reactive strategy is also likely to be ineffective with street crimes "in those parts of cities where confidence in the police has eroded to such a degree that the citizens no longer call when they are victimized" (Moore, Trojanowicz, and Kelling, 1988:6). In these situations, police adopt a **proactive policing** strategy. The police find out about crime by uncovering it themselves. Various methods have been employed.

proactive policing Police take an active role in uncovering crime and in trying to prevent it.

- *Use of decoys.* Sometimes police pretend to be participants in crime, thereby inviting the real offenders to commit crimes in their presence. This strategy has been used for consensual crimes involving prostitution, homosexual activity in semi-public places such as highway rest areas and park restrooms, and in sting operations against the money-laundering activities of drug traffickers and the transactions of fences and thieves. In some situations, as when a rash of assaults has been taking place in a certain neighborhood, undercover police act as inviting victims, hoping to lure potential rapists and muggers into committing a crime.
- *Directed patrols.* When crimes reach epidemic proportions, or when citizen complaints become politically embarrassing, police may turn to the "directed patrol." This involves concentrating patrol officers in particular locations or in surveillance of particular individuals or groups. This sort of saturation policing has been used successfully against youth gangs. Yet departments that adopt this strategy run the risk of merely moving crime to another neighborhood, outside the area of saturation. Such "displacement effects" are an age-old problem in crime prevention,

Proactive policing is needed to find crime in seemingly legitimate places—such as businesses that launder money on behalf of organized criminal groups.

Illustration by John Overmyer

and they undermine proactive policing. The strategy of directed patrols has also been criticized for targeting black inner-city communities (Fishman, 1998:116).

- *Special units.* The police response to some crimes—for example, sexual assault—must be especially sensitive, while the response to others is complicated or dangerous. The police have developed special units to deal with such situations. Sex crime and domestic assault units are now commonplace in larger cities, and SWAT, organized crime, white-collar crime, and repeat offender teams have sprung up around the country. Since these special units often employ undercover methods and recruit informants, they may not be widely known in the community, and so have little deterrent function. However, they generate intelligence for proactive police enforcement.
- *Crime-focused community relations programs.* One form of proactive policing is represented by the "gun buyback" programs that have sprung up around the country in recent years. Police departments ask citizens owning firearms, particularly handguns, to sell them to police with no questions asked. The idea is to get guns off the street, thereby cutting down on the number of gun crimes. Thousands of guns have been turned in, often quickly exhausting the available buyback funds. But the success of buyback programs in actually reducing violent crimes committed with firearms is not proven (Rosenfeld, 1996). An alternative, but more controversial, proactive strategy for reducing gun violence is used in Harlem to combat gun use by gangs and drug dealers. This program is discussed further in Chapter 8.

POLICE AND CRIME DETERRENCE

deterrent effect A reduction in crime resulting from an increase in the risks and costs of offending relative to its benefits.

Aggressive policing such as that advocated in some proactive strategies is believed to contribute to crime reduction through its **deterrent effect**. The idea is that proactive policing raises the risks and costs of committing crime relative to its benefits, and this reduces the appeal of offending: "By stopping, questioning, and otherwise closely observing citizens, especially suspicious ones, the police are more likely to find fugitives, detect contraband (such as stolen property or concealed weapons), and apprehend persons fleeing from the scene of a crime" (Wilson and Boland, 1978:373). Deterrence is working if potential offenders see these outcomes as too costly, and therefore refrain from committing crimes.

Aggressive policing may also lower crime rates by influencing the perceptions people hold of the likelihood of being arrested. As a rule, people have only a vague notion about the actual probabilities of arrest, which are low even for serious crimes. This means that potential offenders will rarely witness an arrest occurring, and if they do, they won't necessarily know what the person is being arrested for. But if the police engage in a rigorous proactive program of arrests, even if this is mostly for relatively minor offenses such as drunkenness or traffic violations, "this is a very visible indicator of police activity . . . [and it may] send a signal to potential offenders that one's chances of getting caught are higher than they actually are" (Sampson and Cohen, 1988:165). Thus proactive policing may have a direct deterrent effect on crime by causing potential criminals to reconsider, even when the actual risks of being arrested for a particular offense may not have changed.

This idea was tested in a study relating police arrest rates for disorderly conduct and driving under the influence (DUI) to the armed robbery rates for 171 American cities (Sampson and Cohen, 1988). The study found that aggressive policing of the public order offenses directly reduced robbery rates in general, but most significantly in the case of robberies committed by adult offenders and by black offenders. Why? The authors suggest that proactive policing of public order offenses may be more visible to black citizens than to white citizens because black citizens see it not only in their own neighborhoods, but also in downtown and commercial areas, where most white suspects are arrested. This may explain why proactive policing of white areas influenced robbery rates among black offenders more than did proactive policing of black areas. Overall, the authors concluded that aggressive police patrolling of public order crimes did have a deterrent effect on adult robbery.

DRAWBACKS OF PROACTIVE POLICING

The first drawback to proactive policing is that it intrudes too much into the lives of citizens and may violate their civil rights. A case in point is the experience in New York City, where a program of aggressive field interrogations and "pat-downs," mostly of minority youths, has reportedly been largely responsible for the city's 30 percent drop in murders and shootings from 1994 to 1995. Second, some people contend that surveillance and other offender-oriented practices raise serious constitutional questions. For example, the decoy technique raises the issue of entrapment: Are the police encouraging people to commit crimes who would not normally do so? Third, since the proactive role is one of seeking out crime, there are worries that police might actually manufacture evidence for it. Finally, some critics argue that aggressive policing helps create a self-fulfilling prophecy, since individuals who have repeated contact with the police are at greater risk of continued offending.

In addition to these drawbacks with proactive policing, three others have been raised as well (Moore, Trojanowicz, and Kelling, 1988):

1. Police are reluctant to build explanations of crime into enforcement strategies. This means that proactive policing strategies are rarely driven by an understanding of the causes of crime.
2. Police are reluctant to encourage neighborhoods and communities to develop their own self-defense capability—block watch programs and property-marking campaigns were token efforts, but police strongly resisted inroads from private security forces and from volunteer groups such as the Guardian Angels.
3. Police often fail to realize that community support is vital to the success of police anti-crime efforts. Since the police rely heavily on the public for information about crime, all aspects of the police function deteriorate when citizens are reluctant to communicate with police or to encourage their activities. Intelligence gathering is at the heart of much proactive policing, and this rests upon solid community support of the police. Community support in turn rests upon how the police behave in their everyday encounters with the public (Kinsey, Lea, and Young, 1986). An overly aggressive strategy of proactive policing, or one that is thought to show bias against a particular group or neighborhood, may end up undermining community support of the police.

COMMUNITY POLICING: A REALISTIC SOLUTION?

Some forms of proactive policing are designed to meet the criticisms outlined earlier (Moore, Trojanowicz, and Kelling, 1988:8–10). These initiatives are sometimes referred to as *team, neighborhood,* or **community policing**. The basic idea is to foster closer collaboration between the police and the public in the fight against crime. The following are among the new techniques:

community policing Proactive policing strategies based on close collaboration between the police and the public.

Community policing can take many shapes, but it always includes getting citizens involved in crime prevention. Here an officer lectures school children on drug resistance.

PHOTO BY BOB STRONG, COURTESY OF IMAGE WORKS

- Enhanced police presence, including conspicuous foot patrols and routine contacts between police and all (not just suspect) citizens.
- Close surveillance of dangerous or repeat offenders—suspects in current crimes and even parolees are placed under continuous surveillance, and the public is canvassed by local police for information about them (which in itself may deter potential offenders who learn from others that the police are keeping tabs on them).
- Shoring up community institutions, as when local police participate in efforts to strengthen schools, churches, neighborhood and community organizations, local businesses, and family relations.

Although there is little consensus on what exactly community policing is (Mastrofski, Wordon, and Snipes, 1995:541), the idea has been "intensely and professionally" marketed not only in the United States, but also in Britain and Canada (Koch and Bennett, 1993). Here is an illustration of community policing at work:

> A local school is plagued by dropouts who continually hang around the school intimidating both students and teachers. Crime has increased in and around the school. The principal decides to crack down on the problem. The neighborhood police officer becomes involved in the efforts. He teaches a course in youth and the law, increases his surveillance of the grounds, consults with teachers about handling problems, and invokes other agencies to become involved with youths who have dropped out of school. (Moore, Trojanowicz, and Kelling, 1988:10).

Note that what is *not* emphasized here is the traditional police tool of arrest. Community policing "rejects law enforcement as the single, core, function of police" (Mastrofski, Worden, and Snipes, 1995:557).

It remains to be seen how well community policing works in reducing crime and disorder and in building communities—the research so far shows mixed results (Greene, 1989; Rosenbaum, 1994; Moore, 1992). In many ways, community policing represents a return to the neighborhood-centered social control of the nineteenth century, except that modern technology, bureaucratization, and a more impersonal society complicate the picture. Indeed, one study of large urban police departments found that the organization and structure of departments with community policing programs were largely indistinguishable from those without such programs (Maguire, 1997). The success of community policing strategies thus rests only partly on the initiative and willingness of patrol officers. Also important is the willingness of high-ranking police officials to decentralize command and decision-making structures. But this has not happened, because some police managers fear losing control in day-to-day affairs, and it is hard for many of them to reduce the operational emphasis on the reactive mode of policing, which has long dominated police operations. Neither the support of beat officers nor of the brass can be taken for granted when it comes to community policing. Furthermore, community policing also places considerable emphasis on the public's willingness to be partners in the effort—something else that cannot be taken for granted (see Box 6.5).

Other resistance to community policing has come from middle management—lieutenants and captains—who see their authority and discretion undermined by giving more decision-making freedom to patrolling officers. This resistance may be overcome with careful planning, clear specification of department goals, and encouragement of innovation and creative problem solving at all levels of police organization (Kelling and Bratton, 1993; Sadd and Grinc, 1996).

Overcoming the resistance of patrol officers, whose practical experiences with community policing have left them disillusioned because crime and disorder have not declined in the neighborhoods they patrol, is another matter. Although officers may help bring about improvements in the physical condition of neighborhoods—cleaner streets, fewer broken windows, fenced-in lots, murals instead of graffiti—patrol officers want to be seen as successful crime fighters. In interviews with community policing officers, some also spoke of the limits of their policing role: "Although the neighborhood was clean, residents still expressed fear about crime. Community police officers would visit apartments and listen to tenants express fears about known criminals, drugs dealers, violence next door, the inability of families to provide children with adequate care, and many other social ills" (Ryan, 1994:132).

Despite these criticisms and concerns, community policing success stories are beginning to appear around the world (Bayley, 1998:142–158). Some show greater citizen involvement and satisfaction with the police, a lower crime rate, and increased job satisfaction among the officers selected for the project. In an experiment with community policing in Madison, Wisconsin, police officers felt a sense of participation in organizational decision making, participated more in investigations and had more contacts with detectives, and were more satisfied with working conditions and supervision (Wycoff and Skogan, 1994). Meanwhile, a survey of residents found perceptions that officers were more visible and more helpful in solving problems, and that violent crimes had decreased—although there was also an increased perception that the project area had a big problem with drugs and parking.

The success of community policing programs seems to be rooted in the commitment of both police managers and the officers assigned to the programs, and in two other features: (1) decentralization, with officers working in teams physically housed within the beat areas; and (2) training in "problem-oriented" policing. This approach requires officers to establish the exact nature of a problem, to seek input from other officers and the public, to base decisions on data

Box 6.5

JUSTICE INNOVATIONS

COMMUNITY POLICING IN EAST ST. LOUIS, ILLINOIS

Community policing strategies are being developed that try to incorporate active participation by the public and by prosecutors and judges. Such a strategy is being tried in East St. Louis, Illinois. This city has the reputation of being crime-ridden, and annually claims one of the highest homicide rates in the nation. Citizens are fed up, but until the arrival of riverboat gambling in 1993, the city's treasury was so bare that there was no money to provide working police equipment, let alone staffing and other resources at levels that matched community needs. In July 1994, with new gambling revenues and 23 surplus patrol cars from the state, East St. Louis began an ambitious plan of crime fighting in cooperation with state and federal prosecutors, educators, and community leaders.

The plan involves regular meetings between police, neighborhood leaders, educators, and the public. The effort involves youth-oriented programs to educate them about drugs, violence, and other problems, as well as the following measures (*St. Louis Post-Dispatch*, July 9, 1994, p. B1):

- Relying on residents to turn in crack dealers and make anonymous calls to the police.
- Making frequent, high-visibility sweeps of neighborhoods to root out drug dealers and shut down crack houses.
- Making high-profile sweeps regularly to serve federal and state arrest warrants.
- Sharing computerized information so that various agencies know what others are doing and where the problems are.
- Holding weekly meetings involving all the agencies to plan the next week's attack.
- Using tougher federal sentencing, where possible.
- Engaging in extensive undercover detective activities.

It is too early to tell whether this program will make a significant difference to crime in East St. Louis. The plan incorporates various proactive strategies but also relies heavily on cooperation across law enforcement agencies. The plan's success will depend on active participation by citizens, including their willingness to keep an eye on their neighbors and to report troublemakers to the police. Even if participation levels are high, the plan faces an obstacle that may be impossible to overcome: the future for many young males in East St. Louis looks extremely dim—there are few jobs, and even fewer jobs with sufficient wages to sustain a family.

instead of on emotions, to establish and follow a strategy for dealing with the problem, and to keep the complainant and/or other residents informed of progress.

If community policing is truly the "new orthodoxy" of law enforcement, as some believe (Sadd and Grinc, 1996:1), then its long-term success will rest not only on how it is implemented but also on adequate funding. Many police departments developed limited community policing initiatives in the early 1990s only to find that the money dried up after six months or a year. A long-term commitment of resources is needed, and this will require the support of both the public and politicians, which at present is mixed. A cautionary observation about the future of community policing has been expressed this way:

> What will happen after we have built a public expectation that the police can do all things for all people? What will happen when . . . unemployment starts to creep up, the economy shrinks, inflation builds, cut-back management highlights the federal budget, and the new "boom" generation hits the criminal justice system? Will tension further increase between minorities and police and erupt in frustration and riot? During these times, will the police still be able to afford storefront operations, graffiti patrols, crime watch, DARE programs, and other community policing projects? Or will the police be mandated to respond more effectively to 911 calls? (Taylor, Fritsch, and Caeti, 1998:5)

These authors, who support innovations in policing, believe that police should continue to refine the concept of what good policing is, and "should continue to press forward in a positive manner." In their view, community policing is a worthy attempt to respond to the connections between crime and the quality of life in neighborhoods and towns across America. But it should not be thought of as the last step in the evolution in American policing: New challenges will require new innovations.

SUMMARY

In this chapter we learned that people who go into police work are just like anyone else, although historically white males are much more likely to have been recruited than women or minorities. Affirmative action programs coupled with political gains by minorities and women have helped improve their opportunities in hiring and promotion, although there is still a long way to go in dismantling decades of racism and sexism in policing. Some of the gains made in recent years may be in jeopardy as public opinion, a conservative Supreme Court, and a Republican Congress chip away at the policies and practices of affirmative action. Being black, Hispanic, Native American, or female seems to have no bearing on how well an individual performs as a police officer; however, the attitudes and actions of a few thoughtless and prejudiced members of a police department or community can make the job a lot more difficult than it need be.

Once on the force, novice police soon learn to think, act, and respond like their fellow officers. The demands of the job and a "cop culture" help create a "working personality" among police, in which defensiveness, suspicion, danger, and depersonalization mix with professionalism, authority, and efficiency to shape responses to everyday actions and events. Past and current experiences, shared expectations, and a concern for self-preservation lead police to develop stereotypes of suspicious people and places and concentrate their resources accordingly. Regrettably, these stereotypes are tinged with the prejudices and myths of the larger society in which police operate, serving to reinforce patterns of police activity that target black and Hispanic citizens far more than white citizens, the young far more than the old, and poorer parts of town far more than the richer suburbs. The Rodney King incident was examined in that context.

Different styles of policing reflect the historical, social, and political characteristics of a community, as well as departmental history, the demands of professionalism, and the expectations of high-ranking officers. We saw that the different styles had implications for the way officers carry out their duties, and even define them.

Proactive policing is the new trend in police circles, although vice and narcotics officers have been doing it for years. Proactive strategies attempt to root out crime and criminals before they are a problem, rather than afterward. Community policing is a neighborhood-based strategy that seeks to encourage closer ties between citizens and the officers who patrol their neighborhoods. Close surveillance and an enhanced police presence are combined with attempts to shore up community institutions such as schools, churches, local businesses, and community organizations. Community policing has many supporters both inside and outside police circles, but there are detractors as well. The future of community policing rests on adequate funding, decentralization of police organization, appropriate training, and, perhaps above all, on the willingness and ability of patrol officers to tear down the barriers between the police ("Us") and the people ("Them"). This will require commitment, support, and understanding from supervisors and most of all from the public itself.

WHAT DO YOU THINK *NOW*?

- Are police recruits different from other people? What motivates them to become police officers?
- Judging from what you've learned, do you feel that prejudice still exists toward hiring and accepting women and minorities as police officers? Why or why not? What steps can be taken to prevent this? What are the dangers of not preventing this?
- How do the three main functions of policing interact? Do you feel they should be evenly balanced, or are some functions more important to police than others?

KEY TERMS AND CASES

police culture
job-related exercises
defeminization
Plessy v. Ferguson
affirmative action
quotas
United States v. Paradise
reverse discrimination
diversity training
police perspective
defensiveness
professionalization
depersonalization
working personality
reasonable suspicion
code of police conduct
styles of policing
proactive policing
deterrent effect
community policing

ACTIVE LEARNING CHALLENGES

1. Discuss the screening procedures for police recruits. Do they ensure the selection of high-quality recruits? What improvements could be made to improve the selection process?
2. Divide the class into two groups. Have each group select opposing positions on this statement: "Affirmative action programs have outlived their usefulness and should be terminated." Research the issue as it pertains to the police and debate it in class.
3. More education is proposed as one strategy for improving the quality of policing. In pairs, find out what your state's education standards are for police, and investigate how these have changed over the years. See if you can find evidence of the benefits or costs of these changes in your state.

4. Invite experienced officers from your nearest urban police department to describe their version of the cop's code and how it has influenced the way they and fellow officers do their job.
5. Break into small groups and have each select a particular example of proactive policing. Find out the theory behind the approach, how it is used by local departments, and whether it has been successful in preventing or reducing crime.

INTERNET CHALLENGES

The Web pages mentioned here can all be accessed through the Web site for this textbook at **http://www.prenhall.com/barlow/.**

1. To learn more about the police culture, explore the unofficial home pages of law enforcement officers from around the world at the Police Officer's Internet Directory. Find out what cops think about police issues such as danger, use of force, community policing, diversity, and family relationships. Is cop culture the same everywhere?
2. Check out the current selection and training requirements for police officers in state and federal law enforcement agencies. The U.S. Department of Justice home page is a good place to start for the federal system, while state governments can generally be reached at their home pages.
3. Job-related jokes are passed around by cops just as they are in most other professions. Like war stories, jokes help promote camaraderie and sometimes teach important lessons. Many jokes are about criminals who have done stupid things, and sometimes they are about stupid cops, too. For examples and links to cop sites on the Web, check out America's Dumbest Criminals. Bring a joke back to class and see if your classmates can figure out the messages it contains.
4. Explore how community policing is being practiced in the United States and in other countries. The best place to start is with the Community Policing Consortium. You can follow its many links to individual departments and check out their community policing programs.

CHAPTER 7

THE EXERCISE OF DISCRETION

LEARNING OBJECTIVES

- Explain the reasons police officers sometimes do not make arrests or issue traffic tickets.
- Distinguish among the legal, behavioral, subjective, and official elements of arrests.
- Understand how field stops and interrogations reflect the exercise of discretion.
- Explain how the interrogation process is vulnerable to abuses by police officers.
- Describe how the police response to calls for assistance is influenced by discretion and stereotyping.
- Distinguish between elective and non-elective shootings, and describe how departmental policies and cultures of violence influence shootings by and of police.

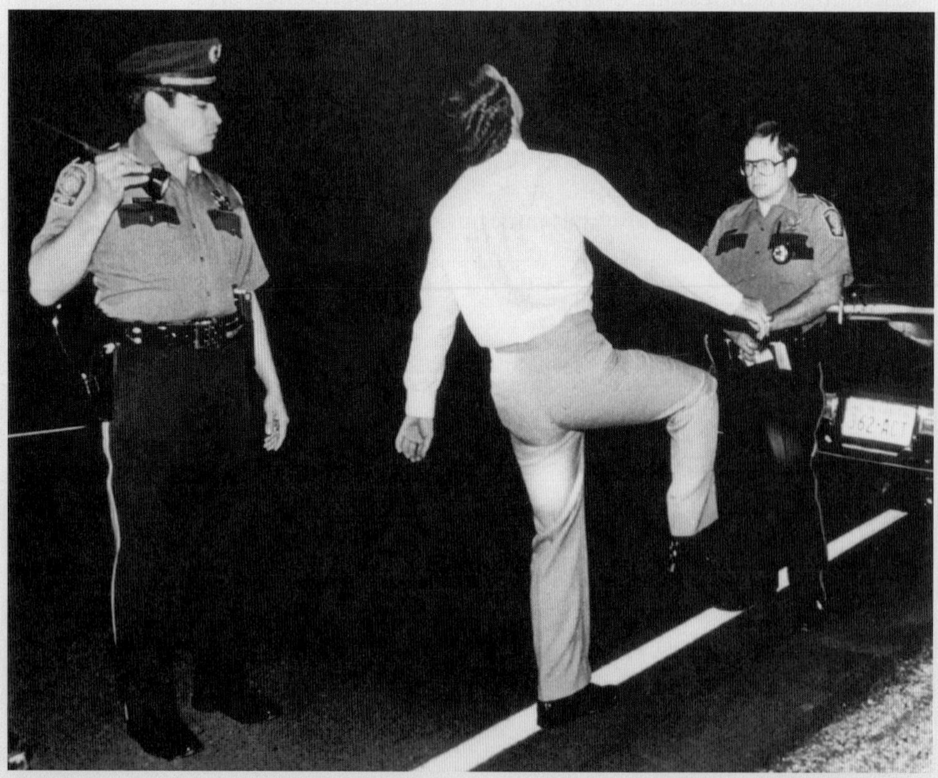

At any point, these officers could release the driver taking the sobriety test; that decision would reflect the exercise of discretion. The scope of discretion is enormous, and deciding who not to arrest is as important as deciding who to arrest.

PHOTO COURTESY OF AP LASERPHOTO

You do the right thing and somebody who sits behind a desk—somebody who's supposed to be on your side—doesn't back you up!

NEW YORK CITY PATROLMAN ON A PROSECUTOR'S REFUSAL TO ISSUE A CHARGE

Where the suspect poses no immediate threat to the officer and no threat to others, the harm resulting from failing to apprehend him does not justify the use of deadly force to do so.

U.S. SUPREME COURT, IN *TENNESSEE V. GARNER ET AL.*, 1985

Officers Linda James and Brian Kelso had joined their department in the same year. They had become acquainted during their training at the police academy and now found themselves assigned to patrol duties in the same district, although on different shifts. Each week they would meet over coffee to discuss how things were going and to share information about their beat.

During their conversation one day, Brian described two young men he had noticed hanging around a busy street corner around noon each day. "They'd be gone within twenty or thirty minutes," Brian told Linda. As far as he could tell they were not waiting for anyone, but something just didn't seem right. He asked Linda what she would do. Linda thought the two men could be on a lunch break, or they could be waiting for someone who never showed up. Or perhaps they were watching someone or something else. Could they be "casing" one of the corner businesses, or checking on the movements of someone in preparation for a robbery? Had Brian noticed anyone talking to them? Perhaps they were selling drugs under cover of the lunchtime crowd.

As they thought about all the criminal exploits the men could be up to, it occurred to Brian that the next time he saw them he could make his presence known and see what would happen. If they were up to no good they might see Brian's presence as a warning and leave the area for good. If they ignored Brian and continued to hang around the street corner then he would have to consider whether to be more intrusive, perhaps even talk to them. Brian considered the men's behavior suspicious, but he doubted whether he had legal grounds to interfere with their movements. He had no grounds to believe they were armed, but they could be. To confront them might pose a danger to passersby, as well as to himself.

Linda wondered whether Brian had considered asking one of the undercover officers to put the men under surveillance. "They'd laugh at me," Brian replied, "And anyway, they are always complaining about how understaffed they are and the long hours they put in. I can't see them putting someone on this, especially since I'm a rookie. No, I think I'll just keep an eye on them myself. Hopefully, they'll disappear."

Brian avoided taking decisive action over the two men, but his intuition would not let him ignore the situation altogether. Every day police officers are faced with two decisions whenever they enter a situation: whether to take any action at all, and what kind of action to take. Much of the time, the choice of action reflects the exercise of **discretion:** decisions made on the basis of professional judgment. How many times have you seen a law broken in the view of a police officer, who did nothing? Or consider what happens to many juveniles caught committing offenses: They are lectured by the cops and then sent home, or perhaps their parents are called to pick them up; no report of the incident is ever made. These are examples of police using discretion; the alternative in these cases would be to make an arrest and start the relevant paperwork. The exercise of discretion lies at the heart of police work; it is how the police create order out of the everyday uncertainty that characterizes their work environment.

discretion Criminal justice officials may choose one action over another on the basis of their professional judgment.

Of course, the police are not the only ones to exercise discretion in the criminal justice system. Discretion is exercised at all levels: by police, by prosecutors, by judges, by probation and parole officials, and by prison personnel. When suspects pass into the system as a result of police decisions, some are then sifted out while others are handed over to the next step, where the process is repeated. Criminal justice officials at each stage find that preceding discretionary decisions have placed limits on their own choices: If the police do not make an arrest, there is no one to prosecute; if prosecutors drop charges, there will be no trial; and so on.

In the daily routines of criminal justice, the police are typically the first officials to exercise discretion. Their decisions shape law in action, and "through the exercise of discretion patrolmen define and redefine the meaning of justice" (Brown, 1988:7). In similar circumstances one citizen may be arrested while someone else is let go; or perhaps one suspect's refusal to cooperate is handled in a different way than another's. Yet the exercise of discretion is by no means a free-for-all. As we shall see, there are rules, expectations, and understandings governing its use, and police officers who ignore this may risk their jobs, if not their lives.

The scope of discretion—that is, the range of choices of action that can be made in a given situation—is enormous. Consider the case of traffic stops. There are at least 770 different combinations of actions that officers could appropriately take (Bayley and Bittner, 1989:98–99). This number is calculated by multiplying ten different actions officers could choose when making initial contact by seven strategies used during the stop and by eleven options for exiting the encounter ($10 \times 7 \times 11 = 770$). Here are some of the exit options that officers could select when dealing with the driver (Bayley and Bittner, 1989:98):

- Release the car and driver.
- Release the driver with a warning.
- Release the driver with a traffic citation.
- Arrest the driver for a prior offense.
- Arrest the driver for being drunk.
- Arrest the driver for actions during the stop.
- Insist the driver proceed on foot.
- Transport the driver somewhere without making an arrest.

Needless to say, dealing with traffic offenses is only one part of the police job; *all* routine police work involves choosing among alternative courses of action. Discretion is the core of policing.

WHAT DO YOU THINK?

- Do police officers use discretion more often today than they did in the past?
- What are the most important factors influencing police decisions to make an arrest?
- Do the police treat women or minorities differently than other groups? If yes, in what ways?

DECISIONS TO ACT UNOFFICIALLY OR TO DO NOTHING

selective enforcement Police enforcement of some laws and not others, or enforcement of laws in some situations but not in others.

Of necessity, the police engage in **selective enforcement** of the law. This means that "the police do not enforce all the laws all the time against every single violator" (Doerner, 1998:152). Some experts believe that the most important discretionary decisions are the *negative* ones, such as not to make an arrest, not to investigate a complaint, or not to make deals. These decisions establish the line between people "getting into trouble" and "getting away with it." They define the limits of the law.

There is a strong incentive for police officers to avoid taking official action: Once they decide to take such action, whether it is responding to a complaint, writing a report, or making an arrest, that decision is subject to review by others. A review can mean a rewarding pat on the back, perhaps even a promotion; but it may also bring criticism, suspension, even dismissal. Decisions to act unofficially or to do nothing, on the other hand, are rarely reviewed because they are usually of low visibility (Gottfredson and Gottfredson, 1988:50). By their very nature, "do nothing" decisions will not be scrutinized by third parties except in extraordinary circumstances. Negative decisions contribute an element of mystery to the routine actions of police officers while lessening both internal (departmental) and external (public and legal) controls.

Given the low visibility of police decisions not to invoke the criminal process, information about such discretionary actions has generally been hard to find. However, recent research on police decision making, including autobiographical accounts by police, has uncovered clues as to why, how, and when nonenforcement decisions are made (Brown, 1988; Bayley and Bittner, 1989; Ragonese, 1991; Fletcher, 1991; McNulty, 1994; Doerner, 1998). Let us review some of the major reasons why police take no action or choose not to enforce a law.

First, police may believe that the *legislative purpose* behind a particular law "would not be served by arresting all persons who engage in the prohibited conduct" (Kadish and Kadish, 1973:74). Examples are gambling laws, traffic laws, and consensual sexual offenses. Imagine how tied up traffic would become if the police stopped every violator they saw; the purpose of traffic laws is to *help* the orderly flow of traffic, not to disrupt it.

Second, some enforcement selectivity is inevitable given the *limitations of police resources.* These resource limitations involve more than simply the time, money, personnel, or equipment available to the police: If there is not enough jail space, sooner or later the police will reduce the number of arrests they make. This will be experienced first with misdemeanors (Wiseman, 1970:71), but it could extend to more serious offenses. This happened in California following the introduction of tougher drunk driving laws in 1982 (Kinkade and Leone, 1992). So many people were being jailed on DUI charges that there was less room for felony suspects, and fewer felony arrests were made.

When this happens, the public may become agitated enough to pressure public officials to do something. This happened some years ago in St. Louis, Missouri, after jail beds had been full to overflowing for some weeks. An injunction was handed down by a local judge requiring that jail occupancy not exceed federal standards. Faced with the choice of letting felony suspects out or not arresting them in the first place, or finding new facilities, local jail officials bowed to public pressure and decided to house the jail overflow in a local hotel. Needless to say, the news media quickly broke this story!

Third, police may be aware that some laws prohibit behavior that is acceptable and expected among some groups in society, and they decide to treat violators selectively because of it. *Subcultural approval* of illegal behavior does not inevitably result in the police doing nothing, for that decision usually depends on how serious, disruptive, or blatant the offenses are. For example, youths who vandalize or spray graffiti on school buildings, deal drugs, or gang-bang may claim significant group support for their behavior, but it is often an unsuccessful defense against police action. At Grateful Dead concerts, however, all manner of infractions escape enforcement, even with police present.

Fourth, in some situations, victims are more interested in *restitution* than criminal sanctions, and the police bow to victim interests. This often happens in shoplifting incidents. In such cases, getting back what was taken satisfies the immediate interests of many victims, who can then also avoid the hassle of giving depositions or court testimony. For their part, the police can treat the case as resolved to the satisfaction of the real victim, and they, too, avoid the hassle of paperwork, further investigation, tracking down witnesses, and going to court—not to mention review of their actions by superiors.

Fifth, police shape their enforcement patterns to some extent on the basis of *community preferences.* A classic illustration of this deals with police enforcement practices in a run-down river town (Alix, 1969:332–339). Rather than bust taverns and other commercial violators of liquor and vice laws on each violation, the police responded to community pressures by rotating their raids, thus keeping offending businesses open and revenue flowing into the town's meager bank account.

Sixth, the police routinely use informants (Rubinstein, 1973; Fletcher, 1990, 1991; Pogrebin and Poole, 1993). Many of these informants are known offenders whom the police decide not to arrest or charge in view of their potential usefulness. By not taking official action, the police have an opportunity to turn a suspect into a *police asset.* The grateful suspect becomes a steady source of information that street cops and detectives use to develop other, more important cases, or simply to stay abreast of what is happening on the street.

Seventh, there are some occasions when officers do not invoke the criminal process because "the personal harm the offender would suffer on being arrested outweighs the law enforcement gains . . . achieved by arresting" (Kadish and Kadish, 1973:75). Such *relative gain* decisions usually have to do with the status of offenders—for example, their age, occupation, or standing in the community. People with more to lose may be given a break, particularly if their offenses are considered petty by police. "Do nothing" discretion is less likely to be followed with suspects who are stereotypically linked with serious crime, such as lower class and minority males.

Eighth, discretionary nonenforcement sometimes reflects the importance of maintaining good *working relationships* among police and with other criminal justice personnel. Police rarely give tickets to other police, even those from faraway states. Leniency confirms the special bond among police. In addition, police work closely with prosecutors, judges, and other officials in the system. Decisions are sometimes influenced by what is likely to happen later on: If the choice is whether or not to arrest a suspect, "the police will often not wish to 'waste' time on arresting individuals who may subsequently be given a merely nominal sentence by the court" (Bottomley, 1973a:41).

In addition to these eight reasons for not enforcing the law, police discretion is also influenced by worries about personal safety and, more generally, the symbolic threat posed by certain citizens (Box, 1981:162–163). These are people who police believe will go over their heads and appeal to higher-ups if street decisions anger them. Denver police interviewed in one study held a clear image of who those citizens are: the wealthy, the connected, and those in professional jobs (Bayley and Mendelsohn, 1968:102).

MAKING ARRESTS

In the minds of many people (and some police officers), the image of suspects being handcuffed defines routine police work. But the daily work of patrolling rarely involves making arrests, or even contact with criminal suspects: "The most cursory observation of patrol officers on the job overturns the imagery of people who make their living parceling citizens into jail" (Black, 1971:1088). Across the nation, the average number of arrests made in any given year is under 40 per patrolling police officer, and only around 8 per officer if serious offenses alone are considered! Even in urban areas, where crime is concentrated, police officers make relatively few arrests. A study of arrests by officers in Chicago, Los Angeles, Detroit, New York, Houston, and Philadelphia found that, on average, they made under 10 felony arrests per year (Pate and Hamilton, 1990). Box 7.2 (pages 246–247) illustrates a typical day in the life of a patrol officer.

THE MEANING OF ARRESTS

Infrequent as it may be from day to day, the decision to **arrest** someone is arguably the most significant discretionary step police officers will take while working the street. To deprive people of their liberty, even for a short time, is no trivial matter. In the opening pages of his partially autobiographical treatise on the terrors of life under the totalitarian regime of Joseph Stalin, *The Gulag Archipelago,* Aleksandr Solzhenitsyn provides a stark account of the "blinding flash" of an arrest. An arrest "is an instantaneous, shattering thrust, expulsion, somersault from one state into another." The statement "You are under arrest" instantly transports an individual from a state of physical freedom to physical restraint. Furthermore, the arrested person is now an official criminal suspect. Somewhat like a young child, he or she is restricted in making even basic decisions—to speak, to go to the bathroom, to sit down, to eat.

arrest A person is physically detained by an authorized agent of the state and is not free to leave.

Next to life, liberty is our most cherished possession. Procedural laws and departmental rules governing arrest are therefore of great importance. They help establish when it is appropriate and inappropriate for the police to make an arrest; they also provide rules governing how arrests are to be made, including the amount of force that can be used. It might look straightforward on TV, but what we call an "arrest" is actually quite a complex event, with much room for discretionary decision making.

Four Dimensions of an Arrest. There are four different dimensions of an arrest: legal, behavioral, subjective, and official (Erez, 1984; Walker, 1992:152–153). In *legal* terms, an arrest is made when someone lawfully deprives another person of liberty; in other words, that person is not free to go. The actual word *arrest* need not be uttered, but the other person *must* be brought under the control of the arresting individual. The *behavioral* element in arrests is often nothing more than the phrase "You're under arrest." However, that utterance is usually backed up by a tight grip on the arm or collar, or the drawing of an officer's handgun. Handcuffs are used to disable the person being arrested, and many departments require the use of handcuffs during field interrogation and search, as well as during transportation to the police station.

Whenever people believe they are not free to leave, to all intents and purposes they are under arrest. This is the *subjective* dimension of arrest. In any case, the arrest lasts only as long as the person is in custody, which might be a matter of a few minutes or many hours. Many people are briefly detained on the street and then released. These brief **field interrogations,** or stops, are similar to arrests in that the individual is not free to go. But the rules of "probable cause"—discussed in detail in Chapter 9—are relaxed for stops.

field interrogation Police stop citizens for brief questioning; also called "stops."

Terry v. Ohio Police may stop people whose behavior leads them to conclude, in the light of their experience, that a crime is being or is about to be committed.

In its landmark decision ***Terry v. Ohio*** (1968), the U.S. Supreme Court ruled that police should be able to stop people whose behavior leads them to conclude, in the light of their experience, that crime is being or is about to be committed. However, *the police have no authority to stop and question unwilling people whom they have no reason to suspect of a crime.* People who are stopped and briefly interrogated by the police may believe that they are in fact under arrest. This apparently happens quite often and largely explains why arrest figures based on self-reports exceed official arrest figures. Thus, when people in Philadelphia were asked about their arrest histories, they reported being arrested more often than was recorded in official arrest records (Erez, 1984).

Official arrests are those detentions that the police record in an administrative record. When a suspect is "booked" at the police station, a record is made of the arrest. However, considerable variation exists among departments (and among individual officers) regarding recording practices at other stages in the arrest process. The significance of paperwork is a factor here. Police officers at all ranks are well aware of the potential benefits and drawbacks of accurate record keeping. If a department wants to impress city hall, one way to do it is to record all arrests as early as possible in the process so that the clearance rate is high (Skolnick, 1966; Walker, 1992:153). Recall that the clearance rate is based on the number of recorded offenses that are cleared or "solved" by arrest. Police consider a case solved for statistical purposes when *any* arrest has been made for that offense. When the clearance rate is relatively high, the police look good. On the other hand, if a department or precinct wants more resources, lowering the clearance rate creates the impression that the police are overwhelmed by crime.

THE ARREST DECISION

Police making arrest decisions have many discretionary choices open to them, based on circumstances surrounding the situation and on events that unfold during the encounter itself. These include whether to make an arrest in the first place; how to conduct the arrest; how to deal with the reactions of those being arrested;

The police are more likely to arrest suspects who are disrespectful to them. This is one of the most widely replicated findings in police research: Any challenge to the police is taken personally, and is seen as an attempt to take away their control of the situation.

PHOTO BY RICK FRIEDMAN, COURTESY OF BLACK STAR

whether to make a report, and what to put in it; whether to release the person or to proceed through to the booking process. Research on arrests supports the following generalizations about the use of discretion (Piliavin and Briar, 1964; Black, 1971; Sanders, 1977; Lundman, 1979; Fletcher, 1991; Doerner, 1998):

1. *The police are lenient.* They use their arrest powers far less often than they could according to the letter of the law. To put it another way, when the police are in a position to make lawful arrests they often refrain from doing so. "An arrest is a decision of last resort" (Crank, 1998:257).
2. *The police are more likely to arrest suspects who are disrespectful toward them.* Although challenged by some recent studies (Klinger, 1994, 1996), this is one of the most widely replicated findings in police research (Worden and Shepard, 1996:83). Any challenge to police authority is a challenge to their ability to control a situation, to show who is boss. Police take respect and its perceived relationship to control very seriously, indeed: "Police officers must be *respected.* In every encounter police officers must gain *control* in the sense of initiating and orienting each part of the situation and maintain that control; they must prevail; psychological and strategic advantages must be maintained" (Strecher, 1995:217). In particular, if suspects are perceived as making encounters especially difficult for the police, an arrest is more likely (Lundman, 1994:647–649).
3. *Arrests are more likely when the evidence of a crime is strong.* Arrest is most likely when the police witness a crime themselves and when there are victims and/or witnesses available and willing to testify against the suspect. It should be noted that arrests for vice or drug offenses are rare among patrolling officers who witness them. These offenders are generally left for specialized—usually undercover—police units. In large cities, traffic offenders are left to the traffic detail.
4. *Arrests are more likely if suspect and victim are strangers.* Police are more likely to think of crimes among intimates and close friends as a

Box 7.1

CAREERS IN CRIMINAL JUSTICE

STATE TROOPER

State police are responsible for statewide enforcement of traffic and criminal laws, and they perform many specialized services as well, including accident reconstruction, drug investigations, safety programs, and search-and-rescue operations. Here are the salary, qualifications, duties, and conditions of employment of a state trooper in Oregon, as advertised in September 1998.

Salary Range: $32,664 to $47,040

Qualifications: High school diploma or GED; pass an entry-level test consisting of a written exam and a physical abilities test; successfully complete two interviews and a background investigation.

Duties: Enforce criminal laws, fish and wildlife regulations, and traffic laws throughout the state; investigate motor vehicle accidents, crimes, and other violations of state law; preserve the peace and engage in the prevention and detection of crime; respond to a variety of emergency situations, some of which may be life-threatening. Working conditions include varied hours of the day or night, weekends, and holidays, and inclement weather; troopers are subject to call-back duty in case of emergencies or court appearances.

Conditions of Employment: Include U.S. citizenship, 21 years of age, possession of a valid driver's license, and no felony convictions or misdemeanor convictions involving violence, sex, drugs, fraud, or moral turpitude.

private matter. However, as we shall see in Chapter 8, many departments now restrict the discretion allowed officers in handling domestic violence.

5. *The likelihood of an arrest increases with age, at least through age 35.* Most police encounters with juveniles who have committed offenses do not result in an official arrest. In cases of runaways, curfew violations, loitering, and intoxication, police officers often frame their discretionary decisions around the course of action best suited to the needs and welfare of the child. Many times, officers merely tell a child to go home and "not do it again," or they take the child home themselves. Sometimes, however, police elect to turn a child over to juvenile authorities; this happens most often when the charges are serious, or when officers suspect that a child is in danger of being assaulted or abused at home.
6. *The single most important factor influencing the arrest behavior of the police is the legal seriousness of an offense.* The more serious the offense, the more likely a suspect will be arrested.

It is helpful to keep in mind that the choices individual police officers make when it comes to arrests are shaped to a large extent by departmental decisions about appropriate order-maintenance and crime-fighting strategies. For example, urban police tend to concentrate their peacekeeping and enforcement activities in poor and minority neighborhoods. These areas become "overpoliced" relative to other parts of the city (Hagan, Gillis, and Chan, 1978; Smith, 1986; Fishman, 1998). To some extent this reflects the concentration in inner-city areas of violent crimes such as robbery, aggravated assault and homicide. However, because the increased police presence results in more arrests, it also reflects and reinforces stereotypes of the origins, characteristics, and dangers associated with "real" crime and "real" criminals. The result is that arrest data

Interrogations involve skillful questioning and requestioning of suspects. A seasoned interrogator knows how to look for lies, contradictions, and other signs that the suspect is hiding something. Today, interrogations are often recorded and sometimes videotaped.

PHOTO COURTESY OF GAMMA

in general include more poor and minority individuals than would otherwise be the case. Even in overpoliced neighborhoods, however, the probability of any particular individual being arrested is low.

INTERROGATING CRIMINAL SUSPECTS

Not surprisingly, from a police perspective the interrogation of suspects is perhaps the single most important process in "working up" a case. When it fits the facts of a case that police have developed, a confession virtually guarantees conviction. The police know it, and so does the person being interrogated. This helps explain why interrogations are viewed with great apprehension by people suspected of crimes. Another reason for the apprehension, however, is fear about what will happen during the interrogation. "If they get me alone in a room, they could do anything!" says the frightened suspect.

Indeed, the history of interrogations is not a pretty one. One of the very first uses of jails and prisons was to confine suspects who could then be interrogated at will. Torture was widely used to get people to confess to crimes well into the eighteenth century. Some of the methods are described in Chapter 15. Although such cruelties disappeared many years ago, ingenuity has not. There are plenty of ways suspects can be put in fear of death or unthinkable pain without actually experiencing either. When actor Laurence Fishburne put his police revolver in the mouth of a suspect during an interrogation in the 1995 film *Just Cause,* there was great tension in the movie audience. Despite constitutional guarantees and modern Supreme Court rulings outlawing any form of coercion during interrogations, people watching that scene may have worried that a similar event could happen today in some police department, somewhere in the United States.

EXPERT INTERROGATORS INTIMIDATE AND WEAR DOWN SUSPECTS

The advent of electronic recording and videotaping of confessions, now widely used in larger police departments, coupled with a rash of court cases over the past few decades, has significantly curtailed the freedom allowed officers when interrogating suspects. Yet most experts would probably agree with this comment, made nearly 40 years ago: "[I]n dealing with criminal offenders, and consequently also with criminal suspects who may actually be innocent, the interrogator must of necessity employ less refined methods than are considered appropriate for the transaction of ordinary, everyday affairs by and between law-abiding citizens" (Inbau, 1962:150).

When police interrogate suspects, the goal is to get them to incriminate themselves or others. Skilled interrogators chip away at the resistance of the suspect, looking for weaknesses and fears that can be turned into information about the case and the suspect's involvement in it. Murders are often solved through confessions, some willingly given, others cleverly drawn from suspects unable to resist their interrogators. Many times, interrogations succeed through a gradual wearing down of the suspect over many hours of questioning. Sometimes interrogators are contemptuous of the suspect, sometimes they are threatening, and sometimes they are understanding. In general, the police interrogator is an expert at seeing through lies and gauging when a suspect is about to break. This is accomplished without thumbscrews or threats of physical violence, and often without hostility. The officer is calm and professional.

Yet there are times when this is not the case. When officers are emotionally involved in a case, when the investigation has taken longer than expected, or when suspects or witnesses have been especially uncooperative, it is sometimes difficult for police interrogators to maintain a high level of professionalism. Tactics are used that interrogators believe will get the job done, even if they depart from the normal routine. The following excerpt from a taped interrogation of a suspect in the killing of a police officer will no doubt seem harsh and degrading to some people; yet the language is used to underscore the interrogators' power over, and contempt for, the suspect, and to suggest that they *know* who and what he is, and that they *will* get what they want.

Detective: OK. Do you know why you are here?
Suspect: They said robbery.
Detective: Robbery first degree, assault first degree. Now, I'm going to tell you a little secret, right here and right the fuck now. I don't like you. I think you're fucking puke. Do you understand me?
Suspect: (inaudible)
Detective: And I'm going to tell you something else that somebody's told me. Do you know what that is?
Suspect: (inaudible)
Detective: You know what that is? Don't fuck around with me, puke breath! You were there the night my sergeant got killed. Don't, don't fuckin' play.
Suspect: I ain't playing.
Detective: Hey, listen to me, shithead! You're probably wondering what took them so long to get your fucking black ass up—
Suspect: I ain't, I wasn't—
Detective: No, you lying piece of self-shit, motherfucking cocksucker, whore dog! Turn around here. Let me see your ear. Did you ever wear an earring?
Suspect: No. Never.
Detective: Never, huh? What happened to your fucking schnoz?

Suspect: I did this when I was—
Detective: How come you stink so bad? Don't you take a fucking shower? . . . OK. I'm going to tell you a little fucking secret. You know and I know you were there that night.
Suspect: You're fucking lying. . . .
Detective: And you're a fucking killer.
Suspect: No. . . .
Detective: Oh, fuck you, punk. Stand the fuck up.
Suspect: You think I'm lying, huh?
Detective: Get over here! Turn the fuck around. Don't look back here. Don't look fucking back here! Man. . . .
Suspect: I didn't did nothing, sir.
Detective: I'm talking about murder! You getting mad at me, boy? You want to fucking hit me?
Suspect: No.
Detective: Because you ain't fucking man enough to come at me straight on, head on, are you, boy?
Suspect: Now, I don't give you any problems. Now don't give me no case.
Detective: Shut the fuck up. I don't give nobody no case. I'm a nice man. If everybody was like me in this fucking world, it would be a lot better. Wouldn't be no scumbags like you out there. Rob . . . hey, you robbed somebody, bitch!
Suspect: That was six years ago.
Detective: That makes him a good man now. That makes him a good man now.
Suspect: Oh, you ain't never, you ain't never made a mistake in your life. Just say that.
Detective: Nah, I've made one fucking mistake all right. Taking this fucking job and having to deal with—
Suspect: I'm talking other than your job.
Detective: I've made a mistake before, but I've never put a gun in somebody's face and robbed them.
Suspect: Man, that was six years ago. . . .
Detective: Oh, yeah, that's right, you went to prison, you went to prison, now you're reformed. Right.
Suspect: Not exactly.
Detective: You're reformed, right. You went to prison. Everybody that goes to prison, everybody that goes to prison never does another crime.
Suspect: Not everybody.
Detective: Let me ask you this, though. Detective will give you a polygraph. Are you going to take a polygraph? Do you think you can pass a polygraph?
Suspect: What do you mean, pass? I ain't getting nothing. As long as I got a lawyer here, you know.
Detective: You can't have a lawyer there. It would just be in your own free will. Otherwise we keep investigating.
Suspect: No, I would like to have a lawyer then. Cause, you know, I don't understand about the polygraph.
Detective: You're going to need a lawyer if you killed the policeman.
Suspect: I didn't kill the policeman.
Detective: Then what do you need a lawyer for?

(*The Riverfront Times,* October 2, 1991, pp. 12–13; reprinted with permission of Hartmann Publishing Company)

It turned out that the suspect was indeed innocent of the murder, and the interrogators recognized this by the end of their interview. Do you think they went too far?

While most interrogations end in innocent suspects being released or guilty ones confessing, false confessions occasionally surface. A study of over 60 false confessions made to police during questioning reports that poor police training is largely to blame (Leo and Ofshe, 1998). The possibility of a false confession is greatest when suspects are suffering from mental illness or retardation or feel isolated and alone. Such people are less capable of dealing with the pressure of an interrogation, and less likely to understand the consequences of what they are saying. Better training will help ensure that the police bring the right suspect to justice.

THE FIELD INTERROGATION

Police officers may choose to question individuals in the field, either while on routine patrol or as part of an investigative assignment. *Field interrogations* may be a simple question or two or they may be quite involved. The field interrogation is an integral part of the job, and another area in which discretion comes into play. Deciding whether to stop and question someone is an important decision for police as well as for the general public. It not only determines whether a citizen will be detained, if only for a short time, but it could also turn out to determine the outcome of a case. How the interrogation is handled may also determine whether citizens later complain about the police officer's behavior.

The police question people they regard as suspicious or who they believe would not willingly divulge information that could help them in their investigation. The police anticipate noncooperation. They must also be prepared to turn a stop into a full arrest, and the possibility of an armed suspect raises the stakes, and the danger. If patrolling alone, an officer must also contend with the added difficulties and dangers posed when more than one suspect is present.

Studies of police field work show that officers are often very casual in their interviewing behavior, rarely taking detailed notes, sometimes none at all (Greenwood, Chaiken, and Petersilia, 1977; Sanders, 1977). Police carry information in their heads, often for many hours, sifting and sorting it until a picture forms that guides their subsequent decisions. Throughout the process, they are trying to establish what really happened and who really "did it." Interrogations are primarily designed to develop information, but they often help officers decide what actually happened and what to call it. Here is an illustration from a study of detectives at work:

> Shortly after ten, Bert and I went over to a junior high school to talk to some boys about an incident involving an assault and a stretched 211 [armed robbery]. What had happened was that a gang of boys had jumped a kid, taking a can of spray paint away from him, and sprayed him with it. A knife was supposedly involved in the incident, and since property had been forcefully taken, this was an "armed robbery."
>
> Bert had no intention of laying a 211 on these kids for the incident, but he said he might use it to scare some of them. During the interview the boys said they had caught a kid defacing a wall with a can of spray paint and had taken the can away from him and sprayed him and his bicycle. By their account, they had struck a blow for law and order by dissuading a vandal from further mischief.
>
> Bert decided they weren't really bad, and instead of referring them to probation, warned them and had them make restitution to the boy for the shirt that had been ruined by the spray paint. One of the boys

> would not admit what had happened and was told that technically he could be charged with armed robbery. After hearing that, the boy began to cry and explained what had happened. (Sanders, 1977:95)

Verbal information secured during field interrogation may point to inconsistencies or inaccuracies in the accounts of victims or witnesses, and it may also be used to "trip up" suspects in subsequent interrogations. Minor inconsistencies may be ignored, even in homicide cases, but a major inconsistency will be taken seriously and investigated further, perhaps during future questioning or through the collection of new evidence. Throughout the process, police categorize and sort the verbal information they receive, combining it with impressions—such as that the suspect is acting "guilty"—and with evidence from the scene or from witnesses.

FIELD INTERROGATIONS OF WOMEN AND MINORITIES

It is often heard that police unfairly target women and members of minority groups when conducting field interviews and traffic stops. One British study of ethnic differences in field interrogations found that more blacks than whites reported (1) being stopped while in a vehicle or on foot; (2) being questioned about an offense, having their house searched, or being arrested; and (3) being asked for documents or to provide a statement (Bucke, 1997). In this country, complaints that police are unfairly targeting black motorists along Interstate 95 has led to investigations in six East Coast states (Newhouse News Service, February 28, 1999).

In response to charges of ethnic or racial bias, police often argue that they are responding to proven stereotypes of "suspicious" persons. For example, "A police officer's experience indicates that young black men engage in robbery at a higher rate than young white men. Data on participation in crime supports this perception" (Walker, 1992:235). Sometimes ethnic groups are believed responsible for periodic crime waves, and the police take these stereotypes as a commonsense basis for targeting their field interrogations. According to a New York City police officer,

> One of the worst days in the police department is Good Friday. An awful lot of Gypsies steal on Good Friday. . . . Christ on the cross is supposed to have said, "From now on and forevermore, Gypsies can steal and it's not a sin."
>
> Good Friday is a big day for them. When I was working the Gypsies, we worked them for ten years, we would never take Good Friday off because it was a day we'd have to get up early and be on the run with them because they would be everywhere. (Fletcher, 1990:222)

As for field interviews of women, a study in Miami uncovered evidence suggesting that some male police officers went out of their way to stop women drivers for traffic violations (Fyfe, 1989). Opportunities for sexual harassment are clearly present in the practice of field interrogation.

Sex Is One of the Seductions of Police Work. Opportunities for sex with female suspects has been called one of the "seductions of police work" for some male officers (Crank, 1998:141–145). It is part of the excitement, the thrill that always lies around the corner. Although undercover cops who work the drug and vice details may have more routine contact with women in settings that promote sexual opportunities, patrolling officers find such opportunities in a variety of situations: during traffic stops of lone women, when dealing with a female victim, when offering a runaway girl a ride or a meal, when making a field interrogation of a female suspect, when responding to calls from lonely women. Not only do police have tremendous power by virtue of their job, including the

Box 7.2

INSIDE CRIMINAL JUSTICE

A DAY IN THE LIFE OF A PATROL OFFICER

The account that follows is from a former student of mine who has spent over ten years patrolling the streets of a growing Illinois city that is a university town as well as part of the St. Louis metropolitan area. In police work, no day is exactly like another; this is a composite of many days. Notice that there is relatively little "action" during the eight-hour shift.

1:30 P.M.	Iron uniform, polish boots, check equipment, load 9mm pistol, dress and double-check belt.
2:30 P.M.	Leave for work.
2:45 P.M.	Load squad car with personal equipment; check mailbox for returned incident reports that need corrections or follow-up, and for court appearances, upcoming special events such as football games, parades, in-service training; check today's patrol assignment and any special assignments or problems.
2:55 P.M.	Talk with off-going shift to see what happened during previous tour.
3:10 P.M.	Check over equipment of assigned squad car, including lights and sirens; check prisoner compartment for contraband that might have been dropped during earlier shift.
3:15 P.M.	Go to service station for gas, car wash, oil check, and other vehicle maintenance.
3:25 P.M.	Assume patrol of assigned area.
3:40 P.M.	Check subdivision for complaint of teenagers speeding after school.
4:00 P.M.	Complete initial run-through of assigned area; look for any stand-out problems that need immediate attention.
4:44 P.M.	Dispatched to traffic accident; park car to ensure safety of scene; check for injuries; call for EMS if necessary; call for additional squad cars if needed; attempt to clear roadway; interview those involved and exchange information; call for tow trucks if necessary; issue citations if warranted.

power to overlook crimes in exchange for favors, they spend much of their time dealing with highly vulnerable and marginal populations. It is easy to be seduced by the opportunities for pleasure. Here is the story of one officer:

> When I first went on patrol, I was surprised to hear some of the other officers talking about the sex they got on duty or as a result of on-duty calls. Seems like everyone talked about it. I really didn't have any offers or even really think about it until I was assigned to a one-man car and one night I stopped a female subject for running a traffic light. She was really first class and the way she acted I just kind of hinted that maybe we could reach an understanding and she picked right up on it. Well, she had enough moving violations that another one could take her license and I guess she didn't want that to happen. Anyway, I met her later that night and had a wild session. I called again a few days later and she wouldn't even talk to me. Yeah, I've had a few similar type experiences since but I'm real careful. (Sapp, 1994:195)

Box 7.2 (continued)

5:30 P.M.	Leave scene; complete accident report at a location where the squad car is visible to motorists and serves as a traffic control.
5:45 P.M.	Resume patrol.
6:30 P.M.	Respond to complaint of barking dog; advise resident to take dog in house, and that repeated complaints could result in charges.
7:10 P.M.	Run radar in area known for speeding.
7:15 P.M.	Stop motorist for speeding; do license check, check proof of insurance, and check for warrants against driver. Issue citation or warning.
7:30 P.M.	30-minute lunch break at fire station.
7:40 P.M.	Interrupt lunch for call on a domestic disturbance in progress.
7:45 P.M.	Arrive at scene with assisting officer; evaluate scene for officer safety, separate participants; interview each separately to evaluate the problem; arrest one or both participants if physical violence has occurred; if not, look for a "cooling off" solution to keep the peace.
8:30 P.M.	Write report while finishing lunch.
9:00 P.M.	Resume patrol; do foot patrol through various businesses and shopping centers; speak with employees and management.
9:45 P.M.	Check subdivisions for out-of-place people and cars.
9:55 P.M.	Stop subjects after complaint of illegal door-to-door soliciting; identify subjects; advise them of city ordinances regulating the activity and how to sell legally.
10:10 P.M.	Stop for coffee at local convenience mart.
10:20 P.M.	Check bar parking lots for intoxicated people and make walk-through of crowded bars.
10:35 P.M.	Drive through shopping center parking lots.
10:45 P.M.	Head to stationhouse to be relieved.
10:50 P.M.	Speak with oncoming shift; turn in completed reports; leave for home.

Source: Officer Todd Ramirez, Edwardsville, Ill., police department, May, 1998 personal interview.

Studies on the extent of police sexual activity on the job are few and far between, although one analysis of recent surveys of municipal and county police officers suggests that it may be widespread. For example, it has been estimated that as many as 1,520 incidents of sexual harassment *witnessed by other officers* occurred in Ohio and 3,175 in Illinois during a one-year period (Crank, 1998:143, citing research by Martin, 1994, and Knowles, 1996). Presumably far more occurred that were not witnessed or not reported in the surveys.

How Police Justify Field Interrogations. In general, the police justify field interrogations on the grounds that someone or something is suspicious. However, the authors of one analysis of field interrogations point out that the police are faced with a dilemma in explaining adequately to others why they behave the way they do. "If an officer has developed an ability to see and attend to features of scenes that most other persons do not notice, how can he show that it is 'reasonable' to stop and question a citizen?" (Daudistel, Sanders, and Luckenbill, 1979:90). The authors continue:

> The fact that officers often cannot explain the reasons for their actions does not mean that they are always covering up for one another or that they always capriciously stop citizens on the street. It appears that most of the time, those who stop and question persons do so only if they feel that an interrogation might lead to the discovery of a crime. The concern with clearing crimes and making many arrests, however, has led to stopping some persons more frequently than others. . . . So, although the frequent stopping of blacks and Chicanos, for example, may be viewed by the police as legitimate and necessary, this practice has also generated conflict in our society. . . . Most often the police do not see the complaints as legitimate, frequently responding to them by commenting, "If you were in our shoes you'd understand why we, the police, did what we did." (Daudistel, Sanders, and Luckenbill, 1979:91)

When officers stop and question citizens under dubious circumstances they will sometimes attempt to "cool out" cooperative "suspects" before letting them go. One method of cooling out is to provide a justification for the interrogation that sounds reasonable under the circumstances. Cooling out helps prevent complaints from being filed, and it also confirms the authority of the officer to make the stop and warns subjects that they should expect it to happen again. Here is an illustration:

> Driving down a residential street an officer noticed some people, Mexican-Americans, moving some belongings from a house to a truck parked adjacent to the curb. It was about 9 o'clock in the evening. The patrolmen asked what was going on and was told that the people were moving. The patrolman frisked several of them and then checked one of them for warrants. The man had no warrants and the officer decided to stop [the interrogation]. Before leaving he told the people that burglars often tell the police they are moving and this was why they were questioned. (Brown, 1988:173)

"Action" and Stereotypes of "Bad Guys." Police stops are sometimes contrived events to overcome boredom. As Box 7.2 illustrates, a lot of hours during a typical patrol shift are spent doing unexciting, routine things. Getting a little "action" spices things up while reaffirming the active, masculine culture of policing. But police do not target just anyone for this activity; they tend to choose individuals who belong to marginal groups in society and pose less risk of complaints or other negative repercussions. The following account from Memphis, Tennessee, illustrates:

> Occupants of a police car actively looked for "deviants" on their beat to break the monotony of a quiet evening. To these officers, deviants included anyone whose clothes, hair length, mannerisms, or race did not conform with an officer's standards of acceptability. Thus, youths with long hair or garish dress—"hippies," as defined by the policemen—transvestites, and blacks were stopped and questioned at the pleasure of the patrolmen.
>
> A typical scenario in a two-man squad car during periods of prolonged inactivity went something like this: Patrolmen Harry and Jack have had an uneventful evening when a car driven by some teenagers goes by. One of the youths stares (or smiles, or grimaces, or sneers, etc.) at the police car. Patrolman Jack turns to his partner and says, "Harry, let's pull that car over. Those kids are guilty of 'contempt of cop'!" Or one of the officers spots a pedestrian who appears likely to provide some "activity" and turns to his partner saying, "Jack, let's stop the fag (or hippie, or whore, or nigger, etc.) and ask him a few questions. That ought to liven things up." (Bent, 1974:17–18)

Lying scarcely beneath the surface of practices such as these are stereotypes of "bad guys," and beneath the stereotypes often lies racism. The Christopher Commission, which investigated the Rodney King incident in Los Angeles, concluded that racism was rampant in Los Angeles and that a confrontational street posture and even excessive use of force received implicit support from the police hierarchy, notably Chief Daryl Gates himself (*Los Angeles Times,* July 10, 1991, p. 1). Although racism among police may be less blatant in other communities, black citizens are often characterized as prone to crime (Brown, 1988; Rome, 1998).

To make matters worse, the stereotypes held by police are reinforced by the media, in such popular shows as *COPS, America's Most Wanted, Stories from the Highway Patrol,* and *Super Cops,* and in routine news coverage of crime (Rome, 1998:91). Since the public constructs its picture of crime and criminals largely from the media, the many visions of police stopping, looking for, or arresting minority individuals leads the public to associate minorities with trouble. In 1990, following the beating of Rodney King and the subsequent riots in Los Angeles, a sample of white Americans were asked how violence-prone black and white Americans were on a scale of 1 to 7, 1 being the most violent (Morris and Jeffries, 1990); 51 percent put black Americans in the most violent categories (1–3), but only 16 percent put white Americans in the same categories.

A confrontational street posture and images of bad guys are also fostered by people who make a living from violence. One company that produces training videos for the criminal justice community recently distributed a flyer advertising "action-filled" self-defense videos for use at home. The flyer speaks authoritatively of "knife culture" offenders and identifies members as "new immigrants from Latin and Asian countries," and "crazies on the streets." The knife culture "has you [police] as its target," the flyer asserts, and in a highlighted box adds: "For any gift-giving occasion or just to say 'I Care,' Surviving Edged Weapons makes an ideal present. ORDER TODAY."

CRIME VICTIMS AND THE EXERCISE OF DISCRETION

One important area in which the police exercise considerable discretion is in their dealings with people who consider themselves victims of crime and call for police assistance. Studies of the relationship between citizens' calls to police and police discretionary practices are rare, however. The difficulty and expense of conducting good research on this issue partly explains this situation. In addition, close observation of police discretionary practices chips away at the veil of mystery surrounding police behavior, and may be resisted by some police authorities for that reason.

What little we know suggests that police decisions are often influenced by factors that have little or nothing to do with legal issues; for example, the complainant's demeanor, preference for action, and ties with the suspect have been found to influence whether responding officers make an official report. Recall from Chapter 2 the path-breaking research undertaken in Washington, D.C., Boston, and Chicago by Albert Reiss and his student, Donald Black. These authors rode around with police as they responded to calls for assistance from the public. After taking into account the legal seriousness of an incident, police were more likely to write official reports when complainants (1) showed them respect and deference, (2) expressed a preference for formal action, and (3) were strangers to the people suspected of committing the offense in question.

Another important set of factors concerns victim decisions to appear as prosecution witnesses and to sign formal complaints when needed. The police are more likely to refuse to pursue complaints from people they believe will not undertake these responsibilities. For one thing, police realize that without the

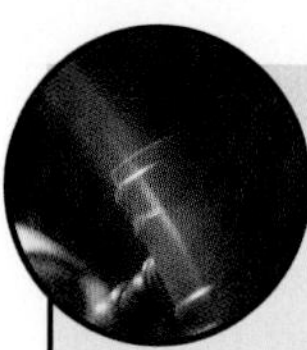

Box 7.3

JUSTICE PROFESSIONALS AT WORK

RULES AND PROCEDURES FOR THE POLICE DISPATCHER

Police dispatchers are the vital link between citizens and patrolling police. They classify calls according to their importance, then assign squad cars to go to the location. Some calls, such as ones in which no suspect or physical evidence is present, are not assigned squad cars but are referred to the Report Deck. In what ways do police judgments about "real crime" and "real victims" sometimes affect the actions of dispatchers?

PHOTO BY J. PICKERELL, COURTESY OF THE IMAGE WORKS

Most police departments have a set of rules and procedures governing the activities of police dispatchers. Here is an example from the Tallahassee, Florida, police department. It shows how calls are to be classified as they come in, and what dispatchers should do if a squad car is unavailable to respond. Note that the rules seem to assume that there will always be a car available for Priority 1 and 2 calls. Since this cannot possibly be true every time, dispatchers presumably seek assistance from other agencies, such as county or state police.

testimony of victims or witnesses, prosecutors are likely to dismiss the charges, if they even bother to file any. This is a frustrating experience for police officers, and one they learn to avoid if at all possible.

DISCRETIONARY ACTIONS BY POLICE DISPATCHERS

When citizen complaints come in on police switchboards, the responsibility for directing the police reaction rests on police dispatchers. Most police departments have a set of rules and procedures governing the work of dispatchers, an example of which is shown in Box 7.3. However, dispatchers are in a position

Box 7.3 (continued)

SUBJECT: COMMUNICATIONS

1. CALL CLASSIFICATION
   A. **Priority Calls** [The Communications Center assigns all calls for service a priority ranking of 1 through 4.]
      1. **PRIORITY 1.** Those calls requiring immediate dispatch (for example, felony-in-progress calls and accidents with injuries).
      2. **PRIORITY 2.** Those calls requiring dispatch within five (5) minutes from receipt of the call (all hazardous traffic situations, accidents without injury, nonfelonious in-progress calls, missing persons involving individuals unable to care for themselves, and the like).
      3. **PRIORITY 3.** Routine calls for police service involving other than the above priority calls and requiring the presence of a police officer.
      4. **PRIORITY 4.** All calls to be referred to the Report Deck where no suspect or the possibility of physical evidence is present.
   B. **Call Stacking**
      When a beat car is not available to respond to a Priority 3 call, dispatch will advise the field supervisor, who will decide whether or not the call will be held until a unit is available. If the call is to be held it may be held for a period not to exceed thirty (30) minutes. Once this period of time expires or a second Priority 3 call for the beat unit is received, the most important call or the call that has been holding the longest will be dispatched to the closest available unit within a two-beat radius. If no such car is available, the dispatcher will advise the field supervisor of the situation. The field supervisor will designate a unit to be dispatched or authorize the call to be held longer. The complainant or victim will be notified of the delay in response at the time the call is received by the communications center.

Source: William G. Doerner (1998). *Introduction to Law Enforcement: An Insider's View* (p. 159). Boston: Butterworth-Heinemann.

of considerable power and responsibility. Their decisions often determine whether there will be any official action, what it will initially be, and the time lag between call and response. Their discretion has a profound effect on enforcement efforts. Today, however, police departments typically have 24-hour tape recording of incoming and outgoing communications; this means the decisions of dispatchers can be more easily reviewed by supervisors—and the courts. Although this surveillance does not directly affect the range of actions open to dispatchers, it may affect the choices they make. Seasoned dispatchers may feel they have less discretion than they used to.

Even though technology is affecting the exercise of discretion in police work, police culture remains an important influence. This is seen in the construction of meanings attached to the communication between citizens, dispatchers, and patrol officers. Police culture constitutes a resource of unwritten symbols used to organize and to justify police activity. As it guides the interpretations and specific acts of individual officers, police culture provides definitions and meanings that influence how technology affects police work and that modify or even subvert departmental rules and official police codes. Despite sophisticated technology, and regardless of the availability of resources, citizen calls for assistance may end up unanswered, responses may be delayed, or complainants may simply be "put off."

Needless to say, sending a patrol to every call for assistance—even those coming in on emergency numbers—would result in absolute chaos. There are simply too many calls, and many of these turn out not to be emergencies.

KVCC KALAMAZOO VALLEY COMMUNITY COLLEGE LIBRARY

Box 7.4

CAREERS IN CRIMINAL JUSTICE

DISPATCHER/CALLTAKER

As we have seen, dispatchers are a critical component of policing, often being the first point of contact between the police and the public. Most urban areas have 911 emergency call systems, and many rural counties do too; these systems direct calls according to the service needed, which include ambulance, firefighting, and police. In some jurisdictions, the 911 calltaker acts as police dispatcher but reroutes calls for fire or ambulance services. Here are the salary, qualifications, duties, and conditions of employment of a 911 calltaker for the Kansas City, Missouri, police department.

Salary Range: $21,108 to $38,652

Qualifications: High school diploma or GED; pass keystroke test with minimum score of 80 percent; ability to learn Kansas City street system; ability to communicate effectively and tactfully; ability to handle tasks in rapid succession and in conditions that may be stressful and confining.

Duties: Serve as contact between citizens who need assistance and the systems designed to provide that assistance; receive various types of calls from assaults involving shootings and cuttings to reports of illegally parked automobiles; reroute 911 emergency calls for fire departments or ambulance assistance; acquire information from callers and determine the best way to meet the caller's need; assist citizens who do not require police response, such as giving directions and making referrals to other governmental agencies.

Conditions of Employment: 5 weeks of intensive classroom training plus 8 weeks on-the-job training in the Communications Unit.

Police are asked to deal with barking dogs, lost cats, personal problems, and all sorts of other things that have nothing to do with "real" police work (Cumming, Cumming, and Edell, 1965). Police often consider these services a drain on resources and a hindrance to their crime-fighting mission. "Most patrolmen define their task largely as the responsibility for controlling crime, and include almost nothing else" (Brown, 1988:135). Dispatchers are well aware of this view, and often attempt to deal with service calls without sending an officer.

"REAL" CRIME AND "REAL" VICTIMS

Another view held by some police officers is that certain groups do not deserve their service (Grossman, 1974). A six-month study of the communications center of a large Canadian police department illustrates this view and its impact on the exercise of discretion (Shearing, 1979). After observing and recording thousands of communications between citizens and the police and among police officers themselves, it was discovered that police officers "made a fundamental distinction between 'the public' on the one hand, and 'third- and fourth-class citizens,' 'the dregs,' or more expressively, 'the scum,' on the other. . . . The public were people the police felt duty-bound to serve and protect" (Shearing, 1979:6). The scum, on the other hand, were troublemakers; they needed police control rather than assistance and were viewed as an enemy of the police. Not surprisingly, police tended to ignore or delay responding to calls for assistance from callers identified as scum or as "stupid" or "ignorant" and therefore only marginally part of the "public."

Here is one exchange between a dispatcher and a citizen calling for assistance in another study:

> "Hello, is this the police?"
> "Yes, Madam, what is the problem?"
> "He is coming up to get me."
> "Where are you Madam?"
> "At home."
> "Where?"
> "230 Sutton Avenue."
> "Who's coming to get you?"
> "George."
> "How do you know?"
> "He just telephoned and said he would take the kid."
> "Is it his child, Madam?"
> "Yes."
> "Is he living with you?"
> "Yes."
> "When is he coming?"
> "Now."
> "Why would he want to kill you?"
> "I don't know."
> "Does he have a weapon?"
> "I don't know."
> *Pause by dispatcher.*
> "Madam, if George arrives and causes any trouble, you call the station and we will send a car."
> *Dispatcher hangs up.* (Grossman, 1974:67)

It turned out the woman was subsequently assaulted by George, just as she had feared. Why did the dispatcher decide not to activate an official police response? After discussing it with the dispatcher, it became clear that the dispatcher chose not to treat the call as a "lights and sirens" emergency (a "real" crime) because the caller sounded as if she was a member of a minority group that local police culture had defined as making too much, and often unnecessary, use of police resources.

This incident is an example of discretionary police action anchored in stereotypes and prejudice that reflect judgments about "real" crime and "real" victims. This is not an isolated problem. Systematic underrecording of crime by police has been documented both in the United States and abroad. There seems to be little question that the practice is related to both the crimes themselves and to their victims. In England, for example, police disparagingly refer to certain offenses as "rubbish" crimes (Kinsey, Lea, and Young, 1986). Rubbish crimes typically involve poor, minority, or female victims who are assaulted in a domestic setting by a friend, relative, or lover or by an offender whom the police regard as an amateur. In an American study (Sanders, 1977:80–81) detectives said that they hated "monkeying around" with "nickel and dime" cases, preferring to deal with crimes "worth investigating," which they called *righteous* crime.

The unresponsiveness of some police to crimes against certain classes of victims, particularly minorities, women, and the poor, is not confined to petty offenses and minor acts of aggression, although this is where it is found most often (Elias, 1986:133–146). Today, largely because of civil rights activists and the women's movement, many police officers are more sensitive about minority victimization, and departments are trying to address racism and prejudice in their hiring and training programs.

Such positive steps must overcome three things:

- The police receive little reward for catering to victims, especially those with no political clout (Elias, 1986:140–141).
- It is likely that stereotyping will endure in police culture despite the enlightenment of some officers and their supervisors.
- Previous unresponsiveness of police may contribute to the reluctance of vulnerable people to call police after they have been victimized—let alone before.

A related complaint is that when police officers *do* respond to calls for assistance, they frequently appear to do very little. According to victim accounts in one investigation of police practices in the field, police asked few questions, even in cases of violent crimes; in the case of burglaries, they did not even "look around" in half the incidents (Whitaker, 1989:6). Even if these victims totally misunderstood good police practice, which is possible, the fact that many felt little was done indicates room for more effective communication between police and civilians.

POLICE AND DEADLY FORCE: SHOOT OR DON'T SHOOT?

Police exercise of discretion is inevitable and desirable. The system of policing—indeed, the criminal justice system as a whole—would simply collapse without it. It also carries with it enormous responsibility. Exercised humanely, cautiously, and in the service of all the people, discretion makes for law enforcement that is just and responsive to social needs. Exercised inhumanely, carelessly, or in the service of prejudice or special interest, discretion becomes intolerable and must be curbed. Nowhere is the problem of discretion more acute than in the decision to use deadly force.

GUNS AND POLICE CULTURE

To understand the use of deadly force by police, it helps to understand the role of guns in police culture. Guns are part of the police uniform in the United States and in many other countries—but not in all. For example, officers on routine patrol in the United Kingdom do not carry guns. Each police constabulary, or jurisdiction, does have a number of Armed Response Vehicles (ARVs), although they are rarely used. ARVs are police cars with armed officers; they are called in as a backup for unarmed officers in life-threatening situations. The decision to call for an ARV is a discretionary one usually made by officers at the scene. It is widely believed in the United Kingdom that arming the police will encourage criminals to arm themselves, and an escalation of gun crimes would surely follow.

In America, guns are a central theme of police culture; they are an important part of the training experience, and throughout an officer's career they are never far from his or her thoughts. Guns have important practical and symbolic meaning:

> In the culture of policing, guns transform police work into a heroic occupation, providing both a bottom line and an unquestionable righteousness that pervades all police-citizen encounters. From training ceremonies to funeral rites, guns symbolize the danger of police work. The gun is the ultimate arbiter of the dangerous unknown. With the gun, the capacity of the police to deal with problems is not bounded by the physical strength or wiliness of an individual officer, though both are desired traits. With guns, police are not just good guys, but good guys with *stopping power,* a distinction that celebrates the use of all necessary force to resolve any dispute, however violent. (Crank, 1998:82)

In addition, there is some evidence that a more militaristic orientation is taking hold in municipal police departments across the country (Kraska, 1996; Kraska and Kappeler, 1997; Crank, 1998:71–75). This new militarism has been supported by the spread of specialized **paramilitary units** (called PPUs). PPUs were originally organized during the 1970s as antiterrorism, antiriot, or SWAT (special weapons and tactics) teams. Their use declined somewhat during the 1980s but appears to be enjoying a resurgence today, particularly in the enforcement of drug laws. It is estimated that one in five police departments in cities of over 50,000 population use PPUs (Kraska and Kappeler, 1997).

paramilitary units Specialized police units trained in the use of military equipment, weapons, and tactics.

While the increasing use of paramilitary units has not been linked to any increase in gun violence by or against police, in fact quite the opposite, some experts worry that it is promoting a "warrior" mentality among police. "It is a vision that celebrates firepower, and PPUs occupy high status within police organizations. . . . [T]he criminal is seen as the *enemy*, and the mission as search and destroy" (Crank, 1998:74). President Lyndon Johnson spoke of the "war on crime," and 30 years later U.S. Attorney General Janet Reno revived the concept in a speech before military and law enforcement officials: "Let me welcome you to the kind of war our police fight every day. And let me challenge you to turn your skills that served us so well in the Cold War to helping us with the war we're now fighting daily on the streets of our towns and cities" (Kraska, 1996:419). It is possible that the militarism represented by the language, training, and weaponry of warriors may dominate policing as the 21st century unfolds. The importance of guns and firepower as themes in police culture will likely grow as a result.

Force Need Not be Deadly. Firearms are not the only way to stop a citizen committing, or about to commit, a crime, nor are they the only means of inflicting deadly force. There are varying degrees of force that police officers learn to apply in routine police work, from *mere presence* to *deadly force* (Skolnick and Fyfe, 1993:37–40). Police may take control of dangerous situations by using a firm *command voice:* "Sir, I asked you for your vehicle papers once. Now I'm *telling* you that you have to give them to me *now.*" Or, cops may subdue a suspect through *pain compliance*—that is, by causing temporary pain without lasting physical injury. Deadly force may be inflicted by the "sleeper (or "choke") hold," which cuts off blood to the brain by choking off the carotid artery in the neck; by the "bar arm control hold," which prevents a person from breathing through pressure on the neck; or by shooting. The first two are not primarily intended to kill, but to render a suspect unconscious. Needless to say, they also require the officer and suspect to be at close quarters.

Guns Are Rarely Fired in Routine Police Work. Although the gun is the symbolic and practical basis of a police officer's power to use force, police officers rarely fire their weapons at civilians, and most officers will never injure or kill anyone in the line of duty. For example, it has been estimated that the average police officer working in Jacksonville, Florida—a city with a relatively high rate of police-citizen confrontations—would have to work 139 years before shooting and killing a citizen, 42 years before injuring one. In New York City, guns are fired in only 1 of every 352 encounters with criminal suspects (Geller and Scott, 1991:449). Furthermore, a 1996 national survey of 6,421 people aged 12 or older found that only 14 said the police had used or threatened force during a face-to-face encounter, and *none* mentioned being shot at by the police (Greenfeld, Langan, and Smith, 1997:12).

For many years, the guiding rule for use of deadly force was the **fleeing felon rule,** based in English common law. Simply, this rule allowed officers to use deadly force whenever they encountered felony suspects and reasonably believed such force was necessary to stop them escaping. The rule made sense in the days of the hue and cry, when virtually all felonies were in any case punishable by

fleeing felon rule Police may use deadly force to stop felony suspects from escaping.

death. However, it vested modern, well-armed police with tremendous discretionary power, and by the 1980s the rule was under attack by civil rights groups as well as from within police circles. In 1982 the U.S. Justice Department and the International Association of Chiefs of Police issued a joint report that rejected the fleeing felon rule in favor of a more restrictive rule that emphasized the need of police to protect themselves or others from "immediate threat of death or (near death) critical bodily harm" (Matulia, 1982:34). The U.S. Supreme Court, in ***Tennessee v. Garner*** (1985), gave constitutional backing to the new emphasis by formally overturning the fleeing felon rule. "The use of deadly force," the Court wrote, "to prevent the escape of all felony suspects, whatever the circumstances, is constitutionally unreasonable." The laws of most states now require that deadly force be used only to protect life.

Tennessee v. Garner
Declared the fleeing felon rule unconstitutional.

Yet the *Garner* decision left considerable discretion in the hands of the police, for it did not adequately define acceptable occupational behavior in the varied situations in which police find themselves. Nor did state laws do any better:

> Even post-*Garner,* no state law tells officers whether it is advisable to fire warning shots into the air on streets lined by high-rise buildings. The law provides no direction to officers who must decide quickly whether to shoot at people in moving vehicles and thereby risk turning them into speeding unguided missiles. The law related to police use of force, in short, is simply too vague to be regarded as a comprehensive set of operational guidelines. (Fyfe, 1988:169)

Shootings by police officers require justification before the public and sometimes before the courts. However, the use of deadly force must also be justified before one's fellow officers. Here there is a difference: Whereas the public and the courts expect the justification to be couched in terms of legal rules or formal procedures, the police themselves allow for negotiating the meanings of rules and procedures so that they are protected from censure and allowed flexibility in applying the rules to any given situation (Waegel, 1984; Hunt, 1991). This helps them "cover their butts" (Barker, Friery, and Carter, 1994). The use of deadly force is understood as a discretionary judgment based on the officer's professional interpretation of the situation.

Most of the relevant research comes from the 1970s and 1980s, and supports the following conclusions about police shootings during that period:

1. *Rates of police shootings varied considerably from one jurisdiction to the next.* In a comparison of nine American cities, a 1,500 percent variation was found even after taking account of the level of community violence and the number of arrest incidents involving violent felonies and, therefore, increased risk to arresting officers. Another study found police shootings to be twice as high per 1,000 police officers in Memphis as in New York.
2. *Rates of police shootings varied considerably over time within the same jurisdiction.* In Philadelphia, for example, while shootings showed a generally downward trend from 1970 to 1983, they shot up during some years and declined equally precipitously in others. Since the number of police shootings tends to be small anyway, it does not take much to move the rate sharply up or down. One author speculates that the peaks in that city were the result of an almost totally unrestrictive shooting policy under Mayor Frank Rizzo (Fyfe, 1988). Variations in other cities may reflect changes in policy, fluctuations in violent crime itself, improvements in the availability and competence of medical care, or simply unpredictability in the actions of cops and suspects during encounters.
3. *The percentage of shooting incidents involving black suspects was disproportionately high.* In the case of fatal shootings, black suspects were any-

where from 5 to 13 times more likely than white suspects to be killed by police action. When one looks at the young (age 10 to 14) and the elderly (age 65 and older), the disproportionate representation of black suspects was even more stark: "black youngsters and old men have been killed by the police at a rate 15 to 30 times greater than that of whites at the same age" (Takagi, 1979:34).

4. *There was a dominant shooting situation:* Most commonly, civilians were shot by on-duty, white officers who encountered an armed black male in connection with an armed robbery.

Two cautions must be considered in regard to these findings. First, they were based on data and methodologies that in most cases cannot be compared. Since there are different ways to compute rates of police shootings, studies using different measures—for instance, calculating the rates in terms of population or number of police personnel—should not be lumped together. Another important difference among studies was the source of information on police shootings. Some studies relied only on official police accounts, whereas others included recollections of witnesses and survivors.

Second, it is probably safe to say that no two shooting situations are ever the same, and decisions are often made on the basis of split-second judgment. Rarely will the pressure leave an officer unaffected, and it may push the event in unpredictable directions. The same is true of the other people involved, including the suspect who also may be armed.

Jurisdictional variations and racial issues in police shootings cannot properly be evaluated in the absence of detailed incident-by-incident information, both in situations in which officers fire and in those in which they do not fire their weapons. In fact, different police departments may experience similar rates of shootings but vary considerably in terms of the situations in which those shootings occurred.

Elective versus Nonelective Shootings

One of this country's foremost authorities on police shootings is James Fyfe, a former police lieutenant in New York City and now a well-known criminologist. Fyfe (1982, 1988) makes an important distinction between police-citizen encounters in which use of deadly force is elective and those in which it is nonelective. **Elective shootings** are "those in which the officer involved may elect to shoot or not to shoot at little or no risk to himself or others." While fleeing felon rules were still in place, the prototypical elective shooting involved a fleeing, unarmed, nonthreatening property crime suspect who posed no apparent danger to anybody and was shot in the back. Fyfe calls elective shootings "real exercises in discretion." **Nonelective shootings** are "those in which the officer has little real choice but to shoot or to risk death or serious injury to himself or others."

elective shootings When a police officer can exercise discretion in deciding whether to use deadly force.

nonelective shootings When the situation leaves the officer no choice but to use deadly force.

The elective and nonelective situations are polar extremes. Any shooting situation falls somewhere along a continuum from elective to nonelective. By hindsight an officer may put an encounter closer to the elective end than he or she actually did when in the situation; similarly, observers of a shooting may later interpret the situation differently from how they saw it at the time; finally, persons who later hear the reconstructed "facts" may define the situation differently than either the officer involved or any witnesses. This shows how difficult it is to create an objective picture. Nowhere is this problem more critical than when an officer shoots a suspect who is actually unarmed and no one was in mortal danger.

Fyfe believes that elective shootings are influenced by a variety of things. These include departmental rules and policies, the attitudes and prejudices of officers, and their level of training in firearms. These factors are *internal* to

Situations like this, in which officers must shoot or risk their own deaths, are known as nonelective shooting. *Situations in which officers can decide not to shoot are* elective shootings. *Deciding how to categorize each new situation is a key discretionary challenge for police, who must wisely choose when to shoot and when not to shoot.*

PHOTO COURTESY OF ARCHIVE PHOTOS

police organization and work. Nonelective shootings, in contrast, are more likely to be influenced by factors *external* to police work and organization. These include the amount and type of crime in a police jurisdiction, and the tendency of different groups to engage in behavior that precipitates shootings—for example, violent crime.

Comparing police shootings in New York and Memphis during the 1970s, Fyfe (1982) found that the elective/nonelective distinction was very useful in contrasting the two cities. In New York, over 60 percent of the shootings that occurred between 1971 and 1975 were interpreted by officers to have been in "defend life"—that is, nonelective—situations. In contrast, police in Memphis were fourteen times more likely to shoot at property crime suspects in elective situations than were officers in New York. That difference was explained mainly by the much more liberal shooting rules in effect at the time in the Memphis police department.

ARE MINORITIES MORE LIKELY TO BE SHOT BY POLICE?

Although there has been little published research on this question in the last few years, earlier studies have shown that African Americans are more likely to be shot at by police than members of other groups, especially whites; but the reasons for this difference are not easy to pin down. In the Memphis study, for example, 85.7 percent of those shot at were black and 14.3 percent were white. Rates of shooting per 1,000 officers showed that blacks were 6 times more likely than whites to have been shot at and missed, 13 times more likely to have been shot at and wounded, and over 3 times more likely to have been shot at and killed (Fyfe, 1982:712–721). Differences by race existed whether shooting rates were calculated in terms of population or felony arrests. In Memphis, the probability of blacks rather than whites being shot was greatest in the case of elective shootings, where discretion is exercised. Half of the blacks killed were shot in nonviolent situations, versus only 12.5 percent in the case of whites.

The Memphis study showed that lenient department shooting policies and racial attitudes among police were major factors accounting for the frequency and character of police shootings. However, a later study in Chicago found other possible explanations for racial differences in police shootings.

Police Shootings in Chicago. The Chicago study is noteworthy because it represented the first time a major American police department opened up its shooting files to outside investigators (Geller and Karales, 1981; 1982). In Chicago, the most common shooting situation occurred when a suspect used or threatened to use a gun. When calculated in terms of their numbers in the population, blacks were 3.8 to 6.6 times more likely to be shot than were whites. However, when calculated in terms of forcible felony arrests—which takes the criminal situation into account—blacks were only slightly more likely to be shot. In fact, black suspects were more likely than whites to be involved in gun use and threat situations. Although 70 percent of all shootings involved white officers, the rate per 1,000 officers was higher for blacks, and black officers were much more likely to shoot black suspects than were white officers. Black officers were more likely than white officers to shoot while off duty and 29 times more likely to shoot civilians in high-crime areas than were off-duty white officers.

Two major conclusions emerged from the Chicago study. First, most of the shootings in Chicago were nonelective, at least according to police accounts. Second, the greater involvement of black victims and off-duty black police officers suggested that Chicago police shootings were patterned according to the residency of black officers. These officers tended to live in areas where the risks of violent crime were highest. In short, the study found no evidence of a significant racist factor in police shootings in Chicago. While Memphis and Chicago both showed higher rates of police shootings of African Americans, the circumstances of the shootings led to different interpretations of this situation.

If there is a general tendency for minority Americans to be shot by police because of who they are rather than what they are doing, this tendency should surface as well when the police use less potentially lethal force. We have already seen evidence that minorities—and other devalued groups such as gays and lesbians—may be unfairly targeted for field stops by patrolling officers. There is recent evidence from Los Angeles that police dogs are deployed more often in minority neighborhoods than elsewhere, and that African Americans are more likely to be bitten when police dogs are used (Campbell, Berk, and Fyfe, 1998). Does this reflect racist practices among police? Not necessarily, as the authors explain: The Los Angeles canine officers are "relatively free to concentrate their efforts where they choose, within the broad requirements of police common sense." They go on:

> A relatively benign implication is that canine officers may overestimate the relationship between race/ethnicity and reported crime and honestly believe that they are deploying in a professional manner. However, they may also believe that complaints of police abuse from minorities are less likely to be taken seriously. As a result, deploying dogs in minority neighborhoods is far less risky, and canine officers may feel less constrained in how they go about their job. There remains, of course, the far more ugly possibility of direct racial animus of the Mark Fuhrman variety, and that, too, could affect how deployment unfolds. (Campbell, Berk, and Fyfe, 1998:556)

Violence Reinforces Violence. It is possible that many police shootings involve the clash of two violent cultures. On the one hand there is the legitimized police culture of enforcement, with its emphasis on force, guns, and danger, and on the other is an inner-city subculture of the streets—a largely outlawed subculture at odds with the establishment and considered a threat by them. Many inner-city minority youths expect violence in their daily lives and are prepared for it. Police who live in or enter these same areas also expect and come prepared for violence.

There are compelling reasons to believe that violence reinforces violence. Surveys have shown that respondents who would accept relatively high levels of police violence are themselves more likely to have been involved in violent situations and are more accepting of it in general (Blumenthal et al., 1972). Public support for use of force in dealing with criminals is bound up with a theme we all recognize: Catch the criminal at all costs. This theme has a cherished image: the cop hero felling a fast-disappearing crook with one shot from a handgun. What may be especially dangerous about this image is its impact on impressionable youths, especially those who expect confrontations with the police. In short, "catch the criminal at all costs" is hardly a sound doctrine for either the police or the public to support. One consequence is police fatalities and injury, the subject of the next section. Another is the mass killings that oc-

Box 7.5

JUSTICE PROFESSIONALS AT WORK

ARE MASS DEATHS FROM SHOOT-OUTS AVOIDABLE? THE SLA INCIDENT AND THE WACO TRAGEDY

Surely, a police officer's worst nightmare is to be caught up in a shoot-out with well-armed adversaries in which many people are killed and the police are later blamed for the way they handled things. Thankfully, this unhappy event is a rare occurrence; yet it is an event that is difficult to anticipate or predict. Although those actually involved may see the event and their role in it differently, it seems that the burden of responsibility for the outcome rests as much with the police as with their adversaries. Two incidents illustrate.

The SLA Shoot-Out. On May 14, 1974, 29 members of the Los Angeles Police Department's Special Weapons and Tactics (SWAT) unit accompanied by FBI agents gathered outside a house. Holed up in the house were six suspected members of the Symbionese Liberation Army (SLA), a self-proclaimed revolutionary group known to the world for kidnapping newspaper heiress Patty Hearst and committing a series of violent robberies. Tear gas was fired into the house and a blazing shoot-out ensued that engulfed the house in fire and left all six SLA members dead. No police officers or innocent bystanders were killed.

The Waco Tragedy. On February 28, 1993, agents from the Bureau of Alcohol, Tobacco, and Firearms (ATF) raided the 77-acre compound of Branch Davidian leader David Koresh and his followers outside Waco, Texas. Agents believed that Koresh was hoarding weapons illegally, and they had been curred in Los Angeles in 1974, and in Waco, Texas, in 1993. These events are briefly described in Box 7.5.

One important conclusion from the various studies of police use of deadly force is that police exercise of discretion can be controlled most effectively by the formulation of explicit departmental rules and procedures governing occupational behavior (Fyfe, 1988; Dunham and Alpert, 1995). Even while guns and control are dominant themes in cop culture, it is the department that is in the best position to reinforce or constrain the behavior of its employees. This applies to police use of deadly force just as it does to relations with the public and with fellow officers.

One practice with the potential to result in someone's death is the high-speed chase. Of late, more and more police departments have been reviewing their policies as a result of chases that have ended up killing innocent bystanders, the fleeing suspect(s), or the pursuing officers. High-speed driving by police is commonplace not only in chase situations but also when officers respond to some calls for assistance, particularly those in which other officers have called for backup. Even though most departments have rules governing speeding and the use of lights and sirens, it appears the rules are often violated with impunity. Like elective shootings, the decision to speed is generally a discretionary one, and the same sort of care and restraint should be exercised with patrol cars as with guns.

BOX 7.5 (CONTINUED)

planning to raid the compound when they learned that he knew of their intentions. The raid failed, and four ATF agents and six sect members were killed in the subsequent shoot-out. A 51-day stand-off ensued, during which negotiations with Koresh were held. Deadlines passed repeatedly, and on April 19, 1993, agents from ATF and the FBI, aided by local police departments, stormed the buildings under cover of tear gas. A giant fire erupted, and the buildings burned to the ground, killing Koresh and 85 followers, including 17 children. It was later determined that the fire had been set by people inside the compound.

Both of these highly publicized incidents sparked considerable controversy. In each case, many citizens and some local community leaders argued that the police dealt with the situation incorrectly. They questioned whether it was necessary for the police to engage in a shoot-out. When it appears that many people will be killed, they asked, why not withdraw and reconsider strategy? Why jeopardize the lives of innocent people? Couldn't the offenders have been captured later without bloodshed? The view of many police was that deadly force was the only way to effectively deal with the situation at hand, which required overpowering any possible resistance.

Subsequent official inquiries largely exonerated the police in the Los Angeles incident, but it was a different story in Waco. Reports by the Treasury and Justice Departments found significant errors in police judgment, including the ATF decision to make the initial raid after they learned that Koresh had been tipped off to their presence. Besides charges of ineptness, federal agents were criticized for trying to cover up their errors, and for lying to and misleading the public. High-level ATF and FBI officials resigned following release of the reports.

The high-speed chase is discretionary but always full of danger. Although more and more departments are implementing policies to increase care and restraint in pursuit situations, the rules are often violated with impunity.

ILLUSTRATION BY JOHN OVERMYER

SHOOTINGS OF POLICE

Relatively few police officers are killed in the line of duty—around 0.01 percent, or less than 100 a year. Compared to some other occupations, police work is actually much safer: Deaths and injuries are far more common among workers in agriculture, mining, construction, and transportation (U.S. Bureau of the Census, 1994:436). Table 7.1 shows the most common circumstances in which police officers have been killed since 1986.

The shooting *of* police officers is understandably very important for the criminal justice community and for society as a whole. Police may be trained and prepared for violence—they may even expect it—but when it happens to one of their own, they all share in the pain. Coping with the threat of danger is at the heart of the police officer's working personality. A national memorial to police killed in the line of duty was unveiled in Washington, D.C., in 1991. As of May 1998, there were 14,622 names of federal, state, and local police officers etched on its walls (*St. Louis Post-Dispatch,* May 13, 1998, p. B2).

A study in Chicago showed that nearly half of the 187 police officers shot—though not necessarily killed—between 1974 and 1978 were off duty; an additional 27 percent shot themselves, mostly by accident, and 11 percent were suicides and attempted suicides (Geller and Karales, 1982). Twenty officers (11 percent) were shot by fellow officers, nearly all accidentally.

The shooting of black officers was disproportionately high: While more than half of the off-duty officers shot were black, black officers represented only 17.5 percent of the Chicago police department as a whole. All but one of the black off-duty officers shot were shot in medium- and high-crime districts where they lived. Off-duty black officers were thirteen times more likely to be shot in high crime areas than were off-duty white officers; by contrast, off-duty black officers were only twice as likely to be shot in low-crime areas as white officers. These findings reflect the residency patterns and routine activities of black and white officers.

Table 7.1 Situations in Which Police Officers Were Killed, 1986–1996

The killing of police officers is relatively rare. However, from 1986 to 1996, a total of 762 federal, state, and local police were killed in the line of duty. This table shows the situations in which they were killed.

Situation	Totals	1986–1996
Disturbance Calls	118	
Bar fights, etc.		51
Domestics		67
Arrest Situations	284	
Robbery-related		96
Drug-related		55
Other arrests		133
Handling Prisoners	35	
Investigating Suspicious Persons/Circumstances	134	
Ambush Situations	76	
Mentally Deranged Attack	15	
Traffic Stops/Pursuits	101	
TOTAL	762	

Source: Kathleen Maguire and Ann L. Pastore (1998). *Sourcebook of Criminal Justice Statistics* (Table 3.154). Washington, D.C.: U.S. Department of Justice.

Officers shot by civilians had a better chance of surviving than civilians shot by police—an 86 percent survival rate versus a 74 percent rate for civilians. This is probably due to factors such as the higher caliber of weapons carried by police, better police marksmanship, a greater number of shots fired by police, and the type of ammunition used—police sometimes used hollow-point bullets, a more lethal form of ammunition because the bullet causes damage to a wider area than conventional bullets.

Geller and Karales (1982:373–374) made some recommendations that they believe will help reduce off-duty shootings of and by police. Among them were these:

- Off-duty officers should generally be prohibited from carrying guns when they anticipate drinking alcohol.
- Greater restrictions should be imposed on the types of weapons and ammunition officers carry, and the minimum standards of proficiency required of officers with these weapons should be tightened.
- Police officers should receive additional guidance in responding to incidents when off duty, including special reminders about the dangers of getting involved if they have no radio with which to summon backup.

The importance of better police training and minimum standards of proficiency is illustrated by recent events in Washington, D.C. For example:

> An off-duty police officer walking his dog in August 1995 fired 11 times while making a traffic stop of an unarmed motorist who hit a utility pole and left the scene. An off-duty police officer fishing in May 1995 shot an unarmed man three times after arguing with him on the banks of Rock Creek. In August, an officer ended a police chase of an irrational truck driver who had rammed several cars by firing 38 times into the truck's cab, killing the unarmed driver. (*Washington Post,* November 15, 1998: A01).

Although these incidents represent some of the worst cases of bad judgment uncovered by investigative reporters, in the period 1993 to 1998, Washington,

Death is an ever-present risk of police work, although fatalities are less common than in some other occupations. Police are most often killed when attempting to make arrests. The National Police Memorial in Washington, D.C., lists the names of over 14,600 officers killed in the line of duty over the years.

LEFT PHOTO BY MIKE ALEXANDER, COURTESY OF AP PHOTO; RIGHT PHOTO BY REINSTEIN, COURTESY OF THE IMAGE WORKS

D.C., police shot and killed 57 people—three more than Chicago police, which has three times as many officers and five times the population. They were also involved in 640 shooting incidents—40 more than the Los Angeles police department, which has twice as many officers and six times the population. While some of these incidents could be justified by any standard, some were also reckless and some were quite possibly criminal. Over 70 lawsuits are pending.

The shootings in Washington, D.C., are partly explained by the city's rising level of violent crime, particularly shootings, which increased everyone's anxiety, including that of patrolling police. In addition, however, the rash of police shootings involved disproportionate numbers of officers who had been on the force less than five years and came on the heels of the department's decision to adopt a new, light-trigger, rapid-fire, 17-bullet handgun—the Glock 17—as its service weapon. The department has now vowed to provide its officers with the skills and philosophy necessary to make the best decision in shoot–don't shoot situations.

The overriding consideration in exercising police discretion should be *outcome,* and this is especially critical in the decision to use force. If society clings to the goal of catching the criminal at all costs, then that outcome is almost inevitably going to include severe injury or death to someone.

SUMMARY

This chapter has explored the exercise of discretion in policing. Patrolling officers, detectives, traffic cops, federal agents, and other law enforcement officers are faced with making important decisions every day. The decisions are important because they may deprive someone of liberty or may result in innocent people getting hurt or a criminal going free. They are important because they define for the public what to expect when they deal with the police, and what the consequences are likely to be. The decisions are important because they describe the character and tone of law enforcement in a community. The decisions are also important for the officers making them. They define each officer's understanding of what police do in a given situation, and they determine what is likely to happen next: nothing, perhaps, or more paperwork, trouble with citizens or supervisors, a successful arrest, a case solved, a pat on the back or promotion, or a shoot-out. Occasionally, the decision may determine whether an officer lives or dies. This is police work.

Because the police are armed and have the authority to act forcefully if need be, we expect their decisions to be guided by rules and regulations and to be applied thoughtfully and fairly. In the real world, however, things are not so simple. In learning and carrying out their jobs, police soon discover that no situation is exactly like another, that in the same situation one officer's decision might be quite different from another's, and that in practice they have broad discretion in exercising their police powers.

The most important decisions police make are arguably the negative ones: not to file a report, not to make an arrest, not to shoot. Such decisions define the outer boundaries of law in action. We saw that all sorts of things influence those decisions, from concerns about the purpose of law itself to administrative pressures and the welfare of victims and offenders. We also learned, however, that in the course of exercising their discretion, the police sometimes target people—or do nothing—more because of who they are than what they have done from a legal standpoint. Evidence shows that minority groups and poor people have borne the brunt of selective enforcement, including being disproportionately targeted for surveillance, field interrogation, arrest, and elective shootings. When they are victims, these same people are more likely to be ignored than victims higher up the social ladder.

The exercise of discretion is structured by departmental policies as well as by informal police traditions, practical considerations (how best to do the job with the least amount of danger and hassle), and the dominant values and norms of the larger society. On balance, police exercise of discretion leads them to behave far more leniently than the law allows, as many erring juveniles and considerable numbers of adult offenders and victims have discovered. Doing nothing or letting people go is probably the dominant mode of behavior for patrolling officers in most situations, and it corresponds with their primary peacekeeping role, discussed in Chapter 5. It is interesting to imagine what life would be like (let alone the justice system) if police suddenly started enforcing the letter of the law.

We found that when it comes to using deadly force, the exercise of discretion has raised many questions. Not least of these are how society and the police can better protect themselves from the clash of two violent subcultures: armed law enforcers on the one hand and armed criminals on the other. While it has been documented that prejudice and racism have colored police use of deadly force in some places and at some times, the bottom line is this: Can society afford to accept the idea, reinforced in movies, novels, and television shows, that catching dangerous criminals at all costs is a profitable strategy for the police to follow?

WHAT DO YOU THINK *NOW*?

- What changes have forced police officers to use discretion more often in their duties? Are some of these changes social? Political? Practical?

- Why do police use arrests as a last resort? Is it advantageous to make as many arrests as possible? Why or why not?
- What changes would need to occur to ensure that all Americans are treated equally by the police?

KEY TERMS AND CASES

discretion
selective enforcement
arrest
field interrogation
Terry v. Ohio
paramilitary units
fleeing felon rule
Tennessee v. Garner
elective shootings
nonelective shootings

ACTIVE LEARNING CHALLENGES

1. Imagine that you have been stopped by police who say they are looking for a burglar who fits your description. Discuss with another student how you would feel and act. Would you cooperate? Would you refuse to answer questions? If the officer asked you to go to the police station for further questioning, what would you do and why?
2. Divide the class into groups. Assign each group to research and develop arguments either for or against this statement: "The police have far too much discretion." A week later, have a class debate and poll the students for the most convincing positions.
3. Have the class consider strategies to ensure that field interrogations and arrests do not unfairly target minorities and women.
4. TV cop shows present a version of policing that departs in many ways from routine police work. Alone or in pairs, have students watch an episode of a popular cop show and report to the class how well its depiction of discretion matches the discussion in the text. Give specific examples from the show and the text as illustrations.
5. In pairs or small groups, find out how local police departments address the use of deadly force by officers. For example, what are their operating rules? Do they allow for elective shootings? What procedures does the department follow if an officer shoots someone?

INTERNET CHALLENGES

The Web pages mentioned here can all be accessed through the Web site for this textbook at **http://www.prenhall.com/barlow/**.

1. Interrogation of suspects is a key aspect of police investigations. Many police departments offer special training in interrogation techniques, and private companies have sprung up to meet the demand. To learn more about these companies and their services, start with the Behavioral Analysis Training Institute. What are the basic elements of their training?
2. Sometimes police decisions can have deadly consequences. One of the most controversial issues concerns high-speed pursuits. See how the U.S. Supreme Court views pursuits in *Sacramento v. Lewis* (1998). Then see how others view them by entering "police chases" in any search engine. What do you learn from all this?

3. Learn about the police officers who have been killed in the line of duty. Visit the Officer Down Memorial Page, which was started in 1991 by a freshman at James Madison University in Virginia; it now includes information from the international police community as well. Who was the first recorded law enforcement officer to be killed? Who is the most recent—and under what circumstances was he or she killed?

CHAPTER 8

Six Crime Challenges for Police Today

LEARNING OBJECTIVES

- Describe how current laws, attitudes, and practices affect the police response to drug use and explain the strategy of supply-side policing of drugs.
- Understand the strategy of problem-oriented policing.
- Understand why transnational crime presents unusual difficulties to law enforcement and how police might overcome them.
- Explain the conventional approach to policing domestic violence and describe the experimental and innovative approaches that law enforcement agencies are now using to police domestic violence.
- Understand the similarities and differences between hate crimes and terrorism and the U.S. trends in both.
- Explain why intelligence, technology, training, and cooperation are crucial factors in policing organized crime, terrorism, and hate crimes.

Individuals can be classified as gang members if they admit to membership and meet one or more criteria such as wearing gang clothing or tattoos, or displaying gang hand signals.

PHOTO BY A. RAMEY, COURTESY OF PHOTOEDIT

Improving the quality of life is not a destination. You never get there. It's a work in progress. But along the way, you keep making things better. And that's what we are determined to do.

RUDOLPH GIULIANI, MAYOR OF NEW YORK CITY, ON HIS CITY'S ANTIDRUG POLICING INITIATIVES

[D]espite the progressive changes that have taken place during the past two decades, law enforcement still does not address domestic violence in the same way it addresses other violent crimes.

LIEUTENANT DOUGLAS MARVIN, PROVIDENCE (NEW JERSEY) POLICE DEPARTMENT

After an eight-year career in banking, Jack Fox spent three years as a city cop, rising to the rank of detective. During this time he dealt with a full range of crimes, from shoplifting to homicides. While most of his arrests involved common thieves, drug offenders, and batterers, he had always been intrigued by the more complex financial crimes involving counterfeiting, money laundering, and international conspiracies. These crimes were almost always handled by federal agencies, and at age 29 Fox decided that he would make a career change. He became a special agent of the U.S. Secret Service, the Treasury Department's primary enforcement agency.

After a three-year tour with the White House detail, protecting President Carter, Fox moved on to other responsibilities, including the investigation of financial crimes. Much to his surprise he discovered that the work was arduous and plodding, following paper trails and traveling extensively. Cases often took months or years to develop, and getting the necessary cooperation from corporations, banks, and foreign countries was often difficult, and sometimes impossible. Fox learned quickly that the growing global economy was providing all sorts of illegal opportunities for enterprising criminals with ties to legitimate business. He saw that the key to many international crimes was organization, yet penetrating organizations was no easy task, especially if their activities were protected by favorable foreign laws.

Fox also discovered that new forms of criminal transactions were constantly appearing, driven by changes in information technology. High-speed personal computers, new forms of interactive software, the Internet, and electronic encryption devices that scrambled communications were turning money launderers, terrorists, and hate groups into high-tech organizations that required a high-tech police response. But one thing didn't change: Cases were still made through the kind of dogged persistence common to all investigative police work.

Special Agent Fox knows that society demands a lot from its police forces and that this demand has increased over the years with the increasing complexity of society and its criminal laws. Policing today is a more difficult job than it was 100, 50, or even 25 years ago. Some crime problems seem to be growing as well, suggesting that the police are overwhelmed and their responses ineffective. To judge from newspapers and television—and from the police themselves—American cities are currently besieged by gangs, drugs, and organized crime.

To these three crime challenges for the police we can add three more: hate crimes, terrorism, and domestic violence. At first glance, these three crimes appear to have little in common. Reactions to the three types of crime are also quite different: Domestic violence tends to be regarded as a private matter and kept quiet; terrorism, in contrast, is everyone's concern and is given considerable press; hate crimes seem to be somewhere in between, invoking cautious and inconsistent reactions, perhaps because some of its targets—gays and lesbians and minorities in particular—are themselves devalued groups in American society.

Yet there are some marked similarities among domestic violence, hate crimes, and terrorism: All three are perpetrated against vulnerable victims; the violence usually comes as a surprise attack, and is therefore extremely difficult to predict and prevent; there is an unsatisfied rage on the part of the attacker and a claim of righteousness to justify it; the crimes are rarely perpetrated only once, although weeks, months, and even years may separate each attack. There is also an intergenerational aspect to these types of crime: Families caught up in domestic violence tend to reproduce the offense in subsequent generations, and hatemongers and terrorists pass on the fervor of their beliefs to their children. (This *intergenerational aspect* is also a common feature of the drug trade and organized crime, and, to a lesser extent, of gangs as well.) Finally, and perhaps more so than with most other crimes, these offenses represent displays of power: The enemy may be within themselves, but the offenders are making a statement about their ability to "get back at" those they consider responsible for their troubles.

All six crimes pose special challenges for the police, although not necessarily the same type of challenge. For example, domestic violence is a particular challenge for officers on routine patrol; hate crimes and terrorism pose special challenges to investigators. However, all three of these pose a stiff challenge when it comes to protecting potential victims. The enormous impact, scope, and complexity of terrorism, drug trafficking, hate crime, and organized crime create special challenges for effective cooperation among local, state, federal, and international police agencies. In the sections that follow, these crime problems are discussed in terms of the challenges posed to police, the nature of the police response, and the success of that response.

? WHAT DO YOU THINK?

- What do you think are the toughest challenges facing police officers today? Why?
- How can police combat these special crime problems? What established techniques would work well? What new ones should be used?
- What are the similarities and differences between hate crimes and terrorism? What are the similarities and differences in how police address these issues?

URBAN GANGS

Among many other activities, gangs fight among themselves and prey on the weak and vulnerable. They delight in demonstrating ownership and control of their "turf," and they sometimes turn neighborhoods into war zones in defense of it. Once gangs form, their graffiti soon adorn buildings and alleyways, and membership is displayed through hand signs, clothing, and special colors. As a newly formed gang grows in reputation and confidence, it soon finds itself attracting "wanna-bes" and "claimers"—nonmembers who would like to be members or who pretend that they are in order to reap the benefits: safety, or girlfriends, or a reputation for toughness.

Today, most cities, even quite small ones, claim to have youth gangs, although not necessarily a gang "problem." The most comprehensive national assessment of gangs in America was conducted in 1995 (National Youth Gang Center, 1997). Over 3,400 police departments across the country reported a total of 23,388 gangs with an estimated 664,906 members. More than 80 percent of the reported members were in three states: California, Illinois, and Texas. The city and county of Los Angeles had an estimated 118,197 youth gang members. Since around 12,000 police agencies were not surveyed at all, the national totals of gangs and members are certainly higher. Furthermore, the influence of any particular gang may spread well beyond its birthplace or current headquarters. Thus, the Latin Kings surfaced in Chicago in the early 1960s, but their influence now stretches into 34 states (Knox and McCurrie, 1996:43).

While the numbers are large, and while half the police agencies surveyed thought that the youth gang problem was getting worse, nobody claims that all these gangs are wreaking havoc or even that they are heavily involved in criminal activity. Yet that is exactly the image most people have of youth gangs today. Since violence is the most widely publicized and feared aspect of urban gangs, let us take a closer look at it.

THE NATURE AND PURPOSE OF GANG VIOLENCE

Gangs have always been associated with violence. In the waning days of ancient Rome, violent bands of strong-arm thugs committed their crimes of theft, extortion, and murder on orders from wealthy Romans who hired them to protect their interests (Lintott, 1968). In the 19th and early 20th centuries, union organizers and striking workers in the coal and auto industries were harassed, beaten, and even shot by gangs of strikebreakers hired by management and owners. The idea that gangs are inevitably anti-establishment or opposed to mainstream norms and values is simply not true. Since they can be bought by anyone, however, their true allegiance is perhaps immaterial.

Today, gangs are the setting in which some young urban males explore the meaning and uses of violence. The ideals of masculinity, toughness, excitement, and reputation are stressed in gang activities (Jankowski, 1991; Dawley, 1992). Members must show that they can take care of themselves when threatened or provoked, and much emphasis is placed on the conquest and dominance of women. Not only does violence help gang members gain a tough reputation for themselves and their gang, but it helps protect that reputation (Daly and Wilson, 1988:129; Goldstein, 1993). During one observational study, members of a gang "gathered in an alley to discuss how they could regain the reputation they had lost when [two of their] members were beaten" (Horowitz, 1987: 447). All favored some sort of violent response. In another study, gang members justified drive-by shootings as a means of promoting the reputation of the gang while protecting its territory and interests (Sanders, 1994). From their vantage point, there is nothing irrational about gang violence.

Drug dealing and periodic shootouts contribute to tensions on the street and reinforce gang violence. The following paragraph summarizes the plight of African Americans living in the inner city and gives a warning:

> The hopelessness and alienation many young inner-city black men and women feel, largely as a result of endemic joblessness and persistent racism, fuels the violence they engage in. This violence serves to confirm the negative feelings many whites and some middle-class blacks harbor toward the ghetto poor, further legitimating the oppositional culture and the code of the streets in the eyes of many poor young blacks. Unless this cycle is broken, attitudes on both sides will become increasingly entrenched, and the violence, which claims victims black and white, poor and affluent, will only escalate. (Anderson, 1994:94)

There is evidence that an escalation of gun violence among inner-city gangs may already be taking place. From 1988 to 1992 the number of gun homicides among juveniles ages 10 to 17 tripled, while nongun homicides remained steady (Blumstein and Heinz, 1995). However, although gang membership in itself appears to promote crime (Battin et al., 1998), it is easy to overstate the "bad" side of contemporary urban gangs, particularly the connection between gangs, drugs, and violence. A three-year study of four of the largest street gangs in Chicago found that of 288 gang-motivated homicides, only 8 were related to drugs (Block and Block, 1993); most were to protect gang turf, which makes them a kind of self-defense to gang members.

Drive-by shootings and other gang violence have claimed many lives over recent years, including those of innocent bystanders. Police are under great pressure to do something. Directed patrols are one promising answer, although critics worry that citizens' civil rights may be in jeopardy.

Illustration by John Overmyer

POLICING GANGS AND GANG VIOLENCE

The job of policing gangs could hardly be more difficult. When there is overpolicing, residents and gang members alike may believe that they are being victimized by oppressive, insensitive police on orders from city hall and the white middle class. On the other hand, police are criticized if they seem unresponsive to the conditions and needs of impoverished neighborhoods and underpolicing results. There is no effective police strategy in dealing with gangs that does not include the cooperation of the public. This is one reason why it is important for police and city officials to communicate honestly about the gang "problem." It is also why many police departments take a proactive strategy in communicating with residents about gang-related problems. Let us take a closer look at one police department's response to gangs, developed in the early 1990s.

The Police Response in St. Louis. Police departments in many cities have recognized that a specialized police response is needed in dealing with gangs. The 1995 National Youth Gang Survey found that 63 percent of police departments and 48 percent of sheriff's departments allocated personnel to special **gang crime units** or **"gang squads"** (National Youth Gang Center, 1997:18). Like the others, the primary task of the St. Louis Police Department's unit is to develop intelligence on gangs and gang activities. This information can then be made available to patrolling officers and to those investigating criminal incidents suspected of gang connections. According to the department's *Gang Manual 1994,* individuals are classified as core gang members if they admit membership in a street gang *and* meet one or more of the following criteria (individuals not admitting affiliation must meet at least two):

gang crime units Specialized police units that track the membership and activities of gangs; also called "gang squads."

- wear gang-type tattoos and/or clothing that is associated with a specific gang
- engage in criminal acts with known gang members or commit gang-related crimes
- are known or observed by police to associate closely with known gang members
- are implicated as a gang member by a reliable police informant
- are observed displaying gang hand signals, writing gang graffiti, or possessing items containing gang graffiti
- appear in photographs indicating gang affiliation
- have written jail or prison letters in which they identify themselves as gang members

In mid-1993, a computerized gang crime tracking system was established; by the end of that year the squad had recorded 69 drive-by incidents and 254 other crimes attributed to gang activity. A computerized regional Gang Tracking System was developed that can be accessed by local police departments, the Missouri Highway Patrol, area prosecutors and court and correctional systems, and all other agencies subscribing to REJIS (Regional Enforcement Justice Information System).

Another innovative step taken by St. Louis police in conjunction with the board of education and other city agencies is the use of a "notification letter" delivered by hand or sent by certified mail to parents whose child is suspected of gang involvement. The official police letter informs parents that a child has "been displaying one or more of the warning signs directly associated with gang-type behavior." A list of gang behaviors follows with items checked that apply to the child. The letter goes on to inform parents of resources that are available to help them steer their child away from gangs, and on the reverse side are listed the names and phone numbers of public and private agencies, including the police department's gang hotline. Gang squad members believe the letter has produced positive feedback from many parents, although no systematic evaluation of its use has yet been made.

POLICE STRATEGIES FOR COMBATING GUNS AND VIOLENCE

What most concerns residents and officials in cities where gang activity is prevalent is the growing incidence of handgun crimes and the rising rates of youth homicide associated with it. Nationwide, from 1987 to 1996, weapon offenses such as carrying or possessing a firearm increased 69.5 percent among youths under age 18; homicides for the same age group increased 50.5 percent (Maguire and Pastore, 1998:333).

directed police patrols Concentrated uniformed patrols that target specific places or special crime problems within a target area.

Directed Police Patrols. In response to concerns about rising gun crimes among youth, the National Institute of Justice funded an experiment in **directed police patrols** aimed at confiscating firearms that are illegal or illegally carried. Directed patrols involve uniformed patrol units that target specific areas or special problems within a target area. When concentrated around gun crime hot spots, directed police patrols appear to reduce both the presence and use of guns at relatively modest cost. And it appears, initially at least, that the patrols do not result in a displacement of gun crime to other areas, where risks of police intervention are lower (Sherman, Shaw and Rogan, 1995). However, repeated tests of the strategy are needed, and some possible hazards still need to be addressed. One of these is the possibility that intensified gun patrols provoke more violence "by making youths subjected to traffic stops more defiant of conventional society" (Sherman, Shaw, and Rogan, 1995:9).

This problem does not seem to have occurred in New York City, whose police claim that directed patrols have significantly reduced gun crimes (*New York Times,* July 30, 1995, p. 15). New York police first flooded a zone consisting of nine streets in northwest Harlem with plainclothes officers and detectives. Then the precinct moved many beat and uniformed narcotics officers from less violent streets to the "hot zone" to arrest low-level drug lookouts and dealers, often initially for minor violations. Meanwhile, patrolling officers in cars looked for legal excuses such as lane changes without signaling so they could stop and question drivers of cars with out-of-state licenses. When approaching suspects in the target zone, officers first looked for a bulge that might be a gun. If they thought the suspect was carrying a gun or responding to their questioning in a suspicious or nervous way, they frisked for a weapon. In June 1995, 30th Precinct officers frisked 450 people, a 150 percent increase from June 1994. The frisks produced only a handful of gun arrests, but shootings began to decline. The police believe that potential offenders were leaving their guns at home in anticipation of encounters with police.

Aggressive police patrolling may be part of the answer to gang-related crimes, as well as to street violence associated with drug trafficking. However, there may be a cost in civil liberties that some Americans will find objectionable. The strategy also tends to target minority and poor neighborhoods, which raises the problem of overpolicing discussed earlier. In cities with large minority populations, there may be a political cost that elected authorities are reluctant to bear. This may explain why some police departments across the country have been reluctant to copy New York City's program.

POLICING THE DRUG PROBLEM

A second area of specialized policing involves the world of illegal drugs. Although there is overlap in the areas of gangs and drugs, much drug use and drug trafficking goes on outside the world of urban youth gangs. A number of factors make enforcement of drug laws extremely difficult. For one thing, the

Box 8.1

JUSTICE AND THE LAW

A REDESIGNED LOITERING LAW IS PROPOSED AS AN AID TO DRUG ENFORCEMENT

Belleville, Illinois. A new city ordinance says the police can arrest people seen loitering in a way that suggests they are buying or dealing illegal drugs. The ordinance lists other criteria police may use in determining intended drug-related activity, such as whether a person:

- "is a known unlawful drug user, possessor or seller"
- is prohibited by court order from being in a high drug activity area
- raises reasonable suspicion by such behavior as "acting as a lookout or hailing or stopping cars"
- is identified by police as a member or associate of a gang that deals drugs
- furtively transfers small objects or packets
- flees or tries to hide when police show up
- tries to hide an item that could be involved in drug dealing
- possesses drug paraphernalia "such as, but not limited to, crack pipes, push wires, chore boys, hand scales, hypodermic needles, razor blades or other cutting tools"

But City Attorney Larry Brockman says Belleville itself may end up in court. Brockman said he is concerned that the ordinance is unconstitutional. The ordinance "is replete with potential problems which I believe could be attacked as being vague and over broad," Brockman said. The ordinance says, for example, that police may consider whether a loiterer "displays physical characteristics of drug intoxication or usage such as 'needle tracks,' burned or calloused thumb or index fingers, underweight, nervous and excited behavior. . . ." Proponents said an identical law in at least one other Illinois municipality had withstood court challenges. (However, in December, 1998, the U.S. Supreme Court agreed to hear challenges to a similar law in Chicago that targeted gangs.)

Source: St. Louis Post-Dispatch, August 23, 1995, pp. 1A, 15A; *USA Today,* December 10, 1998, p. 1.

possession, sale, and use of illegal drugs are often called **victimless crimes** because they usually involve willing participants. Police must typically discover drug law violations on their own.

victimless crimes Illegal activities that involve willing participants, such as drug use, prostitution, and gambling.

To make enforcement more difficult, an individual can easily violate a drug law without being detected. Who is to know that a person is carrying two or three joints, some illegal pills, or a day's supply of heroin? The police can expect little help from the public, partly because of concerns about privacy, but also because of fear of reprisals. Besides, some Americans remain unconvinced that the best strategy for dealing with the drug problem lies with the criminal law. The more proactive the police become, the more people begin to worry about their constitutional rights. Take a look at Box 8.1 and see if you agree.

THE LAW ENFORCEMENT RESPONSE TO ILLEGAL DRUGS

Although the percentage of Americans claiming to be current users of illicit drugs declined from 12 percent in 1985 to less than 6 percent in 1992 (Maguire and Pastore, 1997:269), the president and the United States Congress

One of the biggest challenges facing undercover narcotics officers, or narcs, is living among drug addicts and dealers and pretending to be part of the drug culture. Narcs may have difficulty separating themselves from that world, and some fall victim to temptation.

Photo by Tony Savino, courtesy of The Image Works

continue to treat drug use and abuse as an urgent problem whose solution requires a major police role (Office of National Drug Control Policy, 1998). The law enforcement response to drugs emphasizes the supply side of the problem: Make illegal drugs more difficult to obtain by eradicating crops, disrupting smuggling, seizing drugs at the border, arresting dealers and pushers, and shutting down crack houses and clandestine laboratories. This is the core of the war on drugs, and some experts believe it is destined to fail (Blumstein, 1993). This is largely because a strong market for drugs persists even after the supply is interrupted. This rather pessimistic view is all the more disturbing when one considers how much is spent on the war on drugs: over $28 billion by federal, state, and local governments in 1996. Around half of all the money is spent on the enforcement activities of federal, state, and local police.

Street Enforcement: The Narc and the Informant. Because illicit drug offenses are mostly consensual crimes and because they are not readily observed, police enforcement strategies emphasize undercover work and the use of police informants. By infiltrating the ranks of users, undercover narcotics officers—or **narcs**—are able to develop trusting relationships with users and pushers and thus keep tabs on the people and places associated with the illegal drug industry.

narcs Undercover police officers who specialize in the street-level drug trade.

To maintain their cover, narcs must often live among the "enemy" and to all appearances become one of them. This is a difficult role that carries various risks and costs beyond the obvious one of personal danger. A firsthand investigation of the junkie's world in New York, Houston, Austin, and Los Angeles found that narcs often had difficulty separating themselves from that world, even though they despised it and their goal was to destroy it (Jackson, 1969). Some officers succumbed to temptation; others ended up with severe stress disorders. Keeping their lives separated, remembering "who I really am, and what I am really doing here" sometimes took tremendous willpower and self-confidence. This picture hasn't changed, as we see from a narc's observation in a more recent study of undercover police work:

> I identified very strongly with the bad guys. . . . Even though these people were breaking the law . . . I realized everything wasn't black and white . . . . It didn't take me long to get into the way of thinking like the crooks I was running with. I started identifying with these people very quickly. (Pogrebin and Poole, 1993:388)

Helping law enforcement are **police informants,** known pejoratively as "snitches." Usually drug abusers or sellers themselves, informants are cultivated by police, who use the information they pass on to develop cases. The informants' own crimes are often used as a means to induce them to work for the police. Under threat of arrest and a jail sentence, would-be informants find they have little choice. If they don't cooperate, police can spread word on the street that they are snitches.

police informants People who provide police with information about crimes and criminals in exchange for money or favors; also called "snitches."

"Buy-Busts," "Straight Buys," and "Sting" Operations. Attempts to control street-level drug trafficking in Oakland, California, and Birmingham, Alabama, illustrate various proactive police strategies involving narcotics officers (Uchida, Forst, and Annan, 1992). In Oakland, police used a **buy-bust** strategy. Two hand-picked, specially trained undercover officers made up a "buy" team that drove around in a dilapidated car, making buys from dealers on street corners, in front of motels, houses, and small stores in residential areas. An arrest team composed of other officers wearing police identification was stationed four or five blocks away. If a buy was completed, the arrest team swooped in and arrested the seller and any buyers in the vicinity. "The entire operation lasted 5 to 10 minutes and was visible to the citizens in the immediate area" (Uchida, Forst, and Annan, 1992:18). The teams then moved on to another target area.

buy-bust Undercover police buy drugs from street dealers who are arrested immediately afterward.

In Birmingham, police used two undercover operations. The first was a **straight-buy** strategy, with two officers constituting a buy team. The buy team made purchases over a four-month period, and arrest warrants were later served on the sellers en masse during a three-day operation. (These mass raids are a common way that police mop up their drug investigations, and they usually involve a mixture of plainclothed and uniformed officers from local, state, and federal agencies [Dighton, 1998a]. It is not clear whether they have much impact on the drug business, but they do receive a lot of media attention.)

straight buy Undercover police buy drugs from dealers over a period of months; the dealers are then arrested en masse.

The second strategy involved a **reverse-buy** or "sting" operation. Undercover officers posed as street-corner drug dealers and waited for buyers. Video and audio equipment was concealed in a "boom box" cassette player, which was held by another officer pretending to listen to music. The video camera recorded the transaction and the officer's headset received instructions from a surveillance team stationed nearby in a nondescript van. When approached by a potential buyer, the officer asked what he wanted, and if a drug was named, he then asked to see his money. Under Alabama law, actual exchange of money for drugs does not need to take place to satisfy drug conspiracy laws. The narcotics officer "then said something like, 'Hey, I see a cop down the street. Go around the block and come back and get your stuff.' This forced the buyer to drive around the corner [where he would then be arrested]" (Uchida, Forst, and Annan, 1992:36).

reverse buy Undercover police pose as dealers and sell to buyers who are arrested immediately afterward; also called a "sting" operation.

Evaluation of these strategies showed mixed results. The concentrated six-month buy-bust effort in Oakland significantly reduced trafficking in the target areas, but in Birmingham, drug trafficking was not noticeably reduced by

Box 8.2

CAREERS IN CRIMINAL JUSTICE

SPECIAL AGENT OF THE DEA

Enforcement of the nation's federal drug laws is the primary responsibility of the Drug Enforcement Administration (DEA). Created in 1973 when several drug enforcement agencies were consolidated, the DEA employs over 4,200 special agents, with a 1998 budget of $1.2 billion. From its earliest days, the DEA has targeted international drug trafficking, and its agents often work directly with foreign governments in identifying and prosecuting criminal organizations involved in trafficking. The salary, qualifications, duties, and conditions of employment of a DEA special agent are as follows:

Salary Range: Around $30,000 (entry level) to over $70,000 (senior special agents)

Qualifications: U.S. citizen, 21 through 36 years of age, with valid driver's license; excellent physical condition, uncorrected vision of at least 20/200, and corrected vision of 20/20 in one eye and 20/40 in the other (radial keratotomy disqualifies); college degree with 2.95 GPA or better; successful completion of polygraph examination, psychological suitability assessment, and exhaustive background check.

Duties: Enforce all federal drug laws; investigate drug-related crimes; arrest suspects involved in violation of federal drug laws; assist state and local law enforcement agencies in drug enforcement activities; engage in surveillance and undercover infiltration of suspected drug dealers and traffickers; confiscate illegal drug supplies; present testimony in court; assist foreign agencies in drug interdiction efforts.

Conditions of Employment: DEA special agents must be willing to accept assignments anywhere in the United States; required screening for drugs and random testing throughout their career; required physical fitness screening; formal sixteen-week training at the FBI Academy in Quantico, Virginia; required to complete a probationary/trial period of three to four years.

either the sting or straight-buy operations. On the basis of these experiments and other research, the authors concluded that buy-busts should be part of a police strategy that includes aggressive patrols, community policing efforts, and door-to-door contacts between police and citizens in areas where drug activity is rampant.

Stopping Drug Smuggling: The Federal Interdiction Effort. A major federal enforcement effort is directed at the interdiction of drug trafficking at the border, on the high seas, or in countries involved in production or trafficking. The U.S. Customs Service deals with land border smuggling with the cooperation of other federal agencies, while the U.S. Coast Guard employs more than 135 seagoing vessels and 180 aircraft in its marine interdiction efforts. Smuggling by air is handled by the Department of Defense, although the military is prohibited from making arrests (Bureau of Justice Statistics, 1993d:146). The DEA is also involved, primarily as an investigative and intelligence gathering agency, which includes posting agents in foreign countries.

Combining the seizures of the major federal agencies involved in drug interdiction suggests the staggering magnitude of international drug trafficking.

The seized drugs represent merely the tip of the iceberg. Figure 8.1 shows the figures on cocaine and marijuana seizures from 1992 through 1996 compiled through the Federal-wide Drug Seizure System (FDSS). These figures do not include drug seizures from street arrests and the domestic eradication programs of state and local police. Concerning the latter, state and local police eradicated over 422 million marijuana plants in 1996 alone (Maguire and Pastore, 1997:412). Most of the plants were "ditchweed," which grows wild, but over 3 million cultivated plants were also seized and burned. The four states with the largest number of cultivated plants eradicated were Hawaii, Kentucky, Tennessee, and California.

Why Interdiction Has Not Curbed Drug Trafficking. Despite the massive cost and the thousands of pounds of drugs that are seized, interdiction efforts have generally been unsuccessful in curbing drug trafficking. The General Accounting Office of the U.S. Congress reported in 1989 that the $100 million spent on antidrug efforts in Bolivia and Colombia alone had been "almost entirely useless" (*NCTAP News,* January, 1989:4; Moore, 1990). Another strategy, called **alternative development,** encourages peasant opium and coca growers to switch to legal crops such as cacao, coffee, or tea. Despite claims of successes in Peru and Thailand (Guia and Padilla, 1996), this strategy does not appear to have reduced the worldwide availability of cocaine or heroin.

alternative development
A drug war strategy that encourages peasants to grow legal crops instead of opium and coca.

The drug pipeline is tough to breach, not only because the major importers, wholesalers, and distributors are well organized and equipped, but also because the profitability of small quantities of these drugs make large shipments unnecessary. It is like looking for a needle in a haystack. The diversity of drugs also contributes to the difficulties facing police: "Crack, powder cocaine, heroin, PCP, 'pills'—each drug type has a different volume, different user demographics, and a different relationship to dealer and user crime" (Kleiman and Smith, 1990:73).

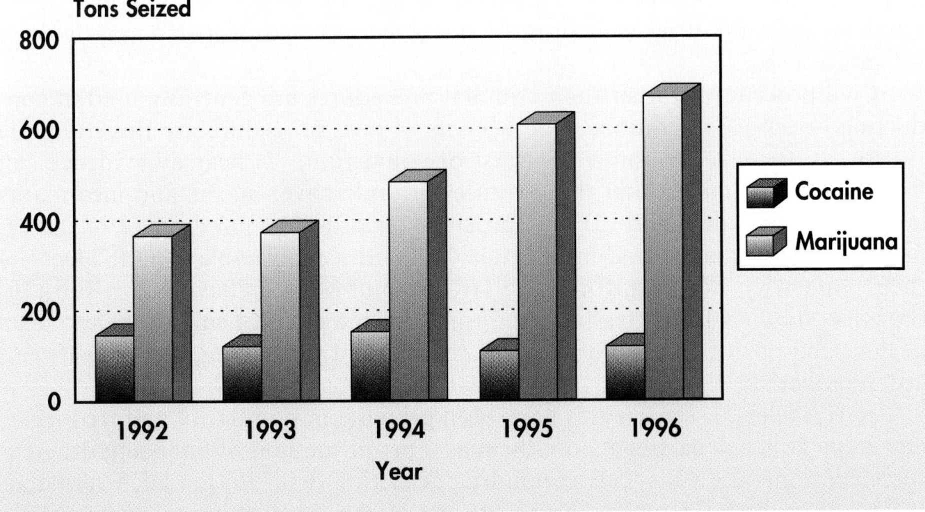

FIGURE 8.1 DRUG SEIZURES BY FEDERAL AGENCIES, 1992–1996 (IN METRIC TONS ROUNDED TO NEAREST TON)
Contributing Agencies include DEA, FBI, Customs, and the U.S. Coast Guard

Source: Office of National Drug Control Policy (1998). *The National Drug Control Strategy.* Washington, D.C.: U.S. Government Printing Office (p. 89).

Asset forfeiture is one of the weapons used in the war against drugs. These cars have been confiscated by police because they were used in the commission of crimes or bought with the proceeds.

PHOTO BY STEVE STARR, COURTESY OF STOCK BOSTON

asset forfeiture Property and cash are confiscated if they have been used in the commission of crimes or are the fruits of such activities.

Asset Forfeiture: Another Weapon in the Drug War. All states and the federal government have passed laws that enable officials to confiscate various types of property assets if these have been used in drug trafficking or manufacture or are the fruits of such activities. This is called **asset forfeiture.** The idea behind asset forfeiture is to raise the costs of drug trafficking by hitting traffickers in the pocketbook and then to use the seized assets to help governments fight the drug war. In most states, confiscated property may be kept for police use.

Civil procedures rather than criminal procedures are generally used in conducting forfeiture operations. The benefits of civil procedure are threefold: (1) Assets can be seized without an arrest or conviction; (2) hearsay evidence can be used—which means that the identities of undercover agents and informants need not be revealed; and (3) the burden of proof is "preponderance of the evidence," rather than a finding of guilt "beyond a reasonable doubt." Despite their popularity, however, forfeiture laws do not seem to have had a substantial effect on illegal drug trafficking. From the viewpoint of smugglers and drug dealers, the risk of forfeiture is one of the costs of trafficking, unfortunate but accommodated.

Nevertheless, asset seizures have been growing in popularity and frequency, and some police departments use them as a major method of financing drug enforcement operations as well as nondrug activities. In 1996, the DEA seized almost $38 million in assets during its marijuana eradication program alone (Maguire and Pastore, 1997:412). Overall, the DEA annually seizes around $500 million worth of nondrug assets, roughly half forfeited to the federal government. This figure does not include state and local seizures not involving the DEA. The assets seized by the DEA in 1997 include the following (Maguire and Pastore, 1998:371):

ASSETS	NUMBER OF SEIZURES	VALUE
Currency	8,123	$284,680,029
Other financial assets	507	73,602,092
Vehicles	3,695	47,379,874
Property	748	108,833,498
Vessels	111	5,884,754
Airplanes	24	8,945,000
Other Conveyance	172	1,734,731

The popularity of asset forfeiture among law enforcement officials is understandable: Here is a material reward for their drug enforcement efforts.

The major obstacle to effective control of drug trafficking at home and abroad is the simplest to identify and the hardest to overcome: Illicit drugs are in high demand, and people are willing to pay the price. The lure of high profits means there will always be plenty of people willing to pit themselves against authorities. Even as the authorities become more organized and sophisticated in their enforcement efforts, so do the traffickers.

Drug and Alcohol Arrests: A Major Police Activity. The police make many drug arrests (see Figure 8.2). In fact, when combined with alcohol-related arrests in any given year, more arrests are made for drug-related offenses than for any other category of crime. Over the past 20 years, drug and alcohol-related arrests have made up around 30 percent of all arrests. Despite the downward trend in self-reported drug use during the 1980s, police agencies did not slow down in making arrests; leaving out alcohol offenses, the number of drug arrests as a percentage of all arrests grew from 5.7 percent in 1983 to nearly 10 percent in 1997. From 1988 to 1997 the number of drug arrests grew by nearly 50 percent (Federal Bureau of Investigation, 1998:221).

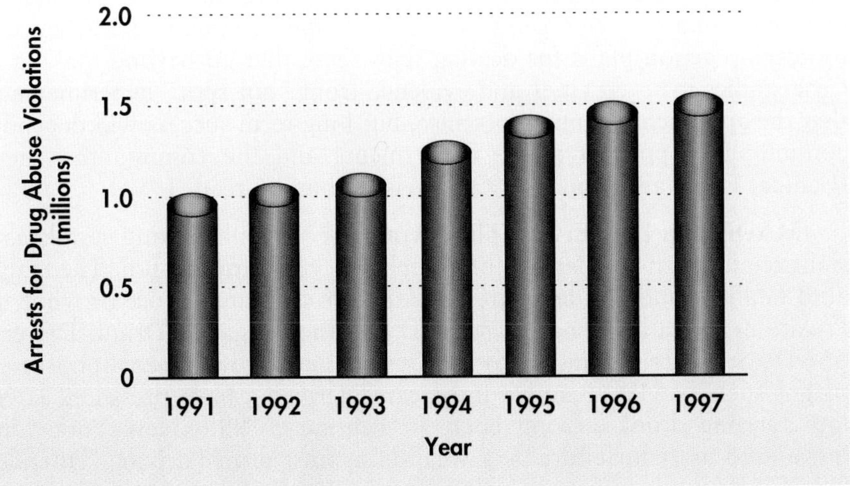

FIGURE 8.2 ARRESTS FOR DRUG OFFENSES, 1991–1997
There has been a generally upward trend in the numbers of arrests on drug-related charges (not including alcohol). Most of the arrests are for possession rather than trafficking.

Source: Federal Bureau of Investigation (1998 and previous years). *Crime in the United States.* Washington, D.C.: U.S. Department of Justice (p. 222).

Arrests on alcohol-related charges far outnumber other drug arrests. Over 65 percent of more than 4 million drug/alcohol arrests in 1997 were alcohol related. The offenses are usually public drunkenness, violation of liquor laws governing sale and consumption, or driving while intoxicated—the most common alcohol offense. Alcohol-related offenses constitute this country's number one law enforcement problem, representing almost a quarter of all police arrests.

Over the past few years, drug arrests of African Americans have been rising faster than those of whites. The spread of crack in inner-city neighborhoods certainly accounts for some of the difference, but the complete story is not that simple. Many drug arrests are incidental to other police actions, and when police target minority neighborhoods with a reputation for crime and social disorder, such actions are likely to uncover many drug violations that might have escaped detection in other neighborhoods (Klofas, 1993). In fact, most drug arrests are not made by specialized narcotics units but by police on routine patrol, whose nondrug stops and searches reveal evidence of drug-related crimes.

Problem-Oriented Drug Enforcement. Many police departments are discovering that increasing the number of drug arrests by itself is an ineffective way of dealing with the drug problem in their communities. Some departments have adopted what are called **problem-oriented policing** strategies that go beyond arrests. Box 8.3 describes a problem-oriented drug enforcement program used by police in Tulsa, Oklahoma. The four primary objectives of problem-oriented drug enforcement are the following:

problem-oriented policing The identification, analysis, and solution of a crime problem by patrol officers in cooperation with the public.

- to increase the effectiveness of police in battling local drug problems by addressing the underlying community problems that spawn them
- to increase reliance on the knowledge and creative approaches of patrolling officers to analyze problems and develop solutions
- to encourage police to tap diverse public and private resources in a cooperative effort to solve community problems
- to develop a closer involvement with citizens and let them see that police address the needs of the public (Bureau of Justice Assistance, 1993:6).

Under this model, patrolling police officers are trained in problem-solving methods and are encouraged to assess and analyze situations as they arise and to develop action plans for dealing with them that go beyond making arrests. Case studies in seven cities and evidence from "hot spot" experiments suggest that the approach has much promise, but long-term success will depend on the continuing support of police departments and the communities they serve (Uchida, Forst, and Annan, 1992; Weisburd and Green, 1995).

MADD and DARE: Are They Working? Drunk driving stands as a constant reminder of the dangers of complacency toward alcohol. The majority of auto fatalities and accidents are attributed to drinking before or while driving. Private organizations such as MADD (Mothers Against Drunk Drivers), and SADD (Students Against Driving Drunk), and government-sponsored campaigns such as RID (Remove Intoxicated Drivers), have pressured lawmakers into revising drunk driving laws. In February, 1999, New York City even introduced asset forfeiture as a weapon against drunk driving. Offenders risk losing their cars.

So far the results are not promising: DUI arrests have actually gone down from their peak in the mid-1980s. The risks of being arrested while driving intoxicated are less than 1 percent, and even when people are stopped by the police, violations continue (Lanza-Kaduce, 1988; Linsky, Colby, and Straus, 1986).

Declines in drug and alcohol use among young people during the 1980s made good press for groups such as Mothers Against Drunk Driving. However, one study tells a different story (Lundman, 1991). City police in the early

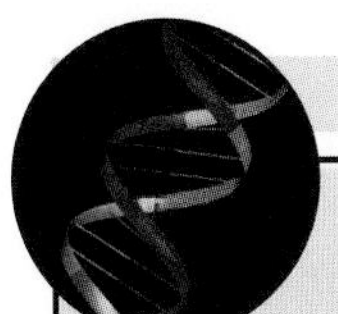

Box 8.3

JUSTICE INNOVATIONS

PROBLEM-ORIENTED DRUG ENFORCEMENT IN TULSA, OKLAHOMA

Throughout the 1980s, North Tulsa experienced consistently higher crime rates than the rest of the city. Almost half the city's violent crime occurred in North Tulsa, as well as most of the city's drug arrests. Much of the crime and most of the drug arrests occurred in and around several low-income housing complexes. A special management team of police officials decided to do something about the drug problem.

Patrol officers were assigned to the target area. They noticed large groups of school-age youths who appeared to be selling drugs during school hours. "As officers approached drug hangouts within the complexes, young lookouts (aged 12 to 16) would call out, 'Rollers!' to alert the dealers to discard their drugs and disperse." Arrests were sometimes made after a chase, but the offenders usually reappeared in the complex the following day.

The officers found that traditional enforcement practices such as surveillance and arrests did little to improve the situation. They also saw that the housing complexes offered few recreational opportunities or programs that might offer alternatives to crime and drug trafficking for youths with nothing to do. The patrolling officers devised a variety of strategies for diverting the youths from drug-related activities: Boy Scout troops were formed; private funds and volunteers were secured to help needy residents, who in turn promised to participate in job skills programs; programs to teach young women job interview skills, help in résumé writing, and improve personal appearance and hygiene were started; sessions on goal setting and self-esteem building were initiated through a government program called the Private Industry Training Council; volunteers from the Oklahoma Highway Patrol were brought in to teach driver's education; a day camp was established on a 20-acre ranch confiscated by police from a convicted drug dealer; ten youths ages 11 to 16 were given individual garden plots, with police and community volunteers providing help and encouragement; a Drug Abuse Resistance Education (DARE) program was initiated; a high-ranking police official arranged for 60 youths to be sent to a summer day camp at the north side YWCA. As a result of its efforts, the Tulsa police department "noted a decline in street sales of illegal drugs in the five target complexes. Youth reacted positively to the officers' efforts to help them, and the programs seemed to deter them from drug involvement. . . . Other social service agencies began working with the police department, establishing satellite offices on the north side of the city, scheduling programs, and requesting police support in their efforts."

Source: Bureau of Justice Assistance (1993). *Problem-Oriented Drug Enforcement* (pp. 45–47). Washington, D.C.: U.S. Department of Justice.

1970s were not much interested in drunk driving and made DUI arrests infrequently. With the founding of MADD in 1980, DUI arrests initially grew, but then actually declined from 1984 through 1989. Apparently, while MADD inspired initial increases in arrests, it turned out that the criminal justice system often could not handle the influx of new offenders, and the police soon discovered there was no point in making arrests since offenders were quickly released (Kinkade and Leone, 1992). Experiences such as these leave the police and public understandably frustrated. In light of the massive increases in incarceration of drug offenders, they also reinforce the view that alcohol-related offenses such as drunk driving are not all that serious. A lesson to learn is that policy changes do not necessarily have the effects that are intended.

Another area of controversy concerns the DARE (Drug Abuse Resistance Education) programs that target fifth and six graders. The typical program includes seventeen weekly lessons taught by uniformed police officers trained by Los Angeles–based DARE America. The officers give lectures and assign homework on the dangers of drugs, alcohol, and gangs. Some schools offer DARE lessons to younger children as well, while others offer a supplemental curriculum for junior high and high school. In 1997 the DARE program received $750 million in federal funding (Glass, 1997).

Despite generally favorable responses from teachers, parents, and young children alike, there are two major problems with DARE: (1) The bulk of research indicates that it does not work in the long run, and some suggests that it may even have a "boomerang" effect: "DARE graduates are *more* likely to use marijuana" (Glass, 1997:20); and (2) a fierce lobby exists, coordinated by DARE officials and backed by the White House and the U.S. Justice Department, that is resisting the research evidence and any attempts by school districts to scale back or end DARE programming. Instead, DARE supporters are calling for *more* DARE (and therefore more DARE funding) on the grounds that its messages need repeating and reinforcement throughout a child's school years.

ORGANIZED CRIME AND THE POLICE

Turning to our third challenge for the police, what exactly *is* organized crime? Five key elements have been identified:

- Those involved associate for the purpose of engaging in criminal activity on a sustained basis.
- They engage in enterprise crime, namely (a) illegally providing goods or services and (b) seeking to maintain and extend market share.
- Like any business, the more sophisticated organizations are hierarchical and also have an overarching structure that involves mechanisms for leadership succession, membership recruitment, and dispute resolution.
- They use violence and corruption to facilitate their economic activities, for self-protection, settlement of disputes, and the carrying out of illicit activities.
- They have a reputation (based on violence or trust) of "being able to deliver" and of "getting things done" (for example, providing protection from other crime groups, the law, and so on). (Steffensmeier, 1995: 270)

Criminal organizations that fit this pattern vary considerably. They differ in terms of size, degree of formal structure, scope of criminal activities, geographic scope, and degree or scale of impact on the communities and nations in which they operate. However, many organized crime groups are composed of members who share a common ethnic or racial identity; Italian Americans, Hispanics, Asian Americans, African Americans, Russian immigrants, and Jamaicans are examples. In the nineteenth century, Irish gangs flourished in New York City.

WHY ORGANIZED CRIME PROSPERS

Law enforcement efforts against organized crime are impeded by various mechanisms that protect the interests of organized crime (Barlow, 1996:260–264). These *survival mechanisms* include codes of conduct, role imperatives, the legislation of morality, professionalization, and public attitudes and behavior. Let us briefly examine each of these survival mechanisms.

The Code. There is a veil of secrecy surrounding organized crime that hinders policing. Secrecy is part of the code of conduct that members of organized crime groups subscribe to. However, there is no evidence that one particular code is shared by all criminal organizations. While the code of La Cosa Nostra—a large-scale Sicilian-Italian crime organization—emphasizes such things as loyalty, teamwork, honor, and secrecy (Cressey, 1969:175–178), research on individual crime families as well as African American and Hispanic groups shows that the specific codes differ from group to group (Ianni and Reuss-Ianni, 1973; Ianni, 1975). For example, various codes stress "Don't be a coward," "Fit in with the group," "Be smart" (know when to conform but also when to beat the system), or "Don't cheat your partner." The existence of all such codes makes police infiltration more difficult.

Role Imperatives in Organized Crime. Three essential survival mechanisms internal to crime organizations are the roles of enforcer, buffer, and corrupter. The *enforcer* makes sure rules are obeyed; methods of enforcement range from verbal warnings to maiming and sometimes even murder. The *buffer* is similar to a corporation's assistant to the president, whose tasks involve internal communication and the flow of decisions in the hierarchy of an organization. The buffer also reports on what lower-level members do and say, passes down important messages from the top, and forewarns of problems with day-to-day operations.

Corrupters "put the fix in." Their job is to bribe, buy, intimidate, negotiate, persuade, and sweet-talk themselves "into a relationship with police, public officials, and anyone else who might help 'family' members maintain immunity from arrest, prosecution, and punishment" (Cressey, 1969:251–252). Corrupter roles emerge in response to the organization of policing itself. For example, if one police agency has jurisdiction over a particular illegal activity, then a centralized corrupter role will tend to develop. If many agencies have jurisdiction, however, corruption will have to occur on more "local" levels to be effective (Moore, 1986).

Corruption can spread throughout a city's political system and reach state and federal levels as well. A study of organized crime in Seattle during the 1960s describes a crime network that extended from street hustlers, bookmakers, pimps, drug dealers, and gamblers to businesspeople, politicians, and law enforcement officials. Hotel, restaurant, club, and bingo parlor operators were fronts for gambling and vice; police officers and prosecutors took bribes and offered protection, falsified reports, and covered up investigations; politicians took campaign contributions of "dirty money" and exercised their licensing and legislative powers in support of the rackets, "one of the largest industries in the state" (Chambliss, 1978:54). This crime network depended for its survival on corruption at all levels of government.

The Legislation of Morality. Organized crime makes the bulk of its profits by supplying illegal commodities and services desired by large numbers of people. Drugs, gambling, and prostitution are profitable precisely because criminal laws have the effect of driving the services underground. This pushes the price up and attracts enterprising people willing and able to meet the demand. In this way, criminal laws that attempt to legislate morality actually help bring about the emergence and spread of organized crime—and the things they are trying to suppress.

Apart from encouraging black marketeering, laws that prohibit vices also help give "a kind of franchise to those who are willing to break the law" (Schelling, 1967:117; Packer, 1964). This "crime tariff" protects the profits of people who break the law by supplying drugs, gambling opportunities, or other illegal services to those who want them but are unwilling to obtain them themselves (Packer, 1964). The legislation of morality promotes the interests of organized crime while hindering effective enforcement.

professionalization of deviance When organizations hide their criminal activities behind legitimate activities and a carefully cultivated image of respectability.

Professionalization of Deviance: Outlaw Motorcycle Gangs. Another factor in the persistence of organized crime is what we might call the **professionalization of deviance.** This occurs when groups submerge their deviance in legitimate-looking organization and activity. Thus, from relatively unsophisticated, unrestrained, and rebellious beginnings, some organized crime groups eventually distance themselves from serious crimes that are likely to draw attention and result in arrests and prosecutions. Their ongoing criminal activity is overshadowed or hidden by legitimate work activities and a carefully cultivated corporate image.

Surprising though it may seem, some outlaw motorcycle gangs in the United States have gone through this kind of evolution since the 1950s (Loves, 1992). They progressed from social rebellion and a stereotypical image as hard-riding, hard-drinking, sexually perverse and crazed partiers, to money-laundering drug traffickers frequenting bike repair shops and tattoo parlors, and eventually to more legitimate-looking social clubs with accountants, lawyers, and real estate experts on the payroll, meetings conducted under *Robert's Rules of Order,* and more sophisticated drug trafficking and money-laundering operations:

> They take over whole industries and launder money through investments as diverse as overseas property development and share investment. The outward trappings of wealth are used to impress professionals and attract potential customers. They think more in terms of a corporate image and structure than of a "biker gang." (Loves, 1992:13)

Not all biker gangs have followed this path. In general, they vary in their degree of professionalism, organization, wealth, and influence. However, the

Surprisingly, many outlaw motorcycle gangs successfully hide their illegal activities in legitimate-looking enterprises, such as motorcycle repair shops and tattoo parlors. This professionalization of deviance varies from gang to gang, and helps gangs survive longer and less conspicuously.

PHOTO COURTESY OF UPI/CORBIS-BETTMANN

claim that professionalization of deviance contributes to the prosperity and long-term survival of criminal groups is not disputed.

Attitudes and Behavior of the General Public. Finally, the survival of organized crime depends on widespread demand for its goods and services by the general public. It also benefits from perceptions people hold of what the real crime problems are. Public perceptions and attitudes about organized crime are fuzzy and mixed, but overall organized crime is not seen as a real problem deserving stringent police control.

The lack of a rigorous public opposition to organized crime reflects the fact that use of its services is widespread, and also that few people are convinced these services are particularly harmful. Moreover, many people have only a vague idea of what organized crime really is, and popular films like *The Godfather* series and *Goodfellas* present a distorted picture full of excitement and mystery. Indeed, the mystery surrounding organized crime gives it the appeal—tinged with fear—of the unknown. Even when people use products and services supplied by organized crime, they rarely come in contact with members of a crime syndicate.

POLICE STRATEGIES IN COMBATING ORGANIZED CRIME

We see from the foregoing that obstacles to the policing of organized crime are considerable. If the aim is to get at lower-level "soldiers" and street criminals at the edges of organized crime, then proactive policing such as undercover work and directed patrols probably will work as well as any in uncovering routine and petty offenses. However, if the aim is to identify and arrest upper-level participants or groups engaged in large-scale criminal operations, then the police turn to high technology for help.

Electronic Surveillance. Electronic surveillance involves a variety of different techniques, some of which require cooperation from at least one party being monitored, and some of which are done without consent. *Wiretapping* is usually nonconsensual. Here police connect listening devices to telephone wires in order to intercept and record conversations. Another form of nonconsensual surveillance is the use of hidden transmitters or "bugging" devices attached to phones or hidden in walls or furniture. Consensual eavesdropping comes in various forms; for example, an undercover agent may use a concealed tape recorder or video camera, or an informer may wear a body transmitter.

While the technology of surveillance is becoming more sophisticated by the day—see Box 8.4—the reasons behind police use of electronic surveillance have not changed. They include the following (Kenney and Finckenauer, 1995:337):

- developing strategic intelligence in which the people and criminal enterprises to be targeted for investigation are identified
- setting up specific investigations
- developing witnesses by, for example, approaching individuals who have been overheard to become informers;
- corroborating witness testimony;
- as a substitute for witness testimony.

Electronic surveillance is also important because criminal organizations rarely keep written documents, and members usually communicate orally, over the telephone or in meetings in homes or businesses.

Perhaps the most famous recently publicized case of police surveillance of organized crime was disclosed in Rudolph Giuliani's successful prosecution of John Gotti. Gotti was head of the Gambino crime family of New York City, one of the so-called Five Families of the New York/New Jersey area and part of La Cosa Nostra, and he had a reputation for cruelty. The FBI received a court's permission to eavesdrop in and around Gotti's club and the private

Box 8.4

JUSTICE INNOVATIONS

ELECTRONIC SURVEILLANCE AND THE CLIPPER CHIP

The technology of electronic surveillance is changing rapidly, and so it must if police are to keep abreast of sophisticated criminals with access to high technology. *Encryption* technology protects sensitive information by concealing it from people without authorized access. The "Clipper Chip" is a tamper resistant encryption—or scrambling—device that allows police to decrypt—or unscramble—communications encrypted by a particular chip. It uses secret keys for encryption and decryption. It plugs into an ordinary telephone between the handset and the base, and the party at either end of a conversation can press a button to initiate a secure conversation. When used in a court-ordered wiretap, communications are intercepted and the Clipper Chip computes a Law Enforcement Access Field (LEAF) that is transmitted over the phone line before encrypted communications take place. If police encounter scrambled messages over the intercepted line, a specially designed personal computer containing a decrypt processor then locates the LEAF transmitted in each direction and identifies the device ID of the encryption chip belonging to the subject of the wiretap. The message can then be decrypted though the special key in the LEAF.

Source: Dorothy E. Denning (1994). "Data Encryption and Electronic Surveillance." *SEARCH Technical Bulletin* 4:1–6.

apartment above it. The resulting tapes supplemented the eyewitness testimony of Gotti's "underboss" Salvatore "Sammy the Bull" Gravano and were instrumental in bringing about his conviction on racketeering and murder charges.

Electronic surveillance is controversial because it always involves invasion of someone's privacy. Democratic societies rest on the privacy of communications and the right to dissent, both of which are undermined by surveillance. Concerns about abuses are heightened as the technological capabilities and sophistication of surveillance increase: "We now have miniaturized equipment, voice-activated equipment, parabolic microphones, lasers, and other highly sensitive devices that vastly increase the capacity for invading people's privacy. These serve to emphasize and reemphasize questions about their legitimate use" (Kenney and Finckenauer, 1995:338).

The Witness Protection Program. Another police weapon against organized crime actually protects many criminals from prosecution: the Witness Protection Program run by the U.S. Marshals Service. Although criticized by some as a "haven for criminals" (Kenney and Finckenauer, 1995:334), the Witness Protection Program provides law enforcement officials with a way to reward organized crime members for their testimony against other members. Apart from avoiding prosecution themselves as co-conspirators or collaborators in crime, organized crime figures receive a new identity for themselves and their families as well as money, housing, and assistance in finding work. In its use against organized crime, the program has been praised by a former administrator as highly successful. He writes: "The testimony of just one witness helped to convict five underworld bosses, severely crippling organized criminal activity on the west coast and in the mid-west" (Safir, 1989:22). Independent evaluations by the General Accounting Office of the United States Congress confirm the positive results.

Even so, there is also plenty of evidence that criminal witnesses protected by the program often return to crime while under its protection. Henry Hill is a case in point. Hill's exploits are detailed in Nicholas Pileggi's popular book *Wiseguy* (1985) and became the subject of the successful movie *Goodfellas*. While Hill's testimony was instrumental in bringing about the convictions of many of his organized crime associates, he subsequently continued his criminal activities while in the Witness Protection Program. He was eventually dropped from the program but continues to live under his new identity.

International Challenges: BCCI and Other Transnational Crime. Working across the boundaries of organized crime and legitimate business are corporations and individuals who make fortunes taking advantage of a global business environment. The more restrictive the laws are at home, the more appealing a foreign country becomes as a place to do business. That appeal is increased if the country also has a large population of poor but able-bodied workers or an abundance of natural resources. This growing area of transnational activity is creating new challenges for law enforcement.

Transnational corporations (TNCs) do business across international boundaries and thus thrive on these conditions. As legitimate businesses find opportunities abroad, so, of course, do shady businesses and enterprising criminals. Consider the advantages that organized criminal groups can find in the Caribbean, particularly the Bahamas (Block and Scarpitti, 1986):

- secrecy in banking laws
- low or nonexistent taxes
- geographic proximity to the United States
- involvement in large-scale criminal enterprises
- secrecy in laws governing ownership, control, and operation of corporations
- dependence on foreign investments and cooperation of public officials

Transnational crime is criminal activities such as money laundering and gun running that cross the borders of nation states. Typically, they draw legitimate businesses and organized crime into networks of collusion, and eventually blur the boundaries between the two. So it was with the Bank of Credit and Commerce International (BCCI). Established in 1972 by Pakistani financier Agha Hassan Abedi, BCCI became the first multinational bank originating out of the Third World. Headquartered in London, regulated (in a very loose way) by Luxembourg, and backed by Middle East oil revenues, BCCI had over $20 billion in assets in 75 countries by 1990, with more than 400 branches and subsidiaries (*Newsweek*, July 22, 1991:37; *Time*, July 29, 1991:42). It gained a reputation for offering first-rate service to its large depositors, and for asking no questions. In its sixteen years of expansion, however, various banking and government officials in the United States, England, Peru, and Argentina knew that BCCI was not the legitimate operation it appeared to be. Yet nothing was done.

transnational crime Criminal activity such as money laundering and gun running that crosses the borders of nation states.

Drug trafficking was BCCI's downfall. Indicted by a federal grand jury in 1988 for laundering millions of dollars in drug money, BCCI eventually pleaded guilty and was fined $14 billion in 1990 (*Time*, July 22, 1991:46). Subsequent investigations produced an incredible array of charges: gun running, bribery and corruption, smuggling, terrorism, securities theft, property theft of all sorts, influence peddling, insurance fraud, covert operations for the CIA, bank fraud, espionage, extortion, kidnapping, and violation of many other domestic and international laws. The bank was closed down in July

1991, its assets frozen. In January 1992, BCCI pleaded guilty to racketeering; many more indictments and convictions followed.

To combat money laundering and other transnational crimes, experts are calling for improved intelligence gathering, more rigorous enforcement of reporting laws on large bank transactions, and the development of a nationwide database available to law enforcement agencies.

Developing a Law Enforcement Strategy. Four lines of law enforcement defense against organized crime have been suggested:

> The first is a vigilant media and an informed public which demands that law enforcement and public officials be held accountable both (a) for treating organized crime as a "serious" crime problem; and (b) for corruptive or complicitous behaviors. The second line of defense . . . is a research and intelligence program that serves to better understand the causes and consequences of organized crime and that discerns racketeers and their corruptive effects. A third line is effective coordination and cooperation of criminal justice resources. Fourth, those resources should place a premium on identifying and chasing "dirty money" and ruining the criminals or the "organization" financially. (Steffensmeier, 1995: 291–292).

These strategies clearly extend beyond the normal realm of policing. But it is just this sort of multifaceted approach that promises the most gains in any se-

Box 8.5

CAREERS IN CRIMINAL JUSTICE

CIA CLANDESTINE SERVICE TRAINEE

Because the mission of the Central Intelligence Agency (CIA) is to develop foreign intelligence and conduct counterintelligence activities to protect national security, it is not generally considered part of America's criminal justice system. However, it does engage in many of the same kinds of activities that are associated with domestic law enforcement, particularly the gathering of intelligence and the investigation of suspicious activities. The CIA employs thousands of people in a wide variety of jobs, from psychologists, engineers, computer scientists, and military analysts to statisticians, language instructors, attorneys, and theatrical effects specialists. Perhaps its most glamorous job is that of spy, referred to as the Clandestine Service. The primary task of the Clandestine Service is to gather information in foreign locations that helps the U.S. government design and implement its foreign policy. Here are the salary, qualifications, and conditions of employment for the entry-level position of Clandestine Service Trainee:

Salary Range: $32,507–$49,831

Qualifications: Bachelor's degree with excellent academic record; ability to write clearly and accurately; a burning interest in international affairs. A graduate degree, foreign travel, foreign language proficiency, previous residency abroad, and military experience are pluses. The CIA is particularly interested in candidates with backgrounds in East Asian and Middle Eastern languages and those with degrees and experience in international economics, international business, and the physical sciences.

Conditions of Employment: Include U.S. citizenship, a thorough medical examination, a polygraph interview, and an extensive background check.

rious effort to combat organized crime. Two things stand out in this approach: first, its emphasis on causes and consequences, which enlists the knowledge and skills of criminology, and second, its awareness of the vulnerability of modestly paid police officers to the corrupting influence of money and the connections that come with it.

HATE CRIMES, TERRORISM, AND THE POLICE

Hate crimes and terrorism will be discussed together. They share many similarities, among them an underlying anger against individuals or groups perceived as responsible for real or imaginary ills. They also pose similar challenges to the police. Nevertheless, they are not the same thing. "Not all acts of terrorism can be considered hate crimes, and hate crimes are not necessarily terrorism unless such prejudicial violence has a political or social underpinning" (Hamm, 1993:107). **Hate crime** is involved when a person assaults or kills an individual or group solely out of hatred of that person's race, religion, ethnicity, or sexual preference. If the same act were committed for political purposes, with or without hatred or prejudice, it would be an act of **terrorism.** They both involve traditional crimes such as assault or murder; it is the *motivation* that distinguishes hate crime and terrorism from other acts of violence. Interestingly, even though counterterrorism is one of the responsibilities of the FBI, there is actually no specific federal crime of terrorism (Smith and Damphousse, 1998:75).

hate crime Violence or threats against people solely because of such things as their race, religion, ethnicity, or sexual preference.

terrorism Violence or threats against individuals, organizations, or governments in furtherance of political or social objectives.

TRENDS IN HATE CRIME

Hate crimes do not necessarily involve violence, but physical assaults are their hallmark. In 1991, under the Hate Crime Statistics Act, the FBI began a program of systematic data collection on hate crime, which it defined as "[a] criminal offense committed against a person or property which is motivated in whole or in part by the offender's bias against a race, religion, ethnic/national origin group, or sexual orientation group" (Federal Bureau of Investigation, 1992:1). The Southern Poverty Law Center and the Civil Rights Division of the Anti-Defamation League of the B'nai B'rith (ADL) also have collected data on hate crimes for many years.

Hate Crime in the United States. Few experts doubt the extensiveness of hate crimes. One of the biggest difficulties in gathering information is that many victims of hate crimes do not report the attacks, often out of fear. Another problem is that wide discrepancies exist between the numbers reported by law enforcement agencies and those compiled by private organizations (Bureau of Justice Assistance, 1997:8). For example:

- In 1991, the FBI reported 421 hate crimes against gays, while the National Gay and Lesbian Task Force listed 1,822 such incidents in Boston, Chicago, New York, San Francisco, and Minneapolis/St. Paul alone.
- In 1994, the FBI reported 908 anti-Semitic incidents, while the ADL documented 2,066 such incidents, the highest number in its history.
- In 1994, the FBI reported 209 hate crimes against Asian Americans and Pacific Islander Americans, while the National Asian Pacific American Legal Consortium reported 452 such crimes.

In addition, most nonpolice observers believe that hate crime has been increasing in the United States, particularly crimes against gays and lesbians (Levin and McDevitt, 1993; Herek and Berrill, 1992). The growth of gay and lesbian activism, coupled with fear of AIDS and its association in people's minds with the gay community, largely explain the upsurge in "gay bashing." Gays are blamed for the spread of AIDS, even though sexual preference in itself has nothing to do with the disease; in Africa, for example, most AIDS cases are found among heterosexuals.

The Southern Poverty Law Center publishes the quarterly *Intelligence Report,* which monitors the activities of hate groups. The SPLC says that hate violence rose to record levels during the 1990s. Since 1990, for example, its Klanwatch program has documented over 100 murders and hundreds of assaults motivated by hate. The offenders are often linked to white supremacist groups, some of which are described in Table 8.1. But whites certainly have no monopoly on hate crime, and homophobia and racism are only two of the many underlying motivations for hate. Besides, hate does not have to be organized to result in violence. More or less spontaneous incidents of gay bashing and assaults on members of immigrant and minority groups have been widely documented. A notorious recent case involved three white men who dragged an African American, James Byrd, Jr., to his death in Jasper, Texas. One defendant has been sentenced to death; the other two are awaiting trial.

Hate crime also appears to be increasing on college campuses and in the nation's high schools. The targets of college hate groups include African Americans, Jews, Hispanics, women, Middle Eastern students, and most of all, gays and lesbians—including people who simply "look" gay (Levin and McDevitt,

TABLE 8.1: Prominent Right-Wing Hate Groups in the United States

The following hate groups are among those currently active in the United States. They generally espouse philosophies of right-wing extremism and of white supremacy.

1. Aryan Nations. Operating primarily in the northwestern United States, with headquarters in Hayden Lake, Idaho, Aryan Nations maintains a doctrine of white supremacy and believes that control of the United States government should be returned to white Christian Americans. Its membership is estimated at around 5,000. The group runs a computer network that links various right-wing groups.

2. Christian Patriots' Defense League. Located in the midwestern United States around southern Illinois and Missouri, this group supports white supremacy, survivalism, and the Christian Identity movement, which spawned Aryan Nations. The group has close ties with conservative Christian groups, and its rhetoric has been extremely violent.

3. Ku Klux Klan. The basic philosophy of the Klan is white supremacy. The organization was originally formed by Confederate veterans immediately after the Civil War. In one month in 1871, the Klan lynched 297 blacks in New Orleans. In 1872, Congress passed the Ku Klux Klan Act, making it a crime for groups like the Klan to deprive citizens of their constitutional rights. In one week in 1874, white supremacists killed 200 blacks before elections in Vicksburg, Mississippi. In 1925, about 40,000 Klansmen marched through Washington, D.C. During the Great Depression, Klan membership reached between 4 and 5 million.

The Klan's fortunes soon declined, however, due to internal squabbling and the widespread reporting of its connections with the Nazi party. Authorities began arresting Klan members for civil rights violations and nonpayment of taxes. The movement enjoyed a modest resurgence during the 1950s and early 1960s, until open and violent confrontations with the FBI and other federal authorities during the civil rights movement turned the tide. Today, a more moderate version of the Klan, which does not espouse violence, appears to be trying to make a comeback, and public rallies and street marches have been held in a number of midwestern towns. There are usually far more onlookers and demonstrators than Klansmen.

4. The Order. Based in Idaho, Colorado, and northwestern states, The Order espouses white supremacy and right-wing extremism. The group has been linked to robberies, assaults, bombings, and arson. Many of its members have been arrested, and

Paramilitary survivalist groups that distrust the federal government, disapprove of gun control, and generally support extreme right-wing causes enjoy playing soldier on weekends.

PHOTO COURTESY OF AP PHOTO/TRAVERSE CITY RECORD-EAGLE, RICH BACHUS

while in prison have helped recruit new members. It is also believed that prison ministry programs run by right-wing Christian groups have (perhaps unwittingly) encouraged inmates to seek membership in The Order after conversion to Christian Identity.

5. Posse Comitatus. Primarily active in the Midwest, the Posse Comitatus is a right-wing, white supremacist group that also wages an ongoing struggle against taxes and the federal government. The group is highly decentralized, with several leaders of local organizations claiming to be spokespeople for Posse Comitatus. Members believe that the U.S. government has been taken over by Jews, and that the highest level of government should be at the county level. Records of prayer services and political meetings reputedly show that the Posse Comitatus endorses violence in the service of its ideals. Federal law enforcement officers have been killed by Posse Comitatus members in Nebraska and Arkansas.

6. Michigan Militia. Various paramilitary survivalist groups operate around the country, but they seem to be concentrated in the Midwest, Texas, and the Pacific Northwest. They are not as overtly racist as the other groups in this box. The Michigan Militia came to national prominence following the Oklahoma City bombing in 1995 because two of its members were connected with the prime suspect, Timothy McVeigh. Like most other militias, the Michigan Militia is a right-wing group that believes the country must be saved from a government that has run amok. They especially dislike attempts to restrict gun ownership and to relax search-and-seizure laws. Militias often play soldier on weekends, and claim that they are only interested in preserving the "American Way." They have enjoyed a lot of support in rural areas, where traditions of independence and gun ownership and declining standards of living pit people against government and taxes. Even though militia spokesmen quickly denied any connection with the Oklahoma City bombing, it brought them a lot of mainstream media and law enforcement attention, and may have cooled support for their activities and their rhetoric.

Sources: Jonathan R. White (1991). *Terrorism: An Introduction.* Pacific Grove, Calif.: Brooks/Cole; James M. Poland (1988). *Understanding Terrorism: Groups, Strategies, and Responses.* Englewood Cliffs, N.J.: Prentice-Hall; Ted Quant and John Slaughter (1980), *We Won't Go Back: The Rise of the Ku Klux Klan.* Atlanta, Ga.: Equal Rights Congress; *St. Louis Post-Dispatch,* April 27, 1995, pp. 1A, 11A; Federal Bureau of Investigation (1997). *Terrorism in the United States 1995.* Washington, D.C.: U.S. Department of Justice.

1993:126). A dramatic increase in membership in American Skinhead groups has also been observed. By one count, in a mere two years the number of Skinheads around the country increased from a 1988 estimate of 1,500–2,000 to 15,000–20,000 in 1990 (Hamm, 1993:11).

Figure 8.3 shows the type of hate crimes reported by the FBI in 1996.

Hate Crime Is a Global Problem. Hate crime is not a distinctly American problem. The Australian National Committee on Violence (1989) reported that racist attacks are on the increase in that country, and that much of it is organized. The Skinheads originated in Britain, where for many years they operated as a loosely knit national group of young racist thugs. During the 1980s, Skinheads were largely responsible for the racial attacks occurring in Britain each year (Hamm, 1993:xvi). Skinheads are now found in Germany, Canada, the Netherlands, and other parts of Europe.

The problem of hate crime violence may currently be worse in Germany than anywhere else in the world, and by all accounts it is growing. In 1997, over 11,700 known offenses were committed by neo-Nazis and other right-wing groups alone (*Associated Press,* May 7, 1998). The fall of the Berlin Wall and subsequent unification of Germany created enormous economic, social, and political pressures, and neo-Nazi groups quickly found growing support for their agenda (Hamm, 1993). The spread of hate crime is a growing concern across the globe, and politicians and the public are looking to the police for answers. The same can be said of terrorism.

TRENDS IN TERRORISM

There is little agreement on how to define terrorism, largely because it is a complex subject that hinges on interpretation of the motives of participants: One person's terrorism is another's selfless act of loyalty to a higher cause. When

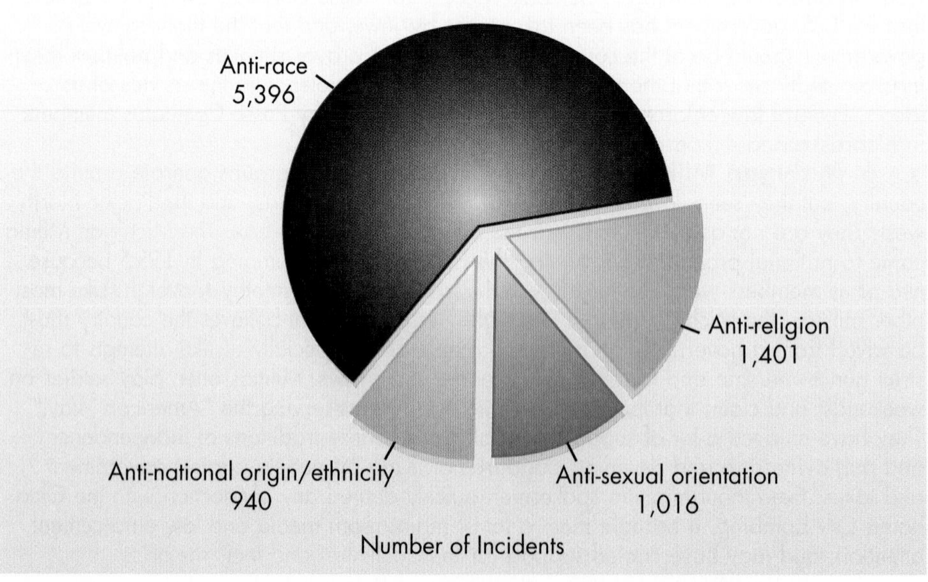

FIGURE 8.3 HATE CRIMES CLASSIFIED BY BIAS MOTIVATION, 1996
Since 1991, local police agencies have reported growing numbers of hate crimes to the FBI. In 1996, the FBI recorded 8,759 such incidents, which were classified by motivation as shown here.
Source: FBI Press Release, January 8, 1998.

Terrorism against America occurs at home and abroad. The 1995 Oklahoma City bombing was the worst mass murder in U.S. history; more people but fewer Americans were killed in the 1998 bombing of the U.S. Embassy in Nairobi, yet the similarities could not be missed. The FBI shoulders the burden of coordinating the police response to terrorism; its main weapon is intelligence gathering.

LEFT PHOTO BY SAYYID AZZIM, COURTESY OF AP PHOTOS
RIGHT PHOTO COURTESY OF AP/WIDE WORLD PHOTOS

members of the Palestinian organization Hamas blow themselves up along with a bus full of Israelis, they consider their deaths honorable and praiseworthy in the eyes of God. For purposes of our discussion, terrorism is defined simply as violence or threats against individuals, organizations, or governments in furtherance of a political or social objective. This is essentially how the FBI defines terrorism (Federal Bureau of Investigation, 1997b). Examples include bombings of abortion clinics, the Oklahoma City bombing by Timothy McVeigh and Terry Nichols, and the violence of Theodore Kaczynski, known as the Unabomber.

The methods of terrorism tend to be the tactics of war: bombings, arson, hijacking, ambush, kidnapping, and hostage taking (Jenkins, 1984; White, 1991:17). And just as in war, the larger the army and the better equipped it is, the more extensive the damage is likely to be. In recent years, much concern has been expressed over the possibility that terrorists will get their hands on nuclear, chemical, or biological weapons, and this concern has driven the attempts of the United States and some European countries to limit the proliferation of weapons of mass destruction. When India secretly detonated five nuclear devices in May 1998, the world was reminded that nuclear bombs can be assembled undetected by even the most sophisticated surveillance devices.

The underlying objective of terrorism is to create fear. The following characteristic features or elements have been identified (Nettler, 1982:228–234):

- *No rules.* Terrorists reject moral limitations on the type or degree of violence that can be used.
- *No innocents.* Terrorists make no distinctions between soldiers and civilians. Children, and even members of their own group, can be quite consciously killed if it serves their purpose.
- *Economy.* Kill one, frighten 10 million. An aim of terrorists is to "achieve grand results from the small investment of lives" (Nettler, 1982:232).
- *Publicity and provocation.* Publicity is important to terrorists. It gives them an audience they couldn't otherwise purchase.

Terrorism in and against the United States. The 1988 bombing of Pan Am Flight 103 over Lockerbie, Scotland, left many Americans outraged but probably thinking: "It couldn't happen here." Scarcely five years later, a bomb damaged the World Trade Center in New York City in 1993. This and the 1995 bombing of the Alfred P. Murrah Federal Building in Oklahoma City showed that mass murders by terrorists can happen at home, at any time, and in any place. Still, Americans are correct in thinking that the threat of terrorism against Americans is greater abroad than at home (Mickolus, 1993). Yet law enforcement authorities do not regard domestic terrorism as any less important or potentially dangerous than that occurring abroad.

Theodore Kaczynski, the Unabomber, is an infamous example of the problem. He constructed small bombs over a seventeen-year period; some were sent through the mail, while others were left inside shopping bags or disguised as bits of lumber. He killed 3 people and injured 23. Box 8.6 outlines the case

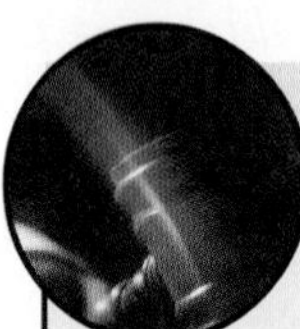

Box 8.6

JUSTICE PROFESSIONALS AT WORK

PURSUING THE UNABOMBER

After 17 years of hard work and the help of key informants, in April 1996 the UNABOM Task Force (UTF) finally arrests the notorious Unabomber, Theodore Kaczynski, in rural Montana. Kaczynski received four life sentences plus 30 years in May 1998.

PHOTO BY BRUCE ELY, COURTESY OF GAMMA LIAISON

On May 25, 1978, a package is mailed to Northwestern University in Evanston, Illinois; it explodes and a security guard is injured. Seventeen years later, on April 24, 1995, timber industry lobbyist Gilbert Murray opens a brown paper package in his office at the California Forestry Association. It explodes in his face, killing him instantly.

Although almost two decades separated these two incidents, the FBI connected both to the same individual, the "Unabomber," so called because the first targets were universities and airlines. Later in 1995, a rambling letter against the Unabomber, the police response, and the final chapter in this extraordinary case.

POLICING HATRED AND TERRORISM

A survey of state police and emergency management officials in 39 states and 148 communities showed that many respondents felt overwhelmed by hate crimes and terrorism (*St. Louis Post-Dispatch*, April 27, 1995 p. 5B). Although this survey, conducted by the Rand Corporation, found that interagency cooperation and local preparedness was reasonably good in larger cities, rural areas were another story. Small police departments with a large territory to cover find it impossible to investigate every suspicious activity or group. However, it is in just such areas that many extremist groups have their home base; rural areas are also the site of many nuclear power plants and military bases, possible targets of terrorist attacks.

BOX 8.6 (CONTINUED)

was mailed from Oakland, California, to the *New York Times* with the signature "FC." The initials FC had first appeared on fragments of the bomb mailed to the president of United Airlines on June 10, 1980. Along with a threat that FC could build more powerful and destructive bombs, the letter offered to stop the bombings in return for publication of a political manifesto. This manifesto, around 30,000 words, was published in September 1995 by the *Washington Post* and the *New York Times*. Authorities hoped that someone would recognize the hand behind the manifesto, and indeed that was the case: David Kaczynski, Theodore's brother, eventually contacted the FBI and the case was broken. The Unabomber was sent to trial in Sacramento, California, on a ten-count federal indictment. A plea bargain eventually ended the case in January 1998, and on May 4, Kaczynski received four life sentences plus 30 years.

The Unabomber was highly successful in eluding the FBI. Despite his use of a trademark and the meticulous hand-building of his bombs, he was extremely cautious. Even with the letter in hand, the FBI had no clue to his identity. According to Director Louis Freeh, the FBI had made an "unprecedented" effort to break the case, involving "thousands of FBI Special Agents and support personnel" and the assistance of the Bureau of Alcohol, Tobacco and Firearms (ATF), the U.S. Postal Inspection Service, and numerous state and local police agencies. In 1993, a UNABOM Task Force (UTF) was set up in San Francisco to provide overall direction for the investigation. Between 1993 and 1995 the UTF investigated more than 2,400 suspects, and was supported by squads of special agents in Chicago, Salt Lake City, and Sacramento.

Although in the end the crime was solved like so many others—through an informer—the UTF still had to coordinate Kaczynski's capture in a remote area of Montana and then prepare the evidence tying Kazcynski to the bombings. The FBI's laboratory used DNA tests, handwriting comparisons, and a host of other tests. It tied the materials and devices recovered from Kaczynski's cabin to the sixteen explosive devices used by the Unabomber. The seventeen years of arduous and plodding work now paid off.

Source: Based on reports by the Associated Press, Reuters, *Newsweek*, and various other news media, and a January 23, 1998, news release by the FBI National Press Office.

The Importance of Intelligence Gathering. The first and most important police tactic in meeting the challenge of terrorism and hate crime is intelligence gathering. The success of any reporting program depends on the cooperation and participation of local police. The job of coordinating this effort falls on the FBI, which is the natural lead agency since its responsibilities include domestic security and it controls the Uniform Crime Reporting program. A training guide was developed, and the FBI held training sessions for state and local police agencies around the country during 1991 (Federal Bureau of Investigation, 1992). These data collection efforts were a first step in mapping a national strategy for the policing of hate crime and terrorism. Along with other federal and state agencies, the FBI also participates in Joint Terrorism Taskforces (JTTFs), which gather intelligence, conduct investigations, and neutralize terrorist groups. By 1996 there were 14 JTTFs around the country (Federal Bureau of Investigation, 1997b:21).

Surprise is a crucial element in terrorism, not only because it prevents adequate preparation by the intended targets and by the police, but also because it creates disarray and even panic in the aftermath of an attack, lessening the effectiveness of emergency and security forces. Intelligence gathering helps authorities anticipate terrorist actions, and occasionally results in the detection and arrest of would-be assailants before they can carry out their mission. The best intelligence comes from covert operations that place agents within terrorist organizations. However, the work is extremely dangerous, and getting information into the right hands without blowing an agent's "cover" is not easy. In addition, "the fanaticism and intensity of terrorist groups today make covert penetration . . . especially difficult" (Poland, 1988:196).

A second intelligence-gathering tactic is common to policing the world of drugs: the development of informers. This tactic was used successfully against the IRA in Northern Ireland, resulting in some arrests and arms seizures. Like covert operators, informants play a dangerous game, and they know it. According to trial testimony, the bombing of the World Trade Center in New York City in 1993 was solved through an informer who was paid $1 million. With his help the FBI used hidden cameras and other electronic surveillance devices to bug a garage in Queens, New York, where handmade car bombs were being assembled by Muslim extremists under the leadership of cleric Sheikh Omar Abdel-Rahman (*The Economist,* July 3, 1993; Associated Press, September 24, 1995).

Much intelligence gathering is neither dangerous nor exciting. It is mundane and routine. Newspapers, periodicals, radio and television broadcasts, libraries, and other "open" sources are analyzed for content that sheds light on terrorist or hate groups and can help authorities build defenses against them. Shortwave radio broadcasts, and now the Internet, are also monitored for leads on the membership, activities, and plans of extremist groups. Thousands of hours must be spent listening and reading for each fragment of information likely to be useful to police intelligence gatherers.

Even after the most extensive and careful analysis of information, it is often pure luck that provides the key to preventing an attack or cracking a case. This is exactly what happened in the Oklahoma City bombing. Shortly after the bombing, Timothy McVeigh was pulled over in a routine traffic stop by an Oklahoma state trooper for driving without a license plate; he was arrested because he was carrying a concealed weapon. It was not until days later that local jail officials realized they had the bombing's prime suspect in their hands.

Technology versus Terrorism and Hate Crime. Neither the Oklahoma City bomb nor the Unabomber's devices were very sophisticated. Nonetheless, there is a widespread fear among authorities that technological advances are providing all sorts of new opportunities for terrorists and hate groups, increasing the nation's vulnerability to their crimes (White, 1991:267–277). At a Congressional hearing in 1991, counterterrorism experts from the FBI, the U.S. Secret Service, and other agencies identified some of the key terrorist threats facing the United States today, including biological attacks, chemical contamination of air and water, and the use of nuclear weapons. One Secret Service witness spoke of other, less obvious, threats:

> These include: penetrating an attack on our financial system through counterfeiting currency or credit cards; monitoring our security by using technological surveillance equipment to observe secured facilities; penetrating our databases such as bank accounts or security information by using computer viruses; and penetrating our borders by traveling with forged travel documents. (U.S. Senate Hearing, 1991:47–48).

The police would like to be one step ahead of terrorist threats, but often find themselves playing catch-up. The development of effective countermeasures requires that the police also take advantage of new technologies. In light of the prominent use and destructive capability of bombs, a major initiative was undertaken in the mid-1980s to develop explosives detectors that could be used in aircraft and other transports, as well as in federal buildings and other likely targets of terrorist attack. By 1991 no acceptable device had been developed, however, and inadequate funding coupled with confusion over appropriate testing procedures hardly helped. Even so, experts doubt whether a single technology would be an adequate defense.

Training and Interagency Cooperation. Arguably the biggest obstacle to effective policing of extremists is lack of adequate coordination and cooperation among police agencies, a problem we discussed in Chapter 5. The problem is not limited to policing across federal, state, and local jurisdictions, but confronts federal agencies in their dealings with one another. In September 1990, for example, the U.S. Department of Justice complained that the National Security Agency (NSA) was not sharing important secret intelligence data on terrorist activity with the department's Command Center, which maintains a database on potential terrorist attacks (U.S. Senate Hearing, 1991:184).

Cooperation between military and police agencies is important when confronting the threat of terrorist and hate attacks inside the United States. The technological sophistication of the U.S. military is unsurpassed, and this includes its intelligence-gathering functions. The use of aircraft, ships, radar, and reconnaissance satellites is crucial to the military's role in international peacekeeping efforts, but it also plays an important part in domestic counterterrorism efforts. High-tech satellite imaging devices can zero in on a small object from many miles away, and computer technology permits operators to track the movement of people and vehicles day or night. And sophisticated electronic listening devices permit police to hear and record conversations from miles away.

Ensuring the Protection of Individual Rights. All of this raises questions about how far the government should go in protecting the country against extremists. Democratic societies are justly proud of their restraints against government excesses. But a delicate balance must be maintained between protecting individual rights and freedoms and enforcing laws, which includes providing security for the larger society. The U.S. Constitution requires the government to provide security, while at the same time the Bill of Rights protects citizens against abuses of that authority. The police, some say, are caught in the middle when faced with a course of action that could prevent a crime but that also infringes upon someone's constitutional rights.

The democratic dilemma is heightened in the context of extremism because extremism threatens the very fabric of society, including the democratic institution itself. The terrorist threat is especially frightening because there are so many causes for fanatics and militant idealogues to take up, and the potential for death and destruction is immense. Another element creating fear is the perception that terrorist attacks are random and unpredictable. For these reasons, people want the government to protect them against terrorism and hate—but they may not be willing to pay the cost in rights and freedoms.

In the aftermath of the Oklahoma City bombing there were calls from many quarters, including President Clinton, to expand police powers. Such a move will not go unchallenged because history has taught Americans that their freedoms and rights, and the laws that support them, can be easily breached in the name of security. Many people were horrified by the conduct of police during civil rights and antiwar protests in the 1960s and 1970s. The 1971 demonstrations in Washington, D.C., by anti-Vietnam War protestors are a case in point: During a four-day period, more than 13,000 people were arrested, many of them peaceful demonstrators and some merely in the wrong place at the wrong time. With nowhere to put them, thousands were herded into R.F.K. Stadium, which served as a makeshift jail. In the end, few people were actually charged with any crime, and the federal courts subsequently ruled the arrests unconstitutional.

Many people would probably dismiss such events as mere overreaction by government authorities caught up in the hysteria of mass protest. Other people might see a darker side—a conspiratorial police bent on eradicating protest, thereby weakening American democracy itself. In the fight against hate crime and terrorism, citizens of democratic countries must decide how much they are willing to sacrifice in order to protect themselves and others, if not democracy itself. The police, meanwhile, will continue to gather intelligence and to monitor the activities of groups that threaten the lives and property of others or the foundations of our democratic society.

THE CHALLENGE OF DOMESTIC VIOLENCE

domestic violence Acts or threats of physical harm that occur among members of the same family, intimate friends, or residents of the same household.

Although commonly used to refer to spousal abuse, the term **domestic violence** refers to acts or threats of physical violence that occur among members of the same family, among relatives, among people living in the same household, and among people who are in intimate relationships. Estimates of the extent of domestic violence show that it is widespread and can be found among all social classes. Nationally, as many as 4 million children are physically abused by family members or relatives each year, and over 3 million women are beaten or threatened by their husbands or lovers. "Females at every age are much more likely than males to be murdered by an intimate" (Greenfeld et al., 1998:9). Of the 5,745 women murdered in the United States in 1991, half were murdered by their spouse or lover (Smolowe, 1994:21). Overall, "a person is more likely to be hit or killed in his or her own home by another family member than anywhere else or by anyone else" (Gelles and Straus, 1979:15).

Characteristics of Domestic Violence

Women are much more likely than men to be victims of domestic violence (Dawson and Langan, 1994; Greenfeld et al., 1998:4). The typical assailant is a husband, the next most common an ex-husband. When a woman is victimized, the degree of injury equals or exceeds that in 90 percent of all rapes, robberies, and aggravated assaults (Bureau of Justice Statistics, 1988:17). There is a tendency for incidents within a family to escalate in frequency and severity with the passage of time.

In households where there is spousal abuse, abusive relationships among other family members are also likely, including abuse of children (McKay,

Victims of domestic violence must deal with physical abuse, the psychological side-effects of such abuse, and sometimes indifferent treatment by the criminal justice system as well. Attempts to improve police handling of domestic violence cases have so far met with mixed success, but most observers believe the effort should continue, and should include better education of victims as well.

Photo courtesy of Uniphoto

1994:32). This provides an intergenerational link for domestic violence among family members, and helps explain why violent adults often recount experiencing abuse as children.

When women kill, the victim is usually the male they are living with. The reasons why women kill and the circumstances surrounding female violence are different from those attributed to males. For example, female homicides are often precipitated by the violence of the men they kill (Browne, 1987). Wives who eventually become murderers have often been physically abused by their husbands over a long period of time.

Women who resort to lethal counterforce do so because alternative solutions have failed and because they feel hopelessly trapped. In one study, 59 percent of interview subjects also reported that they had been raped by their husbands (Browne, 1987:95). Compared to other battered wives, those who killed their spouses reported more severe sexual assaults. Often the women would wake up to find they were being beaten or raped. All the women believed they would be killed, and the fear grew as the husband's battering became more frequent and more severe. Ironically, the batterers were usually killed by their own weapons.

Reasons for Reluctance in Policing Domestic Violence

The conventional police response to domestic disturbance calls—usually called "domestics"—has been a reluctant one. This mirrors a civilian reluctance to get involved in family disputes: When men were asked by researchers what they would do if a friend was hitting his partner in front of them, this reply was typical: "Nothing . . . it's none of my business is it? . . . it's between those two. I'd tell him he was out of order afterwards and that he should go back and make sure she's alright and that but I wouldn't interfere" (Bush and Hood-Williams, 1995:13). Even many victims feel that domestic violence is a private matter (Bureau of Justice Statistics, 1988a). For this reason, police may be considered intruders even though they are there because someone called for help.

There are other reasons why the traditional police response to domestic disturbance calls has been reluctant. Many officers believe that responding to domestic disturbances is not real police work. It is often seen as "uninteresting and unexciting, ranking alongside lost dogs, rowdy youth and bothersome drunks" (Grace, 1995:1). Even when serious violence is involved, a recent study of police actions in Chester, Pennsylvania, found support for a **leniency hypothesis:** police there treated men who beat their wives more leniently than men who committed similar violence in other contexts (Fyfe, Klinger, and Flavin, 1997). These results may not generalize to other departments, but they support longstanding claims that female victims of domestic violence are devalued victims. Forty-five years ago, a police commander from Britain's Scotland Yard is reputed to have put that sentiment into words: "There are only about 20 murders a year in London and not all are serious—some are just husbands killing their wives."

leniency hypothesis The idea that police treat men who beat their wives more leniently than men who are violent in other contexts.

When police are called repeatedly to deal with domestic disturbances in poor and lower-class neighborhoods, resentment rises among some officers, who see their crime-fighting role undermined by having to waste time on trivial matters that other classes of people avoid or handle privately. A study of the police response in London during the 1980s found that it was often slow, and that when police did arrive it was not uncommon for them to side with the assailant, who was rarely arrested (Edwards, 1986; cited in Grace, 1995). This picture also fits the situation in Australia, Canada, and the United States.

Besides being reluctant, the conventional police response to domestic violence is a *reactive* one (Sherman, 1992:208). This is largely because domestic disturbances are considered unpredictable events—and this includes the type and degree of violence involved. This unpredictability discourages the development of proactive policing strategies. Furthermore, although few people would question police who invaded a home because they thought someone was about to be stabbed, raped, or murdered, they would probably be alarmed if police routinely monitored and inspected homes or planted informants so as to prevent domestic disputes from occurring.

Indeed, there are uncertainties as to what kind of domestic violence merits a police response in the first place. For example, when does parental disciplining of a child constitute abuse or crime? If a husband and wife or two brothers get into a fight, at what point does it become police business? Police find domestic incidents on the whole to be frustrating because they feel there is nothing constructive they can do about them (Manning, 1994:47), and many officers are convinced that arrests are not worth the effort (Walker, 1992:118). To make matters worse, domestic incidents are frequently the source of complaints against officers.

Although the majority of disturbance calls do not involve actual use of violence (Black, 1980)—the most prevalent calls involve neighbors complaining about noise—all domestic disputes have the potential for turning violent, and the police don't know exactly what to expect when they arrive on the scene. This uncertainty adds to the tension police feel whenever they move from the comparative safety of the street and their patrol car into someone's private territory.

Cooling Down the Parties and Avoiding Formal Action. Aside from being reluctant, the traditional police response to most domestic incidents is either to do nothing, or to "cool down" the parties involved. Cooling down the parties might mean talking to them for a few minutes, acting as a mediator, or separating them by telling one person—usually the male—to take a walk and come back "when you have cooled down." If police believe that more time apart would be beneficial, they might suggest that one party spend the night with a

Historically, the criminal justice system has tended to treat domestice violence as not "real crime." Largely through the efforts of women's groups, police in many jurisdictions are now required to make arrests whenever there is evidence of violence, no matter how minor, and "no-drop" laws are resulting in prosecutions even when victims do not press charges.

ILLUSTRATION BY JOHN OVERMYER

relative or friend. Sometimes police recommend that the parties seek professional help, although they cannot compel them to do so, and apparently few disputants follow the advice (Walker, 1992:117). If alcohol is involved, which is often the case, the police might take one person—again, usually the male—into custody for the night to sleep it off.

Unfortunately, many domestic incidents fester but do not blow over. An hour later, the next day, or after the next bout of drinking, the anger once more boils over, and the dispute returns, sometimes resulting in serious injuries, or even a murder. In one incident studied by the present author, two officers were called by neighbors to a house where a man and his estranged wife had been yelling threats at each other in the woman's front yard. By the time police arrived the couple had stopped yelling and the officers left after inquiring whether everything was okay. A second call came barely 30 minutes later. Again the two officers drove to the woman's house. The woman wanted the man to leave; he said he had come to collect some clothes and wouldn't leave without them. The officers told the man to take a walk around the block and come back in half an hour; the woman agreed that she would let him get his clothes at that time. The officers left, and the man came back an hour later. Another argument ensued and the man ended up stabbing his estranged wife to death. Should the officers have done things differently? If so, what?

The conventional police response to domestic disturbance calls is an excellent illustration of the police exercise of discretion: In most cases the judgment leans toward informal action, a disposition that was actively encouraged by the International Association of Chiefs of Police for many years (Walker, 1992:119). By taking an informal approach, police officers also avoid the paperwork associated with arrests. Like most people, the police tend to follow the line of least resistance, and if an incident can be handled informally it will be.

NEW DIRECTIONS FOR POLICING DOMESTIC VIOLENCE

During the 1980s, largely in response to publicity about the extent of domestic violence and its excessive victimization of women, state legislatures began to relax the rules governing arrest procedures in domestic disputes. The women's movement can claim much of the credit for bringing domestic violence into the open. Police departments around the country found themselves being sued for denying female victims of domestic violence equal protection of the law. From 1984 to 1986, the proportion of urban police departments encouraging officers to make arrests grew fourfold and several states made arrests mandatory (Sherman, 1992:203). Special prosecution units were also established in some states to ensure vigorous prosecution (Fagan, 1996).

Experiments with Policing Domestic Assaults. Recognizing the need to take a hard look at the police response to domestics, criminologists began conducting research into the problem. The most influential was an experiment conducted with Minneapolis police in 1981–1982 to see whether police actions affected the likelihood of future domestic assaults (Sherman and Berk, 1984). Officers were randomly assigned to three experimental conditions: In one they used mediation, in another they ordered the assailant out of the house, and in the third they arrested the assailant, who spent a night in jail. The police officers were given no special training, being instructed to apply their existing knowledge and experience.

The Minneapolis domestic violence experiment found that those assailants who were arrested were less likely to commit repeat violence over the six-month period. As a result, some major cities adopted the position that officers should always make an arrest whenever a victim alleges that an assault has occurred, even if there are no obvious injuries and the victim does not want to press charges.

However, replications of the Minneapolis experiment in six other jurisdictions (Dade County, Florida; Atlanta, Georgia; Charlotte, North Carolina; Milwaukee, Wisconsin; Colorado Springs, Colorado; and Omaha, Nebraska) have not uniformly confirmed the earlier findings. In the Omaha study, for example, random assignment of domestic assaults to three conditions—mediation of the dispute, separation of the disputants, or arrest—produced no differences in the occurrence of domestic assault six months after intervention (Dunford, Huizinga, and Elliott, 1990). Another study found that a policy of always arresting offenders may backfire in the long run despite short-run benefits (Sherman et al., 1991): The long-term effect of short-duration arrests was *more* violence later on.

Clearly, the troublesome issue of how police should normally react to incidents of domestic violence not involving injury is far from being resolved. The criminologist whose Minneapolis study prompted the rash of experiments concluded: "These mixed results suggest that arrest is certainly no proven panacea and that mandatory arrest may not be justifiable on the grounds of crime control" (Sherman, 1992:206).

Are Proactive Police Strategies an Answer? Could proactive police strategies offer hope of a better way to deal with domestic violence? Would they help reduce its incidence and perhaps also the homicides that sometimes result from it? There are reasons to be pessimistic that proactive strategies will get much support in police circles. Many experts believe that police have neither the time, personnel, or money to mount a serious proactive campaign. Nor is it likely that police management will be eager to take the political risk associated with the more intrusive actions needed to monitor domestic disputes in middle- and upper-class homes. At the same time, the probability that any successful

Box 8.7

GLOBAL JUSTICE

THE BRITISH APPROACH TO DOMESTIC VIOLENCE

In 1990, the British Home Office—roughly equivalent to the U.S. Department of Justice—issued a series of recommendations that united reactive and proactive policing methods. The Home Office recommended that police take a more "interventionist" approach to policing domestic violence. A domestic assault was to be treated as seriously as an assault by a stranger.

The response of many police forces in England and Wales was to establish a Domestic Violence Unit (DVU) or to assign an officer as a Domestic Violence Officer (DVO). The task of these specialized units and officers was to provide information and support for beat officers as well as for victims and other agencies. By 1992 just over half the 43 police forces had a specialist unit with some responsibility for domestic violence; however, only five had a DVU dedicated solely to this offense (Grace, 1995:vii). Most of the officers interviewed in a 1992 survey felt that policing of domestic violence had improved and that incidents were being taken more seriously than in the past. Nevertheless, very few officers outside DVUs had actually received any specialized training in domestic violence.

After two years it appeared by some measures that the British program was not faring particularly well. Most beat officers appeared to have changed their behavior little, even though they were aware that arrest should be a priority and that continuous monitoring of domestic violence cases was an important element of the new strategy. Although strongly committed to their task and very positively received by victims, Domestic Violence Officers seemed to have had little impact on the general police response, and in fact had become rather marginalized in their own departments: beat officers had little to do with them, and this in turn undermined the information sharing that was crucial to proper monitoring and surveillance of households and neighborhoods experiencing domestic violence.

On the bright side, the attempt to establish a proactive police policy involving a more specialized police response to domestic violence has resulted in greater awareness among many police officers of domestic violence issues. Although the decision to make an arrest was still heavily influenced by an officer's perception of how cooperative complainants would be, many officers showed a greater understanding and sympathy for victims. If this attitude spreads, and officers' routine responses can be further shaped through regular training sessions and improved information sharing, the British model may yet prove to be a worthwhile strategy for policing domestic violence.

Source: Sharon Grace (1995). *Policing Domestic Violence in the 1990s.* London: HMSO.

proactive strategy could be devised for preventing serious injury or death in domestic disputes is extremely low.

For example, experimental evidence from Kansas City and Minneapolis showed that homicides could not be predicted on the basis of prior police knowledge of repeated domestic violence. In fact, if police acted on the theory that repeated calls to an address signaled a high risk of domestic homicide, they would have been wrong 99 percent of the time. In Milwaukee, where more than 15,000 police reports of assaults among named couples were studied, only in *one* couple did a homicide later occur; police had had no prior contact with the 32 other victims of domestic homicide (Sherman, 1992).

Yet the possibility exists that a proactive police strategy might be developed for identifying and controlling high-risk couples. By keeping track of calls to specific addresses, police can identify "hot spots" of domestic violence. In Milwaukee, for example, the police found that couples with seven or more prior reports over a three-year period will have another one before the three years have passed. If police acted on that prediction, they would be wrong in only one out of four cases. In addition, there are various other ways proactive policing might be conducted. For example, high-risk couples or families with repetitive police visits might be sent letters via mail or beat officers that threaten more severe penalties the next time an incident occurs. This sort of approach could be tested experimentally. Another idea is repeat random visits by patrolling police to households with a specified number of prior domestic violence calls. Such visits could be made part of a problem-oriented policing strategy (Goldstein, 1990:104–114). Families would be notified that police would be calling periodically to see how things were going. Box 8.7 illustrates yet another approach that is being tried in Great Britain—with mixed success.

Even if successful policing strategies could be developed for dealing with domestic violence, there will probably be little change in the people most likely to be targeted. The policing of domestic conflicts will continue to focus on the lower classes. Apart from the fact that lower-class people are stereotypically linked with violence, their lack of resources and their self-help traditions make it difficult to solve personal problems through counseling, mediation, education, or restitution—forms of social control that are available to the middle and upper classes (Manning, 1994:89). In other words, the policing of domestic violence will remain concentrated in neighborhoods where there is already a disproportionate police presence.

SUMMARY

In this chapter we have journeyed through six problems that constitute tremendous challenges for the police. Gang violence has escalated over the past few years, especially among juveniles, and guns are playing an ever larger role. The police are under pressure to devise effective strategies for reducing gang violence, if not for eradicating gangs altogether. The police have had mixed success in dealing with urban youth gangs. Many city police departments have established special gang crimes units, whose major task is to collect intelligence on gangs. The information collected is then used to help shape the police response.

If the police have their hands full trying to combat gang crimes, the policing of drugs and alcohol is even more difficult. Illegal drugs are not confined to inner-city streets, and much of the trafficking occurs in far more exotic places and involves people and organizations with economic and political power. The war on drugs has pumped millions of dollars into law enforcement agencies, and thousands of federal, state, and local police spend most of their time and energy dealing with drug users and pushers. Even though illegal drugs can be found in middle-class, upper-class, and rural homes, the brunt of policing efforts is borne by the inner city. This is reflected in the sharply rising arrest and incarceration rates of African Americans on drug charges.

Over the past 20 years, eradication programs and interdiction efforts at the borders and on the high seas have collectively resulted in the destruction of millions of pounds of illegal drugs, yet there is little evidence that these costly efforts have resulted in decreases in the availability of marijuana, cocaine, or heroin. *Problem-oriented policing* is now the buzzword in urban drug enforcement circles. Under this model the police combine traditional law enforcement strategies with attempts to address underlying community problems. Early results of these efforts are encouraging, but the greatest improvements have been in the attitudes and support of the public rather than in the prevalence of drug crime itself.

Organized crime draws a major part of its income and influence from trafficking in drugs. Although the American public as a whole stands firmly behind the war on drugs, attitudes toward organized crime are often ambivalent. Organized crime supplies many of the goods and services that people want, and for which they are willing to pay inflated prices. Organized crime is a tough challenge to police for this reason, but also because it enjoys secrecy and loyalty from its members, because its wealth and muscle help it buy the cooperation of officials willing to be corrupted, and because many of its activities are hidden behind a cloak of legitimacy and respectability. The law enforcement task is simply enormous, and even though multi-agency cooperation and all sorts of advances in electronic technology have helped police topple major crime rings from time to time, they still rely heavily on three age-old helpers: luck, informants, and the mistakes of greedy criminals.

There is considerable support among both public and police for doing something about hate crimes and terrorism. These unpredictable and ruthless crimes undermine the very fabric of democratic society. Neither type of crime shows a consistent pattern over time, and after a decline during the 1980s, the 1990s may be witnessing an upsurge in both, especially gay bashing and terrorist attacks within the United States.

The central element in policing these crimes is intelligence gathering. Shadowy hate groups and terrorist organizations do not advertise when they are about to undertake an attack, so police use informants and expert data analysts to uncover evidence of criminal plans. Undercover work is another way to gather intelligence, and this technique has been used extensively by the FBI to monitor the activities of hate groups and militant organizations from both the political left and right. Yet the overall police response to hate and terrorism seems to be quite muddled, and despite its importance, interagency cooperation is not as strong as it could be. And there is yet another difficulty facing police: maintaining the delicate balance between protecting people from crimes of violence while also protecting everyone's rights and freedoms. This problem is discussed in detail in the next chapter.

The police face many difficult problems in dealing with domestic violence. Many people don't even want to talk about it, let alone call the police. Violence among intimates is regarded as a private affair. There has been a tendency among police officers here and abroad to treat domestic violence as not worthy of serious police activity. Considering that women and children are the most common victims of domestic violence, this sends a strong message that it's okay for adults, men in particular, to use physical force against other family members. Men who persist in using violence generally escalate the seriousness of the attacks, sometimes to the level of homicide; at the same time, some victims turn the tables and murder their assailant.

During the 1980s and 1990s, largely thanks to the women's movement, police departments around the country looked for ways to improve their responses to domestic violence. Some established mandatory arrest policies, thereby changing the long-standing tradition of informal police responses in instances where no serious injuries had been inflicted. Some departments have looked for more proactive strategies for dealing with domestic violence. However, because the problem is so easily hidden, and because there is much resistance to police invasions of privacy, proactive policing has so far not shown a great deal of promise.

WHAT DO YOU THINK *NOW*?

- Based on what you have read, what do you now think are the toughest challenges for police officers today? What larger social problems are related to these challenges?
- Out of the different crime-fighting strategies you have read, which ones seem most successful? Which address the problems of society? Which address the criminals themselves?
- How are hate crimes and terrorism domestic problems? International ones? What can police do to combat their growth?

KEY TERMS

gang crime units
directed police patrols
victimless crimes
narcs
police informants
buy-bust
straight buy
reverse buy
alternative development
asset forfeiture
problem-oriented policing
professionalization of deviance
transnational crime
hate crime
terrorism
domestic violence
leniency hypothesis

ACTIVE LEARNING CHALLENGES

1. Divide into small groups and list all the factors, *apart from law enforcement*, that might affect gang behavior and illegal drug use in a neighborhood. Can you think of ways that these factors might be incorporated into prevention strategies involving the police?
2. Discuss the media images of gangs, drugs, and organized crime. Identify the core features of these images and discuss how these make the job of policing more difficult.
3. Break the class into two groups: those who think supply-side efforts are the best way to curb drug use, and those who think demand-side efforts are more important. Have each side present arguments to the class to support their view.
4. Assign groups the task of finding out the policies and procedures of five or six local police departments for dealing with hate crime and terrorism. Invite police representatives into class to discuss the issues and problems they face.
5. Break the class into small groups. Have each group design a strategy for policing domestic violence. Then discuss as a class what is important about each approach and how it departs from current practices.

INTERNET CHALLENGES

The Web pages mentioned here can all be accessed through the Web site for this textbook at **http://www.prenhall.com/barlow/.**

1. Visit the home page of the DEA and find out what the agency is currently doing in its war on drugs. Learn about the Cali Cartel and other international groups doing business in the drug trade.

2. For comprehensive current information on gangs in America, check out the home page of the Department of Justice's COPS Anti-Gang Initiative. Find out what the experts have to say about gangs, and check out the many links to gang-related sites.
3. The DARE program has come under attack in recent years. Find out what DARE officials themselves say about the program, and visit the police departments that use DARE for a police perspective. Start at Ottawa County, Ohio, Sheriff's Office.
4. Terrorism is a greater problem abroad than at home. Check out the current travel warnings at **http://travel.state.gov/travel warnings.html**. Where is it not safe to go? What implications do the warnings have for the interests of Americans and the citizens of the countries involved?
5. The Institute for Law and Justice maintains a Web site with lots of current information and links regarding domestic violence. Find out about current law and use the links to see how police departments around the country are dealing with this problem. Briefly summarize the commonalities and differences you find among these domestic violence strategies.

CHAPTER 9

THE POLICE AND THE LAW

LEARNING OBJECTIVES

- Understand the purpose of the Bill of Rights and its application to policing.
- Identify the important Supreme Court decisions regulating searches and seizures.
- Understand the exclusionary rule and explain how and why it has been modified over the years.
- Understand probable cause and the law of arrest.
- Describe how the Supreme Court has both tightened and loosened the rules governing police interrogations.
- Understand and distinguish the types and contexts of police corruption.
- Explain the differences between reasonable force, misuse of force, and brutality.
- Describe the strategies for controlling police corruption and their chances for success.
- Understand the importance of balancing police powers and democratic freedoms.

Most police deviance consists of minor abuses of occupational authority, which are considered "perks" of the job. The fear that small abuses will escalate into larger ones leads some departments to prohibit police perks. Do you agree with this policy?

ILLUSTRATION BY JOHN OVERMYER

The Constitution should not be read to permit [police] to order innocent passengers about simply because they have the misfortune to be seated in a car whose driver has committed a minor offense.

JUSTICE JOHN PAUL STEVENS, DISSENTING IN *MARYLAND V. WILSON* (1997)

The police must obey the law while enforcing the law.

EARL WARREN, FORMER CHIEF JUSTICE, U.S. SUPREME COURT

I am still waiting for the day when the honest cop is feared by the crooked cop.

FRANK SERPICO, TESTIMONY BEFORE NEW YORK CITY COUNCIL, SEPTEMBER 1997

In 1970, frustrated at the lack of progress in the war on drugs, the U.S. Congress passed the Comprehensive Drug Abuse Prevention and Control Act. One of its provisions allowed federal law enforcement officers armed with appropriate search warrants to forcibly enter private dwellings without knocking or announcing their presence. At the time, Joe Barnes was a special agent with the Office of Drug Abuse and Law Enforcement (ODALE), forerunner of the Drug Enforcement Administration, and he welcomed the new "no-knock" law. Over the next three years Barnes participated in a number of no-knock raids, usually in the company of plainclothed city and state police.

Unfortunately, a number of these raids were botched, leading the late U.S. Senator Charles Percy of Illinois to call for the law's repeal. Percy described one such raid: "[S]habbily-clad, unshaven raiders barged in on two homes. . . . They kicked in the doors without warning, while shouting obscenities and threatening the inhabitants with drawn weapons. . . . At no time during the raids did the agents satisfactorily identify themselves as federal narcotics agents or explain the nature of their authority. When they discovered they had raided the wrong houses, they simply left—no apologies, no explanations. . . ." (Percy, 1974:5).

The law was repealed in 1974. However, the war on drugs began to escalate in the late 1980s and early 1990s, and police authority to make unannounced entry in searches of private dwellings once again became an issue. The U.S. Supreme Court entered the picture with two important decisions that pleased Joe Barnes, even though he was now retired. In **Wilson v. Arkansas** (1995), the Court ruled that there is no blanket knock-and-announce rule, and "countervailing police

Wilson v. Arkansas There is no blanket rule covering when the police may or may not enter a private dwelling without knocking and announcing their presence.

Richards v. Wisconsin
The circumstances at the time of an unannounced entry may justify it even if a judge has refused to issue a no-knock search warrant.

interests" may establish the reasonableness of an unannounced entry. Then in ***Richards v. Wisconsin*** (1997), the Court ruled that even when a judge has refused to issue a no-knock search warrant, the reasonableness of a decision by police to enter a private dwelling unannounced can be validated by the circumstances *at the time of entry.*

The no-knock issue in police searches is part of the larger tension that surrounds the relationship between a democratic society and its police forces. Society expects the police to do many difficult things on its behalf, and to do them efficiently, fairly, and with minimal disruption to daily life. Yet the occupational environment of policing makes it difficult for police to fully meet this expectation. Police culture, politics, a highly inquisitive news media, and periodic boredom encourage behavior that sometimes brings police into conflict with the public, their own superiors, and even the law itself.

In this final chapter on policing, we shall explore the legal environment of modern policing. The central question is this: How does a democratic society such as ours maintain order and protect lives and property while ensuring individual rights and freedoms? Another way of putting this question is: How does society regulate its police? The police have considerable authority and the power to back it up. How does society deal with the so-called "dark side" of policing—corruption and brutality (Kappeler, Sluder, and Alpert, 1994)? What mechanisms are available for controlling the police so that citizens are not abused or laws undermined? A good place to start examining these questions is the U.S. Constitution, particularly the Bill of Rights.

? WHAT DO YOU THINK?

- What are the legal rights of police? What are the main areas in which their rights must be clearly defined?
- When is force justified? What are some of the guidelines for determining the justification of force, and how much should be applied in a given situation?
- Are corrupt police officers "rotten apples" or are there better explanations of corruption and brutality?

CONSTITUTIONAL PROTECTIONS

Not all democracies have a written constitution, but one benefit of the American form is that citizens have a lasting record of their rights and obligations. The Constitution of the United States can be modified only through the addition of amendments. These require passage by two-thirds of the members of both houses of the U.S. Congress *and* the legislative bodies of three-fourths of the states. However, the existence of a written document does not guarantee that everyone will agree on its meanings or application. As we know from Chapter 4, this is where the federal appellate courts come in. These courts rule on legal cases arising from differences over the interpretation of the articles and

The Magna Carta, the most famous document in British constitutional history, has also had great influence on American law. One of its most important features is its emphasis on due process. Due process means that legal procedures are made and followed to protect individual rights and freedoms.

PHOTO COURTESY OF THE GRANGER COLLECTION, NEW YORK

amendments of the U.S. Constitution. The nine justices who sit on the U.S. Supreme Court are the final judges in these matters.

In its original form, the seven articles of the U.S. Constitution had only a few provisions of relevance for the administration of criminal law. However, in 1791, ten amendments were added, constituting a **Bill of Rights.** These amendments specify basic rights that all citizens of the United States enjoy. The ten amendments that make up the Bill of Rights are shown in Box 9.1. Although written over 200 years ago, these ten amendments are one of the world's most important statements of rights. Their roots can be found in the Magna Carta of England.

Bill of Rights Ten amendments added to the Constitution in 1791 that specify the rights of citizens.

The Magna Carta. The **Magna Carta** (Latin for "Great Charter"), signed in 1215, set out the terms of an agreement between King John and the English barons. The barons felt that the king was undermining their authority and depriving them of certain feudal rights, including control of land and of the peasants living on it. Fearing an armed confrontation with the barons, which he would not win, King John signed the document in a ceremony at Runnymede, a few miles outside London.

Magna Carta A charter of rights signed by King John of England in 1215 that established principles of due process.

The Magna Carta is now the most famous document of British constitutional history. It is widely agreed that the Magna Carta established the fundamental importance of "due process of law" as a cornerstone of democracy. **Due process** means that legal procedures are designed and followed in a way that protects individual rights and freedoms. It is rooted in King John's promise that "no man shall be arrested, or imprisoned, or disseized [deprived of his lands], or outlawed, or exiled, or in any way molested; nor will we proceed against him unless by the lawful judgment of his peers or by the law of the land." Amendments IV, V, and VI of the Bill of Rights show the influence of the Magna Carta.

due process Laws are written and applied in a way that protects individual rights and freedoms.

Federal and State Jurisdictions Clash over the Bill of Rights. Although the Bill of Rights was enacted in 1791, it was a long time before its provisions had much affect on law in action. For nearly 100 years, the provisions of the Bill of

Box 9.1

JUSTICE AND THE LAW

THE BILL OF RIGHTS

The Bill of Rights was added as ten amendments to the U.S. Constitution in 1791. It lays out the rights that U.S. citizens enjoy. Here are the ten amendments:

Amendment I: Congress shall make no law respecting an establishment of religion, or prohibiting the free exercise thereof, or abridging the freedom of speech, or of the press; or the right of the people peaceably to assemble, and to petition the Government for a redress of grievances.

Amendment II: A well regulated Militia, being necessary to the security of a free State, the right of the people to keep and bear Arms, shall not be infringed.

Amendment III: No Soldier shall, in time of peace be quartered in any house, without the consent of the Owner, nor in time of war, but in a manner to be prescribed by law.

Amendment IV: The right of the people to be secure in their persons, houses, papers, and effects, against unreasonable searches and seizures, shall not be violated, and no Warrants shall issue, but upon probable cause, supported by Oath or affirmation, and particularly describing the place to be searched, and the persons or things to be seized.

Amendment V: No person shall be held to answer for a capital, or otherwise infamous crime, unless on a presentment or indictment of a Grand Jury, except in cases arising in the land or naval forces, or in the Militia, when in actual service in time of War or public danger; nor shall any person be subject for the same offence to be twice put in jeopardy of life or limb; nor shall be compelled in any criminal case to be a witness against himself, nor be deprived of life liberty, or property, without due process of law; nor shall private property be taken for public use, without just compensation.

Amendment VI: In all criminal prosecutions, the accused shall enjoy the right to a speedy and public trial, by an impartial jury of the State and district wherein the crime shall have been committed, which district shall have been previously ascertained by law, and to be informed of the nature and cause of the accusation; to be confronted with the witnesses against him; to have compulsory process for obtaining witnesses in his favor, and to have the Assistance of Counsel for his defence.

Amendment VII: In Suits at common law, where the value in controversy shall exceed twenty dollars, the right of trial by jury shall be preserved, and no fact tried by jury, shall be otherwise re-examined in any Court of the United States, than according to the rules of the common law.

Amendment VIII: Excessive bail shall not be required, nor excessive fines imposed, nor cruel and unusual punishments inflicted.

Amendment IX: The enumeration of the Constitution, of certain rights, shall not be construed to deny or disparage others retained by the people.

Amendment X: The powers not delegated to the United States by the Constitution, nor prohibited by it to the States, are reserved to the States respectively, or to the people.

Rights placed limits only on the *federal* government; states were free to develop their own laws of procedure for policing and other criminal justice activities.

This was no accident. In establishing an independent system of government, the framers of the U.S. Constitution tried to balance the needs of the federal system against the right of states to govern their own affairs. America prides itself on a democratic system of governance that operates as close to the daily lives of its citizens as possible with minimal federal interference. Articles II and III of the Constitution explicitly restrict federal authority in criminal matters, reserving the bulk of that responsibility to the states.

We should also keep in mind the nature of American life in the early 1800s. The country was young and mainly rural, communications were primitive, slavery was an acceptable practice, and law enforcement was rudimentary in the cities and even weaker on the frontier. The law enforcement interests of the federal government rested primarily in the hands of U.S. marshals, which TV westerns and movies have raised to a level of dignity and prestige they rarely attained in real life. Most of their time was spent guarding and transporting federal prisoners. Meanwhile, local sheriffs and city constables handled the bulk of crimes and offenders—with members of the clergy sometimes acting as judges—and neither the Bill of Rights nor federal rules of criminal procedure applied to them. This changed formally in 1868.

Recognition of the Bill of Rights. In 1868, a new Amendment to the Constitution was added that effectively extended the Bill of Rights to the actions of *state* governments. Section 1 of the **Fourteenth Amendment** reads in part as follows: "No State shall make or enforce any law which shall abridge the privileges or immunities of citizens of the United States; nor shall any state deprive any person of life, liberty, or property, without due process of law; nor deny to any person within its jurisdiction the equal protection of the laws. . . ."

Fourteenth Amendment Extended the Bill of Rights to dealings between citizens and their state government.

The mention of "due process of law" implied that the provisions of the Fourth, Fifth, and Sixth Amendments now applied to states. For state and local police this would mean that the act of searching someone's home or seizing evidence could now be challenged on the grounds that it violated the Fourth Amendment prohibiting unreasonable searches and seizures.

But judicial recognition that the Bill of Rights applied to the actions of states did not occur overnight. It was not until 1925, in fact, that the U.S. Supreme Court began this process. The landmark decision in *Gitlow v. New York* (1925) established that freedom of speech and of the press were fundamental rights guaranteed by the First Amendment and applicable to all citizens in both state and federal jurisdictions through the due process clause of the Fourteenth Amendment. This was the first provision of the Bill of Rights to be applied to states. Later, in *Palko v. Connecticut* (1937), the Court ruled that the due process clause of the Fourteenth Amendment could be used as a basis for the *selective incorporation* of those federal rights, such as freedom from unlawful searches and seizures, that were "implicit in the concept of ordered liberty." With this decision, the Court laid the groundwork for incorporation of the entire Bill of Rights into all dealings between U.S. citizens and their governments.

Let us now examine some of the important ways in which the Bill of Rights has helped American society control its police forces.

THE LEGAL BOUNDARIES OF POLICE ACTION

The Bill of Rights, as interpreted by the courts, has had a tremendous impact on policing; in practical terms, it has established the legal boundaries of police action. Nowhere is this more evident—or important—than in the area of **search and seizure,** when police look for evidence of a crime and take it under their control.

search and seizure Police look for evidence of a crime and take it under their control.

THE RULES OF SEARCH AND SEIZURE

In police work, nothing is more important than the power to seize evidence of a crime following a search of suspects, their homes, their cars, their businesses, or other private premises. Yet the Fourth Amendment gives Americans a right to privacy, which includes protection against unreasonable intrusions by government agents, including the police. How, then, are the police to exercise their powers of search and seizure without violating the Fourth Amendment? And what happens if they do violate it?

search warrant An order issued by a judge and signed by police indicating what is to be seized and where it is expected to be found.

probable cause The constitutional standard for determining whether a search or an arrest is lawful.

The Search Warrant. The Fourth Amendment stipulates that people and their possessions may not normally be searched or seized without a **search warrant** stating clearly what is to be seized and where it is expected to be found. A search warrant is issued by a judge or magistrate upon presentation of a sworn affidavit by the requesting police officer. Search warrants are not issued on a whim but must be supported by **probable cause.** This is the constitutional standard for determining whether a search—or an arrest—is lawful. There is probable cause when the available facts would lead a reasonable person exercising professional judgment to believe that particular evidence of a crime will be found in a certain place. A police officer needs more than a hunch or intuitive feeling to support a request for a search warrant. Even so, police investigators who suspect that incriminating evidence can be found in a certain location usually have little difficulty getting a judge to approve their request for a search warrant. An example of a search warrant is shown in Figure 9.1.

The police often get their information about crimes from informants. We have seen how crucial this information can be in investigating drug offenses, gangs, organized crime, and terrorism, but the police make use of informants whenever they can. All sorts of crimes are solved because of an informant's tip,

The no-knock search has always been surrounded by controversy. Today, there is no blanket no-knock rule; police who feel that circumstances validate a no-knock search can go ahead with it even when a judge has refused to give them permission for it.

PHOTO BY A. RAMEY, COUTRESY OF PHOTOEDIT

COMPLAINT FOR SEARCH WARRANT

[A police officer], COMPLAINANT, now appears before the undersigned Judge of the Circuit Court of the Third Judicial Circuit of Illinois, and requests the issuance of a Search Warrant to search the following described premises:

> the premises at [this specific address] including residence, unattached garage and addition to the unattached garage located on the premises; the residence is a two story beige sided residence, with a covered front porch, green shingles, with a chain link fence around the side and back of the home and a stockade fence between the main residence and the unattached garage, the unattached garage has an addition. The residence is commonly known as [this specific address],

and there to seize, secure, and review including the use of any necessary techniques to open and examine computer files, tabulate and make return thereof according to law, the following property or things:

> Any electronic data processing and storage devices, computers and computer systems (including any electronic, magnetic, optical, electrochemical, or other high speed data processing device performing logical, arithmetic or storage functions); central processing units; internal and peripheral storage devices such as fixed disk, external hard disk, floppy disk drives and diskettes, tape drives and tapes . . . optical storage devices or other memory storage devices. . . . Any and all files contained in the drives, disks, peripherals, tapes, printouts or recordings, including data documents, photographs, email . . . telephones, cellular telephones, pagers. . . . Cameras, including still, Polaroid, moving and video, and any photographs, movies, video tapes, negatives, slides and/or undeveloped film depicting nudity and or sexual activities involving children or children with adults. . . .

And any instruments, articles, or things which have been used in the commission of or which may constitute evidence of the offenses in connection with which this warrant is issued, being Child Pornography. The following facts having been sworn to by Complainant in support of the issuance of this warrant (see attached Affidavit).

WHEREFORE, your Complainant requests that the Court issue a Search Warrant directing a search for and seizure of the property described above at the premises described above.

[signed by Complainant] ________________

[signed and dated by judge] ________________

FIGURE 9.1 EXAMPLE OF A SEARCH WARRANT
While the specific wording of search warrants may differ from jurisdiction to jurisdiction, the Fourth Amendment requires that they be specific as to what is to be searched for where, and that the officers applying for the warrant have probable cause to believe that the particular evidence of a crime will be found in a certain place. Here is an abbreviated example of a search warrant filed on March 9, 1998, in Madison County, Illinois, in a case involving alleged child pornography.

from murders, robberies, and rapes to political bribery and computer crimes. Can an informant's tip be probable cause for police to seek, and a judge to issue, a search warrant?

In *Anguilar v. Texas,* (1964), the U.S. Supreme Court ruled that an informant's tip could be sufficient grounds to issue a search warrant only if the police can show (1) why they believe the information is reliable, and (2) how the informant came by the information. In later cases, the Court relaxed this two-pronged test, favoring an evaluation of the "totality of circumstances" involved in a request. If this led a police officer, and subsequently a judge, to reasonably believe that the information was accurate, then a warrant and search based on it would be legal. Under these circumstances, even anonymous tips may provide probable cause for a judge to issue a search warrant. In *Alabama v. White* (1990), the Court ruled that even in the absence of other information, police could regard an anonymous tip about a suspect's criminal activities as reliable if the tip included accurate predictions about the suspect's future movements.

warrantless search Police search people or their possessions without the authorization of a judge.

Warrantless Searches. There are a number of situations in which the police may search people and their possessions without a warrant. In fact, police make far more **warrantless searches** than they do searches with a warrant. The major circumstances in which warrantless searches are allowed include the following:

1. *Consent searches.* If a police officer requests permission to conduct a search and the person being asked voluntarily consents, then the police do not need a warrant. If the person is drugged, drunk, mentally disabled, or otherwise unable to give intelligent consent, that is a different matter. It could also happen that the person being asked has no authority to consent to a particular search. If a friend is visiting you in your apartment, and in your absence the friend allows the police to search the apartment, would the search be legal? No. But if the friend is also your roommate, considered in law to have "common authority" to control access to the shared property, then the friend's consent would make the search legal. The principle of common authority also applies to spouses living in the same home, as well as to employers and employees, and landlords and renters. One can imagine times when consent given under these conditions causes considerable friction. In *Illinois v. Rodriguez* (1990), furthermore, the Supreme Court took the position that even if it later turns out that a person giving consent to a search no longer had common authority, the search is still legal if the police reasonably believed at the time that consent was lawfully given.
2. *Plain view.* If the fruits of a crime (or the tools to commit one) are seen by police officers, they may not need a warrant to seize them. The *plain view doctrine* holds that if the police inadvertently see incriminating evidence when they are lawfully going about their business, they are not in violation of the Fourth Amendment if they seize it. But there are some additional conditions that restrict plain view seizures: The police cannot move objects around to get a better view of suspect evidence, or look behind curtains, walls, or other partitions. The evidence to be seized must be directly visible, and its incriminating character immediately apparent. Most applications of the plain view doctrine have emphasized that the evidence must be seen inadvertently or by accident. This is to ensure that the police do not claim a plain view exemption when all along they planned it that way. Nevertheless, in *Horton v. California* (1990), the Supreme Court decided that inadvertence was not a *necessary* element for lawful plain view searches. In the *Horton* case, police had applied for a warrant to search the defendant's home for jewelry stolen in a robbery. In the affidavit supporting the warrant request, the police mentioned an Uzi submachine gun and other weapons used in the robbery. However, the weapons were not listed on the search warrant. As it happened, the search revealed no stolen jewelry but officers did come across various guns, including an Uzi. These were seized and used as evidence against Horton. Horton's appeal claimed the police believed all along that the weapons might be there, and therefore their seizure was not inadvertent. The Court rejected the appeal.

3. *Hot pursuit and other exigent circumstances.* Suppose you have just committed an armed robbery and police are chasing you. You duck into your house, slam the door shut, and throw the loot and gun into a desk, which you then lock. Moments later the police burst into your home and proceed to search all over the place, looking for evidence of the crime. They find the loot and gun, which is seized and later used to convict you of the crime. Was this a lawful search and seizure? The answer is yes. In various decisions since the 1960s, the Supreme Court has held that certain emergency situations, or **exigent circumstances,** make warrantless searches permissible. Since you are a suspected felon, thought to be armed and to present a danger to the police or others, the answer is yes. The Court has been particularly careful to emphasize that these emergency exemptions are made in order to protect lives rather than simply to make it easier for police to make warrantless searches and seizures.

exigent circumstances Emergency situations in which warrantless searches are permissible in order to protect lives or prevent the destruction of evidence.

Yet the Court is also aware that there are certain types of evidence that a suspect can easily destroy before police can obtain a warrant. Drugs and drug paraphernalia are examples. Thus, another exigent circumstance is when police have reason to believe delay would result in destruction of criminal evidence. In all exigency situations that result in prosecution, however, the police have to justify their warrantless search to the satisfaction of the court. A mere claim of exigency is not enough. Any decent defense attorney will demand that the police provide a detailed and compelling explanation of their actions. Since 1995, the Supreme Court has left it up to state courts to determine the reasonableness of the explanation.

4. *Exigent motor vehicle searches.* By their nature, vehicles are mobile and both contents and occupants are more or less in public view. Add to this the fact that vehicle use is already regulated by the government, and we see why the Supreme Court has traditionally held a more relaxed view of the privacy doctrine when applied to them. Even so, the baseline requirement of a warrant still governs police actions when it comes to searches and seizures. Realistically, however, there are so many situations in which warrantless searches are permissible that police rarely seek or use a warrant.

The special character of motor vehicles has given rise to some interesting compromises on search and seizure. For example, the requirement of probable cause is relaxed because police may stop a vehicle for a minor traffic infraction (not a crime) and *during questioning* of the driver or occupants establish probable cause to conduct a search or make an arrest. Plain view limitations may be relaxed if during an initial search of the passenger compartment police turn up incriminating evidence of a crime. For example, the police may open a bag in the trunk of a car when information obtained in an initial search gives them reason to believe the bag contains contraband.

When permission is given to police to search a vehicle, the search is likely to be a *complete* search unless the person giving permission expressly limits the extent of the search. If the police are given permission to search a stopped vehicle and they find incriminating evidence in a closed container during the search, a warrantless search and seizure would be legal if police reasonably believe they had permission to search the whole car. Students often express amazement when they hear of huge drug finds in cars that have been stopped for routine traffic offenses, and the driver gave police permission to search the vehicle! In 1996, the Court made it more difficult for drivers to successfully appeal such consent searches: Police officers do not have to tell drivers they are free to leave in order for the search to be considered voluntary.

Maryland v. Wilson Police may order passengers out of a car during traffic stops.

In an interesting recent case, ***Maryland v. Wilson*** (1997), the Supreme Court extended the powers of police in traffic stops by permitting them to order passengers out of the car. The new rule, which Justice Stevens in dissent called "groundbreaking," could have far-reaching implications because it applies the same standard to everyone in a vehicle. Through other Supreme Court decisions, the Fourth Amendment requirement of a search warrant is now relaxed for *all* types of vehicles: motor boats, sailboats, houseboats, and motorhomes may be searched without a warrant if the police have probable cause to believe a crime has been or is being committed—or if they are given permission.

The Supreme Court has also ruled that people riding buses, trains, planes, or other public transport may be subject to a warrantless "sweep" by police searching for contraband, provided the police (1) ask passengers individually for permission to search, (2) do not coerce them into consenting, and (3) do not give the impression that compliance is mandatory. However, the police are not required to tell passengers they have the right to leave or the right to refuse permission. The justices apparently believed that reasonable people would understand that a police request for permission to conduct a search implies a right to say no or to leave. Do you think most Americans would agree with the Court?

5. *Searches incidental to arrest.* An arrest constitutes a seizure—in this case of a person. Anytime a police officer makes an arrest, the suspect is liable to a personal search and a warrantless search of the area under the suspect's *immediate control.*

Chimel v. California Police may search the area under an arrested suspect's immediate control.

An arrest requires probable cause, and that fact establishes the probable cause for a search. Two landmark cases before the U.S. Supreme Court established the guidelines for searches incidental to arrest: *United States v. Rabinowitz* (1950), and ***Chimel v. California*** (1969). The *Rabi-*

Warrantless searches are common in traffic stops. In a recent case in Maryland, the Supreme Court permitted police to order passengers out of the car. This law applies to everyone in a vehicle. What do you think of this law?"

PHOTO BY JAMES NUBILE, COURTESY OF THE IMAGE WORKS

nowitz case involved a stamp collector whom police arrested on suspicion of defrauding other collectors by selling altered stamps. Police arrested the man at work and searched his small office, including his safe, and discovered many altered stamps. Police had no search warrant, and eventually Rabinowitz appealed his conviction in federal court on that basis. The Supreme Court allowed the conviction to stand, arguing that the search was reasonable considering all the circumstances, especially that it was incidental to a lawful arrest.

The *Chimel* case established more clearly exactly where police may search during an arrest. Chimel was arrested at his California home under a warrant charging him with burglary of a coin shop. After his arrest, police asked if they could look around, and when Chimel objected they pointed out that a warrantless search would be lawful since he had just been arrested. Police proceeded to search the whole house, accompanied by Chimel's wife. She was asked to open drawers, and even to move contents around so that police might better spot stolen coins. In the end, police seized coins from various places in the home.

Chimel was convicted in state court, and subsequently appealed on the ground that the search had been unlawful. The U.S. Supreme Court agreed, arguing that the scope of the police search was far greater than could be justified on the grounds of danger or destruction of evidence. In its decision, the Court established that the area of a warrantless search should not extend beyond an area under the "immediate control" of the arrested suspect. However, in subsequent decisions, the Court has given the police some degree of latitude in deciding what "immediate control" really means as a practical defense against danger or destruction of evidence. For example, a search may be made beyond the arm's length of a suspect if police reasonably believe themselves to be in danger.

6. *Stop and frisk.* One of the most common occasions for warrantless searches by police is the *field interrogation,* discussed earlier in Chapter 7. In that discussion it was observed that field interrogations are an important part of police discretionary practice, and that abuses of police power are not uncommon. It is particularly important, therefore, that we understand just what is permissible and what is not when citizens are temporarily detained by the police. The **stop and frisk** rules apply here.

stop and frisk A warrantless "patdown" search of a person's outer clothing during a field interrogation.

The most important case regarding stop and frisk is *Terry v. Ohio* (1968). The *Terry* case involved two men whom a veteran police officer had observed hanging around a street corner, and in his view acting suspiciously. The officer approached the men, and fearing they might be armed, spun them around against a wall and patted them down. He found a gun on Terry, who was later convicted of carrying a concealed weapon. Terry appealed, arguing that the officer had no probable cause to search him. In its 8-to-1 decision, the Court ruled that a police officer may stop and frisk a person when the officer "observes unusual conduct which leads him reasonably to conclude in the light of his experience that criminal activity may be afoot and that the persons with whom he is dealing may be armed and presently dangerous."

Field interrogations involving patdown searches are common police practice, and the *Terry* decision established their lawfulness when reasonable suspicion exists that a subject may be armed. What if the police officer doing a frisk feels something suspicious that is clearly not a weapon; can he or she remove it? It depends. Applying the plain view doctrine, it could be seized if a lawful frisk revealed nonthreatening but obviously incriminating evidence. However, in ***Minnesota v. Dickerson*** (1993), the Supreme Court ruled that squeezing, moving around, and otherwise manipulating a pocket's contents if it is clearly not a weapon goes beyond

Minnesota v. Dickerson Police are not permitted to manipulate objects in a person's pocket during a patdown search if they are clearly not a weapon.

both *Terry* and the plain view doctrine, and therefore constitutes an unconstitutional search and seizure. In the *Dickerson* case, the police officer admitted that he never thought that a small lump in Dickerson's pocket was a weapon, but neither did he immediately recognize it as cocaine, which it turned out to be.

These examples of warrantless searches are the most common situations in routine police work. However, mention should also be made of two others: *border searches* by customs and immigration officials and *roadblock searches,* in which police search for escapees and fleeing felons, or check on the sobriety of drivers passing by—a strategy not uncommon on some university campuses. The justification for these searches is that public safety and the practical difficulty of establishing probable cause on an individual basis leave the police little alternative. In the case of border searches, customs officials may use intuition or gut feelings in picking out someone to search, but the U.S. Supreme Court has ruled that searches must involve reasonable suspicion based on a suspect's actions and/or the professional experience of the officer. It is lawful for customs and immigration officials to use offender profiles of smugglers, drug traffickers, terrorists, and illegal immigrants to guide their search decisions.

The Consequences of Unlawful Searches: The Exclusionary Rule

Weeks v. United States Established the "exclusionary rule" that evidence unlawfully obtained cannot be used to convict a defendant.

We have reviewed the various criteria under which police may conduct searches and seize people or possessions. What happens if these searches and seizures are unlawful? The Supreme Court's first clear statement on this issue came in ***Weeks v. United States*** (1914). Federal agents had suspected Freemont Weeks of selling lottery tickets, a violation of federal law. The police decided to search Weeks's home, and they did so without a search warrant, which was not unusual. They seized many things as evidence, including some of Weeks's personal belongings. Most of the personal items were subsequently returned on the request of Weeks's defense attorney, who argued that they had been seized illegally. However, the remaining evidence was sufficient to convict Weeks, who was sentenced to prison. Weeks appealed the conviction, and his case was eventually heard by the U.S. Supreme Court. His attorney argued that if some of the seized "evidence" had been obtained illegally, then the rest of it was also obtained in violation of the Fourth Amendment. The Court agreed, and overturned the earlier conviction.

The case was a landmark decision that established what is known as the **exclusionary rule.** Simply put, the exclusionary rule means that evidence obtained illegally cannot be used to convict a defendant. The *Weeks* case also affirmed that the police cannot simply barge into someone's home and seize whatever they want even if they do suspect that person of a crime. A search warrant must first be obtained from a judge, specifying the place to be searched and the nature of the evidence police expect to find there.

precedent A feature of common law in which prior court rulings guide future judgments; also called *stare decisis.*

Court rulings apply only to the particular case in front of the court, and other incidents like it. However, the decision sets a **precedent** that may influence judges' rulings on subsequent, but somewhat different cases. The particulars of these later cases may be considered extensions of the initial ruling or exceptions to it. For example, in a case shortly after *Weeks,* police had made an illegal search but later returned all illegally seized evidence. However, they had secretly made copies of some incriminating papers, and these were later introduced in court as evidence against the defendant, who was convicted. The Supreme Court extended the exclusionary rule to cover it, ruling that the copies were tainted by the illegal search. This became known as the *fruit of the poisoned tree doctrine.* Illegal police actions may thus come back to haunt prosecutors later on.

Mapp v. Ohio* (1961).** Despite the direction being taken by the U.S. Supreme Court, many states continued to reject the idea that the exclusionary rule applied to criminal procedures at state and local levels. In 1961, a landmark case, ***Mapp v. Ohio, brought the Supreme Court back to the issue.

Mapp v. Ohio Evidence obtained illegally is inadmissible in state courts.

These were the facts: A Cleveland landlady named Dolree Mapp was arrested, charged, and convicted of possession of obscene materials. On May 23, 1957, police went to Mapp's home, ostensibly looking for a person wanted in connection with a bombing. After first being denied entrance because they had no warrant, police returned three hours later with reinforcements and forcefully entered Mapp's home waving a paper they claimed was a search warrant. Mapp grabbed the paper and stuffed it down her dress; a struggle followed as police retrieved it and then handcuffed Mapp for being belligerent. Mapp's attorney arrived, and police refused to let him into the house or speak with his client. Police searched high and low and eventually discovered "obscene" magazines in a locked suitcase belonging to a boarder.

The U.S. Supreme Court reviewed the case and rendered its decision in 1961. Rather than consider the possibility that Mapp had been wrongfully convicted—the pornographic materials were not hers, nor was there any evidence of criminal intent—the Court focused instead on the procedures followed by the police. In effect, a majority of the justices decided, *when police break the law, the criminal must go free.* The Court held that "all evidence obtained by searches and seizures in violation of the Constitution is, by that same authority, inadmissable in a state court." It had taken nearly 50 years for the exclusionary rule to be applied to state prosecutions.

THE EXCLUSIONARY RULE TODAY

The exclusionary rule has been controversial since its inception. A major objection is that it results in criminals getting off. Even if the police break the law in digging up incriminating evidence, the argument goes, why let the guilty person get away with a crime? Punish the police by all means, but let the conviction stand. The Supreme Court had considered this argument when debating the *Mapp* case, and decided that neither criminal nor civil actions against the police had been used very often or very effectively since *Weeks.* It might mean more to the police if they were deprived of a criminal conviction. Besides, the Court reasoned, it hardly reflects well on the judicial process if courts are allowed to convict people on the basis of evidence tainted by illegal police actions. The courts themselves become tainted.

Once again, let us place things in perspective. The 1960s and early 1970s were a period of great struggles in the United States: over civil rights and individual liberties, over the war in Vietnam, over the proliferation of nuclear weapons and technology. Under Chief Justice Earl Warren, the U.S. Supreme Court threw itself into the fray on the constitutional front, earning the reputation of being "liberal" and staunchly opposed to government intrusions on individual liberties. Under the Warren Court, the Bill of Rights became a very real constraining force in the day-to-day operations of the criminal justice system at all levels. The *Mapp* decision was quickly followed by other important procedural rulings affecting police work, some of which will be discussed in the next section.

Landmark rulings are always controversial, and this virtually guarantees they will continue to be reviewed by the Court, especially as its membership changes through retirements or deaths. From the 1970s onward, under chief justices Warren Burger and William Rehnquist, the Court grew increasingly conservative, and its decisions slowly chipped away at the due process doctrines established by the Warren Court. The exclusionary rule is no exception. Indeed, by the early 1980s some legal scholars were arguing that it was time to abandon the rule altogether (Goodpaster, 1984).

The Good Faith Exception. Such an abandonment has not happened, but there is no question that the exclusionary rule has been weakened by the Supreme Court's adoption of various exceptions to the rule. Three of the most important decisions came in one year. In *United States v. Leon* (1984) the Court established what is called the **good faith exception.** In this case, a confidential police informant had tipped his handler that Leon was trafficking in drugs. Leon was put under surveillance, and police subsequently applied for a search warrant, which was reviewed by government prosecutors and issued by a magistrate in the usual manner. The search turned up drugs and other evidence of trafficking. At a subsequent trial, a federal district judge suppressed the evidence on the grounds that the information supplied by police in support of the original search warrant was insufficient to establish probable cause.

good faith exception Evidence obtained illegally by police who nevertheless believed that a search warrant had been properly issued may be used to convict a defendant.

Government prosecutors appealed the case, arguing that the police believed the warrant was valid; the evidence police collected should not be suppressed simply because a magistrate had erred in issuing a search warrant without probable cause. The Supreme Court agreed, ruling that the evidence obtained by police acting in "objective good faith" that the warrant had been appropriately issued by a detached and neutral magistrate should not be suppressed. A subsequent ruling in *Massachussetts v. Sheppard* (1984) repeated the idea of "good faith." Here, the Court argued that although the police in this case were aware that the details of a search warrant were not completely accurate, evidence they seized was still admissible at trial because a good faith effort had been made to obtain assurance from a judge that the warrant was still valid.

Inevitable Discovery Exception. Another exception to the exclusionary rule was established in *Nix v. Williams* (1984). Although this case revolved around a violation of the *Miranda* ruling, which will be discussed shortly, the Supreme Court's decision further weakened the exclusionary rule by creating the **inevitable discovery exception.** The *Nix* case originated with the 1969 murder conviction of Robert Anthony Williams. While being transported by police during the investigation, Williams had led them to the 10-year-old victim's body apparently because a clever and persistent detective had told Williams that it would be "the Christian thing to do" since Christmas was just around the corner. However, Williams's lawyer had specifically requested the police not to question Williams. Furthermore, the police had not reminded Williams of his right to have a lawyer present during any questioning. In 1975 the U.S. Supreme Court overturned his conviction and sentence of life imprisonment, ruling that the evidence—the body—had been obtained illegally.

inevitable discovery exception Evidence obtained through illegal questioning of a suspect may be admissible if the police were close to finding it even without the suspect's help.

In 1977 Williams was retried for the murder. Although the girl's body was once again part of the evidence used against the defendant, his statements to police were not. He was convicted a second time, and the case was again appealed. In its 1984 *Nix* ruling, the Court declared that the girl's body was admissible as evidence, since police were close to finding it even without Williams's help. It was inevitable, the Court found, that police would have discovered the body in the same condition it was in when Williams led them to it.

Compelling Interest versus the Right to Privacy. In two 1989 rulings, the Court decided that there may be instances when the need to protect public safety overrides any individual right to privacy. Even without reasonable suspicion that crimes have been or are being committed, this **compelling interest** in public safety moved the Court to allow mandatory drug testing of employees

compelling interest Occurs when public safety concerns override an individual's right to privacy.

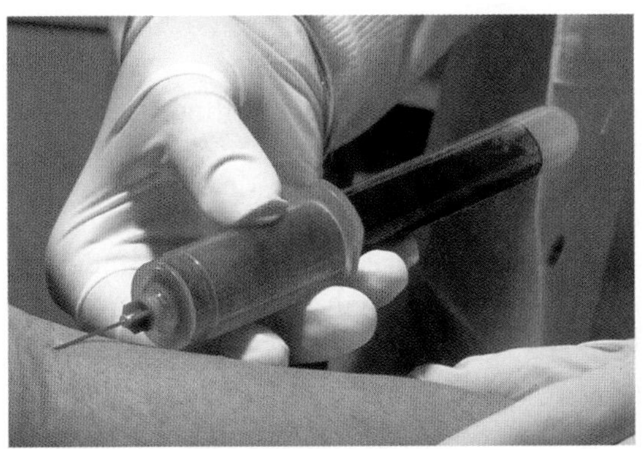

The exclusionary rule, *which says that evidence illegally obtained cannot be used to convict a defendant, has been weakened by Supreme Court decisions in recent years. This trend began in the early 1980s and continued with the 1995 ruling that high school athletes may be given random drug tests. What do you think of this trend?*

PHOTO BY TOM MCCARTHY, COURTESY OF PHOTOEDIT

by law enforcement agencies and by railway companies. In 1995, that ruling was extended to high school athletes, who may be subjected to random, suspicionless drug testing without violating the Fourth Amendment.

THE LAW OF ARREST

In Chapter 7 we discussed the police decision to make an arrest. Here we shall be discussing the legal issues relating to arrests. From a legal standpoint, an arrest occurs when a person is *lawfully detained and not free to leave.* The power of arrest is given to law enforcement personnel who have taken an oath to uphold the laws of the jurisdictions in which they serve. To back up that power, police are provided with handcuffs, a nightstick (or truncheon), and—in many but not all countries—a firearm. Private citizens also have arrest powers, although these are rarely exercised. With the rise of modern policing, the citizen role in law enforcement diminished, and today civilians are discouraged from detaining other citizens. If they do make an arrest, it is generally because the offense was committed against them, or because they witnessed a crime in progress and intervened; in either case, the suspect must be turned over to a law enforcement officer as soon as possible.

PROBABLE CAUSE: THE BASIS FOR AN ARREST

Police may not lawfully arrest someone unless they have probable cause to believe that the arrested person has committed or is committing an offense. An arrest is a seizure, and like other seizures generally requires a warrant. However, in practice the police rarely get warrants before making arrests. Many crimes are witnessed directly, resulting in an arrest on the spot. There is usually no time, nor does the law require that police get a warrant in such situations. Warrantless arrests in situations involving misdemeanors require that the offense occur in the arresting officer's presence; warrantless arrests of felony suspects do not have this requirement, but they must be based on probable cause.

Many felony arrests occur on the street during field interrogations. This can happen when police are called to the scene of a crime and turn up a suspect during questioning, or it may occur during a routine stop. In either case, police must later demonstrate that probable cause existed to make the arrest. In some states police are required to secure an arrest warrant from a judge. The judge reviews the police account and issues an arrest warrant if probable cause existed to make the arrest. It may seem backward, but the idea is to ensure that the coercive decisions of police are reviewed by an impartial court official. In practice, police requests for felony arrest warrants after the fact are rarely denied.

Arrests may seem clear-cut on television, but in real life things are often more complicated. People are sometimes unaware that they are under arrest—or they think they are when in fact they are not. To add to the uncertainty, it is not necessary for the police to actually say "You're under arrest." People who have reason to believe they are being arrested should ask "Am I under arrest?" If the officer answers "Yes," then the suspect has certain legal rights, which we will discuss in a moment. If the officer answers "No," it is generally within a person's rights to leave. As mentioned in earlier chapters, however, police officers are sensitive to how citizens react to their exercise of authority; belligerent challenges to police rarely succeed, and attempts to flee or prevent someone else's arrest could bring charges of obstruction of justice. It should not be forgotten that the fundamental rule police are taught over and over is that they must maintain control of a situation, if not for their own safety then for the safety of others.

Once a person is arrested, further police actions are governed by provisions of the Fourth, Fifth, Sixth, and Fourteenth Amendments. We have already seen that a limited search is permissible, primarily to protect the police and any bystanders from danger and to prevent the destruction of evidence. If the arrested suspect is driving a car or other vehicle, the police may impound the vehicle, which may subsequently be seized under the asset forfeiture laws mentioned in Chapter 8. When a vehicle is impounded, many police departments will make a routine warrantless search of it for inventory purposes—ostensibly to protect the owner—but any incriminating evidence found during such a search may subsequently be admitted into evidence against the defendant.

Confessions and Police Interrogations

The Fifth Amendment provides that "no person" shall be "compelled in any criminal case to be a witness against himself, nor be deprived of life, liberty, or property without due process of law." The Sixth Amendment provides that "in all criminal prosecutions" the accused shall "have the Assistance of Counsel for his defence." In effect, the Fourteenth Amendment applies these provisions to state proceedings, as discussed earlier in the chapter.

These provisions have clear implications for how the police deal with suspects once they have been arrested. Confessions usually make a police officer's job much easier—as long as the person confessing actually committed the crime, of course. Prosecutors also like confessions, because a confession usually means a guilty plea. Even if a defendant subsequently denies the confession, the prosecution can usually introduce it into evidence at a trial, and confessions carry considerable weight with judges and juries.

Confessions Must Be Voluntary. All this places pressure on police to get suspects to confess. Many suspects seem eager to confess the minute they are arrested, and this does not mean that their crimes are minor. Many murderers confess, especially if they have killed a friend or relative, and some even call police themselves. Yet police cannot assume a suspect will confess, and whenever they confront a suspect or execute an arrest warrant, they will be thinking about ways to get the suspect to talk about the crime. Getting a suspect to talk is thus a key element in solving crimes, and all sorts of frightening and painful methods could be used—as indeed they were during the colonial period. For example, heavy weights were pressed on a suspect's chest so as to make every breath excruciatingly painful. This so-called *peine forte et dure* (strong and hard pain) was usually used against people who refused to speak at their trial. At least one American colonist is known to have died under the presses during the Salem witch hunt (Erikson, 1966:149). Any confession obtained this way was obviously not voluntary, to say nothing of whether it was true. The Fifth Amendment was written to ensure that people were not forced into making confessions that could later be used to convict them.

The Right to Counsel and the Miranda Warnings. It was not until the Warren Court made its landmark rulings in *Escobedo v. Illinois* (1964) and *Miranda v. Arizona* (1966) that the full implications of the Fifth and Sixth Amendments for police interrogations were spelled out for state courts. The *Escobedo* case involved a claim that the defendant, Danny Escobedo, had been forced to make incriminating statements during interrogation. These statements led to his conviction on charges of murdering his brother-in-law. The Supreme Court noted that despite repeated requests to see his lawyer, Escobedo did not have an attorney present during questioning, and therefore his confession was made without the advice of counsel, in violation of the Sixth Amendment. The Court ruled that suspects have the right to the advice of counsel during police questioning to ensure that any confession they make is voluntary.

The Court went further in the *Miranda* case. This 1966 case was decided along with three others, all of which dealt with the admissibility of statements obtained from suspects during police interrogations after they had been arrested. Ernesto Miranda's name happened to be at the top of the list, and he became famous because of it.

In deciding *Miranda* and the other cases, the Court ruled not only that arrested suspects have the right to counsel, but also that the police must clearly inform them of that right before any questioning begins. Ernesto Miranda had been convicted of rape and kidnapping largely on the basis of a confession he made following nearly two hours of intense police interrogation. The Court took into account the ability of experienced police interrogators to induce confessions from intimidated suspects; with his attorney present, Miranda might not have succumbed to the menacing interrogation. The right to have counsel present during questioning undergirds the Fifth Amendment right against self-incrimination.

In its decision, the Court ruled that police must inform arrested suspects of certain rights *before* any interrogation begins. The **Miranda warnings** resulted. Television and films have made them famous around the world; many children can probably recite them from memory:

Miranda warnings Before questioning begins, police inform arrested suspects of their rights and the implications of waiving them.

1. You have the right to remain silent.
2. Anything you say can and will be used against you in a court of law.
3. You have the right to talk to a lawyer and to have a lawyer present while you are being questioned.
4. If you cannot afford a lawyer and wish to have one present during questioning, one will be appointed to represent you at no cost.
5. You may stop answering questions at any time.

The suspect is then asked three questions:

6. Do you understand each of these rights I have explained to you?
7. Keeping them in mind, do you wish to answer questions at this time?
8. Do you wish to answer questions without a lawyer present?

If suspects answer "Yes" to *all three* of these questions, they are considered to have waived their Miranda rights. In many jurisdictions, juveniles are also asked if they wish to answer questions without their parents or guardians present.

The Importance of *Miranda*. The *Miranda* decision is probably the single most significant statement of suspect rights in the entire field of policing. It tells the police that even though they have probable cause to arrest someone, they cannot begin any interrogation until they have assured the suspect that he or she doesn't have to say anything. In the absence of compelling evidence or witnesses, a suspect's decision not to talk may mean the end of an effective police investigation. At the least, it means much more effort, much more legwork, much more time and expense—and the longer it all takes, the greater the likelihood the suspect will get off.

The fear that *Miranda* would undermine the law enforcement–crime prevention role of the police led to immediate criticism of the Supreme Court's ruling. Efforts were soon launched in Congress to get the ruling changed, but to no avail. Studies of police use of *Miranda* found that many police officers were not following the rule properly, if at all (see Box 9.2).

Miranda in the 1990s. As the years passed, the reading of *Miranda* rights became an accepted police practice—and most suspects probably anticipate it. But there still remain uncertainties about what the police can and cannot do when questioning suspects. Periodic appeals based on *Miranda* provide continuing review and reconsideration of the constitutional limits to police interrogation. For example, in *New York v. Quarles* (1984), the Court ruled that police may question an arrested suspect in a limited way without giving the *Miranda* warnings in order to protect public safety. In this case, the police had chased an armed rape suspect into a store, and before reading the Miranda rights they asked him where the gun was. The suspect pointed to a shelf where he had hidden the gun. In another case, the Court allowed questioning of a suspect by an

Box 9.2

JUSTICE IN HISTORY

HOW SOME POLICE GOT AROUND MIRANDA

The initial reaction among many police officers to the 1966 *Miranda* decision was not positive. Some soon figured out how to get around it. One investigation of how cops subverted the constitutional protections against self-incrimination built into the Miranda warning described one popular method used by officers in a large metropolitan police department (Lewis and Allen, 1977). The procedure was known as "Participating Miranda" and it operated in the following manner:

> Suppose the police, with probable cause, arrest a suspect ("Sam") at his house or on the street for murder. Sam is transported in a patrol car to the police station. The ride to the police station is made in silence; Sam has not been given any Miranda warnings and he has not been questioned. The *Miranda* rules have apparently not been violated—there has been no custodial interrogation. As soon as the booking process is completed, the suspect is taken into a room and a "friendly" officer begins to give the *Miranda* warnings: "Sam, you have a right to remain silent and anything you say can be used against you." The officer then says calmly and casually (almost as if talking out loud to himself) that often the police arrest the wrong person; that it is understandable why a person might carry a gun for self-protection (suggesting a legal justification for the suspect's actions); that the victim was probably responsible for his own demise, etc. At this point as much as fifteen to thirty minutes may have passed since the first warnings were given. At no time has the suspect been directly questioned or asked to confess.

undercover police officer posing as a cellmate in jail. This ruling came in *Illinois v. Perkins* (1990); the Court decided that Perkins chose to talk freely with someone he thought was a fellow inmate, and given that he was not compelled or coerced into talking, his statements were admissible in court.

At the time of its *Miranda* ruling, the Supreme Court realized the importance of routine questioning of citizens as the police carry out their duties. The decision was never intended to bar all questioning, and it even allows for some kinds of questioning when citizens feel they are not free to leave. One common situation in which police question people is during traffic stops. Police are not required to warn motorists of their rights during routine questioning pertaining to the traffic stop. Even when a person is arrested, it is not required that the police give the Miranda warnings right away. The general interpretation is that citizens must be notified of their rights whenever they are confined in a potentially coercive police environment—for example, at the police station or in a squad car—or whenever the questioning takes on the tone of an interrogation, which means the questioning is designed to elicit an incriminating response. These guidelines leave room for varied interpretations in their application, and for that reason appeals will continue to come before the Supreme Court for clarification of the constitutional limits to this aspect of policing. However, the core issue that is unlikely to change is the requirement that a confession be voluntary. The Supreme Court has reaffirmed that *Miranda* "safeguards a fundamental right by protecting a defendant's Fifth Amendment privilege against self-incrimination."

Box 9.2 (continued)

> Next, Officer Friendly informs the suspect that he has a right to the presence of an attorney during any custodial interrogation. Officer Friendly continues his narration by indicating that retained counsel is often a needless expense and that a suspect with nothing to hide does not need professional service. The narration continues a few more minutes and finally the suspect is informed that counsel will be appointed for him at the state's expense if he cannot afford one. The soliloquy may continue several more minutes. "Participating Miranda" may take from thirty minutes to a full hour. (Lewis and Allen, 1977:67–68).

The authors learned that most suspects would make statements implicating or clearing themselves before the final *Miranda* warnings were given. "As soon as the officer is certain that the suspect is willing to discuss the events leading up to his arrest, the officer will remind the suspect that he has been given his full constitutional rights (sometimes they are given in rapid succession when it is clear that the suspect will talk)." Then the suspect is asked whether he understands his rights—most say they do—and is willing to sign the waiver—which most do. Once the waiver is signed, the real interrogation begins, with officers looking for any discrepancies in the suspect's story. These are explored with the suspect in order to obtain a full confession.

Through this clever process, suspects end up convinced that they were given their constitutional rights and that they voluntarily waived them—which the signed waiver confirms. When later questioned by their own attorneys, suspects reassert the voluntariness of their confession. The police have successfully subverted the *Miranda* rules.

Source: Peter W. Lewis and Harry E. Allen (1977). "Participating Miranda": An Attempt to Subvert Certain Constitutional Safeguards." *Crime and Delinquency* 75: 61–73. Copyright © by Sage Publications. Reprinted by permission.

THE DARK SIDE OF POLICING: CORRUPTION AND BRUTALITY

Constitutional law attempts to constrain police in the exercise of their duties so that the rights of citizens are protected. However, there are other ways in which police may overstep the boundaries of lawful conduct in carrying out their work. Corruption and brutality are part of the "dark side" of policing (Kappeler, Sluder, and Alpert, 1994), and no account of policing in America would be complete without a discussion of them.

The problem of police corruption has followed the police from their earliest origins. An 1816 report to England's House of Commons described corruption among constables and sheriffs' deputies:

> [The] deputies in many instances are characters of the worst and lowest descriptions; the fine they receive from the person who appoints them varies from ten shillings to five pounds; having some expense and no salary they live by extortion, by countenancing all species of vice, by an understanding with the keepers of brothels and disorderly alehouses, by attending courts of justice, and giving there false evidence to ensure conviction when their expenses are paid, and by all the various means by which artful and designing men can entrap the weak and prey upon the unwary. (Pike, 1968:464)

The practices referred to in this report, including extortion and perjury, are merely a few of the activities included under the rubric of police corruption. The term also covers brutality, neglect of duty, sexual harassment, racism, and bribery.

Historically, concern about corruption has been focused on blatant abuses of police authority such as forcing suspects to confess, extorting money through threats, taking bribes, and lying while under oath, although many less serious police practices could be added to the list of corrupt practices. Examples are "police perks" such as free meals and discounts at certain restaurants or stores, the use of abusive or profane language, and paying for favors granted by other police employees. In 1972, the Knapp Commission report to the mayor of New York added another dimension of corruption in arguing that "even those who themselves engage in no corrupt activities are involved in corruption in the sense that they take no steps to prevent what they know or suspect is going on about them" (Knapp Commission, 1972:3).

No one expects the police to be saints or believes that they will never make mistakes. However, most feel they should be called to account for their actions. Unfortunately, many police actions occur "out of sight"; routinely monitoring the police for improper actions, mistakes, or errors of judgment is nearly impossible, nor is it easy to reconstruct such actions after the fact. Ultimately, the cooperation of the police themselves is needed to uncover the dark side of policing. Unfortunately, cooperation is likely to be reluctant since evidence of corruption tarnishes the badges of all police officers, not just those directly involved.

It is sometimes difficult to separate corrupt practices from "mere" mistakes or errors of judgment. Consider police interrogations. A study in Great Britain found, for example, that the practice of allowing a defense attorney present during questioning suspects varied widely from city to city (Brown, Ellis, and Larcombe, 1992). Not only were suspects not treated equally with respect to this legal right, but among those who did have an opportunity to get legal advice, many were not told that their legal consultation could be in private, and 25 percent were not told that the legal consultation was free. Do you think that frequent neglect or omission such as this should be considered a corrupt practice? Some would say it is little more than laziness, but others have questioned the underlying motives of the neglectful officers and whether something more ominous might be involved.

TYPES OF POLICE CORRUPTION

One of the few systematic studies of police corruption identifies eight types of police corruption (Roebuck and Barker, 1974):

1. *Corruption of authority* means receiving unauthorized, unearned material gains by virtue of police officer status. This includes free liquor and meals, discounts, and payments by merchants for more police protection. The corrupters are respectable citizens, there is considerable peer group support, there is little adverse departmental reaction, little organization is required, and the violation involved is primarily that of departmental regulations. If confronted about the practice, businesses and police simply write it off as "just being friendly." This form of corruption is widespread, and most police officers will have encountered it—if they have not actually participated themselves. Inasmuch as the practice results in officers giving more police service to businesses that provide perks—surely an expectation if not an explicit understanding—it undermines the obligation police have to serve all members of the community equally.
2. *Kickbacks* involve receipt of goods and services in return for referring business to a variety of patrons—doctors, lawyers, bondsmen, garages, taxicab companies, service stations, and so on. Corrupters are usually respectable persons who stand to gain from the scheme. Departments tend to ignore it, or actually condone it, depending on the respectability of the corrupter; however, this practice also usually violates formal departmental rules. Peer group support is often substantial, though its degree may depend on the reputation and trustworthiness of the patron. If it is known that the person kicking back to police is involved in criminal activities, an officer's peers may take a more serious view of it. The organization involved is relatively simple, consisting basically of the ongoing relationship between the business and the police officer.
3. *Opportunist theft* consists of stealing goods or money from arrestees, victims, crime scenes, or unprotected property. It involves no corrupter and is clearly in violation of criminal laws as well as departmental rules. Reaction from departments is usually negative, and the reaction is likely to be more severe if the value of goods or cash taken is high, if the public knows about the theft, and if the victim is willing to prosecute. Peer group support depends on informal norms governing distinctions between "clean" and "dirty" money. Dirty money is money that comes from crime, especially drug trafficking; some police officers treat this as fair game. Little organization is involved in opportunistic theft; as the term implies, it is a spontaneous act that occurs when an appropriate situation arises.
4. *Shakedowns* are also opportunistic behaviors. They occur when the police know about a crime but accept money or services from suspects in exchange for doing nothing. The corrupter may be either respectable or habitually involved in criminal activities. Shakedowns violate legal and departmental norms, and though peer group support is necessary for shakedowns to become a routine part of police activities—which happens from time to time—that support is often contingent on the suspect's criminal activity; bribes from drug dealers and armed robbers are frowned upon. Secrecy in peer group relations is a prime element of shakedowns.

5. *Protection of illegal activities* arises when corrupters want to continue illegal activities without risk of being arrested. Since they are doing something illegal, they purchase "protection" from police officers willing to be corrupted. Protection violates criminal and departmental rules and involves considerable collusion, peer group support, and organization. Participating officers have to know which businesses are protected, which employees and which police know about the scheme, and how often, where, and what payoffs are to be made. Though departmental reaction usually results in suspension, dismissal, or criminal charges, the severity and consistency of negative reactions may depend on the degree of community support of the illegal activities being protected. If there is community pressure for strong enforcement activity against a certain crime, the police chief would find it politically risky to ignore or play down any protection scheme that came to light.
6. *"The fix"* refers to either quashing legal proceedings or "taking up" traffic tickets. Corrupters are suspects attempting to avoid arrest. Of course, the fix can occur anywhere in the criminal justice system—even in prison, where guards are paid not to "write up" an incident that could result in an inmate losing credit toward time served. Within policing, patrol officers, detectives, and even dispatchers may accept bribes to look the other way. The fix violates legal and departmental rules, and reaction is usually severe when cases are brought to light. In departments where the fix occurs frequently and with considerable regularity it is a highly organized activity.
7. *Direct criminal activities* involve no corrupter, as the police alone are involved in the activity. Direct criminal activities include crimes of robbery, extortion, and other violence by police officers against suspects, victims, and citizens generally. Lack of peer group support and severe departmental reactions generally underscore the blatant criminal character of these practices.

   Drug enforcement provides a major opportunity and strong incentives for police crime (Pogrebin and Poole, 1993:388; Luttwak, 1995). Pocketing drugs seized from suspects on the street or from smugglers is reputedly a routine occurrence (Abadinsky, 1990:401–402), but these incidents rarely come to the attention of police officials, criminologists, or the public. Not so with some other drug-related crimes: For example, the theft of 57 pounds of heroin from the property office of the New York City police department made headlines around the country. The stolen heroin was among that confiscated during the famous "French Connection" case. More recently, 38 officers of the same city's 77th Precinct—known as the "Buddy Boys"—were implicated in extensive criminal activity, including trafficking and use of drugs (Kappeler, Sluder, and Alpert, 1994:188–212).
8. *Internal payoffs* involve bribes within the police department for such things as assignments, hours, promotions, control of evidence, and credit for arrests. By virtue of their job assignments, some officers are in a particularly good position to take payoffs, as this comment on the police dispatcher shows:

   > He has numerous little favors he can grant a man that will ease the burdens of the tour. For instance, the patrolman can go to "lunch" (policemen [in Philadelphia, at least] refer to all their meal breaks as lunch, regardless of the hour) only with the dispatcher's permission. If the dispatcher wants a man to remain in service, he simply tells him that he cannot go. The men are not supposed to eat to-

> gether and the dispatcher is responsible for seeing that they do not gather. A sympathetic dispatcher will allow several men to share their lunchtime by permitting one man to give a location where the dispatcher knows the police do not eat. (Rubinstein, 1973:85)

The internal payoff system is usually highly organized, particularly in departments under pressure to produce and in those where shakedowns and protection are regular aspects of police work. For the payoff system to work smoothly, extensive peer group support is necessary. Departments where other group-centered corrupt practices thrive have an established informal network of collusion, and those involved in the buddy system would hardly object to this far more benign form of corruption. Departmental reaction to payoffs is tolerant if it means a more satisfied workforce. If officers involved in the payoff system are also in violation of high-priority regulations or the criminal law, the department's reaction is likely to be less tolerant.

Needless to say, these categories are not mutually exclusive in the life of any given police officer: He or she could be found engaging in more than one type at the same time. Furthermore, it is not uncommon to find progression from corruption of authority to more serious violations. This is why some police departments have outlawed perks and have made it a suspendable offense—what begins as "just being friendly" may end up as bribery, kickbacks, payoffs, and direct criminal activities. Such was the case with ex–New York City police officer Michael Dowd. On July 12, 1994, Dowd was sentenced to fourteen years in prison on racketeering and drug charges. According to his own testimony, what began as petty perks taken on the job ended in ongoing criminal activities, shakedowns, and regular use of the fix.

A Second Model of Police Corruption

Recognizing that improper police actions include various dysfunctional behaviors not clearly encompassed by the preceding typology—for example, sexual harassment, discrimination, violation of civil rights, and verbal mistreatment—there is an alternative way of looking at police deviance (Barker and Carter, 1994:3–11). It rests on the distinction between two types of police conduct: occupational deviance and abuse of authority. **Occupational deviance** concerns activities made possible by the nature and organization of normal work activity. Some are occupation specific:

occupational deviance Forms of deviance that are made possible by the nature and organization of work.

> [M]any forms of deviance may be committed only by those who are in a given occupation. For example, only physicians can write fraudulent drug prescriptions and college professors may publish "research results" from false data in order to gain promotion, merit, and tenure. Similarly, only police officers can threaten to arrest in exchange for sexual favors or accept money in lieu of issuing a traffic ticket. The common elements in all of these acts is that they are committed by "normal" persons during the course of their occupational activity and the behavior is a product of the "powers" inherent in their occupation. (Barker and Carter, 1994:7)

Occupational deviance thus includes many corrupt practices as well as misconduct such as sleeping on the job. The key element is that occupational deviance has an internal locus: "It is concerned with how an officer performs as an organizational member, rather than the method by which the officer discharges his/her police duties" (Barker and Carter, 1994:9).

abuse of authority Forms of deviance that relate to how the police exercise their authority in dealings with the public.

The second element in this model, **abuse of authority,** encompasses physical abuse such as brutality and misuse of force, psychological abuse, and legal abuse such as the violation of a person's constitutional rights. Unlike occupational deviance, abuse of authority has an external locus because it addresses the authority relation linking the police to the public—who make up the police "clientele"—and concerns the manner in which the police carry out their lawful function.

In addition to the distinction of locus, three other distinctions are noted by the authors. One concerns motivation, a second concerns police department liability, and the third involves peer tolerance. Abuse of authority is less likely to be motivated by personal gain or gratification, and, largely because of this, is more likely to be tolerated by police peers. But it is also more likely to result in lawsuits claiming civil rights violations. This occurs because the police have exceeded their lawful exercise of authority and may have violated constitutional protections.

We can see that corruption of authority, kickbacks, shakedowns, and the fix are examples of the occupational deviance made possible by the nature of police work; on the other hand, illegal searches and seizures and misuse of force (described in the next section) are abuses of police authority.

Brutality and Misuse of Force

Two aspects of police behavior that continually appear in public discussions of policing are brutality and misuse of force. The notorious beating of Rodney King by members of the Los Angeles Police Department certainly comes to mind here, but other examples could be cited and many more will remain hidden from public scrutiny.

What are meant by brutality and misuse of force? As one might guess, there is hardly consensus on their meaning. It has been suggested by one well-known authority on policing that almost any routine police action could be interpreted by *someone* as an instance of police brutality (Reiss, 1970). Even the police themselves have no clearcut guidelines on the issue. Police training films deal with when and how to use deadly force, but most officers will never be in situations where deadly force is authorized or used.

reasonable force Force necessary to achieve a legal goal without endangering innocent citizens.

At lesser levels of violence, police rely on the notion of **reasonable force.** But what does that mean? A rule of thumb adopted by most police agencies, and supported by the courts, is that reasonable force is *force necessary to achieve a legal goal without endangering innocent citizens.* Any unnecessary force is therefore unreasonable and may be illegal. But these are difficult distinctions to apply in practice, particularly when an officer is under pressure.

Although some experts apply the term *brutality* only to those situations involving force, others include situations of psychological violence, resulting in loss of self-respect and other emotional pain. Although "third degree" techniques are no longer condoned, the questioning of suspects may seem unnecessarily brutal, as we saw earlier in Chapter 7. Some criminal justice observers condemn the use of psychological tricks by police interrogators. They think such tactics can produce intense disorientation and even fear in suspects, in effect making any self-incriminating information or confession coerced and therefore involuntary. Such tactics may also encourage suspects to tell interrogators what they think the police want to hear, even if the information is untrue. Other observers, however, believe that effective police interrogation depends upon giving interrogators latitude in questioning techniques so long as they do not involve use or threats of physical violence. Besides, many streetwise suspects expect police interrogators to "mess with their heads" during questioning, and the interrogation process turns into a test of will and skill on both sides.

Although police brutality is an episodic and unpredictable occurrence, its victims tend to come from marginal groups in society. The Rodney King beating is the most famous recent example of a complex problem that refuses to go away despite widespread negative publicity.

PHOTO BY ROB CRANDALL (COPIED CNN 3/91), COURTESY OF STOCK BOSTON

Distinguishing Brutality from Misuse of Force. The line between brutality and misuse of force is hazy. Though all brutality may well be a misuse of authorized force, not all misuse of force is brutality. An officer who fires at a fleeing robber and hits instead an innocent bystander would probably be considered to have used deadly force inappropriately, but is this police brutality? The term *brutality* is best used in reference to situations in which police knowingly and intentionally use force to satisfy whims, prejudices, and personal goals. *Misuse of force,* then, can be applied to situations in which police use force that exceeds the law or department policy, although the intent is to satisfy those rules and obligations.

THE UGLY FACE OF POLICE BRUTALITY

Brutality occurs when the police physically assault citizens who offer no resistance or who cannot resist—for example, they are handcuffed—or when a number of officers join in the assault of a lone citizen who clearly could be subdued with less forceful means. The Rodney King incident is a well-known example. Similar examples can be found in the history of almost any big-city police department, as in this account from Philadelphia nearly 30 years ago. A man suspected of sexually molesting a child was severely beaten by police captors:

> Any squad member who wished was allowed to beat the suspect from the ankles to the armpits with his stick. Men came in off the street to participate in the beating and then returned to patrol. Before he was taken downtown, the suspect had been severely battered, although he had no broken bones. At no time did he utter a complaint, ask for mercy, or curse the police. Without a murmur he absorbed a brutal

> beating, which caused him to foul himself and drew the admiring comments of several men who admitted he could "really take it." (Rubinstein, 1973:183)

Police brutality is most likely to be an episodic and unpredictable problem. If it occurs persistently word soon gets around, and offending officers and their superiors risk public censure, dismissal, and criminal charges. In larger departments, Internal Affairs units quickly investigate complaints and keep tabs on officers suspected of such behavior. "Bad apples" are weeded out, and in this way the department as a whole avoids being tarnished. Sometimes it works, though in other cases, including the Rodney King incident, the rot extends far up the apple tree. This situation cannot be explained by the bad apply theory, and therefore cannot be as easily remedied, as we shall see in a moment.

MISUSE OF FORCE: AN OCCUPATIONAL HAZARD?

Police misuse of force, although less outrageous, may actually be more detrimental to effective policing because it arises from within the organization and performance of routine policing. Misuse of force is more likely to surface when police are under pressure, when they are acting overzealously, or when they have misinterpreted actions they have witnessed. In addition, excessive force is more likely to be used by poorly trained and inexperienced police officers. Firing warning shots in the air or shooting at fleeing suspects, practices not officially condoned by most police agencies, may be triggered by these factors.

The Need to Gain Control. Misuse of force and, on occasion, police brutality can be linked to a police officer's need to gain control in encounters with citizens. If that control is resisted it will be perceived by officers as a challenge to their authority—and a threat to their safety. It comes as no surprise, then, that excessive use of force is more likely to surface when police believe their control of a situation is threatened. However, these situations are relatively infrequent if one considers the huge number of encounters police have with the citizenry. An estimated 45 million Americans had face-to-face contact with police during 1996 (Bureau of Justice Statistics, 1998b:20). In one percent of these contacts, the police were alleged to have used or threatened force. Even in encounters regarded as potentially violent—for example, dealing with drunks, traffic stops, intervening in fights—mere arrival of the police usually brings a situation under control (Bayley, 1988b).

Police authority to use force is most often invoked when an arrest is taking place. In addition to actual arrests, however, police also exercise this authority whenever they stop a citizen for questioning. Stops and field interrogations are routine events in high-crime areas. They also occur frequently in well-to-do neighborhoods as a method by which police can keep tabs on strangers and people who look different from the typical resident. The general public may not realize that failure to heed an officer's command to stop makes them liable for arrest on charges of refusing to obey the lawful command of a police officer. (They also may not know that once stopped, refusing to answer questions is not an offense). Behind the officer's authority to make the stop lies the authority to use force if needed.

As noted in Chapter 7, boredom is a large factor in routine police work, and field interrogations are sometimes contrived events (Brown, 1988:143). Police actively look for "deviants" on their beat to break the monotony of a quiet evening. During field interrogations an encounter may turn unpleasant as resentful citizens complain about being picked on or harassed by police. As the officer feels control slipping away, an overreaction may result in excessive use of force.

CONTROLLING CORRUPTION AND ABUSE OF FORCE

The extent of corruption, police brutality, and misuse of force is unknown and unknowable. To remove the "blue curtain of secrecy" (Crank, 1998:56), also known as the **blue code** (or "wall") **of silence**, that surrounds police operations, particularly the unlawful ones, requires powers beyond the control of police chiefs, police commissions, and even committees of the U.S. Congress. Serious investigations are also hampered because the time and money required for indepth research are beyond the grasp of most criminologists, assuming they could penetrate the veil of secrecy. Even police officers themselves find it difficult, if not dangerous, to bring corrupt practices to light.

blue code of silence Police officers do not snitch on each other or volunteer potentially damaging information to higher-ups.

The Blue Code of Silence in New York City. New York City has been the site of two extensive investigations into allegations of corruption among police officers. First, the 1972 Knapp Commission found a widespread and "strikingly standardized" pattern of corruption involving police officers who patrolled areas of the city frequented by gamblers, pimps, and drug dealers. Regular monthly payments were made to officers, with supervisors getting somewhat more of the "pad" than lower-ranking patrolmen. Some officers—called "meat-eaters"—actively looked for opportunities to shake down criminals, while others—called "grass-eaters"—did not search out payoffs but took advantage of them if the opportunity arose. Then, in 1994, the Mollen Report detailed an extensive system of shakedowns and direct criminal activities by police, that bore "an uncanny resemblance" (Doerner, 1998:30) to the earlier situation. In the later scheme, officers not only engaged in shakedowns of drug dealers, but also stole contraband and resold it to other dealers.

Both commissions reported on the code of silence and the protection it gave the corrupt officers. "Otherwise honest and law-abiding officers tolerated unscrupulous coworkers and tacitly endorsed their misdeeds by adhering to 'the unwritten rule that an officer never incriminates a fellow officer'" (Dorner, 1998:31, citing the Mollen Report, p. 51). If an officer thought of "ratting" on another officer, he or she faced ostracism from the group, which could be almost a death sentence when officers are called upon to back each other up in life-threatening situations on the street. Indeed, back in 1970, officer Frank Serpico was nearly killed when fellow New York City officers found out that he had "ratted" them out.

Hear no evil, see no evil . . . The Blue Code of Silence.
ILLUSTRATION BY BARRIE MAGUIRE, COURTESY OF THE CREATIVE WORKSHOP

Just as rank-and-file officers protected themselves through the blue code of silence, upper-level police managers enjoyed the protections of the code as well. "The brass were reluctant to uncover corruption because they wished to avoid any embarrassment whatsoever to the department. Their goal was to avoid all negative publicity at any cost" (Doerner, 1998:31). As an extreme example, the Mollen Report noted the case of one officer who had been using drugs and alcohol on the job daily, driving a red Corvette, and otherwise living an openly lavish lifestyle, and who had not made a single arrest although he was assigned to one of the most crime-ridden precincts. His supervisors gave him a "meets standards" evaluation.

Combating Misuse of Force: The Use of Profiles. Police departments around the country are now recognizing that misuse of force among patrol officers is a serious problem that needs more attention than it has received in the past. Police psychologists are being pressed into service to identify possible profiles of officers who are prone to violence, and it is hoped that prevention strategies may be developed from these profiles. A survey of police psychologists helped one researcher create a number of different profiles, discounting the stereotype that claims a few "bad apples" are responsible for most incidents where excessive force is used. Rather, there are several types of bad apples, and any combination can turn up in a police department. The profiles were as follows (Scrivner, 1994):

- *Officers with personality disorders.* Considered a small but high-risk group, these officers display antisocial, paranoid, or abusive tendencies that are enduring personality traits not acquired on the job.
- *Officers whose previous job-related experiences place them at risk.* Traumatic experiences such as shootouts or being wounded in the line of duty become part of the "baggage" that an officer carries around. These experiences may contribute to "burnout" or an officer's feelings of isolation from his or her peers. Such officers often come to light when they lose control in a situation and resort to excessive force.
- *Officers who have problems at early stages in their careers.* Some young and inexperienced officers are seen as "hot dogs," "badge happy," or "macho"; they are highly impressionable and impulsive, and they are strongly influenced by police culture. Their low tolerance of frustration makes them susceptible to edginess and anger in dealings with citizens.
- *Officers who develop inappropriate patrol styles.* A heavy-handed policing style is used to show who is in charge; they are sensitive to challenge and provocation, and their "command and control" style tends to become more and more rigid as they progress through their police career.
- *Officers with personal problems.* Although most officers with personal problems such as divorce, separation, or recurring money difficulties do not use excessive force, these problems seem to be the last straw with some officers, undermining their confidence and making it "more difficult for them to deal with fear, animosity, and emotionally charged patrol situations" (Scrivner, 1994:3). The most common group, according to the psychologists surveyed, these officers exhibit erratic patrol behavior that signals the possibility that they will lose control in a confrontation.

Although they have yet to be applied and evaluated systematically, these profiles may be helpful in directing attention to individual officers who may be susceptible to misuse of force. On the other hand, it is difficult to see how their use will help in addressing the influence of organizational aspects of police work itself, of the cop culture, or of the larger social and cultural environment within which police operate. In the last analysis, abuse of force by police is a social problem rather than an individual one, and its solution requires identification of the social conditions and rewards that encourage it.

The Internal Affairs Unit. Most large police departments, and some much smaller ones, assign sworn personnel to an **Internal Affairs unit,** whose mission is to respond to allegations of corruption and police misconduct and to investigate the circumstances surrounding use of force involving death or serious injury or when suspects are in custody. It is through Internal Affairs that the police police themselves. In response to arguments that the police should not be policing themselves, departments are quick to point out that only the most trustworthy and competent officers are assigned to Internal Affairs. Visit the Web sites of police departments and you will see the public relations effort made on behalf of Internal Affairs.

Internal Affairs unit A squad of experienced police officers who investigate allegations of corruption and misconduct, and the circumstances surrounding use of deadly force.

Many citizens are understandably reluctant to complain *to* the police *about* the police. In addition, making a complaint often entails a great deal of effort (Wagner and Decker, 1989:279). Some departments have taken steps to make the complaint process less intimidating. For example, the Reno, Nevada, police department has placed Internal Affairs in a building separate from the police department, with nonuniformed staff. The department also provides a citizen suggestion phone line so that informal complaints—or praise—can be made anonymously. However, whether formal or informal, every complaint is reviewed by the chief of police and the command staff before Internal Affairs is assigned to investigate. Complainants who request it receive a letter advising them of the outcome of the investigation and the action taken.

There is wide agreement among police experts that the manner in which top police administrators support and respond to the work of Internal Affairs is crucial to the unit's effectiveness in dealing with police corruption and citizen complaints (Alpert and Dunham, 1988:104–105). If Internal Affairs is perceived to be a mechanism by which department brass can validate whatever their officers do, then rank-and-file officers will have no respect for its work or decisions. Nor can there be questions about the integrity of officers assigned to Internal Affairs. A New York City undercover narcotics officer testified in Bronx Superior Court in 1997 that an Internal Affairs inspector had thwarted an investigation because his own son was among the officers accused of leaking confidential information to drug suspects (*New York Times,* April 8, 1997, p. A20). Pending the outcome of a federal grand jury hearing, both father and son remain in their jobs, but the episode has damaged the faith of both public and police in the NYPD's Internal Affairs Bureau.

Some arguments favor a police-only review process (Wagner and Decker, 1989:282). These include the special expertise in law and procedure that experienced officers bring to an investigation; the idea that the process would lack credibility among officers and its outcomes would carry less weight if it included civilians; and the argument that citizen involvement is proof that the organization cannot solve its own problems—and therefore cannot do the job the public expects of it. However, many cities have not been swayed by these arguments, choosing instead to include some sort of civilian review of complaints about police corruption and misconduct.

An example is Santa Cruz, California. In 1994 this city established a Citizens' Police Review Board that reviews investigations by the department's Internal Affairs unit of complaints regarding Santa Cruz police officers. According to the board's Web site (*http://www.ci.santa-cruz.ca.us/cm/cprb/cprb.html*), the review board has jurisdiction over "any allegations of police misconduct, including excessive use of force, discrimination, sexual harassment, improper discharge of firearms, illegal search or seizure, false arrest, false reporting, rude behavior, criminal conduct or misconduct." The review board evaluates reports made by Internal Affairs and can ask for further information, call for an independent investigation, hold hearings, subpoena witnesses, or make a ruling on the case. Its report and recommendations are sent to the complainant and to the chief of police, who determines the final outcome of the case. The review board may also make recommendations to the city council and city manager regarding police policies. This innovative review process provides oversight while protecting the command authority of the police chief.

The Recommendations of the Commission on Police Integrity. In 1960, following a series of corruption investigations, Chicago mayor Richard J. Daley established a five-person Civilian Police Board to oversee the Chicago police department. He also appointed Orlando Wilson, whose story opened Chapter 5, as superintendent of police. Wilson issued General Order 16, which created formal procedures for handling complaints against the police and to control corruption. However, corruption and other police misconduct continued to surface, much of it connected to drug trafficking. In 1997, Daley's son, Mayor Richard M. Daley, appointed a Commission on Police Integrity in response to the indictment of seven police officers from the city's west side on charges of racketeering, conspiracy, and extortion. After meeting with dozens of police officials, visiting ten U.S. cities to learn of their anti-corruption efforts, conducting hundreds of confidential interviews with Chicago police officers, and reviewing the scholarly literature on police misconduct, the Commission made the following recommendations to deal with police corruption:

- Improve hiring standards by increasing minimum requirements to a bachelor's degree and at least one year of work history.
- Use polygraph testing as part of the initial screening process.
- Increase the number and pay of field training officers, overhaul the field training program, and extend the probationary period from twelve months to eighteen months.
- Implement mandatory continuing education programs, including in-service training and external course work. Merely adding courses on ethics is not enough.
- Establish an "early warning system" to alert command personnel when an officer or police unit may be involved in a pattern of misconduct. The system should include opportunities for counseling and should be fully computerized. Its purpose is to stop small problems from becoming big ones.
- Increase the number of staff assigned to Internal Affairs so that each complaint or inquiry receives the attention it needs.
- Improve the management process so that an appropriate balance is kept between the police officer's exercise of discretion on the street and the department's need to ensure that officers are doing what they are supposed to be doing.

It remains to be seen whether these recommendations will be implemented by the Chicago police department, and, if they are, whether they will succeed in preventing police corruption in that city. One obstacle is that "the opportunity structure inherent in the nature of policing presents officers with virtually unlimited chances to engage in deviant activity" (Kappeler, Sluder, and Alpert, 1994:290). Second, some police practices, whether illegal or merely unethical, are functional for middle-class society to the extent that they help the police maintain order, and this in itself reinforces their use as part of police culture. Finally, public opinion is generally favorable toward the police, and no fundamental restructuring of police organization, culture, and behavior can be expected without a corresponding restructuring of the social order itself. The public will be rightly outraged by much-publicized cases such as the Rodney King beating and the drug-dealing cops of New York City's 77th Precinct, but that indignation is unlikely to turn into support for a wholesale restructuring of society and its police.

SUMMARY

This chapter has examined the legal environment of policing in America with two questions in mind: How does a democratic society maintain order and protect lives and property while ensuring individual rights and freedoms? And how and why do the police overstep their authority or engage in other corrupt practices? In America the U.S. Constitution reserves the bulk of criminal matters for state control, and yet that same Constitution has become the primary guidepost for demarcating the boundaries of lawful police activity. The Bill of Rights, comprising the first ten amendments to the Constitution, established over 200 years ago that U.S. citizens enjoy certain rights. These include the right to be free of unreasonable searches and seizures, the right not to be arrested without probable cause, the right against self-incrimination, and the right to have an attorney present during questioning. Although it took many years to accomplish, the provisions of the Fourteenth Amendment applied the Bill of Rights to the actions of state governments.

The chapter reviewed various of the key U.S. Supreme Court decisions pertaining to the routine activities of the police, especially searches and seizures and making arrests. We saw that many things we now take for granted—for example, the reading of a suspect's rights upon being arrested—were unheard of a mere 40 years ago. It was not until the 1960s, when Chief Justice Earl Warren guided the Supreme Court to some of its most controversial decisions in favor of due process, that American citizens finally enjoyed the right to protections against unreasonable searches and seizures, to have counsel present during questioning, and to have unlawfully seized evidence excluded at trial in their dealings with state and local police. Since that time, an increasingly conservative Supreme Court has modified many of the Warren Court's rulings, thereby relaxing constitutional restraints on some police activities. Although as a general rule the police must still have probable cause to make searches or arrests, and although a suspect must still be given the Miranda warnings when arrested, all sorts of exceptions are now allowed, leading some observers to complain that the clock is being turned back to an era when the police functioned with minimal legal restraints, and enjoyed little risk of punishment for practices that made a mockery of the Bill of Rights. Some fear that America is moving in the direction of totalitarian regimes, where the police are allowed virtual free rein in support of the party line.

On the other hand, the loosening of restraints on police practice is being hailed in some quarters as a fitting change in response to growing public concern about the problem of crime, especially drugs and violence. The police need more leeway, it is argued, to effectively combat crime and to maintain order. The pendulum has swung too far in favor of the rights of criminals, supporters of this position often say; now it is time to favor the interests and rights of the police and law-abiding citizens.

Between these two extremes of opinion lie most moderate observers, who believe that some relaxing of restraints on police conduct, when coupled with superior training of police and a diligent public oversight, will not inevitably result in a loss of freedoms for the average citizen, and may make it more difficult for criminals to escape detection and arrest.

And yet there remain some seemingly intractable problems in policing, made glaring by sensational news coverage but nonetheless real. Corruption is one problem with quite broad scope, and police brutality is a specific and horrible version of it. Thankfully, brutality is a relatively rare event engaged in by a few police officers who are at great risk of censure by the public and courts, as well as by their police co-workers. Its episodic and unpredictable character help make it news when it occurs, although there can be little question that many incidents remain hidden. Police misuse of force is far more commonplace, and is fostered by the organization and routine norms and expectations of policing, including police concerns with gaining and maintaining control in police-citizen encounters. For these reasons, misuse of force is a more difficult problem to control than police brutality, which more commonly stems from the self-centered prejudices of a few hateful individuals; once identified they can be excised from the force. It is harder to control overzealousness, to combat inexperience and fear, and to ensure that actions and events will not be misinterpreted by police officers who are armed and authorized to use force. Superior police recruitment, superior training, close mentoring and supervision of officers who work the streets, and an operational commitment to realistic performance goals all may help reduce corruption and related problems, and many big-city departments are pursuing such tactics. In the last analysis, a just and effective system of policing will depend upon the social and political climate in which police officers do their work, and upon the expectations, costs, and rewards that officers perceive are associated with their actions. A cornerstone of any just and effective model of policing is surely a strong public and judicial commitment to the protection of individual rights and liberties; and this brings us back to the Supreme Court and the Bill of Rights.

WHAT DO YOU THINK *NOW*?

- Describe the importance of following guidelines when the police conduct searches and seizures. What are the correct ways to conduct them? What are the consequences if they are conducted incorrectly?
- Describe the different times when it is acceptable to use force, and the general guidelines for how much force to use. When is too much force being used?
- What aspects of police culture encourage corruption and brutality? How do departments both encourage and discourage these problems?

KEY TERMS AND CASES

Wilson v. Arkansas
Richards v. Wisconsin
Bill of Rights
Magna Carta
due process
Fourteenth Amendment
search and seizure
search warrant
probable cause
warrantless search
exigent circumstances
Maryland v. Wilson
Chimel v. California
stop and frisk
Minnesota v. Dickerson
Weeks v. United States
exclusionary rule
precedent
Mapp v. Ohio
good faith exception
inevitable discovery exception
compelling interest
Miranda warnings
occupational deviance
abuse of authority
reasonable force
blue code of silence
Internal Affairs unit

Active Learning Challenges

1. Break the class into two groups: one that feels that police are too restricted in their ability to perform searches and make arrests, and another that feels they have too much authority in these areas. Have each group present evidence to the class that supports their position.
2. As a class, discuss possible alternatives for minimizing police corruption and misuse of force. Consider how the proposals from the class would affect overall police effectiveness.
3. Have pairs of students investigate how local police departments handle complaints against their officers. Report back to the class on the procedures and provide a brief summary of an illustrative case.
4. Watch the movie *Serpico* and discuss how things have or haven't changed since the early 1970s.

Internet Challenges

The Web pages mentioned here can all be accessed through the Web site for this textbook at **http://www.prenhall.com/barlow/**.

1. Explore the U.S. Supreme Court's most recent decisions regarding arrests and searches and seizures. See if you can find a case that enlarges police powers and one that restricts them. Check any of these Web sites: Findlaw or Northwestern University's wonderful site that includes audio chips on some Supreme Court decisions.
2. Read the complete report of the Chicago Commission on Police Integrity. Based on the material in this chapter, do you think that police corruption in Chicago is worse than, better than, or merely different from that in New York City? Using a search engine such as Yahoo or Lycos, see if you can find recent accounts of police corruption in other large cities. How do they compare?
3. Imagine that you are aware of corrupt practices among some members of your local police department, but the department has no formal mechanism for handling public complaints. Using the resources of the Internet, see if you can design a complaint process that protects both the complainant and innocent police officers. Start by learning how different departments around the country deal with complaints; the Web site of the Louisville, Kentucky, police department's Internal Affairs unit is a good place to begin.

Part III

The Criminal Courts

The Judicial Process in Action

Lawyers control the judicial process, so Part III begins with an exploration of lawyering in America and examines who criminal lawyers are and what they do as prosecutors and defense counsel. Chapter 10 also examines the right to counsel and the defense of poor suspects who cannot afford a lawyer. Most criminal defendants never go to trial and Chapter 11 shows why, along with how they are dealt with. The chapter also explains the bail process and the ways that court officials try to protect society from dangerous offenders awaiting trial. Chapter 12 explains the judge's role in criminal matters and takes readers through a criminal trial. Jury selection is examined in detail, as is the presentation of evidence by attorneys for the prosecution and the defense. Finally, recent changes in the criminal court are explored, including technological innovations and the growing use of drug courts.

For most defendants, the culmination of the judicial process is when the judge passes down a sentence. Sentencing is the subject of Chapter 13; here the concept of punishment is explored and possible sentences examined. A major portion of the chapter deals with sentencing disparities and the methods used to reduce them. Two modern sentencing trends are also explored: the use of harsher penalties for some groups of offenders, including "three strikes" laws, and the growing use of intermediate sentences such as boot camps and home confinement for others. The role of victims in sentencing and the rise of restorative justice are also discussed.

CHAPTER 10

THE CRIMINAL LAWYERS

LEARNING OBJECTIVES

- Describe how the legal profession has changed over the years, and explain why it became stratified.
- Explain the low status of criminal lawyers within the legal profession.
- Identify common problems that criminal lawyers face in defending clients.
- Describe what prosecutors do and some of the difficulties they face in carrying out their duties.
- Understand the constitutional right to counsel and its relationship to the defense of poor criminal suspects.
- Distinguish among the various systems of indigent defense.
- Describe what public defenders do and some of the difficulties they face in carrying out their duties.

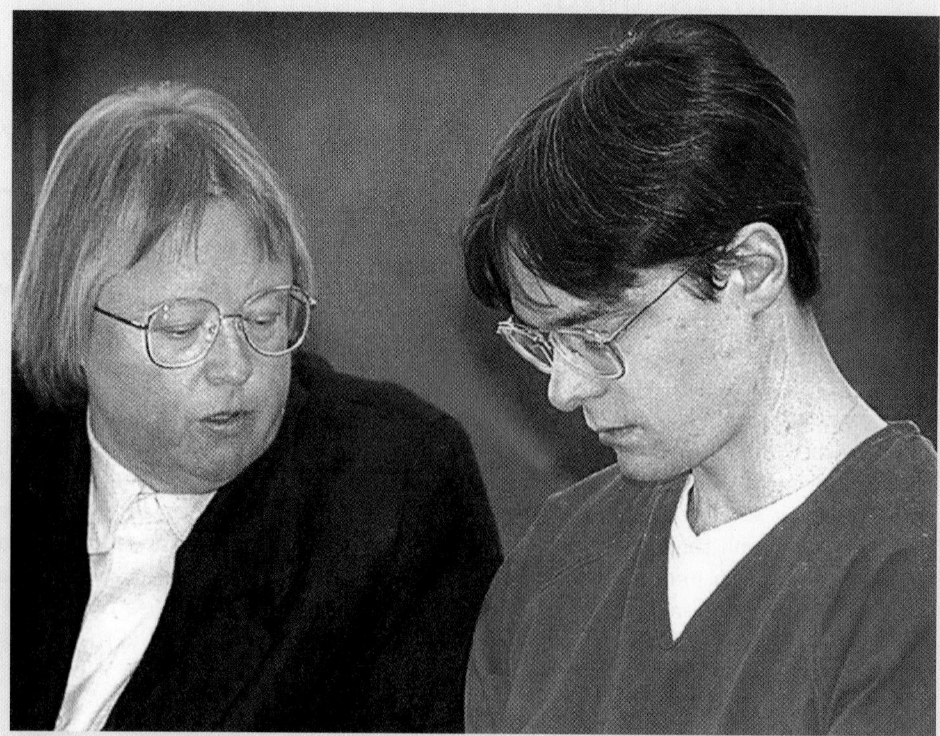

It has taken two centuries for the Sixth Amendment guarantee of right to counsel to be broadly enforced. Today, a criminal defendant who has been denied counsel cannot be sent to prison even if convicted.

PHOTO BY JIM MAENTANIS, THE DAILY TRIBUNE, COURTESY OF AP PHOTO

We are more casual about qualifying the people we allow to act as advocates in the courtroom than we are about licensing electricians.

FORMER U.S. SUPREME COURT CHIEF JUSTICE
WARREN E. BURGER

If you look at the Yellow Pages today and show me the people that claim to be a criminal lawyer, I will show you that a good percentage have never been in a courtroom in their life. They merely advertise that they're criminal lawyers along with everything else.

DONALD WOLFF, CRIMINAL ATTORNEY AND MUNICIPAL JUDGE

When Frances Caldwell graduated from law school in 1998, the realization that the bar exam was still to come quickly dulled the excitement of graduation. In the United States all attorneys must be admitted to the bar. Being interested in criminal law, Caldwell had spent the preceding summer as an intern with the county prosecutor, and this had led to the offer of a full-time position as an assistant prosecutor upon graduation. The job was appealing even though the pay was only $28,000 to start and the position carried little prestige in the legal profession. The prosecutor's office was a good starting point for someone interested in practicing criminal law, and it provided opportunities to develop skills and connections that would be useful in private practice. Caldwell knew of assistant prosecutors who had eventually made successful careers in politics, and this possibility was also appealing.

Most appealing was the challenge of the courtroom itself. Although Caldwell had no illusions about serving the cause of justice—the internship experience had shown firsthand that most criminal cases are resolved by making deals and following the line of least resistance—the idea of taking some defendants to trial and convincing a jury or judge to accept your version of the facts in a contest of persuasion was exciting. Luckily, the law school had a good reputation in trial practice, and Caldwell had spent many hours preparing briefs and arguing her case in mock trials in front of faculty, students, and practicing attorneys. But none of this would matter if she did not pass the bar exam. Caldwell sighed as the vision of a relaxing summer disappeared.

Frances Caldwell is about to become a key player in the judicial processing of criminal suspects. It is through the decisions and activities of people working in the nation's criminal courts that suspects find out whether or not they are legally a criminal, and the official punishment they face if they are. The next four chapters provide a detailed examination of these criminal justice decisions and activities. We will look at the factors that influence how decisions are made, as well as the impact those decisions have on the shape of American justice. We will examine the processing of criminal cases from the vantage point of the participants themselves and also the larger system that their decisions and actions bring to life.

Recalling our discussion of the courts in Chapter 4, the key decision points during the court phase of the criminalization process are the following:

- Filing charges
- Arranging prosecution and defense counsel
- Granting or denying bail
- Entering formal charges through a grand jury indictment or through an information at an arraignment
- Entering a plea—with or without plea negotiations
- Determining guilt
- Filing an appeal
- Determining the sentence

At the center of all these important decisions are the lawyers. What better place to begin our journey through the criminal courts than with the criminal lawyers themselves? From the criminal defendant's vantage point, the selection of defense counsel is one of the most important decisions that will be made. Defendants who can afford to pay legal fees have much more control over this decision than those who cannot. Since many criminal defendants are indigent—unable to pay legal fees—their defense has become an important aspect of criminal lawyering in the United States. The characteristics and implications of indigent defense will also be examined in this chapter.

? WHAT DO YOU THINK?

- What is a popular reason for becoming a criminal lawyer? A prosecutor? Does the work seem exciting or glamorous?
- How well are women and minorities represented in the legal profession? Do you think that the situation has changed much in recent years? If so, how?
- Do you think that Frances's job as a prosecutor will carry different status from that of the public defenders she works against in the courtroom?

AN OVERVIEW OF LAWYERING IN AMERICA

Of the three core functional areas of the criminal justice system—police, courts, and corrections—the courts are where people most often look to see how American justice works. The criminal justice system revolves around the criminal court, and therefore around the people who work there. Although the typical courthouse employs people with diverse skills and responsibilities—from clerks and secretaries to guards, bailiffs, stenographers, office managers, and victim advocates—the special qualifications and authority of prosecutors, defense attorneys, and judges set them apart from the rest. Together with probation officers, these are the criminal justice professionals who make up the **courthouse work group**. Its members handle the daily business of the criminal court, and if an outsider wants to learn about the rules, traditions, and expectations of any particular court, these are the people to ask.

courthouse work group Criminal justice professionals who handle the daily business of the criminal courts.

Whereas in Part II of this book we dealt with a world that most people have some direct personal experience with, the criminal court is a place that many Americans only experience vicariously, mostly through novels and television. Although the O. J. Simpson trial opened up the judicial process to millions of people who had never been inside a criminal court, the scene was quite unlike the typical felony trial—except in one important respect: Lawyers dominated the proceedings. Christopher Darden, Marcia Clark, Johnnie Cochran, and DNA expert Barry Scheck became household names, at least for a time. To help viewers understand what was going on, the media hired other lawyers as on-camera commentators.

The message many viewers take away from highly publicized trials may simply be this: In the hands of skillful lawyers, the "facts of the case" are reconstructed so that two quite different pictures are presented in court. This is what prosecutors and defense counsel are paid to do when a criminal case comes to trial. The judicial process in the United States, as in many other countries, is an **adversarial process**: On one side stands the state and on the other side stands the defendant. The defendant is represented by defense counsel, the state by the prosecutor. Both attorneys attempt to convince the jury that their version of the facts is the correct one. This is the heart of the criminal trial, which is the subject of Chapter 12.

adversarial process During a trial the prosecution and the defense are on opposing sides, each seeking to persuade the judge or jury to accept their version of the truth.

It will help us understand the role and importance of the criminal attorney in modern criminal justice if we first take a brief look at the legal profession in America, including its history.

A Brief History of Lawyering

Law schools are the modern route to a legal career, yet a law school education was almost unheard of until the mid–nineteenth century. Before then, lawyers in America and England gained their training through being apprenticed to a practicing attorney. There were two types of lawyers: *Solicitors* advised clients and prepared cases for court; *barristers* represented clients in the courtroom. In England, barristers were traditionally of noble birth and received their training at the famous Inns of Court in London; solicitors came from more humble backgrounds and gained their training through apprenticeship as *articled clerks*. They worked long hours for little pay, learning the law through assisting in its practice and, when time permitted, reading up on it. Not surprisingly, solicitors far outnumbered barristers, who enjoyed much higher prestige. It was from the ranks of barristers that all higher court judges were drawn, a situation that continues today.

In the American colonies, law was a devalued profession at first. This may have been because of its historical connection with the British system. Lawyers were banned in Massachusetts and Connecticut; Pennsylvania, Virginia, and the Carolinas enacted legislation severely restricting the practice of law (Pound, 1953; Friedman, 1973). Inevitably, though, the growth of the colonies led to more laws and regulations, which in turn created an increasing demand for people trained in the law. By the eighteenth century, a widespread system of legal apprenticeship had emerged, combining the roles of solicitor and barrister.

In England there are two types of lawyers: solicitors, *who handle a broad range of legal matters and sometimes prepare cases for court, and* barristers *(above), who receive training at London's famed Inns of Court and represent clients in the courtroom.*

Photo courtesy of AP/Wide World Photos

Lawyers were prominent among the signers of the Declaration of Independence and the delegates to the Constitutional Convention.

An alternative to practicing law was to teach it. One prominent judge in Litchfield, Connecticut, established an independent law school in 1784. Until its closure in 1833, the Litchfield law office/law school of Judge Trapping Reave trained nearly 2,000 lawyers, from whose ranks came 28 U.S. senators, 101 congressmen, 14 governors, 3 vice-presidents, and 3 justices of the U.S. Supreme Court (Corsi, 1984).

In the meantime, major universities began to establish professorships in law, among them the College of William and Mary and the Universities of Pennsylvania and Maryland. Students didn't receive a law degree; instead, they took courses in law along with courses in classics and the sciences. In 1817, Harvard University established an independent law school, with power to grant degrees in law. Students did three years of undergraduate study and if they successfully passed their exams, they were awarded a Bachelor of Letters in Law, or LL.B. degree.

Fifty years later, most lawyers were still trained through the apprenticeship system. Not only was cost a significant factor, but by the 1870s there were still only a handful of law schools and admissions were tightly controlled. Despite a doubling in the numbers of law schools to over 60 during the next 20 years, in 1900 more than a dozen states still had no formal law school education at all (Friedman, 1973).

Key Innovations in Legal Education. Harvard University had established the first formal university law school, and it was again Harvard that led the way in reforming law school education itself. In 1870, Christopher Columbus

Langdell was appointed dean of the law school. During the next 25 years, Langdell revolutionized admission standards, requiring either a college degree or successful completion of an entrance exam, and he established a system of written final exams covering the core courses in the school's two-year curriculum. Another innovation was his introduction of the **case method** of instruction. The case method brings actual court decisions into the classroom that can then be analyzed and discussed. Previously, students relied on textbook analysis of past legal decisions. The case method remains at the center of the law school curriculum today.

case method Instruction that involves classroom analysis of real courtroom decisions.

Even though it occurs after students have graduated, the **bar exam** is the capstone experience for modern law students because graduates must pass it before they can practice law. The exam was an outgrowth of Langdell's attempts to raise the standards of legal education. In 1921, the American Bar Association (ABA) formally adopted a resolution that "graduation from a law school should not confer the right of admission to the bar, and . . . every candidate should be subject to an examination by public authority to determine his fitness." According to the ABA, the benefits of a bar examination include these:

bar exam An examination that law school graduates must pass before they can practice law.

> They encourage law students to study subjects not taken in law school. They require the applicant to review all he has learned in law school with a result that he is made to realize the interrelation of the various divisions of the law—to view the separate subject courses which he took in law school as a related whole. This the curriculum of most law schools does not achieve. Also, it is the first time many of the applicants will have been examined by persons other than those who taught them, a valuable experience in preparation for appearing before a completely strange judge. (American Bar Association, 1998, **http://www.abanet.org/legaled/Prior.html**)

The Stratified Structure of Legal Education. Whenever the demand for a service grows, the organizations providing the service tend to proliferate. As new organizations appear, some try to emulate the best of existing ones, providing equivalent services, but most cannot and some do not even try. As a result, a system of stratification tends to develop, with the most profitable, respected, or successful organizations at the top and others grouped below into various strata. This process has occurred with legal education.

The growing complexity of American life and the countless economic and technological changes that occurred spawned all sorts of new laws and regulations, and that in turn created a growing demand for lawyers. Law schools sprang up around the country. But not all law schools were created equal. Well-established law schools connected to the nation's most prestigious universities were very expensive and remain so today. These schools have extremely high admission standards; typically, the professors are themselves graduates of highly prestigious and expensive law schools. Needless to say, the competition for admission is fierce and only a handful of prospective lawyers make it. Those who graduate in the top half of their class in an elite law school such as Harvard, Yale, Chicago, Duke, Michigan, or Stanford are virtually assured high salaries, and their success reinforces the reputation of the law school.

The bulk of university law schools, public and private, provide a perfectly competent legal education but fall short of the top-flight schools in reputation. Their curriculum and teaching methods look very similar to those of the top-ranked schools, but their less restrictive admissions policies and the lack of a historical claim to elite stature keeps them in the middle ranks. Even so, their best graduates may still be pursued by prestigious law firms and major corporations.

Besides university-based law schools, many large cities also have privately operated law schools whose primary function is to produce lawyers for local

Law schools such as Harvard's have exceptional reputations. Their graduates are guaranteed high-paying jobs upon graduation, and are more likely to have distinguished careers: four of today's nine Supreme Court Justices graduated from Harvard, two from Stanford, and one each from Columbia and Yale.

Photo by Shopper, 1989, courtesy of Stock Boston

practice. Many of these law schools sprang up to meet the needs of working-class and lower-middle-class students whose educational backgrounds, economic status, and family circumstances precluded admission to most university-based law schools. The John Marshall Law School in Chicago is an example of one of the best stand-alone law schools—yet a 1996 survey by *U.S. News & World Report* placed the school in the fourth tier (see Table 10.1). John Marshall has day and evening divisions, enabling the school to attract and serve nontraditional students who often have families and jobs. Besides the traditional core curriculum in civil procedure, criminal law, constitutional law, torts, contracts, and property, the school also provides two years of study in "lawyering skills," which include handling clients and setting up practice. The school also offers a program in courtroom practice that is taught by a faculty of trial lawyers and judges. Most graduates of these stand-alone law schools work in the local community, many in small or solo private practice, others in local government or the criminal justice system.

The overall reputation of a law school may obscure the fact that a lower-ranked school has achieved a high reputation in a particular branch or specialty of law. For example, the same *U.S. News & World Report* survey of accredited law schools found that faculty experts in the field of *trial advocacy*—courtroom practice—included among their top ten schools some institutions from the fourth and fifth tiers. Thus, along with such first-tier schools as Harvard University and the University of Texas at Austin, other first-rate trial advocacy schools included Stetson University (Florida—a fourth-tier school) and South Texas College of Law (a fifth-tier school). Graduates of top-flight law schools rarely go into criminal law—for reasons we shall discuss later—but they are major figures in the nation's economic and political life, and some end up on the highest courts of the land. In these roles they have a hand in the creation and interpretation of law, and therefore influence the complex

Table 10.1 Rankings of Accredited Law Schools: Samples from the First to the Fifth Tier

Rankings are based on five measures: Student admissions criteria, placement success after graduation, faculty resources, and reputation among (a) 4 deans and 4 faculty members per school and (b) 2,167 practicing lawyers. True rankings are provided for the first two tiers, while the last three tiers are alphabetical samples.

First Tier
Yale University
Harvard University
Stanford University
University of Chicago
Columbia University
New York University
University of Michigan at Ann Arbor
University of Pennsylvania
University of Virginia
Duke University (NC)

Second Tier
Boston College
University of Georgia
Fordham University
Boston University
College of William and Mary (VA)
Washington University (MO)
Brigham Young University (Utah)
University of Iowa
University of North Carolina at Chapel Hill
Wake Forest University (NC)

Third Tier
American University (DC)
Baylor University (TX)
Florida State University
Loyola University of Chicago
St. Louis University
Temple University (PA)
University of Alabama
University of Cincinnati
University of Nebraska at Lincoln
University of San Diego

Fourth Tier
Creighton University (NE)
Howard University (DC)
John Marshall Law School (IL)
Pepperdine University (CA)
Syracuse University (NY)
Texas Tech University
University of Maine
University of Mississippi
University of Oklahoma
University of Wyoming

Fifth Tier
Detroit College of Law
Golden State University (CA)
Loyola University at New Orleans
New England School of Law (MA)
Northern Kentucky University
South Texas College of Law
University of Akron (OH)
University of Baltimore
University of Memphis (TN)
Whittier Law School (CA)

Source: Excerpted from "America's Best Graduate Schools." *U.S. News & World Report,* March 18, 1996, pp. 82–86.

process of criminalization. However, their professional lives are generally far removed from the daily grind of the criminal courts.

Professional Standards and the Bar Association

The rise of university law schools and particularly Langdell's innovations at Harvard promoted a growing belief that the practice of law required a sound education as well as extensive specialized knowledge and training. By the late nineteenth century, there were more than 100,000 practicing lawyers. As their numbers swelled, bar associations began a vigorous campaign to raise standards for admission to the bar. The formation in 1878 of the American Bar Association (ABA), a national organization of lawyers, brought additional clout to the movement. The ABA subsequently developed accreditation standards for law schools, which most states now rely on in controlling admissions to the bar. Today, before an attorney may practice law he or she must be admitted to the bar. As of June 1998, there were 181 ABA-accredited law schools; a complete list with links to the schools themselves is found at the ABA's Web site: **http://www.abanet.org/legaled/approved.html.**

The national ABA and state bar associations have not only created the rules of modern lawyering in the United States, but in a broader sense they have also helped construct a social identity around the practice of law. Today, local and state bar associations have many functions: They define who lawyers are, what lawyers do, how lawyers judge each other, and who lawyers are accountable to; like most professional groups, they discipline errant members and at the same time protect the profession from unwanted scrutiny by outsiders; they maintain continuity across generations of lawyers and promote homogeneity in membership.

The Status of Women and Minorities in the Legal Profession

Relating to the theme of diversity laid out in Chapter 1, the criminal justice system in this country has a long way to go achieve a proper balance in the diversity of its personnel. Like policing, the legal profession has historically been dominated by white men. Women and minorities have had little to say about the content of law or the policies and procedures for enforcing it. In the late nineteenth century, lawyering was like a private club: entrance was limited by race and gender, and also by wealth and connections (Friedman, 1973; Corsi, 1984). Indeed, the American Bar Association began as a "gentleman's club." Law schools are expensive places, but even applicants with money sometimes found the doors locked because they had the wrong surname—many prestigious law schools refused to admit Catholics, Jews, or first-generation immigrants—or had no influential relatives or friends to sponsor them. Less strenuous resistance remains today, but some white males are still reluctant to share the many advantages offered by the legal profession, including opportunities for status, wealth, and power.

Female Lawyers. Although there were rare cases of women being allowed to practice law as early as 1684, the first woman trained in law through an apprenticeship and officially admitted to the bar was Arabella A. Mansfield. She was admitted to the Iowa bar in 1869. Washington University in St. Louis was the first law school to admit women, although not the first to graduate one; that honor went to Chicago's Union College of Law (now Northwestern University Law School), whose first graduate was Ada Kepley in 1869. African American women also began to break into law during the nineteenth century. Howard University, a predominantly black institution, graduated the first black woman, Charlotte Ray, who was admitted to the bar in Washington, D.C., in 1872 (Feinman, 1994:124).

Many of the women who entered law during this period were married to lawyers or came from families involved in the profession. They often trained in the family law office. However, the tightening of professional standards discussed earlier, coupled with the growth of university law schools, meant that by the end of the nineteenth century women seeking a career in law had also to seek a formal legal education. Many of the more prestigious schools began reluctantly to open their doors, some following bitter court battles. However, the Harvard, Yale, and Columbia law schools refused to admit women until Columbia broke ranks in 1928. The Washington and Lee law school held out until 1972, the last to finally admit women (Feinman, 1994:125). In 1986, Columbia Law School appointed a woman, Barbara Aronstein Black, as its dean. In her acceptance speech, Black illustrated the plight of many women who compete in a male-dominated profession while raising a family: "Where I am today has *everything* to do with the years I spent hanging on to a career with my fingernails" (*New York Times*, January 2, 1986).

Although women gradually became more accepted in the legal profession, explosive growth in their numbers did not occur until the last quarter of the 20th century. By the early 1990s the number of female attorneys practicing in the United States had grown from less than 10,000 in 1970 to nearly 200,000. This means that extraordinary growth took place during that period in the number of women seeking a legal education. Indeed, by 1993, nearly half of all law school students were women, and over 60 percent of all the undergraduate degrees in law-related fields were awarded to women—up from around 5 percent in 1971 (U.S. Bureau of the Census, 1994:210). Today, all major American law schools have women among their faculty, although their representation is lowest in the higher ranks: Unpublished data from the American Bar Association showed in 1993 that 65 percent of instructors and lecturers were women, but only 15 percent were full professors (Feinman, 1994:130). This will change as younger women move up the ranks.

The Status of Racial and Ethnic Minorities. African Americans and Hispanics have not fared nearly so well as women. Figure 10.1 shows the percentage of practicing lawyers and judges in 1983 and 1997 who were female, black, or Hispanic. In 1983, African Americans and Hispanics each accounted for less than 3 percent of American attorneys. It remains to be seen whether the

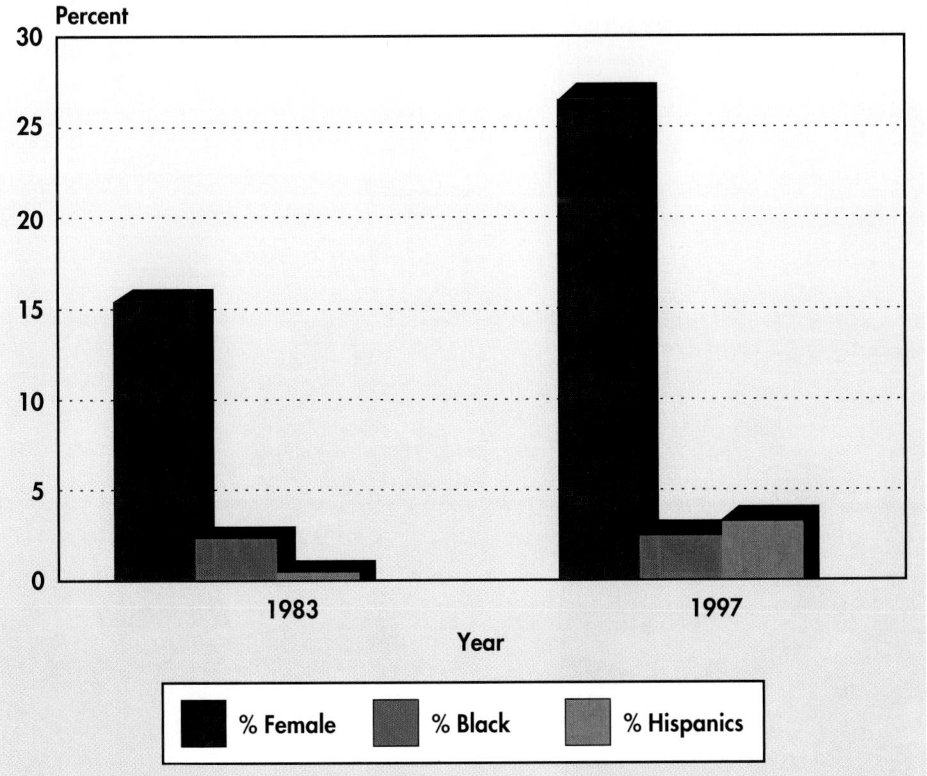

FIGURE 10.1 SEX AND ETHNICITY OF U.S. LAWYERS, 1983 AND 1997
Representation of female lawyers is greater than that of black or Hispanic lawyers, but is still not equal to that of men. Representation of Hispanics is growing, but black representation is stagnant.

Source: U.S. Bureau of the Census, (1998). *Statistical Abstract of the United States 1998* (table 672). Washington, D.C.: U.S. Government Printing Office.

gains made by Hispanics (from 0.9 percent in 1983 to 3.8 percent in 1997) will continue through the next the decade, but the outlook for black lawyers does not seem promising. Their representation remained virtually stable over the 14-year period shown in Figure 10.1. The gains throughout higher education made by African Americans during the 1970s and early 1980s have not continued through the nineties due in large part to rising costs and the increasing challenges to affirmative action plans (Farley, 1995:438–453). To put things in perspective, if over the past 25 years black representation in the legal profession had grown at the same rate as that of women, there would now be around 100,000 African American attorneys in the United States, instead of approximately 22,000. Yet among African Americans and Hispanics that go to law school, from 80 to 88 percent eventually pass the bar exam, according to a Law School Admission Council survey of 27,000 students who entered law schools in 1991 (*New York Times*, May 20, 1998, p. B9). Though somewhat lower than the rate for white law students (97 percent), this finding undermines persistent claims in some quarters that affirmative action programs that have helped minorities gain access to law schools have merely set them up for failure.

Although the nation's jails and prisons house large numbers of minorities, and persistent charges of racism are made throughout the criminal justice system, few African Americans and Hispanics have gained entry to a profession that offers significant opportunities for addressing these very issues. Despite the successes of a few black attorneys, of the more than 30,000 judges nationwide less than 1,000 are African Americans. Also, in 1992 African Americans made up only 4 percent of the nation's prosecutors, Hispanics just 5 percent (Bureau of Justice Statistics, 1993:3).

Law school faculty and lawyers in general are dominated by white males, although women have been gaining ground in recent years. Blacks and Hispanics have not done as well, comprising less than six percent of American lawyers.

PHOTO BY J. GREENBERG, COURTESY OF THE IMAGE WORKS

Anyone who still believes there is no place for women and minorities in the legal profession must have been stunned by the O. J. Simpson trial. Not only was the trial presided over by an Asian American, but the lead attorneys for both prosecution and defense were female or black. What is more, CNN, which televised the entire trial, and the major TV networks used female and minority attorneys among their legal experts. While some of the Simpson trial lawyers have reportedly made millions from lucrative book deals and public appearances, this point should not be lost: The public saw the criminal trial of a minority defendant in which many of the major players were also minorities, including the jurors. That is certainly not the usual picture, and it may encourage more minority Americans to seek a career in law. As more minorities become part of society's formal social control apparatus, it will be more difficult for other participants in the criminal justice system to discriminate against them on the basis of their race or ethnicity (Hawkins, 1994).

THE CRIMINAL ATTORNEY AND THE LEGAL PROFESSION

The **criminal attorney** engages in the practice of criminal law, defending or prosecuting people suspected of criminal offenses, or handling their appeals. Most attorneys do not work in criminal law, and certainly not on a regular basis. Criminal law is the least well paid, least prestigious, and most public realm of legal practice. This largely explains why so much was made of the O. J. Simpson defense team. His "dream team" represented the cream of attorneys working in criminal law. These elite attorneys pick and choose their cases, often command fees in excess of $500 an hour, and are supported by a large staff of junior attorneys, investigators, and expert consultants.

criminal attorney Prosecutes or defends criminal defendants or handles their appeals.

STRATIFICATION OF THE LEGAL PROFESSION

The stratification in legal education discussed earlier is mirrored by stratification among practicing lawyers. The practice of law in the United States has been profoundly influenced by two trends: urbanization and specialization. Not surprisingly, lawyers are attracted to the places and people who need their services; as work and people concentrated in the growing cities, so did lawyers. However, life has also grown increasingly complex, and it is no longer possible or desirable for lawyers to be generalists; no competent attorney would dream of trying to keep up with changes in the many areas of the law. Of necessity, lawyers, like physicians and educators, have become specialists.

Specialization in law affects not only what a particular lawyer is likely to know, but also the context in which that knowledge is used. Some attorneys never set foot in a courtroom, while others become expert trial lawyers; among lawyers who spend a lot of time in the courtroom, some specialize in arguing constitutional issues before appellate judges, while others concentrate on the trial itself. So it is with the practice of criminal law. Long before the O. J. Simpson trial ended, Harvard law professor Alan Dershowitz was preparing post-trial motions and appeals on Simpson's behalf; this was to be Dershowitz's primary role on the "dream team," for his specialty is the appellate side of the judicial process.

Figure 10.2 depicts the stratification of the American legal profession. At the top are the elite law firms. These are the inner circle of law; they are retained by Fortune 500 corporations, foreign governments, and large and wealthy institutions. These corporations and institutions usually have their own in-house attorneys, sometimes hundreds of them, but they hire the elite firms as outside counsel. The elite law firms draw from the top graduates of the best law schools, and they pay first-year graduates salaries approaching six figures. Rarely, if ever, do they handle criminal cases.

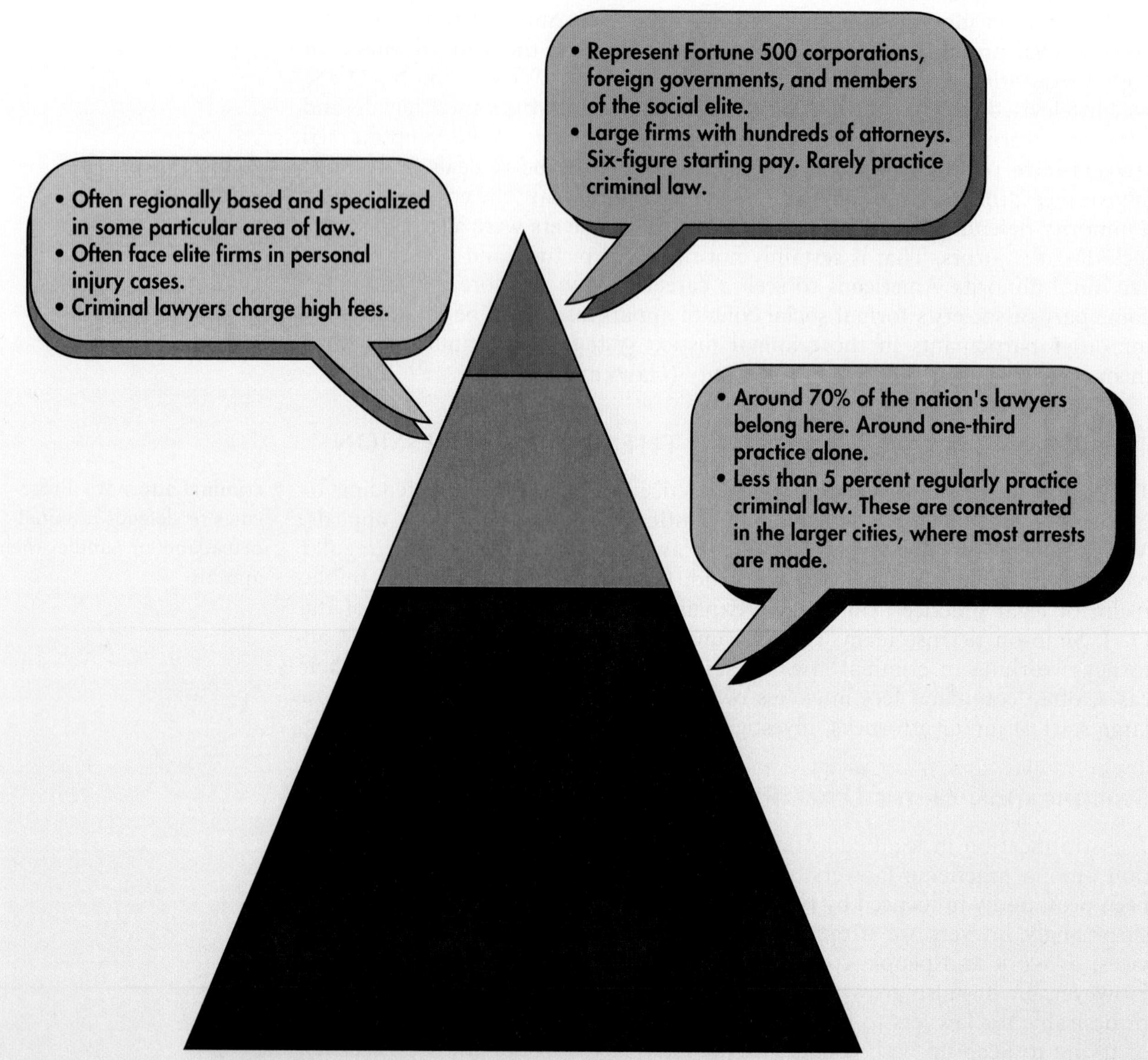

FIGURE 10.2 THE STRATIFICATION OF THE LEGAL PROFESSION

A second stratum or circle of legal practice is composed of medium-sized and some smaller firms that gain regional and sometimes national reputations for expertise in various areas of law, almost always including personal injury. Their clients are often the injured party in suits against corporations, and this sometimes pits them against an elite law firm. Included in this circle are in-house corporate lawyers, and attorneys who have achieved high rank in government service—federal judges, U.S. attorneys representing populous districts, and state supreme court judges. Many of the private law firms in this group will have at least one expert trial lawyer, and some may gain a regional reputation in criminal litigation. Criminal cases are not their bread and butter, but if they do take on the defense of a criminal suspect, their fees are substantial.

Finally, the third and largest stratum is composed of the vast majority of the nation's 820,000-plus licensed attorneys. Around 70 percent of all practicing lawyers work in firms of less than a dozen members; there are approximately 275,000 attorneys working alone, as solo practitioners (American Bar Association Foundation, 1994). Only 30,000 to 40,000 lawyers make criminal law their regular business, and most of these are solo practitioners or members of two- to three-person firms. Most of these lawyers are located in large cities, where most criminal arrests are made. Their offices are located close to the courthouse, and many gain business through connections with bonding services, jail and court personnel, and the police, or through word of mouth. Referrals from other lawyers is an important source of business, and some advertise their services in local newspapers or on TV.

Many lawyers are drawn to criminal practice by internship experiences during law school or by their early postgraduate employment in the offices of prosecutors or public defenders. A study of criminal lawyers in nine cities found that over 50 percent had moved into criminal law via initial employment (Wice, 1978). They gain firsthand experience in criminal practice, including extensive trial work. Once they set up private practice it is natural that their experience would draw them into criminal defense work, and referrals by other attorneys are bound to come their way. In addition, they have become known to many criminal defendants and their friends, who subsequently become a major source of business.

Problems Facing the Criminal Lawyer

It is no wonder that criminal attorneys as a whole are at the bottom of the pecking order. They represent a small minority of lawyers, their clients are often society's misfits, and except for those who are retained by professional criminals, drug dealers, and organized criminal groups, they take on cases for low to modest fees. Most struggle to make a decent living, and the competition from younger attorneys and from salaried public defenders has made criminal practice even more difficult for older solo practitioners, and even less appealing to law students.

Law schools themselves contribute to the low status of criminal practice by offering little more than one or two courses in criminal law and procedure. For example, a survey of law school Web sites shows that during the 1995–1996 school year, Emory University School of Law in Atlanta offered one required first-semester course in criminal law, and three elective courses in the third year; the John Marshall Law School in Chicago offered one core course in criminal law and one elective course in criminal procedure, but did not list criminal practice among its areas of concentration; and the University of Cincinnati College of Law listed two courses in criminal law or procedure and one elective course in juvenile justice. Seattle University School of Law offered two required courses in criminal law during the first year, more than most schools.

The Lack of Appreciation for Criminal Lawyers. What things about the practice of criminal law contribute to its low standing among attorneys? First, their clients are often of low social standing themselves, and the troubles that have brought client and attorney together are usually unpleasant and sometimes downright ugly. Defending suspected rapists, child molesters, batterers, muggers, thieves, and murderers draws the criminal lawyer into a depressing world. Among some prosecutors, defendants are referred to as "shitbums." Like the undercover drug cop, criminal attorneys may find it difficult to separate their own identity from that of the criminals they defend. As one criminal attorney told me, "the dirt is hard to rub off when you're in it every day." As we shall see later, it hardly helps the image of criminal defense attorneys when they are forced to take on poor clients under some systems of indigent defense.

This is another reason why the practice of criminal law has low status within the legal profession.

The public image of criminal defense attorneys as sly and callous, with no regard for "the truth" or the suffering of victims, also contributes to their reputation. So does the fact that most of the time a defense attorney mounts no defense at all. Around 90 percent of criminal cases are decided either by prosecutors who drop charges or by a guilty plea. Most of the time criminal defense attorneys earn their fees by encouraging their clients to plead guilty. This means that defense attorneys are technically on the losing side in most of their cases—their client is convicted—and they will often hear complaints after the fact that they were incompetent or didn't try hard enough.

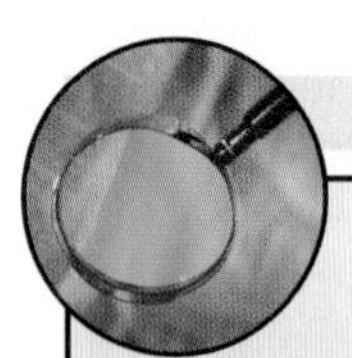

Box 10.1

INSIDE CRIMINAL JUSTICE

AN ATTORNEY RECALLS A CAREER IN CRIMINAL LAW

Donald Wolff is a highly respected criminal lawyer who is also a municipal judge. He practices primarily in the St. Louis area, but has defended clients throughout the United States and in the military. I interviewed him in April 1997 and he shared some observations on his career and law practice. In the next three chapters I draw on some of Wolff's insights when discussing such things as trial preparation, the guilt or innocence of defendants, cross-examination, and sentencing.

Following undergraduate school and an ROTC commission, Wolff entered law school at the University of Missouri in 1959 with the idea of being a criminal defense lawyer. "The school did not encourage people to get into criminal law. In fact, they only offered one course. I think they didn't want their students associated with the bad reputation that criminal law seems to carry with it." On graduation Wolff entered the army, was stationed in Germany, and became a trial lawyer, or *judge advocate*. "Since you know nothing, they make you a defense lawyer." Eventually he became a prosecutor as well. It was not uncommon for him to prosecute a case in the morning and defend another in the afternoon. He tried over 50 courts-martial.

This was important trial training for Wolff, and he believes he gained a balanced perspective on criminal justice as a result of working both sides. After three years he left the army and became an assistant prosecutor in St. Louis for the next three years. His boss was a one-term elected prosecutor who invited Wolff to join him in private practice. He did so, eventually branching out on his own.

Wolff's practice grew through referrals from prosecutors and judges, and from "hustling" to find clients. He joined bar associations, started teaching civil lawyers how to represent indigent (poor) criminal defendants—there were no public defenders in Missouri at that time—and served on the boards of local charities. He also became active with the American Civil Liberties Union (ACLU), eventually serving 25 years as one of its general counsel. As his paying clients grew in number, so did the number of *pro bono* (nonpaying) clients he took on. "You charge those who can afford to pay, and you give charity to those who can't." The bulk of Wolff's business came from other lawyers.

Some other features of criminal practice add to the negative image of this branch of law. For example, attorneys spend a lot of time visiting jails and prisons, and often find that they must hang around the courthouse waiting for their cases to be called. Not only unpleasant, these aspects of the job take time away from other activities and deprive attorneys of the comforts and services of their office. Until the advent of the cellular phone, it was hard for attorneys to keep in contact with their office staff, with other attorneys, and with prospective clients. Since much of an attorney's business is done by phone, the cellular phone has been a tremendous boon.

A problem peculiar to the private practice of criminal law is collecting fees. Most clients are not wealthy, so the fee will be modest; but even a modest fee

BOX 10.1 (CONTINUED)

When Wolff started out it was common for criminal lawyers to take cases from bail bondsmen and "kick back a third of the fee to the bondsman, which was unethical, and perhaps illegal, and you couldn't report it as a business expense on tax day. There were a lot of lawyers who got cases in those days in that way. I always refused." Wolff did pay referral fees, but only to lawyers, and only if they participated in the case. As Wolff's reputation as a defense attorney grew, lawyers stopped charging him fees, glad that he would take their referrals.

Wolff confirmed that getting fees is often a problem for criminal attorneys. "I've had clients that have taken years to pay me fees." This can affect how cases are handled. Like other lawyers, Wolff charges a retainer fee and additional fees for court time. Rather than reject some clients because they could not afford to pay the up-front retainer all at once, he might allow them a few weeks or months to pay it, but he would also delay the case rather than dispose of it as quickly as possible. This way the client got an expert defense attorney and Wolff got his fee.

Over the years Wolff has tried cases against all prosecutors in the St. Louis area, and has worked on cases with lawyers from around the country. He once tried a case in Louisiana involving 32 defendants and lawyers from Florida, Texas, and Louisiana. He has been in the same courtroom with F. Lee Bailey and the late Melvin Belli—known as the "King of Torts" but a terrible criminal defense lawyer, according to Wolff.

Unlike some high-profile criminal attorneys, Wolff has kept his practice small, and except for a few years in partnership with a civil lawyer, has remained without partners. He currently has two associates. Yet he has defended many high-profile cases, including dozens involving the death penalty. No client of his has ever been executed, however. But the pressure is so great, and the work so exhausting, that Wolff decided recently that he would handle no more capital cases. He also feels that defendants facing the death penalty are actually better off with a public defender. They are better qualified, he believes, have more resources to call upon, and can bring a colleague in for the sentencing phase if the client is convicted. "I don't think one lawyer like me doing the whole trial is any longer fair to the client. After spending a whole week telling the jury the defendant is not guilty, you have to say, okay, now he is guilty, but don't kill him. You lose all credibility."

Source: Donald Wolff, personal interview, April 1997.

of $500 to $1,000 is sometimes difficult to collect. Many urban attorneys require an "up front" fee of $500 just to take on a misdemeanor case such as petty theft or drunk driving; a felony charge will cost more, especially if a trial is anticipated. When the client cannot afford the fee, but the attorney needs the business, a payment schedule may be worked out, coinciding with court appearances. If the client cannot pay at the next appearance, the defense attorney may ask the judge to postpone the case (called a *continuance*) saying the client "has not yet arrived" but meaning "I'm still waiting for my fee" (Wice, 1978:111).

There Are Many Good Criminal Lawyers. The foregoing discussion has perhaps left the impression that criminal suspects cannot expect much from their attorney. On the whole this is true, and economics has a lot to do with it. Private criminal lawyers and public defenders are under great pressure to process as many cases as possible, and neither the training, fees (or salary), and work environment are comparable with any other type of legal practice.

Yet it is unfair to lump all criminal attorneys into one group, even excluding elite trial lawyers such as F. Lee Bailey and Johnnie Cochran. In any part of the country one can find highly competent, ethical, and conscientious criminal attorneys who do their very best for their clients and are unlikely to get rich doing so. These attorneys are most likely to be younger lawyers who have made a conscious choice to enter criminal defense work and are employed in the public defender's office. Even though caseloads are often heavy, and in the end most cases are decided through plea negotiations, the public defender's office provides a training ground where hard-working committed attorneys can do a great deal to further the cause of justice while learning the intricacies of criminal investigation, case development, and courtroom practice. As their experience grows, these attorneys filter up to the top of the public defender's staff, gaining reputations for high-quality service. Some will stay, but others eventually leave, some joining existing firms as expert criminal defense attorneys, some returning to law school as professors of criminal procedure and trial advocacy. Box 10.1 summarizes an interview conducted with a prominent St. Louis criminal attorney who has spent most of his professional life defending clients against criminal charges. He addresses some of the highs and lows of life as a criminal attorney.

One of the lows must surely be hearing the criticism "How can you defend such a person!?" The implication is that there must be something bad about criminal attorneys who conscientiously defend people who have committed heinous crimes. However, even if the defense attorney is convinced of a client's guilt, the ethics of the legal profession require that the client be defended to the best of the attorney's ability. Once a client is accepted, guilt or innocence should not influence the effort the attorney puts in on behalf of the client. Nor should personal distaste of a defendant be a reason for defense attorneys or prosecutors to shirk their professional obligations. A conscientious attorney may—indeed, should—turn down a case if he or she believes that personal distate for a defendant would make it impossible to mount a proper defense. But taking on an unpopular defense may be equally difficult. When attorney Stephen Jones was appointed to defend Oklahoma bomber Timothy McVeigh, he said: "We honor the memory of the victims by granting the accused effective assistance of counsel, due process, a vigorous defense and trial by jury, not hysteria" (Associated Press, May 12, 1995).

REPRESENTING THE STATE: THE PROSECUTOR

prosecutor Files charges and represents the state in criminal trials.

The primary role of a **prosecutor** is to represent the state in criminal matters. The prosecutor is probably the single most important player in the courthouse work group: It is the prosecutor who decides whether to bring formal charges in the first place; it is the prosecutor who decides what those charges will be; it is the prosecutor who decides whether to alter or drop charges; it is largely the prosecutor who determines what the range of penalties will be if a defendant is convicted; and it is the prosecutor's decisions that largely determine which criminals are executed, which criminals fill the nation's prisons, and which criminals are slapped on the wrist or ignored altogether.

There are just under 2,400 state prosecutor's offices in the United States, and 93 federal offices. Together, these offices employ over 70,000 support staff, and their activities cost the taxpayers around $6 billion a year. The typical prosecuting attorney—sometimes called district attorney (DA), state's attorney, or circuit attorney—runs a small office of eight staff members with an annual budget of around $300,000 and three assistant prosecutors to help with the caseload. A 1996 survey of state prosecutors found that the average office closed approximately 250 felony cases and 825 misdemeanors a year (DeFrancis and Steadman, 1998:5). "Closed" cases are those that prosecutors pursued until a judgment was entered in court. Of these, almost 90 percent of all felony and misdemeanor cases resulted in some type of conviction.

Although the typical district attorney runs a small office, the nation's 75 largest counties account for more than half of all the felony cases handled by state prosecutors. Los Angeles County is the largest; its district attorney heads a staff of 2,700 with a total budget in excess of $200 million. Like other large county operations, the district attorney of Los Angeles County uses most of the office budget for felony prosecution (Bureau of Justice Statistics, 1993:2–3). The size of population served is the most important determinant of workload, and therefore budget; on average, prosecutors serving populations over 500,000 closed nearly 24,000 cases in 1994, compared with 1,200 cases among prosecutors serving less than 500,000 people. Table 10.2 compares the average population served, staff size, felony caseload, and prosecution budgets of the nation's full-time and part-time state prosecutors' offices.

DUTIES OF THE PROSECUTOR

The formal duties of a prosecuting attorney are established by federal and state statutes. To illustrate, Table 10.3 summarizes some sections of the relevant Florida statutes. Florida selects its chief prosecutors through local elections, as do all but four states. Alaska, Connecticut, and Delaware place responsibility

TABLE 10.2 Size, Caseloads, and Budgets of State Prosecutors' Offices, 1996

Although the average full-time state prosecutor's office has a staff of only eight employees, those serving populations over 500,000 have hundreds of employees and budgets in the millions of dollars. They handle thousands of criminal cases each year. Here are some of the relevant figures from a 1996 survey of prosecutors' offices around the nation.

		Full-Time Offices (population served)			
	All Offices	1,000,000 or more	250,000–999,999	Under 250,000	Part-Time Offices
Number of offices	2,343	34	180	1,516	613
Average size, caseloads, and budget					
Population served	32,866	1,427,827	506,420	40,767	16,855
Felony cases closed	250	11,197	2,928	260	57
Staff size	9	414	103	10	3
Budget for prosecution	$254,000	$25,500,00	$4,800,000	$293,000	$90,000

Source: Carol J. DeFrancis and Greg W. Steadman (1998). "Prosecutors in State Courts, 1996" (pp 1, 5). *BJS Bulletin,* July.

TABLE 10.3 Selection and Duties of the State Attorney in Florida

The criminal procedure laws of each state establish the requirements and responsibilities of the prosecutor, usually called *state's attorney* or *circuit attorney.* The specific legal provisions vary from state to state. Here again is an example from the state of Florida.

Selection of State Attorney
Each court circuit is required to employ a State Attorney who is elected by popular vote and serves for a term of four years.

The State Attorney is not allowed to engage in private law practice while in office.

Duties
The State Attorney:

- Prosecutes or defends all suits or motions, civil or criminal, in which the state is a party.
- Attends grand juries to examine witnesses, give legal advice in any matter before them, and prepare bills of indictment.
- Summons any witnesses required by the court and administers oaths to all voluntary witnesses in criminal cases.

Assistant State Attorneys
The State Attorney of each circuit appoints assistant state attorneys. Salaries for Assistant State Attorneys come from state funds.

Assistant State Attorneys are authorized to sign indictments, informations, and other official documents.

Salaries for State Attorneys
Starting salaries vary by size of the circuit, from $28,000 to $32,000.

State Attorneys determine the compensation of the Assistant State Attorneys of their jurisdiction. This salary must not exceed 100 percent of the State Attorney's salary.

Source: Florida State Statutes (1993), Chapter 27.

for criminal prosecutions in the hands of the state's attorney general; in New Jersey, the governor appoints a prosecutor for each county (Dawson, 1992:2).

The duties of a district attorney are not confined to prosecuting felony cases, although this is where more and more are concentrating the bulk of their work according to a nationwide survey (Dawson, 1992). Other duties include extradition (where suspects are surrendered to officials in other jurisdictions), family matters and nonsupport, consumer protection, traffic offenses, paternity suits, juvenile delinquency, mental commitments, and environmental protection. They also represent the state in appeals and in civil suits brought against it by private citizens and corporations.

In their primary role representing the state in criminal matters, prosecutors have a variety of duties, including the following:

- Investigating suspected violations of criminal law
- Interviewing victims and witnesses
- Reviewing police requests for arrest and search warrants
- Determining whether and what charges to bring
- Presenting the state's case to a grand jury (in many but not all states)
- Issuing subpoenas
- Engaging in plea negotiations
- Representing the government before, during, and after a trial
- Recommending sentences

Why Become a Prosecutor? With all these important tasks to perform, the prospect of becoming a prosecutor must surely be a daunting one. Considering also that the practice of criminal law and government service are both given little prestige or pay, one might wonder why anyone would join the DA's office. A 1992 survey of 290 chief prosecutors across the country found that most assistant prosecutors are hired directly from law school, with an average starting salary of $26,000. The average salary for a chief prosecutor in 1996 was around $70,000 (DeFrances and Steadman, 1998:1).

Like their counterparts in the public defender's office, many criminal lawyers who work as assistant prosecutors see the job as a stepping stone to something else. After a few years on the job gaining experience and connections, they head out into private practice as seasoned criminal lawyers. Some assistant DAs will remain on the job as career prosecutors, perhaps specializing in certain types of crime or as trial advocates. For the chief prosecutor, who must be elected, the job is often a stepping stone to higher public office—a judgeship, perhaps, or election to the state or federal legislature or the governor's mansion.

The Politics of Prosecution. The prosecutor has a high-profile job in which politics plays a major role. Not only is the prosecutor the chief legal officer responsible for protecting the state's interests, but the prosecutor largely controls the reach of the criminal law and the outcomes associated with it. By deciding what crimes to prosecute, what charges to bring, and what penalties to seek, the prosecutor establishes a community's official tolerance of crime and criminals. When highly publicized cases come along, or when the prosecutor takes a stand on a controversial issue, the potential rewards may be high, but so too are the potential risks.

Prosecutors are arguably the most powerful members of the courthouse work group, but their decisions are constrained by a variety of organizational and political forces. Decisions about which cases to prosecute, and how vigorously, are sensitive to political influence. After all, the chief prosecutor is an elected official who usually rides into office on promises that appeal to the electorate because they reflect local concerns. The impact of public opinion is especially powerful in smaller communities, where crime rates are low and district attorneys are closer to the people they serve. Drug enforcement is a major priority of the 1990s, reflecting widespread concerns over the spread of crack cocaine and evidence that rates of teenage drug use are once again on the rise. Prosecutors have responded by increasing the resources put into drug prosecutions and by implementing new techniques and strategies, including aggressive use of forfeiture laws (Barlow, 1996:297–298).

Once a prosecutorial priority is established, the impact is felt throughout the courthouse and on the street. Police soon discover, for example, that there is little point in making lots of arrests for offenses that are not given priority in the DA's office; charges will be refused, and offenders will go free. Police are encouraged to make arrests in high-priority crimes, and this in turn produces considerable pressure on the organizational resources of the criminal justice system. Over the past few years, in fact, drug arrests have increased as a percentage of all arrests, from less than 6 percent in 1982 to over 10 percent in 1995 (Federal Bureau of Investigation, 1996:217). The percent increase may seem small, but in absolute numbers it represents nearly 500,000 more cases that prosecutors must deal with each year.

The interdependence of police, prosecutor, courthouse, and jail means that a decision made at any one level can have a significant impact on decisions made elsewhere. We encountered this issue earlier in our examination of police work and the exercise of discretion. From a prosecutorial perspective, potentially winnable cases must often be rejected because of circumstances beyond the prosecutor's control. Sometimes the police make avoidable mistakes—witnesses are "lost," evidence contaminated, or suspects' rights violated. Sometimes the required paperwork has not been completed or is of poor quality. For example, one investigation found that police records of interviews with suspects were "inadequate" almost a third of the time (Hooke and Knox, 1995). Aside from poor-quality work, organizational pressures such as heavy caseloads, overcrowded jails and prisons, and inadequate resources often force prosecutors to make decisions they are uncomfortable with. To make matters worse, these decisions sometimes conflict with public opinion, putting the prosecutor in a no-win situation.

These decisions may also conflict with the prosecutor's personal and professional interests. A former prosecutor I interviewed pointed out that if an elected prosecutor hopes to survive more than one term, the interests of justice must be balanced against the next election. "A state's attorney has a terrible time fending off all the people who want favors," he told me. This is true in big counties and little counties, he said. There is no simple solution for a prosecutor, and no proven formula exists that can brought into play. On balance, "the long-termers are probably the ones who go easy on the favors. Gaining a reputation as a 'straight shooter' is good for the long haul" (Joseph Brown, personal communication, September 1997).

The Role of Prosecutor as Independent Counsel. It is sometimes necessary for a prosecutor to initiate a criminal investigation of a high government official who may also have close political or economic ties to the prosecutor or may even be the prosecutor's immediate boss. This creates a possible conflict of interest. Federal law and the laws of some states have created the role

Perhaps the best known independent counsel in recent years is Kenneth Starr, who to date has spent over $40 million investigating the alleged misdeeds of President Bill Clinton. Some believe that Starr went beyond the scope of his authority by investigating the Monica Lewinsky affair, but his work was approved by a panel of judges and U.S. Attorney General Janet Reno.

ILLUSTRATION BY DEAN ROHRER

of **independent counsel** to deal with this situation. An independent counsel is a private attorney who conducts the investigation and brings charges if they are warranted. Chapter 40, Section 594, of Title 28 of the United States Code lays down the authority and duties of an independent counsel in federal investigations. These include "full power and independent authority to exercise all prosecutorial functions and powers of the Department of Justice, the Attorney General, and any other employee of the Justice Department. . . ."

independent counsel A private attorney hired to investigate possible crimes by government officials when a conflict of interest exists.

Over the past 30 years independent counsel have been used to investigate possible presidential crimes, including the Watergate scandal under Nixon, the Iran-Contra affair under Reagan, and now, most recently, the Whitewater and Lewinsky affairs under Clinton. During the Clinton administration, independent counsel have been used for seven different investigations at a reputed cost of well over $50 million. Apart from President Clinton, the targets of investigation included the late Commerce Secretary Ron Brown, former HUD Secretary Henry Cisneros, Interior Secretary Bruce Babbitt, and Agriculture Secretary Mike Espy. The charges included influence peddling, lying to Congress, perjury and obstruction of justice, and fund-raising and other financial improprieties.

Criticism of the independent counsel statute includes the argument that the law infringes too much on the president's authority and therefore violates the constitutional separation of powers. However, the U.S. Supreme Court declared the law constitutional in *Morrison v. Olson* (1988). Other criticisms have been directed more at the independent prosecutors themselves than at the law. For example, independent counsel Kenneth Starr came under attack from many Democrats and the White House for taking too long, spending too much money, and expanding investigations beyond the scope of his authority. Starting with the Whitewater land deal in 1994, Starr later expanded the investigation to include possible obstruction of justice, perjury, and subornation of perjury stemming from an alleged sexual affair between President Clinton and former White House intern Monica Lewinsky. However, the expansion of Starr's investigation had been approved by Attorney General Janet Reno, and by a special three-judge panel along the way. Although independent counsel laws help take conflicts of interest out of the investigation and prosecution of high-ranking government officials, they cannot take the politics out of prosecution.

Changing Sides: When Prosecutors Become Defense Attorneys. The skills and connections gained through working in the prosecutor's office can be put to good use as a defense attorney, and many assistant prosecutors eventually change sides. Most do so by entering private practice as a criminal attorney, although they may take on other kinds of cases as well. Their trial experience and familiarity with the judges, court reporters, and prosecutors makes them attractive to firms wishing to enter or expand criminal defense. Former prosecutors also find that their previous position is helpful in securing clients. In his early days as a defense attorney, Donald Wolff, whom we met in Box 10.1, had cases sent to him by judges and former colleagues. And some of the people he had successfully prosecuted in the past now asked him to defend them.

When it comes to defending clients, firsthand knowledge of a prosecutor's perspective can be an advantage. Not only does the ex-prosecutor know the biases of former colleagues, but familiarity with office policies and the relations between the different prosecutors and court personnel, especially judges, can help in the formulation of a defense strategy. On the other hand, an ex-prosecutor may sometimes find that relations with old colleagues become strained after the switch. A former prosecutor told me that prosecutors look upon many defense attorneys as "shysters" who play tricks and cannot be trusted. When he switched there was a brief honeymoon period with his former office colleagues, although "overnight I seemed to have lost IQ points and no one laughed at my jokes anymore" (Joseph Brown, personal communication, September 1997). Eventually, of course, the new professional identity is accepted by the courthouse work group, but relations with prosecutors are never the same.

SPECIALIZED PROSECUTION UNITS

In large urban circuits, with many criminal cases and a large staff, the DA's office is highly bureaucratized, with distinct departments responsible for specialized activities. The most frequent specialized units are those for drug enforcement, juvenile offenders, asset forfeiture, and child abuse; some of the largest districts also have units specializing in homicide, domestic violence, gangs (see Box 11.3 in the next chapter), career criminal prosecutions, arson, and white-collar crime (Bureau of Justice Statistics, 1993:4). As Table 10.4 indicates, part-time offices are rarely able to provide specialized prosecution services, although most reported prosecuting at least one family-related crime such as domestic violence, child abuse, and nonpayment of child support. These are relatively new areas of activity for many prosecutors. They arose from the women's movement of the 1970s and gained considerable public and political support as nationwide reports in the 1980s showed the problems to be widespread.

Many district attorneys participate in task forces that unite various government agencies in the investigation, arrest, and prosecution of complex or high-profile criminals. These have been successfully used to prosecute frauds, organized crime, transnational crimes, and environmental crimes. Los Angeles

TABLE 10.4 Special Types of Felony Offenses Prosecuted by Prosecutor's Offices

In a 1994 National Survey of Prosecutors, chief prosecutors were asked, "Did your office prosecute any of the following types of felony offenses during the year?" The results show that full-time offices serving large populations prosecuted a wide range of special cases, while few part-time offices did so.

		Full-Time Offices (Population Served)		
Prosecutors reporting at least 1 case of:	All Offices	500,000+	Under 500,000	Part-Time Offices
Domestic violence	88%	100%	92%	79%
Child abuse	88	100	91	80
Stalking	68	94	73	50
Nonpayment of child support	57	58	43	45
Elder abuse	41	82	50	15
Parental abduction of children	41	81	54	6
Bank/thrift fraud	34	58	43	11
Hate crime	29	85	32	13
Environmental pollution	26	68	28	13
Health care fraud	21	49	27	4
Gang membership	12	46	15	0
HIV exposure	10	27	13	0
Computer crime	16	64	19	0
Number of offices	2,336	120	1,533	683

Source: Carol J. Defrances, Steven K. Smith, and Louise van der Does (1996). "Prosecutors in State Courts." *BJS Bulletin* (October):3.

County, for example, has initiated an Environmental Crimes Strike Force. Police, prosecutors, and public health officials from five adjacent cities and the State of California deal with 130 to 140 incidents involving hazardous waste each month—about 1,500 a year (Hammett and Epstein, 1993). Many of these result in negotiated settlements, but far more are prosecuted than in the past. The increasing sophistication of environmental crimes, coupled with increasingly complex and stringent laws, have made prosecution of environmental crime both more difficult and more expensive. Most prosecutors are ill equipped to tackle the problem, and they are further constrained by fears that even if they had the resources to do it, the local economy could be hurt by vigorous enforcement of environmental laws (Benson et al., 1988). The task force approach disperses not only the cost, but also some of the criticism.

Prosecuting Criminal Enterprises. Some ongoing criminal activities are sophisticated operations that cut across state lines and come under the primary jurisdiction of the federal government. These operations function like businesses and hide behind a cloak of respectability. They sometimes have ties with organized crime groups, and many legitimate businesses are drawn into their money-making schemes. The range of crimes is extensive: from illegal gambling and drug trafficking to money laundering, interfering with employee pension funds, labor racketeering, tax law violations, and extortion.

Two federal statutes have given prosecutors a powerful weapon in dealing with such crimes. One is RICO, the Racketeer Influenced and Corrupt Organizations Act, the other is CCE, the Continuing Criminal Enterprise Act. RICO focuses on patterns of racketeering activity in an enterprise engaged in interstate or foreign commerce; CCE is limited to illegal drug activity and makes it

Ninety percent of all criminal cases end either with the prosecutor dropping charges or by a guilty plea. Plea bargains are among the most misunderstood procedures in the court system: although disliked by many victims and some defendants, they are necessary to keep courts from overcrowding, and they entice the defendant to admit guilt without tying up resources, including time, on a trial.

Photo by A. Ramey, courtesy of PhotoEdit

a crime for five or more people to commit or conspire to commit a series—courts have said three or more—of felony drug violations. These statutes permit prosecutors to link individual offenses into a group of crimes that can be prosecuted as one, for which a longer sentence applies than for the individual offenses. The sentences are indeed stiff: RICO permits fines up to $25,000, imprisonment up to 20 years, or both, and requires forfeiture of ill-gotten gains and any interest in the enterprise; RICO also permits prosecutors and civilians to sue for damages if business or property losses resulted from a pattern of racketeering activity—in this case the stakes are triple the damages plus the costs of the suit. A CCE conviction carries a mandatory minimum 20 years' imprisonment, a fine of up to $2 million, and forfeiture of profits and any interest in the enterprise. Probation, parole, and suspension of sentence are prohibited.

REPRESENTING THE CRIMINAL DEFENDANT

Prosecution represents the state's obligation to enforce its laws; defense represents a constitutional obligation to provide legal assistance to criminal suspects. Most lawyers in private practice pick and choose their clients and set their own fees. Elite law firms and those medium-sized firms that have criminal defense specialists charge very high fees and are very selective in the cases they take on. The bulk of firms engaged in the practice of criminal law are not so lucky. Not only are their clients generally unable to pay high fees, but many defendants are so poor that they cannot afford even modest legal fees. Such defendants are called **indigent defendants**. As we shall see in a moment, they have a right to counsel even though they cannot afford a lawyer. On occasion, criminal attorneys may be forced to defend poor clients they otherwise might not accept.

indigent defendant A person charged with a crime who does not have the financial resources to hire a private attorney.

DEFENDANT'S RIGHT TO COUNSEL

Private lawyers generally avoid taking on clients who cannot pay their fees, so a system of private lawyering inevitably leaves most poor citizens without the tools to defend themselves against criminal charges. Two hundred years ago, the framers of the Bill of Rights appeared to recognize the unfairness of this situation, for the Sixth Amendment to the U.S. Constitution states that "[i]n all criminal prosecutions, the accused shall enjoy the right to . . . have the Assistance of Counsel for his defence." In 1868, the due process clause of the Fourteenth Amendment extended this right to defendants in state prosecutions. However, it took many years for the **right to counsel** to be extended to the bulk of criminal defendants, many of whom are indigent. The important Supreme Court cases are summarized in Table 10.5.

right to counsel A defendant's constitutional right to the assistance of an attorney during prosecution.

Early Rulings on Right to Counsel. It is one thing to stipulate the right to counsel and quite another to define exactly what that means and to apply it in practice. All sorts of issues are involved, from the competency of counsel to whether assistance of counsel is required at every stage of the criminal process. For many years very little was done to address these issues, and then only in the federal system. The dominant thinking was that the assistance of counsel was not a fundamental right, but should be assured in cases where conviction was likely to result in severe punishment. This argument became the centerpiece of ***Powell v. Alabama*** (1932), a case that involved a man convicted of a capital crime and sentenced to death. He appealed on the grounds that he was denied effective counsel in violation of the Sixth and Fourteenth Amendments. In deciding the case, the U.S. Supreme Court agreed that Powell's right to counsel had been violated, but it stopped short of any blanket application of the

Powell v. Alabama Defendants charged with a capital crime have the right to counsel.

Table 10.5 Evolution of the Constitutional Right to Counsel

The Sixth Amendment of the U.S. Constitution seems to require that no person face criminal prosecution without counsel. Original interpretations of this amendment said that no person should be denied counsel if he or she could pay for it. Over the years, this interpretation was challenged numerous times in light of the many defendants who cannot afford counsel. This table highlights the most important Supreme Court decisions leading to the modern interpretation of the right to counsel.

***Powell v. Alabama* (1932):** All persons facing capital punishment should be provided access to counsel.

***Betts v. Brady* (1942):** All indigent defendants have a right to counsel if they can demonstrate that their case was "prejudiced" by lack of counsel. Poverty alone is not a sufficient reason to provide counsel.

***Gideon v. Wainwright* (1963):** All felony defendants must be provided access to counsel. Lawyers in the courtroom are "necessities, not luxuries."

***In re Gault* (1967):** Juveniles are given the right to counsel in any hearing that might result in commitment to an institution.

***Argersinger v. Hamlin* (1972):** Courts cannot impose a sentence of imprisonment on any defendant convicted of any offense unless the defendant was granted access to counsel.

***Scott v. Illinois* (1979):** Distinction is drawn between "actual imprisonment" and "authorized imprisonment." Indigent defendants in misdemeanor cases are not constitutionally guaranteed a right to counsel if the case does not result in actual imprisonment.

rule. Instead, the Court stated that due process protections do exist for capital cases but might not for other prosecutions.

Ten years later, in ***Betts v. Brady*** (1942), the Supreme Court specifically addressed the issue of indigency but again refused to provide an overarching interpretation that assistance of counsel was a fundamental right protected by the Fourteenth Amendment. This time, the Court argued that indigent defendants claiming protection had to demonstrate that their defense had been "prejudiced" by the absence of counsel, or that some "special circumstances" existed that warranted assistance of counsel, such as a defendant's low intelligence. Poverty alone was not a reason to provide counsel.

Betts v. Brady Poverty alone is not a reason to provide indigents with counsel.

Gideon v. Wainwright:* Establishing a "Fundamental Right" to Counsel.** The prevailing view that right to counsel was not guaranteed merely because a defendant was indigent changed in 1963. In that year, the U.S. Supreme Court under Chief Justice Earl Warren made one of the most important decisions of the 20th century. The account of this case, ***Gideon v. Wainwright, has been read by millions in the book *Gideon's Trumpet*, and the late Henry Fonda gave a masterful performance in the movie version.

Gideon v. Wainwright Defendants in felony cases have a fundamental right to counsel.

Clarence Gideon was charged by Florida prosecutors with breaking and entering a poolroom with the intent to commit a crime. Under Florida state law the offense was a felony. Gideon had no money and appealed to the court to appoint him counsel. The judge refused, citing a Florida law that restricts court-appointed counsel to cases involving the death penalty. Gideon then conducted his own defense, during which he made an opening statement, presented and cross-examined witnesses, and made a brief statement proclaiming his innocence. He did not take the stand. The jury found him guilty, and Gideon was subsequently sentenced to five years' imprisonment.

Like many prisoners, Gideon continued to proclaim his innocence, but he also did more than most. He filed appeals on his own behalf to the Florida appellate courts, and when these failed, to the U.S. Supreme Court. His appeal to the U.S. Supreme Court focused on the fact that he could not afford a lawyer and none was appointed for him. On the grounds that this violated the due process protections of the Sixth and Fourteenth Amendments, Gideon asked the Court to overturn the conviction and appoint him an attorney. The Court agreed, and asserted that all defendants have a fundamental right to counsel. Justice Hugo Black wrote the majority opinion. He spoke of the "obvious truth" that "any person hauled into court, who is too poor to hire a lawyer, cannot be assured a fair trial unless counsel is provided for him." Pointing out that governments spend vast sums of money trying defendants, and that defendants with money hire the best lawyers to defend them, Black suggested lawyers in the courtroom are "necessities, not luxuries." The "noble idea" of a fair trial, Black concluded, "cannot be realized if the poor man charged with a crime has to face his accusers without a lawyer to defend him."

Argersinger v. Hamlin Defendants have a right to counsel if they could be imprisoned upon conviction.

Later Cases on the Right to Counsel. The Gideon case involved a felony, so questions remained as to whether the right to counsel extended to misdemeanors or to criminal cases not involving imprisonment or other loss of liberty. In ***Argersinger v. Hamlin*** (1972), another Florida case, the Supreme Court made it clear that the rationale in *Gideon* also extended to any criminal trial where an accused could be deprived of liberty. In the majority opinion, Justice William O. Douglas wrote:

> We hold . . . that absent a knowing and intelligent waiver, no person may be imprisoned for any offense, whether classified as petty, misdemeanor, or felony, unless he was represented by counsel at his trial. Under the rule we announce today, every judge will know when the trial of a misdemeanor starts that no imprisonment may be imposed, even though local law permits it, unless the accused is represented by counsel. . . .

Scott v. Illinois Indigent defendants without counsel cannot be sent to jail or prison if convicted.

Important as it was in broadening the application of defendant's right to counsel, the *Argersinger* case still did not extend the right to counsel to cases where imprisonment was not an issue. Indeed, in ***Scott v. Illinois*** (1979), the Court upheld the conviction of a man charged with shoplifting less than $150, a crime under Illinois law punishable by a fine, one year in jail, or both. Scott, an indigent defendant, was convicted and fined $50. Despite the fact that the defendant was not provided with counsel, the Court concluded in a 6-to-3 decision that the Sixth and Fourteenth Amendments "require only that no indigent criminal defendant be sentenced to a term of imprisonment unless the State has afforded him the right to assistance of appointed counsel in his defense." In misdemeanor cases, in other words, an indigent defendant without counsel could not be sent to prison ("actual imprisonment"), but it would still be permissible for a state court to try an indigent defendant without counsel if imprisonment was merely "authorized" in such cases but would not actually be imposed. In his dissenting opinion, Justice William Brennan called this splitting of hairs "intolerable," and called for the Court to make right to counsel applicable in all cases where imprisonment was a possibility.

State Law and the Right to Counsel. The *Scott* decision meant that many indigent defendants still could not be assured counsel, despite the Court's earlier pronouncements about the "necessity" of having a lawyer in order to get a fair trial. It should not be forgotten that the Supreme Court is an interpretive body whose rulings act as constitutional checks on the decisions of lower courts and on the statutory actions of legislative bodies. If those decisions and actions are believed to restrict or violate constitutional rights, the Supreme Court will have something to say about it if the case reaches it. However, this leaves the federal government and individual states free to pass legislation that *broadens* citizens' rights beyond the limits acceptable to the Supreme Court.

Many states have in fact enacted legislation that extends the right to counsel to *all* criminal defendants, regardless of the punishment that might be imposed if they are found guilty. The State of Colorado has such a law, although part of it provides that law students, rather than fully qualified attorneys, may be appointed in any misdemeanor case. The federal code of criminal procedure also takes a less restrictive view of the right to counsel than the Supreme Court. Title 18, Section 3006A of the United States Code contains a provision allowing federal courts in "the interests of justice" to provide indigent defendants with counsel in misdemeanor cases for which imprisonment is a possible penalty.

Costs of Indigent Defense. Today, approximately 80 percent of all felony defendants rely on counsel paid for by the state (Bureau of Justice Statistics, 1996). Although government expenditures on public defense of indigent suspects have grown continuously over the past few years (see Figure 10.3), legislatures are reluctant to provide indigent defendants with unrestricted access to counsel. The argument seems to be: "Why spend increasing amounts of money if the stakes for a defendant are not that high anyway, and the Supreme Court won't object?"

This argument falls apart in the face of the huge amounts of money states and the federal government spend prosecuting criminal defendants. The most

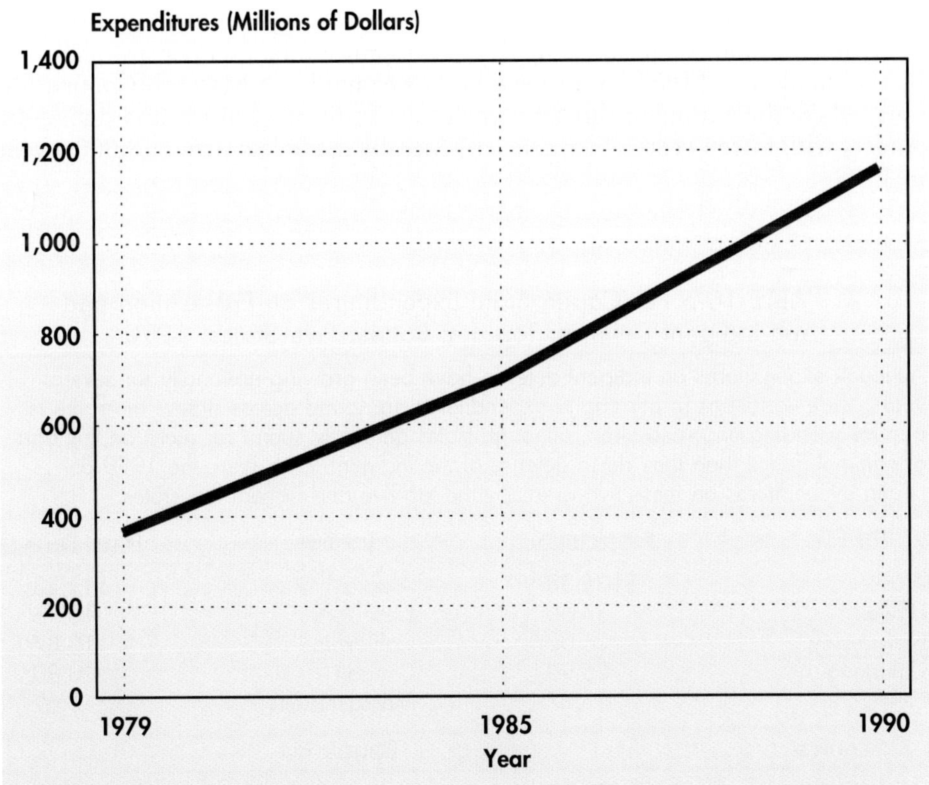

FIGURE 10.3 State and Local Expenditures for Public Defense, 1979–1990

The cost of indigent defense has been steadily rising. By 1988, expenditures for this purpose had reached over $1 billion.

Source: Steven K. Smith and Carol J. DeFrancis (1996). *Indigent Defense* (p. 17). Washington, D.C.: U.S. Department of Justice.

recent survey showed that in 1990, federal, state, and local governments spent approximately $5.5 billion on prosecuting criminal defendants, but less than one-third of that on public defense. When all judicial expenditures are considered, only 10 percent of over $16.5 billion was spent on public defense; if police protection and correctional services are added in, then only 2.3 percent of total criminal justice expenditures went to the defense of indigents. On a per capita basis, the 1990 average for all state and local governments—where most criminals are processed—was $16.01 for prosecution and $5.37 for indigent defense.

These nationwide figures obscure the tremendous state variations in expenditures on judicial services, including indigent defense. For example, the 1990 per capita expenditures of the five states at the top and the five at the bottom were as shown in Table 10.6. While all states spent much more on prosecution than on indigent defense, per capita spending on indigent defense by Alaska and New York was more than ten times that spent in Louisiana and Arkansas.

One of the reasons public prosecution costs more than public defense is simply that not all criminal defendants are indigent, but prosecutors must be assigned to all cases. If you are wondering whether another reason is that prosecutors are paid more, the answer is complicated. In jurisdictions where private counsel are assigned to indigent defense, the per-case fees may be less than what the salaried prosecutor would receive for an equivalent amount of work, but the fees are in addition to the fees paid by private clients. It is difficult to compare fees with salaries. In the case of salaried public defenders, their actual pay is usually set by the chief public defender, just as the pay of prosecutors is set by the chief prosecutor. Salaries depend on experience and the kind of cases assigned. A prosecutor or public defender who is assigned to felony cases generally makes more than one assigned to misdemeanors. Neither are paid well by the standards of the legal profession. For example, in Madison County, Illinois, where the author of this text works, assistant prosecutors and public defenders with fifteen years of experience generally made less than $58,000 a year in 1998.

TABLE 10.6 Per Capita State Expenditures on Prosecution and on Indigent Defense: Top and Bottom Five States, 1990

Although expenditures on indigent defense have been growing nationally for several years, wide variations in per capita expenditures are found across states. The same is true for spending on prosecution, although states generally spend far more on this part of criminal justice than they do in defense of the indigent. Here were the 1990 per capita expenditures on these two areas by the top five and bottom five states.

TOP FIVE	PROSECUTION	TOP FIVE	PUBLIC DEFENSE
Alaska	$135.33	Alaska	$11.23
Hawaii	34.60	New York	10.96
New Jersey	26.03	California	10.87
California	25.90	Oregon	10.80
New York	25.67	Massachusetts	8.62
BOTTOM FIVE		BOTTOM FIVE	
West Virginia	$5.80	Louisiana	$0.11
South Carolina	5.99	Arkansas	0.88
Arkansas	6.46	Mississippi	1.02
Mississippi	6.91	South Carolina	1.04
North Carolina	7.01	Oklahoma	1.14

Source: Kathleen Maguire and Ann L. Pastore (1994). *Sourcebook of Criminal Justice Statistics 1993* (p. 5). Washington, D.C.: U.S. Department of Justice.

Systems of Indigent Defense

Three basic systems of indigent defense can be found in the United States: assigned counsel, contract counsel, and public defenders. Among state court districts in 1992, 23 percent used assigned counsel only, 8 percent used contract counsel only, and 27 percent used the public defender only, while 23 percent had a mix of public defenders and assigned counsel (Bureau of Justice Statistics, 1993:6).

Assigned Counsel. Prior to the *Gideon* decision, most states provided indigent defense through **assigned counsel**. Under this system, private criminal lawyers represent indigent defendants on a case-by-case basis. The presiding judge or magistrate picks a name from a list of attorneys. Sometimes the list includes all attorneys practicing before the court, sometimes only those lawyers who have volunteered to represent poor defendants. There is no guarantee that the defendant will get an attorney with experience in criminal law. Since most attorneys spend little or no time in the criminal court, the chances are good that a random appointment from such a list will result in the assignment of counsel with much more experience in handling divorce, personal injury, or real estate transactions than in handling criminal cases.

assigned counsel Private lawyers appointed by judges to represent indigent defendants on a case-by-case basis.

Under the volunteer system of assigned counsel, many attorneys on the list will be young and inexperienced, some with no trial experience at all. By taking such cases, young lawyers hope to build experience and develop name recognition around the courthouse and on the street. Established attorneys do not need either, and the fees for handling indigents are little incentive for them to volunteer. Most jurisdictions set fees along a range, depending on the nature of the case. In any case, even at the high end—around $100 an hour—the allowable fees will rarely match those charged by an experienced criminal attorney. And some jurisdictions provide no fees at all, arguing that indigent defense is simply one of an attorney's professional responsibilities. If established criminal attorneys volunteer to be on the list of indigent defense lawyers, it is out of commitment to the principles behind the system, because they are doing the court a "favor" and expect something in return, or because state law or the local court requires it.

The assigned counsel system is subject to abuse as well:

> Most state judges are elected or subject to recall votes. Faced with crowded lists, they have little incentive to . . . ensure that the hundreds of impoverished defendants who pass through their courts . . . are represented by well-paid or zealous lawyers. Judges in Houston, Texas, have repeatedly appointed one local lawyer who is famous for hurrying through trials like "greased lightning" to represent indigent defendants. Ten of his clients have been sentenced to death. During one death-penalty case, he fell asleep on several occasions. Nevertheless, the death sentence was upheld on appeal and the defendant has since been executed. (*The Economist*, April 11, 1998 p. 22).

Running an effective assigned counsel system may sound simple, but it is not. Cases vary considerably in the amount of time and effort they require, and lawyers on the list have widely differing commitments at any given time. In addition, many jurisdictions do not pay for investigators and other support services that are often necessary if an attorney hopes to mount a decent defense. These factors, coupled with the low (or nonexistent) fees and the pressure of other commitments, are strong incentives for quickly pleading clients guilty.

The Contract System. A few counties have adopted a **contract system**, in which private law firms enter into an agreement with the court to provide legal services to indigents. Contract attorneys handle almost 90 percent of all

contract system Private lawyers enter into an agreement with the court to provide legal services to indigents.

indigent cases processed in Seattle, Washington (Hanson and Chapper, 1991). Sometimes contracts specify that members of the firm will be available to assist in the defense or prosecution of cases when there are conflicts of interest, when the caseload gets too high, or when an indigent defendant is facing the death penalty. Usually, contracts run for a specified time or until the allotted money runs out, at which time they may be renegotiated. In some counties, the contract specifies that the private lawyer will handle a certain number of cases on a flat fee-per-case basis. An alternative method is to request bids for a one-year contract, with the contract going to the lowest bidder. This system was used in Mohave County, Arizona, until the Arizona Supreme Court found it to be in violation of the Fifth and Sixth Amendments. This was because it did not take into account the time an attorney is expected to spend with a client, provide for support costs such as investigators and paralegals, or take into account the competence of the attorney or the complexity of a case (Kaplan, Skolnick, and Feeley, 1991:354).

Notwithstanding these challenges, a growing body of evidence suggests that contract systems have advantages over the assigned counsel method of indigent defense: The services offered are more comprehensive, the firm makes a commitment to indigent defense that is ongoing and not sporadic, and both costs and coordination of services are better controlled (Houlden and Balkin, 1985; Spears, 1991). To date, there have been few studies of the growth or extent of contract services, but their popularity has been growing over the years (Bureau of Justice Statistics, 1988; 1996). However, it is estimated that only about 8 percent of counties use a contract system exclusively.

The Public Defender

public defender A criminal lawyer and state employee who represents indigent defendants.

Today, the office of public defender is the major system of indigent defense in the United States. The **public defender** is an attorney employee of the county, state, or federal government who is assigned exclusively to indigent defense.

In small counties with small criminal caseloads, the office of public defender may consist of only one full-time attorney and a single legal secretary with perhaps a part-time clerk. In large urban counties and large cities where criminal prosecutions run into thousands of felony cases a year, the public defender's office will have a large staff supporting from 50 to over a 100 full-time lawyers. The Cook County, Illinois, public defender's office is the largest law firm in the state, with over 250 employees.

In most states the public defender's office is administered at the county level, though some states such as New Jersey and Colorado have a statewide administrative and funding structure. All public defender systems are regulated by statute, however, with each state legislature determining the characteristics and responsibilities of the office, whether it is administered at the county or state level. Most states provide some portion of the funding, and a few even prohibit counties or municipalities from providing any funds at all, except under extreme circumstances. The reason for this is unclear, but may reflect two things: (1) concern that indigent defendants facing prosecution in wealthier counties would receive better services than defendants in poorer counties; and (2) concern that indigent defense financed at the local level would enable local lawyers to control the fee structure, perhaps to their own benefit. State statutes also define who qualifies as an indigent defendant. Table 10.7 shows a sample of the relevant rules for the state of Florida.

The Public Defender at Work. In most jurisdictions, public defenders are full-time criminal attorneys. They quickly become specialists in criminal law and in trial advocacy. Furthermore, because they are salaried state employees, they are evaluated by how efficiently they handle their caseload rather than by the

A public defender, overloaded and overworked, speeding off to another case. Heavy caseloads can prevent public defenders from spending the time needed to mount successful defenses for indigent clients.

Illustration by John Overmyer

outcome of individual cases or the fees they bring to the office—performance measures that are important to attorneys in private practice.

The emphasis on efficiency reflects not only heavy caseloads and budget pressures, but also the interdependency among court officials. The courthouse work group, mentioned earlier in the chapter, is composed of defense counsel, prosecutors, bailiffs, jail personnel, and judges—all of whom must work together in a cooperative and efficient manner. Anything that undermines the smooth operation of the courthouse is frowned upon, as one young public defender discovered when he decided to take many of his cases to trial rather than negotiate a plea. The chief justice of his state called him in and "read him the riot act" for not cooperating with the prosecution and the bench (Chambliss and Siedman, 1971:402). Public defenders cannot forget that they are paid by the government. This fact puts them in an odd situation, considering that their job is to defend clients whom their employer prosecutes. They are sworn to do their best for their clients, but they are paid by their judicial adversary.

The Defendant's View of the Public Defender. Streetwise defendants know all about these negative aspects of the public defender's status and role. "Did you have a lawyer when you went to court? No, I had a public defender" sums up the view from the street. One well-researched study of the defendant's perspective found that few clients had positive feelings about their experiences at the hands of their public defender (Casper, 1972). Most said they typically met their public defender in the court hallway or jail lockup for five or ten minutes of hushed conversation, and among the first words uttered were: "I can get you ________ if you plead guilty."

The public defender is seen as an agent of the state in cahoots with the prosecutor. In the words of two defendants:

TABLE 10.7 Rules Governing Indigent Defense in the State of Florida

The criminal procedure laws of each state establish the requirements and responsibilities of public defense of the indigent. The specific legal provisions vary from state to state. Here is an example from the state of Florida.

Public Defender

- Each circuit court is required to employ a Public Defender who is elected by popular vote and serves for a term of four years.
- The Public Defender represents all indigent defendants who are arrested and charged with a felony or a misdemeanor which carries a possible prison term. The Public Defender also represents indigents who are threatened with involuntarily classification as mentally ill or involuntary admission to a residential facility for the mentally disabled.
- The Public Defender is not allowed to engage in private law practice while in office.
- The Public Defender's office shall be able to access and counsel all incarcerated persons at all times. However, these same provisions do not apply to private counsel.

Determination of Indigence

- Defendants are required to request the court to classify them as indigent.
- Defendants are considered indigent if they are unable to pay for the services of an attorney (including costs of investigation), "without substantial hardship to self or family."
- A defendant is not indigent if: (1) the defendant has been released on $5,000 bail or more, or (2) if personal income exceeds $100/week (plus $20/week for two dependents and $10/week for each additional dependent), or (3) if the defendant owns cash in excess of $500.
- Parents or legal guardians who are not indigent are responsible for providing counsel to delinquents. However, if parents or guardians fail to do so, the court may appoint legal counsel.
- Should the court learn within one year that the classification of indigence was improper, the state may try to recover the cost of legal services from the defendant.

Source: Florida State Statutes (1993), Chapter 27.

> A public defender is just like the prosecutor's assistant. Anything you tell this man, he's not gonna do anything but relay it back to the . . . [prosecutor]; they'll come to some sort of agreement, and that's the best you're gonna get. You know whatever they come to and he brings you back the first time, well, you better accept it because you may get more [time].
>
> He just playing a middle game. You know, you're the public defender, now you don't care what happen to me, really. You don't know me, and I don't know you; this is your job, that's all; so you're gonna go up there and say a little bit, make it look like you're trying to help me, but actually you don't give a damn. (Casper, 1972:106–108)

Positive and Negative Aspects of Being a Public Defender. The feelings of frustration and resignation seen in these comments are widespread according to the many attorneys and defendants I have spoken with over the years. Yet are the criticisms leveled against public defenders fair? We have noted some of the drawbacks of the public defender system, but there are also positive aspects that should be noted. The fact that public defenders specialize in criminal law is one; they know the law, they know how it is practiced, they usually know their adversary well, and they know how different judges are likely to react in given situations. They also know the deals that will fly and those that won't. This is a crucial aspect of the art of negotiation, which in most cases is how

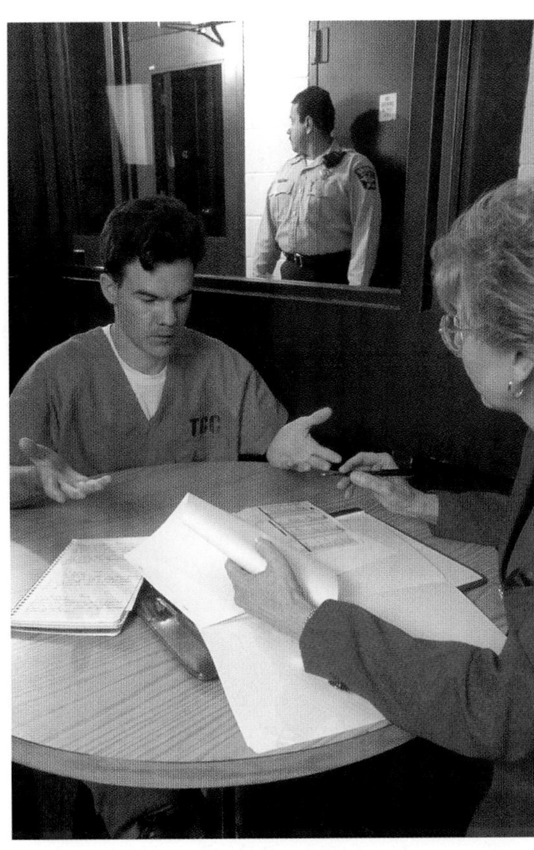

One of the negative aspects of being a criminal defense attorney is having clients who are skeptical, ungrateful, and untruthful. On the other hand, defendants often feel that defense attorneys do not spend adequate time on them, or that they are in league with the prosecution and the judge.

© BOB DAEMMRICH/ THE IMAGE WORKS

criminal cases are settled. Chapter 11 looks at plea bargaining in detail; for now, consider that competent defense attorneys look for the best outcome for their clients, and this usually means getting the lightest possible sentence. Box 10.2 shows us how one veteran public defender views his job and his clients.

For their part, defendants are often distrustful, ungrateful, and not above lying to their attorney. Their past experiences with public defenders may have something to do with this, but it is hardly helpful to their cause. This is another of the unpleasant aspects of the public defender's job—and a reason some lawyers give for quitting the job (Platt and Pollock, 1974). Given the facts of a case—for example, the seriousness of the charge, the nature of the evidence, the presence of witnesses, and the defendant's prior record—competent public defenders must warn often hostile clients that they stand a good chance of going to prison. This bad news is unlikely to go down well, even if the client knows it to be true. When an attorney who knows the score starts talking prison time, the sensible defendant starts thinking "how long" rather than about getting off. To reach this point, where both lawyer and defendant are thinking along the same lines, requires skillful manipulation by the public defender. In the end, the defendant does not have to accept the advice of counsel, but most will because a frail bond of trust has been established.

The difficulties faced by indigent defendants and their public defenders are reinforced in both the dynamics and the bureaucracy of courthouse justice. If you cannot afford a lawyer, you often cannot afford bail either; you come into the courtroom at a disadvantage from the beginning, and everyone knows it. The representative of the public defender's office—overworked, underpaid, and low in status—has probably had little time to investigate and prepare the case, and everyone knows that too. All the players anticipate a deal, and nine times out of ten they get it. The hardest-working, most competent public defender must eventually succumb to this reality.

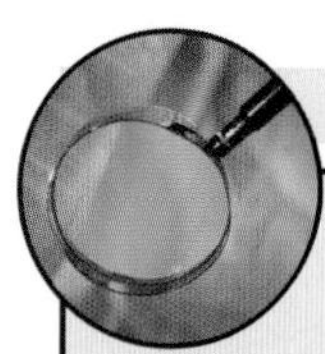

Box 10.2

INSIDE CRIMINAL JUSTICE

A PUBLIC DEFENDER REFLECTS ON HIS JOB AND HIS CLIENTS

A ten-year veteran of the public defender's office, Billy Hahs has done it all. Right after law school he assisted in a death penalty case; since then his clients have included shoplifters, burglars, drug traffickers, robbers, child molesters, murderers, con artists, and rapists. Currently, he handles only felony defendants.

Hahs began his career in 1988 as an assistant public defender in Spartanburg, South Carolina. In South Carolina cases were assigned randomly, so a defendant facing life in prison might find himself assigned to a young, inexperienced public defender. The typical workload was 300 open cases at any one time. Hahs usually met the client in the courtroom at docket call; they would have ten to fifteen minutes to talk. He always read the file before meeting this client, but sometimes only minutes before while walking down the corridor. Many young lawyers cycled through the office, most on their way to private practice. Few showed any commitment to public defense.

Hahs now works in Madison County, Illinois, where his caseload is 25 to 50 open cases. "To do them right keeps me busy five days a week, and I take files home almost every evening." He sees criminals as "astonishingly unsuccessful, poor people, many with addictions. Their crimes are spur-of-the-moment, and most are very sorry for what they have done. They see themselves as flawed and their own worst enemy. It's rare that I don't feel empathy for the defendant, weighing what they did against what the state is getting ready to do to them."

He never asks his clients whether they committed the crime. "They are usually guilty of something, but often not the actual crime they are charged with." Prosecutors overcharge from the beginning because it gives them leverage in making deals, Hahs says, and a prior record always raises the stakes. "It is the single most important issue in plea negotiations. A person with previous prison time is going to go back; the only question is, for how long?"

Hahs spends most of the day negotiating plea bargains. "A prosecutor will say 'Okay, your client committed this armed robbery,' and I say, 'Okay,

SUMMARY

When suspects enter the court system for processing as criminal defendants, they find that many of the most important decisions affecting them are in the hands of lawyers—defense attorneys, prosecutors, and judges. Prosecutors represent the interests of the state, while defense attorneys represent the interests of the person charged with a crime. If the case gets to trial—and most do not—prosecution and defense are pitted against each other in a contest to see who can persuade the judge or jury to accept their representation of the facts.

The legal profession is stratified, as are the law schools that train its members. On the whole, criminal attorneys are underappreciated and underpaid for their work. Law schools tend to discourage criminal practice, offering few relevant courses. The typical criminal attorney works alone or in a small firm, and often has a diversified practice, handling divorces, wills, real estate, and other civil matters as well as criminal cases.

Box 10.2 (continued)

let's look at his life and circumstances.' This is what I negotiate every day. I never want my clients in prison, and as their advocate I try my hardest to keep them out. I make the deal, not my clients, and this is why they have to trust me. It's their life, but I am the one doing the negotiating. I get the best deal I can." Sometimes a deal ends in probation instead of a prison term; at other times a deal shaves years off the sentence the client would have received if convicted at trial. Good deals are difficult to make if the police have put in a bad word against the defendant, such as "We want him off the street."

Out of every 100 cases Hahs handles, only two or three go to trial. He has tried trivial cases for days because he knew the client was innocent. "Some I won, some I didn't." Some defendants insist on going to trial, which is generally very risky. "The system exacts a terrible penalty for those who insist on going to trial and end up being convicted. I've known clients who turned down probation and got natural life in prison. In ten years I can think of only one case I tried and lost and the defendant didn't get the maximum." The word soon gets around the jailhouse, and in Illinois Hahs has found that few clients talk about trials.

Hahs finds that his best allies in working up a case are jailers. "They come from the same background as the police, but whereas the police uniformly despise my clients, the jailers will call me up and say that so-and-so looks stressed, or if there is a favor I need, the jailers will do it. They deal with them day in and day out, and come to know them as human beings, just like the rest of us."

What would Hahs tell a criminal justice student thinking about a career as a public defender? "Let's walk over to the jail and meet some of these folks, and you will see what this job is all about. Like teachers, we make a difference in people's lives. The job is high stress but very rewarding. People who do this for any length of time are committed to it. Public defenders believe passionately that they are the thin line between the rule of law and an unwitting slide into a police state. The willingness of public defenders to stay in a low-pay, high-stress job is critical to the survival of the American constitutional system."

Source: Billy Hahs, personal interview, August 1998.

Before 1963, many poor felony defendants were not represented by counsel because they could not afford a lawyer. This situation had been unsuccessfully challenged on a number of occasions as a violation of the right to counsel guaranteed by the Sixth Amendment. In 1963, however, the U.S. Supreme Court ruled in *Gideon v. Wainwright* that all felony defendants have the right to counsel whether they can afford it or not, and this right was subsequently extended to misdemeanor defendants sentenced to imprisonment. These rulings required states to provide counsel for indigent defendants, resulting in three systems of indigent defense: assigned counsel, contract counsel, and the public defender, which is the most common one.

Chief prosecutors are usually elected employees of a county, but their duties include any legal matters in which the state is a party. Prosecutors are the most powerful members of the courthouse work group, for they decide most matters related to charging defendants, and therefore have a major hand in determining sentences. The typical prosecutor runs a small office of eight staff members, although large counties employ dozens of assistant prosecutors. As changing social conditions have given rise to new crime problems, prosecution has of necessity become more specialized, especially in large counties. Like their counterparts in public defense, assistant prosecutors often move into private practice after a few years, as specialists in criminal law. Many chief prosecutors eventually become judges or move to higher political office.

Chief public defenders are generally elected employees of a county who are assigned exclusively to indigent defense. In larger counties they have assistants who handle the bulk of felonies and misdemeanors. These assistants are often inexperienced young attorneys just out of law school. Many move on to private practice after a few years, taking their experience and connections with them. In larger counties, the workload is heavy and there is an emphasis on efficient disposal of cases. Defendants are often distrustful of their public defender, although experienced public defenders have far more trial experience than their private counterparts, and they know how the system works.

WHAT DO YOU THINK NOW?

- Based on what you know now about criminal lawyers and prosecutors, how do you feel about their jobs? Have your views changed?
- What could be done to improve minority representation in the legal profession?
- Why do criminal lawyers and prosecutors appear to have such different levels of status? Do you feel that the criminal lawyer is underappreciated? Why or why not?

KEY TERMS AND CASES

courthouse work group
adversarial process
case method
bar exam
criminal attorney
prosecutor
independent counsel
indigent defendant
right to counsel
Powell v. Alabama
Betts v. Brady
Gideon v. Wainwright
Argersinger v. Hamlin
Scott v. Illinois
assigned counsel
contract system
public defender

ACTIVE LEARNING CHALLENGES

1. Invite a local prosecutor and a defense attorney into class to discuss their roles and responsibilities, and how they interact as part of the courthouse work group.
2. Discuss the benefits and drawbacks of the three major systems of indigent defense. If you were in need of an attorney and could not afford one, which system would you prefer?
3. *Gideon v. Wainwright* was only one of the notable due process decisions of the Warren Court. Divide into small groups and have each group research a different decision bearing on defendant rights from the Warren Court. What was the case about? What were the important prior Supreme Court decisions that paved the way for this one? What was the core argument of the majority, and of the dissenting justice(s)? Has the decision been weakened or strengthened by more recent cases?

4. Find out if there are any special prosecution units in your area. How long have they been in place? How many cases have they handled? Which cases do they regard as most significant? Will they continue in operation? If not, why not?

INTERNET CHALLENGES

The Web pages mentioned here can all be accessed through the Web site for this textbook at **http://www.prenhall.com/barlow/**.

1. Many sites on the Internet deal with the practice of law. Visit Law World site for an interesting tour of law in the USA and abroad. Follow the link marked "International" and find two or three examples of how the practice of law differs around the world.
2. The American Bar Association is the national organization representing lawyers in the United States; the National Association of Criminal Defense Lawyers is a more specialized organization of lawyers. For the latest developments in trial law and criminal defense check the Web sites of the ABA's Criminal Justice Section and the NACDL. What do you learn about the interests and goals of these legal associations?
3. The Southern Poverty Law Center, co-founded by attorney Morris Dees, is a leader in the fight for legal rights for minorities and poor people. The center has represented clients in many pioneering cases. Look for their recent legal activities at the center's home page. What recent cases dealing with constitutional issues has the SPLC handled? What are some of its landmark cases? Recalling the discussion of hate crime in Chapter 8, what new developments in this area does the SPLC report?

CHAPTER 11

PRE-TRIAL DECISIONS IN THE JUDICIAL PROCESS

LEARNING OBJECTIVES

- Understand what happens to felony suspects from the time of arrest until their case is dismissed, is disposed of through a guilty plea, or comes to trial.
- Explain why some suspects are released from custody before trial and others are not.
- Distinguish among the various types of pre-trial release.
- Understand the problem of pre-trial offending and describe reforms designed to curb it.
- Understand the factors that influence prosecutors in their decisions to proceed or not to proceed with prosecution.
- Describe how the victims' role in prosecution is changing.
- Explain the benefits and costs of plea bargaining for the criminal justice system as a whole and for defendants, prosecutors, defense attorneys, judges, and victims.

Financial release, or bail, is a common form of pretrial release. Often defendants need only post 10% of the bail's cash amount, or they can hire a bail bonds company to post a surety bond. Either way, the defendant can avoid jail time.

PHOTO BY RICK FRIEDMAN, COURTESY OF BLACK STAR

American liberty is premised on the accountability of free men and women for what they have done, not for what they may do.

JON NEWMAN, JUDGE, U.S. COURT OF APPEALS

Plea bargaining, when properly administered, is to be encouraged.

SUPREME COURT, STATE OF ILLINOIS

As she walked from her office to the courthouse, assistant prosecutor Marjorie Stevens was thinking about a comment one of her fellow prosecutors had made earlier that day. Many criminal cases are won or lost, he had said, because of decisions made early in the prosecution process. Stevens had agreed with him, pointing out that pre-trial decisions could significantly affect not only the fortunes of a defendant but those of the community as well. Now she was remembering times when she had not contested the release of clients pending trial, only to have the defendants commit a serious crime such as robbery while free on bail. She knew what the problem was: It is virtually impossible to predict who will pose a danger to the community if released, yet it is neither practical nor fair to keep all suspects in jail.

Plea bargaining was another problem. Personally, Stevens disliked bargaining because defendants usually ended up with a lighter sentence than they deserved, but she was resigned to its importance for an overburdened system that cannot try everyone nor imprison all those offenders whose crimes justify it. Stevens had long since made herself a promise that any deal she approved would always be in the best interests of the state. Nevertheless she had found it a difficult promise to keep.

As Stevens mulled over these problems, she thought of the crime victim, long forgotten in the criminal justice system. Nowadays, the victims of crime are being given more influence, even to the point of participating in plea negotiations and sentencing hearings. Stevens thought that was a good thing, even if it allowed the emotions and personal agendas of victims to become part of judicial decision making. Crime victims had a right to be heard, she believed, because they were the ones most directly affected by the offender's actions.

Stevens pushed open the door to the judge's chambers, clearing her head of these thoughts. She sat down with a nod to the defense attorney and a smile to the judge. "Okay, everyone," the judge began, "have you two reached an agreement or is this case going to trial?"

The daily responsibility facing prosecutors like Marjorie Stevens, as well as judges and defense attorneys, consists of making important decisions so that the judicial process can be completed and a defendant released from the court's authority or passed on for punishment. As we know from previous chapters, the most important pre-trial decisions concern (1) a suspect's release pending trial, (2) prosecution and the determination of formal charges, and (3) plea negotiations. Lawyers are the major players in all these decisions; defendants and victims have relatively minor roles.

? WHAT DO YOU THINK?

- Do you think that most criminal suspects pose a threat to society if released pending trial? Why or why not?
- What are the chances that a felony case will be tried in court, rather than plea bargained?
- What are the state's interests when prosecuting criminal defendants? How can prosecutor Stevens try to protect those interests during plea bargaining?

PRE-TRIAL RELEASE

Within a reasonable time after arrest—usually no more than 48 hours—suspects must be given the opportunity to apply for release from custody, pending future proceedings against them. In most felony situations, defense counsel formally requests a judge or magistrate to grant release during the defendant's **initial appearance** in court. Suspects arrested on misdemeanor charges or for violations of local ordinances are usually released by the police. Sometimes a standard form is used that has been pre-signed by a judge.

initial appearance A defendant's first appearance in court after arrest; usually involves a bail hearing in felony cases.

TYPES OF PRE-TRIAL RELEASE

There are various types of pre-trial release, depending on the circumstances of the case and the laws of the jurisdiction in which the court sits. These are summarized in Table 11.1. **Financial releases** involve the payment or promise of payment of money or property. The most commonly used are deposit bonds, where defendants pay 10 to 20 percent of the full amount of the bail. *Bail* is the term for financial releases, but it is commonly used to cover almost any kind of pre-trial release. **Nonfinancial releases** involve no money or property, and are instead based on threats of what will happen if defendants fail to appear when their case is scheduled in court. Figure 11.1 shows that the most common form of nonfinancial release of felony defendants is **release on recognizance**, where defendants merely promise to appear in court as required.

financial release Defendants are released from jail after payment or promise of payment of money or property, called *bail*.

nonfinancial release Defendants are released from jail without having to put up bail.

release on recognizance A nonfinancial release in which the defendant promises to appear in court as required.

Thousands of release decisions are made every day in the United States. In fact, most criminal defendants are released—many without ever having seen a judge or magistrate. If a financial bond is required, the amount is determined according to a schedule set by the courts. The process is quite simple: The desk sergeant or booking officer merely fills out a release order previously signed by a magistrate or judge. The order usually includes a court appearance date. If a money bond is required, the suspect is rarely required to put up the full amount; most jurisdictions require defendants to put up 10 percent of the full amount. Box 11.1 describes the work of the bail bond companies that operate in some states and provide defendants the bond amount in exchange for a fee.

The pre-trial release decision is an important one for the defendant, and also for the community. For the defendant it means the difference between free-

TABLE 11.1 Types of Pre-trial Release

There are a number of different mechanisms for gaining pre-trial release. They can be broadly categorized into financial and non-financial releases.

FINANCIAL RELEASE	DESCRIPTION	NONFINANCIAL RELEASE	DESCRIPTION
Full cash bond	The defendant posts the full amount of bail in cash. The cash is returned only if the defendant makes all required court appearances.	*Unsecured bond*	The defendant pays no money but is liable for the full amount of bail if a court appearance is missed.
Deposit bond	The defendant posts a percentage (commonly 10 percent) of the full bail amount in cash. The cash is returned (often minus processing fees) when the case is disposed of. Failure to appear makes the defendant liable for the full amount.	*Release on recognizance*	The court releases the defendant on the promise of appearance in court as required. Failure to appear may result in the issuing of an arrest warrant (as with all other types of pre-trial release), but the defendant faces no criminal penalty.
Surety bond	A bail bond company promises to pay the court the full amount if the defendant fails to appear. The defendant is charged a fee for this service (commonly 10 percent of the full bail). The bail bond company buys insurance to protect itself against heavy losses.	*Citation release*	This commonly occurs in traffic situations. When the police issue a ticket, they are in effect arresting and releasing the suspected offender. The ticket usually includes a court date, should the suspect plead not guilty. During the 1970s, a number of cities used citation releases for minor drug offenses.
Property bond or collateral bond	The defendant puts up property, usually real estate, valued at the full bail amount. The property is forfeited if the defendant fails to appear.	*Conditional release or supervised release*	Defendants are released under specified conditions; compliance is usually monitored by a pre-trial service agency.
		Emergency release	This usually occurs in response to a court order that has placed limits on jail populations. There is nowhere to house additional defendants while they await the disposition of their case.

dom and jail while the case winds its way through the system, perhaps taking months if not years. For the community it may mean the difference between security and endangerment.

What Happens If You Don't Make Bail? Regardless of their actual innocence or guilt of the crime(s) they are arrested for, all suspects are technically innocent unless they plead guilty or are convicted. Well over half of all jail inhabitants are innocent in this sense. Most are there because they couldn't make bail. Defendants who cannot afford bail are punished for their lack of financial resources in a variety of ways: They are deprived of freedom; many find themselves in overcrowded and understaffed jails; young suspects or those accused of sex crimes are in danger of being assaulted by other inmates; they are deprived of supportive social relationships; they lose the advantages of freedom when preparing their defense; they are often forced to spend hours, days, and even months in the company of strangers and people they might ordinarily

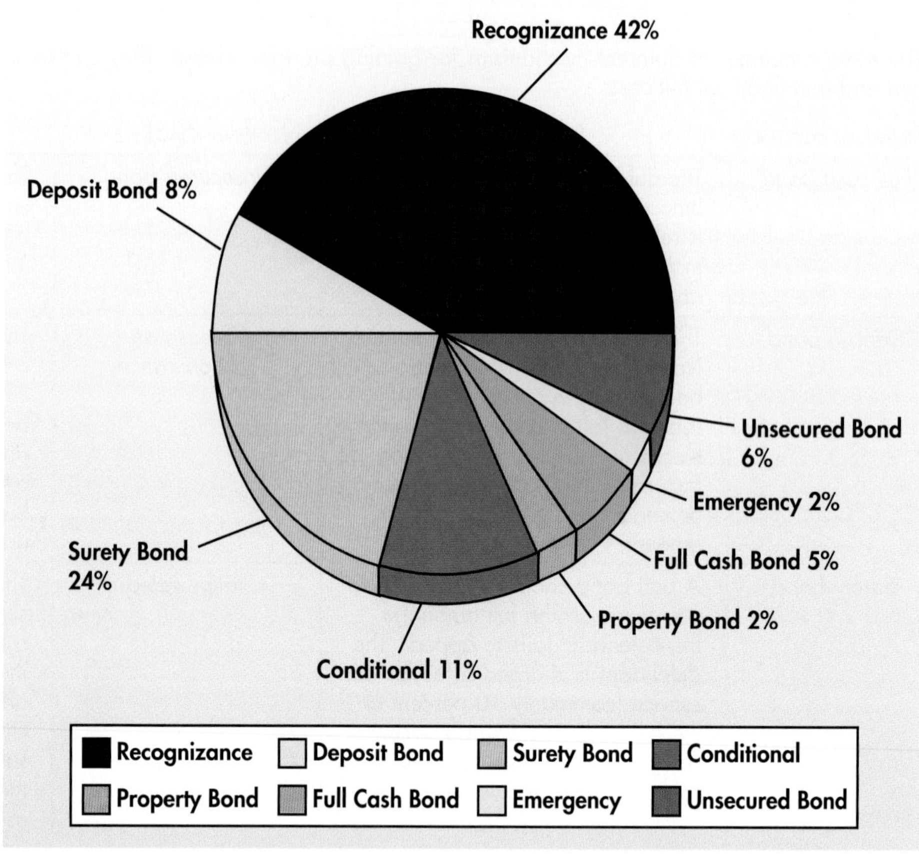

FIGURE 11.1 TYPES OF PRE-TRIAL RELEASE, 1994
Release on one's own recognizance is the most common form of pre-trial release. This graph gives a visual look at some of the many types of pre-trial release for felony defendants in the 75 largest U.S. counties.

Source: Brian A. Reaves (1998b). *Felony Defendants in Large Urban Courts, 1994* (p. 17). Washington, D.C.: U.S. Department of Justice.

avoid; they are forced to follow a regimented daily routine that strips them of ordinary decision-making opportunities and undermines their identities; they are deprived of their privacy. Defendants who are detained before trial are more likely to be convicted (Reaves, 1998b:24). In addition, national surveys have found that suspects detained until case disposition are twice as likely to go to prison if convicted. This is true regardless of their offense (Reaves, 1992; Reaves and Perez, 1994).

DO DEFENDANTS HAVE A RIGHT TO BAIL?

People commonly speak of a constitutional "right to bail," but legal scholars have hotly debated whether there is actually any such thing. The U.S. Constitution does not designate bail as a right, but some experts believe that such a right is implied by the Eighth Amendment (Gottfredson and Gottfredson, 1988:88–89). Federal laws of criminal procedure have held since at least 1789 that defendants charged with crimes not involving the death penalty shall be allowed bail if they provide adequate assurance that they will appear in court. So argued Chief Justice Vinson of the U.S. Supreme Court in ***Stack v. Boyle*** (1951). Justice Vinson also wrote that the practice of requiring a forfeitable financial bond before release "serves as additional assurance of the presence of an accused."

Stack v. Boyle Defendants should be allowed bail if there is adequate assurance that they will appear in court.

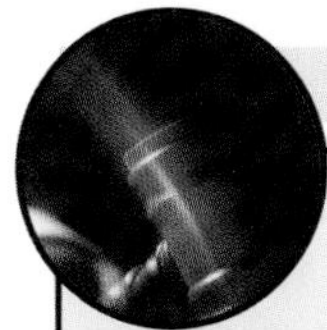

Box 11.1

JUSTICE PROFESSIONALS AT WORK

THE BAIL BOND COMPANY

Most states allow bail bond companies to guarantee the full bail amount should a defendant fail to appear in court. (Illinois, Wisconsin, Kentucky, Oregon, and Nebraska are among those that do not permit the practice.) The bonding company provides a surety bond in exchange for a fee, usually 10 to 15 percent of the bail amount. In some states, bonding companies are allowed to hunt down and bring back defendants who have fled, and some hire professional "bounty hunters" to do the job.

Bonding companies are generally small operations run out of homes or modest offices located near the courthouse. Some companies share offices with lawyers, bringing each other work. Bondsmen—which women are also called—find much of their business through referrals by police, lawyers, and even judges. They are included in the courthouse work group, and successful bondsmen make sure they are on good terms with the other members. Because they help get defendants out of jail pending trial, they help relieve congestion in the jail and courthouse, while also benefiting defendants.

Bail bond companies have endured a lot of criticism, deserved by at least some of them. The main complaints are accusations of corruption. But corruption involves both a corrupter and a corruptee, so other courthouse players bear some of the blame. Bonding companies often pay under-the-table "referral fees" to lawyers, police, and even judges who send business their way. In most states these fees are illegal. One reason is that they easily turn into kickbacks for favors that involve bending the law. For example, a judge may set bail in all cases, regardless of seriousness; or a prosecutor may refrain from pressing for preventive detention. These illegal practices appear to have diminished in recent years, partly as a result of bail reforms and partly because of declining profit margins for bonding companies.

Sources: Malcolm M. Feeley (1979). *The Process Is the Punishment* (pp. 97–108). New York: Russell Sage Foundation; Paul B. Wice (1974). "Purveyors of Freedom: The Professional Bondsmen." *Transaction* (July/August) pp. 21–23; D. Alan Henry and Bruce D. Beaudin (1990). "Bail Bondsmen." *American Jails* 4:8–16.

Here is where the Eighth Amendment clearly does come in. It begins "Excessive bail shall not be required. . . ." When bail is set at a figure higher than that reasonably calculated to assure the presence of an accused, then the figure is excessive, according to Chief Justice Vinson. Unfortunately, applying this idea in practice is no easy matter. How is a judge supposed to know exactly what amount is sufficient to assure that the accused will appear in court? The ability to pay varies widely among defendants: Many cannot afford even a modest bail amount, while some suspects—particularly high-level drug dealers and organized crime figures—have access to millions. In actuality, many criminal suspects cannot even raise the bonding fee. According to one national study, five of every six suspects detained in jails would have been released if they had come up with the necessary money (Reaves, 1998b:16).

Two Important Bail Reforms

Throughout most of the 20th century, bail decisions have been largely on-the-spot determinations in which prosecutors and judges had considerable discretion. Even with the recommendations of police, prosecution, and probation officials, the final decision was often not well informed (Gottfredson and Gottfredson, 1988:87). Judges rarely learned what happened to defendants they had released, and little effort was made to learn how other judges in the same circuit made their bail decisions. Many courtroom observers felt that the system needed tightening up. In addition, the argument that a money bail system is inherently unfair to indigent defendants continued to surface, gaining strength in the 1960s as the civil rights movement grew and America entered a period of critical self-examination. Two important bail reform acts were eventually passed by Congress.

The Bail Reform Act of 1966. The 1966 Bail Reform Act leaned in favor of releasing defendants, either on a simple promise to return to court—release on recognizance—or else under the least restrictive conditions possible—for example, a 10 percent cash bond. The popularity of release on recognizance (or ROR) can be traced to the **Manhattan Bail Project**, run by the Vera Institute of Justice in New York City during the 1960s. The project was inspired by the observation that a money bail system is fundamentally unfair to poor defendants because it virtually guarantees they will be detained pending trial—something non-indigent defendants can avoid. As part of the project, local law students interviewed defendants before their initial appearance in court. The students were looking for evidence of community ties—for example, residential stability, a steady employment history, family in New York City—that researchers believed would reduce the risk of defendants failing to appear in court. Suspects charged with murder, rape, and robbery and those with extensive prior criminal histories were excluded. Over 10,000 eligible defendants were interviewed in a three-year period. Of the more than 2,000 accepted for ROR, less than 1 percent failed to appear in court—a success rate of 99 percent (Freed and Wald, 1964; Ares, Rankin, and Sturz, 1963). The project's findings were hailed as proof that most defendants could be released on their word and they would return to court. Within a year or two many other jurisdictions had made release on recognizance a significant part of their pre-trial options, and by the late 1970s over 120 ROR programs were in operation (Eskridge, 1983). Today, virtually all jurisdictions have some form of ROR among their pre-trial release alternatives.

Manhattan Bail Project
A program in New York City during the 1960s showing that most defendants could be released on a simple promise to return to court as required.

The 1984 Bail Reform Act. The 1984 Act retained ROR as a key alternative for all bailable suspects and mandated that no federal defendants should be detained in jail simply because they cannot afford bail money. However, the act also authorized denial of bail for various classes of defendants. For example, bail would now be denied to defendants charged with violent crimes involving firearms, drug offenses carrying a prison sentence of ten years or more, and capital crimes or offenses carrying the possibility of life in prison, and to defendants on parole or pre-trial release when arrested. The idea behind these distinctions is that danger to community safety, as well as nonappearance, should be addressed as part of the bail decision. Although the 1984 Bail Reform Act directly affected only federal offenders, many states soon came up with similar reforms.

The Prosecutor Has the Most Power in Bail Decisions. Today, bail decision making is largely under the control of the prosecuting attorney. Magistrates and judges look to the district attorney for guidance in making decisions about pre-trial release, and generally place greater weight on the recommendations of the DA than on the requests of defense counsel. Even when judges and prosecuting attorneys disagree, the prosecutors can still have their way simply by manipulating the charges. If the law calls for mandatory pre-trial detention when suspects are charged with certain offenses, a DA can charge a lesser offense, or the most serious one, leaving the judge little discretion.

WHO IS RELEASED AND WHO ISN'T?

In both state and federal courts, close to two-thirds of all felony defendants are released prior to final disposition of the charges. This figure includes many burglary and robbery suspects, and also people arrested on suspicion of weapons offenses, child molesting, and selling drugs. Over half of these felony suspects are released within one day of their arrest. Not surprisingly, defendants who do not have to post a financial bond are generally released sooner than those who have to put up money or property. As Figure 11.2 shows, the defendants least likely to be released before trial are those charged with murder. In large urban state courts, three out of four murder suspects are detained in jail until final disposition of their cases (Reaves, 1998b). Even so, while nearly half of these murder suspects were ordered held without bail, the remainder would have been released if they could have paid the bond set by the court.

Over the years, one of the most important factors determining who gets released and who doesn't is concern about the safety of the community into which a suspect is released. The accumulated evidence from national studies (e.g., Reaves, 1994; 1998b) shows that defendants with the following characteristics are least likely to be granted bail:

- Those charged with violent offenses
- Those who are on parole, probation, or pre-trial release when arrested
- Those with a history of prior court appearances
- Those who have prior convictions in state or federal courts

These findings are based on the experiences of almost 150,000 felony defendants in state and federal courts during the early 1990s. They show decision making that is influenced by the prior criminal justice experience of defendants

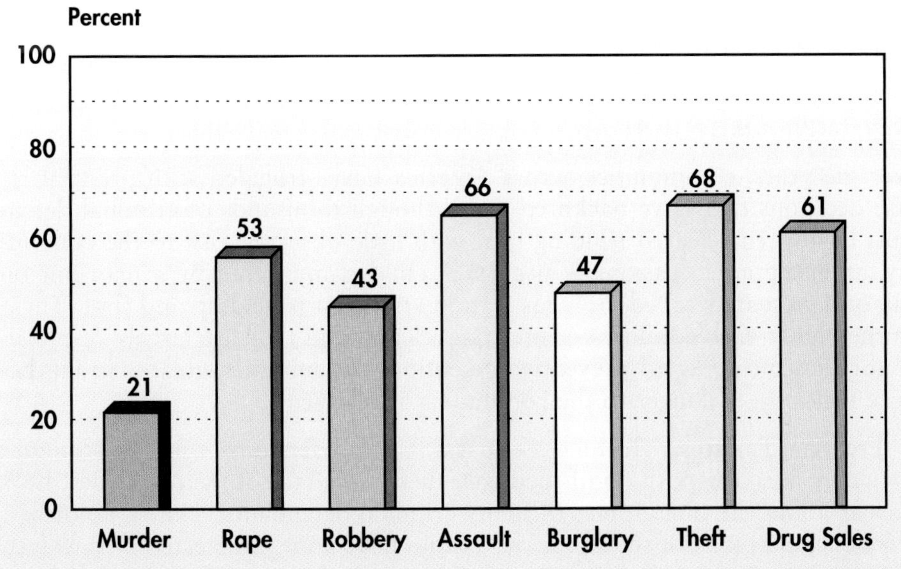

FIGURE 11.2 PERCENT OF STATE FELONY DEFENDANTS RELEASED BEFORE TRIAL, 1994

Most people charged with felonies are released pending trial. However, murder suspects are much less likely to be released. These figures are for defendants in the 75 largest U.S. counties.

Source: Brian A. Reaves (1998b). Felony Defendants in Large Urban Counties 1994 (p. 16). Washington D.C.: U.S. Department of Justice.

Some high-risk suspects are ineligible for bail.

ILLUSTRATION BY JOHN OVERMYER

and to the seriousness of their current offense. However, keep in mind that significant variations in pre-trial practices can exist within states, and even across two neighboring counties that are subject to the same state laws and have similar experiences with crime.

PREVENTIVE DETENTION AND THE DANGEROUS OFFENDER

Over the years, communities across America have struggled with pre-trial release decisions that have backfired. Even though thousands of criminal defendants have been released pending trial with little observed risk to the community, an exception occasionally occurs. A child is murdered by a man out on bail, or a woman is raped, or a gas station attendant is held up and shot. These are the highly visible failures of pre-trial release, and they are largely responsible for the emergence of **preventive detention**: detaining defendants in jail because they pose a danger to the community if released.

preventive detention Defendants are detained in jail because they are believed to pose a danger to the community if released.

Pre-Trial Failures. To imagine that all such defendants will "go straight" while they await disposition of their case flies in the face of their histories. Let's be clear about the biographies of many criminal defendants: They are not first offenders, and many of their previous crimes have gone undetected or unsolved by the police. Time and again, the courts are asked to consider bail for defendants who have been arrested, charged, and convicted for prior offenses. The National Pretrial Reporting Program, run by the Bureau of Justice Statistics, shows that in 1992 around three in eight felony defendants had an active criminal justice status at the time of their arrest: They were on either probation, parole, or pre-trial release (Reaves and Smith, 1995:8). Two-thirds had been arrested previously, and 36 percent of these had at least five prior arrests. Most had a felony record.

Even so, court officials are faced with a dilemma: Many, if not most, defendants probably will go straight for a while—or at least until the present case is over, and among those who do not, the crimes will probably be petty rather than dangerous. So a judge who does not release a defendant chooses a tough option that probably makes life worse for the defendant—whose guilt has not yet been determined—and does little to improve public safety.

It appears that the best that judges can hope for is to reduce the probability of pre-trial failure. To do this, judges have to be aware of the characteristics and circumstances that are associated with failure. A review of the relevant research (Gottfredson and Gottfredson, 1988:94–99) shows that the probability of crime increases with the following factors:

- The length of time that defendants remain on bail
- The extensiveness of their criminal records
- Their involvement with drugs
- Age—younger defendants are at greater risk
- Employment status—unemployed defendants are at greater risk

Relating these variables to the defendant at hand may help prosecutors and judges reduce the probability of pre-trial failure.

Yet in many jurisdictions, overcrowded jails are forcing judges and jail administrators to release defendants whose current offenses and prior criminal records put them at risk of reoffending while awaiting trial. An extensive study of this problem was undertaken in Cook County, Illinois, with defendants who were released because of jail overcrowding (Morison, 1992). The findings are sobering. A random sample of 2,000 defendants released pending trial were tracked during their time at liberty. If they failed to appear in court as scheduled, if they were arrested for new offenses, or if they were reincarcerated in the county jail, this was considered evidence of pre-trial failure. Around half of the defendants released because of jail overcrowding fell into one or more of these three categories.

This failure rate is among the highest in the country, and it represents a heavy burden for the community. The toll is seen in new crimes—an estimated 1,640 new victimizations for violent and property crimes by the 5,816 defendants released in Cook County during a 70-day period (Morison, 1992). Adding to this toll are the additional criminal justice resources and time needed to process bond forfeitures, arrests, and new jail admissions, and the additional costs associated with them—in excess of $20 million.

It Is Difficult, If Not Impossible, to Predict Dangerousness. Government officials are understandably concerned about the financial and workload costs associated with pre-trial failures. Taxpayers also have a stake in reducing these burdens, but their main concern is the danger to their safety and property posed by the release of defendants who then commit new crimes.

The heart of the problem is accurate prediction of a defendant's dangerousness. When a judge releases a defendant, the decision amounts to a prediction that that person will not pose a danger to the community if released. On the other hand, when a judge detains a suspect without bail, or sets bail beyond the reach of a defendant, this amounts to a prediction that if released, the person *will* pose a danger to the community. Unfortunately, there is very little evidence that either prediction can be made with accuracy for the bulk of felony defendants.

Conventional wisdom is little help in predicting dangerousness. This is illustrated by a study conducted a few years ago (Chaiken and Chaiken, 1991). Believing that a small core of dangerous offenders might be identifiable, researchers distinguished "high-rate dangerous" offending from mere repetitive, or habitual, offending and from periodic crimes of violence (see Figure 11.3).

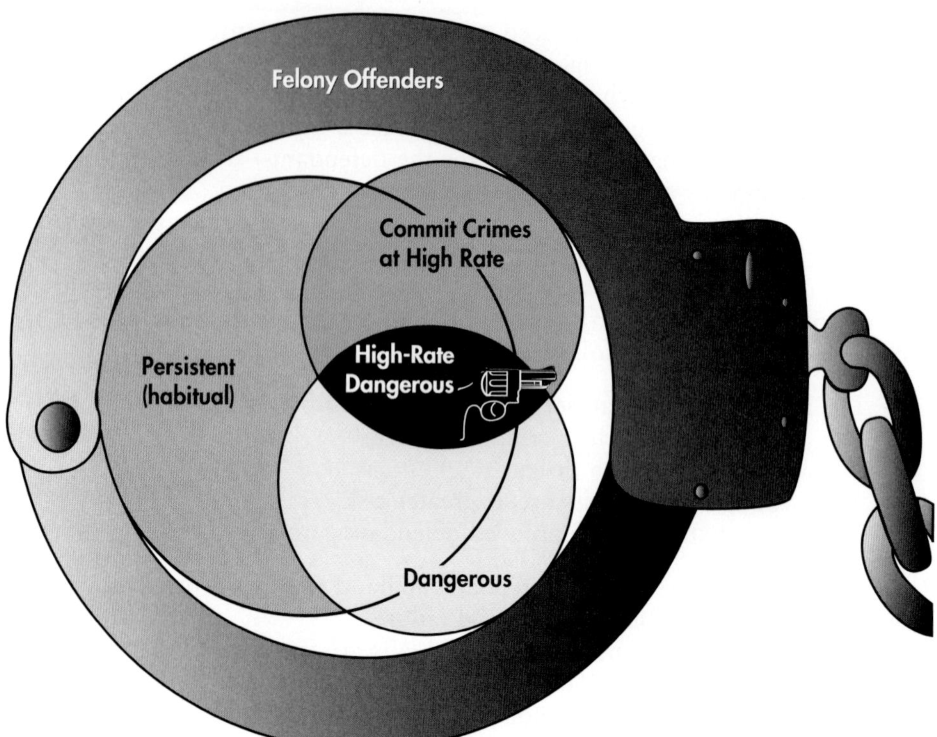

FIGURE 11.3 HIGH-RATE DANGEROUS OFFENDERS: CANDIDATES FOR PREVENTIVE DETENTION?
Persistent felony offenders commit crimes habitually; some persistent offenders commit many crimes over a short period of time; some of these high-rate persistent offenders commit many violent crimes, making them "high-rate dangerous" offenders. These are high-priority candidates for preventive detention.

Source: Marcia R. Chaiken and Jan M. Chaiken (1991). "Priority Prosecution of High-Rate Dangerous Offenders (p. 1)." *NIJ Research in Action* (March).

High-rate dangerous offending is illustrated by offenders who commit combinations of serious felonies over a short period of time. For example, a person who has committed three assaults, two robberies, and a burglary in one month would be considered a high-rate dangerous offender.

Drawing their data from interviews with 452 defendants and official police and court records, the authors found that behaviors conventionally thought to predict dangerousness did not do so in their sample. Thus, displaying or using a gun to threaten a victim, alcoholism, prior arrests for drug distribution or possession, previous imprisonment, previous parole or probation revocation, and previous adult convictions showed *no* association with high-rate dangerous offending. Nor did age at first arrest, race, or employment status.

However, high-rate dangerous offending was more likely under certain other circumstances: when the victim was female; when a knife was used or brandished; when the defendant was wanted for failure to complete a previous sentence; when the current offense was committed in a public place; and when the defendant had one or more juvenile convictions for robbery. It is not at all obvious why this group of factors, and not the first, should predict high-rate dangerous offending. The authors regard their findings as a step toward constructing preventive detention policies, but they stop short of proposing solutions to this controversial problem. Indeed, it is hard to imagine how a useful policy could be constructed out of this array of diverse characteristics and situations.

Some people say that if pre-trial detention can prevent even one predatory or violent act, preventive detention will have served a useful purpose. Other people are concerned that the basis of pretrial detention decisions will be a combination of fear, speculation, stereotypes, and politics. This problem arises because criminal justice authorities have so far been unable to predict accurately which suspects will in fact commit crimes upon release. Failing this ability, suspects are often released if they "look right" and detained if they do not.

Two New Approaches to Pre-Trial Release

Many people recognize that it may be impossible to achieve a truly rational basis for making pre-trial release decisions that are fair to defendants and promise reasonable protection for the public. Nevertheless, two new approaches to pretrial release show promise.

The Judicial Guidelines Approach. Judges in Philadelphia have tried to achieve a rational approach to bail decisions by adopting a set of **bail guidelines** based on an in-depth study of 4,000 release decisions made by their colleagues (Goldkamp and Gottfredson, 1985). The guidelines give judges various release options they can use, from release on recognizance to a high cash bail. These options are weighed against the seriousness of the charges and various characteristics of a defendant, including prior criminal record, community ties, and age. These characteristics are identified as either "positive"—having ties to the community would be positive—or "negative"—such as young age, or prior criminal record.

bail guidelines Standardized instructions to help judges make rational bail decisions based on positive and negative risk factors.

Pre-trial Service Agency staff determine the level of risk and the appropriate charge dimension, and together these produce a guideline bail decision: release on recognizance, low to medium cash bail range, or medium to high cash bail range. Judges may depart from the guideline bail decision, but if they do they must note the reason for departure. Various reasons are listed on a guidelines form that accompanies the case file—for example, a judge might check potential interference with a witness or the mental condition of a defendant as reasons for departing from the guideline decision.

The Philadelphia guidelines make bail decisions both more visible and more equitable because judges can see how each of them treats defendants with similar charges and backgrounds. These important advances in pre-trial decision making benefit both the system and the defendant. Defendants benefit because they are less subject to the whims and biases of officials grinding their own axes; the system benefits because information sharing and goal-directed collaboration are the hallmarks of rational decision making, and because defendants who perceive their treatment as open and fair are more likely to cooperate with authorities. Unfortunately, what is not yet established is whether the guidelines approach really improves the predictive accuracy of bail decisions.

Pre-Trial Intensive Supervision—An Answer to Pre-Trial Offending and Jail Overcrowding? In response to jail overcrowding and rising fears about releasing criminals into the community, the Vera Institute recently experimented with a new model of **pre-trial intensive supervision** (Vera Institute of Justice, 1995). Pre-trial intensive supervision places released defendants under the close monitoring of a probation officer. The model is designed to conserve jail resources, prevent pre-trial offending, and assure that defendants do not evade justice.

pre-trial intensive supervision Released defendants are closely monitored by a probation officer.

The experiment was conducted in two New York counties—Essex and Nassau—and the Bronx. It targeted defendants who were bailable but would have been kept in jail for at least 90 days. The defendants were supervised by Vera staff on a daily basis. Drug and alcohol use was restricted; participation in education, employment, or drug programs was required; and the defendants' whereabouts were monitored constantly. People who violated the conditions of their release were subject to even more restrictive supervision or were returned

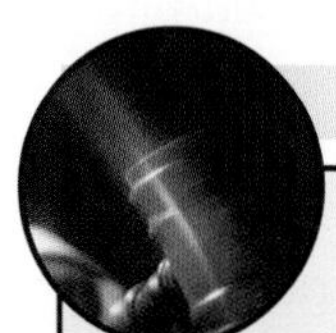

Box 11.2

JUSTICE PROFESSIONALS AT WORK

PRE-TRIAL INTENSIVE SUPERVISION

The Vera Institute of New York has established a program of pre-trial intensive supervision in which released defendants are closely monitored by Vera staff. Here is an account from the daily log of two staff members.

Day Shift

7 A.M. Report to the office; read night shift log.

8 A.M. Visit Mark M. and Yolanda S. at home because they violated yesterday evening's curfew. Impose earlier curfew.

10 A.M. Return to the office. Telephone participants to verify their presence on the job or at service program sites.

11 A.M. Call Rick L. at home because he's absent from work. He seems to be high again.

12 P.M. Go to Rick's house. Convince him to return to the residential treatment facility.

1 P.M. Admit Rick to the residential facility.

2 P.M. Meet Jamie E. at court. Give judge progress report on Jamie's performance.

4 P.M. Return to office and sign out for day.

Night Shift

4 P.M. Report to the office and read day log. Drive to the jail to wait for two new participants to be released.

6 P.M. Transport new participants Lawrence A. and Regina S. to the residential facility.

7 P.M. Wait while they are admitted.

8 P.M. Visit Paul A. and Danny W. at home and collect urine samples. Both test negative.

9 P.M. Return to the office. Call participants on community release to check that they have complied with their curfews. Eat dinner.

10 P.M. Visit Mark M. and Yolanda S., who violated curfew yesterday. Both are at home.

11 P.M. While out, receive call on beeper from residential facility. Regina S. is fighting with staff and is about to be discharged.

12 A.M. Drive to residential facility. Talk with Regina and tell her that if she's forcibly discharged I will return her to jail. She agrees to stop fighting. Negotiate with staff to allow Regina to stay. Leave facility at 1:15 A.M. and go home.

Source: Vera Institute of Justice (1995). *Bail Bond Supervision in Three Counties* (pp. 9–12). New York: Vera Institute of Justice. Reprinted with permission.

to jail. The project's staff members had the authority of bail bondsmen, which means they could arrest and return a violator to jail without a court order. This turned out to be an important factor in the program's success. Also important was the availability of beds in a residential facility; the facility was used both to orient newly released individuals to the program and to control noncompliant defendants. An illustration of the daily routine from a staffer's perspective is shown in Box 11.2.

The program was designed for short-term use, each defendant being supervised for a few months at most. As the time of supervision lengthened at the Bronx site due to court delays, the project's staff found that defendants became increasingly frustrated and likely to violate program rules, reoffend, or attempt to flee. Reducing these risks required more resources and pushed up the costs of the program. Attempts to improve operations were unsuccessful and the Bronx site was closed. Overall, however, the project was considered a success. Pre-trial intensive supervision was much more successful in preventing re-arrest, flight, and nonappearance than release on recognizance or unsupervised release on bail.

Some jurisdictions, including U.S. district courts, are now using home confinement with electronic monitoring of defendants on pre-trial release as a cost-effective alternative to jail. In its newsletter, *The Third Branch*, the Administrative Office of the federal judiciary reported in March, 1997 that over 2,000 defendants were supervised under this program in 1995, at a saving of over $40 per defendant per day. Rates of pre-trial offending and failure to appear among federal defendants under home confinement are reported to be low, which is arguably more impressive—and important—than the cost savings. It will be no surprise if this approach to pre-trial release continues to grow in popularity.

THE PROSECUTION OF CRIMINAL SUSPECTS

We have seen that the bail decision is an important one for defendants and for criminal justice officials—as well as for the community at large. Even more important, however, is the decision to go ahead with prosecution. For defendants, a decision to prosecute usually guarantees conviction; the only remaining question is whether something can be done to reduce the gravity of the punishment. For police, the decision to prosecute vindicates their judgment and efforts, although it opens their methods to scrutiny by the defense, and by the judge and jury if the case reaches the courtroom. For the prosecutor, the decision to proceed with prosecution formally establishes the state's interest in bringing the defendant to justice, and it signifies the prosecutor's belief that the defendant is in fact guilty. For criminal defense attorneys, a decision to prosecute means a client must be defended.

THE DECISION TO PROCEED WITH PROSECUTION

Prosecutors do not proceed against all felony suspects brought to them by the police. Instead, they exercise considerable discretion, not only in deciding whether to proceed, but also in selecting the particular charges that will be presented to the grand jury or at the preliminary hearing in open court.

One important factor affecting the decision to proceed with prosecution is the prosecutor's evaluation of the probability that the defendant will be convicted. Prosecutors avoid investing time and resources in prosecuting defendants who are likely to be acquitted. Prosecuting only those suspects who stand a good chance of being convicted helps serve the state's interest in convicting guilty people. It also confirms that the prosecutor's judgment is sound and that the taxpayers' money is not being wasted.

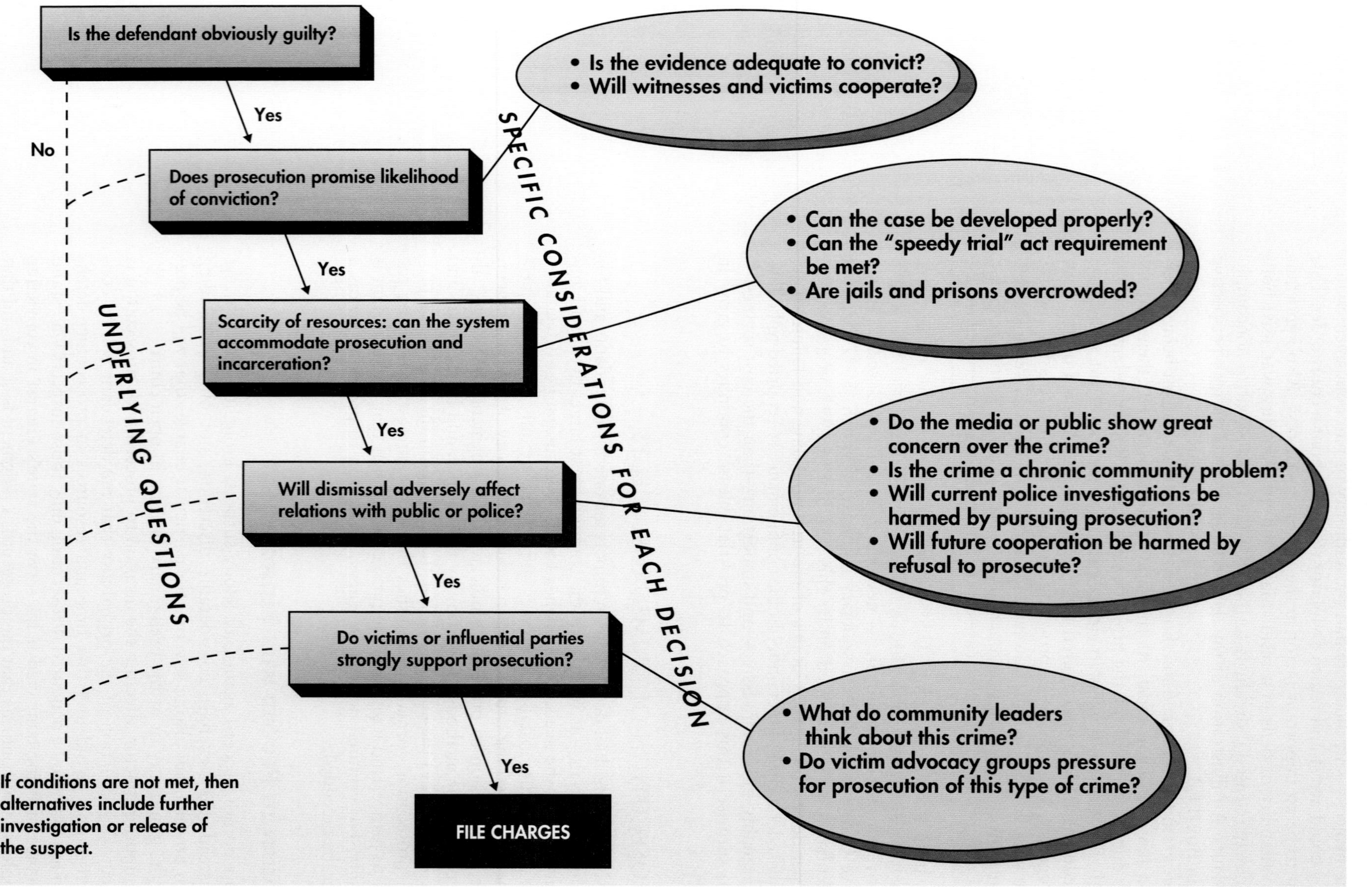

FIGURE 11.4 THE DECISION TO PROSECUTE
Prosecutors face a variety of questions when determining whether to proceed with the prosecution of a criminal suspect. This chart represents the prosecutor's decision tree in the early stages of the judicial process.

The Complex Nature of the Decision to Prosecute. Important as these considerations are in making the decision to proceed with prosecution, this is by no means the whole story. Figure 11.4 presents a diagram showing that the decision to prosecute is often very complex. The prosecutor's exercise of discretion is influenced by many considerations, some of which we touched on in Chapter 10. Some are bound up with questions of justice; some with practical matters involving resources, evidence, and witnesses; some with politics and community interests; and yet others with the organization and culture of the criminal justice system itself. Let us review each of these in turn.

First, a prosecutor often worries about questions of justice. There may be times when a conviction is virtually guaranteed but the prosecutor has doubts about the suspect's actual guilt. Despite a prosecutor's obvious professional interest in obtaining guilty verdicts, conviction of an innocent person does not serve the interests of justice, which prosecutors are sworn to uphold. Concern that a defendant may actually be innocent would lead most prosecutors to delay prosecution pending further investigation. The defendant may have to be released, but this does not stop the prosecutor from coming back later with new charges.

Now consider the problem of resources. It is rarely feasible to prosecute all defendants that prosecutors believe can be convicted, and so a choice must be made among them. A prosecutor may therefore focus resources on the prosecution of people suspected of more serious crimes, or of people with extensive prior arrests, or of people suspected of specific types of crime—for instance, drug offenses or violent crimes.

The decision to prosecute is sometimes influenced by private individuals and groups who put pressure on the district attorney. The fact that chief prosecutors are usually elected officials helps explain their responsiveness to public opinion. It would not be in their interest to spend time prosecuting crimes the public does not care about. In many cities, police and prosecutors have been under pressure to do something about the rising levels of gang violence and drug trafficking. In response, prosecutors are beginning to devise innovative strategies to deal with gang crimes, as Box 11.3 illustrates.

Maintaining Good Relations with the Police and Courthouse Work Group. Prosecution decisions are also influenced by the need to maintain good working relations with police and other members of the courthouse work group, including those who work directly with the victims of crime. In some communities, for example, victim advocacy groups strongly favor the prosecution of certain types of offenders, who previously may have been screened out—for example, those suspected of domestic violence, or people arrested for spraying graffiti or other vandalism. Many police departments have special units to handle sex crimes. These units often work closely with victim advocacy groups to develop "prosecutable" cases.

Sometimes evidence will come to light that the police made legal errors in their handling of a case, such as violations of search-and-seizure rules. This puts prosecutors in a difficult position and can cause strained relations with the police. When cases have been compromised in this way, prosecutors may still proceed with prosecution, but their chances of winning in court are significantly reduced.

THE DECISION NOT TO PROCEED WITH PROSECUTION

The boundaries of the criminalization process in any society are largely determined by negative decisions—that is, decisions to do nothing. In effect, negative decisions establish what people can get away with. As Figure 11.5 shows, many criminal cases that come before prosecutors are screened out at an early

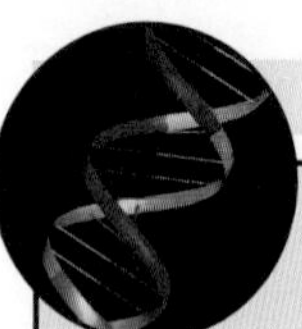

Box 11.3

JUSTICE INNOVATIONS

PROSECUTION OF GANG CRIMES IN THE 1990s

National surveys by the National Institute of Justice and by the National Gang Crime Research Center at Chicago State University conducted in the early 1990s show that drugs and violence involving urban gangs are taking up more and more of prosecutors' time. Most prosecutors do not have specialized gang crime units, and many believe that the lack of a coordinated national policy has itself contributed to the gang problem.

Prosecutors cited problems in prosecuting youth gang crimes because juvenile codes were not designed for the serious violence that characterizes street gang crime. They favored new legislation to cover drive-by shootings, witness protection, gang recruitment activities, weapons offenses, and accessibility to juvenile records. Victim and witness cooperation were cited as a major problem, because in gang crime today's victim may be tomorrow's perpetrator seeking revenge. Effective state and local programs require special efforts to build trust and address victims' needs for protection.

In offices with specialized gang units, the most common arrangement is to have one assistant prosecuting attorney handle a case from beginning to end. This is called **vertical prosecution.** The strategy is found in a third of large urban jurisdictions, and even in some small counties with populations from 50,000 to 250,000. New gang prosecution strategies now being evaluated across the country include the following:

vertical prosecution One assistant prosecutor handles a case from beginning to end.

victim advocate Employee of the prosecutor's office who assists crime victims during the prosecution of their case.

- In Suffolk County, Massachusetts, a prosecutor's gang task force includes a **victim advocate** who maintains extensive contacts with victims and witnesses, working hard to develop and maintain trust; the victim advocate is available by voice mail 24 hours a day.
- Five states (California, Florida, Georgia, Louisiana, and Illinois) have initiated Street Terrorism Enforcement and Prevention (STEP) acts. These acts provide for enhanced penalties and civil forfeiture when crimes are linked to street gang activity. They provide prosecutors with a comprehensive legal framework for prosecuting street gang crimes.

  In Riverside, California, the STEP approach guides intelligence gathering on gangs. The police compile three notebooks on a targeted

stage or end up being dismissed later on. The decision not to prosecute is often made at an initial screening before the case is forwarded to the felony court. In most larger cities, this initial decision is handled by assistant prosecutors who staff a **warrant office.** Besides determining whether initial charges will be filed or the case screened out, the warrant office is the major liaison between the district attorney and the public and will also routinely advise the police on legal matters.

warrant office An office staffed by assistant prosecutors who screen cases and advise police on legal issues.

Problems with Evidence and Witnesses. Among the practical considerations that persuade prosecutors not to proceed with a case, the two most important are problems with the evidence and problems with witnesses. As a rule, evidence problems are most likely to be either insufficient corroboration—willing witnesses could not substantiate the accusations—or lack of physical evidence, such as stolen property or weapons. Witness problems include the failure of witnesses to appear in court or to make themselves available for interviews by investigators.

Box 11.3 (continued)

gang. The first contains copies of all incident, arrest, investigative, and field interrogation reports; the second contains personal records of gang members, including pictures, prints, and rap sheets; the third contains pictures of gang members and their associates, including colors, tattoos, gang slang and hand signals, graffiti, and gathering places. The prosecutor provides police with written notices that identify specific gangs as a criminal street gang under the STEP act, and that participation in the gang can result in a sentence of one to three years. This notification is kept on record and destroys any subsequent claim that a defendant did not know of the street gang's criminal activity. Prosecutors report that the notice itself has an inhibiting effect on many gang members.

- Also in Riverside County, California, the district attorney combines vertical prosecution with a proactive approach in which ten prosecutors are on call and go out with police to interview victims and witnesses and to talk with gang members. In this way the prosecutor participates in efforts to prevent crimes from occurring in the first place, and is involved in the initial investigation when they do occur.
- In Los Angeles, the policy is to seek the maximum penalty if it is established that a person is a gang member through evidence of affiliation, wearing gang colors, or the testimony of witnesses. This strategy is guided by the belief that gang members commit a greater variety of crimes than non–gang members, over a longer period of time, and with more violence.

Most of these strategies involve close cooperation with the police, and complement many of the efforts underway in the nation's larger police departments. Some of these were reviewed in Chapter 8. Many criminal justice officials believe that they are having a positive effect, and they cite declining rates of violent crime as evidence. As the size of the nation's youth population grows over the next decade, however, it will be interesting to see whether this optimism is born out by declines in rates of juvenile violence and drug-related crimes.

Sources: National Gang Crime Research Center (1995). "A Research Note: Preliminary Results of the 1995 National Prosecutor's Survey." *Journal of Gang Research* 2:59–71; Claire Johnson, Barbara Webster, and Edward Connors (1995). "Prosecuting Gangs: A National Assessment." *NIJ Research in Brief* (February):1–10.

A 1994 survey of state prosecutors found that 74 percent cited victim reluctance to testify and 58 percent cited witness reluctance as reasons for declining, diverting, or deferring cases (Maguire and Pastore, 1997:78). As a rule, more cases are screened out or later dismissed because of witness problems than evidence problems (Brosi, 1979). However, the relative importance of witness and evidence problems varies from jurisdiction to jurisdiction. For example, a 1982 survey found that in murder cases, witnesses were more of a problem in St. Louis than in Los Angeles or in New Orleans (Bureau of Justice Statistics, 1983). In drug cases, witness problems were cited as the reason for 80 percent of dismissals in Washington, D.C., but for less than 10 percent in most other jurisdictions.

Finally, in the case of gang crimes, another nationwide survey found that obtaining the cooperation of victims and witnesses was more likely to be considered a "major problem" by prosecutors in large cities than by those in smaller ones (Johnson, Webster, and Connors, 1995). Unfortunately, none of

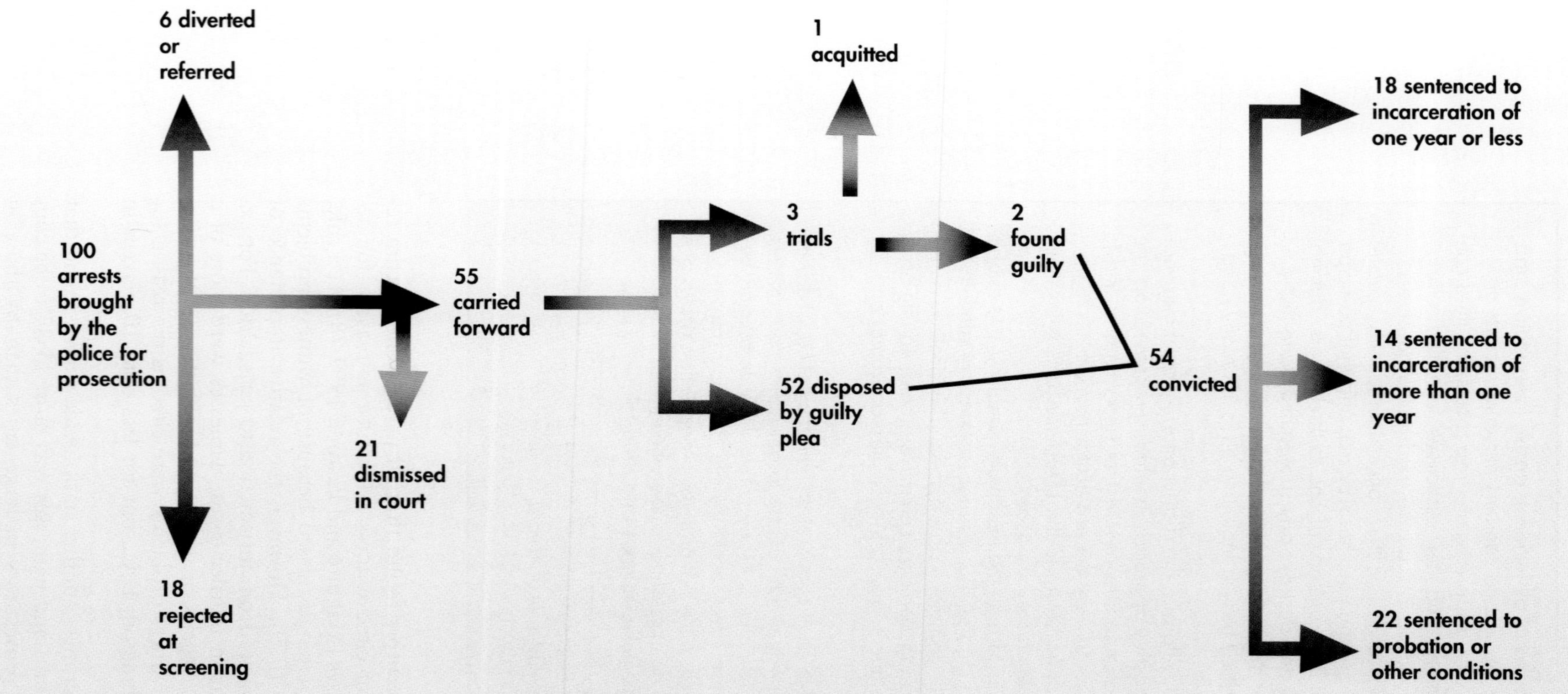

FIGURE 11.5 TYPICAL OUTCOME OF 100 FELONY ARRESTS BROUGHT BY POLICE FOR PROSECUTION

The criminal justice system is like a funnel that leaks. This figure shows that almost half of the felony suspects brought to prosecutors are not convicted of any crime, and less than a third of those who are convicted are sent to prison for one year or more. Only three defendants had a trial.

Source: Bureau of Justice Statistics (1992). *The Prosecution of Felony Arrests* (p. 3). Washington, D.C.: U.S. Department of Justice.

these studies attempted to explain the differences they found. Remembering that the police are primarily responsible for collecting evidence and for initial interviews with witnesses, can you think of some possible reasons for the variations?

Designation of Witnesses as "Uncooperative." Prosecutors know that witnesses to a crime may be uncooperative for a variety of reasons: Some may be afraid that the offender will victimize them again; some may have had unpleasant past experiences with the police or courts; some may not want the offender to be punished, especially if it involves prison time; some may simply want to avoid the hassle, and perhaps the publicity, that may result from being involved as a witness; and some would rather "take care of business" themselves. An uncooperative witness not only hampers the investigation of a case, but is likely to make a poor showing in the courtroom if the case is taken to trial. It is therefore important for both prosecutors and defense attorneys to determine as quickly as possible whether victims and witnesses are likely to be cooperative. If it seems likely that a key witness will not cooperate with the prosecution, any decent defense attorney will be quick to capitalize on the prosecutor's dilemma and push for a dismissal.

Stereotypes sometimes play a role in the designation of witnesses as uncooperative. For example, prosecutors—and police—consider certain offenses more likely to involve uncooperative witnesses; this is a "normal" feature of the crime (Sudnow, 1965). An example is assault. Victims of assault often consider the offense a personal matter, especially if it involves relatives or friends. Many domestic violence victims fail to follow through with official complaints or to appear as witnesses for that reason. Faced with a domestic violence case, prosecutors *expect* to have witness problems, and this expectation is subsequently reinforced by the decision to drop the case. In a number of cities, including New York and New Orleans, prosecutors were three times as likely to screen out assault cases within families, compared to those involving strangers (Forst, 1995:367).

If prosecutors regard witness problems as a normal condition of certain crimes, they may drop cases on the *incorrect* assumption that a witness will be uncooperative. A rare study of witness cooperation concluded that "prosecutors were apparently unable to cut through to the true intentions of 23 percent or more of those they regarded as uncooperative and, therefore, recorded the existence of witness problems when these were premature judgments at best and incorrect decisions at worst" (Cannavale, 1976:50). Armed with stereotypes about how witnesses "normally" behave in certain crime situations, prosecutors may feel justified in dropping a case and citing lack of witness cooperation, even though no serious effort was made to find out whether witnesses would be uncooperative if given the chance to testify.

Relations with the Police. When prosecutors believe that evidence or witness problems will affect the handling of a case they may request further assistance from the police. On most occasions police and prosecutors cooperate with each other as participants "on the same side" in the criminal process. But that cooperation cannot be taken for granted. Prosecutors sometimes complain that cases have to be dropped because of poor work by police investigators. It is easy to explain the heavy reliance prosecutors place on good police work. Their own experience as well as scientific research tells them that the cases most likely to result in convictions are those in which police have produced good physical evidence and two or more witnesses, and have made an arrest quickly (Forst, 1995:367).

Since the police cannot be forced to provide additional information, and since prosecutors rarely have sufficient investigative resources to investigate every case on their own, tensions inevitably arise between police and prosecutors. As

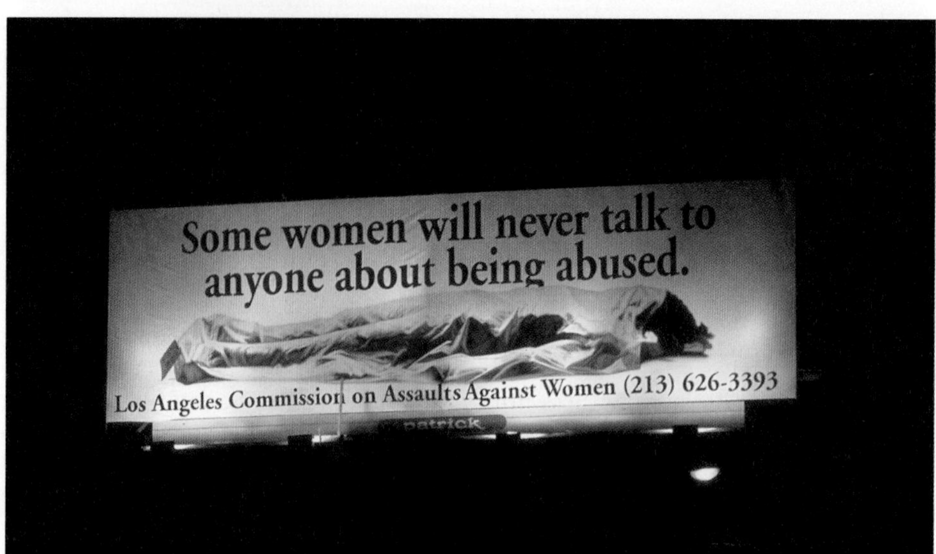

Uncooperative witnesses are not necessarily hostile to police or prosecutors, but may be justifiably afraid of retaliation. In Milwaukee, Wisconsin, new "no-drop" policies in domestic violence cases have resulted in more trials but no significant increase in convictions.

Photo by Michael Newman, courtesy of PhotoEdit

one prosecutor put it, "you can recognize that it's sometimes down to a lack of evidence or care on the part of the police" (Crisp and Moxon, 1994:38). Each side blames the other, however, with police often complaining that prosecutors fail to keep them informed about their decisions.

One way prosecutors can try to improve their relations with police—and therefore the pool of prosecutable cases—is to concentrate on fostering communication and information sharing between themselves and the police. This strategy appears to have worked well in Britain (Crisp and Moxon, 1994:39). Authorities put on special training sessions for police and prosecutors that focused on enhancing mutual understanding; both groups claim the sessions improved relations as well as the proportion of prosecutable cases.

no-drop policy Prosecutors are not allowed to reject cases merely because the victim refuses to cooperate.

The Introduction of Tougher Prosecution Policies. Prosecution policies in many jurisdictions have turned tougher during the past decade, largely in response to public concerns over rising rates of violent crime in the home and by juveniles. One change has been the adoption of **"no-drop" policies** that forbid prosecutors to drop a case merely because a victim declines to cooperate. Milwaukee, Wisconsin, has adopted this policy in regard to domestic violence arrests (Davis and Smith, 1995). As we learned in Chapter 9, domestic violence has received a lot of public attention in recent years, and one result has been the introduction of more stringent prosecution policies. Under the old system, Milwaukee prosecutors pursued cases only when victims showed up at a charging conference held the day after arrest. Few victims showed up, and as a result 80 percent of cases were screened out. The new policy, adopted in January 1995, virtually ignores the behavior—and desires—of the victim, and the prosecution rate has jumped from 20 to 60 percent.

This strategy is yet to be evaluated, but early signs indicate that the results are not as promising as expected. For one thing, many victims do not want to prosecute family members, for reasons listed earlier; forcing them to testify increases the likelihood that they will not cooperate, and this reduces the likelihood of successful prosecution. In addition, defendants who sense that the prosecutor is going ahead regardless of the victim's wishes will tend to "tough it out" rather than enter a plea of guilty. In Milwaukee this has resulted in a considerable increase in the number of misdemeanor domestic assault cases going to trial. An additional strain has been placed on an already overburdened court system with no significant increase in convictions. A policy with good intentions is likely to be in jeopardy if these findings continue.

A second change around the country is that prosecutors are taking a tougher line with some juvenile suspects. As we saw in Chapters 1 and 4, the rates of juvenile offenses involving guns and violence have been increasing over the past few years, and new laws have made it easier for prosecutors to take a hard line with juvenile defendants charged with violent crimes. This is reflected in the rising numbers of juveniles who are being prosecuted as adults (Snyder and Sickmund, 1995:154). From 1985 to 1992, the number of such cases grew from 7,200 to 12,300 (Butts, 1997a:1).

In cases involving juvenile suspects, prosecution decisions have usually been influenced by a child's family circumstances—and this has not changed. As we recall from Chapter 4, family circumstances have been a central issue in juvenile justice for a century. However, it appears that when prosecutors take family circumstances into account in deciding to drop a case, they tend to emphasize the conventional middle-class definition of "good" family circumstances: two parents at home. Thus, suspects from a two-parent family are less likely to be prosecuted than those from single-parent families (Singer, 1993). Apparently, this difference reflects the belief among some prosecutors that two-parent family structures provide better discipline and supervision and are less crime-prone than single-parent families. Sending children home is therefore considered less risky.

Bringing Victims back into the Prosecution Process

For centuries, victims were the forgotten players in the judicial process. The state prosecuted, the state adjudicated, and the state determined the penalty. To be sure, rich and powerful victims have always had influence, with access to key officials guaranteed by their standing in the community. But only in the last couple of decades have victims begun to exercise any real influence. Victims have had to overcome at least three things:

- The legal tradition that it is the state, not the individual, that is officially the victim of crime
- Fear that if victims are invited to play a more formal role, their lack of impartiality will undermine objectivity and due process
- Concern that victim frustration with the ponderously slow and complicated process of justice will result in them opting out at some key point in the proceedings

An international effort is now under way to study the victimizing effects of crime and other social problems and to bring the real victims back into the judicial process. For years victims were "twice victimized"—first by the criminal, and then by the very system to which they turned for help. Crime victims were commonly given the runaround or kept in the dark; they often had their property taken and not returned; and they often found themselves verbally abused and ridiculed in court. To make matters worse, the people most likely to be twice victimized were the very people least equipped to deal with it, and least able to change their situation: the poor, the elderly, minorities, women, and members of single-parent families.

Meeting the Needs of Crime Victims. A variety of constructive responses are now being directed to the needs of crime victims. Some of these responses seek to reduce the probability of victimization and in that sense are part of

Box 11.4

CAREERS IN CRIMINAL JUSTICE

VICTIM-WITNESS ASSISTANT

Although almost unheard of 25 years ago, victim-witness services are offered by prosecutors' offices around the country and in the federal system as well. Most victim-witness services are small operations, some employing only part-time assistants. In larger cities the office may employ five or six full-time assistants and a number of part-time assistants, depending on the workload. Here is a partial job description for the position of *Victim-Witness Assistant,* advertised by the federal government in July 1998:

Salary Range: $26,075 to $28,878 (permanent part-time position, 20 hours per week).

Duties: Include determining eligibility for victim-witness services; maintaining resource materials that identify available counseling and treatment programs; referring victims to available compensation programs and help with the application process; referring victims and witnesses to other agencies that provide medical, psychological, legal, financial, shelter, child care, and employment services; maintaining a calendar of active cases, tracking hearings, trial dates, and sentencing dates; coordinating witness notification of trial appearances.

Qualifications: Prior experience directly related to the job; one year of specialized experience at the next lower grade level; knowledge of applicable victim and witness laws; knowledge of general legal principles including how the judicial system works; ability to communicate orally with victims, witnesses, and employees of federal, state, and local agencies.

Conditions of Employment: Bachelor's degree from an accredited school; graduate work in criminology, criminal justice, social sciences, or related fields such as law.

crime prevention efforts. Neighborhood crime watch programs and "Operation Identification" are examples. Other responses seek to improve the treatment of victims by the judicial process, and others seek to put right the harm caused by crime. For example, the 1984 federal Victims of Crime Act specified that a portion of the fines and other monetary penalties assessed on federal offenders be distributed to states for improved victim/witness services. Other legislative initiatives around the country have focused on victim rights, including the right to be informed of, present at, and heard during all criminal proceedings.

Table 11.2 shows the type of victim services that prosecutors' offices around the country were required to provide in 1994, the date of the most recent survey (Maguire and Pastore, 1997:78). The most common requirements were to notify victims and witnesses of important dates and decisions, to assist victims in seeking restitution or compensation, and to assist victims in preparing victim impact statements for sentencing (these are described in Chapter 13). As might be expected, victim assistance by part-time prosecutors is least widespread.

There is much evidence that victims feel better about criminal justice proceedings if they are present when crucial decisions are made. Yet there is concern in some quarters that the victim movement has been co-opted and manipulated by politicians and criminal justice officials whose real agenda is to secure more resources and public support for cracking down on criminals rather than reducing the pains of victimization (Elias, 1993; Mawby and Walklate,

TABLE 11.2 Victim Services That Prosecutors Say They Are Required to Provide

Over the past fifteen years the services offered to crime victims have expanded so that now most of the country's prosecutors provide at least some services to victims. A 1994 survey asked prosecutors, "Does your jurisdiction require your office to provide any of the following services to victims?" Here are their responses, expressed as a percentage of the prosecutors surveyed.

TYPE OF SERVICE	ALL OFFICES	FULL-TIME OFFICES	PART-TIME OFFICES
Number of offices	2,282	1,599	683
Notification/alert			
Notify victim	82%	86%	73%
Notify witness	55	60	42
Restitution assistance	60	62	55
Compensation assistance	58	66	41
Victim Impact Statement*	55	61	40
Explain court process	41	49	24
Escort victim	23	29	9
Escort witness	17	20	9
Property return	38	40	35
Referral	32	39	18
Crisis Intervention	10	15	0

*The Victim Impact Statement (VIS) is a statement prepared by or on behalf of the victim that tells the court how the victim's life has been affected by the crime. It is discussed more fully in Chapter 13.

Source: Compiled from Kathleen Maguire and Ann L. Pastore (1997). *Sourcebook of Criminal Justice Statistics, 1996* (Table 1.90, p. 78). Washington, D.C.: U.S. Department of Justice.

1994). The true picture is somewhere in between: Victims *are* more significant players than they used to be, and they *are* receiving more services and support than they used to receive. But the reforms have been piecemeal, and the social injustices that underlie much victimization—and that victimization makes worse—have not really been addressed. Many victims who seek justice may find that participation in the process does not ease their frustration with either the process or the outcome.

"Cooling Out" the Victim. This frustration often surfaces early in the judicial process, when victims learn of the formal charges being brought against a defendant. The prosecutor exercises considerable discretion when deciding what to charge suspects with, so the actual charge may be far different from what the victim hoped for or expected. In such situations prosecutors will often attempt to "cool out" victims in the hopes of preserving them as witnesses and allies rather than turning them into adversaries. Cooling out means making victims feel less upset and more accepting of things that have happened to them. Prosecutors may enlist their own victim-witness services personnel to help them in the cooling-out process.

Prosecutors realize that a successful reputation depends in large part on efficiently processing as many guilty defendants as possible. For this reason alone we should expect the cooling out of victims to be taken seriously by most prosecutors. Many prosecutors do all they can within their limited budgets to help ease the pain of crime for victims and to support them in the quest for justice. Yet this is far from promoting a formal role for victims. Since the stakes are often high in terms of time, money, and outcome, it is inevitable that prosecutors will look for the line of least resistance; the lack of a formal role for victims clears one potential obstacle from that path.

Pre-Trial Diversion: An Alternative to Prosecution

Prosecutors justify their existence by securing the convictions of as many defendants as possible. However, a competent and conscientious prosecutor may decide not to prosecute a case because there are favorable alternatives that better serve the cause of justice or that enable the system to concentrate its resources on more important cases. **Pre-trial diversion** is the term used to describe programs that allow prosecutors to send defendants to a community-based program instead of formally prosecuting them. Prosecution is suspended until defendants successfully complete the program, at which point the case is dropped. Defendants who do not complete the program are eligible for prosecution on the original charge(s). The practice gained momentum during the 1970s, and is often cited today as an important way to reduce overcrowding in the criminal justice system.

pre-trial diversion Defendants avoid formal prosecution if they successfully complete a community-based treatment or counseling program.

The History and Purpose of Pre-Trial Diversion. When it first appeared in the early 1970s, pre-trial diversion was seen as a promising alternative to the formal and highly stigmatizing criminal process for the many offenders who commit less serious crimes. Its proponents hoped that diversion would not only remove the stigma of prosecution, but would also reduce the relapse into crime—called **recidivism**—that is common among criminal offenders.

recidivism Committing new offenses after being punished for crime.

There are various reasons to divert a defendant from the court system: Some defendants are found to be mentally ill; others may be addicted to alcohol or drugs; yet others may be victims of unfortunate social or economic circumstances who should be helped rather than punished. Prosecutors look to community agencies rather than the criminal courts as a way of handling such defendants. A large variety of community agencies exist in most urban areas, and many of them provide treatment, counseling, employment opportunities, and family assistance to people in trouble with the law.

Not all defendants are eligible for pre-trial diversion, and the circumstances and settings of some crimes virtually rule out diversion in many jurisdictions. Crimes involving weapons and injuries are two examples; child sexual abuse is another (Gray, 1993). The National District Attorneys' Association (1991) has established guidelines for the use of diversion. The most likely candidates for pre-trial diversion are first offenders charged with nonviolent crimes who also have family ties and are willing to cooperate with the diversion program. The guidelines also recommend that decisions about pre-trial diversion take into account its probable impact on the community and the wishes of the victim.

Problems with Pre-Trial Diversion. Pre-trial diversion has been beset by a variety of problems, some practical and others relating to its purpose. The major practical problem is a financial one. At first, pre-trial diversion programs were supported largely by the federal government. However, local communities were eventually forced to take the reins as federal funding dried up during the late 1980s. This was a financial burden many communities could not afford, so programs dwindled in many smaller counties.

Problems relating to the purpose of pre-trial diversion are more complex. Although diversion suspends formal prosecution of a defendant pending successful completion of the program, some research suggests that pre-trial diversion does not significantly reduce the stigma associated with criminal prosecution, nor does it result in lower rates of recidivism (Rausch and Logan, 1983). In fact, judging from what happens to many defendants who are not diverted from the system, those who are spend more time under the authority of social control agents—the others are often given a small fine or a warning and let go.

This criticism of pre-trial diversion is consistent with the argument that the net of social control has actually been widening in recent years, resulting in more and more people being drawn into it who formerly would have been excluded (Cohen, 1985; Barlow, 1987). Nevertheless, the formal system of prosecution and an overburdened courthouse cannot possibly handle all the prosecutable cases that police bring in, so the decision not to prosecute will continue to loom large in a prosecutor's range of alternatives.

Even though the experience with pre-trial diversion may not have been entirely as promised by its early advocates, the commitment it represents to finding alternatives to formal prosecution should perhaps not be given up. The better strategy is surely to find ways to make it work. There is reason to be optimistic, even for heinous crimes: For example, in intrafamily child sexual abuse cases involving first-time offenders, a study of 384 cases found that pre-trial diversion coupled with treatment *before* charges were actually filed was the most promising of three alternative diversion strategies (Skibinski, 1994).

PLEA BARGAINING AND THE DECISION TO PLEAD GUILTY

In the United States, all criminal defendants have the right to plead not guilty and to ask for trial by a jury of their peers. In theory, the trial is the heart of the Anglo-American judicial process. Yet fans of *Perry Mason, L.A. Law*, and *Court TV* may be surprised to learn that most criminal defendants never go to trial. Instead, they plead guilty because their attorney recommends it. By pleading guilty they convict themselves. In fact, around 90 percent of all convictions are the result of guilty pleas, though the actual percentage varies from place to place (Brown and Langan, 1998:3). This means that only about 10 percent of criminal convictions occur in a public trial. To understand how criminal convictions usually come about, one must examine the pre-trial phases of the judicial process, where prosecutors and defense attorneys search for the line of least resistance in pursuit of their goals. A lot of bargaining goes on, as each side offers the other a "deal" in search of a compromise both can accept.

The Nature of Plea Bargaining

When guilty pleas are entered as a result of a bargain struck between the prosecutor and the defense attorney, it means that both sides see themselves as better off with the plea than they would have been without it. Since defendants whose cases are not dismissed or who do not plead guilty usually end up being

Plea bargaining is the main way in which criminal cases are decided. Here a defense attorney and assistant prosecutor discuss options as they try to settle a case without trial. Without plea bargaining, the courts in most jurisdictions would quickly grind to a halt—and many guilty defendants would be released.

Photo by Donna Hales, Muskogee Daily Phoenix; courtesy of AP Photo convicted, one might think that prosecutors would prefer to prosecute rather than plea bargain. This is not the case, however; 73 percent of chief prosecutors in a national survey said they willingly pursue guilty pleas and often place no time limits on the negotiations once they begin (Dawson, 1992:6). This is vastly different from other countries, where plea bargaining is either illegal, (as in Japan) or severely curtailed, as in Germany (Feeney, 1998).

Types of Plea Bargains. From a defendant's point of view, a number of different "bargains" are possible. A guilty plea may be exchanged for any of the following:

- A reduction in the charge(s)
- A promise of leniency in sentencing
- Concurrent consideration of multiple charges—the defendant serves one sentence for a number of different crimes
- Dropped charges—the defendant pleads guilty to (usually) the major charge, and other lesser charges are dismissed

These bargains are found in every state and the federal system, although a study conducted in 1985 showed that different concessions are emphasized in different jurisdictions (McDonald, 1985). In New Orleans and Tucson, for example, deals involving the combination of sentence recommendations and manipulation of charges were almost non-existent, while they were fairly common in Seattle, Norfolk, and Delaware County. These differences reflect traditions within each jurisdiction and the preferences of prosecutors and judges. There is no reason to believe that this situation is any different today.

In addition to these bargains, the defendant might exchange a guilty plea for release on bail or in order to avoid some other problem. For example, a prosecutor in one jurisdiction will sometimes offer a deal to a defendant who is also wanted in another jurisdiction, using the threat of returning the defendant to that jurisdiction to induce a guilty plea.

Finally, there is the so-called tacit or implicit bargain. Though no explicit negotiation is involved, defendants may plead guilty because they believe the court will show greater leniency if they do. Apparently, many prosecutors and judges agree that guilty pleas should be rewarded (Mendelsohn, 1956; Vetri, 1964; Bottomley, 1970:120–122; Rosett and Cressey, 1976; McDonald, 1985). Among other things, a guilty plea saves the state time and money and suggests that the defendant is ready and willing to pay for the crime. It should come as no surprise to learn that defendants who go to trial receive much longer prison sentences when convicted than those who plead guilty. In the most recent national study, felons convicted by a jury trial received an average sentence of 12 years, versus only 5 years for felons who pled guilty (Brown and Langan, 1998:41).

Additional Incentives for Defendants to Plea Bargain. A reduction in the eventual punishment for an offense is a strong incentive for defendants to plea bargain. Each of the four deals listed earlier offers this incentive. But defendants may feel pressure to "deal" for other reasons: (1) They may want to avoid the stigma of a public trial—an important consideration for offenders who are employed or have families; (2) they may want to avoid the unknowns of a trial; and (3) a guilty plea usually gets things over with more quickly than a trial does, and some defendants—particularly those detained in jail—may feel this is important.

While the incentives for pleading guilty may be similar among defendants charged with different crimes, the actual result may vary considerably, with some defendants benefiting much more than others. For example, a study of 619 defendants indicted for murder, rape, aggravated assault, and robbery in

Alabama found that the offense played a significant role in determining the benefits of a guilty plea (McCarthy and Lindquist, 1988). Rapists and murderers received the greatest gains by pleading guilty, while only slight gains were made by offenders charged with assault. In general, the more serious the crime, the greater the potential benefit of a deal.

When a plea agreement is made, for whatever reason, most states now require that the agreement be in writing and signed by all parties involved. This protects the lawyers, the judge, and the defendant, and ensures that there is a record that can be produced in court should the agreement be denied or contested. In signing the agreement, the defendant is also attesting to the fact that he or she entered a guilty plea voluntarily and knowingly.

When the Prosecution Encourages Guilty Pleas

Prosecutors often use the advantages and incentives considered by defendants as bargaining chips in plea negotiations. One particularly effective method used to encourage guilty pleas is to bring up the defendant on as many charges as possible. These "multiple-count" indictments include the major offense and any additional crimes that were committed in association with that offense. For example, an armed robbery indictment might include various assault, larceny, and weapons charges as well as the major offense. An offer to drop the lesser charges could save the defendant many years in prison, a deal hard to refuse.

Donald Wolff, the criminal attorney we met in Chapter 10, points out that prosecutors sometimes initiate the plea bargaining in an aggressive manner that causes problems for the defense:

> There are many occasions where the prosecutor not only initiates the plea bargain, but initiates it immediately, and says "if you don't take advantage of this offer at this time, the offer goes down. . . ." So in order to get this tremendous offer, you have to waive a preliminary hearing where you may get the defendant discharged. Or you'll have to waive a pretrial motion to suppress a confession or illegal search. In other words, the prosecutor is negotiating you into bypassing a constitutional right that you have so that you can take advantage of their initial offer. . . . If I get that kind of plea bargain I just put it in writing and then use it later when I go before the court. I will just tell the judge that I could not take the offer because as a lawyer I cannot waive my client's constitutional rights. (Personal communication, April, 1997)

Why Prosecutors Like Plea Bargains. If a guilty plea favors the defendant, why would the prosecutor encourage it? One reason mentioned earlier is that with current budgets and personnel, it is virtually impossible to prosecute and try every case police bring in. Most of the time court calendars are full, with cases set months or even years in advance. Under such conditions, prosecutors have little choice but to divert cases from the courtroom.

Another incentive for prosecutors to plea bargain is that convictions are a measure of how productive a prosecutor is, and a productive track record may be important when it comes to re-election:

> Because prosecutors are elected to their positions, they want to show the public that they are making a worthy effort in protecting them against the criminal element. This is likely to take precedence over concerns about due process and social justice. Prosecutors strive, therefore, for high rates of conviction, and correspondingly low rates of acquittal and dismissal once cases are accepted. This can be accomplished through plea bargaining. (Pontell, 1984:35)

Prosecutors can also take advantage of the fact that plea bargaining also benefits other participants in the criminal justice system. By doing favors they help the courthouse work group and ensure that organizational goals are met. As noted earlier, the organization of criminal justice consists of interdependent roles connected by obligations and expectations. When the police produce arrests that hold up in court, this benefits the prosecutor. When the prosecutor speeds cases through the system so that police are not tied up in court, police work is made easier.

Prosecutors are also attracted to plea bargaining when they believe the defendant is guilty but their case is weak. Little is to be gained by taking weak cases to trial, and doing so may actually be counterproductive to the cause of justice. For one thing, a defendant who is found not guilty cannot be tried again for the same offense; this is double jeopardy, which is prohibited by the Fifth Amendment to the Constitution. Even when prosecutors are reluctant to make deals because of the nature of a crime, they may anticipate difficulties at the trial stage, and a deal is the only way to ensure that the defendant is convicted. Many child sexual abuse cases fall into this category (Gray, 1993:100): Such cases are notoriously difficult to successfully prosecute in court, for there is often little physical evidence and there are usually no witnesses. It is the child's word against that of the defendant. Despite the horror of the crime, plea negotiations are commonplace, and trials rare.

Prosecutors who insist on bringing weak cases to trial sooner or later find their conviction rates slipping and with them their reputations. No one is impressed by a loser, least of all those paying the bills. Long before it gets to the point where a prosecutor's job is in jeopardy, however, other members of the courtroom work group will step in with warnings and advice. Even judges have been known to pressure prosecutors to keep weak cases out of the courtroom.

Asset Forfeiture: A New Bargaining Incentive for Prosecutors. A fairly recent development in criminal justice has made plea bargains even more attractive to prosecutors. This is the practice of seizing the assets of criminal suspects with a view to initiating forfeiture proceedings against them. We have already seen that asset forfeiture has become a major weapon in the war against drug trafficking waged by the police. Yet prosecutors have the burden of pursuing asset forfeiture through the courts. There are many stages between identifying the property to be seized and the final judgment of forfeiture where things can go wrong for the prosecutor. Even after a valid forfeiture, a claimant may successfully petition the court for return of the property. This result can make the most seasoned prosecutor cynical and discouraged. So prosecutors try to avoid it through a plea agreement that includes the disputed property.

When asset forfeiture is at stake, a well-crafted plea agreement can eliminate many of the steps where things can go wrong, while also providing an opportunity for investigators to establish more accurately the nature and amount of assets under the control of the defendant. Defendants accused of drug trafficking or racketeering usually face stiff sentences if convicted, so a plea bargain naturally appeals to them. But if substantial assets are also at stake, most defendants will be inclined to lie about the extent of their drug activities and their holdings in property and cash. Through a **contingent plea agreement**, prosecutors can specify that defendants must forfeit or surrender any assets received from their criminal activity before a deal can be struck.

contingent plea agreement The defendant agrees to forfeit or surrender certain assets in exchange for a negotiated plea.

In cases such as *Libretti v. United States* (1995), the U.S. Supreme Court has generally upheld the practice of incorporating asset forfeiture in plea agreements. However, in a 1998 case it did reduce the potential profitability of some forfeitures by linking the value forfeited to the gravity of the actual crime committed. This case, *United States v. Bajakajian* (1998), involved $357,144 seized in 1994 at Los Angeles International Airport. Hosep Bajakajian was attempting to take the money to Cyprus to repay a family debt. Since federal law requires reporting of all currency in excess of $10,000 being taken out of the country, officials confiscated the money under forfeiture laws. The Supreme Court ruled that this constituted an "excessive fine" in violation of the Eighth Amendment.

Plea Bargains Are Useful in Prosecuting White-Collar Crime. White-collar crimes such as complex corporate frauds and antitrust violations pose special dilemmas for prosecutors. Following the line of least resistance, a plea bargain may seem particularly attractive to prosecutors in cases that are likely to involve considerable time, money, and effort. Bear in mind, however, that if prosecutors have already made a significant investment in the investigation stage of these cases, they may have a substantial personal commitment to seeing the case go to trial. "When this happens, there is a tendency to become overcommitted to prosecution" (Mann, 1985:15).

The value of a contingent plea bargain becomes evident again. There are often multiple participants in many sophisticated white-collar crimes, especially in the areas of corporate and political crime. In exchange for dropped charges or leniency in the sentence, participants in a complex crime may be induced to cooperate with prosecutors and turn against their former partners in crime. This deal would be especially appealing to prosecutors if it turns a less important offender into an informant against principals in the crime, or against an offender whose conviction would be a major political coup. A recent application of this strategy occurred in the infamous Whitewater case, which involved shady land deals in Arkansas and possible links to President and Hillary Clinton. The late James McDougal, a central figure in the scandal and longtime Clinton associate, eventually cooperated with Whitewater Independent Counsel Kenneth Starr and received a reduced sentence of three years on eighteen charges of fraud and conspiracy (*Washington Post*, April 15, 1997, p. A01). He could have received 84 years in prison.

WHEN THE DEFENSE ENCOURAGES GUILTY PLEAS

Defense attorneys are often the first to suggest a guilty plea. In many cases they persuade defendants to change initial not guilty pleas to guilty (Casper, 1972). Though this means their client will be convicted of a criminal offense, defense counsel recognize a professional obligation to do what is best for the defendant. If this can be accomplished by copping a plea, then the defense attorney will recommend it. The plea bargain is attractive, if not obligatory, when the client is guilty and the case is strong enough to produce a conviction. If a lighter sentence can be achieved through a deal, then this is the route any responsible defense attorney will take.

Protecting Membership in the Courthouse Work Group. Yet this is not the whole picture. Defense attorneys are subject to some of the same organizational pressures as prosecutors. Whether a public defender or a private attorney, the defense counsel's career is dependent on good relations with other actors in the system. The result is that defendants are often manipulated to serve the professional interests of those working within the criminal justice organization (Chambliss and Siedman, 1971:402). For example, if defense attorneys violate courthouse norms or challenge the expectations of prosecutors and judges, they risk losing their insider status, their access to information, and the cooperation of other officials. Where plea bargaining is heavily emphasized, defense attorneys are expected to conform to that norm.

Economic Advantages of Guilty Pleas. There are also economic advantages to pleading a client guilty. It is widely acknowledged that a criminal attorney's saleable product is influence rather than technical proficiency in the law. For example, attorneys in King County, Washington, "hold the belief that clients are attracted partially on the basis of the attorney's reputation as a fixer, or as a shrewd bargainer" (Cole, 1970:340). In addition, private criminal attorneys usually make money in their offices, on the phone, or in the prosecutor's office, but rarely in the courtroom. Time is money, and except in rare circumstances, the time spent in court is the least profitable. The more clients attorneys can handle in a given day, the more money they can make and the wider their business contacts will become.

Routine use of plea bargaining may be particularly attractive to less competent and less ethical lawyers. These lawyers are often found among the so-called *lawyer regulars*. These criminal attorneys are ". . . highly visible in the major urban centers of the nation; their offices—at times shared with bondsmen—line the back streets near courthouses. They are also visible politically, with clubhouse ties reaching into judicial chambers and the prosecutor's office. The regulars make no effort to conceal their dependence upon police, bondsmen, jail personnel, as well as bailiffs, stenographers, prosecutors, and judges" (Blumberg, 1967:18). In the hands of these attorneys, the true interests of clients may be secondary to those of the attorneys, and the bargain that is struck may actually be no bargain at all.

Plea Bargaining and the Defense of White-Collar Criminals. Notwithstanding this unflattering portrayal of the lawyer regular, attorneys are legally and morally obligated to do their best for their clients, and many try hard to do this. The moment a criminal case is received, an experienced defense attorney such as Donald Wolff begins to form a plea strategy and takes steps to exert as much control as possible over the negotiation process.

This is particularly important in sophisticated white-collar cases, where success at the bargaining table is determined largely by steps taken early on to keep important evidence out of the hands of the opposing attorney and to influence the testimony of witnesses. "When negotiations are begun, the defense attorney will already have done a substantial amount of fieldwork" (Mann, 1985:14). Unlike the situation with street crimes, where the longer a case drags on the more likely the defendant will be acquitted, the experienced white-collar defense attorney knows that an early effort at plea negotiation may pay off in significant concessions from the prosecutor. "At an early point in the investigation the government may falsely assume that necessary evidence is inaccessible. . . . The longer the defense attorney waits to start negotiations, the harder it will be to find flexibility in the government's position" (Mann, 1985:15).

Early in the case, the defense attorney must assess the strength of the government's case, and decide whether a plea negotiation is called for; if it is not, or if there is doubt, a defense strategy of noncooperation will most likely be followed, especially if the prosecutor shows no signs of wavering or no interest in a contingent plea agreement. Noncooperation essentially means keeping information out of the hands of the prosecutor. The experienced defense attorney will spend considerable time advising the defendant and potential witnesses on how to do this. Here is how one attorney advised his client prior to a grand jury hearing (Mann, 1985:145):

Atty A: They are going to ask you questions about the whereabouts of the records, and probably other questions which we can't predict at this time.

Client: What am I supposed to tell them?

Atty A: There are a few questions that you will have to respond to, but in almost every instance you will tell them nothing. . . . At the beginning of the session you will be asked to identify yourself, and you will do that. Give your name and identify yourself as chief executive of the company.

Client A: Just my name, or something else?
Atty B: Nothing else.
Client: But what if they say, "State your name, address, and telephone number"?
Atty B: Give them your name and stop. Take the Fifth [Amendment right not to incriminate oneself] to anything else. . . . Finally, . . . they are going to ask you something like, "Have you made a 'diligent search'?" We will decide later how to handle that question. If you are asked that or any other questions, you come out and talk to me. You can always come out and talk to me; you can be excused for a conference with your attorney at any time. I'll be waiting outside the grand jury room.

Bringing Plea Bargaining into the Open

Complex white-collar crimes are not typical of crime in general, and most criminal defendants spend little time consulting with their attorneys. However, the traditional picture of deals and negotiations hurriedly carried on in courthouse corridors may no longer be as accurate as it once was. The U.S. Supreme Court stands behind plea bargaining, and the whole process is much more open than it used to be. Furthermore, while prosecutors and defense attorneys may prefer to avoid the adversarial formality of the courtroom (Maynard, 1982), they do place greatest weight on strictly legal issues in their plea negotiations—for example, the seriousness of the crime, the criminal past of the defendant, and the strength of the evidentiary case (McDonald, 1985).

Judges Are Getting More Involved in Plea Bargaining. The increasing role played by judges may have a lot to do with bringing plea bargaining out of the closet. Nowadays, judges quite often take an active part in bargaining. In some states a judge's participation is mandated by statute. It should come as no surprise that judges are routinely involved in bargained justice. After all, they are players in the same criminal justice drama, and they are as interested in the line of least resistance as anyone else. Judges are also subject to direct pressures from outside the immediate courthouse work group. Their continued appointment or re-election depends on how well the court's business flows. When things get bogged down, pressure from the media, from politicians, and from the higher judiciary can weigh heavily on their shoulders. In large urban court systems, it is not unusual for judges to order a continuance on the day of trial, encouraging prosecutor and defense counsel to try to negotiate the case (Dawson, 1992:6). Like the roles of prosecutor and defense attorney, the judge's role in the judicial process often leads to an administration of the law that is designed to produce speedy, predictable confirmation of a suspect's guilt.

This does not mean that plea bargaining poses no difficulty for judges, quite the contrary. Just as the public wants cases to be processed as quickly as possible, it also wants to believe that justice is being served. When word gets around that a judge is agreeing to lighter sentences in exchange for guilty pleas, protests are likely to surface, especially when the charges involved are considered serious. Judges have to live with the shifting tides of public opinion—they come with the territory.

A more difficult problem faces judges in jurisdictions that have sought to curb the sentencing discretion of judges through the implementation of sentencing guidelines (discussed in the next chapter). Plea agreements heavily influence the final sentence, since judges are rarely in a position to do independent fact finding. Yet the U.S. Sentencing Commission has urged judges to review plea bargains carefully to make sure they do not undermine the sentencing guidelines. In the end, judges' decisions rest heavily on how prosecutors exercise their discretion: A fair and honest system in which defendants who plead guilty in similar circumstances receive similar treatment in the charging and plea process makes judges much more comfortable in accepting plea agreements.

THE FUTURE OF PLEA BARGAINING

In recent years there has been more and more criticism of plea bargaining, both inside and outside legal circles. One of the most often heard complaints is that plea bargaining leads to unreasonably light sentences. Another criticism is that plea bargaining may result in offenders being convicted of crimes they did not commit. Under pressure from attorneys, including threats of what will happen if they don't make a deal, defendants may buckle and plead guilty when in fact they are innocent of any crime. Most experts believe that this problem is relatively rare. Unfortunately, it is most likely to occur with defendants who are inexperienced with the court system or unable to understand what is happening to them.

Should Plea Bargaining Be Banned? On the heels of increasing criticism, some jurisdictions moved to abolish plea bargaining altogether. Alaska was one of the first, with a complete ban in 1975. Other jurisdictions adopted partial restrictions—for example, banning its use in cases involving career criminals, repeaters, and serious violators, or in cases involving specific heinous crimes such as rape or the killing of law enforcement personnel.

It appears that the effects of reduced bargaining were not exactly as expected, at least in Alaska (Rubinstein, Clarke, and White, 1980). After the prohibition went into effect the number of court trials remained small, the court docket did not bog down (actually, cases were processed faster than before), and the proportion of defendants pleading guilty remained pretty much the same as before the ban. The overwhelming modes of case disposition continued to be dismissals and guilty pleas. Lawyers simply did not perceive any better alternative.

These findings suggest caution in anticipating the consequences of abandoning plea bargaining. The Alaska experience shows that a ban may simply end up being circumvented. Furthermore, what occurs in one jurisdiction may not in another. For example, even though Alaska's experience showed that court dockets did not become clogged, a study of the experience in El Paso, Texas, found that a ban there did adversely affect the ability of courts to process felony cases efficiently (Holmes, Daudistel, and Taggart, 1992). Perhaps lawyers took the ban more seriously in El Paso.

Can Alternatives to Plea Bargaining Be Found? Doubts and cautions about the consequences of plea reforms should not prevent the contemplation and testing of alternatives to the present situation, where bargains are the rule rather than the exception. When the movement to ban plea bargaining first took shape, one critic demanded: "What is so inconceivable about a process which includes a trial (perhaps a shorter and neater trial) for every defendant?" (Griffiths, 1970:397). Perhaps the judicial process would seem less like a game to the participants, including many defendants:

> The system as it operates in practice is seen by defendants in this study as an example of their life on the street. Outcomes do not seem to be determined by principles or careful consideration of persons, but by hustling, conning, manipulation, luck, fortitude, waiting them out, and the like. . . . How well you do in this world depends upon what you've got and how well you use it. The criminal justice system, like the streets, is a game of resource exploitation. The defendant typically

> has little in the way of resources and doesn't win. He can, though, with luck and skill, lose less than he might. (Casper, 1972:18)

Perhaps some lessons can be learned from other countries. For example, although plea bargaining is illegal in Japan, most criminal cases are not seriously contested (Westermann and Burfeind, 1991:111). To deal efficiently with the bulk of less serious cases, Japan allows two shortcuts. In one, the prosecutor provides the lower court judge with a written summary of the evidence, a penalty recommendation, and a signed form from the suspect indicating willingness to waive a formal court hearing. The judge then determines the penalty without the prosecutor, defendant, or complainant ever appearing in court. This procedure is restricted to minor offenses for which the penalty is 20,000 yen or less (around $1,000). Most traffic offenses, but also some street offenses such as public indecency, gambling and liquor law violations, simple assaults, and less serious weapons offenses are handled this way.

The second procedure involves a modified public trial. Again, the facts are essentially undisputed. If all parties agree, the evidence is presented to the court without contest. The judge may ask questions of the parties, and a judgment is then entered. Both these systems increase the efficiency of the court process, but of course they rely on the cooperation of all parties. They work well in Japan partly because a cultural tradition exists in which a great deal of emphasis is placed on an offender's expression of remorse, repentance, apology, and desire to make amends to the victim (Westermann and Burfeind, 1991:110). Japanese prosecutors quite commonly drop cases even when the evidence against a contrite suspect is strong. Critics may assert that such a system would never work in America, where crime rates are high and where cultural emphasis on remorse and shame was lost long ago. But others believe that conferencing and other informal group processes are preferable to formal court hearings for the bulk of criminal cases—and that they will work in America (Braithwaite, 1995). We shall return to this issue in Chapters 13 and 17, when we discuss the process of reintegrative shaming as an alternative to traditional punishments.

SUMMARY

Three important decisions in the judicial process typically occur before trial: (1) whether to grant or deny the release of a defendant pending further proceedings; (2) whether to proceed with prosecution; and (3) whether to negotiate a guilty plea.

Pre-trial release is an important decision for both defendants and the community. Defendants who are denied bail or cannot afford it will languish in jail until their case is closed. Those who are released can continue working and living at home, and they have more and better opportunities to interact with their attorney. Defendants held in jail lose all those advantages and also have to live among convicted criminals under conditions that deprive them of privacy and independent decision making. Other things being equal, detained defendants are more likely to be convicted and to receive sentences of imprisonment than defendants released on bail.

Most defendants are detained before trial for one of two reasons: They cannot afford the bail amount or they are considered a danger to the community if released. Both reasons are the basis for complaints. Because the first reflects lack of sufficient financial resources, critics point out that requiring money bail discriminates against the poor defendant. This argument was articulated in the bail reform acts of 1966 and 1984, which helped established release on recognizance as an alternative to money bail for many classes of crime. The second reflects the belief that a defendant's future conduct can be predicted on the basis of current and past behavior. We saw that it is virtually impossible to predict whether a given defendant will commit dangerous crimes if released. In these days of overcrowded jails and heightened public concern about crime, a promising answer to pre-trial offending is pre-trial intensive supervision, in which defendants are closely monitored by probation officers.

The decision to proceed with prosecution is an equally complex one. Prosecutors must weigh many things, from the likelihood that the defendant will be convicted to the attitudes and opinions of the police, the public, and community leaders. Because there are simply insufficient resources in the criminal justice system to prosecute all defendants, prosecutors must establish priorities. Defendants suspected of violent crimes and drug offenses and those with extensive criminal histories are most likely to be prosecuted—and this strategy is supported by public opinion. When prosecutors decide to screen out or drop a felony case, two of the most important reasons are problems with the evidence and problems with witnesses. They believe that the case will be lost at trial and they recognize that defense attorneys will not be willing to plead their client guilty under those circumstances. An alternative to both prosecution and dismissal is pre-trial diversion, which permits the court to retain jurisdiction in a case while the defendant completes a program of work, study, counseling, and/or treatment under the supervision of a probation officer.

We learned in this chapter that most defendants are convicted because they plead guilty. Most of the time a guilty plea is the result of negotiations between the prosecutor and defense attorney. Such plea bargains are inevitable in an overburdened system, but there are other reasons why lawyers on both sides pursue them. For the prosecution, guilty pleas are a measure of productivity, and they also speed up cases through the system; a guilty plea is also attractive when the prosecution's case is weak; and plea bargaining is useful in cases involving asset forfeiture and white-collar offenses because it provides otherwise complex, time-consuming prosecutions with productive results.

When defense attorneys try to do their best for their clients, they often push for plea bargains. A guilty plea usually means a lighter sentence, which benefits the defendant. Like other members of the courthouse work group, defense attorneys also conform to the norms of the jurisdiction in which they practice. Wherever plea bargaining is commonplace and expected, everyone participates in it. A more unscrupulous but equally practical incentive is that plea bargaining helps a defense attorney dispose of more cases in a shorter time and therefore earn more money. Plea bargaining is much more open than it used to be, and one reason is the participation of judges. While that participation will not blunt all criticism, it may take some of the hustle out of plea bargaining.

WHAT DO YOU THINK *NOW?*

- Can you think of ways that the interests of defendants, victims, and society can all be met in pre-trial release decisions?
- Since plea bargains are frequently inevitable, what would be a prosecutor's best strategy toward plea bargaining? What would happen if defense and prosecution refused to cooperate?
- How can plea bargaining have drawbacks to both prosecution *and* defense?

Key Terms and Cases

initial appearance
financial release
nonfinancial release
release on recognizance
Stack v. Boyle
Manhattan Bail Project
preventive detention
bail guidelines
pre-trial intensive supervision
vertical prosecution
victim advocate
warrant office
"no-drop" policy
pre-trial diversion
recidivism
contingent plea agreement

Active Learning Challenges

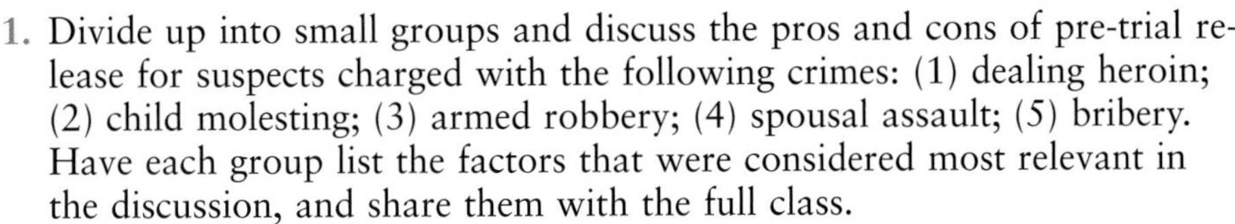

1. Divide up into small groups and discuss the pros and cons of pre-trial release for suspects charged with the following crimes: (1) dealing heroin; (2) child molesting; (3) armed robbery; (4) spousal assault; (5) bribery. Have each group list the factors that were considered most relevant in the discussion, and share them with the full class.
2. The prosecutor has most of the power in determining what happens next to suspects arrested by the police. Is this situation inevitable? Should the prosecutor's power be curbed? If so, how?
3. Most criminal defendants are convicted without trial. Contact the nearest prosecutor's office, and see if you can find out what the current policies and practices are regarding plea bargaining. If possible, invite a prosecutor and a defense attorney to discuss their views on plea bargaining in front of the class.
4. Here is a topic for a class debate: "Money bail should be abolished."

Internet Challenges

The Web pages mentioned here can all be accessed through the Web site for this textbook at **http://www.prenhall.com/barlow/.**

1. Find out what criminal justice practitioners are doing to improve pre-trial release services around the country. Check out the National Association of Pretrial Services Agencies. Report on an innovative program that you think is particularly interesting.
2. Appellate courts have upheld the practice of asset forfeiture, but grassroots opposition is increasing. Find out what opponents are currently saying and doing by visiting the home page of FEAR (Forfeiture Endangers American Rights).
3. Type "plea bargain" in the Search box of any search engine. You will find all sorts of interesting sites to visit, from newspapers to government documents, legal opinions, and chat rooms where the pros and cons are debated and personal experiences shared. See how many pros and cons you can come up with.

CHAPTER 12

THE COURTS AND THE CRIMINAL TRIAL

LEARNING OBJECTIVES

- Describe the organization of criminal courts in America and the role of judges within them.
- Understand the jury selection process, including the role of voir dire and the growing use of scientific jury selection.
- Explain how the composition of a jury may affect its impartiality.
- Distinguish between the types of evidence presented in court and describe ways that attorneys may challenge the evidence used by their opponents.
- Understand the methods of persuasion used by lawyers in the courtroom, including the use of expert witnesses.
- Explain what jury nullification is and its implications for justice.
- Describe how technology is changing courtroom practice, and understand the debate over its impact on justice.
- Describe and explain the development of the community court.

A typical criminal court in session. The judge presides at his raised desk overlooking everyone else. A witness testifies while lawyers listen and the court reporter makes a record of the proceedings.

PHOTO BY PETER D. BYRON, COURTESY OF PHOTOEDIT

Justice is a difficult ideal, vulnerable to attack by benevolence on one side and vengeance on the other.

JAMES Q. WILSON, PROFESSOR OF MANAGEMENT AND PUBLIC POLICY

Jury selection is best based upon seat-of-the-pants instincts. . . .

U.S. SUPREME COURT CHIEF JUSTICE WILLIAM H. REHNQUIST

All sides in a trial want to hide at least some of the truth.

ALAN DERSHOWITZ, DEFENSE ATTORNEY AND PROFESSOR OF LAW

At 8:30 A.M., defendant John Springer entered the courthouse through the back door, shackled to four other men and accompanied by three guards. The shackled men were dressed in orange jumpsuits, regulation jailhouse attire. Under close watch, they were allowed to change into civilian clothes. Springer's case was due to be called at 10:30 A.M. His lawyer had promised to meet for a last-minute review of strategy. Springer was anxious to know whether he would have to testify. The idea scared him, for jail gossip said the prosecutor knew how to break a man on the witness stand. And no matter what you said, it would be turned against you. When his lawyer arrived a few minutes later, Springer was relieved to learn that he would not take the stand. But then another question worried him: "Won't the jury think I have something to hide if I don't testify?"

In another room down the hall, Jenny Carlson, a victim advocate employed by the state attorney's office, was walking the victim through the procedures that would soon take place in the courtroom. Many victims have not experienced criminal court, and what they see on TV hardly prepares them for the real thing. Carlson knew it was important for victims to understand how the trial process works, who the key participants are, and what to expect from them. The fact that suspect and victim would be in the same room is also disquieting to many victims, and Carlson generally stayed close to them during the first day of a trial, when the verdict came in, and during sentencing.

Both Carlson and the prosecutor had already talked with the victim about testifying and the importance of giving clear and concise answers to questions. Carlson was confident this victim could handle cross-examination by the defense attorney, or any questions from the judge. But just to be sure, she spent a few moments going over the procedures for examining witnesses, and what could be expected from these particular lawyers and this particular judge. The victim seemed more relaxed when she had finished, and that was a good thing. Springer, on the other hand, appeared very nervous when he entered the courtroom accompanied by his attorney.

The defendant's apprehension about what will happen during trial is natural enough. And so is the victim's. In many cases there is a lot riding on the outcome. Lawyers also have much riding on the outcome of a trial. The trial is a test of their knowledge of procedural law and their skills of persuasion. It is also a test of their ability to succeed in a setting that is formal and restrained, but also emotional and public. They have to lead witnesses and jurors through the reconstruction of an event that happened weeks, months, or even years before, and do this in a haze of legal jargon, with interruptions, arguments, and distractions at every turn. And they must not offend the judge or they risk being held in contempt.

In this chapter we will explore the criminal courts and various aspects of the criminal trial. We will focus on jury trials because these are the most common form of felony trial. After examining the size, selection, and representativeness of juries, we shall turn to presentation of evidence and the dynamics of courtroom behavior. Since closing arguments, judge's instructions to the jury, and jury deliberations bring the typical trial to a close, these will be discussed last. Finally, we shall consider changes in the criminal court as a result of technological advances and new ideas about dispute resolution.

WHAT DO YOU THINK?

- Does jury selection guarantee a defendant "a jury of his or her peers"?
- Can an attorney reject a potential juror for any reason whatsoever, including race, gender, or class status?
- What factors influence jury decisions? How do lawyers' and judges' communication skills affect the way that juries process evidence?

THE CRIMINAL COURTS

There are two court systems handling criminal complaints in the United States: federal courts, and state courts. Figure 12.1 illustrates the federal system, and Figure 12.2 the typical state system. Some other countries have both federal and state, or provincial, court systems, but unlike the United States, they operate with only one criminal code. In China, private citizens play a much greater role in the court system than is typical of Western nations. Box 12.1 gives a brief description of the Chinese court system.

The lower courts are usually very busy places. If you visit one on a typical morning you will discover a crowded courtroom with all sorts of people milling around. Some are lawyers, some are victims, a few are onlookers and relatives of defendants, and there may be a police officer or two. But most are defendants waiting for their case to be called. At the front of the courtroom it is not uncommon to see the judge engaged in three or four conversations at once. People come and go constantly, and there is a lot of talking going on around the room. A plea of "Order in the court!" would probably be unheard,

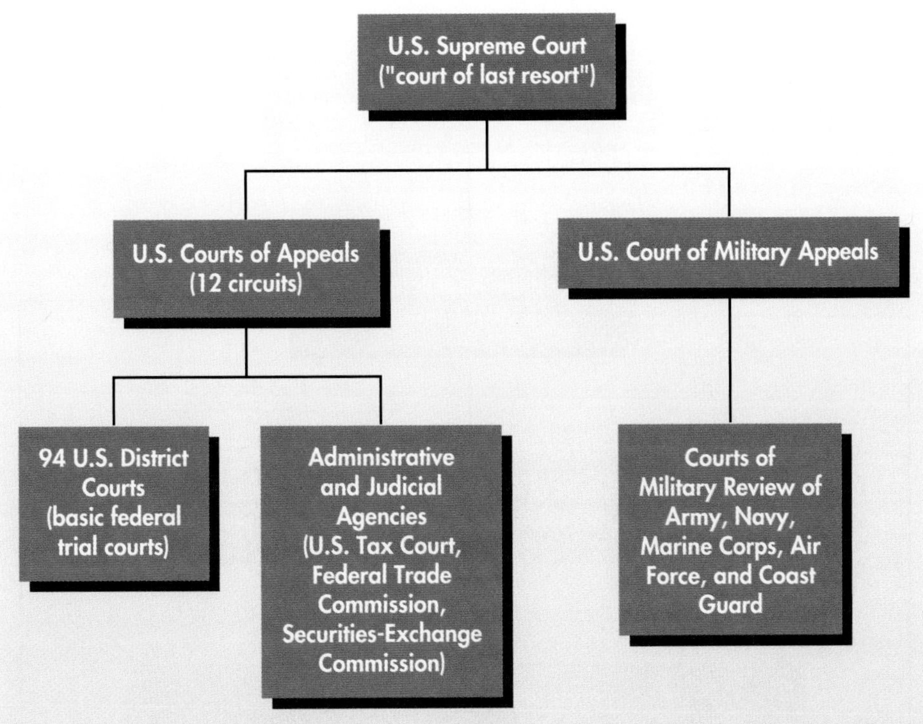

FIGURE 12.1 ORGANIZATION OF FEDERAL COURTS HANDLING CRIMINAL COMPLAINTS

and court bailiffs have learned to overlook the apparent disorder so long as the day's business gets done.

As noted in Chapter 1, most state felony complaints are handled in **courts of general jurisdiction**, sometimes called *superior court* or *circuit court*, while misdemeanors are dealt with in **courts of limited jurisdiction**, often referred to as *lower courts*. All told, state courts process millions of criminal cases each year, and produce nearly 1 million felony convictions (Maguire and Pastore, 1996:497). Nearly one in five felony convictions is for drug trafficking. In the federal system, U.S. district courts handle federal criminal complaints, with the exception of tax matters, which are handled by the U.S. Tax Court, and violations of military law, which are dealt with by the Courts of Military Review of the Army, Navy, Marine Corps, Air Force, and Coast Guard. Depending on the offense, military courts may impose sentences ranging from brief periods of imprisonment to death.

courts of general jurisdiction Also called *superior courts* or *circuit courts*, these courts handle most felony trials and sentence hearings.

courts of limited jurisdiction Also called *lower courts*, these courts handle arraignments and preliminary hearings, misdemeanor trials, and less serious felony trials.

APPELLATE COURTS

The decisions of criminal courts may be appealed. Except in death penalty cases, where an appeal is usually automatic, appeals are based on claims that a decision or procedure violated federal law, a provision of the U.S. Constitution, or the laws or constitution of the state involved. Appeals are most commonly filed on behalf of a defendant who has been convicted, but prosecutors sometimes appeal on points of law and they occasionally appeal the sentence. If a prosecutor files an appeal after a defendant has been acquitted, and the appellate court finds in favor of the prosecutor, the defendant may not be retried because the Fifth Amendment prohibits it; however, the appellate court's ruling may be useful to the prosecutor in future trials.

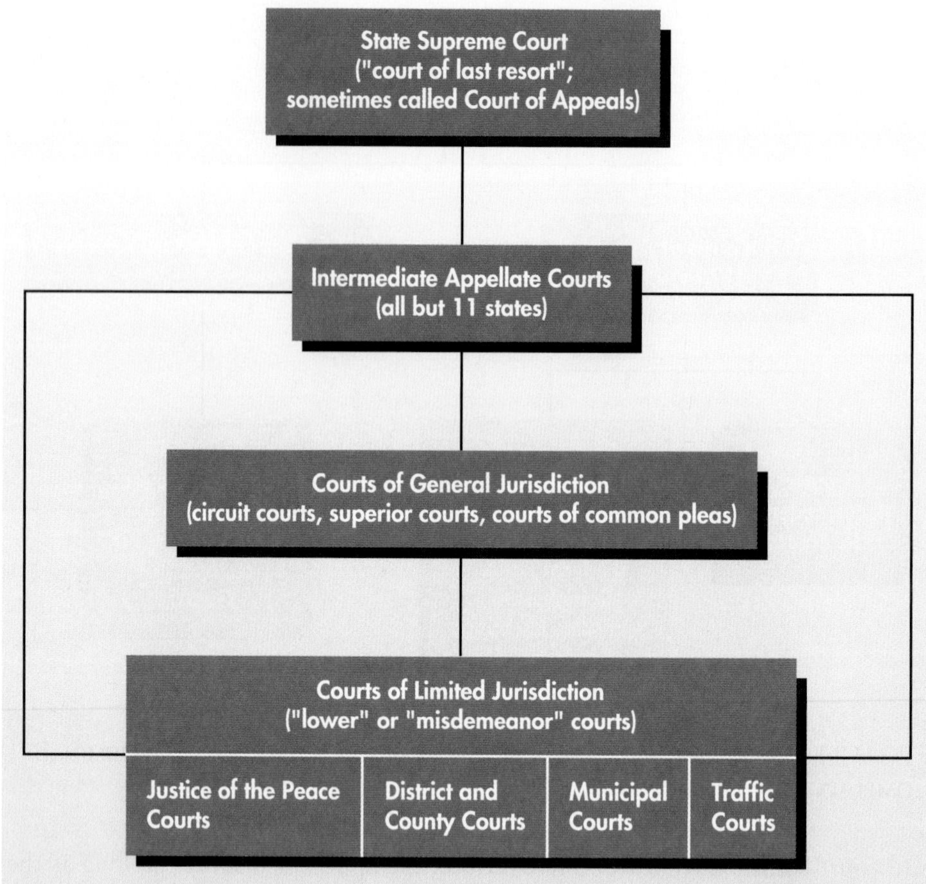

FIGURE 12.2 ORGANIZATION OF STATE COURTS HANDLING CRIMINAL COMPLAINTS
There are different state court structures. This figure shows the most widely used structure.

As shown in Figure 12.2, the court structure in all but eleven states allows for an intermediate appellate court, usually called the *court of appeals*. If a party does not receive a favorable ruling by the intermediate appellate court, the case may be taken to the state's "court of last resort," usually the state supreme court. Disappointed parties may then petition to have their case heard by a federal appeals court. Not surprisingly, federal courts will only consider hearing cases in which violations of federal law are claimed.

In the federal system, the intermediate appellate courts are the twelve regional U.S. Courts of Appeals, the Court of Military Appeals, and the U.S. Court of Appeals for the Federal Circuit (which mainly hears specialized cases on patent and trademark law). The Courts of Appeal hear cases as three-judge panels. They are divided into *circuits*, so named because early in the nation's history the judges visited each of the courts in one region in a certain order, traveling by horseback and riding "the circuit." In 1997, over 50,000 new cases were commenced, representing 940 cases per panel (Maguire and Pastore, 1998:443).

The highest court in the land is the U.S. Supreme Court. It is the court of last resort for all appeals. Its current members, their date of appointment, and background are shown in Table 12.1. The 1998 annual salary of a Supreme Court justice was $167,900, plus an extra $7,500 for the Chief Justice.

If at least four justices vote in favor of hearing a case, a *writ of certiorari* is issued, requesting the lower court to send case records for review. After re-

Box 12.1

GLOBAL JUSTICE

THE COURT SYSTEM IN CHINA

Following the establishment of Communist rule in 1949, the People's Republic of China abolished old systems of law and developed unified codes of criminal law and criminal procedure. After many revisions over the years, in 1979 the Fifth National People's Congress finally adopted nationwide criminal codes.

There are four levels of courts used in criminal cases. The highest court in China is the Supreme People's Court. This court handles major criminal cases of national significance and it is the court of last resort for appeals. It also supervises lower courts such as the 31 Higher People's Courts. These courts handle serious criminal matters and appeals from courts at lower levels. They are situated in various provinces and cities around the country. Intermediate People's Courts are found within provincial cities and towns; in 1991 there were 377 such courts. They also deal with criminal matters, including initial prosecutions, appeals, and transfers from the Primary People's Courts. There are 3,057 Primary People's Courts; they handle the bulk of criminal cases. In addition to these courts, local "people's tribunals" are set up by the Primary People's Courts to help when caseloads become unmanageable, which is a common problem. In 1991, there were actually more people's tribunals in operation than People's Courts.

While appeals are handled by a panel of judges, most initial criminal trials in China are tried by a panel consisting of one to two judges and two to four people's representatives, called *assessors* in the higher courts. The exception is private criminal prosecutions, which are also allowed in China. These are carried out in a more informal justice system, the People's Mediation of Disputes. Chinese procedural law limits private prosecutions to a narrower range of crimes, but allows victims to enter public criminal prosecutions as third parties.

Sentencing is carried out by the trial panel. There are four kinds of penalties:

1. *Guanzhi* (control), rather like supervised probation, is imposed for minor offenses and usually allows the offender to continue working and living at home; it can be imposed for up to two years.
2. *Juyi* (detention), which can be imposed for up to six months, also for minor offenses. Offenders are held in a detention house rather than a prison, and may be allowed to go home one or two days each month.
3. Fixed-term imprisonment, for up to 15 years, and possibly 20 years when combined with other sentences.
4. Life imprisonment.
5. Death by shooting.

Where relevant, all sentences include return of any illegally obtained property, and offenders must make restitution and pay compensation to victims. Detention and imprisonment in China are designed to "reform through labor," which means every able-bodied prisoner must work. Education, including vocational training, is also provided. People can be sentenced to death for murder, rape, and a variety of other crimes. In some cases the sentencing panel suspends the sentence for two years; if during that time the offender repents and demonstrates "meritorious service," the penalty is reduced to a fixed prison term between 15 and 20 years.

Source: Jianan Guo, Guo Xiang, Wu Zongxian, Xu Zhangrun, Peng Xiaohui, and Li Shuangshuang (1996). "China." In Graeme Newman, Adam C. Bouloukos, and Debra Cohen, eds., *World Factbook of Criminal Justice Systems.* Washington, D.C.: U.S. Department of Justice.

TABLE 12.1 Membership of the Current U.S. Supreme Court

Members of the U.S. Supreme Court today: Ruth Bader Ginsburg, David H. Souter, Clarence Thomas, Stephen G. Breyer, Antonin Scalia, John Paul Stevens, William H. Rehnquist, Sandra Day O'Connor, and Anthony M. Kennedy.

PHOTO BY J. SCOTT APPLEWHITE, COURTESY OF AP PHOTO

William H. Rehnquist, Chief Justice, b. 1924, grad. Stanford Law School, 1952. Appointed by President Nixon in 1971. A conservative Republican, known on the court as a staunch advocate of law and order. Appointed Chief Justice by President Reagan in 1986. Estimated net worth in 1997: $210,000 to $590,000.

Stephen G. Breyer, b. 1938, grad. Harvard Law School, 1964. Appointed by President Clinton in 1994. The Court's newest member, with considerable experience in regulatory law, white-collar crime, and sentencing. Considered a moderate with strong academic interests. Net worth in 1997: $3.8 to $14.9 million.

viewing the records the Court may change its mind, but it usually does not. Many Supreme Court cases are reviewed and opinions issued without any oral arguments (Maguire and Pastore, 1998:455). The justices and their law clerks review the material and the justices then meet to discuss their opinions. For other cases, the Court arranges a period of time, called a *sitting*, during which it will hear oral arguments. The nine justices hear oral arguments together. The attorneys representing each side usually have no more than 30 minutes to present their case, and they can expect the justices to ask questions. Parties must then wait several weeks or months for the Court to issue its ruling.

JUDGES: THE COURTROOM IS THEIR DOMAIN

Judges are lawyers; their domain is the courtroom, although many of their decisions are made in the privacy of their chambers. Some judges who handle criminal cases spent most of their prior legal career dealing with criminal law; but this is not a prerequisite, and some judges have had very little experience

Ruth Bader Ginsburg, b. 1933, grad. Columbia Law School, 1959. Appointed by President Clinton in 1993. Taught law and was women's rights advocate before appointment to U.S. Court of Appeals in 1980. Considered moderate. Net worth in 1997: $4.59 to $15.4 million.

Anthony M. Kennedy, b. 1936, grad. Harvard Law School, 1961. Served on U.S. Court of Appeals from 1975 until appointment to the Supreme Court in 1988 by President Reagan. Regarded as a political and legal conservative. Net worth in 1997: $45,000 to $360,000.

Sandra Day O'Connor, b. 1930, grad. Stanford Law School, 1952. The first woman ever appointed to the Court, in 1981 by President Reagan. An Arizona state appellate judge for two years before her appointment to the Supreme Court, she is regarded as a conservative who leans toward preserving and strengthening state powers. Net worth in 1997: $2 to $4.9 million.

Antonin Scalia, b. 1936, grad. Harvard Law School, 1960. Appointed by President Reagan in 1986, Scalia was an assistant attorney general in the U.S. Justice Department from 1974 to 1977, and served from 1982 to 1986 on the U.S. Court of Appeals for the District of Columbia. A conservative who has taken libertarian positions on some issues. Net worth in 1997: $630,000 to $1.37 million.

David H. Souter, b. 1939, grad. Harvard Law School, 1966. Served New Hampshire as attorney general and superior court justice, then as associate justice of the New Hampshire Supreme Court. Appointed by President Bush in 1990. A more moderate justice than many expected, especially his recent opinions on affirmative action. Net worth in 1997, $1.13 to $5.3 million.

John Paul Stevens, b. 1920, grad. Northwestern Univ. School of Law, 1947. Appointed in 1975 by President Ford, he had previously served five years on the U.S. Court of Appeals for the Seventh Circuit. Regarded as independent and moderately conservative. Net worth in 1997: $1.24 to $2.59 million.

Clarence Thomas, b. 1948, grad. Yale Law School, 1974. Headed Equal Employment Opportunity Commission for seven years prior to his appointment in 1990 to the U.S. Court of Appeals for the District of Columbia. Appointed to the Supreme Court in 1991 by President Bush, he is the only African-American justice. Arguably the most conservative member of the court, whose appointment and opinions have been surrounded by controversy. Net worth in 1997: $80,000 to $275,000.

Sources: Cornell University Law School (1998). Available online at **http://www.supct.law.cornell.edu/supct/**; *USA Today*, June 2, 1997, pp. 1–2.

with criminal court. In most courthouses, judges (like trial lawyers) deal with all kinds of legal cases. They are sometimes rotated among various divisions, such as family court, traffic court, probate court, misdemeanor court, felony court, small claims court, and juvenile court. When a criminal defendant appears before a judge, the judge may have plenty of trial experience but little experience with the criminal law.

The Selection and Duties of Criminal Court Judges. Some judges are appointed to the bench while others are elected. U.S. District Court judges are appointed by the president and confirmed by the Senate, and they serve for life. For the past century, three characteristics of those appointed have been predictable: Almost all appointees have been white males who belong to the same political party as the president. However, the judicial appointments of President Clinton show a distinct break with tradition: By the end of his first term in 1996, 30 percent of his 169 appointments were women, and nearly another 30 percent were minorities (Maguire and Pastore, 1997:62). Around half of U.S. District Court judges have prior experience as a state or municipal judge, and around 40 percent have prior experience as a prosecutor.

At the state level, distinctions are generally made between circuit (or superior court) judges who sit in courts of general jurisdiction—including the felony division—and those who sit in courts of limited jurisdiction, such as traffic and misdemeanor court. The latter are sometimes called *associate judges*. In Illinois, as in many other states, associate judges are selected by a vote of the circuit judges. States vary as to how circuit judges are initially selected and later retained (Maguire and Pastore, 1997:75–76). Some use a partisan public election; others use a nominating commission of attorneys and judges; and still others use a nonpartisan public election. In most states, circuit judges serve for a term of at least six years, and they are retained for subsequent terms through a partisan or nonpartisan public election.

What Criminal Court Judges Do. Judges who handle criminal cases are involved in activities that range far beyond presiding over criminal trials. Here are some of them:

- Review and approve search and arrest warrants requested by police
- Review and approve requests for wiretaps
- Preside over bail hearings, initial appearances, preliminary hearings, and arraignments
- Preside over preventive detention hearings
- Preside over hearings to determine whether juveniles should be tried as adults
- Rule on pre-trial motions, including requests for continuances
- Participate in pre-trial conferences with opposing attorneys, including plea negotiations
- Hold sentencing hearings and hand down sentences
- Review post-conviction motions, including petitions from prisoners

A judge's work is mostly a mixture of highly technical problem solving, routine administrative paperwork, courtroom management, and discretionary decision making. The job requires "people skills," including the ability to communicate clearly and decisively, the ability to listen, the ability to handle emotionally charged outbursts (of defendants, attorneys, victims, and courtroom observers), and the ability to keep people on task and to the point. Above all, a judge is expected to be impartial. For all these talents, the pay is modest but comfortable. In 1998, judges in U.S. District Courts made around $137,000 per year (Maguire and Pastore, 1998:56); most state court judges make between $80,000 and $100,000 (National Center for State Courts, 1997).

In the courtroom, judges manage the proceedings with the assistance of a court bailiff, a stenographer, and often an armed guard to watch over defendants and onlookers. No two courtrooms are alike, for no two judges are alike. Some judges maintain a high level of formality, while others are quite informal; in some courts you can hear a pin drop, while in others the atmosphere seems chaotic and loud. While the chief judge in a circuit may attempt to influence how other judges behave, the individuality of judges is shown by how they run their own courtroom.

CRIMINAL TRIALS AND THE JURY SYSTEM

The Sixth Amendment to the Constitution guarantees all defendants the right to a public trial. A public trial offers citizens some protection against the many abuses that might occur if people could be convicted without trial or if the trial were held in secret. Secret trials are the hallmark of dictatorships and totalitarian governments, not of democracies. Yet as Figure 12.3 shows, only a small percentage of criminal cases ever make it to trial, and less than 10 percent of felony convictions occur through a trial. In federal courts, for example, of over 55,000 criminal defendants convicted in 1997, less than 4,000 went through

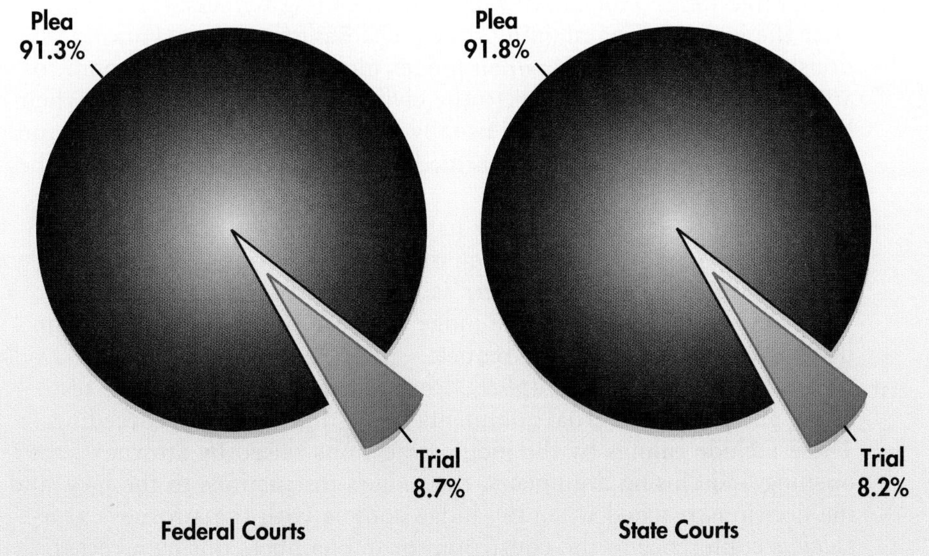

FIGURE 12.3 Criminal Convictions Obtained through Trials
The vast majority of defendants do not go to trial. Most cases that are not screened out in the pre-trial stages are disposed of through guilty pleas. The graphs show the percentage of trials and pleas in federal (1994) and state (1992) courts.

Sources: Kathleen Maguire and Ann L. Pastore (1995). *Sourcebook of Criminal Justice Statistics, 1994* (p. 462). Washington, D.C.: U.S. Department of Justice; Patrick A. Langan and Helen Graziadei (1995). "Felony Sentences in State Courts, 1992." *BJS Bulletin* (January):1–16.

a complete trial (Maguire and Pastore, 1998:397). In state courts in 1994, of the nearly 900,000 felony convictions, only 98,833 were obtained through trial (Brown and Langan, 1998:43). The trial is clearly the exception rather than the rule of American judicial procedure; the vast majority of criminal cases are screened out, dismissed, or handled through plea negotiations.

Even so, the public trial remains the cornerstone of our justice system, and every year thousands of Americans charged with crimes find themselves facing judge and jury. Most criminal trials are held in state courts; misdemeanors and petty offenses, most initial appearances, and less serious felonies are usually handled in lower courts, also known as courts of limited jurisdiction, as discussed earlier. Most felony defendants who go to trial find themselves in a court of general jurisdiction. The typical criminal felony trial is a **jury trial.** In a jury trial, a judge is in charge of the courtroom, but a jury composed of private citizens is reponsible for determining the guilt or innocence of the defendant. However, some criminal defendants choose a **bench trial**, which means a trial in which the presiding judge determines guilt or innocence. There is no jury. Bench trials are favored when the case is so shocking or complicated that the defendant fears a jury would not, or could not, render a fair and impartial verdict. Even though trial by jury is the most common practice in felony cases, bench trials produce nearly half of all felony convictions in state courts—nearly 47,000 guilty verdicts in 1994 (Brown and Langan, 1998:43).

jury trial Evidence is presented to a panel of citizens, who try to determine the defendant's guilt or innocence.

bench trial Evidence is presented to a judge, who determines the defendant's guilt or innocence.

There are various participants in the typical felony trial. Aside from the judge and jury, and the lawyers representing the prosecution and defense, the following occupations are also represented:

- *Bailiff.* Responsible for making sure the trial proceeds smoothly; duties include announcing the judge's entry (for example, "All rise, the

Honorable Judge Jane Smith presiding"), calling witnesses, looking after the jury, and maintaining order. The bailiff's closest working relationship is with the judge; when judges move from one courtroom to another or from the criminal to the civil division, they often take their bailiffs with them. Bailiffs are usually authorized to carry firearms and will make sure that additional armed security guards are present if they feel circumstances warrant it.

- *Court clerk.* Responsible for the paperwork associated with a trial, including defendant files, and for marking and recording exhibits used during testimony. The court clerk is also responsible for swearing in witnesses, and will provide the judge and trial attorneys with information or other assistance they request.
- *Court reporter (or stenographer).* Responsible for recording the testimony and all other verbal comments made during court proceedings. These include rulings by the judge, objections raised by attorneys, the opening and closing arguments, the judge's instructions to the jury, and the decisions reached when the judge confers with the attorneys at a *sidebar* conference in the courtroom or in chambers during a recess. New computer software has made the transcription process simpler and faster.

JURY TRIALS

As well as providing the right to a public trial, the Sixth Amendment also stipulates that criminal defendants have the right to a trial by an impartial jury. Many countries have no jury system at all, and those that do, such as the

Box 12.2

CAREERS IN CRIMINAL JUSTICE

COURT MANAGER

Many court systems employ a court manager or administrator to supervise the operations of the courtroom and its staff. Some systems offer special training in court management through paid internships. Here are the salary, qualifications, and duties for the position of Judicial Management Intern in the Los Angeles Municipal Court, as advertised in June 1998. Upon successful completion of the training program, interns are eligible for appointment as Court Manager. Among the duties of court managers are control and coordination of court calendars, supervision of data processing, preparation and dissemination of reports and procedural manuals, supervision of court security, and assisting the chief judge in the overall operation of the court.

Salary Range: $33,377 to $41,328

Qualifications: (minimum) Master's degree in public administration, political science, business administration, or closely related field; valid California Class "C" driver's license, or ability to obtain transportation for essential job-related functions.

Duties: Participate in training program of up to one year; receive instruction and practical experience in the supervision of court clerks, operation of courtrooms, and administrative activities associated with court management. Interns rotate through line and staff positions and attend specialized training classes.

United Kingdom and France, use it sparingly. Japan established a jury system in 1923, and then abolished it 20 years later (Terrill, 1984).

The jury trial is usually traced back to the Magna Carta of 1215. King John of England agreed that "no man shall be . . . proceeded against . . . unless by the lawful judgment of his peers or by the law of the land." However, it was not until 1968 that the U.S. Supreme Court held that the right to a jury trial applies to state trials through the Fourteenth Amendment. In ***Duncan v. Louisiana*** (1968), the Supreme Court spoke of the protections offered by jury trials: "A right to jury trial is granted to criminal defendants in order to prevent oppression by the Government. . . . Providing an accused with the right to be tried by a jury of his peers gave him an inestimable safeguard against the corrupt or overzealous prosecutor and against the compliant, biased, or eccentric judge. . . ."

Duncan v. Louisiana The right to a jury trial exists only for "serious criminal cases."

This is strong support for the jury system, but in the same ruling the Supreme Court also claimed that the right to a jury trial should extend only to "serious criminal cases." The Court pointed out that "there is a category of petty crimes or offenses which is not subject to the Sixth Amendment jury trial provision." Crimes carrying a penalty of six months or less in jail would be excluded. In ***Blanton v. Las Vegas*** (1989), the Court reasserted this position. It ruled that the defendant in a drunk driving case facing a maximum of six months imprisonment, a possible fine of $1,000, and other penalties did not have a right to a jury trial. Other challenges to the Court's position on the right to a jury trial will doubtless be made, for the Court can—and does—revise its rulings.

Blanton v. Las Vegas Defendants facing imprisonment of six months or less do not have a right to a jury trial.

Size of Juries and the Unanimity of the Verdict. Felony trials are usually conducted before a jury of 12 citizens, although use of smaller juries appears to be on the rise. However, there is no constitutional statement specifying the appropriate number, and the size of juries in misdemeanor cases is often less than twelve. The U.S. Supreme Court has ruled on the matter various times, and the legal minimum for noncapital crimes is now set at six jurors; death penalty cases require twelve jurors, and the jurors must be unanimous in their verdict. Most states and the federal system require that jury verdicts in circuit courts should be unanimous in noncapital cases as well.

Pre-Trial Motions. Once the court bailiff has called the court to order and the judge has entered, the prosecution and defense counsel will be asked by the judge if they are ready to proceed. Sometimes various **pre-trial motions** will have been offered by counsel, and these must be dealt with first. A pre-trial motion is simply a written or oral request that attorneys make before the trial itself begins. Five of the most common pre-trial motions are as follows:

pre-trial motion A written or oral request made to the judge by prosecution or defense before the trial begins.

- *Motion for discovery,* which is a request by defense counsel to see the evidence that the prosecutor intends to present at the trial, including a list of witnesses
- *Motion to suppress evidence,* which requests that certain evidence not be allowed in court
- *Motion for continuance,* which asks the court to delay the start of the trial, usually because counsel are not ready, the defendant or counsel is ill, or there has been a recent change of counsel
- *Motion for change of venue,* which requests that the trial be moved to another location because pre-trial publicity has made it unlikely that the jury will be unbiased
- *Motion to dismiss,* which requests that the case be dismissed. A motion to dismiss may come from either the defense or the prosecution, the latter most often when important witnesses have died or evidence has been destroyed, or when a plea agreement has been reached.

Once pre-trial motions have been settled the judge will turn to one of the most important steps in any jury trial: the selection of the jury. Many lawyers believe that jury selection is the most important part of the trial. In high-profile cases this step may take weeks or even months.

Selection of the Jury

Most felony trials in the United States formally begin with the selection of the jury. According to the Sixth Amendment, defendants have a right to an *impartial* jury. This does not mean that the jury knows nothing about the case. It means that the members should not have formed an opinion about the case before they hear it, nor should they be prejudiced for or against the defendant because of gender, race, social class, or other personal characteristics.

Qualifications for Jury Duty. Potential jurors are normally selected from a master list (sometimes called a *pool* or *wheel*). In most states the master list is created from vehicle registration lists, driver's licenses, or voter registration lists, or some combination of the three. The use of such lists is not without controversy, because they exclude many otherwise eligible people. In the 1996 trial of Arkansas governor Jim Guy Tucker on fraud and conspiracy charges, defense counsel showed that nearly 40 percent of eligible Arkansas residents were excluded from the jury pool, constructed from voter registration lists (Associated Press, January 26, 1996).

Far less controversial are these requirements for jury service: Jurors must be citizens of the United States, and must normally reside in the county in which the trial is to be held; they must be at least 18 years old (in Alabama and Nebraska it is 19; in Mississippi, 20); and they must be able to understand English (Bureau of Justice Statistics, 1995:256–263). Generally, convicted felons are ineligible to serve, and eligible citizens must not have served on a jury within the past year (in some states the past two or three years).

Once the master list is created, citizens are randomly selected from it for jury service, which usually lasts no more than a week or two. Sensational or highly complex cases, and those involving two or more defendants, may last much longer. The O. J. Simpson jury served for more than a year.

Sometimes, individuals who are summoned for jury duty request that they be excused. In many states some people are automatically exempted from serving—for example, people on active military duty, public officials, physicians, and police and fire officials. The decision to excuse a potential juror who is not exempt is largely left up to the judge. Most states allow excusals if the juror shows that serving would constitute undue hardship, extreme inconvenience, a risk to public security, or if the juror is ill or suffering from a physical or mental disability.

Voir Dire: How Individual Jurors Are Selected. The process of jury selection is called *voir dire;* translated from old French, it means literally "to speak the truth." During voir dire the defense and prosecution question each potential juror from the pool. In most states, the judge also participates in the questioning. The voir dire process usually lasts a day or two at most, but again there are exceptions: In the O. J. Simpson trial, a jury pool of more than 1,000 individuals was created, and it took nearly three months to select twelve members and twelve alternates. In many other countries, such a lengthy process would be unimaginable. Box 12.3 describes the jury selection process in England.

Voir dire is designed primarily to establish a juror's impartiality. Some studies suggest that the process can be successful in eliminating jurors who are biased against the prosecution or the defense (Johnson and Haney, 1994).

Box 12.3

GLOBAL JUSTICE

JURIES ARE RARELY USED IN ENGLAND, AND JURY SELECTION IS RELATIVELY SIMPLE

Americans take the jury system for granted, but in many countries there is no such thing as a jury trial; in others juries are permitted, but they are used sparingly. In England, where the modern jury system originated, criminal trials rarely involve juries. Most criminal cases are heard in the nation's 900 magistrates' courts. All but about 50 of the nation's 21,600 magistrates are lay volunteers called justices of the peace. They have little legal training, but a lawyer serves as clerk of the court and advises the magistrate on legal matters. Magistrates usually hear cases in pairs, and one day every two weeks (which explains why there are so many of them). Magistrates' courts do not have juries.

Juries are used in the Crown Courts, where *indictable offenses* are heard. Indictable offenses are roughly equivalent to our major felonies: they carry the possibility of prison terms of five years or more. Only about 1 in 20 eligible criminal defendants in England chooses a jury trial.

To serve on a jury in England, a person must have been a resident of the country for at least five years, must be a registered voter, and must be at least 18 years old but not older than 65. People with prison records are generally excluded, as are lawyers, police and probation officers, courthouse staff, people who have held judicial office such as judges and magistrates, the clergy, and the mentally ill. Other people have the right to be excused from jury duty; these include physicians, nurses, members of the military, and members of Parliament.

Jury selection is usually a simple process of taking the first twelve names out of a box containing the names of all those in the jury panel for that day. Any challenges must be made before trial. Once people are accepted for the jury panel, names drawn from the box cannot be challenged. As in the United States, there are challenges for cause and peremptory challenges. However, only the defense is allowed to make peremptory challenges, and not more than seven per defendant. Even when challenges are made, the judge can order a potential juror to "stand by," which may mean that person would have to serve on the jury if there are not enough eligible jurors in the panel.

Sources: Richard J. Terrill (1984). *World Criminal Justice Systems: A Survey.* Cincinnati, Ohio: Anderson; James Q. Wilson (1997). "Criminal Justice in England and America." *The Public Interest* (Winter):3–14.

However, as we shall see, voir dire is often criticized as a means of "stacking" the jury. During voir dire, counsel are permitted a variety of juror challenges. Sometimes the defense or prosecution will challenge the entire array of potential jurors on the grounds that the pool is not representative of the community in which the alleged crime occurred. This is rare, and usually occurs before the trial begins.

challenge for cause Counsel believes that a potential juror cannot be impartial and asks the judge to remove the juror from the panel.

Challenge for Cause. One of the most common challenges is a **challenge for cause.** This challenge is based on counsel believing that a particular juror would not be impartial. As a result of a prospective juror's answer to their questions, prosecution or defense counsel might conclude that the juror has already formed an opinion about the case or is prejudiced for or against the defendant. Or perhaps the juror believes that defendants are guilty until proven innocent, or that a defendant who did not take the stand was "obviously" guilty. Any of these conditions would be grounds for excusing a juror, although counsel are required to make the case for cause unless it is self-evident to the judge. There is no limit to the number of challenges for cause that defense or prosecution can make. However, judges soon tire of continuous challenges, especially if they believe they are frivolous.

peremptory challenge Counsel are allowed to remove a certain number of potential jurors without giving their reasons.

Peremptory Challenges. The second major challenge is a **peremptory challenge**. Peremptory challenges require no explanation, and counsel make them whenever they think the excusal of a particular juror will help their side or hurt their opponent's. Counsel are restricted in the number of peremptory challenges they can make. In federal criminal trials, each side has 20 peremptory challenges, and the judge has discretion to allow more. Among state courts, the number varies considerably, with fewer challenges generally allowed in misdemeanor trials than in felony cases. In felony trials that do not involve the death penalty, the number of peremptory challenges ranges from three in Hawaii to fifteen in New York (Bureau of Justice Statistics, 1995:269–273). Most states allow from six to ten peremptory challenges for each side.

jury consultant An expert on the relationship between the characteristics of jurors and their verdicts.

Jury Consultants: Adding Science to Jury Selection. Many attorneys now use **jury consultants** to help them in the voir dire process. A jury consultant is usually a social or behavioral scientist who has studied the relationship between

Historically, peremptory challenges have been used to exclude black or female jurors on the basis of their race or sex alone. In Batson v. Kentucky (1986) and most recently in J. E. B. v. Alabama (1994), the U.S. Supreme Court has declared this practice unconstitutional.

ILLUSTRATION COURTESY OF CULVER PICTURES

the characteristics of jurors and their verdicts. Since the composition of a jury is so important to the prosecution and the defense, many lawyers are glad to have objective data to back up their subjective impressions of prospective jurors. The jury consultant brings the perspective of *science* to what used to be called the *art* of jury selection. Jury consultants are used most commonly in high-profile cases, and when the defendant can afford to pay the fees, which may run into hundreds of thousands of dollars. Jury consultants were prominent in the O. J. Simpson case, as well as in the rape trial of William Kennedy Smith. There are an estimated 500 jury consultants nationwide, receiving up to $4,000 a *day* for in-court work (*St. Louis Post-Dispatch*, January 21, 1996, p. E1).

The use of jury consultants first gained national attention in the 1975 trial of Joan Little (Robin and Anson, 1990:323–327). While in a North Carolina jail awaiting an appeal on burglary charges, Little, an African American, killed a 62-year-old white jailer by stabbing him eleven times in the neck with an icepick. She escaped from jail, but eight days later she surrendered to state police. She claimed the jailer had threatened her with the icepick, demanding oral sex. When found, the jailer was naked from the waist down, and semen was discovered on his leg. These facts were interpreted by the prosecution to indicate that Little had lured the jailer into her cell by offers of sex, while all along she intended to escape. Little was charged with first-degree murder, the penalty for which was death.

The incident took place in a small, predominantly white rural community, and defense counsel thought it would be impossible to empanel an impartial jury. They wanted to move the case to another county. So they hired two psychologists to conduct a random survey of residents of a 24-county area surrounding the scene of the crime. They discovered high levels of prejudice and found that African Americans, women, and younger adults were grossly underrepresented in the jury pool. Coupled with testimony on pre-trial publicity, this evidence persuaded the judge to agree to a change of venue. The trial was held in Raleigh, some 100 miles away.

Even after the change of venue, defense counsel still needed answers to two questions: First, was the jury pool representative of the population in the Raleigh area? Second, could jurors potentially sympathetic to the defendant be identified from the pool? The psychologists conducted another random survey and constructed a profile of a "friendly" juror. During voir dire, defense counsel used the survey questions and profile to examine 150 prospective jurors. The prosecutor made an unsuccessful attempt to disqualify all black jurors; the defense, meanwhile, tried to exclude elderly white men who might identify with the dead jailer. In the end, the jury consisted of six white and six black members, mostly middle-aged Democrats. Little was acquitted after a relatively short 78-minute jury deliberation. The total cost of Little's defense was put at $325,000, most of it paid by the Southern Poverty Law Center, a nonprofit organization that fights racial injustice and represents the interests of oppressed groups.

Criticisms of Scientific Jury Selection. Criticisms of scientific jury selection are not hard to find. Some concern its use, rather than its nature or impact. For example, the case is often made that jury consultants are used only in the small minority of cases that involve wealthy defendants or high-publicity crimes. Typically, the resources of public defenders and most defendants with private attorneys do not permit the hiring of consultants, so the question arises: Is it right that only a minority of defendants should have access to their services? There is no adequate answer to this question.

A different sort of criticism is that scientific jury selection seeks to manipulate the partisanship of the jury in favor of the defendant or the state rather than to assure impartiality, as specified in the Constitution. Juries end up being packed with certain kinds of people rather than with a representative sample of the community. Not only may prospective jurors be challenged because of their age, gender, race, family status, and occupation, but also, some critics fear, simply because they are well educated, intelligent, and thoughtful. Not only are such people less likely to be ruled by their emotions, they are also more likely to be critical thinkers, to comprehend complex material, and to be influential arguers in the jury room. In the minds of defense attorneys looking out for their client's best interests, these conditions increase the risks of conviction.

Despite these criticisms, scientific jury selection is probably here to stay. Jury consultant firms are now advertising their services on the Internet, and workshops are being held around the country for attorneys interested in learning more about the science of jury selection. As more and more trial lawyers use jury consultants, more of those defendants with adequate resources will expect them to be part of the defense team. Since scientific jury selection appears to increase the chances that a trial will result in a favorable outcome for the client (Diamond, 1990), anything that increases the chance of success in the adversarial drama of the courtroom will be attractive to both defense and prosecution.

Notwithstanding the reputed benefits of scientific jury selection and the growing interest in it, the bulk of everyday felony trials conducted by the bulk of criminal lawyers will not involve jury consultants. Most lawyers will do their best to select a jury they feel comfortable with using only their experience to guide them. Respected defense attorney Donald Wolff explained how the art of jury selection works for him, and recounted this interesting incident:

> I think I've learned what to look for in picking a jury. Some of the bases on which I say that are eye contact with the potential juror, with how they answer my questions, with their body posture, with some of the questions I'm able to ask about what they read, what they think. I mean, in a capital case once I had a prospective juror reading a John Grisham book, *The Chamber*. Well, the book happens to be anti–death penalty. But instead of assuming "Oh good, here is a very good juror for me," I asked the right questions and found that she was very pro–death penalty, and didn't like the book. I struck her from the jury. So I think it is experience in trying cases that counts more than anything else. (Donald Wolff, personal communication, April, 1997)

Even if it became common in routine criminal cases, scientific jury selection using consultants would not, and could not, replace trial experience and the skills derived from it. At best it is a complement to that experience.

Diversity and the Composition of Juries

The United States is a diverse society whose citizens come from different backgrounds and hold different opinions and beliefs. If only some groups of people were allowed to serve on juries, that breadth of experience, opinion, and belief would be lost; inevitably, juries would not be impartial but would be biased in one direction or another. Many defendants could not expect a fair trial, which is guaranteed by the U.S. Constitution.

The U.S. Supreme Court ruled in *Strauder v. West Virginia* (1880) that a statutory requirement that only white men could serve on a jury—common among Southern states at the time—was unconstitutional because it denied due process of law to black citizens. And over half a century later, in *Thiel v. Southern Pacific Railway Company* (1945), the Court ruled that while a jury of one's peers does not mean that every possible group in a community has to be represented, systematic and intentional exclusion of jurors because of their social characteristics is unconstitutional. The Court repeated this opinion in *Taylor v. Louisiana* (1975). In that case, Justice Byron White wrote that "restricting jury service to only special groups or excluding identifiable segments playing a major role in the community cannot be squared with the constitutional concept of a jury trial."

The Use of Peremptory Challenges to Exclude Black and Female Jurors. Despite these rulings, trial lawyers have used the peremptory challenge throughout the 20th century as a way to exclude black and female jurors. Racial exclusions through peremptory challenges have been commonplace, and the practice still continues today (Bauman and Ottenad, 1994; Ogletree, 1994). Many black defendants have been tried by all-white juries even though black citizens were included in the jury pool. Because no explanation need be given when a peremptory challenge is made, it is difficult to establish that intentional systematic exclusion of black (or white) jurors is involved.

The U.S. Supreme Court accepted the practice of using peremptory challenges to exclude African Americans when it decided ***Swain v. Alabama*** (1965). In this case, a black man was convicted of rape by an all-white jury. Using peremptory challenges, the prosecutor had succeeded in excluding African Americans from the jury. The Court reasoned that the distinction between peremptory challenges and challenges for cause was an important one, and any effort to limit the use of peremptories would muddy the distinction.

Swain v. Alabama Counsel may use peremptory challenges to exclude members of certain groups.

Twenty years later the Court changed its mind. In ***Batson v. Kentucky*** (1986), the Court reversed the lower court conviction of a black man charged with burglary and receipt of stolen property. During the earlier trial, the judge had excluded some jurors for cause and then permitted counsel to use peremptory challenges. The prosecutor used his challenges to exclude all four black people in the jury pool, resulting in an all-white jury. The Court wrote: "Selection procedures that purposefully exclude black persons from juries undermine public confidence in the fairness of our system of justice. . . . [T]he Equal Protection Clause [of the Fourteenth Amendment] forbids the prosecutor to challenge potential jurors solely on account of their race or on the assumption that black jurors as a group will be unable impartially to consider the State's case against a black defendant."

Batson v. Kentucky Counsel may not use peremptory challenges to exclude potential jurors simply because they are black.

The Court did not advocate banning peremptory challenges altogether, though the late Justice Thurgood Marshall, the Court's only African American justice at that time, suggested that it should. A series of Supreme Court cases in the early 1990s have moved the Court closer to Marshall's position, although it seems unlikely that peremptory challenges will disappear entirely. Although a recent case, ***J. E. B. v. Alabama*** (1994), extended restrictions on peremptory challenges to include gender (the Supreme Court argued that "gender, like race, is an unconstitutional proxy for juror competence and impartiality"), protections against race and gender discrimination in jury selection are easily undermined by judges who uncritically accept attorney claims that a particular challenge is not about race or gender.

J. E. B. v. Alabama Counsel may not use peremptory challenges to exclude jurors simply because of their sex.

The Social Class Composition of Juries. The U.S. Supreme Court has specified that social groupings based on race and gender are **cognizable groups** for the purpose of constructing a jury. This means that they are recognized in law as a distinct social category. But what about the social class of potential jurors? Decades of sociological research has demonstrated that people with similar standing or class in a community, based on such things as education, occupation, income, and wealth, tend to display similar attitudes and behavior. Research suggests that class may be even more important than race or ethnicity

cognizable group People sharing a specific characteristic such as race or sex who are recognized in law as a distinct social category.

in organizing social attitudes and behavior (Farley, 1995:458–463). If this is true, the social class of prospective jurors should be taken into account in jury selection as well.

A study of jury panels in Orange County, California, discovered that social class was actually a more significant factor in jury selection than race or ethnicity (Fukurai, 1996). African Americans and Hispanics with relatively high social class position were significantly more likely than their lower-status counterparts to be represented on jury panels. If this finding is duplicated in other studies and reflected in jury selection strategies in the courtroom, social class may soon join race and gender as a cognizable group in jury trials.

Using Change of Venue to Influence Jury Composition. Despite restrictions on the use of peremptory challenges, there are other ways that attorneys can effectively exclude certain groups of citizens from juries. One is to request a **change of venue**. This moves the trial to another location, often many miles from the community where the crime occurred.

change of venue Moving a trial to another location.

The change of venue strategy paid off for the prosecutors in the 1992 trial of the police officers accused of beating Rodney King. No one doubts that the change of venue was driven by considerations of race rather than pre-trial publicity alone. The four police officers accused of beating King were tried in Simi Valley, not in Los Angeles where the assault occurred and where many African Americans live. Simi Valley is a predominantly white, middle-class community. By successfully moving the trial to Simi Valley, defense counsel had significantly increased the chances of getting a jury sympathetic to their side. The all-white jury eventually found the four white officers not guilty. The verdict touched off three days of deadly rioting in Los Angeles. Two of the four officers were later found guilty of violating King's civil rights in a federal court in downtown Los Angeles.

Some legal experts believe that too much emphasis is placed on the biasing effects of pre-trial publicity (Flynn, 1993). However, extensive behavioral research shows that pre-trial publicity that is prejudicial to a defendant is likely to influence the verdict (Kerr, 1994; Otto, Penrod, and Dexter, 1994). One of the ways it does this is by affecting jurors' initial judgments, which in turn influence the way they view the evidence later presented in the trial.

THE ATTORNEYS PRESENT THEIR EVIDENCE

Once a jury has been selected, the trial begins in earnest. The bulk of the trial consists of presentation of evidence by attorneys for the prosecution and the defense. The evidence becomes the "facts" of the case that the jury or judge must consider in reaching a verdict. "Facts" is in quotation marks because a trial is not so much about facts as about interpretations of evidence that is presented as factual. As noted earlier, the trial is an adversarial process in which the prosecution and defense try to convince the jury that their version of reality is the most believable one. The very same "facts" are given a different twist by each side in an effort to influence the interpretations made by the jury. Even something as concrete as a bloody glove can take on different meaning and significance as it moves from the hands of the prosecutor to those of the defense.

Opening Statements by Prosecution and Defense

opening statement Counsel introduce the jury to some of the evidence and counterevidence that will be presented during the trial.

The judge begins the trial by signaling that the court is ready to hear the prosecutor's **opening statement**. An opening statement provides the judge, jury, and defense counsel with a brief overview of the "facts" the prosecutor hopes to prove through presentation of the evidence. After the prosecution has made its

In a criminal trial, lawyers present their version of the "facts."
Illustration by John Overmyer

opening remarks, the defense follows. Both sides usually treat opening statements as an important opportunity to gain the sympathy and support of the jury. The statements are not obligatory, and sometimes the defense will wait until after the prosecution has rested its case before making its own opening remarks. This way the defense counsel can directly attack the evidence that has so far been presented, and can attempt to discredit those parts of the prosecution's case that may have impressed the jury. The risk in waiting is that the jury may interpret the absence of an opening statement by the defense early in the trial as a sign of weakness, preferring to react rather than to lead.

Just as it is risky for counsel not to make an opening statement, it is also risky to get carried away with all sorts of promises of what counsel will "prove." Generally, a good opening statement will be a brief yet engaging account of the major arguments and evidence that counsel plans to introduce. A professional expectation exists that limits this account to evidence that will actually be presented; attorneys who talk about evidence they have no intention of introducing or of fictitious witnesses may find themselves accused of professional misconduct. They may be punished by the judge and possibly by the local bar association, as well.

Types of Evidence Presented in Court

The outcome of a trial usually hinges on the presentation of evidence. Attorneys for the prosecution and defense have two major types of evidence they can offer in support of their case: **demonstrative evidence** and **testimonial evidence**. Demonstrative evidence consists of physical objects—for example, the bloody glove presented in the O. J. Simpson trial, a weapon, fingerprints, blood samples, DNA, stolen property, tire or shoe prints, business records, computer files, and written or videotaped confessions. Testimonial evidence consists of oral evidence given under oath either in the courtroom or in *depositions* taken before attorneys for both sides and recorded by a court reporter.

demonstrative evidence Physical objects, including confessions, that can be shown to the judge or jury.

testimonial evidence Oral statements given under oath.

direct evidence Eyewitness accounts or other evidence that demonstrates a fact about the case at hand.

circumstantial evidence Any evidence that requires the judge or jury to infer a fact about the case at hand.

There are two types of testimonial evidence. Testimony by an eyewitness to the alleged crime is called **direct evidence**. In the Rodney King case, the videotape of the beating qualified as direct evidence. Any testimony or other evidence that requires the jury to infer a fact about the crime is called **circumstantial evidence**. Had Andrew Cunanan, the man accused of murdering fashion designer Gianni Versace and four other men, not committed suicide before he could be arrested, the evidence at his trial would have been primarily circumstantial—there were no eyewitnesses to the murders.

DIRECT EXAMINATION AND CROSS-EXAMINATION OF WITNESSES

United States v. Reynolds A judge is not required to define "reasonable doubt" in instructions to the jury.

Evidence is presented first by the prosecution, and then by the defense. The witnesses called by the prosecution are known as *witnesses for the prosecution*, and those called by the defense are *witnesses for the defense*. Witnesses are questioned, or *examined*, by the attorneys representing each side. When thinking about the examination process, it is important to remember that the defense needs to sow a "reasonable doubt" in the mind of at least one juror to achieve a mistrial. No one has yet come up with an explicit definition of what "reasonable doubt" means, however. In fact, the U.S. Supreme Court has repeatedly ruled that a trial judge is not required to define for the jury what the phrase means. The most recent ruling was in ***United States v. Reynolds*** (1995), where the Court agreed with the Seventh Circuit that "the phrase 'reasonable doubt' is self-explanatory and is its own best definition. Further elaboration tends to misleading refinements which weaken and make imprecise the existing phrase." Perhaps the best way of thinking about reasonable doubt is that doubts are reasonable if the average person hearing the same evidence would come to the same conclusion. In felony cases, as we saw earlier, the prosecution must prove its case *beyond a reasonable doubt* in the minds of *all* jurors. The burden of proof lies with the prosecutor. This tradition in Anglo-American law recognizes the imbalance of power between the individual and the state and allows defendants to benefit from the least possibility that they may be innocent.

direct examination Counsel questioning its own witnesses.

Direct Examination of Witnesses. Each side questions its own witnesses in a process called **direct examination**. Attorneys usually know beforehand what the witness is likely to say under direct examination, because they will have discussed the testimony beforehand. The testimony of witnesses called to the stand by each attorney is usually "friendly" to that attorney's side of the case. This does not necessarily mean that these witnesses want the defendant convicted or acquitted, although they might. Rather, attorneys put witnesses on the stand because they have information the attorneys believe will be useful for their side.

cross-examination Counsel questioning the other side's witnesses.

Cross-Examination of Witnesses. Each side is given the opportunity to question the other side's witnesses. This process is called **cross-examination**. The attorney who has just finished direct examination might end with the words "your witness," signifying that with the judge's approval the opposing attorney may now conduct cross-examination. Or the the attorney might indicate to the judge that direct examination is over, and the judge then asks the opposing attorney if he or she wants to cross-examine the witness. If the attorney declines to cross-examine the witness, the other lawyer may then call the next witness for direct examination.

Although a good adversarial lawyer must be adept at both direct and cross-examination, it is skill at cross-examination that distinguishes great trial lawyers from the rest. In their hands, what was damning evidence or proof of innocence a moment ago becomes the exact opposite. Attorneys learn the fundamentals of cross-examination in law school, often in mock trials. Here are some of the "commandments" that law professors who teach trial advocacy like to emphasize (Asbill, 1994):

- Ask short questions using plain words.
- Ask only leading questions (those likely to draw comments from witnesses that you want them to make).
- Do not ask a question if you don't know the answer.
- Listen to the answer.
- Do not quarrel with the witness.
- Do not allow the witness to repeat his or her direct testimony.
- Do not permit the witness to explain.
- Avoid asking one question too many.
- Save the explanation for the closing statement.

The main focus of the advice is getting information from the witness in a manner that does not confuse, overload, or anger the jury—or produce something unexpected that hurts the attorney's case. These commandments may be sound advice, but cross-examination is a trial skill that is learned and modified through experience in the courtroom. Techniques vary widely from one lawyer to another.

CHALLENGING THE ADMISSIBILITY OF EVIDENCE

Since trial is an adversarial process, both the prosecution and the defense attempt to get each other's best evidence thrown out. This process often starts early, in pre-trial motions to suppress evidence. One argument the defense may make is that the evidence was acquired illegally—for example, in violation of search-and-seizure laws. Such challenges may also occur during the preliminary hearing, if one is held. During trial, lawyers for each side will be heard on occasion to object that evidence is "incompetent, irrelevant, and immaterial." If the judge agrees, the evidence is disallowed and the jury is instructed to disregard it.

Discovery: How Lawyers Find Out about the Other Side's Evidence. Readers who remember the *Perry Mason* TV series starring the late Raymond Burr will remember that many of his cases were won by the last-minute appearance of surprise witnesses or evidence. This always caught the prosecutor off guard. In most states, however, there are rules of **discovery** that require each side to present information to the other about the evidence it intends to produce during the trial. In some states discovery does not apply to defense counsel, so Perry Mason's actions would be permissible. Even in states where discovery rules apply to both sides, new evidence may be admitted provided the other side is given reasonable time to review it and to prepare a response. If either side violates discovery rules, the judge may throw the evidence out and may even fine the offending attorney(s).

discovery A process in which opposing counsel inform each other about evidence they will produce during trial.

SOCIAL STATUS AND THE SUPPORTIVENESS OF EVIDENCE

As argued earlier, a trial is not so much about proving facts as about creating and managing the impressions jurors develop of the evidence presented. The more supportive, or *partisan*, the evidence is, the more likely your side is to win.

A recent study of the production of evidence by seven prosecutors in a medium-sized Georgia town shows that the social status of defendants and victims affects the supportiveness of the evidence (Cooney, 1994). Three processes involving the collection and presentation of evidence were examined:

- The amount of investigative effort lawyers put into a case
- The willingness of people to testify or "come forward"
- The supportiveness, or "quality," of the actual testimony

The Impact of Investigative Effort. The study found that "big cases" involving important people or extraordinary events produced detailed, time-consuming, and costly investigations by both prosecution and defense. The defense of corporate offenders illustrates how the social status of a defendant influences the effort put into an investigation: In one case, a lawyer reported that "three associates worked on the accounts for over two months"; attorneys in another corporate case related that "we billed over 150 hours in three months . . . all in the investigation stage" (Mann, 1985).

In contrast, consider the other end of the spectrum, where defendants are relatively poor and powerless but where the consequences of a conviction may be just as costly, if not more so. Their cases often receive scant attention even when serious felonies are involved, including crimes carrying the death penalty (Elias, 1993; Coyle, Strasser, and Lovelle, 1990; Redlich, Coleman, and Waglini, 1994). Put low-status suspects and low-status victims together and the level of investigative effort tends to be low as well. Arguably the least effort is displayed when known criminals are victims. A case involving a drug dealer suspected of killing another drug dealer illustrates the point: After seven months detectives had still not taken a statement from the defendant (Cooney, 1994:840). Although a murder had been committed, the most serious crime under state law, the case was not considered a priority.

The Willingness of Witnesses to Testify. The willingness of witnesses to come forward is very important for the prosecution and the defense, because their cases are built around testimony in court. However, the willingness of witnesses to testify is often influenced by the social status of the parties involved. The higher the social status of a defendant or victim, the more willing people are to testify on their behalf. This does not mean that lawyers will invite them all to testify, but it expands the pool from which they can pick witnesses—and they might come across useful new evidence while screening them. Corporate offenders and the rich and famous such as O. J. Simpson and Claus von Bulow even received unsolicited offers of help from people wishing to testify on their behalf (Dershowitz, 1986). Every offer will be considered, but most unsolicited offers are refused because the testimony is irrelevant or suspect.

The Supportiveness of Testimony. Even though higher-status defendants and victims are likely to reap the benefits of greater investigative effort and greater numbers of willing witnesses, the outcome of a trial still rests on the supportiveness—or quality—of the testimony for each side. Social status has an impact here as well. All else being equal, "the testimony of high-status witnesses is more credible and has a greater impact on the outcome of a case than that of low-status witnesses" (Cooney, 1994:848).

The same is also true of the testimony of people who are not relatives or intimate friends of the defendant. It is generally accepted that people who are very close to a defendant will be influenced by emotions and biased in favor of the defendant. The testimony of strangers is thought to be more objective and less biased. Since higher-status defendants are in a better position to attract testimony from strangers, including respected attorneys and expert witnesses, they stand to benefit from both higher quantity and quality of supportive testimony. A Georgia case that resulted in acquittal illustrates:

> The defendant, a wealthy businessman well known in his community, was charged with child molestation. He called ten character witnesses. They included an assistant district attorney, a clergyman, a school administrator, a businessman, a police officer, a school teacher, a librarian, and an elderly neighbor with deep roots in the community. Though low-status defendants can sometimes attract the support of one, or maybe two, high-status individuals, support of this standing and volume is largely confined to those who enjoy the twin advantages of high social stature and many strong connections. (Cooney, 1994:850)

Since they influence the quantity and quality of evidence presented at trial, these patterns affect the information received and the impressions drawn by judge and jury. In large measure, testimonial evidence acquires its impact from the social characteristics of the people presenting it. Jurors are more inclined to believe evidence presented by someone they admire and respect than by someone they do not.

The Use of Persuasion in the Courtroom

The key to winning in the courtroom is the ability to persuade the jury to see things your way. Persuasion is a social-psychological phenomenon in which one person induces another to form a belief or opinion, or engage in a behavior, when they are not inclined to do so. Even when criminal cases appear cut

Most criminal defendants cannot afford to hire expert witnesses. Those who can do so because they know that juries tend to hold experts in high regard, and tend to consider their expertise alone as persuasive. Here Dr. Cyril Wecht testifies at the Menendez brothers' murder trial in Los Angeles, California.

Photo by Boris Yaro, courtesy of AP Photo

and dried, good attorneys may still be able to turn the tables against their opponents through persuading the jury to accept their version of the "facts." There are various methods of persuasion commonly used in the courtroom; they include use of expert witnesses, focusing attention on the victim, and "stealing thunder." We will consider each in turn.

expert witness A person with specialized education, training, or accomplishments in a particular field who testifies on behalf of the prosecution or defense.

The Expert Witness. One way to persuade the jury to see things your way is to hire **expert witnesses** whose testimony either contradicts that of witnesses for the other side or puts a different light on the physical evidence. Expert witnesses are people with specialized education, training, and accomplishments in a particular field. They may be experts in criminalistics and other areas of forensic science, or they may be experts in any other field or discipline relevant to the case at hand. Their expertise is not taken for granted, however, but must be established to the satisfaction of the court before they are allowed to testify. In the Timothy McVeigh trial, criminalists from the FBI's crime lab were subject to hours of withering cross-examination by the defense in an effort to show that mistakes had been made in the way the lab handled evidence for the trial.

To make the most of expert witnesses, prosecutors and defense attorneys will sometimes arrange to have the questioning done by attorneys who are themselves experts in the relevant area. However, the prosecution usually has an advantage when it comes to expert witnesses because most criminal defendants cannot afford to hire them, and those represented by public defenders often find there is little or no room for expert witnesses in the office budget. The most a defense lawyer can usually do is to cross-examine the state's expert witnesses in the hopes that some jurors will be persuaded through the questions and replies to doubt the credibility of the state's evidence. Most of the time this is difficult to do, for people tend to hold experts in high regard. The very idea of expertise is persuasive.

Focusing Attention on the Victim. A powerful strategy of persuasion that defense attorneys sometimes use is to create doubts that a crime ever occurred. This strategy is unlikely to work well in the face of overwhelming physical evidence of a crime, but it may be tried nonetheless, especially if there are no eyewitnesses. The core of this strategy revolves around the victim of the alleged crime. The goal is to persuade jurors that the alleged victim was no victim at all. If jurors believe there is no victim, it is harder for them to accept that there was ever a crime.

victim blaming Responsibility for a possible crime is shifted from the defendant to the victim.

In cases such as these it is crucial for the defense to persuade the jury that the victim was a *willing* participant in the alleged crime. The defense can sometimes successfully shift the focus of the jury from the character of the defendant to that of the victim. The attorney has then engaged in **victim blaming,** a technique that diverts responsibility for the incident from the offender to the victim. This is a common ploy in sexual assault trials, even those involving child victims—and quite often it succeeds (Thomas, 1967; MacKinnon, 1989; LaFree, 1989; LaFree, Reskin, and Visher, 1991). Why?

The answer lies not simply with the trial skills of the attorney, although these are certainly important. We must also recognize the influence that social structure and culture have in making jurors—and judges—receptive to defense interpretations that blame or in other ways deny victims of sexual assault. In American society men dominate women in most, if not all, areas of life. As a result both genders are socialized to expect and to prepare for male domination. The question of what constitutes too much—or criminal—domination has traditionally been answered *by* men, whose rules and laws usually allow considerable leeway *for* men. For example, the conventional image of the true rapist is of a stranger who physically attacks a woman and forces her to have sexual intercourse against her will. Historically, a rape conviction required not just evidence of penile penetration of the vagina, but also evidence of victim resistance and physical injury; even with these elements, however, the case was likely to be lost if the victim was not a virgin, if she knew the alleged offender, or if they had been dating—and especially if they had had sex before (Brownmiller, 1975; Russell, 1982; Stanko, 1990). In these situations, the moral character of the victim is questioned, and therefore the credibility of her accusation.

Victim blaming seems to be a generalized response to rape in our culture, and it should come as no surprise that defense attorneys take advantage of this in court. In the extreme, victim blaming becomes a denial that women are rapable. As one male juror put it when interviewed after a trial: "I don't think a woman can be raped. . . . I ask why are they out at that time of night? What did they do to provoke it? . . . A judge over in Ohio told me that a woman can run faster with her pants down than a man, and I believe that. . . . If you want to say rape, then she must be unconscious. She can scream and kick if she's awake and doesn't want it" (LaFree, 1989:225).

During sexual assault trials, the defense attorney will seek to transform the woman's rape into an act of consensual sex. If jurors hold the attitudes of the man just quoted, the task shouldn't be too difficult. Of course, many jurors are less blatantly sexist, but they also recognize that the penalties for rape and other sexual assaults are among the most severe. It is difficult to send someone to prison for many years if there is a hint that the victim may have been a willing participant. Small—and possibly unreasonable—doubts about a defendant's guilt may become convincing doubts in jurors' minds if they believe the victim's behavior was in some way improper.

The courtroom transformation of rape into a consensual act may not be as easy as it once was because most states and the federal government have passed **rape shield laws** that generally bar evidence of a victim's prior sexual conduct. Even so, some states with rape shield laws still allow testimony about the prior sexuality of women if that testimony (1) bears on the question of consent by showing prior sexual conduct between victim and defendant, and (2) shows that the defendant was not the source of semen or a sexually transmitted disease or pregnancy (Allison and Wrightsman, 1993; Matoesian, 1995).

rape shield laws Laws that generally bar the introduction of evidence about a victim's prior sexual conduct.

An analysis of the verbal exchanges between prosecution, defense attorney, judge, defendant, victim, and witnesses during trials shows how attorneys succeed and fail in convincing the jury that the rape victim was really no victim at all (Matoesian, 1993). The strategy is to challenge the victim's sexual/moral character, even though rape shield laws forbid this. Here is an illustration: In pre-trial motions in one case, the judge ruled that the marital status of an unmarried pregnant victim could not be introduced during the trial. In order to obey this ruling and yet make the point that she was single, the defense attorney consistently referred to her as "Miss" when the case came to trial. Through this strategy the attorney hoped to convince the jury that sex with the woman was not rape. In the William Kennedy Smith rape trial, the defense attorney made repeated covert references to the woman's sexual history in an attempt to persuade jurors that the woman was open to impersonal sex with Smith (Matoesian, 1995). Indeed, his questioning suggested that Smith and the woman had developed a consensual sexual relationship in the period immediately before the alleged attack. The strategy was successful: Smith was acquitted.

"Stealing Thunder": Reducing the Impact of Negative Evidence. There are other strategies of persuasion that expert lawyers use to get jurors to see the facts their way. While there is not room to explore them all here, they generally have one underlying purpose when used by the defense: to reduce the impact of negative—incriminating—evidence. Since the prosecution puts its case on first, the defense is playing "catch-up" in terms of jury persuasion. For this reason, the defense may try to steal the prosecution's thunder by bringing up seemingly negative evidence before the prosecution does. Studies of stealing thunder in simulated jury trials suggest that it can be an effective way of devaluing the prosecution's evidence in the eyes of jurors (Williams, Bourgeois, and Croyle, 1993).

A good time to steal the prosecution's thunder is when the facts are not in dispute because eyewitnesses and physical evidence show that the defendant committed the crime. If the defense successfully undermines the prosecution's evidence before it is given, the jury may return with an acquittal, or find the defendant guilty of a lesser offense. In a capital murder case, for example, this strategy may convince the jury that the defendant is guilty of manslaughter, an offense that does not carry the death penalty. Commonly, the defense will focus the jury's attention on the emotional state of the defendant prior to the crime in the hope that jurors will doubt that the offense was a cold-blooded, premeditated killing.

In recent years, defense attorneys have enjoyed some success in getting defendants acquitted on the grounds that their clients suffered from psychological trauma brought about by various kinds of abuse (Dershowitz, 1994). "Battered woman syndrome," "abused child syndrome," and "rape trauma syndrome" are examples of psychological conditions recognized in the medical literature as having a profound effect on the emotional state of the sufferer. One such defense has been called the "urban survival syndrome," and it draws on the characterization of the inner city as a jungle where the rule of survival is "Kill or be killed." The urban survival defense was first used in a Texas case involving an 18-year-old black youth who killed two unarmed men with whom he had had an earlier dispute and who the defense claimed "jumped" the youth in a parking lot. The prosecution claimed the defendant could have run away, but the defense portrayed the shooting as self-defense conditioned by the pervasive violence and fear of inner-city life.

Although some believe that defenses such as urban survival syndrome legitimize violence and therefore send the wrong message, others believe that a defendant's biography, including experiences with violence and the meanings attached to it, should be relevant in evaluating the motives behind the alleged crime. Perhaps it is not inappropriate for a defense attorney to attempt to convince the jury that the crime is caused by environmental conditions that induce fear, stress, and violent countermeasures in some people. What do you think?

JURY NULLIFICATION

Even the most effective presentation of evidence by prosecutors or defense attorneys will be pointless if members of a jury have decided on a verdict before the presentation of evidence has been completed. When this happens, the purpose of a jury is undermined. This problem has been called **jury nullification** and it is a topic that has received a lot of attention of late—even a segment on the CBS news program *60 Minutes* (March 10, 1996). The jury system rests on the premise that it is possible to select twelve citizens who are prepared to be impartial in reviewing the circumstances of a case, and honest and fair in reaching their verdict. The jury system itself is nullified, or abrogated, when verdicts are predetermined or unrelated to the evidence of guilt or innocence.

jury nullification A jury decides on a verdict before all the evidence is presented, without regard for the evidence, or because it wants to make a point despite the evidence.

Jury nullification is particularly important in the case of acquittals because the law gives juries the power to acquit defendants regardless of overwhelming evidence of guilt. The state has no recourse because the Fifth Amendment protects defendants against **double jeopardy**—being tried twice on the same charges after a verdict has been declared. It is in the jury's power, then, to acquit defendants for reasons not directly related to the case at hand.

double jeopardy Being tried twice on the same charges after a verdict has been declared.

It may come as a surprise that jury nullification is actually supported in some quarters as both a community self-help strategy and a political statement. This is the position of law professor Paul Butler. Butler is a black former prosecutor who believes that the justice system is helping to destroy the black community by arresting, prosecuting, and incarcerating large numbers of African Americans for essentially victimless crimes involving drugs and public order offenses (Butler, 1995). He supports black jurors' taking the law into their own hands by acquitting black defendants charged with nonviolent, largely victimless crimes.

The explosive growth in the nation's prison population is largely due to the crackdown on drug offenses during the 1980s, and much of this crackdown has focused on black offenders (Blumstein, 1993; Hagan, 1995). By 1993, for every eleven black men in the workforce, one was in prison; and 12 percent of all black men age 25 to 34 were incarcerated (Freeman, 1995:26). This is a disheartening vision for any American, but especially for the black community. Yet is jury nullification the solution, even if only a temporary one? The answer is surely no. The result will leave criminal defendants without the right to trial by an impartial jury, which is the cornerstone of our system of justice, even if it is rarely used in the typical criminal case. In the long run, as Alan Dershowitz (1994:89) has observed, minority defendants, and the minority community in general, will suffer the most if jury nullification becomes widespread. For instance, do you think that the all-white jury that acquitted Rodney King's white police assailants was engaged in jury nullification?

CLOSING ARGUMENTS

Once the prosecution and defense have presented their cases and have had an opportunity to challenge each others' evidence, each side is given time to make **closing arguments**. Closing arguments are very important because they provide attorneys with an opportunity to emphasize all the evidence and any inferences drawn from it that support their side. An indication of how seriously closing arguments were viewed by O. J. Simpson prosecutors is that Christopher Darden had a team of five colleagues help compose them, and he then practiced delivering them in front of the team (Darden, 1996:358). Attorney Donald Wolff believes that closing arguments are very important when the jury is "flip-flopping" on the defendant's guilt: "If you ever sit on a mock trial you'll find yourself going from I heard this, now I'm on this side, to I heard that, now I'm on that side, and you flip-flop back and forth" (Donald Wolff, personal communication, April, 1997). An effective closing argument can bring the jury back to your point of view.

closing arguments Counsel summarize the evidence they want the jury to remember and explain how it supports their version of the facts and not that of their opponent.

In many jurisdictions (although not California) the defense goes first, followed by the prosecution. This reverses the order in which opening statements are made, and some believe it gives an advantage to the prosecutor, who has "the last word." To remedy this criticism, some states and the federal rules of criminal procedure allow the defense an opportunity to respond to the prosecutor's closing argument. At the O. J. Simpson trial in California, the prosecution made closing arguments first, followed by the defense, and then a final rebuttal by the prosecution.

Lawyers are allowed greater leeway in their closing arguments than in the direct and cross-examination of witnesses. This is their final opportunity to present their version of what the evidence presented during the trial means—and sometimes this is done with great theatrics and emotion. Ironically, closing arguments are one of the few times that media portrayals of criminal justice at work come close to the real thing. Although the jury will be asked to judge only the facts of the case, we already know that these facts are better viewed as impressions, and lawyers want the closing impressions they create to stick in the jurors' minds when they finally sit down to deliberate.

For example, as part of his closing arguments, Simpson defense attorney Johnnie Cochran reviewed in detail the racist behavior and perjured testimony of detective Mark Fuhrman and passionately called on jurors to make a statement with their verdict about racism in the criminal justice system. Cochran had made race an issue throughout the trial, and he used his closing arguments as a way to drive home the point that prosecution evidence provided by racist cops was just another example of bias and obviously could not be trusted. For their part, prosecuting attorneys Marcia Clark and Christopher Darden, himself black, sought desperately to discredit Cochran's position, pointing out that many separate pieces of physical evidence were sufficient to place Simpson at the scene of the crime, and that race had nothing to do with it. In his rebuttal, Darden also resorted to emotional and moral appeals, citing verses from the Bible, and entreating jurors not to resort to jury nullification despite Cochran's encouragement: "You can't send a message to Fuhrman, you can't send a message to the LAPD, you can't eradicate racism within the LAPD or the LA community or within the nation as a whole by delivering a verdict of not guilty in a case like this" (Darden, 1996:372).

Although attorneys are allowed leeway in their closing arguments, opposing counsel may object to specific comments that are made, and the judge may order the jury to disregard them—although everyone realizes the damage has already been done. Judges have broad discretion in how they deal with closing arguments, but appellate court decisions have rendered some tactics plainly unlawful, and the basis for reversal on appeal (Vorhees, 1990:142–147). For example, a prosecutor cannot do any of the following:

- Make direct or indirect reference to a defendant's failure to testify, since this violates the defendant's privilege against self-incrimination
- Imply that the government would not have brought the case unless the defendant was guilty
- Comment on the courtroom appearance or behavior of a defendant who has not testified
- Ask jurors to put themselves in the defendant's shoes and ask themselves what they would have done in that situation
- Argue that in order to acquit the defendant the jury must find that the government's witnesses lied under oath
- Make race-conscious or racially biased arguments—for example, to suggest that it is unreasonable to believe that a black undercover officer would give false testimony against a black defendant

There are closing arguments that neither the prosecution nor the defense should make. For example, neither side may suggest to the jury that evidence supporting its case exists but has not been introduced in the trial. All closing arguments must be derived from the record of the trial, and it is improper for either attorney to draw inferences that are so unreasonable that they amount to the presentation of new evidence. All these rules are essentially designed to safeguard the constitutional rights of individual defendants and the fairness of the trial process at the moment when opposing attorneys are inclined to let loose in a last-ditch effort to win over the jury.

Judge's Instructions to the Jury

jury instructions Laying out the law the jury must follow in deciding on its verdict.

The judge has the last word on the legal elements in a case. Through **jury instructions** following closing arguments, the judge lays out the law that the jury must follow in deciding the case. Judges try to ensure that jurors understand the charges and the type of evidence required to prove them. Some judges also explain what "beyond a reasonable doubt" means, although as noted earlier, there is no constitutional requirement that they do so. Jurors will be told that if they are uncertain or wavering, then they must acquit the defendant. They will also be informed of alternative verdicts they could legally choose. For example, in a homicide case, the jury might decide that the evidence was insufficient to prove the premeditation and intent required for a first-degree murder conviction, but that it did support the lesser offense of manslaughter.

Jury instructions can have a profound effect on the outcome of a trial for two reasons: They are instructions (not suggestions) uttered by the most important official in the court, and they are the last words the jury hears before beginning deliberations. Still, not being lawyers, jurors sometimes have difficulty understanding the judge's instructions. They may also get bored and end up paying little attention.

When judges instruct juries to disregard certain evidence or to avoid drawing unwarranted inferences from testimony, some jurors may actually do the opposite (Kassin and Wrightsman, 1988). This is partly because forbidden information takes on added importance precisely because it is forbidden, and partly because jurors have a tendency to hang on to any evidence—admissible or not—that they believe will help them make the right decision. Research shows, nevertheless, that judges can overcome many of these problems if they provide jurors with clear explanations of their instructions (Diamond and Casper, 1992; Kassin and Wrightsman, 1988). The goal is to treat jurors as active thinkers.

Jury Deliberation

Everyone who watched the O. J. Simpson jury deliver its verdicts sensed the tension in the courtroom; a lengthy trial had finally arrived at the moment everyone involved—and most of the country—had been waiting for: Would the jury find Simpson guilty or not guilty?

We all know the verdict, and it came quickly. There were apparently no lengthy and heated discussions among the jurors, as might have been expected. After being required to sit passively month after month through the most sensational criminal case in U.S. history, the jury rendered a speedy verdict that was simultaneously broadcast on televisions throughout America and the world. Although untypical of criminal trials in many respects, the Simpson trial apparently had one thing in common with the vast majority of jury trials (Kalven and Zeisel, 1966; Hastie, Penrod, and Pennington, 1983): the jurors had reached an opinion about guilt or innocence long before they entered the jury room to deliberate.

Jury deliberations are guided by a **jury foreperson** selected or elected from among the jurors. This juror is responsible for leading the discussions in the jury room, conducting votes, requesting clarification from the judge or other information, and reading the verdict in court. Juries have a tendency to pick better-educated, higher-status individuals as forepersons, and males are more often picked than females (Deosarian, 1993; Strodtbeck and Lipinski, 1985).

jury foreperson A person selected or elected from among the jurors who leads the deliberations, communicates with the judge when necessary, and in some courts announces the verdict.

Jury deliberations have been studied extensively, at first through observation and questioning of real juries at work (Kalven and Zeisel, 1966), and more recently through experiments with mock juries (Tanford and Penrod, 1986; Visher, 1987), and through interviews with real jurors after trials have concluded (Costanzo and Costanzo, 1994). These studies show that *nonlegal* factors often have a significant impact on jury decisions. These range from the courtroom behavior and demeanor of defendants to the behavior of witnesses on the stand; from the gender, class, and race of jurors themselves to the gender, class, and race—and even attractiveness—of defendants. In fact, just about anything that is seen or heard in the courtroom can influence a juror's opinion of the case, and sometimes the verdict of the entire jury.

Most juries take no more than a few minutes or at most an hour or so to reach a verdict. Often, a straw poll will be taken quickly to determine the degree of initial consensus. If the resulting vote is unanimous for acquittal, the jury will quickly take a formal vote and so inform the judge. Any other vote means further discussion (Hastie, Penrod, and Pennington, 1983). Even a unaninimous guilty vote will be further discussed to ensure that all jurors are in agreement as to the exact charge and that the judge's instructions regarding alternative verdicts have been understood and correctly applied.

Should the jury be unable to reach a verdict it is called a *hung jury*. The jury foreperson will inform the judge that the vote is split and that repeated discussions have not removed the deadlock. The trial judge has the discretion to request that the jury continue its deliberations. Despite leaving things unresolved, a hung jury is considered in law to be a legitimate outcome of a trial, and a judge may not browbeat the jury into reaching a verdict or continuing their deliberations for an unreasonable length of time. If the issues are highly complex and the trial has been lengthy, then the judge may feel it appropriate for the jury to spend more time in search of a compromise verdict. When all reasonable efforts fail to produce a verdict, however, the judge declares a **mistrial** on the basis of the hung jury. A mistrial means that the defendant goes free unless the prosecution decides to start the trial process all over again. Since there was no verdict, double jeopardy is not an issue.

mistrial Declared when the jury cannot reach a verdict or when the trial is stopped due to a prejudicial error by counsel or by the death of a juror or attorney

A verdict of not guilty means that the trial is over and the defendant cannot be retried on the same charges. By law, a judge *must* accept a jury's not guilty verdict. The jury's decision is the end of it. Not guilty does not mean that the defendant is actually innocent of the crime; rather, it means that the prosecution failed to prove its case beyond a reasonable doubt. To ignore the jury's verdict would make a mockery of the very idea of trial by jury. However, a defendant found *guilty* by a jury may be acquitted if the judge believes that the evidence did not support the guilty verdict beyond a reasonable doubt. The result is the same as if the jury had found the defendant not guilty. A guilty verdict may also be appealed, and sometimes an appellate court will reverse the conviction or order a new trial.

CHANGES IN THE CRIMINAL COURT

Recent years have witnessed a number of significant changes in the way criminal courts do business. The technology explosion of the past 25 years explains some of the changes; others have more to do with changes in the volume and type of defendants being processed by the criminal justice system, and attempts to find better ways to handle them. Let us look at technology first, with special focus on television in the courtroom.

TECHNOLOGY IN THE COURTROOM

Over the past few years all sorts of technological innovations have appeared in the courtrooms of America (see Box 12.4): arraignments and witness examinations using two-way video; televised evidence display; banks of computers at the attorneys' elbows for immediate data retrieval and communication with their offices via modems; computer monitors for judge, jury, and witnesses; wall-mounted monitors to display testimony or images from outside the courtroom; automated court scheduling; multi-camera video recording of proceed-

Box 12.4

JUSTICE INNOVATIONS

NEW TECHNOLOGY IN THE COURTROOM

It is inevitable that technological advances will find their way into the courtroom, and judges and lawyers generally welcome the efficiency and other practical benefits associated with them. Maintenance and training in the new technology is now a routine part of the trial court administrator's responsibilities—although complaints about insufficient funds and staff are routine.

To better prepare law students for the new technology, some law schools have outfitted their mock courtrooms with the latest devices. One of the world's most technologically advanced mock courtrooms is Courtroom 21 at the Marshall-Wythe School of Law of the College of William and Mary. Among the devices in Courtroom 21 are the following:

- Videoconferencing facilities using two-way television so that defendants can be arraigned and witnesses examined even though they are not present in court; this technology may also allow juries to be formed in other venues without having to move the physical location of the trial.
- Multiple computer-controlled cameras focused on the judge, witness stand, counsel tables, and courtroom as a whole. Use of a multiframe video system that permits simultaneous display of multiple images, such as picture-in-a-picture (PIP) television sets. These images can be recorded to provide appellate courts with a complete audiovisual record of a trial.
- An automated trial presentation system converts trial exhibits into digital form so that they can be called up and projected instantaneously onto large screens or video monitors in the courtroom. Such a system was used in the Exxon Valdez trial and in the copyright infringement suit brought against Michael Jackson for his song "Dangerous."
- Real-time transcription systems, which use stenographic machines linked to personal computers. Lawyers and judges can review an electronic copy of the testimony almost as soon as it is given.

We can expect courtroom technology to continue to advance, especially in the area of electronics. However, like most change, it will not occur without controversy.

Sources: Hugh Nugent and J. Thomas McEwen (1988). "Judges and Trial Court Administrators Assess the Nation's Criminal Justice Needs." *NIJ Research in Action* (August):1–6; Alan Gahtan (1997), "Courtroom 21: The Courtroom of the Future." Available online at **http://www.gahtan.com/alan/articles/court21.htm**.

ings; deposition playback facilities and law firm voice mail; and computer graphics and animation (Lederer, 1994). Even the long-suffering court reporter clicking quietly away during trial may soon be a thing of the past: Sixteen states now authorize use of videotape as the trial record, and an additional ten states are experimenting with it (Bureau of Justice Statistics, 1995:221). A far less encouraging use of technology is also on the rise: X-ray devices and metal detectors at entrances and exits and security cameras peering down from walls and ceilings are now a common sight (Carter, 1993; Greenstone, 1994). They

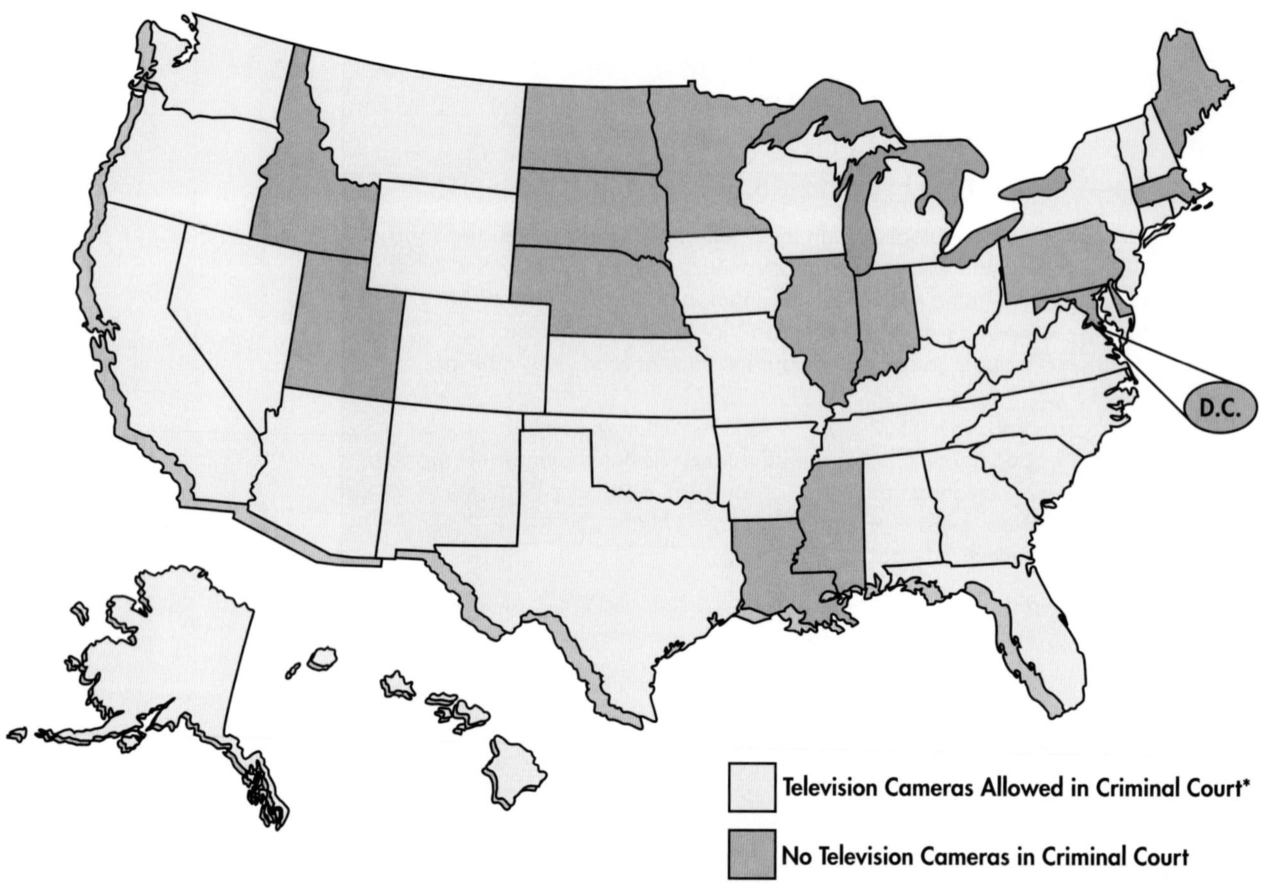

FIGURE 12.4 TELEVISION CAMERAS IN THE CRIMINAL COURTS
Colorado was the first state to allow television cameras in the courtroom, in 1956; Alabama followed in 1976. As of 1997, 35 states allow cameras in a criminal trial. Cameras are not allowed in federal criminal trials.
**Some states require that the judge and/or the defendant consent to the presence of cameras.*

Source: Map created from data supplied by the Information Service of the National Center for State Courts. Available online at **http://www.ncsc.dni.us/is/clrhouse/tv-cams.htm**.

have been installed because courtrooms are increasingly the scene of violent outbursts, as noted earlier.

Television Cameras in the Courtroom. A relatively old technology that continues to make headlines when it is used in the courtroom is television. Many judges and trial lawyers have not been receptive to the presence of television cameras in the courtoom. This controversial issue gained national attention through the O. J. Simpson trial, although appellate courts have been wrestling with the issue for decades. The most current data show that states vary widely in their rules governing television cameras in the courtroom. Some states allow cameras only in appellate courts, some only in civil courts, some in all courts, and some in none. Nearly all states prohibit TV coverage of court cases involving juveniles, victims of sex crime, and domestic relations. Some states require that parties consent to the presence of cameras. Figure 12.4 shows the states that permit television cameras in criminal trial courts as of March 1997.

The U.S. Supreme Court has long maintained that the constitutional guarantees of a public trial (Sixth Amendment) and freedom of the press (First

TV trials have HUGE juries.
ILLUSTRATION BY BARRIE MAGUIRE, COURTESY OF THE CREATIVE WORKSHOP

Amendment) require that criminal trials be open not only to the public but also to the press. However, the presence of television cameras was thought to pose special problems for the defendant's right to a fair trial. Among the concerns expressed by the Court and other critics was that participants in televised trials would be unduly distracted and stressed by the cameras and lights. Jurors would concentrate less on the proceedings, and "lawyers would play up to the cameras rather than to the jury" (Surette, 1992:17). Furthermore, the television audience would receive a distorted picture of the courtroom process, especially if only short edited excerpts of the proceedings were televised. In as much as this selective coverage will tend to highlight the dramatic and usually exceptional moments in the courtroom, it turns justice into a commodity—more viewers means more TV advertising dollars—and devalues the entire process.

Do TV Cameras Prevent a Fair Trial? Nonetheless, between 1965 and 1981, research on the impact of television in the courtroom had not confirmed the earlier fears of the U.S. Supreme Court and many other critics. The State of Florida had spent considerable time and effort studying the impact of cameras after it introduced them experimentally in 1977. After carefully reviewing the evidence, which included interviews with witnesses, judges, jurors, and trial attorneys who had participated in televised trials, the Florida Supreme Court approved television coverage in the courtroom, but also issued strict guidelines. Research since 1981 also supports the conclusion that Court TV and television news coverage of criminal trials does not have a significant negative impact on trial participants (Lancaster, 1984; Barber, 1987; Borgida, DeBono, and Buckman, 1990).

The O. J. Simpson trial caught the nation and many people around the globe in its grip. CNN carried every moment live, and who could forget the carnival atmosphere outside the courtroom and the dozens of cameras and reporters monitoring the comings and goings? Whenever something dramatic happened, the major networks kept the public informed during prime-time news broadcasts. The delivery of the verdict was carried live by all networks, preempting regular broadcasting. Millions watched, and the reactions of the

Box 12.5

GLOBAL JUSTICE

THE FAMILY GROUP CONFERENCE IN NEW ZEALAND

New ideas about how to involve the community in the criminal justice process have given rise to a search for alternatives to the formal court trial for all defendants. One interesting alternative described by Australian criminologist John Braithwaite (1995) is based on the "family group conference" of the Maori, the indigenous people of New Zealand.

The family group conference was invented by the Maori tribes hundreds of years ago. Today, the state has incorporated the idea in the Children, Young Persons and their Families Act of 1989. This statute permits both white and Maori juvenile offenders to be dealt with through family group conferences instead of juvenile courts. A youth justice coordinator invites the offender, the offender's family (including aunts, grandparents, and even cousins), other significant others in the offender's life (for example, a teacher the youth particularly respects), the victim and the victim's family, the police, and sometimes other officials to attend a conference. There may be 20 or more participants.

The family group conference involves two special ingredients that make it different from Western-style mediation, which is typically one-on-one with a disinterested person acting as mediator. First, both victims and victim supporters confront the offender with the harm they suffered; this process is designed to make the conference a *shaming experience*. Second, by inviting offenders to bring in people who care about them, and whom they most respect, the conference builds in *reintegration*: these supporters can demonstrate to offenders that they are not rejected but are still cared about.

Shaming and reintegration are also emphasized in the conference agenda. Shaming is evident in in the first part of the conference. Offenders

victims' families and groups of ordinary citizens—selected, it appeared, mostly along racial lines—were immediately broadcast around the world.

The Simpson trial reopened public discussion of TV in the courtroom, and it remains to be seen how things will develop. Many issues are still unresolved, and some new ones have surfaced. For example, the experiences of the television trial analysts and commentators have produced a new perspective. Each major TV news organization and many local stations hired expert commentators to provide views and analysis of the trial. Erwin Chemerisky, an attorney and professor of law, was legal analyst for CBS during the Simpson trial; he cautions that "[b]ecause the role of trial commentator is new, a great deal of thought should be given to the ethics and craft of being an analyst. Perhaps a voluntary code of ethics should be drawn because neither the lawyer's rules of professional responsibility nor the journalist's ethical standards really apply" (Chemerisky, 1995:100).

THE COMMUNITY COURT: BRINGING JUSTICE TO THE NEIGHBORHOOD

New thinking about the role of neighborhood and community in the fight against crime has given rise to another line of innovation in the court system. Community policing, discussed in Chapter 6, is an example of this new think-

BOX 12.5 (CONTINUED)

describe the incident in their own terms. Then victims, victim supporters, and the families of offenders have the opportunity to describe the harm the incident caused them. Making offenders face the people who have suffered often brings home to them the hurtfulness of their actions. "Sometimes a shaft of shame from the victim will be deflected by the offender, only to spear like a stake through the heart of the offender's mother, sitting beside him, causing her to sob. Then it can be the tears of the mother—her disappointment, her shame, her public ordeal—that pierces the offenders' defenses against shame" (Braithwaite, 1995:178).

Reintegration follows. Once offenders have confronted the consequences of what they have done, the others present in the conference invite them to take responsibility for their actions. "In every conference I have observed," Braithwaite writes, "this has evoked an apology to the victim. Most victims then reciprocate with some gesture or utterance of forgiveness. It is in fact rather hard for human beings who receive a face to face apology in public not to respond with some sort of gesture of forgiveness. Hence, the agenda also structures reintegration into the conference through the simple device of being victim-centered."

The goal of these family group conferences is to come up with a solution to the problems victims have suffered while ensuring that the problem does not occur again. Sometimes offenders pay some form of restitution to the victim. A plan of action is then agreed upon, with the offender taking responsibility for major parts of it, but all parties contribute. The conference seeks to avoid the stigmatization typical of Western justice through being problem centered rather than offender centered.

Source: John Braithwaite (1995). "Reintegrative Shaming, Republicanism, and Policy." In Hugh D. Barlow, ed., *Crime and Public Policy: Putting Theory to Work*. Boulder, Co.: Westview Press.

ing. Here, partnerships between patrolling police and local neighborhoods are developed to address local crime problems. On another level, correctional authorities and communities are forging partnerships in new efforts to reduce prison overcrowding and correctional costs, to devise effective alternatives to incarceration, and to address the correctional needs of special populations such as juveniles, the mentally ill, and the physically disabled. These innovations are discussed in Chapters 16 and 17.

Many of these innovations are based on the idea that just as most rule breaking within families is best handled within the family, many criminals can best be handled within the neighborhoods in which they reside and where, generally, they commit their offenses. Bringing a more informal court into the neighborhood, and involving local residents—especially victims and the offender's family—in the proceedings is a more logical and potentially more effective way of judicial processing than the traditional formal courtroom that is physically and symbolically removed from the neighborhoods where defendants and victims reside. The idea is certainly not new, for a version of it existed in the traveling courts of the Old West; in non-Western cultures, "communitarian" forms of judicial processing have existed for centuries (Braithwaite, 1989, 1995). Box 12.5 provides an illustration that will be discussed further when we consider the theory of reintegrative shaming in Chapter 13.

Drug Court: Innovation in the Processing of Drug Offenders. *Drug court* is a contemporary American example of innovations in court processing that draw upon the resources and involvement of the local community. First developed in Miami, Florida, in 1989, the drug court provides defendants charged with drug offenses with direct access to drug treatment, and monitors them to ensure compliance. Although specific drug court practices vary around the country, the Miami model works as follows: Upon arrest, the suspect is screened by the prosecution for eligibility. A history of violent crime, drug trafficking, or two previous nondrug felony convictions means a defendant is not eligible for diversion to drug court. If eligible, the defendant appears before the drug court judge, accompanied by defense counsel and prosecutor, all of whom participate in explaining the program and outlining the defendant's obligations. Defendants who accept the conditions enter the program, and progress is monitored continually by the judge. The defendant is assigned a primary counselor, a treatment plan is developed that begins with detoxification, urine tests are periodically performed, and attendance at counseling and education sessions at the local community college is required. If the defendant successfully completes the program, which lasts approximately a year, criminal charges are dropped (Finn and Newlyn, 1993a; 1993b).

The Miami drug court is run by Judge Stanley Goldstein, who is famous for his personal touch. He makes every effort to see each defendant—or "client"—successfully through the program, and only rarely has he expelled anyone. Still, approximately six out of every ten graduates of the program have spent at least two weeks in jail for failing to cooperate, and some even longer. They experience many ups and downs before they finally recover and graduate, but this merely convinced Goldstein that conventional criminal prosecution is not the answer. The emphasis in drug court is help. But that does not mean anything goes:

> Arrestees and program participants find they cannot manipulate the court system in the way they anticipate or may have done in the past. They cannot ask the public defender to get them off on a technicality, lie to the probation officer, or get away with feigning innocence to the judge. Defendant to judge: "I couldn't make it to the treatment center. I work odd hours and I got domestic problems. Also, I . . ." Judge, interrupting: "*I* got domestic problems, too. We *all* do! Doesn't mean you go do cocaine!" (Finn and Newlyn, 1993b:4)

According to its advocates, the strengths of the drug court program are fourfold: (1) Comprehensive services are made available that target underlying problems linked to drug abuse—"illiteracy, lack of acedemic credentials, unemployment or lack of work experience, need for job search skills, and inadequate housing" (Finn and Newlyn, 1993a:14); (2) community agencies are involved, including community colleges, treatment centers, and residential care facilities; (3) the judge provides personal attention, and defendants see and appreciate the energy and time he invests in them; and (4) defendants want help in getting off drugs, and many graduates remain involved in the program and the court.

Many jurisdictions have followed Miami's lead, including Madison County, Illinois. There, a commitment has been made to the treatment side of the program, as well as to careful monitoring of defendants' progress, and to a personal touch on the part of the judge. These features bode well for the program's success—which includes reducing pressure on the traditional court structure (Goldkamp, 1994). However, when drug courts are seen *primarily* as a means to greater efficiency and cost reductions for urban court systems, there are risks to be considered. When Cook County, Illinois, introduced five drug night courts in

The Midtown Community Court in Manhattan is the first in the nation to combine court, social services, health care, education, and drug treatment under one roof. To carry out these goals, it combines the elements of mediation, assessment, resource coordination, on-site services, judicial monitoring, and the latest technology.

Photo courtesy of Midtown Community Court, Center for Court Innovations

1989 as a way to alleviate the pressure on the court system posed by 28,000 felony case filings a year, the local public defender—now a law professor at the University of Chicago—suggested that judges and prosecutors were encouraged to dehumanize the process in the name of efficiency. "Justice," he wrote, "is not a by-product of an efficient court system; justice must be the goal of the system" (Randolph Stone, cited in Bureau of Justice Assistance, 1994:4).

It will be some time before the impact of drug courts can be fully assessed. Meanwhile, they continue to spring up around the country. Although they appear to be helping keep some drug offenders out of prison, there is a possible unintended consequence of drug court: Will more drug offense suspects now be arrested by police who beforehand would have been ignored or let go because a prison sentence was almost inevitable if they were convicted? As yet there has been no serious examination of this possiblility, but if true, drug court would extend the reach of the criminal justice system, in effect criminalizing more people.

The Midtown Community Court in Manhattan. A second court innovation in the processing of criminal defendants also emerged as a response to the question, "Is there a better way?" In a three-year experiment launched in 1991 by the Unified Court System of the State of New York, the Midtown Community Court was designed to bring community and court closer together, while helping alleviate pressure on the existing court system posed by the thousands of quality-of-life offenses experienced in Manhattan (Feinblatt and Sviridoff, 1995).

The court, serving three Manhattan precincts, has plenty to do: Of the 21 Manhattan precincts, the court's precincts account for 43 percent of misdemeanor arrests (Feinblatt and Sviridoff, 1995:84). A community advisory committee composed of local residents, businesspeople, social service administrators, and local officials keeps the court in touch with the community, promoting trust and encouraging a proactive approach to problem solving. Local police receive ongoing information about the arrests they have made, and the courthouse is used for regular police meetings with citizens. Community service is the primary punishment given defendants, and the court is provided with daily feedback on their progress. The Midtown Community Court is the first in the nation to combine court, social services, health care, education, and drug treatment under one roof. Thus a large number of defendants and offenders are likely to be found in the courthouse at any one time.

The new way of conducting business exemplified in the Midtown Community Court experiment includes the following elements (Feinblatt and Sviridoff, 1995:90–92):

- *Mediation.* Mediators at the court not only help resolve disputes involving violations of the law, but also mediate disputes between neighbors and between businesses and their customers.
- *Assessment.* Interviews are conducted with defendants to develop information about their backgrounds, including medical histories, and to determine whether they have a place to sleep. The information is recorded with notebook computers and downloaded to the court's computer to aid the court's deliberations.
- *Resource coordination.* A resource coordinator helps the judge and lawyers match each defendant with the appropriate program and provides feedback from social service providers about how a defendant is doing.
- *On-site services.* Individual and group counseling rooms are provided, as well as space for conducting community service business and meetings.
- *Judicial monitoring.* Offenders are required to come before the judge every two weeks at first, then once a month, as part of the court's monitoring strategy. Judges sometimes give offenders a pat on the back, or they may warn them about the consequences of not following the court's orders.
- *Technology.* The court uses computer technology to conduct all its business, permitting judges, prosecutors, defense attorneys, and social service staff to work on a case simultaneously, to quickly access relevant information, and to communicate with each other electronically.

The initial results of the project indicate that the Midtown Community Court is living up to its ambitious agenda of providing swift and sensitive justice to a large number of defendants and victims, as well as to the community at large. It appears that the project has also produced cost savings over the traditional court. This has been achieved through reductions in the time from arrest to arraignment—meaning that police can spend more time on the street—as well as in the extensive use of noncustodial sentences. The high rate of compliance associated with community-based sentences not only means less repeat offenses, but also cuts down on the time police and prosecution must spend dealing with new arrest warrants.

SUMMARY

The U.S. Constitution guarantees all criminal defendants a public trial and the right to have their case heard by an impartial jury. Yet few defendants choose a trial, with most pleading guilty after a negotiation between their attorney and the prosecution. For those who go to trial, most elect to have a jury trial. The trial is an adversarial process in which the prosecution and the defense each try to persuade the jury to accept their version of the facts. Verdicts must be unanimous in all but two states.

The course of a trial is fairly predictable: Pre-trial motions are followed by jury selection, questioning and cross-examination of witnesses, closing arguments, the judge's instructions to the jury, and the jury's deliberations and verdict. In high-profile cases, attorneys often use expert consultants to help with jury selection and presentation of the evidence. For many years, juries were not representative of the populations served by criminal courts; some groups of Americans were systematically excluded because their race or gender either disqualified them from the jury pool or was used as a basis for challenge during the voir dire process. Various decisions by the U.S. Supreme Court beginning in 1880 and culminating in *Batson v. Kentucky* (1986) and *J. E. B. v. Alabama* (1994) helped ensure the impartiality of juries by opening up the pool and outlawing the use of peremptory challenges based on race or gender. Even so, an attorney bent on excluding certain groups might still accomplish this through a change of venue, as in the Rodney King beating trial.

The trial itself is a contest in persuasion. The contest begins with the attorneys' opening statements and continues through questioning and cross-examination of witnesses and closing statements by both sides. The prosecution tries to convince the jury that the evidence is sufficient to convict the defendant, while the defense tries to sow a reasonable doubt in at least one juror's mind. Attorneys use various methods of persuasion, from calling on expert witnesses to reducing the impact of negative evidence by stealing the opposing side's thunder. One powerful strategy of persuasion sometimes used by defense attorneys is blaming the victim. If this strategy is successful, jurors will question whether a crime ever happened.

Most felony jury trials last only a day or two, and most result in guilty verdicts. High-profile cases, which often involve the death penalty, generally take much longer, and the outcome is less predictable. Mistrials are not uncommon, the jury being unable to reach a unanimous verdict. Recent high-profile cases have showcased many of the technological innovations finding their way into the nation's courts, from videoconferencing to almost instantaneous audiovisual playback of testimony. The use of television cameras in the courtroom remains controversial, although a majority of states now allow it.

Technological innovations are changing the face of the courtroom, but some other innovations are changing courts in a more fundamental way. Community courts are helping to bring justice into local neighborhoods. They are less formal and adversarial than regular criminal courts, and offer a variety of services to defendants, victims, and their families. Drug courts are springing up around the country, offering alternatives to prison for many offenders. They reduce pressure on an overburdened criminal justice system, but they may also result in more people getting arrested for drug violations. That possibility deserves close attention.

WHAT DO YOU THINK *NOW*?

- How does jury selection sometimes deny defendants a jury of their peers? How can this be prevented? If it is not prevented, what may be the consequences?

- How are peremptory challenges used to exclude minorities and women? What other types of jurors might attorneys wish to exclude? Why?
- After reading this chapter, do you believe that juries always judge cases based on the evidence alone? How do judges and lawyers influence a jury's decision?

KEY TERMS AND CASES

courts of general jurisdiction
courts of limited jurisdiction
jury trial
bench trial
Duncan v. Louisiana
Blanton v. Las Vegas
pre-trial motion
challenge for cause
peremptory challenge
jury consultant
Swain v. Alabama
Batson v. Kentucky
J. E. B. v. Alabama
cognizable group
change of venue
opening statement
demonstrative evidence
testimonial evidence
direct evidence
circumstantial evidence
United States v. Reynolds
direct examination
cross-examination
discovery
expert witness
victim blaming
rape shield laws
jury nullification
double jeopardy
closing arguments
jury instructions
jury foreperson
mistrial

ACTIVE LEARNING CHALLENGES

1. Contact local court officials for their views on the benefits and drawbacks of scientific jury selection. See how their views compare with the discussion in this chapter. Do their comments raise any new issues?
2. Conduct a mock voir dire, using the class members as potential jurors. The defendant in the case before them is a single mother accused of leaving three young children alone while she went shopping. While she was gone the children accidentally set the house on fire. One died. The mother is charged with negligent homicide, neglect, and endangering the life of a child. You must select twelve jurors from the class. What questions do you ask? Which potential jurors do you challenge? Why?
3. Trial is all about persuasion. Have the class members visit a trial in progress and report back to the class on the techniques of persuasion they observed in use.
4. Discuss the claim that TV in the courtroom undermines a defendant's right to a fair and impartial proceeding.
5. Since most criminal defendants are convicted without trial, we could get rid of the jury system and it would not significantly affect the quality of justice in America. Debate this claim.

INTERNET CHALLENGES

The Web pages mentioned here can all be accessed through the Web site for this textbook at **http://www.prenhall.com/barlow/**.

1. Follow a real case from the crime through prosecution, trial, and outcome. Check out Anatomy of a Murder, a neat Web site created by three university students that takes you through a criminal murder trial.
2. Court TV has covered many trials, both civil and criminal. For more information on some of these trials, check their Web site. What elements in these trials make them newsworthy?

3. Trial consultants and trial research firms are springing up around the country, offering services that are designed to help criminal attorneys win their tough cases. An example is Quo Jure Corporation of San Francisco; visit their Web site. Find out what sorts of services are currently available through firms such as this. In what ways, if at all, will they improve the quality of American justice?

CHAPTER 13

SENTENCING THE CRIMINAL OFFENDER

LEARNING OBJECTIVES

- Understand the difference between the justice model of punishment and the crime prevention model.
- Describe how incapacitation, reformation, rehabilitation, and deterrence may prevent crime.
- Describe sentencing and the major causes of sentencing disparities.
- Understand how sentencing is influenced by the race, social class, and gender of offenders and victims.
- Explain why and how the sentencing discretion of judges has been reduced in the past 25 years.
- Describe how the victim's role in sentencing has changed in recent years.

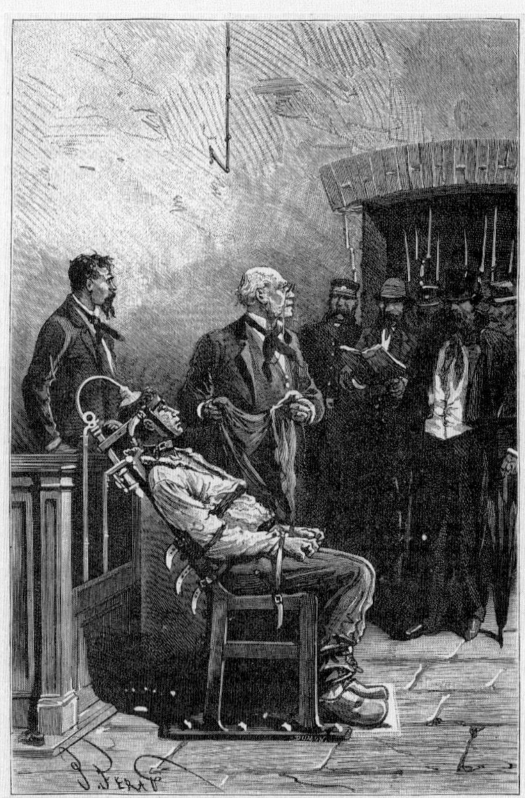

Some supporters of the death penalty believe that executions are a deterrent to crime. However, most research does not support this view. What might be another justification for the death penalty?

PHOTO COURTESY OF THE GRANGER COLLECTION, NEW YORK

Many people have strong common sense beliefs about sentencing and punishment, but it is often common sense uninformed by knowledge. . . . No sentencing system will ever be perfect or free from risks of injustice in individual cases.

MICHAEL TONRY, PROFESSOR OF LAW AND CRIMINOLOGY

Something inside of me says, "We're going to teach you a lesson, Sunshine," and you tend to be more punitive.

AN ANONYMOUS JUDGE ON SENTENCING A REPEAT OFFENDER

Denver, Colorado. Counsel for the defense stood beside her client, Joan Short, awaiting the sentence of the court. They had talked about the possible sentence numerous times, but the moment of truth was now at hand, and everyone was tense. There had been no plea bargain; Short was taking her chances with a jury trial. She had been found guilty of manslaughter for stabbing her ex-boyfriend to death during an argument. The prosecution had sought a murder conviction, so things could have been much worse. Now she faced a maximum sentence of twelve years in prison, but the judge could impose as little as two years if he found that there were mitigating circumstances.

Judge Harold Black had been on the bench for six years, but only three of these had been in criminal court. He had never before had to sentence a defendant convicted of manslaughter, let alone a woman. He found sentencing the most difficult part of his job, even though Colorado, like most other states, had progressively reduced the sentencing discretion permitted judges. Some judges in the circuit were known as hard-liners, while others had reputations for leniency; Black saw himself falling somewhere in between. He tried hard to fit sentences to the merits of each individual case. He believed in making the penalty fit the crime, and for him this meant taking into account the offender's background and circumstances, as well as the experiences and wishes of the victim.

As always, Judge Black had read the probation officer's presentence report on Joan Short very carefully. He found out that Short was a single mother with two small children, that she had been intermittently on welfare and in low-paying service jobs, and that she was regarded by employers, co-workers, and neighbors as a good worker and a caring parent. She had been arrested once before, for shoplifting; she had pleaded guilty and served six months on probation. The probation report indicated past involvement with drugs, but nothing recent. In court, Judge Black had found Short to be respectful and attentive. During the sentencing hearing the victim's mother and sister had spoken of the gravity of the crime and the loss they had suffered, but they had also requested leniency.

Judge Black could see no justice or benefit in a lengthy prison term, but he also felt strongly that two years was too light a sentence for killing someone, even in the heat of an argument. The children would have to be without their mother for around three years if he sentenced Short to a four-year term. They would still be young children when she returned, time enough for them to be a family again. Black had reached his decision, and was ready to explain it to the defendant and her counsel.

For Joan Short, as for most defendants and victims, sentencing is what matters; it is the culmination of the judicial process. Yet even though, in a technical sense, sentencing occurs only after someone has been convicted of an offense, in many cases the sentence has been largely determined beforehand. So when the Queen of Hearts in *Alice in Wonderland* tells Alice, "Sentence first—verdict afterwards," Alice's topsy-turvy world is much closer to reality than Lewis Carroll's readers probably thought.

To illustrate, consider these ways in which the sentence precedes the conviction: First, criminal statutes often specify the exact penalties attached to a crime before it has even occurred; they indicate the seriousness with which an offense is viewed under the law. Second, the discretionary judgments of police officers and their supervisors are sometimes affected by knowledge of the sentences typically handed down in court. Police may decide not to report a crime or not to make an arrest because they anticipate a certain sentence. Third, the typical sentences handed down by a particular judge are known before the criminal trial begins. As we saw in Chapter 12, prosecutors and defense attorneys base many of their decisions on knowledge of the likely sentence. Fourth, it is often the prosecutor who has determined early in the process what the likely sentence will be, because it is the prosecutor who is in control of the charges. A prosecutor can reduce the possible sentence by reducing the charge, and the defendant often knows in advance of sentencing what the penalty will be.

Since the sentence that is handed down specifies a particular punishment for the offense, the best place to begin our discussion of sentencing is with an examination of the concept of punishment and the goals assigned to it in relation to crime. Then we can turn to the sentencing process itself to find out how it works. We shall learn that a lot of important changes have occurred over the past 30 years, almost all of which have reduced the discretion formerly enjoyed by judges. The chapter concludes with a discussion of another recent trend: bringing victims back into the sentencing process.

? WHAT DO YOU THINK?

- Do you feel that Joan Short deserves a lengthy prison sentence? Why or why not?
- What sort of things influence a judge when it comes to sentencing a felony defendant?
- Do you think that legislators should restrict the range of penalties that judges can impose for different offenses? Why or why not?

THE CONCEPT OF PUNISHMENT

Punishment is any action designed to deprive someone of things of value because of something the person is believed to have done. Valued things include freedom, civil rights, money, health, identity, personal relationships, and life itself. Throughout the ages, rulers have devised all manner of punishments for people guilty of wrongdoing. The more serious an offense was considered to be, the harsher the penalties attached to it. Many people consider the harshest penalties to be those that cut offenders off from their families. Today, when a judge formally announces a sentence in a felony case, the penalty could be as little as twelve months on probation, or as severe as life in prison; in 38 states and the federal system, the penalty may be death.

TYPES OF PENALTIES FOR CRIME

There are three major types of punishment that criminals face: official criminal penalties, extralegal penalties, and illegal penalties. Official criminal penalties are punishments established by law and imposed by a jurisdiction according to legal procedures. Over the past century in the United States, the most commonly used official penalties for felony crimes have been imprisonment, fines, probation, and—least often—death.

Extralegal penalties are best thought of as informal punishments. They are not illegal, but nor are they specified in law as penalties for crime. Extralegal penalties may be imposed by all sorts of people, and they come in many forms. Examples are loss of friendship, rejection by family or community, divorce or refusal to marry, and various forms of harassment. Some of these may occur in the context of official criminal penalties. For example, when guards humiliate or insult prisoners or are slow in responding to requests for assistance, those actions are extralegal punishments even though they occur in conjunction with official criminal punishment.

Extralegal penalties are usually imposed *in addition to* official criminal penalties, and they may be imposed even when a defendant has been acquitted of a crime. Consider how O. J. Simpson was treated after his acquittal on murder charges. Many of his past business associates severed ties with him, and he has been the butt of jokes and sarcasm throughout the popular press, television, and radio. One can imagine, too, that some former friends now give him a wide berth. All these actions are punishing to the extent that they deprive Simpson of valued things.

Illegal penalties are punishments that are against the law—such as torture or mutilation—or that are applied illegally—such as the lynching of a convicted murderer or the use of excessive fines. It is not always clear whether a particular penalty is or is not illegal, and so appeals courts will sometimes be asked to decide. For example, a penalty may be appealed to the U.S. Supreme Court as a violation of the Eighth Amendment prohibition against cruel and unusual punishment; if the Court agrees, that particular penalty becomes illegal for the offense charged. However, subsequent statutory changes to the criminal code may override the Court's objection, reinstating the penalty. As Chapter 14 explains, this is exactly what happened with the death penalty after the Supreme Court ruled it unconstitutional in *Furman v. Georgia* (1972).

JUSTIFICATION AND AIMS OF PUNISHMENT

justice model Punishment is justified by the offender's guilt and matches the gravity of the offense.

crime prevention model Punishment is justified by its capacity to reduce crime.

Over the years, two major arguments have been offered as justifications for the punishment of criminals. The first is called the **justice model**; according to this view, punishment is justified in terms of an offender's guilt and the appropriateness of the penalty in light of the crime committed. The second justification of punishment is the **crime prevention model**; it justifies punishment in terms of its capacity to reduce crime. Both models justify punishment in general as well as in its application to specific offenders. Let us look at the two models in more detail.

proportionality The severity of punishment matches the severity of the crime.

The Justice Model of Punishment. According to the justice model, punishment is justified (1) when people are guilty of willfully violating the laws of the society in which they claim membership, and (2) when the guilty person has received a punishment matching the gravity of the offense. The combination of guilt and making the punishment fit the crime—called **proportionality**—make a particular legal punishment a "just dessert."

But how does society achieve proportionality? Various possibilities have been suggested: (1) Make the punishment mirror the crime itself (*lex talionis*, "an eye for an eye"); (2) adjust the severity of penalties according to the social harm caused by different offenses; and (3) link the penalty to the moral outrage felt by a majority of citizens.

From a practical standpoint, none of these proposals is easy to implement. For example, what kinds of penalties accurately mirror robbing a bank of $20,000 or possessing two grams of heroin? On what basis is smoking marijuana socially harmful, and who makes that judgment? Moral outrage may offer more hope, in that public sentiments can be tapped through surveys. As we learned in Chapter 1, wide agreement was found in a national survey rating the seriousness of 141 offenses (Wolfgang, Figlio, Tracy, and Singer, 1985). Even so, a practical problem arises: Two identical acts might generate different degrees of outrage, depending on their circumstances and on who you asked. We can hardly expect judges to poll the public before they sentence an offender.

utilitarianism A philosophy founded on the principle of the greatest happiness of the greatest number.

Reductivism: Punishment as Crime Prevention. The key to reductivism is the idea that punishment can prevent crime. This view was first developed by the so-called classical school of criminology during the eighteenth and early nineteenth centuries. The classical school borrowed heavily from the philosophy of **utilitarianism**. Utilitarians hold that the social value of something is found in its contribution to the greatest happiness of the greatest number. Although crime may produce pleasure for the criminal, it produces pain for others—considered a bad or evil thing by utilitarians. Yet punishment also brings pain, and so it, too, is a bad thing. However, if punishment prevents crime, the group as a whole is given more pleasure at the expense of the criminal. One can justify the use of punishment along utilitarian lines, then, if the group as a whole is better off.

One of the first to apply the utilitarian view was the Italian philosopher Cesare Beccaria (1963 [1764]), who wrote in the second half of the eighteenth century. Beccaria wanted to reform the justice system in Italy. He was especially concerned about the practice of throwing suspects in jail for months without trial, and about the widespread torturing and starving of prisoners. Yet he was also aware that crime was increasing, and he felt that something had to be done. He concluded that a rigorous but fair use of criminal punishment was the answer.

An ideal punishment, in Beccaria's view, is one that is both proportionate to the offense *and* sufficient to outweigh the pleasure derived from it. The second part is important, for it distinguishes the reductivist model from the purely retributivist view, and it helps explain how punishment prevents crime. Crime is prevented when people refrain from offending so as to avoid the pain of punishment. This prediction is the central idea behind deterrence theory, discussed in more detail in the next section. But deterrence is only one way that punishment might prevent crime. Table 13.1 shows that there as many as *ten* different ways that punishment may prevent crime. However, only the first four on

TABLE 13.1 Ten Ways Punishment May Prevent Crime

Deterrence, incapacitation, reform, and rehabilitation are conventionally regarded as the most likely ways that punishment may prevent crime. However, there are at least ten ways that punishment could conceivably prevent crime. Each is listed below with a brief description. A more detailed discussion can be found in Barlow (1996) and Gibbs (1975).

1. *Reformation.* Punishment conveys a sense of shame and remorse to some offenders, and this promotes subsequent conformity. In the original penitentiary, discussed in Chapter 15, offenders were placed in solitary confinement so they could reflect on the evil of their ways and through penitence be reformed.
2. *Incapacitation.* Offenders cannot commit crimes because the opportunity or ability to do so has been removed or reduced. Imprisonment is considered an incapacitating penalty, and so are some forms of mutilation.
3. *Rehabilitation.* Rehabilitation alters behavior by nonpunitive means so that the individual no longer commits crimes. While not punishment in itself, rehabilitation is often attempted within the context of punishment. Work release and prison education programs are examples.
4. *Deterrence.* People are scared away from criminal activity by fear of the consequences if they are caught.
5. *Surveillance.* When people are watched closely or monitored by electronic means, their behavior is made visible to others. This may prevent some crimes from occurring. Obviously, deterrence may be involved here, too.
6. *Normative validation.* Punishment confirms and reinforces the view that an act is wrong. When a teacher or a judge says, "I'm going to make an example out of you," it reminds the offender and others how they ought to behave and what will happen if they do not.
7. *Retribution.* Punishing offenders in a just manner may prevent other crimes such as private vengeance or armed vigilantism. The "subway vigilante" Bernard Goetz is a real-life example. He shot three young men that he claimed were about to rob him. He blamed his behavior on the inability of society to protect him from criminals.
8. *Stigmatization.* Punishment marks people as offenders, and the label *criminal* may stick to them long after the punishment is over. An individual may refrain from crime not because of the punishment itself, but because of the anticipated stigmatization that is associated with it. Laws requiring that neighbors be informed of convicted sex offenders in their midst are designed partly for their stigmatizing effect and partly to encourage surveillance.
9. *Normative insulation.* People tend to be influenced by the people they associate with. If people could somehow escape the influence of criminals, there would be less crime. Parents who keep tight reins on their children may contribute to normative insulation—which children undoubtedly see as a punishment! Electronic monitoring of offenders on probation may contribute to normative insulation as well.
10. *Habituation.* Punishment can lead to the development of habitual behavior that conforms to the law. For example, driving tends to be slower in places where police routinely use speeding traps to catch violators. Habituation differs from deterrence because conforming behavior may persist long after enforcement has ended.

The retribution model has seen many variations. In some societies today, a public execution is considered fair punishment; in others, such as the United States, it is not. Are there certain times when this may be appropriate and certain times when it may not? What do you think?

PHOTO COURTESY OF REUTERS/ARCHIVE PHOTOS

the list have received much attention in criminal justice circles; these are reformation, incapacitation, rehabilitation, and deterrence.

reformation Punishment that builds consciences and promotes conformity.

Reformation: Punishment Builds Consciences. Essentially, the idea behind **reformation** is that punishment conveys a sense of shame and remorse to some offenders, building their consciences and thus promoting conformity to the law. The original penitentiary, described in Chapter 15, was an early application of the idea that reformation occurs through punishment. Offenders were placed in solitary confinement so that they could reflect on the evil of their ways and be reformed through penitence. Even an arrest may have a reformative impact with some criminal offenders. Some amateur shoplifters and many people charged with white-collar crimes experience a sort of moral jolt when arrested. The arrest demonstrates that they have slipped from law-abiding citizen to thief and prompts a return to lawful behavior—at least for a time. While true reformation implies a permanent change in behavior, even a temporary return to law-abiding behavior will have prevented some crime.

incapacitation Punishment that removes or reduces the opportunity to commit crime.

Incapacitation: Punishment Reduces Opportunities for Crime. Some forms of punishment render offenders no longer able to commit crimes. This consequence of punishment is called **incapacitation**. Potential offenders are incapacitated because punishment removes or diminishes their opportunities to commit crimes. Incapacitation is absolute when an offender is executed, but it is relative for other forms of punishment. Consider imprisonment: Although putting someone behind bars reduces the opportunity to commit crimes, it does not rule out all offenses and may actually encourage some that the offender never before committed—for example, homosexual rape.

Capital punishment is the surest way to prevent future crime through incapacitation. But it is not foolproof, because offenders might still commit crimes while awaiting execution. Indeed, an infamous murderer awaiting execution in Illinois has found a way to delay his execution more than once—he has killed fellow prisoners, forcing new criminal investigations and trials, thereby postponing his own scheduled execution. It is surely preposterous to suggest execution as an incapacitation remedy for all types of offenses. A study of persistent thieves found that imprisonment encourages a "rationalization of crime" (Shover, 1995). Inmates learn from others how and why they were "busted," and this encourages a more calculating approach to their own criminal activity. In addition, many inmates leave prison reassured by the fact that they survived the ordeal, claiming in retrospect that prison was no big deal: "For too many of those who pass through it once, the prison experience will leave them less fearful and better prepared for a second trip if that should happen" (Shover, 1995:241).

Rehabilitation: Helping Offenders during Punishment. It is traditional to think of the terms *reformation* and rehabilitation as interchangeable, but this is incorrect. Reform is a direct consequence of punishment, whereas **rehabilitation** is the alteration of an offender's behavior by nonpunitive means so that he or she no longer violates laws. While it is not in itself punishment, rehabilitation is usually attempted side-by-side with punishment. For almost a century the nation's correctional system has included some efforts at rehabilitation while offenders are confined. Work release, prison educational and vocational programs, and halfway houses for offenders about to return to the community are examples. How much effort is put into rehabilitation generally depends on the security level of the prison, as we shall see in Chapters 15 and 16. The higher the security level, the less the emphasis on rehabilitation.

rehabilitation Alteration of attitudes and behavior through training, education, work release, and other programs administered along with punishment.

Deterrence: Fear of Punishment Prevents Crime. The **deterrence doctrine** justifies punishment on the basis that people refrain from crime because they fear the punishment that might follow. The deterrence doctrine has probably received more attention from the scientific community than any other perspective on punishment, and many important people believe in it. For this reason we will spend a little more time discussing it.

deterrence doctrine People refrain from crime because they fear being punished for it.

It is conventional to distinguish between two classes of potential offenders who may refrain from crime because they fear punishment:

1. People who have directly experienced punishment for something they did in the past. If these people refrain from future criminal activity because they fear being punished again, this is **specific deterrence**.
2. People who have not experienced punishment themselves, but are deterred from crime by the fear that they might get the same punishment experienced by others. This is **general deterrence**.

specific deterrence People who have experienced punishment in the past refrain from crime because they fear they will be punished again.

general deterrence People refrain from crime because they fear the punishment that others have received.

The distinction is important because the deterrent effect of experienced punishments may be quite different from that of threatened punishments. When a judge hands down a sentence and tells the offender, "This ought to make you think twice next time," the judge is thinking of the penalty as a specific deterrent; if the judge says, "I intend to make an example of you," the penalty's general deterrent value is being emphasized.

A second important distinction in deterrence research concerns three properties of punishment—severity, certainty, and speed. Beccaria (1963 [1764]) and the English philosopher Jeremy Bentham (1948) believed that the deterrent impact of punishment is greater when it is applied with greater certainty, greater severity, and more swiftly. Beccaria and Bentham considered severity to be less important as a deterrent than the others. Their view was not based on scientific analysis, but fit a growing belief that penalties were too harsh and were being applied inconsistently and unpredictably. Under these conditions, the utilitarian ideal of a just system of punishment that deterred potential offenders could never be realized. So Beccaria and Bentham called for moderation in the severity of punishment, coupled with efforts to increase the certainty and speed of punishment.

Over 200 years have passed since Bentham and Beccaria laid the foundation of the deterrence theory of punishment. During that time a conventional wisdom emerged that punishment deters if it is certain, swift, and reasonably severe. But science has not confirmed that wisdom, and many experts would agree that "probably not" is the best answer to the question "Does punishment deter?" (Nagin and Paternoster, 1991).

The inability of the scientific community to substantiate—or reject—the conventional wisdom that punishment deters crime must be difficult for many people to understand. Most of us can think of anecdotal illustrations of deterrence—from our own personal experience, perhaps, or from hearing about other people who refrained from committing a crime because they were fearful of the consequences. But serious researchers find that the complexities of the subject present formidable obstacles to developing conclusive answers (Gibbs, 1975; Gibbs and Firebaugh, 1990; Stafford and Warr, 1993).

Most surprising, perhaps, is the fact that more than 50 years of research has yet to uncover a deterrent effect for capital punishment (Beyleveld, 1980; Archer and Gartner, 1984; Peterson and Bailey, 1991). There is no good research that supports the oft-heard claim that there would be fewer murders if more killers were executed rather than sent to prison. Murders are often unplanned, spur-of-the-moment attacks, and alcohol is usually a factor in them. But even among hardened criminals who may think about risks in planning their crimes (Horney and Marshall, 1992), fear of punishment does not seem to be a major factor in their decisions (Shover, 1995).

On balance, the threat of formal punishments is much less worrisome to potential offenders than the threat of informal punishments imposed by relatives, friends, coworkers, or other close acquaintances (Tittle, 1980; Paternoster, Saltzman, Waldo, and Chiricos, 1983, 1985; Braithwaite, 1989). The average law-abiding citizen "is afraid of losing his job, of being ostracized by his business associates and friends, of the possible alienation of members of his family, of having to leave his neighborhood or even his town" (Shoham, 1970:9).

One criminologist has argued that punishment may backfire under certain circumstances, and this may explain the lack of a deterrent relationship between crime rates and punishment (Sherman, 1993). Sherman suggests that if punishment is seen as unfair or excessive, an attitude of "defiance" emerges. This defiance undermines any deterrent effect the threat of punishment might have had. It can also undermine any lingering respect for the law—a consideration in the sentencing of youthful and first-time offenders.

To summarize, deterrence clearly does not score high marks as a basis for the formulation and implementation of sentencing policy. Yet the lack of strong evidence does not mean that deterrence theory is disproved. The prospect of swift, certain, and relatively severe punishment may deter some individuals from committing crimes under some circumstances. The difficulty is figuring out who those individuals are, and which circumstances count. Still, rather than rejecting the deterrence doctrine, more research on these complex issues would seem the more prudent course. It would also seem appropriate for politicians, judges, and other court officials to refrain from claiming that harsher punishments will deter crime. The bulk of deterrence research simply does not support this claim.

SENTENCING THE CRIMINAL OFFENDER

sentence The specific penalty for a specific crime.

It is against this background of debate and uncertainty regarding the purpose, justification, and effects of punishment that sentencing of criminal offenders takes place. Over the years, judges have relied heavily on past practice and personal intuition to guide them. For their part, legislatures have specified the type and range of penalties, but until recently left it up to the individual court to decide on the **sentence**—the specific penalty for a specific crime. The result was considerable variation in the sentences handed down, even within the same jurisdiction. This is a problem we will return to in a later section.

A sentence specifies the official criminal penalty that will be imposed on a defendant convicted of a crime. In felony cases, the sentence is usually handed down by the trial judge following a sentencing hearing that takes place a few days or weeks after the offender has been convicted. In misdemeanor cases, the sentence is often imposed at the same time that guilt is established. In very minor cases—and most traffic offenses when the driver admits guilt—the offender may never appear before a judge for sentencing; instead, the offender pays a predetermined fine plus processing costs.

Today, judges may impose a large variety of criminal penalties in most states, from probation to the death penalty. The actual sentence received is tied directly to the conviction offense. Even if the offender actually did something

Box 13.1

CAREERS IN CRIMINAL JUSTICE

COURT ANALYST/ RESOURCE COORDINATOR

Many court systems employ court analysts/resource coordinators who assist the judge and courtroom staff in carrying out their duties. In larger systems, the analyst/resource coordinator is usually assigned to work in a particular court, while in smaller systems the individual might be assigned to work wherever needed within the system. The Criminal Court of New York City, serving Bronx, Queens, and Kings Counties, advertised for a Senior Court Analyst/Resource Coordinator for domestic violence cases in July 1998, describing the salary, qualifications, and duties as follows:

Salary: $39,771 (starting), plus location pay of $798

Qualifications: One year as a court analyst or a bachelor's degree from an accredited college or university and two years of relevant experience; or a master's degree in public or business administration, criminal justice, or social work and one year of relevant experience; preference will be given to candidates with a bachelor's degree in social work or criminal justice who have experience within the courts.

Duties: Include reviewing and recommending alternative sentence plans; providing ongoing information and technical assistance to staff on program issues; overseeing submission of required reports; serving as liaison between judge, courtroom staff, attorneys, victim advocates and service providers, and the public; participating in program planning and development; working on research, confidential analysis, and planning related to budgets, personnel administration, resource allocation; and court management.

else, it is the conviction offense that counts. This is why so much of the bargaining between prosecutors and defense attorneys centers on the formal charges. An offender who actually commits an armed robbery but is convicted of a nonviolent theft offense will receive a sentence appropriate for the theft, not the armed robbery.

Offenders convicted of felonies face a possible sentence of at least a year in a state or federal prison. Despite this generalization, the actual sentences handed down in felony cases vary considerably. With the exception of drug offenses, prison sentences received in federal courts are generally shorter than the average sentence in state courts (Langan and Brown, 1997b:8). Table 13.2 shows the average sentences imposed on felony offenders in state courts in 1994, the most recent year for which published data are available. Reading across the table, we see that violent offenders were most likely to be sentenced to prison and least likely to be sentenced to probation. In 1994, the average length of prison sentences varied widely: 300 months for murder, 120 months for rape, 84 months for robbery, 49 months for burglary, and 36 months for drug possession (Langan and Brown, 1997a:2). Although excluded from the table, fines are sometimes imposed, often together with prison time. Some felony offenders end up with a sentence of probation and no fine or prison time. The death penalty is reserved for crimes considered to be the most heinous of felonies, including some forms of murder, sexual assault, and kidnapping. Crimes carrying the death penalty are called **capital offenses**, and they will be the focus of Chapter 14.

capital offense A crime for which the penalty may be death.

intermediate sanctions Penalties that lie between simple probation and imprisonment.

The four traditional sentences in felony cases—probation, fines, imprisonment, and death—have been joined in recent years by a new class of penalties called **intermediate sentences**, or **intermediate sanctions**. These sentences in-

TABLE 13.2 Percentage of Felony Offenders Sentenced to Prison, Jail, or Probation in State Court, by Conviction Offense

Felony offenses carry possible sentences of one year or more in a state or federal prison. While many felony offenders avoid jail or prison, violent offenders are least likely to do so. This table shows the percentage of felony offenders sentenced to prison, jail, or probation by the nation's state courts in 1994 for different types of conviction offenses. Read the table from left to right. For example, 62 percent of violent offenders were sentenced to prison, 20 percent to jail, and so on.

MOST SERIOUS CONVICTION OFFENSE	PERCENT OF OFFENDERS SENTENCED TO:		
	PRISON	JAIL	PROBATION
All Offenses	**45%**	**26%**	**29%**
Violent Offenses	**62%**	**20%**	**18%**
Murder	95	2	3
Rape	71	17	12
Robbery	77	11	12
Aggravated assault	48	27	25
Property Offenses	**42%**	**26%**	**32%**
Burglary	53	22	25
Larceny and auto theft	38	28	34
Fraud	32	28	40
Drug Offenses	**42%**	**27%**	**31%**
Possession	34	32	34
Trafficking	48	23	29
Weapons Offenses	**42%**	**27%**	**31%**

Source: Jodi M. Brown and Patrick A. Langan (1998). *State Court Sentencing of Convicted Felons, 1994* (p. 5). Washington, D.C.: U.S. Department of Justice.

volve penalties that fall in between probation and imprisonment. They include shock incarceration—also known as boot camp—electronic monitoring, restitution, and intensive supervision. These sentences will be described later in this chapter, and discussed in detail in Chapter 17.

SENTENCING DISPARITIES

For centuries, sentencing statutes allowed judges considerable discretion in the actual sentence they handed down in any given criminal case. This produced variation in sentencing from judge to judge, giving rise to **sentencing disparities**, meaning that offenders convicted of essentially the same offense received different sentences.

sentencing disparities Imposition of different sentences on offenders convicted of essentially the same offense.

INDIVIDUALIZED JUSTICE AND THE INDETERMINATE SENTENCE

The discretion enjoyed by judges—and the resulting sentencing disparities—became even greater during the late nineteenth and early 20th centuries, when penal reforms gave rise to the **indeterminate sentence**. An indeterminate sentence involves sending an offender to prison for an unspecified amount of time between some minimum and a maximum. For example, an indeterminate sentence for burglary might be two to five years in prison. The maximum is usually some multiple of the minimum, in this case two and one-half times the minimum. All states and the federal government sooner or later adopted indeterminate sentences.

indeterminate sentence Imposition of an unspecified amount of prison time between some minimum and maximum.

Under an indeterminate sentence, the state's **parole board** determines when the offender will actually be released. Parole board members are usually appointed by the governor. The board's function is to establish whether an offender seeking release has been "reformed" or "rehabilitated" (some might say "cured") and can therefore be released. The indeterminate sentence and use of parole boards was an attempt to *individualize* justice—to match sentences to the circumstances of individual offenders and their crimes. The law helped judges do this by allowing broad judicial discretion. Studies over the past 25 years have found wide variations in the sentences that judges said they would impose in identical cases (Austin and Williams, 1977; Robin, 1987).

parole board A group that determines when inmates under indeterminate sentences may be released from prison.

Criticism of Indeterminate Sentences. The considerable sentencing discretion allowed judges through the individualization of justice led to charges that sentencing practices were not only unfair but lacked the predictability, and in some cases the severity, necessary to meet the goal of a just penal system. A 1971 book called *Struggle for Justice: A Report on Crime and Punishment in America*, published by the American Friends Service Committee, a Quaker organization, documented the sentencing disparities associated with indeterminate sentences. The book also pointed out that offenders sentenced to prison never knew how long they would actually stay there. This situation imposed unnecessary hardship on offenders and their families.

STATUTORY SOURCES OF SENTENCING DISPARITIES

It is not only judges who vary in the sentences they impose for similar offenses. Sometimes statutory distinctions are drawn between essentially similar behavior, ensuring that some criminals will be given harsher sentences than others despite the similarity of their crimes. The penalties for crack versus powdered cocaine are a case in point.

Under recent federal law, the possession of only 1 gram of crack is considered equivalent to the possession of 100 grams of powdered cocaine, a distinction mirrored in many state statutes (Tonry, 1994b:488). Possession of 5 grams of crack cocaine carries a minimum sentence of five years in prison, while

Basketball star Len Bias, shown here in better times, fell victim to crack cocaine and died in 1986 as a result of his drug use. Since that time, the U.S. government has passed strict laws regarding any drug violation involving crack cocaine—sentences that are consistently harsher than ones involving powdered cocaine. What has been the impact of this policy?

PHOTO COURTESY OF UP/CORBIS-BETTMANN

possession of the same amount of powdered cocaine is a misdemeanor, punishable by a *maximum* of one year. A dealer caught selling 50 grams of crack gets a mandatory minimum of ten years in prison, while a dealer in powdered cocaine would have to sell 100 times that amount to receive the same penalty.

The distinction appears to have arisen as a direct result of the 1986 crack cocaine–induced death of basketball star Len Bias. "Almost immediately after Bias died, then Speaker of the House Tip O'Neill led a charge in Congress to impose strict mandatory minimums for possessing or selling crack cocaine" (Donziger, 1996:118). A sensational media event stimulated a policy change that resulted in gross disparities in sentencing. Furthermore, as we shall see in a later section of this chapter, this policy change contributed to unprecedented growth in the incarceration rate of African Americans. In 1997, the Clinton administration proposed to reduce the disparity between crack cocaine and powdered cocaine sentences to a 10-to-1 difference; however, the American Civil Liberties Union charged that this change was "woefully inadequate" if its goal was "to eliminate racial injustices in the prosecution of drug crimes" (ACLU news release, July 27, 1997).

COMMUNITY INFLUENCE AND SENTENCING DISPARITIES

Another factor producing differences among judges in their sentencing practices can be summarized as community influence. All people are affected by the immediate social environment in which they live and work, and judges are no exception. Studies of judicial sentencing behavior show that it makes a great deal of difference where a judge lives and works. For example, one study found that judges living in rural or smalltown communities were more inclined to sentence offenders to prison. The more-punitive practice reflected community sentiments about deviance that violated the "peaceful" lifestyle and solidarity of rural communities (Hood, 1962; Durkheim, 1964). The relationship between community characteristics and sentencing is probably more complex than this, however. One researcher found that sentencing in rural areas was less, not more, severe than in urban areas (Hogarth, 1971).

Sentencing behavior is clearly influenced by the attitudes of individual judges, but in a complex way that reflects not only community influences but also how judges define their role and responsibilities. For example, judges who believe that deterrence is the primary goal of punishment may react differently to a given case than judges who see rehabilitation as the primary goal. Likewise, judges who see themselves as *the* authority when it comes to sentencing may be less responsive to outside influences, including attempts to curb their discretion. The sentences they hand down may be consistently more or less harsh than those of their colleagues on the bench—or they may simply be less predictable. Whenever wide sentencing discretion is allowed judges by law or because they insist on it, we should expect to find more room for the impact of different attitudes and philosophies. To generalize, judges will attempt to organize their sentencing behavior to match their perceptions of the legal, situational, and social pressures they are required to face on a daily basis.

Sentencing Disparities and the Pre-Sentence Investigation

Another influence in the sentencing process, and therefore another possible source of sentencing disparities, is the **pre-sentence investigation.** Conducted prior to sentencing in most felony cases—but rarely in misdemeanors—a pre-sentence investigation compiles information about the convicted offender that is supposed to help the judge select an appropriate sentence within the jurisdiction's statutory framework. In some states, a pre-sentence investigation is mandatory; in others it is available at the request of the judge. The information is usually collected by probation officers or by trained social workers employed by the state or county. In theory, the pre-sentence investigation report is a neutral, unbiased document containing information on the offender's character, personal and family history, work habits, and prior record.

pre-sentence investigation Collects information on the offender's character, family life, work habits, and prior record to guide the sentencing judge.

The Content of Pre-Sentence Reports. In practice, pre-sentence reports are sometimes neither neutral and accurate nor filled with relevant information. Furthermore, probation officers are hardly immune to the stereotypes and prejudices characteristic of the community in which they work or the larger society. This may explain why some probation officers are less likely to recommend probation for minority individuals and the unemployed (Gelsthorpe, 1992).

According to a rare study of pre-sentence investigations, reports quite often contain misinformation, prejudicial statements, hearsay, and rumor. Here are some real-life illustrations (Remington et al., 1969:697–698):

- "In my opinion he is the type of person who, if not checked soon, will kill somebody someday."
- "There is a broad, deep base of sexual psychopathy in this boy. His offense may technically be burglary but he is basically a sex deviate."
- "He is a loser, plain and simple. He is sexually inadequate, vocationally inadequate, and mentally inadequate. He has failed in everything—school, jobs, military service, with his family, and with his wife. He has even failed as a crook. There is absolutely no reason to think he can make it on probation and probably prison won't help him much. The only thing I can recommend is incarceration for as long as possible and then hope for the best."

Such liberties as these may not be typical today, although the quality of reports is known to vary widely (Gelsthorpe and Raynor, 1995). There are three reasons why pre-sentence investigation reports are likely to contain more than factual, objective information:

1. Many jurisdictions and administrative policies require or encourage investigators to recount feelings and attitudes and to present opinions and recommendations.
2. Despite little formal training, pre-sentence investigators see themselves as experts, professionals whose opinions should be taken seriously.
3. Probation officers are part of the courthouse work group. Thinking about their job security and promotion prospects, probation officers who feel pressured to bias their pre-sentence reports will find it difficult to be objective and factual.

The Impact of Pre-Sentence Reports on Judges' Decisions. All this may not matter if pre-sentence reports have little impact on the actual sentences that judges hand down. The question is, are judges influenced by pre-sentence reports and, if so, to what extent?

Findings on the impact of pre-sentence reports provide few conclusive answers. Some studies show that pre-sentence reports are influential in the sentencing process. A pioneering study in California found that judges and probation officials were in broad agreement about major sentencing criteria and that judges accepted 86 percent of investigators' recommendations (Carter and Wilkins, 1967). Other studies have found similar evidence of strong associations between sentencing recommendations and actual sentences (Frazier and Bock, 1982; Kingsnorth and Rizzo, 1979).

On the other hand, one of the complaints lodged by some judges against pre-sentence reports is that they are too lenient in their recommendations. Probation officers are seen as advocates of probation and other sentences that do not involve prison time, even though the severity of the offense and the offender's past record lead the judge to favor a prison term. Here are some quotes from magistrates and judges in England:

> "Presentence reports never or very rarely propose a custodial sentence, or put another way, they go for a soft option!"
> "Reports tend to only emphasize the use of probation or community service; other disposals seem to be ignored."
> "Reports are often wholly unrealistic in sentence, often ignoring the victims and the public concern for an offence. . . ." (May, 1995:53–57)

With the movement toward harsher sentences that has occurred within the past few years, it is likely that a survey would uncover similar comments from American judges. More than anyone else, probation officers see the human side of offenders and acquire intimate knowledge of their backgrounds, family, friendships, and neighborhood experiences. The fact that they are expected to make sentence recommendations implies that there are alternatives to doing hard time—and suggests that they should support and justify those alternatives if they can.

SENTENCING DISPARITIES AND DIVERSITY

Sentencing disparities could be the result of bias on the part of judges. For many years, criminologists have documented sentencing disparities by race (Sellin, 1935; Wolfgang and Cohen, 1970; Thornberry, 1973) and class (Hood, 1972; Thornberry, 1973), and the question of gender bias has been receiving increased attention in recent years (Datesman and Scarpitti, 1980; Morris, 1987; Chesney-Lind and Shelden, 1992). This section reviews some of the evidence on the role of prejudice in sentencing.

Race and Sentencing. Nationwide surveys of adult sentencing in state felony courts show that, overall, African American men and women are more likely to be sentenced to prison than their white counterparts who have been convicted of similar offenses (Brown and Langan, 1998:24). This finding does not in itself prove racial bias in sentencing because other factors that affect sentencing such as prior record and offense circumstances are not taken into account. Yet the picture it paints calls attention to racial disparities as a national issue in criminal justice, one that also affects juvenile offenders.

One study of juvenile court sentencing practices looked at a sample of 159 counties in 17 states (McGarrell, 1993). Minority youths were more likely than whites to be referred to court, to be detained, and to be placed outside the home. This disparity increased over the five-year period studied, although the increase varied significantly among the counties. On the whole, nonwhite referrals to court rose 38.5 percent, versus only 4.3 percent for whites. The bulk of this increase can be attributed to the growing emphasis on drug enforcement during the 1980s: Juvenile drug referrals showed a 147 percent increase over the period.

The so-called war on drugs has had a greater impact on African Americans than any other group. As already noted, the stiff penalties for crack cocaine offenses have resulted in a huge increase in the incarceration rate of African Americans. This has been called a "hidden effect" of the criminal law (Barnes and Kingsnorth, 1996). It has also been described as "politicized sentencing" to reflect the political character of drug enforcement (Hagan, 1994:164). Politicians and high-ranking government officials have been enthusiastic supporters of harsh measures against illicit drugs at least partly because it means votes at the ballot box and more resources for their home state or county, or the agency they head. When the war on drugs is examined from the perspective of race, however, a startling picture emerges.

Figure 13.1 shows some of the relevant data. Data on illicit drug use compiled through nationwide household surveys shows slight differences between overall drug use patterns by race: White Americans are somewhat more inclined than black Americans to have ever used an illegal drug. The second panel of Figure 13.1 shows that imprisonment rates bear little relationship to use rates. The rate at which black defendants were sentenced to prison for drug offenses was over *six times higher* than that for white defendants. The trend over the past decade has been for black imprisonment rates for drug offenses to increase, while those for white offenders have remained stable or decreased (Tonry, 1994a;b). Though some of this difference is probably explained by legal factors such as prior record and the severity of the current charge—for example, "selling" versus mere "possession"—much of it reflects the tough sentencing of crack cocaine offenders, who are mainly black.

When sentences for drug trafficking and drug possession are compared, black offenders still receive harsher sentences than white offenders. For example, in 1994, the average sentences imposed by state courts on white and black felony drug offenders were as follows (Brown and Langan, 1998:21):

White: possession, 20 months; trafficking, 33 months
Black: possession, 31 months; trafficking, 54 months

It is not possible to tell whether some of this disparity is due to black drug offenders having worse criminal records than white drug offenders, but even if that were true, the records themselves could reflect the cumulative impact of bias, which is discussed in a later section.

Race and Social Class and Sentencing. Race and social class are intertwined in American society, as are gender and class. Black Americans and women tend on the whole to have lower socioeconomic status and power than

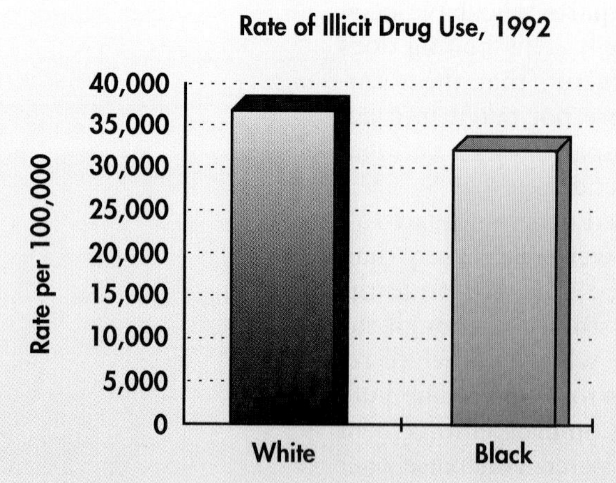

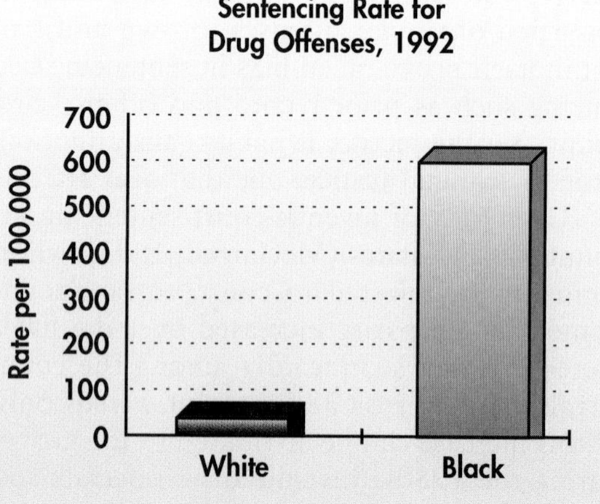

FIGURE 13.1 RACIAL DISPARITY IN THE WAR ON DRUGS
White and black Americans have similar overall rates of drug use, according to national surveys. However, this figure shows that black offenders are six times more likely than white offenders to be sentenced to prison for drug offenses.

Source: Seven R. Donziger, ed. (1996). *The Real War on Crime: The Report of the National Criminal Justice Commission* (p. 118). New York: HarperCollins.

white Americans and men. This makes distinguishing their individual relationship to sentencing more difficult.

It has been shown, for example, that the sentences given to juvenile offenders are affected by both race and class. In one study, the records of 9,601 juvenile court dispositions in Philadelphia were analyzed. Even when legal variables such as severity of offense and prior record were taken into account, black offenders were more likely than white offenders to be prosecuted and institutionalized, and offenders of low socioeconomic status were more severely penalized than others (Thornberry, 1973). More recent studies of the sentencing of juveniles have also shown class and race disparities (Leonard, Pope, and Feyerherm, 1995).

A study of early releases from prison in Ohio found race to be the most important factor in determining releases in certain situations (Peterson and Friday, 1975). For example, when the probation department had recommended against early release, white prisoners were twice as likely as black prisoners be released, even after controlling for criminal record, current offense, and other variables.

Although much of the research on case dispositions appears to show that race and class influence sentencing, a review of numerous studies found ten studies showing no association between class and disposition and seventeen studies showing no association between race and disposition (Box, 1981). Many of these studies used different methods, so caution must be exercised in any search for generalizations. Nevertheless, the author of a recent review of the relevant research raises a thought-provoking question: "Even a single verified case of unequal sentencing because of racial status serves to illuminate flaws in the criminal justice system, and indeed ample research demonstrates that there are thousands of such cases—can we dismiss the real world issue of judicial injustice toward minorities because of a lack of the precise methodological rigor demanded by some quantitative researchers?" (Mann, 1993:196).

Reanalysis of the evidence in some of the earlier studies has shown that the race and class effects on sentencing diminish when other factors such as prior record and circumstances of the offense are taken into account (Hagan, 1974:379). One study focused on racial bias in both capital (death penalty) and noncapital cases and reviewed more than 55 studies, mostly from the 1960s and 1970s (Kleck, 1981). It concluded that there was little evidence of any general, overt racial discrimination in noncapital cases, but strong evidence of discrimination in capital cases in the South when the offense was rape. However, black defendants sometimes were treated more leniently than white defendants, especially when their victims were also black. Various explanations for the more lenient treatment of black-on-black offenders were suggested: (1) Black people are devalued crime victims, hence offenses against them are considered less serious; (2) there exists a sort of white paternalism that promotes an "understanding" and forgiving attitude in dealing with conflicts within the black community; and (3) some judges may feel guilty about past discrimination or may be compensating for institutionalized racism or for any prejudice they might have.

Table 13.3 compares death penalty requests for various racial combinations of offenders and victims (Paternoster, 1983). It clearly shows that when black defendants killed black victims, their offenses were least likely to be classified as capital murders, and when they were, the prosecutor was least likely to request the death penalty.

Other research on sentencing in capital cases confirms that the killing of white victims results in harsher sentences than the killing of black victims. One study found that defendants convicted of killing white victims were over four times as likely to receive a death sentence than defendants who killed black victims (Baldus, Pulaski, and Woodworth, 1983). This finding could not be explained by conventional legal factors, such as the circumstances of the crime or offenders' past records. A later study of death penalty sentences in eight states—Florida, Georgia, Illinois, Oklahoma, North Carolina,

TABLE 13.3 Death Penalty Requests by Prosecutors in South Carolina, 1997–1981

Over the years may experts have claimed that minorities, especially African Americans, have been discriminated against in the imposition of the death penalty. A key player in any decision relating to the death penalty is the proesecutor, who decides in the first place whether to change a defendant with capital murder, in effect requesting the death penalty. The figures below show that during a four-year period in South Carolina, death penalty requests were most likely when a black person killed a white person, and least likely when a black person killed another black person.

CATEGORY OF OFFENSE	NUMBER OF HOMICIDE ACTS	NUMBER OF HOMICIDES ELIGIBLE FOR THE DEATH PENALTY*	NUMBER OF ACTUAL DEATH PENALTY REQUESTS	PERCENTAGE OF ELIGIBLE HOMICIDES IN WHICH PROSECUTORS REQUESTED DEATH
Black killed white	148	111	54	48.6%
White killed white	580	113	44	38.9%
Black killed black	894	76	8	10.5%
White killed black	54	16	7	43.8%

*Capital murder cases are the only homicide cases for which the death penalty may be sought. They involve the commission of the willful homicide in conjunction with at least one other aggravating circumstance as defined by South Carolina's death penalty statute.

Source: Raymond Paternoster (1983). "The Decision to Seek the Death Penalty in South Carolina." *Journal of Criminal Law and Criminology* 74:754–787.

Mississippi, Virginia, and Arkansas—found a "clear pattern" of victim-based discrimination "unexplained on grounds other than race" (Gross and Mauro, 1989:110).

In one study, disparities in sentencing based on the race of offenders and victims were most dramatic when the offenses were more serious. An analysis of 2,858 felony cases ranging from assaults to robberies and murder found that marked racial disparities were present in the sentences received only in the cases of murder and sexual assault (Spohn, 1994). Why this should be so is unclear. Two possibilities are (1) that judges see black-on-white sexual assaults and murders as a serious threat to the power structure, of which they are a part; and (2) that the violent intimacy of the crimes themselves gives rise to racial bias. Yet a recent Florida study of decisions to increase penalties by use of habitual-offender laws shows that racial disparities were more common for *less* serious offenses (Crawford, Chiricos, and Kleck, 1998). The authors surmise that less serious offenses allow judges more room for flexibility in sentencing, including allowing nonlegal factors such as race to enter the picture. Only continued research will clarify the complex relationship between race and sentencing.

Gender and Sentencing. A review of research on juvenile court dispositions concludes that girls receive harsher treatment than boys for lesser crimes but not for more serious offenses (Barlow and Ferdinand, 1992:130–134). To some extent this reflects the impact of gender on referrals to juvenile court. A national study of juvenile court data found that girls were three times as likely as boys to be referred to juvenile court for status offenses—that is, acts that would not be crimes if committed by adults (Snyder and Finnegan, 1987). Once there, however, girls charged with status offenses were also more likely than boys to be incarcerated. This difference is a historical one (Chesney-Lind, 1987a, 1987b, 1988).

What explains this difference in the treatment of boys and girls? One study looked at gender bias in 36,680 juvenile court dispositions in Nebraska over a nine-year period (Johnson and Scheuble, 1991). Hypotheses were derived from two competing theories: sex-role traditionalism and chivalry (or paternalism). The perspective of sex-role traditionalism predicts harsher punishment for females based on the argument that girls and women who commit crimes violate the traditional female role—being gentle, passive, and dependent. The chivalry model predicts an opposite gender bias: Female offenders will be given more lenient sentences because males—who dominate the criminal justice system—try to protect the "fairer sex."

The findings of this study support both models of gender bias. Overall, girls received more lenient dispositions than boys, suggesting a chivalry effect. Yet harsher penalties for girls were found in the case of repeat offenders who committed more serious offenses, suggesting a sex-role effect. Over the nine years, however, the trend was toward greater leniency for females—"higher odds for girls being dismissed and higher odds for probation and lockup for boys" (Johnson and Scheuble, 1991:695).

One interesting study looked at sentencing practices as they take place in the courtroom (Daly, 1989). Courts in New York City and Seattle placed considerable weight on the family ties of defendants. Thus, black women with spouses, dependent parents, or children benefited most from sentencing leniency, and single and married men with children or dependent parents also did better than other men. Likewise, a study of 61,294 criminal cases in Pennsylvania in the late 1980s found that gender had only a small impact on prison sentences; interviews with judges and courtroom observation showed that sentencing was influenced most by perceptions of a defendant's blameworthiness and by the practical consequences of incarceration (Steffensmeier, Kramer, and Streifel, 1993). When defendants had families to support and good jobs to lose, judges tended to be more lenient. This conclusion has also been reached in a study of the sentencing of women in England (Hedderman and Gelsthorpe, 1997).

THE CUMULATIVE IMPACT OF BIAS IN THE CRIMINAL PROCESS

A number of authors have pointed out that an offender's criminal record is a cumulative product of discretionary judgments that may have been influenced by bias or prejudice. The argument is that racial and class injustices permeate the criminal justice system, and the effects of earlier discrimination—for example, by the police—affect the later choices open to prosecutors and judges (Box, 1983:194; Kleck, 1981:799; Morris, 1988; Mann, 1993; Donziger, 1996:114). When introduced as a factor in court deliberations, a prior record also influences sentencing indirectly by affecting a defendant's ability to secure bail and competent private counsel, and to negotiate a reduced charge. In sum, the common finding that legal variables such as prior criminal record account for much of the variation in sentences may actually reflect the accumulated disadvantages of being black and/or lower class.

Consider this:

> If after arrest there were *no* racial bias in the criminal justice system, the racial makeup of the prison population should at least roughly reflect the racial disparity in arrest rates—if three times as many African-Americans get *arrested* for less serious crimes, then there should be roughly three times as many African-Americans per capita in prison for those crimes. But the racial difference among African-Americans and whites in prison is overwhelmingly wider than arrest rates suggest it should be absent racial bias. *There are seven African-Americans to each white in prison.* (Donziger, 1996:108; italics in original).

The evidence on discrimination in sentencing is inconsistent and difficult to interpret, but it would be hard to refute the conclusion that discrimination is a problem, and that minority and lower-class defendants are its main targets. This conclusion also appears justified in regard to the sentencing of offenders in Britain (Hood, 1992). Yet even if there were absolutely no evidence of sentencing discrimination, the fact is that statutory penalties for predominantly lower-class crimes—for instance, robbery, burglary, gun assaults—and those committed most extensively among black offenders—for instance, crack cocaine offenses (McDonald and Carlson, 1993:13)—are generally higher than those for predominantly upperclass crimes—corporate fraud, misrepresentation in advertising, restraint of trade, or environmental crimes. This represents a *built-in* bias against lower-class and minority offenders within the penalty structure itself.

CURBING SENTENCING DISCREPANCIES

Most experts acknowledge the need for some judicial discretion, but many also support efforts to curtail it in the hope of reducing sentencing disparities and excesses. These efforts have resulted in a variety of sentencing reforms. Some of the reforms, appearing in the 1960s and before, dispersed some of the responsibility for sentencing away from the individual judge. For example, in Arkansas, Missouri, Oklahoma, Texas, and Virginia, the same jury that decides guilt or innocence in noncapital cases also sets the sentence. Only in Texas,

Sentencing guidelines require judges to keep sentences within prescribed limits and make them accountable for going outside them. Supporters of this approach believed it would reduce sentencing disparities among judges. However, guidelines have not been a total success, and there have been some unanticipated consequences.

PHOTO BY JEFF JANOWSKI, COURTESY OF AP PHOTO

however, is the trial judge required to accept the jury's sentence (Bureau of Justice Statistics, 1993d:308). Arizona, Indiana, Kentucky, and West Virginia allow juries to make sentence recommendations. In death penalty cases, juries are more widely involved in the sentencing process. In 25 states the trial jury determines the sentence, which in most cases cannot be altered by the judge; in 7 other states, the jury makes a sentence recommendation to the judge.

THE SENTENCING GUIDELINES APPROACH

sentencing guidelines A standardized set of penalty options based on information about the offense and the offender.

A major reform specifically designed to address sentencing disparities is the use of **sentencing guidelines**. The actual sentencing practices of judges within a jurisdiction are used as a basis for developing a standardized set of sentencing options or guidelines for any particular class of crimes. In this way, the sentencing discretion of judges is both narrowed and structured.

Exploratory research in the 1970s showed that the two most important factors influencing sentences were the seriousness of an offense and the offender's prior record. Reference tables, or *matrices*, were devised showing the average or model sentence given by judges in cases with similar offense and offender circumstances (Wilkins et al., 1978). The tables were reproduced on cards distributed to judges for use during the sentencing phase of a trial. Following experiments in Denver and in the state of Vermont, Minnesota was among the first states to adopt the guidelines approach, and their guidelines have served as a model for other states (see Table 13.4).

Using information about the seriousness of the offense and the prior record and "social stability" of the offender, judges can determine scores for offense and offender according to the prearranged formula. To find the model sentence for any particular combination of offense/offender scores, the judge simply

TABLE 13.4 Minnesota Sentencing Guidelines: Presumptive Sentence Length in Months[1]

Sentencing guidelines provide the judge with a fairly narrow range of alternatives when sentencing an offender to prison. This chart shows the judge what the statutory sentence and range are for each combination of offense severity level and offender criminal history. The judge merely locates each score and looks at the corresponding cell.

	Criminal History Score						
Severity Levels of Conviction Offense	0	1	2	3	4	5	6 or more
Level I: Unauthorized use of motor vehicle, possession of marijuana	12[3]	12[3]	12[3]	13	15	17	19 18–20
Level II: Theft-related crimes ($150–$2,500), sale of marijuana	12[3]	12[3]	13	15	17	19	21 20–22
Level III: Theft crimes ($150–$2,500)	12[3]	13	15	17	19 18–20	22 21–23	25 24–26
Level IV: Burglary-felony intent, receiving stolen goods ($150–$2,500)	12[3]	15	18	21	25 24–26	32 30–34	41 37–45
Level V: Simple robbery	18	23	27	30 29–31	38 36–40	46 43–49	54 50–58
Level VI: Assault, second degree	21	26	30	34 33–35	41 42–46	54 50–58	65 60–70
Level VII: Aggravated robbery	48 44–52	58 54–62	68 64–72	78 74–82	88 84–92	98 94–102	108 104–112
Level VIII: Assault, first degree; criminal sexual conduct, first degree	86 81–91	98 93–103	110 105–115	122 117–127	134 129–139	146 141–151	158 153–163
Level IX: Murder, third degree	150 144–156	165 159–171	180 174–186	195 189–201	210 204–216	225 219–231	240 234–246
Level X: Murder, second degree[2]	306 299–313	326 319–333	346 339–353	366 359–373	386 379–393	406 399–413	426 419–433

[1]A presumptive sentence is the sentence an offender would get if there were no mitigating or aggravating circumstances. The presumptive sentence is the first, single number in each cell of the chart. If the judge goes outside the range of numbers this is considred a departure from the guidelines, and must be justified in writing.
[2]First-dgree murder is excluded from the guidelines by law and continues to have a mandatory life sentence.
[3]One year and one day.
Source: Bureau of Justice Assistance (1996). *National Assessment of Structured Sentencing* (p. 64). Washington, D.C.: U.S. Department of Justice.

finds the cell that lines up with the two scores in the table. Suppose an offender in Minnesota has been convicted of simple robbery (severity level V) and has four prior offenses. What would be the model sentence, and what would be the range of sentence the judge could impose without departing from the guidelines? The model sentence would be 38 months, within a range of 36 to 40 months.

Sentencing Commissions. As of 1994, the sentencing guidelines approach is the primary sentencing model in operation in sixteen states and the federal system (see Table 13.5). By 1995, Missouri, Ohio, Oklahoma, and Massachusetts were developing guidelines. Most of these states and a few others have established sentencing commissions to help in the formulation and review of guidelines and other sentencing policies. The membership of these commissions varies from state to state, but most include trial lawyers and judges, with some including representatives of law enforcement, the legislature, education, corrections, and victim advocacy groups. Commissions vary in size, most having 13 to 16 members, all of whom serve part-time. North Carolina has the largest number of voting members (28), followed by Texas (25); Virginia's sentencing commission has the fewest members—7, all of them judges. The U.S. Sentencing Commission (USSC), established in 1987, is composed of three judges and four private citizens. Though small compared to state commissions, the USSC employed 100 full-time staff members in 1991 and had a budget of over $8 million. Most state commissions operate with between five and seven full-time staff members (Bureau of Justice Assistance, 1996:48).

Not surprisingly, the mandate and membership of a sentencing commission directly affects its philosophy and actions. A study of efforts by the New York State Sentencing Guidelines Committee to develop sentencing policy in the mid-1980s shows how difficult it is to bring different philosophies and interests to a point where agreement can be reached. After months of haggling, the committee's final recommendations were universally rejected: "Liberals said the sentences were too long; conservatives claimed they were too short. Judges, prosecutors, defense attorneys, prison administrators, and advocacy groups all found something to criticize, as did the New York media, which had long supported the switch to determinacy" (Griset, 1994:545). Not surprisingly, the New York state legislature refused to act on the committee's sentencing recommendations.

Politics plays an important role, since commission members are generally appointed by elected officials. But some commissions are more closely tied to

TABLE 13.5 Jurisdictions Using Guidelines as Primary Sentencing Practice*

Arkansas (1994)**	North Carolina (1994)
Delaware (1987)	Oregon (1989)
Florida (1979)	Pennsylvania (1982)
Kansas (1993)	Tennessee (1989)
Louisiana (1992)**	Utah (1985)
Maryland (1983)**	Virginia (1991)**
Michigan (1984)**	Washington (1984)
Minnesota (1978)	Wisconsin (1985)**
Federal (1987)	

*As of February, 1994. Dates indicate when sentencing guidelines were first adopted.
**Voluntary or Advisory, meaning judges are not required to follow the guidelines.
Sources: Bureau of Justice Assistance (1996). *National Assessment of Structured Sentencing* (p. 23). Washington, D.C.: U.S. Department of Justice; Bureau of Justice Statistics (1995). *State Court Organization, 1993* (Table 44). Washington, D.C.: U.S. Department of Justice.

legislative and judicial interests than others. Pennsylvania's sentencing commission was specifically authorized to address the concerns of legislators and judges, which included a growing perception that sentences for many offenses were too lenient; eight of the commission's eleven members were judges or legislators. Minnesota's commission, on the other hand, was established to provide input on a broad range of sentencing issues and to research and implement sentencing guidelines for the state, including ways to hold down the number of offenders sent to prison; its commission included representatives from corrections and the parole board, as well as three private citizens.

Comparative studies of the two commissions showed that Pennsylvania's resulting guidelines were far more punitive than Minnesota's, which emphasized the least restrictive penalties necessary to meet sentencing objectives (Martin, 1983). As noted, Minnesota's commission was also mandated to take prison capacity into account in developing its sentencing guidelines. This "capacity-based" approach has been adopted by other states, most recently North Carolina, whose sentencing commission is required to take prison, jail, and community resources into account (*Criminal Justice Newsletter*, November 15, 1994, pp. 3–5; Bureau of Justice Assistance, 1996:44).

Supporters of the sentencing guidelines approach consider it to be a middle course between the lack of consistent practice represented by wide sentencing disparities and the much more restrictive system of mandatory flat sentencing described in a later section. In some states, the model or guideline sentence is considered advisory, while in others judges are required to follow the guidelines. In either case, most states insist that judges give written reasons if they decide to go outside the guidelines in a particular case.

Aggravating and Mitigating Circumstances. Most sentencing guidelines provide various **aggravating** and **mitigating circumstances** that allow departure from the guideline sentence. An aggravating circumstance is one that makes an offense more serious; a mitigating circumstance is one that lessens the seriousness of an offense. Aggravating factors that judges might use to justify a harsher sentence include the offender's role in the offense—a leader versus a follower, for example—the amount of force used and degree of injury to the victim, whether the offender was on parole or probation at the time of the new offense, and the defendant's lack of remorse. Mitigating factors that judges might cite as a basis for reducing a sentence include pleading guilty, good family supports, good employment history, willingness to cooperate with the police or prosecution, and evidence of remorse. States differ in the number and type of extenuating circumstances they list—some as few as 4, others as many as 50. Of the seventeen jurisdictions that currently use sentencing guidelines as their primary sentencing practice in felony cases, all but Pennsylvania and Florida list extenuating circumstances that judges may cite when they depart from the presumed sentence recommended by the guidelines (Bureau of Justice Assistance, 1996:78). These lists are not exclusive, and judges may cite additional reasons for departure.

aggravating circumstance An aspect of a crime that makes it more serious, deserving a harsher penalty.

mitigating circumstance An aspect of a crime that makes it less serious, deserving a more lenient penalty.

Impact of Sentencing Guidelines on Sentencing Disparities. The federal sentencing guidelines adopted in 1987 have resulted in a changed profile of offenders sentenced to prison. In particular, the proportion receiving longer prison terms has gone down, as has the proportion of inmates convicted of violent crimes. However, the proportion of inmates with drug offense convictions has gone up, and now constitutes a majority of the federal prison population (Federal Bureau of Prisons, 1991). The sentences for some specific crimes have gone up; for example, the typical term for robbery is now 78 months, up from 48.8 months prior to 1987.

Although not a formal goal of sentencing guidelines, reductions in crime rates were believed by many supporters to be an incidental benefit that would result from their use. The reasoning was that if longer terms of incarceration are reserved for persistent offenders who commit serious crimes, then the incapacitation aspect of imprisonment should drive felony crime rates down. Yet there is little evidence this has happened. In fact, sentencing guidelines may actually have worked against this result (Bureau of Justice Assistance, 1996:115). This is because the system tends to be lenient toward first-time youthful offenders who may be at the beginning of a career in crime, and harsh toward older offenders with long criminal histories who may be "burning out" of their criminal careers. Filling prisons with less risky and older inmates diminishes the incapacitation that might result from imprisonment.

There is some evidence that the use of sentencing guidelines is producing, not reducing, racial disparities. For example, in Pennsylvania nonwhite offenders were found to have slightly higher incarceration rates and longer average minimum sentences than white offenders (Kramer and Lubitz, 1985). Some authors point out that sentencing guidelines are supposed to reduce discrimination, but not the disparities due to different rates of offending (Petersilia and Turner, 1985). Since black offenders have higher rates of violent crime than white offenders, the guidelines will tend to generate longer sentences for black offenders compared with their white counterparts. If crack cocaine convictions are excluded, it appears that federal sentencing guidelines do not in themselves result in significant differences by race (McDonald and Carlson, 1993). Furthermore, racial (and gender) disparities in guideline sentences can be linked to earlier decisions in the criminal process, particularly bail and charge decisions (Gottfredson and Jarjoura, 1996). We shall examine this issue further when we discuss mandatory minimum penalties.

If the major purpose of sentencing guidelines was to reduce sentencing disparities among judges, then the appropriate question is "Has it worked?" Extensive research conducted in Minnesota, Washington, and Oregon shows mixed results (Stolzenberg and D'Alessio, 1994; D'Alessio and Stolzenberg, 1995; Parent, 1988; Bureau of Justice Assistance, 1996). While sentencing guidelines appeared initially to produce reductions in disparities, these early gains have eroded (Tonry, 1993). The most common explanation for this is that judges are departing from the guidelines. Indeed, a majority of federal judges surveyed by the American Bar Association in 1993 thought that sentencing guidelines worked poorly or not at all; many criticized what they saw as the inflexibility of guidelines (Miller, 1995:182). Some federal judges have even removed themselves from the random draw by which criminal cases are assigned in order to avoid having to impose what they believe are excessive penalties in drug cases (*Washington Post*, May 17, 1996, p. F7).

When judges depart from the guidelines, it is most often in the direction of greater leniency. U.S. District Judge Vincent Broderick gives three illustrations of situations where downward departures held up under appellate review:

> Where a proprietor of a small candy store accepted illegal bets [amounting to] $20,000 a year, a downward departure from sentences intended for kingpins who supervised large illegal operations was found appropriate.
>
> Where rehabilitation of an offender in a nondrug case appeared likely because family members and community leaders were willing and able to supervise the defendant, home confinement was ordered rather than imprisonment.
>
> Where voluntary participation in shock incarceration ("boot camp") appeared likely to succeed in assisting a violator to turn his life around, this was substituted for a prison term (Miller, 1995:182).

When judges depart from the guidelines, they open the door to sentencing disparities, including disparities by race and gender. There is perhaps a natural inclination among judges to protect their discretionary powers from statutory restrictions, especially if they are strong believers in individualized justice. U.S. District Judge William Beatty falls into this category, and he shares some of his views on sentencing in Box 13.2. Of course, exercising discretion may mean that judges open themselves to the influence of all sorts of extralegal factors, including their own biases and prejudices, and those of the people who advise them.

SELECTIVE INCAPACITATION: TARGETING HIGH-RISK OFFENDERS

In developing their sentencing guidelines, sentencing commissions in some states looked to policy-based research for guidance. One influential study gave rise to the idea of **selective incapacitation** (Greenwood and Abrahamse, 1982; Greenwood, 1984). Recall that one of the ways punishment may prevent crime is through the incapacitation of offenders, that is, taking them out of circulation. Imprisonment does this. Selective incapacitation is based on the idea that sentencing policies can be constructed to maximize this function for offenders who are most likely to commit crimes if released. Incapacitation would therefore be selective: "[S]ome offenders would be imprisoned for a longer period than others convicted of the same offense, because of predictions about their future criminality" (Cohen, 1983:3).

selective incapacitation Imposition of longer prison terms for people most likely to commit crimes if released.

A study of prison inmates in California found that robbers who had four or more of the following characteristics committed an average of 31 robberies per year while free, compared with an average of 2 robberies per year for inmates with only one of these characteristics:

1. Prior convictions for robbery or burglary
2. Being incarcerated for more than half of the preceding two years
3. Juvenile conviction prior to age 16
4. Commitment to a state or federal juvenile facility
5. Current heroin or barbiturate use
6. Heroin or barbiturate use as a juvenile
7. Employed less than half of the preceding two years, excluding jail time (Greenwood,1984:6)

Selective incapacitation policy would use this seven-item "scale" as the basis for setting prison terms at sentencing.

Supporters of selective incapacitation believe use of this scale will enable judges to form risk-based sentencing decisions. The idea of selective incapacitation and the accompanying scale appeals to policymakers because it formalizes a widely accepted justification for incarceration—incapacitation of high-risk offenders—while providing tools to put it into practice. But pragmatic and moral objections were soon raised (Cohen, 1983; von Hirsch, 1984). A common ethical objection is that two persons convicted of the same offense deserve a similar punishment. Another questions whether it is fair to send a person to prison for crimes not yet committed.

On the practical side, there are serious doubts whether accurate predictions of future criminality can be made. Indeed, the errors that have appeared in past efforts suggest that around half the offenders evaluated as high risk in fact are not. A methodological objection to the Greenwood approach helps explain why many experts lack confidence in it: He studied only incarcerated offenders and based his predictions largely on self-reported information. It has not been established that the same results would hold with offenders at large.

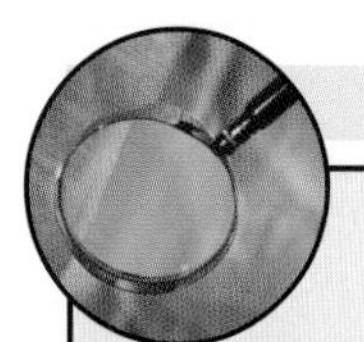

Box 13.2

INSIDE CRIMINAL JUSTICE

A JUDGE TALKS ABOUT HIS CAREER ON THE BENCH AND THE TASK OF SENTENCING OFFENDERS

I interviewed Senior U.S. District Judge William Beatty in August 1997. His experiences in both state and federal courts give us an insider's view of judicial discretion, responsibility, and power.

Judge Beatty has been on state and federal benches for over 20 years. After eighteen years in a successful private law practice, Beatty was elected to the circuit court of Madison and Bond Counties, in southern Illinois. He was eventually elected chief circuit judge by his colleagues. "It wasn't a great honor because it was mostly a rotation at the time. Nobody really wanted the job. It was primarily administrative . . . and you did no actual judging." The chief circuit judge ran the courthouse, a job often performed by a civilian court administrator in larger circuits. Like other judges, Beatty rotated through the various court divisions, from juvenile to civil to criminal. He recalls that in his eighteen years in private practice he had handled only two criminal cases, so "I had to do a lot of boning up for the criminal division."

In 1979 President Carter appointed Judge Beatty to the federal bench for the Southern District of Illinois. His appointment was confirmed by the U.S. Senate. U.S. District judges serve for life; when they retire their salary continues until death. They can be removed from office only through impeachment, although there are disciplinary mechanisms within the federal court system that can be used to sanction judges who stray from accepted practices.

Beatty believes that sentencing is the most difficult and unrewarding task facing a judge. He believes sentences should contain a punishing element so they act as a deterrent, but they should also be tailored to each individual. However, "federal sentencing guidelines have, for all practical purposes, taken the discretion out of the hands of the judge, and put it in the hands of the prosecutors." If a judge strays "the least little bit you're going to get reversed," Beatty observed. He believes that the individualization of justice requires a certain amount of sentencing flexibility, and therefore disparity. For this reason

A different line of attack focuses on the scale itself. According to the scale, unemployment carries the same weight as prior-conviction offenses and all the other items. The objection is to the possibility that a person's unemployment could make the difference between jail or prison (Walker, 1985:62–63): "The policy would take us back 300 years to the days of imprisonment for debt. . . . The way to deal with [the relationship between unemployment and crime]—the rational, effective, and humane way—is to provide employment."

Despite these objections, the ideas behind selective incapacitation received a lot of attention, and many states incorporated the scale items in their lists of mitigating and aggravating circumstances.

Among the modern forms of structured sentencing, the guidelines approach has the broadest potential impact on criminal penalties because it need not be restricted to sentences of incarceration. Although originally designed to guide judges in setting prison terms, some guideline states have incorporated noncustodial sentences in response to growing interest in alternatives to prison (Morris and Tonry, 1990). For example, in Oregon and Louisiana, the available

Box 13.2 (continued)

Beatty doesn't like mandatory minimum sentences either. "It's a way of Congress interfering with the judicial branch of government."

Nevertheless, Judge Beatty has come up with some creative sentences on occasion. He recalled a commercial fisherman on the Mississippi River who carried a shotgun on his boat to shoot snakes in the river. A game warden stopped the fisherman one day and found that he had a felony record, making possession of the gun a federal felony offense. He was arrested and wound up in front of Judge Beatty for sentencing. Beatty put him on probation and ordered him to provide 50 pounds of fish every week to a nearby children's home. "To me that did a lot more than putting the guy in the penitentiary." On another occasion he made several public officials cut the grass at various charitable organizations after they were found guilty of fraud involving city lawn-cutting contracts.

The biggest part of Judge Beatty's criminal work is taken up by drug cases, principally involving cocaine. He regrets the much harsher federal sentences for crack over powdered cocaine, and has on occasion expressed regret to defendants he has had to send to prison for lengthy terms. Judge Beatty takes his sentencing responsibilities very seriously, and reads all presentence investigation reports very carefully before coming to a decision. "There's a nugget in there someplace that may make a big difference." He always tells his law clerks how the 1963 *Gideon v. Wainwright* decision on the right to counsel might never have been made "had it not been for a law clerk who took the trouble to read everything that came across his desk, saw the significance of Gideon's handwritten letter, and passed it on to his boss."

Since becoming a judge, Beatty has seen many changes in the courthouse. Among the most notable is the greater presence of women, both as lawyers and as defendants. Beatty believes that both situations reflect changing attitudes toward gender. A change Beatty would strenuously resist is any reduction in the centrality of the jury system: "The one thing that we've got to hang on to is the jury system. Take lifetime tenure, take away anything you want, but not the jury. I tell jurors they are the most important people in this whole system."

Source: Judge William Beatty, personal communication, August 1997.

penalties range from probation to house arrest, community service, work release, jail time, and imprisonment (Bureau of Justice Assistance, 1996:74–75).

DETERMINATE SENTENCING

A second form of structured sentencing is restricted to penalties involving incarceration. **Determinate sentencing** refers to "flat" or "fixed-term" sentences to prison. For example, under determinate sentencing an offender may be sentenced to a flat term of six years. However, provisions are usually made for reductions in the time actually served: The defendant serves a specified term with time off for good behavior. The parole board is abolished, although post-release parole supervision is retained in most states.

determinate sentencing Imposition of flat or fixed terms in prison.

The first state to enact fixed-term sentencing was Maine, in 1975. California, Illinois, Indiana, New Mexico, and Washington (in its 1977 juvenile code) soon followed suit. Currently, 20 states have some form of determinate sentencing, sometimes in combination with other systems. An example of a determinate sentence from the current Indiana penal code is that state's penalty for murder: "A person who commits murder shall be imprisoned for a fixed term of fifty (50) years, with not more than ten (10) years added for aggravating circumstances or not more than ten (10) years subtracted for mitigating circumstances. . . ."

Determinate sentencing was supported in many quarters as a solution to excessively lenient penalties as well as sentencing disparities. It was seen as meeting both fairness and "get tough" agendas. In fact, determinate sentencing usually reduces judicial discretion only after the judge has decided on imprisonment. In other words, a judge may still be free to decide whether an offender should receive probation or some other penalty; however, once the judge decides on prison, the law sets the term of imprisonment.

If the idea was to reduce judicial discretion, the way in which determinate sentencing structures were originally developed in Illinois and Indiana virtually doomed the process from the start. These states used wide ranges of confinement options for given classes of offenses, in effect permitting judges considerable discretion. For example, in Illinois a defendant convicted of armed robbery or rape—a "Class X" felony—could be given a sentence anywhere from 6 to 30 years. This situation did little to reduce disparities, but it did result in offenders generally receiving longer sentences than under the previous indeterminate system. Both states subsequently revised their sentences, and Indiana now uses fixed-term sentences as in the preceding illustration.

MANDATORY MINIMUM SENTENCES

mandatory minimum sentence Imposition of a minimum term in prison.

A different structured sentencing reform, designed as a get-tough measure that also reduces judicial discretion, and therefore sentencing disparities, is the **mandatory minimum sentence.** Under this system, a minimum sentence is required for certain offenses, usually those involving armed, violent, repeat, or drug offenders. For example, a convicted armed robber may be required to serve a minimum of five years in prison. All 50 states and the federal system now have mandatory minimum sentencing (Bureau of Justice Assistance, 1996:20–21). In 41 states, imprisonment is mandatory for repeat or "habitual" felony offenders and for offenders convicted of crimes involving possession of a deadly weapon. All but 18 states have also included mandatory minimum sentences for certain drug possession and trafficking offenses.

Nonviolent property offenses have not escaped mandatory minimums. In Illinois, for example, burglary of a residence now carries a mandatory minimum four-year sentence. In 1991, over 1,000 offenders were sentenced to prison under this rule (Joyce, 1992:365). Twenty-seven states have made drunk driving an offense for which incarceration is mandated. However, this is usually for relatively short periods in a local jail rather than a state prison.

All states have some form of mandatory sentencing, and the penalty structures in some are quite complicated. For example, Maine and Illinois have combined mandatory and fixed-term sentencing. Some states have retained combinations of mandatory and indeterminate sentencing or have made some sentences fixed term but not mandatory. Yet others have combinations of sentencing guidelines and mandatory minimums.

"three strikes" laws Mandate life in prison if convicted of a third felony.

"Three Strikes and You're Out." This baseball metaphor has become the catch-phrase for a reform that has taken mandatory minimum sentencing to a new level. Embraced by state legislators, the U.S. Congress, and President Clinton, the so-called **"three strikes law"** gives offenders life imprisonment without parole if they are convicted of a third felony offense. As of 1995, 24 states had enacted "three strikes" laws. However, Table 13.6 shows that there is little consensus among the states on which offenses qualify as strikes. Some states include only violent felony offenses; a few include any felony. Other variations exist around the country: In New Mexico only 5 crimes are eligible for "three strikes" consideration, while in Washington State 51 offenses are eligible; Washington also includes some offenses that public opinion surveys have ranked low in seriousness; promoting prostitution is one.

From all the attention it has received, "three strikes" appears to represent a major change in sentencing policy. It is more correctly viewed as a small incremental addition to the long-standing determinate sentencing agenda, one that has dominated sentencing reform for the past 30 years: "three strikes" extended the established practice of linking length of sentence to both the severity of the offense and the past criminal history of the offender (Saint-German and Calamia, 1996:66; Turner, Sundt, Applegate, and Cullen, 1995).

Despite their appeal to politicians, the news media, and many members of the public, "three strikes" laws have garnered criticism from many quarters, including criminologists, lawyers, police and correctional officials, and civil libertarians. In 1997, the American Civil Liberties Union published a commentary condemning the laws at its Web site on the Internet (www.aclu.org). Among other things, the ACLU claimed there would be an increase in violence from criminals who would resist arrest, kill witnesses, or attempt prison escapes in efforts to avoid life in prison. There is no reliable evidence that this is occurring, but some of the ACLU's other claims have merit.

For example, "three strikes" is having a disproportionate impact on minority offenders, in part because many states include felony drug offenses as prior strikes. Data collected from the Los Angeles County public defender's office show that black offenders are targeted in 57 percent of third-strike prosecutions. Furthermore, they are charged with third-strike offenses at thirteen to seventeen times the rate of white defendants (Schiraldi, 1995; American Bar Association, 1997). The American Bar Association (1997) claims that in California, 25 percent of those sentenced under "three strikes" are sentenced for nonviolent offenses, and the practice is resulting in many more jury trials. These are clogging the system and costing taxpayers more, another criticism of "three strikes" made by the ACLU.

Concerns raised by criminologists about "three strikes" include its potential impact of on prison populations, its costs, and its disproportionate impact on minority offenders. A task force established by the American Society of Criminology has called for further research into the impact of "three strikes" and other mandatory sentencing laws (*The Criminologist*, 1995, Vol. 20: 15). The task force believes such laws run counter to existing knowledge on criminality, and "they cannot take into account all the circumstances affecting individual cases or their various factual permutations." For all the criticism, "three strikes" enjoys considerable support among politicians and the public; it is unlikely to go away in the near future even if evidence shows it to be yet another example of how criminal justice negatively impacts minority populations. Although the U.S. Supreme Court refused to hear a California case involving "three strikes" in January 1999, the court noted some serious concerns about its use, and encouraged continued review of this controversial law. (Associated Press, January 19, 1999).

Truth-in-Sentencing: Targeting Early Release from Prison. Good-behavior time allowances and severe prison overcrowding associated with determinate and mandatory sentencing mean that many offenders serve only a portion of their prison sentence. For example, in state courts the average sentence in 1994 was 71 months, but the average time served was expected to be only 27 months, or 38 percent of the sentence (Brown and Langan, 1998:8). From

TABLE 13.6 Variations in State Three Strikes Laws

Between 1994 and 1995, 24 states adopted so-called three strikes laws (although some allow four strikes, and some only two). This table shows that there are significant variations among the states in offenses included, number of strikes needed, and in the meaning of "Out," i.e., the mandatory penalties imposed.

STATE	MAJOR OFFENSES INCLUDED	STRIKES NEEDED TO BE OUT	MEANING OF *OUT*
Arkansas	Murder, kidnaping robbery, rape	Two	At least 40 years in prison; no parole
California	Any felony if one prior conviction for one of 27 listed felonies	Two	Twice the usual term for offense involved
	Any felony if two prior convictions for one of 27 listed felonies	Three	Indeterminate life with no parole eligibility for 25 years
Colorado	Any Class 1 or 2 felony, or any Class 3 if violent	Three	Life in prison with no parole eligibility for 40 years
Connecticut	Murder, arson, kidnapping, aggravated sexual assault, robbery	Two	Up to 40 years in prison
		Three	Up to life in prison
Florida	Any forcible felony, aggravated child abuse, lewd or indecent conduct	Three	Up to life in prison
Georgia	Murder, armed robbery, rape, kidnapping, aggravated sodomy	Two	Life without parole
	Any felony	Four	Maximum sentence for the charge
Indiana	Murder, rape, child molestation, robbery, drug dealing	Three	Life without parole
Kansas	Any felony against a person	Two	Double term listed in guidelines
	Any felony against a person	Three	Triple term listed in guidelines
Louisiana	Murder, rape, kidnapping, drug offense punishable by more than 5 years	Three	Life in prison with no parole eligibility
Maryland	Murder, rape, burglary, kidnapping, carjacking, use of firearm in felony	Four	Life in prison with no parole eligibility
Montana	Deliberate homicide, sexual intercourse without consent	Two	Life in prision with no parole eligibility
	Aggravated assault, kidnapping, robbery	Three	Same
Nevada	Murder, robbery kidnapping, arson	Three	Up to life without parole

1992 to 1994, even violent offenders served less than half of their sentence on the average (Bureau of Justice Statistics, 1995c). A 1991 survey of state prison inmates found that prisoners were generally aware they would serve just under half their sentences; and 69 percent of those given life sentences expected to be released (Beck and Greenfeld, 1995:2).

Considering the growing public concern over crime and all the talk of getting tough on criminals, findings such as these provoked an outcry when they became widely publicized in the early 1990s. In response, a number of other states and the U.S. Congress have passed **truth-in-sentencing laws**. These laws stipulate that convicted offenders *must* serve most or all of their sentence before being released. The impact on time served will be dramatic. For example, in 1994, the average prison sentence for felony offenders convicted in federal courts was 80 months; it is estimated that the average time served will be 85 percent of that, or 68 months (Langan and Brown, 1997:9). This is more than twice the number of months served on average by state felony offenders.

truth-in-sentencing laws State that offenders must serve most or all of their sentences before being released.

Truth-in-sentencing laws have been hailed by prosecutors, many of whom were at the forefront of the drive to enact them. For example, St. Louis County prosecutor Robert McCullogh lobbied the Missouri legislature with graphic

State	Major Offenses Included	Strikes Needed to be Out	Meaning of *Out*
New Jersey	Murder, robbery, carjacking	Three	Life in prison with no parole eligibility
New Mexico	Murder, kidnapping, criminal sexual penetration	Three	Life in prison; parole eligibility after 30 years
N. Carolina	Fourty-seven violent felonies	Three	Life in prison with no parole eligibility
N. Dakota	Any Class A, B, or C felony	Two	Up to life in prison
Pennsylvania	Murder, rape, arson, kidnapping, robbery	Two	Up to 10 years in prison
	Same offenses	Three	Up to 25 years in prison
S. Carolina	Murder, rape, armed robbery, drug trafficking, embezzlement	Two	Life in prison with no parole eligibility
Tennessee	Murder and aggravated violent felonies	Two or Three if prison time served for prior offenses	Life in prison with no parole eligibility
Utah	Any first or second degree felony	Three	Up to life in prison
Vermont	Murder, arson causing death, kidnapping, lewd conduct with child	Three	Up to life in prison
Virginia	Murder, kidnapping, carjacking, sexual assault	Three	Life in prison with no parole eligibility
Washington	List of 51 offenses, including murder, arson, and promoting prostitution	Three	Life in prison with no parole eligibility
Wisconsin	Murder, abuse of child, sexual assaults, arson, burglary	Three	Life in prison with no parole eligibility

Source: Compiled from John Clark, James Austin, and D. Alan Henry (1997). "'Three Strikes and You're Out': A Review of State Legislation," *NIJ Research in Brief*, September: Exhibits 9 and 10.

stories of justice gone awry (*St. Louis Post-Dispatch*, May 29, 1994, p. 1B). The stories typically described violent criminals who had served less than half of their sentences, and upon release returned to their violent ways. Legislators responded by designating seven crimes for which defendants will have to serve at least 85 percent of their sentence: second-degree murder (first-degree murder carries either death by lethal injection or life without parole), rape, kidnapping, forcible sodomy, first-degree assault (for example, drive-by shootings or other attacks intended to kill or cause severe bodily injury), and first-degree arson (setting fire to a building, knowing it to be occupied). Arizona, which also enacted truth-in-sentencing laws in 1994, has applied the 85 percent rule to all felonies.

It is too early to tell the full impact of truth-in-sentencing laws, but there is little reason to be optimistic that the reform will have much of an impact on crime. Time and again, studies have shown that criminals who commit serious crimes rarely think about the consequences of getting caught. Where the impact will probably be felt most is in the correctional system: Prisons will have to find room for more prisoners for a longer period of time. The prison population will grow older, producing increased demand and costs for geriatric services.

Truth-in-sentencing laws require offenders to serve most or all of their prison sentence. The laws have been promoted by victim groups and prosecutors, who used examples of criminals like Lawrence Singleton to support their cause. Singleton had raped 15-year-old Mary Vincent in California, then cut off her forearms and left her to die. He was paroled before completion of his sentence and then murdered a woman in Florida.

PHOTO COURTESY OF AP PHOTO

Evaluation of Determinate and Mandatory Sentencing. As with any reform, both determinate and mandatory sentencing systems have their critics. Some claim that discretion is not really curbed but is simply shifted from judge to prosecutor. Indeed, the California determinate sentencing laws were called a plea bargainer's paradise, for they give prosecutors all kinds of leverage in securing guilty pleas (Alschuler, 1978:73). Rather than receiving sentences intended by reformers, offenders escape them through the bargaining process. In addition, some critics argue that the mandatory sentences are uniformly too high and, despite rhetoric to the contrary, will be avoided by prosecutors and judges because correctional resources are inadequate to handle the influx of new prisoners (Foote, 1978:133–141). As already noted, some judges have refused to serve in criminal court because they fear having to send nonviolent offenders to prison for lengthy terms. Others find the sentencing task more painful than ever: U.S. District Judge Lyle Strom even apologized to two men for having to sentence them to a minimum of 30 years in prison for cocaine trafficking (*New York Times*, November 27, 1995, p. B5).

A study of the early Indiana experience with determinate sentencing is instructive. The 1977 penal code included mandatory terms of imprisonment for seven classes of offenses, with enhancement for aggravation (such as use of a weapon or brutality) and reduction for mitigation (such as victim precipitation). Under the code, for example, the maximum possible sentence for a Class A felony such as armed robbery or rape was 30 years plus 20 years' enhancement for aggravation; the minimum would be 30 years minus 10 years' mitigation. Once in prison, the offender would be able to build credit toward future release in the form of good-behavior time, thus reducing the actual time served (Clear, Hewitt, and Regoli, 1978).

The authors of the study point out that the code increased sentencing discretion in two ways. First, enhancement and mitigation rules greatly extended the bargaining flexibility of prosecutors. Under this system, a lesser charge or fewer elements of aggravation would add up to many years off the sentence. Second, the use of credit time as the only way a sentence could be reduced in effect gave sentencing discretion to prison authorities. "Thus, a great deal of effective control over the inmate's sentence has been placed directly in the hands of the correctional officer who watches over him" (Clear, Hewitt, and Regoli, 1978:440).

The popular criticism that structured sentencing systems inevitably result in growth of prison populations is not consistently supported by the available research. An evaluation of determinate sentencing in ten states found that prison populations had substantially increased only in one state, Indiana, while they had decreased substantially in Minnesota and Washington (Marvell and Moody, 1996). However, the declines are largely explained by the fact that prosecutors and judges are allowed to circumvent the system in response to prison overcrowding. As for states that have combined mandatory minimum and sentencing guideline systems, the conclusion is more clear: States that do not incorporate capacity-based controls will experience continued growth in prison populations, and overcrowding will result.

There is no evidence that mandatory minimum sentencing is reducing crime. While mandatory minimums do keep a number of offenders off the streets for significant amounts of time, and therefore have some incapacitation effect, they appear to have no general deterrence effects. In California, for example, despite a 600 percent rise in the state's prison population and a 400 percent rise in its prison budget since 1985, the state's violent crime rate rose by 40 percent (Skolnick, 1995).

Most of the criticism of mandatory sentencing laws has been directed against their use in drug cases. Barred from considering mitigating factors or alternatives to imprisonment, judges are forced to sentence first-time offenders to lengthy prison terms. A backlash has developed. The brother of a man sentenced to a mandatory five-year prison term on marijuana charges established Families Against Mandatory Minimums (FAMM) to increase public awareness and to lobby legislatures to reintroduce proportionality into the sentencing structure (FAMM's home page on the Internet is http://www.FAMM.org/home.htm). FAMM has documented some cases where first offenders with jobs and families have been sentenced to lengthy prison terms, often on the word of people who were themselves involved in the crime. Many of the cases documented by FAMM illustrate another controversial issue: the rule of "substantial assistance."

The Substantial Assistance Rule. Federal law and the laws of many states permit judges to use the **substantial assistance rule** to reduce the sentence imposed on a defendant who has helped the government in its investigation and prosecution of a crime. This obviously appeals to defendants who can reduce a lengthy prison sentence by incriminating someone else. But the rule is open to abuse, and some experts believe it is also unfair: "Prosecutors praise [the rule] as a tool for cracking down on tight-lipped felons. But in real life, it rewards people for higher levels of involvement in the drug trade. The former hippie with 1,000 marijuana plants growing in his basement and no drug ring to rat on gets the full decade in prison, while the savvy dealer bringing in boatloads of pot from south of the border can finger a few friends and be out in half the time." (Steinberg, 1994:33).

substantial assistance rule Defendants who give significant help to police or prosecution may receive a lighter sentence for themselves.

The emphasis on cooperation tends to work against defendants who believe they are innocent, who fear that cooperation will bring harm to themselves or their families, who have nothing to offer, or whose moral code forbids it. A U.S. district judge explains:

> [T]here may be a variety of reasons why an alleged offender does not offer substantial assistance. The defendant may honestly believe he or she is not guilty and will be acquitted; the defendant may be willing to gamble on an acquittal even if guilty; the defendant may not appreciate the consequences of conviction, and counsel may not be able to communicate adequately with the defendant; the defendant's moral sensibilities, however well or poorly formed, may prevent cooperation since cooperation makes an offender a "snitch" or "stoolpigeon"; the defendant may be fearful of retribution against himself or family members; and finally, the defendant may have nothing to offer in the government's view. . . . This is unfair. (Miller, 1995:186)

Although the intent of the substantial assistance rule was to aid law enforcement in bringing organized and serious criminals to justice, its use in practice has often resulted in just the opposite: First-time and casual offenders are getting heavy sentences while more seasoned criminals play the game and save themselves years in prison. There is also evidence that legally irrelevant characteristics such as gender, race, and ethnicity may play a role in who benefits from the substantial assistance rule (Mayfield and Kramer, 1998). There are, in fact, signs that the substantial assistance rule may be in jeopardy. In July 1998 a three-judge panel of the U.S. Court of Appeals declared that exchanging leniency for testimony against others is illegal under federal statutes. This decision was immediately appealed by the Justice Department, and will be reviewed by the full U.S. Appeals Court for the Tenth Circuit, and no doubt ultimately by the U.S. Supreme Court.

INTERMEDIATE SENTENCES: ALTERNATIVES TO PRISON

Sentencing reforms of the past few years have contributed to a "crisis in corrections" that is exemplified by a grossly overcrowded prison system and escalating correctional costs, which will be discussed in Chapter 15. This crisis brought about an urgent demand for alternatives to incarceration, which in turn spawned a variety of innovations known collectively as *intermediate* or *alternative sentences* (Petersilia, 1987:1). These intermediate sentences fall in between probation and imprisonment and were initially aimed at first-time felony offenders and people convicted of nonviolent crimes such as drug and alcohol offenses. Such offenders are considered good prospects for intermediate sentences because they are bad risks for simple probation but not so dangerous that they require imprisonment. Critics of the traditional sentencing choice of probation or prison believe that too many offenders are sent to prison who would be better handled in the community; conversely, too many offenders are given probation who should be placed in a more controlled environment (Morris, 1991). Intermediate punishments are advocated as a solution to these problems.

The number of states that use intermediate sentencing has grown steadily over the past few years. In a 1992 national survey of prosecutors, almost all said that they had had at least some cases that resulted in the imposition of intermediate sentences (Dawson, Smith, and DeFrancis, 1993:6). Today, the most prominent of these sentences are boot camp, electronic monitoring, intensive probation supervision, and restitution. These and other intermediate sanctions will be discussed and evaluated in detail in Chapter 17.

Surveys suggest that the public favors sentencing alternatives that are community based, cost-effective, and secure (Brown and Elrod, 1995; Sigler and Lamb, 1995). As far as costs go, Figure 17.3 in Chapter 17 shows that all currently used intermediate sentences have significant cost savings over imprisonment.

Security is less easy to pin down, and occasional horror stories of offenders committing murder or rape while on electronic monitoring, intensive supervision, or community service naturally raise public fears about the safety risks of intermediate sentences. Although such incidents are largely unpredictable, they are also rare. In any case, the clock does not seem about to be turned back. Judges both here and abroad are finding intermediate sentences an attractive alternative to prison or probation. In Germany, for example, "the number of offenders per 100,000 inhabitants increased by 7 percent in regions where imprisonment was the sentencing norm and decreased by 13 percent in regions that opted for alternative sentencing" (National Institute of Justice, 1996:2).

"Creative" Sentencing. Some judges have made headlines in recent years for their personal innovations in sentencing. Whether this creative sentencing will stand up under appellate review remains to be seen, but it represents an effort by some judges to take back some of the discretion they have lost under sentencing reforms. Many judges undoubtedly have the best intentions, but individualized sentences such as those listed raise the possibility of new disparities in the sentencing process.

- A judge in Charleston, South Carolina, sentenced a drug offender to be whipped by his grandmother (*New York Times,* September 25, 1995, p. A11).
- A Louisiana judge sentenced 400 small-time offenders to church rather than to jail or fines (*Christianity Today*, 1995, Vol. 39:44).
- Another Louisiana judge sentenced a shoplifter to write 10,000 times: "I will not steal other people's property" (*St. Louis Post-Dispatch*, January 4, 1994, p. A4).

By and large, reactions to creative sentencing from the public and from some legislators have been favorable. What do you think?

SENTENCING AND THE CRIME VICTIM

We return, finally, to an issue that was raised in Chapter 11: bringing crime victims back into the judicial process. Since at least the seventeenth century, the tradition in Europe and America has been to play down the individual victimization that accompanies crime (Ziegenhagen, 1977:68). Under Anglo-American criminal law, crimes are public wrongs, and in criminal law the state is the victim. The state prosecutes, the state adjudicates, and the state determines the possible penalties. The real injury to the real victim of a crime has been formally ignored. The result is that punishment has been largely "an abstract measure of justice," because the penalty is not based on the real harm experienced by its immediate victims (Bittner and Platt, 1966:81).

In 1976, the crime victim was described as "forgotten" in the criminal justice system (McDonald, 1976:650); in that same year, at the Second International Symposium of Victimology in Boston, a number of authors began to debate the merits of bringing victims back in. The author of this book suggested that a special role be created for victims, that of "judicial consultant" (Barlow, 1976). The idea sounded new but was borrowed from a study of drunk court judges, who used court helpers, called "knockers" and "rappers" by defendants, to help them with sentencing suggestions. Although they had no formal role in decision making, these "consultants" were paid for their "assistance" (Wiseman, 1970:86–103). But they were not victims of the offenders being sentenced. The term *judicial consultant* emphasizes two things: (1) the role is not itself a decision-making one, but rather one of advice, opinion, counsel, or information; (2) the advice or counsel can always be modified or rejected by the judge—but it must be heard as part of the judicial process.

This idea seemed rather radical at the time, but over the past fifteen years many jurisdictions have moved in that direction. The 1984 federal Victims of Crime Act helped pave the way. This act put victims back into the penalty process by earmarking fines from federal offenders to support states in developing victim services. Later measures gave victims the right to be informed of, present at, and heard during criminal proceedings. Some states have since passed constitutional amendments guaranteeing certain rights to crime victims. On April 1, 1998, a congressional joint resolution (S.J. Res. 44) to protect the rights of victims was proposed as an amendment to the U.S. Constitution. Its

TABLE 13.7 The Provisions of the Proposed 1998 Congressional Resolution Protecting Crime Victims' Rights

On April 1, 1998, a bipartisan joint resolution for a constitutional amendment to protect crime victims' rights was presented to the 105th Congress by U.S. Senators John Kyl (R-Arizona), Diane Feinstein (D-California), and others. Its provisions are as follows:

Article:

Section 1. Each victim of a crime of violence shall have the rights to reasonable notice of, and not to be excluded from, all public proceedings relating to the crime—

- to be heard, if present, and to submit a statement at all public proceedings to determine a release from custody, an acceptance of a negotiated plea, or a sentence;
- to the foregoing rights at a parole proceeding that is not public, to the extent those rights are afforded to the convicted offender;
- to reasonable notice for a release or escape from custody relating to the crime;
- to consideration for the interest of the victim in a trial free from unreasonable delay;
- to an order of restitution from the convicted offender;
- to consideration for the safety of the victim in determining any release from custody; and
- to reasonable notice of the rights established by this article.

Section 2. Only the victim or the victim's representative shall have standing to assert the rights established by this article. Nothing in this article shall provide grounds for the victim to challenge a charging decision or a conviction; to overturn a sentence or negotiated plea; to obtain a stay of trial; or to compel a new trial. Nothing in this article shall give rise to a claim for damages against the United States, a State, a political subdivision, or a public official.

Section 3. The Congress and the States shall have the power to implement and enforce this article within their respective jurisdictions by appropriate legislation, including the power to enact exceptions when necessary to achieve a compelling interest.

Section 4. The rights established by this article shall apply to all proceedings that begin on or after the 180th day after ratification of this article.

Section 5. The rights established by this article shall apply to all federal and State proceedings, including military proceedings to the extent that Congress may provide by law, juvenile justice proceedings, and proceedings in any district or territory of the United States not within a State.

provisions are shown in Table 13.7. If passed by Congress, the resolution becomes part of the Constitution only if ratified within seven years by three-fourths of the states.

A similar resolution had failed in 1996, despite intense lobbying by the National Organization for Victim Assistance (NOVA) and the support of President Clinton. As was the case in 1996, the major objections to S.J. Res. 44 are likely to came from trial lawyers, judges, and critics who say the U.S. Constitution is not the appropriate place to define the legal rights of victims. They reject arguments that an amendment is necessary to counterbalance the rights of defendants, a claim made by Clinton and other supporters (Associated Press, June 26, 1996). In any case, the procedural laws of many states now cover most of the rights listed in Section 1 of the new resolution. Furthermore, it is unclear whether a victims' rights amendment would allow victims to appeal decisions by criminal justice officials on constitutional grounds. Section 2 suggests that victims would not have this right. Finally, some critics object that the new resolution does not go far enough: It is largely symbolic and ignores victims of nonviolent crimes. What do you think?

THE VICTIM IMPACT STATEMENT

In 1986, the state of Maryland passed a statute authorizing that a **Victim Impact Statement (VIS)** be compiled in all felony cases prior to sentencing. The report must list the identification of the victim, the economic losses resulting from the crime, the nature and permanence of any physical injuries, any change in the victim's welfare or family relationships because of the crime, and any other information indicating the crime's impact on the victim. The VIS is an advisory document that the judge is expected to take into account when deciding the sentence. In *Payne v. Tennessee* (1991), the U.S. Supreme Court ruled 6 to 3 that the VIS is constitutional.

Victim Impact Statement (VIS) A report to the sentencing judge listing the effects of a crime on the victim.

Crime victims generally feel better about criminal justice proceedings if they are present when crucial decisions are made. The spread of VIS now

Until recently, crime victims were largely forgotten by the criminal justice system. Today a variety of programs and services exist to help victims, yet ensuring fair treatment remains a problem because the typical victim has low social status.

PHOTO BY BOB DAEMMRICH, COURTESY OF THE IMAGE WORKS

means that judges must consult, through written statements and sometimes orally, facts and opinions about a crime, from the victim's perspective. Whereas for generations victims were left out of the picture, now they are formally part of the sentencing proceedings. This is very important when one considers that the typical victim is poor, often black, and very likely looks, speaks, and acts like the typical offender. These are not the attributes usually held in high esteem by court officials, or for that matter, the general public. Small wonder, the voice of victims has been weak.

How successful these reforms will be is still uncertain. The tendency throughout America and Europe has been for crime victims to leave things up to the "proper authorities," even when they could play an active role (Joutsen, 1994). And the reforms are controversial in legal circles. Some believe the impartiality and objectivity of the law is threatened; many fear the emergence of vengeful sentencing. Yet the idea that victims would be vengeful and advocate harsher sentences than judges or the general public has not materialized in practice (Erez, 1994). On balance, this relatively modest step toward bringing victims back in seems to have stirred up more debate than its results justify.

RESTORATIVE JUSTICE: PENAL PHILOSOPHY FOR THE NEW MILLENNIUM?

The victims' movement of the 1970s and 1980s helped redefine the assumptions underlying society's response to crime, especially the purpose of the criminal sentence. Although, legally speaking, crime is still a violation of state law, the new emphasis on victims and their rights led to a broader conception of justice, which emphasized that the state, criminal offenders, victims, and the larger community should all be included in the response to crime. This is the so-called **restorative justice model**, developed by Howard Zehr (1985; 1990) and others. Restorative justice is "concerned with repairing the harm done to victims and the community through a process of negotiation, mediation, victim empowerment, and reparation" (Bazemore and Umbreit, 1994:6).

restorative justice model A system that brings together offenders, victims, and the community in attempts to repair the harm done by crime.

According to the restorative justice model, punishment alone is ineffective in addressing the problem of crime; it also tends to disrupt the community and further strain relationships between victims and offenders. Victims are central to the process of resolving a crime, since the goal in sentencing is to restore all parties through a process of reconciliation and an emphasis on the future. Along with dispute resolution and victim-offender mediation, community service and restitution are key aspects of the restoration process. In addition, the input of victims is used to determine whether justice—in the restorative sense—could be achieved (Zehr, 1990). Questions relevant for crime victims are as follows:

- Do victims have sufficient opportunities to speak about the crime and its impact to those involved in the judicial process?
- Do victims receive needed compensation or restitution?
- Are victims sufficiently protected against further violation?
- Do victims have a voice in the legal process?
- Does the outcome adequately reflect the severity of the offense?
- Do victims' families receive adequate assistance and support?
- Is there an opportunity for victims and offenders to exchange information and feelings about the event and about one another?

The restorative justice model is currently being tested in the juvenile justice systems of selected counties in Oregon and Texas (Bazemore and Umbreit, 1994). Although many states and local jurisdictions have expressed interest in restorative justice, relatively few courts have adopted the significant changes in policies and procedures that a fully developed program would require. Time will tell whether this new approach to achieving justice will find widespread support among legislators, judges, and community leaders in the 21st century.

SUMMARY

After a defendant is found guilty of a felony offense, a date is set when the judge will pronounce the sentence. For convicted offenders and their victims this is the climax of the judicial process, although the approximate sentence is often known beforehand through plea negotiations or because it is set by law. A criminal sentence specifies the penalty to be paid by the offender—whether prison, a fine, probation, or an intermediate sanction such as restitution. The justification of punishment is generally of two kinds: retribution, which involves making the guilty person pay a penalty proportional to the seriousness of the offense, or prevention of crime, known as reductivism. There are at least ten ways that punishment may prevent crime, the four best-known being deterrence, incapacitation, reformation, and rehabilitation. We have seen that each of these has implications for sentencing policy and practice, and none is free of controversy.

Over the years there has been little consistency in the sentences actually handed down by the courts—even within the same jurisdiction. The resulting sentencing disparities have been the focus of much debate. The disparities originated in the considerable sentencing discretion allowed judges, and they were later fueled by efforts to individualize justice through the use of indeterminate sentences. These allow considerable variation in the prison time actually served by different offenders convicted of similar crimes. In addition, sentencing disparities have been tied to the race, class, and gender of offenders and victims. Although criminological research has produced inconsistent findings on this issue, there is little debate that African Americans have tended to bear the brunt of the disparities, most recently as a result of the war on drugs.

Attempts to curb sentencing disparities have resulted in a number of reforms, including the development of sentencing guidelines. Guidelines reduce the sentencing discretion of judges, who must justify any departure from them. Even more restrictive is the recent passage of mandatory minimum sentencing laws, including "three strikes and you're out"; these laws leave judges few, if any, sentencing options. Meanwhile, prosecutors continue to wield considerable power in the sentencing process: They can negotiate sentences through the bargaining process and they can control the sentence by manipulating the charges.

New ideas about sentencing have surfaced in recent years in response to growing concern that existing practices are not serving justice well, especially from the vantage point of crime victims. A movement to bring victims back into the sentencing process has resulted in a greater role for victims, including the use of victim impact statements during sentencing hearings, and even the development of a new penal philosophy: restorative justice. Restorative justice seeks to repair the harm done by crime, and therefore includes a central role for victims in the determination of penalties.

- Judging from what you now know about criminal sentences, would you give Joan Short a lengthy prison sentence? Has your opinion changed since before you read this chapter? Why or why not?

- Do you think that judges allow nonlegal factors such as gender, class, or race to influence their sentencing decisions? If so how, and to what extent?
- In recent years, state and federal legislatures have restricted the discretion allowed judges when sentencing offenders. What do you think of this now?

KEY TERMS

justice model
crime prevention model
proportionality
utilitarianism
reformation
incapacitation
rehabilitation
deterrence doctrine
specific deterrence
general deterrence
sentence
capital offense
intermediate sanctions
sentencing disparities
indeterminate sentence
parole board
pre-sentence investigation
sentencing guidelines
aggravating circumstance
mitigating circumstance
selective incapacitation
determinate sentencing
mandatory minimum sentence
"three strikes" laws
truth-in-sentencing laws
substantial assistance rule
Victim Impact Statement (VIS)
restorative justice model

ACTIVE LEARNING CHALLENGES

1. Divide into groups. Randomly assign each group one or two of the ten ways in which punishment may prevent crime, listed in Table 13.1. A week or so later, have the groups present arguments (backed by outside reading, if possible) for and against the claim that their way(s) actually prevent crime.
2. Discuss the view that justice requires sentencing disparities.
3. Have class members break off in pairs. Each pair must come up with a sentence for an offense and present their justifications to the class. Here is an interesting example: A local chemical company has been found guilty of burying toxic waste near the plant. This is the company's first conviction of any sort. After the presentations the class is told the statutory penalty for this offense (if one can be found).
4. Discuss the idea that the typical felony sentence should be an intermediate one.

INTERNET CHALLENGES

The Web pages mentioned here can all be accessed through the Web site for this textbook at **http://www.prenhall.com/barlow/**.

1. Compare the felony sentences established by law in your state with those in a neighboring state. Pick five felony offenses and use the Criminal Code section of Cornell University's Topical Index to State Statutes as your link to the relevant state statutes.

2. Find out what is currently being done in your state and around the country to help victims of crime find justice. Check the Web site of the U.S. Department of Justice's Office for Victims of Crime.
3. Truth-in-sentencing laws are supported by Congress and by many states. Check out the reasons why. To start, visit the home page of the National Criminal Justice Association (NCJA), a special-interest group that works closely with the National Governor's Association and other policymaking groups.

Part IV

Punishment and Corrections

Dealing with the Criminal Offender

What happens to criminal defendants who have been convicted and sentenced? The range of modern punishments is quite extensive, from probation and fines to boot camps and community service, from jail time to years in prison—sometimes in solitary confinement 23 hours a day. And some criminals are executed. Part Four begins with the ultimate punishment—death—and moves through successively less incapacitating punishments. Chapter 14 explores the use of punishments ending in death through exile or execution. Capital punishment is examined in detail, including a discussion of the law, methods of execution, Death Row, and the charge that use of the death penalty in America discriminates against the poor and minorities. The next two chapters examine the use of jails and prisons for punishing criminals; the modern history of imprisonment is discussed in Chapter 15, along with the controversial issues of privatization and prison overcrowding. Chapter 16 looks at life in prison from the vantage point of male and female inmates and the people who guard them; the chapter concludes with a discussion of three challenges in corrections: AIDS, older inmates, and prisoner rights. The last chapter of Part Four, and of the text, explores the growing field of community corrections, particularly the use of intermediate sanctions such as boot camps, house arrest with electronic monitoring, restitution, and community service. Parole is also discussed as a form of community-based punishment, as is shaming, which has a long history but is being revived in new forms.

CHAPTER 14

CAPITAL PUNISHMENT

LEARNING OBJECTIVES

- Describe the historical use of capital punishment, and alternative punishments such as banishment and transportation.
- Explain why public executions have been abandoned in most countries.
- Describe and explain trends in the use of the death penalty in the United States.
- Explain how states have revised their death penalty statutes to meet Supreme Court objections and to reflect "get tough" attitudes on crime.
- Explain what a death-qualified jury is and why is it controversial.
- Understand how the race of offenders and victims enters into the use of capital punishment.
- Understand the relationship between politics, public opinion, and the death penalty.

This execution of murderer Billy Calder in Montana on March 16, 1900, reflected the executioner's concern with avoiding a flawed execution. A sheriff adjusts the noose for the correct fit, and if the weight-operated pulley failed to lift Calder from his feet, the wooden plank beneath him (which covered a foot-deep hole) could be removed.

PHOTO COURTESY OF THE MONTANA HISTORICAL SOCIETY, HELENA

The modern rituals of execution attest to this double process: the disappearance of the spectacle and the elimination of pain. . . .

MICHEL FOUCAULT, FRENCH PHILOSOPHER

My eyes slowly traced the contours of his body . . . searching for signs of life, a cough, a twitch, a moan, a second thought. None came. . . . The show was over; the passage from life to death was horrifyingly invisible, a silent and efficient erasure. . . .

SUSAN BLAUSTEIN, ON WITNESSING THE EXECUTION OF ANTHONY COOK IN HUNTSVILLE, TEXAS, NOVEMBER 10, 1993

The event itself is cruel and unusual punishment, and everything surrounding it is, too. The whole process is cruel for the families of the victims, for the families of the executed and for the prison staff, who get to know the executed person as a human being. . . .

REV. HUGH BEHAN, CHAPLAIN TO MISSOURI DEATH PENALTY INMATES

Juror number eight looked out at Timothy McVeigh. She felt completely drained. The trial had been long, and the media presence was a constant source of pressure even though there were no live broadcasts from the courtroom as in the O. J. Simpson trial. It had not been difficult to find McVeigh guilty of the Oklahoma City bombing in which 168 people died. The prosecution had done a good job, and even though questions were raised about police procedures, the jurors were confident in their verdict. There were no reasonable doubts.

Now it was time for them to announce the sentence. Juror number eight had never imagined that one day she would be condemning someone to his death. She had no strong feelings about the death penalty, believing it right under some circumstances, but not under others. In this case she had no qualms whatever. She reasoned that if the death penalty was ever appropriate, it was in a case like this. So many people died, without warning, without a chance to escape. In earlier times this would have amounted to an act of rebellion, and justice would have been swift and terrible. The execution would have been public, a spectacle of bloodcurdling terror, the condemned man's mutilated body carried through the city, and his head impaled on a stake for all to see. She understood that McVeigh would be executed by lethal injection before a handful of witnesses in the dead of night.

But not before he had spent many years on Death Row as his lawyers pursued his right to appeal. Although the U.S. Supreme Court had recently curtailed death penalty appeals, hoping to shorten the time between conviction and execution, McVeigh would probably not be executed for at least six or seven years. That was a long time for the families of victims to wait for justice. There was always the chance that an appeal might succeed, but McVeigh still faced murder charges brought by the state of Oklahoma, and few doubted that he would eventually be executed.

Juror number eight felt no pity for McVeigh, but she wondered how she would feel if this were a more typical death penalty case. She had had a hand in imposing the ultimate penalty, and this placed her in the history books along with jurors who had allowed their decisions to be guided by prejudice and vengeance. A mere handful of murderers are ever executed, and the ones who are often had poor, uneducated backgrounds, and were defended by overworked and underpaid attorneys with little experience in capital cases. Although the outcome was the same, these cases seemed a far cry from McVeigh. Where do you draw the line?

Timothy McVeigh and over 3,000 other Americans currently face the ultimate punishment for a criminal offense: death. Through execution society rids itself of the offender. Execution incapacitates forever: *That* offender, at least, will commit no more crimes. This chapter explores capital punishment, but we begin with a brief historical journey back to the days of banishment and transportation. Although they were lesser punishments than execution, they were also designed to remove offenders from society. As we shall see, exile penalties such as banishment often resulted in death.

? WHAT DO YOU THINK?

- Would you have sentenced Timothy McVeigh to death? Why or why not?
- Many countries, and some American states have abolished the death penalty. Where do you stand, and why?
- Do you favor a lengthy appeals process in death penalty cases? Why or why not?

EXILE PENALTIES

Imagine that a member of a group to which you belong does something that seriously threatens the well-being and perhaps even the survival of the group. What would the group do? One possibility is to expel the offender from the group. By revoking the offender's membership, the group attempts to protect itself against the threat to its remaining members.

Expelling a person from the group is an *exile penalty*, and the practice is commonplace, occurring in all kinds of groups. However, exile penalties are rarely used today as a form of legal punishment for crimes. The closest parallel is when the government deports illegal immigrants or people whose U.S. residency or citizenship has been revoked because of past crimes. In 1996, an elderly Detroit man, Ferdinand Hammer, was stripped of his citizenship and deported for concealing that he was a Nazi concentration camp guard during World War II. Since 1979, 48 former Nazis have been deported (*The Detroit News*, November 1, 1996, p. 1B). Due to a tightening of immigration laws and the recent crackdown on illegal aliens ordered by the Clinton administration, deportation of illegal immigrants grew from 43,500 in 1992 to 67,000 in 1996 (Associated Press, October 28, 1996). This trend is expected to continue into the 21st century.

Banishment

Under the punishment of **banishment**, offenders were sent away from their homes and villages with orders never to return. Tribal groups and village communities used banishment to rid themselves of people who posed a threat to the leaders or to community as a whole. This may not sound like much of a punishment today, but in ancient times there were many dangers to be faced outside village walls. Not only were wild animals a threat, but the scarcity of food and shelter and the hostility of neighboring tribes made banishment a feared punishment. Anyone caught returning illegally from exile was automatically sentenced to death.

banishment Offenders are expelled from their homes and villages.

Villagers risked execution by offering food or shelter to the banished. Because the banished were considered outside the prevailing moral order, there was no obligation for people to treat them kindly—in fact, quite the opposite: They were obligated *not* to provide assistance. Imagine how other group members would feel if you helped someone the group had expelled. Your actions undermine the rules and decisions of the group and therefore threaten its solidarity. You have committed a sort of treason against the group, and treason always results in the most severe penalties.

During the Middle Ages, landowners from kings to lesser nobility recognized a significant value in banishment: They could outlaw undesirable relatives and political opponents without risking public outcry by executing them. Some rulers, of course, lived to regret the fact that they had imposed exile over death. Their enemies returned from exile with armies or conspired with people at home to overthrow the ruling party from within.

Over the centuries many famous people have been banished into exile, and in some Third World countries the practice still exists. The great Carthaginian general Hannibal chose exile over imprisonment in Rome, and eventually committed suicide in 182 B.C. to avoid capture. Julia, the daughter of the Roman emperor Augustus, was banished and died of starvation in A.D. 14. In the nineteenth century, Napoleon I of France was exiled to Elba, an island off the coast of France, and the French poet Victor Hugo was exiled in 1851 by Napoleon III; both, however, returned from exile in triumph. So did Argentinian leader Juan Perón and Kenyan President Jomo Kenyatta, both banished in the 1950s. Perhaps the most famous recent ruler banished into exile was the brutal African dictator Idi Amin, president of Uganda from 1971 to 1979; he did not return.

Transportation

As distant lands were opened up through European exploration and colonization, banishment was replaced with **transportation**. The punishment of transportation usually meant that a criminal was sent by ship to another country far away. By transporting convicts to their colonies, nations like England and France could achieve two goals with one means: While the home country could rid itself of undesirables, the developing colonies could benefit from a

transportation Offenders are sent by ship to a penal colony in another country.

Convicts landing at Van Diemen's Land.

Both England and France transported many criminals to distant colonies; Georgia and Australia were originally penal colonies. This way, the home country reduced its criminal population while newly-founded colonies, starving for laborers and a large colonist population, received a constant supply of newcomers.

ILLUSTRATION COURTESY OF THE GRANGER COLLECTION, NEW YORK

continuing supply of new laborers to tame the land. The use of transportation grew steadily during the seventeenth and eighteenth centuries. Most of those sent abroad came from poor or working-class backgrounds, leading historian Robert Hughes, author of the 1987 best-seller *The Fatal Shore*, to describe it as "an effort to exile en masse a whole class."

Thousands of convicts were transported from England alone. Offenders were sent to penal colonies in America, and later to Australia, for a term of years—and sometimes for life. Once there they usually served out their sentence "at hard labor," working until they dropped. Much of this labor helped England build settlements and expand the commercial value of the colonies. Needless to say, many prisoners died en route, packed like sardines in overcrowded and disease-ridden ships. Among those who made it across the oceans, many would die before their sentence was served, their place quickly taken by newcomers from the steady stream of replacements. Those who survived the ordeal often remained in the colonies, either because they could not purchase the return passage or because they found life in the colonies a more appealing prospect than returning home.

When considering appropriate places to set up a penal colony, government officials looked not only at the risks of convicts escaping, but also at the likelihood that the colony would be self-sufficient and could eventually become an economic and political asset. In 1779, for example, Sir Joseph Banks's recommendation of Botany Bay as a penal colony in Australia cited the abundant resources of the area, the impossibility of escape, and the likelihood that England would receive "advantageous returns" from the territory (Evans and Nicholls, 1976:23). He was right: Botany Bay, originally discovered by explorerer James Cook in 1770, is where the great city of Sydney now stands.

Increasing criticism of transportation at home and abroad led Parliament to halt the practice during the second half of the ninteenth century (Babbington, 1968). Besides growing complaints from Australia that it should no longer be the dumping ground for England's outcasts, English policymakers came to realize that keeping able-bodied men at home helped stock the supply of labor needed to reap the benefits of industrialization. More and larger prisons could be built to house criminals at home, and, if necessary, work could be extracted from them. As a result, the permament removal of criminals from the land came to rest solely on the shoulders of the executioner.

CAPITAL PUNISHMENT

The only punishment that is absolute in every sense is **capital punishment**, or death by execution. Once inflicted, the punishment is irreversible. If a miscarriage of justice is discovered, a fine can be returned or imprisonment stopped, but there is no turning back after an execution. This has been a long-standing objection to the use of capital punishment, but rarely has it persuaded rulers to abandon the death penalty. If nothing else, the belief that death is the only just and reasonable response to certain crimes generally outweighed this objection. Furthermore, in nations ruled by absolute monarchs or dictators—the case throughout much of human history—the choice of penalties for crime was a decision of the individual ruler and not open to debate. Execution was a quick, simple, and inexpensive way of getting rid of enemies, and rulers used it often.

capital punishment Death by execution.

THE DEATH PENALTY IN HISTORY

Under early criminal codes, offenders were put to death for a wide range of crimes, some of them unheard of today. Both the ancient Mosaic code and the Code of Hammurabi prescribed death for many offenses, including witchcraft, incest, kidnapping, various forms of theft, and negligence that resulted in someone's death. In ancient Greece and Rome and among the Germanic tribes governed by the laws of Tacitus, death was also a common penalty, and it was also used extensively by the ancient Egyptians, Assyrians, and Hindus (Durkheim, 1900:65–93).

There were many gruesome forms of execution among these early civilizations, but one of the most common was public stoning. Stoning is described in the Bible; it took place in public, and ordinary citizens were expected to take part as both witness and executioner. Sometimes, the person who had been wronged threw the first stone, but stoning often became a sort of free-for-all:

> The impression to be gained from the Bible, which includes accounts of a number of stonings, a few of them impromptu, is that those executed in this manner somehow came to terms with their terrifying punishment, bearing their fate with some resemblance of dignity. And terrifying those executions must have been. Following the lead of witnesses, the citizens would arm themselves with stones and surround the offender, perhaps also taunting and ridiculing him before launching their onslaught of bruising rocks; they would only stop when the offender's bloody and lifeless form lay buried under the stones. (Johnson, 1990:6)

With ordinary citizens actively participating in the stoning, the execution was a community event that validated both the law and the punishment; the community was cleansed of the offense and the offender.

Popularity of the Death Penalty. It has been said that during the 37-year reign of Henry VIII, 72,000 people were executed for theft and robbery alone (Calvert, 1971:4). Assuming the figure is correct—and some scholars have challenged it (Newman, 1978:111)—this is the equivalent of nearly 2,000 executions a year, or five each day. Considering that the population of England at the time was less than 2 million, this means an execution rate of 1 per 1,000 citizens. An equivalent figure in the United States today would mean 26,000 executions a year!

The popularity of capital punishment reached a peak during the sixteenth century, when it dropped off only to rise again by the end of the eighteenth century. At that time, England had more than 200 death penalty offenses, many of them relatively trivial (Blackstone, 1962). The list of capital crimes included violent crimes such as arson, rape, murder, mutiny, and highway robbery, but also many nonviolent offenses: forgery, sodomy, pocket picking, shoplifting, burglary at night, stealing farm animals, cutting down trees in a public avenue, destroying silk or velvet in the loom, sacrilege, and returning from exile.

Historians argue that the increase in capital crimes coincided with the weakening of the monarchy and the rise of parliamentary power. Parliament was constantly enacting new laws to shore up the economic and political interests of its members, most of whom were landowners. Nevertheless, despite the large number of capital crimes, relatively few people were executed; indeed, many of those sentenced to death were spared: "It is amazing indeed that judges boomed out their sentences of death with such grandeur and sincerity, yet immediately recommended pardons and commutations for the majority of cases" (Newman, 1978:140).

Such leniency was not because crime was rare or especially petty. On the contrary, street crimes such as robbery and burglary were on the rise in eighteenth-century England. These crimes directly threatened the property interests of landowners and the emerging class of industrial capitalists. It should come as no surprise that robbery and burglary offenses accounted for 70 percent of the death sentences handed out in London during the period 1749–1771 (Newman, 1978:138).

The fact that many death sentences were never carried out reflects the widespread use of bribes to buy off judges and prosecutors, and also the feeling among many judges—and probably the public, too—that death was too harsh a punishment for the particular offense or offender. Judges also took into account such things as the young age of an offender, the absence of weapons, and whether the stolen goods had been returned. Judges were also more likely to commute a death sentence when the conviction was based solely on a confession. This was because confessions were quite often beaten out of suspects or made by defendants who had no idea they would be hanged as a result.

Since street crimes were committed primarily by teenagers and younger adults—as is the case today—the vast majority of executed offenders were under age 21. Indeed, it was not uncommon in Europe for children to be hanged. By the 1840s, however, the use of execution as a principal penalty was in decline. Only 20 offenses were designated as capital crimes in England, and the execution of children was abolished. Table 14.1 shows that today many countries have abolished the death penalty altogether, while fourteen have abolished it for ordinary crimes, the United Kingdom among them.

Executions in American History

Even though the colonists brought English law and legal procedures to the New World, capital punishment was never used as extensively in the colonies as in England. Even so, the death penalty was imposed for a variety of offenses, including witchcraft. During the Salem, Massachusetts, witch trials in 1692–1694, 20 people, mostly women, were condemned as witches or collaborators and hanged. Gravestones commemorating the executions are now a major tourist attraction in Salem. A total of 35 alleged witches were hanged in colonial times, but far more met their death in Europe: an estimated 30,000 in England, 75,000 in France, and 100,000 in Germany (Newman, 1978:145).

During the Spanish Inquisition, up to 100 witches were burned in a day. The American colonies seemed quite restrained in comparison to most of Europe.

During frontier days, executions increased in popularity and some were carried out with little attention to due process. Fleeing suspects risked being executed on the spot if the pursuing sheriff's posse caught up with them. Lynchings also emerged during this period, especially along the frontier and in the rural South. Caught up in the anger and fear that accompanies violent crime, otherwise law-abiding citizens sometimes took the law into their own hands. The local sheriff or town marshal—if there was one—was usually ill equipped to protect suspects against an unruly mob, and some undoubtedly assisted in the lynchings. In small frontier towns, suspects often had to wait weeks in the local lockup before the traveling judge would arrive to hear their case. Some suspects were transported to larger towns, with more secure jails. But this was no guarantee of safety from a lynch mob, which might set up an ambush along the way.

Since the earliest colonial days, a total of 18,816 executions had been documented in America and its territories as of 1994 (*New York Times*, December 4, 1994, p. E3). And this figure is certainly low, since many county records have been lost. During the two centuries that federal courts have existed, it is estimated that approximately 350 federal executions have occurred, usually in the state where the sentence was imposed. The first person executed by a state under federal law was a sailor, Thomas Bird. Bird was convicted of murdering the captain of his ship; he was executed in Maine in 1790, after President Washington refused a plea for clemency (Keve, 1991:9). The last execution carried out by a state on behalf of the Federal Bureau of Prisons was in 1963, when Iowa executed kidnapper Victor Feguer.

Even if all American executions could be documented, the total number of executions in American history would probably fall far short of the number of beheadings and hangings during the reign of Henry VIII. People often complain about the level of violence in society today, but it is nothing compared to the violence perpetrated in sixteenth- and seventeenth-century Europe through executions carried out in the name of justice.

The Public Execution: Spectacle and Showmanship. For most of human history, **public executions** were standard practice, and often had all the trappings of a sporting event, family picnic, or carnival (Hay, 1975:114; Newman, 1978:125–130). In London during the seventeenth and eighteenth centuries, the condemned were carried by open cart in a procession from Newgate prison to Tyburn, the place of execution. The entertainment in the event included the actual execution, which was often accompanied by cheers from the crowd. However, if the public sympathized with the condemned, the executioner might face an angry, jeering crowd.

public execution Capital offenders are put to death in a public place.

Though usually masked, executioners gained reputations as showmen and for their skill at wielding the sword or axe. During a 23-year career from 1663 to 1686, English executioner Jack Ketch beheaded, hanged, and burned hundreds of criminals—yet also managed to botch a few. Another famous executioner was John Thrift. He held the office of executioner from 1735 until 1752. However, his career started poorly: Thrift's first execution was a mass hanging of thirteen criminals and he forgot to cover the condemned men's heads, the standard procedure in England; later, after hanging Thomas Reynolds, the "corpse" pushed back the lid of the coffin and sat up (Bleackely, 1929; cited in Newman, 1978:259). Thrift immediately hanged him again—and was severely beaten by the crowd for doing so.

Public executions matched the level and intensity of violence that was characteristic of society in general. For offenders charged with the most serious capital crimes such as treason or the murder of a member of the nobility, a simple,

TABLE 14.1 Use of the Death Penalty around the World, 1999

1. Abolitionist Countries

One hundred and four countries have abolished the death penalty in one of three ways: (1) abolishing it for all crimes; (2) abolishing it for ordinary crimes, but retaining it for some crimes under military law or crimes such as treason or espionage; (3) abolishing it de facto in that no one has been executed in the past ten years, or an international commitment has been made not to use it. Here is a sampling of the countries that belong to each category; the date of the last execution is also listed, when known.

ABOLISHED FOR ALL CRIMES (67 COUNTRIES)

COUNTRY	DATE OF ABOLITION	DATE OF LAST EXECUTION
Angola	1992	
Australia	1985	1967
Austria	1950	1950
Belgium	1996	1950
Canada	1998	1962
Colombia	1910	1909
Costa Rica	1877	NA
Denmark	1978	1950
Ecuador	1906	NA
Finland	1972	1944
France	1981	1977
Germany	1949 (West); 1987 (East)	1949 (West)
Hungary	1990	1988
Ireland	1990	1954
New Zealand	1989	1957
Nicaragua	1979	1930
Norway	1979	1948
Portugal	1976	1849
Romania	1989	1989
Spain	1995	1975
Sweden	1972	1910
Switzerland	1992	1944
Uruguay	1907	NA
Venezuela	1863	NA

ABOLISHED FOR ORDINARY CRIMES (14 COUNTRIES)

COUNTRY	DATE ABOLISHED	DATE OF LAST EXECUTION
Argentina	1984	
Brazil	1979	1855
Cyprus	1983	1962
El Salvador	1983	1973
Israel	1954	1962

speedy execution was not enough. The execution was designed so the crowd would not soon forget the offender or his crime. One particularly gruesome method of execution used in medieval England and some other European countries was "hanging, drawing, and quartering." Offenders were hoisted up by the neck, but before they died the executioner cut out their intestines, which were burned in front of their eyes; the four limbs were then severed from the body—or in some cases torn away by horses tied to each limb. According to witnesses, some victims of quartering remained alive through much of the ordeal (Foucault, 1977). The Academy Award–winning movie *Braveheart* illustrates this sort of execution in gory detail. After execution, the remaining trunk was then either burned or dragged through town. The offender's severed head was usually impaled on a stake for public display.

ABOLISHED FOR ORDINARY CRIMES (14 COUNTRIES) (CONTINUED)		
COUNTRY	DATE ABOLISHED	DATE OF LAST EXECUTION
Malta	1971	1943
Mexico	NA	1937
Peru	1979	1979
South Africa	1995	1991
United Kingdom	1973	1964

ABOLISHED DE FACTO (23 COUNTRIES)	
COUNTRY	DATE OF LAST EXECUTION
Bermuda	1977
Bhutan	1964
Congo (formerly Zaire)	1982
Gambia	1981
Grenada	1978
Madagascar	1958
Mali	1980
Suriname	1982
Sri Lanka	1976
Turkey	1984

2. Retentionist Countries
Ninety-five countries currently retain and use the death penalty for ordinary crimes. These countries include the following:

COUNTRY		
Afghanistan	Iraq	Taiwan
Algeria	Japan	Thailand
Bangladesh	Kenya	Uganda
Bulgaria	Libya	Ukraine
Chile	Morocco	United States
China	Pakistan	Vietnam
Cuba	Poland	Yemen
Guatemala	Russia	Yugoslavia
India	Saudi Arabia	Zambia
Indonesia	Sudan	Zimbabwe
Iran	Syria	

Source: Compiled from Amnesty International (1999). "The Death Penalty: List of Abolitionist and Retentionist Countries" (February 1999). Available online at **http://www.amnesty.org/ailib/intcam/dp/abrelist.htm**. © Amnesty International.

In the eighteenth century, the rise of scientific medicine, especially anatomy, gave a new twist to the English execution: Doctors and their anatomy students needed cadavers, and what better place to find them than at the foot of the gallows. Corpses became valuable, as the family and friends of the condemned competed with the medical community for the remains. Arrangements were sometimes made for surgeons to perform experiments on the body before the condemned were actually dead. It was not uncommon for medical friends of a condemned man to use their skills to try to revive him after the hanging—and some were apparently successful (Newman, 1978:143). This led to some amazing scenes, with relatives and friends pulling frantically on the legs of the executed criminal as he hung from the rope, hoping to relieve his suffering and also keep his body safe. Sometimes the buried corpse of an executed criminal

In eighteenth-century England, it was a capital offense to steal livestock; in the American Old West, stealing a horse could get you hanged (either legally or by a mob, as shown in this drawing). Why were these crimes, which may seem insignificant to us today, considered so important then? Do you think they deserved the death penalty?

ILLUSTRATION COURTESY OF CORBIS-BETTMANN

would be dug up by profiteers in the service of anatomists, only to be stolen back by friends and relatives and reburied. Perhaps the most famous incident was the theft and recovery of the body of Dick Turpin, a notorious highwayman who robbed, raped, and murdered his way to fame in the 1700s.

With the exception of lynchings, public executions in America were generally far more restrained than those in England. This may reflect the important role played by clergy in the American execution, and the emphasis given to the sermon and accompanying hymns during the hanging. Full of fire and brimstone, the sermon quieted the crowd and probably carved fear into the hearts of many onlookers. During the nineteenth century, many American states moved executions inside prison walls, largely in response to growing appeals for the abolition of capital punishment and fears that public executions could too easily turn into riots. For a while, prison wardens nevertheless allowed large crowds to attend executions. The last truly public execution in the United States took place on August 14, 1936, in Kentucky; a 20-year-old black man was hanged before a crowd of over 20,000.

Why Execute in Public? The idea behind making executions public was based on a mixture of moral and practical issues. One moral issue involved proportionality: The most severe penalties should be reserved for the most serious crimes. Proportionality was applied within capital punishment itself, the most torturous forms of killing being reserved for the most serious capital offenses.

A variety of practical benefits were believed to flow from public executions: for example, deterring others, establishing social expectations, and validating the law. Having people witness executions exploits their fear of death, which might deter them from committing capital crimes themselves. It also helps establish and reinforce an expectation that similar crimes should and will receive similar punishment. Finally, public executions validate the law each time they occur and in the long run they are absorbed as part of the cultural response to particular crimes. This outcome also helps establish a moral sense in citizens that the acts involved are rightly condemned by all and thus *deserve* the ultimate punishment. The various rituals involved in public executions helped reinforce the morality of killing offenders while also providing witnesses a way of coping with death (Sturma, 1986). For example, sermonizing during the execution added religious force to the practical and moral lessons of public executions.

Even when most executions were carried out in public, some were occasionally closed to the common citizen. This occurred if an execution was unpopular and the authorities feared a public uprising, and sometimes when the offender was a member of the nobility. High-status offenders were often treated differently from commoners and executed in private, before a small gathering of their peers. Some executions took place with the general public unaware of them until after the fact. The decision to hold an execution in private was thus partly practical and partly a reflection of the importance of class distinctions in European society.

The Decline of Public Executions. Public executions fell out of favor in Europe during the nineteenth century. They had become a spectacle that many observers considered barbaric, and they were incompatible with the penal reforms that were taking hold. In his influential book *Essay on Crimes and Punishments* (1963 [1764]), the Italian philosopher Cesare Beccaria had argued against the cruel public torment of criminals. The emergence of behavioral science, the broadening scope of medicine, and incessant debates over the meaning and purpose of punishment all helped turn attention away from public hanging toward saving offenders' souls through penitence, work, and rehabilitation (Foucault, 1977). Indeed, the death penalty itself was falling out of favor. In 1847, Michigan became the first American state to abolish the death penalty.

Today, in the few Western countries that have retained the death penalty, public executions are almost unheard of. This is not the case in Islamic countries such as Saudi Arabia, where public executions are commonplace. It has been suggested that the modern American execution personifies the art of concealment, thereby losing any deterrent effect it might otherwise have (Lofland, 1977). These essentially private executions also deprive the condemned of the opportunity to publicly display courage and dignity at the time of death—a test of character that observers almost always comment on and see as proof of virtue. Such courage is all the more extraordinary when the execution is prolonged and painful, as in this French execution by burning, drawing and quartering in 1757:

> Monsieur Le Breton, the clerk of the court, went up to the patient several times and asked him if he had anything to say. He said he had not; at each torment, he cried out, as the condemned in Hell are supposed to cry out: "Pardon, my God! Pardon, Lord." Despite all this pain he raised himself from time to time and looked at himself boldly. The cords had been tied so tightly by the men who pulled the ends that they caused him indescribable pain. Monsieur le Breton went up to him again and asked if he had anything to say; he said no. Several confessors went up to him and spoke to him at length; he willingly kissed the crucifix that was held out to him; he opened his lips and repeated: "Pardon, Lord."

> The horses tugged hard, each pulling straight on a limb, each horse held by an executioner. . . . This was repeated several times without success. He raised his head and looked at himself. Two more horses had to be added to those harnessed to the thighs, which made six horses in all. Without success. . . . The executioners gathered round and Damiens [the condemned man] told them not to swear, to carry out their task and that he did not think ill of them. . . . (Foucault, 1977:4).

Modern executions are no match for the brutality and pain of medieval punishments, but someone is nevertheless about to die. There is surely value in allowing the condemned person a public display of dignity and grace at the threshold of death. In some states today, the condemned is even denied an opportunity to say any last words to the witnesses present at the execution.

Public Executions: Deterrence or Brutalization? In recent years there have been calls to make executions more accessible, and perhaps even to televise them (Bedau, 1994). The belief is that greater publicity would have a deterrent effect on some potential killers. The idea of filming executions has not been received well in most states, and federal courts have ruled that the First Amendment guarantee of free speech does not prohibit states from banning filming. At the same time, modern research has cast doubts on claims that highly publicized executions would deter crime (Bailey and Peterson, 1994; Bailey, 1990; 1998; Peterson and Bailey, 1991). These studies suggest that extensive execution publicity has no deterrent effect on homicide rates.

brutalization theory Publicized executions lower inhibitions against violence, thereby promoting more killings.

Some critics of publicized executions believe that they actually encourage homicides (Bowers, 1988). The **brutalization theory** holds that publicized exe-

While some countries have abolished capital punishment, in others it is on the rise. This includes the United States and China (above). In three months of 1996 alone, China executed over 1,000 criminals. The six prisoners shown here were charged with drug offenses; after being sentenced to death, they were quickly taken to a remote place and executed.

PHOTO BY VINCENT YU, AP PHOTO

cutions lower people's inhibitions against using deadly violence, thereby bringing about an increase in killings. Some evidence supports this view: In a study of Georgia executions from 1950 to 1965, highly publicized executions were associated with an increase of 55 homicides over the period (Stack, 1994). However, other research finds mixed support for the brutalization theory (Bailey, 1990; 1998; Cochran, Chamlin, and Seth, 1994). Needless to say, neither the deterrent nor brutalizing effects of live television coverage can be accurately assessed at present in this country, since no state televises its executions.

The Current Status of Capital Punishment

Many nations have abolished the death penalty altogether, while in others the use of capital punishment appears to be on the rise. China, for example, executed over 1,000 criminals in a three-month period in 1996 (*Newsweek*, July 22, 1996, p. 67); Amnesty International reported a total of 4,367 executions for the year (Associated Press, February 2, 1998). Many were killed in mass executions following a public parade. The condemned were taken to a vacant field, where they knelt down in rows and were shot in the head. Ostensibly part of a campaign to crack down on rising crime, some observers of Chinese society see the rise in executions as a deliberate effort by aging Chinese leaders to show strength in the face of economic and political instability, and international concern over China's takeover of Hong Kong in 1997. Unbridled use of the death penalty is perhaps the ultimate demonstration of power, but its use implies a weakening of control.

Furman v. Georgia:* The U.S. Supreme Court Halts Executions.** In 1972, following a 30-year downward trend in executions (Figure 14.1), it looked as if the United States might never execute again. The last execution had been in 1967, and five years later the Supreme Court ruled in ***Furman v. Georgia (1972) that the death penalty violated the prohibition against "cruel and unusual punishment" in the Eighth Amendment. In the 5-to-4 decision—Justices Burger, Blackmun, Powell, and Rehnquist dissented—the justices did not agree on which aspects of the death penalty were unconstitutional. Only two—Brennan and Marshall—voted to abolish capital punishment outright; the other three objected not to the death penalty itself but to the way in which states had applied it. The justices objected to the lack of standards, the broad discretion permitted trial judges, and the often discriminatory manner in which death sentences had been given out (von Drehle, 1995). This last point is discussed further in a later section of the chapter. Suffice it to say that the ruling left the door open for state legislatures to enact new statutes and develop procedures promising safequards and limiting discretion. Florida was the first to do so, and other states quickly followed suit, including Georgia.

Furman v. Georgia Death penalty was ruled cruel and unusual punishment as it had been applied.

The question of whether the death penalty *in itself* constitutes cruel and unusual punishment came up again in ***Gregg v. Georgia*** (1976), the first constitutional test of the new Georgia statute and others like it. Gregg was convicted of robbing and killing two men. He was sentenced to death under a revised Georgia death penalty statute. Gregg appealed the death sentence as cruel and unusual punishment. The U.S. Supreme Court rejected the appeal. In two separate but concurring opinions, six of the justices declared that capital punishment is not in itself cruel and unusual punishment, that it can be an appropriate penalty for certain murders, and that the new Georgia statute met the intent of the *Furman* decision.

Gregg v. Georgia Death penalty in itself is ruled to be not cruel and unusual punishment.

However, murder is one thing, rape is another. Although rape had long been a capital offense among Southern states, in ***Coker v. Georgia*** (1977), the

Coker v. Georgia Death penalty declared cruel and unusual punishment in a rape case.

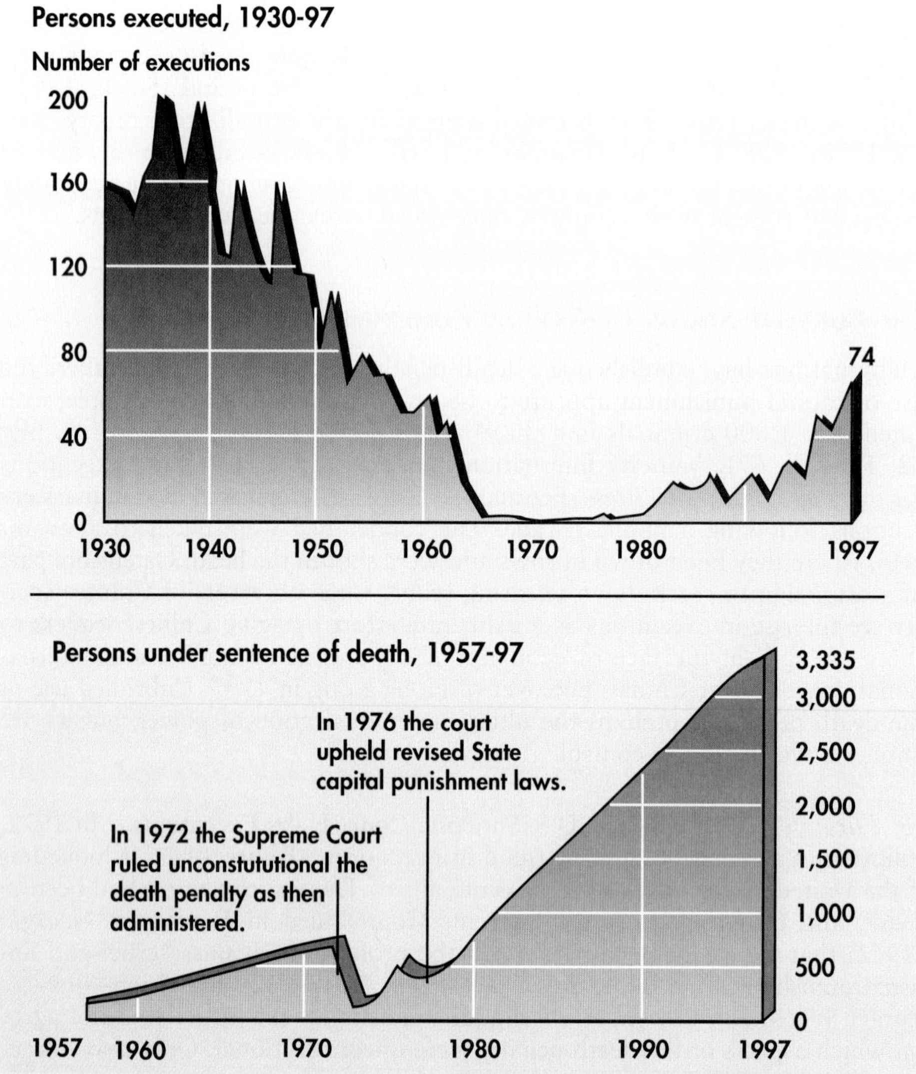

FIGURE 14.1 TRENDS IN DEATH SENTENCES AND EXECUTIONS
The top graph in this figure shows the dramatic decline in executions over a 30-year period and the rise that has occurred since 1980. The bottom graph tells us to expect many executions as growing numbers of Death Row inmates exhaust their appeals.
Source: Tracy L. Snell (1998). "Capital Punishment 1977," *BJS Bulletin*, December; Figures 1 and 3.

Supreme Court overturned a death sentence for rape on the grounds that it is cruel and unusual punishment. The Court's ruling incorporated a variety of opinions, however. Justices White, Stewart, Blackmun, and Stevens considered death for the crime of rape "grossly disproportionate and excessive" because the offender has not killed anyone; Justices Brennan and Marshall reaffirmed their *Furman* position—that death is always cruel and unusual punishment; and Justice Powell felt that death was excessive in this case because the crime was not committed with excessive brutality, and the victim did not sustain "serious or lasting injury."

The first person executed after *Furman* was Gary Gilmore, killed by firing squad in a shed outside the Utah State Prison in January 1977. Amnesty International (1997) reported that over the following 20 years, 358 executions took

TABLE 14.2 Number of People Executed by States, 1930–1998

The federal government began collecting death penalty data in 1930. From 1930 to the end of 1998, 4,359 people had been executed, over half of them in eight southern states. Since 1977, when the death penalty was reinstated, six southern states were responsible for 67 percent of the 500 executions: Texas (164), Florida (43), Virginia (59), Louisiana (24), Georgia (23), and South Carolina (20).

STATE	SINCE 1930	SINCE 1977	STATE	SINCE 1930	SINCE 1977
U.S. Total	4,359	500	U.S. Total	4,359	500
Texas	461	164	West Virgina	40	
Georgia	389	23	Nevada	36	7
New York	329		Federal System	33	
California	297	5	Massachussetts	27	
North Carolina	274	11	Connecticut	21	
Florida	213	43	Oregon	21	2
Ohio	172		Iowa	18	
South Carolina	182	20	Utah	18	5
Mississippi	158	4	Delaware	20	8
Louisiana	157	24	Kansas	15	
Pennsylvania	154	2	New Mexico	8	
Alabama	152	17	Wyoming	8	1
Arkansas	135	17	Montana	8	2
Virginia	151	59	Nebraska	6	3
Kentucky	104	1	Idaho	4	1
Illinois	111	11	Vermont	4	
Tennessee	93		New Hampshire	1	
Missouri	94	32	South Dakota	1	
New Jersey	74		Alaska	0	
Maryland	71	3	Hawaii	0	
Oklahoma	73	13	Maine	0	
Washington	50	3	Michigan	0	
Colorado	48	1	Minnesota	0	
Indiana	47	6	North Dakota	0	
Arizona	50	12	Rhode Island	0	
District of Columbia	40		Wisconsin	0	

Sources: Tracy L. Snell (1998), "Capital Punishment 1997 (Table 10)." *BJS Bulletin*, December; Critical Criminology Division of the American Society of Criminology, "1998 Executions in the U.S.," at **http://www.smu.edu/~deathpen/**.

place in 26 states, over 100 of them in Texas alone. Southern states accounted for most of the remainder, a dubious honor they have held throughout the 20th century (see Table 14.2). Today, over 3,000 inmates are on Death Row. As appeals run out we can expect a continued rise in the numbers of Americans executed each year. Figure 14.1 shows clearly what has been happening over the past 25 years: a steep increase in death sentences and a reversal of the downward trend in executions that began in the mid-1930s.

CAPITAL PUNISHMENT AND THE LAW TODAY

As of January 1998, 38 states and the federal criminal code allowed capital punishment for certain crimes, called **capital offenses**. The most common capital offenses are murder during a sex offense, murder for gain, murder of a police officer, and murder during a kidnapping. Twenty states authorize the death penalty for offenders who have a previous murder conviction. All states but Arkansas—and federal death penalty procedures—allow automatic review of all death sentences regardless of a defendant's wishes (Snell, 1996:4). In the federal system, the crime bill passed by Congress in September

capital offense A crime for which the penalty may be death.

1994 extended the death penalty to over 20 new offenses, including drug-related killings.

In the grip of the "get tough on criminals" fervor of the early 1990s, many states have also expanded their death penalty statutes to include more offenses and additional categories of victims. These included murder arising from drug violations, murder of a kidnapping victim, murder of a child following torture or injury, aircraft hijacking, forcible rape of a child under 14, and drive-by shootings. Two states with extensive death penalty offenses are Alabama and Colorado, as shown in Table 14.3.

Methods of Execution. Over the past decade or so many states have modified their method of execution; the favored method is now lethal injection, used in 32 states (Table 14.4). It is regarded as more humane and less painful than other methods, such as electrocution and lethal gas. Three states—Idaho, Oklahoma, and Utah—permit execution by firing squad. Sixteen states authorize two methods of execution—lethal injection and one other—and most of these states allow the condemned to choose which one. In the years 1977 to 1997, 284 individuals were killed by lethal injection, 134 by electrocution, 9 by gas, 3 by hanging, and 2 by firing squad.

Thompson v. Oklahoma Stanford v. Kentucky Two cases in which the U.S. Supreme Court ruled that the execution of people under age 16 at the time of their offense would be cruel and unusual punishment.

Juveniles and the Death Penalty. It is possible for children to be sentenced to death in some states. In 8 states there is no specified minimum age at which a person may be sentenced to death; in 13 states and the federal system the minimum age is 18, while the law in 16 states specifies either 16 or 17 years of age. Arkansas, Mississippi, and Virginia allow the death penalty to be imposed on 13- or 14-year-olds. However, the U.S. Supreme Court implied in ***Thompson v. Oklahoma*** (1988) and ***Stanford v. Kentucky*** (1989) that the execution

TABLE 14.3 Capital Offenses in Alabama and Colorado

Some states now have extensive lists of offenses that carry the death penalty. Here are two examples from different regions of the country:

Alabama. Murder during kidnapping, robbery, rape, sodomy, burglary, sexual assault, or arson; murder of a peace officer, correctional officer, or public official; murder for gain or contract; aircraft piracy; murder by a defendant with a previous murder conviction; murder of a witness to a crime; murder of a victim who has been subpoenaed in a criminal proceeding, when the murder is related to the role of the victim as a witness; murder when a victim is less than 14 years old; murder in which a victim is killed while in a dwelling by a deadly weapon fired or otherwise used from outside the dwelling; murder in which a victim is killed by a deadly weapon while in a motor vehicle; murder in which a victim is killed by a deadly weapon fired or otherwise used in or from a motor vehicle.

Colorado. First-degree murder; felony murder; intentionally killing a peace officer, firefighter, judge, referee, or federal law enforcement officer or agent; intentionally killing an elected state, county or municipal official; kidnapping or taking a person hostage, by either the defendant or an associate of the defendant; being party to an agreement to kill another person; murder committed while lying in wait, from ambush, or by use of an incendiary or explosive device; murder for gain; murder in an especially heinous, cruel, or depraved manner; murder for the purpose of avoiding or preventing a lawful arrest or prosecution or effecting an escape from custody, including the intentional killing of a witness to a criminal offense; killing two or more persons during the same incident; murder of a child less than 12 years old; treason.

Source: Bureau of Justice Statistics (1996). "Capital Punishment 1994." *BJS Bulletin* (February):3–4.

TABLE 14.4 Methods of Execution, by State, 1997

LETHAL INJECTION		ELECTROCUTION	LETHAL GAS	HANGING	FIRING SQUAD
Arizona	New Hampshire	Alabama	Arizona	Delaware	Idaho
Arkansas	New Jersey	Arkansas	California	New Hampshire	Oklahoma
California	New Mexico	Florida	Mississippi	Washington	Utah
Colorado	New York	Georgia	Missouri		
Connecticut	North Carolina	Kentucky	North Carolina		
Delaware	Ohio	Nebraska	Wyoming		
Idaho	Oklahoma	Ohio			
Illinois	Oregon	Oklahoma			
Indiana	Pennsylvania	South Carolina			
Kansas	South Carolina	Tennessee			
Louisiana	South Dakota	Virginia			
Maryland	Texas				
Mississippi	Utah				
Missouri	Virginia				
Montana	Washington				
Nevada	Wyoming				

Source: Tracy L. Snell (1998). "Capital Punishment 1997," *BJS Bulletin*, December, (Table 3).

of offenders who were under 16 years of age at the time of their offense would constitute cruel and unusual punishment, in violation of the Eighth Amendment. In practice, therefore, the effective minimum age for a capital sentence is 16 years of age.

Since 1990, five countries are known to have executed prisoners who were under 18 years old at the time of the crime: Iran, Pakistan, Saudi Arabia, Yemen, and the United States, where there have been six such executions (Amnesty International, 1997). The United Nations and various international human rights organizations have called for a universal minimum age of 18 at which a person may be sentenced to die. Even so, many American states are debating *lowering* the minimum age in the face of highly publicized killings involving juvenile offenders. Public opinion on the issue appears mixed, however. One survey found that residents of Cincinnati and Columbus, Ohio, were generally opposed to the execution of juveniles (Shovron, Scott, and Cullen, 1989). However, a more recent nationwide survey found that 60 percent of those polled felt that a teenager found guilty of murder by a jury should not be spared the death penalty "because of his youth" (Maguire and Pastore, 1995:184).

Aggravating Circumstances as the Basis for a Death Sentence. Traditionally, a legal distinction has been drawn between capital murder and other killings; capital murder, which carries the death penalty, has usually required that the prosecution prove **premeditation.** A finding of premeditation means that the offender contemplated the crime before committing it. In most death penalty states, a death sentence may now be permitted when an otherwise noncapital offense contains certain special elements. These elements are called **aggravating circumstances**—aspects of the crime that make it worse. Missouri is among 23 states that have identified specific aggravating circumstances. Box 14.1 describes the aggravating circumstances used in Missouri. They include prior murder convictions, murder for pay, murder of a police officer, and murder in the course of a hijacking.

premeditation The offender thinks about the crime before committing it.

aggravating circumstance An aspect of a crime that makes it more serious, deserving a harsher penalty.

The highly publicized kidnapping and sexual murder of 12-year-old Polly Klaas in California illustrates the aggravation rule in that state. Although

Box 14.1

JUSTICE AND THE LAW

AGGRAVATION REQUIREMENTS FOR THE IMPOSITION OF THE DEATH PENALTY IN MISSOURI

The laws of 23 states specify various aggravating circumstances that make a crime eligible for the death penalty. In most of these states, the crime of murder must be aggravated by at least one of a specified list of circumstances. For example, under the 1977 capital murder law of the State of Missouri, the death penalty is prohibited unless one of fourteen specific aggravating circumstances is found to be part of the offense or the offender's criminal history. The fourteen aggravating circumstances are as follows:

- Prior capital murder convictions, or a history of serious assault convictions
- A second capital murder being committed at the same time
- Using a device, such as a motor vehicle, bomb, or chemical, in a public place that endangered persons other than the victim
- The murder was committed for pay
- The victim was a judicial officer or prosecutor, or had been one, and the murder occurred during or because of the victim's exercise of his or her duties
- The defendant hired another person to commit the murder
- The crime was "outrageously or wantonly vile," involving "torture, or depravity of the mind"
- The victim was a working police officer, corrections officer, or firefighter
- The murder was committed while the accused was in custody, or attempting to escape from custody
- The murder was committed to avoid, interfere with, or prevent the lawful arrest or custody of the offender or another
- The murder was committed during the commission or attempted commission of certain specified felonies, such as robbery or rape.
- The murder victim was a witness or potential witness in any past or pending investigation or prosecution
- The murder victim was a correctional employee or an inmate of a correctional institution
- The murder victim was killed as a result of hijacking an airplane, train, ship, bus, or other public conveyance

Sources: Missouri Revised Statutes, Section 656.032; Tracy L. Snell (1998). "Capital Punishment 1997." *BJS Bulletin* (December):2–4.

defense attorneys did not contest the murder charge, they did contest the claim that Klaas had also been sexually assaulted. A successful defense against this element of aggravation would have spared their client the death penalty under California law. The defense failed, and her killer, Richard Allen Davis, was convicted of "first-degree murder with special circumstances" in June 1996. He received the death sentence four months later.

Death penalty statutes are routinely challenged in the courts as part of the appeals process. In recent years attention has focused on the aggravation circumstances required for death sentences. One such case challenged Idaho's aggravating circumstance—that the defendant exhibited "utter disregard for human life"—as unconstitutionally vague. The case at hand involved an inmate serving life terms for several first-degree murders. While in prison he smashed the skull of a physically handicapped inmate with a sock full of batteries and kicked him repeatedly about the head and throat. The trial court sentenced him to death in part because he exhibited "utter disregard for human life."

The Idaho Supreme Court rejected an appeal on the grounds of vagueness, finding in part that the petitioner was a "cold-blooded, pitiless killer." However, a federal appeals court declared the aggravating circumstance unconstitutionally vague and reversed the conviction partly on that basis. In ***Arave v. Creech*** (1993), a 7-to-2 decision by the U.S. Supreme Court reversed the federal court of appeals. The Court held that the aggravating circumstance "provides clear and objective standards and minimizes the risk of an arbitrary and capricious application of the death penalty." This decision was a blow to death penalty opponents, who believed that it would encourage states to use broad aggravation language, thereby extending the potential reach of the death penalty.

Arave v. Creech Use of aggravating circumstances as a basis for imposing the death penalty was ruled constitutional.

"Death-Qualified" Juries: Controversial but Legal. Some people are so strongly opposed to the death penalty that if they found themselves on a jury in a capital case they would automatically vote against the death penalty regardless of the facts of the case. They might vote to acquit the defendant for fear that a conviction would lead to a death sentence; or they might agree to convict the defendant, but refuse to vote for the death penalty during the sentencing phase of the trial. In a death penalty state their principles threaten to undermine the legislative intent of the death penalty statute, not to mention the goal of the state prosecutor who has charged a defendant with a capital crime. Understandably, the prosecutor will try to remove such individuals from the jury during the voir dire process that we explored in Chapter 12. By seating only those prospective jurors who can accept the idea of imposing the death penalty according to the law, the prosecutor creates what is called a **death-qualified jury**.

death-qualified jury All members of a jury can accept the possibility of imposing the death penalty.

This practice has been challenged because it would disqualify a section of the public from jury service solely because of its moral views. As we shall see later, opinion polls show that black Americans are more likely to be opposed to the death penalty than white Americans, so some critics also assert that by excluding death penalty opponents, prosecutors may deny black defendants a jury of their peers.

The U.S. Supreme Court has ruled that death-qualified juries are not unconstitutional. However, the Court has drawn an important distinction between having "qualms" or "conscientious scruples" about the death penalty and being so opposed to it that a person feels compelled to vote against its imposition regardless of the law and the facts of the case. In ***Witherspoon v. Illinois*** (1968), Justice Potter Stewart wrote that it would be improper to exclude for cause jurors who "simply voiced general objections to capital punishment or expressed conscientious or religious scruples against its infliction." To remove such jurors from a case, it would be necessary to convince the trial judge that their objections or scruples would interfere with their ability to be impartial. For example, prospective jurors whose opinions would automatically lead them to vote against a death sentence would be in violation of the impartiality required of a juror. Nearly 20 years later, in ***Wainwright v. Witt*** (1985), the Court clarified its position, and established the standard under the Sixth and Fourteenth Amendments for determining when jurors may be excused for cause because of their views on the death

Witherspoon v. Illinois A distinction was drawn between jurors with qualms about the death penalty and jurors whose opposition would automatically lead them to vote against imposing it.

Wainwright v. Witt Jurors may be excused for cause if their views on the death penalty would "substantially impair" their role as jurors.

penalty: whether these views would "substantially impair" the performance of their duties in accordance with the trial judge's instructions and their oath.

These cases dealt with death penalty appeals based on the exclusion of prospective jurors who indicated that they opposed the death penalty. A more recent case, *Morgan v. Illinois* (1992), addressed the other side of this issue: excluding jurors because they *support* the death penalty. The case involved a capital trial in Illinois, which requires the same jury to determine a defendant's guilt and then to determine whether the death penalty should be imposed. During jury selection, the court had asked prospective jurors whether they would vote against the death penalty, regardless of the facts.

This was an appropriate question, given the *Witt* standard. However, defense counsel requested the court to also ask jurors if they would automatically vote *for* the death penalty if the defendant was convicted. The trial court refused, saying that it had asked substantially that question when asking jurors whether they could be fair and impartial. Morgan's conviction and death sentence were upheld by the Illinois State Supreme Court, which ruled that a trial court is not required to ask a "life-qualifying" or "reverse *Witherspoon*" question. The U.S. Supreme Court saw it differently, however. Justice Byron White wrote the 7-to-2 opinion, noting that the impartiality requirement would be violated if a juror would automatically vote for a death sentence. "The defendant's right not to be tried by those who would *always* impose death would be rendered . . . as meaningless as the State's right . . . to question those who *never* do so."

Neither *Witherspoon* nor *Witt* directly addressed another issue that death-qualification raises: the prospect that death-qualified juries would be more predisposed to find a defendant guilty. This would also violate a defendant's right to an impartial jury. In addition, death-qualified juries might actually encourage executions through their role in sentencing. In most death penalty states, juries recommend the sentence in capital cases, and in some states judges are bound by the jury's recommendation. If death-qualified juries are prone to convict and also prone to sentence capital offenders to death, their use would artificially increase both capital conviction rates and execution rates.

Over the years, numerous capital defendants have filed appeals in lower courts—a few of them successfully—based on claims that death-qualified juries are unconstitutionally prone to convict. The U.S. Supreme Court did not explicitly address the issue until nearly 20 years after *Witherspoon*. In ***Lockhart v. McCree*** (1986), the Court concluded that empirical evidence on the issue was fragmentary and inconsistent. Going further, the Court said that even if there were good evidence that death-qualified juries are generally conviction prone, each jury must be judged on its individual merits; no blanket constitutional ruling would therefore be appropriate. This means that the burden of proving that a death-qualified jury was biased in favor of conviction lies with the defendant in each particular case.

Lockhart v. McCree The burden of proving that a death-qualified jury is biased in favor of conviction lies with the defense.

***Harris v. Alabama* (1995): The U.S. Supreme Court Confirms Its Reluctance to Interfere with State Courts in Death Penalty Cases.** In recent years, the Supreme Court has shown considerable reluctance to interfere with how states run their criminal courts. This reluctance is surfacing more and more in death penalty cases, where defendants are inclined to appeal over and over again in the hopes of staving off their execution. The Court made its position quite clear in a 1995 death penalty appeal involving a judge who refused to accept a jury's sentence recommendation. As noted earlier, some states require judges to follow a jury's sentencing recommendation in death penalty cases, while others do not. For example, Georgia does, but Alabama does not require judges to follow the jury recommendation, nor do its statutes specify how much weight a judge should place on the recommendation. This led to appeals claiming that the death penalty has been imposed in an arbitrary manner, in violation of the Eighth Amendment.

The U.S. Supreme Court dealt with this claim in ***Harris v. Alabama*** (1995). In this case, the jury recommendation of life imprisonment for a woman convicted of capital murder was ignored by the trial judge, who sentenced her to death. After the conviction was upheld in state courts, the U.S. Supreme Court ruled in an 8-to-1 decision that the Supreme Court should not be in the business of "micromanaging" state courts, and that the Alabama statute need not specify the weight assigned to jury recommendations in order to comply with the Eighth Amendment.

Harris v. Alabama Death penalty statutes need not specify the weight assigned to jury sentence recommendations.

By and large, Supreme Court rulings in recent years have tended to make imposition of the death penalty easier, despite the outspoken opposition of some of its own members. Now-retired Justice Lewis Powell and the late Justices William Brennan and Thurgood Marshall all believed that the death penalty was cruel and unusual punishment, and therefore unconstitutional. Justice Harry Blackmun came to the same position shortly before retiring in 1994. These justices are gone, and the likelihood of getting *five* justices who all agree that capital punishment is unconstitutional, and who are serving on the Court at the same time, is small indeed. As a constitutional issue, the death penalty appears here to stay. But this does not mean that individual states could not decide to abandon this form of punishment. The American Civil Liberties Union, the American Society of Criminology, the NAACP, Amnesty International, and a host of other national and international organizations are hopeful that they will.

Awaiting Execution: Death Row in America

Most defendants sentenced to death can expect to spend many years in prison awaiting execution. In 1997, 74 inmates were executed in the United States; they had been under sentence of death an average of 11 years and 1 month (Snell, 1998:12). In four states—Florida, Texas, California, and Georgia—58 inmates were still awaiting execution on January 1, 1998, more than *18 years* after their death sentences were handed down. The reason for the delay is the lengthy appeals process that generally follows a capital conviction. Not only is there an automatic review by a state supreme court, but lawyers for most convicted capital defendants initiate appeal after appeal in the hopes of saving their client's life. Nearly half the time they succeed.

The Writ of *Habeas Corpus*. One method of challenging a capital sentence—strictly speaking, it is not itself an appeal—is to file a **writ of *habeas corpus*.** *Habeas corpus* is Latin for "you have the body"; during the tumultuous seventeenth century, it was used by British courts to free enemies of the crown who had been locked away in the Tower of London without benefit of a trial. Sir William Blackstone called the writ of *habeas corpus* "the Great Writ," by which name it has been known ever since. It is a core procedure in Anglo-American law, for its use enables independent courts to review the detention of citizens and to release them from illegal imprisonment.

writ of *habeas corpus* A legal procedure that forces courts to review the legality of a person's imprisonment.

The use of *habeas corpus* in capital cases has come under challenge because lawyers often invoke the writ over and over again, stalling an execution that has been repeatedly reviewed for legality. A 1989 report by a commission set up by Chief Justice Rehnquist of the U.S. Supreme Court to study the use of *habeas corpus* recommended that there should be "one complete and fair course of collateral review in the state and federal system. . . . When this review has concluded, litigation should end" (*Criminal Law Reporter*, September 27, 1989, p. 3240).

McCleskey v. Zant U.S. Supreme Court moved to limit repeated use of *habeas corpus* appeals in capital cases.

The Supreme Court moved in this direction with its decision in ***McCleskey v. Zant*** (1991). The appeal claimed that prosecutors had deceived the defense as to the nature of the state's evidence against McCleskey. Apparently, they had secretly planted an informant in an adjoining jail cell solely for the purpose of eliciting incriminating statements from McCleskey that could be used against him during trial. However, this was not McCleskey's first *habeas corpus* appeal, and the Court ruled 6 to 3 that the evidence in this latest appeal should have been brought into McCleskey's previous appeal. The current appeal was denied. The Court's minority opinion was that the defense found out about the informant only after "years of demands and denials," for which the state should be held responsible. McCleskey was executed in September 1991, after thirteen years on Death Row.

In 1992 the Supreme Court continued its path toward curtailing *habeas corpus* appeals by forbidding other federal appeals courts from issuing any more stays of execution for Robert Alton Harris. The Ninth Circuit Court of Appeals had issued a fourth stay of execution after Harris was strapped into the gas chamber with less than a minute to go. Just hours prior to this last appeal, Harris's lawyers had claimed that gas chamber executions were cruel and unusual punishment in violation of the Eighth Amendment. This tactic clearly frustrated the Court, which said the claim could have been brought "more than a decade ago." The Court continued: "There is no good reason for this abusive delay, which has been compounded by last-minute attempts to manipulate the judicial process." The Court's extraordinary 7-to-2 decision to bar further appeals in the Harris case—Justices Harry Blackmun and John Paul Stevens dissented—put the legal community on notice that frivolous appeals would not be tolerated and that those sentenced to death could expect time to execution to be shortened. Harris became California's first execution in 25 years.

Anti-Terrorism and Effective Death Penalty Act A 1996 law establishing strict time limits for filing federal *habeas corpus* appeals.

Although condemned by some critics as a "rush to kill" (*New York Times*, April 17, 1992, p. 14), the Supreme Court decisions restricting *habeas corpus* challenges received support from the U.S. Congress. In 1995, the House voted 297 to 132 in favor of the Effective Death Penalty Act establishing a one-year limit on filing of *habeas corpus* appeals by Death Row inmates. After the act failed in the Senate, a modified version was tacked onto an anti-terrorism bill and signed into law by President Clinton in May 1996. The new **Anti-Terrorism and Effective Death Penalty Act** provides strict time limits for the filing of federal *habeas corpus* appeals (*Newsweek*, May 6, 1996, p. 72). Once all appeals in state courts have been exhausted, death penalty inmates must now file federal appeals within one year (or within six months if they have a state-appointed attorney). However, in addition, the new law requires federal judges to place more weight on earlier state court decisions in the case—which have usually gone against the inmate—and to issue their own ruling within strict time limits. The current U.S. Supreme Court is likely to view this law favorably when the inevitable challenges arrive before it, and the result will be a speeded-up death penalty process.

Life on "The Row." Inmates awaiting execution are usually housed in a special section of a maximum security prison apart from other inmates. This is Death Row—or just "The Row." Only Missouri has no Death Row; in that state, people under sentence of death are housed with the general inmate population of the Potosi Correctional Center. The typical inmate of this prison is serving more than 25 years; many are serving life terms with no possibility of parole. The capital punishment inmate is removed to segregation about 36 hours before the execution is scheduled to take place.

Life on Death Row can be a time for a condemned person to make peace with himself and with his fate—or it can be a constant torment. What are some ways that people on Death Row cope with their impending death?

Illustration by John B. Overmyer

Death Row is rarely discussed as part of capital punishment, yet only people condemned to death experience it. It is indeed part of capital punishment, and a very significant part for condemned prisoners. "Most capital cases consume only a few weeks of court time; the act of killing takes only a few minutes. Death Row is years and years" (Jackson and Christian, 1980:ix).

What is The Row like? What does it mean to those awaiting execution and to those who work there? To answer these questions, researchers Bruce Jackson and Diane Christian (1980) interviewed 26 men on Death Row in Texas and also spoke with two custodial officers, four porters or "hall boys"—inmates themselves who have earned the trust of prison officials—and one medical assistant. The inmates and workers describe a special society, different in many ways from the prison life experienced by other inmates in the same prison. The condemned men, all with violent pasts, are confined in three tiers of four-by-seven-foot cells; every move they make is monitored, and the physical space is tightly controlled. Most of the time, Death Row inmates are either in their cells or in a day room no bigger than a living room. They have far less freedom than other inmates, and the potential for violence is even greater than among the general inmate population. Death Row inmates often feel they have nothing to lose: A provocation, whether real or imagined, is virtually guaranteed a violent response.

Death Row inmates get mad over little things. As one porter explained:

> "You're locked up with a sentence like they have—it's a small world. Teeny things tend to become big things. Like 'I don't like potatoes. How come you're giving me potatoes?' Or, 'There's a bean on my potato!' Their world is real small right now and it's a small place for them to live, and they do get angry over little things that I wouldn't get

> angry over. But when they do get angry, they are impatient. . . . They want things to happen faster. . . ." (Jackson and Christian, 1980:142)

A typical week on Florida's Death Row has been described as follows:

> A typical day begins at 5:45 A.M., when the lights are turned on. Breakfast is brought to inmates by a "runner," an inmate who lives on Death Row but is not under a death sentence, at approximately 6:30. . . .
>
> Lunch is served at 11:30 A.M. and supper at 4:30 P.M. The diet is heavy in carbohydrates and starches, emphasizing potatoes, rice, and bread. . . . One inmate has gained fifty pounds since he began living on Death Row; others exercise in their cells and manage to keep shape. . . .
>
> Inmates are permitted to exercise in the recreation yard for two hours, two times per week. . . . Every other night, each inmate is permitted to take a five-minute shower. Inmates may receive visitors on either Saturdays or Sundays from 9 A.M. to 3 P.M. in a special visitor's room. . . . Except for special occasions, inmates spend the remainder of their time inside their cells.
>
> Each inmate is allowed to spend up to fifteen dollars a week for canteen items (e.g., soda, cigarettes, toilet articles), although the sum is converted to prison stamps since money itself is contraband. Each inmate is given ten packs of nonfilter "Florida Division of Corrections Industries" cigarettes per week; the quality of these cigarettes is unmatched on the commercial market. . . .
>
> While one would expect the atmosphere on Death Row to be grim and depressing, this is not the case. The noise level is unusually high, for television sets and radios blare all day long. Doors at the end of each row are constantly slamming, and the conversation among inmates is often so loud that one has to shout to be heard. . . . (Lewis, 1979:208–209)

Lewis describes the atmosphere on The Row as optimistic, perhaps because in the late 1970s many inmates fully believed that the reinstatement of capital punishment would be short lived. Condemned prisoners expected to live, not to die in the electric chair. Today, the picture is different; the status of the death penalty is as strong as ever, and executions are a weekly event.

An optimistic atmosphere does not mean a peaceful one; violence has always been an ever-present danger on The Row. Lewis (1979:209) reports being threatened by an entire row of inmates because he spoke briefly to an unpopular child killer. Assaults on other inmates and Death Row workers are commonplace, and there are ritualized ways of carrying them out: "The way you usually get somebody here is to heat up some water boiling hot and when he comes by your cell, you scald him. Or take a mayonnaise jar and throw it through the bars and let it cut people up. I got cut up over there yesterday when someone threw a glass through the bars at the floor boy. That glass, hitting the bar, it's got a lot of momentum and it will cut you bad." (Jackson and Christian, 1980:115)

There are many ways in which life on The Row differs from life elsewhere in the same prison. One notable difference is the absence of deals and agreements between convicts and prison officials and between convicts themselves. "On Death Row, none of the usual bargains apply. . . . On Death Row, there is little the wardens can do for the men, and equally little the men can do to or for the prison. They don't work, so they can't strike. They don't get good time, so their behavior is meaningless" (Jackson and Christian, 1980:23–24). Many convicts on Death Row spend most of their time trying to get out, fighting their case through appeal after appeal. This is what keeps them going. In the end, some will win, some will lose, and some will demand that the ordeal be ended, that they be put to death. Gary Gilmore, executed in Utah by firing squad in 1977, demanded to be put to death, and so did Gerald Smith, executed in 1990 by lethal injection in Missouri.

THE MODERN EXECUTION

The modern execution bears little resemblance to executions throughout most of recorded history. In America today, the time of execution makes death inconspicuous—it is usually in the middle of the night or very early in the morning; the place of execution is secluded from public view; few witnesses are allowed; the technique is generally reliable, fast, and relatively quiet; the executioner is anonymous and impersonal; the announcement is terse and made without fanfare; and the body is removed quietly and quickly. The emphasis on quiet orderliness and efficiency is consistent with modern middle-class values of civilized order and good breeding: "Rather than a demonstration of power, the modern orchestration of death lends assurance that everything is in order, everything is humane and civilized, and that we aren't, after all, barbarians. In other words, the rituals of capital punishment are now *defensive* rather than *demonstrative* in intent." (Haines, 1992:126).

By past practices, the modern execution probably appears humane. However, some critics believe this is nothing more than an illusion—the dispassionate, ritualistic, impersonal, assembly-line procedures "actually make modern executions distinctively brutal and dehumanizing" (Johnson, 1990:25). Certainly, execution today is a very clinical procedure, formalized and rehearsed down to the last detail to ensure that the killing process is carried out quietly and without a hitch. This is not to say that the staff who carry out a modern execution minimize the significance of what they are about to do. As Box 14.2 illustrates, the job of executioner is stressful and full of fears, and taken very seriously by those who volunteer for it.

Lethal Injection: The Modern Method of Execution

A "medicalization" of the execution process has occurred in recent years, illustrated best in death by lethal injection. As we saw earlier, execution by lethal injection is now the primary method of capital punishment in America. Texas was one of the first states to introduce lethal injection, doing so in 1964. Executions take place at the Texas State Prison in Huntsville, called "The Walls":

> The killing room is not large. A gurney is now where the [electric] chair used to be. When an execution takes place, the gurney will be taken through the control room into the row of death cells, and the man to be killed will be strapped to it. The gurney will be quickly moved back to the killing room. . . .
>
> Three intravenous tubes will be inserted in the condemned man's arm. They lead through a wall to three petcocks and three bottles. One tube and one bottle . . . will contain water or some other harmless fluid; a second will contain sodium pentothal; the third will contain the killing fluid. . . .
>
> There are no chairs for witnesses. A visitor, being shown the room for the first time, said to the guide, "You should have chairs. People may get faint."
>
> "No," the guard said, "that won't be a problem. It will be very quick. And it will look just like the guy is going to sleep. That's the reason for the pentothal. There won't be time for people to get sick. It will be over in seconds." (Jackson and Christian, 1980:4–5).

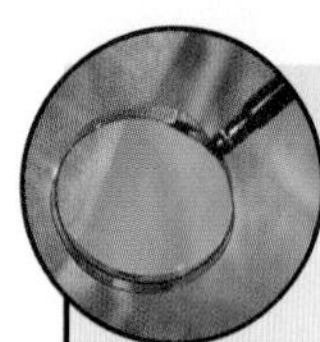

Box 14.2

INSIDE CRIMINAL JUSTICE

THE EXECUTIONER AT WORK

With all the publicity given victims and offenders in capital cases, little thought is given to the job of executioner. Criminologist Robert Johnson spent time with an execution team before, during, and after the electrocution of a man convicted of the gruesome murder of an elderly woman. His book *Death Work* documents the modern execution process from the vantage point of the people who carry it out. These are some of his insights.

The modern execution is a highly bureaucratized and impersonal process. Every aspect of the execution is planned and routinized. The execution team, drawn from volunteers among the prison staff who are carefully screened for maturity and dependability, rehearses its job carefully. The members of this "death watch" team look upon themselves as professionals dedicated to the service of criminal justice. The responsibility they are asked to fulfill is a premeditated killing. The team will spend hours with the condemned prisoner before the execution, comforting and calming the individual when it becomes necessary—as it usually does. At the same time, the leader of an execution team is expected to be a calming influence on the other team members, to help keep them in a state of mental readiness for their task. Even though they may care little for the condemned, the emotional strains are felt by everyone and escalate as the hour of death approaches.

The "on again, off again" nature of many executions can be a source of stress for the team. Adrenaline builds as the tension mounts, then orders come to stand down. Sometimes within minutes the team is told that the execution is back on. This process may be repeated in the final hour before the scheduled execution. Everyone is exhausted by the emotional roller coaster and the toll it takes on the condemned.

While every step of the execution is carefully planned, mistakes can occur. Equipment may malfunction, or something or someone may slip. The biggest worry is that emotions will overtake the prisoner or a team member, causing loss of control in the execution chamber. Prisoners are carefully walked to the place of execution because even tripping on a step may trigger a violent or desperate outburst. As one executioner put it, "You don't want to get in a situation where you have to fight a man to the chair. I think that would leave a mental scar on you worse than anything."

During the moments before an execution, the execution team avoids eye contact with the condemned. Yet the need to say goodbye, to reach out and touch the condemned in a gesture of goodwill from one human being to another, sometimes overcomes an executioner. One officer mopped the brow of a condemned man as he sat in the electric chair awaiting death and briefly touched his hand farewell. "This personal touch in the midst of an impersonal procedure was, in the warden's opinion, an attempt to help the officer himself live with the death penalty. The warden noted that it also by implication helped the team of which he was a part. 'It's out of our hands,' the gesture seemed to imply. 'We're only doing our job'" (Johnson, 1998:176).

Source: Robert Johnson (1998). *Death Work: A Study of the Modern Execution Process.* 2nd Edition, Belmont California: Wadsworth.

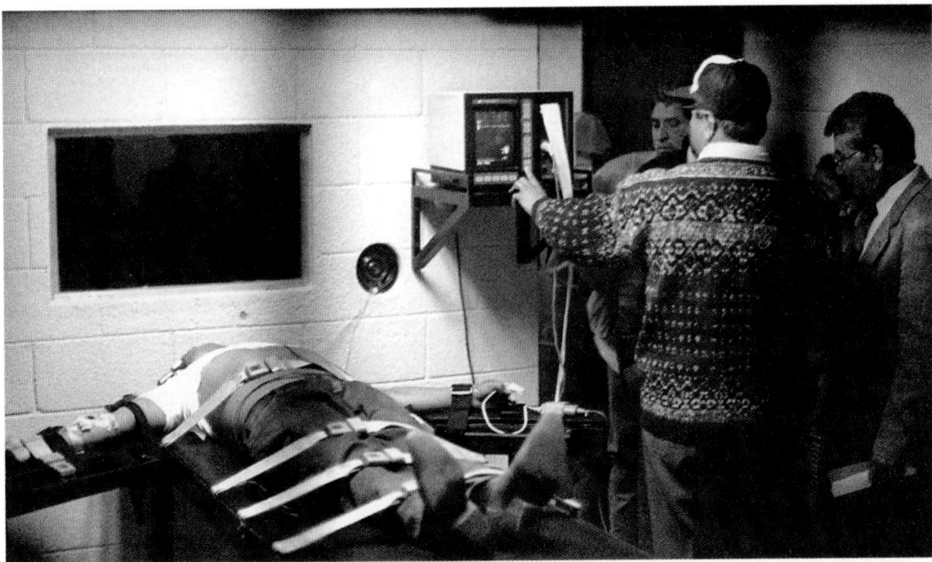

Witnesses at an execution can include state's witnesses, who attest that the execution did take place; members of the press; and the families of both the victim(s) and the condemned. Here, medical technicians check for vital signs after Manuel Martinez was executed by lethal injection Tuesday, February 10, 1998, at Pavon Prison just outside Guatemala City, Guatemala.

Photo by Moises Castillo, courtesy of AP Photo

The claim that death by lethal injection is "like going to sleep" is often used to calm the condemned and to reassure witnesses that what they are about to see will be painless, quiet, and dignified. But does anything adequately prepare people for the moment of execution, whether their own or someone else's? Most of us have had little to guide our thinking as we grew up. The recent film *Dead Man Walking* may help change that, and even more important will surely be the increasing rate at which Americans are being executed and the debate this is sparking.

Witnessing the Execution of Thomas Battle. To become more informed about the process of execution from the perspective of a modern-day witness, on August 7, 1996, I attended an execution by lethal injection at the Potosi Correctional Center in Missouri. I went as a *state's witness*. States with the death penalty usually require executions to be observed by independent citizens who can attest that the execution in fact occurred, and if necessary, testify in court as to what happened. Citizens volunteer for this duty.

The experience confirmed much of what I had read of modern executions, but I came away with a greater appreciation of the clinical, impersonal aspects of the process, and the emphasis on efficiency and formality. Every effort was made to ensure that no problems would occur. The staff carried out their duties in a calm and respectful manner. Security inside and outside the prison was high. I was twice stopped and questioned outside the prison by heavily armed guards, and once inside went through a metal detector more sensitive than any I had experienced at an airport.

The execution was scheduled to occur at 12:01 A.M., and I was required to arrive by 10:30 P.M. Witnesses were carefully segregated in four groups: press, victim's family, offender's family, and state's witnesses. I sat for approximately 50 minutes in a lunchroom with four other state's witnesses and a Department of Corrections security officer. I felt overdressed. My plain suit and tie were in stark contrast to the T-shirt and jeans, colorful pantsuit, Hawaiian-style shirt, and other casual clothes worn by the other witnesses. I wondered if, like me, they had worried over what to wear for an execution. My decision had rested on two thoughts: There could hardly be a more formal event, and a display of respect seemed appropriate for what was about to take place—if not for the process, then for the last moments of a person's life.

After about five minutes, an uncomfortable, strained silence gave way to small talk among some of the witnesses, and eventually all of us. People talked about the condemned man's crime, a little bit about themselves, and about various aspects of the criminal justice system. No one mentioned their reasons for volunteering to be a state's witness, nor was there much talk about the execution we were about to watch. At one point our security escort commented that lethal injection makes death "easy." Occasional light humor broke the tension we could all feel, but there were no jokes about executions. The security officer joined in, and was generally helpful in responding to questions, though more polite than friendly. She, like most other correctional officials involved with the execution, had volunteered for the detail; unless state law or policy requires a person's presence, participation in an execution is strictly voluntary.

At approximately 11:35 we were joined by two more correctional officers, one wearing a dark suit and a two-way radio headset and carrying papers and a pad on which he periodically jotted things down. He had three members of the press with him, who then joined our group as state's witnesses. We were escorted through a seeming labyrinth of hallways and locked doors until we ended up in a room that looked like a small courtroom. Here we were greeted by another official in a dark suit and wearing headphones, and by the director of the Department of Corrections, who thanked us for fulfilling this important and somber responsibility. The second official read the execution order and gave us a brief explanation of the killing process itself: first, sodium pentathol would be administered through an IV to produce unconsciousness, then pancromium bromide (Pavulon) to stop the respiratory system, and finally potassium chloride to stop the heart. He and the director then left the room. The two uniformed officers stayed outside the room, leaving us with the dark-suited officer, who from time to time checked his watch and wrote things down, sometimes after hearing something (indecipherable to us) through his headphones.

Further hushed small talk resumed among the witnesses, now seated in rows. Some read packets of information provided for the news media, and eventually made available to all of us. The packet included information about Battle and the crime for which he was about to be executed, as well as other information about the death penalty in Missouri. We learned that Battle was born in 1962, and had two previous offenses: making a false police report, and failing to appear, for which he had been fined a total of $330. He was arrested on July 16, 1980, for capital murder, and sentenced to death on September 18, 1981. Battle had participated in the burglary and rape of an 80-year-old neighbor, and court testimony established that he had repeatedly stabbed the woman with a twelve-inch butcher knife, finally plunging it under her left eye. Battle became a capital punishment inmate on October 10, 1981; by the date of his execution he had been the longest-serving death penalty inmate in Missouri. Various state and federal appeals were made, three reaching the U.S. Supreme Court, the last one rejected on June 3, 1996. Three days later the Missouri Supreme Court set the execution date for August 7, 1996. Battle was about to become the 60th person executed in Missouri since 1938, and the 33rd African American.

Noises in the hallway alerted us to the presence of other people we could not see. At 11:55 P.M. we were led out of the small courtroom, across a courtyard and into another wing of the prison. Passing through two more locked doors, we arrived at the death chamber. Many correctional officers were in attendance, senior officials wearing headsets. Three walls of the small, square chamber each had two windows whose blinds were closed. If anything was going on behind the blinds, we could neither see nor hear it. We were escorted through one viewing area to three elevated rows of seats—nine in all—facing the windows of the middle wall. As we took our seats, an accordion-fold wall was pulled shut to our right, separating us from the viewing area we had passed through; a similar wall to our left separated us from the third viewing area. We could hear people taking their places in the other viewing areas—one for the victim's family, one for Battle's relatives.

Our viewing area was crowded: There were eight state's witnesses, two senior correctional officers—also with headsets—standing at the sides of the front seats holding rods that controlled the window blinds, the two suited officers who had escorted us, and five uniformed officers, including the guard from the lunchroom.

At approximately midnight we could see that someone was raising inner blinds on the windows, and at 12:01 A.M. we heard through the officers' headsets that the "procedure" was about to begin. The two officers in front of us raised the blinds on our side.

Through the smallish windows and past the people in front of me I could see that Battle was lying on a gurney facing us, all but his face covered by a white sheet. Only the act of killing remained, for all other preparations had been made. I was surprised that the condemned man would apparently have no opportunity for "last words" before public witnesses. A black tube snaked through the wall behind him. The IV was in place, as were the devices used to monitor his vital signs. Battle had already said goodbye to his family and to prison staff. He had, I soon realized, already uttered his last words. He was alone in the room.

A spectacled Battle raised his head from the pillow, looked around, and gave a vague smile to people I could not see. As he did so a voice announced through all the headsets that the first procedure had begun. The official who had earlier explained how death would occur now told us the first drug was being administered. Battle's head suddenly jerked twice and he fell gently back, eyes closed. From that moment on I could detect no real movement, although I thought I saw brief twitches at the corners of Battle's mouth and a slight flaring of his nostrils. Some published accounts of execution by lethal injection have mentioned brief but heavy breathing. I saw none.

A few moments later, the headset voice announced that the second procedure had commenced, and this information was again relayed on to us. There was little movement in our viewing area. I noticed that most of the correctional officials could not see into the death chamber, and those who could were mostly looking down at their feet or at each other. One official at the window paid close attention to the proceedings; he would close the blinds if anything unexpected happened. We had been told earlier that if it was necessary for prison officials or the attending physician to enter the chamber, the blinds would be closed to protect their anonymity.

I could detect no change in Battle, though I knew that his breathing must have ceased. At about 12:04 A.M. the third drug was administered, and now Battle's heart was stopped. Again there was no discernible movement or change. I knew that Battle's vital signs were being monitored continuously by the attending physician in an adjoining room. At 12:07 A.M. the headset voice announced that the physician had declared Battle deceased. Again the information was relayed to us, and almost immediately the blinds were closed. Before leaving the area the eight state's witnesses concluded their somber duty by signing the official record of the execution.

We were escorted out of the area, which turned out to be located in the prison hospital—a perverse but practical arrangement. When I left the prison at 12:35 A.M., there were few signs of the heightened security I had witnessed on arrival. The brightly lit facility was very quiet. Our escort said it always is the night of an execution, and would be again two weeks later, when the next execution was scheduled. There were 94 death penalty inmates in Missouri as of August 8, 1996, 24 of whom had been awaiting execution for more than ten years. The prospect of at least one execution per month in Missouri was fast becoming a reality.

Flawed Executions

Executions may be flawed in one or more of three ways: (1) Something goes wrong with the act of killing itself; (2) the person executed did not commit the crime for which the death sentence was given; or (3) the ceremony surrounding the execution is disrupted or undermined.

In the days of beheading and hanging it was not unusual for an execution to go wrong: the head was not severed on the first blow, the rope broke, or the trapdoor stuck. These events gave ammunition to death penalty abolitionists, who questioned the morality of capital punishment. But even today, despite all the preparations and precautions, executions are sometimes flawed. Between 1977 and 1989, at least 12 of 150 executions in the United States were marred by technical hitches—the injection system didn't work properly, for example, or electrical connections came loose (Radelet, 1990). The most famous recent case involved Pedro Medina, executed in Florida in March, 1997. Medina was

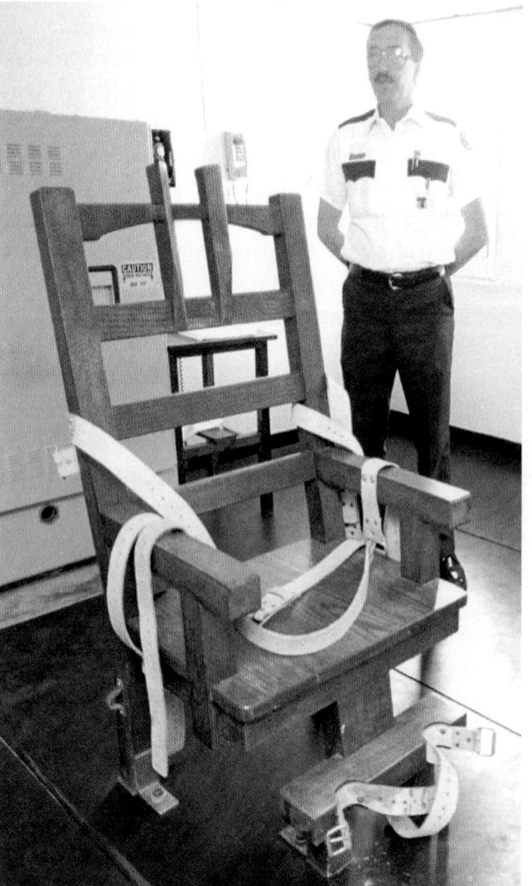

The March 1997 execution of Pedro Medina in Florida is a recent example of a flawed execution. Medina, sentenced to die in Florida's "old Sparky"—an electric chair that was 74 years old at the time—was successfully executed, but not before a foot-long flame shot up from his head.

Photo by Mark Foley, courtesy of AP Photo

electrocuted in Florida's 74-year-old electric chair. During the procedure a foot-long flame shot up from his head because a dry sponge had been incorrectly used in the headpiece (*Jacksonville Times-Union*, September 9, 1997, p. 1). Although medical experts claimed Medina suffered no pain and was killed instantly, Florida temporarily halted all executions while it debated the merits of electrocution.

Over the years, irregularities in sentencing or conviction have come to light after some executions, showing that the imposition of the death penalty itself is sometimes a mistake. Between 1900 and 1985 in the United States, at least 350 people were sentenced to death for crimes they did not commit, and 23 were actually executed (Radelet and Bedau, 1988). Between 1972 and 1993, 48 condemned men were freed from Death Row; in Illinois alone, 8 Death Row inmates were released between 1988 and 1998 after being found innocent (*St. Louis Post-Dispatch*, April 12, 1998, p. A7). There is, in short, a "high risk that [some innocent Death Row inmates] will be executed" (Amnesty International, 1997:3).

In 1997, the U.S. Supreme Court unanimously ruled that an Illinois Death Row inmate, William Bracy, was entitled to investigate whether his 1981 murder conviction was "fixed" by a corrupt judge (*Chicago Tribune*, June 17, 1997, p. 1). The ruling may have implications for at least five other Death Row inmates convicted in murder trials under the former judge, Thomas J. Maloney. However, it is unlikely that Bracy will escape execution, because he is under a death sentence for two murders in Arizona!

The third way in which executions may be flawed is neither technical or legalistic but involves violations of the execution ritual itself. Onlookers may become hysterical or unruly, or the condemned may not cooperate with officials. Although death chamber outbursts and struggles are rare, when they do occur they disrupt the orderly and efficient dispatching of the condemned. "Almost no one seems to want to watch prisoners being dragged screaming to their deaths" (Haines, 1992:129). In one well-known incident in 1986, Daniel Thomas appeared relatively calm as he was being taken to the electric chair. But once there he began kicking and screaming, and it took six prison officials to strap him into the chair. The fact that such incidents are rare may reflect psychological exhaustion, and even a sense of relief now that years of waiting for death are over (Johnson, 1990). In addition, Death Row guards and execution teams often go out of their way during the final hours before an execution, catering to the needs of the condemned, and helping them deal with their fears.

WHO IS EXECUTED IN THE UNITED STATES?

Of the 4,291 executions between 1930 and 1998, over 90 percent were for murder, with rape accounting for most of the remainder. Nearly 2,300 executions occurred in the South, as did all but 12 of the 455 executions for rape. Over 90 percent of the nation's executions were of men. Overall, more black prisoners than white prisoners have been executed, and nearly 90 percent of those who died for rape were black. Homicide is usually intraracial—white on white, or black on black—but when it comes to the penalty, black offenders who kill white victims are more likely to have been executed than any other offender-victim combination. Out of more than 16,000 documented executions on the U.S. mainland, only 30 have involved a white person sentenced to death for killing a black person (*Time*, April 4, 1991, p. 68). The NAACP Capital Punishment Project reports that from 1977 to April 1995, of 289 executions, only four involved white offenders who killed black victims, while 94 involved black offenders who killed white victims.

Very few women have been executed in the United States. Since 1977, only 3 women have been executed, although nearly 50 women are currently awaiting execution. Karla Faye Tucker is perhaps the best-known recent case. Tucker and her boyfriend killed two people with a pickax during a robbery in 1983 when Tucker was 23. She underwent a Christian conversion while awaiting trial; she expressed remorse for her crime and testified against her boyfriend but received no leniency in return. While on Death Row, she was a model prisoner and spent a great deal of time counseling other prisoners with her prison chaplain husband (Associated Press, January 12, 1998).

As her execution date neared, well-known leaders spoke out for mercy, including evangelist Pat Robertson. To some people, Tucker simply did not fit the image of the Death Row inmate. To others, her good works since conversion and the strong likelihood that she would continue them for the rest of her life seemed justification enough to let her live, despite her terrible crime. Yet others believed that the sentence was just, considering the crime, and anything less would violate the principle of proportionality—and perhaps send the wrong message: Death Row inmates who behave in exemplary ways may earn a reprieve.

Unswayed by all the publicity, Governor George W. Bush refused to commute her sentence, and Tucker was executed by lethal injection on February 3, 1998. She was the first woman executed in Texas since 1863; yet since 1976, Texas has executed 155 men, one-third of all the executions in the country. Tables 14.5 and 14.6 summarize the demographic picture of the people on Death Row as of December 31, 1997, and of the people executed since 1977.

Discrimination and the Death Penalty. The racial imbalance in the imposition of the death penalty has fueled charges of discrimination. This has been the central issue in the NAACP's long fight to have the death penalty abolished. Analysis of data going back as far as 1890 led one researcher to conclude that the findings point "unmistakably to a pattern of racial discrimination in the administration of capital punishment in America" (Bowers, 1974:102). Other criminologists have made similar charges (Wolfgang and Riedel, 1973).

Discrimination appears to have been concentrated in the South, where black offenders have been executed for less serious crimes, as well as for crimes less often punished by death (such as rape) when committed by white offend-

TABLE 14.5 Composition of the U.S. Death Row Population, 1997

This table shows the race/ethnic and sex composiiton of the 3,335 Death Row inmates as of December 31, 1997. Almost all Death Row inmates are males, and African Americans are also overrepresented.

	NUMBER	PERCENT
Total number on Death Row	3,335	100%
Race/Ethnicity Males		
White Male	1,846	55.4%
Black Male	1,392	41.7
Hispanic Male	274	8.2
Females		
White Female	30	0.89
Black Female	14	0.4
Hispanic Female	2	0.06

The Death Row population also included 28 American Indians (0.8%) and 17 Asian Americans (0.51%).

Source: Tracy L. Snell (1998). "Capital Punishment 1997," *BJS Bulletin*, December: p. 8.

Table 14.6 Americans Executed from 1977 to 1996: A Demographic Picture of Who They Were and Who They Killed

This table shows the race/ethnicity and gender of most of the people executed in America during the past quarter-century, and of their victims. Those executed were almost always male; their victims were almost always white, but almost half the time women.

	Number	Percent
Race/Ethnicity		
Offenders		
White	187	55.82%
Black	128	38.21
Latino/Latina	17	5.07
Native American	2	.60
Asian	1	.30
Victims		
White	370	82.04
Black	57	12.64
Latino/Latina	17	3.77
Native American	0	0
Asian	7	1.55
Sex		
Offenders		
Male	334	99.70%
Female	1	.30
Victims		
Male	257	56.98
Female	194	43.02

Source: NAACP Legal Defense Fund (1996), *Death Row, USA*. New York: National Association for the Advancement of Colored People.

ers (Marquart, Ekland-Olson, and Sorensen, 1993). Further, the black offenders who have been executed were generally younger than their white counterparts and were more often executed without appeals. A study of who gets the death penalty in Kentucky found that "blacks who killed whites were significantly more likely to end up on Death Row," and this finding held regardless of seriousness and other aspects of the crime (Keil and Vito, 1989:527). Similar findings emerged in a study of more than 600 murder cases in Georgia (Barnett, 1985).

A finding of racial discrimination at the aggregate level does not inevitably mean that the practices of individual courts are discriminatory. The U.S. Supreme Court ruled in *McClesky v. Kemp* (1987) that while the link between the victim's race and the death penalty has been well documented for the country as a whole, this does not mean that in an individual case the death sentence was given only because the victim was white. Nevertheless, civil rights advocates are concerned that the preponderance of white prosecutors and white judges and the relative rarity of black-on-white homicide raise the risks of discrimination on the basis of race.

In Columbus, Georgia, for example, prosecutorial discretion to seek the death penalty has long been held in the hands of four white men, who have exercised it most often (78 percent of the time) when victims were white. This is despite the fact that in Columbus, homicide victims are black 65 percent of the time (*Time*, April 4, 1991:69). A similar prosecutorial bias showed up in Kentucky (Keil and Vito, 1989), and studies of capital sentencing in Louisiana, New Jersey, Illinois, Mississippi, Florida, Arkansas, North Carolina, and Oklahoma

Historically in America, use of the death penalty has been biased against poor and black Americans. Almost all those executed for rape have been blacks charged with assaulting white women. Here Rainey Bethea is hanged for rape in 1936 in front of a crowd of over 20,000 spectators. Note his body dangling beneath the scaffold.

PHOTO COURTESY OF UPI/CORBIS-BETTMANN

generally confirm that the race (and gender, in Louisiana) of the victim in homicide cases is strongly related to imposition of the death penalty (Smith, 1987; Gross and Mauro, 1989; Marquart, Ekland-Olson, and Sorensen, 1993).

Four Conclusions about Use of the Death Penalty in America. The following conclusions can be drawn from research into the use of the death penalty in this country:

1. There is "overwhelming uncertainty" as to which killers will actually be executed (Berk, Boyer, and Weiss, 1993:92); when a murder occurs, the outcome in court and the eventual penalty cannot be predicted.
2. However, very few people who kill others actually end up being executed. Around 25,000 Americans were murdered in 1997, but less than 1 percent of these cases will result in the killer being executed.
3. The chances of being executed are influenced more by characteristics of the victim than by characteristics of the offender.
4. The history of the death penalty in America is a history of bias that has favored white offenders over nonwhite offenders, and the rich over the poor.

THE FUTURE OF CAPITAL PUNISHMENT

The future of capital punishment in America will be determined by a combination of three things: public opinion, court decisions, and politics. Public opinion today favors the death penalty, at least for certain crimes. A 1997 poll by the Louis Harris organization found that 75 percent of respondents "believed in" capital punishment, up from only 38 percent in 1965 (Maguire and Pastore, 1998:138). When asked, "Are you in favor of the death penalty for a person convicted of murder?" 77 percent of respondents in a 1995 Gallup poll said "yes," a significant increase from the 1950s and early 1960s, when fewer than half of those polled answered yes to the same question (see Figure 14.2). The high level of support for the death penalty in recent years reflects more conservative attitudes toward crime in general, and violent crime in particular. And it has undoubtedly been fanned by media coverage of high-profile murders. There was much publicity during the late 1970s and the 1990s about rising rates of violent crime, and highly publicized reports of serial killers and mass murderers hardly eased a worried public's fears.

To say that opinions regarding capital punishment are overwhelmingly positive in the United States ignores important differences. For example, men, white people, those under age 30, people with incomes over $30,000, and Republicans are more likely to favor the death penalty than women, nonwhite people, people over age 50, those earning less than $20,000, and Democrats (Bohm, 1991). Furthermore, when there is a choice between execution or life in prison without parole, the proportion of people favoring the death penalty tends to decline (Maguire and Pastore, 1995:181). Apparently, some people support the death penalty only because they believe there are no defensible alternatives.

A recent proposal for an alternative has sparked considerable debate but as yet little legislative support. The idea is to offer Death Row inmates an

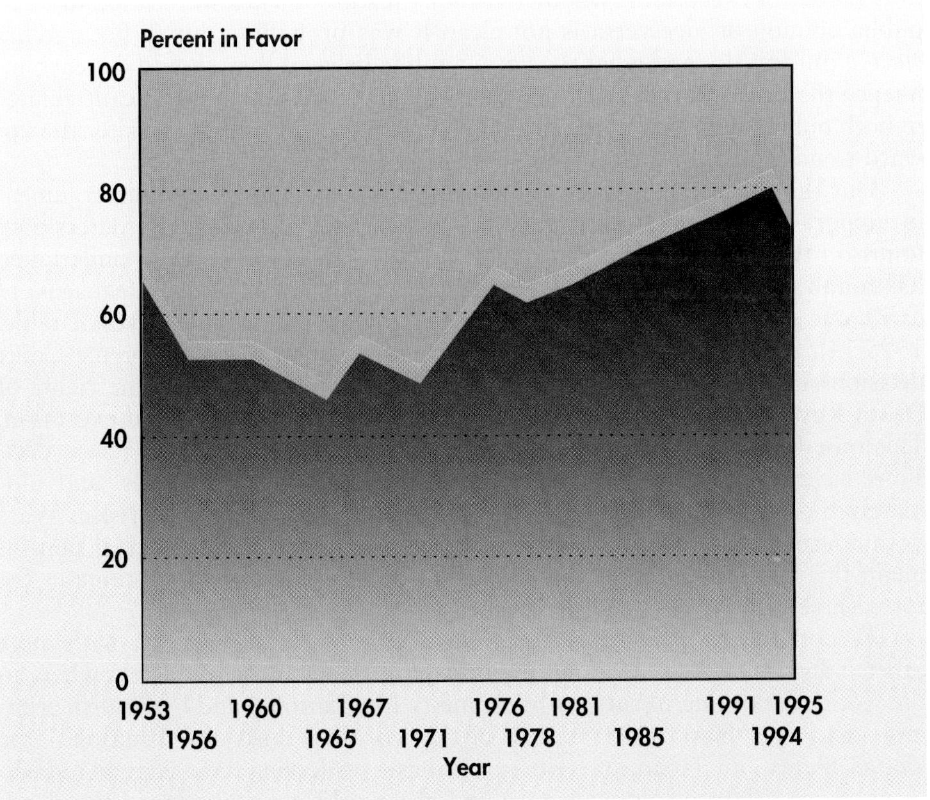

FIGURE 14.2 PUBLIC ATTITUDES TOWARD THE DEATH PENALTY, 1953–1995

The graph shows the percentage of those surveyed who answered yes to the question, "Are you in favor of the death penalty for people convicted of murder?"

Source: Kathleen Maguire and Ann L. Pastore (1998). *Sourcebook of Criminal Justice Statistics, 1997* (p. 142). Washington, D.C.: U.S. Department of Justice.

opportunity for life in exchange for donating bone marrow or a kidney so that someone else may live. At least two lives would be saved. Some transplant surgeons support the idea, but others argue that "organ donation must be a purely altruistic gift," and the proposal would be a "loophole where the Death Row inmate would be trading it, bartering an organ" (*St. Louis Post-Dispatch*, February 6, 1998, p. C3).

Other distinctions also warn against making blanket statements about how Americans favor the death penalty. For example, a study of 307 prison inmates found that while there was general support for the death penalty, this did not include their own crimes! (Stevens, 1992). There is also the possibility that attitudes favorable to the death penalty reflect emotions such as fear, anger, and frustration rather than an informed consideration of the issues. However, in one study, the commonly heard idea that a more informed public would end up opposing the death penalty received little support (Bohm, Vogel, and Maisto, 1993). In another study, when subjects were asked if they would still support the death penalty even if research proved conclusively that executions did not deter crime, a slight majority still said yes (Finckenauer, 1988:83).

The fact that many Americans support the death penalty is noted by policymakers, and most politicians—including President Clinton—also say they support capital punishment. Politicians and government officials are influenced by the opinions of voters, and through the media they in turn influence the opinions of the general public. Figure 14.1 showed that as favorable opinions regarding the death penalty waned during the 1950s and 1960s, so, too, did the number of executions; whether criminal justice officials were responding to public opinion or vice versa is not clear. It was probably a bit of both: What elected officials do, and what the voting public believes they *should* do, each influence the other. Because of this relationship, it will take a significant change in both public opinion *and* the behavior of government officials to alter the upward trend in death sentences and executions.

One thing that might bring about change is cost. A long-standing argument in support of the death penalty was that it is cheaper to execute murderers than imprison them. This has turned out to be false: "Every cost study undertaken has found that it is far more expensive, because of added legal safeguards, to carry out a death sentence than it is to jail a killer for life" (von Drehle, 1995:14). Appellate court decisions have had an impact here. Supreme Court decisions in the late 1950s and throughout the 1960s protected the rights of Death Row inmates and extended the time between conviction and execution. This raised the costs of providing services to them. However, more recent decisions have moved in the opposite direction, reducing the appeals, and ultimately the time and costs of keeping inmates on Death Row. In recent years both courts and legislators have renewed their commitment to capital punishment; this is reason enough to believe that current trends will continue in the foreseeable future.

As noted earlier, this puts the United States in stark contrast with most other industrialized countries and with capital punishment trends elsewhere in the world. According to surveys by Amnesty International and by English criminologist Roger Hood (1989), most of the world's industrialized nations—the United States and Japan are two exceptions—no longer have capital punishment. Since 1989, 21 countries around the world have abolished the death penalty for common crimes or for all crimes; among them are Namibia, Gambia, Paraguay, Hungary, Romania, Greece, Italy, Switzerland, and New Zealand. Regardless of their moral position on the death penalty, abolitionist nations have a compelling practical argument on their side: There is absolutely no good evidence that abolitionist countries—or abolitionist American states, for that matter—have experienced greater problems with violent crime because they have rejected capital punishment.

SUMMARY

Death is the ultimate punishment for crime. Capital punishment has a long past, stretching back to the earliest days of recorded history. Societies and powerful rulers have used it to rid themselves of enemies and other undesirables. Exile penalties such as banishment and transportation have also been used for the same purposes, and often with the same result: death.

The popularity of capital punishment among European nations grew during the medieval period, and by the eighteenth century it was the designated penalty for hundreds of crimes. Public executions were the rule, both in Europe and America, and these often had a carnival atmosphere. However, penal reforms led to a general decline in the use of capital punishment during the nineteenth century, and executions were moved inside prison walls. Execution as a painful, public spectacle gave way to execution as an efficient, clinical procedure carried out as inconspicuously as possible. Death by lethal injection is now the method favored in most states.

Reversing a 40-year trend, the 1980s and 1990s saw an upsurge in executions in America. A "get tough" penal policy swept the nation in the face of rising rates of violent crime; an increasingly conservative Congress and U.S. Supreme Court paved the way for more death sentences and more executions. States and the federal government expanded death penalty statutes, and the appeals process was curtailed. Inmates awaiting execution can expect to spend less time on Death Row, which is getting more and more crowded as the number of death sentences rises.

America's current embrace of capital punishment flies in the face of worldwide trends over the past few decades. Many countries have abolished the death penalty—some completely, others for all crimes but treason and certain wartime military offenses. Since few murderers are actually executed, it is difficult to claim that capital punishment stands as a moral or practical protection against killing. Further, research generally has not supported claims that capital punishment deters crime. Among the more compelling arguments against the death penalty is the claim—supported by considerable evidence—that it has been applied in an arbitrary and discriminating manner. After *Furman v. Georgia* (1972), state legislatures tried to fashion death penalty statutes that would help alleviate these problems, but in practice those criminals most at risk of being executed are black offenders who kill white victims. The U.S. Supreme Court said in *McKlesky v. Kemp* (1985) that even if there is racial bias in the imposition of the death penalty on black offenders as a whole, this does not constitute grounds for overturning a death sentence in any particular case, nor for declaring capital punishment unconstitutional. The degree of racial bias was on the whole tolerable, the Court ruled. Unless public opinion, political support, and court rulings change fairly radically, the future of capital punishment in America seems secure.

WHAT DO YOU THINK *NOW?*

- After reading this chapter, in particular the section about the execution of Thomas Battle, have your views on capital punishment changed? Explain.
- After reading about appeals, and typical conditions on Death Row, do you think reform is necessary? Do you agree with the U.S. Supreme Courts attempts to curb appeals? If so, why?

KEY TERMS AND CASES

banishment
transportation
capital punishment
public execution
brutalization theory
Furman v. Georgia
Gregg v. Georgia
Coker v. Georgia
capital offense
Thompson v. Oklahoma
Stanford v. Kentucky
premeditation
aggravating circumstance
Arave v. Creech
death-qualified jury
Witherspoon v. Illinois
Wainwright v. Witt
Lockhart v. McCree
Harris v. Alabama
writ of *habeas corpus*
McClesky v. Zant
Anti-Terrorism and Effective Death Penalty Act

ACTIVE LEARNING CHALLENGES

1. Debate this statement: Executions should be public.
2. Break into groups and identify as many arguments as you can for and against capital punishment. Assign the arguments to members of the group, then search for evidence in support of each argument and report your findings to the class.
3. Find out whether your state has a Death Row; if so, see whether it is possible to communicate with inmates and prison officers to learn more of life on Death Row.
4. Racial bias in the imposition of the death penalty has a long history in America. What steps do you think would put an end to it once and for all?
5. Divide the class into two groups: those who support the death penalty and those who oppose it. Have each group discuss why members take the position they do, and then share their arguments with the entire class. At the end of the session see if opinions have changed at all, and how.

INTERNET CHALLENGES

The Web pages mentioned here can all be accessed through the Web site for this textbook at **http://www.prenhall.com/barlow/**.

1. Many Web sites contain information, discussion, and court cases dealing with the death penalty. A good place to start for a worldwide perspective is Amnesty International's home page. Find out the latest death penalty statistics from around the world; what is Amnesty International doing to promote its position on capital punishment?
2. For U.S. Supreme Court cases dealing with the death penalty, including full transcripts, visit the USSC+ home page and find *Furman v. Georgia* (1972) as a start, then check out more recent rulings. (Simply look for "death penalty" in the list of key words cited with each case for the year you are searching; then click on the appropriate format for viewing the case.) What sorts of issues bring appeals to the Court?
3. The Critical Criminology section of the American Society of Criminology is opposed to the death penalty and has links to interesting death penalty sites. See what you can find out about cases where the wrong person has been—or would have been—executed. What do these cases have in common?

4. There are many commentaries for and against the death penalty on the World Wide Web. One of the best ways to access these is to type in "death penalty" in Yahoo, Excite, or other search engines. This will connect you to hundreds of sites on the subject. Look for sites where the death penalty is supported. What are some of the major arguments used in favor of the death penalty? How do these compare with your views?

CHAPTER 15

The History and Use of Prisons

LEARNING OBJECTIVES

- Describe the origins of imprisonment and the significant penal reforms that shaped modern prisons.
- Understand the nature and influence of the reformatory movement of the late nineteenth and early 20th centuries.
- Explain what is meant by the rehabilitative ideal.
- Describe the rise, decline, and rebirth of prison labor over the last 100 years.
- Explain the different levels of security in prisons today, and understand why warehousing has replaced rehabilitation in maximum-security prisons.
- Understand the origins of community corrections and why they have grown in popularity as an alternative to prison.
- Understand the development of privatization and its pros and cons.
- Explain how criminal justice policies have driven up prison populations.

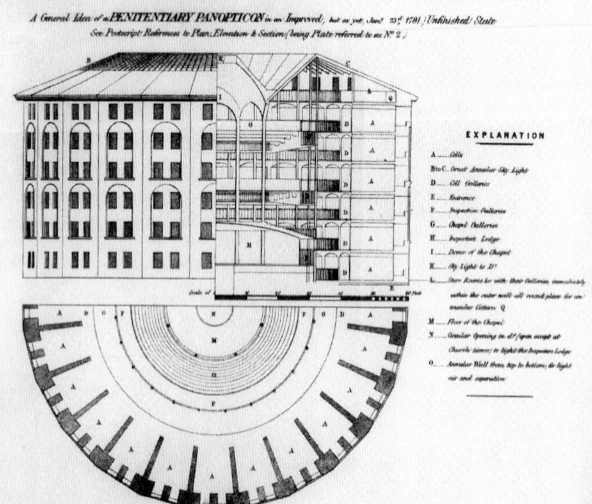

Eighteenth century English philosopher Jeremy Bentham introduced the Panopticon Prison as a new design that allowed no communication between prisoners, who could be observed at all times by the guards located in the hub of the wheel-like tiered structure. A living example is Joliet Correctional Center in Illinois.

Photo courtesy of AP Photos; drawing courtesy of The Bodleian Library

No one has ever come out of prison a better man.

JACK HENRY ABBOTT, *IN THE BELLY OF THE BEAST* (1981)

Under our new laws, all inmates must work, get a basic education, and get treatment. We're not going to let them sit idly in their cells. They're going to use their time working and developing job skills.

MISSOURI GOVERNOR MEL CARNAHAN, STATE OF THE STATE ADDRESS, 1996

When Dr. Charles Lambie joined the staff of Seaview Penitentiary in 1930, he was the only psychologist in the state working full-time for the correctional system. The idea that even hardened criminals could be rehabilitated through a combination of classification, treatment, education, and work was beginning to take hold around the country, and civilian experts such as Lambie were among the first to bring behavioral science into maximum-security prisons.

Lambie soon found that building relationships with the custodial staff was not easy. The traditional emphasis in corrections was on custody and control, and even though the idea of rehabilitation had been around for 60 years, there was tremendous resistance to it. Lambie spent much of his first five years at Seaview helping the warden and custodial staff see the benefits of tailoring treatment to the needs of individual inmates. Security need not be sacrificed, he convinced them, and might actually be improved.

Thirty-five years later, Lambie was ready to retire. By 1965, all sorts of civilians were working in prisons, and even the most secure facilities had a staff of counselors, therapists, teachers, and doctors working for the benefit of inmates. However, Lambie could sense that attitudes were once again changing. Crime rates were on the rise, and in Lambie's view politicians were looking for something or someone to blame. To make matters worse, large percentages of ex-inmates were being returned to prison for new crimes. The easy explanation: Rehabilitation was not working. Lambie could see the writing on the wall. It was a good time to retire.

Lambie's professional life spanned some of the most important developments in the modern use of prisons as punishment. However, prison history goes back much further, although by no means as far as capital punishment. In this chapter we explore the history of imprisonment as a form of criminal punishment. Our objective will be to understand why and how prisons came into existence, and to understand the various forms they have taken. We will investigate the important developments in penal policy that shaped prisons in the 20th century and will suggest what prisons and jails will look like in the 21st century. In Chapter 16 we take an in-depth look at what life is like inside correctional institutions today.

? WHAT DO YOU THINK?

- Is rehabilitation currently a major goal of prisons? Do all prisons even have the same goals?
- Many maximum-security prisons currently "warehouse" felony offenders with little concern about rehabilitation. Is a situation like this dangerous for inmates? Staff? Society?
- Prison populations have been changing over the past thirty years. What do you think are some of the most significant changes?

THE DEVELOPMENT OF THE PRISON

Although prisons are used extensively today, ancient societies and even medieval Europe rarely used incarceration as a way of punishing their criminals. Most offenders were fined, beaten, publicly shamed, banished, or executed. Some people were confined or locked up, but not as a punishment in itself. Rather, physical custody served three other purposes: (1) as a means of detaining people until they could be tried; (2) as a way of dealing with offenders who had not paid their fines; or (3) as a method of holding offenders who were to be punished in some other way—for example, by torture, banishment, or execution; the offender was placed in a dungeon or other secure place to receive punishment, but not *as* punishment.

EARLY PRISONS AND THE USE OF TORTURE

Prisons first emerged with the growth of cities and the development of a suitable construction technology (Durkheim, 1900). One of the earliest-known prisons was built by the Romans around 64 B.C. The Mamertine Prison was a vast system of dungeons attached to the main sewer of Rome (Johnstone, 1973:5). Most early prisons were inside or attached to royal palaces, fortresses, or temples, and the stone walls and towers that surrounded them.

The ancient Tower of London is a good example. Today it houses the crown jewels of English royalty and is a major tourist attraction. For over 900 years, however, one of its uses was as a prison. Originally built in 1078 as a strategic fortress and royal residence for William the Conqueror, the tower soon housed traitors, religious heretics, and members of the nobility who had fallen out of favor. Many prisoners were brought to the tower by boat under cover of darkness and admitted through the infamous "Traitor's Gate" directly from the River Thames. Many formerly powerful people were beheaded on Tower Hill right outside the fortress, and others were tortured or murdered inside. One of the most infamous killings was of two young princes, Edward IV and his younger brother, who were murdered in the tower in 1483. It was widely believed—but never proven—that their murderer was an ambitious uncle who later became King Richard III. The great explorer Sir Walter Raleigh was imprisoned in the tower for thirteen years, until his execution in 1618.

Little is known about the functioning of early prisons, except that they soon gained reputations for their horrors: Prisoners lived with filth and vermin, they were fed barely enough to keep them alive, and they were often restrained by shackles and iron collars. Dungeons and prisons were suited to the growing use of physical torture in medieval Europe. Untold numbers of people, including members of the nobility and even priests, such as the Jesuit Edmund Campion, were tortured in an effort to get them to confess to treason or heresy.

The Torture of Prisoners, Past and Present. Campion was put on the rack three times before being hanged, drawn, and quartered in 1581. The rack stretched its victims; another torture device, the "scavenger's daughter," rolled them up into a ball:

> On the rack the prisoner seemed in danger of having his fingers torn from his hands, the toes from his feet, the hands from the arms, the feet from the legs, the forearms from the upper arms, the legs from the trunk. Every ligament was strained, every joint loosened in its socket; and if the sufferer remained obstinate when released, he was brought back to undergo the same cruelties with the added horror of past experience and with a diminished fortitude and physical power. In the Scavenger's Daughter, on the other hand, the pain was caused by an ingenious process of compression. The legs were forced back to the thighs, the thighs were pressed onto the belly, and the whole body was placed within two iron bands which the torturers drew together with all their strength until the miserable human being lost all form but that of a globe. Blood was forced out of the tips of the fingers and toes, the nostrils and mouth; and the ribs and breastbone were commonly broken by the pressure. (Pike, 1968:87–88)

Although torture has been outlawed in America and most of Europe for over 150 years, cruel and vicious forms of physical abuse occur from time to time inside prisons. Beatings and floggings administered as discipline are the most widespread form of abuse, but reports occasionally surface of more extreme forms of torture. When criminologist Tom Murton was appointed head of the Arkansas prison system in the late 1960s, he discovered that physical torture was commonplace in that system (Murton and Hyams, 1969). In the Tucker prison farm, for example, officers used the so-called Tucker telephone to punish inmates. Electrical wires from the "telephone" were attached to the feet and genitals of inmates, who were then "rung up" with an extremely painful electrical charge.

There are other forms of punishment in today's prisons that some call torture. Here is how one inmate describes life in the "Hole"—a special unit of solitary confinement cells separated from the main cell blocks—at Graterford Penitentiary in Pennsylvania. Is it torture, or is it merely discipline?

> The Hole represents a penal institution's harshest form of legalized punishment short of the death penalty. . . . Whenever possible, the cells in solitary were kept either shivering cold in winter or stifling hot in the summer. . . . [M]eals were often served cold and in the most cruel manner. And, while corporal punishment was prohibited, "goon squads" were formed by the guards to administer unofficial physical punishment. These goon squads were often comprised of guards who were not assigned to the general population, so inmates could not recognize them. They never wore name tags and their activities were never reported, at least not by the staff. (Hassine, 1996:100–101)

We shall examine prison discipline in more detail in Chapter 16. Suffice it to say that while in general modern prisons and prison discipline are genteel in comparison with that of the sixteenth century, the prison environment and the emphasis on control invite abuses. Torture may be too strong a word, but what else would you call the Tucker telephone?

WORKHOUSES, HOUSES OF CORRECTION, AND GAOLS

workhouse A dwelling where poor and homeless people lived and worked under strict supervision.

The sixteenth century produced two institutions of incarceration that were forerunners of the modern prison. They grew in popularity until the eighteenth century. The **workhouse** was a place where a dozen or more people lived and worked under guard and supervision. It was established during the mid-sixteenth century as a humanitarian strategy to deal with the growing number of poor people. At that time, the church was the traditional relief agency, and its resources were stretched to the limit. The workhouse was designed to address two things: (1) a practical problem—the poor needed food and shelter, and (2) a prevalent belief—that poverty is caused by idleness. Beggars, vagrants, and the homeless poor were given a place to live under a regimen of hard work and strict discipline. When there was no work, some institutions even introduced treadmills to keep the residents busy.

house of correction A residential penal institution emphasizing hard work under strict discipline.

The **house of correction** emerged during the same period to serve the many criminals whose offenses were not serious enough for the gallows, banishment, or transportation. The house of correction was designed as a residential penal institution, but the regimen was identical to that of the workhouse: hard work under strict discipline. Neither place was designed to teach specific work skills; rather, inmates were expected to learn the value and habits of work. As time passed, the workhouse and house of correction became virtually indistinguishable; vagrants, the poor, beggars, prostitutes, and petty criminals were mixed in together.

gaol (jail) A secure lockup for holding prisoners awaiting trial.

The **gaol**, or **jail**, also appeared around this time in towns and villages throughout England. Gaols were primarily designed to house criminal suspects while they awaited trial. Conditions in the larger gaols were dreadful, and during the eighteenth century diseases such as typhus (called "gaol fever") spread

Like workhouses for adults, the "house of refuge" was an attempt to instill the virtues of hard work and discipline into juvenile delinquents. Unfortunately, they became centers of exploitation and misery. Some children were sent there simply for having poor or insane parents who could not care for them; all worked long hours for no pay and pitifully small meals.

ILLUSTRATION COURTESY OF STOCK MONTAGE

Box 15.1

CAREERS IN CRIMINAL JUSTICE
DETENTION DEPUTY, OR JAILER

Most jails are run by the sheriff's department, whose staff maintain security and sometimes provide specialized services as well. The work is potentially dangerous, requires physical strength and endurance, may involve the use of firearms or other weapons, and is often carried out in a confined area with limited access to freedom. Here are the salary, qualifications, duties, and conditions of employment of a detention deputy, or jailer, as advertised by the Polk County, Florida, Sheriff's Department in July 1998.

Salary: $25,524 (entry level, after training)

Qualifications: High school graduate or GED; previous experience in corrections, security, or social work fields preferred.

Duties: The Detention Deputy monitors, controls, and accounts for incarcerated inmates and civilian visitors; provides jail security; controls and subdues inmates; executes emergency procedures during escape attempts or medical situations; conducts searches of cells and inmates; provides housing management by moving inmates in and out of cells; supervises inmates during outdoor recreation periods; resolves inmate disputes; maintains responsibility and integrity for collection of inmate property, mail, and money; testifies in court; operates transport vehicles; and monitors visitors. The Detention Deputy may be rotated into specialty areas such as booking, Disciplinary Review Board, farm supervisor, and trusty supervisor.

Conditions of Employment: Include valid Florida driver's license and satisfactory completion of training leading to Basic Recruit Certificate of Corrections Compliance, or comparable out-of-state training.

through the inmate population and into the surrounding town (Allen and Simonsen, 1995:27). Sheriffs who controlled the gaols apparently cared little about the conditions within them, and some even found ways to make money off inmates—for example, through bribes for better treatment or early release, or by allowing prostitution to flourish.

The Penal Reforms of Beccaria, Bentham, and Howard

It was not until the end of the eighteenth century that imprisonment began to take shape as the cornerstone of modern penal systems. "Doing time" *as punishment for crime* was the key element in eighteenth-century penal reform. Two prominent philosophers in Italy and England, Cesare Beccaria (1738–1794) and Jeremy Bentham (1748–1832), wrote important works that tried to address the problem of crime in a way that ensured the best benefits for society while treating criminals humanely. Torture was condemned, but so, too, were the many excesses of power associated with eighteenth-century justice. These included the buying and selling of judgeships, the many loopholes in the laws that allowed the rich and powerful to escape justice, and the freedom enjoyed by courts when sentencing offenders. Penal reformers such as Bentham and Beccaria were searching for a "more finely tuned justice" (Foucault, 1977:78).

As we saw in Chapter 14, the penal philosophy of Beccaria and Bentham was based on two main ideas: (1) **proportionality**, or making the punishment fit the crime, and (2) **utilitarianism**, a philosophy based on the greatest happiness

proportionality The severity of punishment matches the severity of the crime.

utilitarianism A philosophy founded on the principle of the greatest happiness of the greatest number.

of the greatest number. Both authors believed that punishment should and could be designed to deter crime so that society as a whole would benefit.

In his influential book *Essay on Crimes and Punishment*, Beccaria proposed that imprisonment be used more widely as the penalty for serious crimes. He also proposed that life imprisonment replace the death penalty. An execution, he asserted, could not be undone; there was therefore no way to rectify a mistake. Beccaria was not content merely to advocate greater use of prisons; he also proposed changes in the way prisons worked. There should be better physical quarters, he said, and attempts should be made to separate and classify prisoners by age, sex, and degree of criminality.

Bentham's important contributions to penal reform came in the development of more humane laws, including the abolition of torture, and in his attempts to design and implement punishments that would outweigh the expected gains from crime. Bentham was particularly keen to rid England of criminal laws and policies that favored the ruling classes. A just penal system would treat offenders who committed similar crimes in the same way, regardless of their station in life.

Panopticon Plan A prison designed by eighteenth-century philosopher Jeremy Bentham.

Bentham's Panopticon Plan. In his later years Bentham even designed an entire prison, which he called the **Panopticon Plan**. The Panopticon consisted basically of tiers of cells arranged along the rim of a larger circular structure. Guards would be housed in a central tower like the hub of a wheel. This would permit them to observe every cell. The cells, in contrast, would be separated from each other by walls; only the front of each cell is open to observation. The prisoner "is seen, but he does not see; he is the object of information, never a subject in communication. . . . [A]nd this invisibility is a guarantee of order . . ., there is no danger of a plot, an attempt at collective escape, the planning of new crimes for the future. . . ." (Foucault, 1977:200).

Besides the innovative architecture, Bentham included plans for heating, care of prisoners, health and educational services, and food and clothing as well. Despite extensive public debate and his use of the family fortune to promote the idea, Bentham found few supporters for his prison in England. However, there are living examples in the United States, one at Joliet, Illinois, and another in Pittsburgh, Pennsylvania.

John Howard's Four Principles. Joining Beccaria and Bentham in pressing for reform of the penal system in England was John Howard (1726–1790). Howard was appointed sheriff of Bedfordshire in 1773, a position that gave him firsthand exposure to the jails and prisons of England. Appalled by the filth, overcrowding, and other inhumane conditions he found, he proposed a variety of reforms in *The State of Prisons in England and Wales*, published in 1777. Howard proposed four principles for prison reform:

1. Prisons should be secure and sanitary structures.
2. They should be systematically inspected.
3. Prisoner fees should be abolished.
4. There should be an emphasis on reforming prisoners.

Parliament responded by enacting the Penitentiary Act of 1799, which incorporated Howard's four principles. The plan was to erect one or two national prisons, but the necessary funds were never provided.

Hulks: The Floating Prison. At about the same time that John Howard was proposing his prison reforms, the pains of social change were coming to a head in England. Industrialization and unprecedented population growth were putting the nation's major cities under great stress, and the ranks of the unemployed and homeless continued to swell. Crime rates soared, and even though the newly discovered territory of Australia provided new opportunities for transportation of convicts, the growing demand proved too much for existing prison facilities. Enter the **hulks**.

hulks Abandoned ships converted into prisons in the late 1700s.

Hulks were dilapidated or abandoned ships anchored in rivers and harbors around the British Isles. Criminal justice authorities saw a temporary way out of their problems by turning these ships into jails and prisons. Far from temporary, the hulks remained in use until midway through the nineteenth century.

The hulks were appalling places, and conditions there helped stimulate the reforms of Bentham and Howard. Besides being overcrowded, dirty, and lacking proper sanitation, those in charge of the hulks made no effort to separate serious from minor offenders, the young from the old, or men from women. Beatings and rapes were commonplace. Far from being a solution to the problem of overcrowding, hulks created new misery amid more overcrowding. The only good thing to say about the hulks is that they helped spur reforms.

DEVELOPMENT OF PRISONS IN THE UNITED STATES

While all this was going on in England, America was struggling with penal reform as well. A landmark event was the opening of the Walnut Street Jail in Philadelphia, usually identified as America's first state prison and its first penitentiary. Opened in 1773, the jail received its first state prisoner in 1790.

THE PENNSYLVANIA AND AUBURN PENITENTIARY SYSTEMS

This historic occasion rewarded the hard work and dedication of a group of Pennsylvania citizens, many of them Quakers. These citizens condemned the cruelty and degradation of existing punishments and felt that an alternative could be devised that was both humane and reformative. The group embraced the Quaker view that criminals should be made to contemplate the evil of their ways in solitary confinement day and night. Solitude would force the inmate to turn inward, contemplate his wrongdoing, and become repentant. Work, necessary for regeneration of the spirit, would be performed alone in the prisoner's cell.

Built inside the existing jail structure, the new penitentiary was an awesome place. Crude efforts were made to segregate women; capital offenders; and debtors, vagrants, and other petty criminals. The inmates were housed individually in tiny whitewashed cells measuring six feet wide, eight feet long, and nine feet high. A small grated window could be seen high up on the outside wall, and the toilet amenities consisted of a lead pipe in the corner of each cell. The convicts were preached to on a regular basis but were denied any form of recreation. For their part, the guards were forbidden to use chains, irons, weapons, or canes.

Ten other states soon constructed prisons along the lines of Philadelphia's Walnut Street Jail. Although particular procedures varied somewhat from state to state—in Massachusetts, for example, the guards were issued guns, bayonets, and cutlasses—the basic architectural design was the same, as was the emphasis on solitary confinement. This approach became known as the **Pennsylvania system**. Eventually, overcrowding in most of these early prisons forced administrators to give up the idea of solitary confinement for every inmate. Instead, solitary confinement was used more and more for those who had violated prison rules.

Pennsylvania system A Quaker-influenced system of prison architecture and control, emphasizing solitary confinement and penitence.

Support for a penitentiary system embodying solitary confinement was reaffirmed in the 1820s, when the Pennsylvania legislature authorized two new prisons—Western Penitentiary in Pittsburgh and Eastern Penitentiary in Philadelphia. The structures were monolithic, with small cells ranging along the outside walls. The solitude was almost total. Charles Dickens, on visiting Eastern Penitentiary, wrote of the typical inmate: "He sees the prison officer, but with that exception he never looks upon a human countenance or hears a human voice. He is a man buried alive; to be dug out in the slow round of years; and in the meantime dead to everything but torturing anxieties and horrible despair." (Goldfarb and Singer, 1973:26).

Auburn system A system of prison architecture and control, emphasizing strict regimentation of all movement, silent work in small groups, and one-person cells.

The Auburn System. The Pennsylvania system was tried and soon abandoned in New Jersey and Rhode Island. These states turned instead to what is known as the **Auburn system** after Auburn Prison in New York. In that prison, opened in 1817 but enlarged and modified by 1823, inmates were locked in separate cells at night but worked together in small groups during the day and took meals together—though in strict silence. Complete silence was maintained both day and night, and all movements were strictly regimented. The prison contained tiered blocks of tiny cells with narrow galleries encircling them. All was surrounded by an outside wall of stone over two-and-a-half feet thick. Almost all early American prisons were fashioned after Auburn. In contrast, many European and South American countries adopted the Pennsylvania system.

The Penal Agenda of the New Prisons. During this period of penal reform, the underlying purpose of imprisonment had shifted from prison as a place *for* punishment to prison *as* punishment. Imprisonment removes offenders from society, isolating them from the world outside. This is the punishment. Yet reformers of the eighteenth and early ninteenth centuries believed that prisons should also be places of *correction*: Prisoners should be made into better people by the experience. Strict discipline and hard work became the tools of correction in most prisons.

In his influential book *Discipline and Punish: The Birth of the Prison*, the late French philosopher Michel Foucault (1977:244–255) adds a third, more hidden penal agenda for prisons: control over the quality and content of detention, including its duration. Prison administrators recognized early on that by controlling how prison sentences were actually carried out, they controlled the experience of punishment for each inmate. Most important, that control enabled them to link the prison experience not only to the crime an inmate had committed, but also to how well the prisoner responded to the experience itself. In other words, the actual punishment for crime is determined not only by statutes and the judges who apply them, but also by those in charge of prisons and the supervisors of individual cell blocks within them. Punishment can be truly individualized—shaped not only by the crime a person commits, but by the way a person responds to the process of being punished.

This situation gave prisons an autonomy or independence in the penal process that was probably not intended by most early reformers. Nor does it appear to have been anticipated by lawmakers and judges, who had the legal responsibility for assessing penalties. But as imprisonment emerged as the principal method of punishing criminals, correctional processes within the prison experience received increasing attention.

THE REFORMATORY MOVEMENT

reformatory movement A late nineteenth-century prison movement emphasizing inmate reform rather than suffering, and centered on the indeterminate sentence and classification of inmates.

The **reformatory movement** was an outgrowth of this trend. From around 1870 to the early 20th century, this movement dominated American corrections. The movement's principles were outlined at the first meeting of the American Prison Congress in 1870. Two ideas were most important: (1) that *reform of the inmate* rather than suffering should be the cornerstone of penal practice; and (2) that *indeterminate sentences* should be adopted to enable authorities to release early, or keep longer, those inmates who had succeeded, or failed, in demonstrating rehabilitation. An indeterminate sentence does not specify exactly when the punishment will end.

The Prison Congress proposal included a detailed classification system. Inmates were to be put into three classes, depending on their achievements and conduct: First Grade, meaning that they had earned sufficient "marks" to make them eligible for parole; Second Grade, mostly for new entrants who had not yet shown their true colors; and Third Grade, for those whose disobedience and lack of improvement suggested the need for sterner measures.

The fundamental new idea behind the reformatory movement was that the newly emerging behavioral sciences and continuing education could be applied to the prison experience. In addition, by making careful observations of inmate progress, corrections officials could make continued adjustments in their treatment.

The Elmira Reformatory. The first prison organized to apply these principles was the Elmira Reformatory in New York, opened in 1876. Elmira was used primarily for young first offenders, 16 to 30 years old. Its superintendent was Zebulon Brockway, a confident and determined administrator who by his own admission left no stone unturned trying to prove the success of this new penology (Brockway, [1912] 1969). His approach reflected the mix of evangelism—Brockway was a born-again Christian—and temperance, which dominated late nineteenth-century social reform in America (Jenkins, 1984). Though more impressionistic than scientific, early results appeared encouraging, and this led other states to follow suit. By 1913 some eighteen state reformatories had been established around the country.

Elmira was certainly different from the traditional prison. Some called it a "hospital" or "college on the hill" (Johnson, 1987:41). Although it was mostly styled after the Auburn system, important modifications had been made. These included extensive natural and artificial light; clean and distinctive uniforms reflecting the grades of inmates; a diet designed to promote physical fitness; a gymnasium and facilities for outside recreation; training in crafts and trades; education to the high school level and some college courses; a well-stocked library; periodic entertainment such as theater presentations; religious opportunities; a prison newspaper; and periodic counseling. Treatment was individualized, and prisoners who did well might be released early.

The Failure of the Reformatory Movement. By the 1900s the reformatory movement was on the decline. It failed for a number of reasons:

- Lack of high-quality leadership and staff, especially in the key area of education
- Continued acceptance, despite all the rhetoric, of the idea that imprisonment should be a punishing experience
- Lack of understanding that reformation and architecture might somehow be related—the reformatories were by and large forbidding stone fortresses with few comforts, little light, and nothing to reinforce the lessons reformers were trying to impart
- Overcrowding, which led to a breakdown in classification, grading of behavior, and early attempts at behavior modification
- An overemphasis on the custodial functions of prison by administrators—reform took a distant second place to control
- Perhaps most important, a lack of official commitment to the movement in the form of supporting policy and resources. Although many states built reformatories and adopted indeterminate sentencing, legislators and high-level criminal justice officials often paid little more than lip service to the ideas behind the movement.

Brockway himself may have contributed to the movement's decline. In 1894, the New York State Board of Charities heard testimony from some of Brockway's staff and inmates that showed a pattern of "cruel, brutal, excessive

Zebulon Brockway (left), shown above the prison at which he was superintendent, Elmira Reformatory. As the prison's name suggests, the focus was on reforming criminals rather than punishing them through suffering. However, prisoner testimony revealed that Brockway himself used harsh punishment of those who did not obey him.

PHOTOS COURTESY OF CULVER PICTURES

and unusual punishment of the inmates." One researcher concluded later that "the orderly demeanor of the inmates observed by visitors and attributed to the effectiveness of the Elmira system was largely a result of fear" (Pisciotta, 1983:622–623). An inmate who had failed to complete a work assignment testified to the following events:

> I knew I was in for a beating and as I knew the terrible treatment received by others, I had a terror of what was coming. I refused to leave my cell. They stuck into the cell an iron rod with a two-foot hook on the end, heated red hot, and poked me with it. I tried to defend myself with the bed, but my clothing took fire, and the iron burned my breast. My breast is deeply scarred today from the burn. They also had a shortened hot poker, which burned my hands. I have those scars too. I finally succumbed, was handcuffed and taken to the bathroom. I asked

> Brockway if I had not been punished enough. He laughed at me and said, "Oh yes, we have just fixed you up a little though"; with that a hook was fastened to my shackles, and I was hoisted off the floor. I got half a dozen blows with the paddle right across the kidneys. The pain was so agonizing that I fainted. They revived me, and when I begged for mercy, Brockway struck me on the head with a strap, knocked me insensible. The next thing I knew I was lying in a cot in the dungeon, shackled to an iron bar. . . . I stayed in the dungeon that night and the next day shackled, and received only bread and water. The next day I was again hoisted and beaten, returned to the dungeon, and after one day's rest, beaten again. Then I was put in the cell in Murderer's Row, where I remained for twenty-one days on bread and water. (Pisciotta, 1983:621)

Such stories not only damaged the credibility of Brockway's personal claims of humane treatment of his inmates, but they undermined the entire reformatory movement as well since he was its acknowledged leader.

PRISONS: THE LAST 100 YEARS

By the dawn of the 20th century, prisons in America were a mixture of penitentiaries and reformatories. In both systems, the key words were *discipline* and *control*. Prisons were—and still are—custodial institutions housing people who are not voluntary residents. To the staff who run them, and the politicians who fund them, maintaining an orderly, peaceful prison has always been the primary custodial challenge (Johnson, 1987:35). It is against this background that reforms must be understood.

It has been said that compared with the previous century, little change in penal systems occurred in the first nine decades of the 20th century (Hawkins and Alpert, 1989:53). Nevertheless, five important developments involved (1) use of prison labor, (2) growth of inmate classification and the rise of minimum- and medium-security prisons, (3) development of community corrections, (4) emergence of "warehousing" and the supermaximum-security prison, and (5) privatization of corrections. Let us explore each of these developments before turning, finally, to the population of prisons and jails today.

THE RISE, DECLINE, AND REBIRTH OF PRISON LABOR

During the latter half of the nineteenth century, growing crime rates, rising prison populations, and escalating costs were problems that some experts believed could be solved by importing the ideals and practices of the factory system. Get prisons involved in industrial production, and prisons might even pay for themselves. The private sector also saw benefits: To the industrial entrepreneur, the unique advantage of prisons was the large supply of cheap labor housed in one place. A new source of profits could be found by turning prisons into factories. However, this would also mean significant changes to the way prisons were run, including the end of the silence rule, hallmark of the penitentiary. Communication among inmate workers would be essential in a factory environment.

The Industrial Prison. Turning prisons into factories meant that goods could be produced for consumption within the prison or for sale elsewhere. Prison officials were quick to seize on this new opportunity, and many states turned their new facilities into **industrial prisons** where all manner of goods were produced. Some prisons even looked like large factories with high walls

industrial prison A prison that functioned largely as a factory, producing goods for consumption and for sale.

around them; in many respects the only difference with other factories was that the workers could not leave.

Penal officials and factory owners believed that the discipline learned in prisons would work well in the factory, and the work rules and hierarchy of authority experienced in the factory would work well in prison (Scull, 1977; Melossi and Pavarini, 1981) For both the state and the capitalist, the key word was *profits*: the larger the pool of confined and disciplined workers, the more money that could be made. It didn't matter where they came from. Anxious to take advantage of these opportunities, authorities built large industrial prisons at San Quentin, California; Sing Sing, New York; and Stateville, Illinois.

The Lease and Contract Systems Come under Fire. Despite the promise of the industrial prison, problems surrounding prison labor kept surfacing. This probably surprised no one, because the history of prison labor had rarely been calm. Even the early houses of correction had experienced problems—often there was not enough work, and when there was, local businesses complained of unfair competition.

By the late 1800s, the emerging labor union movement brought tremendous pressure to bear on states to end the common lease and contract systems of convict labor (Allen and Simonsen, 1995:55). Under the **lease system**, prisoners were leased to private contractors who used them as cheap labor for whatever jobs they wished; under the **contract system**, prisons provided inmates to complete particular jobs or contracts. These often involved working on roads, railroads, canals, or mines. In either case, the cheap prison labor was condemned as unfair competition by unions seeking job security, better pay, and improved working conditions for their members.

lease system The leasing of prisoners to private contractors.

contract system Using prisoners to complete work contracts for outside employers.

The lease and contract systems were also criticized for the many abuses that flourished. In the South, especially, prisoners were "brutally and callously exploited for their labor" (Keve, 1991:20). After the Civil War, the vast majority of southern convicts were black, and they were put to work in the plantations at cotton-picking or cane-cutting time. A New Orleans newspaperman named George Washington Cable brought many abuses to light. Cable focused on the convict lease system across twelve southern states, documenting how prisoners gave up their health and their lives to convict labor, while the owners and operators made a handsome profit. There were virtually no standards of care, and black prisoners once again found themselves living as slaves.

Opposition to Prison Industries and the Rise of State-Use Systems

Opposition to prison industries reached its height during the Great Depression, from 1929 to 1940. With millions of American workers unemployed, the very idea that prisoners were working—and in some cases getting paid for it—made many people angry. Thirty-seven states passed laws prohibiting the sale of prison products on the open market, and in 1940, Congress completely prohibited all interstate shipment of prison products. The industrial prison was essentially dead, and the only productive work being performed in most prisons was labor related to running the prison system itself or other state agencies. As two examples, vehicle license plates in many states were manufactured through prison industries, as were the metal desks and chairs used in state offices.

state-use system Prison industries supply goods for use by state agencies.

This type of prison labor is known as the **state-use system**, and it is still around today. Perhaps the best-known state-use system is actually run by the federal government through a government-owned corporation called Federal Prison Industries, Inc., also known as UNICOR. Various states have created similar corporations: CORCRAFT in New York State, for example, and PRIDE,

Inc., in Florida. PRIDE was launched in 1981 with a $200,000 donation from Florida businesses, and by 1985 it managed over 22 types of prison industries in Florida, including an optical lab, print shops, metal fabrication, and agricultural industries (Mullen, Chabotar, and Carrow, 1985:22). These organizations have purportedly saved state and federal governments millions of dollars. In addition, new civilian employment opportunities have resulted, particularly in the manufacturing of raw materials and in transportation of products to and from prisons.

JOINT VENTURES: A NEW ERA IN PRISON INDUSTRIES?

During the late 1970s, Congress attempted to restore private involvement in prison industries while maintaining some protection for the external labor market. It lifted the ban on interstate transportation and sale of prison-made goods and brought inmate pay into line with the local labor market. It also specified that proposed joint ventures between prisons and the private sector should not have a adverse impact on those local markets. To help achieve these protections, the Private Sector/Prison Industry Enhancement Certification Program authorized joint ventures, provided that:

- Inmates working in private-sector prison industries are paid at a rate not less than the rate paid for work of a similar nature in the locality in which the work takes place.
- Local unions are consulted prior to the initiation of a project.
- The employment of inmates does not result in the displacement of employed workers outside the prison, does not occur in occupations in which there is a surplus of labor in the locality, and does not impair existing contracts for services.

The appeal of joint ventures involving prison industries and the private sector can be summarized as follows (Sexton, 1995):

1. Private companies are attracted because prisons can provide a readily available and dependable source of entry-level labor that is a cost-effective alternative to workforces in the Third World.
2. The retention of jobs in the United States—some in prison, but others among civilians in a company's other plants and support operations—improves the marketability of the products produced by the venture, and helps other workers accept the idea of prison-based labor.
3. Correctional administrators like the fact that joint ventures can provide meaningful, productive employment that gives inmates a purpose to their daily routine and helps reduce idleness.
4. Joint ventures result in direct benefits to society in the form of taxes, victim compensation, family support payments, and room and board fees that are deducted from inmates' wages. For example, from 1979 to 1992, the wages paid to inmates through joint ventures totaled over $28 million. However, during that time the following deductions were made from inmate wages:

   - $5,068,909 to offset the cost of their incarceration
   - $3,243,011 in federal and state taxes
   - $1,713,043 in victim compensation
   - $1,862,867 toward the support of their families

5. The job training and experience gained by inmates and the company's opportunity to assess their performance and job habits open the way to an inmate's postrelease employment with the company. For example, of

> 300 inmates hired by TWA at the Ventura Training School for Youthful Offenders in California, 55 continued their employment at TWA's Los Angeles reservation center after their release from prison.

Since the late 1980s, many joint ventures have sprung up around the country, and all kinds of correctional facilities are involved, from the youth training school in California mentioned previously to a women's prison in Arizona and a maximum-security men's facility in Connecticut. In some cases, the workers are employed, supervised, and trained by the prison; in others they are employed, supervised, and trained by the private company; in yet others they are employed and trained by the prison, but supervised by the company. Because of the flexibility of the ventures and the documented benefits to public and private sectors, joint ventures may become the dominant mode of prison labor in the 21st century.

Yet joint ventures are not without controversy. Some critics say that giving private-sector jobs to prison inmates constitutes unfair competition for the civilian workforces. However, this claim of job loss has proved difficult to assess, especially considering the thousands of jobs that have already moved overseas as a result of the globalization of economic activity. Some prison jobs would undoubtedly have moved abroad had joint ventures not been available. A more fundamental criticism of the economic marriage between the criminal justice system and private corporations says that prisoners have become the raw material for long-term corporate growth (Christie, 1993). Private corporations in the prison business will try to keep prisons full, even if crime is decreasing. This controversial argument will be explored in more detail in the section of the chapter dealing with the privatization of corrections.

CHAIN GANGS

chain gang A group of prisoners shackled together by chains, working the fields or highways under armed guard.

During the nineteenth and early 20th centuries, it was not uncommon in the South to see groups of prison and jail inmates shackled together by chains and working at hard labor in the fields or along highways. These **chain gangs** worked for the local county authority on public works projects or for private farmers during planting and harvesting seasons. They grew in popularity during the period of Reconstruction following the Civil War. Southern states had been devastated by the war, and crime and disorder were on the rise. Race tensions were also high, with newly freed slaves seeking new opportunities and the white establishment resisting them at every turn. Georgia, the Carolinas, and Alabama increasingly turned to chain gangs as a way to solve their economic and social problems (McKelvey, 1936; Myers, 1993).

The chain gang was commonly used for less serious felons and for people sentenced to the county jail. The chain gangs who worked the roads were usually housed in cages made out of railroad boxcars, and surrounded by dogs and armed guards. They worked twelve to fourteen hours a day, year-round. Disproportionate numbers of chain gang offenders were black, giving the practice racist overtones. In Alabama, prisoners who refused to work on the chain gang were chained to a metal bar called "the hitching post" for as many as twelve hours a day (Morrison, 1995). (In 1998, a U.S. district court declared this practice unconstitutional as applied, and set another hearing to determine its constitutionality in any form). The use of chain gangs on farms was closely tied to the value of the year's harvest. If prices were high and crops good, farmers could afford to hire labor at market price, which meant work for able-bodied white and black workers. However, when economic conditions were depressed, farmers turned to cheaper convict labor. Coupled with the demand for new roads, this added pressure for convict labor led local courts to sentence increasing numbers of minor offenders to the chain gang (Myers, 1993).

Chain gangs had largely disappeared by the 1950s; they were condemned in many quarters for their cruelty and racism, including by a federal judge who refused to send an escaped prisoner back to Georgia. Based on testimony from prisoners and from articles in national magazines, the judge concluded "that it was the custom of the Georgia authorities to treat chain-gang prisoners with persistent and deliberate brutality [and] that Negro prisoners were treated with a greater degree of brutality than white prisoners" (Goldfarb and Singer, 1973:373). Nevertheless, as Box 15.2 illustrates, chain gangs have reappeared in some states as a "get tough" response to prison and jail overcrowding and rising correctional costs. Alabama was the first state to reestablish chain gangs, in 1995; however, opposition was so strong that the state legislature banned them a year later (*New York Times*, June 21, 1996, p. A14).

Prison Security Levels, Inmate Classification, and the Rehabilitative Ideal

Not all prisoners require the same level of control, nor do all pose the same threat to a community if they escape. Yet it was not until the 20th century that serious attempts were made to provide a systematic classification of security levels for the nation's prisons and to match inmates with them. Today, state and federal correctional facilities vary considerably in their level of security; the higher the level of security, the less freedom allowed inmates and the more difficult it is to escape. In addition, as security levels go up, the emphasis on treatment and rehabilitation of inmates goes down. Table 15.1

Table 15.1 Security Classifications of Federal Prisons

The facilities of modern correctional systems differ in their security levels; as the security level of a prison increases, the freedom allowed inmates and the work and treatment programs offered decrease. The security levels of the prisons within the federal system are as follows:

Security Level	Characteristics	Examples
High	Walled or double-fenced perimeter, 18 to 25 feet high, armed guards in observation towers, multiple and single cells, close staff supervision and movement controls	USP* Atlanta, GA USP Leavenworth, KS USP Lompoc, CA USP Terre Haute, IN USP Florence, CO USP Allenwood, PA USP Marion, IL
Medium	Double-fence perimeters with electronic detectors, cell or cubicle housing, wide variety of work and treatment programs, highest staff-to-inmate ratio to ensure internal controls	FCI* Englewood, CO FCI Estill, SC FCI Greenville, IL FCI McKean, PA FCI Oakdale, LA FCI Phoenix, AZ
Low	Double-fence perimeters, dormitory housing, strong work and program components, lower staff-to-inmate ratio	FCI Bastrop, TX FCI Butner, NC FCI La Tuna, NM FCI Milan, MI
Minimum	Dormitory housing, lowest staff-to-inmate ratio, no fences, work and program oriented, often located near larger facilities or on military bases where inmates perform work	FPC* Boron, CA FPC Bryan, TX FPC Duluth, MN FPC Pensacola, FL FPC Yankton, SD

*USP = United States Penitentiary
FCI = Federal Correctional Institution
FPC = Federal Prison Camp

Source: Federal Bureau of Prisons (1997). *State of the Bureau 1996* (pp. 23–40). Washington, D.C.: U.S. Department of Justice.

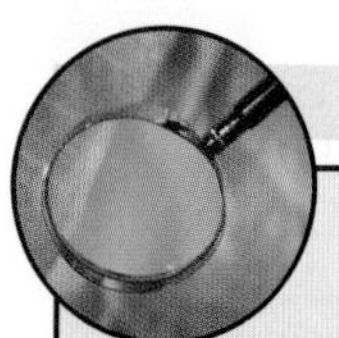

Box 15.2

INSIDE CRIMINAL JUSTICE

WORKING ON THE CHAIN GANG IN THE 1990s

Arizona features the country's first female chain gang, the brainchild of controversial Maricopa County Sheriff Joe Arpaio. Some think that the Chain gang constitutes cruel and unusual punishment. Others, like the 34 prisoners who applied for the first Arizona female chain gang, see it as a welcome relief from overcrowded jails. What do you think?

PHOTO BY JEFF ROBBINS, COURTESY OF AP PHOTO

shows the security classification now used in the Federal Bureau of Prisons' 85 correctional facilities. It has four levels: high, medium, low, and minimum. As of June 1998, the Federal Bureau of Prisons housed over 117,000 inmates: 14 percent in high-security facilities, 23 percent in medium security, 35 percent in low security, and 28 percent in minimum security (Bureau of Prisons, 1998, **http://www.bop.gov/**). Most state systems have three levels—maximum, medium, and minimum—although "supermaximum" prisons are becoming popular, as we shall see. There are currently no regularly published national state data on security levels of inmates.

inmate classification A system for identifying similarities and differences among inmates.

Inmate Classification. Because prison inmates differ in terms of backgrounds, personalities, dangerousness, and needs, prison authorities have developed systems of **inmate classification**. Classification results in groupings that reflect the similarities and differences among inmates. For example, a system of classification based on security concerns might group inmates according to

Box 15.2 (continued)

In the mid-1990s, Alabama, Arizona, Iowa, Georgia, and Florida reintroduced the chain gang. Similar legislation was also introduced in Illinois and a handful of other states, but remains pending as this is written. Alabama subsequently halted the practice in June 1996 after a prisoner was shot dead by a guard who said the inmate was trying to attack another inmate on the work detail. This incident and a great deal of negative publicity persuaded the legislature to ban chain gangs altogether.

In the states that have implemented chain gangs, they are primarily for offenders charged with less serious felonies and those serving time in county jails. Most counties use chain gangs to pick up refuse by the side of the road. Some use them as a form of special punishment when inmates violate jail rules. Reactions from inmates and officials are mixed:

- In Florida, members of the chain gang, called a "restricted labor squad," clear brush and repair roads and fences on prison property. Florida prisoners are not shackled together but are restricted by chains on their legs. "Of course I don't want to be out there with my legs chained," said one inmate. But some Florida legislators believe the prisoners should be chained together to reduce risk of escape and to increase the harshness of the punishment.
- In Phoenix, Arizona, prisoners are housed in tents and fed bologna. Sheriff Joe Arpaio believes that inmates should be made to suffer "in a humane sort of way." There are male and female chain gangs. One is composed of fifteen women who have chosen it in preference to punishment in the jail's disciplinary cells. They are chained together at the ankles while they clean up downtown streets. Thirty-four women had applied for the chain gang.

It remains to be seen whether chain gangs will survive long into the 21st century. Challenges that the practice constitutes cruel and unusual punishment have been filed in appellate courts, but the U.S. Supreme Court has not ruled on the issue as of this writing.

Sources: Associated Press, June 24, 1996; Peter Morrison (1995). "The New Chain Gang States' New 'Get Tough' Prison Policies Are Gaining Support from Politicians and the Courts." *National Law Journal* (August):1–7; Associated Press, September 19, 1996.

their potential for violence or escape; a system based on inmate needs might group inmates according to their educational levels or medical condition.

Inmate classification was in use at the Walnut Street Jail as early as 1797. It was based on the risk that inmates posed to the internal security of the jail. The most dangerous inmates were placed in solitary confinement, and the least dangerous were allowed the greatest freedom. Dangerousness was determined largely by the inmate's behavior while in prison. Prison inspectors kept track of the conduct of each inmate in an attempt to uncover "the potentiality of danger that lies hidden in an individual" (Foucault, 1977:126).

In 1870, the reforms advocated at the first Prison Congress included the foundations of a new approach to imprisonment, stressing individualized treatment. The approach has become known as the **rehabilitative ideal**, and it consisted of these revolutionary ideas:

rehabilitative ideal Foundation of the reformatory movement, stressing individualized treatment and use of indeterminate sentences.

- Punishment should be individualized, taking into consideration the characteristics and needs of each offender.

- Prison sentences should be indeterminate rather than fixed so that prisoners have an incentive for participating in their own reform: Inmates showing evidence of rehabilitation can be released early and incorrigible inmates confined longer.
- Prisons should classify and separate inmates on the basis of characteristics such as age, sex, and criminal background.
- Education, industrial training, and rewards rather than punishment should be used whenever possible to change behavior.
- Treatment received inside prison should be supplemented by further assistance and supervision once inmates are released into the community—this became known as **parole**.

parole Supervised release of inmates prior to the full completion of their prison term.

It took more than 50 years for the various components of this ideal to come together in practice, however. Prison authorities were not prepared for such drastic changes to conventional practice, so reform proceeded in a haphazard manner, with tremendous variation from state to state. Some states adopted only one or two elements of the proposed reforms, and their reasons had little to do with indivualized treatment. In California, for example, parole was adopted initially as a means of reversing excessive sentences and controlling prison population growth (Hawkins and Alpert, 1989:187).

maximum-security prison Emphasizes custody and control and is used to house felons who have committed more serious crimes or are escape risks.

The Era of the "Big House": Maximum-Security Prisons. Although prison reform was in the air, the early 1900s became known in penal circles as the era of the **maximum-security prison**, where inmates went "stir crazy" from the monotony and lack of diversions. Custody, not treatment, was emphasized. Prison administrators and their custodial staff focused their efforts on maintaining control and preventing escapes. With security risk driving the process, inmate classification was generally based on a prisoner's offense. Most felony

The phrase Big House *conjures up a bleak, violent place, epitomized by institutions such as the federal prison in Leavenworth, Kansas. A Big House can hold thousands of inmates in a relatively secure, but potentially explosive, environment.*

PHOTO COURTESY OF ARCHIVE PHOTOS

offenders were sent to the "Big House," the prisoners' term for the maximum-security prison.

At that time, the cornerstone of the American penal system was the large, maximum-security prison. Over 30 such prisons were built during the period 1870–1930, and most of these are still in use today. The term "Big House" reflected their size and architecture. John Irwin, a criminologist and ex-inmate of a maximum-security prison, describes them as follows: "The Big House was a walled prison with large cell blocks that contained stacks of three or more tiers of one- or two-man cells. On the average it held 2,500 men. Sometimes a single cell block housed over 1,000 prisoners in six tiers of cells. Most of these prisons were built over many decades and had a mixture of old and new cell blocks." (Irwin, 1980:3).

"Big Houses" were known also for the bleak monotony of life within their walls, and for the threat of violence that hung constantly in the air. Over 25 "Big Houses" are still operating today; they include Leavenworth in Kansas, San Quentin in California, Menard in Illinois, and Graterford in Pennsylvania. Behind the high walls, armed guard posts, and razor wire of these prisons, however, lurk the dinosaurs of correctional practice. Yet even the "Big House" prisons were eventually touched by the rehabilitative ideal. This occurred in the form of a medical model of corrections.

The Medical Model and the Emerging Emphasis on Corrections. The goal of "Big House" prisons was secure custody of a large number of criminals. During the 1940s and 1950s, however, the various elements of the rehabilitative ideal began to merge. State officials responded to the growing influence of the behavioral sciences, especially psychology, which linked crime to the antisocial personalities of "sick" individuals. An individual-centered **medical model** of offender rehabilitation emerged that focused on diagnosis and treatment.

medical model Emphasizes rehabilitation through diagnosis and treatment of antisocial personalities.

Inmate classification shifted from security alone to include the appropriate plan of treatment for each newly arrived prisoner. Security concerns were not ignored, but they were now coupled with the selection of a rehabilitation program for each inmate. In the California system, for example, new inmates were placed in a Guidance Center, undertook a variety of medical and psychological tests, and then faced the Classification Committee. Here is how one prisoner later remembered the Committee:

> The Classification Committee was made up from representatives of the various prison departments. The real power was shared by two cooperative branches—Care and Treatment, and Custody. At this time Custody had the final clout . . . because they feared these [treatment] programs might threaten their fundamental responsibility which was simply to keep us locked up until the Adult Authority said we could go. Roughly, Custody was the old way, Care and Treatment the new. Custody was usually represented by a captain or lieutenant of the guards, and Treatment sent an associate warden. One of the chaplains would be present, as well as a psych, or sociologist, or, later on, a correctional counselor, and, usually, someone from Education came in. (Braly, 1977: 166)

The growing acceptance of the rehabilitative ideal represented a major shift in orientation: from prison as a place of punishment to prison as a place for *correction.* This term had been used 300 years earlier—remember the "houses of correction"—but now the emphasis was on providing scientific programs of planned intervention. A new field of corrections emerged, and the National Prison Association, founded in 1870, changed its name to the American Correctional Association. A set of correctional standards for the operations of prisons and treatment of inmates was developed, and a growing number of correctional experts emerged from across the behavioral sciences and education. Words denoting an emphasis on custody, such as *prison*, *warden*, and *guard*, began to be replaced by more neutral or therapeutic terms such as *correctional facility*, *superintendent* or *administrator*, and *correctional officer*. The term *correctional treatment* became the buzzword of the 1950s, and the progressive prison contained more humanized living conditions for inmates, a more educated staff, and expanded treatment and training programs coordinated with inmate classification.

The coupling of rehabilitation and custody was by no means easy, however. This was particularly true in maximum-security facilities. In some prisons, guards and wardens actively resisted the efforts of case workers assigned to classification units (Morris, 1979). In general, the medical model was not easily absorbed by existing prison organization. The influx of civilian therapists, counselors, teachers, and researchers with no experience of prison life and little awareness of security issues created new problems for prison administrators: Whom should they report to? Where should they be housed in the prison? Should they work shifts, like guards, or a standard nine-to-five day? Who should control treatment budgets?

Relations with custodial staff were strained, in part because each side tended to define the work of the other as in conflict with their own:

> On the one hand, behavior routinely performed by guards in the past was now open to charges of being antitherapeutic. Furthermore, treatment personnel frequently felt that the guards were purposefully undermining their work. On the other hand, guards sensed that their duties were being made more difficult. Their authority with inmates was being undercut. Prisoners, sensing the conflict, could play off the differences between the two camps. (Hawkins and Alpert, 1989:196)

Such strained relationships between custodial and treatment staff contributed to the growing view that rehabilitation and maximum security were incompatible. Even as authorities struggled with the implications of bringing behavioral science into the prison, the diversity among inmates was impossible to ignore. It simply made no sense to assign all felony offenders to maximum-security prisons. As the rehabilitative ideal took hold, prisons were constructed to better accommodate its practice. Enter the medium- and minimum-security prisons.

The Medium-Security Prison. Despite the newly embraced emphasis on treatment, custody and security nevertheless remained the primary concern of prison systems. The **medium-security prison** offered two benefits: (1) security could be protected without the oppressive and dehumanizing atmosphere of the big maximum-security institutions, and (2) a medium-security prison is cheaper to build and operate. Today, for example, it costs between $75,000 and $100,000 to construct each maximum-security unit, or bed, for one inmate, versus approximately $58,000 for each bed in a medium-security facility (Camp and Camp, 1993:46; Donziger, 1996:49).

medium-security prison Places high priority on security within a more relaxed environment that also emphasizes treatment and rehabilitation.

The medium-security facility places high priority on security but provides a more relaxed environment for inmates, who are often housed in dormitories or cubicles. Medium-security prisons also provide more extensive treatment and rehabilitation services to inmates. Even so, the medium-security facility is usually surrounded by double fences topped by razor or "concertina" wire that engulfs anyone who attempts to climb over it.

Around 90 percent of all the nation's medium-security prisons have been built since 1925, most in the last 25 years (Allen and Simonsen, 1995:605). They now house around 30 percent of all state inmates, and around a quarter of federal inmates (Federal Bureau of Prisons, 1997:45). Together, the newer medium-security prisons and older "Big Houses" form the core of the correctional system in America, housing nearly two-thirds of all prison inmates.

The Minimum-Security Prison. Many criminals pose no danger to other inmates or to the outside community when they are sent to prison. These offenders can be housed in **minimum-security prisons** without fences, walls, or armed guards. They may even be allowed to leave prison grounds for work and family visits. Often housed in dormitories, and sometimes even private rooms, inmates of minimum-security prisons interact freely with one another, participate in a variety of group treatment and educational programs, and are subject to minimal control by staff. The emphasis is on treatment and rehabilitation, not security. In many facilities, inmates work outside prison grounds on public works projects. Prison uniforms generally look little different from civilian clothes, and although prisoners returning from work or family visits may be frisked for contraband, they are rarely subjected to stripping and intrusive body cavity searches unless officials suspect them of trying to smuggle in drugs or weapons.

minimum-security prison Usually has no walls or fences, uses minimal control by staff, and emphazes treatment and rehabilitation programs.

In the federal system, around 30 percent of all inmates are housed in minimum-security prisons (Federal Bureau of Prisons, 1997:45); national figures for states are unavailable, but they are probably much smaller, in the region of 15 to 20 percent of all offenders incarcerated in prisons. The states make greater use of community corrections, described later in this chapter and in more detail in Chapter 17.

Minimum-security facilities are often located adjacent to medium- and maximum-security prisons so that inmates can provide work and other services to their more secure neighbors. They are generally small facilities, housing fewer than 200 inmates. However, a wide variety of offenses will be represented among these inmates, from property crimes to murder. Some nonviolent offenders are sent to minimum-security institutions immediately following conviction, while other inmates arrive later, after they have first served time—sometimes many years—in medium- or maximum-security prisons. Good behavior during these early years of incarceration allows some violent offenders to "graduate" to a minimum-security facility.

No, the Minimum-Security Prison Is Not a Country Club. Some people say that modern prisons are nothing more than country clubs. They object to the recreational opportunities in some prisons, or to perceived inmate "perks" such as free TV, access to computers, conjugal visits permitting sexual intimacy wth spouses, or work release programs. They hear stories of inmate abuse of privileges, supported by prison staff who look the other way. I heard such a story recently: An ex-inmate of a minimum-security federal prison recalled how he regularly visited his girlfriend at a motel in a nearby town. He would spend the night and get back just in time to sign out for his work release. Prison officials knew what was going on but allowed it, he believed, because of his good reputation among staff and other inmates.

For all the freedoms and privileges that are allowed inmates in some minimum-security facilities, these prisons are nevertheless places where adults are held under restrictive rules. If they violate the rules, inmates risk immediate transfer to a secure, even more restrictive facility. At the same time, the programs and perks of the minimum-security facility are designed to help prepare inmates to be responsible, constructive members of a freer society when they are released. The institution that most minimum-security prisons probably come closest to is the single-sex boarding school—without the "punishment" of being sent home if unruly.

With the exception of Colorado, Georgia, Illinois, and Missouri, states have furlough programs that allow inmates to leave a minimum security facility temporarily (Maguire and Pastore, 1998:513–514). Most furloughs are granted for family reasons—to visit a terminally ill relative, attend a funeral, or simply to maintain family ties—or for medical treatment. Sometimes inmates are given furloughs for educational or employment purposes, or a part of a prerelease program.

RECIDIVISM AND THE RISE OF COMMUNITY CORRECTIONS

recidivism Commision of new offenses after being punished for crime.

Despite its promise, the rehabilitative ideal was falling into disfavor by the 1970s. Instead of declining, crime rates were continuing to rise; to make matters worse, in some states nearly 70 percent of released felony offenders were being returned to prison for new crimes—a relapse that criminologists call **recidivism**. A published review of 231 studies of prison rehabilitation in the mid-1970s added fuel to the growing discontent (Martinson, 1974; Lipton, Martinson, and Wilkes, 1975). The authors were unable to find any treatment program that had successfuly reduced recidivism. Although the findings were subsequently heralded as evidence that "nothing works," and that rehabilitation efforts in prisons should be abandoned, the report did not rule out "a more full-hearted commitment to the strategy of treatment" (Martinson, 1974:49). Since then debate over rehabilitation in prisons has remained vigorous in academic circles (Cullen and Gilbert, 1982; Whitehead and Lab, 1989; Andrews, et al., 1990; Lab and Whitehead, 1990, Mair, 1991), and prison wardens can still be found who support it (Cullen et al., 1993).

Why Rehabilitation in Prisons Was Failing. There were, in fact, several schools of thought concerning the connection between correctional efforts and recidivism. Some people argued that reform and rehabilitation simply would not work in a prison setting. Part of the problem relates to prison organization and management: "Wardens are paid for running quiet prisons, not for reforming inmates," wrote one criminologist. "Any attempt to establish rehabilitation programs in prison are opposed by both staff and inmates because it makes life more difficult for all concerned" (Jeffery, 1977:88). Furthermore, prisons isolate inmates from the communities into which they will later return, often by hundreds of miles. Many prisons are located in sparsely populated areas, far from the largest cities in their states, where most offenders live. This is largely because the benefits to inmates of being close to home are downplayed in the economic and political battles surrounding prison construction.

pathology of imprisonment The prison environment encourages staff and inmates to view each other with contempt, according to psychologist Philip Zimbardo.

Adding to the critique of prison-based rehabilitation is the argument that the world of incarceration breeds contempt among inmates and staff for the rights and well-being of others. Stanford psychologist Philip Zimbardo has called this contempt the **pathology of imprisonment**. It flows, he believes, from the influence of the prison environment over the behavior of guards and prisoners. Zimbardo (1972) conducted a controversial experiment in the basement of a Stanford University building, which was turned into a temporary jail. In this experiment, 24 emotionally stable and otherwise normal college students from middle-class homes were arbitrarily assigned as prisoners or guards. The guards were instructed to prepare rules for maintaining law and order, and were allowed to improvise new ones as they saw fit throughout the course of the experiment. Without warning, the prisoners were picked up by real policemen at their homes, taken to the Palo Alto police station, stripped, searched, handcuffed, fingerprinted, and then blindfolded for the trip to the "jail."

The experiment was called off at the end of six days because "it was no longer apparent to most of the subjects (or to us) where reality ended and their roles began" (Zimbardo, 1972:5). The student-guards and student-prisoners adopted their respective roles in "every aspect of their behavior." Initial solidarity among the prisoners eventually gave way to each man for himself; some guards became tyrannical, while "good" guards stood by and did nothing. The power of the social situation—in this case, the roles and expectations associated with being a guard or an inmate—overwhelmed whatever prior inclinations subjects had to treat other people with dignity and respect.

Another manifestation of the pathology of imprisonment that received considerable attention during the 1970s involved the use of prisoners in research involving drugs, shock therapy, and even psychosurgery. In "Clockwork Orange in a California Prison," R. T. Trotter (1972) described three brain operations performed in 1968 on inmates of Vacaville State Penitentiary. Another author documented the systematic use in prisons of powerful depressants such as Thorazine and Prolixin (Speiglman, 1976). Whether in this form or in the daily routines of prison life, which we shall explore in the next chapter, the realities of incarceration were viewed by many critics as inconsistent with rehabilitation. No amount of behavior modification, drug therapy, group counseling, or other "correction" can overcome the pathology of imprisonment. "Prisoners adjust to the environment of the prison, not to the environment of free men," one criminologist claimed (Jeffery, 1977:86); like growing numbers of other experts, he advocated the community, not the prison, as the proper locus of rehabilitation.

Deinstitutionalization and Community-Based Corrections. The most prominent view emerging from the debate over rehabilitation during the 1970s was that while prison is the proper place for custody, the community is the proper place for correction and rehabilitation. Most inmates will eventually be returned to freedom, and prison is not the best place to prepare them for the independence and responsibilities associated with freedom. The new view held that a more promising solution to rising crime rates, high levels of recidivism, prison overcrowding, and the pathology of imprisonment itself was to get as many people out of prison as quickly as possible, and to provide them with community-based treatment and rehabilitation services. The process of emptying institutions was called **deinstitutionalization**, or decarceration. Massachusetts took the first significant step toward deinstitutionalization in 1972, when it closed all its juvenile reform schools and replaced them with group homes in the community. Other states did not go as far, but in virtually every jurisdiction a variety of programs were initiated to provide correctional opportunities within local communities. These **community-based corrections** programs included halfway houses, work-release programs, and residential treatment centers. Many inmates of minimum-security prisons participated in the programs, and some offenders avoided prison altogether, being "diverted" to a community center instead.

deinstitutionalization Large-scale movement of people out of prisons, mental hospitals, and juvenile detention centers into the community during the early 1970s.

community-based corrections Criminal penalties that reduce or eliminate time in prison or ease the transition from prison to freedom.

In its various forms, community corrections offered two major advantages to its clients: (1) offenders were able to maintain or re-establish relationships with family, employers, and significant others that are important in binding individuals to a social community; and (2) they avoided lengthy interruption of the normal cycles of life, especially those involving family and work. If free, many first-time prison inmates would have been embarking on a series of important economic and social transitions to ensure that they would "make it" in life: finishing school, getting a job, raising a family, and so on. It is easy to fall behind when imprisoned, and many ex-offenders never recover.

Warehousing of Violent and Repeat Offenders

In the face of steeply rising crime rates and high levels of recidivism, it is easy to agree that "nothing works." During the late 1970s and early 1980s the "be tough while being fair" justice model discussed in Chapter 13 began to replace the treatment model as the cornerstone of penal policy. Determinate sentencing and mandatory minimum prison terms were popular sentencing reforms.

Deterrence and incapacitation replaced rehabilitation as the buzzwords in correctional circles.

This was especially true with respect to violent and repeat offenders. The dominant view was that such offenders should be taken off the streets and held in secure prisons for lengthy periods of time. The term **warehousing** aptly describes the role of many maximum-security prisons during the 1980s. Forget treatment and other prison-based efforts to rehabilitate inmates, supporters of warehousing argued, but make sure that prisons are professionally run, humane places where society can place the thousands of violent, high-risk criminals who require maximum control (Fleisher, 1989:236–238).

warehousing Housing large numbers of violent and repeat offenders in maximum-security prisons with minimal privileges and few, if any, rehabilitation programs.

Unfortunately, warehousing has been anything but humane, and many prisons suffered from mismanagement, overcrowding, and neglect. Prison violence became epidemic, from everyday assaults and gang fights to full-blown riots. Administrative reforms invariably followed high-profile violence, but they were often short lived; tight budgets, high rates of staff turnover, continued overcrowding, growing racial tensions, and the proliferation of gangs all served to undermine real reforms.

Warehousing That Works: USP–Lompoc. This pessimistic picture of warehousing during the 1980s is rarely challenged, but one exception may be the United States Penitentiary in Lompoc, California, observed firsthand by anthropologist Mark Fleisher (1989). USP–Lompoc is regarded as cleaner, less tense, and—despite the killing of a correctional officer in April 1997—less violent than many other maximum-security prisons. And yet its role is primarily to warehouse violent and repeat offenders. Among the things that makes Lompoc different from other warehousing prisons is a staff-inmate culture that stresses peace:

> Staffers and inmates share the pursuit of peace: Staff members work peacefully toward retirement, and inmates are given the chance to work peacefully toward parole. . . . Doing "easy time" is important. Convict Slim says: "I just want to do my time and get out. If you fuck up in a federal joint, they'll never let you out." Staff utter similar sentiments. "We do time along with the inmates, and you have to be willing to talk to them," said Jim Farley. (Fleisher, 1989:49)

Though occasionally broken by fights and by disciplinary actions by staff, peace was established at Lompoc through effective managerial control of overcrowding, drug smuggling, and gang activity, problems plaguing most maximum-security prisons that we will discuss further in Chapter 16.

The New Supermaximum-Security, or Maxi-Maxi, Prisons. Peace has been elusive at many maximum-security prisons. Prison escapes, killings, and riots have taken their toll on inmates, staff, their families, and society at large. To combat these problems, federal and some state correctional systems have constructed so-called **supermaximum-security prisons**, sometimes referred to as *maxi-maxi prisons*. As the name suggests, maxi-maxi prisons operate at the highest levels of security. They are built solely to house inmates regarded as too dangerous or too likely to escape from "regular" maximum-security institutions. Inmates are kept under tight control at all times, often under *lockdown*. Lockdown means that inmates must stay in their cells for almost the entire day, and few privileges are allowed. One of the primary goals of lockdown is to keep inmates from interacting with each other.

supermaximum-security prison A facility with the highest legal levels of security and inmate control.

The Experience at U.S. Penitentiary–Marion. The idea of a super-secure prison facility actually goes back to the establishment of Alcatraz as a federal penitentiary in 1934 (see Box 15.3). Alcatraz was closed in 1963 after 29 years of operation. The search for a suitable replacement had begun eight years ear-

Alcatraz, the nation's first super-secure prison, was opened in 1934 and closed in 1963. Today so-called supermaximum-security prisons include the U.S. Penitentiary in Florence, Colorado; Pelican Bay State Prison in California; Tamms Correctional Center in Illinois; and Riker's Island jail (Rose Singer center shown) in New York City.

TOP PHOTO COURTESY OF UNIPHOTO; BOTTOM PHOTO BY SARAH LEEN, COURTESY OF MATRIX INTERNATIONAL INC.

lier. In the end, a site was selected near Marion, Illinois, a town close to Southern Illinois University at Carbondale, and bordering on Crab Orchard Lake, a large federal wildlife refuge. In a speech to the university, Myrle Alexander, assistant director of the Federal Bureau of Prisons, gave four reasons for its selection: (1) a supportive community environment, including recreational and educational facilities, that would help in staff recruitment; (2) the active interest and support of a major university; (3) the availability of suitable federal land; and (4) the economic need of the area. As is usually the case with new prison construction, a combination of politics, economics, and community support had determined the location of the new penitentiary.

The United States Penitentiary–Marion was called a supermaximum-security prison, although the Federal Bureau of Prisons itself does not use that term. No Alcatraz prisoners were actually transferred to Marion, but

Box 15.3

JUSTICE IN HISTORY

ALCATRAZ, THE NATION'S FIRST SUPERMAXIMUM-SECURITY PRISON

Located in the middle of San Francisco Bay, Alcatraz Island had been a fort, a military barracks, and for 20 years a military prison. The small rocky outcrop was regarded as impenetrable. By 1900 the island housed 400 military prisoners, and in 1912 a permanent cell block was constructed.

The U.S. military found Alcatraz excessively expensive and inconvenient to run—drinking water, supplies, and any visitors had to be brought across an often treacherous stretch of water. By 1933 the army was ready to abandon the island. As luck would have it, then–U.S. Attorney General Homer S. Cummings had been proposing that the federal government build a new type of tough prison for tough criminals. An internal memo written by Cummings spoke of the importance of building a "special prison for racketeers, kidnapers, and others guilty of predatory crimes. . . . in a remote place—on an island or in Alaska, so that persons incarcerated would not be in constant communication with friends outside" (Keve, 1991:174). The criminals he had in mind were people like Al Capone, John Dillinger, Frank Nash, and "Machine Gun" Kelly, all making headlines during the 1920s and 1930s with their racketeering, killings, and kidnappings.

Opened in July 1, 1934, the new federal prison at Alcatraz was the talk of the land. The nation's most dangerous federal prisoners were moved there from prisons around the country, including McNeil Island near Tacoma, Washington, and the United States Penitentiaries at Atlanta and Leavenworth. Al Capone was among them.

From the beginning, security came first at Alcatraz, and rules "were strict, privileges minimal, and treatment programming virtually nonexistent." Furthermore, "[n]o other federal prison was ever so determined to shield its operation from outside scrutiny" (Keve, 1991:178). The press was unwelcome; prisoners had limited opportunities for visitors; and, when visitors were allowed, a thick steel-and-glass wall separated visitor from inmate. All incoming and outgoing mail was censored, and inmates received copies of incoming mail rather than the originals to prevent the possibility of communication by secret code or ink. In the early years a rule of silence was also imposed. Even the nation's most powerful gangster, Al Capone, lost all the influence and privilege he had enjoyed in the Atlanta penitentiary.

Riots and escapes were rare at Alcatraz, although when they occurred excited crowds would gather along the mainland shore in an attempt to catch sight of something. In 1946, they were rewarded with a spectacular naval and marine bombardment of a cell block building that six inmates had taken over after killing two guards and taking seven others hostage. Grenades dropped from above eventually killed three inmates. The surviving three were charged with murder, and two were subsequently executed in San Quentin prison.

Although there is no proof that anyone ever escaped from Alcatraz and survived, the most notorious attempt, of which there are two highly successful film versions, involved two brothers and another inmate who laboriously chipped away at their cell walls, and when the hole was big enough climbed into a ventilation shaft, leaving cleverly constructed dummies behind in their beds. The three men made it to the water but were never seen again, and were presumed drowned.

Source: Paul W. Keve (1991). *Prisons and the American Conscience* (pp. 174–177) Carbondale and Edwardsville, Ill.: Southern Illinois University Press.

the intent was to make Marion the bureau's number one prison in terms of security and the close custody of inmates. High-risk prisoners from around the federal corrections system were to be housed at this "prison of last resort" (Keve, 1991:193).

In all, from 1965 to 1983, inmates at Marion murdered 3 corrections officers and 21 inmates, attempted various escapes, and participated in countless serious but nonfatal assaults. Prison officials introduced periodic lockdowns and severely curtailed services. Violence continued to erupt, and other measures were taken, including hiring more guards, introduction of more permanent control measures—including leg irons for the movement of prisoners—and use of random shakedowns for weapons and contraband (Karacki, 1987).

The "Marionization" of Prisons: USP–Florence and Pelican Bay. In 1994, the Bureau of Prisons opened a new maximum-security penitentiary in Florence, Colorado, at a cost of $60 million. This prison is nestled in the foothills of the Rocky Mountains, some 90 miles south of Denver. Newspaper reports describe the prison as a "super-controlled environment that enforces a hard-edged solitude to contain the risk of social mixing and violence. Even the cell windows deny them all views of the outside except the sky above" (*New York Times*, October 17, 1994, p. 1).

In what has been termed the "Marionization" of prisons (*Criminal Justice Newsletter*, November 1991:1), new supermaximum-security wings have been built at various state prisons, and entirely new maxi-maxi prisons have been proposed. This activity has generated concern among human rights supporters and prison watchdog groups. They argue that permanent lockdown, lack of treatment programs, and harsh security measures deprive inmates of basic rights and may even contribute to the violence within prisons, putting inmates unnecessarily at risk. Such claims were made when Marion introduced its control unit, and again when security was further tightened in the 1980s. A number of class action suits have been filed on behalf of inmates in supermaximum prisons, one of the latest against California's Pelican Bay State Prison (*New York Times*, January 13, 1995, p. 21).

Pelican Bay is actually three prisons in one: a minimum-security facility housing around 200 inmates, a regular maximum-security prison with 2,000 inmates, and a supermaximum-security facility called the Security Housing Unit, housing up to 1,500 inmates. The class action suit, ***Madrid v. Gomez*** (1994), was directed against the supermaximum-security unit. The plaintiffs alleged many abuses in the unit, comprising of windowless one-man cells in which inmates lived for 22½ hours each day with very little human interaction, virtually no privileges, and minimal medical care. It is important to note here that while the Pelican Bay suit drew considerable attention to supermaximum-security prisons, it was more about the treatment of inmates by correctional staff than the high level of security itself. At Pelican Bay, some prison officials apparently used the emphasis on security as an excuse for abuses. For example, the court found excessive and unnecessary use of firearms by prison officers, resulting in numerous injuries and three deaths. Based on testimony by inmates, correctional staff, and various expert witnesses, the court concluded that the use of force by staff was not driven by security concerns but by the desire to inflict pain on inmates.

Madrid v. Gomez A successful class action suit alleging physical abuse of inmates by staff at the Pelican Bay maximum-security prison.

With violent crime very much on the public's mind these days, it is unlikely that supermaximum-security prisons will disappear. The general feeling among experts and laypersons alike is that society needs somewhere absolutely secure to house dangerous criminals who cannot be allowed to mingle with the general inmate population, who pose a special threat to prison staff, or who are an escape risk. The problem is that no prison can be absolutely secure—prisoners have even escaped from the Marion penitentiary—and the further we move toward that elusive goal, the more abusive and inhumane life will be for inmates. So the practical difficulty facing correctional officials seeking security is to find the appropriate balance between control and the rights of inmates.

PRIVATIZATION OF CORRECTIONS

privatization Handing over activities and agencies traditionally run by the government to the private sector.

During the past two decades, more and more states, as well as the federal government, have turned to private companies to help them run their correctional systems. This is part of a broader trend called **privatization**, in which activities and agencies traditionally run by the government are turned over to the private sector. Today, one finds privatization at work in all aspects of the criminal justice system, from policing to prisons.

Private Correctional Facilities. In 1983 there were virtually no privately run prisons; by 1994 there were nearly 45,000 beds in private correctional facilities (Figure 15.1). This phenomenonal growth can be largely explained by three things: rising prison populations, rising correctional costs, and the potential for profits. Rising inmate populations and rising costs go hand in hand. We shall see in a moment just how much the inmate population has grown, but the connection should be obvious: More inmates means more beds—and ultimately more prisons, more correctional personnel, more correctional services (such as health care, counseling, and work and recreational activities), and more wear and tear on existing facilities. Someone has to pay for all this, and the cost to

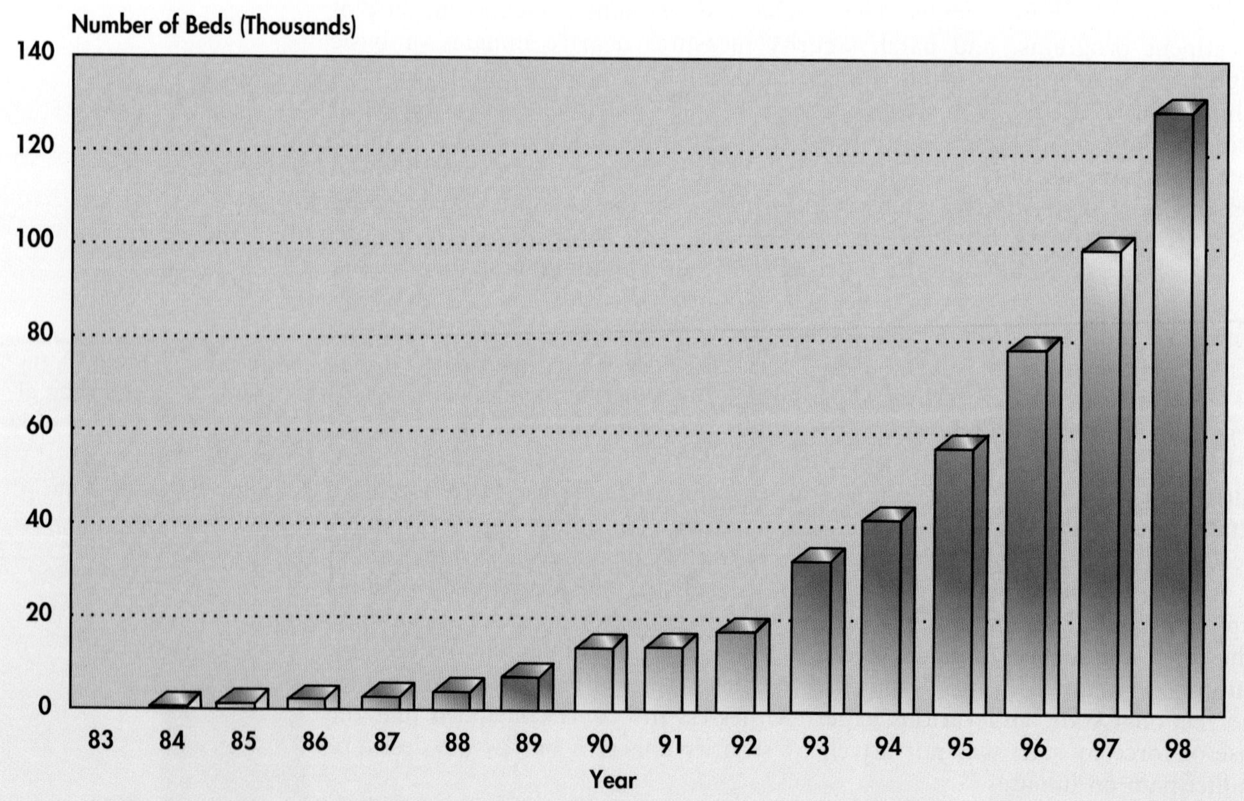

FIGURE 15.1 THE RISE IN PRIVATE CORRECTIONAL BEDS, 1983–1998
This figure shows the rise in the use of prison beds owned or managed by private companies since the early 1980s.

Source: Charles W. Thomas and Dianne Bolinger (1999). *Private Adult Correctional Facility Census* (12th ed.). Gainesville, Fla.: University of Florida Center for Studies in Criminology and Law.

taxpayers has been increasing at an astounding pace. For example, in 1981, state governments spent just over $500 million on prison and jail construction; ten years later they spent $2.2 billion on construction. States spent $3.2 billion running prisons and jails in 1981, and $12.5 billion in 1991. Figure 15.2 shows the escalating expenditures in prisons and jails in more detail. Prisons are now the fastest-growing item in almost all state budgets (*New York Times*, June 2, 1996, p. 12E).

Prisons Are Big Business. All this growth makes prisons big business, and private companies are anxious to get a piece of the action. The largest private correctional company is Corrections Corporation of America (CCA). In 1993, CCA reported profits of $4 million on $100 million in revenue, and just over 13,000 beds in operation or under contract (*New York Times*, August 14, 1994: 1C; Thomas, 1995). By 1997, the capacity of CCA's facilities had grown to over 50,000 beds (Thomas and Bolinger, 1999). This represents almost a 300 percent increase in a mere four years. The next largest correctional firm is Wackenhut Corrections Corporation, with an estimated capacity in 1997 of over 22,000 beds. There are at least 11 other firms operating correctional facilities for a profit. There are more private correctional beds in Texas than anywhere else—over 26,000 in 1997.

Apart from the huge incomes to be made from construction and management of private correctional facilities, many other entrepreneurial opportunities exist (Lilly and Knepper, 1993). Private companies supply a vast array of goods and services to prisons and jails, including food, furniture, clothes, security systems, and personnel management services. Of course, these goods and services are needed no matter who is building and running the nation's prisons. But they are another major reason private businesses have an interest in corrections. Table 15.2 shows a sampling of the correctional facilities currently run by private companies.

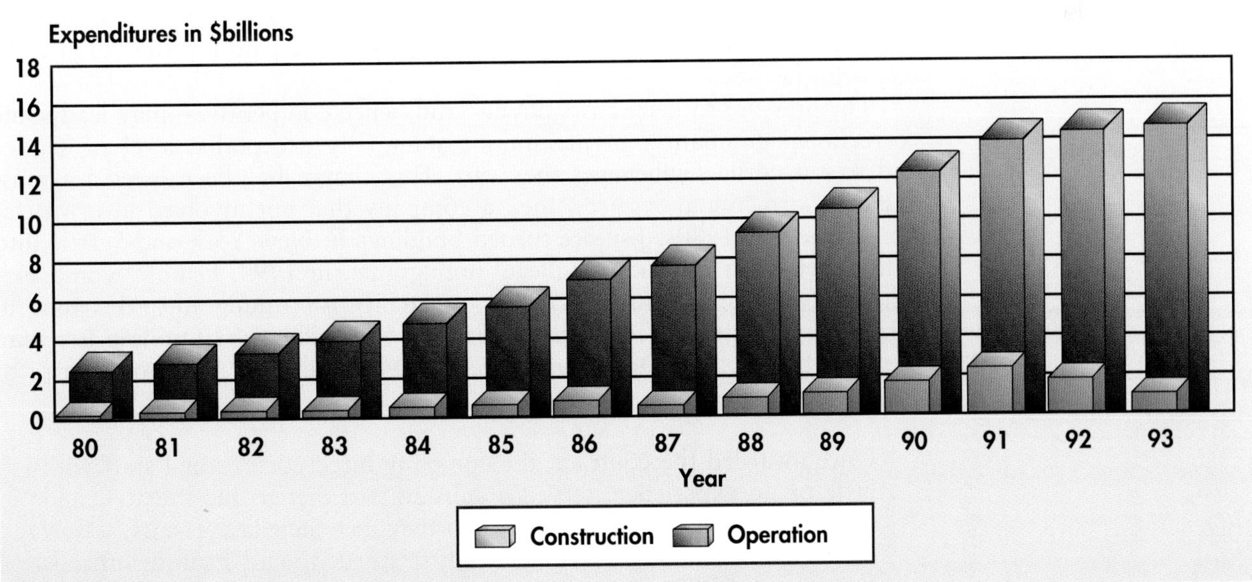

FIGURE 15.2 ESCALATING STATE EXPENDITURES ON PRISONS AND JAILS, 1980–1993
This figure shows the constant escalation of state expenditures on prisons and jails between 1980 and 1993.
Source: Kathleen Maguire and Ann L. Pastore (1998). *Sourcebook of Criminal Justice Statistics*, 1997 (p. 12). Washington, D.C.: U.S. Department of Justice.

TABLE 15.2 A Sampling of Private Correctional Facilities Across the Nation

Corrections has become big business and many private corporations have sprung up around the country to take advantage of opportunities. Here is a sampling of some of those companies and the prisons and jails they manage.

LOCATION	MANAGEMENT COMPANY	RATED CAPACITY	SECURITY LEVEL
Adelanto, CA	Maranatho Production Co.	500	min/medium
Bay County, FL	Corrections Corporation of America	750	medium
Draper, UT	Management and Training Corporation	400	min/medium
Eden, TX	Corrections Corporation of America	1,225	min/medium
Eloy, AZ	Corrections Corporation of America	1,250	medium
Granada, MS	Correctional Services Corporation	160	all levels
Gretna, FL	U.S. Corrections Corporation	768	min/medium
Joplin, MO	GRW Corporation	60	maximum
Kinder, LA	Wackenhut	1,474	med/maximum
Leavenworth, KS	Corrections Corporation of America	327	med/maximum
Live Oak, CA	Cornell Correction	270	minimum
Phoenix, AZ	Correctional Services Corporation	400	minimum
Ponce, Puerto Rico	Corrections Corporation of America	1,500	medium
Taft, CA	Wackenhut	2,048	minimum
Venus, TX	Corrections Corporation of America	1,000	minimum

Source: Charles W. Thomas and Dianne Bolinger (1999). *Private Adult Correctional Facility Census* (Table 3). 12th Edition. Gainesville, FL: University of Florida Center for the Study of Criminology and Law.

The Pros and Cons of Privatization. Most observers agree that there are benefits to the taxpayer from privatization. The most obvious is financial: It is generally more costly for a government to build and run a prison than it is for the private sector. For example, the Washington, D.C., Department of Corrections will save approximately $11 per day per inmate under its 1996 agreement with Corrections Corporation of America (Associated Press, October 7, 1996). But some critics point out that the main reason privatized prisons and jails are cheaper is that they are non-union and employees are paid less than in government-run facilities.

The pressure to keep costs down—and hence competitive—may lead some correctional companies to maintain a minimally acceptable level of service and to cut corners whenever they can. This charge has been leveled against Esmore Correctional Services, Inc., a company that got involved in privatization in the late 1980s. Esmore turned buildings in New York and Seattle into federal detention facilities for illegal immigrants. In 1994, Esmore won a bidding war to manage another detention facility for immigrants, this time in Elizabeth, New Jersey. The Esmore bid was $54 million, $20 million less than the next highest bid (Donziger, 1996:91). What followed was no surprise to critics of privatization:

> Once awarded the contract, the company hired correctional staff with little or no experience, served a substandard diet to the inmates, and shackled detainees in leg irons when they met their lawyers. . . . Carl Frick, who served as the facility's first warden, said Esmore officials had instructed him to lie to [Immigration and Naturalization] officials about conditions at the facility. He said he was instructed to renegotiate a food service contract because $1.12 per day was considered too expensive for an inmate's meals. "They don't want to run a jail," said Frick, referring to Esmore officials. "They want to run a motel as cheaply as possible. Money, money, money, that's all that was important to them. . . ." (Donziger, 1996:92)

Some private companies offer specialized services to correctional agencies; medical care is one such service. Investigative reports by news media around the country suggest that some of these companies are offering mediocre care at best, and at worst are responsible for unnecessary suffering—and even death—among inmates. One company, Correctional Medical Services (CMS), provides health services to more than 268,000 inmates at 341 sites in 30 states (*St. Louis Post-Dispatch*, September 27, 1998: G1–G12). CMS has been criticized for its level of care by the U.S. Justice Department and by corrections officials in Arkansas, Georgia, Ohio, Nevada, and Virginia. Former employees of the company, including doctors and nurses, say the medical decisions are influenced by pressures to cut costs and maintain profits. Some critics believe that those in the private correctional industry who provide poor health care or other substandard services are taking advantage of the public's ill will toward criminals in general and prison inmates in particular. What do you think?

Considering the pressures to cut corners when company profits are at risk, governments must be prepared to write tough privatization contracts from the outset, and to provide the necessary regulation and oversight to make them work. But this may be asking too much, for many states are faced with a correctional crisis that needs solving *now*.

Illinois is a good example. A 1993 Illinois Task Force on Crime and Corrections began: "The crowding of inmates in the Illinois prison system has reached crisis proportions—and the crisis is growing worse by the day. . . . The latest projections . . . indicate that the state's prison population will grow by nearly 8,500 inmates over the next three and one-half years. . . . By June of 1996 the prison population will surpass 40,000—leaving more than *4,000 offenders* whom the department will not be able to incarcerate" (*Final Report*, p. 4). Yet nowhere in the report did the Task Force recommend privatization as a solution. But this is exactly what Governor Jim Edgar proposed in August 1995. He ordered the state to contract with private companies to spend nearly $130 million on new prison beds. His chief of staff explained how the state would save money: "We don't intend to shackle the builders with all of the red tape and all of the procedures that [would be in place] if we were building [the medium-security prison]. And it won't in any way adversely affect the project" (*St. Louis Post-Dispatch*, August 24, 1995, p. 1B).

One of the ways some states are dealing with overcrowding is by sending jail and prison inmates to other states. The transportation of inmates to facilities in other states may offer an immediate solution to overcrowding, but it is not without risks and costs. For example, 500 Missouri inmates transferred to Texas in 1996 were sent to privately run jails that were not designed or staffed for dangerous felons or escape-risk inmates. A Missouri inmate who had escaped from the jail said, "The place is a joke. The security down here isn't much at all" (*St. Louis Post-Dispatch*, June 23, 1996, p. 1A). Other inmates complained of the mixing of violent felons with nonviolent offenders, and pointed out that they were denied counselors, adequate medical care, and even hot meals. One of the most common complaints is that inmates are denied access to their families back in Missouri.

The complaints of Missouri inmates housed in privately run Texas jails came to a head in the summer of 1997 with the release of a videotape showing inmates being attacked by guards and sheriff's deputies using stun guns and attack dogs as the inmates were forced to crawl across the floor. Capital Correctional Resources, Inc., ran the jail in question, and denied that excessive force had been used, calling the incident a training exercise. Missouri eventually cancelled its $6.2 million contract with the company, and shipped its prisoners back to Missouri. Texas lawmakers are now reviewing state regulations governing the housing and treatment of prisoners. Meanwhile, numerous lawsuits are making their way through the courts as a result of the incident.

THE POPULATION OF PRISONS AND JAILS TODAY

As noted at the beginning of this chapter, the vast majority of convicted felons are sentenced to some form of incarceration. The size of the incarcerated population today may surprise you: On January 1, 1998 there were 1,244,554 prisoners serving time in state or federal correctional institutions (Gilliard and Beck, 1998:3). This represents an **incarceration rate** of 445 prisoners per 100,000 U.S. residents. This incarceration rate is over three times the 1980 rate of 139 per 100,000 residents. In that year, the nation's prisons held 329,821 inmates.

incarceration rate The number of prison inmates per 100,000 U.S. residents.

Since 1980 the number of prison inmates has grown every year, increasing by an average of 8.7 percent. Figure 15.3 shows the trend. On a state-by-state basis, the largest percentage increases in the ten-year period 1986–1996 occurred in Texas, Colorado, and New Hampshire; the smallest increases occurred in Maine, Kansas, and Oregon (Table 15.3). On a regional basis, western states showed the greatest increase (151.0 percent), followed by the South (121.7 percent), the Midwest (114.4 percent), and the Northeast (116.9 percent).

Not surprisingly, states with larger populations tend to have larger inmate populations, while smaller states have smaller inmate populations. A useful way to compare prison populations across states is to compute incarceration rates, which take population into account. If we do this then the following pic-

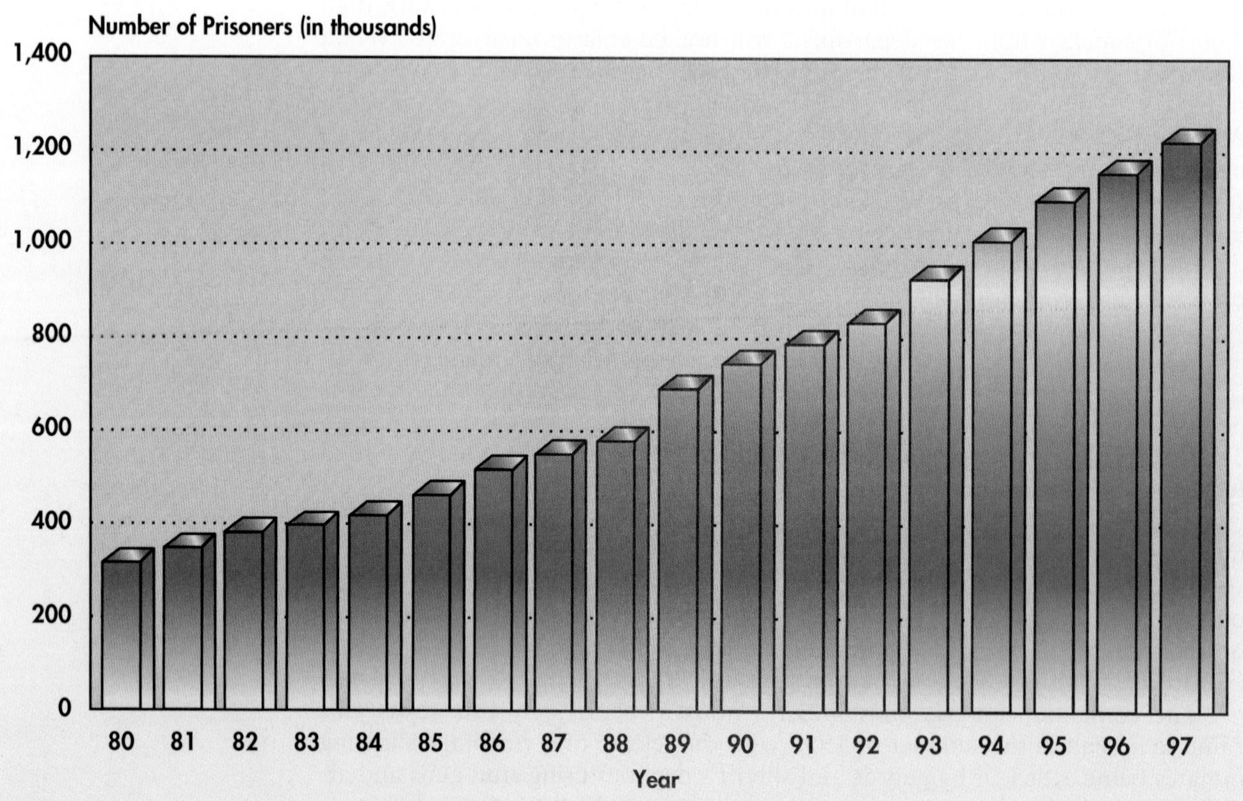

FIGURE 15.3 TRENDS IN THE U.S. PRISON POPULATION, 1980–1997
The U.S. prison population grew fourfold between 1980 and 1997. This accounts for much of the increase in prison expenditures noted in Figure 15.2.
Sources: From Darrell K. Gilliard and Allen J. Beck (1996). "Prisoners in 1994," *BJS Bulletin* August, p. 2; and Darrell K. Gilliard and Allen J. Beck (1998), "Prisoners in 1997," *BJS Bulletin* August, p. 3.

Table 15.3 States with Largest and Smallest Increases in Prison Populations, 1986–1996

Prison populations have grown dramatically over the past two decades throughout the country. During the decade 1986–1996, even most of the smallest increases were over 40 percent; some state prison populations more than doubled.

Largest Increases		Smallest Increases	
State	Percent	State	Percent
Texas	243.5	Maine	12.8
Colorado	227.0	Kansas	45.1
New Hampshire	164.8	Oregon	53.4
Kentucky	144.1	Delaware	59.5
Arizona	139.0	Nebraska	64.4
Connecticut	138.1	Maryland	67.1

Source: Christopher J. Mumola and Allen J. Beck (1997). "Prisoners in 1996," *BJS Bulletin* (June):4, Table 4.

ture emerges, shown in Table 15.4: In 1997 Texas ranked number one, with 717 inmates per 100,000 residents, followed by Louisiana (672) and Oklahoma (617). States with the lowest incarceration rates were North Dakota (112), Minnesota (113), and Maine (124).

Prison Overcrowding: A Correctional Crisis

As noted in the preceding section, prison overcrowding is a real problem in the nation's correctional systems. In Illinois, for example, the prison population is projected to increase from 28,000 in 1992 to 45,900 in 2000 (Joyce, 1992). Assuming no significant change in policies and crime, Illinois will have to build 23 new prisons at a cost of $1.2 billion and an annual operating budget of $391 million. Other states are facing a similar crisis. At the beginning of 1996, 39 states, the District of Columbia, and the federal prison system reported operating at 100 percent or more of the capacity they were designed or approved for (Bureau of Justice Statistics, 1996:8).

Jail Populations Are Growing, Too. Most states have turned to local jails as one way of dealing with prison overcrowding. By January 1, 1998, almost 34,000 prison inmates were being held in local jails. In some states the numbers are large: During 1997, New Jersey sent nearly 3,000 felons to jails, Virginia sent nearly 4,000 and Louisiana over 10,000 (Gilliard and Beck, 1998:6).

Table 15.4 States with Highest Incarceration Rates, 1996

Incarceration rates represent the number of prisoners per 100,000 residents in a jurisdiction. The number of prisoners in a county, state, region, or country is divided by the total resident population and the result is multiplied by 100,000. Rates take population size into account and, therefore, allow large and small jurisdictions to be compared. Here are the 10 states with the highest incarceration rates in 1997.

1. Texas	717	6. Nevada	518
2. Louisiana	672	7. Alabama	500
3. Oklahoma	617	8. Arizona	484
4. South Carolina	536	9. California	475
5. Mississippi	531	10. Georgia	472

Source: Darrell K. Gilliard and Allen J. Beck (1998). "Prisoners in 1997." *BJS Bulletin* (August):5, Table 5.

By the early 1990s, America's jails and prisons were severely overcrowded and the prison population continued to grow. This led to the construction of new or expanded facilities.

ILLUSTRATION BY BARRIE MAGUIRE, COURTESY OF THE CREATIVE WORKSHOP

In 1994 alone, Texas sent nearly 21,000 to jails because of prison overcrowding; however, by 1995 the state had significantly increased its prison capacity through new construction, and no prisoners were transferred to jails that year.

In midyear, 1997, the nation's 3,304 local jails were operating at 97 percent of capacity, with 567,079 inmates (including over 9,000 juveniles). This total was the largest number ever recorded. Although the nation's overall jail capacity was slightly greater than the jail population, this obscures the fact that some individual jails have been operating well over their rated capacity in the mid-1990s. In 1994, for example, jail facilities in Los Angeles County were operating 50 percent over capacity, with a daily population of 20,113; Dallas County Jail in Texas was 46 percent over capacity. In 1995, jail facilities in Philadelphia and in Orange County, California, were operating 35 percent over capacity (Gilliard and Beck, 1996:12).

Overcrowding adds to the already long list of problems facing the nation's jails (Perkins, Stephan, and Beck, 1995). It should be remembered that jails perform a variety of functions; detention is only one of them, although it is the central purpose of a jail. Jails detain the following people:

- People awaiting trial, conviction, or sentencing
- Juveniles pending transfer to juvenile authorities
- Probation, parole, and bail-bond violators
- Mentally ill people awaiting transfer to mental health facilities
- People wanted by the military, under protective custody, for contempt of court, or as witnesses

Jails also do the following:

- Release inmates into the community after completion of their sentence
- Transfer inmates to state and federal authorities
- Operate community-based programs involving electronic monitoring, community service, or other types of supervision

In 1993, 413 jurisdictions were under court order to address specific conditions of confinement (Cornelius, 1997). In descending order of severity, these conditions included the following:

- Crowded living units
- Inadequate recreational facilities
- Inadequate medical services or facilities
- Too restrictive visitation policies or procedures
- Inappropriate disciplinary policies or procedures
- Inadequate food service
- Inappropriate mixing of inmates (e.g., by age, gender, or offense)
- Inadequate training and education programs
- Inadequate counseling services

Critics of jails contend that jail time is generally more punishing, dangerous, and degrading than time in a maximum-security prison. There is, in addition, the mixing of technically innocent people, petty offenders, and sometimes juveniles with hardened criminals. Experienced convicts often say they would rather do time in prison than in jail.

If we add the jail and prison populations together, then over 1.7 million Americans were held in prisons or jails at midyear 1997. This represents a total U.S. incarceration rate for adults of 645 per 100,000 U.S. residents. Figure 15.4 shows how the United States compares with other industrialized countries. Only Russia, whose figure is regarded as an estimate, comes close.

Policies Drive Prison Populations Up. Some of the variation in international and domestic incarceration rates may be explained by variations in crime rates: Places with higher rates of serious crime will tend to have higher rates of imprisonment. However, there is evidence that much of this variation is explained by differences in crime policy rather than differences in crime itself. For example, the United States sends more people to prison for lesser crimes, and keeps them there longer (Donziger, 1996:37–38). The recent increases in American prison populations are also explained largely by policy, not by crime (Irwin and Austin, 1994).

To illustrate, the rise in Illinois crime during the 1980s accounts for only 9 percent of the growth in the Illinois prison population; another 20 percent was caused by demographic shifts such as increasing numbers of young adults (Joyce, 1992). Yet a toughening of drug enforcement beginning in 1984 resulted in a 742 percent increase in the number of drug offenders sent to prison (from 518 to 4,361). This policy change was the single most important factor accounting for growth in the Illinois prison population. A similar situation exists nationwide, as shown in Figure 15.5. From 1986 to 1991 the state prison population grew 58 percent; nearly half of this increase was accounted for by drug offenders (Bureau of Justice Statistics, 1993c).

The Demographics of Imprisonment

It has been estimated that the lifetime probability of any particular American between ages 13 and 84 serving time in a state prison is 1 chance in 20 (Bonczar and Beck, 1997). However, the risks are not equal for all groups of

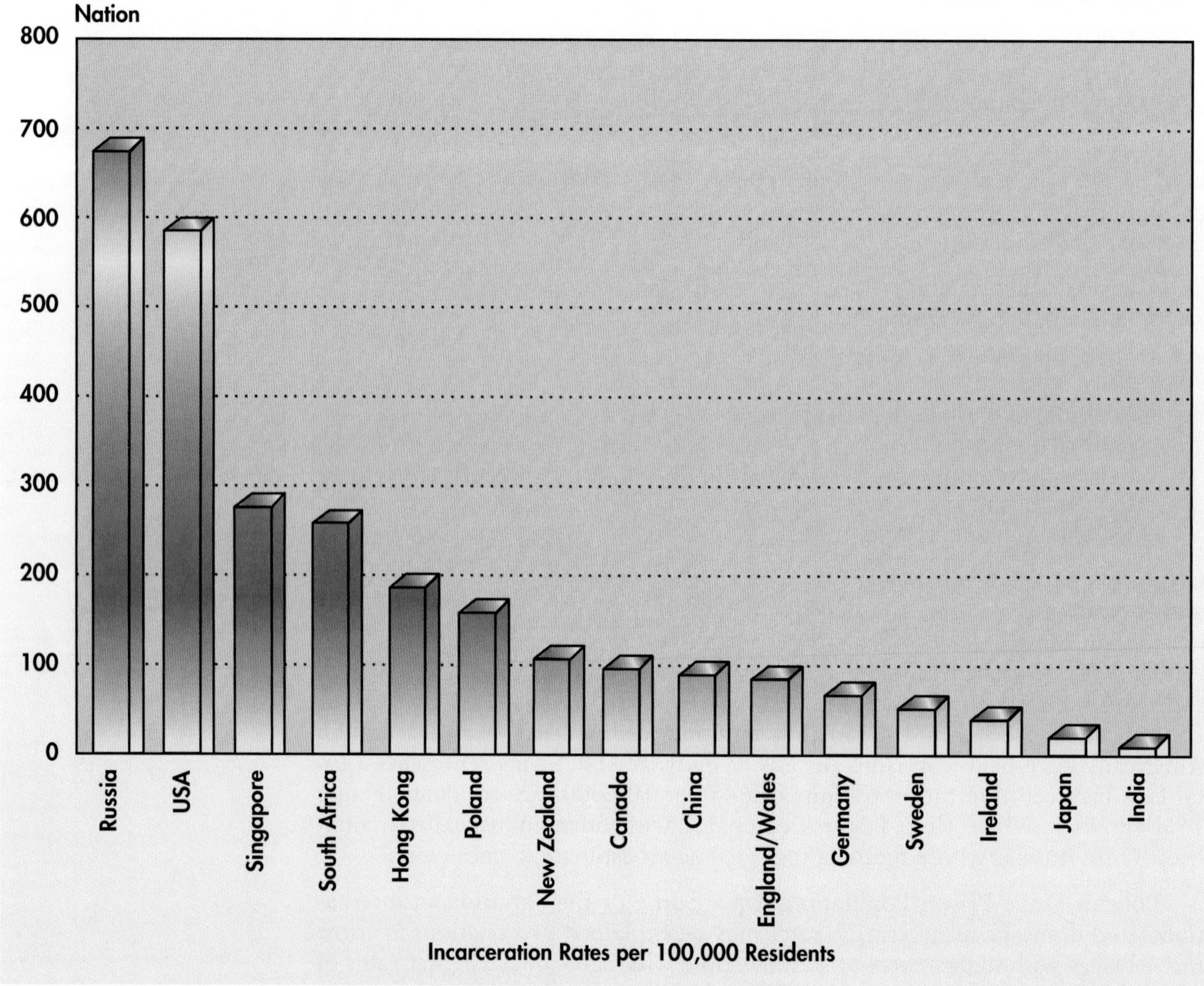

FIGURE 15.4 Incarceration Rates of Various Nations, 1995
The U.S. incarceration rate is much greater than the rate in most other nations, and it is surpassed only by Russia's.

Source: Marc Mauer (1997), *Americans Behind Bars: The International Use of Incarceration, 1995*. Washington, D.C.: The Sentencing Project.

Americans. The highest probabilities of imprisonment are for black males—1 chance in 4—and the lowest for white females, who have 1 chance in 200 of going to prison during their lifetime. Table 15.5 shows the lifetime probabilities of imprisonment for different groups of Americans.

Overall, the incarceration rate for black Americans is 1,860 per 100,000 black residents compared to only 289 white Americans per 100,000 white residents. Although the racial disparities may not be the same, this is not just an American phenomenon. Race-based differences are also found in Great Britain, Australia, and Canada: black people, aboriginal people, and native Canadians, respectively, are incarcerated at far higher rates than whites (Tonry, 1994b; Rothman, 1994). In all these countries, the crackdown on drug offenders and tougher sentencing policies seem responsible for much of the disparity, but racial prejudice and discrimination within criminal justice are undoubtedly contributing factors as well. And in America, the rising rates of violent crime among black males during the past three decades have also contributed to the higher incarceration rate.

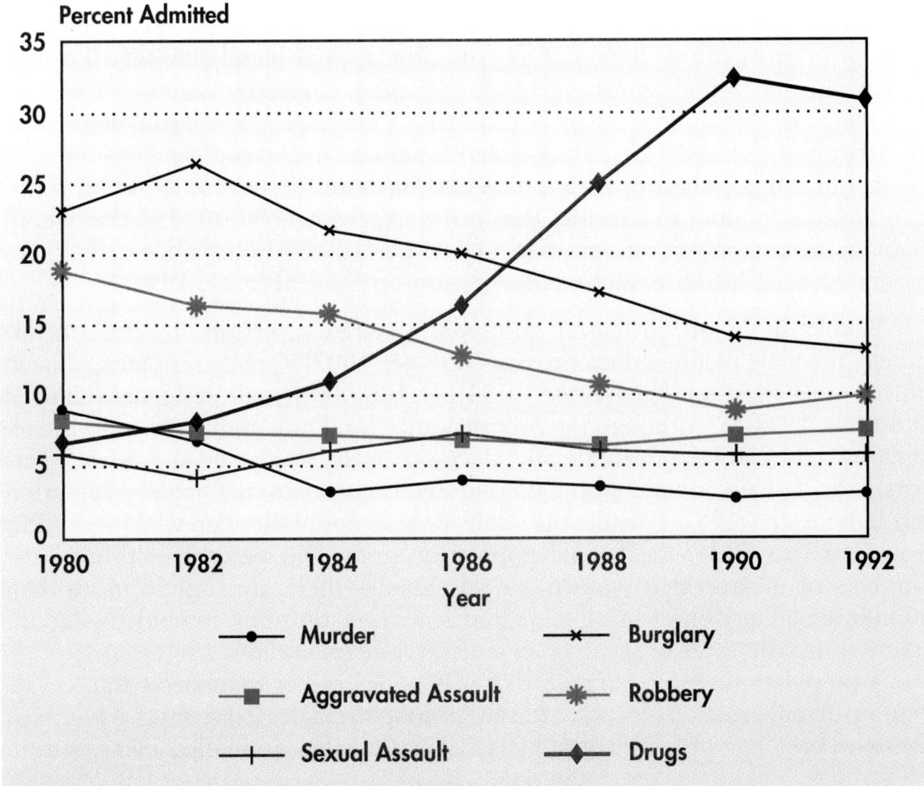

FIGURE 15.5 Commitments to State Prisons, 1980–1992
The percentage of new prisoners admitted for drug offenses dramatically increased between 1980 and 1992. Admissions for other offenses declined or remained stable over this time period.

Source: Darrell K. Gilliard and Allen J. Beck (1994). "Prisoners in 1993," *BJS Bulletin* (June):10.

Table 15.5 Lifetime Probability of Going to Prison for Different Groups of Americans

The risk of being sent to prison during a person's lifetime varies from one group of Americans to another. Based on 1991 incarceration rates, here are the most recent calculations based on sex and race.

Group	Lifetime Probability of Going to Prison
Sex	
Male	1 chance in 11
Female	1 chance in 91
Race/Ethnicity	
White	1 chance in 40
Male	1 chance in 23
Female	1 chance in 200
Black	1 chance in 6
Males	1 chance in 4
Female	1 chance in 28
Hispanics	1 chance in 11
Males	1 chance in 6
Females	1 chance in 67

Source: Thomas P. Bonczar and Allen J. Beck (1997). "Lifetime Likelihood of Going to State or Federal Prison." *BJS Special Report* (March):2.

Figure 15.6 shows that white and black prison admissions have been converging for most of the 20th century, and now approximately half of all prison inmates in the United States are black. Yet there is concern among Hispanics that their rates of imprisonment are starting to increase even faster than those of African Americans. Hispanics are the nation's most rapidly growing and most youthful population, with the highest birth and fertility rates and a tradition of large families (Martinez, 1987). In fact, from 1980 to 1993 the overall Hispanic incarceration rate grew from 163 per 100,000 Hispanics to 529. An estimated 163,500 Hispanics were in prison on December 31, 1993.

Women in Prison. Men far outnumber women in prison. In 1997, for instance, the male incarceration rate was 853 per 100,000 male residents, sixteen times higher than the female rate of 54 per 100,000 female residents (Gilliard and Beck, 1998:5). Although the proportion of total prison inmates who are female has not changed dramatically since the early 1970s (from 4 to 5.9 percent), the female inmate population grew faster than the male population throughout the 1980s: while the male prison population grew 214 percent from 1980 to 1994, the female population grew 386 percent. Although the numbers of incarcerated women are still small—there are slightly more than 60,000 female prisoners in all state and federal institutions combined—the increase in female rates of incarceration deserves explanation.

It should come as no surprise that it is policy rather than crime that is driving up female rates of incarceration. Although female arrest rates have risen over the past few years, suggesting a rise in female criminality, incarceration

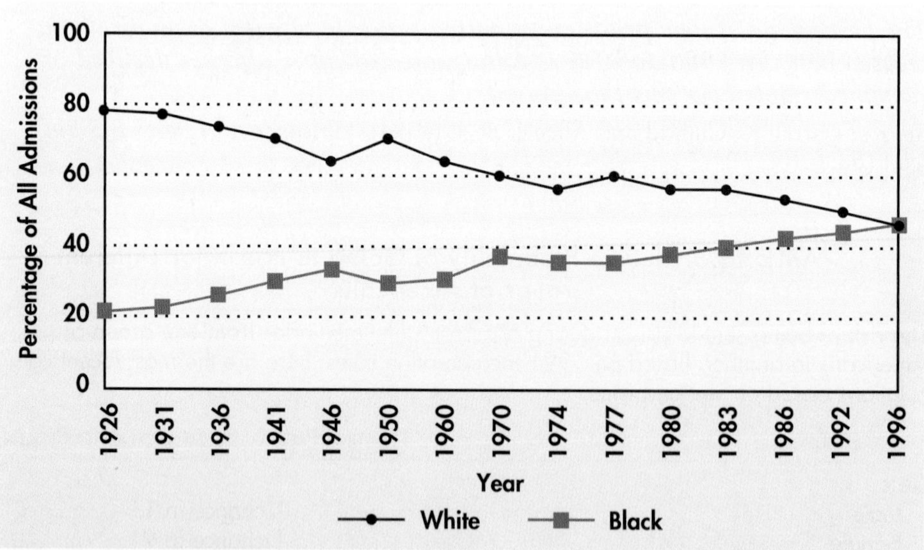

FIGURE 15.6 CONVERGENCE OF BLACK AND WHITE INMATES IN THE ADULT MALE PRISON POPULATION, 1926–1992

Today, there are slightly more black inmates in prison than white inmates. This new situation is the culmination of changes that began a long time ago and have continued to the present day. This graph shows the convergence of the two races over a 70-year period. Although black Americans make up less than 15 percent of the U.S. population, they represent half of the prison population. The reasons are explained in the text.

Sources: Compiled from Patrick A. Langan (1991). *Race of Prisoners Admitted to State and Federal Institutions, 1926–1986* (p. 5). Washington, D.C.: U.S. Department of Justice; Darrell K. Gilliard and Allen J. Beck (1998). "Prisoners in 1997." *BJS Bulletin* (August):9.

rates for women have risen even faster. The reason is drug law violations. Although the incarceration rate for women has increased since the 1980s, the percentage of women in prison for violent crimes has declined, while the percentage of women in prison for drug offenses has more than doubled, to over 30 percent.

According to a 1993 survey of corrections departments in 45 states, there were more women in prison on drug or alcohol offenses than for either violent crimes *or* property crimes in 14 states and the District of Columbia (Maguire and Pastore, 1995:550).

There is no sign that this trend will change over the next few years. This means that more and more jail and prison administrators will come under pressure to address the needs of a rising population of female inmates. Female prisoners have special needs that require unique services, and yet there is mounting evidence that correctional authorities have been slow to meet this challenge. This topic is discussed in detail in the next chapter, which considers what prison life is like for inmates and staff.

SUMMARY

The use of imprisonment as a form of punishment dates from the seventeenth and eighteenth centuries; before then, prisons were used to hold people awaiting trial or who had not paid their fines, and as a place where branding, torture, or other punishments could be administered. The forerunners of the modern prison were the sixteenth-century workhouses and houses of correction, providing food and shelter and a regimen of hard work and strict discipline to the homeless poor and criminals whose offenses did not merit execution or exile.

Penal reforms of the late eighteenth century led to the spread of imprisonment as a punishment in itself, and architectural innovations accompanied new ideas about how prisoners should be treated during confinement. Torture was out, and influential Quakers advocated silent penitence in solitary confinement as a means to reform criminals. Adopted as the Pennsylvania system after the first penitentiary in Philadephia, silent penitence in solitary cells soon gave way to the Auburn system of reformation through work—though silence was still enforced most of the time. The reformatory movement of the late 1800s expanded on the idea that the prison experience should reform inmates, and promoted individualized treatment as its cornerstone. However, faced with overcrowding, insufficient resources, and continued belief that imprisonment should be a punitive experience, the movement was in decline by 1900.

The last 100 years have seen five major developments in the use of prisons:

1. At first, the use of prison labor expanded until many prisons were like large walled factories crammed with workers. However, prison labor soon came under fire from labor groups concerned with unfair competition and from others concerned about the many abuses of inmates, especially black inmates in the South whose labor was leased out to private companies. Except for inmate work done on behalf of the state or prison itself, a 30-year lull in prison industries followed. The 1970s saw a rebirth, however, with new protections for both inmates and workers on the outside, and now joint ventures between prisons and the private sector are all the rage.
2. Attempts to classify inmates grew in popularity along with the behavioral sciences, and prison populations were divided up according to the levels of security needed to ensure their confinement and control. Maximum-, medium-, and minimum-security prisons emerged, and a new emphasis was placed on correcting and rehabilitating all but the most dangerous and escape-prone inmates.

3. As time passed, rehabilitation remained more an ideal than a reality. By the 1970s people were questioning whether anything worked. Growing inmate populations and periodic rioting resulted in warehousing of violent and repeat offenders and the emergence of the supermaximum-security prison.
4. Rehabilitation in prisons was not working, so a new idea emerged: community corrections. Many states moved large numbers of children and adults—including criminal offenders—out of institutions for treatment in the community. This subject is covered in detail in Chapter 17.
5. The idea of making money out of prisons was not a 20th-century invention, but it emerged with renewed vigor in the 1980s, partly in response to overcrowding. Privatization is now extensive, with more than 80 prisons and jails constructed and/or managed by private companies. Some private prisons make their money by taking in prisoners from other states, and this is just one point of controversy surrounding privatization.

The prison and jail population today is growing at an astounding pace. If it keeps up there will be nearly 2 million prisoners by the year 2000. America already has the highest incarceration rate among Western industrialized nations, and one of the highest in the world. Changes in policies rather than in crime itself are largely responsible for this growth. The rise in mandatory sentencing, the call for longer sentences, "three strikes" laws, and harsh drug policies are all factors in the recent growth of prison populations. The next chapter explores some of the implications of these policies for prison life.

WHAT DO YOU THINK NOW?

- Now that you've read about different types of prison movements, were you surprised by the variety? What are the different goals of prisons?
- How did USP–Lompoc avoid the traditional problems associated with warehousing? How might prison staff encourage this sort of atmosphere?
- You have seen that prison inmates are disproportionately drawn from certain groups of Americans. Explain why this is so and how the picture has changed.

KEY TERMS AND CASES

workhouse
house of correction
gaol (jail)
proportionality
utilitarianism
Panopticon Plan
hulks
Pennsylvania system
Auburn system
reformatory movement
industrial prison
lease system
contract system
state-use system
chain gang
inmate classification
rehabilitative ideal
parole
maximum-security prison
medical model
medium-security prison
minimum-security prison
recidivism
pathology of imprisonment
deinstitutionalization
community-based corrections
warehousing
supermaximum-security prison
Madrid v. Gomez
privatization
incarceration rate

ACTIVE LEARNING CHALLENGES

1. Debate the pros and cons of using prisoners to produce goods and services for sale on the open market.
2. Divide the class into four groups and have each group find out as much as they can about one of the following types of prisons: supermaximum-security, maximum-security, medium-security, and minimum-security. Then have the groups report back to the class on the nature, benefits, and drawbacks of each type.
3. Discuss the pros and cons of privatization of corrections.
4. The incarceration rates of men, women, African Americans, Hispanics, and non-Hispanic white people are significantly different. Find the most recent numbers from the Bureau of Justice Statistics, and discuss the reasons for the differences. What conclusion does the class reach?

INTERNET CHALLENGES

The Web pages mentioned here can all be accessed through the Web site for this textbook at **http://www.prenhall.com/barlow/**.

1. Learn about great prisons of the past and see how they differ from those of today. In what ways has imprisonment *as punishment* changed? Begin with a visit to England's Tower of London.
2. For links to the American Correctional Association and all sorts of other corrections-related sites, check out the Corrections Connection. Find out what issue is the current topic for discussion in the "Corrections Think Tank."
3. Visit the home pages of companies in the business of corrections. What do they offer? How do they promote their products and services? What new ideas in privatization can we expect in the 21st century? A good place to start your investigation is at prisons.com, the Web site representing the corrections industry.

CHAPTER 16

LIFE IN PRISON

LEARNING OBJECTIVES

- Explain the primary goal of maximum-security prisons, and describe the methods used to control inmates.
- Describe how inmates adapt to prison life and the different ways they attempt to survive.
- Describe the guard's perspective on use of discipline and control of inmates.
- Understand why prisons are stressful places for inmates and correctional officers, and the problems that surface as a result.
- Understand the special problems facing women in prison, including motherhood and health care among female inmates, and relations with men among female staff.
- Explain the three challenges in corrections: HIV/AIDS, geriatric inmates, and prisoner rights.

A total institution such as prison envelops the lives of both inmates and guards. In this situation, guards may feel they are "doing time" just as the inmates are.

ILLUSTRATION BY BARRIE MAGUIRE, COURTESY OF THE CREATIVE WORKSHOP

The days are all the same—just a blur—and looking back a year ago . . . it seems like only yesterday because yesterday was just like it was a year ago.

JIMMY DUNN, FORMER INMATE OF VARIOUS "BIG HOUSE" PRISONS

Gangs run everything. They rape, they rob, they extort.

FRANKIE MACK COLBERT, FORMER ILLINOIS INMATE

You can't show weakness or else they will devour you, eat you alive. I change when I walk in there. I can feel my neck and shoulders tense up as soon as I'm in the parking lot.

MICHAEL THEBERGE, CORRECTIONAL OFFICER AT A MAXIMUM-SECURITY STATE PRISON IN MISSOURI

John Martin was headed back to prison for the second time. As he rode the Department of Corrections bus from the county jail to the prison, he thought about what was ahead. The first time he was incarcerated, he was in a medium-security prison. That was not so bad, since he had opportunities to work and to entertain himself. And there were no gangs at that facility. This time he was headed to the "Big House." He had heard plenty of stories of life in the "Big House," and although he thought he was pretty tough, his mouth went dry with anxiety and fear as the bus drew into the prison courtyard. The whole bus went very quiet, he noticed.

Martin knew he was in for a miserable time and that his ten-year sentence would seem like an eternity. He had made himself a promise to keep out of trouble, but he knew there were lots of ways a new inmate, or "fish," could be drawn into disputes with staff and other inmates. Even making eye contact with some guys would be taken as a challenge. Since he was older than many inmates and had done a prior stretch, he did not fear sexual assault. More likely, his tattoos—remnants of gang membership in his youth—would draw the attention of gang members looking for recruits or identifying potential enemies. He had heard of fish with gang connections being killed on their first day among the general inmate population.

Martin's strategy for survival was simple: Do your own time. He would find out who the troublemakers were and try to stay clear of them. He would be polite to the guards but not friendly; you needed to know the lay of the land before you made any friends in prison, and being too friendly with guards made other inmates suspect you of being a snitch. That could spell lots of trouble. He would try to find a routine that kept his mind busy but did not draw attention to himself. There were people inside that he knew from the street, so he would not be completely alone; they might be useful connections if he needed them. Ten years is a hell of a long time.

It is almost certain that some of your fellow students know someone like John Martin or have a close relative who has spent time in prison; one or two students may even have been incarcerated themselves. Imprisonment is affecting an increasing number of Americans each year. When you add up the inmates, the correctional staff, and all their relatives and friends, 30 to 40 million people are probably touched by some aspect of prison life every day in the United States.

This chapter explores the organization and culture of prisons, and examines the experience of imprisonment from the vantage point of those who live and work there. We shall also examine the controversial issue of prisoner rights. Many of the changes that have occurred within prisons over the years resulted directly or indirectly from lawsuits brought by inmates against those who run the nation's jails and prisons.

At the outset it is important to keep in mind that correctional institutions vary considerably in terms of size, location, characteristics of inmates, nature and range of services offered, and security level. You should therefore be suspicious of generalizations about prison life. On the other hand, *no* prison allows its inmates to come and go as they please, and *all* prisons restrict inmate access to family and friends, and regulate how inmates are to interact with each other and with the staff. This generalization is worth remembering: *All forms of imprisonment deal with involuntary populations whose behavior is closely regulated and may be controlled by force.*

Most of the discussion in this chapter concerns life in maximum-security prisons for men. There are five reasons for this:

1. Imprisonment in a maximum-security facility is the most severe form of *common* punishment for crime; it is important to know what the bulk of society's most serious offenders experience as punishment.
2. The maximum-security prison has been around for 200 years and as such is a continuous thread linking present correctional practice with the early days of penal reform.
3. The maximum-security prison has been the site of most of the killings and other violence that has plagued corrections in America, but which has worsened in the past 30 years.
4. Inmates of maximum-security prisons have generally been incarcerated more often, and for longer periods of time, than inmates of other facilities. Moreover, more and more maximum-security inmates are "lifers" who will get old before they get out—if they ever do. This has serious implications for our prisons and the people who run them.
5. Finally, life in maximum-security prisons has been studied more closely than that in any other type of correctional facility. One of the first studies was by sociologist Hans Reimer, who in the

1930s voluntarily served three months in prison so he could explore prison life through participant observation. His work stimulated later studies (Clemmer, 1940; Sykes, 1958), and these classics in turn spawned others (Jacobs, 1977; Fleisher, 1989).

These studies examined maximum-security prisons for men and can tell us nothing about life in correctional facilities for women. There have been important studies of life in female prisons, and these have uncovered unique problems that confront incarcerated women (Ward and Kassebaum, 1965; Giallombardo, 1966; Heffernan, 1972). A later section of the chapter will explore the character and problems of prison life for women.

? WHAT DO YOU THINK?

- What are some of the new challenges facing prisons today? How has prison life changed over recent decades?
- What is the best way for inmates to deal with trouble-making inmates, such as gang members, frequent fighters, and those dealing in contraband? What is the best way for guards to handle them?
- What are the keys to solidarity among prison staff? What can undermine it?
- What are some of the special challenges facing female inmates?

THE ORGANIZATION AND CULTURE OF MAXIMUM-SECURITY PRISONS FOR MEN

Two sociological concepts will help us understand what is going on behind prison walls. First, there is the distinction between formal and informal organization. **Formal organization** refers to a social structure that is deliberately created to achieve one or more specific goals, and whose positions and roles are governed by written rules. The different units and lines of authority within a formal organization are often depicted in the form of a hierarchical chart. Your university or college is a formal organization, as is General Motors, IBM, the New York Yankees, and your local supermarket chain. Prisons are also formal organizations.

formal organization A social structure created to achieve specific goals with written rules governing how activities are carried out and how authority is exercised.

Informal organization arises within formal organizations. It develops from two things: (1) the adjustments individuals make to the experience of being members of the formal organization, and (2) the impact of their personalities and backgrounds on their activities and relations with other members, including the people in charge. Examples are friendship networks, work cliques, and other informal groupings that emerge as members develop shared routines.

informal organization Friendship networks and work cliques that arise in formal organizations as members respond to their experiences and to the impact of their backgrounds and personalities.

Sometimes this informal organization helps the larger organization achieve its goals, as when workers develop informal strategies for getting work done more efficiently; sometimes informal organization hinders formal goal achievement, as when workers “go slow” on the job. In correctional facilities, we find a prison culture that is partly universal—found in prisons everywhere—and partly unique to each particular facility. Later sections of the chapter explore prison culture in detail.

PRISON AS A "TOTAL INSTITUTION"

Most people participate in more than one formal organization, moving back and forth between them, and between these organizations and other aspects of their lives. Formal organizations often exert significant influence over the attitudes and behavior of participants, yet individuals can still go home and "be themselves." They have a life apart from the organization.

total institution A closed social system such as a prison, the military, or a mental hospital that completely envelops the lives of the people living or working in it.

Things are different for people living or working in prisons, military bases, and mental hospitals. These are examples of what sociologists call a **total institution.** This is the second important concept that will help us understand life in prison. A total institution envelops the lives of its participants. They have no life apart from the institution. Here are the classic characteristics of a total institution (Goffman, 1961:6):

1. All aspects of life are conducted in the same place and under the same single authority.
2. Each phase of the member's daily activity is carried on in the immediate company of a large batch of others, all of whom are treated alike and required to do the same thing together.
3. All phases of the day's activities are tightly scheduled, with one activity leading at a prearranged time into the next, the whole sequence of activities being imposed from above by a system of explicit formal rulings and a body of officials.
4. The various enforced activities are brought together into a single rational plan purportedly designed to fulfill the official aims of the institution.

Total institutions are closed social systems that exclude outsiders, even the spouses of participants. This binds members together and creates informal customs for establishing belonging and "worth." In the maximum-security prison for men, many of these customs involve displays of toughness or "machismo." Total institutions also isolate some insiders from others: for example, officers from enlisted soldiers, medical staff from patients, correctional staff from inmates. In maximum-security prisons, inmates often find themselves isolated from each other, both physically and socially. Sometimes this isolation is by design—physical separation in cells, for example, or as a form of punishment—and sometimes it arises from the informal organization created as inmates adapt to the ordeal of imprisonment. Prison culture is not a sharing culture (Fleisher, 1989:209), so close personal relationships are difficult to establish and maintain. The loss of personal relationships is one of the "pains of imprisonment," discussed later in the chapter.

THE PRIMARY GOAL AND FORMAL STRUCTURE OF MAXIMUM-SECURITY PRISONS

As we saw in Chapter 4, the individual prison is part of a larger correctional structure within the state or federal bureaucracy. In the federal system, for example, the Federal Bureau of Prisons manages the government's correctional facilities as an agency within the U.S. Department of Justice. The director of the bureau reports to the attorney general of the United States, a presidential appointee who must be approved by the U.S. Congress. In most states, the Department of Corrections is a state agency whose director is appointed by the governor and approved by the state legislature. In theory, the organization and operation of individual facilities is governed by laws and administrative regulations, and by the policies and procedures approved at the system level and passed on to the prison warden or administrator. In practice, the formal structure and informal organization of the individual prison largely determine what goes on inside its walls.

Custody Is the Primary Goal. Custody—confining people within a physical space—is the prison's primary reason for being, and the first concern of correctional management. However, as danger and risk of escape increase, the importance of custody increases; maximum-security prisons are designed, built, and managed so as to keep prisoners from escaping and to minimize the risks that they will injure or kill staff or other inmates. Yet even minimum-security prisons must guard against inmates walking out before they are released. This is accomplished primarily by restricting the population of minimum-security prisons to short-term, nonviolent offenders who pose little escape risk. Armed guard towers, high walls, and razor wire are not needed, and the facility looks more like a college campus than a prison.

The Custodial Hierarchy. For most of modern correctional history, the custodial goal has been accomplished through a military-style organization of prison guards, now usually called *correctional officers*. These officers also have day-to-day responsibility for inmate and staff safety. A hierarchical structure of uniformed officers reports to the prison warden or superintendent via assistant wardens, captains, lieutenants, sergeants, and—at the bottom—line officers. In most prisons the line correctional officer reports up through the chain of command to the assistant or associate warden responsible for daily operation of the prison. Even with the rise of rehabilitation and new management techniques after World War II, military-style custodial management has remained in one form or another at virtually all maximum- and medium-security prisons. Uniforms are still commonplace—although less formal-looking—and so is the system of hierarchical ranks, although sometimes without the militaristic emblems and labels.

CONTROLLING THE BEHAVIOR OF PRISON INMATES

Custody and safety involve controlling the behavior of inmates. All sorts of inanimate forms of control are found in prisons, the most obvious being bars and locks. However, to work properly, all these security devices depend on the behavior of human beings.

Correctional officers with direct responsibility for custody and security are assigned to cell blocks, perimeter towers, catwalks, workshops, and common

A prison guard in a guard tower, which gives guards view of all comings and goings in the prison's outdoor areas. Indoors, guards are also stationed on the cellblock floor, on catwalks, and in dining rooms and other places where prisoners interact.

PHOTO BY A. RAMEY, COURTESY OF PHOTOEDIT

areas of a prison where inmates and staff move about. In many state prisons and the federal system, these officers are unarmed when in direct contact with inmates, but may be armed with handguns, shotguns, or automatic rifles at other times. In the Menard penitentiary in Illinois, for example, the tiered cell blocks are overseen by officers armed with automatic rifles who patrol a catwalk above the cells; guards in the perimeter towers are also armed with rifles. However, the correctional officers who move inmates from place to place or have other direct contact are unarmed for their own safety and that of the inmates.

Security Classification of New Inmates. One of the first steps taken to ensure control and safety is the *security classification* of new inmates. Prison administrators recognize that some inmates are likely to be more trouble than others, and therefore inmates are assigned to different custody levels even within the same maximum-security prison. At USP–Lompoc, for example, inmates are assigned a custody score when they first arrive based on such things as involvement with drugs and alcohol, mental stability, current and prior offenses, and—when relevant—prior behavior while in prison. The highest security level is VI, and these inmates are MAX custody (Fleisher, 1989:66). MAX prisoners are confined to only certain cell blocks, and they may be excluded from certain types of work. If they are moved outside the secure perimeter for any reason, they are placed in full restraints—leg irons and a *Martin chain*, which wraps around the waist and to which handcuffs are padlocked.

If an inmate has previously assaulted or killed correctional staff, has made successful or repeated unsuccessful attempts to escape, or is thought to be a high-ranking gang member or gang hit man, his picture and criminal histories are filed in a "blue book" that all staff are expected to read and remember. These inmates are carefully watched, especially by the line guards with whom they have most interaction. In most prison systems, high-risk inmates such as these are kept in special cell blocks or transferred to supermaximum facilities. Sometimes elaborate steps are taken to keep gang leaders apart. In Illinois, for example, known gang leaders are often transferred from one prison to another, with no warning and in the middle of the night.

Looking for Weapons and Other Contraband: Searches and Shakedowns. One of the major ways that correctional officers ensure their own and the inmates' safety is by looking out for hidden weapons. In 1991, I visited the Dartmoor prison in England, situated in the middle of a desolate region 175 miles southwest of London. On the wall by the main entrance were two display cases full of handmade weapons confiscated from inmates. In prisons, weapons are fashioned from just about anything, but pens, combs, cutlery and utensils, and toothbrushes are popular. A retired prison warden remarked, "I've had 'em murdered in there with T-shirts, shoe strings, blankets—anything at all can be used" (*St. Louis Post-Dispatch*, August 18, 1996, p. B5). In prison, weapons have special names that become part of a unique language, or *argot*, characteristic of prison culture. Prison argot is found in various forms around the world. Box 16.1 illustrates some of the terms and their meaning; they are drawn from the various prison studies cited in this chapter.

Since most weapons are easily concealed, prisoners in maximum- and many medium-security institutions are patted down and sometimes strip-searched when they enter or leave secure areas, when they return from work assignments, and both before and after meeting visitors. Officers are looking for weapons and popular contraband such as drugs, alcohol, matches, or food. Similarly, officers might "shake down," or search, an inmate's cell searching for weapons, drugs, or homemade alcohol, usually called "brew." Brew is commonplace in prisons, but an inmate caught with it is usually punished. The reason is simple: Alcohol is a dangerous substance inside a prison because prison

Box 16.1

GLOBAL JUSTICE

PRISONERS SPEAK THE SAME LANGUAGE IN MANY DIFFERENT PLACES

Prison culture everywhere produces a special language, or argot. Inmates and staff of different prisons across America, and even across English-speaking countries generally, share some of the same argot. Argot serves various purposes: It is a shorthand for more complicated words and phrases; it often replaces official words and phrases—so in a sense it is "owned" by inmates and staff; it carries special meanings, some of which are derogatory, some complimentary. Above all, prison argot is the language of "belonging"—it separates insiders from outsiders since only those who have experienced prison life understand it.

The slang used for inmate weapons is an example of prison argot. A "sissy shank," for example, can be made by attaching a razor blade or other sharp metal edge to the end of a toothbrush. "Stickers" are thin, pointed weapons like an ice pick. They can be easily made out of bedsprings. Inmates or guards who are assaulted with such weapons are "stuck" or "shanked."

Inmates and guards are referred to with special names. Guards are "pigs," or "hacks," or "screws." New inmates are called "fish," new guards "fish pigs," or "rookie hacks." Inmates who take things from others by force are called "gorillas"; inmates who give information to guards or other inmates are "rats"; inmates from the same town or neighborhood are "home boys."

Not surprisingly, there are prison terms to cover illicit activities. Alcohol, banned in prisons but smuggled in or made by inmates, is known as "brew." "Punks" are male inmates who are forced into submissive homosexual activities, while "fags" are considered homosexual by nature. In women's prisons, a "Cherrie" is a female inmate not yet initiated into lesbian activity, while a "femme," "Mommy," or "fox" plays the female role to a "stud broad," "butch," or "pimp" in lesbian relationships.

is a world of anger, threats, frustration, and resentment. In 1983, for example, a Missouri prison guard was stabbed to death with a metal ruler by drunken inmates (*St. Louis Post-Dispatch*, August 18, 1996, p. B5). Sometimes an entire cell block will be searched by a shakedown team of ten to fifteen officers, and every unauthorized piece of property, however harmless, is removed.

During a shakedown, "nooks and crannies are combed in every cell. Hacks check inside every cardboard box; look inside, under and behind every footlocker; open every book; inspect and feel every article of clothing; check inside toilets, and so on . . ." (Fleisher, 1989:190). If they are present, inmates stand outside their cells, watching and sometimes complaining bitterly about the intrusion. By removing objects that inmates have collected to personalize their cells but that are technically against the rules, prison staff establish their authority and power to enforce rules and to control the most personal aspects of an inmate's life.

DISCIPLINING INMATES

Whenever an inmate breaks a rule and is caught by prison staff, some sort of disciplinary action is likely to follow. Formal procedures generally distinguish among levels of seriousness. In the federal system, for example, there are four levels of prohibited acts, rather like college course numbers, but in reverse.

Thus, 100-level infractions are the most serious, and include murder and assault, escape, rioting, or setting fires (Fleisher, 1989:81). 200-level offenses include fighting or threatening staff, and engaging in sex; 300-level offenses include refusing to work, being insolent to staff, and drunkenness; 400-level offenses include tattooing and being unsanitary.

The penalties for rule infractions vary according to the seriousness of the infraction. Box 16.2 shows the penalties used in Graterford Penitentiary in Pennsylvania. Of course, a list of penalties is one thing, enforcement is another. In fact, prison officials have wide discretionary power in the enforcement of most rules. Without doubt this power is enhanced by the vague and subjective wording of some of the offenses. Unfortunately, this invites abuses of the disciplinary system, which in turn extend enforcement beyond the point necessary to ensure control and safety.

The Discretionary Side of Prison Discipline. Prison staff have wide discretionary power in the enforcement of most rules. Without doubt, this power is enhanced by the vague and subjective wording of some of the infractions. This invites abuses of the prison disciplinary system, and these in turn extend enforcement beyond the point necessary to ensure control and safety. In Scotland during 1986, for example, an analysis of inmate offenses committed in men's prisons showed that serious offenses against discipline such as assaults and property damage were less than 10 percent of the total (Scraton, Sim, and Skidmore, 1991:81). By far the most common offenses were violations of "good order and discipline" (31.5 percent), disobedience and refusal to work (22.2 percent), disrespect and improper or indecent language (13 percent), and committing a nuisance (11.5 percent). In other words, inmates were largely be-

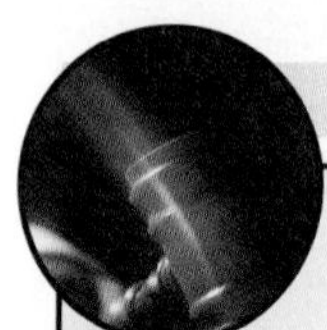

Box 16.2

JUSTICE PROFESSIONALS AT WORK

DISCIPLINING INMATES

When prison inmates violate the rules, there are various responses that correctional staff may make. The response depends on the seriousness of the infraction. The more serious the infraction, the more formal the response and the more severe the penalty. Here is a list of disciplinary penalties in use during the 1980s at Graterford Penitentiary in Pennsylvania:

1. *Reprimand and warning*: A warning from the Hearing Examiner not to do it again, "or else!"
2. *Loss of privileges*: Suspension of privileges for a given period of time. Privileges include visitation, phone calls, access to the commissary or yard, work, and television.
3. *Cell restriction*: Confinement to cells except for meals and recreation, and loss of job. All other privileges are left intact unless specifically suspended.
4. *Double-lock feed-in*: Confinement to one's cell except for two hours' recreation in the cell block, and three showers per week. Loss of job, all privileges suspended or curtailed, and three full meals in the cell.
5. *Disciplinary custody*: The Hole, or "Siberia." Solitary confinement in the isolation unit with all privileges suspended or curtailed. Three full meals in the cell, and two hours' recreation per day.

Source: Victor Hassine (1996). *Life without Parole* (pp. 16–17). Los Angeles: Roxbury.

ing punished for petty offenses. The comments of inmates at one prison suggest both frustration and resentment:

> Discipline is so bad in here you can only breathe when told to.
>
> These petty rules and the way they are enforced are surely going to cause a major incident again.
>
> It's one-sided. A prisoner can't put up any defence. If an officer says coal is white, it's white. (Scraton, Sim, and Skidmore, 1991:82–85)

This situation creates bad feelings among inmates, and it may produce spiraling confrontations between inmates and staff, as well as festering resentments that may explode into violence against other inmates. Ironically, this is precisely what prison officials don't want.

Informal Discipline. Many more infractions are handled informally by prison staff. Informal discipline can be an effective tool of control, particularly when the punishment is the result of a negotiated settlement between staff and inmate: "It is to both parties' advantage to come to terms on the spot. Staffers reinforce the fact that *they* are in charge and that *they* control inmate behavior. Staffers also reduce their paperwork this way—an important incentive not to be overly punitive, lest inmates refuse the negotiation and lodge their own complaint against them. By the same token, violations that are resolved informally . . . don't become part of the inmate's official dossier" (Fleisher, 1989:81).

Any time a correctional officer confronts an inmate, it is an opportunity for each to test the other's resolve and to evaluate the kind of prisoner or guard he or she is. Officers who enforce rules strictly but fairly may gain reputations as hard-nosed, but they are also likely to be respected *and obeyed.* Guards know that their position gives them the right to expect obedience, but they also know that prisoners are more likely to follow an order when they agree that the guard's authority is legitimate (Hepburn, 1985). Guards who compromise over petty rule infractions but are strict with important ones exercise greater control over inmates, especially if inmates see them as exercising skilled professional judgment in their decisions. Just as in any other job, a reputation for competence and good judgment is a plus in prison work.

Control and the Role of the Warden. Although the everyday actions of inmates and prison staff shape the climate of a prison, the warden bears ultimate responsibility for the conditions under which inmates live and correctional officers work. Some wardens have gained reputations for tyrannical rule, as in the case of Warden Ragen of Stateville Penitentiary in Illinois (Jacobs, 1977:28–54). Ragen ran Stateville with an iron hand from 1936 to 1961; both guards and inmates were controlled by a system of snitching, or informing, that resulted in suspensions and demotions of staff, and segregation and transfers of inmates. Officers' rooms as well as inmate cells were subjected to periodic shakedowns. Regan limited outside involvement in his prison, even refusing federal assistance to train his custodial staff.

Today, federal lawsuits, unionization of prison staff, and increasingly complex administrative rules have left most wardens little room or incentive to run prisons this way, even if they wanted to. However, this does not mean that conditions in the cell block are unaffected by decisions made at the top. Quite the contrary; prison regimes strongly influence the behavior and relationships of inmates and staff. The conclusion reached in one exhaustive review of research was that control in prisons is enhanced if guards are trained in interactive skills and more emphasis is placed on rehabilitative and other noncustodial aspects of their work (Ditchfield, 1990).

A different conclusion was reached in a study of management styles in Michigan, California, and Texas prisons, although it, too, confirmed the link between how prisons are managed and effective control of inmates (DiIulio, 1987). The study identified a general management philosophy that many prison managers shared, called the **keeper philosophy**. As keepers, managers believe that prisoners should be treated humanely but also in accordance with how they behave while incarcerated. If they break rules, they should be denied privileges or placed in segregation. However, beyond this basic philosophy, management styles varied greatly between the prison systems.

keeper philosophy Humane treatment of inmates is linked with imposition of penalties when rules are broken.

In Texas, for example, prison administrators subscribed to a **control model**, in which strict enforcement of rules, quick resort to discipline, and only those inmate rights required by law are emphasized. This style exerts the most control over the daily lives of inmates. In the Michigan system, a **responsibility model** is emphasized, with restraint exercised over inmates only for protection of staff or other inmates. The prison staff act as facilitators of inmate decision making rather than as controllers. In California, a **consensual model** has been developed, in which inmates agree to be governed by staff and cooperate voluntarily in creating order in the institution.

control model Rules are enforced quickly and strictly.

responsibility model Staff facilitate inmate decision making and restrain inmates only to protect themselves or other inmates.

consensual model Inmates cooperate voluntarily with staff in creating order within the prison.

The author concludes that neither the Michigan nor California styles are as effective in maintaining control as the Texas approach. The responsibility model leaves inmates too much freedom, and the consensual model allows them to manipulate the system to their own advantage. As a general rule, of course, the security level of a prison dictates to a large degree how much freedom or responsibility inmates will be allowed in practice. I doubt that either the consensual model or the responsibility model would work well in a supermaximum-security prison, where life is highly regimented and controlled.

Discipline and Control through Segregation. Most prisons have a place set apart from the main cell block where inmates can be isolated from the main inmate population and held under more restrictive conditions, often in solitary confinement. This is the isolation unit, commonly referred to as **segregation** or the "hole." Some inmates are in segregation for their own safety—and may

segregation A secure unit within the prison that keeps an inmate isolated from other inmates.

In most prisons, segregation serves two purposes: a form of punishment for inmates who have broken the rules, and a way of protecting inmates from other inmates. In either case, contact with other human beings is severely restricted and the psychological toll on inmates can be extreme.

ILLUSTRATION BY JOHN OVERMYER

even have requested it—while others are there as punishment for violations of prison rules. Many stories are told by inmates of days, even months, spent in the hole for minor infractions of the rules. Generally, however, isolation is reserved for serious or repeat offenders, and for prisoners who are a danger to fellow inmates. In some prisons, the hole is also used as a way of punishing inmates considered "difficult" or "subversive" by correctional staff (Scraton, Sim, and Skidmore, 1991:85).

Different prisons have different versions of the hole. Many segregation units are composed of solid-walled cells, sometimes without windows. Some sound terrifying: "When you step into the cell you see a box. That's the silent cell. Around this is all their strip-lights and big heaters. Also metal straps to keep the heat in. The inside is about three square yards. There are two spy-holes and two small air vents. It's a human furnace. I've had headaches all week. Sitting here in this cell is like having a hand clasped around your throat" (Scraton, Sim, and Skidmore, 1991:84–85).

In Pennsylvania during the 1960s, state courts ruled that inmates in segregation must have some light. Officials at one prison responded by constructing a cell built of transparent Plexiglas, known as the "glass cage," into which bright lights were shone 24 hours a day (Hassine, 1996:100).

Such brutal places are rare today. The long-standing **hands-off doctrine**, under which wardens enjoyed virtual free rein in running their prisons, had disintegrated during the 1970s and 1980s as court rulings severely curtailed the use of authoritarian control strategies (Jacobs, 1977; Johnson, 1987). In most American prisons today, inmates placed in segregation are fed the same food as other inmates, their cells allow in natural light, and they are permitted an hour of exercise per day. The main variation is in the amount of time an inmate can be placed in the hole. Some states limit time in the hole to days or weeks, while others specify no time limit but require regular review of the inmate's case. A positive review means release back into the general population.

hands-off doctrine Wardens were free to run their prisons without external interference.

Objections to the Use of Segregation. Although the hole may be a more humane place than it once was, the practice of disciplining by segregation is not without controversy. For example, some people object that solitary confinement violates the Eighth Amendment's prohibition against cruel and unusual punishment. However, the U.S. Supreme Court has consistently ruled that solitary confinement is not in itself unconstitutional. Yet lower appellate courts have occasionally ruled that the way disciplinary segregation is carried out may violate the Eighth Amendment. For example, an inmate of a Tennessee prison was placed in a five-by-eight-foot unlighted cell and made to sleep nude on the floor; disposal of his wastes down a hole in the floor was controlled by a guard. A federal court ruled this treatment unconstitutional (Rudovsky et al., 1988:4). But predicting what courts will do in a given case is difficult: A federal court in Texas upheld solitary confinement even though the inmate was held in complete darkness and given a full meal only every 72 hours.

Another objection concerns the procedures for returning inmates to the general population. Appellate courts have ruled that inmates must be provided with clear criteria for working their way out of the hole. Yet how is "successful" behavior to be evaluated? It is difficult to see how inmates held in segregation can show that they are ready to be mixed in with others.

A third objection concerns the distinction between *problem inmates* and *inmates with problems*. Problem inmates are prisoners who repeatedly break the rules; inmates with problems have physical or psychological difficulties that hinder their adjustment to prison life. Sometimes correctional staff may put an inmate in the hole not realizing that the inmate is in psychological distress rather than simply disobeying the rules. The experience of segregation might very well turn such an inmate into a problem inmate, thus making things worse. There is also the risk that isolation will turn a merely difficult inmate into an inmate with psychological problems. Unfortunately, it is often difficult for staff to establish during disciplinary hearings whether a particular inmate is of one kind or the other—or *both*.

These are all troublesome issues that have no easy answers. Despite the problems, however, the use of disciplinary segregation will continue because prison officials have found no satisfactory alternative to dealing with inmates who repeatedly break the rules or whose behavior makes them a danger to other inmates or to corrections staff. The best hope is that segregation will be used sparingly and in the most humane manner possible.

INMATE CONTROL AND THE CORRECTIONAL OFFICER

Day-to-day control of inmates rests with correctional officers. Formerly called guards and today sometimes called custody or discipline staff, we saw in Box 16.1 that in prison argot they are "hacks," "pigs," or "screws." All these terms suggest an animosity or hostility on the part of inmates—the kept—toward the prison staff—the keepers. This view is summed up by one long-term state prison inmate as follows: "Among themselves, the guards are human. Among themselves, the prisoners are human. Yet between the two the relationship is not human. *It is animal*. . . . What I am saying is that the prisoner is closer to humanity than the guard: because he is *deprived* by the guard. That is why I say that evil exists—not in the prisoner, but in the guard" (Abbott, 1981:70–71).

While many inmates may subscribe to this negative characterization, the truth about prison guards is much more complex. Most guards, like most prisoners, want to do their "time" with a minimum of trouble. They will avoid danger and disruption if they can. If forced to discipline an inmate for a rule infraction or to control a situation, most experienced officers will try to minimize negative repercussions for themselves, whether from inmates or from their superiors.

Beyond this observation, the truth about prison guards remains rather obscure. This is mainly because they have received comparatively little attention. As research has grown, however, it now seems clear that "the keepers and the kept are not necessarily at odds with one another; they are not locked into oppositional roles . . ." (Johnson, 1987:123). In many prisons, "an unwritten agreement has been established between inmates and guards: inmates get what they want by being friendly and nonaggressive, while guards ensure their own safety by not strictly enforcing the rules" (Hassine, 1996:117–118).

Inmates Confront and Test Their Guards. There are, nevertheless, aspects of prison life that inevitably bring inmates and guards into conflict and that test a guard's abilities. One is disobedience. An inmate who refuses to obey an instruction from a correctional officer presents a challenge that cannot be ignored. Failure to deal with the situation quickly and decisively is one of the worst mistakes a guard can make. Rookie officers hear plenty of horror stories during training, but nothing adequately prepares them for the reality. As one experienced guard put it:

> Working in this penitentiary is just babysitting a bunch of thugs, until the shit hits the fan. . . . [N]ew men don't know what's going on, for the first few months, but they better learn in a hurry. If a hack doesn't respond to an emergency, or if he backs away from action at the scene, he's a wimp, a coward, a chicken-shit. . . . Rookies have to prove that you can trust them: his actions, his willingness to work; he isn't bash-

Box 16.3

CAREERS IN CRIMINAL JUSTICE

CORRECTIONAL OFFICER

Correctional officers, often referred to as guards, perform a variety of tasks in prisons and other detention facilities, but their main duty is to supervise and control inmates, thereby protecting the security of the facility, the staff, visitors, and inmates. As with other criminal justice jobs, specific duties and requirements differ from place to place. Here are the salary range, qualifications, duties, and conditions of employment of a correctional officer as advertised by the State of Oregon in September, 1998.

Salary Range: $26,100 to $36,696

Qualifications: High school diploma or GED, or other proof of education at same or higher level; possess reading comprehension, report writing, and retention abilities.

Duties: Include maintaining security and enforcing discipline; preparing and writing reports about inmate conduct; restraining violent inmates; lifting and carrying injured inmates; sighting and firing weapons; walking cell blocks and performing searches, including strip searches; listening for whispers and conversations at a distance; reacting instantly to emergencies.

Conditions of Employment: Include U.S. citizenship within a year of hiring; minimum age 21; valid driver's license; no felony convictions or evidence of substance abuse; no misdemeanors relating to sex, violence, drugs, fraud, or moral turpitude.

> ful, he'll give orders; how he looks and how he acts when inmates are around. (Fleisher, 1989:209)

An incident some years ago at Graterford Penitentiary illustrates what can happen when a guard fails to effectively control a situation. According to inmates, the incident marked a turning point in relations between guards and inmates at the prison, leading to loss of staff control over the prison. The incident also illustrates the significance of informal controls, and the dangers that can follow when they break down.

On Super Bowl Sunday, 1983, an inmate openly defied a rule forbidding inmates from taking food from the dining room to their cells. "While violations of this rule were commonplace, the usual practice was to hide one's food before leaving the dining hall. To accommodate this minimal demand for obedience, most inmates smuggled out food in anything from trash-bag liners to empty potato-chip bags, often stashed in the split lining of one's institutional prison coat. Guards never searched for food, and no harm was done" (Hassine, 1996:43–44).

This particular inmate blatantly challenged convention by carrying out a plate piled high with food. A guard saw him and ordered him to either eat the food in the dining hall or throw it away. The inmate refused and the guard grabbed the plate out of his hands.

> What ensued became known as the Super Bowl Sunday Chicken Riot. . . . Every inmate related to the incident as if the guard had tried to take something of *his*. The chicken was more than just food—it represented each man's hustle, and its confiscation challenged everyone's livelihood.

Prisons are dangerous places and correctional officers must control difficult inmates and situations as quickly as possible. Failure to act quickly and decisively will ruin a guard's reputation among fellow guards and inmates—and perhaps cost him his life.

PHOTO BY CAESAR MARAGNI, COURTESY OF AP PHOTO

> Dozens of men swarmed to the aid of the inmate and beat the guard. Dozens more mobbed the dining room to defiantly take chicken dinners back to their cells. In quick order, every guard on the block was assaulted and some were even locked in cells. (Hassine, 1996:44)

The incident was quickly defused when inmates dispersed to watch the Super Bowl and allowed staff to attend to the guards, none seriously injured. Later, the men responsible for the "riot" were put in segregation, but the damage had been done: "Inmates had joined together to beat the guards fair and square. . . . If you ask any staff member or inmate who runs Graterford, the answer will always be the same: 'The inmates run Graterford'" (Hassine: 1996:44–45).

It is doubtful that inmates run any prison; rather, in many maximum-security facilities there is an uneasy alliance between line staff and inmates, each periodically testing the others' tolerance levels. From the prison guard's perspective, the older and simpler days of authoritarian rule, when hacks gave orders and inmates obeyed or else, have been replaced by court-ordered restraints, bureaucratic interference, and a growing sense of powerlessness (Hawkins and Alpert, 1989:350–353). The dominant adaptation of correctional officers is to keep a low profile and "cover your ass." You're on your own: Trust no one. This situation is ironic, because trust is a valued commodity for correctional officers: At any moment a guard may need the emotional or physical assistance of fellow officers. But as one line officer puts it: "Trust in fellow officers is a fragile thing" (Fleisher, 1989:209). It is easily undermined in a world where snitching is actively promoted as a means of maintaining control by staff—and by inmates over other inmates.

Alienation and Stress among Correctional Personnel. Trust is also undermined by the growing alienation felt by many line personnel. Guards recognize the many similarities between the inmates' situation and their own working conditions—for example, the dangers, distrust, loneliness, and physical isolation—and many guards see themselves as "uniformed prisoners" (Johnson, 1987:124). The daily stress of working the cell blocks of a maximum-security prison is made worse by the sense that neither the public nor their superiors understand or care about their situation.

The assistant superintendent of the Illinois correctional officer training academy has found that officers usually start out talking about how inmates cause problems, but soon turn to "what's really bothering them: dealing with other staff and the administration. They don't feel like they're getting enough support. . . . They don't feel that anybody else understands what the problems are" (*Copley Newspapers*, 1992:8). Such alienation encourages the emergence of a battle mentality: "Us" versus "Them."

Under these conditions, violence by guards against inmates and by inmates against guards is likely to rise. In prisons where a warlike mentality has taken hold, the "Us" and "Them" distinction even extends to relations among line officers (Marquart, 1984): The more violence-prone "smug hacks" and "goon squads" actively exclude their nonviolent fellow officers from their ranks, further damaging the fragile trust among correctional officers. Recent research suggests that this work environment of conflict and distrust is worse in older rural penitentiaries with large minority populations drawn from urban areas and a mostly white staff with rural backgrounds (Britton, 1997:100). Correctional officers in these locations tend to be less satisfied with their jobs, to feel more stress, and to believe that they are less effective in dealing with inmates.

When Control Fails: Inmate Attacks on Correctional Officers. In any prison, the line officer's worst fear is that he or she will be attacked by inmates. Experienced officers in maximum-security prisons have no trouble articulating their fears, even if they have never been personally attacked. As one ten-year veteran of a state prison put it: "What do I fear most? Being a hostage. After being raped, I'd probably be tortured. There are a lot of people in here, angry people, that think I'm just a redneck. . . . If I ever *am* held hostage, I hope the officers come in shooting" (*St. Louis Post-Dispatch*, August 18, 1996, p. 5B).

Rookie correctional officers quickly find out the meaning of fear: "My partner that first night [on the job] was Bill Hill, a soft-spoken six-year veteran who immediately told me to take the cigarettes out of my shirt pocket because the inmates would steal them. Same for my pen, he said—or 'They'll grab it and stab you. . . .'" (*St. Louis Globe-Democrat*, November 13, 1978:B6).

This rookie had been assigned to the third tier of the segregation unit of the Pontiac prison in Illinois. At meal time, inmates were served through their locked cell doors. Everything went smoothly for the first 20 cells. "Suddenly, a huge arm shot through the bars of one cell and began swinging a metal rod at Hill. As he ducked away, the inmate snared the cookie box." The rookie guard tried to grab the cookies back and he was held from the cell behind him, and struck in the back by a metal can.

> Until that moment I had been apprehensive. Now I was scared. The food cart virtually trapped me, blocking my retreat.
>
> Whirling around, I noticed that mirrors were being held out of every cell so inmates could watch the ruckus. I didn't realize that the mirrors were plastic, and became terrified that the inmates would start smashing them to cut me up.
>
> The ordinary din of the cell house had turned into a deafening roar. For the length of the tier, arms stretched into the walkway, making grabbing motions. Some of the inmates swung brooms about. . . . Wheeling the food cart between us, we made a hasty retreat. My heart was thumping, my legs felt weak. Inside the plastic gloves, my hands were soaked with sweat. Yet the attack on us wasn't considered unusual

> by other guards, especially in segregation. This was strictly routine, and we didn't even file a report. (*St. Louis Globe-Democrat*, November 13, 1978, p. B7).

In prisons where officers and inmates are locked in a battle for control, even severe acts of violence may be seen as routine: Neither side is prepared to back down, and both the expectation and level of violence are high. This hostile prison environment is most likely to develop in prisons with racially mixed populations of younger inmates and high concentrations of violent criminals. A climate of violent confrontation develops—of inmate against inmate, guard against inmate, and inmate against guard. Predatory inmates, preying on the weak and vulnerable, are met by repressive guards doing essentially the same thing. This seems to have been the case in the Marion federal penitentiary during the 1970s and 1980s (Keve, 1991) and in many other "warehousing" state prisons across America.

Nevertheless, in most maximum-security prisons, inmate attacks on correctional officers have been relatively rare and not particularly severe. Most inmates are happy to do their time peacefully, and most guards appreciate this fact—and do the same thing. But violence of all sorts appears to be on the rise. Up until 1989, for instance, the entire 55-year history of the Federal Bureau of Prisons had seen only five staffers killed by inmates, but three of these occurred in the five years between 1980 and 1985 (Fleisher, 1989:214). Violent prison riots, almost unheard of before, plagued the 1970s and 1980s, and many prisons are described as powder kegs in the 1990s. Ohio's maximum-security prison in Lucasville erupted in violence on Easter Sunday 1993, leaving one correctional officer dead.

There is no adequate information to document rising inmate violence against prison staff in this country, but a recent study in England shows a generally upward trend since the 1970s that has risen more steeply since the late 1980s (Ditchfield and Harries, 1996), as shown in Figure 16.1. The explanation for the recent trend suggests that a combination of factors may be at work:

- Higher levels of inmate-on-inmate violence
- Higher concentrations of young inmates
- Higher concentrations of minority inmates
- Higher concentrations of younger, more inexperienced staff

Much more research needs to be done to identify trends and causes of inmate attacks on staff. From the vantage point of line officers, experience and prison lore tell them that attacks can occur without warning, and for that reason staff must always be on guard against them. Don't trust anyone; always be suspicious; never let inmates get the upper hand.

Why Inmates Assault Staff. Considering that the penalties for assaulting staff are generally severe, including additional prison time, why do inmates attack staff? According to a Lompoc inmate, the reasons are often petty:

> An officer could have disrespected you or the officer could be an asshole and you get fed up with it, and it get to the point where you want to do something to him. Some of them have a shitty attitude or think you a lower form of dude 'cause you're on this side of the wall. It's petty stuff, really. Let's say the phone. You call your people, they accept the charges, then hacks cut you off. If they're so tough, let them take off that radio and let's step in that little room, then they not be tough. (Fleisher, 1989:217)

Inmates know that doing their time quietly is the best solution to incarceration, but the dominance of masculine themes in prison culture draws many men to react to frustrations and confrontations with violence. When hacks are

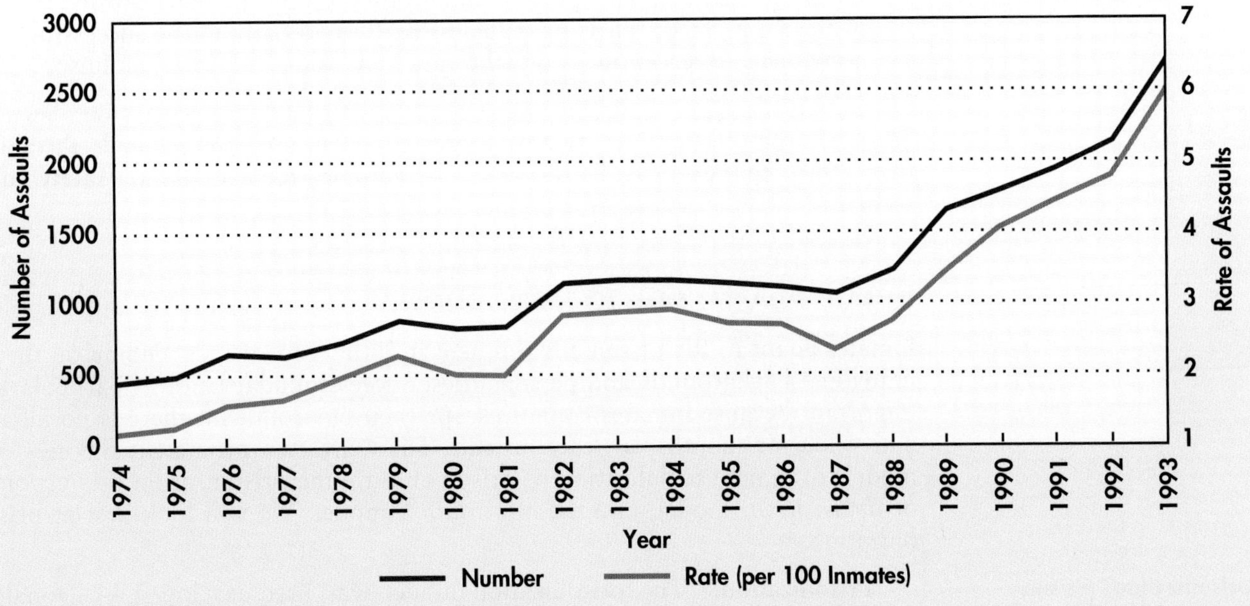

FIGURE 16.1 Assaults on prison Officers in England, 1974–1992
Life in American and British prisons has been getting more dangerous for inmates and staff alike. Much of the problem can be accounted for by increasing numbers of young inmates, by growing racial tensions as minority populations have increased, and by the rise of gangs. Even though it is still relatively rare for staff to be assaulted, this graph shows the upward trend in English prisons. There are no comparable data for American prisons; however, between 1987 and 1990, yearly assaults on federal correctional officers went from 33 to 185.

Sources: John Ditchfield and Richard Harries (1996). "Assaults on Staff in Male Local Prisons and Remand Centres." *Home Office Research Bulletin* 38:16; Kathleen Maguire and Ann L. Pastore (1998). *Sourcebook of Criminal Justice Statistics, 1997* (p. 307). Washington, D.C.: U.S. Department of Justice.

brutal, inmates respond in kind: "My views on violence are simple enough: if they [staff] have a license to inflict brutal beatings—then you must do likewise at the earliest opportunity as a defensive act to show them you're prepared to stand none of it. I don't believe in abusing or assaulting warders just because they are locking me up. I treat them as they do me" (Scraton, Sim, and Skidmore, 1991:75).

This inmate expresses a major theme in prisons and on the street: Aggression requires counteraggression. Ironically, the motive for counteraggression is often to end someone else's aggression, to show others that you will not be "messed with." This rarely works in practice, despite a vast masculine lore that says it does. Being a tough inmate is an invitation to others to challenge you.

The relationship between inmates and correctional officers is tense, but not inevitably a violent one. Many prison guards, in fact, are oriented toward helping and supporting inmates, in the belief that their role should be more than merely custodial. They are searching for a constructive work niche:

> They hunger for opportunities to improve the quality of life in the prison community and grasp them when they can. Like most of us, they want to be people who matter. In the prison the skills that matter are human relations and human services skills. These are the skills that can be used to develop relationships, and hence to reduce tension, defuse crises, and conduct daily business in a civilized (and potentially

> civilizing) manner. This point is often obscured by the macho-worship of the smug hack, but is nevertheless reaffirmed daily in the successful nonviolent interventions on the part of some officers. (Johnson, 1987:138)

These are the officers that inmates appreciate most, and it is arguably through their efforts that everyone in the prison community achieves greater safety and security.

INMATE ADAPTATIONS TO IMPRISONMENT

Inmates adapt to the prison environment in different ways, depending on their individual backgrounds and personalities. Successful adaptation is particularly important because inmates cannot escape their environment; there is no alternative life for months or years on end. There are two prominent theories or models of inmate socialization to prison culture: the prisonization *(indigenous* or *deprivation)* model, and the *importation* model. We will look first at prisonization.

prisonization Prison culture is adopted by inmates as they adapt to imprisonment.

Prisonization. The **prisonization** model was first developed by Donald Clemmer (1940) in his study of Menard Penitentiary in Illinois. Clemmer defined prisonization as "the taking on in greater or lesser degree of the folkways, mores, customs, and general culture of the penitentiary." Through prisonization, inmates learn how to behave and even how to think like other inmates. Most important, prisonization implies a *change* in the attitudes, values, and behavior of inmates: They become more antisocial and criminal as time passes. It is a variation of the long-standing view that prisons are "schools for crime."

A core element in prisonization is acceptance of the *inmate code* that shapes how men relate to each other and to the staff. At Menard, the code emphasized loyalty and cooperation among inmates; it was pro-inmate and anti-authority, but not to the extent of promoting open conflict. In fact, the code helped organize the prison community, providing cohesion and stability where anarchy might otherwise reign.

A study of Trenton State Prison in New Jersey also found evidence of an inmate code (Sykes, 1958). Convicts were expected not to interfere with the interests of other inmates and never to rat on another con; to stay cool and do their own time; to be a "right guy," in other words, don't steal from, exploit, or break your word to another inmate; to be a real man, not a whiner; and to be wary and distrustful of prison staff. Right guys served their time with a minimum of fuss and played an important role in promoting cohesion and stability so inmates and staff could deal with the pains of imprisonment.

pains of imprisonment Rejection, lack of goods and services, deprivation of sexual intimacy, deprivation of autonomy, and loss of physical security.

Sykes identified five **pains of imprisonment**. Most apply in maximum-security prisons today just as they did in the 1950s. First, there is a *deep sense of rejection* by the free community. Every day an inmate remains cut off from society, he or she is reminded of this rejection, and the psychological toll is heavy. Second, *prisons lack goods and services* that free people take for granted. Third, inmates are *deprived of sexual intimacy* with the opposite sex. The inmate is "figuratively castrated by involuntary celibacy" (Sykes, 1958:523). Fourth, there is the *deprivation of autonomy*, the lack of independence that is typical of total institutions. There are rules and regulations to cover virtually everything. The inmate's most trivial actions are brought under control day after day. A typical prison day might go something like this:

6:30 A.M. Loud bell rings; inmates dress.
7:00 A.M. Cells unlocked; some inmates go to mess hall for breakfast; those in lockdown eat in cells.

8:00 A.M.	Inmates counted; those with work or education assignments proceed to their job or classroom; others remain in cells.
11:30 A.M.	Lunch in mess hall or cell.
1:00 P.M.	Exercise (weather permitting).
2:00 P.M.	Inmates counted; those with work or program assignments proceed to their job or program group; others remain in cells.
4:00 P.M.	All inmates returned to cells; inmates counted.
5:00 P.M.	Evening meal; some inmates proceed to mess hall; others eat in cells.
6:00 P.M.	Recreation activities in cell block or gym; visiting with relatives; theater; many inmates stay in their cells.
9:30 P.M.	Inmates returned to cells.
10:00 P.M.	Cells locked; inmate count.
11:30 P.M.	Lights out.

Finally, the fifth pain of imprisonment is *loss of physical security*. Fear is everywhere: "Jails and prisons . . . have a climate of violence which has no free-world counterpart. Inmates are terrorized by other inmates, and spend years in fear of harm" (Toch, 1977:53).

Inmate adaptation to the pains of imprisonment varies considerably. Some respond with hostility and violence; others cope by finding niches that meet their needs—work assignments, the gym, building ties with other inmates, or finding a quieter, more relaxed cell block; others throw themselves wholeheartedly into the underground economy, becoming wheelers and dealers of prison contraband. Some find a home in gangs. Some simply keep to themselves and mark time in the prison yard. "There is no typical niche, just as there is no typical prisoner. . . .The safest and potentially most rewarding way to live in prison . . . is to avoid the predatory world of the convicts and evolve a smaller more congenial world of one's own" (Johnson, 1987:111).

Importation. The prisonization perspective on inmate adaptation stresses the role of conditions inside prison. Adaptation grows out of prison life itself. The **importation** model, on the other hand, suggests that inmate adaptation is strongly influenced by pre-prison experiences. Rather than constructed out of conditions within prisons, prison culture is largely imported from outside. One of the first sociologists to propose this idea was Clarence Schrag, whose research showed that inmates' criminal backgrounds influenced the types of roles they took on in prison.

importation Prison culture is molded by the pre-prison experiences of inmates and their connections to the outside world.

James Jacobs's (1974, 1977) study of gangs in the Stateville penitentiary also lent support for the importation model. Rather than create gang structures and behavior, prison preserved and strengthened already existing street norms and gang organization. Gang members imported the essential features of the parent street gangs; the same people who were the leaders on Chicago streets were the leaders in prison. In fact, gang leaders continued to *run* their street gangs from their prison cells.

The importationists are skeptical about the long-term effects of prison life suggested by the prisonization model. After reviewing the literature, one expert concluded that the experience of imprisonment does not significantly affect the attitudes or behaviors of inmates (Hawkins, 1976). Another has concluded that the "Big Houses," where most early prison research was carried out, "did not reform prisoners or teach many persons crime" (Irwin, 1980:21).

Nevertheless, the prisonization model had a certain appeal to correctional authorities because it gave them some hope of constructing a better prison environment: If conditions within prisons largely determined inmate behavior, then one could change those conditions in order to improve that behavior. The prisonization view also linked up nicely with the rehabilitative ideal. Rehabilitation supports the idea of a partnership between inmate and staff that might actually change the criminal through treatment and educational programs, while at the same time counteracting the process of prisonization.

So what molds prison culture—prisonization or importation? In the final analysis, both contribute to inmate adaptation and the characteristics of prison culture. During the past 30 years, however, the balance has swung in favor of importation for three reasons: (1) The decline of the hands-off doctrine opened prisons to outsiders and introduced many changes to conditions in prisons; (2) the influx of minority inmates with street gang connections brought new structures of influence and power, and linked inmate lives to forces and tensions external to the prison community; and (3) the influx of professional prison managers and new management styles helped dismantle the old authoritarian regimes in which the inmate code had flourished.

Sex in Men's Prisons. Lack of sexual intimacy is one of the pains of imprisonment. Inmates make up for it in various ways, ranging from masturbation to homosexual activity. In 1988, a lurid videotape showing mass murderer Richard Speck doing drugs and having sex with other inmates of the maximum-security Stateville Correctional Center in Illinois caused a national outcry. The tape had been made by inmates who hoped to profit from its sale. Although the taping was called a one-time aberration by authorities, they also acknowledged that the sexual activities themselves were commonplace in every prison system.

In men's prisons, sex between inmates occurs primarily in two contexts:

1. As consensual behavior motivated by sexual frustration and the desire for gratification, if not feelings of love; in this context, prison sex is little different from homosexual activity on naval ships or in monasteries (Allen and Simonsen, 1995:440). Since younger inmates and inmates willing or desiring to take on the passive role in anal or oral sex are most desirable, they often become the object of jealousies, which can turn to violence if their affections are transferred to someone else. This aspect of consensual sexual relations helps explain why the second context of sexual activity also flourishes.
2. As an integral part of a larger system of dominance and exploitation in which some inmates are victimized by others; sex is a commodity that is purchased, taken by force, stolen, sold, and even traded. Weaker inmates, often younger ones, become the boys, or "punks," of more aggressive inmates. One ex-inmate recalls how prisoners sometimes bet "their boys" during poker games when they had run out of cash (*St. Louis Post-Dispatch*, February 8, 1998, p. D12).

It is in the context of exploitation that most of the sexual violence occurs in prisons. Sexual aggression is encouraged by two things (Bowker, 1980; Scacco, 1982). First, prison denies men their masculine role by curtailing decision making and suppressing independent behavior. Prisoners have little control over their daily lives. Sexual aggression, in which weaker inmates are made to submit, helps some prisoners preserve a masculine identity. They get what they want because they are tough. The last thing prison rapists want is to be thought of as homosexuals. Second, the act of sexual violation makes a statement about power and domination. This feature explains the most common pattern of sexual assault in many prisons: Black inmates, alone or in groups, force sex on young white inmates. As one black inmate put it, "It's a new ego thing. He can show he's a man by making a white guy into a girl" (Carroll, 1982:124; Hawkins and Alpert, 1989:277). This process encourages racial violence in prisons: "Fighting and forced sex become the testing ground for racial power and definitions of manliness in men's prisons. The entering inmate, especially if he is white, is likely to face several masculinity tests. He must either defend himself, become a punk, or try to leave the scene. In deciding whether to "Fight, Fuck, or Flee," the most desirable response may be to fight" (Hawkins and Alpert, 1989:278).

Gangs and Changing Race Relations in Prison. The rise of ethnic gangs and deteriorating race relations throughout the nation's maximum- and medium-security prisons lent support to the importation model of inmate adaptation. The gangs in the Stateville penitentiary closely reproduced their Chicago-based namesakes on the street. The Black P. Stone Nation, the Devil's Disciples, and the Vicelords were black gangs; the Latin Kings were Hispanic. The reputation and power of these gangs radiated throughout Stateville and dominated relations among the races. Recognizing the power of gangs over members and nonmembers alike, prison officials negotiated unofficially with gang leaders, thereby giving up some of their own power. This tended to undermine the authority of line staff and contributed to decreasing staff morale and increased tension.

The presence of ethnic gangs accentuates the racial tensions that have grown along with the increasing numbers of black and Hispanic inmates that we documented in Chapter 15. Today, gangs dominate life in many maximum-security prisons. In Texas, for example, several prominent prison gangs operate (Fong, 1990; Fong, Vogel, and Buentello, 1992): The Mexican Mafia is the largest and fastest-growing; its members are all Hispanic, as are the members of Nuestro Carnales and Hermanos De Pistolero. Black gangs include the Mandingo Warriors, and the Aryan Brotherhood of Texas is all-white. There

Prison violence is a nonending cycle of aggression and counteraggression. Prisoners often feel they have to avenge even the smallest insults. This proves a disturbing fact: Incapacitation does not prevent some forms of crime; it merely displaces them behind prison walls where they are out of sight.

Illustration by John Overmyer

are mixed-race/ethnicity gangs, too: The Self-Defense Family is predominantly black, the Texas Syndicate predominantly Hispanic, and the Texas Mafia predominantly white. Variants of these gangs are found in California prisons and throughout the federal system.

In the Graterford penitentiary during the 1980s, black Philadelphia street gangs such as the 21st and Norris gang and the 60th and Market gang competed for control of cell blocks and contraband sales. Whenever a new black Philadelphian inmate arrived, gang scouts checked him out to see if he was a "homey," from the same neighborhood or community, and therefore a likely recruit (Hassine, 1996:62). White gangs existed, too, but they were smaller and usually originated in prison to provide members with protection. Notable exceptions were outlaw motorcycle gangs such as Hell's Angels. Like the black gangs, their strong street connections and reputations for violence made them powerful forces in prison.

The number of gang members in the nation's prisons is unknown and probably unknowable, though some observers claim that as many as 80 to 90 percent of inmates in some prisons are affiliated with gangs. It is not hard to see why gangs are flourishing: They offer protection, financial rewards, access to drugs and other contraband, connections to the street when inmates are released, and a family for the inmate. In some prisons, they are believed by other inmates to be so powerful that they virtually run the prison. The claim of a former inmate of Illinois prisons is not uncommon: "[Gangs] try to recruit you as soon as you get off the bus. It's terrible. The gangs run everything. They rape, they rob, they extort. . . . They have their own places to eat in the cafeteria. You can't go where you want. You sit where they tell you. And the officers let it go on." (*Southern Illinoisian*, June 9, 1996, p. 7A).

This inmate was assaulted in 1993 by a white supremacist gang member who wanted to store prison brew in the victim's cell. When prisons were predominantly white, it was commonplace for minority black inmates to be victimized by white prisoners and guards. But now it appears that in many prisons it is white inmates, especially younger, middle-class whites incarcerated on drug charges, who are victimized by minority inmates. The fact that some maximum-security prisons now house more black inmates than white inmates may explain this trend. However, some recent research suggests that since black Americans have higher rates of violence both inside and outside prison, it is prior exposure to violent street culture among black Americans that explains their significantly higher levels of prison violence (Harer and Steffensmeier, 1996:342).

Racial and ethnic conflicts are commonplace outside prison, and these conflicts are reproduced inside prison. Some of the aggression of minority inmates toward white inmates may be explained as a reaction to their treatment by some correctional officers, especially white officers. Reviews of the available research document unfair and abusive treatment of minorities by guards, and racial prejudice appears to explain at least some of it (Mann, 1993:230–236). In some prisons, minority inmates are cited for rule infractions more often than white inmates, are assigned less desirable and more menial prison jobs, and are more restricted in the exercise of their religious and cultural practices, including language. There seem to be no prisons in which the reverse is true.

In addition, certain offenders are singled out for special victimization by other inmates. Child molesters and homosexuals are at the bottom of the pecking order and consequently receive the most systematic victimization by other inmates as well as by guards. This includes beatings and rapes as well as nonphysical abuse, such as the "silent treatment," where no one will speak to them, and exclusion from group activities. In contrast, violent offenders who commit murder, adult rape, and robbery stand at the top of the hierarchy; their reputations for being tough and cool are valuable in this world dominated by streetwise felons.

An Illinois Task Force on Crime and Corrections reported in 1993 that violence against other inmates as well as guards had been growing in scope and intensity. As we saw in Chapter 15, it recommended that the state build a supermaximum-security prison just to house dangerous and predatory inmates. In 1998, the Tamms Correctional Center took in the first of its 500 inmates (Associated Press, March 9, 1998). Inmates will spend 23 hours a day locked up alone in a 67-square-foot cell; guards in a high-tech control room will let them out, one at a time, to shower or spend up to one hour in a concrete-sided exercise yard with a fenced roof.

Will this help? Probably not. Experience with "lockup" and segregation units in the Marion penitentiary in Illinois (Keve, 1991) and in the California system suggests that while there may possibly be some gains in control, the more likely result is a self-fulfilling prophecy: Inmates "become serious troublemakers, committed revolutionaries, or gang members" (Irwin and Austin, 1994:105).

Some years ago, ex-inmate John Irwin described a new prison hero that has emerged amid the rising violence, fear, and hopelessness found in many maximum-security prisons: the "convict."

> The convict or hog stands ready to kill to protect himself, maintains strong loyalties to some small groups of other convicts (invariably of his own race), and will rob and attack or at least tolerate his friends' robbing and attacking other weak independents or their foes. He openly and stubbornly opposes the administration, even if this results in harsh punishment. Finally, he is extremely assertive of his masculine sexuality, even though he may occasionally make use of the prison homosexuals or, less often, enter into more permanent sexual alliance with a kid. . . . To circulate in this world, the convict world, one must act like a convict and, with few exceptions, have some type of affiliation with a powerful racial clique or gang. (Irwin, 1980:195)

Interviews with California inmates have confirmed the serious deterioration in prison life that Irwin and others have written about. Correctional policies themselves may have something to do with it, for they have emphasized segregation and lockdowns as ways of dealing with trouble (Hunt et al., 1993). Efforts to eradicate gangs during the 1980s appear to have led to a vacuum that has been filled by larger, more aggressive new gangs such as the Crips, Bloods, and 415s. Further, an increased splintering of prison groups has occurred, contributing to a prison climate of uncertainty and unpredictability. Finally, mandatory sentences, tougher parole policies, and truth-in-sentencing laws have reduced the stakes that inmates have in remaining nonviolent. Being passive, quiet, obedient, and nonaggressive is no longer good for an early release.

Prison overcrowding has been blamed for some of these problems, but some prison experts warn that overcrowding is rarely the sole cause of serious inmate problems (Cavadino and Dignan, 1992). One study found that overcrowding had no significant effects on inmate health, violence, or recidivism (Gaes, 1991). While this controversial finding may fuel claims that the overcrowding "problem" has been promoted by special-interest groups—prison administrators, guards and their unions, prisoner rights activists, reformers, and inmates themselves (Bleich, 1989)—there is still no definite answer.

The discussion so far has focused primarily on maximum-security prisons for men. But women are imprisoned, too, and we should certainly not forget the women who work at all levels of the correctional system. The next section addresses the women who live and work in prisons.

Box 16.4

CAREERS IN CRIMINAL JUSTICE

CORRECTIONS RECREATION SPECIALIST

Many prisons offer recreational opportunities for inmates, which may be part of formal treatment therapies or simply a way to help ensure the general well-being of inmates and the security of the facility. Oregon is among states that employ correctional personnel with skills and experience in designing and coordinating recreation programs for inmates. Here are the salary range, qualifications, duties, and conditions of employment of a corrections recreation specialist as advertised in July 1998.

Salary Range: $28,296 to $37,944

Qualifications: Two years of full-time experience assessing, developing, coordinating, and implementing recreational programs and leisure time activities; bilingual skills desirable.

Duties: Include designing, coordinating, and implementing large multiprogram recreational therapy and leisure time activities; gathering information and determining activities appropriate for diverse inmate groups; assessing availability of funding, equipment, facility space, and community resources and designing appropriate activity programs; inspecting recreation equipment and supplies entering the facility to ensure absence of contraband; recording inmate progress and providing input to inmate counselors and review committees.

Conditions of Employment: Include valid driver's license and a thorough background investigation.

WOMEN IN PRISON

The number of incarcerated women in the United States grew at a faster rate during the 1980s than the number of incarcerated men. Figure 16.2 shows the trend up to 1997. During the 1980s, the nation built 34 new prisons to house female inmates. The number of women held in the nation's jails has also increased substantially over the past decade. In 1985, 19,077 women were in jail on any given day; in 1997, the figure was 59,296, an increase of over 200 percent (Gilliard and Beck, 1998b:16).

WOMEN BEHIND BARS: PROFILES AND PROBLEMS

Despite the considerable increase in female inmates, the profile of incarcerated women has not changed much since the 1960s (Feinman, 1994:44–46; Snell, 1994; Donziger, 1996). The average female offender is black or Hispanic, between the ages of 25 and 35, and a single parent with one to three children. She is typically a high school dropout with a background of drug or alcohol use; most women are unemployed or only marginally employed before being sent to prison. Most female inmates have been incarcerated at least once before. However, female violent offenders are much less likely to have had prior incarcerations than their male counterparts (Bureau of Justice Statistics, 1991d). Fewer than one in five women are serving time for a violent offense; those who are most likely murdered or assaulted an abusive mate. The most common crimes for which women are serving time in the 1990s are drug offenses or nonviolent property crimes.

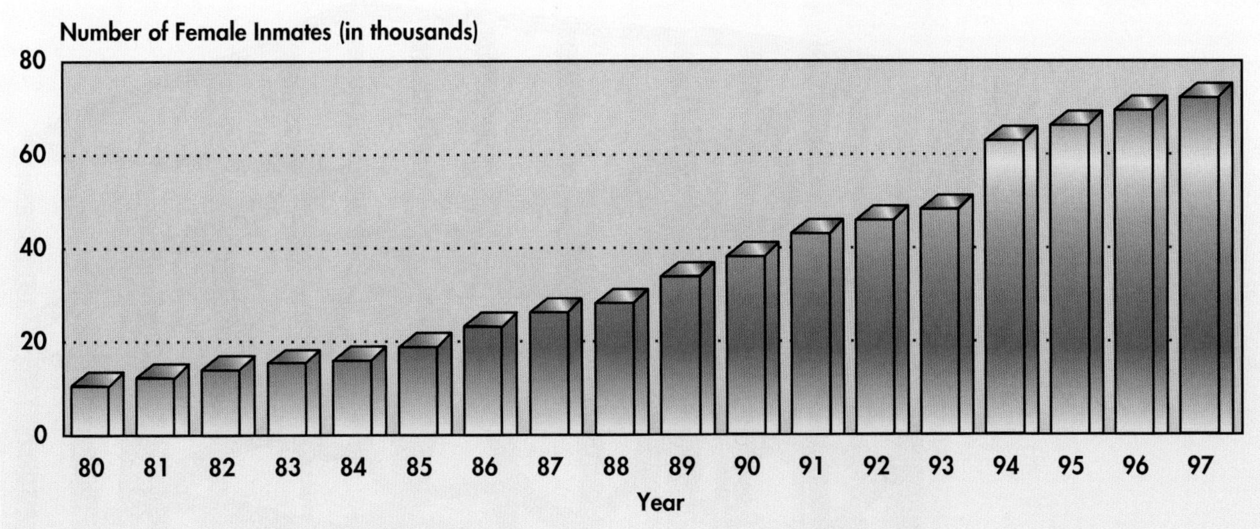

FIGURE 16.2 WOMEN BEHIND BARS: TRENDS FROM 1980 TO 1997
In recent years, the number of women in prison has grown faster than the number of men.

Sources: Kathleen Maguire and Ann L. Pastore (1995). *Sourcebook of Criminal Justice Statistics 1994* (p. 540). Darrell K. Gilliard and Allen J. Beck (1998). "Prisoners in 1997" (p. 5). *BJS Bulletin* (August):5.

Although they share many of the problems of white female prisoners—for example, poor health, drug or alcohol addiction, and difficulty in finding and keeping a job—minority women in prisons and jails have a more difficult time than white women: "They are more likely to be single, poor, and responsible for dependent children" (Feinman, 1994:51). They are also more likely to be pregnant when imprisoned.

Pregnancy and Motherhood in Prison. Most incarcerated women leave children behind, and some are pregnant when imprisoned. A survey of state and federal correctional authorities in 1993 found that over 600 inmates were pregnant (Contact Publications, 1994:8–10). This figure is low because it excludes California and New York, which together hold 20 percent of the nation's female inmates, but apparently do not track pregnancies. Also, during the same year over 760 incarcerated women gave birth, a figure likely to be more accurate for obvious reasons.

Pregnancy and motherhood create special problems for female inmates. One concerns relationships with their children. When a father is incarcerated, responsibility for his children is generally assumed by the mother; when a mother is incarcerated, on the other hand, the father rarely assumes primary care of his children (Donziger, 1996:153). That responsibility is most often assumed by the grandparent (Moses, 1995). One study found extreme separation anxiety among incarcerated mothers, made worse by the physical distance between home and prison and by a lack of transportation (Baunach, 1979). Most women tried to keep in contact with their children and planned to live with them after release. But they were plagued by such questions as, would the children accept them? Would they be able to support them? For their part, children with mothers in prison suffer from insecurity, lack of trust, anxiety, and loneliness (McGowan and Blumenthal, 1978). In this respect, prison punishes the children as well as the mothers.

Pregnant inmates face special difficulties. In the "old days"—a mere 20 years ago—pregnant inmates were often forced to deliver their child inside

Because of limited resources available to female prisoners, they are sent to prisons in other states more often than men. Separation from their families (the typical female prisoner is a single parent with one to three children who depend on her) can breed anxiety and depression.

ILLUSTRATION BY JOHN OVERMYER

prison, and the infant's birth certificate would record the fact that the mother was incarcerated. Today, many states allow women to give birth in community facilities or local hospitals, and birth certificates do not mention the legal status of the mother. Yet problems remain. For example, some states retain the right to declare the inmate an unfit mother, placing her children in foster care or putting them up for adoption. New York was one of the first states to abandon this policy, in 1983, and its department of corrections encourages family visits and assists inmates in dealing with family responsibilities.

One of the most controversial issues concerns what to do with an infant born to an inmate. The conventional approach is to remove the infant immediately or within days of its birth. This is devastating to many mothers, and no amount of prior warning adequately prepares them for the loss of contact. Finding denial of mother-infant visitation to be cruel and unusual punishment, a federal judge wrote in 1994: "Few events could be more stressful than the forced separation of a parent from his or her child" (*Women Prisoners of the District of Columbia Dept. of Corrections v. District of Columbia*, 1994). But many correctional officials believe that prison is no place for children, even if their budgets could accommodate them.

No one advocates a blanket policy that would keep a newborn child in prison until the mother is released; that idea is absurd, since some women will spend many years behind bars. But advocates of reform do suggest keeping an infant with its mother for the first year or so of life, and then providing regular opportunities for close interaction. Such a policy has been adopted by the Bedford Hills Correctional Center in New York City. "There is a nursery on a floor of the prison hospital where each mother and her baby share a room. During the day the mother goes to classes or works, and her baby is cared for by specially selected and trained inmate child care workers" (Feinman, 1994:61). The center also has a fully equipped playroom where visiting children and their mothers spend time together. Some other states, and foreign countries such as Germany, Israel, Finland, Australia, and England, have also implemented live-in programs and daylong visits between inmate mothers and their children. In the United States, a new partnership between Girl Scout councils and correctional facilities for women shows promise for a brighter future for incarcerated mothers and their children. This program has so far been tried in Maryland, Ohio, Arizona, Delaware, New Jersey, Kentucky, and California. It is briefly described in Box 16.5.

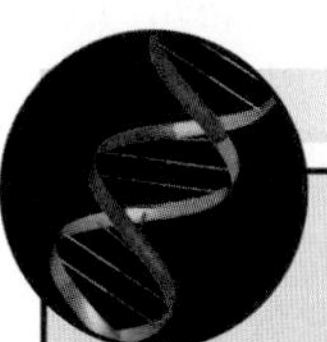

Box 16.5

JUSTICE INNOVATIONS

GIRL SCOUTS BEYOND BARS

Around two-thirds of the nation's female inmates have children under age 18. Most of these children are residing in the homes of grandparents or other female relatives; under one-third are living with their fathers. Correctional authorities are struggling to find innovative ways to keep imprisoned mothers connected with their children. Here is one promising program.

In 1992, a pilot program was designed at the Maryland Correctional Institution for Women to keep mothers and daughters connected and to enhance parenting skills. More than 30 daughters meet their mothers at the prison two Saturdays a month, and on alternate Sundays they meet in a Baltimore church with Girl Scout volunteers to work on Scouting projects. The Girl Scouts serve as mentors and friends. Sometimes the group goes on outings or camping trips.

The mothers participate in planning the mother-daughter meetings, and they meet periodically with Girl Scout staff. They receive training in parenting skills from a licensed social worker, and engage in role playing and other group activities. In a Florida program, implemented in 1994, mothers meet four times a month for two hours. The sessions are a mixture of parenting instruction and planning for upcoming Girl Scout troop meetings, which their daughters will attend. In an Ohio version, mothers and daughters meet on Tuesday evenings and eat a family-style meal together. "It enables families to talk around the table like you and I might do at home," said Girl Scout leader Mary Ann Binder.

These programs are in their infancy, and have not yet been evaluated as to their long-term effectiveness. As programs go, the cost is relatively low, around $30,000 to $50,000 a year. However, implementation and maintenance require leadership, motivation, management skills, and fund-raising expertise. These are likely to vary from one Girl Scout council to another—but there is no reason other youth service organizations could not be involved as well.

Sources: Marilyn C. Moses (1995). "Keeping Incarcerated Mothers and Their Daughters Together: Girl Scouts beyond Bars." *NIJ Program Focus* (October):1–12; Tracy L. Snell (1994). "Women in Prison." *BJS Bulletin* (March):1–18.

Special Health Problems of Women Inmates. Another area in which female inmates have experienced special problems is physical and mental health. Gynecological and obstetric care and special lab tests to detect cervical and breast cancer are now provided in most prisons, but the rural location of many prisons raises questions about the adequacy of care and the availability of medical specialists. In addition, many incarcerated women come from backgrounds where malnutrition, dental disease, alcohol and drug addiction, and spousal abuse are common problems. The physical and mental toll associated with these problems is bad enough outside prison; inside prison the difficulties are often compounded by lack of adequately trained staff and separation from family support systems.

Although most states have taken steps to address the health problems of women, the fact that the prison system is largely designed for, funded by, and run by males continues to hamper reforms. This is particularly true in the area of rehabilitation and prison programs. A 1990 Task Force Report on the Female Offender undertaken by the American Correctional Association reported that very few work assignments were available to female inmates. Furthermore, the prison programs that exist have generally been designed to conform with the values of middle-class white males, not the realities of life for mostly poor, minority women, who are also single mothers (Feinman, 1994). Compared with men, the adult female inmate "has been ignored in terms of facilities, programs, and security" (Gordon, 1991:3). What women need most is training and education that will help improve their life chances; what they generally receive is training in low-paying service and clerical skills: food services, sewing, cosmetology, and clerking. These programs provide needed services to the prison community, but do little to improve the chances that ex-inmates will ever be able to move above the poverty level.

Types of Women's Prisons. Just as men's prisons vary considerably, so do women's prisons. It is therefore impossible to describe a generic prison for women. However, when the classic studies of women's prisons cited at the beginning of this chapter were undertaken in the 1960s, women's institutions were undoubtedly the backwater of American corrections. In 1962, there were only 35 correctional facilities for women in the entire country (Freedman, 1981:144), and many of these also housed male inmates. Fifteen years later, only 34 states had separate institutions for women (Hawkins and Alpert, 1989:303). In the other states, women were usually housed in special sections of male prisons.

co-correctional prison A correctional facility that houses both men and women.

Eighteen states and the Federal Bureau of Prisons have developed **co-correctional prisons** that house both men and women under one administration, and permit varying degrees of interaction between the sexes (Maguire and Pastore, 1995:101). Many of these prisons house both medium- and minimum-security inmates, and some have a maximum-security section as well. Some of these facilities allow considerable interaction between male and female inmates, while others restrict contact to work and education programs. Many co-correctional facilities were opened to cut costs or to deal with overcrowding. Some states needed a place to house aging and infirm male offenders, and so converted minimum-security women's facilities to house both sexes. Occasionally, the motivation for co-corrections was more idealistic: to create a more normal environment in which rehabilitation and pre-release programs would be more effective.

Co-corrections remains a controversial issue, and there is no sign that states are rushing to build more such facilities. Some of the benefits of co-corrections include a more relaxed atmosphere, a broader array of educational and treatment programs, and opportunities to develop positive relations with the opposite sex. However, there is evidence that there are also serious drawbacks for female prisoners (Hawkins and Alpert, 1989:331–333; Feinman, 1994:77–79), including the following:

- Falling into traditional sex roles, in which male inmates tend to become the leaders and to take the best jobs, and women assume more subordinate roles
- Discouragement from entering nontraditional vocational training
- Pressure from men for sexual favors (although it is the women—who are usually in the minority—who suffer greater restriction and surveillance because of it)

In January 1995, about half of all female prisoners were held in minimum-security facilities (Figure 16.3). Only 11 percent were classified as maximum-security inmates. The only strictly maximum-security women's facilities are run by the military—at Fort Leavenworth, Kansas, and in San Diego, California. Most maximum-security inmates are held in special units of mixed-security prisons. But as a rule, inmate security classification seems to mean less in a women's facility than in one for men. There are three reasons for this: (1) Since the number of female inmates is relatively small, the per-inmate costs of providing different types of facilities and programs are relatively high; (2) women at all security levels tend to be more closely supervised than their male counterparts; and (3) the requirements for managing maximum-security inmates shape the prison environment for all other inmates housed in the same facility.

"MAKING IT" IN A WOMEN'S PRISON

As noted at the beginning of the chapter, far more research has been undertaken on life in men's prisons than on the social structure and culture of women's prisons. The participant observation studies by Giallombardo (1966,

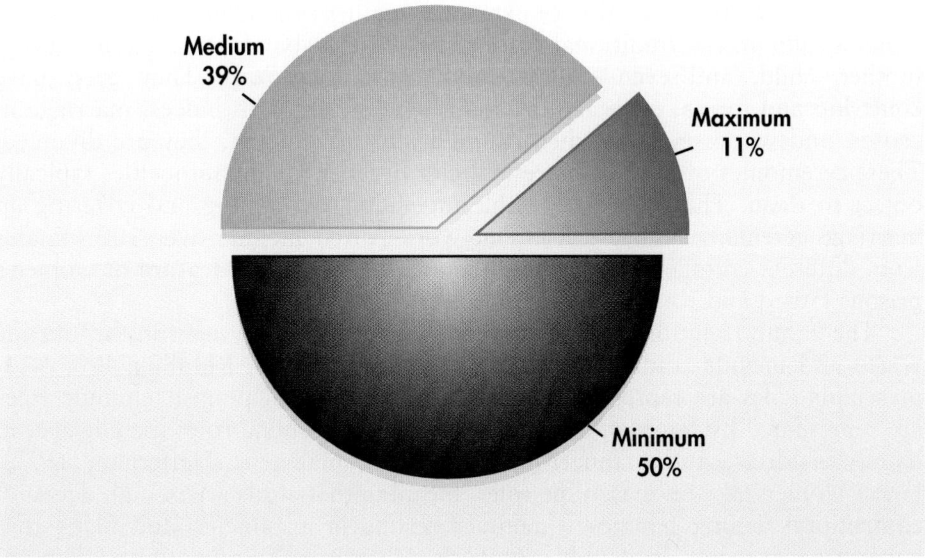

FIGURE 16.3 SECURITY CLASSIFICATIONS OF FEMALE PRISONERS, 1994
Half of all female prisoners in the United States are held in minimum-security facilities. The smallest proportion is held in maximum-security facilities. Data are unavailable for California, Colorado, Maine, Texas, Utah, and Vermont.

Source: Kathleen Maguire and Ann L. Pastore (1995). *Sourcebook of Criminal Justice Statistics, 1994* (p. 550). Washington, D.C.: U.S. Department of Justice.

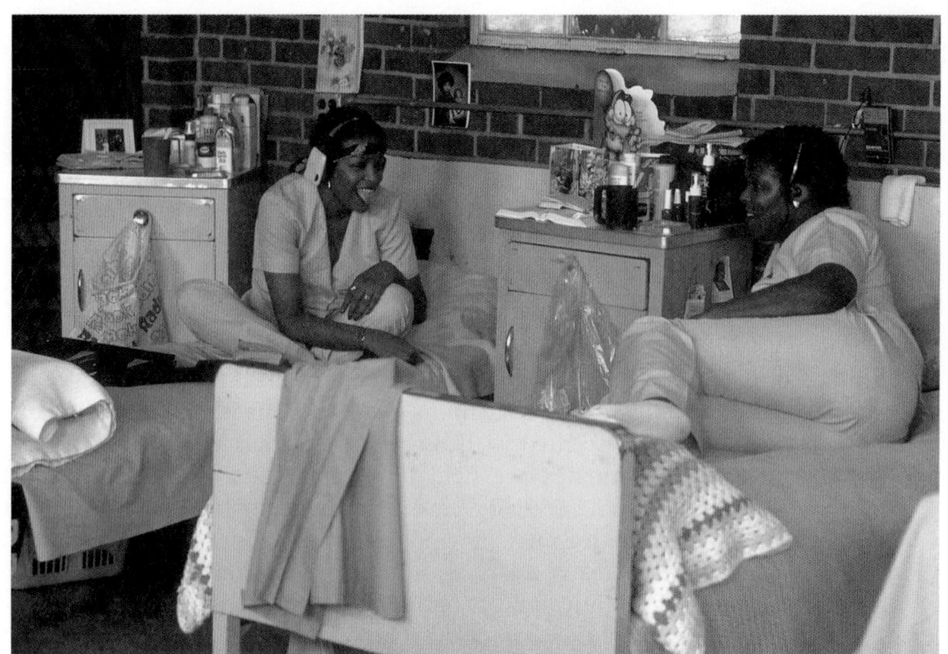

Women's prisons have elaborate social systems called kinship systems, *in which inmates take on the roles of parents, spouses, children, grandchildren, and even in-laws. Pseudo-marriages are common and are often accompanied by elaborate secret ceremonies.*

PHOTO BY A RAMEY, COURTESY OF PHOTOEDIT

1974) and Heffernan (1972), in particular, have helped open up the correctional backwater of women's prisons, and their work remains significant today.

The Importance of Kinship. The inmate social system in women's prisons is dominated by the formation of extended families or *kinship systems* in which inmates take on the traditional roles of mother, husband, father, aunt, grandmother, child, and even in-laws (Giallombardo, 1966). They even have courtship and formal marriage ceremonies, complete with judges, marriage licenses, and witnesses; and when married inmates fall out, they are divorced. These ceremonies often take place in secret because prison authorities typically object to them. There is considerable ingenuity in planning and covering up marriage ceremonies since kinship networks often include over 100 inmates from different cottages or dorms, and snitching is a major feature of women's prisons (Ward and Kassebaum, 1965).

The family relationships created in women's prisons mirror the outside world and include traditional gender-based social roles. Recalling Box 16.1, masculine roles are represented by studs, butches, and pimps; feminine roles are represented by femmes, broads, and foxes. Masculine roles include special hairstyles, dress, and mannerisms to indicate maleness (Heffernan, 1972). Fewer women take on masculine roles, meaning that studs are in high demand; competition among femmes sometimes results in arguments and fights that have to be mediated by family members. Adding to the potential conflict are "chippies" and "tricks," women who serve as prison prostitutes seeking sex with studs. They may break up marriages, disrupting family relations. Disruption is also caused by married studs falling for each other, which produces role-switching, as one stud now becomes a femme. Frequent role switching is disapproved of and results in loss of status (Giallombardo, 1974:190).

Prison families provide a sense of belonging and identification and provide all sorts of social and emotional supports for inmates. This helps women do their time. However, there is evidence that kinship may be declining in women's prisons (Fox, 1982). The opening of previously closed prisons to outsiders—volunteers, service providers, and educators—has helped reduce idleness and the heavy reliance on kinship as a solution to adjustment problems. In addition, changes in the outside world have produced changing ideas about women's roles. These changes may reduce the importance of kinship structures, but they probably will not disappear.

Homosexual Activity. Homosexual activity is widespread in men's prisons, where it is often associated with aggression, power, domination—and bartering. Homosexual activity also occurs in women's prisons, but it more often takes place in the context of romantic attachments and inmate marriages. Sometimes, sexual activity is unrelated to romance but is associated with loneliness—sex brings women together and the momentary companionship and physical pleasure makes them feel good:

> When I was with my man outside I felt big and strong and like a woman . . . and, you know, I was aware of being a real woman. . . . But inside this place, when I do something with a girl, usually I feel like a little girl and someone's comforting me and just making me feel good. It's not really a sex thing, even when it's sex, because in here you feel so damn little and alone. And you don't feel like a woman, because when you feel that little, you don't know anything about sex. All you know is it feels good. (Burkhart, 1976:362)

Like men in prison, women rarely continue their homosexual activity after release. Homosexual activity is situational, and many ex-inmates disapprove of "true" homosexuality just as they did before going to prison.

WOMEN IN CORRECTIONAL WORK

Corrections has always been dominated by men, and that characterization remains true today. Although women have long worked in the field, they worked almost exclusively in women's facilities, or as clerical and medical staff in men's prisons. In 1972, Congress enacted Title VII of the Civil Rights Act. This law prohibited sex discrimination in hiring by state and local governments. The new law opened the door to the employment of women in all aspects of corrections in all types of institutions. Despite progress, by 1996, women still held far fewer positions than men, especially in higher-level managerial positions. Figures 16.4 through 16.6 show the representation of women and minorities in corrections employment in 1996 in adult and juvenile facilities. Women are underrepresented compared to men in both adult and juvenile corrections facilities, and this is true regardless of race or ethnicity. In fact, the representation of black and Hispanic men in corrections jobs equals or exceeds their representation in the U.S. population as a whole. The employment of women is most disproportionate among wardens and superintendents of prisons. Only 18 percent of these jobs were held by women in 1996.

Women as Correctional Officers in Male Prisons. There has been long-standing resistance to hiring women as correctional officers in male facilities. The situation is similar to the resistance encountered in police work that we discussed in Chapter 6. The conventional wisdom is that women will be less effective as guards because (1) they lack the strength and assertiveness needed

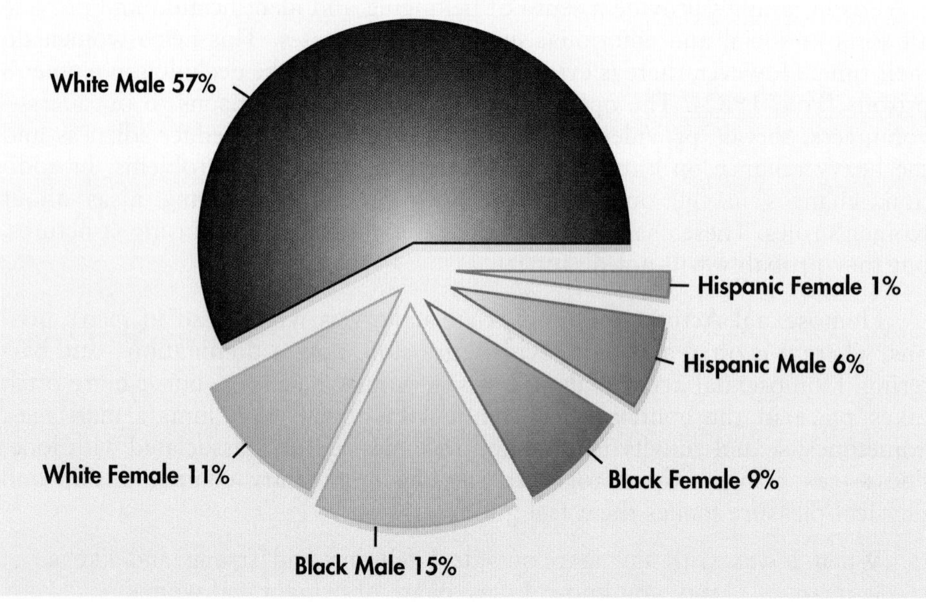

FIGURE 16.4 PROPORTION OF MALE AND FEMALE CORRECTIONAL OFFICERS
By race/ethnicity in adult facilities in June, 1996.

Source: American Correctional Association (1998), *1998 Directory: Juvenile and Adult Correctional Departments, Institutions, Agencies, and Paroling Authorities* (pp. xliv-xlv). Laurel, MD: American Correctional Association.

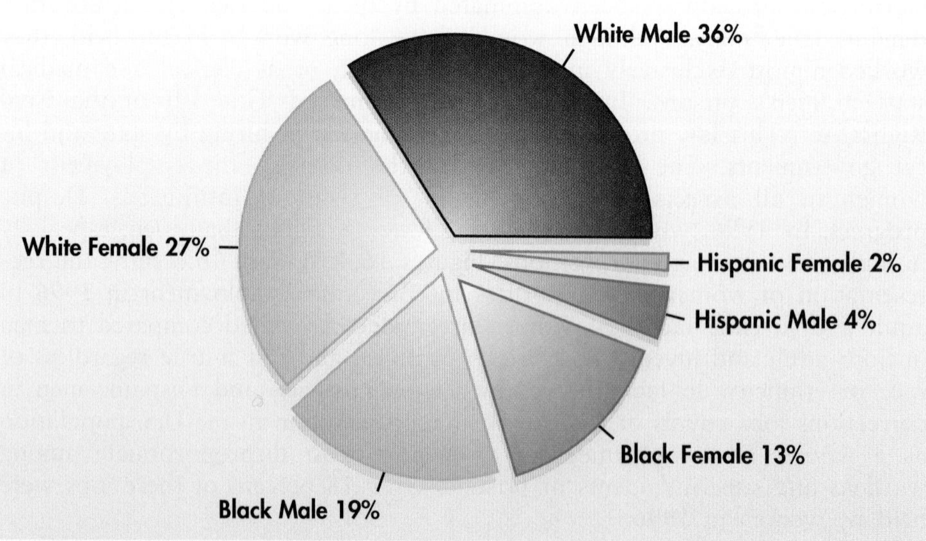

FIGURE 16.5 PROPORTION OF MALE AND FEMALE CORRECTIONAL PERSONNEL IN JUVENILE FACILITIES
By race/ethnicity in juvenile facilities, June, 1996.

Source: American Correctional Association (1998), *1998 Directory: Juvenile and Adult Correctional Departments, Institutions, Agencies, and Paroling Authorities*, (pp. xlii-xliii). Laurel, MD: American Correctional Association.

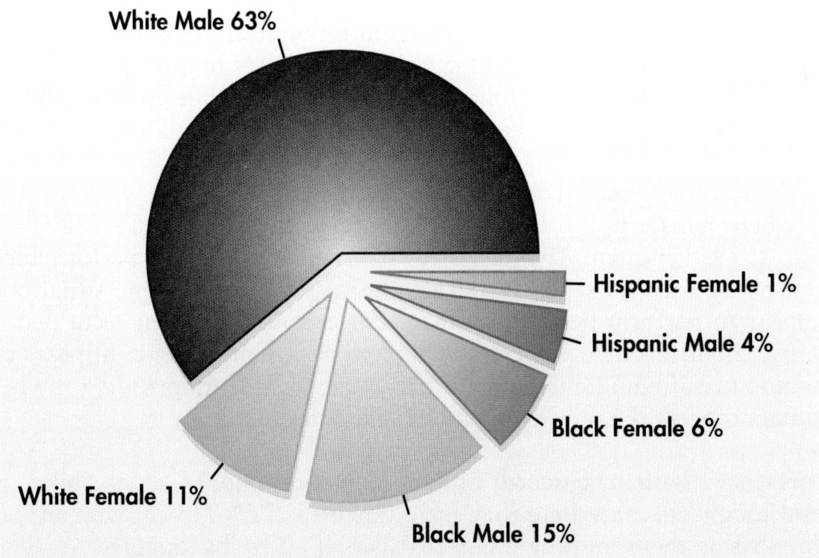

FIGURE 16.6 PROPORTION OF MEN AND WOMEN IN SUPERINTENDENT AND WARDEN POSITIONS IN ADULT PRISONS
By race/ethnicity in June, 1996.

Source: American Correctional Association (1998), *1998 Directory: Juvenile and Adult Correctional Departments, Institutions, Agencies, and Paroling Authorities*, (p. xlvi). Laurel, MD: American Correctional Association.

More and more women are applying for jobs as correctional officers, but they have a long way to go before their representation matches that of men. Female guards who work in male prisons generally have a difficult time and, like female police officers, must contend with rejection and even harassment from male colleagues.

PHOTO COURTESY OF UPI/CORBIS-BETTMANN

to deal with male inmates; (2) they are vulnerable to sexual assault by inmates; (3) they must observe and interact with males in intimate circumstances, for example, during showers or strip searches, and this increases tensions; and (4) inmates are considered less likely to follow their orders, and male guards will feel compelled to protect them from violence, thereby increasing danger to themselves.

Research on these issues tends to disprove this conventional wisdom, just as it does where female police officers are concerned (Alpert, 1984; Hawkins and Alpert, 1989; Feinman, 1994:177–187). When it comes to performance tasks, women and men do equally well on the whole, and in some situations women appear to perform better than men. For example, women seem better able to defuse situations before they turn violent, and their presence appears to have a calming or softening effect on the prison environment, including the behavior of male officers. Here is how one female guard explains it:

> [The presence of a female guard] forces male officers not to act as "big, bad and tough" because here they have this little 5'2" 115 lb. woman standing beside them, putting a guy that is 6'4", 230 lbs. in cuffs . . . saying, "Come on now, act right," and not having any problem doing

Box 16.6

INSIDE CRIMINAL JUSTICE

"THE BLEAKER IT SOUNDED, THE BETTER IT SOUNDED": A TOP CORRECTIONS OFFICIAL DESCRIBES HER CAREER AND ACCOMPLISHMENTS

This is a summary of an interview conducted with Dr. Dora Schriro, director of the Missouri Department of Corrections, and one of the first women appointed to head a state corrections agency. She describes her life as "a series of happy accidents with many mentors along the way." In high school, a one-day lecture on criminology convinced her that "that's what I want to do." During the 1960s there were not many females embarking on a career in criminal justice, and Schriro believes she received extra attention and support because of it. She studied sociology at Northeastern University, then after graduating tried to get into corrections but couldn't because state agencies at that time only hired people age 25 or older. After completing a master's degree she was hired at a medium-security prison in Massachusetts to run an educational program; she had no training in education, and her hiring is indicative, she believes, of the low standing in which rehabilitation and treatment were held by corrections administrators at the time. Her program was located outside the prison, and inmates were ferried back and forth each day.

Her lack of experience in education led her to seek a doctor of education degree at Columbia Teachers College in New York. She supported herself by working in correctional services for New York City, administering a variety of educational programs in local prisons and jails. She later became coordinator of criminal justice for the mayor's office, and in 1984 was invited to be assistant commissioner for corrections in New York City.

In 1989 she was invited to become superintendent at a medium-security facility in St. Louis. She arrived at an institution with substantial problems, in-

> it. Whereas he might have to go in there with 2 or 3 other guys and tackle him down to cuff him. It also forces them to recognize that they can't go home and talk about how bad and mean they are and what a tough day they have had because some little chickie can do the same thing that he is doing. (Owen, 1985:158)

There are, nevertheless, problems that are associated with female correctional officers in male prisons—and, in some cases, male officers in women's prisons. One problem concerns the issue of inmate privacy. Here, the courts have generally supported the policy of **least restrictive means**. Under this policy, the least restrictive steps must be taken to ensure both women's right to employment and inmates' right to privacy. In prisons, this might mean prohibiting female guards from conducting strip or body cavity searches of male inmates but allowing them to conduct pat-down searches. Another solution is to construct screens or windows that permit the inmate to be seen, but not entirely; some prisons have put half-doors on toilets. These steps are also taken in female prisons where male guards work.

least restrictive means A policy that protects a woman's right to employment in a male prison and the male inmate's right to privacy.

Another problem concerns resentment or hostility of male guards toward the women who work with them. The resistance of male correctional officers

Box 16.6 (continued)

cluding drug use by staff. Yet, "the bleaker it sounded, the better it sounded." Her work in St. Louis brought her to the governor's attention, who in 1991 appointed her to be director of the Missouri Department of Corrections.

Schriro finds it difficult to assess how gender may have been an issue in her career. Others have characterized her work as innovative and point to her gender as the explanation: She was not confined by the "old boys" network and traditional practice. She is proud to be known for not choosing between public safety, staff advocacy, and inmate welfare; she believes that to do one you have to do all. She approaches problem solving in a collaborative way and believes in empowering staff and inmates while treating the community as the customer of correctional services.

Dr. Schriro is particularly proud of her work to reduce lawsuits by inmates. "Every state continues to experience an increase in prisoner litigation, but in my state I have cut it by 62 percent." Schriro did this by establishing dispute resolution mechanisms within correctional facilities, and providing inmates with speedy responses to their complaints. More times than not the response is no rather than yes, Schriro points out, but the process validates the right of inmates to be heard, and remedies are often found that help to address some aspect of the inmate's complaint. Inmates feel they have been treated with respect, and they can still file suit in the courts if they wish to pursue a complaint further. The process has been helped by providing better medical services to inmates, including health education and faster diagnosis of medical symptoms.

When asked for advice to students contemplating careers in corrections, her answer was, "Do it. It's some of the most important work that one could pursue." And since crime and victimization show no signs of abating, "the opportunity for innovation is greater now than ever before."

Source: Dr. Dora Schriro, personal communication, July, 1996.

to the presence of women has been most pronounced in maximum-security prisons for men. In some cases, female guards report being ostracized by their colleagues, and even fear being "set up" so that they can be fired or even sexually assaulted: "There is a mind set of officers here who feel that women don't belong at Stillwater [a maximum-security prison in Oklahoma] and they are waiting for one of us to get sexually assaulted because then we will all leave. They think that we will make a mass exodus. And what concerns me is that they (the male officers) might in some way, inadvertently, set it up or allow the situation to escalate" (Fox, 1982:70).

The fear of rejection, noncooperation, and even abuse by male colleagues contributes to tensions among prison staff and can seriously undermine security. So it is clearly important for prison administrators—who are mostly male—to recognize that there is a place for women in all aspects of corrections, and to see to it that proper training and support systems are put in place.

There is reason to feel optimistic. As I write this, women have begun to appear in corrections at the highest level. For example, the director of the Federal Bureau of Prisons is a woman, Kathleen Hawk. And so is the director of the Missouri Department of Corrections, Dr. Dora Schriro. These women have helped break the gender barrier in administration of correctional bureaucracies, and while that does not guarantee that more women will find work in corrections, it does mean that males no longer have a monopoly on policymaking.

Consider as you read Box 16.6 that Dr. Schriro is head of an agency whose facilities include an old "Big House" prison built in 1836 and a new maximum-security facility opened in 1988. The old Missouri State Penitentiary is known as "The Walls," and was tagged "the bloodiest 47 acres in America" following a 1954 riot in which four inmates died. The new prison, the Potosi Correctional Center, houses the state's death chamber.

THREE CHALLENGES IN CORRECTIONS: AIDS, GERIATRIC INMATES, AND PRISONER RIGHTS

Three new and important challenges confront those who live and work in prisons. The first two issues emerged as pressing concerns only in the past decade or so; the issue of inmate rights has a much longer history, although in practical terms inmates had little recourse to the courts until the 1940s.

HIV/AIDS IN PRISONS

In prisons today, inmates and correctional staff alike are faced with a new hazard: HIV infection and AIDS. Since 1985, when the Centers for Disease Control (CDC) first tracked AIDS cases in the correctional system, the cumulative total of AIDS cases among U.S. inmates had grown to 11,565 by 1993. A 1995 end-of-year survey of correctional facilities found 5,099 confirmed AIDS cases and 18,165 inmates who had tested positive for HIV infection. The rate of confirmed AIDS among prisoners is six times higher than that among the general population (Maruschak, 1997:4). In 1995, 1,010 state inmates died of AIDS-related diseases while in custody; this is a third of all inmate deaths. Figure 16.7 shows the cumulative trend in inmates deaths since 1986.

The incidence of AIDS is much higher in correctional populations than in the general population: 518 cases per 100,000 state or federal inmates and 706 per 100,000 jail inmates, compared with 41 per 100,000 for the population at large. Half the prison AIDS cases are concentrated in New York and New Jersey, but this proportion has been dropping as the epidemic has spread throughout the country. Today, despite widespread publicity about the importance of

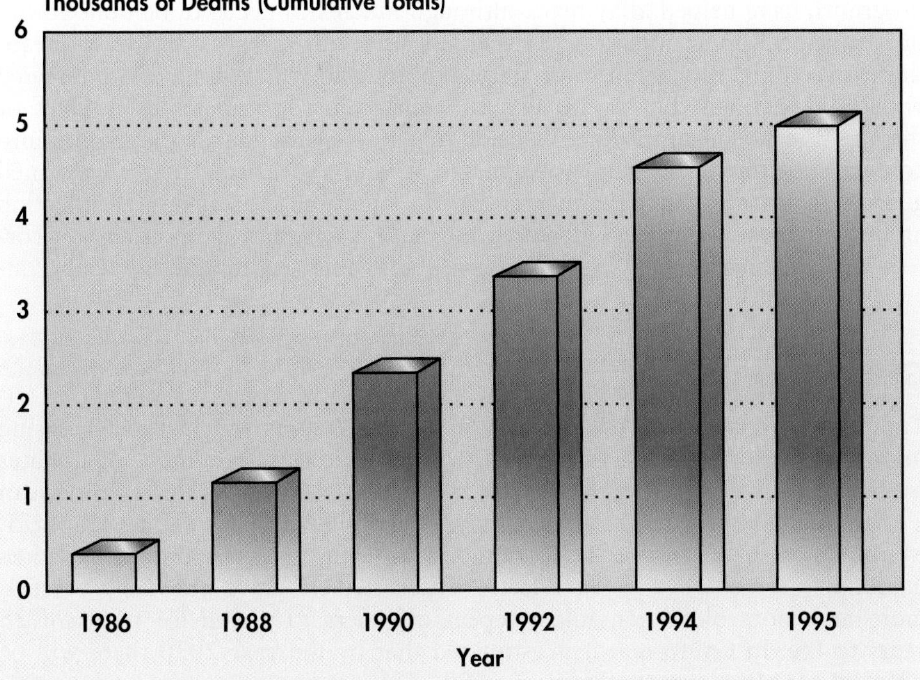

FIGURE 16.7 Cumulative AIDS Deaths Among Prison and Jail Inmates, 1986–1995
Prevalence of AIDS is rising in the correctional population. In the ten-year period, 1986-1995, the total number of AIDS-related deaths rose from around 500 to over 5,000.

Sources: Theodore M. Hammett, et al. (1995), *1994 Update: HIV/AIDS and STDs in Correctional Facilities* (p. 5). Washington, D.C.: U.S. Department of Justice; Laura Maruschak (1997). "HIV in Prisons and Jails, 1995". *BJS Bulletin* (August):1.

safe-sex practices and the difficulties of treating HIV infection, it appears that many, if not most, arrested men and women have not practiced safe sex (Decker and Rosenfeld, 1995). The implications of this for jail and prison populations are painfully obvious.

Although most prison AIDS patients are male, the rate of infection is actually higher among female inmates, and this applies to jail populations as well (Maruschak, 1997). This reflects the fact that larger proportions of female inmates have a history of intravenous (IV) drug use, and that women are more often incarcerated for drug and prostitution-related offenses. When race is considered, black and Hispanic rates of HIV infection are three times the rate for white inmates. This difference is most likely explained by the higher rates of IV drug use associated with the street drug culture among black and Hispanic Americans.

AIDS poses all sorts of problems for prison populations and for those who manage them. Short of segregating HIV/AIDS inmates, many correctional systems are restricting the ways infected inmates have contact with others. California, for example, prohibits HIV-infected inmates from working around food, and appellate courts have upheld this restriction (*Criminal Justice Newsletter* 1994, Vol. 25:2–3). Alabama and Mississippi segregated all HIV-infected inmates as late as 1994, although states that have mainstreamed their HIV-infected inmates have generally not experienced the dire consequences anticipated in some quarters. In fact, not one case of HIV transmission from an inmate to a correctional officer had been reported as of 1994 (Hammett et al.,

1995:4). Careful training and education of staff and inmates, including peer programs, have helped allay fears, although much still needs to be done to improve medical and counseling services. In addition, privacy laws have meant that correctional officers in some states are not told which inmates are infected with HIV—though they eventually find out from the inmates themselves or through the prison grapevine. Considering how easily guards may come into contact with the bodily fluids of inmates, it is not surprising that uninformed guards feel unnecessarily endangered by this situation. If rates of HIV infection among inmates continue to increase, one can be sure that the pressure on correctional systems to deal effectively with HIV-infected inmates will also increase.

GERIATRIC INMATES

The punitive trend toward longer prison sentences is producing an increasing number of older inmates. From 1990 to 1994 alone, the number of inmates over age 55 increased nearly 50 percent, from 19,160 to 27,674 (American Correctional Association, 1995). Today, over 1,000 inmates are over age 75. Many of these older inmates committed violent crimes later in life, when mandatory sentences were in effect. "Three strikes" laws are likely to send more and more older nonviolent repeat offenders to prison for terms of 25 years to life. In California, it is estimated that by the year 2020 there will be 126,400 geriatric inmates (Donziger, 1996:53).

From the vantage point of inmates who have grown old in prison, the idea of leaving may actually be frightening—they are used to prison life. How would they survive outside? Many of their relatives and friends have died. Who would look after them? The elderly inmate represents "a growing underclass of dependents in a world of change" (Hassine, 1996:97).

Geriatric prisoners present unique problems in today's corrections system. In California alone, by the year 2020 there will be an estimated 125,000 geriatric inmates.

ILLUSTRATION BY JOHN OVERMYER

From the vantage point of correctional administrators, a growing geriatric population means growing costs for special services. According to a California study, 80 percent of elderly inmates have a chronic health condition, 38 percent have hypertension, 28 percent have heart disease, and 16 percent have cataracts (Zimbardo, 1994). The average national cost of housing a state inmate is around $22,000 per year; an elderly inmate costs around $69,000 a year (Donziger, 1996:54).

The dilemma of what to do with elderly inmates will become part of the debate over prison costs, which is likely to escalate since many states cannot afford to run the new prisons that governors and legislators have rushed to build. Many observers believe that elderly inmates are unlikely to pose a threat to the community if released, especially if they have family on the outside. Nevertheless, the widely held sentiment that gave us mandatory minimums and truth-in-sentencing laws may not be satisfied with early release, even for elderly inmates. If the California projections mentioned previously are indeed correct, and similar trends occur in other states, the challenge of the geriatric inmate can only get worse.

PRISONERS' RIGHTS

Until the 1960s, the prevailing rule on the rights of inmates was that they had only those rights jailers were willing to allow them. The courts largely took a "hands-off" position. Some even argued that when convicted of a felony, people should suffer a **civil death:** They lose many, if not all, of the rights that come with citizenship, including the right to seek a redress of grievances in a court of law. As for what went on inside prisons, the prevailing view was that prison administrators knew what they were doing and would balance the security needs of their facilities with a reasonable concern for the humane treatment of inmates (Rudovsky et al., 1988). In practice, the hands-off doctrine helped keep prisons closed to outside scrutiny, and the treatment of prisoners inside was often inhumane.

civil death Loss of citizenship rights if convicted of a felony.

The first step toward abandonment of the hands-off doctrine was taken in the 1940s (Hawkins and Alpert, 1989:367–368). In ***Ex parte Hull*** (1941) the U.S. Supreme Court declared that prisoners have the unrestricted right of access to federal courts. In ***Coffin v. Reichard*** (1944) a U.S. Sixth Circuit Court of Appeals ruled that inmates had the right of court review when challenging the conditions of confinement. The cases applied only to federal prisoners, but they opened the door—at least a small crack—to challenges involving the constitutionality of conditions in state and local prisons.

Ex parte Hull Prisoners have unrestricted right of access to federal courts.

Coffin v. Reichard Federal prisoners have the right to challenge conditions of confinement in federal court.

From the 1960s to the 1980s more and more inmate grievances appeared before the courts. A significant case occurred in 1962, when Black Muslim inmates at the Stateville penitentiary in Illinois sued for the right to practice their religion. The inmates brought their suit under Section 1983 of the federal Civil Rights Act. In ***Cooper v. Pate*** (1964), the U.S. Supreme Court ruled that denial of the inmates right to practice their religion was a violation of their First Amendment rights. Section 1983 lawsuits became the avenue of choice for inmates seeking to change the conditions of their confinement (Hanson and Daley, 1995).

Cooper v. Pate Prisoners have a constitutional right to practice their religion while confined.

During the 1970s and 1980s other significant cases occurred. Many concerned complaints that prison conditions amounted to cruel and unusual punishment under the Eighth Amendment. In a 1977 case, a U.S. district judge found "overwhelming" evidence that conditions as a whole in a Rhode Island prison were unconstitutional: "The judge had found leaking and inadequate plumbing, filth, roaches and rodents, and an inadequate maintenance program. The amount of lighting was less than that necessary for reading. The noise level was maddening, the heating and ventilation systems were not minimally adequate, and there were numerous fire hazards" (Rudovsky et al., 1988:3)

As a result of suits such as these, conditions in prisons improved, and the rights of prisoners were slowly established. Today, prisoners' rights and protections include the following:

- The right of religious freedom, including a place to worship and the right to wear religious insignia
- Freedom of speech, including the right to communicate with people outside the prison
- The right to medical treatment, including sanitary conditions and necessary medication
- The right to be protected from foreseeable attack or sexual assault
- The right to due process before being punished by prison officials
- Freedom from sexually offensive behavior by prison staff of the opposite sex, including being strip-searched
- The right to equal treatment in provision of jobs and vocational, educational, and other services within the prison or jail

It is important to note, however, that these rights and protections are properly understood as *conditional.* They are to be weighed against the control and safety needs of the prison, including its staff and inmates. A curtailment of rights and protections is generally allowed when it is reasonable in light of security concerns.

The number of prisoner lawsuits continues to increase, in large measure because the prison population itself has increased. From 1986 to 1996, for example, the number of suits charging violations of inmate rights grew from around 21,000 to over 41,000 (Scalia, 1997:4). Some critics charge that many suits are frivolous claims brought by inmates who have time on their hands and a vague hope of early release. Dan Lungren, California's attorney general, spoke for many critics when he said: "Relatively few lawsuits have merit. Many lack substance and only waste the court's time and the taxpayers' money" (*National Prison Project Journal*, 1996, Vol. 11:1). Now that some states have passed laws permitting prisoners to request DNA testing of evidence used to convict them, there is concern that a rash of motions for testing will flood the courts. Illinois has responded to that possibility by threatening inmates with having up to 180 days of "good time" added back into their sentence for frivolous requests (*St. Louis Post-Dispatch*, July 26, 1997, p. 8).

The truth is that while some suits are frivolous, objectionable and possibly unconstitutional conditions are still found inside prisons. Inmates' voices need to be heard by outsiders if only to protect society's interest in the fair and humane treatment of all its citizens. Consider the issue of gender. Since most prison litigation has involved male inmates and male staff, and has been decided by male judges, the rights of female inmates and female staff have been largely ignored. A variety of reasons can be given (Feinman, 1994:72): Women are more accepting; women have less access to the resources needed in litigation; women's prisons are usually in rural areas, cut off from law libraries, lawyers, and the courts; female inmates are assumed to be better off than male inmates, and are therefore ignored. Although courts have ruled that the rights of female inmates generally coincide with those of men, it appears that gender discrimination still exists in the treatment of women. The excuse used in ***Klinger v. Nebraska Department of Correctional Services*** (1994) and some other recent cases is that the prison experience is not the same for men and women and therefore women are not entitled to the same access to programs and other opportunities. But is it trivial or frivolous for female inmates to continue to seek a clear standard on the important issue of equal rights?

Klinger v. Nebraska Department of Correctional Services Men and women are not entitled to the same access to prison programs because their prison experiences are different.

SUMMARY

Life in maximum-security prisons is full of fears and tensions for both inmates and staff. Although modern correctional facilities and management techniques have changed the prison environment for many inmates in a positive way, prisons are still largely closed systems where every aspect of an inmate's life is regulated and tightly controlled. Prisons are "total institutions," and people who live and work there have little or no life apart from the institution.

The primary goal of prisons is custody. A military-style custodial hierarchy exists in maximum- and medium-security prisons, with line officers (or guards) in closest daily contact with inmates. Safety issues are paramount, and correctional officers ensure their own and the inmates' safety by close monitoring of inmates, periodic shakedowns for contraband and weapons, and disciplinary measures when rules are violated. Staff have considerable discretion in applying the rules, and many staff and inmates find that informal discipline works best in many situations. Segregation (the "hole") is a formal punishment commonly used for dealing with serious discipline problems. While courts have ruled that the use of segregation is constitutional, the practice remains controversial.

As inmates and staff adapt to life inside, a prison culture emerges that helps them cope with the rigors of incarceration and the expectations of superiors. The prisonization model of inmate adaptation stresses the influence of actual conditions inside prison; the importation model stresses pre-prison experiences. Debate over which model best describes inmate adaptation has seen more support for importation than prisonization, especially in light of the reproduction of street gangs among inmates in many prisons. Racial tensions have been growing in prisons along with increasing gang involvement, and both trends are partly due to the increased imprisonment of young black and Hispanic offenders with gang connections and violent pasts.

Women in prison face special problems that still are not adequately addressed. Although improvements have occurred—often as a result of inmate lawsuits—women inmates still find themselves denied adequate health care and equal access to correctional programs and services. The implications of the fact that most women inmates are poor, minority single mothers seems to have been lost on mostly white, middle-class, male correctional administrators. Personal relationships and mutual support are important in prison, and women achieve these ends through the creation of kinship networks.

Three special challenges face corrections at the dawn of the 21st century: rising numbers of inmates with HIV/AIDS, a growing population of elderly inmates, and the continued clarification of inmate rights. None of these problems has easy solutions, and it is probably safe to predict continued debate but slow progress. Indeed, this is the case with the adequacy and humanity of America's punishment of its criminal offenders generally.

WHAT DO YOU THINK *NOW?*

- Now that you're familiar with the issues of AIDS, geriatric patients, and prisoner rights, can you think of any other new issues that prison staff have to deal with? What about the increasing number of women in prison?

- Based on what you've read, what are the biggest problems for maintaining order in prison? What do new inmates have to fear? Why must guards, especially in maximum-security prisons, always be vigilant?
- How do prison staff stand together to maintain order? What can undermine solidarity among correctional officers?

KEY TERMS AND CASES

formal organization
informal organization
total institution
keeper philosophy
control model
responsibility model
consensual model
segregation
hands-off doctrine
prisonization
pains of imprisonment
importation
co-correctional prison
least restrictive means
civil death
Ex parte Hull
Coffin v. Reichard
Cooper v. Pate
Klinger v. Nebraska Department of Correctional Services

ACTIVE LEARNING CHALLENGES

1. Arrange a class visit to a prison or jail. Make sure that corrections authorities will allow all interested students to participate and that you will be able to talk with inmates about life in prison.
2. Invite ex-inmates to visit the class to describe and discuss their experiences before, during, and after confinement. Most states have organizations that can put you in touch with ex-inmates, and the Internet is a useful resource for addresses and phone numbers.
3. Discuss the view that justice and crime prevention would be better served if prisons were harsh and unpleasant places with few amenities and minimal services to inmates.
4. Divide the class into small groups representing (1) male inmates, (2) female inmates, (3) correctional officers, (3) inmate families, and (4) correctional administrators (for example, state directors, wardens, and superintendents). Each group should then design the ideal prison environment from their perspective.
5. Have each class member select one or two states and report back to the class on the status of prisoner lawsuits challenging conditions inside prisons in those states. A good place to start is with the ACLU's 1995 report, *State Prisons and the Courts*.
6. Spend a week researching the nature and role of homosexual behavior in men's and women's prisons. Explain the differences and then discuss whether such behavior ought to be ignored, allowed but controlled, or prohibited altogether.

INTERNET CHALLENGES

The Web pages mentioned here can all be accessed through the Web site for this textbook at **http://www.prenhall.com/barlow/**.

1. For an update on appellate court cases dealing with prisons and prisoners, start at the Legal Information Institute at Cornell Law School and follow the links to recent U.S. Supreme Court cases. Find two decisions that you believe have special significance for life in prisons.

2. Find out about programs serving families of incarcerated felons; check out the United Nations Crime and Justice Information Network. What are some specific things being done around the world to help inmate families?
3. For inmate home pages and email connections to inmates, visit the Inmate Classified Web site. See if you can make e-mail contact with inmates in your state, and invite them to answer questions from your class.

CHAPTER 17

Community-Based Corrections

Learning Objectives

- Understand the benefits and drawbacks of financial penalties.
- Describe the use of probation, including its history, concern over public safety, probation conditions, and reforms.
- Explain the emergence of intermediate sanctions and describe their appeal to policymakers, the public, and criminal justice professionals.
- Distinguish between various types of intermediate sanctions and understand their benefits and drawbacks.
- Understand why community service and restitution are receiving a lot of emphasis in modern corrections.
- Understand how reintegrative shaming may be a more effective punishment than traditional penalties.

Community-based corrections, which make up the bulk of intermediate sentences, can take many forms. These people have been sentenced to perform community service by shoveling snow. Some offenders sentenced to community service do not expect the hard work and close supervision, and claim that life would have been easier in prison.

Photo by James Nubile, courtesy of The Image Works

I don't feel that I'm under any obligation to balance the budget on the backs of people coming into court. And I won't do it.

A MUNICIPAL COURT JUDGE, ON USING FINES TO RECOVER JUSTICE COSTS

These young men are much better for it. They received a second chance and it's well worth the effort we've put into it. Many will avoid a further life of crime.

JOHN TAYLOR, DIRECTOR OF A BOOT CAMP IN NORTH CAROLINA

On [intensive probation supervision] you see the officer five times a week. Every day—that's outrageous! It's like prison. You spend most of your time with the probation officer.

A TEXAS AUTO THIEF UNDER INTENSIVE SUPERVISION

Jason Platt, convicted burglar, faced a possible prison term when he stood before Judge Harold Black for sentencing. Platt looked across the courtroom and found his wife, who was looking intently at the judge. She knew that the next few moments would determine whether her husband would be led away to prison or be allowed to serve his sentence in the community, perhaps even live at home. She had reason to be hopeful: The pre-sentence report showed some prior nonviolent offenses—a negative factor—but Platt had roots in the community, an employer willing to keep him on the job, and a wife and three children at home. These were usually considered mitigating factors that could lead to reductions in the penalty.

There were other reasons to be optimistic. The prosecutor had not pressed for a prison sentence, and Platt's attorney had made an eloquent case for an intermediate sentence that would keep him out of prison but still be more severe than probation alone. The victim of Platt's latest burglary had favored a penalty that would allow for restitution and keep the offender under close supervision in the community. He had no interest in seeing Platt spend five years in prison. Platt's wife was grateful that the judge would not hear requests for prison time from anyone directly involved in the case. Still, she knew there was a lot of pressure these days to give tough sentences to felony offenders, and this wasn't his first offense. Platt looked back at the judge and held his breath.

If you were in the judge's shoes, what would you do? Would you sentence Platt to prison? Why or why not?

community-based corrections Criminal penalties that reduce or eliminate time in prison or ease the transition from prison to freedom.

What Platt and his wife hoped for was a sentence to **community-based corrections**. Community-based corrections include a variety of criminal penalties that either reduce or eliminate time in prison, or ease the transition from prison to freedom.* By the end of 1996, around 4 million Americans were under some form of community-based corrections (Bureau of Justice Statistics, 1997). Three broad classes of community-based corrections exist:

1. Pre-trial diversion of suspects from the criminal justice system. This takes place after the police make an arrest, usually following consultation with an assistant prosecutor and sometimes a judge. Suspects must agree to participate, and failure to complete the program may result in prosecution on the original charge(s). Pre-trial diversion was discussed in Chapter 11.
2. Criminal penalties that restrict offenders or impose certain obligations on them while maintaining them in the community. Fines and probation are the classic examples, but a long list of alternatives to prison now exists, including intensive supervision, residential treatment centers, electronic monitoring, boot camps, restitution, and community service. These newer forms of community-based corrections are usually called **intermediate sanctions**, signifying that they lie between the most lenient punishments of unsupervised probation and small fines and the harsher punishment of jail or prison time.
3. Procedures and programs designed to smooth the transition from prison to freedom. These include parole and halfway houses, and may also involve forms of surveillance such as electronic monitoring.

intermediate sanctions Penalties that lie between prison and simple probation.

In this chapter we shall explore community-based corrections from the vantage point of offenders, correctional authorities, and the larger community. We will then evaluate community-based corrections and imprisonment as alternative penal strategies. The chapter concludes with some thoughts on criminal justice in the 21st century.

WHAT DO YOU THINK?

- How do fines help the community and punish the offender? How might they not be effective?
- Do you believe that community service is a fair punishment for some crimes? Which crimes should be eligible for intermediate sanctions such as this? Which should not?
- Do you think that boot camps for young offenders will teach them to obey the law, or will they merely toughen them into serious criminals?

*There are some very good books on community-based corrections. Students seeking a detailed treatment of this complex subject should consult one of the following texts: Cromwell and Killinger, 1994; Klein, 1997; Latessa and Allen, 1997; McCarthy and McCarthy, 1997.

EARLY FORMS OF COMMUNITY-BASED CORRECTIONS

The use of community-based corrections as an alternative to imprisonment is largely a product of 20th-century penal reform, as we saw in Chapter 15. Yet over the centuries some offenders have been able to avoid prison time, and even execution. Sometimes a leader—king or queen, president or governor—would grant a pardon or reduce a sentence. Prosecutors and judges sometimes reduced or dismissed charges, or suspended sentences. Juries, too, might have a hand in reducing, or *mitigating*, the severity of sentences. For example, a jury could help a thief avoid the death penalty by reducing the value of the stolen property.

Some defendants avoided the reach of the criminal law entirely by claiming **benefit of clergy**. This was a privilege originally extended to priests and nuns accused of crimes; it allowed them to be tried by ecclesiastical courts instead of secular courts. The accused avoided death, but their punishment might still be severe by modern standards. In the fifteenth and sixteenth centuries, benefit of clergy was extended to all citizens in capital cases who could prove they could read. Courts often used Psalm 51 as a test of literacy, and it became known as the "Neck Verse" (Cromwell and Killinger, 1994:5). Some common criminals memorized it, and then escaped hanging by pretending to read it in court.

benefit of clergy A medieval privilege that allowed clergy and certain other offenders to avoid the death penalty.

Another way harsh punishments were mitigated was through *judicial reprieve*. In this case, a judge would withdraw or suspend the penalty for a certain period of time, during which the offender remained free. This is similar to the modern-day **suspended sentence**, in which a judge postpones the imposition or the execution of a penalty. Today, suspended sentences are commonly given to first-time offenders convicted of local ordinance violations and misdemeanors. Many jurisdictions require the defendant to stay out of trouble for three to six months; after that, the conviction is *expunged*, or cleared, from the defendant's criminal record. An arrest record still remains, however.

suspended sentence The penalty for a crime is not imposed if the offender stays out of trouble for a specified time.

The judicial reprieve became a widespread practice in nineteenth-century England, but in the United States it was entangled in controversy. Some judges left the period of reprieve or suspension open, in effect placing the defendant under the power of the court indefinitely. A defendant who committed an offense years later could be punished for both the new and the old offense.

In 1916, the U.S. Supreme Court reduced judicial discretion in suspending sentences. The so-called **Killits case** involved a first-time offender with a good background and reputation who embezzled $4,700 from a bank in Toledo, Ohio. The offender, John Killits, made full restitution, and the bank declined to prosecute. The federal judge gave Killits an indefinite suspension of sentence. On appeal by the prosecution, the U.S. Supreme Court ruled that federal courts had no inherent power to suspend sentences indefinitely. The ruling confirmed the right of legislatures, not courts, to establish terms of suspension under the penal code. States must specifically grant courts the power to suspend the imposition of penalties before judges can grant reprieves.

Killits case Judges cannot suspend sentences indefinitely without legislative approval.

The Killits ruling reflected the tension between the legislative and judicial branches of government, a tension that has grown in recent years. Nowadays, judges who seek to mitigate the harshness of penalties in individual cases find themselves confronted with mandatory-sentencing laws that prohibit suspended sentences and other noncustodial penalties for increasing numbers of offenses. We saw the results of this development in Chapters 15 and 16.

Another practice used to mitigate the harshness of the law on an individual basis that also predates community-based corrections was the practice of *recognizance*, introduced by Boston judge Peter Oxenbridge Thatcher in 1830. Recognizance was a formal agreement between the court and the defendant, usually backed by a cash bond that was forfeited if the terms were not followed. The agreement might specify that the defendant pay a fine, keep the peace, or appear in court when called. As we saw in Chapter 11, recognizance is mostly used today as a *pre-trial* alternative to detention.

FINES

Although not originally intended as an alternative to jail or prison, the fine is often thought of as a community-based penalty. Fines have been part of the criminal sanctioning process for centuries. Under early law, monetary payments in the form of damages or compensation were made directly to crime victims. By the thirteenth century, payments were diverted to the state treasury, and victims of wrongs could receive compensation only by suing offenders in civil court. This is essentially how things remained until the 1970s.

There are various reasons for the historical popularity of financial penalties:

- They are relatively inexpensive to administer.
- They can be paid back if wrongly imposed.
- They can be adjusted according to the gravity of the offense—the more serious the offense, the larger the fine.
- They can be adjusted, within the limits of the law, according to the financial capacity of the offender.
- They can be substituted for harsher punishments such as imprisonment, thus relieving pressure on overcrowded jails and prisons.
- They can be collected in installments while the offender lives and works in the community.

Despite these various advantages, American judges have generally been reluctant to use fines as the penalty for felony crimes (Cole et al., 1987). This is in marked contrast to many other countries, where fines are the preferred penalty for most offenses, including many violent crimes (Tonry, 1996: 124–125; Tak, 1994). In the Netherlands, for example, the criminal code requires judges to provide a written statement of reasons for *not* imposing fines.

Despite American reluctance, the use of fines for more serious crimes has increased in recent years, mainly as a result of prison overcrowding and heavy probation caseloads. A survey of 126 judges around the country found that most now impose fines on a regular basis. First-time offenders are the people most likely to be fined, and their offenses range from sale of an ounce of cocaine to auto theft, embezzlement, and passing bad checks (Hillsman et al., 1987:2). However, many of these same judges are reluctant to choose fines as an alternative to incarceration or as the *only* penalty in felony cases.

Criticisms of Fines. Like most forms of punishment, financial penalties are not without drawbacks. In justifying why he rarely imposes fines, one judge said, "After paying $56 in court costs, $10 fee to the Crime Victim Compensation Fund, $200 public defender fee, and $100 to $500 in probation supervision fees, the defendant will be sufficiently punished" (Hillsman et al., 1987:3). Yet some judges see a fine as too lenient for many common crimes. Furthermore, many judges feel that it is impossible to set fines high enough to punish and deter while also taking into account the offender's ability to pay. The purpose of a fine is obviously foiled when the offender cannot pay.

Much of the current criticism of fines focuses on two issues: (1) the practice of sending offenders to jail or prison when they fail to pay their fines, and (2) the fact that fining discriminates against offenders who are poor. Nonpayment usually results in harsher punishments that can be avoided by more affluent criminals: Around half of those fined end up in already overburdened jails or prisons for nonpayment. Those who don't pay their fines are often poor offenders, which fuels the second criticism that fines are inherently discriminatory. When corporations and rich white-collar criminals are fined even large amounts, the penalty often causes little economic hardship. Wealthy offenders who avoid prison time by paying fines get to stay in the community, where they can work and enjoy their family and friends. They may have to report to a probation officer, but this hardly matches the pains of imprisonment that many poor defendants face.

Fines and Fees as a Means of Recovering Criminal Justice Costs. However, fines can also have positive effects. Fines are now being used more widely as a way to recover some of the costs of investigating, prosecuting, and punishing offenders. This is called **cost recovery**. The use of fines as cost recovery "fees" is permitted by federal sentencing guidelines and the practice is growing among states, too. Offenders in Texas, for example, were assessed a total of $57 million in 1990 to offset the costs of administering probation services. The average fee collected per probationer was $298. In New Jersey, Ocean County charges jail inmates $200 for the first ten days of their jail sentence, and $10 a day after that (Reuters News, January 5, 1997). This is technically a fee rather than a fine, but it represents a financial penalty automatically added to jail sentences as cost recovery.

cost recovery Using fines to recover some of the costs of catching, prosecuting, and punishing offenders.

Cost recovery programs may sound attractive to budget-minded officials and legislators, but criticisms abound: Many offenders are unable to pay, making it an inefficient way to collect revenue; it is not fair to make people pay for what they are required to receive; there is a risk that states will lose control over local probation departments if the latter achieve fiscal independence (National Institute of Justice, 1992). The American Civil Liberties Union has criticized cost recovery fees as double punishment: Offenders pay once with jail time, for example, and again with the money that goes toward their keep. Despite these criticisms, the growing costs of criminal justice and intense pressures to reduce public spending make it likely that cost recovery programs will grow rather than decline in the foreseeable future.

Day Fines. Another innovation in fining penalties is the so-called day fine. Under this system, widely used in Europe and in South America, fines reflect the nature of the offense and the offender's ability to pay based on his or her daily income. Looking at the offense, judges use a "unit scale" or "benchmark" to determine how many "units of punishment" will be applied—say 2, 5, 10, or 20. These are then translated into a dollar amount based on the offender's daily income. A minor crime might result in a 2-day fine, a more serious one in a 20-day fine. The defendant must pay the equivalent of one day's income for each unit of punishment (Klein, 1997:223). A day's income for a poor defendant might be $50; a millionaire's might be $5,000. The day fine system means that offenders pay the same proportion of their income for the same offense. Nonpayment is punished by the number of day fines not paid. For example, if a defendant fails to pay three day fines, he could be sent to jail for three days.

An evaluation of an experimental day fine project in New York's Staten Island concluded that day fines were fairer, easier for judges to administer, and more likely to be paid in full, and raised more fine revenue than conventional fixed fines (Winterfield and Hillsman, 1993). We can expect to see more use of day fines, although given the widespread use of mandatory sentencing laws, it is unlikely that day fines will divert large numbers of felony offenders from prison.

New Methods of Collecting Fines Ensure Their Future. Technology has increased the likelihood that financial penalties will be around for a long time, despite their drawbacks and despite the traditional reluctance of American judges to use them as alternatives to incarceration. Credit cards, computerized record keeping, and innovations in telephone technology have all found their way into the handling of fines.

Many courts have turned to private collection agencies to handle delinquent accounts, and these agencies use the same methods as they would in collecting any other debt—including notifying credit bureaus (Cole, 1989). The threat of a bad credit rating seems to be a strong incentive for offenders to pay up. In 1995, Massachusetts developed a private collection program for its district courts, following the success of an earlier pilot program (Klein, 1997:225). The initial project collected $6 million in unpaid fines at a cost of $100,000—a pretty good return on the state's investment.

PROBATION

probation An alternative to prison or jail that allows offenders to remain in the community under court supervision.

Probation arose as a true alternative to imprisonment and has become the mainstay of community-based corrections. Instead of going to jail or prison, offenders sentenced to probation are allowed to remain in the community under the supervision of an authorized agent of the court.

A BRIEF HISTORY OF PROBATION

The first person to use the term *probation* was John Augustus, a shoemaker by trade and a crusading member of the temperance movement in Boston, Massachusetts. His interest in combating the evils of alcohol led Augustus to propose an innovative court procedure: In 1841 he asked the court's permission to put up bail for petty offenders, mostly drunkards, who were then released to his custody, which he called "probation." If the defendant remained sober, law-abiding, and industrious during a specified period of time, the original charges were dropped or a modest fine was imposed. Augustus accompanied his charges into court on their return visits and provided testimony on their behavior while on probation. The first man Augustus helped was fined one cent

John Augustus of Boston, Massachusetts, a temperance crusader and the first person to use the term probation. *Offering an alternative to the imprisonment of petty offenders (mostly drunkards), Augustus put up bail for them and had them released into his custody. If the offender stayed sober, law-abiding, and employed during the probationary period, the charges would be dropped or a modest fine would be imposed. Augustus put up an astronomical sum for the probation of nearly 2,000 people, and he died penniless.*

COURTESY OF THE MASSACHUSETTS HISTORICAL SOCIETY

plus court costs of $3.75, which was "immediately paid" (Augustus, [1852] 1939:5). Between 1841 and his death in 1859, Augustus helped 1,152 men and 794 women avoid imprisonment. He put up more than $240,000 of his own money—a huge fortune in those days—and died penniless.

At the same time that Augustus was trying to keep drunks and petty offenders out of jail in Boston, an English magistrate named Matthew Davenport Hill began using suspended sentences together with the supervision of a guardian for certain youthful offenders who came before him in Birmingham, England (Dressler, 1962:12–13). Although separated by thousands of miles, and certainly unaware of each other's activities, both Hill and Augustus were influential in moving their countries' respective penal practices away from the routine imprisonment of petty and youthful offenders. Community-based supervision—the heart of probation—was to become the major alternative to prison on both sides of the Atlantic. But it took nearly 100 years before probation was widely available for both juvenile and adult offenders.

In the United States, Massachusetts was the first state to legislate probation as an alternative to incarceration, doing so in 1878. Massachusetts made probation available for both juveniles and adults. Within 30 years all but a handful of states had followed suit for juvenile offenses, but it took longer for many legislatures to extend probation to adults. By 1923, however, 35 states had established adult probation. By the 1950s, all states and the federal system had some form of probation as an alternative to jail or prison.

Over the years since Augustus, probation has undergone some important changes. Its early development was closely tied to the correctional reform movement of the late nineteenth century and its emphasis on individualized justice and the rehabilitative ideal (see Chapter 15). Another important influence was the juvenile court, established in Chicago in 1899. Under this innovation, juvenile offenders were to be treated differently than adults, with society taking on the role of a caring parent. Probation seemed to fit this more paternalistic, caring system of justice.

Probation and Concern over Public Safety. Community safety was an ever-present concern in the development of probation. Both Augustus and Hill had recognized the risks in allowing criminals to remain in the community, and both therefore used screening and supervision as integral parts of their programs. But to many people, probation was equivalent to allowing lawbreakers to "run loose in the community" (Latessa and Allen, 1997:110). Between 1909 and 1925, 34 bills to establish a federal probation system were introduced in Congress; one finally passed after its sixth introduction, signed into law by President Calvin Coolidge, a former Massachusetts governor familiar with probation in his state.

The philosophy behind the development of probation consisted of two basic ideas: (1) that most criminal offenders do not pose a danger to the community if released under some form of supervision, and (2) that the community is a far better place for them to be than prison. Probation gives offenders a second chance and a helping hand in putting their lives in order. The expectation was that both the offender and the community would benefit from probation. Yet advocates of probation also believed that safeguards should be constructed to ensure public safety.

The safeguards that emerged as probation developed focused on (1) offender eligibility, (2) pre-sentence investigations to guide decision making, and (3) supervision of probationers. Together, these remain today the most important elements in the decision to grant probation.

Eligibility. Courts have consistently ruled that probation is a privilege, not a right. Offenders do not have a constitutional right to probation, nor do state or federal statutes make probation an automatic, sole penalty for any offense. However, offenders do have the right to be *considered* for probation if convicted of an offense for which probation is an option. In general, eligibility for probation is based first on the nature of the current offense (National Institute of Corrections, 1993). More than half of the states currently prohibit probation when weapons are used or the offense is murder; 23 states prohibit it for sex offenses. The past criminal history of offenders may disqualify them from a probation sentence: Offenders are ineligible in 23 states if they have been convicted of a prior felony.

Pre-Sentence Investigations. The pre-sentence investigation (PSI) was discussed in Chapter 13. It is designed to help judges in their sentencing decisions, and has been a formal responsibility of probation agencies for many years.

For much of probation's history, PSIs were geared toward learning as much as possible about offenders and what probation could do for them. While these *offender-based* PSI reports include information about the offense, they emphasize characteristics of the offender, including personality, family history, physical and mental health, financial condition, and prior criminal record. Over the past 30 years, with the rise of determinate sentencing and sentencing guidelines, more and more emphasis has been placed on the offense, giving rise to *offense-based* PSI reports. "The sentencing court is concerned with the offender's culpability in the offense, whether anyone was injured, whether a firearm was used, the extent of loss to the victim(s), and other aspects of the offense" (Cromwell and Killinger, 1994:49). The *Federal Sentencing Guidelines Handbook*, published in 1990, states that the only offender characteristics to be taken into account by federal courts are the defendant's criminal history and the defendant's willingness to take responsibility for the crime.

Supervision of Probationers. When probation is recommended, the PSI will typically also include a recommendation on the level of offender supervision—from minimal to intensive—and any other special conditions such as drug or mental health treatment. A 1986 survey of nearly 80,000 probationers in seventeen states found that just over half of them had a special condition to fulfill (Bureau of Justice Statistics, 1992). The most frequently imposed conditions were drug testing and drug or alcohol treatment.

Traditionally, probation supervision involves two aspects: surveillance of probationers and access to services in the community. Through surveillance, probation officers keep track of the individuals in their charge and make sure that they are fulfilling the conditions of probation. Surveillance may mean little more than a periodic check-in by the probationer, or it may involve much closer monitoring. Providing access to services is the treatment or rehabilitative side of supervision. Generally, a treatment plan is developed by the probation officer in consultation with the offender "client." Progress is monitored and adjustments made according to feedback from the service provider(s) and the probationer.

There are various models of probation supervision. For many years a *casework model* of supervision prevailed, in which the probation officers established one-to-one relationships with their clients and provided counseling and treatment services directly. Under this model, usually associated with social work, emphasis is placed on developing a therapeutic and cooperative relationship between the officer and the probationer. The probation officer is viewed as a primary change agent, helping offenders deal with every problem and guiding them in the modification of their behavior.

Largely as a result of growing caseloads and the imposition of numerous probation conditions requiring specialized resources, a second model of supervision has gained prominence. Under the *resource brokerage model* the probation officer no longer acts as primary change agent, but instead identifies an offender's needs and then matches them with available community resources, such as drug treatment, mental health, educational, employment, and family support agencies. The brokerage approach requires that the probation officer be familiar with available community services and maintain close relationships with agency directors. Since a community may have many different services supplied by a large number of agencies, probation officers in larger probation departments sometimes specialize in particular services, say, drug and alcohol abuse or employment services. One variation of this approach is the development of probation teams consisting of specialists who can address the diverse needs of each probation officer's caseload.

No matter which model of supervision is followed, the probation officer is responsible for evaluating the needs of the offender, developing a treatment or service plan, and following up on the probationer's progress with periodic evaluations and, if necessary, modifications of the plan. Since some offenders will require far more intensive supervision and assistance than others, the caseloads of many probation officers consist of a mix of offenders. However, some larger departments and those with more extensive resources may employ a *specialized caseload system*, in which each officer supervises a group of offenders requiring similar services or sentenced to similar conditions of probation.

CONDITIONS OF PROBATION: WHAT OFFENDERS MUST DO

Most offenders sentenced to probation are expected to fulfill a number of **conditions of probation**. These conditions vary widely, from making restitution to victims, to paying fines or fees, meeting family support obligations, or even spending evenings or weekends in jail. It has become conventional to distinguish between *standard conditions* and *special* or *discretionary conditions* of probation. Standard conditions are conditions that all probationers must generally meet; special conditions are above and beyond standard conditions, and are designed to meet the particular needs of the individual offender or to reflect the nature or severity of the offense. Over 98 percent of adults on probation in 1996 had to meet at least one special condition (Bureau of Justice Statistics, 1998b:33).

conditions of probation Things offenders must do in order to remain on probation.

The primary standard condition is that probationers commit no crimes. The most common special condition is payment of a fee or a fine. Other conditions are shown in Table 17.1. In some jurisdictions, conditions of probation are set by statute, while in others they are set by a combination of statute and judicial discretion. In some states the conditions of probation are largely left up to the probation department. This places considerable power in the hands of probation officials, and opponents of the system object that it has weakened legislative and judicial control of criminal punishment. This argument gains weight when one considers that the activities of probation departments are much less visible than those of legislatures and the courts.

The Federal Sentencing Commission and the American Probation and Parole Association both say that probation conditions should be tailored to the purposes of punishment, yet not be unduly restrictive. The Commission's 1995 *Sentencing Guidelines Manual* lists few standard conditions other than refraining from crime. However, in felony convictions, the guidelines also impose at least one of the following conditions: a fine, restitution, or community service. Where these might be special conditions under state statutes, they are standard conditions for federal probationers convicted of felony crimes.

Three goals are linked to probation conditions: *punishment*, *therapy*, and *protection of the community*. Some conditions of probation are clearly punitive—fines or jail time are examples—while others are meant to be therapeutic and to help the offender develop a healthier, more socially responsible lifestyle. Required drug, alcohol, or mental health treatment are examples of therapeutic conditions. Yet other conditions may reflect a combination of purposes. For example, community service such as clearing trash from highways may be seen

TABLE 17.1 Conditions of Probation

The most important condition of probation is that probationers commit no new crime. If they do, they are usually sent to prison for their original crime and also punished for the new one. On the whole, conditions of probation, like conditions of parole, generally require more from offenders than we expect from law-abiding citizens. Is this (a) fair? and (b) realistic?

PHOTO BY JEFFRY SCOTT, COURTESY OF IMPACT VISUALS

State and federal courts may impose a variety of conditions on the probationer. Standard conditions must be met by all probationers in a jurisdiction, while special conditions are imposed on certain offenders, depending on their needs and on their offense.

Standard Conditions. Probationers must:

- refrain from crime
- not leave the court's jurisdiction without permission
- not change their residence or workplace without notifying the probation officer and (in some jurisdictions) receiving permission
- refrain from associating with known criminals
- report to the probation officer as directed
- allow the probation officer to visit at any time
- stay away from people and places associated with illegal drugs
- contribute to the support of dependent family members

Special or Discretionary Conditions. Depending on state or federal law and discretionary decisions of the court, probationers may be required to:

- pay a fine or cost recovery fee
- make restitution to victim or the community
- perform community service
- participate in drug, alcohol, or mental health treatment
- spend time in jail or prison
- submit to urinalysis or other testing for consumption of controlled substances

as both punitive *and* therapeutic. Restrictions on offenders' movements and associations may have therapeutic benefits when they keep probationers away from "bad influences" or encourage self-control. They also reflect a primary goal of probation conditions: protecting public safety. State and federal laws generally require that the safety of the community be the first consideration in granting probation and specifying its conditions. That is why the nature of the offense and the criminal history of the offender are the key determinants of who gets probation in the first place.

Revocation of Probation

Probationers who do not live up to the conditions of probation risk having their probation revoked. **Revocation of probation** usually means that the probationer will be incarcerated, so the decision to revoke is not taken lightly. A decision to revoke implies failure and it reflects not only on the offender, who has forfeited the benefits of being released to the community, but also on the probation officer and the therapeutic ideals of probation itself.

revocation of probation When the supervising court removes offenders from probation because they have failed to meet its conditions.

Before considering the failures, we should note that most offenders successfully complete their probation sentence. For example, in 1993, 81 percent of the 20,449 federal probationers leaving probation had successfully completed their sentences (Bureau of Justice Statistics, 1996:65). Of the 1,042,242 offenders leaving state probation services in 1993 for whom the information was known, 73 percent were "successful completions" (Snell, 1995:37).

The most frequent basis for revocation of probation is a **technical violation**. Technical violations involve such things as failure to report in, failure to complete a required treatment program, or changing residence without permission. Because they have invested their time and their expertise in supervising their clients, probation officers are understandably reluctant to initiate the revocation process for technical violations. The common practice is to overlook an occasional violation and to seek revocation if violations are persistent or threaten public safety.

technical violation Probationers fail to report in or to complete a required program.

The worst-case scenario is for the probationer to be arrested and convicted of a new crime. Nearly one-third of probation revocations in 1993 were because of new offenses. Traditionally, individuals whose probation is revoked because of a new crime are almost always sent to prison to serve out the remainder of their sentence. In 1993, over 170,000 probationers were incarcerated under the terms of their existing probation sentence (Snell, 1995:37).

Under probation rules in most states, the probation officer can request a revocation hearing even if the probationer has not actually been arrested or convicted of a new crime (Klein, 1997:328). The probation officer is merely required to show that a preponderance of evidence exists that the probationer broke the law. Some appellate courts have expressed concern over this practice, but the Supreme Court has not ruled it unconstitutional. Those who support the practice argue that revocation merely means the imposition of a sentence that has already been pronounced—and the hearing is not a true criminal prosecution, but an administrative hearing brought by the probation department.

The U.S. Supreme Court has nevertheless established certain rights for probationers when it comes to revocation. ***Gagnon v. Scarpelli*** (1973) is the most important procedural case, for the Court ruled that probationers have a right to a two-stage revocation process: first, a hearing to determine whether there is probable cause that a violation has occurred, and then a second hearing to determine whether the facts support a decision to revoke. At both stages, the probationer has the following rights:

Gagnon v. Scarpelli Probationers faced with revocation have certain rights.

1. The right to prior notice of the hearing
2. The right to written notice of the charges

3. The right to be present at the hearing
4. The right to present evidence and witnesses
5. The right to a hearing before a neutral and detached officer

If the probationer requests it, an attorney also may be present. Once it has been decided to revoke an offender's probation, only the court has the power to impose a sentence—and this usually means the original sentencing judge. A variety of possible sentences exist, ranging from continued probation but with new restrictions, to completion of a prison term as specified in the original sentence.

United States v. Granderson Offenders whose probation has been revoked cannot be given a longer prison term than they would have received at the original sentencing.

The U.S. Supreme Court has argued that revocation sentences must be fair in light of the original sentence handed down. For example, in ***United States v. Granderson*** (1994), the Court reviewed a case in which a probationer was sentenced after revocation to 22 months in prison even though the prison term that his original offense carried was only 6 months. The Court ruled that it was unfair to force a probationer to spend more time in prison than he would if he had been incarcerated for the offense in the first place.

RECENT TRENDS IN PROBATION

Probation is the most widely used criminal penalty in the United States today. At the end of 1995, over 3 million adults were on probation, representing 58 percent of all adults under correctional supervision (U.S. Department of Justice press release, August 16, 1998). The largest probation populations were in Texas (429,329), California (286,526), Florida (237,117), New York (174,406), and Michigan (147,598). Just over half of the adults on probation had been convicted of a felony offense; the remainder were found guilty of misdemeanors or driving while intoxicated. A detailed breakdown of felony probationers by offense shows that the most common probation offenses involve assault, theft, or drug possession (Petersilia, 1995). The past few years have witnessed growing numbers of probationers convicted of violent crimes or with extensive criminal histories.

Figure 17.1 shows trends in the adult correctional population from 1980 through 1997. As we know from Chapters 13 and 15, "get tough" sentencing policies and the crackdown on drug offenses have resulted in considerable growth in all correctional populations over the past two decades. The numbers of Americans on probation, in jail, in prison, or on parole after imprisonment grew from 1.8 million in 1980 to over 5.6 million by the end of 1997. The number of adults on probation grew the most—by over 2 million. The prison and parole populations are, of course, closely linked; except in the federal system and the few states without parole, rising prison populations automatically produce rising parole populations. More will be said about parole in a later section of the chapter.

The Demographics of Corrections Today. Table 17.2 shows the adult correctional population by sex and race in 1995, the most recent date for which national information is available. Three things stand out. First, men make up most of the country's correctional population. Second, women make up a much larger percentage of the probation population (21 percent) than of the adults who are incarcerated or on parole (10 percent or less in each case). This undoubtedly reflects a combination of factors, including the tendency of women to commit less-serious felonies, the likelihood that a higher percentage of women than men meet probation criteria, and a nationwide shortage of prison beds for women.

The third point that stands out in Table 17.2 is that while black offenders make up approximately half of the jail, prison, and parole populations, they account for only a third of the probation population. This is still far more than their representation in the U.S. population as a whole—which is just over 12

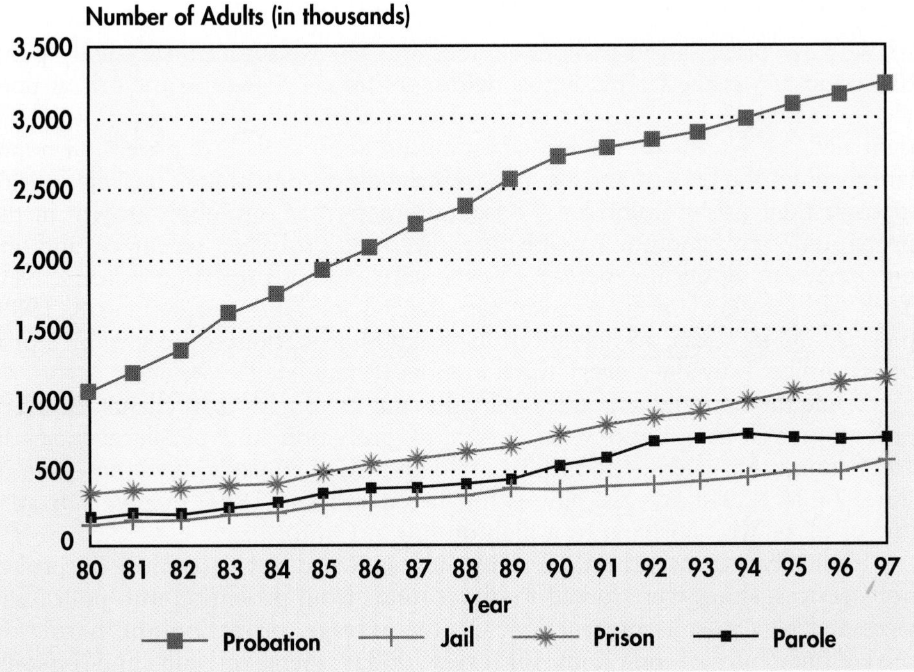

FIGURE 17.1 ADULT CORRECTIONAL TRENDS IN THE UNITED STATES, 1980–1996

This figure shows the number of adults on probation, in jail, in prison, or on parole over a 17-year period. While the figure shows growth in all correctional populations, probation shows the steepest increase.

Source: Kathleen Maguire and Ann L. Pastore (1998). *Sourcebook of Criminal Justice Statistics 1997* (p. 464). Washington, D.C.: U.S. Department of Justice.

percent—but it shows that black offenders are even more overrepresented in the incarcerated populations. Higher violent crime rates among black Americans and the toughening of penalties during the 1980s, especially those related to crack cocaine and gun crimes, help explain the greater overrepresentation of black Americans in the correctional populations.

TABLE 17.2 The Demographics of Corrections: Probation, Jail, Prison, and Parole Populations by Sex and Race, 1995

	PROBATION	JAIL	PRISON	PAROLE
Sex				
Male	2,454,000	448,000	1,014,500	629,900
	79%	90%	94%	90%
Female	642,500	51,300	64,000	70,300
	21%	10%	6%	10%
Race				
White	2,057,600	262,200	522,100	368,300
	66%	53%	48%	53%
Black	999,200	228,500	538,500	324,700
	34%	47%	52%	47%
Totals	3,096,500	499,300	1,078,500	700,200

Note: The "Totals" row slightly exceeds the totals of the individual race figures due to the exclusion of 73,300 offenders classified as "other race."

Source: Compiled from Bureau of Justice Statistics (1997). *Correctional Populations in the United States, 1995.* (p. 5, Table 1.2). Washington, D.C.: U.S. Department of Justice.

CRISIS IN PROBATION AND EMERGING REFORMS

As we have discussed in earlier chapters, the 1980s saw an increasingly punitive trend across the United States, with continuous growth in the prison population as more and more states turned to mandatory-sentencing laws and tightened restrictions on the use of probation and parole. Yet probation populations grew too, as jail and prison overcrowding forced many jurisdictions to increase their use of community-based alternatives. Continuing growth in the probation population put a tremendous strain on probation resources, and one outcome was significant increases in the caseloads of probation officers. New York City caseloads grew to over 250 (*New York Times*, September 8, 1989, p. M2), and in Texas, 95 percent of its 400,000 probationers are seen by a probation officer only once every three months (Petersilia, 1995).

While the national average caseload is put at roughly 150 clients for every probation officer, a nationwide survey of probation and parole agencies in 1994 found that average monthly caseloads varied considerably from state to state. Table 17.3 shows the figures for fifteen states in 1994; they vary from a low of 65 in West Virginia to a high of 400 in California.

Ironically, just as prison overcrowding spawned new pressures on probation services, states were forced to divert funds from probation into police services and new prison construction. On the average, probation and parole received one-tenth of one cent for every dollar spent on jails and prisons. Looking at it another way, "although nearly *three fourths* of correctional clients are in the community, only about *one-tenth* of the correctional budget goes to supervise them" (Petersilia, 1995:484, italics in original). Not surprisingly, probation officer salaries, a sample of which are shown in Table 17.3, are among the lowest in criminal justice.

TABLE 17.3 Number of Probation Officers, Average Caseloads, and Average Annual Salary in Fifteen States, 1994*

As the use of intermediate sanctions grows, caseloads for probation officers are increasing. However, probation officers are among the lowest-paid criminal justice professionals.

	Average Monthly Caseload	Number of Officers		Average Salary
		Male	Female	
Arkansas	197	55	42	$19,058
California	400	5,000**	NA	40,000
Connecticut	199	167	129	50,000
Georgia	211	526	331	31,671
Hawaii	75	42	55	28,500
Illinois	135	1,700**	NA	26,000
Indiana	116	425	437	21,576
Kansas	80	198	143	28,770
Massachusetts	125	676	344	NA
Nebraska	96	118	81	26,572
New York	129	2,304**	NA	25,752 to 35,138
Rhode Island	294	30	18	31,117 to 35,131
South Dakota	125	46	22	26,800
Tennessee	68	203	198	21,528
West Virginia	65	73	62	28,030

*Data come from a nationwide survey; many states reported combined figures for probation and parole and are excluded from the table.
**Includes females; no gender breakdown was available.
Source: Adapted from CEGA (1995). *Corrections Compendium* (pp. 9–16). Lincoln, Neb: CEGA Publishing.

By the early 1990s probation was clearly in a state of crisis, with little sign of improvement on the horizon. Underfunded and overwhelmed—and seemingly unappreciated by politicians and the public alike—the probation officer could see little reason for cheer. Some probation officials contributed to the crisis by clinging to the treatment-based casework ideology, which is labor intensive and works best with small caseloads. By the same token, innovations such as resource brokerage helped with growing caseloads but did little to address the larger question of where probation fits in a "get tough on crime" environment.

One emerging answer to this larger question has been a toughening of the conditions associated with probation. More and more jurisdictions are turning to incarceration as a condition of probation. Georgia was one of the first states to establish a period of imprisonment as a condition of probation, in 1989. In 1993, the state added probation-run detention centers to house probation violators for periods up to 160 days (Klein, 1997:76). California, Florida, Nebraska, and numerous other states now permit judges to sentence offenders to a period of incarceration as a condition of probation. And courts have generally supported the toughening of probation conditions, especially for violent, repeat, and drug offenders. Still, most offenders find probation coupled with some time in prison vastly preferable to the years they would otherwise be spending behind bars.

Another emerging reform ties the traditional treatment goal of probation with larger doses of surveillance. According to opinion polls, many criminal justice officials, researchers, and members of the public believe that a combination of treatment and punishment holds the best hope of dealing effectively with offenders while protecting the community in which they reside (Petersilia, 1995). But neither treatment nor extensive surveillance is cheap, and some experts are calling for a reinvestment in community-based corrections, especially for drug-related offenders. While current expenditures on the supervision of probationers average around $200 per year, effective programs cost from $12,000 to $14,000 per year (Petersilia, 1995). With a commitment of adequate funding, the therapeutic elements of probation can be successfully combined with the more punitive elements of close surveillance and strictly enforced regulations.

INTERMEDIATE SANCTIONS

The reforms that are making probation a tougher alternative to incarceration belong to a parcel of reforms known in court circles as "intermediate (or alternative) sentences" and in correctional circles as *intermediate sanctions* or *community-based alternatives*. These penalties lie between prison and probation in their severity. The most common intermediate sanctions are the following:

- **Boot camps**, where offenders undergo short-term incarceration, living a regimented life of work or study under strict discipline with minimal recreation.
- **House arrest/electronic monitoring**, where offenders stay at home except to go to work or school. Usually, their movements are monitored by electronic devices attached to their wrist or ankle.
- **Intensive supervised probation (ISP)**, where offenders must see probation officers at least once a week; this usually includes mandatory drug testing, counseling or treatment, and unannounced visits by the probation officer.
- **Community service**, where offenders are required to put in so many hours of unpaid labor on public works projects such as picking up litter, clearing debris, painting public buildings, or applying their special skills to benefit the community.

boot camp Short-term incarceration under close supervision and military-style discipline.

house arrest Offenders stay at home unless at work or school.

electronic monitoring Offenders wear wrist or ankle bracelets that trigger alarms if they move beyond a certain area.

intensive supervised probation (ISP) Close monitoring by probation officers, including surprise visits, and completion of required treatment programs.

community service Offenders are assigned to work on projects that benefit the community.

restitution Offenders repay the victims of their crimes, or the community at large, with money or services.

day reporting center Offenders report in daily and their activities are monitored throughout the day.

- **Restitution**, where offenders must pay back the victims of their crime, usually in money, but sometimes in work.
- *Restitution centers*, where offenders work at their regular jobs and pay a portion of their wages in restitution, but are locked in at night and must usually undergo drug treatment, counseling, job training, or high school classes.
- **Day reporting centers**, where offenders must report in person each morning, and their activities are monitored throughout the day.

Figure 17.2 shows the number of states using these various intermediate sanctions in 1993, the most recent date for which nationwide data are available. Intensive supervised probation (ISP) is the most widely used. Since ISP was discussed in Chapter 11 as a type of pre-trial diversion, this chapter focuses on the other major intermediate sanctions: boot camps, house arrest with electronic monitoring, restitution, and community service.

SUPPORT FOR INTERMEDIATE SANCTIONS

Intermediate sanctions appeal to many policymakers, criminal justice practitioners, and academics as a promising response to three developments originating in the 1960s and 1970s and continuing into the 1990s (Tonry, 1996: 100): (1) a declining faith in rehabilitation and individualized punishment; (2) a growing acceptance of the *justice model* of sanctioning, which calls for the scaling of penalties according to a crime's seriousness as well as reductions in the discretion of sentencing judges; and (3) a growing belief—encouraged by cries for "law and order" in political campaigns—that ordinary probation is insufficient punishment for most crimes.

Public Support for Intermediate Sanctions. Intermediate sanctions are promoted as a way to significantly reduce prison overcrowding and correctional costs, while maintaining a continuum of punishments consistent with "just desserts" and attempts to reduce recidivism. Figure 17.3 shows that the

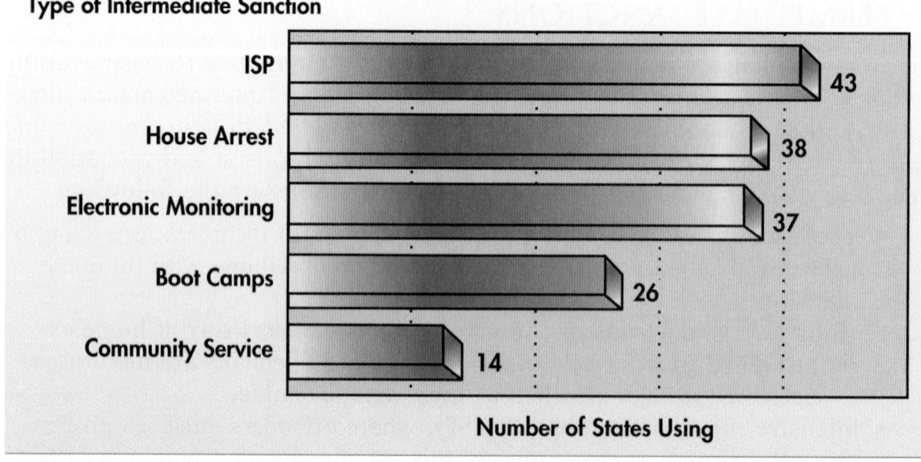

FIGURE 17.2 USE OF INTERMEDIATE SANCTIONS AMONG STATES, 1993
By 1993, most states were using intermediate sanctions. Electronic monitoring is growing faster than other sanctions as technology improves its reliability.

Source: Bureau of Justice Statistics (1994). *State Court Organization, 1993* (p. 312, Table 43). Washington, D.C.: U.S. Department of Justice.

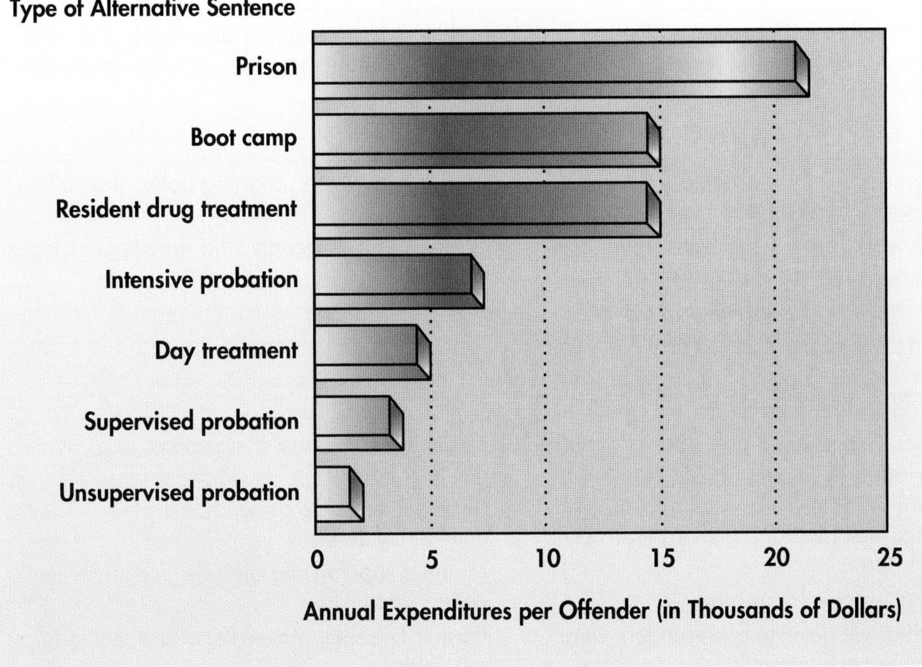

FIGURE 17.3 Costs of Prison and Intermediate Sanctions for Each Offender, 1994

One of the reasons for the development of alternative sentencing is the high cost of imprisonment. These figures show that prison is up to 20 times more costly per offender than alternatives.

Source: Steven R. Donziger, ed. (1996). *The Real War on Crime: The Report of the National Criminal Justice Commission* (p. 58). New York: HarperCollins.

per-offender costs of some alternative sanctions are considerably less than those of imprisonment.

The general public seems to approve of intermediate sanctions, at least for certain offenders. In a 1991 national survey of 1,000 adults, 80 percent of respondents favored nonprison programs in which "nondangerous" offenders are required to hold a job, perform community service, repay their victims, and receive counseling. A second national poll, conducted by the same research team, found that 75 percent of respondents agreed with the statement, "A balanced approach of prevention, punishment, and treatment is better at controlling and reducing crime than imprisonment alone" (American Correctional Association news release, June 4, 1995).

Many citizens associate intermediate sanctions with leniency. Yet in a 1996 Texas survey, almost half of the 1,085 respondents still believed that intermediate sanctions could be effective in protecting citizens against crime (Sims, 1997). Another study examined opinions on a wide range of crime topics, including intermediate sanctions. The views expressed in Oklahoma were fairly typical: Almost 90 percent of the 400 respondents supported greater use of alternative sanctions for nonviolent offenders as a way of solving prison overcrowding (*Oklahoma Criminal Justice Research Center Journal*, Spring 1996).

Table 17.4 shows what Oklahomans wanted and didn't want from the various alternative sentences. It appears that they want punishments that are tough, but fair and constructive. Asked about correctional conditions in general, Oklahomans believed that offenders should be made to work, should be denied perks such as HBO, and should pay for college courses. On the other hand, they did not think that offenders should be breaking rocks, given bread

TABLE 17.4 What Oklahomans Want and Don't Want from Alternative Sanctions

Surveys of Americans generally show that people support the use of intermediate sanctions as an alternative to prison, especially for nonviolent offenders. However, many people also have strong views about what such punishments ought to involve. Here are the views of citizens of Oklahoma

SANCTION TYPE	WHAT OKLAHOMANS WANT	WHAT OKLAHOMANS DON'T WANT
Boot camp	Structure and discipline; offenders get up early and work hard all day Productive work (grow vegetables, reupholster furniture, etc.) to offset cost of incarceration Offenders internalize work ethic, become more likely to get and keep a job upon release Acquire GED, job skills	Meaningless work; digging holes, then filling them in Sadistic drill sergeants who harass or debase offenders
Community service	Hard, productive work to pay back community (e.g., picking up litter, clearing brush, emptying hospital bedpans) Long, tough, meaningful sentences that would deter would-be criminals Supervision, strict enforcement Visibility that will deter (e.g., offenders wearing distinctive clothing while working in public)	Undemanding, easy assignments (e.g., working in a library) Short sentences (e.g., 20 hours of community service) Minimal supervision; offender reports when convenient. Former baseball player Pete Rose teaching a gym class
House arrest	Part of a sentence combined with a work requirement	Offenders sitting around all day, watching television Using or selling drugs from their living room
Strict probation, intensive supervision	Part of a sentence combined with a work requirement	Offenders who are *solely* monitored more closely
Restitution	Offenders must pay back their victims to the best of their abilities	Indigent offenders who cannot make restitution going to prison, debtors' prisons

Source: Compiled from John Doble Research Associates. Reprinted by Dan Lawrence (1997). "Crime and Corrections: The Views of the People of Oklahoma." Oklahoma Criminal Justice Research Consortium. Available online at **http://www.doc.state.ok.us/docs/ocjrc.htm**

and water, be subjected to corporal punishment, or put on a chain gang. How do your views compare?

Professional Support for Intermediate Sanctions. Strong support for intermediate sanctions is found among many criminal justice professionals and their associations. The American Correctional Association, long a conservative organization dominated by prison administrators, is now committed to finding community-based alternatives to incarceration. Its 1996 legislative position urged Congress and the states to "[s]upport community corrections and increased use of intermediate sanctions, including the use of non-incarcerative sanctions for non-violent offenders" (American Correctional Association news release, January 15, 1996).

The International Community Corrections Association (ICCA) has gone even further. Its members believe that:

- Community-based punishment, not prison, should be the *presumptive choice* [that is, taken for granted] for nonviolent offenders.
- America's criminal justice system should do more than punish the offender—it should also rebuild lives, restore victims and communities, and prevent future crime.

- There should be a graduated system of intermediate punishments to deal with offenders along with a continuum of services and treatment.
- The *least restrictive* and *least costly* means of sanctioning offenders should be implemented, as long as they are consistent with *public safety*.

The American Bar Association, which speaks on behalf of the nation's lawyers and is a powerful force in politics, also supports intermediate sanctions as a penalty option. Its Model Adult Community Corrections Act, published in 1994, includes the following goals and objectives:

- To enhance public safety and achieve economies by encouraging the development and implementation of community sanctions as a sentencing option.
- To ensure that the offender is punished in the least restrictive setting consistent with public safety and the gravity of the crime.
- To make offenders accountable to the community for their criminal behavior, through community service programs, restitution programs, and a range of locally developed sanctions.
- To foster the development of policies and funding for programs that encourage jurisdictions to minimize the use of incarceration where other sanctions are appropriate. (American Bar Association, 1994:3).

Although they are a long way from supplanting prison as the cornerstone of modern American corrections, intermediate sanctions have spread across the country and are sufficiently important to warrant careful evaluation. This work is now being done, and the initial results are mixed. Before reviewing the major intermediate sanctions, however, a brief word about "net widening" is in order.

Net Widening: A Criticism of Intermediate Sanctions. Although intermediate sanctions often divert offenders from prison, some critics argue that community-based corrections widen the net of social control (Austin and Krisberg, 1981, 1982; Cohen, 1985). This is because intermediate sanctions are sometimes imposed on offenders who were not in fact prison bound, and would have received a lighter sentence. In addition, by dispersing control mechanisms from custody institutions into the community, a blurring of the boundaries between deviants and nondeviants and between different types of deviants occurs. This enables the control system to camouflage its activities and its broadening scope. The "real awful secret of community control," according to one critic, is that "the same old experts have moved office to the community and are doing the same old things they have always done" (Cohen, 1985:75).

The problem of net widening remains an issue in discussions of intermediate sanctions. One attempt to evaluate net widening effects was undertaken in Florida (Wagner and Baird, 1993). The Florida Community Control Program (FCCP) is an intensive-supervision house arrest program that has placed more than 40,000 offenders on community control from 1983 to 1992. The authors found that net widening did occur—in 1987, for example, 46 percent of offenders were diverted into FCCP from lesser punishments. In addition, about 10 percent of the participants were sent to prison for technical violations such as removing monitoring devices or lying to probation officers. Despite these results, the Florida program seems to have been successful in diverting many offenders from prison, reducing correctional costs, and alleviating some of the prison overcrowding in that state.

Despite the net widening and increased controls associated with intermediate sanctions, even critics such as Stanley Cohen, quoted above, agree that community-based corrections can promote both "good" and "justice," especially in their less coercive forms:

> "Good" comes in the form of rape crisis centers, counseling programs, and shelters for battered women; the teaching of techniques for survival; the providing of talk, friendship and intimacy . . . and the creation of more opportunities [for offenders]. "Justice" comes in the form of emphasizing less severe sanctions for middle-range offenses; providing genuine alternatives to imprisonment for offenders who otherwise would have been released . . . ; extending to lower-class delinquents that to which middle-class individuals have always had access. (Barlow, 1987:439)

SHORT-TERM INCARCERATION IN BOOT CAMPS

A short term of incarceration has long been a condition of probation in some states, and in California since 1927 (Klein, 1997:301). However, the "boot camp" concept is much newer. *Boot camps*, also known as **shock incarceration** programs, are designed to maximize the impact of confinement, particularly on young, first-time, and nonviolent offenders; many states restrict adult eligibility to those serving their first felony sentence as an adult (Mackenzie and Souryal, 1994:1). Called a "tough" intermediate sanction (Mackenzie and Herbert, 1996), boot camps are patterned after basic training in the military.

shock incarceration Short-term incarceration as a way of scaring offenders from more serious crimes; also another term for boot camp.

Box 17.1

CAREERS IN CRIMINAL JUSTICE

BOOT CAMP DRILL INSTRUCTOR

As the name suggests, boot camps are generally patterned after basic training in the military, with strict discipline and arduous physical drills. Boot camps, sometimes referred to as "shock incarceration," belong to the category of criminal punishments known as intermediate sanctions. They are used for both adult and juvenile offenders. The work is potentially dangerous, requires physical fitness, and is often performed outdoors in variable weather conditions. Here are the salary, qualifications, duties, and conditions of employment of a drill instructor in a juvenile boot camp in Florida, as advertised in July 1998.

Salary: $25,524 (entry level)

Qualifications: High school graduate or GED.

Duties: The drill instructor is a certified detention deputy who trains juvenile recruits using a regimen of close order drill (marching), basic daily routine, and physical and classroom training to develop discipline and self-esteem; conducts inspections, counsels recruits, and transports them to required appointments or court appearances; performs periodic physical fitness tests; reviews recruit evaluation files; completes incident reports as necessary; and attends various training classes to maintain certification requirements and enhance professional abilities.

Conditions of Employment: Include valid Florida driver's license and successful completion of training leading to Basic Recruit Certificate of Corrections Compliance.

The Spread of Boot Camps as an Intermediate Sanction. The first boot camps were opened in Georgia and Oklahoma in 1983. By 1996 there were 75 camps with over 10,000 total beds operating in 35 states and the Federal Bureau of Prisons (Maguire and Pastore, 1998:81–83; Gowdy, 1996). Table 17.5 shows where the camps are located, and gives information on program length and average number of inmates.

The rapid spread of shock incarceration is due primarily to its strong appeal with policymakers and the public. Boot camps are also magnets for the media because of their disciplinary aspects, promise of costs savings over longer-term incarceration, and overall "get tough" image. "Images of offenders participating in military drill and hard physical labor make boot camps look demanding and unpleasant, characteristics that crime-conscious officials and voters find satisfying" (Tonry, 1996:110).

Boot Camps Vary Widely. Although boot camps share a militaristic character, the specific components of the programs vary widely around the country (Cronin, 1994; Tonry, 1996). For example, some emphasize community service, education, or counseling, while others are primarily discipline based or include components of intensive probation supervision; some last 90 days, others three times as long (see Table 17.5); in some states admission is controlled by judges, in others by corrections officials; some admit only males, while others, such as New York's program at Lakeview, admit women as well, and yet others have separate facilities for men and women (see Box 17.2); finally, some boot camps have failure rates among inmates of 30 to 50 percent, while others terminate fewer than 10 percent.

At boot camps, young offenders undergo an intense short-term incarceration period, during which they live a strictly regimented life. Boot camps are controversial; some believe their popularity is due to the fact that they "sell well" politically, while critics say that camps might inadvertently harden young offenders into tougher, more disciplined criminals. Some boot camp graduates, however, feel that the experience was helpful.

PHOTO BY MICHAEL GREENLAR, COURTESY OF BLACK STAR

TABLE 17.5 Boot Camps in America, 1996

STATE	YEAR OPENED	NUMBER OF CAMPS	PROGRAM LENGTH (MONTHS)	AVERAGE NUMBER OF INMATES
Alabama	1988	1	3 to 6	120
Arizona	1988	1	4	NA
Arkansas	1990	1	3	160
California	1993	3	4	350
Colorado	1991	1	3 to 4	110
Florida	1987	1	4 (minimum)	94
Georgia	1983	29	4	NA
Idaho	1989	1	6	292
Illinois	1990	3	4	641
Kansas	1991	1	6	95
Kentucky	1993	1	4	42
Louisiana	1987	1	3 to 6	130
Maryland	1990	1	6	272
Massachusetts	1992	1	4	NA
Michigan	1988	1	3	319
Minnesota	1992	1	6	51
Mississippi	1985	2	5	400
Missouri	1994	1	3	45
Montana	1994	1	3 to 4	NA
Nevada	1991	1	6	73
New Hampshire	1990	1	4	NA
New York	1987	4	6	1,450
North Carolina	1989	2	3 to 4	240
Ohio	1991	1	3	NA
Oklahoma	1983	2	3 to 6	202
Oregon	1994	1	6	NA
Pennsylvania	1992	1	6	130
South Carolina	1987	2	3 to 6	164
South Dakota	1996	NA	4	NA
Tennessee	1989	1	3 to 4	142
Texas	1989	2	3	250
Vermont	1993	1	3 to 6	85
Virginia	1991	1	3	57
Washington	1993	1	4	150
Wisconsin	1991	1	6	70
Wyoming	1990	1	4	30

The Federal Bureau of Prisons also runs 2 boot camps, opened in 1991. Program length is 6 months, and there were 321 inmates on average in 1996.

Source: Kathleen Maguire and Ann L. Pastore (1996 and 1998). *Sourcebook of Criminal Justice Statistics* (pp. 95 and 81–83). Washington, D.C.: U.S. Department of Justice.

A Typical Day in Boot Camp. Despite the variations among boot camps, it is possible to outline some typical features of daily life under shock incarceration. The appearance and dress code is usually stringent, including shaved heads in many men's camps and short haircuts among the women. The daily schedule is demanding, with little time provided for relaxation or recreation. Up before dawn, inmates face a ten- to sixteen-hour schedule beginning with an hour or two of physical exercise and drills under the watchful eye of one or more instructors. In many camps, inmates march everywhere, and stand at attention before speaking, eating, or taking lessons. Most inmates work during the day, after which there are more workouts and drills. The work may be community service, such as picking up litter along highways or in parks, or it may be work around the camp itself. After the evening meal, inmates generally

Box 17.2

INSIDE CRIMINAL JUSTICE

THE BOOT CAMP EXPERIENCE SEEN THROUGH THE EYES OF FEMALE INMATES

Most boot camps serve only male offenders; in 1992, only 13 states had boot camp programs for women. Nationwide in 1994, only 930 women had completed a boot camp program, compared with 10,761 men. Two types of boot camps exist for women: One integrates women in facilities designed for and also housing men, although the women usually live in a separate housing area; the second type provides completely separate boot camp facilities for men and women.

In most integrated facilities, men and women participate in the same education, physical training, drill and ceremony, drug education, and counseling programs. However, men and women are often assigned to separate work details. Many female offenders report that integrated boot camps are very stressful, particularly in camps where men far outnumber women. Women report being harassed by other inmates and by male drill instructors; in some cases they are permitted little privacy, with bathrooms and dormitories supervised by members of the opposite sex. In integrated facilities, programs have usually been designed with men in mind, not women. Few integrated camps offer educational, job training, and counseling programs geared specifically to women. The therapeutic needs of many female inmates—whether drug treatment, counseling on sexual abuse and domestic violence, or help with parenting skills—are often ignored.

Some female inmates in both types of boot camps find the military-style regimen and harsh behavior of some drill instructors abusive and frightening. Many have grown up in abusive environments or have experienced past battering by lovers or spouses. The screaming "in your face" posture of instructors reminds them of earlier physical and mental abuse. On the other hand, some women believed that they had learned to stand up for themselves in confrontations.

Many female inmates cite the discipline and physical demands as benefits of the boot camp experience. Some especially appreciate the physical conditioning that regular strenuous exercise promotes. On balance it seems that women in separate programs, away from male inmates, have fewer problems and are more likely to be offered therapeutic programs designed to address their special needs. Yet few boot camp programs for women, whether integrated or separate, offer the kinds of programs likely to help women in the job market or in dealing with domestic abuse once they return home.

Sources: Cherie L. Clark, David W. Aziz, and Doris L. Mackenzie (1994). "Shock Incarceration in New York: Focus on Treatment," *NIJ Program Focus* (August):2–11; Doris Layton Mackenzie, Lori A. Elis, Sally S. Simpson, and Stacy B. Skroban (1996). "Boot Camps as an Alternative for Women." In Doris Layton Mackenzie and Eugene E. Hebert, eds., *Correctional Boot Camps: A Tough Intermediate Sanction.* Washington, D.C.: U.S. Department of Justice.

participate in camp programs such as counseling, skills training, academic education, or drug education and treatment.

Boot Camps for Juveniles: Growing but Controversial. Juvenile camps are growing in popularity around the country; in 1995, states received over $10 million in federal aid to develop new juvenile camps (Klein, 1997:304).

They are similar to adult camps, although some facilities combine the militaristic boot camp philosophy with experiential or adventure programming that challenges the youths physically and mentally while teaching the importance of teamwork (Zachariah, 1996). For example, in an adventure program the youths might have to travel a certain distance through difficult terrain within a certain time and successfully complete different tasks along the way. Yet many juvenile experts have expressed reservations about applying the boot camp concept to children, arguing that juveniles need more intensive educational and counseling programs than are typically available in boot camps. Still, the executive director of one boot camp for juveniles sees much merit in the militaristic routine: "The military structure gives these kids strong motivation and a sense of control and empowerment. They work from early in the morning to late in the evening. The atmosphere here is quite different from the institutions where 20 to 30 kids sit in a day room and watch TV all day. In the boot camp, the kids are emotional and positive" (Zachariah, 1996).

This idea is consistent with the rationale behind the original Georgia boot camp: that many young offenders have never learned basic discipline and respect for authority. The Georgia program was originally designed to shock young offenders who had never experienced life in prison (Erwin, 1996). The 90-day program of intensive verbal confrontation, drill, and rigorous work was supposed to instill respect for authority, physical conditioning, and good work habits. Young offenders exposed to the rigors of prison life—but without the real abuses that occur among a hardened prison population—would be shocked away from crime. The debate over the merits of boot camps for juveniles will certainly continue, although it is likely to be overshadowed by a broader question: Are boot camps in general successful?

Are Boot Camps a Successful Intermediate Sanction? If this question is asked with prison overcrowding in mind, then the answer is a modest yes. The most extensive evaluation, which compared experiences in eight states—Georgia, South Carolina, Texas, New York, Illinois, Louisiana, Florida, and Oklahoma—concluded that boot camps can reduce prison overcrowding. This is especially true when corrections officials, rather than the courts, select participants (Mackenzie and Souryal, 1994). In these cases, the decision to send offenders to a boot camp is geared to prison occupancy rates.

Researchers are much less confident about the impact of boot camps on recidivism among criminal offenders. After an extensive review of available studies, one author concluded that most boot camps have "no discernible effect on subsequent offending" (Tonry, 1996:110). Many probation and parole officials are also skeptical about the crime prevention benefits of boot camps. In a recent national survey, 42 percent of directors of probation and parole agencies said they did not want or need boot camps. One director commented: "I personally feel that boot camps are a silly idea . . . with no demonstrated value in positively impacting our population of offenders" (McEwen, 1995:49).

A recent study of newly formed juvenile boot camps in Cleveland, Ohio; Denver, Colorado; and Mobile, Alabama found that while most youths finished the programs without being any worse off for the experience, all three programs experienced problems during the *aftercare* phase that follows detention (National Institute of Justice, 1996). Disciplinary problems and high levels of absenteeism occurred, and many youths were arrested for new offenses. This is similar to the behavior of many adults who have been through boot camps (Mackenzie and Brame, 1995). The findings raise doubts about the long-term impact of the boot camp experience itself. At the very least, carefully constructed aftercare programs are needed, including more intensive supervision.

Nor is there much evidence to substantiate the huge cost savings claimed by supporters of shock incarceration. Although Figure 17.3 showed that the overall per-offender costs of boot camps are less than prisons, boot camps have actually increased correctional costs in some jurisdictions. This is because they draw their participants from among first-time and nonviolent offenders who would not have gone to prison in the first place. Ironically, if they fail the programs, as a substantial minority of boot camp participants do, these offenders are then sent to prison, which costs the state more money and contributes to prison overcrowding.

Some critics of boot camps question the military-style industrial discipline in light of the backgrounds and likely futures of participants: "Even if the typical 90-day regime of training envisioned by proponents of boot camps is effective in reorienting its subjects, at best it can only produce soldiers without a company to join. Indeed, the grim vision of the effect of boot camp is that it will be effective for those who subsequently put their lessons of discipline and organization to use in street gangs and drug distribution networks" (Feeley and Simon, 1992:464). It is small wonder that many probation and parole experts have little positive to say about shock incarceration.

HOUSE ARREST AND ELECTRONIC MONITORING

Electronic monitoring is part of a "new age of surveillance," according to one criminologist (Lilly, 1990). It is a means by which criminal justice personnel can monitor the movements of offenders who have been released into the community with severe restrictions—the most restrictive being *house arrest*, also called *home confinement*. Offenders under house arrest are confined to the their homes when they are not working or engaged in activities pre-approved by their probation officer. Their movements are monitored through electronic devices described in the following section.

House arrest with electronic monitoring is an intermediate sanction that combines control and restraint with freedoms that promote responsibility and enable offenders to make a living or improve their skills. It is growing in popularity as a low-cost alternative to imprisonment but its overall impact on recidivism and public safety is uncertain.

PHOTO COURTESY OF PHOTOEDIT

The rules of confinement vary, but in some jurisdictions every adult in the offender's house is expected to abide by them. "No alcohol, no parties, and no weapons" is one such rule in Cook County, Illinois (Turnbaugh, 1995a:7).

How Electronic Monitoring Works. The origins of electronic monitoring are traced back to the 1960s, when researchers at Harvard University constructed a belt-worn transmitter and a series of repeater stations in the Boston area that were linked to a central monitoring station (Renzema, 1992). Signals from the transmitter allowed the wearer to be tracked over several blocks.

The most widespread application today consists of a number of computer terminals, or monitoring towers, linked via phone lines to a receiver that resembles a cable TV box in the offender's home. The offender wears a nonremovable ankle band holding a transmitter that sends a signal to the receiver. Beyond a certain range, from 100 to as much as 750 feet, the signal fades and the receiver triggers a violation report, which is printed out at the monitoring station. In the Cook County program mentioned earlier, the monitoring towers are manned by six technicians who constantly check the activity of 180 to 200 individuals under house arrest.

Early experiments with electronic monitoring equipment in the field uncovered various problems, from equipment failures to radio interference and weather-related difficulties. It was found that signals could be masked by simple household products such as aluminum foil. But the idea had caught on by the 1980s and the prospect of growing profits attracted the resources and ingenuity of the private sector. Continued refinements by manufacturers and vendors has resulted in all sorts of innovations: Whereas early electronic monitoring required a phone line to the offender's home, cellular technology has replaced lines and allows for continuous and random checks by probation officers. Today, numerous companies compete for this growing business (Klein, 1997:288).

One company, called Sentencing Alternatives, markets both single-offender and multiple-offender systems—which are capable of monitoring up to 40 offenders with one telephone line and one receiver. They offer "full services" such as free officer safety devices, free expert court witnesses, and 24-hour monitoring done on a sophisticated, powerful mainframe computer system, not a PC. The company claims that "only you will know when or where the offender will be subject to being checked, and at the same time the officer never has to leave the comfort and safety of the automobile" (Sentencing Alternatives, 1997, **http://www.sentalt.com/**).

Support for Electronic Monitoring of Offenders. In 1986, there were only 95 offenders on electronic monitoring in the entire country (Renzema, 1992:41). By 1995 there were an estimated 70,000 people under some kind of electronic monitoring (Lilly, 1995). In Florida alone, more than 13,000 offenders were on house arrest in 1993 (Blomberg, Bales, and Reed, 1993).

Home confinement with electronic monitoring is appealing because it promises so much. Its supporters usually cite four distinct benefits: (1) it protects society; (2) it punishes offenders; (3) it allows offenders to work and to improve their future prospects through counseling and education; and (4) it reduces prison overcrowding and correctional costs. A 1994 national survey of criminal justice professionals found widespread support for electronic monitoring (McEwen, 1995:51–52). One of the few studies of public attitudes toward electronic house arrest found strong yet conditional support for the practice (Brown and Elrod, 1995). Most respondents felt that house arrest was appropriate for low-risk, nondangerous offenders. However, some officials have expressed concern over the criteria for selecting offenders for monitoring. Individual jurisdictions have largely followed a trial-and-error process, with mixed results.

In Mississippi, for example, electronic monitoring was restricted at first to a "very select group" of nonviolent offenders (Gowen, 1995). As time passed, several high-risk offenders with backgrounds of violence, mental illness, or severe drug abuse slipped by the screening yet successfully completed the program. This encouraged officials to widen the class of offenders placed in the program. However, that decision meant an increase in the need for supervision and greater risks to probation officers. The officers adapted by using two-way mobile radios, cellular pages, and bulletproof vests—and many began carrying firearms as well.

Attitudes of Offenders. The attitudes toward electronic house arrest among offenders are mixed. Not surprisingly, offenders like being close to their families and loved ones, and those who work or attend school appreciate the rehabilitative possibilities of this community-based sanction. But some have reacted negatively to the constant surveillance. In an English study, a relative of someone under house arrest emphasized the humiliation associated with wearing the device: "[S]he would not use tagging [a British term for electronic monitoring] on a dog as it was so demeaning" (Mair and Mortimer, 1996:20). In contrast, however, when offenders under electronic surveillance in Indianapolis were asked if they would recommend electronic monitoring to "somebody in your situation," nearly 75 percent said they would (Baumer and Mendelsohn, 1989).

How Successful Is Home Confinement with Electronic Monitoring? Electronic monitoring is still a new practice, and there have been few comprehensive studies of its use. In the earlier days, technological problems compromised its use, and while there is more confidence in the technology today, defects still surface from time to time. Some have come to light as a result of lawsuits filed by citizens who have been robbed, raped, or assaulted by offenders under electronic surveillance (Christianson, 1995).

In a 1994 case, a Chicago firefighter had been murdered by a gang whose members included a convicted armed robber who had escaped from his electronic confinement. The suit alleged that the equipment had failed because it was poorly maintained and improperly used; it was revealed that over a seven-year period, 120 other offenders had cut off their monitors and had not been recaptured. The jury awarded $3 million in damages to the firefighter's estate.

The Cook County sheriff maintained that the incident represented an isolated case, and this appears to be justified. Nevertheless, if only one potentially violent offender escapes from home confinement, questions are raised about public safety. Perhaps the best answer to public safety is to make the selection process an informed and rigorous one. This is also the recommendation of the American Bar Association, in its 1994 Model Adult Community Corrections Act.

Concerning the two other promised benefits of electronic monitoring—reduction of correctional costs and offender recidivism—most case studies show considerable cost savings over imprisonment, even with the increased probation costs associated with electronic monitoring (Gowdy, n.d.). Evidence on recidivism is more mixed. Not surprisingly, the few studies that have been conducted show more success with low-risk offenders, particularly those convicted of drunk driving. However, some experts remain skeptical of the incapacitative benefits of house arrest (Tonry, 1996:120). Electronic monitoring does not prevent offenders from committing domestic crimes, and motivated offenders can steal from the workplace or commit crimes by enlisting the help of others. More research will reveal the benefits and limitations of electronic house arrest. As things stand today, it remains a popular alternative to traditional imprisonment for nonviolent offenders.

RESTITUTION AND COMMUNITY SERVICE

Restitution and community service are old ideas. This is especially true of *restitution*, which refers to the act of restoring something to its original state or ownership. When offenders are sentenced to undertake restitution, it generally means that they must make reparation *to the victim or the victim's family* for the harm resulting from the crime they committed. When an offender is sentenced to perform *community service*, he or she makes reparation to the entire community rather than to the individual victim. This explains why community service is sometimes referred to as *community restitution*. Restitution and community service require that offenders give up something of their own—usually money or time—to help others.

Restitution can be found in the Bible; in the Code of Hammurabi, written around 1760 B.C.; and in the ancient Roman Law of the Twelve Tables. In sixteenth-century England, Sir Thomas More, that country's chief legal authority, recommended that petty thieves and scoundrels pay restitution to victims and work on public projects as punishment for their offenses.

Restitution and community service are sometimes imposed along with other sanctions such as jail time and fines. Community service is often ordered as a condition of probation. Most states place these two punishments at the more lenient end of intermediate sanctions, and reserve them for petty criminals, drunk drivers, and some white-collar offenders.

Restitution as a Modern Punishment. Criminal restitution lay dormant for centuries before being resurrected in the 1970s. The late criminologist Stephen Schafer deserves much of the credit for bringing restitution back into criminal justice. In his book *Compensation and Restitution to Crime Victims*, which was widely read during the 1960s and 1970s, Schafer argued that while

The concepts of restitution and community service are old and can be found far back in English history. Sir Thomas More (1478–1535), philosopher and England's chief legal authority during his lifetime, recommended that petty offenders pay restitution to victims and work on public projects.

PHOTO BY SCALA, COURTESY OF ART RESOURCE

traditional punishments do something *to* or *for* offenders, restitution requires the offender to do something for others. He supported restitution as a way of making victims whole, while also promoting a sense of responsibility in the offender and a feeling of harmony in the community.

Due to the efforts of groups such as the National Organization for Victim Assistance (NOVA), between 1976 and 1990 many states and the federal government adopted new laws recognizing the rights of crime victims. Some states even amended their constitutions to include restitution as a victim right. One of the first to do so was California. In 1982, Californians declared that "all persons who suffer losses as a result of criminal activity shall have the right to restitution from the person convicted of the crimes for losses they suffer" (Klein, 1997:156). Most states have not gone that far, however, choosing instead to make restitution a formal condition of probation or an automatic element of any punishment for certain crimes. In 1996, for example, New Hampshire legislators proposed that all juvenile offenders, or their parents or guardians, repay their victims for any property loss or medical expenses incurred as a result of their crimes (*The Boston Globe*, February 8, 1996, p. 30).

The U.S. Department of Justice encouraged the spread of restitution programs during the 1970s and 1980s by handing out millions of dollars to state and local governments to fund new programs. One of the first programs is described in Box 17.3. Hundreds of individual restitution programs emerged around the country, most administered by courts or probation departments. Today, all states allow local courts to order restitution in both adult and juvenile sentencing. Juvenile restitution programs are rare but apparently on the rise (*Wall Street Journal*, September 20, 1995, p. 1).

Determining the Nature and Amount of Restitution. Three different methods of establishing the nature and amount of restitution are now used around the country:

1. The court determines restitution after hearing from the prosecution and defense, a probation official, the victim, and the offender.
2. The victim is required to file what amounts to a restitution claim with the court, and must provide records relating to stolen or damaged property, medical costs, lost wages, and so on. In fixing the offender's payment, the court may consider any insurance the victim might have. This method is generally regarded as the least satisfactory, since it places considerable burden on victims who often have already suffered physically and emotionally (Klein, 1997).
3. The restitution is established through face-to-face meetings of offenders and victims who work out a mutually acceptable agreement. Twenty years ago, this method was rare; now it is increasingly seen as yet another promising application of dispute resolution techniques. Furthermore, it fits nicely with the growing interest in restorative justice, as we shall see in a moment.

Most jurisdictions allow offenders to pay restitution in installments monitored by court or probation officials. This is critical for the collection of restitution, because many offenders cannot afford to pay the restitution amount all at once, and some find it difficult even when the amount is spread over many months. According to one study of 32 counties, the average restitution order was $3,400 (Langan and Cunniff, 1992). Spread over two years, this would still be a monthly payment of $142. If the offender is earning minimum wage, or employed only part-time, this is a hefty sum each month.

Some restitution orders are for much more, even millions of dollars. These sentences are not given to run-of-the-mill offenders, however, but to corporations and individuals involved in large-scale frauds and thefts. Because the

Box 17.3

JUSTICE INNOVATIONS

THE RESTITUTION CENTER

The nation's first formal restitution program that gave some offenders an alternative to serving out a prison term was established in Minnesota in 1972. The Minnesota Restitution Center took in adult male offenders who had been sentenced to the Minnesota State Prison for up to two years. Offenders had to have served at least four months of that sentence to be eligible for the program. Offenders were ineligible if they had previously served time in prison, if they had been convicted of a violent offense, or if it was determined that they could afford to make restitution without the center's help. A restitution plan was established during face-to-face meetings in the prison between the offender and victim, in the presence of a Restitution Center staff member. If approved by the parole board, the offender was then released to the Restitution Center, where he would live and fulfill the terms of the agreement.

The Minnesota program became a model for other states. Georgia, Texas, and South Carolina established restitution centers—called *Community Diversion Centers* in Georgia, *Rehabilitation Centers* in Texas—serving primarily nonviolent offenders. While at the centers, residents must maintain employment—with a certain portion of their pay going to restitution, room and board, and sometimes child support—and attend individual or group counseling sessions. They may also be required to perform community service work. Because many of the offenders housed at restitution centers have not completed their high school education, have never held a steady job, and have a history of alcohol or drug abuse, many centers offer life skills training and drug treatment as part of their programming.

Sources: Belinda Rodgers McCarthy and Bernard J. McCarthy, Jr. (1997). *Community-Based Corrections*, 3rd ed. (p. 167). Belmont, Calif.: Wadsworth; Paul F. Cromwell and George G. Killinger (1994). *Community-Based Corrections: Probation, Parole, and Intermediate Sanctions*, 3rd ed. (pp. 281–282). Minneapolis, Minn.: West; Andrew Klein (1997). *Alternative Sentencing, Intermediate Sanctions, and Probation* (pp. 170–188). Cincinnati, Ohio: Anderson; Douglas C. McDonald (1988). *Restitution and Community Service*. Washington, D.C.: U.S. Department of Justice.

restitution amounts are so large, they often get considerable publicity. Here are some examples from 1996:

- A Massachusetts psychiatrist who made up diagnoses, session notes, and bills for patients he never saw was sentenced to four years in federal prison and ordered to pay \$1.5 million in fines and restitution (*Boston Globe*, March 23, 1996, p. 19).
- The Prudential Insurance Company was ordered to pay \$100 million in restitution and \$35 million in fines for fraudulent sales practices (*Atlanta Constitution*, July 10, 1996, p. B1).
- A Wall Street securities company agreed to pay \$1 million in restitution to 3,000 customers it overcharged when trading stock (*Wall Street Journal*, July 26, 1996, p. B5).
- A California physician was sentenced to 20 years in prison and ordered to pay \$41 million in restitution for health insurance fraud (*Los Angeles Times*, July 18, 1996, p. B1).

These cases all involved multiple victims, which partly explains why the restitution amounts were so large. What these brief accounts do not tell is that the frauds took place over many years, and restitution came only after a lengthy legal process.

Restitution and Restorative Justice. The spread of restitution as a community-based alternative or supplement to incarceration did not reflect any fundamental change in corrections philosophy, which retained its emphasis on the offender. However, in 1988, the National Council of Juvenile and Family Court Judges challenged judges to rethink the fundamental purpose of punishment, especially in dealing with juveniles. Its publication *Juvenile Probation: The Balanced Approach* called for a system of punishment that attempts to *restore* the victim and larger community, while also improving the chances that offenders will become responsible, productive members of society. The idea of **restorative justice** was born.

restorative justice A response to crime that seeks to restore the well-being of victims and the larger community while promoting responsible and productive behavior in offenders.

This approach appealed to many practitioners and policymakers familiar with restitution. By the mid-1990s, model programs were being tried in Florida, Pennsylvania, and Minnesota. In a 1995 editorial, the commissioner of the Minnesota Department of Corrections called restorative justice a "truly exciting concept" and "not a passing fad or quick fix" (Klein, 1997:163). He predicted that restorative justice would continue to be implemented throughout that state. One of the key elements in these restorative programs is that both offenders and victims are directly involved in the process of restoration. In many cases this is being done through the use of mediation.

Restitution and Victim/Offender Mediation. Although not essential for restitution, many restitution programs now encourage face-to-face meetings of offenders and victims mediated by trained, neutral staff. Such sessions highlight the human side of crime, and help both offenders and victims see the event from the vantage point of the other. Since participation in restitution via mediation is voluntary, the atmosphere, though often tense, is characterized by a desire to work things out. The crime involved an offender and a victim, and now that same offender and victim try to repair the damage together. Many offenders and victims recall the experience in positive terms (Umbreit and Coates, 1993). Typically, they see each other in a new light: Offenders often see a hurt, vulnerable person whom they violated; victims often see a frightened offender who regrets the hurt the crime caused and is ready to accept responsibility for it.

This does not mean that victim/offender mediation sessions are quiet, dignified conversations. In fact, they are often quite the opposite: Angry, heated exchanges can occur between offenders and victims, with blame flying in both directions. Without trained mediators present, such confrontations might easily break down into violence. Instead, they are usually resolved peacefully and to the eventual satisfaction of both victim and offender. Although still rare, restorative programs in some states bring violent offenders face-to-face with their victims. These, too, have shown positive results.

In a January 1994, article, the *Boston Globe* reported on a series of mediation sessions held in a Rhode Island prison between a mother and an inmate who had murdered her son in the course of a robbery that netted \$10. The mediator was Dr. Mark Umbreit, of the University of Minnesota Center for Restorative Justice and Mediation. Although the very thought of the murderer touching her had made her ill, at the conclusion of one session she found herself shaking hands with him. According to the victim, the mediation had helped bring closure to her son's death, and enabled her to get on with her life.

Restitution through Community Service. Many restitution programs combine reparation to the individual victim with community service. All forms of community service are a type of restitution, because the offender pays something back to the community whose laws were violated. Community service is used primarily as a condition of probation or as a punishment for motor vehicle offenses and other less serious nonviolent crimes. Box 17.4 illustrates one such program, used as an alternative to jail in Cook County, Illinois.

Support for Community Service as an Intermediate Sanction. Community service has been called "the most under used intermediate sanction in the United States" (Tonry, 1996:121). In many European countries, community service penalties are authorized by statute and have found widespread use. England and Wales, Scotland, and the Netherlands are in the forefront of this movement. In England, for example, the Criminal Justice Act of 1991 expressly identified community service combined with probation supervision as a way of punishing and deterring offenders as well as assisting in their rehabilitation (Ellis, Hedderman, and Mortimer, 1996:1).

Supporters of community service as an intermediate sanction claim many benefits:

- The experience is punishing and therefore carries the prospect of deterring offenders from committing further offenses.
- It is relatively inexpensive to administer—the SWAP program discussed in Box 17.4 is self-sufficient, and even had a $68,000 surplus in 1994 (Turnbaugh, 1995b).
- It produces a community benefit in the work that is done; its rigor, duration, and degree of supervision can be scaled to the offense and offender.
- The experience can have rehabilitative value in building time management skills, a work ethic, and responsibility; and last, but by no means least:
- Community service receives considerable public approval—it is seen as worthwhile punishment.

American judges, however, are guarded in their support of community service, even in jurisdictions where it has been used for a number of years. A study of 20 California municipal judges, for example, found support for the use of community service sentences for indigent offenders who cannot pay fines or monetary restitution and would otherwise be sentenced to jail (Meyer and Jesilow, 1993). Judges were more skeptical when it came to the use of community service in place of incarceration. Some judges said they combined jail time with community service to meet this objection.

Some judges and probation officials worry about how to deal with offenders who violate the terms of community service orders. On the whole, compliance rates are quite high, around 80 percent in most studies. But over the life of community service programs, compliance rates have had a tendency to slip. No one is quite sure why, but the usual response has been to introduce closer supervision and more rigorous enforcement. This happened in New York City, which in 1979 started the first community service program for repeat misdemeanor offenders in the country. To counteract the problem, the Vera Institute of Justice, a nonprofit agency that operated the program, hired compliance officers to make home visits and track down missing offenders. It also hired "enforcement officers"—mostly retired police and corrections officials—to further encourage completion of the program, and to make arrests as a last resort.

Research in England shows that the compliance aspects of community service orders create something of a dilemma for many probation officers, especially those who have been in the service a long time (Ellis, Hedderman, and Mortimer, 1996). The tendency of many probation officers is to use a

Box 17.4

JUSTICE INNOVATIONS

SWAP, THE COMMUNITY SERVICE PROGRAM FOR COOK COUNTY, ILLINOIS

Many communities are implementing community service programs as an alternative to jail and prison for some offenders. SWAP stands for the Sheriff's Work Alternative Program. Begun in 1984 to alleviate overcrowding in Cook County Jail, the program originally served as an alternative punishment for individuals convicted of a second drunk driving offense. Initially, offenders volunteered for the program, but its reputation as a tough alternative soon had some eligible offenders choosing jail time instead. In 1989 the program was extended to misdemeanor and nonviolent felony offenders. Some judges began sentencing offenders to SWAP regardless of their wishes.

In SWAP the judge first determines how jail time translates into SWAP time. A rule of thumb is "day for day," meaning that for every day offenders might have spent in jail, they spend 24 hours in SWAP. The average time is 15 days, although some offenders serve 180 days or more.

The program is self-sufficient—participants must pay a $25 registration fee and $1 for every hour they work. Within seven days of sentencing, offenders must report to the SWAP office for an interview to determine their schedule and activities. Schedules are built around eight-hour shifts, and are tailored to accommodate an offender's regular job or school schedule. Sentences must be served in consecutive weeks, on the same scheduled days—say, Saturday, from 8 A.M. to 4 P.M. If offenders are even one minute late they are sent home and receive no credit for that day. Yet they are expected to complete their sentence as quickly as possible.

On their scheduled days of work, offenders report to one of seven locations, where they are frisked and checked for contraband. If any is found they are arrested. On a typical day 150 to 300 participants will report for their assignments. Elderly offenders and those with medical problems are assigned less strenuous work details, such as washing county vehicles and doing cleanup work around the sheriff's department. Others will be separated into coed groups of 20 to 25 people and bussed to work locations. During the day they will receive two breaks and 30 minutes for lunch; talking is discouraged, and offenders are "told when they can stand up and sit down." If an officer feels that an offender is not working hard enough, the offender may be denied credit for that day.

Work can be strenuous: cutting and pruning trees; painting picnic tables, benches, and buildings; cleaning all sorts of county property; and picking up trash along interstates and other major streets in Chicago and surrounding Cook County. In 1994 alone, SWAP offenders picked up 18 million pounds of trash, saving an estimated $5 million in sanitation costs. All work is performed by hand, and when an offender has a particular skill such as carpentry, plumbing, or electrical work, this is identified and put to use.

Some participants complain that the rigid schedule, strict supervision, and hard work make SWAP little different from the old-fashioned chain gang. However, there are no shotguns, and offenders are free to leave at any time. In 1994, ten did, but most returned the next day rather than face jail. On another occasion, an offender decided that 90 days in SWAP was more than he had bargained for and asked the sentencing judge to send him to jail instead; the judge refused and doubled his sentence in SWAP.

Since 1984 more than 32,000 offenders have participated in SWAP, and 80 percent of these completed their sentences successfully.

Source: Kristi Turnbaugh (1995). "Sheriff's Work Alternative Program: Paying Back the Community." *The Compiler* (Winter/Spring):4–6.

highly discretionary and informal enforcement approach while they concentrate their efforts on the rehabilitative and therapeutic aspects of community-based corrections. But if community service is to be used as a true intermediate sanction—an *alternative to jail or prison time but harsher than simple probation*—then it makes sense to establish strict standards of compliance and to ensure that they are enforced. In 1992 England adopted national standards to address this issue, but compliance problems still exist. Most stem from the practical difficulty of balancing discretion against rigorous enforcement in the absence of comprehensive and clear-cut guidelines.

Are Restitution and Community Service Orders Successful Alternatives to Prison? There is no doubt that restitution and community service cost far less than imprisonment, so on that count the answer must be yes. In terms of recidivism, available evidence does not show significant advantages over prison, but neither does it suggest that these programs increase recidivism (Tonry, 1996:122–123). To those who say that community service is not tough enough and is too risky for the community, the appropriate answer appears to be that neither view is justified. Regarding toughness, many offenders see community service, with its hard work and close surveillance, as more punishing than jail or prison (Petersilia, 1995; Turnbaugh, 1995b). As for risks to the community, noncompliance and disappearance are generally minimal; in addition, the mainly nonviolent offenders who participate in community restitution present negligible risks of violence.

The generally positive results of community service programs have led some experts to call for their expansion (e.g., Tonry, 1996:123–124; McIvor, 1993). One possible area of expansion is to broaden the range of offenders permitted in such programs; another is to provide work services to specific individuals or groups within a community in addition to the public at large. Both strategies have been employed in Europe, with beneficial results.

In Scotland, for example, the typical offender on community service is a young, single male who is unemployed, has at least one previous conviction, and whose current offense is burglary, theft, or minor assault (McIvor, 1993:387). In the United States, such offenders would more likely be found in boot camps, under intensive probation supervision, or in prison. In addition, many Scottish offenders on community service work in teams that provide practical services to elderly, infirm, or poor individuals who need jobs done around the home but cannot afford to pay outsiders. A 1990 survey of 565 community service recipients in Scotland found high levels of satisfaction with the standard of work carried out, and a general feeling that the service was extremely beneficial; most respondents said they would make future use of the service if possible (McIvor, 1993).

THE FUTURE OF INTERMEDIATE SANCTIONS

Although evidence on the benefits of intermediate sanctions is mixed, they will probably grow in importance during the next few years because they are backed by strong public and professional support. This prediction might be questioned if recidivism rates were significantly higher among offenders given intermediate sanctions compared to those sent to prison, but they are not. In addition, some intermediate sanctions—particularly restitution and house arrest—have shown significant cost savings over imprisonment.

There is another reason for believing that intermediate sanctions are here to stay. There is growing evidence that offenders see some intermediate sanctions as *more* punishing than prison (Petersilia, 1995). This is particularly true of intermediate sanctions that restrict freedoms while imposing obligations such as work, reparation, and intensive treatment. When nonviolent offenders in Oregon were given the choice of prison or intensive probation supervision with drug testing, mandatory community service, and frequent visits by a probation officer, one-third chose prison. In a Minnesota study, offenders and correctional staff rated three years on intensive probation supervision as equivalent in punitiveness to a year in prison (Petersilia and Deschenes, 1994). These opinions reinforce the idea that intermediate sanctions can be a tough alternative to prison, and they may have some deterrent value because of it.

Some policymakers remain reluctant to throw their support behind intermediate sanctions, and they will continue to defend mandatory sentencing, "three strikes" laws, and lengthy prison terms. Intermediate sanctions sound more lenient than prison, even if they are not. Adding fuel to this resistance is the periodic publication of studies claiming that rising prison populations produce reductions in crime and significant economic benefits to society from the crime losses that are thereby averted (DiIulio, 1996:18–19). This has led one prominent economist to claim that "incarceration is a bargain" (*Wall Street Journal*, September 23, 1996, p. 12). But would the benefits to society be even greater if the money spent on prisons were spent on alternatives, including prevention programs targeting at-risk youths and neighborhoods?

In answer to this debate, Austin Turk, a prominent criminologist and past president of the American Society of Criminology, writes:

> The vast majority of incarcerated offenders do not and cannot benefit from their imprisonment, so they eventually come out no better and probably less able to stay out of trouble. Community-based correctional programs encouraging and assisting offenders are . . . far more likely to help them change their behavior. In any case, curtailing the prison-building and prison-filling boom will be a major step toward eliminating the gross disparities in the chances and severity of punishment that exacerbate class and ethnic antagonisms in American society. (Turk, 1995:22–23)

Intermediate sanctions, applied with sufficient resources to provide adequate supervision and decent opportunities for counseling, treatment, and rehabilitation, offer a promising strategy for dealing with the bulk of felony offenders.

PAROLE

In 1997, almost 700,000 Americans were on parole (U.S. Department of Justice press release, August 16, 1998). **Parole** involves releasing inmates from prison into supervised aftercare in the community prior to the completion of a sentence. The practice of parole originated in Britain in the early 1800s, and became popular in America with the rise of the indeterminate sentence. Recalling Chapter 15, indeterminate sentences emerged as part of the reforms of the 1870 National Prison Congress. Under an indeterminate sentence, the state's parole board determines when the offender will actually be released. Parole board members are usually appointed by the governor. The board's function is to establish whether an offender can safely be released into the community under supervision. With the growth of determinate sentences, the participation of parole boards in the release of inmates steadily declined, from 71.8 percent of all prison releases in 1977 to only 40.3 percent by 1988.

parole Supervised release of inmates prior to the full completion of their prison term.

The indeterminate sentence and use of parole boards was an attempt to *individualize* justice—to match punishment to the circumstances of individual offenders, including their behavior while in prison. Prisoners who meet parole board criteria for release may be released long before their prison sentence expires. For example, an offender with a sentence of five to ten years might earn more than a year of "good time" credit and be eligible for parole in just over three years. Unfortunately, one of the criticisms of parole boards is that the process for selecting inmates for parole is highly subjective, and prisoners often do not know what standards will be applied in their case (Allen and Simonsen, 1995:273). Even though inmates soon learn that participation in prison programs generally counts heavily with parole boards, a particular inmate may discover that he or she has not done enough, or has been in programs that do not impress the board. Furthermore, at parole hearings in many states, police, prosecutors, and victims may present written or oral testimony on why an inmate should not be released; the reasons usually have nothing to do with the inmate's behavior while in prison. Thus from the inmate's standpoint, "playing the game" in prison may not help him or her get released.

The key to parole is successful supervision and aftercare in the community, which makes it an appropriate topic for this chapter. Parolees are released from prison under conditions that include no further criminal violations and adherence to the rules laid down by parole officials. They sign an agreement to that effect. In practice, this means following the instructions of a **parole officer**. Parole officers are employees of the state who are assigned a caseload of parolees to supervise and to assist in finding appropriate aftercare, employment, and housing. Since parole failure rates are high—more than 60 percent of parolees are rearrested within three years of their release (Bureau of Justice Statistics, 1989)—parole officers must face the likelihood that most of their clients will end up back in prison.

parole officer An officer responsible for supervising parolees and assisting them in making the adjustment back into the community.

Parole officers have a difficult task, made worse by the fact that they must be a cop and a social worker at the same time: Their cop duties include restricting parolees' activities, detecting violations, making arrests, and initiating proceedings that may lead to revocation of parole; their social work duties include providing counsel and support to parolees and otherwise assisting them in the difficult adjustment back into the community. There is no single key to a successful parole, but one is the development of a trusting relationship between parole officer and parolee. Yet this is difficult to establish, let alone maintain, when parolees see the officer as a cop who could send them back to prison, and officers see the parolee as likely to fail—as most eventually do.

Among other things that contribute to the high failure rate among parolees are (1) large caseloads and inadequate resources to support close and effective mentoring; (2) inadequate educational and vocational skills, and the poor employment histories of many parolees; (3) reluctance of neighborhoods and employers to welcome parolees into their midst; (4) the tendency of parolees to gravitate back to their old neighborhoods and associations; and (5) the expectation that parolees will act like responsible adults and lead exemplary lives, even though their independence is severely restricted and they are treated more like children.

Whereas the future of parole may have seemed in doubt a few years ago as some states abandoned it altogether and others removed much of the discretionary release power of the parole board, the rising prison population and yearly release of thousands of inmates directly into the community will doubtless put pressure on some states to rethink the parole question. However, until new resources are made available and strong public support is kindled, it is unlikely that the rather tarnished image of parole will change for the better.

SHAMING: A COMMUNITY-BASED SANCTION FOR THE 21ST CENTURY?

The dawning of a new millennium would be a wonderful time to announce that the fight against crime was being won, and that humane and effective punishments were partly responsible. While rates of serious crime, especially homicides, have taken a downward turn in many cities across America in recent years, there is no good evidence to suggest that current penal policy is responsible. Despite downward trends, American crime rates remain among the highest in the developed world. Some scholars and criminal justice officials believe that a significant reduction of crime rates will occur only when communities find effective ways of demonstrating their intolerance of criminality.

Shaming and Intolerance of Crime

John Braithwaite, a world-renowned Australian criminologist, believes that societies with low crime rates "are not those that punish crime most effectively, but those that are most effectively intolerant of crime" (Braithwaite, 1995:191). The effective use of shaming is the key to lowering crime, Braithwaite believes. *Shaming* is any social process that expresses disapproval and lowers a person's reputation in the eyes of others:

> It can be subtle: a frown, a tut-tut, a single comment, a turning of the head, a laugh; it can be a direct verbal confrontation in which the offender is admonished about how guilty she should feel or how shocked her relatives and friends are over her conduct; it can be indirect confrontation by gossip which gets back to the offender; it can be broadcast via the mass media or by a private medium (as when the feminist paints a slogan on the front fence of a rapist); it can be officially pronounced by a judge from the bench or by a government which names a wrongdoer in an official report or in the chamber of the legislature; it can be popularized in mass culture by a film which moralizes about a certain act of wrongdoing. (Braithwaite, 1989:57–58)

Shaming is not a new reaction to crime, as some earlier forms of punishment illustrate: Branding and mutilation spelled out "criminal" to everyone the offender encountered. These punishments flourished during the medieval period, and they were used in colonial America for a variety of offenses, including burglary, robbery, religious crimes, and hog stealing (Earle, 1969). Until the nineteenth century, the stocks and pillory were used extensively in England and America for such crimes as drunkenness, disorderly conduct, prostitution, blasphemy, lying, swearing, and threatening. The illustration below shows a

Reintegrative shaming—more than simply a return to the stocks.

Illustration by John Overmyer

common shaming punishment. In Sweden, offenders were sometimes tied backwards on a wooden horse and left there to be ridiculed by their neighbors (James, 1817:236–239).

These punishments made sense in tradition-bound, self-sustaining communities, where people lived close together and continuously interacted with each other over their lifetimes. The power of shaming mechanisms was weakened as industrialization and geographic mobility broke down insular communities (Rothman, 1974). Western societies no longer brand, maim, or pillory their criminals, but many nations still incorporate elements of shaming as part of legal punishment. For example, certain offenses carry automatic penalties—called **collateral consequences**—that deprive offenders of civil rights or common privileges: citizenship, employment, inheritance, and even marriage. In this country, one collateral consequence of a felony conviction is loss of the right to serve on a jury; in Alabama, Arkansas, Delaware, Iowa, Mississippi, Ohio, Rhode Island, and South Carolina, felony offenders are also barred forever from holding public office; under some circumstances, parental rights may even be terminated. These stigmatizing penalties convey permanent social disapproval.

collateral consequences Automatic penalties such as loss of citizenship or loss of the right to serve on a jury or to run for public office.

Even so, Western societies have effectively separated punishment and shaming by removing most of the public aspects from the penal process (Braithwaite, 1989:59–60). This was done partly because of the cruelty of onlookers during whippings, executions, and other public punishments. However, it also removed opportunities for the criminal to receive punishment with courage and dignity witnessed by the community, and for the community to participate in processes of reconciliation.

The Return of Shaming. There are signs that shaming is finding its way back into the criminal process, especially for offenders convicted of less serious crimes such as public order offenses. The decision of Joliet, Illinois, officials to publish the names of male clients of prostitutes was front-page news in the Midwest. Other communities have adopted similar public shaming of drunk drivers, drug traffickers, and people convicted of domestic violence: Their photos, names, and even addresses are printed in the local newspaper.

Some courts are sentencing violent offenders to public shaming as part of their punishment. In Tennessee, a judge ordered the posting of a sign at the entrance to a convicted child molester's home to tell the public of its resident's crime; however, the Tennessee Supreme Court struck down the sentence in 1996 as an unconstitutional extension of judicial authority. In Illinois, meanwhile, a circuit judge ordered a similar sign placed in front of the home of a man twice convicted of aggravated battery (*St. Louis Post-Dispatch*, February 8, 1997, pp. 14–15). That decision is now before the Illinois Supreme Court.

Reintegrative Shaming: From Stigmatization to Reconciliation. Shaming penalties such as these stigmatize people as criminals and encourage neighbors to shun them. At worst, the offenders become outcasts in their own community, with no stake in conformity. They join gangs or participate in other subcultures of resistance. This may encourage them to commit further crimes.

Braithwaite (1989, 1995) believes that a special kind of shaming is necessary to encourage offenders to embrace the rules. He calls it **reintegrative shaming**. In reintegrative shaming the act of shaming is bound up with ceremonies of forgiveness and repentance in which both offenders and the community participate. The idea is that the bonds between individual and community are strengthened. The context for shaming is positive and supportive—even loving—rather than punitive, negative, and destructive. The main characteristics of reintegrative shaming are the following:

reintegrative shaming Punishment that includes forgiveness and attempts at reconciliation.

- Disapproval while sustaining a relationship of respect
- Ceremonies to certify deviance (sent to room) terminated by ceremonies to decertify deviance (forgiving hug)
- Disapproval of the evil of the deed without labeling the person as evil
- Deviance not being allowed to become a master trait (for example, junkie, bully) (Braithwaite, 1995:194).

This is, after all, how children are effectively socialized and disciplined in the family. Close-knit communities where there is active citizen participation in community life are the ideal setting for reintegrative shaming. This hardly sounds like modern-day America, especially in the cities. It is also a far cry from the bureaucratic and impersonal criminal justice system most urban Americans experience. But Braithwaite (1995) believes that reintegrative shaming can be introduced into American justice. For example, community accountability conferences similar to those now adopted in New Zealand and described earlier (see Box 12.5) could be established in crime-torn urban neighborhoods as an alternative to conventional courts. This could have a significant payoff, especially in places like South Central Los Angeles, where stigmatization and gang subcultures of resistance are commonplace.

Reintegrative shaming will not work for all offenders. For example, people who feel no pangs of conscience when others express disapproval will not recognize their own shame. There are also some criminals who must be imprisoned because public safety or the gravity of their offense requires it. But for all petty criminals and the bulk of felony offenders—especially young offenders—reintegrative shaming holds promise. The combined experience of (1) being faced with disapproval from people they care about, (2) being confronted with the consequences of what they have done to victims and the community, (3) being invited to take responsibility and given the opportunity to make reparation and to develop a plan to prevent recurrence, and (4) being forgiven, may be a far more constructive penal policy for the 21st century than the one that dominated the 20th century. What do you think?

SUMMARY

Community-based corrections include fines, probation, and a range of penalties between probation and prison. These include boot camps, house arrest with electronic monitoring, intensive probation supervision, community service, and restitution. Community-based sanctions generally cost taxpayers less than imprisonment, and they allow offenders to retain relationships with family and work while undergoing various treatment options. However, because offenders remain in the community, there are risks to public safety that imprisonment avoids—at least for the period of incarceration. This is why most community-based programs are reserved for misdemeanants and nonviolent felony offenders with few, if any, prior convictions.

Although fines have been used for centuries, American courts rarely use them as the penalty of choice for felony offenders. However, prison overcrowding and heavy probation caseloads have resulted in increasing use of fines. Some states are also using fines as a way of recovering some of the costs entailed in prosecuting and punishing criminals. Credit cards and computer technology have made it easier to collect fines, adding further to their appeal.

There are more Americans on probation than ever before. Most offenders sentenced to probation are expected to fulfill special conditions; these range from refraining from crime to performing community service or spending time in jail. Offenders who do not live up to the conditions of probation may have their probation revoked. Nationally, 70 to 80 percent successfully complete probation; those who fail do so for technical reasons such as failure to report in, or because they have committed a new crime. The growing number of offenders placed on probation has meant growing caseloads for probation officers. Yet resources have not kept pace with demand, a condition made even worse by "get tough" policies requiring closer surveillance and by the growth of intermediate sanctions.

There is widespread professional and public support for intermediate sanctions for nonviolent offenders. However, the support is qualified: people want a clear element of punishment to be present and they want offenders to put out effort in the form of work, training, or education. They also want to ensure the public's safety, and this means close monitoring and supervision of offenders. House arrest with electronic monitoring is growing in popularity, as is community service that involves hard work. A new emphasis on restoration has emerged in recent years, with offenders and victims working together through mediation to bring balance and harmony to themselves and to the community.

New ideas about ways to shame offenders effectively have also surfaced. Reintegrative shaming is based on the idea that the process of punishment should be more than merely stigmatizing. It should also provide opportunities for offenders to see the harm they have caused, to take responsibility for it, and to be forgiven. This is very different from the current emphasis on prisons and jails as the backbone of corrections in America. Yet the American Correctional Association now stands behind a balanced approach to punishment that includes rebuilding lives and restoring victims and the communities in which they live. This is the great correctional challenge for the 21st century.

WHAT DO YOU THINK NOW?

- What are the major benefits and drawbacks of using fines as punishment? Do you feel that some fines should be applied toward restitution? Why or why not?
- How are punishments that force offenders to work within the community beneficial to the community? To the offenders? Are the punishments as easy as you had thought they were? Why or why not?
- How did you feel about the effectiveness of shock incarceration, or boot camps? Do you feel they could be improved? Do you feel they should be more widespread?

KEY TERMS AND CASES

community-based corrections
intermediate sanctions
benefit of clergy
suspended sentence
Killits case
cost recovery
probation
conditions of probation
revocation of probation
technical violation
Gagnon v. Scarpelli
United States v. Granderson
boot camp
house arrest
electronic monitoring
intensive supervised probation (ISP)
community service
restitution
day reporting center
shock incarceration
restorative justice
parole
parole officer
collateral consequences
reintegrative shaming

ACTIVE LEARNING CHALLENGES

1. Discuss ways that probation could be made a more effective punishment without jeopardizing public safety. This requires you to think about the goals of punishment.
2. Find out what types of intermediate sanctions are currently being used in your state or county. If there is a program near you, see if you can interview the people running it, and perhaps also some of its "graduates."
3. Break into small groups and identify as many arguments as you can for and against the intermediate sanctions discussed in this chapter. Then find evidence for each of these arguments and report back to the class.
4. Break into two groups. Imagine that you have caught a student stealing books and videos from the library. Have each group independently design a scenario for reintegrative shaming. Present the scenario to the class, with members of the group acting the roles of offender, victims, and community members. Have class members vote on which scenario they believe would be most effective in crime prevention, and discuss why.

INTERNET CHALLENGES

The Web pages mentioned here can all be accessed through the Web site for this textbook at **http://www.prenhall.com/barlow/**.

1. Many states maintain Web sites describing the community-based programs of their departments of correction. North Carolina has made headlines with some of its programs. Check them out on the Web page of North Carolina's Department of Correction. Then see if other states have similar programs.
2. Restorative justice requires that victims of crime participate in the punishment phase of the criminal justice process. This is particularly important for deciding on restitution. But how do crime victims find out what they are entitled to and how to get it? To find out how restitution works in Iowa, visit Iowa's Restitution and Other Financial Remedies page. See if the rules are different in yours or a neighboring state.
3. Reintegrative shaming may hold promise for improving justice and reducing crime. See if you can find out more about the use of shaming in criminal justice. Visit some of the criminal justice sites you have bookmarked while reading this book, and look for relevant information. Information on the sentencing practices of judges may be found by searching newspaper archives. What sort of shaming do you find? In what contexts is it applied? Is it reintegrative? What is your opinion of its promise?

APPENDIX

Definitions of Offenses from Uniform Crime Reports and from National Crime Victimization Survey

1. UNIFORM CRIME REPORTS

Offenses in Uniform Crime Reporting are divided into two groups, Part I and Part II. Information on the volume of Part I offenses known to law enforcement, those cleared by arrest or exceptional means, and the number of persons arrested is reported monthly. Only arrest data are reported for Part II offenses.

Part I Offenses

criminal homicide a. Murder and nonnegligent manslaughter: the willful (nonnegligent) killing of one human being by another. Deaths caused by negligence, attempts to kill, assaults to kill, suicides, accidental deaths, and justifiable homicides are excluded. Justifiable homicides are limited to: (1) the killing of a felon by a law enforcement officer in the line of duty; and (2) the killing of a felon, during the commission of a felony, by a private citizen. b. Manslaughter by negligence: the killing of another person through gross negligence. Traffic fatalities are excluded. While manslaughter by negligence is a Part I crime, it is not included in the Crime Index.

forcible rape The carnal knowledge of a female forcibly and against her will. Included are rapes by force and attempts or assaults to rape. Statutory offenses (no force used—victim under age of consent) are excluded.

robbery The taking or attempting to take anything of value from the care, custody, or control of a person or persons by force or threat of force or violence and/or by putting the victim in fear.

aggravated assault An unlawful attack by one person upon another for the purpose of inflicting severe or aggravated bodily injury. This type of assault usually is accompanied by the use of a weapon or by means likely to produce death or great bodily harm. Simple assaults are excluded.

burglary-breaking or entering The unlawful entry of a structure to commit a felony or a theft. Attempted forcible entry is included.

larceny-theft (except motor vehicle theft) The unlawful taking, carrying, leading, or riding away of property from the possession or constructive possession of another. Examples are thefts of bicycles or automobile accessories, shoplifting, pocket-picking, or the stealing of any property or article which is not taken by force and violence or by fraud. Attempted larcenies are included. Embezzlement, confidence games, forgery, worthless checks, etc., are excluded.

motor vehicle theft The theft or attempted theft of a motor vehicle. A motor vehicle is self-propelled and runs on the surface and not on rails. Specifically excluded from this category are motorboats, construction equipment, airplanes, and farming equipment.

arson Any willful or malicious burning or attempt to burn, with or without intent to defraud, a dwelling house, public building, motor vehicle or aircraft, personal property of another, etc.

Part II Offenses

other assaults (simple) Assaults and attempted assaults where no weapon is used and which do not result in serious or aggravated injury to the victim.

Sources: Federal Bureau of Investigation (1998). *Crime in the United States, 1997* (p. 407). Washington, D.C.: U.S. Department of Justice; Bureau of Justice Statistics (1997). *Criminal Victimization in the United States, 1994* (pp. 147–149). Washington, D.C.: U.S. Department of Justice.

forgery and counterfeiting Making, altering, uttering, or possessing, with intent to defraud, anything false in the semblance of that which is true. Attempts are included.

fraud Fraudulent conversion and obtaining money or property by false pretenses. Included are confidence games and bad checks, except forgeries and counterfeiting.

embezzlement Misappropriation or misapplication of money or property entrusted to one's care, custody, or control.

stolen property; buying, receiving, possessing Buying, receiving, and possessing stolen property, including attempts.

vandalism Willful or malicious destruction, injury, disfigurement, or defacement of any public or private property, real or personal, without consent of the owner or persons having custody or control.

weapons; carrying, possessing, etc. All violations of regulations or statutes controlling the carrying, using, possessing, furnishing, and manufacturing of deadly weapons or silencers. Included are attempts.

prostitution and commercialized vice Sex offenses of a commercialized nature, such as prostitution, keeping a bawdy house, procuring, or transporting women for immoral purposes. Attempts are included.

sex offenses (except forcible rape, prostitution, and commercialized vice) Statutory rape and offenses against chastity, common decency, morals, and the like. Attempts are included.

drug abuse violations State and/or local offenses relating to the unlawful possession, sale, use, growing, and manufacturing of narcotic drugs. The following drug categories are specified: opium or cocaine and their derivatives (morphine, heroin, codeine); marijuana; synthetic narcotics—manufactured narcotics that can cause true addiction (demerol, methadone); and dangerous nonnarcotic drugs (barbiturates, benzedrine).

gambling Promoting, permitting, or engaging in illegal gambling.

offenses against the family and children Nonsupport, neglect, desertion, or abuse of family and children.

driving under the influence Driving or operating any vehicle or common carrier while drunk or under the influence of liquor or narcotics.

liquor laws State and/or local liquor law violations, except "drunkenness" and "driving under the influence." Federal violations are excluded.

drunkenness Offenses relating to drunkenness or intoxication. Excluded is "driving under the influence."

disorderly conduct Breach of the peace.

vagrancy Vagabondage, begging, loitering, etc.

all other offenses All violations of state and/or local laws, except those listed above and traffic offenses.

suspicion No specific offense; suspect released without formal charges being placed.

curfew and loitering laws (persons under age 18) Offenses relating to violations of local curfew or loitering ordinances where such laws exist.

runaways (persons under age 18) Limited to juveniles taken into protective custody under provisions of local statutes.

2. NATIONAL CRIME VICTIMIZATION SURVEY

aggravated assault Attack or attempted attack with a weapon, regardless of whether or not an injury occurred and attack without a weapon when serious injury results.

with injury An attack without a weapon when serious injury results or an attack with a weapon involving any injury. Serious injury includes broken bones, lost teeth, internal injuries, loss of consciousness, and any unspecified injury requiring two or more days of hospitalization.

threatened with a weapon Threat or attempted attack by an offender armed with a gun, knife, or other object used as a weapon, not resulting in victim injury.

household burglary Unlawful or forcible entry or attempted entry of a residence. This crime usually, but not always, involves theft. The illegal entry may be by force, such as breaking a window or slashing a screen, or may be without force by entering through an unlocked door or an open window. As long as the person entering has no legal right to be present in the structure a burglary has occurred. Furthermore, the structure need not be the house itself for a burglary to take place; illegal entry of a garage, shed, or any other structure on the premises also constitutes household burglary. If breaking and entering occurs in a hotel or vacation residence, it is still classified as a burglary for the household whose member or members were staying there at the time the entry occurred.

completed burglary A form of burglary in which a person who has no legal right to be present in the structure successfully gains entry to a residence, by use of force, or without force.

forcible entry A form of completed burglary in which force is used to gain entry to a residence. Some examples include breaking a window or slashing a screen.

unlawful entry without force A form of completed burglary committed by someone having no legal right to be on the premises, even though no force is used.

attempted forcible entry A form of burglary in which force is used in an attempt to gain entry.

motor vehicle theft Stealing or unauthorized taking of a motor vehicle, including attempted thefts.

completed motor vehicle theft The successful taking of a vehicle by an unauthorized person.

attempted motor vehicle theft The unsuccessful attempt by an unauthorized person to take a vehicle.

purse snatching/pocket picking Theft or attempted theft of property or cash directly from the victim by stealth, without force or threat of force.

rape Forced sexual intercourse including both psychological coercion as well as physical force. Forced sexual intercourse means vaginal, anal or oral penetration by the offender(s). This category also includes incidents where the penetration is from a foreign object such as a bottle. Includes attempted rapes, male as well as female victims, and both heterosexual and homosexual rape. Attempted rape includes verbal threats of rape.

robbery Completed or attempted theft, directly from a person, of property or cash by force or threat of force, with or without a weapon, and with or without injury.

completed/property taken The successful taking of property from a person by force or threat of force, with or without a weapon, and with or without injury.

completed with injury The successful taking of property from a person, accompanied by an attack, either with or without a weapon, resulting in injury.

completed without injury The successful taking of property from a person by force or the threat of force, either with or without a weapon, but not resulting in injury.

attempted to take property The attempt to take property from a person by force or threat of force without success, with or without a weapon, and with or without injury.

attempted without injury The attempt to take property from a person by force or the threat of force without success, either with or without a weapon, but not resulting in injury.

attempted with injury The attempt to take property from a person without success, accompanied by an attack, either with or without a weapon, resulting in injury.

simple assault Attack without a weapon resulting either in no injury, minor injury (for example, bruises, black eyes, cuts, scratches or swelling) or in undetermined injury requiring less than 2 days of hospitalization. Also includes attempted assault without a weapon.

with minor injury An attack without a weapon resulting in such injuries as bruises, black eyes, cuts or in undetermined injury requiring less than 2 days of hospitalization.

without injury An attempted assault without a weapon not resulting in injury.

theft Completed or attempted theft of property or cash without personal contact. Incidents involving theft of property from within the sample household would classify as theft if the offender has a legal right to be in the house (such as a maid, delivery person, or guest). If the offender has no legal right to be in the house, the incident would classify as a burglary.

completed To successfully take without permission property or cash without personal contact between the victim and offender.

attempted To unsuccessfully attempt to take property or cash without personal contact.

GLOSSARY

abuse of authority Forms of deviance that relate to how the police exercise their authority in dealings with the public

actus reus The wrongful conduct, or activity, that constitutes a crime

adversarial process During a trial the prosecution and the defense are on opposing sides, each seeking to persuade the judge or jury to accept their version of the truth

affirmative action A policy requiring employers to take positive steps to avoid discrimination and to remedy past discrimination

affirmative defense A defense raised by the defendant's counsel, who has the burden of proof and tries to present the undisputed facts of a case in a new light

aggravating circumstance An aspect of a crime that makes it more serious, deserving a harsher penalty

alternative development A drug war strategy that encourages peasants to grow legal crops instead of opium and coca

Anti-Terrorism and Effective Death Penalty Act A 1996 law establishing strict time limits for filing federal *habeas corpus* appeals

Arave v. Creech Use of aggravating circumstances as a basis for imposing the death penalty was ruled constitutional

Argersinger v. Hamlin Defendants have a right to counsel if they could be imprisoned upon conviction

arrest When a person is physically detained by an authorized agent of the state and is not free to leave

asset forfeiture Property and cash are confiscated if they have been used in the commission of crimes or are the fruits of such activities

assigned counsel Private lawyers appointed by judges to represent indigent defendants on a case-by-case basis

Auburn system A system of prison architecture and control, emphasizing strict regimentation of all movement, silent work in small groups, and one-person cells

bail guidelines Standardized instructions to help judges make rational bail decisions based on positive and negative risk factors

banishment Offenders were expelled from their homes and villages

bar exam An examination that law school graduates must pass before they can practice law

Batson v. Kentucky Counsel may not use peremptory challenges to exclude potential jurors simply because they are black

bench trial Evidence is presented to a judge who determines the defendant's guilt or innocence

benefit of clergy A medieval privilege that allowed clergy and certain other offenders to avoid the death penalty

Betts v. Brady Poverty alone is not a reason to provide indigents with counsel

Bill of Rights Ten amendments added to the Constitution in 1791 that specify the rights of citizens

Blanton v. Las Vegas Defendants facing imprisonment of six months or less do not have a right to a jury trial

blended sentencing Dispositions that incorporate traditional juvenile treatment strategies with punishments traditionally imposed on adults

blue code of silence Police officers do not snitch on each other or volunteer potentially damaging information to higher-ups

boot camp Short-term incarceration under close supervision and military-style discipline

Bow Street Runners A famous eighteenth-century police unit in London composed of six salaried thief takers who usually ran to crime scenes

brutalization theory Publicized executions lower inhibitions against violence, thereby promoting more killings

Bureau of Justice Statistics (BJS) Collects data, conducts research, and disseminates results on all aspects of criminal justice

buy-bust Undercover police buy drugs from street dealers who are arrested immediately afterward

capital offense A crime for which the penalty may be death

capital punishment Death by execution

case method Instruction that involves classroom analysis of real courtroom decisions

chain gang A group of prisoners shackled together by chains, working the fields or highways under armed guard

challenge for cause Counsel believes that a potential juror cannot be impartial and asks the judge to remove the juror from the panel

change of venue Moving a trial to another location

Chimel v. California Police may search the area under an arrested suspect's immediate control

circumstantial evidence Any evidence that requires the judge or jury to infer a fact about the case at hand

civil death Loss of citizenship rights if convicted of a felony

civil law A body of written law governing the relationships among individuals and organizations

clearance rate The proportion of crimes that result in arrests

closing arguments Counsel summarize the evidence they want the jury to remember and explain how it supports their version of the facts and not that of their opponent

co-correctional prison A correctional facility that houses both men and women

code of police conduct Informal rules covering how police should behave in general and specific situations

Coffin v. Reichard Federal prisoners have the right to challenge conditions of confinement in federal court

cognizable group People sharing a specific characteristic such as race or sex who are recognized in law as a distinct social category

Coker v. Georgia Death penalty declared cruel and unusual punishment in a rape case

collateral consequences Automatic penalties such as loss of citizenship or loss of the right to serve on a jury or to run for public office

common law A body of national laws created by traveling courts in the twelfth century

community-based corrections Criminal penalties that reduce or eliminate time in prison or ease the transition from prison to freedom

community policing Proactive policing strategies based on close collaboration between the police and the public

community service Offenders are assigned to work on projects that benefit the community

compelling interest When public safety concerns override an individual's right to privacy

complainant A person who calls police about a possible crime

conditions of probation Things offenders must do in order to remain on probation

conflict model Emphasizes differences in interests, values, and needs, and the conflicts that arise as a result

conflict perspective Social order rests on the ability of some people to dominate over others in the struggle for scarce resources

consensual model Inmates cooperate voluntarily with staff in creating order within the prison

consensus model Emphasizes cooperation and compromise based on shared values and goals

consensus perspective Social order rests on agreement among people about basic values and appropriate ways of behaving

constable A local official responsible for keeping the peace

contingent plea agreement The defendant agrees to forfeit or surrender certain assets in exchange for a negotiated plea

continuance A request for a delay in trial proceedings that can be made by either defense or prosecution

contract system (1) Private lawyers enter into an agreement with the court to provide legal services to indigents; (2) using prisoners to complete work contracts for outside employers

control model Rules are enforced quickly and strictly

Cooper v. Pate Prisoners have a constitutional right to practice their religion while confined

cost recovery Using fines to recover some of the costs of catching, prosecuting, and punishing offenders

courthouse work group Criminal justice professionals who handle the daily business of the criminal courts

courts of general jurisdiction Also called superior courts or circuit courts, these courts handle most felony trials and sentence hearings

courts of limited jurisdiction Also called lower courts, these courts handle arraignments and preliminary hearings, misdemeanor trials, and less serious felony trials

crime control model Emphasizes the capacity of the criminal justice system to promote order and safety by arresting, prosecuting, and convicting a high proportion of criminal offenders

crime displacement Occurs when crime prevention efforts result in offenders changing the way they commit offenses or shifting from one type of crime to another

crime prevention Teaching people how to avoid becoming victims of crime, aggressive patrolling of trouble spots, or teaching youngsters to resist drugs

crime prevention model Punishment is justified by its capacity to reduce crime

crime rate A measure of crime conventionally expressed as the number of crimes known to the police for a given year divided by the population for the same year and multiplied by 100,000

crimes known to the police The official count of criminal offenses recorded and reported by police agencies

criminal attorney Prosecutes or defends criminal defendants or handles their appeals

criminalization When acts, events, or people are labeled criminal

criminal justice A society's system of roles and activities for defining and dealing with crime

criminal law A body of written law dealing with the definition of crimes and procedures for dealing with them

cross-examination When counsel questions the other side's witnesses

dark figure of crime All the crimes that do not become part of the official police record

day reporting centers Offenders report in daily and their activities are monitored throughout the day

death-qualified jury When all members of a jury can accept the possibility of imposing the death penalty

decriminalization When the criminal label is removed from acts, events, or people

defeminization When male officers neutralize perceived threats to male dominance by calling female officers unfeminine

defensiveness Being alert to the many dangers of police work and building defenses against them

deinstitutionalization Large-scale movement of people out of prisons, mental hospitals, and juvenile detention centers into the community during the early 1970s

demonstrative evidence Physical objects, including confessions, that can be shown to the judge or jury

depersonalization Denying the personal qualities of individuals and avoiding relationships with members of the public

determinate sentencing Imposition of flat or fixed terms in prison

determinism Human beings are pushed or pulled into behaving a certain way by forces over which they have no control

deterrence doctrine People refrain from crime because they fear being punished for it

deterrent effect When policing reduces crime by increasing the risks and costs of offending relative to its benefits

direct evidence Eyewitness accounts or other evidence that demonstrates a fact about the case at hand

directed police patrols Concentrated uniformed patrols that target specific places or special crime problems within a target area

direct examination When counsel questions its own witnesses

discovery A process in which opposing counsel inform each other about evidence they will produce during trial

discretion Criminal justice officials may choose one action over another on the basis of their professional judgment

diversity training Training designed to improve race and gender relations by raising sensitivity to the cultural differences among individuals and groups

domestic violence Acts or threats of physical harm that occur among members of the same family, intimate friends, or residents of the same household

double jeopardy Being tried twice on the same charges after a verdict has been declared

due process Laws are written and applied in a way that protects individual rights and freedoms

due process model Emphasizes the willingness of the criminal justice system to protect the constitutional rights of citizens and the formal fact-finding process

due process reforms Attempts in the 1950s and 1960s to strengthen the constitutional safeguards afforded juveniles, including right to counsel and to cross-examine witnesses

Duncan v. Louisiana The right to a jury trial exists only for "serious criminal cases"

elective shootings When a police officer can exercise discretion in deciding whether to use deadly force

electronic monitoring Offenders wear wrist or ankle bracelets that trigger alarms if they move beyond a certain area

ethnography A descriptive account of a culture or lifestyle that is obtained through participant observation and/or in-depth conversations with the people involved

exigent circumstances Emergency situations in which warrantless searches are permissible in order to protect lives or prevent the destruction of evidence

Ex parte Hull Prisoners have unrestricted right of access to federal courts

expert witness A person with specialized education, training, or accomplishments in a particular field who testifies on behalf of the prosecution or defense

felony A more serious offense punishable by more than one year in a state or federal prison

field interrogation Police stop citizens for brief questioning; also called "stops"

financial release Defendants are released from jail after payment or promise of payment of money or property, called *bail*

fleeing felon rule Police may use deadly force to stop felony suspects from escaping

formal organization A social structure created to achieve specific goals with written rules governing how activities are carried out and how authority is exercised

founding decision When investigating police decide whether a particular incident should be treated as a crime (founded) or not (unfounded)

Fourteenth Amendment Extended the Bill of Rights to dealings between citizens and their state government

frankpledge system A medieval form of policing that required male citizens to form teams ("tythings") to deliver offenders to court

free will doctrine Human behavior reflects free choices that individuals have made from among alternative courses of action

Furman v. Georgia Death penalty was ruled cruel and unusual punishment as it had been applied

Gagnon v. Scarpelli Probationers faced with revocation have certain rights

gang crime units Specialized police units that track the membership and activities of gangs; also called "gang squads"

gaol (jail) Secure lockup for holding prisoners awaiting trial

general deterrence When people refrain from crime because they fear the punishment that others have received

general theories Theories that explain a broad range of facts in varied social or historical settings

Gideon v. Wainwright Defendants in felony cases have a fundamental right to counsel

good faith exception Evidence obtained illegally by police who nevertheless believed that a search warrant had been properly issued may be used to convict a defendant

grand jury A group of citizens, usually 23, who are assembled to determine whether sufficient evidence exists to warrant prosecution

Gregg v. Georgia Death penalty in itself is not cruel and unusual punishment

hands-off doctrine Wardens were free to run their prisons without external interference

Harris v. Alabama Death penalty statutes need not specify the weight assigned to jury sentence recommendations

hate crime Violence or threats against people solely because of such things as their race, religion, ethnicity, or sexual preference

house arrest Offenders stay at home unless at work or school

house of correction A residential penal institution emphasizing hard work under strict discipline

hue and cry Able-bodied citizens chase noisily after fleeing suspects

hulks Abandoned ships converted into prisons in the late 1700s

ideology The beliefs, opinions, and doctrines that influence the way people explain and deal with the world around them

importation Prison culture is molded by the preprison experiences of inmates and their connections to the outside world

incapacitation Punishment that removes or reduces the opportunity to commit crime

incarceration rate The number of prison inmates per 100,000 U.S. residents

inchoate offenses Incomplete or partial acts that could cause harm if they were actually carried out

independent counsel A private attorney hired to investigate possible crimes by government officials when a conflict of interest exists

indeterminate sentence Imposition of an unspecified amount of prison time between some minimum and maximum

index offenses Eight serious crimes that the FBI uses as a measure of crime in America: criminal homicide, forcible rape, robbery, aggravated assault, burglary, larceny-theft, motor vehicle theft, and arson

indigent defendant A person charged with a crime who does not have the financial resources to hire a private attorney

industrial prison A prison that functioned largely as a factory, producing goods for consumption and for sale

inevitable discovery exception Evidence obtained through illegal questioning of a suspect may be admissible if the police were close to finding it even without the suspect's help

informal organization Friendship networks and work cliques that arise in formal organizations as members respond to their experiences and to the impact of their backgrounds and personalities

initial appearance A defendant's first appearance in court after arrest; usually involves a bail hearing in felony cases

inmate classification A system for identifying similarities and differences among inmates

In re Gault Juveniles facing commitment to an institution are given the same formal rights of due process enjoyed by adult defendants in criminal court

intensive supervised probation (ISP) Close monitoring by probation officers, including surprise visits, and completion of required treatment programs

interactionist perspective Social order is a continuous creation based on everyday interactions in which people respond to the actions and reactions of others

intermediate sanctions Penalties that lie between prison and simple probation

Internal Affairs unit A squad of experienced police officers who investigate allegations of corruption and misconduct, and the circumstances surrounding use of deadly force

J. E. B. v. Alabama Counsel may not use peremptory challenges to exclude jurors simply because of their sex

job-related exercises Real-world simulations and other tests that tap problem-solving skills, sensitivity to others, and reactions to stress

jury consultant An expert on the relationship between the characteristics of jurors and their verdicts

jury foreperson A person selected or elected from among the jurors who leads the deliberations, communicates with the judge when necessary, and in some courts announces the verdict

jury instructions Laying out the law the jury must follow in deciding on its verdict

jury nullification A jury decides on a verdict before all the evidence is presented, without regard for the evidence, or because it wants to make a point despite the evidence

jury trial Evidence is presented to a panel of citizens who try to determine the defendant's guilt or innocence

justice model Punishment is justified by the offender's guilt and matches the gravity of the offense

keeper philosophy Humane treatment of inmates is linked with imposition of penalties when rules are broken

Kent v. United States The juvenile court must provide the "essentials of due process" when transferring juveniles to adult court

Killits Case Judges cannot suspend sentences indefinitely without legislative approval

Klinger v. Nebraska Department of Correctional Services Men and women are not entitled to the same access to prison programs because their prison experiences are different

labeling perspective The meaning and social impact of behavior is established by the reactions to it

labeling theory Crime is a consequence of stigmatization

law enforcement Arresting suspects, infiltrating criminal gangs, or giving traffic tickets

lease system The leasing of prisoners to private contractors

least restrictive means A policy that protects a woman's right to employment in a male prison and the male inmate's right to privacy

legalistic definition of crime Crime is a human act that violates criminal law

leniency hypothesis The idea that police treat men who beat their wives more leniently than men who are violent in other contexts

level of explanation Distinguishes between theories that explain the behavior of individuals and those that explain the behavior of groups, communities, or societies

life course The long-term sequences (for example, work or parenthood) and specific life events (for example, first job or going to college) that people experience from birth to death

Lockhart v. McCree The burden of proving that a death-qualified jury is biased in favor of conviction lies with the defense

Madrid v. Gomez A successful class action suit alleging physical abuse of inmates by staff at the Pelican Bay maximum-security prison

Magna Carta A charter of rights signed by King John of England in 1215 that established principles of due process

mala in se Acts that are evil in themselves

mala prohibita Acts that are evil because they are forbidden

mandatory minimum sentence Imposition of a minimum term in prison

mandatory sentencing Occurs when the law requires judges to impose a certain penalty for a given offense

Manhattan Bail Project A program in New York City during the 1960s showing that most defendants could be released on a simple promise to return to court as required

Mapp v. Ohio Evidence obtained illegally is inadmissible in state courts

Maryland v. Wilson Police may order passengers out of a car during traffic stops

maximum-security prison Emphasizes custody and control and is used to house felons who have committed more serious crimes or are escape risks

McCleskey v. Zant U.S. Supreme Court moved to limit repeated use of *habeas corpus* appeals in capital cases

medical model Emphasizes rehabilitation through diagnosis and treatment of antisocial personalities

medium-security prison Places high priority on security within a more relaxed environment that also emphasizes treatment and rehabilitation

mens rea The intent, or "guilty mind," behind the wrongful conduct

minimum-security prison Usually has no walls or fences, uses minimal control by staff, and emphasizes treatment and rehabilitation programs

Minnesota v. Dickerson Police are not allowed to manipulate objects in a person's pocket during a patdown search if the objects are clearly not a weapon

Miranda warnings Before questioning begins, police inform arrested suspects of their rights and the implications of waiving them

misdemeanor A relatively minor offense punishable by up to one year in jail

mistrial Declared when the jury cannot reach a verdict or when the trial is stopped due to a prejudicial error by counsel or by the death of a juror or attorney

mitigating circumstance An aspect of a crime that makes it less serious, deserving a more lenient penalty

M'Naghten Defense The defendant did not know what he or she was doing at the time of the crime or was unable to distinguish right from wrong

moonlighting Off-duty police officers provide security services to private companies

narcs Undercover police officers who specialize in the street-level drug trade

National Crime Victimization Survey (NCVS) An annual survey of 100,000 people age 12 and older to determine the nature and extent of their victimization by crime

National Criminal Justice Reference Service (NCJRS) Responsible for disseminating all justice-related federal publications and federally funded research

National Incident-Based Reporting System (NIBRS) A nationwide database consisting of individual police records on crimes and related arrests, slated to replace the UCR in 1999

National Youth Survey (NYS) A repeat survey of adolescents who were interviewed each year from 1978 to 1981, and then four more times as adults through 1993

"New Police" (Bobbies) A full-time, uniformed, salaried police organization developed by Sir Robert Peel in 1829 to patrol the streets of London

"No-drop" policy Prosecutors are not allowed to reject cases merely because the victim refuses to cooperate

non-elective shootings When the situation leaves the officer no choice but to use deadly force

nonfinancial release Defendants are released from jail without having to put up bail

occupational deviance Forms of deviance that are made possible by the nature and organization of work

Office of Justice Programs (OJP) A Justice Department agency that oversees criminal justice research, data collection, and training programs for the federal government

Office of Juvenile Justice and Delinquency Prevention (OJJDP) Sponsors programs, collects data, conducts research, and disseminates results specifically on juvenile crime and juvenile justice

opening statement Counsel introduce the jury to some of the evidence and counterevidence that will be presented during the trial

order maintenance The peacekeeping function of policing: handling disputes, dealing with troublemakers, keeping things quiet

pains of imprisonment Rejection, lack of goods and services, deprivation of sexual intimacy, deprivation of autonomy, and loss of physical security

Panopticon Plan A prison designed by eighteenth-century philosopher Jeremy Bentham

paramilitary units Specialized police units trained in the use of military equipment, weapons, and tactics

parens patriae The doctrine that the state should take over the role of parent in dealing with problem children

parole Supervised release of inmates prior to the full completion of their prison term

parole board A group that determines when inmates under indeterminate sentences may be released from prison

parole officer An officer responsible for supervising parolees and assisting them in making the adjustment back into the community

pathology of imprisonment The prison environment encourages staff and inmates to view each other with contempt, according to psychologist Philip Zimbardo

Pennsylvania system A Quaker-influenced system of prison architecture and control, emphasizing solitary confinement and penitence

peremptory challenge Counsel are allowed to remove a certain number of potential jurors without giving their reasons

Plessy v. Ferguson Allowed "separate but equal" facilities for white and black citizens

police culture Shared values, activities, and attitudes that are characteristic of people in law enforcement

police informants People who provide police with information about crimes and criminals in exchange for money or favors; also called "snitches"

police perspective A special way of looking at people, things, and events that emerges from training and day-to-day experiences on the job

politicization Occurs when police operations are heavily influenced by politics

posse comitatus A group of able-bodied men assembled to catch criminals or deal with local emergencies

Powell v. Alabama Defendants charged with a capital crime have the right to counsel

precedent A feature of common law in which prior court rulings guide future judgments; also known as *stare decisis*

preliminary hearing A court hearing to determine whether there is sufficient evidence to proceed with prosecution

premeditation The offender thinks about the crime before committing it

pre-sentence investigation Collects information on the offender's character, family life, work habits, and prior record to guide the sentencing judge

pre-trial diversion Defendants avoid formal prosecution if they successfully complete a community-based treatment or counseling program

pre-trial intensive supervision Released defendants are closely monitored by a probation officer

pre-trial motion A written or oral request made to the judge by prosecution or defense before the trial begins

preventive detention Defendants are detained in jail because they are believed to pose a danger to the community if released

primitive law A system of rules and regulations identifying private wrongs and based on self-help justice through retaliation

prisonization Prison culture is adopted by inmates as they adapt to imprisonment

privatization Occurs when activities and agencies traditionally run by the government are handed over to the private sector

proactive policing Police take an active role in uncovering crime and in trying to prevent it

probable cause The constitutional standard for determining whether a search or an arrest is lawful

probation An alternative to prison or jail that allows offenders to remain in the community under court supervision

problem-oriented policing The identification, analysis, and solution of a crime problem by patrol officers in cooperation with the public

procedural criminal law A body of written law that specifies the rules to be followed by the state when dealing with crimes and criminals

procedural defense The claim that a defendant's rights were violated by police or other criminal justice personnel

professionalization Development of specialized techniques, service ideals, shared language, and professional identity

professionalization of deviance When organizations hide their criminal activities behind legitimate activities and a carefully cultivated image of respectability

profiling An investigative technique that develops a behavioral picture of an offender who is not yet caught

Progressive Era A late nineteenth-century period in which criminal justice reforms took place, centered on rehabilitation and treatment

proportionality The severity of punishment matches the severity of the crime

prosecutor Files charges and represents the state in criminal trials

proximate causes Causes of behavior that are closer to the event or more immediate in their impact

public defender A criminal lawyer and state employee who represents indigent defendants

public execution Capital offenders are put to death in a public place

quotas When organizations hire a certain number of women or minorities regardless of their qualifications

rape shield laws Laws that generally bar the introduction of evidence about a victim's prior sexual conduct

reasonable force Force necessary to achieve a legal goal without endangering innocent citizens

reasonable suspicion On the basis of their training and experience, police believe that an illegal act has been or is about to be committed

recidivism Committing new offenses after being punished for crime

reformation Punishment that builds consciences and promotes conformity

reformatory movement A late nineteenth-century prison movement emphasing inmate reform rather than suffering, and centered on the indeterminate sentence and classification of inmates

rehabilitation Alteration of attitudes and behavior through training, education, work release, and other programs administered along with punishment

rehabilitative ideal Foundation of the reformatory movement, stressing individualized treatment and use of indeterminate sentences

reintegrative shaming Punishment that includes forgiveness and attempts at reconciliation

release on recognizance A nonfinancial release in which the defendant promises to appear in court as required

responsibility model Staff facilitate inmate decision making and restrain inmates only to protect themselves or other inmates

restitution Offenders repay the victims of their crimes, or the community at large, with money or services

restorative justice A response to crime that seeks to restore the well-being of victims and the larger community while promoting responsible and productive behavior in offenders

restorative justice model A system that brings together offenders, victims, and the community in attempts to repair the harm done by crime

restricted theories Theories that explain a narrow range of facts occurring at one time or place, or involving specific groups of people

reverse buy Undercover police pose as dealers and sell to buyers who are arrested immediately afterward; also called a "sting" operation

reverse discrimination The charge that preferential treatment of minorities unfairly penalizes equally well-qualified white applicants

revocation of probation When the supervising court removes offenders from probation because they have failed to meet its conditions

Richards v. Wisconsin The circumstances at the time of an unannounced entry may justify it even if a judge has refused to issue a no-knock search warrant

right to counsel A defendant's constitutional right to the assistance of an attorney during prosecution

routine activity approach Looks at how everyday activities create favorable conditions for crime by bringing motivated offenders and suitable targets together in the absence of capable guardians

Scott v. Illinois Indigent defendants without counsel cannot be sent to jail or prison if convicted

search and seizure When police look for evidence of a crime and take it under their control

search warrant An order issued by a judge and signed by police indicating what is to be seized and where it is expected to be found

segregation A secure unit within the prison that keeps an inmate isolated from other inmates

selective enforcement When police enforce some laws and not others, or enforce laws in some situations but not in others

selective incapacitation: When people most likely to commit crimes if released are given longer prison terms

self-report studies Surveys that ask people whether they have committed crimes during a given period of time

sentence The specific penalty for a specific crime

sentencing disparities When different sentences are imposed on offenders convicted of essentially the same offense

sentencing guidelines A standardized set of penalty options based on information about the offense and the offender

service function Providing assistance to citizens with problems

sheriff The top county official authorized to collect taxes and to enforce the king's laws

shock incarceration Short-term incarceration as a way of scaring offenders from more serious crimes; also another term for boot camp

situational crime prevention Attempts to reduce or prevent crimes by removing the opportunities and inducements associated with the situations in which they typically occur

situational defense A defense against criminal charges based on circumstances surrounding the incident

social order The forces that hold society together

social process perspectives Theories of crime based on more proximate causes located in the social experiences of individuals

social structure perspectives Theories of crime based on background causes located in the organization and culture of societies

specific deterrence When people who have experienced punishment in the past refrain from crime because they fear they will be punished again

speedy trial The constitutional right to be tried within a reasonable time after arrest, usually 120 to 160 days

Stack v. Boyle Defendants should be allowed bail if there is adequate assurance that they will appear in court

state-use system Prison industries supply goods for use by state agencies

status offenses Delinquent acts such as truancy and running away that only juveniles can commit

stop and frisk A warrantless "patdown" search of a person's outer clothing during a field interrogation

straight buy Undercover police buy drugs from dealers over a period of months; the dealers are then arrested en masse

styles of policing Characteristic ways that police in different communities respond to the demands of the job

substantial assistance rule Defendants who give significant help to police or prosecution may receive a lighter sentence for themselves

substantial capacity test The defendant is unable to understand the wrongfulness of an act or to conform to the requirements of the law

substantive criminal law A body of written law that defines crimes and specifies the criminal penalties associated with them

supermaximum-security prison A facility with the highest legal levels of security and inmate control

suspended sentence The penalty for a crime is not imposed if the offender stays out of trouble for a specified time

Swain v. Alabama Counsel may use peremptory challenges to exclude members of certain groups

technical violation When probationers fail to report in or to complete a required program

Tennessee v. Garner Declared the fleeing felon rule unconstitutional

terrorism Violence or threats against individuals, organizations, or governments in furtherance of political or social objectives

Terry v. Ohio Police may stop people whose behavior leads them to conclude, in the light of their experience, that a crime is being or is about to be committed

testimonial evidence Oral statements given under oath

thief taker An eighteenth-century version of the American bounty hunter

Thompson v. Oklahoma, Stanford v. Kentucky Two cases in which the U.S. Supreme Court ruled that the execution of people under age 16 at the time of their offense would be cruel and unusual punishment

"three strikes" laws Mandate life in prison if convicted of a third felony

total institution A closed social system such as a prison, the military, or a mental hospital that completely envelops the lives of the people living or working in it

transnational crime Criminal activity such as money laundering and gun running that crosses the borders of nation states

transportation Offenders were sent by ship to a penal colony in another country

truth-in-sentencing laws State that offenders must serve most or all of their sentences before being released

Uniform Crime Reports (UCR) An FBI program that collects and disseminates national data on crimes known to the police and on arrests

United States v. Granderson Offenders whose probation has been revoked cannot be given a longer prison term than they would have received at the original sentencing

United States v. Paradise Alabama is ordered to achieve racial balance in its Department of Public Safety without laying off any white officers

United States v. Reynolds A judge is not required to define "reasonable doubt" in instructions to the jury

utilitarianism A philosophy founded on the principle of the greatest happiness of the greatest number

vertical prosecution One assistant prosecutor handles a case from beginning to end

victim blaming When responsibility for a possible crime is shifted from the defendant to the victim

Victim Impact Statement (VIS) A report to the sentencing judge listing the effects of a crime on the victim(s)

victimization surveys Surveys that ask people whether they have been victims of crime during a given period of time

victimless crimes Illegal activities that involve willing participants, such as drug use, prostitution, and gambling

Wainwright v. Witt Jurors may be excused for cause if their views on the death penalty would "substantially impair" their role as jurors

warehousing Housing large numbers of violent and repeat offenders in maximum-security prisons with minimal privileges and few, if any, rehabilitation programs

warrantless search Police search people or their possessions without the authorization of a judge

warrant office An office staffed by assistant prosecutors who screen cases and advise police on legal issues

watch system The first formal system of policing in which property owners took turns guarding the town during the night

Weeks v. United States Established the "exclusionary rule" that evidence unlawfully obtained cannot be used to convict a defendant

Wilson v. Arkansas There is no blanket rule covering when the police may or may not enter a private dwelling without knocking and announcing their presence

Witherspoon v. Illinois A distinction was drawn between jurors with qualms about the death penalty and jurors whose opposition would automatically lead them to vote against imposing it

workhouse A dwelling where poor and homeless people lived and worked under strict supervision

working personality Develops when elements in police work such as suspicion and danger create a unique way of looking at the world and responding to it

writ of *habeas corpus* A legal procedure that forces courts to review the legality of a person's imprisonment

References

Abadinsky, Howard (1990). *Organized Crime,* 3rd ed. Chicago: Nelson-Hall.

Abbott, Jack Henry (1981). *In the Belly of the Beast.* New York: Vintage.

Agnew, Robert (1990). "Adolescent Resources and Delinquency." *Criminology* 28:535–566.

Agnew, Robert (1992). "Foundation for a General Strain Theory of Crime and Delinquency." *Criminology* 30:47–87.

Agnew, Robert (1995). "Controlling Delinquency: Recommendations from General Strain Theory." In Hugh D. Barlow, ed., *Crime and Public Policy: Putting Theory to Work.* Boulder: Westview Press.

Alix, Ernest K. (1969). "The Functional Interdependence of Crime and Community Social Structure," *Journal of Criminal Law, Criminology, and Police Science* 60:332–339.

Allen, Francis A. (1964). *The Borderland of Criminal Justice.* Chicago: University of Chicago Press.

——— (1974). *The Crimes of Politics.* Cambridge, Mass.: Harvard University Press.

Allen, Harry E., and Clifford E. Simonsen (1995). *Corrections in America.* Upper Saddle River, N.J.: Prentice-Hall.

Allison, Julie A., and Lawrence S. Wrightsman (1993). *Rape: The Misunderstood Crime.* Newbury Park, Calif.: Sage.

Alpert, Geoffrey P. (1984). "The Needs of the Judiciary and Misapplication of Social Research: The Case of Female Guards in Men's Prisons." *Criminology* 22:441–455.

——— (1991), "Hiring and Promoting Police Officers in Small Departments—The Role of Psychological Testing," *Criminal Law Bulletin* 27:250–265.

Alpert, Geoffrey P., and Roger G. Dunham (1988). *Policing Urban America.* Prospect Heights, Ill.: Waveland Press.

Alschuler, Albert W. (1978). "Sentencing Reform and Prosecutorial Power: A Critique of Recent Proposals for 'Fixed' and 'Presumptive' Sentencing," in *Determinate Sentencing: Reform or Regression, Proceedings of the Special Conference on Determinate Sentencing,* University of California, Berkeley, June 2–3, 1977.

American Bar Association (1994). "Model Adult Community Corrections Act." *Community Corrections Report* 1:3–8.

——— *Facts About the American Criminal Justice System.* Chicago: American Bar Association.

American Bar Foundation (1994). *Lawyer Statistical Report: The U.S. Legal Profession in the 1990s.* Chicago: American Bar Association.

American Correctional Association (1998). *1998 Directory of Juvenile and Adult Correctional Departments, Institutions, Agencies and Paroling Authorities.* Laurel, MD: American Correctional Association.

Amnesty International (1997). *The Death Penalty: Facts and Figures, August, 1997.* On line at **http://www.amnesty.org/ailib/intcam/dp**

Anderson, Elijah (1994). "The Code of the Streets." *The Atlantic Monthly* 273:81–94.

Andrews, D. A., Ivan Zinger, Robert D. Hoge, James Bonta, Paul Gendreau, and Francis T. Cullen (1990). "Does Correctional Treatment Work? A Clinically Relevant and Psychologically Informed Meta-Analysis." *Criminology* 28:369–404.

Archer, Dane, and Rosemary Gartner (1984). *Violence and Crime in Cross-National Perspective.* New Haven, Conn.: Yale University Press.

Ares, Charles E., Anne Rankin, and Herbert Sturz (1963). "The Manhattan Bail Project: An Interim Report on the Use of Pre-Trial Parole," *New York University Law Review* 83:68–95.

Asbill, H. W. (1994). "Ten Commandments of Cross-Examination Revisited." *Criminal Justice* 8:2–6, 51–54.

Augustus, John ([1852] 1939). *First Probation Officer.* New York: Probation Association.

Austin, James, and Barry Krisberg (1981). "Wider, Stronger, and Different Nets: The Dialectics of Criminal Justice Reform." *Journal of Research in Crime and Delinquency* 18: 165–183.

Austin, James, and Barry Krisberg (1982). "The Unmet Promise of Alternatives to Incarceration." *Crime and Delinquency* 28:374–409.

Austin, William, and Thomas A. Williams III (1977). "A Survey of Judges' Responses to Legal Cases: Research Notes on Sentencing Disparity." *Journal of Criminal Law and Criminology* 68:306–310.

Babbington, Anthony (1968). *The Power to Silence.* London: Robert Maxwell.

Bachman, Ronet (1994). "Violence and Theft in the Workplace." *BJS Crime Data Brief* (July):1–2.

Bacon, Sheldon (1935). *The Early Development of American Municipal Police.* Ph.D. diss., Yale University.

Bailey, Ronald H. (1976). *Violence and Aggression.* New York: Time Life Books.

Bailey, William C. (1990). "Murder, Capital Punishment, and Television: Execution Publicity and Homicide Rates." *American Sociological Review* 55:628–633.

——— (1998). "Deterrence, Brutalization, and the Death Penalty; Another Examination of Oklahoma's Return to Capital Punishment." *Criminology* 36:711–733.

Bailey, William C., and Ruth D. Peterson (1994). "Murder, Capital Punishment, and Deterrence: A Review of the Evidence and an Examination of Police Killings." *Journal of Social Issues* 50:53–74.

Baker, Michael A., and Alan F. Westin (1987). *Employer Perceptions of Workplace Crime.* Washington, D.C.: U.S. Department of Justice.

Balch, Robert (1977). "The Police Personality: Fact or Fiction?" In David Kennedy, ed., *The Dysfunctional Alliance: Emotion and Reason in Justice Administration.* Cincinnati, Ohio: Anderson.

Baldus, David, Charles Pulaski, and George Woodworth (1983). "Comparative Review of Death Sentences: An Empirical Review of the Georgia Experience." *Journal of Criminal Law and Criminology* 74:661–753.

Banton, Michael (1973). *Police Community Relations.* London: William Collins.

Barber, S. (1987). *News Cameras in the Courtroom.* Norwood, N.J.: Ablex.

Barker, Thomas (1994). "Peer Group Support for Police Occupational Deviance." In Thomas Barker, and David L. Carter, eds., *Police Deviance*, 3rd ed. Cincinnati, Ohio: Anderson.

Barker, Thomas, and David L. Carter, eds. (1994). *Police Deviance*, 3rd ed. Cincinnati, Ohio: Anderson.

Barker, Thomas, Rodney N. Friery, and David L. Carter (1994). "After L.A., Would your Local Police Lie?" In Thomas Barker and David L. Carter, eds., *Police Deviance,* 3rd ed. Cincinnati, Ohio: Anderson.

Barlow, David E., and Melissa H. Barlow (1993). "Cultural Diversity Training in Criminal Justice: A Progressive or Conservative Reform?" *Social Justice* 20:69–85.

Barlow, Hugh D. (1976) "Crime Victims and the Sentencing Process." Paper presented at the 2nd International Symposium of Victimology, Boston, Massachusetts, September.

——— (1987)."Of Secrets and Visions: Stanley Cohen on Crime Control." *Journal of Criminal Law and Criminology* 78:430–441.

——— (1989). "The Good, the Bad, and the Ugly: Perceptions of Policing in a Bankrupt City." Presented at the Annual Meeting of the American Society of Criminology, Reno, Nevada, November.

——— (1991). "Explaining Crimes and Analogous Acts, or The Unrestrained Will Grab at Pleasure Whenever They Can." *Journal of Criminal Law and Criminology* 82:229–242.

——— (1993). "From Fiddle Factors to Networks of Collusion: Charting the Waters of Small Business Crime." *Crime, Law and Social Change* 20:319–337.

——— (1996). *Introduction to Criminology,* 7th ed. New York: HarperCollins.

Barlow, Hugh D., and Theodore N. Ferdinand (1992). *Understanding Delinquency.* New York: HarperCollins.

Barnes, Carole Wolf, and Rodney Kingsnorth (1996). "Race, Drugs, and Criminal Sentencing: Hidden Effects of the Criminal law." *Journal of Criminal Justice* 24:39–55.

Barnett, Arnold (1985). "Some Distribution Patterns for the Georgia Death Sentence." *University of California-Davis Law Review* 18:1327–1374.

Bastion, Lisa (1995). "Criminal Victimization, 1993." *BJS Bulletin* (May):1–6.

Battin, Sara R., Karl G. Hill, Robert D. Abbott, Richard F. Catalano, and J. David Hawkins (1998). "The Contribution of Gang Membership to Delinquency Beyond Delinquent Friends." *Criminology* 36:93–115.

Bauman, M., and M. Ottenad (1994). *Report of the Oregon Supreme Court Task Force on Racial/Ethnic Issues in the Judicial System.* Salem, Ore.: Office of the State Court Administrator.

Baumer, Terry I., and Robert I. Mendelsohn (1989). "The Electronic Monitoring of Nonviolent Convicted Felons." Unpublished report to the National Institute of Justice.

Baunach, Phyllis Jo (1979). "Mothering from Behind Prison Walls." Paper presented to the Annual meeting of the American Society of Criminology, San Francisco, California, November.

Bayley, David H. (1998). *What Works in Policing.* New York: Oxford University Press.

Bayley, David H., and Harold Mendelsohn (1968). *Minorities and the Police: Confrontation in America.* New York: Free Press.

Bazemore, Gordon, and Lynette Feder (1997). "Judges in the Punitive Juvenile Court: Organizational, Career and Ideological Influences on Sanctioning Orientation." *Justice Quarterly* 14:87–114.

Bazemore, Gordon, and Susan E. Day (1996). "Restoring the Balance: Juvenile and Community Justice." *Juvenile Justice* III (December):3–14.

Bazemore, Gordon, and Mark S. Umbreit (1994). *Balanced and Restorative Justice.* Washington, D.C.: U.S. Department of Justice.

Beccaria, Cesare (1963). *Essay on Crimes and Punishments,* trans. by Henry Paolucci. Indianapolis, Ind.: Bobbs-Merrill.

Beck, Allen J., and Darrell K. Gilliard (1995). "Prisoners in 1994." *BJS Bulletin* (August):1–12.

Beck, Allen J., and Lawrence A. Greenfeld (1995). "Violent Offenders in State Prison: Sentences and Time Served." *BJS Selected Findings* (July):1–12.

Becker, Gary S. (1968). "Crime and Punishment: An Economic Approach." *Journal of Political Economy* 76:493–517.

Becker, Howard S. (1963). *Outsiders: Studies in the Sociology of Deviance.* New York: Free Press.

Bedau, Hugo A. (1994). "American Populism and the Death Penalty: Witnesses at an Execution." *Howard Journal of Criminal Justice* 33:289–303.

Bell, Daniel J. (1982). "Policewomen: Myths and Reality." *Journal of Police Science and Administration* 10:112–120.

Bennett, B. R. (1995). "Incoroprating Diversity: Police Response to Multicultural Changes in their Communities." *FBI Law Enforcement Bulletin* 64:7.

Bennett, James (1981). *Oral History and Delinquency: The Rhetoric of Criminology.* Chicago: University of Chicago Press.

Benson, Michael L., William J. Maakestad, Francis T. Cullen, and Gilbert Geis (1988). "District Attorneys and Corporate Crime: Surveying the Prosecutorial Gatekeepers." *Criminology* 26:505–516.

Bent, Alan Edward (1974). *The Politics of Law Enforcement.* Lexington, Mass.: D.C. Heath.
Bentham, Jeremy (1948). *The Principles of Morals and Legislation.* New York: Hofner Publishing.
Berg, Bruce, and Kimberly Budnick (1986). "Defeminization of Women in Law Enforcement: A New Twist in the Traditional Police Personality." *Journal of Police Science and Administration* 14:314–319.
Berk, Richard A., Jack Boyer, and Robert Weiss (1993). "Chance and the Death Penalty." *Law and Society Review* 27:89–110.
Bernard, Thomas J. (1992). *The Cycle of Juvenile Justice.* New York: Oxford University Press.
Beyleveld, Deryck (1980). *A Bibliography on General Deterrence.* London: Saxon House.
Bittner, Egon, and Anthony M. Platt (1966). "The Meaning of Punishment." *Issues in Criminology* 2:81–105.
Black, Donald J. (1970). "Production of Crime Rates." *American Sociological Review* 35:733–748.
——— (1971) "The Social Organizaton of Arrest." *Stanford Law Review* 23:1087–1111.
——— (1980). *The Manners and Customs of the Police.* New York: Academic Press.
Blackstone, Sir William (1962). *Commentaries on the Laws of England,* vol. 4. Boston: Beacon Press.
Bleackely, H. (1929). *The Hangmen of England.* London: Chapman and Hall.
Bleich, Jeff (1989). "The Politics of Prison Crowding." *California Law Review* 77:5–35.
Bloch, Peter, and Deborah Anderson (1974). *Policewomen on Patrol: Final Report.* Washington, D.C.: Police Foundation.
Block, Carolyn Rebbecca, and Richard Block (1993). "Street Gang Crime in Chicago." *NIJ Research in Brief* (December):1–11.
Block, Alan A., and Frank Scarpitti (1986). "Casinos and Banking: Organized Crime in the Bahamas." *Deviant Behavior* 7:301–312.
Blomberg, Thomas G., William Bales, and Karen Reed (1993). "Intermediate Punishment: Retributing or Extending Social Control?" *Crime, Law, and Social Change* 19:187–201.
Blumberg, Abraham S. (1967). "The Practice of Law as a Confidence Game: Organizational Cooptation of a Profession." *Law and Society Review* 1:15–39.
Blumenthal, Monica, Robert L. Kahn, Frank M. Andrews, and Kendra B. Head (1972). *Justifying Violence:* Attitudes of American Men. Ann Arbor, Mich.: Institute for Social Research.
Blumer, Herbert (1969). *Symbolic Interactionism: Perspective and Method.* Upper Saddle River, N.J.:Prentice-Hall.
Blumstein, Alfred (1993). "Making Rationality Relevant—The American Society of Criminology 1992 Presidential Address." *Criminology* 31:1–16.
Blumstein, Alfred, and H. John Heinz III (1995). "Youth Violence, Guns and the Illicit-Drug Industry." In Carolyn Block and Richard Block, eds., *Trends, Risks, and Interventions in Lethal Violence.* Washington, D.C.: U.S. Department of Justice.
Boggs, Sarah Lee (1964). "The Ecology of Crime Occurrence in St. Louis: A Reconceptualization." Ph.D. diss., St. Louis, Mo.: Washington University.
Bohm, Robert M. (1991). *The Death Penalty in America: Current Research.* Cincinnati, Ohio: Anderson.
Bohm, Robert M., Ronald E. Vogel, and Albert A. Maisto (1993). "Knowledge and Death Penalty Opinion: A Panel Study." *Journal of Criminal Justice* 21:29–45.
Bonczar, Thomas P., and Allen J. Beck (1997). "Lifetime Likelihood of Going to State or Federal Prison." *BJS Special Report* (March):1–13.
Borgida, Eugene, Kenneth G. DeBono, and Lee A. Buckman (1990). "Cameras in the Courtroom: The Effects of Media Coverage on Witness Testimony and Juror Perceptions." *Law and Human Behavior* 14:489–509.
Bottomley, A. Keith (1970). *Prison Before Trial.* London: G. Bells and Sons.
——— (1973). *Decisions in the Penal Process.* London: Martin Robinson.
Bottomley, A. Keith, and C. Coleman (1981). *Understanding Crime Rates.* Farnborough, England: Gower.
Bowers, William J. (1974). *Executions in America.* Lexington, Mass.: D.C. Heath.
——— (1988). "The Effect of Executions Is Brutalization, Not Deterrence." In Kenneth C. Hess and James A. Inciardi, eds., *Capital Punishment: Legal and Social Science Approaches.* Newbury Park, Calif.: Sage.
Bowker, Lee H. (1980). *Prison Victimization: A Gruesome Catalogue of Unintended Punishments.* New York: Elsevier.
Box, Steven (1981). *Deviance, Reality, and Society*, 2nd ed. London: Holt, Rinehart, and Winston.
——— (1983). *Power, Crime, and Mystification.* London: Tavistock.
Braithwaite, John (1978). "An Exploratory Study of Used Car Fraud." In P. R. Wilson and J. B. Braithwaite, eds., *Two Kinds of Deviance: Crimes of the Powerless and Powerful.* Brisbane: University of Queensland Press.
——— (1989). *Crime, Shame and Reintegration.* Cambridge, England: Cambridge University Press.
——— (1995). "Reintegrative Shaming, Republicanism, and Policy." In Hugh D. Barlow, ed., *Crime and Public Policy: Putting Theory to Work.* Boulder, Colo.: Westview Press.
Braithwaite, John, and Philip Pettit (1990). *Not Just Deserts: A Republican Theory of Criminal Justice.* Oxford, England: Oxford University Press.
Braly, Malcolm (1977). *False Starts: A Memoir of San Quentin and other Prisons.* New York: Penguin Books.
Brantingham, Paul J., and Patricia L. Brantingham (1981). *Environmental Criminology.* Beverly Hills, Calif.: Sage.
Britton, Dana M. (1997). "Perceptions of Work Environment Among Correctional Officers: Do Race and Sex Matter?" *Criminology* 35:85–105.
Brockway, Zebulon R. ([1912] 1969). *Fifty Years of Prison Service: An Autobiography.* Montclair, N.J.: Patterson Smith.
Brosi, Kathleen B. (1979). *A Cross-City Comparison of Felony Case Processing.* Washington, D.C.: U.S. Government Printing Office.

Brown, David, Tom Ellis, and Karen Larcombe (1992). *Changing the Code: Police Detention under the Revised PACE Codes of Practice.* London: HMSO.

Brown, Jodi M., and Patrick A. Langan (1998). *State Court Sentencing of Convicted Felons, 1994.* Washington, D.C.: U.S. Department of Justice.

Brown, Michael (1988). *Working the Streets: Police Discretion and Dilemmas of Reform.* New York: Russell Sage.

Brown, Michael P., and Preston Elrod (1995). "Electronic House Arrest: An Examination of Citizen Attitudes." *Crime and Delinquency* 41:332–246.

Browne, Angela (1987). *When Battered Women Kill.* New York: Macmillan.

Brownmiller, Susan (1975). *Against Our Will.* New York: Simon and Schuster.

Burbeck, Elizabeth, and Adrian Furnham (1985). "Police Officer Selection: A Critical Review of the Literature," *Journal of Police Science and Administration* 3:58–69.

Bureau of Justice Assistance (1989). *Disclosing Hidden Assets: Plea Bargains and the Use of the Polygraph.* Washington D.C.: U.S. Department of Justice.

——— (1993). *Problem-Oriented Drug Enforcement.* Washington, D.C.: U.S. Department of Justice.

——— (1996). *National Assessment of Structured Sentencing.* Washington, D.C.: U.S. Department of Justice.

——— (1997). *A Policymaker's Guide to Hate Crimes.* Washington, D.C.: U.S. Department of Justice.

Bureau of Justice Statistics (1985). *Special Report: Reporting Crimes to the Police.* Washington, D.C.: U.S. Department of Justice.

——— (1988a). *Crime and Justice in America,* 2nd ed. Washington, D.C.: U.S. Department of Justice.

——— (1988). "Criminal Defense of the Poor, 1986." *BJS Bulletin* (September):1–6.

——— (1989). "Recidivism of Prisoners Released in 1983." *BJS Special Report* (April):1–13.

——— (1991a). *Bulletin: Prisoners in 1990.* Washington, D.C.: U.S. Department of Justice.

——— (1991b). *Jail Inmates, 1990.* Washington, D.C.: U.S. Department of Justice.

——— (1991c). *Pretrial Release of Felony Defendants, 1988:* National Pretrial Reporting Program. Washington, D.C.: U.S. Department of Justice.

——— (1991d). *Special Report: Women in Prison.* Washington, D.C.: U.S. Department of Justice.

——— (1992a). *National Update,* vol. 2. Washington, D.C.: U.S. Department of Justice.

——— (1992b). *The Prosecution of Felony Arrests.* Washington, D.C.: U.S. Department of Justice.

——— (1993a). *Census of State and Local Law Enforcement Agencies, 1992.* Washington, D.C.: U.S. Department of Justice.

——— (1993b). *Highlights from 20 Years of Surveying Crime Victims.* Washington, D.C.: U.S. Department of Justice.

——— (1993c). *National Corrections Reporting Program, 1990.* Washington, D.C.: U.S. Department of Justice.

——— (1993d). *National Update,* vol. 3. Washington, D.C.: U.S. Department of Justice.

——— (1993e). "Prosecutors in State Courts, 1992." *BJS Bulletin* (December):1–8.

——— (1993f), *Recidivism of Felons on Probation, 1986–1989.* Washington, D.C.: U.S. Department of Justice.

——— (1993g). *Survey of State Prison Inmates, 1991.* Washington, D.C.: U.S. Department of Justice.

——— (1994a). *Criminal Victimization in the United States: 1973–1992 Trends.* Washington, D.C.: U.S. Department of Justice.

——— (1994b). *Demonstrating the Operational Utility of Incident-Based Data for Local Crime Analysis.* Washington, D.C.: U.S. Department of Justice.

——— (1994c) "Fact Sheet: Drug Data Summary." *BJS Drugs and Crime Data* (July):1–5.

——— (1994d). *State Court Organization, 1993.* Washington, D.C.: U.S. Department of Justice.

——— (1994e). "Violence Between Intimates." *BJS Selected Findings* (November): 1–10.

——— (1994f), *Violence Against Women.* Washington, D.C.: U.S. Department of Justice.

——— (1995a). *Drugs and Crime Facts, 1994.* Washington, D.C.: U.S. Department of Justice.

——— (1995b). *Felony Sentences in State Courts, 1992.* Washington, D.C.: U.S. Department of Justice.

——— (1995c). "Prison Sentences and Time Served for Violence." *BJS Selected Findings* (April):1–3.

——— (1995d). "Prisoners in 1994." *BJS Bulletin* (August):1–16.

——— (1995e). *State Court Organization, 1993.* Washington, D.C.: U.S. Department of Justice.

——— (1995f). "Violent Offenders in State Prison: Sentences and Time Served," *BJS Selected Findings* (July):1–10.

——— (1996a). "Capital Punishment, 1994." *BJS Bulletin* (February):1–15.

——— (1996b). *Compendium of Federal Justice Statistics.* Washington D.C.: U.S. Department of Justice.

——— (1996b). "Capital Punishment 1994." *BJS Bulletin* (February):1–15.

——— (1996c). *Correctional Populations in the United States, 1994.* Washington, D.C.: U.S. Department of Justice.

——— (1996d). *Federal Criminal Case Processing, 1982–1992.* Washington, D.C.: U.S. Department of Justice.

——— (1996e). *Federal Criminal Case Processing, 1982–1993, With Preliminary Data for 1994.* Washington, D.C.: U.S. Department of Justice.

——— (1996f). *Fiscal Year 1996 at a Glance.* Washington D.C.: U.S. Department of Justice.

——— (1996g). "Indigent Defense." *BJS Selected Findings* (February):1–4.

——— (1996h), "Prison and Jail Inmates, 1995." *BJS Bulletin* (August):1–16.

——— (1997a). *Adults on Probation, 1995.* Washington, D.C.: U.S. Department of Justice.

——— (1997b). *Changes in Criminal Victimization, 1994–1995.* Washington, D.C.: U.S. Department of Justice.

——— (1997c). *Correctional Populations in the United States, 1995.* Washington, D.C.: U.S. Department of Justice.

——— (1997d). *Privacy and Juvenile Justice Records: A Mid-Decade Status Report.* Washington, D.C.: U.S. Department of Justice.

——— (1997e). *Probation and Parole Populations, 1996.* Washington, D.C.: U.S. Department of Justice.

——— (1997f). "Study of NIBRS Reporting to Law Enforcement Agencies." *BJS On-line.*

——— (1998a). *Criminal Victimization in the United States, 1995.* Washington, D.C.: U.S. Department of Justice.

——— (1998b). *Bureau of Justice Statistics Fiscal Year 1998: At a Glance.* Washington D.C.: U.S. Department of Justice.

Burkhart, Kathryn Watterson (1978). *Women in Prison.* New York: Popular Library Edition.

Bush, Tracey, and John Hood-Williams (1995). "Domestic Violence on a London Housing Estate." *Home Office Research Bulletin* 37:11–18.

Butler, Paul (1995). "Racially Based Jury Nullification: Black Power in the Criminal Justice System." *Yale Law Journal* 105:677–725.

Butts, Jeffrey A. (1996). "Offenders in Juvenile Court, 1994." *OJJDP Juvenile Justice Bulletin* (October):1–12.

——— (1997) "Delinquency Cases Waived to Criminal Courts, 1985–1994." *OJJDP Fact Sheet* 52:1–2.

Camp, George M., and Camille Graham Camp (1993). *The Corrections Yearbook 1993: Adult Corrections.* South Salem, NY.: Criminal Justice Institute.

Campbell, Alec, Richard A. Berk, and James J. Fyfe (1998). "Deployment of Violence: The Los Angeles Police Department's Use of Dogs." *Evaluation Review* 22:535–560.

Campbell, Ann (1984). *Girls in the Gang.* Oxford, England: Basil Blackwell.

Cannavale, Frank J. (1976). *Witness Cooperation.* Lexington, Mass.: D.C. Heath.

Canter, David (1994). *Criminal Shadows: Inside the Mind of a Serial Killer.* London: HarperCollins.

Carroll, Leo (1982). "Humanitarian Reform and Biracial Sexual Assault in a Maximum Security Prison." In Anthony M. Scacco, Jr., ed., *Male Rape.* New York: AMS Press.

Carter, David L., Allen D. Sapp, and Darrel W. Stephens (1989). *The State of Police Education: Policy Direction for the 21st Century.* Washington, D.C.: Police Executive Research Forum.

Carter, Robert W. (1993). "Keeping a Secure Courthouse," *Judicature* 76:314–318.

Carter, Robert M., and Leslie T. Wilkins (1967). "Some Factors in Sentencing Policy." *Journal of Criminal Law, Criminology, and Police Science* 58:503–514.

Carter, Ronald L., and Kim Q. Hill (1979). *The Criminal's Image of the City.* New York: Pergamon.

Casper, Jonathan D. (1972). *American Criminal Justice: The Defendant's Perspective.* Upper Saddle River, N.J.: Prentice-Hall.

Cavadino, Michael, and James Dignan (1992). *The Penal System.* Newbury Park, Calif.: Sage.

CEGA (1995). *Corrections Compendium.* Lincoln, Neb.: CEGA Publishing.

Cernkovich, Stephen A., Peggy C. Giordano, and Meredith D. Pugh (1985). "Chronic Offenders: The Missing Cases in Self-Report Delinquency Research." *Journal of Criminal Law and Criminology* 76:705–732.

Chaiken, Marcia R., and Jan M. Chaiken (1991). "Priority Prosecution of High Rate Dangerous Offenders." *NIJ Research in Action* (March):1–8.

Chambliss, William J. (1973). "The Saints and the Roughnecks," *Society* 11:24–31.

——— (1975). *Criminal Law in Action.* Santa Barbara, Calif.: Hamilton.

——— (1978). *On the Take: From Petty Crooks to Presidents.* Bloomington, Ind.: Indiana University Press.

Chambliss, William J., and Robert B. Siedman (1971). *Law and Order.* Reading, Mass.: Addison-Wesley.

Champion, Dean J. (1997). *The Roxbury Dictionary of Criminal Justice.* Los Angeles: Roxbury Publishing Company.

Chandler, Kathryn A., Christopher D. Chapman, Michael R. Rand, and Bruce M. Taylor (1998). *Students' Reports of School Crime: 1989 and 1995.* Washington, D.C.: U.S. Department of Justice.

Chapman, Dennis (1968). *Sociology and the Stereotype of the Criminal.* London: Tavistock.

Charles, Michael T. (1982). "Women in Policing: The Physical Aspects." *Journal of Police Science and Administration* 10:194–205.

Chemerisky, Erwin (1995). "Trial Over, Simpson Analyst Re-evaluates." *ABA Law Journal* (December):99–101.

Chesney-Lind, Meda (1987a). *Girls' Crime and Women's Place: Toward a Feminist Model of Female Delinquency.* Honolulu, Hawaii: University of Hawaii Youth Development and Research Center.

——— (1987b). "Female Status Offenders and the Double Standard of Juvenile Justice: An International Problem." Presented at the Annual Meeting of the American Society of Criminology, Montreal, November 11–14.

——— "Girls in Jail," *Crime and Delinquency* 34:150–168.

Chesney-Lind, Meda, and Randall G. Shelden (1992). *Girls, Delinquency, and Juvenile Justice.* Pacific Grove, Calif.: Brooks/Cole.

Christianson, Scott (1995). "Defective Electronic Equipment May Lead to Further Criminal and Civil Liability." *Community Corrections Report* (July/August):3–4.

Christie, Nils (1993). *Crime Control as Industry.* London: Routledge.

Clark, Cherie L., David W. Aziz, and Doris L. Mackenzie (1994). "Shock Incarceration in New York: Focus on Treatment." *NIJ Program Focus* (August):2–11.

Clark, John, James Austin, and D. Alan Henry (1997). "'Three Strikes and You're Out': A Review of State Legislation." *NIJ Research in Brief* (September):1–14.

Clarke, Ronald V. (1988). "Situational Crime Prevention: Its Theoretical Basis and Practical Scope." In Michael Tonry and Norval Morris, eds., *Crime and Justice: An Annual Review of Research, vol 6.* Chicago: University of Chicago Press.

Clarke, Ronald V., ed. (1992). *Situational Crime Prevention: Successful Case Studies.* New York: Harrow and Heston.

——— (1997). *Situational Crime Prevention: Successful Case Studies,* 2nd ed. New York: Harrow and Heston.

Clarke, Ronald V., and Patricia Mayhew, eds. (1980). *Designing Out Crime.* London: HMSO.

Clear, Todd R., John D. Hewitt, and Robert M. Regoli (1978). "Discretion and the Determinate Sentence: Its Distribution, Control, and Effect on Time Served." *Crime and Delinquency* 24:428–445.

Clemmer, Donald (1940). *The Prison Community.* New York: Rinehart.

Clinard, Marshall B., and Peter Yeager (1980). *Corporate Crime.* New York: Free Press.

Cochran, John K., Mitchell B. Chamlin, and Mark Seth (1994). "Deterrence or Brutalization: An Impact Assessment of Oklahoma's Return to Capital Punishment." *Criminology* 32:107–134.

Cohen, Debra, and Sandra Longtin (1996). "Canada." In Graeme Newman, Adam C. Bouloukos, and Debra Cohen, eds., *World Factbook of Criminal Justice Systems.* Washington, D.C.: U.S. Department of Justice.

Cohen, Jacqueline (1983). *Incapacitating Criminals: Recent Research Findings,* NIJ Reports. Washington, D.C.: National Institute of Justice.

Cohen, Lawrence E., and Marcus Felson (1979). "Social Change and Crime Rate Trends: A Routine Activity Approach." *American Sociological Review* 44:588–608.

Cohen, Lawrence E., and Richard Machalek (1988). "A General Theory of Expropriative Crime: An Evolutionary Ecological Approach." *American Journal of Sociology* 94:465–501.

Cohen, Stanley (1985). *Visions of Social Control: Crime, Punishment and Classification.* New York: Polity Press.

Cohn, Steven F., Steven E. Barkan, and William A. Halteman (1991). "Punitive Attitudes Towards Criminals: Racial Consensus or Racial Conflict?" *Social Problems* 38:287–294.

Cole, George F. (1970). "The Decision to Prosecute." *Law and Society Review* 4:331–343.

——— (1989). "Innovations in Collecting and Enforcing Fines." *NIJ Reports* (July/August):1–6.

Cole, George F., Barry Mahoney, Marlene Thornton, and Roger A. Hanson (1987). *The Practices and Attitudes of Trial Court Judges Regarding Fines as a Criminal Sanction.* Washington, D.C.: National Institute of Justice.

Conly, Catherine H. (1989). *Organizing for Computer Crime Investigation and Prosecution.* Washington D.C.: U.S. Department of Justice.

Cooney, Mark (1994). "Evidence as Partisanship." *Law and Society Review* 28:833–858.

Cordner, Gary (1989). "The Police on Patrol." In Dennis Jay Kenney, ed., *Police and Policing: Contemporary Issues.* New York: Praeger.

Cornelius, Gary (1997). *Jails in America: An Overview of Issues,* 2nd ed. Lanham, Md.: American Correctional Association.

Cornish, Derek B., and Ronald V. Clarke (1986a). "Situational Prevention, Displacement of Crime and Rational Choice Theory." In Kevin Heal and Gloria Laycock, eds., *Situational Crime Prevention.* London: HMSO.

Cornish, Derek B., and Ronald V. Clarke (1987). "Understanding Crime Displacement: An Application of Rational Choice Theory." *Criminology* 25:933–947.

Corsi, Jerome R. (1984). *An Introduction to Judicial Politics.* Upper Saddle River, N.J.: Prentice-Hall.

Costanzo S., and M. Costanzo (1994). "Life or Death Decisions: An Analysis of Capital Jury Decision Making Under the Special Issues Sentencing Framework." *Law and Human Behavior* 18:151- 170.

Coyle, Marcia, Fred Strasser, and Marianne Lovelle (1990). "Fatal Defense: Trial and Error in the Nation's Death Belt." *National Law Journal* (June):11–30.

Crank, John P. (1998). *Understanding Police Culture.* Cincinnati, Ohio: Anderson.

Craven, Diane (1996). "Female Victims of Violent Crime." *BJS Selected Findings* (December):1–3.

Crawford, Charles, Ted Chiricos, and Gary Kleck (1998). "Race, Racial Threat, and Sentencing of Habitual Offenders." *Criminology* 36:481–512.

Cressey, Donald R. (1969). *Theft of the Nation: The Structure and Operations of Organized Crime in America.* New York: Harper & Row.

Crisp, Debbie, and David Moxon (1994). *Case Screening by the Crown Prosecution Service: How and Why Cases are Terminated.* London: HMSO.

Critchley, T. A. (1972). *A History of Police in England and Wales,* 2nd ed. Montclair, N.J.: Patterson Smith.

Cromwell, Paul F., ed. (1996). *In Their Own Words: Criminals on Crime.* Los Angeles: Roxbury.

Cromwell, Paul F., and George G. Killinger (1994). *Community-Based Corrections: Probation, Parole, and Intermediate Sanctions,* 3rd ed. Minneapolis: West.

Cronin, Roberta (1994). *Boot Camps for Adult and Juvenile Offenders: Overview and Update.* Washington D.C.: U.S. Department of Justice.

Cullen, Francis T. (1983). "Paradox in Policing: A Note on Perceptions of Danger." *Journal of Police Science and Administration* 11:457–462.

Cullen, Francis T., and Karen E. Gilbert (1982). *Reaffirming Rehabilitation.* Cincinnati, Ohio: Anderson.

Cullen, Francis T., Edward Latessa, Velmer S. Burton Jr., and Lucen C. Lombardo (1993), "The Correctional Orientation of Prison Wardens: Is the Rehabilitative Ideal Supported?" *Criminology* 31:69–92.

Cumming, Elaine, Ian Cumming, and Laura Edell (1965). "Policeman as Philosopher, Guide and Friend." *Social Problems* 12:276–286.

Cunningham, William C., John J. Strauchs, and Clifford W. Van Meter (1990). *Private Security Trends 1970 to the Year 2000: The Hallcrest Report II.* Boston: Butterworth Heinemann.

D'Alessio, Stewart J., and Lisa Stolzenberg (1995). "The Impact of Sentencing Guidelines on Jail Incarceration in Minnesota." *Criminology* 33:283–302.

Daly, Kathleen (1987). "Structure and Practice of Familial-Based Justice in a Criminal Court." *Law and Society Review* 21:267–290.

——— (1989). "Neither Conflict Nor Labeling Nor Paternalism Will Suffice: Intersections of Race, Ethnicity, Gender and Family in Criminal Court Decisions." *Crime and Delinquency* 35:136–168.

Daly, Martin, and Margo Wilson (1988). *Homicide*. New York: Aldine de Guyter.

Darden, Christopher (1996). *In Contempt*. New York: Regan Books/HarperCollins.

Datesman, Susan K., and Frank R. Scarpitti (1980). *Women, Crime and Justice*. New York: Oxford University Press.

Daudistel, Howard C., William B. Sanders, and David F. Luckenbill (1979). *Criminal Justice: Situations and Decisions*. New York: Holt, Rinehart and Winston.

Davis, F. James (1962). *Law as a Type of Social Control*. New York: Free Press.

Davis, Robert C., and Barbara Smith (1995). "Domestic Violence Reforms: Empty Promises or Fulfilled Expectations?" *Crime and Delinquency* 41:541–522.

Dawley, David (1992). *A Nation of Lords: The Autobiography of the Vice Lords,* 2nd ed. Prospect Heights, Ill.: Waveland Press.

Dawson, John M. (1992). "Prosecutions in State Courts, 1990." *BJS Bulletin* (March):1–9.

Dawson, John M., and Patrick A. Langan (1994). "Murder in Families." *BJS Special Report* (July):1–13.

Dawson, John M., Steven K. Smith, and Carol J. DeFrancis (1993). "Prosecutors in State Courts, 1992." *BJS Bulletin* (December):1–8.

Decker, Scott H., and Richard Rosenfeld (1995). "'My Wife is Married and So is My Girlfriend:' Adaptations to the Threat of AIDS in an Arrestee Population." *Crime and Delinquency* 41:37–53.

DeComo, Robert E. (1993). *The Juveniles Taken Into Custody Research Program: Estimating the Prevalence of Juvenile Custody by Race and Gender.* San Francisco: National Council on Crime and Delinquency.

Defrancis, Carol J., Steven K. Smith, and Louise van der Does (1996). "Prosecutors in State Courts." *BJS Bulletin* (October):1–8.

Delattre, Edwin J. (1994). *Character and Cops: Ethics in Policing*. Washington: American Enterprise Institute Press.

Denning, Dorothy E. (1994). "Data Encryption and Electronic Surveillance." *SEARCH Technical Bulletin* 4:1–6.

Deosarian, Ramesh (1993). "The Social Psychology of Selecting Jury Forepersons." *British Journal of Criminology* 33:70–80.

Dershowitz, Alan M. (1986). *Reversal of Fortune: Inside the von Bulow Case*. New York: Random House.

——— (1994). *The Abuse Excuse*. Boston: Little, Brown.

Diamond, Shari Seidman (1990). "Scientific Jury Selection: What Social Scientists Know and Do Not Know." *Judicature* 73:178–183.

Diamond, Shari Seidman, and Jonathan D. Casper (1992). "Blindfolding the Jury to Verdict Consequences: Damages, Experts, and the Civil Jury." *Law and Society Review* 26:513–563.

Dighton, Daniel (1998). "Isolation and Limited Resources Create Challenges for Rural Law Enforcement." *The Compiler* (Spring):4–5.

DiIulio, John J., Jr. (1987). *Governing Prisons: A Comparative Study of Correctional Management*. New York: Free Press.

——— (1996). "Help Wanted: Economists, Crime, and Public Policy." *Journal of Economic Perspectives* 10:3–24.

Ditchfield, John (1990). *Control in Prisons: Review of the Literature*. London: HMSO.

Ditchfield, John, and Richard Harries (1996). "Assaults on Staff in Male Local Prisons and Remand Centres," *Home Office Research Bulletin* 38:15–20.

Doerner, William G. (1998). *Introduction to Law Enforcement: An Insider's View.* Boston: Butterworth-Heinemann.

Donziger, Steven R., ed. (1996). *The Real War on Crime: The Report of the National Criminal Justice Commission.* New York: HarperCollins.

Dressler, David (1962). *Practice and Theory of Probation and Parole.* New York: Columbia University Press.

Dunford, Franklyn W., and Delbert S. Elliott (1984). "Identifying Career Offenders Using Self-Reported Data." *Journal of Research in Crime and Delinquency* 21:57–86.

Dunford, Franklyn W., David Huizinga, and Delbert S. Elliott (1990). "The Role of Arrest in Domestic Assault: The Omaha Police Experiment." *Criminology* 28:183–206.

Dunham, Roger G., and Geoffrey P. Alpert (1995). "Controlling the Use of Force: An Evaluation of Street-Level Narcotics Interdiction in Miami." *American Journal of Police* 14:83–100.

Durkheim, Emile ([1893] 1964). *The Division of Labor in Society.* New York: Free Press.

——— (1900). "Deux Lois de l'Évolution Pénale." *l'Annee Sociologique* IV:65–93.

D'Alessio, Stewart J., and Lisa Stolzenberg (1995). "The Impact of Sentencing Guidelines on Jail Incarceration in Minnesota." *Criminology* 33:283–302.

Earle, Alice M. (1969). *Curious Punishments of By-Gone Days.* Montclair, N.J.: Patterson Smith.

Edwards, S.S.M. (1986). *The Police Response to Domestic Violence in London.* London: Central London Polytechnic.

Egger, Steven A. (1998). *The Killer Among Us: An Examination of Serial Murder and Its Investigation.* Upper Saddle River, NJ: Prentice-Hall.

Einstadter, Werner, and Stuart Henry (1995). *Criminological Theory: An Analysis of its Underlying Assumptions.* Fort Worth, Tex.: Harcourt Brace.

Elias, Robert (1986). *The Politics of Victimization.* New York: Oxford University Press.

——— (1993). *Victims Still.* Newbury Park, Calif.: Sage.

Ellis, Tom, Carol Hedderman, and Ed Mortimer (1996). *Enforcing Community Sentences: Supervisors' Perspectives on Ensuring Compliance and Dealing with Breach.* London: Home Office.

Erez, Edna (1984). "On the 'Dark Figure' of Arrest." *Journal of Police Science and Administration* 12: 431–440.

——— (1994). "Victim Participation in Sentencing: And the Debate Goes On. . . ." *International Review of Victimology* 3:1–2, 17–32.

Erikson, Kai T. (1966). *Wayward Puritans: A Study in the Sociology of Deviance.* New York: Wiley.

Erwin, Billie S. (1996). "Discipline in Georgia's Correctional Boot Camps." In Doris L. Mackenzie, and Eugene E. Hebert, eds., *Correctional Boot Camps: A*

Tough Intermediate Sanction. Washington, D.C.: U.S. Department of Justice.

Eskridge, Chris (1989). "College and the Police: A Review of Issues." In Dennis Jay Kenney, ed., *Police and Policing: Contemporary Issues.* New York: Praeger.

——— (1983). *Pretrial Release Programming.* New York: Clark Boardman.

Evans, Lloyd, and Paul Nicholls, eds. (1976). *Convicts and Colonial Society, 1788–1853.* New South Wales, Australia: Cassells.

Fagan, Jeffrey (1996). *The Criminalization of Domestic Violence: Promises and Limits.* Washington, D.C.: U.S. Department of Justice.

Farley, John E. (1995). *Majority-Minority Relations,* 3rd ed. Upper Saddle River, N.J.: Prentice-Hall.

——— (1998). *Sociology,* 4th ed. Upper Saddle River, N.J.: Prentice-Hall.

Federal Bureau of Investigation (1992). *Hate Crime Statistics, 1990: A Resource Book.* Washington, D.C.: U.S. Department of Justice.

——— (1994). *Crime in the United States, 1993.* Washington, D.C.: U.S. Department of Justice.

——— (1996). *Crime in the United States, 1995.* Washington, D.C.: U.S. Department of Justice.

——— (1997a). *Crime in the United States, 1996.* Washington, D.C.: U.S. Department of Justice.

——— (1997b). *Terrorism in the United States 1995.* Washington, D.C.: U.S. Department of Justice.

——— (1998). *Hate Crime 1996.* Washington, D.C.: U.S. Department of Justice.

Federal Bureau of Prisons (1991). *State of the Bureau 1990.* Washington, D.C.: U.S. Department of Justice.

——— (1997). *State of the Bureau 1996.* Washington, D.C.: U.S. Department of Justice.

Feeley, Malcolm M. (1979). *The Process is the Punishment.* New York: Russell Sage Foundation.

Feeley, Malcolm M., and Jonathan Simon (1992). "The New Penology: Notes on the Emerging Strategy of Corrections and its Implications." *Criminology* 30:449–474.

Feeney, Floyd (1986). "Robbers as Decision-Makers." In Derek B. Cornish and Ronald V. Clarke, eds., *The Reasoning Criminal: Rational Choice Perspectives on Offending.* New York: Springer-Verlag.

Feinblatt, John, and Michele Sviridoff (1995). "The Midtown Community Court Experiment." In Robert P. McNamara, ed., *Sex, Scams, and Street Life: The Sociology of New York City's Times Square.* Westport, Conn.: Praeger.

Feinman, Clarice (1994). *Women in The Criminal Justice System,* 3rd ed. Westport, Conn.: Praeger.

Feld, Barry C. (1984). "Criminalizing Juvenile Justice: Rules of Procedure for the Juvenile Court." *Minnesota Law Review* 69:141–156.

——— (1993), "Juvenile (In)Justice and the Criminal Court Alternative." *Crime and Delinquency* 39:403–424.

Felson, Marcus (1998). *Crime and Everyday Life,* 2nd ed. Thousand Oaks: Pine Forge Press.

Ferdinand, Theodore N. (1980) "Criminality, the Courts, and the Constabulary in Boston, 1702–1967." *Journal of Research in Crime and Delinquency* 17:190–208.

Fielding, Nigel (1994). "Cop Canteen Culture." In Tim Newburn and Elizabeth Stanko, eds., *Just Boys Doing Business?: Men, Masculinities and Crime.* London: Routledge.

Finckenauer, James O. (1988). "Public Support for the Death Penalty: Retribution as Just Desserts or as Revenge?" *Justice Quarterly* 5:75–84.

Finn, Peter (1997). "Reducing Stress: An Organization-Centered Approach." *FBI Law Enforcement Bulletin* 66:20–26.

Finn, Peter, and Andrea K. Newlyn (1993). "Miami's 'Drug Court:' A Different Approach." *NIJ Program Focus* (June):1–15.

Finn, Peter, and Monique Sullivan (1988). "Police Respond to Special Populations." *NIJ Reports* (May-June):7–8.

Fishman, Laura (1998). "The Black Bogeyman and White Self-Righteousness." In Coramae Richey Mann and Marjorie S. Zatz, eds., *Images of Color, Images of Crime.* Los Angeles: Roxbury.

Fleisher, Mark S. (1989). *Warehousing Violence.* Newbury Park, Calif.: Sage.

Fletcher, Connie (1990). *What Cops Know.* New York: Pocket Books.

——— (1991). *Pure Cop.* New York: Pocket Books.

Flynn, Joseph F. (1993). "Prejudicial Publicity in Criminal Trials: Bringing *Sheppard v. Maxwell* into the Nineties." *New England Law Review* 27:857–882.

Fong, Robert, Ronald E. Vogel, and S. Buentello (1992). "Prison Gang Dynamics: A Look Inside the Texas Department of Corrections." In A. V. Merlo and P. Menekos, eds., *Dilemmas and Directions in Corrections.* Cincinnati, Ohio: Anderson.

Foote, Caleb (1978). "Deceptive Determinate Sentencing." In Proceedings of the Special Conference on Determinate Sentencing, University of California, Berkeley, June 2–3.

Forst, Brian (1995). "Prosecution and Sentencing." In James Q. Wilson and Joan Petersilia, eds., *Crime.* San Francisco: ICS Press.

Foucault, Michel (1977). *Discipline and Punish.* New York: Vintage Books.

Fox, James G. (1982). "Women in Prison: A Case Study in the Social Reality of Stress." In Robert Johnson and Hans Toch, eds., *The Pains of Imprisonment.* Beverly Hills, Calif.: Sage.

Frazier, Charles E., and E. Wilbur Bock (1982). "Effects of Court Officials on Sentence Severity." *Criminology* 20:257–272.

Freed, Daniel J., and Patricia M. Wald (1964). *Bail in the United States: 1964.* Washington D.C.: U.S. Department of Justice.

Freedman, Estelle B. (1981). *Their Sisters' Keepers: Women's Prison Reform in America, 1830–1930.* Ann Arbor, Mich.: University of Michigan Press.

Freeman, Richard B. (1995). "The Labor Market." In James Q. Wilson and Joan Petersilia, eds., *Crime.* San Francisco: Institute for Contemporary Studies.

Friedman, Lawrence M. (1973). *A History of American Law.* New York: Simon & Schuster.

Fukurai, Hirashi (1996). "Race, Social Class, and Jury Participation." *Journal of Criminal Justice* 24:71–88.

Fyfe, James J. (1982). "Blind Justice: Police Shootings in Memphis." *Journal of Criminal Law and Criminology* 73:707–722.

——— (1987). *Police Personnel Practices, 1986.* Washington, D.C.: International City Management Association.

——— (1988). "Police Use of Deadly Force: Research and Reform." *Justice Quarterly* 5:165–205.

——— (1989) "Police/Citizen Violence Reduction Project." *FBI Law Enforcement Bulletin: 58–59.*

Fyfe, James J., David A. Klinger, and Jeanne M. Flavin (1997). "Differential Police Treatment of Male-on-Female Spousal Violence." *Criminology* 35:455–473.

Gaes, Gerald G. (1991). "Challenging Beliefs about Prison Crowding." *Federal Prisons Journal* 2:19–23.

Garry, Eileen M. (1996). "Truancy: First Step to a Lifetime of Problems." *Juvenile Justice Bulletin* (October):1–7.

Geller, William A., and Kevin J. Karales (1981). "Shooting of and by Chicago Police." *Journal of Criminal Law and Criminology* 72:1813–1866.

Geller, William A., and Kevin J. Karales (1982). "Shootings of and by Chicago Police: Uncommon Crises, Part II: Shootings of Police, Shooting Correlates, and Control Strategies." *Journal of Criminal Law and Criminology* 73:331–378.

Geller, William A., and Norval Morris (1992). "Federal and Local Police." In Michael Tonry and Norval Morris, eds., *Modern Policing.* Chicago: University of Chicago Press.

Geller, William A., and Michael Scott (1991). "Deadly Force: What We Know." In Carl Klockars and Steven Mastrofski, eds., *Thinking About Police,* 2nd ed. New York: McGraw-Hill.

Gelles, Richard J., and Murray A. Straus (1979). "Violence in the American Family." *Journal of Social Issues* 35:15–39.

Gelsthorpe, Loraine (1992). "Social Inquiry Reports: Race and Gender Considerations." *Home Office Research Bulletin* 32:17–22.

Giallombardo, Rose (1966). *Society of Women.* New York: John Wiley.

——— (1974). *The Social World of Imprisoned Girls.* New York: John Wiley.

Gibbs, Jack P. (1975). *Crime, Punishment and Deterrence.* New York: Elsevier.

Gibbs, Jack P., and Glenn Firebaugh (1990). "The Artifact Issue in Deterrence Research." *Criminology* 28:347–367.

Gibbs, Jack P., and James F. Short (1974). "Criminal Differentiation and Occupational Differentiation." *Journal of Research in Crime and Delinquency* 11:89–100.

Gilliard, Darrell K., and Allen J. Beck (1994). "Prisoners in 1993." *BJS Bulletin* (June):1–11.

Gilliard, Darrell K., and Allen J. Beck (1998a). "Prisoners in 1997." *BJS Bulletin* (August):1–14.

Gillliard, Darrell K., and Allen J. Beck (1998b). "Prison and Jail Inmates at Midyear, 1997." *BJS Bulletin* (January):1–11.

Gitchoff, Thomas G. (1988). "Privatization and the Criminologist: Some First-Hand Observations." *The Criminologist* 13:14–15, 17.

Glass, Stephen (1997). "Don't You D.A.R.E." *The New Republic* (March 3):18–28.

Glueck, Sheldon, and Eleanor Glueck (1950). *Unraveling Juvenile Delinquency.* New York: Commonwealth Fund.

Goffman, Erving (1961). *Asylums.* Garden City, NY: Anchor Books.

Goldfarb, Ronald L., and Linda R. Singer (1973). *After Conviction.* New York: Simon and Schuster.

Goldkamp, John S. (1994). "Justice and Treatment Innovation: The Drug Court Movement." *NIJ Issues and Practices* (June):1–38.

Goldkamp, John S., and Michael R. Gottfredson (1985). *Guidelines for Bail: The Philadelphia Experiment.* Philadelphia: Temple University Press.

Goldstein, Paul J. (1993). "Drugs and Violence." In Carolyn Rebecca Block and Richard L. Block, eds., *Questions and Answers in Lethal and Non-Lethal Violence.* Washington, D.C.: U.S. Department of Justice.

Goldstein, Herman (1990). *Problem-Oriented Policing.* New York:McGraw-Hill.

Goodpaster, K. E. (1984). "An Essay on Ending the Exclusionary Rule." *Hastings Law Journal* 33:1065.

Gordon, Cyrus H. (1957). *Hammurapi Code: Quaint or Forward Looking?* New York: Holt, Rinehart & Winston.

Gordon, Judy G. (1991). "The Female Offender: ACA's Look to the Future." *Federal Prisons Journal* 2:3–5.

Gottfredson, Michael R., and Travis Hirschi (1990). *A General Theory of Crime.* Stanford, Calif.: Stanford University Press.

Gottfredson, Michael R., and Don M. Gottfredson (1988). *Decision-Making in Criminal Justice,* 2nd ed. New York: Plenum.

Gottfredson, Stephen D., and G. Roger Jarjoura (1996). "Race, Gender, and Guidelines-Based Decision-Making." *Research in Crime and Delinquency* 33:49–69.

Gowdy, Voncile B. (1996). "Historical Perspective." In Doris L. Mackenzie, and Eugene E. Hebert, eds., *Correctional Boot Camps: A Tough Intermediate Sanction.* Washington, D.C.: U.S. Department of Justice.

Gowen, Darren (1995). "Electronic Monitoring in the Southern District of Mississippi." *Federal Probation* LIX:10–13.

Grace, Sharon (1995). *Policing Domestic Violence in the 1990s.* London: HMSO.

Gray, Ellen (1993). *Unequal Justice: The Prosecution of Child Sexual Abuse.* New York: Free Press.

Greene, Jack R. (1989). "Police and Community Relations: Where Have We Been and Where Are We Going?" In Roger G. Dunham and Geoffrey P. Alpert, eds., *Critical Issues in Policing.* Prospect Heights, Ill.: Waveland Press.

Greenfeld, Lawrence A., Michael R. Rand, Diane Craven, Patsy A. Klaus, Craig A. Perkins, Cheryl Ringer, Greg

Warchol, and James Alan Fox (1998). *Violence By Intimates.* Washington, D.C.: U.S. Department of Justice.
Greenstone, James L. (1994). "Violence in the Courtroom: Culpability, Personal Responsibility, Sensitivity and Justice." *Journal of Police and Criminal Psychology* 10:5–17.
Greenwood, Peter W. (1984). "Selective Incapacitation: A Method of Using Our Prisons More Effectively." *NIJ Reports.* Washington, D.C.: National Institute of Justice.
Greenwood, Peter W., and Allan Abrahamse (1982). *Selective Incapacitation.* Santa Monica, Calif.: Rand.
Greenwood, Peter W., Jan Chaiken, and Joan R. Petersilia (1977). *The Criminal Investigation.* Lexington, Mass.: D. C. Heath.
Grennan, Sean (1988). "Findings on the Role of Officer Gender in Violent Encounters with Citizens." *Journal of Police Science and Administration* 15:78–85.
Griffin, Patrick, Patricia Torbet, and Linda Szymanski (1998). *Trying Juveniles as Adults in Criminal Court: An Analysis of State Transfer Provisions.* Washington, D.C.: U.S. Department of Justice.
Griffiths, John (1970). "Ideology in Criminal Procedure, or a Third 'Model' of the Criminal Process." *Yale Law Journal* 79:359–417.
Griset, Pamela L. (1994). "Determinate Sentencing and the High Cost of Overblown Rhetoric: The New York Experience." *Crime and Delinquency* 40:532–548.
Gross, Samuel R., and Robert Mauro (1989). *Death and Discrimination: Racial Disparities in Capital Sentencing.* Boston: Northeastern University Press.
Grossman, Brian (1974). "The Discretionary Enforcement of Law." In Sawyer F. Sylvester and Edward Sagarin, eds., *Politics and Crime.* New York: Praeger.
Groth, Nicholas (1979). *Men Who Rape: The Psychology of the Offender.* New York: Plenum.
Guia, Elizabeth, and Oscar Padilla (1996). "Fighting Drugs at the Source." *The World and I* (November):62–67.
Guo, Jianan, Guo Xiang, Wu Zongxian, Xu Zhangrun, Peng Xiaohui, and Li Shuangshuang (1996). "China." In Graeme R. Newman, Adam C. Bouloukos, and Debra Cohen, eds., *World Factbook of Criminal Justice Systems.* Washington, D.C.: U.S. Department of Justice.
Hagan, John (1974). "Extra-legal Attributes and Criminal Sentencing: An Assessment of a Sociological Viewpoint." *Law and Society Review* 8:357–383.
——— (1994). *Crime and Disrepute.* Thousand Oaks, Calif.: Pine Forge.
——— (1995). "Rethinking Crime Theory and Policy: The New Sociology of Crime and Disrepute." In Hugh D. Barlow, ed., *Crime and Public Policy: Putting Theory to Work.* Boulder: Westview Press.
Hagan, John, A., R. Gillis, and J. Chan (1978). "Explaining Official Delinquency: A Spatial Study of Class, Conflict and Control." *Sociological Quarterly* 19:386–398.
Hagan, John A., R. Gillis, and John Simpson (1985). "The Class Structure, Gender and Delinquency: Toward a Power-Control Theory of Common Delinquent Behavior." *American Journal of Sociology* 90:1151–1175.
Haines, Herb (1992). "Flawed Execution, the Anti-Death Penalty Movement, and the Politics of Capital Punishment." *Social Problems* 39:125–138.
Hakim, Simon, and George F. Rengert, eds. (1981). *Crime Spillover.* Beverly Hills, Calif.: Sage.
Hall, Jerome (1952). *Theft, Law, and Society,* rev. ed. Indianapolis, Ind.: Bobbs-Merrill.
Haller, Mark H. (1976). "Historical Roots of Police Behavior: Chicago, 1890–1925." *Law and Society Review* 10:303–324.
Hamm, Mark S. (1993). *American Skinheads: The Criminology and Control of Hate Crime.* Westport, Ohio: Praeger.
——— (1995). *The Abandoned Ones: The Imprisonment and Uprising of the Mariel Boat People.* Boston: Northeastern University Press.
Hammett, Theodore M., and Joel Epstein (1993). "Prosecuting Environmental Crime: Los Angeles County." *NIJ Program Focus* August:1–16.
Hammett, Theodore M., Rebbecca Widom, Joel Epstein, Michael Gross, Santiago Sifre, and Tammy Enos (1995). *1994 Update: HIV/AIDS and STDs in Correctional Facilities.* Washington, D.C.: U.S. Department of Justice.
Hanson, Roger A., and Henry W. K. Daley (1995). *Challenging the Conditions of Prisons and Jails: A Report on Section 1983 Litigation.* Washington, D.C.: U.S. Department of Justice.
Hanson, Roger A., and J. Chapper (1991). *Indigent Defense Systems.* Washington, D.C.: National Center for State Courts.
Harer, Miles D., and Darrell J. Steffensmeier (1996). "Race and Prison Violence." *Criminology* 34:323–355.
Harlow, Caroline Wolf (1991). *Female Victims of Violent Crime.* Washington, D.C.: U.S. Department of Justice.
Harring, Sydney (1983). *Policing a Class Society: The Experience of American Cities.* New Brunswick, N.J.: Rutgers University Press.
Harris, Richard N. (1973). *The Police Academy: An Inside View.* New York: Wiley.
Hassine, Victor (1996). *Life Without Parole.* Los Angeles, Calif.: Roxbury.
Hastie, Reid, Steven D. Penrod, and Nancy Pennington (1983). *Inside the Jury.* Cambridge, Mass.: Harvard University Press.
Hawkins, Darnell (1994). "Ethnicity: The Forgotten Dimension of American Social Control." In George S. Bridges and Martha A. Myers, eds., *Inequality, Crime, and Social Control.* Boulder, Colo.: Westview Press.
Hawkins, Gordon (1976). *The Prison: Policy and Practice.* Chicago: The University of Chicago Press.
Hawkins, Richard, and Geoffrey P. Alpert (1989). *American Prison Systems: Punishment and Treatment.* Upper Saddle River, N.J.: Prentice-Hall.
Hay, Douglas (1975). *Albion's Fatal Tree: Crime and Society in Eighteenth Century England.* London: Allen Lowe.
Hedderman, Carol, and Loraine Gelsthorpe (1997). *Understanding the Sentencing of Women.* London: HMSO.

Heffernan, Esther (1972). *Making It in Prison: The Square, the Cool, and the Life.* New York: Wiley Interscience.

Henry, D. Alan, and Bruce D. Beaudin (1990). "Bail Bondsmen." *American Jails* 4:8–16.

Hepburn, John R. (1985). "The Exercise of Power in Coercive Organizations: A Study of Prison Guards." *Criminology* 23:145–164.

Herek, G., and K. Berrill (1992). *Hate Crimes: Confronting Violence Against Lesbians and Gay Men.* Newbury Park, Calif.: Sage.

Herrington, Nancy (1997). *"Female Cops—1992."* In Robert Dunham and Geoffrey Alpert, eds., *Critical Issues in Policing,* 3rd ed. Prospect Heights, Ill.: Waveland Press.

Hills, Stuart L., and Ron Santiago (1992). *Tragic Magic: The Life and Crimes of a Heroin Addict.* Chicago: Nelson-Hall.

Hillsman, Sally T., Barry Mahoney, George F. Cole, and Bernard Auchter (1987). "Fines as Criminal Sanctions." *Research in Brief.* Washington, D.C.: U.S. Department of Justice.

Hindelang, Michael J., Travis Hirschi, and Joseph G. Weis (1979). "Correlates of Delinquency: The Ilusion of Discrepancy between Self-Report and Official Measures." *American Sociological Review* 44: 995–1014.

Hogarth, John (1971). *Sentencing as a Human Process.* Toronto: University of Toronto Press.

Holmes, Malcolm D., Howard C. Daudistel, and William A. Taggart (1992). "Plea Bargaining Policy and State District Court Caseloads: An Interrupted Time Series Analysis." *Law and Society Review* 26:139–159.

Homant, Robert J., and Daniel B. Kennedy (1985). "Police Perceptions of Spouse Abuse: A Comparison of Male and Female Officers." *Journal of Criminal Justice* 13:29–47.

Hood, Roger (1989). *The Death Penalty: A World-wide Perspective.* New York: Oxford University Press.

——— (1962). *Sentencing in Magistrates' Court.* London: Stevens.

——— (1972). *Sentencing the Motoring Offender.* London: Heinemann.

——— (1992). *Race and Sentencing.* Oxford, England: Clarendon.

Hooke, Andrew, and Jim Knox (1995). "Preparing Records of Taped Interviews." *Home Office Research Findings* (November):1–4.

Horney, Julie, and Ineke Haen Marshall (1992). "Risk Perceptions Among Serious Offenders: The Role of Crime and Punishment." *Criminology* 30:575–592.

Horowitz, Ruth (1987). "Community Tolerance of Group Violence." *Social Problems* 34:437–449.

Hough, Michael J., and Pat Mayhew (1983). *The British Crime Survey.* London: HMSO.

Houlden, Pauline, and Steven Balkin (1985). "Quality and Cost Comparisons of Private Bar Indigent Defense Systems vs. Order Assigned Counsel." *Journal of Criminal Law and Criminology* 76:176–200.

Hunt, Geoffrey, Stephanie Riegel, Tomas Morales, and Dan Waldorf (1993). "Changes in Prison Culture: Prison Gangs and the Case of the 'Pepsi Generation.'" *Social Problems* 40:398–409.

Hunt, Jennifer (1991). "Police Accounts of Normal Force." In James M. Henslin, ed., *Down to Earth Sociology,* 6th ed. New York: Free Press.

Hunt, Raymond G., and John M. Magenau (1993). *Power and the Police Chief: An Institutional and Organizational Analysis.* Newbury Park: Sage.

Ianni, Francis A. J. (1975). *Black Mafia: Ethnic Succession in Organized Crime.* New York: Pocket Books.

Ianni, Francis A. J., and Elizabeth Reuss-Ianni (1973). *A Family Business: Kinship and Control in Organized Crime.* New York: Russell Sage.

Inbau, Fred (1962). "Police Interrogations: A Practical Necessity." In Claude R. Sowle, ed., *Police Power and Individual Freedom.* Chicago: Aldine.

Inwald, Robin, and Dennis Jay Kenney (1989). "Psychological Testing of Police Candidates." In Dennis Jay Kenney, ed., *Police and Policing: Contemporary Issues.* New York: Praeger.

Irwin, John (1980). *Prisons in Turmoil.* Boston: Little, Brown.

Irwin, John, and James Austin (1994). *It's About Time: America's Imprisonment Binge.* Belmont, Calif.: Wadsworth.

Jackall, Robert (1988). *Moral Mazes: The World of Corporate Managers.* New York: Oxford University Press.

Jackson, Bruce (1969b). "Exile from the American Dream: The Junkie and the Cop." *Atlantic Monthly* 219:44–51.

Jackson, Bruce, and Diane Christian (1980). *Death Row.* Boston: Beacon Press.

Jacobs, James B. (1974). "Street Gangs Behind Bars." *Social Problems* 21:395–409.

——— (1977). *Stateville: The Penitentiary in Mass Society.* Chicago: University of Chicago Press.

James, J. T. (1817). *Journal of a Tour.* London: John Murray.

Jankowski, Martin Sanchez (1991). *Islands in the Street: Gangs and American Urban Society.* Berkeley, Calif.: University of California Press.

Jeffery, C. Ray (1977). *Crime Prevention Through Environmental Design.* Beverly Hills, Calif.: Sage.

Jenkins, Brian Michael (1987). "Will Terrorists Go Nuclear?" In Walter Laqueur and Yonah Alexander, eds., *The Terrorism Reader.* New York: Meridian Books.

Jenkins, Philip (1984). "Temperance and the Origins of the New Penology." *Journal of Criminal Justice* 12:551–565.

——— (1994). *Using Murder: The Social Construction of Serial Homicide.* New York: Aldine De Gruyter.

Jianan, Guo, Xiang Guo, Zongxian Wu, Zhangrun Xu, Xiaohui Peng, and Shuangshuang Li (1996). "China." In Graeme Newman, Adam C. Bouloukos, and Debra Cohen, eds., *World Factbook of Criminal Justice Systems.* Washington, D.C.: U.S. Department of Justice.

Johnson, Cathy, and Craig Haney (1994). "Felony Voir Dire: An Exploratory Study of Its Content and Effect." *Law and Human Behavior* 18:487–506.

Johnson, Claire, Barbara Webster, and Edward Connors (1995). "Prosecuting Gangs: A National Assessment." *NIJ Research in Brief* (February):1–10.

Johnson, David R., and Laurie K. Scheuble (1991). "Gender Bias in the Disposition of Juvenile Court Referrals: The Effects of Time and Location." *Criminology* 29:677–699.

Johnson, Jean (1997). "Americans' Views on Crime and Law Enforcement." *NIJ Journal* (September):9–14.

Johnson, Robert (1987). *Hard Time: Understanding and Reforming the Prison.* Monterey, Calif.: Brooks/Cole.

——— (1990). *Death Work: A Study of the Modern Execution Process.* Pacific Grove, Calif.: Brooks/Cole.

——— (1998). *Death Work: A Study of the Modern Execution Process,* 2nd ed. Belmont, CA: Wadsworth.

Johnstone, Norman (1973). *The Human Cage: A Brief History of Prison Architecture.* Washington, D.C.: American Foundation Press.

Joutsen, Matti (1994). "Victim Participation in Proceedings and Sentencing in Europe." *International Review of Victimology* 3:57–67.

Joyce, Nola M. (1992). "A View of the Future: The Effect of Policy on Prison Population Growth." *Crime and Delinquency* 38:357–368.

Kadish, Mortimer R., and Sanford H. Kadish (1973). *Discretion to Disobey.* Palo Alto, Calif.: Stanford University Press.

Kalven, Harry, and Hans Zeisel (1966). *The American Jury.* Boston: Little, Brown.

Kaplan, John, Jerome H. Skolnick, and Malcolm M. Feeley (1991). *Criminal Justice: Introductory Cases and Materials.* Westbury, N.Y.: Foundation Press.

Kappeler, Victor E., Richard D. Sluder, and Geoffrey P. Alpert (1994). *Forces of Deviance: Understanding the Dark Side of Policing.* Prospect Heights, Ill.: Waveland.

Karacki, Loren (1987). *An Assessment of the High Security Operation at USP Marion.* Washington, D.C.: U.S. Department of Justice.

Kassin, Saul M., and Lawrence S. Wrightsman (1988). *The American Jury on Trial.* New York: Hemisphere.

Keil, Thomas J., and Gennaro F. Vito (1989). "Race, Homicide Severity, and the Application of the Death Penalty: A Consideration of the Barnett Scale." *Criminology* 27:511–535.

Kelling, George L. (1988). *Police and Communities: The Quiet Revolution.* Washington, D.C.: National Institute of Justice.

Kelling, George L., and William J. Bratton (1993). "Implementing Community Policing: The Administrative Problem," *NIJ Perspectives on Policing* (July):1–11.

Kenney, Dennis J., and James O. Finckenauer (1995). *Organized Crime in America.* Belmont, Calif.: Wadsworth.

Kerr, Norbert L. (1994). "Effects of Pretrial Publicity on Jurors." *Judicature* 78:120–127.

Keve, Paul W. (1991) *Prisons and the American Conscience.* Carbondale and Edwardsville, Ill.: Southern Illinois University Press.

King, Harry (1972). *Boxman: A Professional Thief's Journey,* William Chambliss, ed. New York: Harper & Row.

Kingsnorth, Rodney, and Louis Rizzo (1979). "Decision-Making in the Criminal Courts: Continuities and Discontinuites." *Criminology* 17:3–14.

Kinkade, Patrick J., and Matthew C. Leone (1992). "The Effects of 'Tough' Drunk Driving Laws on Policing: A Case Study." *Crime and Delinquency* 38:239–254.

Kinsey, Richard, John Lea, and Jock Young (1986). *Losing the Fight Against Crime.* Oxford: Basil Blackwell.

Kleck, Gary (1981). "Racial Discrimination in Criminal Sentencing: A Critical Evaluation of the Evidence with Additional Evidence on the Death Penalty." *American Sociological Review* 46:783–805.

Kleiman, Mark A. R., and Kerry D. Smith (1990). "State and Local Drug Enforcement: In Search of a Strategy." In Michael Tonry and James Q. Wilson, eds., *Drugs and Crime, vol. 13 of Crime and Justice: A Review of Research.* Chicago: University of Chicago Press.

Klein, Andrew (1997). *Alternative Sentencing, Intermediate Sanctions, and Probation.* Cincinnati, Ohio: Anderson.

Klinger, David A. (1994). "Demeanor or Crime? Why 'Hostile' Citizens are More Likely to be Arrested." *Criminology* 32:475–493.

——— (1996). "More on Demeanor and Arrest in Dade County." *Criminology* 34:61–82.

Klockars, Carl B. (1974). *The Professional Fence.* New York: Free Press.

——— (1985) "The Dirty Harry Problem." In Frederick A. Elliston and Michael Feldberg, eds., *Moral Issues in Police Work.* Totowa, N.J.: Rowman & Allanheld.

Klofas, John M. (1993). "Drugs and Justice: The Impact of Drugs on Criminal Justice in a Metropolitan Community." *Crime and Delinquency* 39:204–224.

Knapp Commission Report on Police Corruption (1972). New York: George Braziller.

Knox, George W., and Thomas F. McCurrie (1996). "Gang Profile: The Latin Kings." *Journal of Gang Research* 4:43–72.

Kobetz, Richard W. (1978). *Criminal Justice Education Directory, 1978–1980.* Gaithersburg, Md.: International Association of Chiefs of Police.

Koch, Brigitte, and Trevor Bennett (1993). "Community Policing in Canada and Britain." *Home Office Research Bulletin* (Summer):36–42.

Kramer, John H., and Robin L. Lubitz (1985). "Pennsylvania's Sentencing Reform: The Impact of Commission-Established Guidelines." *Crime and Delinquency* 31:481–500.

Kraska, Peter B. (1996). "Enjoying Militarism: Political/Personal Dilemmas in Studying U.S. Paramilitary Units." *Justice Quarterly* 13: 405–429.

Kraska, Peter B., and Victor E. Kappeler (1997). "Militarizing American Police: The Rise and Normalization of Paramilitary Units." *Social Problems* 44:101–117.

Kuykendall, Jack, and David Burns (1980). "The Black Police Officer: An Historical Perspective." *Journal of Contemporary Criminal Justice* 4:103–113.

Lab, Steven P., and J. T. Whitehead (1990). "From 'Nothing Works' to 'The Appropriate Works': The Latest

Stop on the Search for the Secular Grail." *Criminology* 28:405–417.

LaFree, Gary D. (1989). *Rape and Criminal Justice: The Social Construction of Sexual Assault.* Belmont, Calif.: Wadsworth.

LaFree, Gary D., Barbara F. Reskin, and Christy Visher (1991). "Jurors' Responses to Victims' Behavior and Legal Issues in Sexual Assault Trials." *Social Problems* 32:389–407.

Lancaster, D. (1984). *Cameras in the Courtroom: A Study of Two Trials.* Bloomington, Ind.: Indiana University Press.

Lane, Roger (1967). *Policing the City: Boston, 1821–1885.* Cambridge, Mass.: Harvard University Press.

——— (1992). "Urban Police and Crime in Nineteenth-Century America." In Michael Tonry and Norval Morris, eds., *Modern Policing.* Chicago: University of Chicago Press.

Langan, Patrick A. (1991). *Race of Prisoners Admitted to State and Federal Institutions, 1926–1986.* Washington, D.C.: U.S. Department of Justice.

——— (1994). "Between Prison and Probation: Intermediate Sanctions." *Science* 264:791–793.

Langan, Patrick A., and Jodi M. Brown (1997). "Felony Sentences in State Courts, 1994." *BJS Bulletin* (January):1–15.

Langan, Patrick A., and M. Cunniff (1992). *Recidivism of Felons on Probation, 1986–1989.* Washington, D.C. U.S. Department of Justice.

Langan, Patrick A., and Helen A. Graziadei (1995). "Felony Sentences in State Courts, 1992." *BJS Bulletin* (January):1–16.

Lanza-Kaduce, Lonn (1988). "Perceptual Deterrence and Drinking and Driving among College Students." *Criminology* 26:321–334.

Latessa, Edward J., and Harry E. Allen (1997). *Corrections in the Community.* Cincinnati, Ohio: Anderson.

Laub, John H., and Robert J. Sampson (1988). "Unraveling Families and Delinquency: A Reanalysis of the Gluecks' Data." *Criminology* 26:355–380.

Laub, John H., Robert J. Sampson, Ronald P. Corbett, Jr., and Jinnie S. Smith (1995). "The Public Policy Implications of a Life-Course Perspective on Crime." In Hugh D. Barlow, ed., *Crime and Public Policy: Putting Theory to Work.* Boulder, Colo.: Westview Press.

Lawrence, Dan (1997). "Crime and Corrections: The Views of the People of Oklahoma." *Oklahoma Criminal Justice Research Center Journal.* On line at **http://www.doc.state.ok.us/docs/ocjrs.html**

Lederer, Frederick I. (1994). "Revolution in Courtroom Technology Presents Opportunity and Risk." *Trial* 30:86–90.

Lemert, Edwin M. (1951). *Social Pathology.* New York: McGraw-Hill.

Leo, Richard A., and Richard J. Ofshe (1998). "The Consequences of False Confessions: Deprivations of Liberty and Miscarriages of Justice in the Age of Psychological Interrogation." *Journal of Criminal Law and Criminology* 88:429–496.

Leonard, Kimberly Kempf, Carl E. Pope, and William H. Feyerherm, eds. (1995). *Minorities in Juvenile Justice.* Thousand Oaks, Calif.: Sage.

Leshin, Cynthia (1997). *Internet Investigations in Criminal Justice.* Upper Saddle River, N.J.: Prentice Hall.

Levi, Michael (1987). *Regulating Fraud: White-Collar Crime and the Criminal Process.* London: Tavistock.

——— (1995). "White-Collar Crimes and other Crimes of Deception: Connecting Policy to Theory." In Hugh D. Barlow, ed., *Crime and Public Policy: Putting Theory to Work.* Boulder, Colo.: Westview Press.

Levin, Jack, and James Alan Fox (1985). *Mass Murder: America's Growing Menace.* New York: Plenum Press.

Levin, Jack, and Jack McDevitt (1993). *Hate Crimes: The Rising Tide of Bigotry and Bloodshed.* New York: Plenum Press.

Lewis, Peter W. (1979). "Killing the Killer: A Post-Furman Profile of Florida's Condemned: A Personal Account," *Crime and Delinquency* 25:200–218.

Lewis, Peter W., and Harry E. Allen (1977). "'Participating Miranda:' An Attempt to Subvert Certain Constitutional Safeguards." *Crime and Delinquency* 75:61–73.

Lilly, J. Robert (1990). "Tagging Reviewed," *Howard Journal of Criminal Justice* 29:229–245.

——— (1995). "Electronic Monitoring In the U.S." In Michael Tonry and Kate Hamilton, eds., *Intermediate Sanctions in Overcrowded Times.* Boston: Northeastern University Press.

Lilly, Robert J., and Paul Knepper (1993). "The Corrections-Commercial Complex." *Crime and Delinquency* 39:150–159.

Linsky, Arnold S., Jr., John P. Colby, and Murray Straus (1986). "Drinking Norms and Alcohol-Related Problems in the United States." *Journal of Studies on Alcohol* 47:384–393.

Lintott, A. W. (1968). *Violence in Republican Rome.* Oxford, England: Clarendon Press.

Lipton, Douglas, Robert M. Martinson, and Judith Wilkes (1975). *The Effectiveness of Correctional Treatment: A Survey of Treatment Evaluation Studies.* New York: Praeger.

Little, Dorscine Spigner (1997). "Comments on Diversity Training in the Criminal Justice System." *The Criminologist* (January/February):1–3.

Lofland, John (1977). *The Dramaturgy of State Executions.* Montclair, N.J.: Patterson Smith.

Loves, Mark F. (1992). "Organized Crime on Wheels: The Evolution of the Outlaw Motorcycle Gangs in the United States and Canada." *Criminal Organizations* 6:9,13.

Luckenbill, David F. (1977). "Criminal Homicide as a Situated Transaction." *Social Problems* 25:176–186.

Lundman, Richard J. (1979). "Organizational Norms and Police Discretion: An Observational Study of Police Work with Traffic Law Violators." *Criminology* 17:159–171.

——— (1980). *Police and Policing.* New York: Holt, Rinehart & Winston.

——— (1984). *Prevention and Control of Juvenile Delinquency.* New York: Oxford University Press.

——— (1991). "Police and Drunk Driving: Baseline Data and DUI Arrests, 1960–1989." Presented at the Anuual Meeting of the American Sociological Association, Cincinnati, August 22–26.

——— (1994). "Demeanor or Crime? The Midwest City Police-Citizen Encounters Study." *Criminology* 32:631–656.

Luttwak, Edward N. (1995). "Going Dutch: The Unending Cost of the Drugs War." *Times Literary Supplement* 1 (September):4–5.

Mackenzie, Doris Layton, and Robert Brame (1995). "Shock Incarceration and Positive Adjustment During Community Supervision." *Journal of Quantitative Criminology* 11:111–142.

Mackenzie, Doris Layton, Lori A. Elis, Sally S. Simpson, and Stacy B. Skroban (1996). "Boot Camps as an Alternative for Women." In Doris Layton Mackenzie and Eugene E. Hebert, eds., *Correctional Boot Camps: A Tough Intermediate Sanction.* Washington, D.C.: U.S. Department of Justice.

Mackenzie, Doris Layton, and Eugene E. Hebert, eds. (1996). *Correctional Boot Camps: A Tough Intermediate Sanction.* Washington, D.C.: U.S. Department of Justice.

Mackenzie, Doris Layton., and Claire Souryal (1994). *Multisite Evaluation of Shock Incarceration.* Washington, D.C.: U.S. Department of Justice.

MacKinnon, C. (1989). *Toward a Feminist Theory of the State.* Cambridge, Mass.: Harvard University Press.

Maguire, Edward R. (1997). "Structural Change in Large Municipal Police Organizations During the Community Policing Era." *Justice Quarterly* 14:547–576.

Maguire, Kathleen, and Ann L. Pastore, eds. (1994). *Sourcebook of Criminal Justice Statistics, 1993.* Washington, D.C.: U.S. Department of Justice.

——— (1995). *Sourcebook of Criminal Justice Statistics, 1994.* Washington, D.C.: U.S. Department of Justice.

——— (1996). *Sourcebook of Criminal Justice Statistics, 1995.* Washington, D.C.: U.S. Department of Justice.

——— (1997). *Sourcebook of Criminal Justice Statistics, 1996.* Washington, D.C.: U.S. Department of Justice.

——— (1998). *Sourcebook of Criminal Justice Statistics, 1997.* Washington, D.C.: U.S. Department of Justice.

Maine, Sir Henry Sumner (1905). *Ancient Law,* 10th ed. London: John Murray.

Mair, George (1991). "What Works: Nothing or Everything?" *Home Office Research Bulletin 30: 23–29.*

Mair, George, and Ed Mortimer (1996). *Curfew Orders with Electronic Monitoring.* London: Home Office.

Makkai, Toni, and John Braithwaite (1994). "Reintegrative Shaming and Compliance with Regulatory Standards." *Criminology* 32:361–383.

Maloney, Dennis, D. Romig, and T. Armstrong (1988). "Juvenile Probation: The Balanced Approach." *Juvenile and Family Court Journal* 39: 1–56.

Mann, Coramae Richey (1993). *Unequal Justice: A Question of Color.* Bloomington: Ind.: University Press.

Mann, Coramae Richey, and Marjorie S. Zatz, eds., *Images of Color, Images of Crime.* Los Angeles: Roxbury.

Mann, Kenneth (1985). *Defending White-Collar Crime: A Portrait of Attorneys at Work.* New Haven, Conn.: Yale University Press.

Manning, Peter K. (1977). *Police Work: The Social Organization of Policing.* Cambridge, Mass.: MIT Press.

——— (1992). "Economic Rhetoric and Policing Reform." *Criminal Justice Research Bulletin* 7:1–8.

——— (1994) "The Police, Symbolic Capital, Class, and Control." In George S. Bridges and Martha A. Myers, eds., *Inequality, Crime, and Social Control.* Boulder, Colo.: Westview Press.

Manson, Don (1997). "Presale Firearms Check." *BJS Selected Findings* (February):1–5.

Marquart, James W. (1984). "Prison Guards and the Use of Physical Coercion as a Mechanism of Prisoner Control." Paper presented at the Annual meeting of the American Sociological Association, August.

Marquart, James W., Sheldon Ekland-Olson, and Jonathan Sorensen (1993). *The Rope, The Chair, and The Needle.* Austin, Tex.: University of Texas Press.

Martin, Susan E. (1983). "The Politics of Sentencing Reform: Sentencing Guidelines in Pennsylvania and Minnesota." In Alfred Blumstein, Jacqueline Cohen, Susan Martin, and Michael Tonry, eds., *Research and Sentencing: The Search for Reform, vol. 2.* Washington, D.C.: National Academy Press.

——— (1989). "Female Officers On the Move? A Status Report on Women in Policing." In Roger G. Dunham and Geoffrey P. Alpert, eds., *Critical Issues in Policing.* Prospect Heights, Ill.: Waveland Press.

——— (1997). "Women Officers on the Move: An Update of Women in Policing." In Roger G. Dunham and Geoffrey P. Alpert, eds., *Critical Issues in Policing,* 3rd ed. Prospect Heights, Ill.: Waveland.

Martinez, Orlando (1987). "Minority Youth and Crime." *Crime and Delinquency* 33:325–328.

Martinson, Robert (1974). "What Works? Questions and Answers about Prison Reform." *Public Interest* 35:22–54.

Maruschak, Laura (1997). "HIV in Prisons and Jails, 1995." *BJS Bulletin* (August):1–12.

Marvell, Thomas B., and Carlisle E. Moody (1996). "Determinate Sentencing and Abolishing Parole: The Long-term Impacts on Prisons and Crime." *Criminology* 34:107–128.

Marx, Gary T. (1988). *Undercover: Police Surveillance in America.* Berkeley, Calif.: University of California Press.

Marx, Karl, and Friedrich Engels ([1846] 1947). *The German Ideology.* New York: International Publishers.

Masters, Ruth, and Cliff Roberson (1990). *Inside Criminology.* Upper Saddle River, N.J.: Prentice-Hall.

Mastrofski, Stephen D., Robert E. Worden, and Jeffrey B. Snipes (1995). "Law Enforcement in a Time of Community Policing." *Criminology* 33:539–563.

Matoesian, Gregory (1993). *Reproducing Rape: Domination Through Talk in the Courtroom.* London: Polity Press.

Matoesian, Gregory M. (1995). "Language, Law, and Society: Policy Implications of the Kennedy Smith Rape Trial." *Law and Society Review* 29:669–701.

Matulia, K. J. (1982). *A Balance of Force: Executive Summary.* Washington, D.C.: U.S. Department of Justice.

Mauer, Marc (1997). *Americans Behind Bars: The International Use of Incarceration, 1995.* Washington, D.C.: The Sentencing Project.

Mawby, R.I., and S. Walklate (1994). *Critical Criminology.* Thousand Oaks, Calif.: Sage.

Maxfield, Michael A., Dan A. Lewis, and Ron Szoc (1980). "Producing Official Crimes: Verified Crime Reports as Measures of Police Output." *Social Science Quarterly* 61:221–236.

Maxfield, Linda Drazga, and John H. Kramer (1998). *Substantial Assistance: An Empirical Yardstick Gauging Equity in Current Federal Policy and Practice.* Washington, D.C.: U.S. Sentencing Commission.

May, Chris (1995). *Measuring the Satisfaction of Courts with the Probation Service.* London: HMSO.

Mayhew, Pat, Natalie Aye Maung, and Catriona Mirrlees-Black (1993). *The 1992 British Crime Survey.* London: HMSO.

Mayhew, Patricia, Ronald V. Clarke, and David Elliott (1989). "Motorcycle Theft, Helmet Legislation and Displacement." *Howard Journal* 28:1–8.

Maynard, Douglas W. (1982). "Defendant Attributes in Plea Bargaining: Notes on the Modeling of Sentencing Decisions." *Social Problems* 29:347–360.

McCarthy, Belinda Rodgers, and Charles A. Lindquist (1988). "The Impact of Guilty Pleas on the Sentencing Process: A Crime-Specific Analysis of Prosecutorial, Defendant, and Judicial Behavior." Paper presented at the Annual Meeting of the Academy of Criminal Justice Sciences, Chicago, November.

McCarthy, Belinda Rodgers, and Bernard J. McCarthy, Jr. (1997). *Community-based Corrections,* 3rd ed. Belmont, Calif.: Wadsworth.

McCorkle, Richard C. (1993). "Research Note: Punish and Rehabilitate? Public Attitudes toward Six Common Crimes." *Crime and Delinquency* 39:240–252.

McDonald, Douglas C. (1988). *Restitution and Community Service.* Washington, D.C.: U.S. Department of Justice.

McDonald, Douglas C., and Kenneth E. Carlson (1993). *Sentencing in the Federal Courts: Does Race Matter?* Washington, D.C.: U.S. Department of Justice.

McDonald, William F., ed. (1976). *Criminal Justice and the Victim.* Beverly Hills, Calif.: Sage.

McDonald, William F. (1985). *Plea Bargaining: Critical Issues and Common Practices.* Washington, D.C.: U.S. Department of Justice.

McEwen, Tom (1995). *National Assessment Program: 1994 Survey Results.* Washington D.C.: U.S. Department of Justice.

——— (1996). *National Data Collection on Police Use of Force.* Washington, D.C.: U.S. Department of Justice.

McGarrell, Edmund F. (1988). *Juvenile Correctional Reform: Two Decades of Policy and Procedural Change.* Albany, N.Y.: State University of New York Press.

——— (1993). "Trends in Racial Disproportionality in Juvenile Court Processing: 1985–1989," *Crime and Delinquency* 39:29–48.

McGowan, Brenda, and Karen Blumenthal (1978). *Why Punish the Children? A Study of Women Prisoners.* Hackensach, N.J.: National Council on Crime and Delinquency.

McIvor, Gill (1993). "Community Service by Offenders: How Much Does the Community Benefit?" *Research on Social Work Practice* 3:385–403.

McKay, Mary M. (1994). "The Link Between Domestic Violence and Child Abuse." *Journal of Child Welfare League of America* 1:29–38.

McKelvey, Blake ([1936] 1977). *American Prisons: A History of Good Intentions.* Montclair, N.J.: Patterson Smith.

McMullan, John L. (1998). "Social Surveillance and the Rise of the 'Police Machine.'" *Theoretical Criminology* 2:93–117.

McNeely, R. L., and Carl E. Pope (1981). *Race, Crime, and Criminal Justice.* Beverly Hills, Calif.: Sage.

McNulty, Elizabeth W. (1994). "Generating Common-Sense Knowledge Among Police Officers." *Symbolic Interaction* 17:281–294.

Meier, Robert F., and Gilbert Geis (1997). *Victimless Crime? Prostitution, Drugs, Homosexuality, Abortion.* Los Angeles: Roxbury.

Melossi, D., and M. Pavarini (1981). *The Prison and the Factory: Origins of the Penitentiary System.* Trans. by G. Cousin. Totowa, N.J.: Barnes and Noble.

Melton, Ada Pecos (1998). "Traditional and Contemporary Tribal Justice." In Coramae Richey Mann and Marjorie S. Zatz, eds., *Images of Color, Images of Crime.* Los Angeles: Roxbury.

Mendelsohn, Alan J. (1956). "The Influence of Defendant's Plea on Judicial Determination of Sentence." *Yale Law Journal* 66:204–222.

Mennel, Robert M. (1973). *Thorns and Thistles.* Hanover, N.H.: University Press of New England.

Merton, Robert K. (1938). "Social Structure and Anomie." *American Sociological Review* 3:672–682.

Messerschmidt, James W. (1986). *Capitalism, Patriarchy, and Crime.* Totowa, N.J.: Rowman & Littlefield.

Messner, Steven F., and Richard Rosenfeld (1994). *Crime and the American Dream.* Belmont, Calif.: Wadsworth.

Mickolus, Edward F. (1993). *Terrorism, 1988–1991: A Chronology of Events and a Selectively Annotated Bibliography.* Westport, Conn.: Greenwood Press.

Miller, Marc. (1995). "The Importance of Flexibility in Sentencing." *Judicature* 78:182–188.

Miller, Ted R., Mark A. Cohen, and Brian Wiersema (1996). *Victim Costs and Consequences: A New Look.* Washington, D.C.: U.S. Department of Justice.

Miller, Walter B. (1973). "Idealogical and Criminal Justice Policy: Some current issues," *Journal of Criminal Law and Criminology* 64:141–162.

Milton, C. (1972). *Women in Policing.* Washington, D.C.: Police Foundation.

Mirrlees-Black, Catriona (1995). "Estimating the Extent of Domestic Violence: Findings from the 1992 BCS." *Home Office Research Bulletin* 37:1–9.

Mirrlees-Black, Catriona, Pat Mayhew, and Andrew Percy (1996). "The 1996 British Crime Survey." *Home Office Statistical Bulletin* September: 1–78.

Monkkonen, Eric H. (1992). "History of Urban Police." In Michael Tonry and Norval Morris, eds., *Modern Policing*. Chicago: University of Chicago Press.

Moone, Joseph (1997). "Juveniles in Private Facilities 1991–1995." *OJJDP Juvenile Justice Bulletin* (April):1–3.

Moore, Mark H. (1986). "Organized Crime as a Business Enterprise." Paper presented at the annual meeting of the American Society of Criminology, Atlanta, November.

——— (1990). "Supply Reduction and Drug Law Enforcement." In Michael Tonry and James Q. Wilson, eds., *Drugs and Crime,* vol. 13, *Crime and Justice: A Review of Research*. Chicago: University of Chicago Press.

——— (1992). "Problem-Solving and Community Policing." In Michael Tonry and Norval Morris, eds., *Modern Policing*. Chicago: University of Chicago Press.

Moore, Mark H., Robert C. Trojanowicz, and George Kelling (1988). *Crime and Policing*. Washington, D.C.: National Institute of Justice.

Morash, Merry (1986). "Understanding the Contribution of Women to Police Work." In Louis A. Radalet, ed., *The Police and the Community,* 4th ed. New York: Macmillan.

Morash, Merry, and Jack R. Greene (1986). "Evaluating Women on Patrol: A Critique of Contemporary Wisdom." *Evaluation Review* 10:230–255.

Morison, Kevin P. (1992). "Feeling the Effects of Pretrial Failures." *The Compiler* (Summer):6–9.

Morris, Allison (1987). *Women, Crime and Criminal Justice*. Oxford: Basil Blackwell.

Morris, David, G. (1979). *Reception and Classification: Organizational Processing in a Maximum Security Prison*. Masters Thesis, Southern Illinois University at Edwardsville.

Morris, Norval (1988), "Race and Crime: What Evidence Is There That Race Influences Results in the Criminal Justice System?" *Judicature* 72:105–114.

——— (1991). "The Case for Intermediate Punishments." *Federal Prison Journal* 2:11–14.

Morris, Norval, and Michael Tonry (1990). *Between Prison and Probation: Intermediate Punishments in a Rational Sentencing System*. Oxford: Oxford University Press.

Morris, Richard, and Vincent Jeffries (1990). "The White Reaction Study." In Nathan Cohen, ed., *The Los Angeles Riots*. New York: Praeger.

Morrison, Peter (1995). "The New Chain Gang States' New 'Get Tough' Prison Policies are Gaining Support from Politicians and the Courts." *National Law Journal* (August):1–7.

Moses, Marilyn C. (1995). "Keeping Incarcerated Mothers and their Daughters Together: Girl Scouts Beyond Bars." *NIJ Program Focus* (October):1–12.

Mullen, Joan, Kent John Chabotar, and Deborah M. Carrow (1985). *The Privatization of Corrections*. Washington, D.C.: National Institute of Justice.

Mulvihill, Donald J., Melvin Tumin, and Lynn Curtis (1969). *Crimes of Violence*. Washington, D.C.: U.S. Government Printing Office.

Mumola, Christopher J., and Allen J. Beck (1997). "Prisoners in 1996." *BJS Bulletin* (June):1–15.

Murton, Tom, and Joe Hyams (1969). *Accomplices to the Crime: The Arkansas Prison Scandal*. New York: Grove Press.

Myers, Martha A. (1993). "Inequality and the Punishment of Minor Offenders in the Early 20th Century." *Law and Society Review* 27:313–343.

NAACP Legal Defense Fund (1996). *Death Row USA*. New York: National Association for the Advancement of Colored People.

Nagin, Daniel S., and Raymond Paternoster (1991). "The Preventive Effects of the Perceived Risk of Arrest: Testing an Expanded Conception of Deterrence." *Criminology* 29:561–587.

National Center for Juvenile Justice (1996). *State Responses to Serious and Violent Juvenile Crime*. Washington D.C.: U.S. Department of Justice.

National Center for State Courts (1997). *Survey of Judicial Salaries*, Vol. 22. Williamsburg, Va.: National Center for State Courts.

National Committee on Violence [Australia] (1989). "Racist Violence." *Violence Today* 8:1–7.

National District Attorneys' Association (1991). *National Prosecution Standards*. Alexandria, Va.: NDAA.

National Gang Crime Research Center (1995). "A Research Note: Preliminary Results of the 1995 National Prosecutors' Survey." *Journal of Gang Research* 2:59–71.

National Institute of Corrections (1993). *State and Local Probation Systems in the United States: A Survey of Current Practice*. Washington, D.C.: U.S. Department of Justice.

National Institute of Justice (1991). *Research in Brief*. Washington, D,C.: U.S. Department of Justice.

——— (1992). *Making The Offender Foot the Bill: A Texas Program*. Washington, D.C.: U.S. Department of Justice.

——— (1993). *Project to Develop a Model Anti-Stalking Law*. Washington, D.C.: U.S. Department of Justice.

——— (1996). *Boot Camps for Juvenile Offenders: An Implementation Evaluation of Three Demonstration Programs*. Washington, D.C.: U.S. Department of Justice.

National Youth Gang Center (1997). *1995 National Youth Gang Survey*. Washington, D.C.: U.S. Department of Justice.

Nettler, Gwynne (1982). *Killing One Another*. Cincinnati, Ohio: Anderson

Newman, Graeme R. (1978). *The Punishment Response*. Philadelphia: Lippincott.

Newman, Graeme R., Adam C. Bouloukos, and Debra Cohen, eds. (1996). *World Factbook of Criminal Justice Systems*. Washington, D.C.: U.S. Department of Justice.

Newman, Oscar (1972). *Defensible Space: Crime Prevention Through Urban Design*. New York: Macmillan.

Niederhoffer, Arthur J. (1967). *Behind the Shield: The Police in Urban Society*. New York: Anchor.

Nugent, Hugh, and J. Thomas McEwen (1988). "Judges and Trial Court Administrators Assess the Nation's Criminal Justice Needs." *NIJ Research in Action* (August):1–6.

O'Brien, Robert M. (1991). "Sex Ratios and Rape Rates: A Power Control Theory." *Criminology* 29:99–114.

——— (1996). "Police Productivity and Crime Rates: 1973–1992." *Criminology* 34:183–207.

Office of National Drug Control Policy (1998). *The National Drug Control Strategy, 1998.* Washington, D.C.: U.S. Government Printing Office.

Office of Juvenile Justice and Delinquency Prevention (1995). *Juvenile Offenders and Victims: A National Report.* Washington, D.C.: U.S. Department of Justice.

——— (1997). *Proposed Comprehensive Plan for Fiscal Year 1997.* Washington, D.C.: U.S. Department of Justice.

Ogletree, Charles J. (1994). "Just Say No! A Proposal to Eliminate Racially Discriminatory Uses of Peremptory Challenges." *American Criminal Law Review* 31:1099–1151.

Otto, Amy L., Steven D. Penrod, and Hedy R. Dexter (1994). "Biasing Impact of Pretrial Publicity on Juror Judgements." *Law and Human Behavior* 18:453–470.

Owen, Barbara A. (1985). "Race and Gender Relations Among Prison Workers." *Crime and Delinquency* 31:147–159.

Packer, Herbert L. (1964). "The Crime Tariff." *American Scholar* 33:551–557.

——— (1968). *The Limits of the Criminal Sanction.* Stanford, Calif.: Stanford University Press.

Parent, Dale G. (1988). *Structured Criminal Sentences: The Evolution of Minnesota's Sentencing Guidelines.* Stoneham, Mass.: Butterworth.

Pate, Anthony, and Edwin Hamilton (1990). *The Big Six: Policing America's Largest Cities.* Washington, D.C.: The Police Foundation.

Paternoster, Raymond (1983). "The Decision to Seek the Death Penalty in South Carolina." *Journal of Criminal Law and Criminology* 74:754–787.

Paternoster, Raymond, Linda E. Saltzman, Gordon P. Waldo, and Theodore G. Chiricos (1983). "Perceived Risk of Social Control: Do Sanctions Really Deter?" *Law and Society Review* 17:457–479.

Paternoster, Raymond, Linda E. Saltzman, Gordon P. Waldo, and Theodore G. Chiricos (1985). "Assessments of Risk and Behavioral Experience: An Exploratory Study of Change." *Criminology* 23:417–433.

Percy, Charles H. (1974). "The Legacy of No-Knock: Drug Law Enforcement Abuse." *Contemporary Drug Problems* 3:3–20.

Perkins, Craig A., James J. Stephan, and Allen J. Beck (1995). "Jail and Jail Inmates, 1993–94. *BJS Bulletin* (April):1–16.

Petersilia, Joan (1987). *Expanding Options for Criminal Sentencing.* Santa Monica, Calif.: Rand Corp.

——— (1995) "A Crime Control Rationale for Reinvesting in Community Corrections." *The Prison Journal* 75:479–496.

Petersilia, Joan, and E. P. Deschenes (1994). "Perceptions on Punishment: Inmates and Staff Rank the Severity of Prison Versus Intermediate Sanctions." *The Prison Journal* 74:306–328.

Peterson, David M., and Paul C. Friday (1975). "Early Release from Incarceration: Race as a Factor in the Use of 'Shock Probation.'" *Journal of Criminal Law and Criminology* 66:79–87.

Peterson, Mark A., Harriett B. Braiker, and Suzanne M. Polich (1980). *Doing Crime: A Survey of California Prison Inmates.* Santa Monica, Calif.: Rand Corp.

Peterson, Ruth D., and William C. Bailey (1991). "Felony Murder and Capital Punishment: An Examination of the Deterrence Question." *Criminology* 29:367–395.

Pfohl, Stephen J. (1985). *Images of Deviance and Social Control.* New York: McGraw-Hill.

Phillips, Coretta, Gemma Cox, and Ken Pease (1996). "England and Wales." In Graeme Newman, Adam C. Bouloukos, and Debra Cohen, eds., *World Factbook of Criminal Justice Systems.* Washington, D.C.: U.S. Department of Justice.

Pike, Luke Owen (1968). *A History of Crime in England,* vol. 2. Montclair, N.J.: Patterson Smith.

Pileggi, Nicholas (1985). *Wiseguy: Life in a Mafia Family.* New York: Pocket Books.

Piliavin, Irving, and Scott Briar (1964). "Police Encounters with Juveniles." *American Journal of Sociology* 70:206–214.

Pisciotta, A. W. (1983). "Scientific Reform: The 'New Penology' at Elmira." *Crime and Delinquency* 29:613–630.

Platt, Anthony M. (1969). *The Child Savers: The Invention of Delinquency.* Chicago: University of Chicago Press.

Poe-Yamagata, Eileen and Jeffrey A. Butts (1996). "Female Offenders in the Juvenile Justice System." Washington, D.C.: OJJDP.

Pogrebin, Mark R., and Eric D. Poole (1991). "Police and Tragic Events: The Management of Emotions." *Journal of Criminal Justice* 19:395–403.

Pogrebin, Mark R., and Eric D. Poole (1993). "Vice Isn't Nice: A Look at Working Undercover." *Journal of Criminal Justice* 21:383–394.

Poland, James M. (1988). *Understanding Terrorism.* Upper Saddle River, N.J: Prentice-Hall.

Pontell, Henry N. (1984). *A Capacity to Punish.* Bloomington, Ind.: Indiana University Press.

Pope, Carl C., and William Feyerherm (1991). "Minority Status and Juvenile Justice Processing." *Criminal Justice Abstracts* 22:327–336 (Part 1); 22:527–542 (Part 2).

Post, James E., and Edwin Baer (1978). "Demarketing Infant Formula: Consumer Products for the Developing World." *Journal of Contemporary Business* 7:17–37.

Pound, Roscoe (1953) *The Lawyer from Antiquity to Modern Times.* St. Paul, Minn.: West Publishing.

Poveda, Tony (1990). *Lawlessness and Reform: The FBI in Transition.* Pacific Grove, Calif.: Brooks/Cole.

Pringle, Patrick (n.d.). *Stand and Deliver: The Story of the Highwayman.* New York: Norton.

Radelet, Michael L. (1990). "Post-Furman Botched Executions." *Lifelines* (September/October):7.

Radelet, Michael, and Hugo Bedau (1988), "Fallibility and Finality: Type II Errors and Capital Punishment." In

K. C. Haas and James Inciardi, eds., *Challenging Capital Punishment: Legal and Social Science Approaches.* Newbury Park, Calif.: Sage.

Ragonese, Paul (1991). *The Soul of a Cop.* New York: St. Martin's Press.

Rand, Michael (1993). "Crime and the Nation's Households, 1992." *BJS Bulletin* (August):1–12.

Rausch, Sharla, and Charles Logan (1983). "Diversion from Juvenile Court: Panacea or Pandora's Box." In James Kluegel, ed., *Evaluating Juvenile Justice.* Beverly Hills, Calif.: Sage.

Reaves, Brian A. (1992). "Pretrial Release of Felony Defendants, 1990." *BJS Bulletin* (November):1–14.

——— (1994). "Pretrial Release of Federal Felony Defendants." *BJS Special Report* (February):1–11.

——— (1996). *Campus Law Enforcement Agencies, 1995.* Washington, D.C.: U.S. Department of Justice.

——— (1998). "Federal law Enforcement Officers, 1996." *BJS Bulletin* (January):1–11.

Reaves, Brian A., and Andrew L. Goldberg (1998). "Census of State and Local Law Enforcement Agencies, 1996." *BJS Bulletin* (June):1–15.

Reaves, Brian A., and Jacob Perez (1994). "Pretrial Release of Felony Defendants, 1992," *BJS Bulletin* (November):1–16.

Reaves, Brian A., and Pheny Z. Smith (1995). *Felony Defendants in Large Urban Counties, 1992.* Washington, D.C.: U.S. Department of Justice.

Reaves, Brian A., and Pheny Z. Smith (1996). *Sheriffs' Departments, 1993.* Washington, D.C.: U.S. Department of Justice.

Redlich, N., J. E. Coleman, Jr., and S. S. Waglini (1994). "Politics and the Death Penalty: Can Rational Discourse and Due Process Survive the Perceived Political Pressure?" *Fordham Urban Law Review* 21:239–298.

Reiman, Jeffrey H. (1984). *The Rich Get Richer and the Poor Get Prison,* 2nd ed. New York: Wiley.

Reiss, Albert J., Jr. (1970). "Police Brutality: Answers to Key Questions." In Michael Lipsky, ed., *Law and Order: Police Encounters.* Chicago: Aldine.

Reiss, Albert J., Jr., and Jeffrey A. Roth, eds. (1993). *Understanding and Preventing Violence* Washington, D.C.: National Academy Press.

Remington, Frank J., Donald J. Newman, Edward L. Kimball, Marygold Melli, and Herman Goldstein (1969). *Criminal Justice Administration.* Indianapolis, Ind.: Bobbs-Merrill.

Renzema, Marc (1992). "Home Confinement Programs: Development, Implementation and Impact." In Lames M. Byrne, Arthur J. Lurigio, and Joan Petersilia, eds., *Smart Sentencing: The Emergence of Intermediate Sanctions.* Newbury Park, Calif.: Sage.

Reuss-Ianni, Elizabeth (1983). *Two Cultures of Policing: Street Cops and Management Cops.* New Brunswick, N.J.: Transaction Books.

Robin, Gerald D. (1987). *Introduction to the Criminal Justice System,* 3rd ed. New York: Harper & Row.

Robin, Gerald D., and Richard H. Anson (1990). *Introduction to the Criminal Justice System.* New York: Harper & Row.

Robinson Daniel N. (1996). *Wild Beasts and Idle Humours: The Insanity Defense from Antiquity to the Present.* Cambridge, Mass.: Harvard University Press.

Rockwell, Robin (1990). "The Advent of Computer Related Crimes." *Secured Lender* (July/August): 40–42.

Roebuck, Julian B., and Thomas Barker (1974). "A Typology of Police Corruption." In Ronald L. Akers and Edward Sagarin, eds., *Crime Prevention and Social Control.* New York: Praeger.

Rome, Dennis (1998). "Murderers, Rapists, and Drug Addicts." In Coramae Richey Mann and Marjorie S. Zatz, eds., *Images of Color, Images of Crime.* Los Angeles: Roxbury.

Roncek, Dennis W., and Pamela A. Maier (1991). "Bars, Blocks, and Crimes Revisited: Linking the Theory of Routine Activities to the Empiricism of 'Hot Spots.'" *Criminology* 29:725–753.

Rosen, Marie Simonetti (1997). "An LEN Interview with Edwin J. Delattre." *Law Enforcement News* (May 15): 10–13.

Rosenbaum, Dennis P., ed. (1994). *The Challenge of Community Policing.* Thousand Oaks, Calif.: Sage.

Rosenfeld, Richard (1996). "Gun Buy-Backs: Crime Control or Community Mobilization?" In M. Plotkin, ed., *Under Fire: Gun Buy-Backs, Exchanges, and Amnesty Programs.* Washington, D.C.: Police Executive Research Forum.

Rosett, Arthur, and Donald R. Cressey (1976). *Justice by Consent.* Philadelphia: Lippincott.

Rossi, Peter H., Emily Waite, Christine E. Bose, and Richard E. Berk (1974). "The Seriousness of Crimes: Normative Structure and Individual Differences." *American Sociological Review* 39:224–237.

Rothman, David, J. (1994). "The Crime of Punishment." *New York Times Review of Books* XLI:34–38.

Rowe, Alan, John H. Lindquist, and O.Z. White (1989). "A Note on the Family and Crime in the United States." *Psychological Reports* 65:1001–1002.

Roy, Calvert E. (1971). *Capital Punishment in the Twentieth Century.* New York: Kennikat Press.

Rubin, Sol (1949). "The Legal Character of Juvenile Delinquency." *The Annals* 261:1367–1400.

Rubinstein, Jonathan (1973). *City Police.* New York: Farrar, Straus & Giroux.

Rubinstein, Michael L., Stevens H. Clarke, and Teresa J. White (1980). *Alaska Bans Plea Bargaining.* Washington, D.C.: U.S. Department of Justice.

Rudovsky, David, Alvin J. Bronstein, Edward I. Koren, and Julia Cade (1988). *The Rights of Prisoners: The Basic ACLU Guide to Prisoners' Rights,* 4th ed. Carbondale, Ill.: Southern Illinois University Press.

Russell, Diana E. H. (1982). *Rape in Marriage.* New York: Collier.

Ryan, Joseph F. (1994) "Community Policing: Trends, Policies, Programs, and Definitions." In Albert R. Roberts, ed., *Critical Issues in Crime and Justice.* Thousand Oaks, Calif.: Sage.

Sadd, Susan, and Randolph M. Grinc (1996). "Implementing Challenges in Community Policing." *NIJ Research in Brief* (February):1–18.

Safir, Howard (1989). "The United States Witness Protection Program." In H. Smith, ed., *Transnational Crime:*

Investigative Responses. Chicago: University of Illinois at Chicago, OICJ.

Saint-Germain, Michelle A., and Robert A. Calamia (1996). "Three Strikes and You're In: A Streams and Windows Model of Incremental Policy Change." *Journal of Criminal Justice* 24:57–70.

Sampson, Robert J., and Jacqueline Cohen (1988). "Deterrent Effects of the Police on Crime: A Replication and Theoretical Extension." *Law and Society Review* 22:163–189.

Sampson, Robert J., and John Laub (1990). "Crime and Deviance Over the Life Course: The Salience of Adult Social Bonds." *American Sociological Review* 55:609–627.

——— (1992). "Crime and Deviance in the Life Course." *Annual Review of Sociology* 18:63–84.

——— (1993a). "Structural Variations in Juvenile Court Processing: Inequality, the Underclass and Social Control." *Law and Society Review* 27:285–312.

——— (1993b). *Crime in the Making.* Cambridge, Mass.: Harvard University Press.

Sanders, Wiley (1970). *Juvenile Offenders for a Thousand Years.* Chapel Hill, N.C.: University of North Carolina Press.

Sanders, William B. (1977). *Detective Work: A Study of Criminal Investigations.* New York: Free Press.

——— (1994). *Gangbangs and Drive-bys.* New York: Aldine de Gruyter.

Sapp, Allen D. (1994). "Sexual Misconduct by Police Officers." In Thomas Barker and David L. Carter, eds., *Police Deviance,* 3rd ed. Cincinnati, Ohio: Anderson.

Scalia, John (1997). *Prisoner Petitions in the Federal Courts, 1980–96.* Washington, D.C.:U.S. Department of Justice.

Scacco, Anthony M., Jr., ed. (1982). *Male Rape.* New York: AMS Press.

Schafer, Stephen (1969). *Theories in Criminology.* New York: Random House.

Schelling, Thomas D. (1967). "Economic Analysis of Organized Crime." In President's Commission on Law Enforcement and the Administration of Justice, *Task Force Report: Organized Crime.* Washington, D.C.: U.S. Government Printing Office.

Schiraldi, Vincent (1995). "Blacks are Targets of 57 Percent of 'Three Strikes' Prosecutions in Los Angeles." *Overcrowded Times* 6:7–8.

Scott, Eric J. (1981). *Calls for Service: Citizen Demand and Initial Police Response.* Washington, D.C.: U.S. Government Printing Office.

Scraton, Phil, Joe Sim, and Paula Skidmore (1991). *Prisons Under Protest.* Milton Keynes, England: Open University Press.

Scrivner, Ellen M. (1994). "Controlling Police use of Excessive Force: The Role of the Police Psychologist." *NIJ Research in Brief* (October):1–6.

Scull, Andrew T. (1977). *Decarceration: Community Treatment and the Deviant—A Radical View.* Upper Saddle River, N.J.: Prentice-Hall.

Sellin, Thorsten (1935). "Race Prejudice in the Administration of Justice." *American Journal of Sociology* 41:212–217.

——— (1938). *Culture Conflict and Crime.* New York: Social Science Research Council.

Sellin, Thorsten, and Marvin E. Wolfgang (1964). *The Measurement of Delinquency.* New York: Wiley.

Sexton, George E. (1995). "Work in American Prisons: Joint Ventures with the Private Sector." *NIJ Program Focus* (November):1–15.

Shannon, Lyle W. (1982). *Assessing the Relationship of Adult Criminal Careers to Juvenile Careers: A Summary.* Washington, D.C.: U.S. Department of Justice.

Shaw, Clifford R. (1930). *The Jack-Roller: A Delinquent Boy's Own Story.* Chicago: University of Chicago Press.

Shearing, Clifford D. (1979). "Subterranean Processes, the Maintenance of Power: An Examination of the Mechanisms Coordinating Police Action." Paper presented at the Annual Meeting of the American Sociological Association, New York, August.

Shearing, Clifford, and Richard V. Ericson (1991). "Culture as Figurative Action." *British Journal of Sociology* 42:481–506.

Sherman, Lawrence W. (1992). "Attacking Crime: Police and Crime Control." In Michael Tonry and Norval Morris, eds., *Modern Policing.* Chicago: University of Chicago Press.

——— (1993). "Defiance, Deterrence, and Irrelevance: A Theory of the Criminal Sanction." *Journal of Research in Crime and Delinquency* 30:445–471.

Sherman, Lawrence W., and Richard Berk (1984). "Specific Deterrent Effects of Arrest for Domestic Assault." *American Sociological Review* 49:261–272.

Sherman, Lawrence W., Patrick R. Gartin, and Michael Buerger (1989). "Hot Spots of Predatory Crime: Routine Activities and the Criminology of Place." *Criminology* 27:27–55.

Sherman, Lawrence W., and Dennis P. Rogan (1995). "Effects of Gun Seizures on Gun Violence: 'Hot Spots' Patrol in Kansas City." *Justice Quarterly* 12:673–693.

Sherman, Lawrence W., James W. Shaw, and Dennis P. Rogan (1995). "The Kansas City Gun Experiment." *NIJ Research in Brief* (January):1–11.

Sherman, Lawrence W., Janell D. Schmidt, Dennis P. Rogan, Patrick R. Gartin, Ellen G. Cohn, Dean J. Collins, and Anthony R. Bacich (1991). "From Initial Deterrence to Long-Term Escalation: Short-Custody Arrest for Poverty Ghetto Domestic Violence." *Criminology* 29:821–850.

Schneider, Ann L. (1977). *The Portland Forward Check of Crime Victims: Final Report.* Eugene, Or.: Oregon Research Institute.

Shoham, Shlomo (1970). *The Mark of Cain.* Dobbs Ferry, N.Y.: Citadel.

Short, James F., Jr. (1997). *Poverty, Ethnicity, and Violent Crime.* Boulder, Colo.: Westview Press.

Shover, Neal, and Belinda Henderson (1995). "Repressive Crime Control and Male Persistent Thieves." In Hugh D. Barlow, ed., *Crime and Public Policy: Putting Theory to Work.* Boulder, Colo.: Westview Press.

Shovron, Sandra Evans, Joseph E. Scott, and Francis T. Cullen (1989). "The Death Penalty for Juveniles: An

Assessment of Public Support." *Crime and Delinquency* 35:546–561.

Sigler, Robert T., and David Lamb (1995). "Community-based Alternatives to Prison: How the Public and Court Personnel View Them." *Federal Probation* LIX:3–9.

Silver, Allan (1967). "The Demand for Order in Civil Society." In David Bordua, ed., *The Police: Six Sociological Essays.* New York: Wiley.

Simon, Rita, and David Aaronson (1988). *The Insanity Defense.* New York: Praeger.

Sims, Barbara (1997). "Questions of Corrections: Public Attitudes Toward Prison and Community-Based Programs." *Corrections Management Quarterly* 1:49–56.

Singer, Simon I. (1993). "The Automatic Waiver of Juveniles and Substantive Justice." *Crime and Delinquency* 39:253–261.

Skibinski, Gregory J. (1994). "Intrafamilial Child Sexual Abuse: Intervention Programs for First Time Offenders and Their Families." *Child Abuse and Neglect* 18:367–375.

Skolnick, Jerome H. (1975). *Justice Without Trial,* 2nd ed. New York: Wiley.

——— (1994). *Justice Without Trial: Law Enforcement in a Democratic Society,* 3rd ed. New York: Wiley.

——— (1995). "What Not to Do About Crime—The American Society of Criminology Presidential Address." *Criminology* 33:1–15.

Skolnick, Jerome H., and James J. Fyfe (1993). *Above the Law: Police and the Excessive Use of Force.* New York: Free Press.

Slater, Harold, and Martin Reiser (1990) "A Comparative Study of Factors Influencing Police Recruitment." *Journal of Police Science and Administration* 16:168–176.

Smith, Brent L, and Kelly R. Damphousse (1998). "Terrorism, Politics, and Punishment: A Test of Structural-Contextual Theory and the 'Liberation Hypothesis.'" *Criminology* 36:67–92.

Smith, Douglas A. (1986). "The Neighborhood Context of Police Behavior." In Albert J. Reiss, Jr., and Michael Tonry, eds, *Communities and Crime.* Chicago: University of Chicago Press.

Smith, M. Dwayne (1987). "Patterns of Discrimination in Assessments of the Death Penalty: The Case of Louisiana." *Journal of Criminal Justice* 15:279–286.

Smolowe, Jill (1994). "Sleeping With the Enemy." *Time* (July 4):18–25.

Snell, Tracy L. (1994). "Women in Prison." *BJS Bulletin* (March):1–18.

——— (1995). *Correctional Populations in the United States, 1993.* Washington, D.C.: U.S. Department of Justice.

——— (1996) "Capital Punishment 1995." *BJS Bulletin* (December):1–16.

——— (1998), "Capital Punishment 1997." *BJS Bulletin* (December):1–16.

Snodgrass, Jon (1982). *The Jack-Roller at Seventy.* Lexington, Mass.: Lexington Books.

Snyder, Howard N. (1997). "Juvenile Arrests 1995." *OJJDP Juvenile Justice Bulletin* (February):1–12.

Snyder, Howard N., and Terrence A. Finnegan (1987). *Delinquency in the United States, 1983.* Washington, D.C.: U.S. Department of Justice.

Snyder, Howard N., and Melissa Sickmund (1995). *Juvenile Offenders and Victims: A National Report.* Washington, D.C.: U.S. Department of Justice.

Sparks, Richard F. (1980). "Criminal Opportunities and Crime Rates." In Stephen F. Feinberg and Albert J. Reiss, eds., *Indicators of Crime and Criminal Justice: Quantitative Studies.* Washington, D.C.: U.S. Government Printing Office.

Spears, Lawrence (1991). "Contract Counsel: A Different Way to Defend the Poor—How it's Working in North Dakota." *American Bar Association Journal on Criminal Justice* 6:24–31.

Speiglman, Richard (1976). "Building the Walls Inside Medicine: Corrections and the State Apparatus for Repression." Ph.D. diss., University of California, Berkeley.

Spergel, Irving (1964). *Racketville, Slumtown, Haulberg: An Exploratory Study of Delinquent Subcultures.* Chicago: University of Chicago Press.

Spohn, Cassia (1994) "Crime and the Social Control of Blacks: Offender/Victim Race and the Sentencing of Violent Offenders." In George S. Bridges and Martha Myers, eds., *Inequality, Crime, and Social Control.* Boulder, Colo.: Westview Press.

Stack, Steve (1994). "Execution Publicity and Homicide in Georgia." *American Journal of Criminal Justice* 18:25–39.

Stafford, Mark C., and Mark Warr (1993). "A Reconceptualization of General and Specific Deterrence." *Journal of Research in Crime and Delinquency* 30:123–135.

Stahl, Anne L. (1998). "Delinquency Cases in Juvenile Courts, 1995." *OJJDP Fact Sheet* (May):1–2.

Stanko, Elizabeth (1990). *Everyday Violence.* London: Pandora.

Steffensmeier, Darrell J. (1986). *The Fence: In the Shadow of Two Worlds.* Totowa, N.J.: Rowman & Littlefield.

——— (1995). "A Public Policy Agenda for Combatting Organized Crime." In Hugh D. Barlow, ed., *Crime and Public Policy: Putting Theory to Work.* Boulder, Colo.: Westview Press.

Steffensmeier, Darrell J., John Kramer, and Cathy Streifel (1993). "Gender and Imprisonment Decisions." *Criminology* 31:411–446.

Steinberg, Neil (1994). "The Law of Unintended Consequences." *Rolling Stone* (May 5):33–34.

Stevens, Dennis J. (1992). "Research Note: The Death Sentence and Inmate Attitudes." *Crime and Delinquency* 38:272–279.

Stolzenberg, Lisa, and Stewart J. D'Alessio (1994). "Sentencing and Unwarranted Disparity: An Empirical Assessment of the Long-term Impact of Sentencing Guidelines in Minnesota." *Criminology* 32:301–310.

Strecher, Victor (1995). "People Who Don't Even Know You." In Victor Kappeler, ed., *The Police and Society.* Prospect Heights, Ill.: Waveland Press.

Strodtbeck, Fred, and Richard Lipinski (1985). "Becoming the First Among Equals: Moral Considerations in Jury

Foreman Selection." *Journal of Personality and Social Psychology* 49:927–936.

Sturma, Michael (1986). "Death and Ritual on the Gallows: Public Executions in the Australian Penal Colonies." *Omega* 17:89–100.

Sudnow, David (1965). "Normal Crimes: Sociological Features of the Penal Code in a Public Defender Office." *Social Problems* 12: 255–268.

Sullivan, Peggy S. (1989). "Minority Officers: Current Issues." In Roger G. Dunham and Geoffrey P. Alpert, eds., *Critical Issues in Policing*. Prospect Heights, Ill.: Waveland Press.

Sullivan, Peggy S., Roger G. Dunham, and Geoffrey Alpert (1987). "Attitude Structures of Different Ethnic and Age Groups Concerning Police." *Journal of Criminal Law and Criminology* 78:177–193.

Surette, Ray (1992). *Media, Crime, and Criminal Justice.* Pacific Grove, Calif.: Brooks/Cole.

Sutton, John R. (1990). "Bureaucrats and Entrepreneurs: Institutional responses to Deviant Children in the United States, 1890–1920s." *American Journal of Sociology* 95:1367–1400.

Sykes, Gresham M. (1958). *The Society of Captives.* Princeton, N.J.: Princeton University Press.

Tak, Peter J. P. (1994). "Sentencing in the Netherlands." *Acta Criminologica* 7:7–17.

Takagi, Paul (1979). "Death by 'Police Intervention.'" In U.S. Department of Justice, *A Community Concern: Police Use of Deadly Force.* Washington, D.C.: U.S. Government Printing Office.

Tanford, Sarah, and Steven Penrod (1986). "Jury Deliberations: Discussion Content and Influence Processes in Jury Decision Making." *Journal of Applied Social Psychology* 16:322–347.

Taylor, Robert W., Eric J. Fritsch, and Tory J. Caeti (1998). "Core Challenges Facing Community Policing: The Emperor *Still* has no Clothes." *ACJS Today* XVII:1–5.

Terrill, Richard J. (1984). *World Criminal Justice Systems: A Survey.* Cincinnati, Ohio: Anderson Smith.

Thomas, Charles W., and Dianne Bolinger (1999). *Private Adult Correctional Facility Census,* 12th ed. Gainesville, Fla.: University of Florida Center for the Study of Criminology and Law.

Thomas, D. A. (1967). "Sentencing: The Basic Principles." *Criminal Law Review* 25:514–520.

Thomas, Kenneth R. (1993). "How to Stop the Stalker: State AntiStalking Laws." *Criminal Law Bulletin* (March–April):124.

Thornberry, Terence P. (1973). "Race, Socioeconomic Status, and Sentencing in the Juvenile Justice System." *Journal of Criminal Law and Criminology* 64:90–98.

——— (1987). "Toward an Interactional Theory of Delinquency." *Criminology* 25: 863–891.

Tittle, Charles R. (1980). *Sanctions and Deterrence.* New York: Praeger.

——— (1995). *Control Balance: Toward a General Theory of Deviance.* Boulder, Colo.: Westview Press.

Tjaden, Patricia, and Nancy Thoennes (1998). "Stalking in America: Findings from the National Violence Against Women Survey." *NIJ Research in Brief* (April):1–19.

Toch, Hans (1977). *Police, Prisons, and the Problem of Violence.* Rockville, Md.: National Institute of Mental Health.

Tonry, Michael (1993). "Sentencing Commissions and their Guidelines." In Michael Tonry, ed., *Crime and Justice: A Review of Research,* vol. 17. Chicago: University of Chicago Press.

——— (1994a). "Racial disproportion in US Prisons." *British Journal of Criminology* 34:97–115.

——— (1994b). "Racial Politics, Racial Disparities, and the War on Crime." *Crime and Delinquency* 40:475–494.

——— (1996). *Sentencing Matters.* New York: Oxford University Press.

Trasler, Gordon (1986). "Situational Crime Control and Rational Choice," In Kevin Heal and Gloria Laycock, eds., *Situational Crime Prevention: From Theory into Practice.* London: HMSO.

Trotter, R. T. (1972). "Clockwork Orange in a California Prison." *Science News* 101:174–175.

Tunnell, Kenneth D. (1992). *Choosing Crime: The Criminal Calculus of Property Offenders.* Chicago: Nelson-Hall.

Turk, Austin (1995). "Transformation versus Revolution and Reformism: Policy Implications of Conflict Theory." In Hugh D. Barlow, ed., *Crime and Public Policy: Putting Theory to Work.* Boulder, Colo.: Westview Press.

Turnbaugh, Kristi (1995a). *"Electronic Monitoring." The Compiler* (Winter/Spring):7–9.

——— (1995b). "Sheriff's Work Alternative Program: Paying Back the Community." *The Compiler* (Winter/Spring):4–6.

Turner, Michael G., Jody L. Sundt, Brandon K. Applegate, and Francis T. Cullen (1995). "'Three Strikes and You're Out' Legislation: A National Assessment." *Federal Probation* LIX:16–35.

U.S. Bureau of the Census (1994). *Statistical Abstract of the United States 1994.* Washington, D.C.: U.S. Government Printing Office.

——— (1997). *Statistical Abstract of the United States 1997.* Washington, D.C.: U.S. Government Printing Office.

U.S. Department of Justice (1976). *The LEAA: A Partnership for Crime Control,* Washington, D.C.: U.S. Government Printing Office.

——— (1995). "The Nation's Two Crime Measures." BJS Document NCJ–122795.

U.S. Senate Hearing (1991). *Countermeasures against Terrorism: The Federal Effort.* Washington, D.C.: U.S. Government Printing Office.

Uchida, Craig, Brian Forst, and Sampson O. Annan (1992). *Modern Policing and the Control of Illegal Drugs: Testing New Strategies in Two American Cities.* Washington, D.C.: U.S. Department of Justice.

Umbreit, Mark S., and Robert Coates (1993). "Cross-Site Analysis of Victim-Offender Mediation in Four States." *Crime and Delinquency* 39:565–585.

United States Commission on Civil Rights (1981). *Who Is Guarding the Guardians: A Report on Police Practices.* Washington, D.C.: U.S. Government Printing Office.

van Maanen, John (1973). "Observations on the Making of Policemen." *Human Organizations* 32:407- 418.

Vera Institute of Justice (1995). *Bail Bond Supervision in Three Counties.* New York: Vera Institute of Justice.

Vetri, Dominick R. (1964). "Guilty-Plea Bargaining: Compromise by Prosecutors to Secure Guilty Pleas." *University of Pennsylvania Law Review* 112:896–908.

Vila, Bryan J. (1994). "A General Paradigm For Understanding Criminal Behavior: Extending Evolutionary Ecological Theory." *Criminology* 32:311–359.

Visher, Christy A. (1987). "Jury Decision-Making: The Importance of Evidence." *Law and Human Behavior* 11:1–17.

von Drehle, David (1995). *Among the Lowest of the Dead.* New York: Times Books.

von Hirsch, Andrew (1984). "Selective Incapacitation: A Critique." *NIJ Reports.* Washington, D.C.: National Institute of Justice.

Vorhees, Donald S. (1990). *Manual on Recurring Problems in Criminal Trials.* Washington D.C.: Federal Judicial Center.

Waegel, William B. (1984). "The Use of Lethal Force by Police: The Effect of Statutory Change." *Crime and Delinquency* 30:121–140.

Wagner, Dennis and Christopher Baird (1993). "Evaluation of the Florida Community Control Program." *NIJ Research in Brief* (January):1–6.

Wagner, Allen E., and Scott H. Decker (1989). "Evaluating Citizen Complaints Against the Police." In Roger G. Dunham and Geoffrey P. Alpert, eds., *Critical Issues in Policing: Contemporary Readings.* Prospect Heights, Ill.: Waveland.

Walker, Samuel (1985). *Sense and Nonsense about Crime: A Policy Guide.* Monterey, Calif.: Brooks/Cole.

——— (1992). *The Police in America: An Introduction,* 2nd ed. New York: McGraw-Hill.

Walker, Samuel, and Susan E. Martin (1995). "Through the Looking Glass Ceiling: Patterns in Hiring and Promotion by Race, Ethnicity and Gender in American Policing, 1982–1992." Paper presented at the Annual Meeting of the American Society of Criminology, Chicago, November.

Ward, David A., and Eugene Kassebaum (1965). *Women's Prisons: Sex and Social Structure.* Chicago: Aldine.

Weiner, Norman (1974). "The Effect of Education on Police Attitudes." *Journal of Criminal Justice* 2:323–330.

Weis, Joseph G., Robert D. Crutchfield, and George S. Bridges, eds. (1996). *Readings: Juvenile Delinquency.* Thousand Oaks, Calif.: Pine Forge Press.

Weisburd, David, and Lorraine Green (1995). "Policing Drug Hot Spots: The Jersey City Drug Market Analysis Experiment." *Justice Quarterly* 12:711–735.

Weisheit, Ralph A. (1993) "Studying Drugs in Rural Areas: Notes From the Field." *Journal of Research in Crime and Delinquency* 30:213–232.

Weisheit, Ralph A., David N. Falcone, and L. Edward Wells (1994). "Rural Crime and Rural Policing." *NIJ Research in Action* (October):1–15.

Weisheit, Ralph A., and L. Edward Wells (1998). "In A Rapidly Changing World, What Lies Ahead for Law Enforcement in Rural Areas?" *The Compiler* (Spring): 8–10, 18.

Werthman, Carl, and Irving Piliavin (1967). "Gang Members and the Police." In David Bordua, ed., *The Police: Six Sociological Essays.* New York: Wiley.

Westermann, Ted D., and James W. Burfeind (1991). *Crime and Justice in Two Societies.* Pacific Grove, Calif.: Brooks/Cole.

Weston, Paul B., and Kenneth M. Wells (1972). *Law Enforcement and Criminal Justice.* Pacific Palisades, Calif.: Goodyear.

Whitaker, Catherine J. (1989). *The Redesigned National Crime Survey: Selected New Data.* Washington, D.C.: U.S. Department of Justice.

White, Jonathan R. (1991). *Terrorism: An Introduction.* Pacific Grove, Calif.: Brooks/Cole.

White, Mel (1994). *Stranger at the Gate.* New York: Simon & Schuster.

Whitehead, J. T., and Steven P. Lab (1989). "A Meta-Analysis of Juvenile Correctional Treatment." *Journal of Research in Crime and Delinquency* 26:276–295.

Wice, Paul B. (1978). *Criminal Lawyers: An Endangered Species.* Newbury Park, Calif.: Sage.

Wilbanks, William (1983). *Murder in Miami.* New York: University of America Press.

Wilkins, Leslie T., Jack M. Kress, Don M. Gottfredson, Joseph C. Calpin, and Arthur M. Gelman (1978). *Sentencing Guidelines: Structuring Judicial Discretion.* Washington, D.C.: U.S. Government Printing Office.

Williams, Hubert, and Patrick V. Murphy (1990). "The Evolving Strategy of Police: A Minority View." *Perspectives on Policing,* 13:1–23.

Williams, Kipling. D., Martin J. Bourgeois, and Robert T. Croyle (1993). "Effects of Stealing Thunder in Criminal and Civil Trials." *Law and Human Behavior* 17:597–609.

Wilson, James Q. (1968). *Varieties of Police Behavior.* Cambridge, Mass.: Harvard University Press.

——— (1997). "Criminal Justice in England and America." *The Public Interest* (Winter):3–14.

Wilson, James Q., and Barbara Boland (1978). "The Effect of the Police on Crime." *Law and Society Review* 12:367–390.

Wilson, James Q., and Richard J. Herrnstein (1985). *Crime and Human Nature.* New York: Simon & Schuster.

Winterfield, Laura A, and Sally T. Hillsman (1993). "The Staten Island Day-Fine Project." *NIJ Research in Brief.* (January):1–7.

Wiseman, Jacqueline P. (1970). *Stations of the Lost: The Treatment of Skid Row Alcoholics.* Upper Saddle River, N.J.: Prentice-Hall.

Wolf, Daniel R. (1991). *The Rebels: A Brotherhood of Outlaw Bikers.* Toronto, Canada: University of Toronto Press.

Wolfgang, Marvin E., and Bernard Cohen (1970). *Crime and Race.* New York: Institute of Human Relations Press.

Wolfgang, Marvin E., Robert M. Figlio, Paul E. Tracy, and Simon I. Singer (1985). *The National Survey of Crime Severity.* Washington, D.C.: U.S. Department of Justice.

Warchol, Greg (1998). "Workplace Violence, 1992–1996." *BJS Special Report* July: 1–9.

Wice, Paul B. (1974). "Purveyors of Freedom: The Professional Bondsmen." *Transaction* (July/August):21–23.

Worden, Robert E., and Robin L. Shepard (1996)."Demeanor, Crime, and Police Behavior: A Reexamination of the Police Services Study Data." *Criminology* 34:83–105.

Wortham, Sarah Dowse (1993). "Juvenile Justice in Illinois: An Overview." *The Compiler* (Summer):3–10.

Wright, Benjamin, William Doerner, and John Speir (1990). "Pre-employment Psychological testing as a Predictor of Police Performance during an FTO Program." *American Journal of Police* 9:65–79.

Wright, Kevin N., and Karen E. Wright (1994). *Family Life, Delinquency, and Crime: A Policymaker's Guide.* Washington, D.C.: Office of Juvenile Justice and Delinquency Prevention.

Wright, Richard T., and Scott H. Decker (1994). *Burglars on the Job: Streetlife and Residential Break-ins.* Boston: Northeastern University Press.

Wycoff, Mary Ann, and Wesley G. Skogan (1994). "Community Policing in Madison: An Analysis of Implementation and Impact." In Dennis P. Rosenham, ed., *The Challenge of Community Policing.* Newbury Park, Calif.: Sage.

Zachariah, John K. (1996), "An Overview of Boot Camp Goals, Components, and Results." In Doris L. Mackenzie, and Eugene E. Hebert, eds., *Correctional Boot Camps: A Tough Intermediate Sanction.* Washington, D.C.: U.S. Department of Justice.

Zawitz, Marianne W. (1995). "Guns Used in Crime." *BJS Selected Findings* (July):1–7.

——— (1996). "Firearm Injury from Crime." *BJS Selected Findings* (April): 1–7.

Zehr, Howard (1985). *Retributive Justice, Restorative Justice.* Akron, Pa.: Mennonite Central Committee.

——— (1990). *Changing Lenses.* Scottsdale, Pa.: Herald Press.

Ziegenhagen, Eduard A. (1977). *Victims, Crime, and Social Control.* New York: Praeger.

Zimbardo, Philip G. (1972). "The Pathology of Imprisonment." *Society* 9:4–8.

——— (1994). *Transforming California's Prisons into Expensive Old Age Homes for Felons.* San Francisco: Center on Juvenile and Criminal Justice.

Zupan, Linda L. (1992). "Men Guarding Women: An Analysis of the Employment of Male Correction Officers in Prisons for Women." *Journal of Criminal Justice* 20:297–309.

NAME INDEX

SUBJECT INDEX

Note: Page numbers in bold refer to illustrations; page numbers followed by the letter t refer to tables.